Glass
A to Z

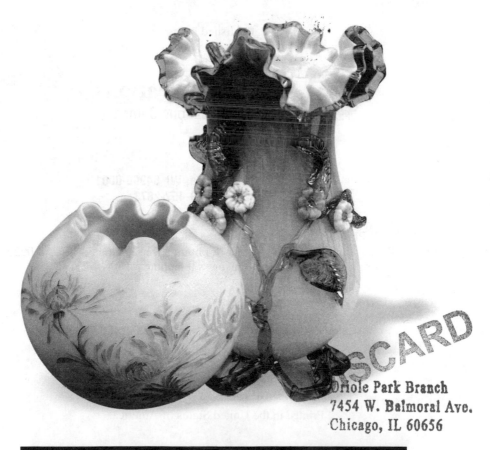

David J. Shotwell

Published by

krause publications
An F&W Publications Company

700 East State Street • Iola, WI 54990-0001
715-445-2214 • 888-457-2873
www.krause.com

Please call or write for our free catalog of publications.
Our toll-free number to place an order or obtain a free catalog is 800-258-0929
or please use our regular business telephone 715-445-2214.

Library of Congress Catalog Number: 2002105772

ISBN: 0-87349-385-0

Printed in the United States of America

Table of Contents

INTRODUCTION

The primary objective of this book is to describe the types and kinds of glass; the tools, materials, and processes related to its manufacture and embellishment; and brief histories of numerous glass manufacturing facilities and biographies of glass designers, decorators, and artisans.

While there are naturally occurring forms of glass, the origins of man-made glass date back only about 5,000 years to ancient Mesopotamia, where it is believed to have been discovered quite by accident and used as a coating on beads and stones. It was first used by itself to make amulets and beads about 2,500 B.C. Egypt appears to have been the first to establish a glass industry about 1,500 B.C., making core glass vessels. Over the next several centuries, glassmaking centers sprang up and declined throughout northern Africa and southwestern Asia as centers of power changed and craftsmen migrated with the conquerors. The first great advance in glass-making came during the early first century B.C. when Phoenicians discovered that glass could be blown. This innovation spread eastward throughout the Roman Empire, becoming the norm within 100 years, then declining with the Empire in the west as the capital moved eastward to Constantinople.

Over the next 1,000 years the industry was all but nonexistent. While glass had been made in Venice as early as 450, the industry came into its own in the 13th century, moving to Murano in 1292. The formulation of a clear glass, *cristallo*, in the 14th century helped the industry maintain its supremacy until 1676 when lead glass was made on a commercial basis. The next great advance in glassmaking was the mechanical pressing of glass in the 1820s. Since then advances have been made in the commercial production of glass and glassware, while at the same time handcrafted glass-ware has enjoyed periods of great popularity.

The first permanent settlement by Europeans in what is now the United States was at Jamestown, Virginia, in 1607. The first industry established there, in 1608 or 1609, was glassmaking. While short-lived, another was established in 1621, operating until 1625. For the next 100 years, the industry was virtually dead; a few unsuccessful attempts were made. The first successful facility was built by Casper Wister in 1739, making bottles and window glass—the staples of the early glass industry.

As time went on, more facilities were built, most short-lived. The life span was dictated by finances, governmental controls, tax levies and tariffs, fuel supply, labor problems, innovations, etc. Because of this, the workers often seemed to be nomads, moving from facility to facility when one closed, when new ones were built, or when they felt like it. Their plight is not unique. As the history of facilities, are reviewed, it is not unusual to find an individual involved with several facilities as well as numerous owners of the same facility, as partnerships and corporations were created and dissolved. This led to numerous name changes and, because of the confusion created, the use of local names. Further confusing the issue is the fact that sources do not always agree on the facts. There is often disagreement with respect to years of operation, owners or sequence of owners, products, name, or existence.

Then there is the glass itself. It can be classified in many ways, such as by manufacturer, country, state region, city, decoration, decorator, type, use, finish, style, composition, color, pattern, etc. A single piece may fall in several categories. Because workers frequently moved from facility to facility, wares produced at one location may be similar to those in another. This is further compounded by the fact that patterns were copied, molds were sold, facilities moved, different facilities had different names for the same pattern or the same name for different patterns, etc.

This work represents only a portion of 30 years of research in the area and is certainly not all-inclusive; in fact, it merely scratches the surface. I hope to be able to expand it in the future.

David J. Shotwell (shotwell@goes.com)

abatjour A candle shade or hurricane glass.

Mosser ABC plate, vaseline glass, 6" d. Davanna Collection

ABC plates (Aka *alphabet plates*) Plates designed for use by children, not only to eat from, but as teaching aids. They had printed (usually around the rim) letters and/or numbers, and were popular from 1780 to 1860.

aborigene, vetro *(Italian)* Ornamental glassware developed by Ercole Barovier at Barovier & Toso in the mid-1950s. It has an overall haphazard pattern of small pieces of opaque, colored glass of various shapes embedded in colorless glass.

abrasion Decorating a glass object by grinding with an abrasive wheel or by using particles conveyed by air or water or some other medium.

Abrogast & Kaplahn See *Birmingham Flint Glass Company.*

acanthus scroll A decorative motif resembling an acanthus leaf in profile (normally curled downward or coiled under) at the top.

accelerator A substance, such as arsenic and antimony oxides, sodium and barium sulfates, and calumite, added to the glass batch to increase homogeneity and reduce seeds.

acetabulum *(Latin)* A small cup, made of Roman glass during the 1st century AD. It has a semi-globular shape, resembling the socket in the hipbone (for which it is named). It has a sloping, or vertical, collar and rests on a foot ring.

achauffern A chafing dish.

achromatic lens A lens made by combining two or more lenses of different focal lengths to eliminate color fringes that tend to distort images.

acid A compound which loses a positive charge (proton) when it reacts chemically. Glass is resistant to most acids with the exception of phosphoric acid (H_3PO_4) and hydrofluoric acid (HF), which attack the glass's surface.

Acid Cutback A product developed by Frederick Carder of Steuben Glass Works and made in limited quantities during the 1920s (only about 1,800 pieces in about 400 different designs). It is made using the same process and techniques as Carder's *Acid Etched* wares and it appears they only differ in name. Pieces are commonly decorated with floral designs, but a few have animal and aquatic designs. Some are marked with the Steuben Fleur-de-lis or signed "F. Carder." See *Acid Etched.*

acid cutback glassware See *acid-etched glassware.*

acid engraving See *etching.*

Acid Etched A registered name for an art glass created by Frederick Carder, in 1932, at Steuben Glass Works. The manufacturing process used is detailed under acid-etched glassware (1). It was cased with two layers of different colors. The design was etched by the acid to the lower layer's depth, so the finished piece had the outer layer's base color while the design was the inner layer's color. See *acid-etched glassware; Acid Cutback.*

Acid-etched Depression Glass champagne, 5-1/2" h. Davanna Collection

acid-etched glassware (1) (Aka *acid cutback glassware*) Glassware decorated by etching its surface with acid, appearing like more expensive cameo glass. The object is covered with an acid-resistant wax into which a design is scratched or, in the case of Carder's Acid Etched or Cut Back wares, a design is transferred to it and an acid-resistant wax placed around it. The piece is then immersed in acid, usually hydrofluoric acid. This process etches the glass where the wax is absent, leaving behind the design. When cased glass is acid etched, the object is immersed in the acid long enough for the acid to etch through the glass's outer layer or layers. The end result is the designs are a different color from the exterior layer of glass. It was popular between the 1890s and 1930s. See *etching.* (2) Glassware made in an acid-etched mold. A design is etched into a mold using acid. Wares produced have designs in relief that appear to have been etched.

acid polishing A procedure used in making cut glass. The finished product achieves a polished surface by dipping it into a bath containing a mixture of hydrofluoric and sulfuric acids. This cost-cutting procedure replaced the time consuming and laborious hand-polishing methods.

acid stamping The process of etching with acid, a manufacturer's or decorator's trademark or signature into previously annealed glass.

acid treating A procedure used in finishing glassware resulting in a dull, lusterless finish. This occurs by treating its surface with hydrofluoric acid.

Acme Cut Glass Company (1916-1922) A glass cutting company established by Charles D. and George Link (creator of the *Bridgeton Rose*) in Bridgeton, New Jersey, during 1916. Over the next three years, the company operated under a variety of names. In 1919, the name was changed to Aetna Cut Glass Company.

Acme Glass Works A glass manufacturing facility established during 1874 in Steubenville, Ohio, by Reddick, McKee & Company. Purchased shortly thereafter by Gill, Mitchell & Company, its name changed to Acme Glass Works. It claimed to be the United States' largest maker of glass chimneys.

acorn bottle Any widemouthed bottle used for sprouting acorns. A popular novelty item in the mid-1800s.

acorn finial An acorn-shaped finial turned upside down with its pointed end upward.

acorn goblet A short-stemmed, covered goblet resembling an acorn turned upside down. The cover is tall and narrow with a beehive shape. The bowl and cover are encircled with glass threads and the stem is lion-masked.

acorn knop An acorn-shaped knop sometimes found alone, with a second acorn reversed, or with other types of knops.

acorn lamp A fairy lamp with a hobnail base and an acorn-shaped shade of swirled glass, made between the 1860s and 1890s by Hobbs, Brockunier & Co.

Actglas A clear glass with coral decoration developed at Loetz, about 1900, by Max von Spaun.

actor/actress glass A type of glassware, first made in 1879, depicting the popular actors and actresses of the period. The name of an actor or actress was affiliated with each of the 26 different characters represented. When an actor or actress lost popularity, his or her name was removed from the mold and replaced with a more popular one—but the portrayal remained the same.

Adams & Company

(1) Prior to 1851, Adams, Macklin & Company established a glass manufacturing facility in Pittsburgh, Pennsylvania. In 1851, it took over the operations of the Stourbridge Flint Glass Works in Pittsburgh. In 1860/1861, it was operated by Adams & Company (aka *John Adams & Company*), and moved to Pittsburgh's Birmingham section. It made pressed and engraved flint glass tablewares, and later on, lime glasswares. In 1891, it joined the U.S. Glass Company, becoming *Factory A*. (2) See *New Hampshire Glass Factory*.

Adams Glass Company

A short-lived window (cylinder) glass manufacturing facility established in Adams, Massachusetts, in 1812, by John Whipple, James Mason, Daniel Shearman, and others.

Addison Mosaic Glass Co.

See *Egginton & Brewster*.

ADNA

A mark of the A. Douglas Nash Associates.

Adlerhumpen (*German*)

Literally, *eagle beaker*. A *Humpen* with enameling depicting a double-headed eagle. The earliest known example dates from 1547. See *Reichsadlerhumpen*.

aeolipile (*Greek*)

A globular or pear-shaped vessel having a narrow neck and mouth. Most are of Islamic origin and are believed to be containers for liquids. The term originated during the 2nd century from a device consisting of a closed, water-filled container that, when heated, was rotated by jets of steam from bent tubes projecting from its surface.

Aetna Cut Glass Company

(1) (1907-1909) A glass cutting company established in Meridan, Connecticut, by Alfred and Joseph Pelerin. (2) See *Acme Cut Glass Company*.

Aetna Glass & Manufacturing Company

(1879-1890) A glass manufacturing facility in Bellaire, Ohio, making goblets initially, later adding all types of pressed, blown, and cut glass.

Aetna Glass Works

See *Johnson Glassworks*.

Two Agata bowls and a tumbler, c. 1886-1888, 3" h.
The Corning Musuem of Glass

Agata glass juice tumbler, 3-3/4" h.
Krause Publications

Agata glass

A mottled, opaque art glass, a variation of the New England Glass Company's *Peachblow* (*Wild Rose*). It was created and patented in 1886 by Joseph Locke, and made for less than a year. The usual shades range from an opaque pink to a moderately dark rose or from an opaque white to a rose; some pieces have gold and blue mottling. To make it, the object was spattered with a metallic stain in a solvent, such as alcohol. As the solvent evaporated, a mottled effect was left on the surface and fixed by firing. All known pieces have a glossy finish, except one having a satin finish with the spatter darkened.

agate glass

(1) A decorative, multicolored opaque glass made by combining and partially mixing metals of different colors before the object is shaped. The primary colors used are green and purple. It looks like any one of a variety of natural semi-precious stones, such as agate, onyx, etc. When agate glass was made in Venice during the late 15th century, it was called *calcedonio*; in England, *jasper*. The earliest known are of Roman glass. (2) A type of glass developed during the 1870s by Eugene Rousseau and later made by other companies. Gold and other metallic oxides were added to the batch, the result being a laminated effect typical of agate stone. (3) An early Louis Comfort Tiffany *Favrile* product made to imitate agate by adding opaque metals of different colors to a pot, mixing them until a striated

mixture resulted. It is called, inappropriately, *laminated glass*. At times some turned a rust color, and when polished, was called *metallic glass*. Some pieces were marked with a paper label, and a few had engraved Tiffany marks. See *Moss Agate glass.*

age lines (Aka *annealing lines, marks, or cracks*) Tiny, perceptible, fissures in milk glass generally caused by the object being cooled too rapidly during the annealing process. See *annealing marks.*

agent A position of power in early United States glass companies; today the equivalent of a general manager.

Ages of Man A decorative motif in which a man, rarely a woman or couple, is shown in various life stages. It is most often depicted in four pictures representing the four periods of a man's life: adolescence, young man, middle age, and old age, but sometimes in up to ten pictures, each illustrating a decade of a man's life. The two most common techniques of presenting it are (1) a man ascending and descending an arched bridge, and (2) a man depicted in a series of panels encircling an object. Enameling and engraving are the most common forms of decoration. It was popular from the 16th through 19th centuries.

aggry bead (Aka *aggri bead*) A bead made by slicing a multicolored glass cane at an oblique angle producing a zigzag pattern. They date to ancient times; the oldest being discovered in Africa.

agitable lamp A whale oil lamp, patented by John Miles of Birmingham, England, in 1787, consisting of a reservoir with a cover having a hole in the center into which a burner with one or more tube wicks was fitted.

Agnew, John, & Co. In 1842, Chambers, Agnew & Company established a glass manufacturing facility in Pittsburgh, Pennsylvania, making vials, bottles and window glass. In 1854, Chambers withdrew and the operating firm became John Agnew & Company, making druggists', green glass and flint glassware. In 1866, Agnew's sons entered the business and the firm became Agnew, Sons & Co. After 1876, it was known as Agnew & Co. It was still operating in 1886.

air bleb See *bleb.*

air locks (Aka *air traps*) A style of embellishment in which small envelopes of air become the motif. They are slightly larger than typical air bubbles or tears, and often arranged in decorative pattern. The process for making them was patented by Benjamin Richardson of W.H., B. & J. Richardson in 1858. They were popular during the late 1800s and Frederick Carder made great use of it at Steuben.

air ring An elongated air inclusion encircling a paperweight near the base, usually above and below a torsade.

air traps See *air locks.*

air twist A twist enclosed within one or more twisted columns of air, made by entrapping air in a rod of glass which is stretched until thin, then twisting it, making a spiral pillar entrapping the air. Multiple series air twists have one twist concentrically within another, the product of one mold becoming the core rod within another. It dates from early 18th century England and is used primarily in stems. See *air twist stem; mercury twist.*

air twist stem A stem in which an air twist is the only, or primary, embellishment. It was one of the earliest stem decorations. See *air twist.*

aisyll bottle A cruet. *Aisyll* or *aisylhe* is a synonym for vinegar.

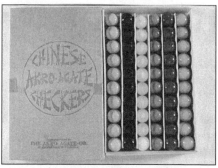

Akro Agate Chinese checkers, 10 each, in six colors of marbles, original box.
Davanna Collection

Akro Agate Glass Company Established in 1911 near Akron, Ohio, it was primarily a jobber, manufacturing children's marbles for an Ohio marble company. In 1914, it moved to Clarksburg, West Virginia, making marbles for sale under its own name. In 1932, it began to diversify, making various types of glassware; among the most popular were children's dishes, floral ware, cosmetic containers and novelties. It closed in 1951, sold to the Clarksburg Glass Company. Most of the glassware was signed either with an eagle flying through the letter "A" or with a circle seal with "AKRO" and a flying eagle carrying marbles in its talons. Also usually added was, "Made in USA," and often a mold number.

alabaster Milk glass.

alabaster glass See *pate-de-riz*.

Alabaster glass A 1920s translucent glass resembling alabaster, made by Frederick Carder at Steuben. It has an iridescence created by spraying it with stannous chloride and reheating it. It is used mainly to create ornamental wares. It also functions as a casing on multi-layered glassware, a background on other wares, and an applied decoration on Aurene glass. It has been sandwiched between two layers of clear-colored glass where the outer layer is etched to reveal the alabaster inner layer.

alabaster quartz See *quartz glass*.

alabastron (Greek) A small bottle or flask designed to hold perfume or oil. Some were made of core glass as early as 300 BC in Alexandria. Early ones were cylindrical-shaped, and later ones tapered inward near the neck, having a hemispherical base. A few have small loop handles or lugs for hanging by a cord from the waist. Those of core glass are from 3 to 4-3/4 inches or more tall.

Alacite A translucent glass varying from pale ivory to pinkish-beige, developed by Henry Hellmers for the Mantle Lamp Company during 1938, and made from 1940 to 1949. It was initially made with a uranium oxide, which the federal government prohibited for commercial use in 1942. After that, alternate chemicals were used resulting in color variations.

Aladdin Industries, Inc. See *Mantle Lamp Company*.

Alba An alabaster white, opaque glass made by MacBeth-Evans beginning in 1903. It was used for electric light shades and globes, and other commercial and household wares. Two lines were made of this glass: *Thebian*, patented in May 1914 and *Decora*, patented in July 1914.

Albany Glass Company Located in Albany, New York, little is known about this window glass manufacturing facility. Its existence is mainly known through its exhibitions at the Franklin Institute's 17th Exhibition in 1847 and at the American Institute of the City of New York's Annual Fair where it exhibited glass water pipes.

Albany Glass House (Works) About 1783, a window and bottle glass manufacturing facility was erected at Dowesborough, New York, failing in 1787. During 1792, McCallen, M(a)cGregor & Co. took it over and named it the Albany Glass House. It made the same products as its predecessor. In 1794, the operating firm was MacGregor & Company, and, in 1795, Thomas Mather & Company. Sometime during the next few years it was renamed the Hamilton (Glass) Manufacturing Company or Hamilton Manufacturing Society, making crown and cylinder window glass, as well as bottles and flasks. It was reported closed in 1815 due to lack of fuel, but it is believed that some glass globes were made as late as 1823. See *Dowesborough Glass Works; Rensselaer Glass Factory*.

albarello A cylindrical, slightly waisted vessel, sometimes with a cover and a short foot, designed to hold various drugs, especially thick, syrupy liquids, or solids.

Albert (drop) A drop, used on lusters during the Victorian period, in the shape of an arrowhead; triangular in section with faceted edges; named for Prince Albert, Queen Victoria's husband.

Albertine glass See *Crown Milano*.

ale glass A drinking glass of English derivation to hold ale or beer, derived from the 17th century short stemmed dwarf ale glass, developed over time into the current version; a tall, thin, stemless tumbler, slightly tapered to a solid base. During the evolutionary process, its capacity has increased from about three ounces to its current twelve ounces. They were popular in England from 1730 to 1750, being embellished with engraving, enameling and gilding, usually with motifs indicative of the ingredients, such as hops and barley. Their different sizes denote the evolutionary stages as follows: *dwarf, small, full,* and *giant.* See *dwarf ale glass; Georgian ale glass.*

ale jug A jug used to serve ale or beer, usually engraved or enameled with ingredient motifs, such as hops and barley.

Alembic(k) (Arabic) A device, dating back to ancient times, for distilling liquids. It was shaped like an inverted bowl with a small tube coming from the side, where vapors condense and exit. It was placed with its mouth down over a vessel called a *cucurbit* containing the liquid being heated. As the liquid was heated, vapors rose, came in contact with the cooler alembic, and condensed. The liquid ran down the sides of the alembic into a duct and was carried through the tube into a receiving receptacle. The alembic and cucurbit were often combined into one piece. See *retort.*

Alexandrit A monochromatic glass made by L. Koloman Moser; the most common rare earth glass, containing four to five percent neodymium by weight. It appears pale, bluish violet under fluorescent light and red violet in natural sunlight or tungsten light. It should not be confused with *Alexandrite.*

Alexandrite An art glass of transparent glass, shading from pale yellow to rose to blue, initially made about 1900, by Thomas Webb & Sons. Webb made it in a single layer with the three merging colors produced by successive reheatings of object parts. Later, Stevens & Williams made it using the *cut-through* method. The body was transparent amber and cased with rose, and then blue glass. The outer layers were cut away to make a pattern on an amber background.

Alford, C.G., & Company (1872-1918) A New York City company which operated a jewelry and watch repair shop, and a glass cutting shop. Some pieces are signed.

alkali Any substance having prominent basic properties (as opposed to acidic properties), i.e. the ability to neutralize acids. It is necessary in making glass, being about 15% to 25% of the batch, serving as a flux, acting to reduce the silica's fusion temperature. It is supplied mainly by soda (sodium carbonate) and/or potash (potassium carbonate) (see *soda; potash*). Soda was used in making Spanish, Roman, Egyptian, Syrian, Venetian, and some English glass, potash in making German and Bohemian glass. Today both are used.

alkali silicates Soluble glasses used only as solutions. Sodium silicates, the most common, are made by simply melting sand and soda ash together. The product varies in composition from $Na_2O.SiO_2$ to $Na_2O.4SiO_2$ and is known as *water glass.* It is widely used as an adhesive in making corrugated paper boxes, for fireproofing and in egg preservation.

allegorical subject Spiritual, abstract, or symbolic figures or subjects used as decorative motifs on glassware, mainly by enameling and engraving.

Allen, William, Cut Glass Co. (1905-1920) A glass cutting company in Johnstown, Pennsylvania.

Allen Glass Co. A glass cutting company in Corning, New York, operating for a few years around the turn of the 20th century. It probably was named for William Allen, a foreman at Hoare & Co., who, in 1905, established the William Allen Cut Glass Co. There are two ownership theories of the Corning facility: (1) William Allen owned and operated it as a part-time business while remaining a foreman at Hoare & Co., or (2) it was a subsidiary of Hoare & Co., named for the foreman (a common industry practice).

almond bossed beaker A mold-blown beaker, normally having six rows of almond or lotus-bud-shaped bosses around it, made in Syria during the 1st and 2nd centuries AD.

almond thumbprint See *thumbprint.*

almorratxa (Spanish) Also spelled *almorrata.* A vessel having a pedestal foot and four tapered spouts extending upward from the shoulder around the neck. They were used as rose-water sprinklers for ceremonial purposes and made in Catalonia, Spain, from the 14th through the 18th centuries. Some were imported into Spain from Damascus during the 14th century and from Venice and Austria during the 16th and 17th centuries.

alms dish A dish or container in which food and/or other provisions for the poor were placed to later be given away.

Almy & Thomas (1903-1918) It purchased the Knickerbocker Cut Glass Company, Corning, New York, making cut glass on blanks from Corning, U.S. Glass, and Pairpoint. Some pieces are signed "A&T" or "Almy & Thomas, Corning, N.Y." within a circle.

alphabet plates See *ABC plates.*

Altare, L' A community near Genoa, Italy, established by glassmakers during the 800s after leaving Normandy or Flanders. By the 1450s, it had become a major manufacturing center, rivaling Venice and emulating its wares.

alternate panels cutting (Aka *cross-cut squares*) A pattern in cut glass made by cutting pairs of mitered diagonal channels at right angles to another pair, and then cutting horizontal and vertical single channels. This results in smooth areas, or panels, in the shape of octagons or squares with beveled corners. It has been erroneously called *hobnail.*

alternate prism cutting See *prism cutting.*

Alton Manufacturing Company In 1907, it reopened the old Boston & Sandwich Glass facility in Sandwich, Massachusetts. While it made some good wares, it closed after a few months. One of its products was *Travaise Ware.*

alumino-silica glass Any glass containing 20% or more of alumina (aluminum oxide, Al_2O_3). It has favorable electrical and chemical properties, extraordinary thermal shock resistance, and high softening temperature. The glass is used in high temperature thermometers, combustion tubes, and stovetop cooking ware.

Alva Glass Manufacturing Company (1890-1899) A bottle glass manufacturing facility established by some unemployed glassblowers in Salem, New Jersey. In June 1899, it was sold to the Philadelphia Pickling Company.

Alvin Manufacturing Company A silver company specializing in making silver deposit glass.

alzata *(Italian)* **Literally,** *elevation.* A tiered serving object consisting of two to four pedestal-footed plates or bowls positioned one above the other, reducing in size as they rise. They were popular during the 19th century.

Ambassador Russian cut glass pattern where the button is crosshatched.

amber glass Any glass with a brownish-yellow or reddish-yellow color.

Amber Onyx An onyx glass made by the Byesville Glass Company. An inner layer of onyx glass is cased by an outer layer of glass containing uranium and iron oxides, which when heated and exposed to gas fumes, causes amber-colored swirls.

Amber Satin See *Klondike (Dalzell, Gilmore & Leighton).*

amber slag glass A white glass streaked with tan to dark brown colored swirls.

amber-stained glass Mainly victorian-era pattern glass partially or completely stained a natural amber color. The tone ranged from light pale yellow to deep golden brown. Made by numerous companies, it was introduced about 1885, and remained popular until about 1905.

Amberette (1) Certain lines of amber-stained pattern glassware made by George Duncan & Sons. (2) See *Klondike (Dalzell, Gilmore & Leighton).*

Ambergris (1) A yellow-colored art glass made by Victor Durand, Jr., at Vineland Flint Glass Works. (2) A transparent pale-yellow glass often used by Tiffany in making his iridescent glass.

Amberina A translucent, uncased art glass shading from light amber to ruby, patented on July 24, 1883, by John Locke for New England Glass Co. The trade name was issued for Amberina on April 4, 1884. This glass was made by placing a small quantity of gold, in solution, in a batch of transparent amber glass. The article formed was allowed to cool below the glowing red point. Then specific parts were reheated at the furnace's glory hole. The reheated parts turned ruby, caused by the gold in the batch. It was made from 1883 to about 1900. The articles were mostly blown or blown molded, but some were pressed; much was made with flint glass and often had air bubbles. True Amberina always had a pontil mark; it being necessary to attach the article to the pontil to reheat it at the glory hole. Generally, the ruby color is at the top because it was usually reheated with the pontil attached to the bottom. When the ruby color is on the bottom of the piece, it is called *Reverse Amberina*. If heated too long, the color changed from ruby to purple. In 1917, to celebrate the company's 100th anniversary, Libbey revived it; about 40 different styles were made over a two year period, each piece bearing their etched trademark. Mt. Washington made a similar product called *Rose Amber* as did Boston & Sandwich (daisy and button pattern). Many Midwestern glass houses made similar products using mass-production methods. Selenium, instead of gold, is used in imitation of Amberina. A later version called *Flashed Amberina* was made by flashing the pieces' tops with an amber glass mix (selenium usually used for flashing) has no pontil mark. *Plated Amberina* is not to be confused with *Flashed Amberina* since the plated is an opalescent glass cased with an outer layer of Amberina glass. See *Rose Teinte; Blue Amberina; Flashed Amberina; Painted Amberina; Plated Amberina; Pressed Amberina.*

ambrosia dish (or bowl) An asymmetrically-shaped, oval dish or bowl, having an irregularly lobed rim, a small curling handle at the small end and a stemmed foot. They have Rococo-style embellishment with faceting and polished and/or unpolished intaglio engraving.

Amelung, Frederick, & Co. See *Baltimore Glass Works.*

Amelung, John Frederick (1739-1798) He came to the United States from Bremen, Germany, in 1784, bringing with him 68 workers, glass making tools and equipment, and purchased land near Frederick, Maryland, erecting a glass manufacturing facility, which he named the New Bremen Glass Manufactory (aka *Etna Glass Works, American Glass Manufactory, New Bremen Glassworks* or *Amelung Glassworks*). By 1790, he erected a second facility on the site. His initial products were window glass and bottles, adding, in 1785, tableware. In spite of his initial success, it failed to make a profit, and a 1790 fire almost wiped him out. In 1795, after two appeals to Congress for financial aid, he offered most of his land and operations for sale, deeded his unmortgaged land to his son, John Frederick Magnus Amelung, and declared bankruptcy, closing his operations. He then moved to Baltimore, Maryland, where he died. It is believed that two of his workers, Adam Kohlenberg and John Christian Gabler, bought the facility in 1799. Shortly thereafter, Gabler sold his interest to Kohlenberg who operated it making window glass and bottles until the 1810s. See *New Bremen Glass Manufactory.*

America in Crystal See *Americana Series.*

American Art Glass Company See *Byesville Glass Company.*

American-Bohemian glass A mid-1800s cut and/or etched flashed or cased glass made at the New England Glass Company. The flashing was mainly ruby red over a clear base.

American Cut Glass Company (1) A glass cutting company established as a subsidiary of Libbey during 1897 in Chicago, Illinois, moving, about 1900, to Lansing, Michigan, and closing about 1920. (2) A small cutting shop, in Corning, New York, operating for a short time in 1905 and 1906. (3) A glass cutting company in Port Jervis, New York, operating during the early years of the 20th century. In 1906, it was a subcontractor for Hawkes. (4) See *Arcadia Cut Glass Company.*

American eagle flask A flask, having a Masonic emblem on the obverse and an eagle on the reverse, made in the United States from about 1813 to 1830.

American Ferroline Company See *New Brighton Glass Company.*

American Flint & Lime Glass Manufacturers Founded in 1874, a voluntary association of 55 tablewares' manufacturers whose goals were to contest the labor demands, reduce the costs of materials, and stabilize prices. It was behind the formation of the United States Glass Company combine established in 1891. The Midwestern section of this group was the Western Flint & Lime Glass Protective Association.

American Flint Glass Works (1) (1850-1851) A pressed-flint and colored-glassware manufacturing facility in Wheeling, West Virginia. (2) See *South Boston Crown Glass Co.* (3) See *Steigel, William Henry.*

American glass(ware) Glassware made in the 48 contiguous states of the United States; the first glassware being made at Jamestown, Virginia, in 1608 (see *Jamestown glass houses*).

American Glass Company (1) (1889-1890) A glass manufacturing facility in Anderson, Indiana, making tableware, vase lamps, table lamps, sewing lamps, night lamps, castors, etc. (2) An affiliate of General Glassware in Carney, Kansas. See *Haley, K.R., Glassware Company.* (3) See *South Boston Crown Glass Co.*

American Glass Manufactory See *New Bremen Glass Manufactory; Amelung, John Frederick.*

American Glass Specialty Company A short-lived, late 1800s glass-decorating firm operating in Monaca, Pennsylvania.

American Glass Works (1865-1905) A glass manufacturing facility established in Birmingham (Pittsburgh), Pennsylvania. In 1871, it was operated by Duff & Campbell and, in 1880, by T. Campbell & Company. It made window and photographic glass, and rough, plate, and stained and enameled glass.

American Lamp & Brass Company See *Ellwood City Glass Company.*

American paperweights Paperweights have been made in the United States from 1851 on by several facilities, including Boston & Sandwich Glass Co., New England Glass Co., Gillinder Glass Co. and Whitall, Tatum & Co. It has also been made by individuals at shops and studios. They are often embellished in a French-paperweight style.

American Plate Glass Company A late 1800s-early 1900s plate glass manufacturing facility in Pittsburgh, Pennsylvania. See *Cayuga Plate Glass Company.*

American System, The (1) A Federal policy, beginning with the War of 1812, designed to protect manufacturers through the establishment of higher tariffs. The money from which was used to improve the internal transportation systems. (2) A pressed glass historical flask, made by Bakewell, with a depiction of a side-wheel steamer flying an American flag on the obverse; the steamer encircled by the inscription "The American System." On the reverse is a sheaf of rye.

American Wholesale Corporation (Aka *Baltimore Bargain House*) In 1922, this retail and mail order house, with stores in Baltimore and Cumberland, Maryland, registered trademarks for cut glass, consisting of the initials "AWC" and name "American Wholesale Corporation (Baltimore Bargain House)." It did no cutting on its own, but acted as a retail outlet for other cutters.

American Window Glass Company A consortium of about sixty window glass manufacturers from the east and Midwest, founded in 1890. See *Cleveland Glass Works; cylinder glass; Dunbarton Glass Works; Durhamville Glass Works.*

Americana Glass Company A 1962 glass-decorating company established by E.B. Willis and D. Grindley whose products were distributed through college bookstores and souvenir markets.

Americana Series A series of 50 engraved bowls, identical in every aspect except for the engraved decorations. A Steuben project, begun in 1948 and completed in 1959, it was originally named *America in Crystal* and exhibited in

Steuben's New York City gallery as *United States in Crystal*. Sidney Waugh did the sketches for each bowl, which represented a state with an engraved picture relating to that state's image in an overall theme of its American historical importance.

amethyst glass Any glass with color ranging from pale, light to deep, dark purple. If the glass appears black and only exhibits a deep purple color when held to strong light, it is commonly called *black amethyst*.

amethyst quartz See *quartz glass*.

amorino (Italian) A child-like depiction of a cupid with wings, often used as a embellishment on glassware. Dating to the 1st century AD, it was first used by the Romans.

amorphous Lacking a definite form. Glass is considered amorphous because it does not return to a crystalline state on cooling.

amphora (Latin) A large egg-shaped jar, used to store oil, wine, or other liquids; some were made of Roman glass in the 2nd century BC. They have two vertical loop handles, the ends attached at the vessel's shoulders. They are usually plain and, on occasion, taper to a point on the bottom. They are of two basic styles: (a) the *neck amphora* where the neck protrudes from the shoulder, meeting the body at an angle; and (b) the *continuous curve amphora* where the neck and body form a continuous curve.

amphoriskos (Greek) A small glass vessel, used to hold oil, in the form of *amphora* and first made in Egypt and/or Cyprus during the 14th century BC and in the eastern Mediterranean region between the 7th and 2nd centuries BC. They are made of core glass with an opaque body, typically turquoise or dark blue, and combed decoration in orange, yellow, light blue, or white. They are 2 to 6 inches in height, have a bulbous or ovoid body, a pointed bottom, and domed foot or disk-based knob.

ampulla (Latin) A small vessel similar to the amphora, of Roman derivation; some made of Roman glass between the 1st and 4th centuries AD. They have an ovoid body with a tall slender neck, usually one or two side loop handles attached to the shoulder and rest on a circular flat base.

amulet An ornament, gem, scroll, etc., worn as a charm to ward off evil spirits and harm, or to bring good fortune. Some of Egyptian glass date from the 15th century BC.

Anchor Cap & Closure Corporation
See *Salem Glass Works*.

Anchor Hocking Corporation See
Anchor Hocking Glass Company; Salem Glass Works.

Anchor Hocking Glass Co. "Classic Snack Set" comprised of four plates and four cups. Made of heat-resistant milk glass with 22 K. gold trim.
Davanna Collection

Anchor Hocking Glass ad, June 1954.
Davanna Collection

Anchor Hocking Glass Company A
company formed on December 31, 1937, through a merger of the Hocking Glass Company of Lancaster, Ohio, and the Anchor Cap (& Closure) Corporation of Long Island City, New York, and several other glass manufacturing facilities already controlled by either one of these two. In 1969, the name became Anchor Hocking Corporation. See *Ohio Flint Glass Company*.

Anchor Glass Company See *Ohio Flint Glass Company*.

ancient glass A term applied to all kinds of glass that pre-dates blown glass and includes all pre-Roman glass, ancient Roman glass and Roman blown glass. The first known use of glass exists in the form of a green glaze on a string of beads and the oldest known glass object is a small, molded-blue Mesopotamian amulet, made about 3000 BC.

Anglo-Irish glassware Lead and other types of glass made in Ireland from about 1780 to 1825 by English glassmakers. See *Irish glassware.*

Anglo-Saxon glass Glassware made in England between 410 AD (the date the Romans withdrew from England) and 1066 AD (the Battle of Hastings) when the Angles, Saxons, Jutes, and other Germanic tribes dominated the area.

Anglo-Venetian glassware (1) Glassware, in the *facon de Venise*, made in 1400s and 1500s England by Venetian glassmakers. (2) Another name for *ice glass*; a type of glassware made in England during the 1850s. See *ice glass.*

Angster (German) A bulbous flask with a slanting neck consisting of several intertwined tubes from which liquids pour sluggishly. See *Kuttrolf.*

angular knop A knop having a flattened spherical shape, and a rounded edge which angles upward and downward to the stem.

animal beaker See *Tierhumpen.*

Animal dish, Boyd hen on nest in pink champagne, 5".
Davanna Collection

animal dishes Covered dishes or bowls in a variety of types of glass having covers representing the upper portion of an animal or an animal on a nest or bed. Animals represented include chickens, dogs, cats, camels, fish, elephants, etc.

Animal figures in frosted glass, most with clear base. Deer signed "Lalique France," buffalo 3-1/2" h. signed "Goebel 1987," bird 3-1/2" h. Davanna Collection

animal figures Animal-shaped objects made from the earliest times in pressed, molded, carved, or blown glass. They may be alone, with a set (often as a family), or as part of another object such as a finial, lid, lamp base, candy container, bank, etc.

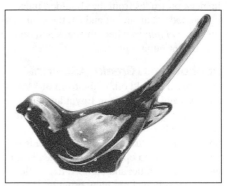

Fenton cobalt-blue bird, 6-1/2" l.
Davanna Collection

animal paperweight A paperweight having as its primary embellishment a portrayal of an animal, including insects, birds, reptiles, etc. The "animal" may be within the dome of the weight, on the dome, or the weight itself may be in the shape of the "animal." They are sometimes included in the general category of *subject paperweights*.

Annagelb *(German)* See *Annagrun (German)*.

Annagrun *(German)* A glass exhibiting fluorescent properties, created by the addition of uranium to the batch, developed by Joseph Riedel in Germany, and made from 1830 to 1848. It was either fluorescent greenish-yellow or yellowish-green depending on the amounts of the other ingredients in the batch. The yellowish-green he named *Annagrun* and the greenish-yellow *Annagelb*, both in honor of his wife Anna Marie.

annealing (Aka *heat tempering*) A process that toughens glass by eliminating internal stress through heating and gradually cooling it in an annealing oven or lehr. If any glass article, regardless of the production method, is left to cool freely in ambient air, internal stresses develop within the article, inevitably leading to its spontaneous breakage. In the annealing process, glass is elevated to a temperature just below that at which flow begins and held there (*annealing point*), until it has reached that temperature throughout. (Stress can also be removed from glass, more slowly, by holding the article within a temperature range, known as the *annealing range*.) It is then slowly cooled to a temperature at which no further flow can take place. The processing time varies greatly, requiring between 45 minutes and several days depending on the glass's type, thickness, and the article's shape. The annealing range for a typical soda-lime-silica glass is from about 900° to 1020° and for glass with a high lead content, about 735° F to 840° F.

annealing cracks See *annealing marks*.

annealing kiln A smaller version of an annealing oven used in the making of studio glass, usually of simple construction and heated by gas or electricity, or waste heat from the furnace.

annealing lines See *annealing marks*.

annealing marks (Aka *annealing cracks, straw marks*) Marks originating during the annealing process as the object passes through the lehr. As cooling glass contracts, small surface fissures sometimes appear. While they may occur anywhere on the piece, the most common area is near the edges. They are really small cracks caused by the same tensions causing glass to crack if cooled too rapidly.

annealing oven See *lehr.*

annular Ring shaped.

annular knop A knop in the form of a ring.

annulate(d) Embellishment consisting of a series of mereses or rings (of uniform size or graduated) positioned vertically. It is frequently found on the article's foot, stem, or knop.

antimony An element of metallic appearance with a crystalline structure, tin white in color, hard and brittle, having several uses in the glass industry. From the 20th to the 6th century BC, it was used to produce opacity in glass. From the 2nd to the 4th century AD, the Romans used it as a decolorant. In more modern times, it has been used as a yellow colorant.

antique glass (1) Glass(ware) old in terms of years. (2) Glass(ware), not necessarily "old" in terms of years, but made using antiquated methods, such as being hand blown. (3) See *Cypriote glass*. (4) Sheets of colored, stained glass of variable thickness, usually having deliberately introduced air bubbles, giving the appearance of medieval glass. See *antique method*.

antique method The process of making sheet glass by handmade methods. Most stained glass windows are still made from sheets of handmade glass, generally using the cylinder method. They are mainly either *pot antique* (made in one pot and of one color) or layered *flash antique*.

AOP Abbreviation for "all over pattern." A piece of cut glass, its entire surface covered with a pattern.

Apostelglas *(German)* Literally, *Apostle glass*. A tall glass embellished with the enameled representation of the twelve Apostles, illustrated separately (each with his name on a banner above) surrounding the glass in two rows. Similar types of glasses depict the Four Evangelists.

apostle wares Any item, such as a mug, glass, plate, spoon, plaques, etc., depicting one or more of the twelve Apostles, popular between the mid-17th and mid-18th centuries.

applicator See *drop stopper.*

applied glass (decoration) A separate gather of glass applied and attached to the main gather. This was done during the blowing and shaping process, or just after the article was pressed. The applied glass may be an integral object part, such as a handle or stem, or decorative.

applique(d) Any type of art glass embellished with applied glass decorations.

apricot A deep yellow color with a pinkish tinge, somewhat lighter than amber glass and having a reddish component.

Aqua Marine An art glass developed at Steuben by Frederick Carder. It resembles *Verre de Soie,* except it has a greenish tint. Very little was made.

Aqua Regia A corrosive liquid composed of one part nitric acid and three or four parts hydrochloric acid, used to dissolve platinum and gold. It was used in a glass batch to impart color.

aquamarine A color, light greenish-blue or bluish-green.

Aquamarine See *Tiffany Aquamarine.*

arabesque (1) In Islamic art, because of the religious ban on the human figure portrayals, a flat embellishment consisting of a fanciful interlacing of lines, bands, geometric forms and abstract designs, principally of classical derivation. In 19th century England, they were termed *Moresque.* (2) In Renaissance art and later European art, an embellishment with flowing curved lines and intertwining foliage, scrolls and animal forms. It was prevalent from about 1760 to 1790. (3) *Grotesques.*

Arbogast & Stackhouse See *Gibbs, Kelly & Company.*

arcaded rim A rim embellished with glass loops or arches, often with a prunt at the joints.

Arcadia Cut Glass Company (1901-1928) A glass cutting company in Newark, New York. In 1902, it changed its name to the American Cut Glass Company, and in 1903, to the Arcadian Cut Glass Company. In 1908, it moved to Lestershire (now Johnson City), New York, operating there until it closed. See *Spencer Cut Glass Company.*

Arcadian Cut Glass Company (1) See *Arcadia Cut Glass Company.* (2) A name used for the Corning branch of the Elmira Cut Glass Co. Some sources place it in Corning, New York, operating about the turn of the 20th century; others believe it never existed.

arched decoration Embellishment on cut glass, consisting of a sequence of contiguous semi-circles or rounded arches. It was fashionable on 1840s English cut glass.

arched rectangle decoration Embellishment on cut glass consisting of a sequence of contiguous semi-circles or rounded arches held up by short upright rectangles; the width identical with the diameter of the rounded arch. It was common on Waterford glassware during the late 1700s and early 1800s.

architectural glass Glass, normally flat, used for utilitarian purposes, such as windows, mirrors, tabletops, solid and hollow blocks, etc. Sometimes the pieces are rounded, or of irregular shape, and embellished by sandblasting, etching, etc.

Argand lamp (Aka *space lamp*) An oil-burning lamp, named for Aime Argand (1750-1803) of Switzerland who invented the tubular wick burner in 1782. It had a hollow tube, open at both ends, extending upward through the burner's center, a woven wick fitted tightly around it, and another cylinder placed around that. Oil from the reservoir was fed into the chamber's side containing the wick, the center tube providing air to the flame's center. The heat from the flame tended to increase the draft, as did the chimney. Fuel was gravity fed to the burner from a side reservoir and slightly above the flame. This lamp remained the standard for lighting until the middle of the 19th century.

argyle Also spelled *argyll*. A vessel used to keep gravy hot at the table. It was actually two vessels; an inner one containing the gravy and an outer containing water, kept hot by placing it above a spirit lamp. It was named for the fourth Duke of Argylle.

Orrefors Ariel glass, aqua-green vase, 5" h. Davanna Collection

Ariel glass A cased glass having embedded air bubbles, arranged in various patterns, either as an actual or abstract representation an object or figure. The process for making it was developed at Orrefors in the early 1930s by Vicke Lindstrand and Edvin Öhrstrom, similar to that used to make *Graal* glass.

armlet A ornamental bracelet or band designed to be worn on the upper arm.

armonica See *musical glasses*.

armorial glassware (Aka *heraldic ware*) Any form of glassware that bears royal, or some other official, coats-of-arms, generally enameled or engraved, made in many European countries from the 1600s through the 1800s.

Armstrong Cork Company See *Whitall, Tatum & Co.*

arrow(head) cane (Aka *crow's foot cane*) A cane used in making paperweights. The cane's middle rod is encircled by pedal-shaped rods, in each of which is a three-pronged (resembling the tip of an arrow); the

tips aimed toward the middle rod, producing a flower-like effect.

Arsenal Glass Works A glass manufacturing facility established in Pittsburgh, Pennsylvania, by Charles Jeremy, operating for only one season, the fall of 1865 through the spring of 1866, making mold-blown jars.

arsenic A solid, brittle, very poisonous substance of tin white to steel gray color with a metallic luster. Arsenic trioxide, A_2O_3, is also commonly called *arsenic* or *white arsenic*. It, in small quantities, is found in almost all modern colorless glass, improving the glass's color, transparency and brilliance by removing the organic matter that carbonizes in the pot during the melting operation (a decarbonizer). It is also used in making opaque white glass and, on occasion, opaline.

Art Cut A line of glassware made by the U.S. Glass Company; a pressed ware in imitation cut glass, advertised as "heavy pure crystal, excellent copy of genuine cut." Much was made as iridized carnival glass.

Art Deco lamp with custard glass globe, German, 8" h. Tri-State Antiques

Art Deco style (Aka *Art Moderne*) This decorative art style began after the Paris Exposition of 1925, and flourished in the last half of the 1920s into the 1930s. It is exemplified by bold styles, streamline contour, and linear geometric patterns, which embrace the use of new materials. It influenced all types of furniture and accessories as well as decorative arts, jewelry, glassware, and even games.

Art Glass (1) Any of an assortment of glassware shapes made by numerous United States and European glass manufacturing facilities and studios from about 1870 to

1910. It was executed in many newly developed surface textures and colors. Some had several colors shading from one to another and with layers of different-colored cased glass. Manufacturing methodologies often involved laborious and complex procedures and were often patented and/or registered. The embellishments were normally elaborate, typically using old Venetian techniques; applied embellishments of contrasting colors were very fashionable. It is not common commercial glass, mass-made in large quantities. Normally it is made in very limited quantities, frequently expensive one-of-a-kind pieces, made by hand methods, most often blown or blown molded. (2) Any glassware made for ornamental rather than utilitarian purposes, with initial consideration being given to the quality of the glass and the artistic nature of the form and embellishment.

Art Manufacturing Company A
glass cutting shop in St. Louis, Missouri, in 1902, at the same site as the Missouri Glass Company and Yall, Clark & Cowan. See *Missouri Glass Company.*

Art Moderne See *Art Deco style.*

Green Art Nouveau vase with gold embellishment, 3-1/2" h.
Tri-State Antiques

Art Nouveau Rebelling against "traditional" or "established" forms of art, a style in fashion from the late 1800s until just prior to the start of World War I. A reaction to the perfectionism and pretentiousness of the Victorian era, it was initiated by two idealists: William Morris and John Ruskin (1819-1900). Morris wanted art and "honest" designs to be available to all at an affordable price while Ruskin loathed machine-made articles, idealizing the "creative craftsman." Its advocates borrowed from the ancient world and Japan, adopting ideas in original manners and arrangements. They used new materials and techniques to create forms of embellishment. The style was adapted to glassware by many artists, including Emile Galle and Louis Comfort Tiffany, who tried to recreate the iridescence and pitted surfaces created by minerals and moisture acting on the glass's surface buried in the earth. The term *Art Nouveau* is from a Paris gallery owned by Siegfried Bing called *Maison de l'Art Nouveau.*

Arte Vetraria *(Italian)* Literally, *Art of Glass.* A standard work on glassmaking written by Antonio Neri, published in Florence, Italy, in 1612 and again in 1661, and in Venice in 1663 and 1678. It was translated and published in several languages through the mid-18th century.

artificial leach See *leach glass.*

Artists in Crystal See *Twenty Seven Artists in Crystal; British Artists in Crystal; Asian Artists in Crystal.*

Arts & Crafts Movement A forerunner to the style later known as Art Nouveau.

aryballos *(Greek)* A small bottle, used to hold bath oil, having a squat, sphere-like body, a short neck and a small orificed flat disk mouth, and one or two scroll or loop handles extending from the shoulder to just below the mouth disk. They were of core glass with combed decoration on a dark blue body, ranging in size from 1-1/5 to 8 inches and made in the Eastern Mediterranean region from the 6th century BC to 1st century AD.

ash pit A space beneath the grate (see *grate*) extending the furnace's full length, into which the ashes from the burned fuel fell. To create a draft, its ends were open to the outside, promoting combustion in the furnace.

"Protecto" ashtray with match pack holder, 3" x 5-1/2". Davanna Collection

ashtray A small vessel in which the ashes of cigars and cigarettes (and even pipes) are deposited.

Ashburton One of the oldest and most famous pressed glass patterns. First made in the 1840s, it was made for several decades by many New England companies and Bakewell, Pears & Company.

ashes The powdery, solid residue that remains when combustible material is burned. In glassmaking, they furnish the necessary alkali. The ashes of marine plants procured in Spain (barilla) and Egypt (roquetta) were used in making early Venetian soda glass; the ashes of kelp as alkali in England, northern France and Scandinavia; the ashes of beechwood in making potash glass in Germany and Bohemia; and the ashes of bracken (fern ash) in France. Bone ash was used as a flux and as an opacifying agent. See *alkali; barilla; roquetta; kelp; potash; fern ash; bone ash; pearl ash; glasswort.*

Asian Artists in Crystal A third in the *Artists Series* made by Steuben. From 130 drawing by various Asian artists, 36 were selected. Completed in 1955, the entire series was made in less than two years. Conceived by Harold Stassen, then Director of the Foreign Operations Administration, after he had viewed Steuben's *British Artists in Crystal*, believed it would improve relations with non-communist Asian countries. It was first exhibited at the National Gallery in Washington, D.C., on January 17, 1956.

askos (Greek) A small receptacle, used in ancient Greece and Rome to hold oil for pouring into lamps, in the form of a low, completely enclosed bowl with an overhead handle and a cylindrical upright or diagonal spout at one end. They range in length from about 2-3/4 to 10 inches. Some were made of Roman glass from the 3rd century BC through the 1st century AD.

aspersorium A shallow bowl with an overhead bail handle used to hold holy water, made in Venice and Spain during the 16th century.

Associated Artists An interior designing and decorating firm founded in 1879 by Louis Comfort Tiffany, Samuel Colman, Lockwood DeForest, and Candice Wheeler, relying greatly on influences of Persia, Byzantine, India, Japan, and North Africa, in a lush surrounding with exotic naturalism.

astragal (1) A die (plural is *dice*) originally made from the astragalus or anklebone in Greece, used in ancient games played with various game pieces. (2) Small convex molding, used as stays to hold windowpanes within a sash (muntins) or as muntins to form a pattern for glass panels. Known in a variety of curved, saltire (X), and geometric configurations, they are often found on bookcase and cabinet doors.

astral glass See *astrale, vetro.*

Astral lamp (Aka *space lamps*) A lamp invented by Count Rumford (Benjamin Thompson, 1753-1814, an English physicist and diplomat, born in the United States). Oil from a central container is conveyed to tubular appendages holding Argand-type burners (see *Argand lamp*). The appendages could be moved over a book or other object to produce a bright light without interference from the lamp base.

astrale, vetro (Aka *astral glass*) Glass objects suggestive of shapes associated with outer space.

at-the-fire The technique of reheating a glass object at a furnace's glory hole to permit it to be reworked with tools to alter its contours or structure or enable additional blowing to take place. Some objects are reheated there to change the color (see *striking*) or surface coloring (see *Aurene glass*). Certain objects are fire polished in this manner.

at-the-flame See *at-the-lamp*.

at-the-lamp (Aka *at-the-flame, lamp-work*) The technique of shaping glass articles over an open flame.

Atco Glass Manufacturing Company (1884-1908) A window glass manufacturing facility founded by John T. Wilcox in Atco, New Jersey, and reorganized in 1893 as the Atco Window Glass Company. It was noted for a unique tradition, called "Girl Night." On Wednesday evenings, during the blowing season, after the second shift ended, workers made novelty items for their wives or girl friends who were invited to watch the operations from a special platform.

Atco Window Glass Company See *Atco Glass Manufacturing Company.*

Atkins, Lloyd An American glass designer who joined the design department at Steuben Glass Works in 1948. He is well known for his ornamental pieces, such as *Quintessence* and *Sea Chase*, which were engraved by others.

Atlantic Coast Glass Company A glass manufacturing facility established during the early 1890s in Barneget, New Jersey. They made pocket bottles and in 1897, were incorporated as the Atlantic Coast Glass Company.

Atlantic Cut Glass Company (1920?-1935) A glass cutting company in Egg Harbor City, New Jersey, making heavy brilliant cut glass, but in its later years, it cut only light wares.

Atlantic Glass Works (1851-1866) A small glass manufacturing facility built by Samuel Crowley, in Crowleytown, New Jersey. In 1852, it was managed by John Huffsey and officially named the Atlantic Glass Works, and made bottles and druggists wares. Clayton Parkes blew the first Mason jars there. (John Landis Mason was never a glassblower, he was a tinsmith who devised the rubber gasket and metal seal, receiving

his first patent on March 7, 1856, and another, more commonly seen on the jars, on November 11, 1858.) In 1858, the Burling Brothers purchased the facility, operating it until it burned in 1866.

Atlas Glass Company See *Consumer Glass Company, Limited.*

Atlas of Oneida Co. See *Dunbarton Glass Works.*

atomizer A device used to dispense a liquid, such as medicine or perfume, in the form of a fine spray or mist. See *perfume atomizer.*

Green glass perfume atomizer with rhinestones set in top, gold overlay, and gold-tone atomizer.
Heartland Discoveries

atrophied edge An incomplete edge on a piece of pattern glass resulting from the mold not being totally filled with molten glass.

Attar of Rose See *scent bottles* (throw-away).

Atterbury & Company See *White House Works.*

Atterbury, Challnor & Hogan See *Pennsylvania Glass Manufacturing Company.*

Aubin See *glass hunt.*

Audubon Plates A series of ten plates made by Steuben in 1947, depicting various birds, one per plate, given to Queen Elizabeth by the United States Ambassador to England as a wedding gift.

Auldjo Jug A jug (*oenochoe*) found, in pieces, in the ruins of Pompeii between 1830 and 1832. It was repaired and refurbished, and took the name of its former owner, Richardson Auldjo. Believed to date to the 2nd or 3rd quarter of the 1st century AD, it is of blue glass encased with white glass, engraved in cameo relief, analogous to that on the Portland Vase. The embellishments consist of vine leaves, grapes, and ivy within a border of doves and foliage. It has a flat base with a molded base ring. The body is globular, the neck short with a short spout and the handle curved up from the body above the neck and downward to the rim.

Aurene glass A blown, iridized art glass developed by Frederick Carder at Steuben, made its debut in 1904 and remained in production until 1933. The name stems from the Latin word *aurum* meaning *gold* and the middle English word *schene* meaning *sheen*. Its satiny iridescence depends upon the ability of certain glasses to keep in solution, in an oxidized state, salts of rare metals. It, when made into various objects and exposed to a reducing flame, becomes coated with a metallic film that may be varied in thickness through flame adjustments. When the reduced metallic coating is of sufficient thickness, it is sprayed with a solution of a tin salt, such as stannous chloride, and heated in an oxidizing flame, resulting in iridescent colors.

If iron chloride is used instead of the tin salt, then followed by the tin salt, a golden color is produced. If the tin and iron sprays are not used, the surface has a high mirror-like gloss. There are only two types of true Aurene: (1) *Gold Aurene* (the earliest, introduced in 1904, had a purplish tinge, successfully eradicated after 1905); and (2) *Blue Aurene* (debut in 1905, having the same formula as Gold Aurene except cobalt was added to the batch, sometimes called *Cobalt Blue Aurene*, shading from dark blue to pale silvery blue); the surfaces of both appear metallic. Sometimes surfaces have wavy lines that were intentional; created when the sprayed areas are enlarged and the glass reheated. Articles fully formed before being reheated have no such lines. From 1904 to 1910, some articles were embellished with lustered applied glass leaves and vines or with trailed, feathered or millefiori decorations. Articles were signed on the base's underside or foot near the pontil mark with either "Aurene" or "Steuben" with a fleur-de-lis (note: articles where the signature or the fleur-de-lis is unusually large are imitations). Paper labels in the shape of large triangles with brown printing were also used.

Many other articles made by Carder resemble Aurene, but are not true Aurene. Various wares called *Red Aurene, Green Aurene,* and *Brown Aurene* were made at Steuben between 1904 and 1910. The name *Red Aurene* is applied to a group of articles made from Calcite or Alabaster glass either partially or totally cased with *Gold Ruby*, having applied Aurene-type embellishments (usually feather motifs or trailed threadings) often combined with floral and leaf shapes. There are also a few solid ruby glass pieces with Aurene-type trailed embellishments and the whole surface slightly iridized that are also called *Red Aurene. Rouge Flambe* is sometimes incorrectly called Red Aurene. *Green Aurene* is usually applied to a group of Calcite or Alabaster glass pieces either totally or partially cased with green glass, having Aurene-type embellishments. *Brown Aurene* is similar to true Aurenes, having an iridescent surface produced by tin chloride sprayed at-the-fire. The glass itself is colored with iron or nickel oxides and cased over Calcite glass. *Platinum Aurene* is a name incorrectly attributed to *Blue Aurene. Ivrene* glass and *verre de Soie* have sometimes incorrectly been called *White Aurene.*

Opaque, iridescent "Aurene" glass cologne bottle, 1920s, 6-1/2" h. x 2-1/2" w.
The Corning Museum of Glass

Aurene Jewels An early 1970s novelty product made by the Imperial Glass Company. It is a dark blue iridized glass.

Aurora A satin and crackle iridescent stretch glass made by the U.S. Glass Company.

Aurora Glass Co. A late 1800s glass manufacturing facility in London, England, which developed a technique for embedding precious metals into a glass object's body, calling it *metallized glass*. It was sometimes coated with flakes of mica, gold, silver, and platinum.

Austin, Charles B., & Co. See *Union Flint Glass Co.*

australite See *tektite.*

Austrian glassware Glassware made in the former Austrian Empire from the 16th century on. In the 16th century, the centers of glassmaking were Vienna, Hall-in-Tyrol, and Innsbruck. The facilities in these cities were operated by Venetians, While those in Graz (Styria) and Henriettental (Carinthia) were operated by natives. From the 16th century through the 19th century, the most prominent centers were in Silesia and Behemia, and in Vienna; those best known today are Lobmeyr, Stolzle, Riedel, Swarovski, and Salzberger.

aventurine glass (1) A translucent glass flecked throughout with oxidized metallic particles, looking like brownish aventurine quartz flecked with mica and other minerals. The earliest known is of Venetian origin, resulting from metallic copper particles being formed chemically by including copper oxide and forge scales in the batch. It was a brownish color, flecked with copper, first recorded in the early 17th century and known as *gold aventurine*. In 1860, a French chemist named Hautefeuille made it by adding to the batch fine iron or brass turnings enclosed in paper. Another method, developed about 1865 by a chemist named Pelouze, produced a greenish color created by adding particles of chromium to the batch (*green aventurine*); made recently by the Fostoria Glass Company. There also was a pink aventurine. The name comes from the Italian words *avventurine* meaning *chance* or *avventurina*, a brown quartz. (2) Small fragments of gold wire sprinkled over the lacquer's surface.

Averbeck Cut Glass Company A retail jewelry store in New York City with a large mail order business in cut glass from 1892 to 1923. Its catalog guaranteed each item to be "Genuine Cut Glass" representing the "labors of skilled artisans." Very few pieces were signed. It purchased its wares from small, relatively unknown cutting shops.

avoider A vessel used to carry items from the table. See *voider.*

Ayotte, Rick A glassworker specializing in lampwork bird paperweights. A native of Nashua, New Hampshire, he studied at the Lowell Technological Institute and worked as a scientific glassblower. In 1970, he established his own business, *Ayotte's Artistry in Glass.* He makes his weights in limited editions of 25 to 75 pieces, each signed with his last name.

Bb

Bacalles Glass Engravers The Bacalles Glass Shop of Corning, New York, sold local glasscutters' wares on a commission basis. The company later hired cutters and engravers to make its own cut and engraved wares, changing its name to Bacalles Glass Engravers. It sold its wares through its own shop, and wholesaled many to Tiffany & Co., the Corning Glass Center, and other retail outlets. It used blanks made in Romania and by Corning Glass and Federal Glass.

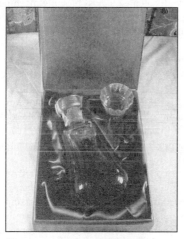

Baccarat crystal decanter, liter capacity. Contents "Bisquit Fine Champagne Cognac," ground stopper, stopper and neck numbered "902."
Davanna Collection

Baccarat Glass Factory A glass manufacturing facility in Baccarat, France, established in 1765, continuing to the present under the following names: 1765, Verreries Renaut & Cie; 1768, Verreries de Baccarat; 1773, Verreries de Sainte-Anne; 1816, Verreries de Voneche a Baccarat; and 1823 on La Compagnie des Cristalleries de Baccarat. While primarily known for its cane and millefiori paperweights from 1860 to 1880, it has made the following: since 1816, crystal; since 1823, agate glass and opaline; since 1824, molded glass bottles with portraits; since 1846, millefiori glassware and paperweights; since 1848, sulfides; since 1851, colored glassware; and since 1867, wheel engraved glass. Today it is famous for its stemware, freely formed cut-glass pieces and paperweights. Bottles with portraits are now made at a branch facility at Trelon. See *Compagnie des Cristalleries de Baccarat; Baccarat paperweight.*

Baccarat paperweights Millefiori and other paperweights were made at Baccarat since 1846. Some are dated between 1846 and 1853; the most common being 1848, the rarest, 1849. In 1848, it made a line of weights called "sulfures," followed by a similar line called "sulfides." It also made *flower, bouquet, subject, and overlay paperweights* and a few *magnum* and *miniature weights,* the majority having a star-cut base.

Baccarat's Amberina See *Rose Teinte.*

Bacchus, George, & Son A glass manufacturing facility in Birmingham, England, specializing in making cameo and flashed glassware. During the early 19th century, it was one of the earliest to embellish glassware with transfer printing.

back painting (1) Painting on the glass's reverse (the side away from that viewed), generally on mirrors, panels, and some Chinese snuff bottles. See *reverse painting on glass; mirror painting; Chinese mirror painting; Chinese snuff bottles; picture engraving.* (2) Painting on stained glass's exterior surface to reproduce a subduing effect like the natural patina on the surface of old glass.

Backus & Fenn See *Peterboro Glasshouse.*

Bacon Goblet A large, colorless goblet, having a rounded funnel bowl on a stem embellished with two knops (each with an enclosed air bubble), a folded foot and is about 12 inches tall. Made in England about 1700, it is named for John Bacon (1886-1948), the Circle of Glass Collectors (London) founder that gave it to the British Museum in his memory.

badging The process of etching a design, name, etc., on glassware with an etching solution.

bag beaker A drinking vessel having a wide mouth, a waisted neck, a pointed bottom, and an overall shape of an extended cloth bag. Made in England in the late 6th century, the majority are embellished with vertical trailing, starting just below the neck and ending at the bottom.

bag wall The wall in an oil or gas fired kiln that prevents the flame from coming in direct contact with the glassware.

Bailey & Dobelmann See *Greenpoint Flint Glass Works.*

bait A tool dipped into molten glass to start a drawing operation. The molten glass sticks to the tool and gravity causes it to trail off, similar to honey on a honey stick.

Baker, Stewart & Co. See *New Boston Glass Works.*

Baker Brothers & Company See *Baltimore Glass Works; Garden Glass Works.*

Bakewell & Company A glass manufacturing facility in Pittsburgh, Pennsylvania, established in 1807 by Robinson & Ensell. In 1808, Benjamin Bakewell, Sr. (1767-1844), purchased Robinson's share, the name becoming Bakewell & Ensell. In 1809, Ensell withdrew and the firm became B. Bakewell & Co., making bottles, flasks, and flint tableware. It added, in 1810, cut and engraved glass. In 1811, Bakewell and Page (joining the firm in 1808) became the sole owners, changing the name to Bakewell & Page. About 1812, it took over the Pittsburgh Flint Glass Manufactory. In 1813, the firm became Bakewell, Page & Bakewell when Benjamin's son Thomas

entered. In 1817, it became the first American glasshouse to supply the White House, making a table service for President James Monroe, followed by another for President Andrew Jackson. At this time, it was recognized as the largest flint glass manufacturer in the western hemisphere. In late 1825, it added pressed glass wares when John Palmer Bakewell, another son of Benjamin's, was granted a patent for pressing glass knobs (the first patent associated with glass pressing in the United States) and began, on a small scale, the first fully mechanical pressing of glass by means of a mold and plunger. In 1827, the name was changed to Bakewell, Page & Bakewells when John Palmer Bakewell entered, and in 1832, Bakewell & Anderson when Alexander M. Anderson entered the firm. Anderson withdrew in 1836, and it reverted to Bakewell, Page & Bakewells. In 1834, John and Thomas Bakewell patented a glass blowing machine. In 1844, Benjamin Bakewell, Sr., died and it became Bakewell, Pears & Co. when John Palmer Pears, a nephew of Benjamin Bakewell, Sr. became a principal. At this time, it offered a complete line of plain, pressed, and cut flint glass wares, and bottles and flasks of all types. In 1845, it burned, and a new facility was built. In 1854, it was moved to the south side of Pittsburgh. On September 29, 1874, Benjamin Bakewell, Jr., received a patent for pressing together glass of two different colors so the two colors bond only where their surfaces contact each other (called *Double Glass*). After several changes of ownership, all including members of the Bakewell family, it closed in 1881 or 1882. It is known for its historical flasks, including "The American System," and for tumblers with sulfides portraying leading citizens in their base. See *American System, The.*

Baldwin, H.C., Cut Glass Shop (1911-1918) A glass cutting shop established by Herbert C. Baldwin in Meridan, Connecticut, moving in 1914 to Wallingford, Connecticut.

ball and claw foot A representation of a talon or claw grasping a ball, frequently made of glass. Used as a foot for chairs, tables, cabinets, etc. It is of Chinese or early Roman derivation.

Ball canning jars, 1/2-pint, pint, quart, 1/2-gallon. Reproductions by Alltrista.
Davanna Collection

Ball Brothers Glass Manufacturing Company
A glass manufacturing facility established in 1880 by the five Ball brothers. Originally it made tin jacketed glass jugs for kerosene and coal oil. In 1884, it began making jars for preserving fruits. The name was changed to Ball Brothers Company, Inc., and, in 1969, to Ball Corporation, before becoming part of Alltrista. The original facility was in Buffalo, NY, later, moving to Muncie, Indiana, and additional facilities in Terre Haute and Greenfield, Indiana, and Coffeyville and La Harpe, Kansas.

ball cover See *ball stopper.*

ball cut See *printie.*

ball knop A knop of spherical shape.

ball mill See *jar mill.*

Variation of the ball stoppered bottle. Ball is in bottle forced against inside of neck. Front: Black & Cox-Manchester w/anchor; back: Aldham Bottle Co., Wombwell; bottom: S & C, 9" h.
Davanna Collection

ball stopper (Aka *ball cover*) A sphere of glass designed to rest on a bottle's mouth. It had three basic purposes: (a) keep contaminants from getting into the bottle, (b) keep the contents fresher by minimizing air contact, and (c) minimizing evaporation. The earliest were made in France between 1700 and 1710. They range in size from about 1/2 inch to one foot.

ball stopper bottle A bottle with a rubber washer in its neck upon which rested a glass ball. The bottle was filled with an effervescent beverage, the ball forced against the washer, secured with a wire or clasp. Hiram Codd is credited with inventing them in England during the early 1870s. They were originally designed to contain a soft drink known as "Codd's Wallop."

Ballinger Glass Pail Works (1878-1883) A glass manufacturing facility in Ravenna, Ohio, making glass pails, buckets, and similar vessels. It was purchased by the Enterprise Glass Co.

balloon A cylinder of glass in the process of being blown.

balloon glass See *brandy glass.*

ballotini Small spheres of glass ranging in size up to 1,500 microns having a variety of industrial uses, including filtering, shot blasting, and grinding. They are used by glassmakers in the various casting processes, mainly *pate de verre* and *cire perdue.*

balsamarium See *unguentarium.*

Balthazar See *wine bottle, sizes.*

Baltic A trademark of the W.P. Hitchcock Company.

Baltimore Bargain House See *American Wholesale Corporation.*

Baltimore Flint Glass Company A flint glass manufacturing facility established in Baltimore, Maryland, in 1820, still operating in 1836, and believed to be the site where John Lee Chapman's bottle manufacturing facility began operations in 1849.

Baltimore Glass Works In 1790, Frederick Amelung & Co. (John Frederick

Magnus Amelung, the son of John Frederick Amelung, and Alexander Furnival, J.F.M. Amelung's father-in-law, were principals) built a glass manufacturing facility in (Spring Garden) Baltimore, Maryland. In 1799, it built another in the city (Federal Hill). They were collectively known as the Baltimore Glass Works, but also the Federal Hill Works, Spring Garden Works, Hughes Street Works, and Patapsco River Glasshouse. It advertised its wares to include "all kinds of white hollow glass, black and green bottles and window glass." It was dissolved in 1802, and Phillip R.I. Friese leased and then purchased the Federal Hill facility. Later George and Jacob Reppert purchased half interest. When Friese died in 1830, Frederick and Lewis Schaum became associated with the Repperts. Later it was operated by Schaum & Everhart. About 1840, Everhart took over the window glass portion. By 1860, the window glass operation was managed by Reitz & Everhart. The Schaum Brothers took over the bottle operations, retaining the name Baltimore Glass Works, closing in 1852. In 1853, Baker Brothers & Company, purchased the Schaum Brothers portion , continuing to make bottles of all kinds, and adding flasks to their line. In 1873, a flint glass facility was constructed that was still operating in the early 20th century.

Baltimore monument flask A United States made, 19th century mold-blown flask picturing the monument commemorating the Battle of North Point of 1815.

baluster An older English drinking glass having a baluster stem, often with internal tears and bubbles; popular in the early 1700s. See *first period baluster; inverted baluster; true baluster; heavy baluster; light baluster; baluster stem; balustroid; balustroid stem.*

baluster stem A stem on a drinking glass or other vessel in the form of a staircase or balcony railing spindle, etc. They are somewhat pear-shaped, swelling some toward the narrow end. When the pear-shaped portion is nearer the bottom, it is a *true baluster*; when nearer the top, it is an *inverted baluster*. Sometimes there are two connecting baluster forms, with either the bulbous ends or the small ends facing each

other. Drinking glasses with such stems are known as *balusters*.

balustroid A baluster drinking glass or other vessel, the stem being more delicate and elongated than the earlier, thicker baluster stem. It has plain knops, or is of inverted baluster form without knops. See *balustroid stem.*

balustroid stem A stem, derived from earlier balusters, that is longer, slimmer and more delicate than the baluster. Most have either a plain single, double, or triple knop, or are of inverted baluster form without knops or, on rare occasion, with one or more knops. They were popular in England from about 1725 to 1760. See *balustroid.*

Bamford Glass Works See *Excelsior Flint Glass Works.*

Bamper-Bayard Glasshouse See *Glass House Company of New York.*

banana boat See *banana bowl.*

banana bowl A bowl, comparable to a berry bowl, except elliptical in shape, similar to a canoe, but with rounded ends. It was used as a fruit server.

Fenton Silver Crest milk glass banana stand, bowl 12" l. x 5" h.
Davanna Collection

banana stand An article that looks like a misshapen cake stand. Instead of a flat glass disk on top of a tall stem, it has a dish that curves up on two sides. They were first imported into the United States in 1804, being made here from about 1865 to 1880.

band, mercury See *mercury band.*

banding (1) The application of bands of enamel or luster to glassware. (2) In stained glass, the process of attaching copper wire to panels of glass.

Bandwurmglas *(German)* Literally, *tapeworm glass.* A beaker that is tall, either cylindrical or club-shaped, has a high kick base, and on its outside a notched spiral or snake-like glass trail or thread. It has been erroneously called a *Passglas,* but a *Passglas* has horizontal, parallel, equidistant dividing lines that the *Bandwurmglas* does not. They were made in the Rhineland during the 15th and 16th centuries.

Banford, Ray & Bob A father and son team that began making paperweights in 1971 in Hammonton, New Jersey. Ray's include bouquets of lampwork roses, irises, lilies-of-the-valley and morning glories; Bob's include single flowers, upright and flat bouquets, dragonflies, bumblebees, salamanders, and snakes. They both made some overlay weights. Bob's are signed with a signature cane with a red "B" within a white ground and a blue rim; Ray's with a signature cane with a black "B" in a white ground. Some of their earlier pieces were signed in a variety of color combinations.

bangle An ornamental, ring-shaped bracelet or anklet made in numerous places from about 300 BC to the present. Glass ones were popular during the 19th century. They are currently being made in Nigeria.

Pale amethyst, colorless glass bank with aquamarine striations, 5-1/2" h.
The Corning Museum of Glass

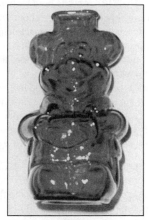

Cobalt-blue glass bank, "Mickey Mouse"-type, 6-1/2" h.
Davanna Collection

bank A receptacle for saving small amounts of money, usually coins. Some were made of glass, particularly in the United States. Earlier ones generally were hand crafted, newer ones pressed. Made by several companies, the two most famous makers were Boston & Sandwich Glass Co. and New England Glass Co.

bar A piece of glass formed by fusing several canes or rods together which may be cut into slices, each having the same design, and used for inlays and mosaic glass.

bar bottle A bottle, essentially an ordinary decanter with a more prominent lip. A decanter has a small lip with a ground neck, fitted with a ground glass stopper; a bar bottle, a heavy rounded lip, fitted with a cork stopper. See *bar lip.*

bar lip A lip on early pressed and mold-blown decanters, with either a thick rolled edge or ring of applied glass. See *bar bottle.*

bar tumblers See *double shot glass.*

Barbara Potters Goblet See *Potters, Barbara, Goblet.*

barbarico, vetro *(Italian)* An ornamental cased glass, developed in 1951, by Ercole Barovier for Barovier & Toso. The base glass has an overall pattern of metallic blue, small blotches, cased with transparent glass.

barber bottle A bottle used by barbers to hold various liquids. First used about 1850, they continued in use after the enactment of the Food & Drug Commission Act of 1906, forbidding re-use of such bottles for sanitary reasons. They were made in every type of glass, with every type of decoration and in a variety of shapes, but usually either quart or fifth size, and often sold in sets that might include a shaving paper vase, a finger bowl, a talcum sifter and a soap sifter. See *tree bark bottle.*

barber pole paperweight A Clichy paperweight formed like a checkered or paneled weight; the difference being the florets are separated by areas of white filigrana glass encircled by a twist of opaque colored glass, generally red, but often blue or other colors.

Barber rose See *Millville Rose.*

Barberini Vase See *Portland Vase.*

barilla A marine plant found in the salt marshes of southeastern Spain and other areas of the Mediterranean. The ash produced from its burning was a source of impure soda used in making both soap and glass. European and English glassmakers, during the 15th and 16th centuries, purchased it for their furnaces. After the development of lead glass, it lost its importance and today, chemically made soda has replaced it.

barium A chemical element occasionally added to the glass batch as an oxide. In mold-pressed glass, it imparts a silvery ice-like appearance. It is also used in some optical glasses. It has been used in making glass in China for over 2,000 years.

barium crown glass An optical glass. See *optical glass.*

barn lantern A lantern, used to light one's way from the house to outbuildings, specifically designed to prevent mishaps caused by errant flames and sparks or drops of hot fuel since they were often near hay, straw, and other flammables.

Barncroft, Barnard Company In April 1905, the company that took over the old Boston & Sandwich facility in Sandwich, Massachusetts. It made glass for a short time before closing.

Barnegat Glass Company (1907-1913) A glass manufacturing company, making glass vials. After 1908, the Co-operative Glass Company took over operations, making green glass bottles.

Barnes, Faupel & Company See *Belmont Glass Works.*

barometer (Aka *weather glass*) An instrument used to determine atmospheric pressure and anticipating weather changes, consisting of a thin, graduated tube in a vertical position. The tube is sealed at the upper end, open at the lower, and partially filled with liquid. The open end is placed in a reservoir of the liquid, subject to atmospheric changes in pressure and, as it fluctuates, the fluid level of the tube rises and falls.

baroque The style of art and architecture prevalent from about 1550 to the late 18th century when it was superceded by the *rococo* style. It is highlighted by the use of curved and contoured forms that appear dynamic and mobile, and by classical symmetrical embellishment.

Barovier, Anzolo (*Angelo*) A master glassmaker and technician from Murano, credited with raising the art of glassmaking to new artistic and technical levels. From 1424, he held official positions of increasing importance in Murano. He introduced to the art of glassmaking and decorating many new processes and techniques, and reintroduced many old ones. He contributed to the development of *cristallo* and was, with Nocolo Mozetto, in February 1457, granted a concession to make it. He died in 1460. See *Barovier, Ercole.*

Mellon rib vase attributed to Barovier, deep teal top to golden amber base, 9-1/2" h.
Tri-State Antiques

Barovier, Ercole (1889-1974) A descendent of Anzolo Barovier, he fostered the development of modern glass varieties, styles, and forms in Venice and was one of the founders of Barovier & Toso. See *Barovier & Toso.*

Barovier, Marie (Marietta) A relative of Anzolo Barovier who, in 1487, was the first woman in Venice permitted to build a glass furnace for cane making and firing of enameled decoration.

Barovier & Toso A glass manufacturing facility established in 1936 by Ercole Barovier and Artemio and Decio Toso, specializing in making custom-made lighting fixtures of industrial quality, chandeliers, and ornamental glass and a leader in the development of many new techniques. See *aborigene, vetro; barbarico, vetro; damasco, vetro; diafano, vetro; gemmato, vetro; primavera, vetro; rugiadoso, vetro; sidone, vetro.*

Barovier Cup A wedding chalice (made about 1475 at Murano) of blue glass with the bowl resting on a hollow spreading base. On opposite sides of the bowl are enameled medallions of the bride and groom, which divide an encircling frieze: one part portraying a procession of horsemen and ladies, the other women bathing at the Fountain of Love. The enameling is mainly dark green with sections in blue, red, and gold. It was believed to have been made by Anzolo Barovier, but now is not because of its Renaissance style predominant in the 1470s, at least 10 years after Barovier's death.

barrel flask A flask in barrel form with hoops of trailed glass, short feet, and neck, to be placed horizontally and used to hold brandy. They were made in the late 2nd and early 3rd centuries of Roman glass and in the 17th and 18th centuries in Spain, Germany, France, and Venice.

barrel lantern A lantern, cylindrical in cross section as opposed to those that are square, rectangular or flat-front, half-round.

barrel-shaped goblet See *hotel goblet.*

Barrett, Henry The inventor and patentee (1872) of the internal screw stopper for bottles.

Barryville Cut Glass Shop (1910-1932) A glass cutting shop established in Barryville, New York, by William H. Gibbs & Company; sold in 1912 to Krantz & Sell Company. See *Krantz-Smith Company; Gibbs, Kelly & Company.*

bars In cut glass, a design made from double or multiple parallel miters.

Barth Art Company An early 1940s association of glass grinders, polishers, and cutters founded by Harry Barth. It also made molds that were assigned to Paden City Glass Company and others. Some of the glassware made by these companies from the molds was returned to Barth for further decorating. In 1950, it sold some animal figurine molds to Viking Glass Company. When Paden closed in 1951, most of the Barth molds were sold to the Canton Glass Company.

Barth Art Glass See *New Martinsville Glass Manufacturing Company.*

Bartlett-Collins (Sapulpa) Glass Company The first facility to make glass in Oklahoma prior to the Depression and, by 1931, the only independent facility making tableware west of the Mississippi. It made hand-crafted glassware until 1941, then began using machines and modern methods.

baryta glass A glass made with barium oxide, baryta (BaO), and lime. It was less brilliant, and cheaper to make, than lead glass, but more brilliant than ordinary glass.

bas relief (French) See *low relief.*

basal rim or ring (1) The ring around the bottom of a concave base of some paperweights. (2) See *foot ring.*

Basdorf glass (Aka *glass porcelain*) Glass made at two facilities near Basdorf, Germany, during the 3rd quarter of the 18th century. It was made of crushed green glass mixed with gypsum and lime, forming an opaque white glass resembling porcelain, often with enameled flowers. It was first made experimentally at the Tornow facility by a glassmaker named Schopp, about 1750, and then at Stennewitz (see *Schopp's glass*).

base (1) The bottom of a vessel on which it stands or rests. See *kick base; splayed base; star cut base; foot.* (2) The bottom of a paperweight. (3) Chemical substances, typically metal oxides, hydroxides, or compounds that give up hydroxide ions in aqueous solutions. They react with protonic acids, neutralizing them, forming salt and water.

base ring A ring of glass applied to an object's base after the body is formed. It is normally flattened somewhat so its edge extends beyond the base, providing an even support. See *coil base; pad base; foot ring.*

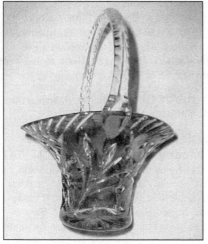

Cut-to-clear basket on figured blank, amber over clear glass with clear glass handle, 8-3/4" h.
Davanna Collection

basket (1) A glass vessel in the form of a basket. Many were made at Murano, and in the Netherlands and Spain during the 18th century. They have been made in every type of glass with every type of embellishment and are solely for ornamental purposes. See *bride's basket; trellis-work basket; Art Glass basket.* (2) A funnel-shaped embellishment surrounding the primary motif of some paperweights. See *basket ground; basket paperweight.*

basket ground A ground in the shape of a funnel made of double swirl canes of filigrana glass. St. Louis weights frequently had a basket ground.

basket paperweight (1) A paperweight whose primary motif is a basket made up of a circle of staves surrounding millefiore canes, all being enclosed inside the dome. They were made in France, mainly by Clichy and St. Louis, and in Bohemia where, in some, the staves are crowned by twisted ribbons. (2) A paperweight shaped like a basket with vertical staves surrounding millefiore canes. Sometimes the rim and the base are covered in an entwined ribbon cable (*torsade*). Some were made by Clichy.

Bassett Glass Works (Aka *Elmer Glass Works*) A glass manufacturing facility established in 1896 by Samuel Bassett in Elmer, New Jersey, making a variety of bottles. In 1898, it was sold to Gilchrist Jar Company, specializing in battery jars. In 1901, the Novelty Glass Company took over, and made fruit jars using patented molds; patent owners sued, forcing it to close. It was later reopened by Isaac Townsend who operated it for about one year before closing in 1908.

Bastow Glass Company (1) Harry Bastow worked for Harry Northwood in Ellwood City, Pennsylvania, in 1895, and succeeded him as chief operating officer of the Northwood facility in Indiana, Pennsylvania. In 1900, he and some fellow workmen from the facility established the Jefferson Glass Company in Steubenville, Ohio. In October 1903, Bastow established his own facility in an abandoned tile factory in Coudersport, Pennsylvania. Frank and John Fenton, who later established their own company, went with Bastow. His products were similar to those made at the Northwood and Jefferson facilities. The Coudersport facility burned in 1904 and was never rebuilt. In 1912, Bastow was working for the West Virginia Optical Glass Company. (2) A company established about 1909, in Weston, West Virginia, making lighting wares.

bat (1) Refractory shelves used in kiln firing to hold wares. (2) The material, usually wood or sheets of plywood, used for mold bases.

batch (Aka *mixture*) The sum of all the different raw materials needed to make a definitive amount of a specific glass type. The raw materials include sand, one or more fluxing agents, decolorizers or coloring agents, stabilizers, refining agents and cullet. See *three, two, one batch.*

batch cart A cart, pushtruck or wagon, generally made of iron, used to transport the batch from the mixing room to the glass furnace, then placed in the pot or tank for melting.

batch room (Aka *mixing room*) A room or area in which a batch's components are mixed in proper proportions by weight. The ingredients, until relatively recently, were hand mixed.

bathroom set See *toilet set.*

Batsto Glass Works The first facility was built in Batsto in 1846 by Jesse Richards, making window glass. The glass quality varied greatly and, as a result, four grades were established. In 1848, these were Union Extra, Union First, Greenbush Patent and Neponset Patent, later named Star & Moon, Jesse Richards, Sterling and Washington. In 1851, there were numerous complaints because the quality of the glass within each grade was not uniform. Further, the glass was not cut to measure, and large sheets were often bowed and broken on arrival at their destination. About three miles away, in what is now Nesco, New Jersey, the New Columbia Glass Works (Aka *New Batsto Glass Works*) (See *New Columbia Glass Works*) was erected, making window glass and panes for street lamps. In 1866, the Batsto Glass Works burned, was quickly rebuilt and placed in operation. However, in February 1867, the workers struck, wanting to be paid in cash rather than scrip, and in June, 1867, it closed. Batsto, completely restored, is now owned by the State of New Jersey.

battle scenes A form of embellishment prevalent during, or as a consequence of, a conflict of some type, depicting military battles or engagements, camp scenes, individual confrontations, etc. It was usually depicted in enameling, gilding, engraving, Schwarzlot, etc.

battledor(e) A flat square or rectangular wooden paddle, with a handle projecting from the center of one edge. It was used to flatten the bottoms of vessels, other articles, and feet while the glass was still hot and pliable. It was always soaked in water so it charred rather than burned when it came into contact with the hot glass.

battleship trays Pressed glass boxes or covered trays shaped like United States Navy marine vessels (ironclads) of the 1890s; made following the end of the Spanish-American War.

battute, vetro *(Italian)* Literally, *beaten glass.* An ornamental glass object, the entire exterior ground lightly (forming countless, minute random marks) with an abrasive wheel, created by Venini. It has the appearance of being battered.

Bavarian glassware Glassware made in Bavaria, in southern Germany, adjacent to Bohemia. Its major glass manufacturing centers are Nuremberg and Ratisbon (now Regensburg).

Bay State Glass Company A glass manufacturing facility established in the late 1840s (or 1853, depending on the source) in East Cambridge, Massachusetts, by Norman S. Cate & Company. Incorporated as Bay State Glass Company in 1857, it made flint glassware, chemical and druggist wares, kerosene and oil lamps and lanterns, lamp chimneys, other lighting wares, tablewares, door knobs and "silver glass reflectors." In 1851, it operated as Cate & Phillips. In 1873, it was purchased by John P. Squires and William W. Kimball who operated it until it closed in 1877.

bay window A window, usually curved or three sided, which projects outward from a building's wall; decorative glass is often found in the transome or upper sash.

Bayard, Samuel, & Company See *New Windsor Glass House.*

Bayot & Cummings See *St. Louis Flint Glass Works.*

bead A small, usually perforated, object, often spherical, but also cylindrical, oblate, polyhedral or irregularly shaped, generally strung on a cord with other beads, either identical, similar, or dissimilar. They have been made for personal use and commercial trade since earliest times and are usually made from a hollow glass tube, solid glass rod or glass ribbon. See *cane eye bead; chevron bead; colored bead; crumb bead; double strip bead; eye bead; flush crumb bead; leech bead; mosaic bead; glass paste bead; ring eye bead; spot bead; stratified eye bead.*

beaded edge An embellishment on an article's edge or rim consisting of a continual series of very small relief beads.

beaded knop A knop blanketed with minute beads in relief.

beaded ware Glassware, the exterior encrusted with miniature multicolored threaded beads forming a design that looks like *petit point* embroidery and fashionable during the second and third quarters of the 19th century.

beading (1) An embellishment consisting of a continuous series of miniature relief beads. (2) A line motif found on cut glass made by cutting two long parallel miters in close proximity and notching the area between them so the end result resembles a string of beads. See *notched prism.*

beak A lip on some pouring vessels extending to a point, like the bottom of a sparrow's beak.

beaker (1) A drinking glass shaped like a tall handless tumbler, often with a flared mouth and tapering sides (some have vertical sides). Some have a stemmed foot or three bun feet, and some have a cover. The present definition of a *beaker* indicates that it has *no* handles; but, it originally applied to a vessel with a handle and spout. (2) A wide cylindrical glass vessel with vertical sides, a slightly flared rim and pouring lip, usually of heat resistant glass used by chemists and druggists. See *animal beaker (Tierhumpen); bag beaker; bell beaker; button beaker (Knopfbecker); claw beaker; Castle Eden claw beaker; concave beaker; Come Again beaker (Wiederkommehumpen); cone beaker; cylinder beaker (Walzenbecker); dolphin beaker; drop beaker (Nuppenbecker); Elector's Beaker (Kurfurstenhumpen); figured beaker; footed beaker; Hope Beaker; Imperial Eagle Beaker (Reichsadlerhumpen); Kempston Beaker; Koula Beaker; medallion beaker (Medaillonbecker); mortar beaker; network beaker (vasa diatreta); Orpheus Beaker; ox head beaker (Ochsenkopf); Reformation Beaker; ring beaker; shellfish beaker; truck beaker (Russelbecher); trunk beaker (claw beaker); Welcome beaker (Willkommhumpen).*

bear jar A 19th century, bear-shaped jar made in the United States to hold bear grease.

beaten glass See *battute, vetro.*

Beatty, A.J. See *Kilgore & Hanna; Beatty-Brady Glass Company; Tiffin (Art) Glass Company.*

Beatty, Alexander J., & Sons See *Beatty-Brady Glass Company.*

Beatty & Stillman See *Kilgore & Hanna.*

Beatty-Brady Glass Company A glass manufacturing company established in Steubenville, Ohio, by Kilgore & Hanna in 1830, with a second built in 1898 in Dunkirk, Indiana (this being moved to Tiffin, Ohio). In 1900, both facilities became part of the U.S. Glass Company; the Steubenville facility as *Factory S* and the Tiffin facility, known as Alexander J. Beatty & Sons, as *Factory R.* See *Kilgore & Hanna.*

Beaumont Glass Company A glass-decorating facility founded in 1895, by Percy J. Beaumont, Harry Northwood's wife's brother, in the old Northwood facility in Martins Ferry, Ohio. It originally decorated glass by staining, etching, gold banding, etc. In 1898, it began making glass and, in 1902, moved to Grafton, West Virginia, selling the Martins Ferry facility to the Haskins Glass Company, a maker of electrical lighting, which, in 1906, moved into the abandoned West Virginia Glass Company facility, also in Martins Ferry. In 1906, Beaumont sold to Hocking Glass, and a new company was formed, the Tygert Valley Glass Company. Beaumont opened another decorating shop in Morgantown, West Virginia, which he operated for only a short time.

Beaver Falls Co-operative Glass Company A short-lived glass manufacturing company founded in Beaver Falls, Pennsylvania, in 1879. See *Co-operative Flint Glass Company.*

Beaver Falls Glass Company A glass manufacturing facility established in Beaver Falls, Pennsylvania, during 1887. It made a variety of pressed glass, and closed in the 1890s. About 1900, the Imperial Glass Company occupied the facility.

Beaver Flint Glass Company A glass manufacturing facility established during 1897 in Toronto, Canada, originally making chemical, pharmaceutical and scientific wares. Soon after it added bottles and jars—mainly preserve jars. In later years, it was a wholesaler of medical glassware and supplies.

Beck, Phillips & Company A window glass and preserving jar manufacturing facility established in 1866 in Pittsburgh, Pennsylvania. In 1874, it was operated by Phillips & Company; still operating in 1886.

Beck, Washington (Aka *"Wash"* *Beck*). Considered to be the most outstanding American mold maker of the 19th century, he made molds for facilities in the United States and abroad. His facility in Pittsburgh, Pennsylvania, founded in 1857/8, is believed to have been the largest in the United States. He received nine patents, inventing the first practical power pressing machine (patent received May 4, 1875).

Becker, Benjamin A glasscutter associated with two glass cutting houses; Becker & Wilson and Becker & Brisbois. After Becker and Brisbois split in 1918, he continued to cut in Brooklyn, New York. In 1920, Charles Becker took over and, by 1923, started another on Long Island, New York. For a brief period both shops operated simultaneously. See *Becker & Brisbois; Becker & Wilson.*

Becker, Charles See *Becker, Benjamin.*

Becker & Brisbois (1912-1918) A glass-cutting house in Brooklyn, New York. Becker was formerly associated with Becker & Wilson. See *Becker, Benjamin; Becker & Wilson: Brisbois, Victor.*

Becker & Wilson A glass-cutting house operating in Brooklyn, New York, from 1889 to 1903, then moving to Montrose, Pennsylvania. In 1908, it opened another in New Brunswick, New Jersey. In 1912, Becker sold to Joseph Wilson who operated it until 1914, as Mahon & Wilson. Becker joined with Victor Brisbois, forming Becker & Brisbois.

Beckett & Fisler See *Fislerville Glass Works.*

bed warmer (Aka *virgin*) A vessel filled with hot water and placed in a bed to heat it before the occupant got in.

Beecher, Thomas, Glassworks A glass manufacturing facility believed to have been founded by Thomas Beecher. It operated for a short period about 1776 in Hartford, Connecticut.

beehive foot A domed foot with external horizontal ridges, having the appearance of a beehive.

beer wagon (Aka *bottle slider*) A wheeled coaster designed to hold bottles on the table. The bottles were placed on it and pushed from guest to guest.

Beilby, William, Ralph, and Mary William, Jr. (1740-1819), Mary (1749-97), and Ralph (1743-1817) were the daughter and sons of William Beilby, Sr. (1715-65), a gold- and silversmith. Mary and William, Jr. were enamellers at Newcastle-upon-Tyne; Ralph was an engraver there. William and Mary worked at the Dagnia-Williams facility from 1762 until 1774, the year Mary had a paralytic stroke. In 1778, they moved to Fife in Scotland. William added "junr" to his signed ware until 1765, when his father died.

Beinglas (*German*) Literally, *bone glass*. Milk-and-water glass.

Belfast glassware Glassware made in, nearby, or attributed to, Belfast, Ireland, since 1776. Initially by Benjamin Edwards, Senior, at Long Bridge. See *Irish glassware.*

Belgian glassware Glassware made from the 5th century to the present in the area today known as Belgium. By the mid-16th century, glassworkers had come from Murano to work at Antwerp and others from L'Altare to work at Liege. See *Frankish glass; South Netherlands glassware; Voneche Glassworks; Val St. Lambert.*

Left: cranberry flashed, pressed glass; right: ruby flashed, cut-to-clear. Both goblets with modified stem and no foot.
Davanna Collection

bell (1) A hollow vessel, usually of inverted cup-shape, with an everted rim, rung by a clapper, hammer, or other object. Glass bells came into prominence in the early 1800s; some functional, but most purely ornamental, such as those made from goblets with no foot and modified stem. Following is a partial list of the types and kinds of glass bells: *Akro Agate bells* (from 1930 in white and other opaque colors); *Avon bells* (from 1967); *Baccarat bells* (late 19th century with shaded swirl pattern); *Bohemian bells* (most common is about 4-1/2 inches in deep ruby with various scenes; other colors included amber, green, blue and black; many reproductions); *Burmese Art Glass bells* (rare, from Mt. Washington Glass Company); *Bristol glass bells* (semi-opaque from the 19th and 20th centuries, often embellished with gold and enamel trim); *Cambridge glass bells* (made off and on from 1901 to 1954); *Carnival glass bells* (made from 1900 to 1925, many reproductions); *custard glass bells* (pressed or mold blown; many made by Northwood); *Durand glass bells* (usually made from goblet molds without the stem from 1920 to 1931); *Fenton glass bells* (clear and satin glass, some with enameling); *Lalique glass bells* (most popular from the Art Deco period); *Mary Gregory glass bells* (several made in the early 1900s; many reproductions); *milk glass bells* (popular in the late 1800s); *pressed glass bells* (made from the late 1820s to date); *Steuben glass bells* (clear, iridescent, controlled bubble and other unusual types); *Tiffany glass bells* (made after 1890, many in Favrile glass, some with gold openwork clappers); *Venetian glass bells* (made since the 13th century). Also see *hand bell; table bell; smoke bell.* (2) The hollow ball-shaped object formed at the end of a blowpipe when the molten glass is first blown.

bell beaker A beaker similar in shape to an inverted bell with concave sides, a wide mouth and curvilinear bottom, often with a center finial. They were made during the Frankish period from about the 5th to the 7th centuries.

bell bowl A bowl on a drinking glass shaped like an inverted bell.

bell decanter A bell-shaped decanter.

bell flask A bell-shaped flask.

bell glass A bell jar.

bell goblet A goblet, having an ordinary bowl, but no stem or foot, with a bell attached to the bottom, rung by the drinker when a refill or service was needed. To place the goblet on a table, it had to be emptied and inverted. They were made in the Netherlands and in Germany.

bell jar (Aka *glass bell, bell glass*) A glass container, open at the bottom and closed at the top, similar to a bell, with a finial or handle at the top to lift it. It is used as a dust cover or enclosure for an item, such as a watch or clock, or display. They exist in many sizes and are frequently used in laboratories to house instruments sensitive to dust or vapors.

bell tone The distinctive tone usually associated with cut glass or other quality glassware. It is generated when the object is struck or tapped lightly. The article's shape is a determining factor. Hemispherical articles, such as bowls and goblets, will produce the best tone (even poorer quality glass will produce a tone) while decanters and other objects with small mouths will not produce one, regardless of the glass's quality.

Bellaire Goblet Company A glass manufacturing facility founded in 1876/1878 in Bellaire, Ohio. It made mainly goblets and stemware before moving to Findlay, Ohio, in 1888. In May 1889, it burned and a new and larger facility was built, beginning operation in August 1889. In February 1891, the United States Glass Company was formed and, on June 27 of that year, it joined the combine (*Factory M*), making stemmed goblets, cordials, and wine glasses; tumblers and mugs in a variety of patterns (pressed, cut and engraved); and novelty items prior to joining the combine. On December 8, 1892, the workers were let go and the furnaces banked. On January 12, 1893, the natural gas was turned off and all machinery, boilers, and the entire mixing room were moved to Gas City, Indiana, where a new facility (*Factory U*) was built.

Belleville Cut Glass Company A glass cutting company established in Ontario, Canada, in 1912, operating for only a short time.

Mid-19th century bellows flask, unknown maker. Museum of American Glass at Wheaton Village, Millville, NJ.

bellows flask A flask having a shape similar to a bellows, with an egg-shaped body, a long tapering upright neck and base resembling bellows' handles. They were made in the United States and England during the 19th century.

belly flagon A vessel used in a barbershop, held by a customer across his stomach as a *catchall*. Their usual shape was quarter-mooned, although some were rectangular.

Belmont Glass Company (1866-1890) A glass manufacturing facility founded by Barnes, Feupel & Company in Bellaire, Ohio, making large quantities of pressed glass. In the late 1860s, it had its own foundry, making its own molds as well as molds for other glass companies.

Belmont Tumbler Company (1915-1935) A facility established in Bellaire, Ohio. Until 1925, it only decorated glass, mainly tumblers. In 1925, it began, on a small scale, to make small glass objects.

belt hook A small oblong article with an openwork orifice for a belt, made in China, originally of jade. During the Han Dynasty (200 BC to 220 AD), many were made of glass in imitation jade.

Beltzhoover, Wendt & Co. See *Pennsylvania Flint Glass Works*.

Benedictus, Edouard Inventor of laminated glass in 1903.

benitier (French) The basin at the entrance of Roman Catholic churches for holding holy water; a holy water stoup.

Benners, H.B. & J.M.; Benners, Smith & Campbell See *Kensington Glass Works*.

bent glass Glass that is not flat, such as that used in china cabinets, lampshades, etc.

Berain motifs An embellishment having as its main feature mythological and grotesque figures and half-figures, also with drapes, scrollwork, urns, balustrades and other objects, having the appearance of floating in space. The style was derived from the design books of Jean Berain and represents a transitional stage between *baroque* and *rococo*.

Bergen & Niland See *Bergen, J.D., Company*.

Bergen & Son See *Bergen Cut Glass Company*.

Bergen, J.D., Company (1880-1916) A glass cutting company established in Meriden, Connecticut, originally operated as Bergen & Niland. In 1885, Bergen bought out Niland and formed the J.D. Bergen

Company. Niland continued to work for Bergen until 1896, leaving to establish Thomas A. Niland & Company. Niland soon sold his interest in this new company, returning to work for Bergen in 1897. It used two signatures: the earlier, two intersecting globes in a circle; the later, and most common, the name "Bergen" in script.

Bergen Cut Glass Company (1912-mid 1930s) A glass cutting company established in St. Louis, Missouri. In 1913, its name became Bergen-Phillips Cut Glass Company, being changed back to Bergen Cut Glass Company in 1914. In 1921, it became Bergen & Son. During its later years the company operated as Bergen Glass Works and Bergen Glass Company.

Bergen, Val, Cut Glass Company A glass cutting company established about 1907 in Columbia, Pennsylvania, closing in the early 1920s, making brilliant-cut patterns on heavy blown crystal blanks.

Bergen Glass Company; Bergen Glass Works; Bergen-Phillips Cut Glass Company See *Bergen Cut Glass Company.*

Bergen & Walter See *Williamsburgh Flint Glass Works.*

Berkemeyer *(German)* A variation of a Romer, made of Waldglas, with a funnel-shaped bowl at the top, becoming cylindrical near the base; the cylindrical portion embellished with prunts. They were made in the Rhineland and the Netherlands during the 16th and 17th centuries.

Berkshire Crystal Window Glass Company A window glass manufacturing facility established in 1853 in Berkshire, Massachusetts. It was still operating in 1880. See *Berkshire Glass Company.*

Berkshire Glass Company A window and bottle glass manufacturing facility incorporated in 1847 in Berkshire, Massachusetts. In 1853, it built another facility at Lanesboro. Operations ceased about 1857 at the Berkshire site. (It may be that this company and the Berkshire Crystal Window Glass Company were the same. It is possible Lanesboro

facility was, in reality, the Berkshire Crystal Window Glass Company since both were reported to have begun operations in 1853 and continued to operate after the Berkshire Glass Company closed in 1857.) The facility in Lanesboro operated until about 1880.

Berleue Cut Glass Company A glass-cutting house established by Floyd Berleue in 1922 in Walnut Grove, Pennsylvania. It closed in 1930, resumed operations in 1934, and closed in 1940.

Berluze A vase introduced in 1900 by Daum Brothers with an egg-shaped body and tall, narrow neck, protruding upright from the body to a height almost twice that of the body. They were often embellished with floral patterns or woodland scenes.

berry bowl One of two types of circular bowls. While the standard size bowl is about 8 inches in diameter, berry bowls range in size from 3 inches in diameter and very shallow (*individual serving dish*) to 10 inches in diameter by 5 inches deep (*serving bowl*). See *berry set.*

berry set A large bowl (*serving bowl*) with matching smaller bowls (*for serving individuals*), used for serving fruit and other desserts. See *berry bowl.*

Best Metal A trade name for blanks of exceptionally high quality made by Corning.

Bethany Glass Works A window glass manufacturing facility established in Bethany, Pennsylvania, in 1818, failing after a few years and closing. In 1829, it was placed back in operation, making window glass until it closed during 1839.

betrothal glass See *marriage glass.*

Better Homes Bureau A trademark registered in 1925, by Abraham & Straus, of Brooklyn, New York, and used on glassware it sold. It was applied with a paper label, on which was represented a house and the words "Better Homes Bureau." It did not make glassware, purchasing it wholesale from various manufacturers and decorators.

Betty lamp A small lamp with an upright handle of varying length used by cooks, being

lowered into a pot or kettle, to determine the condition of its contents; the handle used for lowering and hanging it on the wall. The usual fuel was animal or vegetable fat. They are also known as cruisie, developed during the early 17th century. The *double cruisie* was developed, during the late 17th century, with a pan to catch the drippings. By 1700, the wick holder design was improved so two or more wicks could be used and a drip pan was not needed. During the mid-18th century, the design was again improved by including a spreading hollow foot, weighted with sand.

beveled glass Flat glass where the edges, usually meeting at right angles, are cut away, forming a chamfered corner, introduced about 1676. Beveling is done for two reasons: (1) for decorative effect and (2) to minimize chipping. An additional advantage on mirrors is that they cause light to refract into a rainbow of colors. Very old beveled glass is shallowly beveled while the newer is deeply beveled. See *bevels, hand processed; bevels, machine processed.*

Bever, S.C., & Co. See *New Albany Glass Works.*

beverage set A pitcher with a matching set of tumblers for serving drinks.

bibelots See *objects of vertu.*

biberon A bottle used for feeding, having a spherical or egg-shaped body resting on a flattened bottom or stemmed foot, a single handle (usually in the shape of a scroll loop), and a thin neck with a long, curved spout opposite the handle. Occasionally they have a cover and/or stopper. Some were made in Venice and Spain during the 17th century.

Biblical subjects Subjects based on persons, locations, incidents and/or events found in the Bible, either in the Old or New Testament, depicted in glass or used as embellishment on glassware. The earliest have been found on Roman glass, engraved in the 4th to the 6th centuries. They did not regain prominence again until the 15th and 16th centuries. See *religious subjects.*

Bicheroux A modern mechanized technique for making sheet glass wherein the glass is made, in sheet form, from between rollers. One of the main advantages is, as the glass exits the rollers, it requires little grinding and polishing.

bichrome Embellishment employing two colors.

bicolor See *bichrome.*

bidoro (*Japanese*) *Glass.* Because of the country's early lack of interest in making glass, the Japanese term is derived from either the Spanish (*vidrio*) or the Portuguese (*vidro*).

Biedermeier style A style of embellishment emanating in Germany about 1820. It was fashionable for the next 20 years, succeeding the Empire style on the European continent. Its name comes from two eccentric middleclass characters lacking refinement and culture with petty and materialistic values; created by Ludwig Eichradt and named Biedermann and Bummelmeier. The style in England is similar to the William IV and early Victorian. Vividly colored glass and engraved flashed glass of immense form, but somewhat crude, took the place of clear cut glass. Numerous elaborately cut picturesque engravings were made during this period.

bifocal lens A lens having two distinct focal lengths, to provide the wearer both close and distant vision. In the majority of cases, the lower section of the lens is smaller than the upper and used for close work, such as reading, while the larger upper section is used for distant vision. In a few cases the reverse is true; the smaller section, for closer work, being on top, used by those having an occupation requiring looking up for close work, such as electricians, pipefitters, etc. The bifocal lens is believed to have been invented by Benjamin Franklin (1706-1790) in an effort to save him from changing glasses when looking from distant objects to close ones or viceversa. They were refined in the 1890s by Bosch, fusing a piece of high-density flint glass onto a crown glass blank (*fused bifocal* type). In the early 1940s, British lens maker A.H. Emerson developed a method of grinding two distinct areas of different power on the same lens (*solid* or *one-piece bifocal*); the complete lens made of crown glass, harder than flint, and more resistant to scratches. This was succeeded by another in which the small portion was supplanted by a larger area for reading (*executive lens*). Another breakthrough is one of a graduated lens on which there is no definitive dividing line between sections; the power changing gradually from top to bottom (*graduated bifocals* or *progressive bifocals*).

Big Pine Key Glass Works A glass manufacturing facility established by Lester Cunningham in Big Pine Key, Florida, making paperweights, flasks and giftware items before closing in 1973.

Bigaglia, Pietro The originator of the millefiore paperweight. He exhibited it in Vienna during 1845 at the Exhibition of Austrian Industry. It was a 2-inch cube embellished in white filigranna; some canes possess his initials and the date 1845. Others created by him are in the more traditional spherical form, also being initialed and dated 1845.

biidori-e (Japanese) Glass plaques painted with landscapes or engraved with designs, exhibited as individual works of art or inset into furniture, walls, lacquer trays, combs, fans, etc.

Biltmore A trademark of the W.P. Hitchcock Co.

BIMAL A term for older bottles that were blown in the mold with applied lip.

Hummingbird feeders, at left: amber-glass grape cluster; at right: purple shading to pink with metallic finish.
Davanna Collection

Bird fountain base with a quart Mason/Ball jar containing water inverted over it.
Davanna Collection

bird feeder or fountain A container designed to hold food (solid or liquid) for birds, having a small spout or port at or near the bottom providing them access. During the 18th and 19th centuries, many were made of glass. Specialty feeders, such as those for hummingbirds, are often made of glass.

bird fountain A centerpiece or mantelpiece, entirely of glass, consisting of a tall pedestal with two birds perched on top and two or more shorter pedestals, each with a bird on top. Each bird has a tail of glass fibers. They were popular in England during the mid-19th century.

Birks, House of A glass cutting house that operated in Montreal, Canada.

Birmingham Flint Glass Company (1832-1860) A glass manufacturing facility established in Birmingham (Pittsburgh), Pennsylvania, by O'Leary, Mulvaney & Co., making pressed, cut and plain flint glass. About 1845, the operating firm was Mulvaney & Ledlie(r). After 1850, it was operated: Ledlie(r) & Ulam; Ihmsen & Ulam; Blackburn & Ulam; Abrogast & Kaplahn; and Bryce, Walker & Company. It then made cut, molded, plain flint and fancy colored glassware.

Birmingham Glass Works
See *Pennsylvania Flint Glass Works.*

Bischoff Glass Company A glass manufacturing facility founded in Huntington, West Virginia, in 1922. In the 1940s, it moved to Culloden, West Virginia, and in 1963, was sold to Lancaster Colony, which in turn, sold it to Chuck Sloan in 1968. It made lighting glass, crackle glass, etc.

biscuit box A cracker jar.

bishop's bottle See *coachman bottle.*

bishop's hat A round, shallow bowl with an out-turned rim, its appearance resembling a bishop's hat, usually used as flower holders.

bit A small gather of glass, gathered on a bit iron by a bit gatherer or servitor, attached to a paraison to make a stem, foot, leg, handle, prunt, knop, etc.

bit gatherer The worker who collects small amounts of glass on a bit iron to make small parts (feet, stems, handles, etc.) for attaching to articles being made. These tasks were performed by the servitor at some facilities.

bit iron A steel rod used by the bit gatherer or servitor to gather small amounts of glass to attach to a paraison. See *bit and bit gatherer.*

Bitner, S.K., & Company (1913-1928) A glass-cutting house in Lancaster, Pennsylvania.

Grouping of bitters bottles, Whitney Glass works, Glassboro NJ, c. 1880. Museum of American Glass at Wheaton Village, Millville, NJ.

bitters bottle A small bottle, four to five inches tall, to hold bitters, most having a dropper. They were made in quantity during the 1860s and 1870s.

bittlin A milk bowl.

Black, B.F., & Co. See *New Geneva Glassworks.*

Black, Joseph The operator of a small cutting shop in Corning, New York; a subsidiary of T.G. Hawkes & Company around 1910.

Black & McGrew See *Warne, Parkinson & Co.*

black amethyst (glass) See *amethyst glass.*

black bottle A glass bottle, not black in color, but deep green or brown, safeguarding the contents from damages associated with light (discoloration, decomposition, etc.). The glass was durable, providing protection during transportation. Its introduction corresponded with the use of cork stoppers, providing an airtight seal, and the invention of the corkscrew about 1686.

black carnival glass A solid black (not a color which appears black), opaque glass with an iridescent finish; most made by Fenton or Sowerby (most black amethyst made by Dugan and Diamond).

black diamond See *tektite.*

Black pedestal vase with white enameling, 15" h.
Davanna Collection

black glass (1) Glass that is black in color, made using manganese oxide, blended with iron oxide, in the batch. (2) A very dark green, brown, blue, or purple glass that appears black under normal lighting conditions; the true color determined by placing it between an intense light source and the observer.

Black glass fruit bowl with scalloped rim, Mt. Pleasant.
Krause Publications

black lead See *Schwarzlot.*

black light See *ultraviolet light.*

Blackburn & Ulam See *Birmingham Flint Glass Company.*

Blackburn, Joseph Of English birth and training, a glass cutter who began cutting in Corning, New York, in 1891. He worked for T.G. Hawkes & Co. and other companies. In December of 1901, he started his own cutting shop there, and closed it in the spring of 1905.

Blackfriars Glasshouse A glasshouse established in London's former Blackfriars Monastery during 1598. It was previously leased in 1596 to Sir Jerome Bowes, who assigned his rights to William Turner and William Robson. Turner and Robson then operated it from 1598 to 1614.

blacking bottle A small bottle for holding stove black or polish. Usually, they were small square bottles with squared shoulders, a short neck and wide mouth, with an application sponge beneath the cap or stopper.

Blackmer, A.L., Company (1894-1916) A glass-cutting company established by Arthur L. Blackmer in New Bedford, Massachusetts, trading as Blackmer (Cut) Glass Company. It made high-quality cut glass and, as the Brilliant Cut Period drew to an end, it chose to close rather than put out a cheaper quality product.

blacks (Aka *moil, black moil*) Surplus glass, containing small particles of iron, knocked from the irons and pontils during the various glass making and production processes.

bladed knop A knop in the shape of a narrow ring with an elevated central ridge.

blank (1) An unembellished glass article intended to be embellished by cutting, engraving, enameling, gilding, etc. (2) Specifically, an uncut piece of glass in the form of an object, such as a bowl, dish, plate, etc., made with the intention of being cut or engraved. (3) Any piece of glass or glass object requiring further forming in some manner.

blank, cased glass An unembellished article made of two or more layers, the outer layer(s) to be embellished by cutting or engraving, generally revealing the lower layer(s) of a different color(s).

blank, figured A blank on which a design is made by blowing molten glass into a mold with the design. This design was generally only a part of the entire finished design.

Blankatzung (German) Literally, *bright etching.* A chemical process for polishing glass using a chemical solution of hydrofluoric acid with diluted sulfuric acid.

Blankinsops, McCarty & Torreyson See *Duval, Isaac & Co.*

Blankschnitt (German) Literally, *polished cut.* A style of embellishing intaglio cut or engraved glassware, by polishing the dull surface of the ground with soft discs or brushes of leather, or cork. It is believed to have been invented by Georg Schwanhardt, becoming a common method of embellishing Nuremberg glassware. Using this method, thin glass, especially potash glass, could be engraved and polished, the resultant engraving having the appearance of being more deeply cut with better definition.

Blaschka, Leopold & Rudolf Leopold (1822-1895) and Rudolf (1857-1939) created the famous *Harvard Glass Flowers*, working alone collecting representative specimens of flora and duplicating them in colored glass. See *Harvard Glass Flowers.*

blast The starting of a fire in a glass-melting furnace.

blaze (Aka *fringe*) A cut-glass line motif. The vertical lines, made by the shallow cuts, run parallel, forming a border resembling a fringe. By varying the length of the lines, the cutter could create a semi-circular or wedge-shaped scallop along the edge.

bleb (Aka *air bleb*) A small bubble of air in a glass object.

bleeding bowl (Aka *blood porringer*) A receptacle used by barbers, surgeons, or physicians to "bleed" patients, a practice used during the 18th and 19th centuries to purge patients. It is a bowl with side handles, similar to a porringer or shaving basin. Since the amount of blood drawn was to be exact, a true bleeding bowl will have marks designating quantities. See *bleeding glass.*

bleeding glass (Aka *cupping glass* or *cupping bowl*) A device used by barbers, surgeons, or physicians during the 18th and early 19th centuries to "bleed" patients. It was a small, cylindrical container about 4 inches tall with a rounded rim and stemmed foot. It was of a different shape and used differently than a bleeding bowl. A bleeding glass was used either for *dry cupping* or *wet cupping. Dry cupping* is performed by warming it, pressing its open end to the skin. As it cooled, a vacuum was created pulling flesh into the cup, blood being drawn to the surface of the skin. *Wet cupping* is performed by piercing the skin and repeating the same operations as with *dry cupping.*

Blenko hand-blown cobalt vase, 17" h.
Tri-State Antiques

Blenko Glass Company Born in England during 1854, at age 10, William John Blenko was apprenticed to a London bottle facility where he learned the essentials of glass making. In 1893, he came to the United States

and erected a facility in Kokomo, Indiana. The venture was unsuccessful because of (a) the depression, (b) a lowering of tariffs on imported glass, and (c) Americans favoring imported glass. To counter the last, he is believed to have shipped glass to England, then back to the United States as imported. After ten years, he closed his facility and returned to England. He established a facility, exporting glass to the United States.

In 1909, he returned to the United States, erecting a facility in Port Marion, Pennsylvania. In 1911, it failed. He moved to Clarksburg, West Virginia, and built a new facility. In 1913, it closed because of tariff reductions, high labor costs and inadequate business. Over the next few years, he worked as a chemist, perfecting his colors and making new molds. In 1921, he moved to Milton, West Virginia, where he built another facility, Eureka Art Glass Company. Again he was confronted with major problems, but persisted. His son, William H. Blenko, Sr., joined the company, adding a line of decorative ware and stained glass, used in many churches and cathedrals in the United States and England. When the Depression hit, construction slowed, orders for stained glass diminished and it concentrated on their decorative line. In 1930, it changed its name to Blenko Glass Company. All through the Depression it showed a slight profit. In 1933, William John died and William H., Sr., took charge. In 1936, it received permission to make a line of reproductions for Colonial Williamsburg because its methods of production were similar to those used during the colonial period. The wares had to be replicas of an actual piece found on the Williamsburg site and of the same composition as the original (*Williamsburg* line). After World War II, the decorative line remained popular and, with the building boom that followed, the stained glass production increased dramatically. The business is still operated by members of the Blenko family.

blister A large gas bubble creating an imperfection in glass or glassware. They are normally near the surface producing a bump on the glass. The glass covering the blister is often very thin and may easily break leaving a pit or pocket with a jagged edge.

Blister Glass See *Catalonian.*

blobbed glassware (1) Glassware embellished with haphazard sized and spaced blobs of various colors of glass, giving a mosaic effect, first made using a mold in Egypt during the 14th century BC. (2) Glassware embellished with haphazardly spaced white blobs of glass, irregularly shaped, and of different sizes, made by placing blobs of opaque white molten glass on colored glass and marvering (embedding them in the mass), formed and enlarged by blowing. It should *not* be confused with *encrusted glassware, jeweled glassware,* or *flecked glassware.*

blob (1) (Aka *mascaroon, prunt, seal*) Small globs of glass applied in the molten state to glassware as an embellishment. (2) Mounds of glass of varying color and shape made in a free-form fashion inside a kiln. They are flat on the back and may be integrated, by foiling or leading, in a window or lamp design. They may also be glued to a stained glass design's suface. (3) A lump of molten glass to be used as a paraison.

block (1) (Aka *blocking wood*) A wooden dipper-like implement with a hemi-spherical recess on one side, used, after being immersed in water to inhibit charring, to shape a blob of molten glass into a sphere as the initial step in preparing a globular paraison. (2) A cut-glass geometric motif consisting of raised, flat top squares formed with perpendicular and parallel miters.

block molding (Aka *drop molding*) The most basic, simplest method of pressing glass with a one-piece mold. A gob of molten glass is dropped inside the mold and a plunger brought down on it.

blocker The member of a chair or shop responsible for the initial shaping of a molten glass blob. The gatherer hands him a blowpipe with a gather at the tip. He rolls it on a marver, giving it an initial shape, then blows a puff of air into the paraison to expand it slightly. Alternatively, he might place it in a spot mold, expanding it to impart a simple pattern. Assisting the blocker are a mold boy who opens the spot mold, a warming-in boy who removes and reheats the paraison, and a carrying-over boy who takes the paraison from the blocker to the blower.

blocking wood See *block.*

blood porringer See *bleeding bowl.*

bloom A surface condition often found on old glass, imparting a dull, slightly opaque look, made (a) as the result of excess alkali in the batch (*inherent deficiency bloom*); (b) by the wearing off of gilding or enameling (*fixitive bloom*); or (c) by reheating glass at the glory hole in the presence of sulfur bearing gases (*sulfur bloom*).

Bloomingdale Flint Glass Works (1820-1840) A glass manufacturing facility established in New York City's Bloomingdale section (originally called the New York Glass Works) by John L. Gilliland and John and Richard Fisher. In 1822, the Fishers bought out Gilliland, and it was renamed Fisher's Factory, making plain and cut flint glass table and decorative wares; clear, blue, purple, and red glass; and, chemical glassware, mainly bottles.

blow and blow process A method for making bottles developed in the late 19th century. The paraison is blown by compressed air in the neck-down position, then inverted, suspended by the neck in a final mold, and blown again by compressed air into the final shape.

blow block An iron block hollowed in the shape of a hemisphere, about 18 inches in diameter, used by the blower to blow a paraison when making cylinder glass. It formed the rounded end of a long cylinder. See *second glass block.*

blow iron A blowpipe. See *blowpipe.*

blow over In *blown-in-the-mold* glass, that portion of the bulb which rose above the article's desired height. When the blower senses the article is complete, he brings the blowpipe up and to the side of the mold, blowing a final puff of air, creating the *blow over* which solidifies quickly and is shattered almost immediately.

blow pipe (Aka *blow iron, blowing iron, fistula*) A hollow tube, usually iron, ranging from two to six feet in length, wider (approximately one inch) and thicker at the end on which the gather is obtained than on the blowing end. It is used to take a gather of molten glass from a pot and, by blowing the mass into a bubble, to form and shape articles of hollow glassware. Wooden coverings are often placed at various locations along the pipe to afford the workman a comfortable handhold.

blower The worker, a member of a chair or team, who expanded the gather of molten glass into the desired shape. He was assisted by the servitor.

blower, foot See *foot blower.*

blowing A technique where a paraison of molten glass, after being marvered and reheated, is formed and shaped, with or without a mold, by blowing air through a blow pipe into the mass. The technique is believed to have been developed in Syria/Palistine during the 1st century BC and considered one of the most important developments in the history of glass, not surpassed until the 1820s development of pressing glass by machine. See *free blown glass; mold blown glass.*

blowing iron A blow pipe. See *blow pipe.*

Grouping of South Jersey blown glass, early 19th century. Museum of American Glass at Wheaton Village, Millville, NJ.

blown glassware Glassware made by a technique considered to be the highest level of glassmaking, in talent, artistry, and skill. Glassware so-made is entirely free blown, formed by forcing air through a blow pipe into molten glass and shaped by manual techniques, without the use of molds (see *blowing*).

blown molded glass See *blown-three-mold glass; mold-blown glass; three-section, mold-blown glass.*

blown-three-mold glass (Aka *three-section, mold-blown glass; three-mold glass*) A type of mold-blown glass developed in the United States about 1815 as a low-cost imitation of English cut glass; its popularity lasted until the 1830s. A gather was placed into a full-sized, hinged-metal mold of two or more pieces, on the inside of which was an intaglio pattern. If the mold was made of three or more pieces, one was fastened permanently to the base; the others joined to it by hinges held in place by removable pins. The gather was expanded until it pressed against the sides of the mold, usually opening the seams a bit, often allowing a small amount of glass protruding at the seams on the finished article. Finally it was removed quickly from the mold, and the top and bottom finished by hand. While two- and four-piece molds were used in making this glass, the majority of the molds were three piece. Therefore, the term *blown-three-mold* is misleading, as it applies to molds of other than three pieces.

Blown-three-mold glass has four distinct characteristics: (a) mold marks (the number indicative of the number of mold pieces); (b) the concavo-convex relationship of the glass's inner and outer surface. A protuberance on the outside has a corresponding depression on the inside and vice-versa. Pressed glass and part-size piece or dip molds do not have this. (c) patterns tend to have greater definition than pattern molded and expanded glass (pressed glass shows a comparable exact imprint from the mold throughout whereas blown, three-mold pieces display forms and angles with less sharpness and detail); and (d) the pattern design elements and the patterns themselves. Numerous patterns were unique to blown-three-mold glass and can be divided into three basic types: geometric, arched, and Baroque. The common types of base designs are as follows: ringed; rayed; rayed and ringed; fluted and ringed; or circle of concave dots, or petal-shaped or diamond-shaped indentations. The geometric motifs are as follows: diamond; diamond diapering; sunburst; circles and ovals; fluting; and ribbing. Some arch group patterns are: Roman arch; Roman arch with a sprig of leaves; Gothic arch; Gothic arch with a double spray of leaves; and arch and fern with a snake medallion. Some Baroque-type patterns are: shell and ribbing; shell with diamond; star; heart and chain; horizontal palm leaf; horn of plenty; and trefoil and ribbed. Many blown-three-mold pieces were of clear flint glass, but examples in every shade of green, blue, amethyst, and bottle glass (olive green to olive amber) exist. Blown-three-mold glass is often called *Stiegel glass,* which is misleading as to date and place of origin. Stiegel made no blown-three-mold glass. It is also called *Stoddard glass,* which too is misleading as to origin and date since Stoddard did not make glass until 1842. *Insufflated* and *blown molded* are two terms that have been proposed and used as a simpler means of describing this type of glass. See *three-section-mold-blown glass.*

blowout bowl A bowl with a pincered edge, alternating inward and outward.

Blue Amberina (1) A rare glass made by the Mt. Washington Glass Company, believed to be made from only one small batch. Its coloring is the same as *Rose Amber* with a third color, blue, blending from the top. The only piece known to exist is a jug, 6-5/8 inches high, engraved with a whaling ship. (2) See *Bluerina.*

Blue Aurene See *Aurene glass.*

Blue Burmese A *new* Burmese-type art glass developed by Fenton Art Glass Company in 1984. Using cobalt and gold in the batch, this opaque glassware is pale blue when made, but on reheating, rose tints are brought out.

blue glass Glass having a color from pale to deep blue, made by adding an oxide of cobalt or copper to the batch.

blue milk glass See *milk glass; delphite glass.*

Blue Nugget A deep-blue spangled glass by Sowerby's Ellison Glassworks during the late 1800s, made by rolling a paraison of cobalt blue glass over a marver strewn with flakes of mica, then coated with a clear or pastel-colored transparent glass and blown in a mold for its final form.

Blue Quartz See *Quartz glass.*

blue-tint lead glass A slight bluish tint found in some lead glass caused when lead ore mined in Derbyshire, England is used in the batch. Much old Waterford glass had this characteristic.

Bluerina (Aka *Blue Amberina*) An art glass shading from light blue to ruby.

boat (1) An article of decorative glassware shaped like a boat or galley (those in the form of a ship are described under the terms ship or nef). (2) A piece of utilitarian glassware shaped like a boat, such as a gravy boat.

bobbin knop A knop made up of several small, connected flattened spheres, sometimes graduated in size, in a column.

bobbin stem A stem made of bobbin knops, taking their shape from bobbin turned furniture, popular from the 16th through the 19th centuries.

Bobe & Albietz; Bobo & Albietz See *Eagle Glass Works.*

bobeche (French) The drip pan of a candle nozzle.

bocca (Italian) Literally, *mouth.* A large orifice in the arches of a furnace through which pots are put into the furnace and the batch put into the pots. It is sealed during the melting process with a temporary barrier of clay, having a spy hole through which a worker can observe the melting, remove impurities and/or take samples. See *spy hole; bye hole; glory hole.*

Bochsbeutel (German) A flattened globular bottle with a thin neck, tapering toward the top, and high kick base, used in the Franconian wine region of Germany from the 18th century on, for Steinwein.

Boda Glassworks A glass manufacturing facility established in Sweden in 1864, joining the Kosta Glassworks, in 1970, to become part of the Afors Group.

Bodine, J. & F. See *Bridgeton Glass Works.*

Bodine & Adams See *Tansboro Glass House.*

Bodine & Black; Black & Coffin See *Free Will Glass Manufactory.*

Bodine, Joel, & Sons A company established by Joel F. (father) and Joel A., John F., and William H. (sons), purchasing the

Stratton, Buck & Company glassworks in Bridgeton, New Jersey, in 1846. In 1855, it was sold to Maul, Hebrew & Company, which failed the same year. It was then purchased by Potter & Bodine, who made fruit jars, and patented a wax-seal-type in October 1858, and a clamp-top-type in June 1862. In 1863, Potter sold his interest to J. Nixon Bodine, and Francis L. Bodine, both sons of Samuel Bodine. By 1870, it was known as the Cohansey Glass Manufacturing Company. See *Bridgeton Glass Works; Washington Glass Works; Freewill Glass Manufactory; Cohansey Glass Manufacturing Company.*

Bodine, Thomas & Co. See *Washington Glass Co.; Freewill Glass Manufactory.*

Bodine Brothers See *Freewill Glass Manufactory.*

body The principal part of a vessel as opposed to its minor parts, such as the base, stem, handle, spout, cover, decoration, etc.

Bohemian crystal See *chalk glass.*

Bohemian glass vase, ruby cut-to-clear, 11" h. Davanna Collection

Bohemian glassware (1) Glassware made in Bohemia, a region in Austria, then Czechoslovakia. Glassmaking as an industry originated there in the second half of the 14th century, and by the late 1500s, engraving and enameling were widely practiced. In 1685, with the development of lime glass, an etched overlay glassware, called *Bohemian glassware* [see (2) below], came into being. From about 1700, Bohemia was renowned for its magnificent cut glass and *Zwischengoldglas.* In the first half of the 19th century, a variety of outstanding glass

was made, including cut, engraved, tinted, spun, millefiori, glass painted with transparent enamel, colors, and overlay and cased glass. (2) Glassware originally made in Bohemia, developed in the latter part of the 17th century, continued into the 20th century. It was an ornate overlay or flashed glass; the outer layer often ruby, but sometimes blue, yellow, or green, etc., cut or etched so the subtle color gradations produced exceptional pictorial effects. See *Czechoslovakian glass; Moser, Ludwig: Mattoni, Andreas: Pfeiffer, Anton.*

Bohemian red See *ruby glass.*

bollicine, vetro A decorative glass, developed in Italy by Venini, with many tiny air bubbles just beneath the outer surface made by using a metal base with numerous pointed protuberances upon which molten glass is placed and quickly pulled away. Air bubbles become entrapped where each protuberance had been.

bolts head A glass container having a long neck, tapering to produce a cone.

bomb A container, originally of Islamic glass, generally spherical with a small opening at the top. In Medieval times, they were filled with a flammable liquid, and a wick was inserted in the opening and ignited. Then the bottle was quickly thrown at the enemy or his property. On impact, the container broke; the contents igniting with explosive force, much like a hand grenade. They were an early form of the *Molotov Cocktails.*

bon bon (or bonbon) (Aka *nappy*) A term derived from a French-type of candy, having a creme filling (*bonbonniere*). A candy dish made in a variety of shapes, some with handles, some divided, some footed (also called *comports*) and some covered.

bone ash The ashes of calcined bones (the remains of bones, roasted/oxidized by heat) of animals, used as a flux in making glass and an opacifier in making *opaque white glass*, *milk-and-water glass* and *opaline.*

bone dish A dish kept on the table in which bones removed from meat or fish were placed. Generally cresent-shaped, some were made in unusual shapes.

bone glass See *Beinglas; milk-and-water glass.*

Bonita Glass Co. A facility established in Cicero, Indiana, by Otto Jaeger in late 1898, making a variety of wares, in both decorated and plain clear, opal, and colored glass. John H. Hobbs, of Hobbs, Brockunier, joined the company in 1899, and his son Charles was in charge of the mold department and facility manager. In December 1900, it was sold. Jaeger continued working for glass companies in Fostoria, Ohio, and Wheeling, West Virginia, and later established another facility, also named Bonita Glass Co. The Cicero Glass Co. moved into the Bonita facility in 1902.

bonnet glass A small glass container, usually with a knop stem, used to hold sweetmeats. They were made in numerous shapes; the bowl being either cup- or double-ogee-shaped, either plain or with molded designs. Later examples had an egg-shaped bowl, and cut decoration was common. The base was either flat or hollow, often dome-shaped or terraced, and either circular, square or scalloped. They have been incorrectly called *monteiths.*

boot bottle (1) A boot-shaped novelty bottle of a men's or ladies' high shoe. (2) A small flat or slightly curved flask designed to fit into a boot top while being worn.

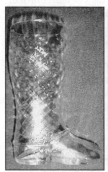 

Pressed-glass boot glass with diamond pattern pressed on inside of boot, 6-1/2" h.
Davanna Collection

Boot glass with design, 6" h.
Davanna Collection

boot glass A boot-shaped drinking glass in a variety of styles, including calf-high, knee, and leg-shaped boots, etc., made during the 1600s in Holland, Italy, and Germany, and also in England during the late 1700s. See *shoe; joke glass.*

bootleg A small secondary furnace used to heat a blowpipe or reheat a piece of glassware for further manipulation.

E.G. Booz Old Cabin whiskey bottle, Whitney Bros., Glassboro, NJ, c. 1860. Museum of American Glass at Wheaton Village, Millville, NJ.

Booz(e) bottle A flask made during the 1860s by the Whitney Glass Works for Edmund G. Booz of Philadelphia, Pennsylvania, an alcoholic beverage manufacturer and dealer. It was shaped like a rectangular two-story house with plain walls and shingled roof; the neck being the chimney. On some flasks the date "1840" appears. This is supposedly the date of the contents, not the date it was made. The flask is mold blown, always with the name "E C Booz." Reproductions are rampant. The term *booze* does not come from these bottles, but from *bouse*, an old English word meaning *to carouse.*

boracic A glass made at Clichy during 1849 using borax, claimed to be free from bubbles and other impurities, as well as strong and resistant to chips and temperature changes.

borax A crystalline, slightly alkaline borate of sodium, with the chemical formula $Na_2B_4O_7$, used originally, as was boric acid, as a flux in making lead glass and, in the 18th century, plate glass. Now it is used extensively in certain types of container glass and in making high index borate glass, having a lower dispersion value and higher refractive index than any known glass. In addition to its high fluxing power, it tends to lower the expansion coefficient and increase chemical durability, strengthening glass against blows, chipping, and temperature changes, and is used in making heat resistant glassware for the laboratory and kitchen and as an optical glass. It replaces part of the silica in the batch. Boric acid is used as a flux in batches where only a small amount of alkali is wanted.

Borden, George L., & Company

A glass-cutting shop in Groveville, New Jersey, operating from 1910 to 1920. In 1912, it opened another in Trenton, New Jersey, "Krystal Krafters." Its trademark, registered on July 25, 1922, placed on the wares with gummed labels, but in use since November 7, 1921, was "Krystal Krafters - Trenton, N.J. - Genuine Cut Glass" encircling two large letters "K."

boric acid

An acid, H_3BO_3, used as a flux in making both ceramics and glass. See *borax.*

borosilicate glass

Boric oxide and silicate glasses are used for optical and scientific work and utensils. They usually contain 13 to 28% B_2O_3 (boric oxide), have low expansion coefficients, superior resistance to thermal shock, excellent chemical stability and high electrical resistance. They are used for baking dishes, laboratory glassware, pipelines, sealed beam headlights, insulators, etc. The 200-inch disc of the Mt. Palomar telescope is cast borosilicate glass. See *pyrex; optical glass; heat-resistant glass.*

borsella *(Italian)*

A tong-like tool used for shaping glass. A *borsella puntata* is a tong-like tool having a pattern imprinted on the jaws that is impressed on the glass.

bosom bottle

A bouquet holder, in miniature, for pinning to buskin (a thick-soled laced boot), a dress just above the breast, or inserted into the "V" of the breasts. Filled with water, they kept a small bouquet of flowers fresh for a fairly long period of time.

boss

Any protuberant or projecting part, as on a finned bowl, the almond-shaped projections.

boss blower

The head of a *team* or *chair* in a glass-blowing operation, having his own pot, tools, and assistants.

Celery vase of colorless glass, Boston & Sandwich Glass Company, c. 1830-1840, 7-1/4" h.
The Corning Museum of Glass

Boston & Sandwich Glass Co. (1)

(1825-1888) Deming Jarves, formerly of the Boston Porcelain & Glass Manufacturing Company & New England Glass Company, erected a glass manufacturing facility at Sandwich, near Cape Cod, Massachusetts, named the Sandwich Manufacturing Company. It made plain, cut, engraved and molded tablewares, lamps, etc. In 1826, the Boston & Sandwich Glass Co. was incorporated (Jarves was agent and general manager) taking over the operations of the Sandwich Manufacturing Company. In 1828, it added pressed glass to its line, making plates, cup plates, etc. in lacy glass, and paperweights and wares in the Venetian and English styles and, after 1830, some opaline wares. In later years, it manufactured overlay, stained, and novelty wares. In 1858, Jarves left. From 1873 on, it suffered from the competition of Midwestern facilities making less expensive wares. In early 1888, after a glass blowers strike, it closed permanently. Its wares from the period 1825 to 1845 are called *Early Sandwich Glass*, the most famous being its early pressed glass. It is best-known for its lacy-patterned pressed glass, so popular, that *Sandwich Glass* became a generic term for it regardless of the source or location of manufacture. See *Jarves, Deming; Electrical Glass Company; Crib, The; Western Glass Company; Bancroft, Bernard Company; Alton Manufacturing Company; Packwood, N., & Company.* (2) (1895-1896) A glass manufacturing facility established by Frederick Shirley and others, operating in the old Boston & Sandwich Glass Company facility [see *(1)* above].

Boston (Crown) Glass Manufactory

Located in Boston, Massachusetts, the original company was organized by Robert Hewes, Charles F. Kupfer, etc., in 1787. The Massachusetts legislature granted it the exclusive right to make glassware within the Commonwealth for a 15-year period. Because of numerous problems, it did not manufacture glass until 1793. It then made window glass and hollow wares and, during the first quarter of the 19th century, became one of the most successful glassworks of its kind, making high-quality crown glass. Because of the delay in opening the facility, the legislature granted it the exclusive right to make window and plate glass and all sorts of hollow ware, for a period of ten years. In 1802, two of its directors built another facility in Chelmsford, then Middlesex Village, making cylinder glass. This was an affiliate of the Boston Crown Glass Manufactory, known as the Chelmsford Glassworks. In 1809, the Boston Crown Glass Manufactory became the Boston Glass Manufactory. In 1811, it built a new facility in South Boston, the South Boston Flint Glass Works, more commonly known as the South Boston Crown Glass Company. The original facility closed during the War of 1812, reopening afterward, but never as prosperous as before. In 1827, it became insolvent and closed. See *South Boston Crown Glass Company.*

Boston Flint Glass Company

An 1830 glass manufacturing facility located in Boston, Massachusetts.

Boston Flint Glass Works

A glass manufacturing facility established prior to 1849 in Cambridge, Massachusetts, by Thomas Leighton, Sr., making all kinds of druggists' chemical and tablewares, lamps and fixtures, paperweights, and lanterns for ship and railroad use. It closed sometime after 1867.

Boston Glass Bottle Manufacturing Company

(1826-1827) A glass manufacturing facility in Boston, Massachusetts, making bottles and other glassware.

Boston Porcelain & Glass Manufacturing Company

Granted a charter by the Massachusetts Legislature in 1787, it began operating during 1792 in East Cambridge.

Deming Jarves was associated with the firm. In 1815, it was leased to Emmett, Fisher & Flowers, and in 1817, closed. The equipment and property was sold at public auction to the New England Glass Company. See *New England Glass Company.*

Boston Silver Glass Company

A company established in Cambridge, Massachusetts, in 1857 by A.E. Young & Haines, making flint glass tablewares, silver (mercury) glass, lamp chimneys, lanterns, and lamps. In 1868, it was operated by Young, Haines & Dyer until about 1871.

botijo *(Spanish)*

A container for holding and pouring water; the body being spherical, resting on a spreading base, having an overhead loop handle and a short, wide spout.

Dark-amber (beer) bottle, frontmarked
"Wm. H. Earl—Newton, N.J."
Davanna Collection

bottle

The most common of all glass wares, it was the primary glass object made in the United States from about 1700 to 1870. It is believed to be the first item made by the glass industry in almost every country. A hollow container with a slender neck and no handles, its basic purpose is to hold liquids. The bottle's manufacture dates from Syrian and Roman times, and since then, they have been made in a great variety of shapes, sizes, and styles. The body may be cylindrical (most common), spherical, pear shaped, etc. or of square, hexagonal, or octagonal cross-section (the first mold-blown square bottles date from about 25 AD, and the first polygonal bottles date from about 70 AD, both in the Roman Empire). The sides may be flat or rounded; the base flat or with a kick. The contents are normally sealed in with stoppers, usually glass or cork, screw caps, or crimp caps.

The initial method for making them was the sand-core process. Since ancient glassmakers could not achieve high temperatures, the glass used was high in alkali and poor in quality; exhibiting an iridescent film, scaling and/or layering. With the invention of the blowpipe, a glassmaker was able to gather a blob of glass at the end of a pipe and blow a bubble, which he could then shape with primitive tools into a bottle. Using the principle of the blowpipe, a semi-automatic process was developed and refined into the highly mechanized and automated, fast production of today. The bottle's neck, intended to receive a stopper or other form of closure, was made after the bottle was shaped and cut from the blowpipe. The neck was then finished; as a result, the top of the bottle became known as the *finish*.

Toward the end of the 19th century, numerous patents were registered, all attempting to imitate the blowpipe process by mechanized means and eventually automated bottle processing was born, but by reversing the mouth-blown process, the finish was made first. The following process was developed along those lines. The blowpipe was removed from the process and the glass was gathered at the end of an plain iron rod and allowed to run from the rod's end into a paraison mold at the bottom of which was the *finish* or *ring* mold. The mold had a little metal plunger sealing the opening through which air was blown.

When sufficient glass had been allowed to enter, the stream was snipped off and a baffle plate positioned over the top of the paraison mold. Compressed air was then blown upward from the bottom. A bubble originated and the glass was expanded upward against the baffle plate and mold walls, forming a paraison. It already had a completed *finish*, but was in the neck-down position. It was turned upside down, suspended by the *finish* in the final mold and blown, by compressed air, into the final bottle shape.

Some of these machines could produce 200 ready-to-use bottles per hour. The process used is known as the *blow-and-blow process*. During the same period, an alternate process known as the *press-and-blow process* was developed. The gather, as in the previous process, was put in a mold, but the paraison was pressed out within the mold using a large plunger. It was then removed and placed into a final mold where it was blown by compressed air into its final shape. Entirely automated glass bottle making was initiated with the invention of the automatic glass feeding device known as the *feeder* (see *feeder*). Several different types of bottle manufacturing machines are in existence, but by far the most prominent one, which has almost entirely replaced all others, is the IS machine (see *IS machine*). Another method of making bottles is the vacuum gather process (see *vacuum gather process*). See the following types of bottles: *bishop's; bitters; black; boot; bosom; cabin; camphor; case; casting. castor; coachman's; cologne; decanter; double; double cone; Elixer of Life; feeding; fire; fish; ink; hexagonal; hogarth; liqueur; Ludlow; Maltese Cross; measuring; medicine; mercury; mermaid; multiple; perfume; pepper; pilgrim; pocket; poison; pomegranate; pouch; rectangular; saddle; sauce; scent; sea horse; serving; shaft & globe; smelling; snuff; square; tea; tear; thread wound; toilet; toilet water; triple; vinegar; wine; and witch.*

bottle, largest Made for the St. Louis Exposition at Whitall Tatum Company, Bridgeton, New Jersey, by Emil Stanger and Marcus Kuntz, aided by Tony Stanger and John Fath, it was blown by compressed air. A special square block had to be built for the bottle, as well as a special pit, pot, and oven. It held a capacity of 108 gallons, but was broken after the Exposition, either at St. Louis or enroute back to Bridgeton.

bottle glass See *green glass*.

bottle green paperweight See *door stop*.

bottle label The painted or engraved name on a bottle or decanter's exterior designating the contents, used mainly on bottles containing alcoholic beverages. They gradually lost favor with the increased popularity of the bottle ticket about 1760.

bottle seal   A seal carrying a monogram or design, frequently molded, and fastened to the bottle to identify either the owner, a tavern, or a factory.

bottle-shaped decanter   A decanter having a cylindrical shape and sloping shoulder lengthening into its neck.

bottle slider   A coaster or beer wagon. See *coaster; beer wagon.*

bottle stand   See *cruet stand; coaster.*

bottle ticket   (Aka *wine label*) A small plaque suspended around the neck of a bottle, decanter, or other container inscribed with the contents, becoming fashionable from about 1740, and eliminating the bottle label by 1760.

Bottletown   See *South Millville Plant.*

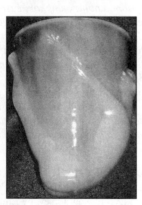

Bottom's up glass, clear at rim to ivory-yellow at base, 3-1/2" h.
Davanna Collection

bottom's up glass   A drinking glass made with a rounded or pointed base so it cannot be put down without spilling the contents. Once emptied, it is placed upside down on its rim. Modern versions frequently have a nude figure of a woman lying across the bottom.

boucher style   See *rococo.*

boudoir clock   A clock mounted within a crystal case or frame. In many instances, the clock would be made in one country and mounted in the case or frame in another (many made in Czechoslovakia). The glass was generally decorated by cutting, often with intaglio decoration; but some was pressed with popular period motifs.

boughpot   A decorated container or vase with a pierced top to hold stems and boughs in an upright position.

bouillottes   A shaded candelabra often placed in a table's center, used for a French card game of the same name.

bouquet   A cluster of flowers. As a decoration, a cluster of flowers with leaves. The flowers, either stylized or natural, fashioned in a bouquet or garland. See *flat bouquet; standing bouquet; upright bouquet; bouquet paperweight.*

bouquet of flowers chandelier   See *ciocche.*

bouquet paperweight   A paperweight having a primary motif of two or more flowers, either natural or stylized. The leaves form a garland, or are arranged in a bouquet, either flat or standing. The weight itself may be the traditional or overlay type. Weights with the flowers tied at the base with a ribbon are called *spray paperweights.*

bouquetiere (French)   (1) A vase to hold cut flowers with several upright tubes for inserting the individual stems and a central orifice for filling with water. See *flower stand.* (2) A glass bowl, mounted on a stem and foot, with a wide, flared mouth having a wavy-edged rim, often with molded fluting, applied ribbing and mascarons. They were originally made in Venice and later on in France during the 18th and early 19th centuries.

bourdalou (French)   (Aka *slipper, coach pot, chamber pot*) A small urinary container used by females, dating from about 1710, remaining in vogue until about 1850. In shape and size, they are often confused with a sauceboat. The dissimilarities are: (a) a sauceboat has a pouring lip, the bourdalou an incurved rim; and (b) a sauceboat sometimes has a stemmed foot, a bourdalou never has one, but has a foot ring or no adornment on the base. The bourdalou has a single handle. See *urinal; chamber pot.*

bousing can   A drinking cup.

bow drill or bow lathe   A drill used in ancient times for hollow and relief cutting. It consisted of a bow with its bowstring looped around a fixed spindle to which was attached one of a variety of discs. The drill was rotated by moving the bow back and forth while the glass being cut was held against the revolving disc.

bowit Also spelled *bowet*. A small lantern having a wooden frame or case

Cut glass bowl, Brilliant Period, 9" d.
Davanna Collection

bowl (1) A concave container, usually hemispherical, used to hold liquids, fruits, etc., normally wider than high, but deeper than a saucer, and often with a foot ring. (2) The depressed part of anything, as of a spoon, ladle, etc. (3) The hollowed part of glasses used to hold wine or other liquids. For more information on bowls as defined by (1) and (3) above, see the following types and kinds of bowls: *Achaemenian; banana; bell; berry; bucket, bucket topped, Buckley; Buggin; Canosa; caviar; chilling; conical; cup; cupped top; cupping; double ogee; drinking; faceted; finger; finned; flex; funnel; fruit; Gazelle; handkerchief; hat shaped; hexagonal; Irish glassware; kettle drum; lipped; Merry Widow; Napoleon's hat; octagonal; ogee; Omphalos; orchid; ovoid; pan topped; peppermint stick; pillar molded; punch; ribbed; rose; saucer topped; shrimp; standing; sugar; tea; thistle; Trivulzio; trumpet; tulip; turn over; U shaped.*

bowl gatherer A member of a chair, shop, or team who assists the gaffer in making such objects as wine glasses.

bowldish A bowl or basin used primarily in the toilet, such as a washbowl. Other spellings are *boledish, boledysshe,* and *boldyche.*

Bowman & Chisholm See *Excelsior Flint Glass Works.*

Bowman, George H., Company Succeeding the C.A. Selzer Company, it was established in 1888 in Cleveland, Ohio. From 1910 to about 1921, it engaged in wholesale and retail sales of china, glass, and pottery. It also maintained a glass-cutting shop in Salem, Ohio. In 1932, the Cleveland store closed and another opened in Salem, under the same name. In 1964, George H. Bowman's daughter still operated the shop under the name "The Fiesta Shop."

Bowman, J.L., & Co. See *New Albany Glass Works.*

box A container with four sides, a bottom, and removable cover or lid, pierced and secured by metal hinges or mounted in a metal frame for the same purpose. They are relatively small; a large one is called a *casket.* They date to Roman times.

boy An unskilled worker at a glass manufacturing facility. See *carrying-in boy; carrying-over boy; warming-in boy; mold boy.*

Boyd, Zack He worked at Cambridge Glass and Crystal Art Glass and created many unique colors, some of which were named after him. He worked at other facilities across the country, returning frequently to Cambridge. He last worked for the Degenhart facility after the death of John Degenhart, working there until a few months before his own death in 1968. He was the father of Bernard Boyd. See *Boyd's Crystal Art Glass.*

Boyd's Crystal Art Glass factory and store.
Anna Shotwell

Boyd's Crystal Art Glass In 1978, Bernard C. Boyd and his son bought the Degenhart factory in Cambridge, Ohio, acquiring 50 of their molds with the "D in heart" trademark removed. Many were used by the Boyds who also made the doll, "Louise"; the pony, "Joey"; and the elephant, "Zack" (after Bernard's father) from their own molds. These were issued each month in a new and different color of crystal or slag glass. The trademark of the company was a "B" in a diamond.

Boyle, John A. A glasscutter who lived in Brooklyn, New York, cutting glass during the 1910s.

Boyle Brothers A glass-cutting shop in Somerville, Massachusetts, operating in the early 1920s.

bracken See *fern ash.*

Bradley, Ernest L., Cut Glass Manufacturer (1904-1906) A glass-cutting shop in Corning, New York.

brain glass An iridescent glass made by Richardsons of Stourbridge, England, having a surface texture resembling that of the brain.

Braintree Glasshouse A glass manufacturing facility established in Braintree, Massachusetts, in 1850, to make bottles, closing before 1852.

brandy bottle A small bottle used to hold brandy. Usually square or rectangular in cross section, they have a short threaded neck and a screw cover.

brandy glass (Aka *balloon glass, brandy snifter*) An oversize drinking glass with a globular bowl, a somewhat inverted rim and short-stemmed foot. The shape of the bowl permits it to be held in the palms of the hands, allowing the brandy to be warmed and its vapors released.

brandy snifters See *brandy glass.*

Brannigan Glass Company A glass manufacturing facility using a method of making stemware developed and patented by Bryce Brothers in 1902. It involves blowing the bowl and attaching it to a previously made molded stem.

brass An alloy of copper and zinc. Brass filings were added to batches of opal glass to produce a turquoise color.

Bread plate, *Last Supper,* frosted grape leaf border, 10-7/8" x 7".
Krause Publications

bread plate A large oval plate, popular from the mid-1800s, that holds a loaf of bread. Often of pressed glass, the designs on the plate popularized people, places, topical items, and events.

bread (and butter) plate (Aka *sherbet plate*) A small plate usually about six inches in diameter which, when part of a table service, to hold bread taken from a serving tray.

breakfast set (1) Specifically, a small sugar bowl and creamer made only in carnival glass. See *dejeuner service.* (2) A sugar and creamer. (3) A set of tableware that includes two to four place settings (plate, bread and butter plate, and cup and saucer), together with a sugar and creamer. It may include a jelly or jam jar, a powdered sugar sifter, syrup jug, or other holder or container.

Breast pump with rubber bulb held on by metal band, 5-1/2"
Davanna Collection

breast glass A hollow glass receptacle designed to fit over the breast of a nursing mother. It is warmed and placed over the breast. As it cools, a partial vacuum is created, drawing milk from the breast into the receptacle. They have attached to them a small tube or curved spout used to drain the milk from the breast glass into another container. See *nipple shield.*

Bremen Pokal See *New Bremen Glass Manufactory.*

Breslin A trademark of the W.P. Hitchcock Co.

Bride's basket in Pioneer pattern with hand-painted roses, 8" w.
Tri-State Antiques

bride's basket A one-of-a-kind, basket-shaped glass curiosity, presented to a bride as a wedding present. They became highly fashionable during the 1880s. During the 1890s, cut-glass baskets were popular. They lost favor about 1905.

bridge fluting A decorative pattern in the form of faceted short, wide vertical fluting. See *flute cutting.*

Bridge of Life A representation of the various periods of a person's (usually a man) or animal's life while crossing a bridge. Normally there are four figures representing: *youth; adolescence; middle age;* and *elderly.* See *Ages of Man.*

bridge set A set of four small dishes, one each in the shape of the four suits from a deck of cards: heart, spade, diamond, and club.

Bridgeport Glass Works (1811-1847) A window glass manufacturing facility established in Bridgeport, Pennsylvania. About 1822, it was purchased by Benedick Kimber and, about 1824, N. & P. Swearer bought or leased it, making green glassware and window glass. By 1837, Kimber & Co. operated the works.

Bridgeton Cut Glass Company A glass-cutting house in Bridgeton, New Jersey, operating during the late 1910s.

Bridgeton Glass Works (1836/7-1917) The commonly accepted name of a glass-manufacturing facility, in Bridgeton, New Jersey, established by Stratton, Buck & Co., starting as a window glass facility, shortly after adding bottles and flasks. In 1841, it burned, Buck died, and in 1842, Stratton retired. It was rebuilt by John G. Rosenbaum who operated it until 1846, when Joel Bodine & Sons, owners of the Washington Glass Works, took over. In 1855, Maul, Hebrew & Company purchased it, but failed in the same year. In 1863, J. & F. Bodine, nephews of Joel Bodine, bought it, operating it until 1867. In 1870, the Cohansey Glass Manufacturing Company took over, making window glass, bottles and hollow ware. See *Bodine, Joel, & Sons*

bridle rosettes Small glass buttons used to embellish a horse's bridle.

Briefbeschwerer (German) See *paperweight.*

bright etching See *Blankatzung.*

Brilliant Cut Glass Company A glass cutting shop in Hawley, Pennsylvania, operating in the late 1910s.

Brilliant Glass Company (1) A glass manufacturing facility in Weston, West Virginia, operating during the 1920s, then changing its name to the Westite Glass Company, operating until 1936. Its molds and assets were sold to the Akro Agate Company. (2) (1889-1896) A glass manufacturing facility in Brilliant, Ohio, not to be confused with the Brilliant Glass Works.

Brilliant Glass Works A glass manufacturing facility established in Brilliant,

Ohio, in 1880; originally as the Novelty Glass Company before moving to Brilliant from La Grange, Ohio. In 1883, Dalzell Brothers & Gilmore leased it, but in 1884, abandoned it to build a new one in Wellsburg, West Virginia. In 1887, the Central Glass Company of Wheeling, West Virginia, rented it, moving, in 1889, to Greensburg, Pennsylvania, operating as the Greensburg Glass Company. See *Greensburg Glass Company.*

Brilliant style See *cut glass.*

brimmer (Aka *bumper*) A drinking vessel, filled to the brim with liquor for a toast, after which it was bumped on the table for emphasis. See *bumper.*

Brinley, George, & Co. (1826-1827) A glass bottle manufacturing facility established in Boston, Massachusetts, also making some flasks, ink bottles, demijohns, carboys and gallon bottles.

Brisbois, Victor (1918-1930) Affiliated with Becker & Brisbois until 1918, he established a glass cutting shop in New York City, moving to Brooklyn, New York before closing.

Bristol blue glass (1) Generic: any dark blue translucent glass. (2) Specific: the intense deep blue translucent glass containing Saxon smalt, made at Bristol and other English cities between 1761 and 1790.

Pair of Bristol vases with gold floral decoration, 8" h.
Davanna Collection

Bristol glassware Glassware made at Bristol, England, in the 17th, 18th, and 19th centuries. Of particular significance were the opaque white glass (when placed in front of a light produces an orange hue similar to that observed in a forest fire) and the translucent Bristol blue glass. The majority of Bristol glassware seen today is a lightweight, opaque glass, frequently blue, made during the Victorian era.

Bristol Roller See *rolling pin.*

British American Glass Works (1855?-1870s) A glass-manufacturing facility established at Pointe a Cavagnol, Hudson, Quebec, manufacturing bottles, chimneys and insulators. It later was called the Montreal Glass Company.

British Artists in Crystal A second artists' series (the first being *Twenty-seven Artists in Crystal*) conceived by Arthur Houghton and made at Steuben. Each of twenty artists selected for the second series submitted a sketch that was engraved on a piece of glassware. The last sketch was submitted in the late spring of 1953. The series was completed in early 1954 and put on display at Steuben's New York shop.

British paperweights (1) *Antique.* Weights made primarily by four companies: (a) Stourbridge (millefiori weights from 1849 in the style of Clichy); (b) George Bacchus & Sons (millefiori weights and some with white filigrana since about 1848); (c) Whitefriars Glass Works (weights with colored florets, and occasionally faceted weights from about 1848); and (d) Islington Glassworks (weights similar to those made at Stourbridge; having a cane with a silhouette of a horse and are marked "IGW"). (2) *Victorian.* Weights made in the traditional shape with a domed, clear magnifying glass and having, on the bottom a colored print. Later, about 1890, a photograph of a well known resort, local site, or street scene of England or the United States became popular. First made about 1850, they were usually made in Belgium or Germany and sent to England for the picture to be affixed. (3) *Modern.* A contemporary weight made in the United Kingdom by such makers as Whitefriars Glassworks; Paul Ysart; Moncrieff Glassworks; Strathern Glassworks; Perthshire Paper Weights, Ltd.; Caithness Glass Co.; and Wedgwood Glassware.

broad glass (Aka *muff glass, cylinder glass*) Flat glass, mainly used for window-panes. To make it, a large glob of molten glass is gathered on the end of a blowpipe and blown into a very large bubble, which is swung on the blowpipe's end until it forms a long cylinder with hemispherical ends. The ends are sheared off, leaving a long cylinder, called a *muff*. The cylinder, up to five feet in length, is cut lengthwise, reheated, and allowed to settle to a flat sheet or pressed flat by a wooden plate. This process is called the *Lorraine Method* because its first recorded use was about 1100 in Lorraine in western central Europe. This process replaced the former, more wasteful crown glass process. It exhibited straight ripples, was much smoother, and required less polishing than crown glass. See *cylinder glass; Lubbers process, float glass.*

broadsheet technique See *cylinder glass.*

Brockway Glass Company A glass manufacturing facility established during 1907 in Brockway, Pennsylvania. In 1933, it acquired the Monarch Glass Company, and in 1964, became part of the Hazel Atlas Division of the Continental Can Company. It is now in Zanesville, Ohio, making containers and bottles.

broken swirl or rib A style of embellishment on glassware combining swirled and vertical ribbing. To make it, a gather of glass was pressed into a ribbed mold, removed, reheated and twisted, then reinserted into the mold to produce the vertical ribbing.

Broncit glassware A style of embellishment on glassware developed by Joseph Hoffman about 1910 and made by J. & L. Lobmeyr. It consists of geometrical patterns painted in a blackish flat pigment on transparent or satin clear glass.

Bronson Cut Glass Company A cutting shop established in 1910 in Painted Post, New York. It is known for its rare cut-glass inkwells made under the Bronson Inkstand Co.'s patent for inkwells known as *Bronson's Ink Stands*. It also made other cut-glass articles for ornamental and table use. The glass blocks for the inkwells were purchased from

T.G. Hawkes & Company. It lasted about 18 months and made about 100 inkwells. See *Bronson Inkstand Co.*

Inkstand with two bottles, colorless glass, c. 1894-1897. Possibly Corning, NY, Bronson Inkstand Co.
The Corning Museum of Glass

Bronson Inkstand Co. A glass-cutting shop established in Corning, New York, in 1898, famous for the *Bronson's Ink Stand*. In 1908, it closed, but in 1910, the Bronsons moved to Painted Post, New York and established the Bronson Cut Glass Company. See *Bronson Cut Glass Company; Drake, George W., & Company.*

bronze, gilt See *gilt bronze.*

Bronze Glass See *Webb's Bronze Glass.*

Bronzite A Lobmeyr product designed by Joseph Hoffman. Clear glass vessels painted in black or dark grey colors.

brooch See *fibula.*

brooch runners A jug made during the 6th and 5th centuries BC in Italy, core-formed in blue, green, and brown glass; some have handles, decorated with trailing; others are of monochrome ribbed glass and have no handles.

Brookfield, James See *Honesdale Glassworks.*

Brookfield & Co. See *Bushwick Flint Glass Works.*

Brookfield Glass Manufacturing Company A glass manufacturing company in business for over a century before closing in 1920. It was one of the nation's largest makers of glass insulators for the telegraph and telephone industry.

Brooklyn Cut Glass See *Haughwout, E.V., & Company.*

Brooklyn Flint Glass Works See *Brooklyn Glass Works; Gilliland, John L.; Corning Glass Works.*

Brooklyn Glass Works (1) John L. Gilliland established the Brooklyn Glass Works in 1823 in Brooklyn, New York, making flint glass tablewares, and by 1830, adding pressed and colored glass. In 1843, it was known as the Brooklyn Flint Glass Works. In 1856, it added lenses, lamps and chandeliers, and signals for railroads and ships. In 1864, Amory Houghton & Son secured controlling interest and, in 1868, moved it to Corning, New York; establishing the Corning Glass Works. (2) A glass manufacturing facility established by Frederick Stanger and John Marshall in (Old) Brooklyn, New Jersey. As it was being completed in mid-1831, Stanger died. John Marshall completed it with the help of Thomas Stanger. Operations began in 1832. In 1839, Marshall retired and the firm became Stanger & Dotterer. It burned in 1856. In 1857, C.B. Tice rebuilt it, operating it until 1868.

Brooklyn Glasshouse About 1754, Lodewyck Bamper is presumed to have operated a bottle manufacturing facility in Brooklyn, New York.

Brown Aurene See *Aurene glass.*

Brownsville Glass Works (1828-1900) A glass manufacturing facility established in Brownsville, Pennsylvania, by George Hogg. In 1829, John Taylor & Co. leased, then purchased it with Edward Campbell, but Hogg retained control of the operations. In 1831, John Taylor & Co., sold its interest to William R. Campbell, and the firm became E. Campbell & Co. In 1831, Edward Campbell sold his interest to Robert Forsyth and the firm became Campbell & Forsyth. In 1834, Forsyth sold his interest back to Edward Campbell. The Campbells, after a short time, sold to Gabler & Gue who operated it until the late 1830s when it was repurchased by George Hogg. Over the next quarter century, the ownership changed numerous times [Burke, Sedgwick & Co.; Carter & Hogg; Benedict Kimber (took over in 1844); Haught, Swearer & Co.; Robert Rogers: and George Wells]. In 1873, it was purchased by Schmertz & Quinby. Originally bottles were made, later window glass and tablewares were added. In 1881, a cooperative took control, operating it until it closed.

bruise (1) A flaw in a paperweight associated with its making, rather than its treatment. It evolves during the making, disclosing itself as a small blemish just below the crown's surface. (2) (Aka *wear mark*) Tiny scratches, usually on the bottom of a piece, where it has rubbed against a surface (table, shelf, etc.), or on the inside (bowls, plates, etc.), where an object, such as a frog, was placed. These are considered a show of age.

Brunswick star A cut-glass motif in the form of a twelve-pointed star, each point being joined by a line to the fifth point in either direction from it. After all the points are joined in this manner, an almost circular outline is produced in the center.

brush pot A receptacle utilized by artists and craftsmen to hold or clean brushes.

Bryce, James A partner in several glass manufacturing facilities such as Bryce, McKee & Co.; Bryce, Richards & Co.; Bryce, Walker & Co.; Bryce Brothers; etc.

Bryce Brothers See *Bryce, McKee & Co.*

Bryce, Higbee & Company (Aka *Homestead Glass Works*) A glass manufacturing facility established in 1879 in Pittsburgh, Pennsylvania, by John Bryce (see *Bryce, Mckee & Company*), John Higbee and Joseph A. Doyle (see *Doyle & Company*), making mainly pressed tablewares and novelties. About 1900, Higbee gained controlling interest, changed its name to J.B. Higbee Glass Company, moving to Bridgeville, Pennsylvania (see *J.B. Higbee Glass Company*). See *Menagerie Set.*

Bryce, McKee & Company A glass-manufacturing facility established in 1850 in East Birmingham (Pittsburgh), Pennsylvania, by brothers Frederick M., James, and Stewart McKee, and brothers James and Robert D. Bryce, making flint tablewares, lamps and other wares. In 1854, the firm became Bryce,

Richards & Co.: in 1865, Bryce, Walker & Company (a brother, John Bryce, joined with his brothers, and William Walker; also see *Birmingham Flint Glass Works*). In 1882, Walker left and Edwin W. Bryce, son of Robert Bryce, entered the firm, the name becoming Bryce Brothers. In 1896, it opened a second facility in Hammondsville, Pennsylvania. In 1899, the Pittsburgh facility was absorbed into the U.S. Glass Company (*Factory B*). In 1900, the Bryce Bothers erected a new facility in Mt. Pleasant, Pennsylvania, eventually moving the Hammondsville operations there.

Bryce, Richards & Co.; Brice Walker & Co. See *Bryce, McKee & Co.*

Bryden's Pairpoint See *Gundersen Pairpoint Glass Works.*

B.T.Co. A trademark of Burley & Tyrrell Co.

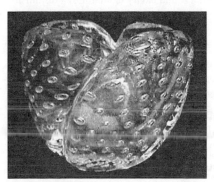

Controlled bubble Murano vase with tulip-petal shape, gold flecks, 2-3/4" h.
Tri-State Antiques

bubble (1) A small globule of air or gas that becomes trapped within a piece of glass either as the result of incomplete ingredient fusing (see *seeds*) or done intentionally to produce a decorative effect. Intentional bubbles were either in controlled or random designs. Controlled bubbles are ordinarily made by one of two methods: (a) rolling molten glass over a wooden slab with protruding spikes in the desired pattern, or (b) blowing molten glass in a dip or hinged mold having protruding spikes in the desired pattern. Random bubbles were made by several methods, one of the simplest known as *sticking-the-pot* (see *sticking-the-*

pot). (2) The paraison of molten glass attached to a blowpipe or a pontil.

bubble ball A spherical glass ornament, having a multitude of air bubbles in a distinct pattern, frequently mounted on a stand and functioning as a luminor. Tiffany and Kimble made many, during the 1930s and 1940s.

Controlled bubble paperweight, laser produced, 1-3/4" h. x 1-3/4" w. x 3" l.
Davanna Collection

bubble paperweight A glass paperweight with bubbles, purposely introduced either haphazardly or in a controlled pattern (see *bubble*).

Bubble Glass See *Catalonian.*

bubbled glass See *puleroso, vetro.*

Buck, E.A., & Company See *Westford Glass Company.*

bucket A container for capturing, holding, or carrying liquids or solids. Usually it has a bail handle and with a cylindrical form or with sides sloping inward toward the bottom (some have curved or ogee-shaped sides). Early ones were made of Roman glass between the 1st and 4th centuries.

bucket (form) bowl A drinking glass bowl of cylindrical shape with sides tapering slightly inward toward the base and a flat bottom at the point of stem contact. There are numerous deviations, including the *square bucket* with vertical sides, the *curved bucket* with slightly curved sides, the *waisted bucket* with waisted sides, and the *lipped bucket* with a lipped rim. They were popular from the 1730s until the 1800s.

bucket-topped bowl A bowl of a drinking glass in the shape of a bucket bowl;

however, instead of a flat bottom, it has a deep, round funnel below.

Buckeye Glass Company
See *Excelsior Glass Works.*

Buckeye Novelty Glass Company
(1888-1904) A glass manufacturing facility in Bowling Green, Ohio, making tableware, lamps, flasks, and some unique glass items.

bucranium *(Latin)*
A decorative motif, originally used during Roman times, the main element being an ox skull embellished with wreaths.

Buddha figure
A figure in the form of a seated Buddha. Those of glass were originally made in China during the second quarter of the 19th century, primarily for export to Siam.

Buffalo Cut Glass Company
(1902-1920) A glass-cutting house in Buffalo, New York, moving, in 1905, to Batavia, New York. Its trademark was a buffalo standing atop a map of the world and the legend "Buffalo Cut Glass Company."

bugle
(1) An bugle-shaped ornament, made at Bristol and Nailsea at the turn of the 19th century. Also see *post horn; fireman's horn; coach horn.* (2) A lengthened, hollow, cylindrical bead used in trimming dresses.

bulb glass
See *hyacinth vase.*

bulbous stopper
A round, nearly round, or globular stopper often with cut designs, frequently found on decanters made in the Pittsburgh, Pennsylvania, area.

bulle de savon *(French)*
Literally, *soap bubble.* A type of French opaline glass, made from about 1822, in an assortment of pastel colors.

bullet resistant glass
Glass, generally between 1-1/2 and 2 inches thick, made of several layers of laminated glass separated by layers of plastic or vinyl.

bullion (glass)
(Aka *pontil of a crown of glass, bull's-eye*) The thickened portion of a crown of glass to which the pontil was fastened after blowing the bubble and, from which, the spinning into a crown was performed.

bull's-eye
(1) A cut-glass motif shaped like a hollowed out circle made by a round edged fluting wheel. If the hollowed out area is an oval, it is called a *round thumbprint*; if surrounded with prism flares, a *sunburst.* (2) See *bullion (glass).*

bull's-eye & diamond point pattern
A pattern used on United States' early pressed glass, consisting of a series of raised *bull's-eyes,* to which is attached a group of raised diamonds in pointed triangular form.

bull's-eye mirror
See *convex mirror.*

bull's-eye pane
(Aka *center boss pane*) Pane glass, cut from a piece of a crown glass' center, having circular ridges radiating concentrically outward from the pontil mark.

bull's-eye stopper
(Aka *target stopper*) A stopper in the shape of an upright flat disc with a round cavity (sometimes a diminishing lens) in the middle. Some are plain; others have cut or molded flutes or ridges radiating outward from the central eye.

Bulltown Glass Works
See *Burlington, Atlantic, Cape May & Philadelphia Glass Manufacturing Company.*

bumper
A firing glass, bumping glass, or brimmer. After the toast, they were bumped on the table. See *brimmer; firing glass.*

bumping glass
See *firing glass.*

bun foot
A foot shaped like a somewhat flattened balloon, generally made separately from the body and fastened to it while hot and plastic, or with an adhesive after cooling.

bung
A stopper used in a kiln, either fitted in the door for viewing purposes or in the roof for releasing fumes resulting from firing lusters, enamels, etc.

burette *(French)*
(1) A cruet, ordinarily used at the altar for serving sacramental wine, having an extended curving spout, usually opposite a loop handle. (2) A small cruet for holding oil or vinegar. (3) A graduated glass tube, usually with a small aperture and stopcock, for delivering measured quantities of a liquid or for measuring the liquid or gas received or discharged.

burgee The waste material resulting from the cutting, grinding, etc., of glass; a sludge consisting of glass particles, abrasives, and liquids and, when dry, becoming hard, similar to concrete.

Burgess, Edward T. An 1880s glasscutter in Corning, New York, who worked at home and patented several cut-glass designs.

Burgin & Pearsall (1844-1910) A glass manufacturing facility established in Kensington (Philadelphia), Pennsylvania, making green glass druggist's wares. It also operated another facility in Millville, New Jersey (see *Whitall, Tatum & Co.*). In 1849, the Kensington facility became Burgin, Fowler & Company, and in 1853, Burgin & Sons.

Burgin & Sons; Burgin, Fowler & Co. See *Burgin & Pearsall.*

Burgin & Wood; Burgin, Wood & Bodine See *Glasstown Factory.*

Burgin, Wood & Pearsall See *Whitall, Tatum & Co.*

Burgundy glass A large wine glass having a stemmed foot, intended for burgundy. The bowl is sometimes globular or sometimes tall and ovoid, with a slightly inverted rim.

burial glassware See *cemetery glassware.*

Burke, Sedgwick & Co. See *Brownsville Glass Works.*

Burling Brothers See *Atlantic Glass Works.*

Burlington, Atlantic, Cape May & Philadelphia Glass Manufacturing Company (Aka *Bulltown Glass Works*) A glass manufacturing facility established by Samuel Crowley in 1858 in Bulltown (Waldo), New Jersey, making mainly bottles and, perhaps, Mason jars until about 1870.

Burlington Glass Works (1874/5-1909) A glass manufacturing facility established in Hamilton, Ontario, Canada, making pressed pattern glass in flint glass, milk glass, and colored glass. It was known for its lamps, lighting equipment, and paperweights. In

1891, it was purchased by the Diamond Glass Company, Montreal, Canada (later the Dominion Glass Company Limited).

Burmese vase, pink and yellow glass, c. 1885-1895, Mt. Washington Glass Co.
The Corning Museum of Glass

Burmese toothpick holder, glossy finish, 2-5/8" h.
Krause Publications

Inverted bell-shaped vase, flared, scalloped, and pinched rim; pedestal base with scalloped rim and acid finish, 4" h.
Krause Publications

Burmese glass An art glass developed by Frederick Shirley in 1881, patented on December 15, 1885, and made at the Mt. Washington Glass Co. Thomas Webb & Sons was licensed in 1886 to make the ware in

England, where it was known as *Queen's Burmese* (see *Queen's Burmese*). It is a homogeneous, translucent ware, shading from salmon pink to lemon yellow; the shading created by subjecting a portion of the lemon yellow piece to heat, causing it to change to pink. The colors are made by adding a small amount of uranium to the batch (uranium oxides cause it to glow yellow-green under ultraviolet light). The ware may be free- or mold-blown, plain, or pattern molded; the primary pattern being the expanded diamond. The satin finish, created using an acid bath, is more common than gloss. The decorations are usually flowers or birds, occasionally lines of poetry are added; some pieces are embellished with pictures or applied flowers of colored glass. It is quite thin, very brittle, and easily broken.

Because of the expense involved in making it, the company discontinued production in 1900. In 1932, Pairpoint made 132 pieces. The Gundersen Glass Co., successor to the Mt. Washington Glass Company, produced it for a short time in 1952 and 1957. The newer ware is heavier and thicker than the original, but embellished in the same ways, except the shapes are more modern. Reproductions have been made. Fenton's are marked on the base (see *Burmese glass by Fenton*). Italian imitations, made in 1960, have a grayish tint and the pontil mark usually shows the two colors mixed in that area.

Burmese Glass by Fenton

On January 1, 1970, Fenton introduced twelve pieces of its Burmese Glass, six undecorated and six in a Maple Leaf Burmese; one of its most expensive wares. Each piece is pressed into its preliminary shape and crimped, stretched and shaped into its final form by hand, constantly reheating it at the glory hole so the metal remains pliable; the reheating causing the portion subjected to the flame to change color from a creamy yellow to blushing pink (the gold causing the uranium based yellow to strike pink when reheated). See *Blue Burmese*.

Burmese glass, white

A name incorrectly applied to Mt. Washington's White Lusterless Glass.

burn out oven

A low temperature oven for melting wax out of a mold in the *lost wax process*.

burner block

Refractory block through which the burner flame is propelled into the furnace.

burning off

The process of separating a glass object from its mold by turning it in the middle of a ring of burners fitted with fine jets.

burning out

(1) The point in the firing process of pots and refractories where the water of plasticity and chemically held water is safely removed. (2) The process of melting the wax out of a mold in the *lost wax process*.

Burns, Thomas

See *Excelsior Flint Glass Works*.

burst-off penny green work

A method of finishing off the tops of bottles by merely knocking them from the blowing iron without further finishing.

Bush, The

See *Pennsylvania Glass Manufacturing Company*.

Bush (Cut) Glass Company

A glass cutting company established by Edgar J. Bush in Lansing, Michigan, in 1911, making fine cut glass from imported lead crystal blanks and a less-expensive line from pressed and figured blanks supplied by McKee Glass Company. In 1916, it stopped making cut glassware, but changed its name to Lansing Cut Glass Works, becoming a distributor of glassware and crockery until 1920. Bush personally continued cutting glass until 1918 using the name Bush Cut Glass Company.

Bushwick Flint Glass Works

A glass manufacturing facility established about 1865 in Brooklyn, New York, making flint glass. Prior to 1884, it was renamed Brookfield & Co. In the 1890s, it made bottles; closing about 1898.

bust

A representation of an individual in full relief that includes the head, neck, and a portion of the shoulders and breast. They date back to 325 A.D. See *head*.

Butcher & Waddington See *Elmer Window Light Company.*

Butland, James, & Co.
See *Kensington Glass Works.*

Butler Glass Company A short-lived glass manufacturing facility operating in Fostoria, Ohio, in the late 1880s.

butter, covered See *covered butter.*

butter ball container or holder (1) A round dish having a flat base and short straight vertical sides, used to serve butter. (2) See *stick dish.*

butter basin See *butter dish.*

Vaseline glass Daisy & Button pattern butter chip, 3" d.
Davanna Collection

Cut glass butter dish.
Davanna Collection

butter chip (Aka *butter pat*) A small dish, round, oval, or square, 1-1/2 to 3 inches in diameter, used to hold a single pat of butter.

Mosser cobalt-blue butter dish, 6" h.
Davanna Collection

butter dish (Aka *butter basin*) A small dish used to serve butter at the table or store it in the refrigerator. The dish used to serve butter at the table is normally round, generally about six inches in diameter, with a domed cover (see *covered butter*), often with two protruding vertical lug handles. Dishes used to store butter in the refrigerator are usually rectangular with a lid or square, cross section designed to hold either one pound or a quarter pound of butter.

butter molds and stamps A mold or stamp to shape and/or imprint butter with a symbol.

butter pat See *butter chip.*

butter receiver See *stick dish.*

butter tub A small bowl, used for serving butter, approximately five inches in diameter and two inches deep; sometimes accompanied by a plate about seven inches in diameter.

butterette A small butter plate, generally about 3 to 3-1/2 inches in diameter; somewhat larger than a butter chip, but smaller than a butter dish.

butterfly blue See *Mohammadan Blue.*

butterfly paperweight A paperweight, the central motif being an embedded glass butterfly, either alone or hovering over a flower. Some have a surrounding fringe of millefiori florets or garlands, others have a muslin ground. Some were made by Baccarat, and St. Louis.

buttermilk glass See *custard glass.*

button (1) A knob, disk, or the like, to be fastened on an article of clothing, either as a fastener or embellishment. (2) A style of wheel cut decoration in the form of raised rings within which is a smaller raised or depressed circle; the rings usually arranged in three rows around the vessel. It is found normally on vessels of Byzantine or Persian origin from the 6th to the 8th centuries or of Syrian origin from the 9th century. (3) The cut-glass motif known as *hobnail.*

button beaker See *knopfbecher.*

button drop A small, circular drop that typically hangs above a larger drop.

button knop A flattened variation of the annular knop, popular throughout the 18th and well into the 19th century.

buzz A geometric cut-glass motif first appearing about the turn of the 20th century, continuing in popularity in various forms until World War I. It received its name from its strong resemblance to a *buzz saw.* The vanes in the motif were miter cuts, either straight or curved, radiating from the edges of a central hobnail. These vanes often had fans cut between them. The first *buzz* patent is believed to be No. 30267, issued on February 28, 1899, to Patrick H. Healy and assigned to the American Cut Glass Co. of Chicago. The *pinwheel* is the most elaborately cut buzz, formed by curved miters and alternating fans; the heavy cutting creating the illusion of a spinning wheel. In the *buzz star,* the number of miters and fans was lessened and the center flattened, to decrease costs. During the "Flower Period," the buzz or buzz saw was further reduced in complexity, with fewer miters and fans, and on occasion, no fans at all.

buzz saw; buzz star See *buzz.*

bye hole (Aka *bocella, nose hole*) A small opening in a furnace wall (a) for extracting specimens of the metal for evaluation, (b) for reheating small articles or parts, (c) for further manipulation of an object during the finishing process, and (d) for heating the blowpipe and pontil. See *glory hole; spy hole; bocca.*

Byesville Glass (& Lamp) Company Located near Cambridge, Ohio, the company, originally known as the American Art Glass Company, began the production of glass in 1901. See *Cambridge Glass Company.*

Byrne, J.J. A blacksmith in Corning, New York, who cut glass on Pairpoint blanks from 1905 to 1907.

Byzantium An ancient Greek city on the Bosporus (a strait connecting the Black Sea and the Sea of Marmara), considered the origin of both gilding and enameling on glass.

C-and-S scroll See *rococo*.

cabbage stalk See *Krautstrunk*.

cabin bottle A flask in the shape of a square or rectangular log cabin with a pitched roof, a chimney (serving as a spout), and usually one door and two windows on the sides. Made in the United States to contain alcoholic beverages, they are often inscribed with the word "Tippecanoe" (part of the campaign slogan of presidential candidate William Henry Harrison).

cable A single twist with closely wound glass threads running through the entire stem length. Normally opaque white, but some colored or air twist. Found in the stems of some English drinking glasses, they may be a single cable or two cables intertwined.

cable decoration A decorative relief pattern normally in the form of a vertical column having a rope-like appearance, found most frequently on American glassware.

cabochon (French) A stone cut in convex form and polished, not faceted. Blobs of glass made to imitate such stones, especially precious and semi-precious stones, were often applied to glassware beginning on Roman glass made during the 4th century AD.

caboret A round, shallow, cut glass bowl with two glass handles, divided into two or more sections by glass dividers.

cachepot (French) In French, *pot hider*. A decorative, rather than functional, pot of opaque glass used to hold, and hide, a common flowerpot.

caddy A small container to hold tea. The term is derived from the Malasian word *Kati*, a weight equivalent to about 21 ounces. When tea was a luxury and quite expensive, it was shipped from the East to Europe in tin boxes, known as *caddies*. Eventually any

container, regardless of size, used to hold tea became known as a *caddy* or *tea caddy*.

cadmium ruby glass See *ruby glass*.

cage cup A cup of the *vasa diatretum* type in the form of a footless egg-shaped beaker, about five inches tall. Secured to the cup by small glass braces is a network of glass circles and sometimes a Latin or Greek inscription. Made by Roman craftsmen in the Rhineland, the body of the cup is of transparent glass and the network and/or lettering is often of colored glass. See *vasa diatreta*.

cagework Ornamental hand cut or pressed metalwork used to encase a glass bottle, fitting around the body, but not applied to it. It is not to be confused with silver overlay.

Cain(e)s, Thomas H. & William Thomas (1779-1865), born in England, worked in the glass industry there before coming to the United States. He arrived in New England during 1812, to work for the South Boston Flint Glass Works. In 1821, he founded the Phoenix Glass Works with his brother, William. Thomas is called the father of the New England flint glass industry. See *Phoenix Glass Works; South Boston Flint Glass Works*.

Caines & Johnston See *Phoenix Glass Works*.

Caithness Glass, Ltd. A glass manufacturing company established in 1960, with facilities at Wick (Caithness) and Oban (Argyll), Scotland, making crystal tableware and ornamental pieces with engraved embellishments, specializing in paperweights. See *Scottish glassware*.

cake (clay) Slabs of clay (used for pots) that come from a filter press. Because of the need to have homogeneous clay for pots, it is often necessary to add water to the clay until it becomes *slip*. The slip is then mixed, sieved, and placed in a filter press to remove much of the water. The cake is placed into a de-airing pugmill to remove more moisture before pot making.

cake (glass) See *glass cake*.

cake plate (Aka *sandwich plate, chop plate, salver*) A large, circular, heavy serving plate.

cake stand A large circular plate on a pedestal base for holding a cake.

Calabash flasks, New Jersey, c. 1860. Museum of American Glass at Wheaton Village, Millville, NJ.

calabash A flask made exclusively in the United States, with an egg-shaped body tapering to a tall neck. In reality, it is a bottle, but is classified with flasks because its production and press-molded patterns are similar to flasks made at the same facilities. Many historical flasks were made in the form of a calabash.

calcar (1) The oven or furnace in which frit was made or silica burnt in a calcining atmosphere. Also spelled *calker* or *caulker*. (2) A reverberatory furnace where heat is reflected from the roof downward toward the batch. The fusion of the basic ingredients of the batch is initiated within.

calcedonio *(Italian)* (1) (Aka *agate glass, chalcedony glass*) A variegated, opaque Venetian glassware made during the latter half of the 15th century. It imitated the earlier Roman agate glass resembling semi-precious stones, such as onyx and agate, with brown, blue, yellow, and green swirls. The art of making it was revived in the second half of the

19th century. See *Schmelzglas*. (2) A Venetian glass having a watery milk appearance.

calcine (1) To make powdery by the action of heat (by removing water of hydration or crystallization). (2) To oxidize, as by heat. (3) To frit (fuse).

Gold Aurene on calcite compote, Steuben Glass Works, Corning NY, c. 1910. Museum of American Glass at Wheaton Village, Millville, NJ.

Calcite glass An art glass, named for the mineral it resembles, developed about 1915 by Frederick Carder at Steuben. It has a creamy white tint with a soft ivory translucency, used mainly in making illuminating fixtures because of the interior surface's excellent reflective qualities and the softness of transmitted light. It is also used for various ornamental objects, tablewares, the inner or outer casing for the gold and blue Aurenes, and the matrix glass for the red, green, and brown Aurenes. The translucency was produced by the inclusion of calcium phosphate (bone ash) into the batch. The glass was gathered in three separate layers, by gathering about a third of the total amount needed and cooling it in a wooden block, covered with a second layer, also cooled, and a third layer added in the same manner. The result was a piece of three fused layers, each having its own reflecting and refracting surface. The outer surface was often sprayed, while still ductile, with stannous chloride, in the same manner as *Aurene* and *Verre de Soie*, giving the glass a slightly iridescent surface. The outer surface was, on occasion, acid etched or engraved with designs. Often a brown oxide, such as burnt umber or ocher mixed with linseed oil and turpentine, was rubbed into the etched surface to accent the design.

calcium phosphate Any of the phosphates of calcium occurring naturally in animal bones and some rocks, used in making translucent, milk-and-water, opaque white, and opal glass.

calico glass Marble or slag glass.

California Glass Insulator
Company A glass manufacturing company making insulators in the early years of the 20th century. In 1916, after it stopped making insulators, it changed its name to the California Glass Works.

calker See *calcar.*

Calla Lily A deeply acid etched design on *Florentine* blanks made by Consolidated Lamp & Glass Company. William Heacock gave it the name *Calla Lily.*

Callet, T.J., Cut Glass Co. (1921-1922) A glass cutting company established by William Allen and Tobias Callet in Corning, New York. See *Allen, William, Cut Glass Co.*

calligraphy Writing in a rather elegant script as a decorative art, often added to glassware by diamond point engraving. It was a popular form of decoration in Holland, perfected by Anna Roemers Visscher, during the second quarter of the 17th century.

cal(l)iper(s) An instrument with two arms, usually curved, fastened together with a rivet or screw or with a spring and pivot, used to determine thickness, dimensions, distance between surfaces, etc. The arms are usually bowed outward with the measuring tips pointing inward for measuring outside dimensions, and bowed inward with the measuring tips pointing outward for measuring inside dimensions.

calm(e) See *came.*

camaieu, en (French) A painting in several tones or hues of the same color. It has been used to embellish glassware, especially opaque white glass.

Camargue A creatively stylized vase, made by Lalique about 1935, with a ribbon-like rim and base, and a frosted glass body with four plaques, each with a representation of a horse set against a background of whirling clouds of dust or smoke and stained with sepia.

"Bashful Charlotte" by Cambridge (signed), peach, 6-1/2" h. Davanna Collection

Cambridge Glass ad from the Crockery and Glass Journal, dated September 1931, showing the #3011 Figured Stem line. Krause Publications

Cambridge Glass Company (1901-1954) A glass manufacturing company established in Cambridge, Ohio, in 1901, by Myron L. Case, Addison Thompson, Casey Morris, Fred L. Rosemond, and Andrew W. Herron (all principals in the National Glass Company). Arthur J. Bennett was the manager and President, gaining controlling interest shortly after it became operational in May 1902. In 1910, it established another facility in Byesville, Ohio, the Byesville Glass & Lamp Co.; which operated until 1917. In 1916, even though successful making pressed glasswares, Bennett redirected its efforts to make high-quality, hand-crafted blown tablewares. In 1939, Bennett sold his interest to his son-in-law, W.L. Orme. It closed in 1954; reopened shortly thereafter and operated, at a reduced capacity, until 1958. Its assets were sold to the Imperial Glass Company, including numerous molds that Imperial continued to use, altering some so they can be distinguished by the maker. When Imperial closed in 1985, the molds were sold to other glass companies, individuals, and National Cambridge Collectors, Inc.

The Cambridge Glass Company used several trademarks; the most common was *Near Cut*, used after 1906, and, after 1916, pressed glass was marked with a "C" in a triangle; many wares marked only with paper labels.

There are some terms that have special meanings to Cambridge glassware: (a) *acid cutback*—a deep etched design resulting from immersion in acid; (b) *Alpine*—clear or satin etched, only on its *Caprice* pattern; (c) *Doped (Carnival) glass*—an acid mist sprayed on hot glass, creating an iridescent finish; *(d) flashed*—the use of a special spray on cold glass reheated in a lehr to a high temperature, fusing the spray and the glass, making it very durable; (e) *floral decorated*—hand enameled flowers; (f) *gold encrusted*—acid etched and inlaid with 22-carat gold; (g) *gold stippled*—a rare embellishment made by daubing with a cloth or sponge; (h) *intaglio*—a very deep etched design obtained by being immersed in acid; (i) *Moonstone*—acid etched on one side; (j) *Pearl Mist*—a special acid etching giving a soft translucent or semi-opaque effect, only on its *Everglades* pattern; (k) *needle etched*—a design deeply etched by an electric powered needle; (l) *silk screen*—a design resulting from spraying enamel through an outlined fine screen and firing in a decorating lehr; (m) *silver deposit*—acid etched, encrusted with silver; and (n) *sponged acid*—a pitted effect obtained by daubing the glass with a sponge soaked in acid. See *Canton Glass Company*.

Camden Glass Works

A glass manufacturing facility established in Camden, New Jersey, by Joseph Wharton, an American pioneer in the production of nickel, and owner of over 100,000 acres of land now comprising the Wharton State Forest in southern New Jersey. It has been reported that it operated from 1877 to 1884 or from 1883 to 1886.

Camden (City) Cut Glass Company

(1911-1924) A glass cutting shop operating in Camden, New Jersey.

came H- or U-shaped lead strips used as muntins to hold small panes or pieces of glass. The H-shaped section is used when glass is fitted on both sides; the U-shaped for outer edges. The old term for *came* is *calm* from the Old English word *calme* meaning "length."

cameo A small carving in relief; the projection of figures, etc., from a background. Originally, a stone or shell carved in low relief showing the design and background in contrasting colors. The same technique, showing the design in two or more colors, is used to make cameo glass. They were popular between 1840 and 1875, having periodic comebacks since then. See *cameo glass*.

cameo engraving See *wheel engraving; wheel engraving, relief.*

Cameo glass vase with blue background and white decoration, etched "Thomas Webb & Sons" in banner, 6" h.
Krause Publications

cameo glass An object formed of cased or flashed glass where portions of one or more of the outer layers are removed either by carving, cutting, etching or other means, leaving a design, in relief, against a background of a different color. The process of making it was used by the ancient Egyptians and Romans, and also by the Chinese during the 18th century BC; some examples from the 1st and 2nd centuries AD have survived. In the 1870s, John Northwood made a replica of the *Portland Vase* in cameo glass. Thomas Webb & Sons retained him to make examples of cameo glass for the International Exposition in Paris in 1878. He made a vase, known as the *Pegasus* or *Dennis Vase*, signed and dated 1882, with a very dark, blue-coated exterior of opalescent glass.

Northwood worked with his brother Joseph, and instructed George and Thomas Woodall, who were quite inventive in making the blanks for it. Instead of layering glass of different colors over the base glass, they selectively applied patches of colored glass on the base relating to the specific cameo design. Emile Galle and the Daum brothers also made some fine specimens of cameo glass, usually in the Art Nouveau style. Frederick Carder was associated with Northwood in making it from 1880 to 1901.

In ancient times, parts of the overlay were cut away by chiseling or by wheel, leaving a design of the overlay color against a background of a different color. In the last quarter of the 19th century, an acid-resistant bituminous coating was put on the surface parts to be developed as a pattern and the unprotected areas exposed to a hydrofluoric acid bath, baring the background. Then a silhouette of the final design is outlined, coated with the bituminous paint, and the piece again subjected to hydrofluoric acid until the unprotected parts are eaten away, exposing still more of the background. The bituminous coating was removed and the worker, using tools, brings the rough pattern to the final desired product. True cameo glass requires much time, skill, and patience. Many imitations are simply painted or entirely acid etched. One should look carefully at items marked *cameo* or *Florentine Art Cameo*; real cameo glass is never so marked. For more information, see the following: *Florentine Art Cameo glass; French cameo glass; Galle cameo glass; Ivory cameo glass; Le Verre Francais(e) cameo glass; simulated cameo glass; Tiffany cameo glass; carving; Portland Vase; Milton Vase; Pegasus Vase.*

cameo incrustation A sulfide; also spelled *sulphide*. See *encrusted cameo; crystallo-ceramie.*

Campbell & Forsyth; Campbell, E., & Co. See *Brownsville Glass Works.*

Campbell, T., & Company See *American Glass Works.*

Campbell, Thomas B., & Company (1905-1918) A glass cutting company established in Brooklyn, New York, moving, about 1913, to Manhattan, New York.

Campbell, Jones & Company See *Shepherd Company.*

campfire theory The theory proposed by Pliny the Elder in his *Natural History* glass' discovery. Supposedly Syrian merchants landed on an island and decided to build, on the beach, a campfire for heat and cooking. Having no rocks to set their kettles on, they used blocks of natron (sodium carbonate) from their ship. After starting the fire, they noticed rivulets of a substance flowing along the sand. Theoretically, the sand, sodium carbonate, and heat made glass. However, the temperature of a campfire is not hot enough to fuse the ingredients.

camphene lamp A lamp, similar to a whale oil lamp, that burned camphene, a mixture of 1.25 parts turpentine and 6.75 parts alcohol. The mixture was occasionally scented with aromatic oils, such as lemon, citron, juniper, etc. They came into use about 1835. However, because of the highly flammable nature of camphene, the wick holders of these lamps were set at about a 45° angle from each other, rather than vertical, as with whale oil lamps.

camphor bottle See *toilet bottle.*

Camphor glass powder jar, green, dog finial, 4-1/2" h. x 4-1/2" w. Krause Publications

camphor glass A glass with a cloudy white appearance created by treating the object with hydrofluoric acid vapors, made in numerous Midwest facilities during the mid-19th century. Blue camphor glass, attributed to the Sandwich Glass Company, is extremely rare.

can A drinking glass in the shape of a cylindrical tankard.

Canada Glass Works Co., Ltd See *Ottawa Glass Works*.

canal lamp See *canalboat lantern*.

canalboat lantern A box-shaped lantern enclosed on three sides and the top and bottom with tinned sheet iron, the remaining side being glass. It has a top ring handle for suspending it from a ceiling or wall hook on canal boats and normally held three to five candles in a row.

canary glass See *vaseline glass*.

candelabrum A large, ornamental piece having two or more limbs with candle nozzles. Often made in pairs, they were often placed on a side table in front of a mirror to reflect the light. Early ones were generally unadorned and rudimentary, having a base, short shaft and limbs with plain candle nozzles. Later ones were taller and more elaborate, embellished with icicles, spires, etc., and festoons of drops. Early English terms were *girandole* or *luster*. The plural is *candelabra*.

candle beaker See *Kerzenbecher*.

candle cover (Aka *candle shade, hurricane shade, abatjour*) A high glass jacket, usually between 18 and 30 inches tall, to be placed around a lighted candle to protect the flame from drafts; some in a cylinder-shaped vase with a flaring mouth, attached to the candleholder through a hole in the rounded bottom; others bulb-shaped with top and bottom openings designed to fit over a single candlestick. See *chimney; hurricane shade*.

candle lustre See *lustre*.

candle nozzle A socket fashioned to hold a candle, normally found on candlesticks, chandeliers, etc. They are occasionally detachable and often have a small tray known as a *drip pan* or *bobeche* encircling it (for catching wax drippings from the candle and either permanently fixed to the nozzle or detachable).

candle shade See *candle cover*.

candle socket See *candle nozzle*.

candlebeam A chandelier.

Bohemian glass candlestick, amber over clear glass, 10" h.
Davanna Collection

Amethyst glass candlestick, New England, c. 1840-1860, 7-1/2" h.
The Corning Museum of Glass

candlestick A device for holding a solitary candle, generally with a flat base of round, square, or ornamental shape, and a central column (*shaft*) that has a socket or nozzle, with a drip pan at its tip. On some, the nozzles and/or drip pans are removable. They came into existence during the 17th century with the creation of small diameter candles, replacing thick candles used on the spikes of pricket candlesticks. Generally, their base and shapes changed with the style of stemmed glassware. Early ones were usually built in parts. One-piece candlesticks came into being in the late 1850s- early 1860s. See the following types of candlesticks: *chamber; column; dolphin; figure; hand; ship; tea; vase*.

candlestick unguentarium An unguentarium having a high, narrow, cylindrical neck tapering outward to a wide, flat base, suggestive of a single candlestick and made of Roman glass.

candlestick vase A vase having a reversible cover; one side being plain and the reverse having an attached candle nozzle. The term *cassolette* is sometimes used for such vases, but it should only be used if there are cover holes allowing scent to escape.

Candlewick #100 pattern candelabrum by Imperial Glass, 4-3/4" h.
Tri-State Antiques

Candlewick Glass A glassware made by Imperial Glass, from 1936 until October 1982, the pattern known as Imperial's No. 400; a plain glassware molded with beading around the rims and bases or stems of most pieces. Several pieces were made without beads; these are hard to identify since Candlewick was marked only with paper labels.

Since originally introduced, over 400 different articles have been made; in latter years only 36 different articles were made; some not for public use; others are rare, such as desk calendars, picture frames, and hand and small standing mirrors. Items were usually offered in clear and colored glass. Proprietary colors such as *Viennese Blue* (pale blue, 1937-38), *Ritz Blue* (cobalt, 1938-41), and *Ruby Red* (red, 1937-41) were used, as were amber, black, emerald green, lavender, pink, and light yellow. From 1977 to 1980, four items of Candlewick stemware were made in proprietary solid colors: *Ultra Blue, Nut Brown, Verde Green,* and *Sunshine Yellow.* At the same time, some black stemware was made on an experimental basis. Sometimes the colored wares are accented with fired-on gold and red, blue and green beads. Other embellishments include silver overlay, gold incrustations, cuttings, etchings, and hand-painted designs. Many items were made in a variety of shapes and styles, i.e., three styles of baskets, five wine sets, five sugars and creamers, 11 ashtray sets, 13 cruets, 26 vases, 65 types of stemware and tumblers, and 71 bowls and bowl sets. The molds were eventually purchased by several companies and individuals. About 200 molds were purchased by Mirror Images of Lansing, Michigan, and 18 small molds by Boyd Crystal Art Glass of Cambridge, Ohio. Many of the articles advertised as Candlewick were made by others; there were numerous other patterns similar to Candlewick made by Heisey, Anchor Hocking, Bryce Brothers, Seneca Glass Co., Libbey, Lotus Glass Co., Duncan & Miller, etc. True Candlewick was made by Imperial and should not be confused with the old Cannon Ball pattern, the Atlas pattern, or the Candlewick pattern made in the 1800s.

candy container (1) *For home use,* primarily a covered dish, jar, etc., used to hold candy; generally in the form of a fairly deep dish or small jar. (2) *For commercial use,* usually large covered cylindrical containers or round, flat-sided containers with an opening offset from the top's center for easy access. (3) *For the retail trade,* made in a variety of shapes (from standard containers to those shaped like animals, vehicles, etc.) and sizes to accommodate specific types of candies. One of the first was made in 1876 for Croft, Wilbur, & Co., Confectioners, filling a small glass Liberty Bell with candy, sold at the 1876 Centennial Exposition in Philadelphia. Jeanette, Pennsylvania, was a focal point for the packaging of candy in containers. The principle manufacturers were Victory Glass, J.H. Millstein, T.H. Stough, and J.C. Crosetti. Some of the earliest were West Brothers; L.E. Smith; and Cambridge Glass. They remained popular until the 1960s when they became too expensive to make.

Cobalt-blue nude candy dish.
Davanna Collection

candy dish A small dish, occasionally covered, used to contain candy.

Miss America pattern covered candy jar, pink glass.
Krause Publications

candy jar A jar used to hold candy, often part of a dinnerware set. They were often footed and stemmed. See *candy container.*

candy paperweight See *scrambled paperweight.*

cane (1) A glass object shaped like a walking stick or staff, for decorative, not practical use. (2) A rod of glass usually cut into slices (*set ups*), used for making millefiori or mosaic glassware or, when uncut, made into stems of drinking glasses. See the following types of canes: *arrowhead; pastry mold; pie crust; shamrock; silhouette; star dust; friendship.* (3) A blowpipe. (4) (Aka *chairbottom*) A cut glass motif imitating the design of the woven cane in chair bottoms, consisting of eight-sided buttons in alternate squares formed by vertical and horizontal cuts. Double diagonal cuts traverse the raised squares at right angles to each other.

cane-on-cane A cut glass motif consisting of the cane pattern, on each button is cut a likeness of a section of the design, including four tiny buttons. It is rare because of the intricate cutting involved.

cane variant (Aka *Russian variant*) A cut glass motif consisting of a group of six buttons surrounding a pyramidal star; the six buttons becoming a part of the adjacent six. It is a variant of the Russian motif in which four buttons are arranged around a pyrimidal star. Martha Louise Swan calls it the *Hexad-*

of-Buttons-and-Star, "hexad" meaning a group or series of six.

canister A container for holding food products, such as cookies, tea, etc.

canne (1) French for blowpipe. (2) Italian for makers of large beads of prepared enamels for exportation. See *perlai.*

cannikin A small drinking cup.

canning jar See *fruit jar.*

Pressed-glass canoe, Daisy & Button pattern 9" l.
Davanna Collection

Cut glass canoe, 13" l. x 4" w.
Davanna Collection

canoe A shallow bowl, long and narrow, tapering upward to points on each end, like a canoe. Generally used to hold flowers, they are often, incorrectly, called *celery holders.* Bowls and saltcellars were made in this shape.

canopy A decorative piece placed at the top of a candelabrum or chandelier, often with festoons of drops attached.

canted corner See *chamfered corner.*

Canterbury The Russian cut glass pattern with the button cut with a single star.

cantir (Spanish) Also spelled *cantaro* or *cantarro.* A closed jug with two nozzles extending vertically from the body; one, short and wide, for pouring and filling; the other, tall and thin, becoming narrower as it rises, for drinking by shooting a stream directly into the mouth. Its body is spherical or egg- or pear-shaped, has a kick base and an overhead vertical ring handle. They were made in Catalonia, Spain, Venice, and southern France in the 17th and 18th centuries.

Canton Collectibles, The
See *Consolidated Lamp & Glass Company.*

Canton Glass Company
(1) A glass company originally founded as the Sneath Glass Company in 1883 in Canton, Ohio, making pressed glass tablewares and fruit jars under the Mason patent and their own, "Canton Domestic Fruit Jar." In 1894, it moved to Marion, Indiana, and, in 1899, joined the National Glass Company. In 1901, it was dismantled and moved to Cambridge, Ohio, becoming known as the Cambridge Glass Company. (2) (1904-1905) A glass manufacturing facility in Canton, Ohio.

cap cover A cover for a jar that is low, flat topped, and typically circular, designed to fit over a cylindrical collar on a jar. See *screw cap; dome cover.*

Cape Cod Glass Company
A glass manufacturing facility established in 1858 in Sandwich, Cape Cod, Massachusetts, by Deming Jarves (after he withdrew from the Boston & Sandwich Glass Co.) and James D. Lloyd. Jarves built it for his son, John (I W.) From January 15, 1863, until October 26, 1863, it was operated by J.W. Jarves & Company (John Jarves dying in 1863), which on the latter date was in liquidation. It was reorganized and incorporated on February 8, 1864, as the Cape Cod Glass Company with Deming Jarves as President. Its wares, including tablewares and lamps, mainly pressed pattern and cut glass, were similar to those of the Boston & Sandwich Glass Co. In the late 1860s, it made some art glass. On April 15, 1869, Deming Jarves died, it closed shortly thereafter. A few years later, a Doctor Flowers bought it, making some paperweights and *vasa murrhina* among other products. In 1882, it closed permanently.

Cape Cod Glass Works See *Cape Cod Glass Company.*

Cape May Glass Company
(1901-1924) (Aka *Upper Factory*) A bottle glass manufacturing facility established in Cape

May Court House, New Jersey. See *Hereford Glass Company.*

Capewell glass Flint glassware made by John Capewell at his Philadelphia facility about 1825.

Capewell, James G., & Company
See *Excelsior Flint Glass Works; Westville Flint Glass Works.*

Capewell, J.G., & Sons; Capewell & Brothers
See *Excelsior Flint Glass Works.*

capstan salt (Aka *spool, pulley, or scroll salt*) A spool- or pulley-shaped salt, often with scroll-shaped rim brackets to hold a plate or napkin to cover it.

capstan stem (Aka *spool stem*) A stem on English ale glasses, popular from about 1800 to 1830, shaped like a ship's capstan, resembling a spool-like cylinder, with a collar below the bowl and a larger ring above the foot.

captain glass (Aka *master glass*) A large sweetmeat dish, placed in the center of a salver, with smaller sweetmeat and/or jelly glasses around it.

captain's decanter A decanter designed to be used aboard ship. They were heavier than those used at home and distinguished by their broad, flat base, providing added stability at sea.

carafe A bottle, used for serving wine or water, with a somewhat spherical or cylindrical body and a thin neck with no stopper. Originally called *water crafts,* they were smaller than a decanter and usually placed between a pair of diners and often accompanied by a pair of matching goblets. Later, accompanied by a matching tumbler, inverted to fit over the mouth, serving as a cover, they served as a bedroom water container.

caramel slag See *chocolate glass.*

carbon amber glass An inexpensive, rich amber-colored glass, the color believed to be imparted by carbon, but later proven to be caused by iron oxide and sulfur in a soda-lime glass batch (melted in a strong reducing atmosphere; carbon being the reducing agent).

Dark olive-green glass carboy, c.
1850-1900, 17" h. x 16-1/2" w.
The Corning Museum of Glass

carboy Derived from the Persian word
qarabah, a bottle of considerable size used
for storage or transportation of liquids.
English ones were originally spherical, but
during the 19th century became pear-shaped
with a tall, narrow neck, and a string rim,
designed to hold about one gallon, but after
about 1830, they were made in larger capacities. Many were enclosed in boxes or
wrapped in wicker to minimize breakage.

Carcel lamp (Aka *patent lamp, mechanical* or *mechanized lamp*) A variation of the
Argand lamp, first made in France about
1800. It used the Argand burner and had a
clockwork pump that controlled the flow of
whale oil. The flame was protected by a vertical chimney and round shade.

Circe Perdue (lost wax) bowl, Frederick
Carder, Steuben Glass Works, Corning NY,
c. 1930. Museum of American Glass at
Wheaton Village, Millville, NJ.

Carder, Frederick (1863-1963) Born in
England, he worked at Leys Pottery, owned
by his father and paternal grandfather. He

then went to work at Stevens & Williams, in
1880, where he began designing original
glass forms. As the demand for cameo glass
intensified, Stevens & Williams, in 1881,
engaged John Northwood, who worked with
him on many artistic and technical projects. In
1888, he won a silver medal in the National
Competition of Schools of Science and Art
for a vase design, *Cupid & Psyche*, modeled
in white wax relief on dark amethyst glass.

In 1889, he won a gold medal for *The Muses*, a
dark blue glass vase with white wax relief. He
became an art instructor at the Stourbridge
School of Art. In 1891, he received his Art
Master's Certificate and the Gold Medal of the
Year for his 30-inch copy of the bronze, *The
Archer*. As a result, he was entitled to study for
three years in Paris, Rome, or London, but
Stevens & Williams disapproved his leave. In
1891, the local government requested Carder
establish an art school in Wordsley where artistic laborers could attend evening courses. In
1902, the Institute sent him on a tour of the
glassmaking centers of Germany and Austria.
In 1903, it sent him on a fact-finding mission to
the United States where he visited several facilities including those in Corning, New York.

On meeting Hawkes in early March 1903,
Carder signed a contract and, in July 1903, he
and his family sailed to New York. His original
objective was to make high-quality blanks for
craftsmen at the Hawkes facility to decorate,
but he persuaded Hawkes to initiate another
venture permitting him more experimental lee-
way. As a result, in late October 1903, the
Steuben Glass Works was created. He ran the
facility almost single-handedly until, in 1918, it
became a division of the Corning Glass Works.
He was retained by the new management as
Managing Director, but soon after, his authority
was diminished when most of the ornamental
glass production was replaced by the bulbs, tubing, and optical glass.

In August of 1919, he had to surrender yet
more of his authority, being demoted to Art
Director. After World War I, the facility had
begun again to make more artistic ware.
Carder's policy from 1903 to 1932 was to
continue to make an object as long as it sold,
adding "designs discontinue themselves." In
February of 1932, he was removed as Art

Director of Steuben and made Art Director of Corning Glass Works, transforming his office into a studio where he installed a furnace and other glassmaking and decorating equipment. Later he was moved to a suite of offices at Steuben. Although he presumably had been delegated to an inactive status as far as Steuben production was concerned, he was regularly consulted by scientists, management, collectors, museums, and others interested in the various aspects of glassmaking.

In 1959, Carder, at age 96, decided to retire and moved his factory studio-office to his home, donating the remaining contents of his office to the Corning Museum of Glass. He specialized in formulating new and different colorings for all kinds of patterns and surface effects and used combinations of modern and traditional techniques to make new wares. He ventured back to every period in history for inspiration and, through his work, Steuben became one of the greatest experimental glasshouses in the country. Many factory-made pieces bear his signature, *F Carder*, but some made during the 1950s and early 1960s also have his signature which indicates the piece was his design (sometimes called his *late signature*). The exceptions to this are castings from his *cire perdue* molds which were usually signed by him and dated. See the following types of glass: *acid cutback; Alabastor; Aqua Marine, Aurene, Calcite, Cintra; Cluthra; Cyprian; Diatreta; Florentia; Grotesque; Intarsia; iridescent; Jade; Moss Agate; opalescent; Plum Jade; Quartz; Rouge Flambe; Ruby; Silveria; Tyrian.* Also see: *Mandarin Yellow; Matsu-no-ke.*

Cardinal Virtues, Twelve See *Virtues, Twelve Cardinal.*

Carmen A line of red glassware made from 1931 to 1942 by the Cambridge Glass Company, and reintroduced in 1950.

Carmen cut A cut-glass pattern consisting of large diamond panels filled with four point stars and fans, alternating with smaller cut diamonds.

carnauba wax A leaf wax from the Brazilian carnauba tree, frequently used, together with beeswax and resin, to lubricate glassmaking tools.

Carnival glass flat bowl, *Grape* **pattern, Northwood Glass Co., Wheeling, WV, c. 1910-1919.**
The Corning Museum of Glass

Vintage carnival glass bowl by Fenton, c. 1911.
Tri-State Antiques

Carnival glass (Aka *Nancy glassware, Taffeta glassware*) An inexpensive imitation of the iridescent glass of Carder and Tiffany, made from about 1895 through the 1920s. It received its current name because it was used as a premium at grocery stores and given away as prizes at carnivals and fairs. It was made in large quantities and is being reproduced today, both in the United States and abroad in some of the popular early patterns. The objects were generally of pressed glass, a few being mold blown. Some pieces have a pattern on both the outside and the inside—sometimes the patterns differ. It was made by subjecting the object, while still hot, to an inexpensive spray, instead of using metallic oxides in the batch as did the more expensive art glass, and sprayed again with hydrofluoric acid and dipped in vinegar to iridize it. Variations in the process include: (a) spraying the ware more than once with different solutions; (b) varying the amount of the spray; or (c) allowing the glass to cool somewhat before spraying (the spray on very hot glass produced a mat surface while on cooler glass, a shiny iridescence, frequently called a *radium finish*). Any manipulation after spraying will create minute breaches in the iridescent surface, creating an onion skin effect. The motifs are generally realistic, derived from plant and animal life and cut glass designs. A variety of colors were used; either the glass itself is colored or flashed. The most popular colors were marigold, green, blue, and purple; pastels were less common; red is rare because of the expenses incurred in production. The leading maker was Northwood Glass, followed by Fenton Art Glass and Imperial Glass, with some of the finest iridescence developed by Millersburg Company. Most reproductions made in the 1950s have an impressed "IG" for Imperial Glass or an "F" for Fenton Art Glass. See *Doped Ware*.

Carothers, George See *Virginia Green Glass Works*.

Carpenter, Edward, & Co. Carpenter & Heston: See *Olive Glassworks*.

carpet ground A ground made of numerous, solidly packed small canes of the same type and color into which a few strategically placed canes are placed of different color for a pattern, floret, or silhouette. The effect was a background resembling a carpet.

carpet (ground) paperweight A paperweight having a carpet ground with strategically placed canes with florets, patterns, or silhouettes. Many were made by Baccarat and St. Louis. They are also called "geometrically arranged millefiore paperweights."

Carrara Ware Jade glass made by the U.S. Glass Company in the following colors: coral, jade, pearl gray, and Chinese yellow.

carriage glass A footless vessel carried in carriages, used for serving travelers.

carriage lights Any of a variety of lamps specifically designed for use in coaches, carriages, or other horse-drawn vehicles.

carrot A cone-shaped formation of glass used in making an opaque twist stem for a drinking glass, made by lining a steel cylinder with rods of opaque white glass and spreading molten glass over them. The cane produced is marvered into a cone, enclosed in another layer of molten glass, and annealed. It is used as needed in making stems by affixing the point of the cone to the bowl of the glass and drawing and twisting the cone to make a stem. Once made, the remainder of the *carrot* is sheared off and placed aside for future use.

Carruthers Glass Company A short-lived glass hollow ware and window glass manufacturing facility established in 1820 in Wheeling, West Virginia, by George Carruthers.

carrying (-in) boy An unskilled laborer who carries a newly formed glass object, or a glass object in a mold to, and inside, the lehr. He is also responsible for counting the objects put in the lehr to ensure his team has met the requirements of the *move* list. Also, if a piece has to be further decorated, he may turn it over to the warming-in boy. It is generally the first job at a facility to be held by a newly hired youth.

carrying-over boy An unskilled laborer who conveys the heated, partially shaped molten glass while still on the blowpipe, from the blocker, or warming-in boy, to the blower.

Carter & Hogg See *Brownsville Glass Works*.

Carter & Woodruff See *Putnam Flint Glass Works*.

cartoon The full-scale design of a picture, ornamental motif, pattern, etc., made on tracing paper and transferred to the piece's body to be embellished. It is also used as a planning tool so various designs and combinations of designs may be reviewed in relation to the object's size and shape to be embellished.

carved glass (1) Glass cut or abraded into a shape or form from a solid piece of glass. (2) Blown, pressed, or cast glass further embellished or shaped by cutting, engraving, and/or grinding. See *wheel engraving; wheel engraving, relief; relief*.

Carved Glass, Tiffany See *Tiffany Carved Glass*.

carving See *wheel engraving; wheel engraving, relief; relief.*

Cascade Glass Works A glass manufacturing facility established in 1859 in Birmingham, Pennsylvania. In 1864, Johnson, King & Company took over, making pressed, blown, and cut glassware, and table and bar wares. In 1869, the operating firm became King, Son & Company and, in 1880, King Glass Company. In 1884, it purchased the burned-out facility of the Crystal Glass Company of Bridgeport, Ohio. In 1891, it joined the U.S. Glass Company (*Factory K*). See *King Glass Company.*

case bottle A bottle of square or rectangular cross section designed to fit with other identical bottles in compartments in a case or box, see *bottle case.* See *whiskey decanter.*

Clear glass cased in blue glass, cut to clear, 14-1/2" h.
Davanna Collection

American cased glass salt and vase.
Krause Publications

cased glass Glassware made of two or more layers of different-colored glass. It is created by blowing a gather of glass, and from this, forming a bowl-shaped object by knocking off the end nearest the blowpipe. This is then placed in a mold and a second gather of metal of a different color is blown into it. The piece, now of two layers, is removed from the mold and heated to a temperature just high enough for the two layers to fuse. The process is repeated for each additional layer desired, called *cup casing* or *cup-overlay method.* Cased glass has a thicker outer layer than flashed glass. The major problem to overcome in making cased glass is ensuring the glasses have compatible coefficients of expansion. It has been made since Roman times and used in making cameo and cut glass, and in paperweights. See *imitation cased glass; multi-layered cased glass; silver glass; overlay glass; cameo glass; flashed glass.*

casket A small chest, box, case, or carton, decorative in nature, to hold jewels or jewelry, or used as a reliquary. Larger ones are usually made of wood or lead, covered with glass embellishments, often with small figures made *at-the-lamp.* Smaller caskets are often made of lead glass with overall cutting and a hinged lid. See *box.*

Cassell & Gallagher (1852-1863/4) A glass manufacturing facility established in Zanesville, Ohio, by Cassell & Gallagher; being purchased shortly thereafter by Kearns, Burns & Carter.

casserole A deep, round dish or bowl, generally covered, for baking and serving food. They are made of heat resistant glass, such as *Pyrex.*

Cassius Purple See *Purple of Cassius.*

cassolette (French) (Aka *essence vase* or *pot*) A covered vase to hold perfume, scented fluids, or solid substances used to freshen a room with a perforated cover or shoulder. They were often mounted in ormolu or gilt bronze with openwork decoration. Similar vases with no cover or shoulder holes, but with a reversible cover with a candle nozzle on one side, have been incorrectly called *cassolettes*; these are *candlestick vases.* A vase with a reversible cover with a candle nozzle on one side is considered a *cassolette* only if it has holes in the cover or shoulder.

cast figure mold A mold making process perfected by Reuben Haley. First, designs were molded or sculpted in clay. Then a plaster casting was made from the clay object, and from this casting, an iron mold was made.

cast glass (1) Glass in sheet form made by the casting process, originally made by the Romans in making mirrors. The process was refined during the 17th century. It involved pouring molten glass onto a sand-covered iron table, rolling it into a flat sheet, and grinding and polishing it on both sides. Cast glass so-made was used almost exclusively for coach and house windows, and mirrors. (2) Glass objects made by pouring molten glass into molds and allowing it to cool. (3) A type of glass made by one of the following two processes: (a) the fusing of powdered glass in a one- or two-piece mold, the resultant products being either open vessels or solid objects, but never hollow objects; or (b) the *cire perdue* process. See *cire perdue.*

cast porcelain An extremely dense white glass, made by adding the mineral cryolite to the batch. In England, it is called *vitro-porcelain.* See *cryolite; cryolite glass.*

castellan See *chatelaine.*

castellated See *crenellated.*

caster See *castor.*

caster place Blown glass objects made without the use of a mold.

casting A technique used in ancient times to make glass objects by simply pouring molten glass into a mold, either open or closed, and allowing it to harden.

casting bottle A scent bottle for dispersing scent about a room. See *springel glass.*

castor (Aka *sifter*) Also spelled *caster.* A vial, cruet, or small container for serving condiments. The term *castor* includes *cruets,* and a *cruet* is regarded as a *castor.* A *castor* is considered a small container, with a perforated lid, for disseminating seasonings such as salt, pepper, sugar, etc. Although sometimes it was not perforated, for holding condiments such as mustard. The exterior or interior of the castor's neck was threaded for a threaded stopper or a threaded screw cap. Some castors are of one piece with holes pierced in the domed top for dispensing and a large hole, usually cork stoppered, for filling at the bottom. See *sugar castor; pepper bottle; cruet; muffineer; castor bottle; castor set.*

castor hole chair When a glass manufacturing facility had more than one *chair,* it was the first *chair,* consisting of a blower or gaffer and three assistants. It made large objects, jugs, decanters, etc., while other *chairs* made less complex objects.

Castor set in silver-plated frame.
Krause Publications

Pressed glass castor set (salt, pepper, and mustard) on leaf tray.
Davanna Collection

castor set A set typically consisting of three to seven condiment or castor bottles within a glass, pewter, silver, or silver-plated frame, usually with a center handle. The individual bottles, usually of different sizes and some of different shapes (depending on the intended contents), have an overall tendency to match others in the set.

Caswell & Co. See *Cleveland Glass Works.*

Catalonian (Aka *Bubble Glass, Smear Glass, Blister Glass*) A line of glassware designed by Reuben Haley who received a patent for the process to create it, made by Consolidated Lamp & Glass and introduced in January 1927. It was an attempt to reproduce the look of 17th century Spanish handmade glass. The original labels read "*Catalonian—A Reproduction of Old Spanish Glass.*" The process for making it was as follows: A rod is dipped into molten glass and an initial gather taken, rolled, cooled, and reheated. Then, raw materials used in the batch were sprinkled onto the gather. The reaction between the hot glass and the cool raw materials caused the gather to have bubbles and blisters, elongated as the glass at the end of the rod was swung back and forth by the worker, before blowing it into its final form. It is distinguished by concentric rings in the design and rough pontil marks. Most wares are either clear or light colored with a light transparent wash; some darker pieces were made (such as red) or a darker wash used. Rainbow highlighting was sometimes used for decorative effect. Infrequently, one or more colors were applied over a portion of crystal glass. Similar wares were made by McKee Glass Company (in 1928), called *Rebecca* (in green, amber, and pink); by Diamond Glass-Ware Company, called *Barcelona*; by Morgantown Glass Works (in January 1933), called *El Mexicano*; and by Dunbar Glass Company (in 1935). Consolidated also made a closely related line called *Spanish Knobs* (see *Spanish Knobs*).

Cate, Norman S., & Co. See *Bay State Glass Co.*

Cate & Phillips See *Bay State Glass Co.*

Cate & Teasdale See *Bay State Glass Co.*

Cate, LaSalle & Company See *Missouri Glass Company.*

cathedral glass (1) A decorative glass used in windows patented by Arthur Schierholz on July 17, 1883. To make it, one of the following initial steps was taken: (a) an entire sheet of glass was covered with a colored or colorless enamel compound, upon which glass beads, either colored or clear, were scattered; or (b) the enamel coating was used over part of the surface in accordance with a predetermined design. The sheet was then placed in a kiln just hot enough to melt the enamel and fuse the beads to its surface (see *Coralene glass*). (2) Machine or hand-rolled stained glass. Machine rolled is *double rolled*; the rollers may be plain and/or embossed with a texture impressed on the glass sheet. It is of uniform thickness, has consistent color and is relatively easy to cut. Cathedral glass is always one color, does not have the brilliance of hand-blown antique glass, and is less expensive. It is made by melting the batch ingredients in large furnaces and extruding the resultant metal through rollers, passing into a lehr. The color is produced by mixing silver nitrate and metallic and non-metallic oxides in the batch. The names of some of the textures are: *Antique, Semi-Antique, Oceanic, Ripple, Moss, Granite, Hammered, Flemish, Florentine, Figure C, Seedy, Pebble, Marine Antique,* etc. Hand rolled cathedral glass is made one sheet at a time on a steel plate. It is not of uniform thickness and is more difficult to cut.

cat's paw opals An opal made of stained glass, having a mottled effect, i.e., *cat's paw*, achieved by reheating glass in the lehr and rolling it over a cool cast iron plate; it contracts instantaneously, creating an irregular surface where it comes in contact with the plate.

caudle cup A vessel, for drinking caudle (a warm drink for ailing individuals; a mixture of wine or ale with eggs, bread, or gruel, sugar and spices), having one or two handles, a baluster or straight-sided form with a flared mouth, and usually a domed lid and finial.

cauliflower ground See *choux-fleur ground.*

caulker See *calcar.*

cave (1) The "cellar" beneath a tank furnace where molten glass, flowing from the furnace, was gathered. (2) The ash pit (see ash pit).

cavetto (Italian) A *piatto da pompa* with a deep center well. See *piatto da pompa; well.*

caviar bowl A large bowl with a stemmed foot in which is a smaller bowl is often supported by a metal frame, for serving caviar. The caviar is placed in the smaller bowl and shaved ice in the larger bowl. Smaller size double bowls of this type are used for serving chilled fruit or seafood cocktails, such as shrimp.

Cayuga Plate Glass Company (1906-1907) A plate glass manufacturing facility established in Cayuga, Haldimand, Canada, by the American Plate Glass Company, Pittsburgh, Pennsylvania.

Clear glass celery vase, c. 1855-1870.
The Corning Museum of Glass

celery (1) (Aka *celery dish*) A long, narrow, rectangular, or oval dish with low vertical or slightly sloping sides for holding celery, the stalks lay *horizontally*. (2) (Aka *celery glass, celery vase*) A vessel for holding celery in which the stalks stand *vertically*. It is tall, usually cylindrical in shape, with the bowl narrowing slightly toward its flat bottom or widening to a bulbous bottom, often resting on a short stem attached to a spreading flat base and often having two side handles.

celery dish, vase, or glass See *celery.*

celery handle A handle that looks like a stalk of celery, made by placing on the handle adjacent, parallel threads of glass, giving a ribbed appearance, spreading outward as they approach the point of contact with the body. They were first made by the Romans about the 1st century AD.

cellular glass See *foam glass.*

cellular technique A glass inlay technique developed in the 6th century BC in the Mediterranean region. Each piece of glass is set within a hollowed-out space or cell.

cemetery glassware (Aka *burial glassware*) Glassware found in the graves, tombs,

and catacombs, regardless of faith or lack thereof. To date, the bulk has been found in the catacombs of ancient Rome, dating from the 4th and first half of the 5th century AD, relating to the Christian faith; some has been found in tombs in ancient Egypt, dating to the Eighteenth Dynasty (1580-1350 BC).

Centennial Set (1876) A cut and engraved decanter (representing the national government) and 38 glasses (representing the 38 states of the Union at the time). It was first displayed at the 1876 Centennial Exhibition in Philadelphia, Pennsylvania.

center boss pane See *bull's-eye pane.*

centerpiece (Aka *table ornament*) A large and impressive decorative piece for display in the center of a sideboard or dining table. On occasion, it is used as a serving piece. See *salver; punch bowl; epergne; compote; sweetmeat stand.*

Central City Glass Co. See *Huntington Glass Company.*

Central Cut Glass Company (1910-1919) A glass cutting house in Walkerton, Indiana. See *Roseen Brothers Cut Glass Company.*

Central Glass Company A glass manufacturing facility established during 1863 in Wheeling, West Virginia, by workmen from South Wheeling Glass Works, making pressed glass, specializing in bar and lamp wares. In 1891, it joined the U.S. Glass Company (*Factory O*). From 1893 to 1895 it was closed due to union-management conflicts. In 1896, U.S. Glass Company sold it to a company that again used the name Central Glass Company. Operations were moved to Summitville, Indiana, in 1898. During the Great Depression in the 1930s, it closed for a short time, and then reopened in 1933, continuing to make all types of bar goods. In 1939, it closed; Imperial Glass Corporation purchased its assets and molds.

Centura See *tempered glass.*

Century Cut Glass Company Commencing operations in the late 1910s in Saugerties, New York, it operated for about two years under the management of the Naugherty Brothers.

Ceredo Pike's Peak A flask made at Ceredo, near Huntington, West Virginia, depicted Pike's Peak on its side.

ceremonial plate See *piatto da pompa.*

cesendello (Italian) A lamp of tall cylindrical form with a slightly everted rim, decorative finial in the center of its rounded bottom, and glass smoke shade above. It was suspended from a ceiling or beam by three metal chains, often used as a sanctuary lamp with enameling in various colors or with *filigrana.* They were made during the late 16th century in Murano, for local use and export to Turkey and the Middle East.

Chade Monogram Glass Company

(1930-1940) A glass cutting company established by Charles H. Gilliland in Valparaiso, Indiana.

chaffern See *chafing dish.*

chafing dish A dish on a legged frame with a heating source beneath it, used to cook or keep foods warm.

chain (1) (Aka *guilloche, chain trailing, trailed circuit*) An applied decorative pattern formed by two parallel threads of glass tooled into chain form, often used as a border. (2) A link chain made of glass. The most difficult part of chain making is to prevent the link being made from adhering to the link to which it is being connected.

chain handle A handle made of two parallel heavy threads of glass tooled into chain form. It was first used on Roman glass during the 3rd century AD.

chain trailing See *chain.*

chair (1) A wide wooden bench with elongated, flat, and slightly slanting arms, used by a gaffer while he formed and shaped glass objects. The arms are used to support the blowpipe with its attached paraison of molten glass. The gaffer rolls the blowpipe back and forth so the paraison retains its symmetrical shape and does not collapse while he works it. (2) (Aka *shop*) The gaffer and a group of assisting craftsmen and apprentices, usually consisting of five or six employees.

chair, wine See *wine chair.*

chairbottom The cut glass motif more commonly known as *cane* and *Harvard.*

chalice A cup used in church for drinking the sacrament of the Lord's Supper, occasionally with a matching paten. In 803, the Council of Rheims banned the use of glass chalices for the Mass because of breakage. The Council of Tribur, in 895, reconfirmed this prohibition. Regardless, glass chalices continued to be made and, on occasion, used.

chalk glass (Aka *Bohemian crystal*) A glass having a large proportion of chalk (calcium carbonate) in combination with potash (potassium carbonate) in the batch. It was first made in Bohemia about 1680. While it had good clarity and brilliance when cut, it did not have lead glass' refractive properties and high level of transparency.

Challinor A family, actually spelled *Challoner,* associated with several glass companies during the last half of the 19th century. For specifics, see *listings under Challoner.*

Challoner & Taylor; Challoner, Hogan & Company See *Pittsburgh Glass Manufacturing Co.*

Chamaleon-Glas (German) Literally, *chameleon glass.* A type of Lithyalin glass made in Bohemia by Friedrich Egermann and introduced in 1835. See *chameleon glass.*

chamber candlestick (Aka *hand candlestick*) A one-piece candlestick fastened with a saucer's center with an attached handle and occasionally a stemmed foot.

chamber pot A lidded vessel to hold body wastes (before the advent of indoor plumbing), kept under the bed or in the closed bottom of a nightstand. If it was designed to fit in a hole inside a commode, called a *closestool,* it was called a *closestool pan.* See *bourdalou; closestool pan; Jordan; oval chamber pot.*

Chambers, A. & D.H. See *Pittsburgh Glass Works.*

Chambers, Agnew & Co. See *Agnew & Co.*

chameleon glass A glass, made with uranium oxides, used as a raw material in making costume jewelry. See *Chamaleon-Glas (German)*.

chamfered corner (Aka *canted corner*) A corner made by cutting away the angle made by two adjacent, right-angle flat surfaces.

champagne glass A glass for drinking champagne. From about 1770 to 1850, fluted glasses were the favored type. From about 1830 and favored about 1850, the shallow saucer-like bowl on a stemmed foot became the traditional champagne glass. Champagne connoisseurs favor the flute glass because the deep bowl and narrow mouth prevent the bubbles from escaping as quickly, allowing the true taste to be savored longer.

Champlain Glass Company (1827-1850) A glass manufacturing facility established in Burlington, Vermont, making cylinder window glass. John S. Foster was its first superintendent, staying until about 1830. In 1834, Frederick Smith leased the facility, purchasing it in 1837. It later made window glass, druggists' wares, and bottles, and was operated by numerous owners over the years, including Loomis, Smith & Co.; Janes, Smith & Co.; Wilkins & Landon; and Smith & Wilkins, closing because of high fuel costs.

Champleve enameling A type of enameling in which the depressions made by cutting and engraving are filled with enamels, set by low temperature firing.

Chandelier with glass center post, arms, chains, and drops; probably Austrian, 24" w. x 24" h.
Davanna Collection

chandelier A candlestick, lamp stand, gas fixture, or other lighting fixture with several branches, especially one to be suspended from the ceiling. Early Venetian ones from the 1700s often had a metal frame embellished with clear and/or colored glass flowers, leaves, and fruits. In the early 1700s England, the metal frames from which crystal ornaments were hung were superceded by a central shaft with glass globes, culminating in a glass bowl from which glass arms extended outward to nozzles. In the mid-1700s, the use of glass pendants began. Later, in the rococo period, faceted drops and spires were fashionable. In the Neo-classical period, urn-shaped decorations and festoons of prismatic drops were common. In the Regency period, all metallic components of the chandelier were hidden beneath glass; the central shaft camouflaged behind a curtain of stings of drops; the nozzles and drip pans often elaborate with deep cut decoration.

Charder A signature found on some rare pieces of Schneider Art Glass.

charge The act of placing the batch into the melting pot or furnace.

charger (Aka *charyowre*) A large dish, plate, or platter used to carry food to the table and serve guests. It is distinguished from the *trencher* from which an individual served himself.

charyowre See *charger*.

Chase Glass Works A glass manufacturing facility in Bay View (Milwaukee), Wisconsin. It operated during the late 1800s-early 1900s making household glassware.

chatelaine The term originated in medieval times when men, living in castles, carried keys to various rooms on chains fastened to their belts. When away they entrusted them to their ladies, referred to as *castellans* or *chatelaines*. During Victorian times, the device holding the keys became an item of jewelry called a *castellan* or *chatelain,* initially single or multiple chains fastened to the belt by a hook or clasp. There were many types. Those for sewing might have attached scissors, a needle case, a tape measure, a thimble and/or related items; those for evening wear, a tiny mesh purse, a scent bottle, a pencil, etc. As time went on, the holder became more decorative, being fastened to a belt or dress itself. Some were made of glass in various designs, embellished with cutting, faceting, enameling, etc. The glass holder was framed with precious metals, hooks, or clasps from which to suspend the chain or chains or had holes cut or drilled in it from which to suspend them.

check A crack (often caused by contact of hot glass with a cold surface or liquid) or imperfection in a piece of glassware.

checker ground A ground of regularly spaced canes placed in a checkerboard pattern separated by a grid of filigree canes.

checker paperweight A geometrically composed millefiore paperweight, in a checkered pattern, consisting of scattered or patterned millefiori or floret canes separated by short canes, usually of filigrana, opaque white, or colored glass. On occasion, there is a border of short canes.

checkered diamond (Aka *strawberry diamond*) A diamond faceting in which four small diamonds are cut in a checkerboard pattern on the upper surface of a large diamond.

checkered spiral trail decoration A relief decoration on some tankards, beakers, etc., in the form of an applied spiral trail, normally thick and wide, being interrupted at short regular intervals by flat and/or slightly concave areas. To make this, the trailing is applied, the piece is subjected to heat and placed in a vertically-ribbed pattern mold. It is then expanded by blowing just enough, so only the vertical ribs were impressed in the trailing. The result is a checkered pattern resembling cut flat diamonds spiraling upward. It was first made in Antwerp, and later in the lower Rhineland and southern Netherlands, from about 1550 to 1650. It has been incorrectly termed *Spechter*.

cheese bell A cover for a cheese wheel, round and domed, usually with a handle in the middle of the top. They served many purposes, including minimizing odor, preventing rodents or other animals from eating it, and preserving *freshness*. It is larger than the dome of a cheese dish.

Cheese dishes.
Davanna Collection

"Sanitary Cheese Preserver" with instructions molded on top, 7" d. x 6" h.
Davanna Collection

cheese dish A dish for storing and serving cheese, consisting of a flat tray and high-domed cover with a top finial, usually in knob form. The tray and dome are flatter and larger than that of a butter dish. It is impossible to tell when such an object ceases to be a butter dish and commences being a cheese dish. The breaking point is regarded by many as six inches tall by six inches dome diameter and eight inches underplate diameter. A smaller size is considered a butter dish; greater, a cheese dish.

Chelmsford Glass Company In 1828, a glass manufacturing facility was erected in Chelmsford, Massachusetts, in the old Chelmsford Glasshouse, making window glass and bottles beginning in the second quarter of 1829. Between 1837 and the second quarter of 1839, operations were gradually moved to Suncook Village in Pembroke, New Hampshire, due to the inferior quality sand and fuel scarcity. See *Suncook Glass Works.*

Chelmsford Glasshouse A glass manufacturing facility established during 1802 in Chelmsford, Massachusetts, making cylinder window glass (adding bottles about 1820), affiliated with the Boston Crown Glass Manufactory. It, and the Boston Crown Glass Manufactory, failed in June 1827. In 1828, a portion of the facility burned. The Chelmsford Glass Company took over the remains, repaired and rebuilt it, and began making window glass and bottles. See *Chelmsford Glass Company; Suncook Glass Works.*

Chemcor See *tempered glass.*

Cheshire Crown Glass Company (1812-1815) A glass manufacturing facility established in Cheshire, Massachusetts, by Captain David Brown, his sons Darius and John, John D. Leland, and a Mr. Hunt, making crown window glass.

Cheshire Glass Co. See *Massachusetts Glass Company.*

Chester Creek Glass Works A glass manufacturing facility believed to have been established in 1683 on Chester Creek in Delaware County, Pennsylvania, by the Free Society of Traders. If, after being built, it operated at all, it was for only a few months or a firing season at most.

Chester Glass Co. See *Chester Glass Works.*

Chester Glass Works (1812-1815) A window glass manufacturing facility in Chester, Massachusetts, owned by the Chester Glass Co., a company formed specifically to finance it and make window glass.

Chesterfield flute See *Scudamore flute.*

chestnut bottle or flask A flask appearing flat when viewed from the side, and circular or ovoid when viewed from the front or back. The body is entirely covered with a pattern of curved ribbing extending from the base, spreading outward and converging around the neck, looking like a shelled chestnut. Originally made in Germany during the 18th and 19th centuries, many facilities in the United States made similar bottles without the ribbing (*Ludlow bottles*). Smaller ones were called *chestnut bottles.*

cheval (glass) (Aka *horse dressing mirror*) A tall, rectangular framed toilet or dressing mirror mounted in a free-standing, four-legged or footed frame, apparently "big enough to picture a horse," made initially during the last quarter of the 18th century; some have candleholders fastened to the frame. In the majority of specimens, the tall mirrors swivel between uprights on screws or pins (*swing mirrors*). Another type has the framed mirror itself balanced by weights within the supporting uprights, allowing it to be moved up or down like a sash window.

Chevaliers See *Gentilshomme Verriers.*

chevron A mark indicating rank and service in the form of an upside-down "V." As a decorative motif, it is often found in a repeated series resembling a zigzag pattern. They are also found as a combed thread pattern.

chevron bead Considered the most significant of all Venetian beads because of its proportions and broad distribution, they are made from canes built up from repeated layers of colored glass, primarily blue, red, and green, separated by thin layers of opaque white glass. The opaque glass is placed so when viewed in cross-section, it forms a star-like pattern.

Chicago Cut Glass Company A short-lived glass cutting shop operating in Chicago, Illinois, about 1918.

Chicago Flint & Lime Glass Company A glass manufacturing facility located in Chesterton, Indiana, operating in the late 19th-early 20th centuries.

Chiddingfold See *Wealden glass.*

chigger bite A small chip on a piece of glassware.

Chihuly, Dale Born in 1941 and raised in Tacoma, Washington, he was graduated from the University of Washington where he became interested in glass blowing. He entered graduate school at the University of Wisconsin, the only school in the United States at that time which taught glassblowing as a serious art. In 1967, he went to the Rhode Island School of Design. Continuing his studies, he began to teach, and became head of the sculptural department.

In 1970, he and some friends established a glassblowing institute, Pilchuck School, at Union Lake, Washington. It was an institute for glassblowers and serious students of art glass. Chihuly's works began to sell and museums began purchasing them. In 1980, he gave up his position in Rhode Island, devoting full time to working in glass. An accident in England during 1976 left Chihuly blind in his left eye. Being unable to do his own glassblowing because of depth perception deficiency, he developed a team method of glass blowing, preparing designs, and supervising operations. His operations have expanded tremendously to four studios and a warehouse; the Lake Union studio being called the Boathouse.

Over the years his works have become more massive, going from a single piece to installations involving hundreds, even thousands, of pieces. One of his most impressive (*Chihuly over Venice*) was the installation of 14 gigantic chandeliers installed temporarily over the canals and palazzos of Venice in September of 1996. They were created, over an 18-month period, in major facilities all over the world, including Finland, Mexico and Ireland. His largest piece is *Fiori di Como* in the Bellagio Hotel and Casino in Las Vegas, Nevada. It, completed in 1998, is suspended from a ceiling, covering 2,100 square feet with over 2,000 pieces, and over 40,000 pounds of hand-blown glass. His works generally have a relationship to the sea: shells, jellyfish, etc., in exotic and unique colors.

chilling bowl See *monteith.*

chimney A tube, usually of glass, placed around a flame, either a cylinder or a tube with a bulge at or near the base, at the flame's height. Its two primary purposes are (a) to prevent drafts from flickering the flame, and (b) to provide additional illuminating power.

chimney (looking) glass A large framed mirror to be hung over a fireplace or mantelpiece. Early ones are mostly rectangular, hung horizontally, with three separate mirrors. The center section is normally twice the width of the two matching side sections; a few have four sections. Later ones were either a single square mirror or a rectangular mirror hung vertically. Some have candle nozzles fastened to both sides of the frame.

Chine Metallique *(French)* (1) An ornamental effect accomplished by applying a layer of gold or other metallic foil either between two layers of glass or on the exterior. (2) An iridescent glass, plain or with craquelled effects, patented in 1878 by Pantin Glass Works.

Chinese mirror painting (Aka *painting on glass, back painting*) Mirror painting as executed in China from about 1766 until the early 19th century. The process involved first tracing the design on the mirror's reverse, removing the silvering within the design area, and painting the picture with oil paints in reverse (frontal details first, background last) within it. They were often painted on the reverse of thin, clear glass since the Chinese perceived colors became more distorted as the glass became thicker. Canton was the focal point of such work, using designs, prints, mirrors, and glass from England.

Chinese snuff bottles Snuff bottles made in China between about 1650 and 1750 at the Manchu Court at Peking and for everyday use from about 1780 to 1800. They were made by three processes; the most common was by *blowing*, followed by *molding*, and then *carving* it from a solid block of glass (*seal* bottles). The majority were flat, round, or ovoid, having a cork or glass stopper with a small spoon attached and categorized as: (a) *monochrome*, of one color, often Imperial yellow, sometimes with carved or engraved embellishment; (b) *enameled* with landscapes, portraits, or floral patterns on opaque white glass; (c) *mottled colors* to replicate precious or semi-precious stones such as jade, turquoise, or aventurine; (d) *interior painted*, see *Chinese snuff bottles with painted interiors*; (e) *cased* or *overlay* with a single overlay, usually turquoise blue, ruby red, shades of green, or multiple overlays with two to four layers of different colored glass usually of the afore mentioned colors; and (f) *variegated*, with single overlays of up to eight colors applied to different areas on the same ground. The glass stoppers are generally of contrasting colors and bottles with the range in size from one to four inches in height. On occasion, two snuff bottles have been joined to form a double bottle. Production of snuff bottles declined after 1850 and revived about 1950.

Chinese snuff bottles with painted interiors
Snuff bottles made in China, embellished by painting in reverse on their interior; painted with watercolors (foreground first, background last) using a very fine pointed angled bamboo pen inserted through the neck of the bottle. The interior surface was roughened so that the paint would adhere better; the painting generally a landscape facing the front of the bottle with an inscription facing the back. The colors used are generally lackluster; black, brown, dark green and dark blue being the primary colors; the exception being a span of twenty years at the start of the 20th century, during which brighter colors were used.

Chinex An ivory-colored glassware having scroll design edges, and occasionally, colored decal decorations. The glass was made by MacBeth Evans, and introduced during the late 1930s.

chinoiserie *(French)* Decoration done in Europe, inspired by oriental sources, mostly Chinese. It has pseudo-Chinese figures, such as pagodas, landscapes, dragons, and other monsters with imaginative fantasy components

Chintz (Aka *2000 Line*) A glassware introduced by Consolidated Lamp & Glass Company in January 1927, using the same blanks as in the Florentine line, having modernistic motifs with an Oriental flavor as decorations.

Chintz glassware An art glass having a pattern of multicolored vertical stripes that look like fabrics initially made in India, called *chintz*. It was made in many colors by a complicated, expensive process; originally developed at Tiffany Furnaces by Arthur W. Nash, but never made there. A. Douglas Nash made some pieces, but it was not patented until Nash

was working at the Libbey Glass Co. Only a few experimental pieces were made.

chip A fragment of glass, having some depth, that has become detached from the object's main body, leaving irregular sharp edges.

chipped See *geschnitzt (German)*.

chipped mold process A process used for cutting a design directly into the mold using various tools to make intricate flat patterns less complicated than the designs made by the mold-etched process. The final product does not appear etched.

chipper A *mold chipper*. One who makes molds for the glass industry.

chipping A process developed and subsequently patented by Wilhelm von Eiffin in the 1930s, involving sandblasting a design onto the surface of a glass object and filling the eroded areas with glue, which, upon reheating and cooling, contracted and fell away with some of the glass particles, leaving a frosted surface. See *Handel Glass Co.*

chocolate glass (Aka *chocolate slag*) A glass made by the Indiana Tumbler & Goblet Company from 1900 to 1903. It was created by Jacob Rosenthal, in late 1900, while he was employed there. The National Glass Company, which bought the company in 1899, purchased the formula from Rosenthal in 1902. It is an opaque brown glass, ranging from a dark, rich chocolate to a lighter "Boston Coffee" shade, introduced in May of 1901 at the Pan American Exposition in Buffalo, New York. The most popular patterns are *cantus* and *leaf bracelet*. It is often mistakenly called *carmel slag*. Reproductions are muddy brown in color. See *chocolate slag*.

chocolate pot A covered pot for serving hot chocolate, generally pear shaped or cylindrical, often with the handle at a right angle to the spout which is usually long, extending upward from near the body's bottom.

chocolate slag See *chocolate glass*.

chop plate A large, flat serving plate or salver, oval (most common), round, or rectangular in shape. See *cake plate*.

chope *(French)* A drinking glass, for serving beer, having the shape of a tall, straight-sided tumbler, such as a Humpen, or a mug.

choux-fleur ground A ground in the style of a carpet ground, except it has white canes shaped somewhat irregularly and loosely set, giving the appearance of a cauliflower.

chrinsie *(French)* A drinking vessel of any kind.

Christensen Agate Company M.F. Christensen developed a semi-automatic marble-making machine in 1901. In 1911, he became a partner in the Akro Agate Company, but withdrew when it moved in 1914, establishing the Christensen Agate Company, in Cambridge, Ohio, to make marbles and novelty glass items.

Christian glassware Glass objects embellished with motifs from the New Testament, made primarily from 200 to 600 AD in the Eastern Mediterranean region, mainly in Syria and in the Roman Empire.

Christmas lights Sources of light, specifically to illuminate a tree, building, or other object as a form of commemoration of Christ's birth. Those for a tree were originally made in the United States by Sandwich and other companies of pressed or mold-blown glass shaped like a common water tumbler. They were partially filled with water and suspended from the tree by a wire handle; oil was floated on the water, serving as fuel for the lighted wicks. Some were designed to hold a small candle and were a fire hazard. Although experiments with electric light bulbs occurred before 1900, it was 1903 before the first socket set was marketed; early sets were expensive and a safety hazard.

By 1910, General Electric was making bulbs for such sets. They were round with a pointed end and, until 1919, hand blown. The first figural bulbs were made about 1910 in Austria; Japan following with ones of lesser quality. American makers first made machine-made figurals after 1919. Bubble lights were popular from about 1945 to 1960 at which time miniature lights were introduced. These took the public by storm and makers stopped making replacement bulbs for the bubblers. In the early 1990s, production of bubble lights was resumed on a small scale. Miniature lights remain popular and, as an added enhancement in addition to blinking, have blinking in time with music and marquee type movement.

Christmas ornaments During the late 1870s, German imported, blown glass ornaments for Christmas trees were introduced in the United States. Over 6,000 designs are recorded from this era, including carrots, cucumbers, clown faces, angel heads, butterflies, stars, etc., all painted inside with silvery colors. From 1890 through 1910, blown glass spheres were often embellished with beads, tassels, and tinsel rope. Ornaments in the form of glass spheres are still made, by machine. Reproductions of older ornaments are now on the market. See *Kugel; Christmas lights.*

Christy, J.F. See *black glass.*

chromium A metallic agent used as a coloring agent in making dark green glass since the early 19th century; previously the main coloring agent was iron oxide. Chromium is introduced into the batch as an acid (chromic acid) or salt (potassium dichromate). If too much is added, it produces a color so dark the glass appears black. Since it does not easily dissolve in the glass batch, when used in overabundance, it will likely form chromates, remaining in the finished product as undissolved specs. Potassium dichromate is yellow, and the color may be imparted to certain glasses. To make an emerald green glass and avoid a yellowish tinge, other agents, such as arsenic or tin oxide, must be added. All glass with chromium has a high transmission in the red part of the spectrum and should never be used for signal glass since the two colors (red and green) will cancel each other. Though associated with green glass, yellow through bluish-red, red to dark green, or even black glasses can be made with chromium when combined with other oxides.

Chrysoprase Alabaster glass An opaque green uranium glass made by Baccarat in the mid-1840s.

Chubb, Lewis W. In 1920, Chubb invented polarized glass while employed at the Westinghouse Electric Co., East Pittsburgh, Pennsylvania.

chunk glass See *dalle-de-verre.*

chunk jewel Large, thick pieces of colored glass used in articles of stained glass to add texture and a three-dimensional quality.

chunked A badly damaged glass object.

church glassware Glassware, including reliquaries, chalices, patens, etc., used mainly in the church for sacred purposes. The Council of Rheims in 803 prohibited the use of glass chalices for Mass. As a result, church glassware production declined dramatically. Glass objects were often used for reliquaries as a result of a medieval papal edict requiring all altars to have a relic.

church warden's pipe A tobacco pipe with a long stem and small bowl.

ciborium A vessel, dating from the 3rd century, to hold and serve Eucharistic wafers. It is cup-shaped with a stemmed foot, an everted rim, and two vertical loop handles

cicada A cicada- (locust) shaped glass funerary object made in China during the Han Dynasty (206 BC- AD 220), to be placed on the tongue of the dead.

Cicero Glass Co. Established in Cicero, Indiana, during 1902, it operated in the facility of the former Bonita Glass Co. and is believed to have made a general line of pressed and blown wares.

cider glass A drinking glass for cider. Most are identified by an engraved motif of a spray of apple blossoms, apple tree branches, or an apple tree with fruit. They are usually flute shaped, having an opaque twist stem with a central knop, set on high spreading foot.

cider pitcher A round bodied pitcher usually with a lid, specially for serving cider.

cigar(ette) holder A holder for a cigar or cigarette; the unlit end held in a cylinder tapering to a flattened mouthpiece. Some are curved or upturned.

Cigar-shaped stem A glassware stem, circular and hollow, which tapers a bit inward toward the bottom, where it joins the base.

Pair of cigarette lighters, cutting on pressed blank, 8" h., gold-plated lighter mechanism. Davanna Collection

cigarette lighter A cigarette lighter within a glass holder. Many were made during the late 1930s.

Cincinnati Glass Manufacturing Co. A glass manufacturing facility established in 1814 by Major Isaac Craig in Cincinnati, Ohio, making window glass, bottles, flasks, and tumblers. In 1817, it failed. Sources disagree on its future; one states the facility closed at that time, while another states it was leased to Henry Teeter who resumed glass making. In 1818, it was purchased by Pugh & Teeter and, closed in 1822.

cinerary urn An urn holding cremated human remains, used extensively during Roman times.

cinque foil A paperweight motif consisting of a garland of canes having five loops.

Cintra perfume bottle, clear, white, and black glasses, c. 1920-1930. The Corning Museum of Glass

Cintra glass An art glass developed by Frederick Carder at Steuben prior to 1917. It was made by rolling a gather of molten crystal glass over pulverized glass of various colors scattered on the marver. Usually, a second gather of crystal glass was applied over the colored particles to encapsulate them, keeping them in apparent suspension. The thickness of the second layer was varied by design; the thicker layer used when air bubbles, either controlled or random, were desired; the thinner layer when no air bubbles were desired. It was made in monochromes, two colors when shaded effects were desired, and variegated colors.

One of the unique Cintra techniques is found in pieces designed with vertical stripings of alternating colors, usually of blue and pink, or blue and yellow. Blue and yellow stripes were made by scattering finely pulverized blue glass on a marver and rolling a gather of molten crystal over it. After the blue glass was marvered in, the gather was reheated and blown into a ribbed mold, which caused the blue glass to form vertical stripes separated by bulges of nearly clear glass (usually with a blue tint). The molded piece was rolled on a marver covered with pulverized yellow glass. The protrusions of nearly clear glass picked up the yellow powder. Then the object was reheated, the surface smoothed and enclosed in a gather of clear glass.

On occasion additional embellishments were applied, including black or blue applied edge rings or threads, frequently pulled by a hook to form feather or leaf borders, or applied colored decoration on a vase's neck and/or shoulder. Although most pieces have an outer crystal glass casing, some do not, leaving a unique surface finish. Cintra glass was made into the 1920s.

Carder created the name Cintra from the verb "to sinter" (to cause to become a coherent solid mass without completely melting). It differs from Cluthra in that it has very small bubbles in the outer casing (if an outer casing and bubbles are present) while Cluthra has a myriad of bubbles of various sizes; and the colored glass used in Cintra is more finely pulverized than in Cluthra since the coarser particles were removed by sifting. See *Or Verre; Lace glass; Cluthra glass.*

ciocche (Italian) Literally, *bouquet of flowers.* A chandelier of Venetian origin made from the 18th century. Its support system is a metal frame decorated with soda glass flowers, leaves, fruit, etc., made *at-the-lamp.* These are unusually large, ranging from 6-1/2 to 8-1/4 feet in diameter.

cipher See *monogram.*

circlet paperweight A paperweight having as its major motif a circle of tiny flowers or florets.

circular faceting See *faceting.*

circus bowl A glass jar, bowl, or beaker having scenes from a Roman arena or circus, with gladiators, chariot races, etc., as an embellishment. Made of Roman glass, mold blown as early as the 1st century AD, some are further embellished with inscriptions. During the 3rd and 4th centuries AD, many were embellished with engraved scenes rather than scenes imparted by the mold.

Carder vase, Cire Perdue technique, c. 1955.
The Corning Museum of Glass

cire perdue (French) Literally, *lost wax.* A process used for pieces too detailed to be made by the usual process of making in a mold. It was originally used in casting bronze works, and later used effectively in making glassware. It involved fashioning a model in wax, encasing the wax model in a mold, heating it causing the wax to melt and drain out. The mold was then filled with molten glass or reheated powdered glass. A more elaborate process was developed by Frederick Carder in 1933/34, and used by him until 1959. It required the following: (a) a model was made in clay; (b) a duplicate made in plaster of Paris; (c) a sectional gelatin mold made from the duplicate; (d) a wax replica made using the gelatin mold; (e) a ceramic mold made over the wax replica; (f) the mold was dipped into boiling water, causing the wax to melt and drain out; (g) small pieces of glass rods were placed into the mold which was then fired; and (h) finally the mold and glass were annealed, the mold broken, and a glass casting of the original clay model remained. The casting was usually one of a decorative nature, such as diatreta glass.

cistern An artificial reservoir or large container, specifically for storing water, frequently in the shape of a deep basin.

Clair-de-Lune Various sources provide two different descriptions of this glass developed by Emile Galle. (a) A slightly opalescent clear-to-blue glass made in 1878 using oxides of potassium and cobalt, turning a brilliant sapphire when struck by light. (b) A transparent glass, colorless or slightly tinted, made during the 1870s. In either case, it won him a gold medal at the 1878 Paris Universal Exhibition.

clam The process of spreading wet clay on bricks to seal up the front of a pot furnace.

clam water glass See *pate-de-riz.*

clambroth glass A glassware, semi-opaque, watery white to grayish white in color, similar in appearance to clambroth; popular during the Victorian era.

clamp A tool often used in place of a pontil to hold a blown glass vessel at its closed end, while the open end is being shaped. It expedites the production process, avoiding the presence of a pontil mark.

clapper A tool, used by a glassmaker, formed of two wooden arms fastened at one end by a curved leather hinge. One of the arms is flat while the other has an opening to fit around the stem of a glass in the process of being made. It was used to compress a blob of molten glass at the base of the stem into the preliminary shape of the foot. See *foot clappers; woods; pucellas.*

Clapperton & Sons A glass cutting company founded by G.H. Clapperton in 1905 in Toronto, Canada. In 1906, he was joined by N.F. Gundy, forming the Gundy-Clapperton Company. About 1916, Gundy left and Clapperton took control, changing the name to Clapperton & Sons and the trademark from "GCCo" in a shamrock to "C" in a shamrock (in the early 1920s, it was omitted from its smaller items). It purchased its

blanks from others and was still making cut glass in 1967. In 1921, Clapperton opened Quinte-Clapperton Amalgamated in Deseronto, Canada, which burned in 1931, and Clapperton returned to Toronto.

claret decanter (Aka *decanter* or *claret jug*) A decanter or jug with a spherical or egg-shaped body, a thin, tall neck with a pouring lip, a curved handle attached near the top of the neck and at the shoulder, and a flat base or a low cone-shaped foot. The majority have a glass stopper.

claret glass A wine glass of medium size, having a stemmed foot.

claret pitcher A pitcher for serving claret, made in a variety of shapes, from classical to Art Nouveau, and often embellished with grapes and vines and mounted in silver or pewter.

Clark, Joseph A., Window Glass Company A window glass manufacturing facility established in 1882, making plate glass while still in the experimental stage.

Clark, T.B., & Company A glass cutting house established in Seelyville. Pennsylvania, by Thomas Byron Clark in 1884. Originally named Hatch & Clark, then Clark & Wood, before becoming, in 1886, T.B. Clark & Company. It purchased blanks primarily from Dorflinger. A few years later Clark established another cutting facility in Hawley, Pennsylvania. In 1895, Clark and Wood established the Wayne Silver Company in Honesdale to make silver mountings for its glassware. In 1904, T.B. Clark & Company took over the Maple City Glass Company. As cut and engraved ware declined in popularity about 1920, it made gold decorated glassware until closing in 1930. See *Hatch & Clark.*

Clark Brothers Glass Company See *Ellwood City Glass Company.*

Clark & Wood See *Hatch & Clark.*

Clark's Glass Works A glass manufacturing facility established in 1837 in Washington, D.C., making hollowware into the 1850s.

Clarke's Patented Pyramid Night Light See *fairy lamp.*

Classics, The A series of pieces of traditional design initiated by Thomas Buechner, President of Steuben, in the 1970s, consisting of ten bowls and vases designed by Don Pollard. They were in the shapes of ancient Chinese vessels, unadorned, and placed on exhibition in September 1977.

claw beaker (Aka *trunk beaker*) A green or blue beaker of conical shape embellished with two or three rows of prunts around it, stretching from the sides in the shape of claws with the trailing edge of each in the upper row falling between the heads of the next lower row. The claws are hollow, allowing the beaker's contents to flow into them. The beakers taper inward toward the bottom to a circular base with a foot ring. Just below the beaker's wide everted mouth and above its foot ring are wide bands of notched trailings of colored glass. Claw beakers are the best known glass vessels made during the Dark Ages. See *Castle Eden claw beaker.*

Clayton Glass Works See *Fislerville Glass Works.*

clear glass Colorless, transparent glass. Ancient glass termed *clear glass* is generally tinged green or yellow, due to impurities in the raw materials.

Clearform Corning's trademark for its transparent multiform glass.

Pitkin-type flask, attributed to Clementon Glass Works, Clementon, NJ, c.1825. Museum of American Glass at Wheaton Village, Millville, NJ.

Clementon Glass Works (1804-1825) (Aka *Gloucester Glass Works; Clement's Glass Works*). Built in Clementon, New Jersey, it first made bowls and pitchers, later changing to bottles and flasks. In the 1810s, it made Pitkin flasks for the Philadelphia market.

Clement's Glass Works See *Clementon Glass Works.*

clepsydra (Aka *water glass*) An instrument used to measure time, similar to an hourglass or sand glass, except water is used as the medium instead of sand. See *sand glass.*

Cleveland The Russian cut-glass pattern where the button is undecorated.

Cleveland Glass Works A cylinder window glass manufacturing facility established by Anthony Landgraff in Cleveland, New York, during 1840. The Landgraff family operated it until 1861 when it was acquired by William Sanders. In 1863, Caswell & Co. purchased it, and later took over the idle Union Glass Works nearby. In 1889, both facilities were purchased and upgraded by the United Glass Company, but failed to make a profit. During 1899, both were sold to the American Window Glass Company, which had little luck, and within a short time, closed them permanently. Some local residents made an attempt to reopen them in 1902, but that also proved a failure.

Clevenger Brothers pitcher, apple green, 6-1/2" h. x 4-1/4" d. at mouth. Obverse reads "Molly Pitcher (6/28/1778 to 6/28/1978)." Reverse reads, "Battle of Monmouth, Limited Edition of 1500." Davanna Collection

Clevenger Brothers A glass manufacturing facility established by Thomas, Lorenzo, and William Clevenger during 1926 in Clayton, New Jersey. Since then, most Clevenger glass has been hand blown by gaffers in the early South Jersey manner. One of the first items made was a reproduction of the Booz bottle, always advertising their reproductions as such. The Depression of the late

1920s-early 1930s did not stop the brothers from making wares that were stockpiled. Their glass was *freehand blown* until the 1940s, when it was *mold blown*. The articles were made in a wide range of colors. In 1964, the family decided to close since experienced glass blowers were scarce. Mr. and Mrs. James Travis arranged to take over, continuing to operate under the Clevenger name.

Clichy Glassworks A glass manufacturing facility established in 1837 at Billancourt (Pont-de-Sevres), France, by M. Rouyer and G. Maes. It was moved, in 1839, to Clichy-la-Garenne (a suburb of Paris). It has been reported, at about this time, it moved to Sevres and then, in 1844, to Clichy-la-Garenne; regardless, by 1846, it was in Clichy-la-Garenne. It made high-quality paperweights from 1846 to 1857 and introduced the use of millefiori canes on other objects. By 1884, it was known as the *Cristalleries de Sevres et Clichy*.

Clichy paperweight A paperweight made at the Clichy Glassworks. Specimens exist from 1846 until 1870, with best quality made from 1846 to 1857. Many weights were signed; some with the letter "C" on an individual cane and some with the full name (Clichy) spelled out, either on a single cane or divided between two adjacent canes. A unique feature of many Clichy weights is the *Clichy Rose* (see *Clichy Rose*). Of the millefiori weights, many have florets forming a design; however, some are scrambled with no apparent design; some have muslin or moss grounds; many have faceting or a star-cut base; and many have swirl patterns and color cushions of brilliant red, green, blue, yellow, and mauve. It also made miniature weights in these same styles.

Clichy Rose A slice or set-up of a cane having the appearance of an open rose, made at the Clichy Glassworks. It is a cane of the floret variety, representing a stylized rose with a central cylindrical motif surrounded by flattened tubes of glass. The colors of the roses range from shades of pink to white and often include amethyst, wine-red, green, yellow, and blue. It was regularly used as a central motif or simply scattered among the canes of various millefiori weights. The rose

was either fashioned after a Venetian plaque dated 1846 or Bohemian paperweights, and was imitated by numerous other glasshouses.

Climax Cut Glass Co. (1911-1912) A glass cutting shop in Corning, New York.

Clinton Cut Glass Co. (1905-1924) A glass cutting facility established in Aldenville, Pennsylvania. In 1918, the name became the Elite Cut Glass Manufacturing Company.

Clinton Glass Works A window glass manufacturing facility established in Wheeling, West Virginia, in 1839 by Ensell & Cuthbert, operating for only a short time.

clippings See *shearings*.

cloche A hollow bell or dome-shaped object used as an airtight cover. Usually, at the top's center is a finial, serving as a handle.

cloche glass A combined hourglass and clock made during the 16th century.

clock case An ornamental piece designed to accommodate a clock.

clock glass The decorative mirror or painted pane of glass below or above the face or dial on many clock cases, quite common during the late 18th-early 19th centuries

clock lamp A device used to tell time at night, popular in the first half of the 18th century. It rests on a brass stand which supports an oil reservoir from the bottom of which protrudes horizontally an opening for holding a wick. Illumination from the burning wick allows the reservoir's graduated time scale to be read. Sometimes, a separate tube adjacent, but connected to, the reservoir is graduated and used to determine the time. Its accuracy depends on a uniform burning rate.

closed handled An object having solid tab handles.

closed millefiori paperweight A paperweight in which millefiori canes are in a random pattern, blanketing its entire base. Because of the dome's magnification, they appear to fill the weight with hundreds of small flowers and, sometimes, an odd shape or two. The maker can often be determined by the inclusion of an identifying cane. See *millefiore paperweight*.

closestool pan A pan or basin designed for use inside a commode, called a *closestool*, to collect human wastes. It is similar to a chamber pot, except it has a wide rim to keep it from falling into the hole into which it sets. See *chamber pot*.

clover cut See *printie*.

club glass See *Keulenglas (German)*.

club shaped A drinking glass, most often a Humpen, or decanter, that is tall and circular, sloping inward slightly from halfway between the mouth and the base to near the base, and then sloping outward to the base. See *Keulenglas; Igelglas*.

cluster paperweight A paperweight having as a primary embellishment a cluster of canes organized in a concentric fashion with a design repeated several times. In each cluster, the canes have a similar floral motif; however, some have silhouettes or piecrust canes.

Steuben vase, c. 1918-1932, grayish bubbly Cluthra glass with acid etching, 8-1/2" h. The Corning Museum of Glass

Steuben vase, Cluthra glass, c. 1920. Museum of American Glass at Wheaton Village, Millville, NJ.

Clutha glass A glass patented in the 1890s by James Couper & Sons, Glasgow, Scotland. The majority of known pieces are greenish in color, but some are turquoise, yellow, brownish green, or smokey black. It has embedded, within air bubbles, streaks of pink and white, and specks of aventurine. It is often confused with Thomas Webb & Sons' *Old Roman Glass*, but recognizable by the bits of aventurine in the metal. See *West Lothian Glassworks*.

Cluthra glass An art glass created at Steuben by Frederick Carder prior to 1930. It is made using a pulverized glass technique similar to that used in making Cintra glass. It is characterized by its larger, random, non-uniform air bubbles, larger, non-uniform glass particles, and thicker casing. The body is monochrome, most often wisteria or green, or shaded or variegated colors. Pieces were cased in crystal, white, and other translucent colors, and often used as blanks for acid etched designs, mainly on lamp bases. A similar glass was made by Kimble Glass Company about 1925.

Clyde Glass Works (1828-1880) A window glass manufacturing facility in Clyde, New York. In 1845, Stokes & Ely operated it. From 1850 to 1868, it was operated by three firms: Stevens & Miller; Stevens, Miller & Co.; and Miller, Roswell & Co. In 1868, Southwick, Reed & Co. operated it and a nearby bottle manufacturing facility established in 1864 by Southwick & Woods. The last firm to operate the facilities was Ely, Reed & Co.

coach(ing) glass A drinking glass designed to be emptied by the drinker and returned to the table in the inverted position with the rim down, like a *stirrup cup*. The bowl is in the shape of an inverted cone, with no handle and, in the place of a foot, a knop or ball at the end of a short, thick stem. They were used by passengers on carriages or at wayside stations.

coach horn An ornamental glass, coach horn-shaped object. Their size is about that of the real horn—up to 40 inches in length. They were usually made of Nailsea or Bristol glass, of clear or deep blue-colored glass.

coach pot See *bourdalou*.

coachman bottle (Aka *bishop's bottle*) A high-hatted coachman-shaped bottle, made mainly in England. Some were made in the United States beginning during the 1840s.

coaster A small tray, usually round, on which to place a bottle, decanter, or drinking glass to prevent scratching or staining a table. The term comes from early coasters that had wheels so a bottle could be pushed from guest to guest; those with polished wooden or papier-mâché bottoms were called *sliders*. They were also known as *bottle* or *decanter stands*. Modern coasters are small, to be used under a single drinking glass. See *beer wagon*.

coated glass Glass to the surface of which has been permanently fire bonded a thin, transparent, metallic oxide coating enabling it to conduct electricity. It is used for residential and industrial heating, lighting panels to reduce interference from fluorescent lights, etc.

cobalt A tough, lustrous, silver-white metal used in the form of its oxides to impart dark and light hues of blue to glass, including a very dark blue, called *cobalt blue* or *Bristol blue*. The oxide of cobalt (see *zaffer*) is blended into some molten glass that is cooled and ground to a product called *smalt*, used as a coloring agent for glass. Glass colored with cobalt is very dense with respect to light transmitted. The deepest blues are obtained with glass containing potash. It may be used as a decolorizer if minute quantities are mixed with sand as a diluent.

cobalt blue glass (1) A very dark blue opaque ware often mistaken for china. (2) A bright dark blue ware, either transparent or translucent, made using an oxide of cobalt as a colorant.

cobbler's lamp See *lace maker's lamp*.

Cockran & Brother See *Mills, Peter & Co.; New Granite Glass Co.*

Cockran & Company See *Excelsior Flint Glass Works*.

Cockran's Glass Factory See *Medford Glass House*.

cocktail glass A small drinking glass used for serving cocktails. Its bowl rests on a stemmed foot. It may be of any shape, but typically is funnel shaped.

cocoon (Aka *roller*) A cylinder of glass made by a blower in the *cylinder method*.

coefficient of expansion The relationship (expressed numerically) between the change in size of a substance and a change in temperature of the same substance. With respect to glass, it refers to its expansion over a specific temperature range.

coelanaglyphic See *intaglio*.

coffee cup A cup, with or without a handle, to hold coffee, generally about 25% larger than a teacup.

coffee pot A covered container in which coffee is prepared and served. Generally, regardless of shape, they have a loop handle, opposite a spout.

coffin A small object, related to burial traditions, in the shape of a coffin or, on occasion, an individual. The earliest known were made in Egypt during the 18th Dynasty, about 1475 BC. They were buried with the deceased, like an *ushabti*. Sometimes they held a miniature figure, often a likeness of the deceased, and were inscribed with the name and title(s).

Coffin, William See *Winslow Glass Works; Greenbank Glass House; Hammonton Glass Works.*

Coffin, William, Jr., & Company; Coffin & Pierce; Coffin, Hay & Bowdle See *Winslow Glass Works.*

Coffin & Hay See *Winslow Glass Works; Hammonton Glass Works.*

Coffin, Pearsall & Company See *Coffin & Hay.*

cog cane A millefiori cane molded with a serrated edge, common on silhouette canes.

cogwheel base A base, often on tumblers, vases, etc., having deep cutting around the edge giving it the appearance of a cogwheel.

Cohansey Glass Manufacturing Company (For previous history of the company, see *Bodine, Joel, & Sons.*) Founded in

Bridgeton, New Jersey, about 1870, by Francis I., Francis L., and J. Nixon Bodine. It patented a fruit jar on July 16, 1872, one of the most successful canning jars, having an all glass top with a single wire bail. It made several types of fruit and canning jars, in addition to window glass, flasks, electrical insulators, and bottles. It had, in 1899, two hollowware and three window glass facilities in Bridgeton. See *Bridgeton Glass Works.*

coil base A base on a vessel made by trailing molten glass around the object's base, forming a ring (on which the vessel stands).

coin glass A drinking glass, tankard, or jug having one or more coins embedded in a hollow knop on the stem, in the base, or in the foot. Its making dates to Roman times. Existing English and Italian ones date to the mid-17th century. In making it, the coin was placed into the knop prior to it being attached to the stem. It is still made today. See *coin pattern glass.*

Fostoria Coin Glass nut dish, blue.
Davanna Collection

Fostoria coin pattern glass ashtray,
olive green, 7-1/2" d.
Davanna Collection

coin pattern glass Originally, a costly pattern of frosted pressed glass made during a five month period in 1892 by the Central and Hobbs glass companies. The molds for this ware were patterned from newly minted coins having an 1892 date. When the government learned of this, it declared it an illegal reproduction of money, ordering them to cease making it and destroy the molds. Other glass companies, realizing the marketability of the pattern, used Spanish coins, renaming the pattern *Columbian Coin.* During the 1960s, a contemporary variation was made; however, there are no dates or names on the coin-like medallions. See *coin glass; Central Glass Company; Fostoria Glass Company.*

coin spot glass Glass having, as a pattern, opalescent spots resembling coins, made in a variety of colors during the mid-1800s by several companies. See *opalescent glass.*

coin weight See *Munzegewicht (German).*

Colburn process A technique invented in 1908 by I.W. Colburn for drawing sheet window glass. The machinery and the process were improved by the Libbey-Owens Sheet Glass Company at Charleston, West Virginia, in 1917.

cold colors Oil paint or lacquer colors, used to embellish glassware, applied to the article without firing (cold), hence the term *cold painting,* and wearing off quite easily. They are more effectively used when applied to the inside surface or rear of the surface being viewed or handled, especially when safeguarded by a layer of varnish or metal foil, or even another layer of glass.

cold cutting The process of grinding or cutting an object from a raw block of glass, not previously molded or cast into a shape. It has been used since early times, but became more common after the 8th century B.C. Often such pieces can be distinguished by the presence of internal spiral grooving made by a tool.

cold gilding See *unfired gilding.*

cold glass decoration or working
Embellishment applied to glass articles while at ambient temperature. See *cold colors; cold*

cutting; cut glass; engraving; etch-ing; gilding; unfired gilding; color etching.

cold painting See *cold colors.*

cold working See *cold glass decoration or working.*

Coliseum Glass Company A short-lived glass manufacturing facility operating in Fostoria, Ohio, during the late 1880s.

collage The technique of cutting and applying pieces of colored paper to a stained glass cartoon.

collar (1) A circular ring around the stem of a glass, often used on three-piece glasses to conceal the weld mark where the stem connects to the bowl or foot, or sometimes between larger knops on the stem. See *merese.* (2) A band of applied glass around the rim of a vessel, frequently found on bottles, used to secure a cork. (3) On the font of a lamp, the threaded metal ring used to secure a screw-in burner.

collar base (Aka *marie*) Located on the base of an object, in the form of a low collar, usually round, but may be oval, hexagonal or multi-sided, following the base's shape.

collar holder An inappropriate term used for a round candy box, candy holder, or covered bon-bon. Some believed they were designed to hold a celluloid collar from a man's shirt.

collared stem A stem embellished with a collar, plain, faceted, or vermicular.

colloid Finely divided particles of a substance dispersed in another substance. Colloidial dispersions, in glass making, are often responsible for colors, in one of two ways: (1) the actual color of the colloid or (2) the interference of waves of light by the very tiny dispersed particles in the colloid, resulting in an opaque effect. See *Lycurgis cup.*

cologne bottle A stoppered bottle for the dressing table to contain *eau de cologne* (toilet water). It is larger than a scent bottle or perfume bottle and generally of square, oval, or circular section. See *toilet water bottle; scent bottle; smelling bottle.*

Colonial Cut Glass Company (1910-1916) A glass cutting company established by C.B. & J. Warner in New York City.

colonial flute See *flute cutting.*

colonial glassmaking The techniques and technology used by the colonial American glassmakers differed little from those used by glassmakers of the ancient Roman Empire. The essential ingredients of their glass were silica, mostly in the form of sand, and alkalis, such as potash, carbonate of soda or lime, plus other ingredients depending on the type and color of glass to be made. Most colonial glass had color to it, either resulting from impurities in the raw materials or by intent. Common bottle and window glass, the primary products, were made of unrefined ingredients and usually green as a result of certain metallic oxides present as impurities in the raw materials. Other oxides were used to produce artificial colors. Clear glass was made by adding to the batch black oxide of manganese (*glass [maker's] soap*). By substituting an oxide of lead for the soda or lime, a softer, more lustrous glass was made (*lead* or *flint glass*).

color A phenomenon perceived by the human eye when it receives light of different wavelengths. The spectrum visible to the naked human eye ranges from about 390 to 740×10^{-9} meters, from violet, indigo, blue, green, yellow, orange, to red. Normal daylight contains a mixture of all wavelengths of light in the visible spectrum (*white light*). Color has three qualities: (a) hue (dependent on wavelength); (b) saturation (dependent on the degree the wavelength moves away from white light); and (c) brightness. Glass may exhibit color in three possible ways: (a) reflecting color from a pigment applied to the glass; (b) reflecting color from particles within the glass; and (c) color resulting from light transmitted through the glass. See *colored glass.*

color etching An embellishing technique where a thin flashing of colored glass is applied over clear glass and etched so the pattern appears in clear glass.

color ground A background on a glass object of transparent or opaque color and on which a design is placed.

color twist A twist in which, at a minimum, one spiral thread is colored; typically opaque but sometimes translucent. At times two colors are combined, but more often at least one opaque white thread is combined with a colored one. Occasionally, an air twist is combined with a colored thread, and rarely an air twist is combined with a colored and white thread (mixed twist). The colors usually found on such twists are blue, green, brown, red, pink, and canary yellow.

color twist stem A stem with a color twist, common on English drinking glasses made from about 1755 to 1775. See *color twist.*

colorband glassware A glass container, such as a bottle or drinking glass, with horizontal loops of stripes or bands of contrasting color.

colored bead A bead of colored glass or clear glass colored on the surface.

colored glass Glass, translucent or opaque, that is colored. Ancient glassmakers knew that by adding certain ingredients to the standard raw materials, color could be imparted to the glass. The color is caused by impurities in the raw materials or by techniques for coloring using one of the following methods: (a) Absorption of distinct light frequencies by specific agents in solution in the molten glass; such coloring agents are oxides of elements such as titanium, nickel, vanadium, chromium, manganese, iron, cobalt, uranium, sulfur, and copper; the color due to the chemical structural environment or by differences in the state of oxidation; examples of colors produced by this method are amethyst or purple with manganese added to the batch, green with iron or copper, dark blue with cobalt, and light or pale blue with nickel; (b) Colloidial particles precipitated within an originally colorless glass by heat treatment; an example is when colloidial gold is used to make ruby glass; (c) Microscopic or larger particles which may be colored themselves, such as selenium reds (SeO_2) used in traffic lights, lantern globes, etc., or particles which may be colorless producing opals. Colored glass has been made since the earliest times in Egypt and favored over colorless glass, and the same was true in all regions making Roman glass until the development of *cristallo* in Venice in the 15th century and of lead glass by George Ravenscroft in England about 1676. The use of colored glass has been revitalized from the early 19th century onward, especially by makers in the Art Nouveau style and during the Depression glass era in the United States. Clear glass is imparted a color when exposed to sunlight, either direct or diffused, for a long period of time (usually ten years or more). Also clear glass buried in the soil will often be imparted a color, in addition to other effects, due to, and depending on, the minerals in the soil. Further, colored glass will also be affected by sunlight.

color man See *hot metal man.*

color mixed twist A color twist in combination with an air and white twist. See *mixed twist.*

coloring (1) The act of producing color in the batch by adding coloring agents. (2) Polishing as the final operation in making fine cut glass; the manual technique whereby the cut design was polished using a wooden or felt wheel with pumice or putty powder to impart the same brilliant look and feel as the remainder of the article.

coloring agent See *colored glass.*

Columbia Cut Glass Company A glass cutting shop in Columbia, Pennsylvania. It opened and closed in 1918.

Columbia flask A flask made in the United States, having on the obverse a bust of Columbia (the oldest "trademark" of the United States) and normally an American eagle on the reverse. They were blown in a two-piece, full-size mold between 1815 and 1870.

Columbia Glass Company A glass manufacturing facility established in 1886 in Findlay, Ohio; the first tableware facility to locate there, it made goblets, lantern chimneys, and sauce dishes; soon adding colored, etched, and decorated wares. [Early in 1891, D.C. Jenkins, Jr., was involved in glass tableware manufacturers' consolidation. He and others applied, for a corporate charter in Pennsylvania as the United States Glass Company. Columbia's stockholders voted to place the facility in the combine in June 1891. Jenkins was on the Board of Directors and supervisor of *Factory J* (as the Columbia Glass Company was known), *Factory M* (Bellaire Goblet Company), and *Factory T* (Novelty Glass Company)]. Factory J made quantities of pattern glass, plain mugs, jelly tumblers, and bar goods. On January 12, 1893, it closed.

Columbia Glass Works
A cylinder glass manufacturing facility established by Francis Myerkoff during 1812 in Columbia, New Jersey. The company began operations in 1813. In 1825, it closed and was sold at sheriff's sale. It was purchased by Abram Piesch, its manager under Myerkoff. He too was forced to suspend operations and sell it. On February 12, 1833, it was taken over by the Columbia Glass Manufacturing Company, established by William Heijberger, O.D. William Lilliendahl, John J. Van Kirk, William Heyberger, Frederick Salade, and John Beck. Lilliendahl managed it with little success. A Mr. Smouth succeeded him and made a serious attempt at glass blowing, making green glass tablewares in addition to window glass. He too failed, and it closed in 1839.

Columbian coin
See *coin pattern glass.*

column candlestick
A candlestick having a nozzle on a support in the form of a column.

columnar vase
A small vase, cylindrical or nearly cylindrical in form, having the general appearance of a column. Usually it has a splayed base or decorative ring projecting outward, and occasionally, a similar ring around the neck.

comb
(1) An implement used to smooth and arrange hair. Some were made of glass, particularly in Japan; the larger ones having inset panels of cut glass. See *biidori-e.* (2) The process by which combed decoration is made, mainly by pulling a toothed metal tool over the molten glass. See *combed decoration.* (3) A tool used to make combed decoration.

combed decoration
An applied embellishment in the form of a wavy, festooned zigzag or feathery pattern. Generally found in two or more colors on glass objects. It is made by applying to a molten object of one color, threads of opaque glass of a different color or colors. The surface is then combed or dragged with a tool to produce the desired decorative effect, which may be marvered into the body. The technique is quite old. Occasionally it is found on Egyptian core glass vessels as early as the 15th century B.C., on Greek vases from the 5th to the 2nd century BC, and on some 16th century Venetian glassware (referred to as *vetro fenici* or *vetro a pettine*, but often referred to incorrectly as *latticino*). See *comb, combing.*

combed fluting
A decorative pattern on cut glass in the form of tightly spaced vertical flutings (see *splits*). Smooth at the bottom, with each split tapering to a point at the top, the overall appearance resembles a comb.

Come Again beaker
See *Wiederkomm (humpen).*

comfit glass
(Aka *comfits*) A small sweetmeat glass used to serve dry sweetmeats, such as chocolates, nuts, etc., about 2-3/4 to 4 inches tall, often with a rudimentary or no stem at all.

commemorative glassware
Glass or decorated glass objects made to commemorate a specific event, person or cause. The object itself may be made to look like an item or symbol associated with the event, person, or cause. Also, it may be an everyday item, such as a drinking glass, decanter, bowl, etc. The objects are embellished with a scene, inscription, portrait, or symbol so associated. Symbols are often used to conceal the true significance of the commemoration. See *presentation glassware.*

Compagnie de Cristalleries de Baccarat
A glass manufacturing facility established in 1764 at Baccarat, a city near Luneville, in Lorraine, France. It was founded by Monseigneur de Montmorency-Laval, Bishop of Metz, as a royal undertaking under the auspices of Louis XV. Initially it was named Verreries Renaut & Cie; after 1768, Verreries de Baccarat; and, after 1773, the Verreries de Sainte-Anne. In 1816, it was

bought by Aime-Gabriel D'Artiques, who moved its operations to his Voneche Glassworks calling it Verreries de Voneche a Baccarat. In 1823, the name became Compagnie de Cristalleries de Baccarat. Since 1816, it has made crystal glass; since 1823, agate and opaline glass; since 1824, molded glass bottles embellished with portraits; since 1839, colored glass; in 1843, uranium glass (*cristal dichroide*) and later a green opaque glass (*Chrysoprase*); since 1846, millefiori glassware and paperweights; since 1848, sulfides; and since 1867, wheel engraved wares. Today, it makes stemware and objects of freely formed cut glass. See *Baccarat Glass Factory; Baccarat paperweight.*

companion piece One of a pair, set, or group of related, matching, or like objects. Examples: a sugar is a companion piece to a matching creamer; a saltshaker to a matching pepper shaker.

Compartmented candy dish, Duncan & Miller, First Love pattern, 6-1/2" d.
Tri-State Antiques

compartment bowl A round shallow bowl, usually with two handles, divided into sections with glass dividers. The cut-glass version is called a *caboret.*

compatibility The characteristic of two or more paraisons of glass with comparable coefficients of expansion. This is usually achieved by use of parasions from the same batch, and is of extreme importance in making cased glassware or glassware with enclosed ornamentation, such as paperweights. If they are not compatible, the object will crack when subjected to a slight change in temperature or mechanical shock. See *pull test.*

comport (1) A stand or salver with a heavy flared foot for holding fruit or jelly glasses. (2) A *compotier*, now called a *compote.* (see *compotier*). (3) A footed bon-bon.

composite stem A stem of an English drinking glass uniting a component of air twist and plain clear glass, the latter often in the form of a knop, made primarily between about 1745 and 1765.

composition of glass

Typical Composition of Soda-Lime Silica Glass

Bottle Glass

Ingredient	Colorless	Amber
SiO_2 (Silica)	72.1 %	72.5 %
Na_2O (Sodium oxide)	13.6 %	14.4 %
Al_2O_3 (Alumina)	2.0 %	2.0 %
Fe_2O_4 (Iron oxide)	0.06 %	0.1 %
CaO (Calcium oxide)	10.4 %	10.2 %
Other ingredients	0.7 %	0.8 %

Other Wares

Ingredient	Window Glass	Lamp Bulbs	Domestic Glassware
SiO_2 (Silica)	72.0 %	72.9 %	70.5 %
Na_2O (Sodium oxide)	14.3 %	16.3 %	16.5 %
Al_2O_3 (Alumina)	1.3 %	2.2 %	2.5 %
Fe_2O_3 (Iron oxide)	0.06 %	0.06 %	—
CaO (Calcium oxide)	8.2 %	4.7 %	5.5 %
MgO (Magnesia)	3.5 %	3.6 %	3.0 %
K_2O (Potassium oxide)	—	0.2 %	1.2 %
B_2O_3 (Boric oxide)	—	0.2 %	—
Other ingredients	0.6 %	—	—

Typical Composition of Lead Glass

Ingredient	Full Lead Crystal	Low Quality Lead Glass
SiO_2 (Silica)	55.55 %	66.0 %
PbO (Lead oxide)	33.00 %	15.5 %
K_2O (Potassium oxide)	11.00 %	9.5 %
Fe_2O_3 (Iron oxide-*unwanted*)	0.025 %	—
Al_2O_3 (Alumina)	—	0.9 %
CaO (Calcium oxide)	—	0.7 %
BaO (Barium oxide)	—	0.5 %
Na_2O (Sodium oxide)	—	6.0 %
B_2O_3 (Boric oxide)	—	0.6 %

Typical Composition of Boro-Silicate Glass

Ingredient	Typical Composition
SiO_2 (Silica)	76.2 - 80.0 %
Al_2O_3 (Alumina)	3.7 - 2.5 %
CaO (Calcium oxide)	0.8 - 0.0 %
Na_2O (Sodium oxide)	5.4 - 4.5 %
B_2O_3 (Boric oxide)	13.5 - 12.2 %

composto, vetro *(Italian)* Glassware developed by Venini, made by placing a very thin flashing of colored glass over a thin different-colored glass object.

compote See *comport; compotier.*

Pattern glass covered compote. Krause Publications

compotier *(French)* (Aka *compote* or *comport*) A bowl, often on a stemmed foot, for serving *compote* (fruit cooked in syrup). They typically have a cover, and are made in numerous designs and types of glass of various quality. In size, they usually range from 6 to 12 inches in diameter and 8 to 15 inches in height. Covered ones are rare; the larger the compotier, the rarer it tends to be.

concave beaker A beaker with sides curved inward from the rim to the bottom, resting on a low base. Generally, the rim's diameter is about twice that of the base. They were made in the 1st century AD of a very dark green Roman glass, which appears black.

concentric (1) An embellishment consisting of circles, one within the other, similar to a *bull's-eye* target. (2) Any spacing scheme in millefiori paperweights having concentric circles of canes around a central cane or cluster of canes.

concentric paperweight A millefiori paperweight in which florets are placed in an overall pattern of concentric circles. They are either "open" (circles spaced relatively far apart), "close" (circles close together) or "spaced" (millefiori canes set equal distances apart in vaguely defined concentric circles).

Con-Cora A line of glassware made by the Consolidated Lamp & Glass Company in the 1950s, consisting of several milk glass items decorated with various motifs. The molds of its *Catalonia* line were used to make it.

Concord Street Glass Works See *Hibbler & Rausch.*

Concord Street Flint Glass Works Founded by Christian Dorflinger in 1852, on Concord Street, Brooklyn, New York. The company made blanks, druggist's bottles, and chimneys for oil lamps. Dorflinger created a "smokeless" chimney that revolutionized production, giving him a virtual monopoly in the field. In 1854, cutting operations were introduced. By 1858, the cutting operations were relocated to his new facility on Plymouth Street which continued cutting for a few years and sold in 1870 to Fowler, Crampton & Co. Within two years, it was enlarged and replaced by a new one at Concord & Prince Street, the Long Island Flint Glass Works.

condenser glass See *water lens.*

condiment box A container used to hold condiments. See *saltshaker.*

condiment set A set of matching containers, customarily with a tray or rack, for holding condiments, such as salt, pepper, mustard, oil, vinegar, etc.

Condon (Cut) Glass Company (1916-1920) A glass cutting facility established by James J. Condon in Toledo, Ohio.

Con-Dor See *Conlow & Dorworth.*

cone beaker A drinking vessel of inverted conical shape. Specimens were made of Roman glass during the 4th century A.D. and similar, but taller ones, later of Frankish glass in northern France and Belgium. They could be placed down only on the rim, since they did not have a flat base. It is the belief of many that they were not necessarily designed to be drained at one time, but used by the drinker, then handed to a servant between sips. Most are made of colorless glass; others of light olive green or amber glass. They are often embellished with glass blobs or glass trailing. See *Kempston Beaker; Spitzbecher.*

cone knop A knop in the shape of an upright truncated cone.

confection dish See *stick dish.*

Congress (& Empire) Spring Co. Glass Works; Congressville Glass Works See *Granger, O.& H., & Co.*

conical bowl A bowl of a drinking glass shaped like an inverted cone with its mouth slightly narrower than the base of the funnel bowl.

conical faceted stopper A stopper in the shape of a cone with overall faceting.

conical foot A foot shaped like a low cone, either solid or hollow. The hollow type prevents the pontil mark from marring the table. Both types provide stability to the object.

conical stopper A stopper, conical in shape, but lacking the height of a spire stopper. See *conical faceted stopper.*

Conlow & Dorworth (1915-1920?) A glass cutting house with locations in Mt. Holly and Palmyra, New Jersey, operating under the trade name *Con-Dor.*

Connell, John, & Co. See *Hewson, Connell & Co.*

console bowl A shallow, circular center piece bowl, generally larger in diameter than in height and normally with a wide flaring rim, often with matching candlesticks.

console set A console bowl together with matching candlesticks, serving as a centerpiece, particularly popular in the 1920s and 1930s.

Consolidated Lamp & Glass Co., Line 700 Reuben blue vase, 6-1/2" h.
Davanna Collection

Consolidated Lamp & Glass Company It came into existence, in 1893, as a result of a merger between the Wallace & McAfee Company (a lamp and glass jobber) of Pittsburgh, Pennsylvania, and the Fostoria Shade and Lamp Company of Fostoria, Ohio. It began operations, in 1894, in both Pittsburgh and Fostoria. When the Fostoria facility burned in 1895, it, in 1896, moved all operations to Coraopolis, Pennsylvania. Its principal products were oil lamps and associated globes and shades.

As electric lamps gained in popularity, it began making glass bases and shades for them. In 1911, it was the largest lamp, globe, and shade manufacturer in the United States. In addition to lighting wares, it, as a result of the *Art Deco* movement, made fashionable lines of pressed and blown tablewares. In 1925/26, the company began a line of giftwares, known as *Martele,* inspired by Rene Lalique. This line was marketed by Howard Selden from his showrooms in New York City, and is often called *Selden Glass.*

Some of its tableware patterns were *Cone, Florette, Guttate,* and *Cosmos.* The *Cosmos* line, made from 1894 to 1915, included lamps and tableware. Other lines of *Martele* quality included *Catalonian,* made beginning in 1926, and, in the next three years, *Florentine, Chintz, Ruba, Shaded Light, Rombic,* and *Line 700* were introduced. Many of its lines closely resemble lines made by the Phoenix Glass Company, because many of the molds were made by Reuben Haley. On Haley's death, in 1933 (Consolidated closed in 1932), the molds were inherited by his son, Kenneth, who was Chief Designer at Phoenix. Kenneth Haley put together a line, called the *Reuben* line, from the most popular of these molds. However, the colors were distinctively different from those made at Consolidated.

Consolidated reopened, during 1936, under McCune family management. At this time, it introduced the *Dancing Nymph* line based on the 8-inch salad plate of its *Martele* line. In the 1940s, it introduced the *Regent* line and, in the 1950s, the *Con-Cora* line of decorated milk glass. In August 1962, it was sold to Dietz Bros. In 1963, it was damaged by fire during labor disputes and, in 1964, it closed. Some of its molds were obtained by Sinclair Glass, which used them for a period. In 1988,

Westclair, a Division of Sinclair, made some wares, *Canton Collectibles*, using these molds.

consommé dish See *cream soup*.

constable glass An English goblet-shaped glass with a funnel shaped bowl, ranging to 15 inches in height, used in one of two ways: (a) a loving cup on ceremonial occasions, or (b) (Aka *serving rummer*) a vessel for holding alcoholic beverages to be transferred to individual serving glasses, usually wine glasses.

Constitution Flint Glass Works

(1865-1886) A glass manufacturing facility in Brooklyn, New York, affiliated with Augustine Thier(r)y & Company, making lead glass perfume bottles, both cut and colored. It claimed to be the largest maker of glass chimneys for kerosene lamps in the United States. In 1876, the name became La Bastie Works, operated by Ernest De La Chapelle & Company.

Constitution mirror Mirrors made in the early 18th century having a gilt eagle cresting. They are long, rectangular mirrors, above which is a reverse painting on glass, and/or thirteen drops (for the thirteen original states) around the frame's upper part.

Consumers Glass Company, Limited

A glass manufacturing facility established by former employees of the Diamond Flint Glass Company (Montreal, Canada) as the Atlas Glass Company during 1913, in Montreal, Canada. The facility was never finished. New financial backers created the Premier Glass Company and continued construction, but again money ran out before glass was made. On October 14, 1917, the Consumers Glass Company, Limited, was formed, the facility completed, and the manufacturing of bottles and containers began.

contact three-section mold glass See *blown three-mold glass; three-section-mold blown glass*.

contemporary glass Art glass made since 1950.

conterie (Italian) (1) Small beads of glass of varied colors, globular or oval, and/ or smooth or irregular in shape, sold on strings or in mass quantity. Sometimes they are used as a raw material, and are remelted to make other glass objects. They are made from thin glass tubes cut in short segments, each rounded by heat. (2) The makers of small beads. See *perlai*.

Continents, The Four

See *Four Continents, The*.

continuous firing triple kiln A kiln with three distinct sections, each maintained at a different temperature. The bottom section is maintained at the highest temperature, for preheating; the central at a moderate temperature, for firing; and the top at the lowest temperature, for cooling and annealing.

contracted neck A vessel with a neck quite slender in proportion to the body.

convex mirror (Aka *bull's-eye mirror*) A mirror having a convex surface reflecting a reduced image. In the 15th century, they were made by blowing a metallic mixture with resin or salt of tartar into a hot glass globe producing a reflecting surface when viewed from the exterior. When the globe had cooled, it was cut into circular convex mirrors.

Cook, Lane & Corning See *Redford Crown Glass Works*.

Cookstown Glass Works A window glass manufacturing facility established in 1844 in Cookstown, Pennsylvania. It had numerous owners over the years, closing during the Civil War. In 1865, it was reopened by D. Harmony & Co. Several owners followed. In 1873, the Iron City Window Glass Co. took over and, in 1877, George Wankoff & Co. acquired it, operating it until it closed in 1882.

cooler jug A decanter jug with an indented side well. The well held ice to cool the beverage in the decanter without diluting it.

Cooper & Townsend See *Eagle Glass Works*.

Co-operative Cut Glass Company

See *McCue & Earl*.

Co-operative Flint Glass Company

(1879-1934) A glass manufacturing facility established in Beaver Falls, Pennsylvania, as Beaver Falls Co-operative Glass Company. In 1889, it became the Co-operative Flint Glass Company. It is best known for its extensive line of gift items, and soda fountain and restaurant wares.

Co-operative Glass Company

See *Barnegat Glass Company.*

copper A metallic agent utilized in coloring glass, dating back to ancient times. Egyptian blue, popular in Roman times, and an opaque red glass made by ancient Egyptians, both derived their color from copper compounds. They are also used to produce shades of green, including turquoise. The blue produced is a transmutation color, appearing red when seen by transmitted light. In a reducing atmosphere (predominantly carbon monoxide), they produce *copper red*. Ruby glass can be made by using a colloidial dispersion of metallic copper. Gold aventurine glass has tiny flakes of metallic copper suspended within the glass. See *Egermann, Friedrich.* Copper is also used in electroplating glass. See *electroplating.*

copper wheel engraving

See *engraving.*

Coralene Embellishment on glass having the appearance of sprays of coral stretching over the surface. The technique used involved coating the surface with an enamel compound having a syrupy consistency, either colored or transparent, usually in coral-like forms. Before it dried, tiny glass beads (solid and/or perforated; colorless, colored and/or opalescent) were applied to it and the object heated to a temperature just hot enough to melt the enamel so the beads were cemented to the glass' surface, usually a satin glass. The designs, other than coral, included fish, birds, flowers, etc. It was made by the New England Glass Company in the late 1800s. Mt. Washington Glass Company also made some and is responsible for naming it. It was made by several other companies in the United States and Europe. Low-cost imitations were made in the late 1800s. True

Coralene beads, fired on, will not rub off. If they rub off, the ware is not true Coralene.

Corbyns See *dispensary container.*

cord An imperfection occurring in glassware, appearing as long strings or lines that are of slightly different composition from the main body and may be caused by: (a) deviation in the temperature of the furnace; (b) inconsistent density of the material used caused by poor stirring; (c) incomplete melting; (d) remelting of stones; (e) unmelted silica in the pot's composition; or (f) a portion of the refractory breaking off and fusing with the batch. Sometimes they are not visible to the naked eye, but can be felt with the fingers.

cordial glass (Aka *liqueur glass*) A drinking glass with a capacity of about 1 to 1-1/2 ounces, used for serving cordials. They are usually in the form of wine glasses, but smaller, with a bowl resting on a tall stem and foot. See *flute cordial glass.*

core (1) A glass cane positioned vertically in the center of the stem of a drinking glass enclosed within a spiral twist. (2) The material upon which core glass is formed into its final shape. See *core forming; core glass.*

core forming A technique used for making core glass. See *core; rod- and core-forming; core glass.*

core glass A glass object made by a process used from about 1500 to 1200 B.C. in Mesopotamia and Egypt, and thereafter in Mesopotamia, Egypt, and the eastern Mediterranean region; declining between 1200 and 800 BC, but revived in eastern Mediterranean region from about 800 to the 1st century B.C.

The primary process used was called *core winding.* It involved making a core in the desired object's shape. It was rotated while molten glass was trailed around it until it was covered. Then the piece was marvered, trailing more glass on it until the desired thickness was attained. It was then marvered again causing the exterior to become smooth, annealed, and the core was removed.

An alternate process used to make core glass was to merely immerse the core into molten glass until covered, then remove the core after the glass was annealed and polish it. Some core glass was made by slumping (see *slumping*). Occasionally glass of more than one color was used with combing being the favored type of embellishment. Originally it was believed that sand was used as a core and, upon drying in the furnace, it could be poured out, but now it is generally accepted that mud or dung bonded with straw or clay formed the core; still, it is often called *sand core glass*. Once glass blowing was developed about 100 B.C., it declined rapidly and then ceased altogether.

core molding See *core forming*.

core winding One of the processes used to make core glass. See *core glass*.

coring The process of making core glass. See *core glass; core forming*.

cork wheel A wheel originally made from cork tree bark, but now from ground cork with a binding agent. It is used with abrasive powders to polish glass.

corkscrew twist A single air twist or opaque tape twisted in corkscrew fashion, or two such intertwined. On occasion the tapes are edged with colored glass thread.

corne (d'abondance) See *cornucopia*.

corner pot A pot or container where the odds and ends of glass (broken or misshapen pieces, glass remaining on the blowpipe or pontil, etc.) were thrown by workers during the course of their daily activities, considered to be for exclusive use by the glass workers.

Corning Cut Glass Co. (1901-1911) A glass cutting company established by James Sebring in Corning, New York, purchasing its blanks from the Pairpoint, Phoenix, Fairmount, and Union.

Corning Flint Glass Works
See *Corning Glass Works*.

Corning Glass Works The Corning Flint Glass Works was established in Corning, New York, by Amory Houghton, Sr. and Jr. (their Brooklyn Flint Glass Works, relocated in an effort to find cheaper fuel, labor, and raw materials). It was in full operation by October 1868. In 1872, it went bankrupt and closed, reincorporated as the Corning Glass Works,

with Amory Houghton, Jr., as President. It placed a high priority on scientific research and development of special products and new areas of applied glass technology.

From 1872 to 1918, Corning continued to make decorative lead crystal blanks, which it sold to the numerous area cutting shops. In 1918, it acquired the Steuben Glass Works. In 1951, it established the Corning Glass Center, housing the Steuben Glass Works, The Corning Museum of Glass, and the Hall of Science & Industry. It is still in operation and, during its history, has made almost every type of glassware. It cut glass from about 1900 to 1929 using *Best Metal* and *Pyrex* blanks.

Some highlights of its history are: in 1879, the bulb for Edison's electric light was blown by Fred Douerlein; in 1912, heat-shock resistant borosilicate glass (trademark *Pyrex*) was developed by Eugene C. Sullivan and William C. Taylor; in 1926, a fully-automatic machine to blow electric light bulbs was developed; in 1931, fiber glass was developed in conjunction with the Owens-Illinois Glass Company; in 1934, it cast the largest piece of man-made glass in the world, the 200-inch, 15-3/4 ton, telescope disc for the Mount Palomar Observatory; in 1936, 96% silica glass was developed by Harrison Hood and Martin Nordberg; in 1945, it developed a method of mass producing optical glass; in 1947, photosensitive glass was developed by S.D. Stookey; in 1951, photochemical glass was developed; in 1957, glass-ceramic crystalline materials were developed by S.D. Stookey (trademark *Pyroceram*); in 1962, chemically-tempered glass was developed; and in 1964, photochromic glass was developed by W.H. Armistead and S.D. Stookey.

Cornucopia, purple flashing on clear glass, cut to clear, 11-1/2" l. x 7" h.
Davanna Collection

cornucopia A receptacle shaped like a cone or animal horn, generally curved slightly. They are used for ornamental purposes and as wall pockets.

Corona A Nash mark.

Corona Cut Glass Company (1905-1920) A glass cutting shop established in Toledo, Ohio, making all types of cut and engraved glassware. By 1911, it was making only light cut wares. On January 23, 1912, it was issued a trademark (used from May 1906) depicting the sun with a fiery corona, in the center of the darkened sun is the name *Corona*.

coronation glassware Glassware commemorating a coronation in England. The earliest known is the Exeter Flute commemorating the coronation of Charles II (1660).

Correia Art Glass A studio founded by Steve Correia in 1974 on the Pacific coast of southern California. It is known for its paperweights with unusual surface designs and its wide assortment of cut and faceted lampwork. It has made many three dimensional animal, floral, and aquatic scenes. Each weight has a frosted outer surface with one large facet cut to reveal the interior motif. Each is signed, dated, and accompanied by a certificate of authenticity.

corroded glass See *corroso, vetro*.

corroso, vetro (Italian) Literally, *corroded glass*. A type of ice glass, developed by Venini about 1933, made using hydrofluoric acid. To make it, the surface of a glass is covered with an acid-resistant resin that cracks when it dries. Hydrofluoric acid is applied on top of the dried resin, penetrating the cracks and attacking the glass, leaving the rest of the glass smooth. If the resin is removed in stages, an array of effects can be produced.

corrugated foot A foot having a series of small steps giving a corrugated effect; a modification of a terraced foot.

Cosmos (Aka *Stemless Daisy*) A patterned glass made from 1894 to 1915 by Consolidated Lamp & Glass Company. Relief molded flowers in a cross-cut background were painted in soft colors of pink, blue, and yellow. Though nearly all items were made of milk glass, a few are of clear glass. Tableware, lamps, and perfume bottles were made in this pattern.

costeril See *costrel*.

costrel Also spelled *costeril* or *costret*. A bottle or flask with ears, tabs, or handles to which a cord was attached for carrying or hanging on the body. See *pilgrim flask*.

costret See *costrel*.

cottle (or cottling) A wall or barrier made of wood, cardboard, or other material, used to hold fluid plaster around a model until it solidified.

cotton dispenser (Aka *cotton picker*) A container for holding cotton, generally used on the boudoir table. They first appeared in the United States in the mid-1930s, in a variety of shapes, always with a circular opening on the side or top.

cotton glass See *filigrana*.

cotton picker See *cotton dispenser*.

cotton twist All types of twists made of opaque white glass. See *opaque twist*.

coulage (French) A process of making plate glass by casting, perfected by Louis Lucas de Nehou about 1675. Molten glass was poured into frames, spread evenly by rollers, annealed, and polished, though small by today's standards, were, at that time, unparalleled in size.

counterfeit A reproduction made to appear genuine with the intent to deceive or defraud the buyer.

counterfeit porcelain See *porcellana contrafatta*.

country market glassware Glassware made for country and artisan markets, for sale at fairs as gifts or souvenirs. Embellishments were normally executed in unfired cold colors and gilding.

Couper, James, & Sons See *West Lothian Glassworks; Clutha glass*.

court cellar glass See *Hofkellereiglas*.

court dish A large goblet referred to as a standing cup or state cup.

courting mirror A mirror with a wide molded frame incorporating glass painted with flowers and foliage, and capped with a stepped crest.

cover An unattached top (as distinguished from a lid, normally hinged) for sealing an open vessel. They vary in shape, being flat, conical, dome shaped, resembling an animal or portion of one, etc., and are usually surmounted by a closed ornamental handle, called a finial or knop. They generally fit within a rim, but, on some, over the rim, resting on an applied ring. See *dome cover.*

Covered butter dishes, above: Imperial's rectangular pressed glass Candlewick pattern; at right: cut glass, round under plate, 7-1/2" d. x 5" h. Davanna Collection

covered butter A two-piece item for serving butter, in bulk. It consists of a flat underplate and a domed cover, generally with a finial or knop to lift it. It is similar to a covered cheese, but smaller. See *cheese dish.*

covered cheese See *cheese dish.*

cowhorns The enlarged end of canes used in the making of mosaic glass.

cowl board A face-shaped wooden mask with eye slits fitted with blue or amber lenses, worn by glass blowers making cylinder glass.

It protected their faces from the furnace's extreme heat and held in place by a mouthpiece held between his teeth. When not in use, it hung by a string around the blower's neck.

crack An actual separation in glass that will potentially continue to lengthen, ruining the piece's value. They are caused by sudden changes in temperature or striking it against another object.

Mt. Washington cracker jar. Krause Publications

cracker jar (Aka *cookie jar*) A receptacle for holding crackers or cookies. Inexpensive ones were often sold with product inside. More expensive ones are often confused with tobacco jars because of the similarity in shape. The most common shapes for cracker jars are: (a) barrel shaped with a glass cover and finial, sometimes with an underplate; (b) basket shaped with a silver rim, handle, and cover; and (c) tobacco jar shaped with a silver or glass cover. See *tobacco jar.*

cracker off A worker who, when making tumblers, chimneys, stemware, etc., would mark the object at the proper height and train a gas flame on the mark, applying water while at the same time rotating the object; thus trimming and smoothing the rim to the proper height.

cracking off (1) (Aka *wetting off*) The process of separating a glass object from the blow pipe or pontil rod after it has cooled. Originally done manually, circumscribing the object with a diamond point, or wet file, and (a) giving a sharp tap to the blow pipe's end or pontil rod so the object breaks off cleanly, or (b) heating it so it breaks off along the scratched line. (2) A process where a glass object, blown in the mold and annealed, is rotated against a diamond or tungsten point for scoring. A fine-tipped flame is applied to the scored line (while it is rotating) until it cracks.

Crackle glass champagne pitcher, c. 1870-1888, 11" h.
The Corning Museum of Glass

crackle glass (Aka *frosted glass, ice glass, iced glass, overshot glass*) Also spelled *craquelle*. Created by the Venetians during the 16th century, it is made by plunging hot glass into cold water and quickly pulling it out, reheating it until pliable and blowing it to the desired size, thus producing a crackled effect (a network of fine cracks covering the entire surface). In addition to clear glass, it was made in several colors. Most of the old surviving crackle glass dates from the 1800s; some of the best made by Sandwich and Hobbs, Brockunier & Co. From the late 1930s to the early 1970s, crackle glass was made by about 500 companies.

crackled iridescent glass
See *iridescent glass.*

Crackleware A pattern popular on glassware during the 1920s and 1930s; the crackled effect made by using a mold with a network of lines on its inner surface.

Craig & O'Hara See *Pittsburgh Glass Works.*

Craig & Ritchie A glass manufacturing facility established about 1825 in Wheeling, West Virginia. It is reported to be the first facility in the United States making pressed glass.

cranberry glassware Objects of reddish-pink transparent glass, made in England and the United States since the mid-19th century and popular as one of the layers in overlay glass, either as the base layer with a white overlay or as an overlay on a clear base. The cranberry color is lighter than gold ruby and not to be confused with Bohemian clear glass flashed with ruby. It was made by adding gold to the batch from which a gather was blown or molded into the desired form, then reheated at a low temperature and the cranberry shade developed. In later years, copper was substituted for gold, creating a harsh amber-red tint.

Crandell, Fox & Co. See *Rensselaer Glass Factory.*

craquelle glass See *crackle glass.*

crater A jar or vase similar to an amphora.

Craven & Brothers A glass manufacturing facility established in 1862 in Salem, New Jersey, by John V. Craven, Henry D. Hall, and Joseph Pancoast, making bottles and chemical apparatus. Shortly thereafter, it was operated by Craven & Brothers. About 1925, it was operated by the Gayner Glass Company. See *Salem Glass Works.*

cream basin (Aka *cream bason*) A small, deep dish, occasionally footed, from which cream was ladled.

cream boat A small boat-shaped vessel for serving cream at the table, usually with a handle at one end and pouring lip at the other, resting on a splayed base. It is similar to a sauceboat, but smaller.

cream bowl A bowl, circular with steeply sloping sides and a pouring lip, for settling milk; the cream rising to the top and poured off.

Creamer cut on pressed blank, 6-1/2" h.
Davanna Collection

cream jug (Aka *cream pitcher, cream pot, creamer*) A small jug or pitcher for serving cream. It is often pear shaped, having a single loop handle and a pouring lip and, on occasion, a cover. It is smaller than a milk jug. See *yacht jug*.

cream pail A small cylindrical cream basin with straight sides and bail handle, resembling a miniature pail.

cream pitcher or pot: See *cream jug*.

cream soup (1) A bowl or nappy, about 5 inches in diameter, usually with two handles near the rim. (2) A two-handled bouillon or consommé dish.

creamer (1) See *cream jug*. (2) Half of the related table set called a *sugar & creamer*.

MacBeth Evans Cremax plate,
Petalware pattern.
Davanna Collection

Cremax A beige glassware made by Macbeth-Evans, introduced in the late 1930s.

Cremona See *Pomona glass*.

crenellated (Aka *castellated*) Notched, in the form of battlements, with equally spaced, perpendicular straight-sided projections.

Crescent Cut Glass Company (1900-1920) A glass cutting company in Newark, New Jersey.

Crescent Glass Company A glass manufacturing facility established in 1908 in Wellsburg, West Virginia, by Henry Rithner and Ellery Worthen, making tumblers, lamp globes, lights for autos. When it burned in

1911, the company purchased the former Riverside Glass facility and the Lobmiller Decorating Co. When Worthen died in 1920, the Rithner family became sole owner; still managing the facility, making novelty items, lamp accessories, etc.

Crescent Glass Works A glass manufacturing facility established in Pittsburgh, Pennsylvania, making flint, green, and window glass and glassware, vials and bottles, beginning sometime before 1867. In 1869, it was known as the Cresent Glass Works, operated by Evans, Sell & Company. By 1886, the operating firm was known as Thomas Evans & Co., specializing in glass chimneys.

cresoline glass Glass having a color resembling a cresol/resin mixture (pale, yellowish-green). Cresol was used mainly as a disinfectant during the late 19th/ early 20th centuries, often burned in sick rooms in lamps specifically designed for that purpose.

cresting A decorative ornament often found projecting from the outer edge of the wings of winged glasses, or a similar ornament on the stem of such glasses. It is in the form of small, tightly spaced tufts, points, or thin semi-circles, pincered with close parallel ridges.

crib A one-man glass shop.

Crib, The A glass manufacturing facility operated for a short time in the early 1890s. It was located in the old Boston & Sandwich Glass Company's facility in Sandwich, Massachusetts, after the Electric Glass Company closed. It made opal lighting wares and was operated by some former employees of the Boston & Sandwich Glass Company.

Cricklight A later modification by Samuel Clarke to his patented Fairy Night Light (trademark registered 1889), highly fashionable until about 1930, for use on dining room tables. The two were similar, except the Cricklight emitted more light because the shade was made of clear uncut glass, rather than the colored shade of the Fairy Night Light. Some were used on chandeliers and candelabra, being held in place by a glass peg inserted into the candle nozzle.

crimp mold A mold made of radiating iron or wood ribs fitted on a base plate. The ribs range in number, thickness, and height depending on the form of crimp desired. To create the crimped edge, the rim of the hot glass object was pressed against the ribs. See *crimper.*

crimper A special tool used to embellish the rim of bowls and other objects with a crimped or wavy effect. It is a metal or wooden device, generally smaller than a crimp mold.

Blue glass bowl with crimped rim, 9″ w. x 5-1/4″ h.
Davanna Collection

crimping (1) Embellishing glassware by pinching the rim, usually with a crimper, to form a wavy edge. (2) The process of drawing in molten glass to shape a neck of a vessel. (3) The process of configuring a glass ornament into a decorative design. (4) The process of finishing the end of a handle by pinching it with a special tool.

crimping boy A laborer that takes hot, partially finished glassware to the furnace, reheating it at the glory hole. The name is derived from the practice used in making chimneys where a laborer takes a partially completed chimney to the glory hole to be reheated before being placed in a crimping machine.

crinze A drinking cup.

crisselling Also spelled *crizzling.* An imperfection in glass caused by an inappropriate ratio of ingredients in the batch, especially an overabundance of alkali, resulting in a maze of delicate internal cracks and beads of sour smelling moisture forming on its surface. Such glass (called *diseased glass*) ultimately deteriorates, decomposes, and/or disintegrates. Glassware made during the late 17th century in England, Holland, Germany, and China where much experimentation took place to find an alternative for Venetian glass often exhibits crisselling. It must be distinguished from decay which results from centuries of being buried in the damp earth. In decayed glass, only the surface is effected, due to dissolved carbonic acid in the soil which draws the alkali from the glass, often producing iridescence. See *sick glass; decay.*

Cristal Dichroide A trade name used by Baccarat for its uranium glass, introduced in 1843. It had a yellow or green tint, dependent on the light source.

cristal superieur See *full lead glass*

cristallai (*Italian*) A division of the Venetian glassmakers guild, which specialized in making hollowware and crystal

Cristalleries du Val-Saint-Lambert A glass manufacturing facility established during 1825 in Liege, Belgium. It was originally operated by English craftsmen, making excellent lead glass. Through the years to the present, it has continued to be a dominant Belgium factory. Artistic strategy changed as English craftsmen were displaced by French and the French style of clear cut tableware with variations having engraved and gilded embellishments.

cristallo (*Italian*) A soda glass formulated in Venice during the 14th century which, as of that date, was the most transparent glass yet made. It was clear or a very pale yellow, made colorless using magnesium.

Made using barilla ashes or natron as the source of alkali, the glass was remarkably ductile, easily manipulated when hot, and conveyed a light fragile appearance, but was thin, brittle, and easily susceptible to breakage. It could not be readily carved, cut or stippled, but was well-suited for diamond point engraving, enameling, gilding, trailing, and filigree embellishments.

Cristallo Ceramie A process used in making sulfides or encasing a small object, such as a cameo, in a solid block of clear glass. Apsley Pellatt perfected the process, completing his best works between 1819 and 1835.

crizzling See *crisselling.*

croquet hoop design A molded decoration on a bowl where separate loops of glass were applied around its edge, the loops resembling the hoops used in croquet.

Crocker Glass Company A short-lived glass manufacturing facility operating in Fostoria, Ohio, during the late 1880s.

Cross-cut diamond A cut-glass motif in which a cut diamond has a cross cut on the flattened tip. See *alternate panels cutting; strawberry diamond (American version).*

cross paperweight A type of close millefiori paperweight divided into quadrants by a cross of similar canes, each having a central floret. Most were made at St. Louis.

crossbill A two-part divided bottle, each having a separate neck. The necks curve and cross over each other, often confusing the pourer.

crosshatching A cut-glass geometric motif, consisting of minute parallel lines intersecting at right angles, used to fill the inner areas of various geometric figures. The English placed four crosshatched squares together, calling the arrangement a strawberry diamond.

crow's foot cane See arrowhead cane.

Crowley, Samuel See *Atlantic Glass Works; Crowley Glass Works.*

Crowley(town) Glass Works (1858-1870) A bottle manufacturing facility established in Bulltown, now Waldo, New Jersey, by Samuel Crowley, who also established the Atlantic Glass Works in 1851. See *Atlantic Glass Works.*

crown (1) An ornamental piece made in the form of a crown. (2) (Aka *dome*) The clear glass dome over and around the decorative motif of a paperweight. (3) A type of paperweight (see *crown paperweight*). (4) The refractory brick arch enclosing the top of a tank furnace.

Crown Cut Glass Company (1) A glass cutting house established in the early 1900s in Pittsburgh, Pennsylvania. Little is known of it, except, in June 1903, it advertised in the *Ladies' Home Journal.* (2) A glass cutting house in Hancock, New York.

crown flint glass An optical glass. See *optical glass.*

Crown Flint Glass Company See *Ravenna Flint Glass Company.*

crown glass Flat pane glass made by first blowing a pear-shaped bubble of glass, rotating it rapidly, forming a flattened globe, transferring it from the blow pipe to a rod, cutting it open, and rapidly rotating it, with repeated reheatings. Centrifugal forces, created by rapid rotation of the cut open bubble, caused the mass to form into a large flat disc, up to four feet in diameter. The disc was cut off the rod, placed on a flat surface, heated, and placed in an annealing kiln where it cooled over a two or three week period. It was then cut into rectangles, squares, or diamond-shaped panes of glass. The disc was fairly thin, showing a slight convexity and concentric wavy lines caused by the rotating process. The center where the rod was attached is called the *center boss* or *bull's-eye* and the thickest part of the disc, excellent for doors, usually being translucent, but not transparent. The technique was first used by the Romans. It was known as the *spinning process* and later, the *Normandy Method.* Its rediscovery has been credited, with uncertainty, to Philippe de Caqueray of Normandy, believed to have used it during the 14th century.

Crown House, Ltd. See *Webb, Thomas, & Sons; Webb's Crystal Glass Co., Ltd.; Edinburgh Crystal Glass Co.*

Crown Milano vase with egg-shaped body, cylindrical neck and flattened bulbous top. Features two applied handles, gold floral decorations, blue highlights, beige flower bud, star mark, 10" h.
Krause Publications

Crown Milano An art glass formulated by Frederick Shirley at Mt. Washington Glass Company in 1884, remaining popular after Mt. Washington merged with Pairpoint in 1894. It is made of opal glass, the body being pale biscuit color and shaped by free blowing, molding, or press molding with a satin finish using an acid bath. There were brown and beige designs embedded in the glass, which was embellished with enameled motifs, often animals, birds, fish, flowers and leaves, and scrolls of gold and occasionally silver. It was originally called *Albertine Glass* and sold as such. Unless the original paper label is intact, one cannot tell if it was made as *Albertine Glass* or *Crown Milano*. Some pieces are marked on the pontil with a five-pointed crown, below which is a "C" over an "M." Some pieces are not acid treated, having a glossy finish, called *Shiny Crown Milano*, and usually embellished with floral motifs in gold, with an enameled red laurel wreath on the base. In the late 1890s, Crown Milano was advertised as *Dresden Decorated* and *Ivory Decorated*.

crown (paper)weight A hollow paper-weight having as its central motif an embedded crown-like pattern of twisted ribbons, often of opaque white glass, alternating with ribbons or twisted ropes of various colors, starting at the base, flowing upward to meet the central millefiori motif near the crown's top. They were made mainly by St. Louis and the New England Glass Company.

crown pot A pot or crucible in which the various ingredients for making glass were fused. It was covered with a domed top having a side opening (*mouth*) at the shoulder, as distinguished from the earlier *skittle pot*. Its creation in the mid-1600s hastened the banning of wood as a fuel in England and was beneficial in making lead glass since it prevented combustion gases from coming in contact with, and discoloring, the molten glass.

Crown Tuscan covered footed candy dish by Cambridge with gold-trimmed pink shell cover, 7" h.
Tri-State Antiques

Crown Tuscan (1936-1954) A pink opaque glass made by the Cambridge Glass Company. It should not be confused with shell pink milk glass.

cruche A jug having one large spout and an overhead handle. A *botijo*.

crucible A glass melting pot, jockey pot, or skittle pot. See *pot*.

Crucifixion candlestick A candlestick having a hexagonal base and nozzle with a molded glass Crucifix applied to the shaft or column. They were made by the New England Glass Co., until 1888, using many types of glass in various colors.

cruciform Shaped like a cross or in quatre-foil section with four equal lobes or foils.

cruciform decanter A decanter, the body having a cross-section resembling a Greek cross. Specimens are known dating from 1740-60.

Mary Gregory stoppered cruet, 5-1/4" h.
Davanna Collection

cruet (Aka *cruet bottle*). A small jug-shaped receptacle, often with a handle, lip, or spout, and stopper or lid. It is used for serving liquid condiments, such as oil, vinegar, etc. Other containers with a pierced cover, also called *cruets*, are for dry condiments, such as pepper, sugar, etc. and should be called *castors*. See *double cruet; setrill; vinaigrette.*

cruet set A set containing from two to five cruets; sometimes each being inscribed with the name of the contents, and accompanied by a cruet stand.

cruet stand (Aka *bottle stand*) A holder, typically part of a dinner service, for two or more cruets (cruet set).

cruisie See *betty lamp.*

crumb bead A bead having very small particles of varicolored glass attached to the surface. It is usually made by heating beads until slightly plastic and covering them with particles of glass. A *flush crumb bead* has the particles marvered into the surface. It is believed they originated in the Aegean Islands, about 1300 B.C., and in Egypt several centuries later.

crushed fruit bowl A bowl, generally of pressed glass, used to hold small pieces of cut fruit. They are about 4 inches high and 9 inches in diameter; most divided into two to four sections, three being the most common. Some have a cover. They were popular in the early 1900s.

crutch A block or cup for shaping a paraison of glass. It had a short handle held by the crutchman while the blower created the initial paraison.

Crutched Friars Glasshouse (Aka *Crotchet Friar Glasshouse*) A glass manufacturing facility established in London in 1568 (some sources state 1549) by Jean Carre to make *cristallo*. It was operated by craftsmen from Murano, including Jacopo Verzelini, who came to London by way of Antwerp and managed the glasshouse after Carre's death. In 1576, it burned. Verzelini rebuilt it.

crutchman The worker who held a tool called a crutch while the blower blew the paraison into it, giving it its initial shape.

cryolite Sodium/aluminum fluoride. When added to a batch, it creates a dense whiteness in the glass and is used in making opal glass or cast porcelain. It, together with a small amount of manganese, was often added to the raw materials for making slag glass. When melted, the glass had a variety of color combinations.

crystal (1) *Rock crystal*. See *rock crystal.* (2) The colorless transparent glass resembling rock crystal. The term is used loosely for all fine glassware, particularly that made for the table. (3) Today *crystal* is usually associated with glass made with lead oxide. Standards for the amount of lead oxide that must be present for it to be called *crystal* vary with location. In the United States, glass must contain at least 1% lead to be called *crystal*. Recently, European Economic Community (EEC) regulations forbid any glass to be called or labeled *crystal* unless it contains over 10% lead oxide and glass with over 30% lead is designated *high lead crystal*. A generally accepted standard for glass to be called *crystal* is that it must contain at least 24% lead oxide, occasionally called as *half lead* and glass with 30% lead oxide as *full lead* or *Cristal Superieur*. See *full lead crystal; half lead crystal.*

Degenhart robin with berry on nest, 5-1/2".
Davanna Collection

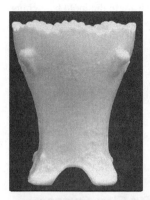

Degenhart custard glass toothpick, Colonial Drape pattern.
Davanna Collection

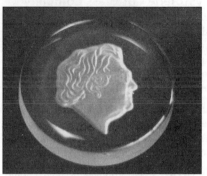

Degenhart portrait of Elizabeth Degenhart, designed by Jack Choko of Millville, NJ, made by Imperial Glass for Crystal Art Co., introduced during 1977.
Krause Publications

Degenhart mug, stork, cobalt blue, carnival, 2-5/8" h.
Krause Publications

Crystal Art Glass A facility opened in 1947 in Cambridge, Ohio, by John (1884-1964) and Elizabeth (1889-1978) Degenhart. When John, highly acclaimed for his paperweights, died, Elizabeth took over, hiring workers from the defunct Cambridge Glass Co., including Zack Boyd (see *Boyd, Zack*). Boyd was responsible for formulating many unique colors, some of which were named for him. From 1964 to 1974, over 27 different molds were created and over 145 original colors developed. When Elizabeth died, some of the molds were sold to Island Mold Company, with the company's signature ("D" in a heart or, on small pieces, just "D") removed; Zack Boyd purchased some of the remaining molds. The facility was eventually sold to Boyd's son, Bernard Boyd (see *Boyd's Crystal Art Glass*).

Crystal (City Cut) Glass Co. These names were supposed to have been used by various Corning, New York, cut glass shops, but they were never used and no company or companies by this or these names existed in Corning, New York.

Crystal Cut Glass Company (1) (1893-1905) A glass cutting house in Chicago, Illinois. (2) (1913-1918) A glass cutting house in Honesdale, Pennsylvania.

Crystal Glass Company (1868/9-1909) A glass manufacturing facility, making crystal tablewares, chimneys and bar goods, established in Birmingham (Pittsburgh), Pennsylvania, moving to Bridgeport, Ohio, in 1882. In March of 1886, it burned, was rebuilt and back in operation in February 1887. In 1888, it purchased the bankrupt LaBelle Glass Company, operating it until about 1908. In 1899, it was purchased by the National Glass Company. In 1902, it burned again and was rebuilt. See *Elson Glass Company.*

Crystal Glass Manufacturing Company A glass manufacturing facility established by the Whitney Brothers in 1886 in Camden, New Jersey, making bottles for alcoholic beverages, flasks, demijohns, pickle jars, and other containers. On March 29, 1889, it was destroyed by fire, rebuilt, and enlarged and operated for a few more years.

Crystal Manufacturing Co. (1) A glass cutting house located in Corning, New York, in 1902, operating a short time. It is believed to have been a trade name of the Bronson Cut Glass Co. (2) In July 1903, a glass cutting house was incorporated in Painted Post, New York, by this name.

Crystal Mirror & Glass Company

See *Simms Modern Cut Glass Company.*

crystal painting See *reverse painting on glass.*

Crystal Palace (1) The immense structure erected in Hyde Park, London, England, to house the Great Exhibition from May 1 to October 11, 1851, and later dismantled and moved to Sydenham. An iron framed building enclosed with about 300,000 panes of glass, it was destroyed by fire in 1936. Among the original exhibits was a large amount of contemporary glassware. (2) A structure erected in New York, as a centerpiece of the United States' first World's Fair in 1853, to house domestic displays. It was smaller than the Crystal Palace in London. It was also iron framed and covered with panels of glass, having a large dome, second in size only to St. Peter's in Rome. After the Fair went bankrupt, it was leased for a variety of purposes. On October 5, 1858, it was destroyed by fire. See *Gunderson (Pairpoint) Glass Works.*

Crystal Window Glass Works A

glass manufacturing facility established in 1873 in Baltimore, Maryland, by William Swindell, Jr., and later operated by his sons as Swindell Brothers. When it closed is uncertain, but it was still operating in 1883. Initially it made window glass, but in 1880, it added green glass bottles and, in 1883, flint glass bottles.

crystalline (1) Consisting of crystals, unlike glass, which is amorphous. (2) A frosty texture on the surface of glass made using hydrofluoric acid. (3) Glass approaching crystal in quality.

crystallo-ceramie (1) A sulfide; also called *encrusted cameo* or *cameo incrustation.* (2) The technique used to encase a small object such as a cameo in a solid block of clear flint glass. The best were made by the creator of the process, Apsley Pellatt, between 1819 and 1835.

crystalography The name given by the Fort Pitt Glass Company to the process of

decorating glassware in the mold by etching. The process was patented by Henry Feurhake and assigned to Washington Beck. See *Feurhake, Henry; Crystaloid.*

Crystaloid A line of etched glassware developed by the Fort Pitt Glass Company, introduced in September 1879. See *crystalography; Feurhake, Henry.*

Crystaltynt A colored glassware developed by Bagley & Co. in the early 1930s and made in a wide range of Art Deco designs, commissioned by various London designers.

Crystolene Cut Glass Company

(1918-1921) A glass cutting house established by Louis Stanner and Hugo Eugelke in Brooklyn, New York. Its trademark, on a paper label, consisted of the name "Crystolene" and a tall glass vase cut in a *chair bottom* pattern.

cucumber trainer A glass tube used as a horticultural aid to keep a growing cucumber straight. It is about 15 inches tall and has a rounded upper end with a small orifice.

cucurbit A glass container to hold a liquid to be distilled. It is supported over a flame and upon it rests the alembic. Sometimes it and the alembic were made in one integrated piece.

Vaseline glass cullet, approx. 5 lbs.
Davanna Collection

cullet Broken pieces or fragments of glass from imperfect, discarded, or broken objects or from a cooled melt. It may come from operations within the plant or outside sources, and, after being cleaned, is melted with the fresh ingredients of a new batch. It melts faster and at a lower temperature, resulting in a savings in fuel costs and raw materials. The amount added to a batch may range from a very low percentage up to 100%, but the standard range is from 25% to 50%. It must be mixed thoroughly with the new ingredients to ensure smoothness.

Cumberland Glass Company (1932-1962)
A glass manufacturing facility established in Mt. Savage, Maryland, making hand-blown objects and tableware.

Cumberland Glass Manufacturing Company
A glass manufacturing facility established during 1880 in Bridgeton, New Jersey, making bottles of all styles and colors. From 1890 to 1908, all *Bromo Seltzer* bottles were hand blown here. In the 1890s, it added opal ware. In 1889, it purchased More, Jonas & More (see *More, Jonas & More*). By 1920, it was purchased by the Illinois Glass Company and a transfer to complete automation was started.

Cumberland Works
See *Marshallville Glass Works*.

Cunningham & Company
It operated two glass manufacturing facilities in Pittsburgh, Pennsylvania. (a) The original was established by Cunningham & Johnson in 1845 on Water Street, making bottles and window glass. In 1849, it was called Pittsburgh City Glass Works, operated by W. Cunningham & Company. In 1857 or 1865, depending on the source, the operating company became Cunningham & Ihmsen, and in 1876, Cunningham & Company, expanding to include druggists wares, convex glass for parlor windows, etc. By 1886, the operating company was D.O. Cunningham & Company. (b) The second was established in 1849 on Brown Street, making green glass and flasks. About 1867, the operating company was Cunningham & Johnson. In 1886, it operated as Cunningham & Company. (Other addresses for these facilities are: (a) Twenty-second Street and (b) Twenty-sixth and Jane Streets.)

cup (1) A small bowl-shaped vessel for drinking. Some have no handle; but may have one or more, and on rare occasions, two handles and a cover. It may rest on a stemmed foot or a foot ring. Usually it is accompanied by a matching saucer similarly decorated.

See *teacup*. (2) Any small bowl-shaped hollow object used as an ornament. (3) A large bowl-like receptacle. See the following cups: *caudle; feeding; lotus bud; loving; Lycurgus; Morgan; palm; procession; pterotus; punch; standing; stirrup; tassaker; tea; Valor, The; Victory; wing-shaped*. Also see *penny mug*.

cup and can Any two companion pieces where the larger vessel (*can*) is used to fill a smaller vessel (*cup*). Examples include a carafe and cup, a decanter and glass, etc.

cup and saucer sets Two companion pieces, a cup and a saucer, used for an individual service of coffee, tea, etc.

cup bowl A bowl on a drinking glass, almost spherical in shape with an inverted rim.

cup casing See *cased glass*.

cup-overlay method See *cased glass*.

Clear glass cup plate, pressed, c. 1930s.
The Corning Museum of Glass

Pairpoint amber cup plate, "G. Washington, 1732-1799."
Davanna Collection

cup plate A plate, about 3 to 3-1/2 inches in diameter, used as a resting place for a cup while tea or other hot beverage was being drunk from its saucer. When beverages were too hot to drink, the custom was to pour the hot beverage into a saucer (to cool more quickly) and drink directly from it. The cup plate was used to rest the cup and protect the table. This was strictly an American custom from about the 1820s to 1860s. They were one of the first mold-pressed objects to be made in quantity by glasshouses in Massachusetts, Pennsylvania and Ohio. The embellishments on them can be divided into three groups: conventional patterns (geometric, flowers, etc.), historical patterns, and colored plates, many of all three groups being of *lacy* design. Over 1,000 designs of historical subjects or conventional patterns are known. The plates were usually circular, often with scalloped or serrated rims, but some were octagonal. They are made of clear or colored glass, rarely of opaque white or opalescent glass. The best were made by Boston & Sandwich (these should ring when plinked). Reproductions were made by the Westmoreland Glass Company in the 1930s (these do not ring). Reproductions are still being made.

cup salt A salt having a wide bowl on a stem with a molded foot.

cupped top bowl A bowl on a drinking glass, the upper part of which has a cup shape with a deep round funnel beneath it.

cupping bowl See *bleeding glass; cupping glass.*

cupping glass (Aka a *ventose*) A glass cup used for *cupping* (a process of drawing blood to the surface of one's body). There are two types: (a) dry cupping, and, (b) if an incision was made, wet cupping. In either case, a partial vacuum was created in the glass by heating it and applying its mouth to the skin. As the air in the cup cooled and contracted, creating a partial vacuum, it drew blood to the surface and into the cup. They were used in Roman times, and, more recently, from the 16th century. The practice has basically been discontinued in the 20th century, except in the more primitive areas.

curious glass (1) Remnants of leftover sheet glass from the production of antique stained glass, sold at a discount by supply houses. It is suitable for bonding with epoxy resin for jewelry, mobiles, etc. (2) Glass made as *one-of-a-kind* runs, not fitting into a regular production schedule.

Curling See *Fort Pitt Glass Works.*

Curling creamer A pressed glass cream jug inscribed with the words "RB Curling & Co., Fort Pitt" (see *Fort Pitt Glass Works*). It is of conventional shape with a heavy handle.

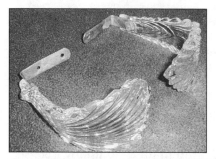

Curtain tie-back with metal brackets, 4-1/2" l.
Davanna Collection

curtain tie-back An ornament, fastened to a wall bracket used for tying back a curtain or drape, especially during the Victorian Era. Some were made of lacy glass by the Boston & Sandwich Glass Co. Older ones are rare today, but reproductions are easily found.

Curtis & Messer See *Granite Glass Works.*

curved cutting A decorative pattern on cut glass, made by diverting the object out of line with the edge of the cutting wheel, rather than cut patterns made in straight lines with the object held in line with the cutting wheel. Various motifs can be produced, but are difficult to make. See *Kugelgravuren; printie.*

curved miter See *miter.*

cushion ground A ground slightly arched and elevated above the base ground so some parts of the motif can be seen in the intervening space, depending on the angle of observation.

cushion(ed) knop A knop of flattened sphere-like shape, positioned on a ring. There is a variation having a ring above and below the knop (*double cushioned knop*).

cushion pad A hollow ornament of flattened spherical shape placed, singly or in a group, between the bowl and the stem of a drinking glass. If in a group, they generally tend to get smaller as they progress downward to the stem. See *cushion(ed) knop; service*.

cusp (1) A pointed end, such as the point at which two branches of two arcs meet and stop. (2) A pointed knop on the stem of a glass.

cuspidor A receptacle into which one would spit tobacco juice. A bow-shaped object narrowing to a short practically non-existent neck (about-half of the diameter of the bowl), flaring out to a wide rim that slopes gently downward toward the neck. The diameter of the bowl is usually from 8 inches to 12 inches. The rim is usually wider than the bowl. See *spittoon*.

McKee Tom & Jerry custard glass punch set (fluoresces under UV light), bowl: 11-1/2" d.; mugs: 3-1/2" h.
Tri-State Antiques

custard glass (1) A small glass bowl for serving custard. Some have a stemmed foot and/or a single handle. (2) Any opaque glass having a smooth creamy white texture, the color of custard. See *Custard glass*.

Custard glass (Aka *Buttermilk Glass*) As early as the 1800s, it was made in England. Migrating glassmakers brought the formulation for the creamy ivory ware to America. In 1886, the LaBelle Glass Works began making it, followed by Northwood, Heisey, Tarentum, Fenton, and McKee, all making souvenirs and dinnerware. Some used uranium salts in the batch, tending to produce the creamy ivory color; the salts causing the ware to glow a yellow-green under ultra-violet light.

custrel A vessel used to hold wine. A variation of the term *costrel*. See *costrel*.

cut & shut A process for making pitchers, cruets, and some bottles using, in part, pressing operations. The object is pressed upside down with the plunger passing through the top. After pressing, it is *snapped up* on the bottom. The top is reheated and the lip and top formed and finished. Next a special *snap*, with a section cut out for the handle, is used to hold the top while the open bottom, is reheated, closed and *cut shut* (cutting excess metal from the base to close the opening in the base).

cut base paperweight A paperweight, its base embellished with a cut pattern, generally a star, strawberry diamond cutting or a small checkerboard pattern. Such cutting is typical on weights having either a translucent colored ground or of clear glass without a ground.

cut glass Glassware embellished with facets, grooves, and depressions made by the process of cutting into its surface using a rotating wheel of iron or stone. It should be differentiated from glassware embellished by wheel engraving and from sculptured glass. The glass, usually lead glass, is ground to form facets, which give a high degree of light refraction. Etched glass is not included because it is made by the application of corroding acid.

History

The art of cutting glass was practiced by the Egyptians as early as 1500 B.C.; the Assyrians as early as 720 B.C.; and the Persians as early as 530 B.C. During the 1st century B.C., Romans embellished (a) glass articles with interlacing grooves by wheel cutting in the tradition of lapidary craftsmen; (b) glass articles with relief designs; and (c) cased glass with crafted pictorial subjects. During the Roman era, it was one of the most common forms of glass decoration. It was done at Cologne during the 3rd and 4th centuries. During the 5th and 6th centuries, pre-Islamic glass from Persia and Mesopotamia was cut with diamond and circular concave faceting, and Islamic glass from the 9th and 10th centuries was cut with facets and arabesque designs. For several centuries, there is no historical evidence that it was practiced. It was revived in Bohemia and Germany in the late 1500s.

In England, from the development, in 1676, of lead glass, cutting became the predominant method of embellishing English and Irish glassware. Glass cutting in what is now the continental United States did not begin until about 1771 and, at this point, this history shall center primarily on the United States, which during the late 19th and early 20th centuries became a world leader in making cut glass; both in quality and quantity. The history of cut glass in the United States is generally divided into four periods: *Early Period* (1771 to 1830); *Middle Period* (1830 to 1876); *Brilliant Period* (1876 to 1910); and *Flower Period* (1905 to 1916); the period from 1905 to 1910 is often referred to as the *Brilliant-Flower Transition Period* (or simply *Transition Period*).

History * United States * Early Period * 1771 to 1830

There are no records (or specimens) of cut glass being made in the future United States prior to 1771. Baron Stiegel, in 1771, was the first to cut glass, followed shortly by Amelung. Like most other glassmakers in America, they came from Europe and, since most Americans during this period considered European glassware superior to that made in America, early glasscutters perpetuated the European designs and styles. Two types of glass were cut: (a) a thin "German" or "Bohemian" lime glass, and (b) a flint or heavy "English" lead glass. The metal was generally inferior to that made later, and some pieces had bubbles and other imperfections. Some 30 glass makers were engaged in cutting and engraving during this period, including the New England Glass Company, Boston & Sandwich and Bakewell & Co.

History * United States * Middle Period * 1830 to 1876

Impetus to the production of cut glass came in 1830 when a tariff on foreign glass was imposed. Strong nationalism created a negative response to European patterns and a strong desire for more unpretentious patterns and designs developed. The trend was toward more etching and engraving, rather than cutting, a characteristic feature on much of the early glass. In mid-century, companies began to favor the heavier-cut patterns such as ovals of pointed diamonds or groupings of cross-hatched squares with fan borders. Since the English formula for making glass was being used, glassware of the period has a slight grayish tint. During the Civil War, because of the demand for materials and manpower, many facilities closed or switched to pressed glass. Some of the major makers of cut glass during this period were: C. Dorflinger & Sons; Brooklyn Flint Glass Works; New England Glass Company; and Boston & Sandwich Co.

Brilliant Period cut glass vase, 15" h. x 10" w. Blank 5/8" thick at top; over 1" thick at widest part. Davanna Collection

History * United States * Brilliant Period * 1876 to 1910

The 1876 Centennial Exposition, in Philadelphia, Pennsylvania, was the initial exposure of a brilliantly cut glass to Americans. Some exhibitors were: C. Dorflinger & Sons; New England Glass Company; Mt. Washington Glass Co.; Hobbs, Brockunier & Co.; and Gillinder & Sons. The period was named for the brilliance associated with it. The excellent quality and prominence of the cut glass during this period was attributed to the following: (a) large deposits of high quality sand relatively free of impurities in the Great Lakes area; (b) discovery and development of natural gas enabling more consistent control over furnace temperatures; (c) refining and elaborating the patterns and designs of the Bohemians, English and Irish, often merging two or more designs to contrive a pattern of overall cutting; (d) originality and individuality of design and deep cutting on thick blanks; and (e) extraordinary clarity of lead glass. Still, many considered imported glass superior. As a result, many labeled their wares as imported from England or other European countries; others were reported to have shipped their product to Europe, reshipping it back as "imported" to realize a higher price.

In 1893, to combat misrepresentation, American glass manufacturers began an advertising campaign to make Americans aware of *"American Rich Cut Glass"* and distinguish it from the inferior type from Europe. From 1895 to 1900, the following cost-cutting measures were initiated: (a) substitution of hydrofluoric acid in the polishing process, allowing one or two people to polish the output of a large factory, previously done by as many as 40 skilled workers; and (b) Owens innovation of fire-polished pressed blanks, cut down on the laborious, time consuming manual task of the rougher and smoother. It also did away with the loss of metal in the first cutting. The blanks coming to the workmen were already pressed with the first deep incisions, so patterns could be reproduced more cheaply and rapidly. This destroyed the refractory surface and the basic brilliance, and the sharp cutting of true cut glass was lost.

By the turn of the century, more than 100 facilities were involved with cutting glass. Some made their own blanks and blanks for other houses. At the beginning of the 20th century, patterns were changing and quality of design began to deteriorate. This, plus the cost-cutting measures, lessened the prestige of cut glass. By 1906, increasing costs of production and declining interest in ornately cut glass caused many facilities and cutting shops to turn to simpler designs or close.

History * United States * Brilliant-Flower Transition Period * 1905 to 1910

During this period, some companies did overall cutting associated with the Brilliant Period while others did engraving associated with the Flower Period. Others cut transitional pieces with both geometric cut designs and engraving. Because of this gradual transition, the

ability to establish time frames becomes complicated. Consequently, transitional pieces must be dated by pattern and depth of cutting rather than by period.

History * United States * Flower Period * 1905 to 1916

This period initiated the copper wheel engraving of glass. Craftsmen used nature (birds, insects, plants, animals, etc.) as an inspiration; flowers dominated the designs. Facilities still used lead in the formulation of their glass, but began to use figured or pressed blanks in place of plain ones. These, while reducing costs, have a slight grayish color, a decrease in brilliance, and a greasy feel to the molded portions. With the outbreak of World War I, the production of cut glass declined dramatically because of the demand for lead in the war effort. Unable to get lead, many companies closed while others survived by making less costly glass.

Cut Glass Blanks

The general ingredients used in America to make glass suitable for cutting are silica, potash, niter (natron), arsenic, manganese, and lead oxide (35% to 50%). The quality of the blank depends on the impurities in the raw materials and the combination of ingredients. The English used more soda and the glass had a yellowish cast, weighing less than the comparable American product. The Irish and Bohemians employed a combination of potash and lime and their blanks had a grayish tint. Potash and soda make glass more fusible, but lime gives it its hardness. Americans combined potash and lead oxide to produce a fusible heavy crystal with high refractory power. Manganese and arsenic are the usual decolorizing agents, removing iron from the silica. The ingredients were mixed, placed in a crucible or pot, covered to prevent products of combustion from coming in contact with the batch. The batch was heated to about 2500° F. The fluid metal had to cool slightly until it became viscous enough to gather. The gatherer inserted the end of a blowpipe into the pot and collected the gather, which was rolled on a marver and expanded by blowing to form a hollow ball. He handed the blowpipe to a blower who, sitting in his special chair, rolled the pipe back and forth on its arms and blowing, made the desired shape. Some pieces were free blown; others were shaped in an iron mold, called a *paste mold*.

As the article was being fashioned, a servitor might reheat it from time to time in the *glory hole*. If the article required a pedestal, handle or foot, a footman or servitor made these from a different gather collected by a bit gatherer. When the blower finished his job, the servitor attached a flat topped iron rod, called a *pontil*, to the base of the vessel with a tiny wad of molten glass, then broke the article from the blowpipe. The gaffer or foreman now gave the vessel its final shape by tooling. Frequently, he applied the handles or pedestals fashioned by the footman or servitor, sheared the lip and removed any tool marks with additional heating.

Upon completion of the blown blank, the gaffer handed it to a taker-in who used asbestos covered pincers to transport it to the annealing oven or lehr. Different-sized objects went into different ovens, cooling the object from about 1400° Fahrenheit to ambient temperature. The oven, once filled, was sealed to prevent drafts that could cause the glass to crack. It was allowed to cool very slowly; heavy, thicker pieces remained in the lehr for as long as a week while lighter, thinner pieces could be removed after as little as 24 hours without fear of shattering. Annealing reduced the brittleness of the glass. If the glass cooled too quickly, it would *fly* or show tiny hairline imperfections or wrinkles.

Cutting and Polishing

The primary reasons for the superiority of American cutting were: (a) electric-powered cutting machines, giving the craftsmen a greater degree of control of wheel speeds; (b) steel cutting wheels giving a smoother, more controlled cutting than wheels of other metals or stone; (c) better brushes which gave a finer polish to the glass; and (d) assembly-line techniques.

True cut glass is cut entirely by hand. All cutting started with a pattern, normally designed by the master cutter. Workmen or the rougher drew the major portions of the pattern on the blanks with a gummy red or black fluid. The rougher, probably an apprentice, cut the deep miter lines of the pattern by pushing the blank against a large rapidly turning stone or steel wheel, watching his work through the glass. Wet pumice dripped from an overhanging funnel onto the steel wheel to keep the glass from overheating and to help cut the blank; a stone wheel only needed water. Later, carborundum was used for the wheel because it cost less, working as well. Cutting wheels came in various thicknesses, diameters, and shapes. The main shapes being: (a) flat edge, for making flat faceting; (b) mitered (V-shaped) edge, for making grooves in straight line patterns; and (c) convex edge, for making depressions or hollow patterns. Both roughing and smoothing demanded a large number and variety of wheels. The smoother or master cutter refined the work of the rougher and composed, freehand, a design on the glass; each requiring the use of from 10 to 12 wheels.

The surface of the glass took on a whitish look when it was cut and, as a result, had to be polished. Before 1900, the polisher used wheels of willow, cherry, or other soft wood along with a mixture of pumice, and/or rottenstone and water to produce the luster. He held the glass against the wooden wheel while it turned through the damp pumice. For a second polishing, he used a brush wheel moistened with the same preparation. Next he brushed the piece with a putty powder consisting of lead or tin. The final polishing required a cork or wooden wheel covered with a fine, moist putty powder. Flat surfaces needed buffing with a thick felt wheel. Lapidary cutting found on stoppers and neck rings required three wheels; a steel wheel for roughing, a stone wheel for smoothing, and a lead wheel for polishing. After the turn of the century, acid baths were used for polishing because it was less expensive in terms of time and manpower. Wax was used to cover areas that did not require polishing or meant to have a frosted appearance.

Pieces polished by hand have a higher brilliancy and a greater value than those polished in an acid bath. After submersion in the acid bath, there was a final washing with water and an employee would acid stamp the signature, if any, on the article. He would also scratch numbers on decanters and bottles fitted with stoppers. Matching numbers were put on the stopper and on the bottle's neck.

Colored Cut Glass

Though produced in greater quantities during the Middle Period than at any other time, colored cut glass was always a small percentage of the total cut glass production. It may be divided as follows: (a) uniformly colored throughout, by far the rarest; and (b) a sandwich of two or more layers, at least one of which is colored and one of which is clear crystal. Colored cut glass of (b) may be further divided as follows: (i) cased, (ii) flashed and (iii) overlay; all three result in a colored surface of varying thickness superimposed on a foundation of clear crystal. The production of colored glass may have been a sideline or done for a presentation piece, special display items or special order gift. American-made colored cut glass has a more vibrant color than foreign glass because of the lead content and was mainly in the following colors: green, ruby, amber, blue, cranberry, amethyst and rainbow (a blending of three or more colors). Very few pieces are signed.

Cut Glass Patterns

A combination of different motifs creates a pattern. As a rule, a pattern incorporates one dominant and one or more minor motifs. A few of the early patterns used only the dominant motif.

As the demand for American cut glass increased in the domestic and foreign market, companies required more patterns. To create new patterns, they often altered their existing patterns or those of other companies, even altering slightly patented patterns to avoid infringement suits. They frequently changed or simplified patterns, but kept the same name, or the same pattern, but changed the name. Often many cut the same pattern, each calling it a different name. Typically when a pattern maker left a company, he made an agreement with the company to take his designs with him, thus supplying his new employer with a large number of designs. Often companies helped each other; when one received multiple orders or a large special order, the work was often farmed out to another. As a result, two different signatures may appear on identical pieces within the same set. Sometimes one company agreed to let another duplicate one of its original patterns, thus giving the pattern greater exposure and aided both financially.

Companies often cut public domain patterns, issuing it under a different name. In adapting a pattern to pieces of different shapes and sizes (bowls, pitchers, compotes, plates, etc.), the artisan took the liberty of adding to or subtracting from the original basic design. The true craftsman cared more about the beauty of the final article and cutting the entire surface than adhering strictly to the basic sketch, so he often cut according to the shape and size of the piece rather than becoming subservient to the design.

Agents or a wholesale house sometimes used a pattern name in their catalog that was different from the one given by the facility that cut the pattern. Therefore, catalogs should be considered only as a secondary reference of identification. A glassmaker or cutting house usually cut a number of sample patterns for a catalog. As the orders came in, the company made only those patterns ordered, not necessarily all patterns appearing in the catalog.

Consequently some of the patterns listed by name in the various catalogs never went into production. Sometimes a facility would advertise to replace broken or lost pieces. Hence, a replacement piece may have been cut by a facility other than the one that cut the original (eg. a lamp base may be cut by a different company than the top or shade). Also some companies made blanks to be cut by other companies. Therefore, the shape of a particular piece cannot necessarily be attributed to a specific cutting house.

Public domain patterns are: (1) patterns that never belonged to a specific company, but were from the beginning in the public domain; or (2) other patterns which had been patented, but when the patent expired, usually after 3, 5, or 7 years, the design went into the public domain to be cut by anyone. Most of the public domain patterns covered the entire surface. Some of the names of the public domain patterns were: *Russian, Honeycomb, Notched Prism, Prism, Harvard, Flute, Block, Cane, Strawberry Diamond,* and *Strawberry Diamond & Fan*. Without a signature on pieces with public domain patterns, no one can positively identify the cutter or house. Because so many patterns have no known names, various authorities often have suggested descriptive names to aid in identifying them.

Identification of Cut Glass

Some of the methods of identifying cut glass are: (a) *Ring*. All good cut glass is made with lead glass and will ring with a bell tone when struck lightly with a finger or pencil. Unfortunately, this does not work on all shapes. Pieces with narrow openings like bottles, rose bowls, candlesticks, etc., will not ring when tapped. The most prolonged ringing with the best tone will be on bowls from the Brilliant Period cut on thick blanks. The quality of the tone often depends on the thickness of the blank; (b) *Pattern*. Most of the patterns cut during the Brilliant Period were produced only in fine hand-cut crystal and have never been reproduced. One exception is the *Daisy & Button* pattern, very similar to the *Russian* pattern in cut glass; (c) *Sharpness*. Edges on cut glass are crisp and sharp to the hand and eye. Pieces pressed or molded have a smooth edge and "greasy" feeling; the edges appearing slightly rounded to the eye and not sharp to the touch. This test will also distinguish the pieces cut at the height of the period from those acid polished or fire polished on pressed blanks. Cut glass imports are made in the latter manner and, therefore, fail to pass the sharpness and prolonged bell tone tests; (d) *Brilliance*. Brilliance or sparkle of fine cut glass is caused by the lead content as well as the hand polishing and coloring. Any fine piece of old cut glass of high quality will contain from 35 to 50% lead; and (e) *Weight*. A true piece of cut glass will weigh considerably more than a reproduction in pressed glass, due to the high lead content.

Signed Cut Glass

Toward the end of the 19th century, makers of cut glass decided that a signature on their wares offered a possible solution to the pirating of patented patterns. In 1895, Libbey and Hawkes took the initiative, announcing they would place an acid-etched signature on all of their cut glass. Soon other companies followed suit. Because of the time period when signatures became commonplace, most signed pieces are from the Brilliant period. To locate a signature on a piece of cut glass, hold it near a strong light and rotate it until there is a mirror-like reflection, which causes the signature to "stand out." Signatures are in various locations on different pieces, so knowing where to look simplifies the task.

On a bowl, nappy, or bonbon, the most likely place to find the signature is on the inside center of the piece, or sometimes, near the top rim. On footed pieces, check the top or bottom of the foot near the edge. For handled pieces, the signature may be on the flat area on top of the handle, under it or on the base. Lastly, on tumblers, decanters, and vases, it is often placed on the bases' edge.

If the piece has a lid, the signature is usually on the inside center of one or both pieces. If a signature cannot be found in the places mentioned, try the unusual places, such as the lip of a jug or pitcher, the neck of a carafe, the side of a deep miter, the rim of a lid, etc. With the increasing emphasis on a signature, especially ones in scrip, forgeries are becoming common. You can easily detect a forgery done with an electric needle by scraping it with your fingernail. Very little colored cut glass is signed.

Damages to Cut Glass

Most dealers list brilliant cut glass as "mint" or "as is." "Mint" means the piece is in perfect condition or with only the most minor defects. "As is" means the piece shows some very obvious damage. Damages most often found on cut glass are: (a) *Chips*. Either a small nick or a sizable hunk broken off a piece of cut glass, appearing particularly along edges; (b) *Flakes*. A thin layer of glass that splits from the glass, most often at or near the rim and generally does not feel sharp at the edges; (c) *Bruises*. A multitude of tiny scratches, producing a cloudiness in the base of a piece or on the inside of a bowl or compote; frequently called *age marks* or *wear marks*; (d) *Fractures*. An abundance of very tiny cracks resulting from the accidental striking of two pieces of glass together or one piece against a hard surface; (e) *Cracks*. An actual cleavage in the glass, which may or may not be felt, caused by any of a variety of reasons—if occurring in and following a deep miter, it may not be visible; however, the piece will not produce a bell tone when tapped; (f) *Heat checks*. Tiny white lines found on handles or applied pieces arising when the applied piece and object are not heated to the same temperature at the time of application, or if the applied piece cools more rapidly than the object; and (g) *Sick glass*. Subdivided into three types—(i) glass with a slightly cloudy or frosted appearance inside, especially on decanters, cruets, and saltshakers resulting from the acidity of the contents, causing a chemical reaction that oxidizes the inner surface; such cloudiness is occasionally associated with too high an alkali content in the batch; if one puts water or other liquid such as oil, Glass Wax, non-stick cooking spray, etc., onto the cloudy area, it will disappear; (ii) another type of sick glass consists of a residue forming in the bottom of vessels that have not been properly cleaned; it can sometimes be removed; (iii) another type of sick glass results when crystals separate as a result of imperfect fusion of the metal; when looked at through strong light, a web of minute fissures can be seen; such sickness may be caused by improper annealing, ie. cooling the piece too quickly.

Cut Glass Corporation of America

See *Quaker City Cut Glass Company; Laurel Cut Glass Company.*

Cut Glass Products Company A

wholesale outlet in Chicago, Illinois, serving several small glass cutting shops in the area. See *Rochester Cut Glass Company.*

cut mold process A process used during the Depression era to make glassware resembling cut glass. It is of poor quality and lacks the brilliance of earlier pressed glass.

cut stem A stem on a drinking glass embellished with cutting or faceting. Before 1777, it was rarely used. Elongated cut diamonds were used in the interests of saving time and labor costs, but subsequently the diamonds became more equilateral, and more detailed cutting became frequent, even extending on to the bowl. Some stems were embellished with a series of encircling vertical connected plane surfaces (*flat cut stems*);

others were embellished with scale faceting or hexagonal faceting, sometimes extended on to the knops.

cut-to-clear The cutting of a design on stained, flashed, or cased glass having a clear glass underlayer so that the design shows clear against a colored background.

Cut velvet diamond quilted opalescent vase, pale peach, 6" h. x 3-1/4" d.
Tri-State Antiques

cut velvet glassware A type of glassware made of two layers of glass, the inner layer (usually white) being mold blown in various patterns reminiscent of those on cut velvet, and the outer layer (usually a pastel color) being acid finished to simulate a velvet texture. The most frequently used pattern was ribbed, but occasionally diamond quilting was used. It was made at several facilities during the late 1800s. The primary locations being Mt. Washington Glass Company and Phoenix Glass Works. Many reproductions are being made.

cutting (1) The act of separating a piece of glass into two parts. In the past, it was done by running a hot pointed iron slowly along the proposed line of fracture; a crack followed the iron. Today, such cutting is done by making a scratch or score on the glass with a small steel, diamond, carborundum, or other type of cutting wheel or point (lubricated with a fluid such as kerosene) mounted on a handle; then tapping the glass along the score causing it to break. (2) The process used to make cut glass. (3) A term used in describing certain cut glass motifs and patterns. See the following *cuttings: alternate prism; ball; checkered diamond; cold; curved; fine line; flat diamond; flute; grey;*

hexagon; hobnail; hollow diamond; pillar; printie; thumb mark; finger; clove.; prism; raised diamond; scale; shallow diamond; strawberry diamond; and triple. (4) See *shearings*.

cutting wheel (1) A wheel on the end of a handle used to scratch or score glass. See *cutting*. (2) A wheel used in the process of making cut glass; derived from lapidary equipment. Those used for cutting motifs and patterns were made of stone, steel and carborundum, and for engraving of copper; each in a variety of sizes, thicknesses, and shapes. There are three basic types or contours: pointed or V-shaped edge for cutting miters or bevel cuts; the flat edge for panel cuts; and the convex edge for hollow cuts. One wheel with two or more V-shaped cutting edges is called a *gang wheel*. There are numerous variations of the three types of wheels. For more information, see *cut glass, Cutting & Polishing; gang wheel*.

Cyathus (Latin) See *kyathos*.

cylinder beaker See *Walzenhumpen*.

cylinder bottle See *wine bottle, shapes*.

cylinder glass (Aka *broad glass*) Made by the *Broadsheet Technique* or *Lorraine Method*, it is believed to have been developed by Lorraine glaziers about 1100 and was used extensively beginning in the early 19th century, because larger panes could be made as opposed to the crown method. The process is as follows: The blower, wearing boots and pants, but stripped to the waist, with a cowl board tied around his neck, ascended a ramp or steps to a platform so he could work at an even level with the furnace doors. Below him was a pit.

The blower clamped the mouthpiece of the cowl board between his teeth and approached the furnace as the gatherer gathered a blob of glass on the blowpipe. With a dipper (*second glass block*), the gatherer shaped a gather to give it a slight form. Molten glass was continually added to this gather by successive trips to the furnace by the gatherer. After each trip the gather was crudely shaped. When about 60 pounds of white hot glass had been gathered, the blower began to blow the paraison into an iron block about 18 inches in diameter (*blow*

block). Sawdust was usually placed in the block to keep the glass from sticking to the iron and the block was set in water to keep it cool.

With the block as a guide, the blower blew a glass balloon until it was a few feet long. He then moved to the *swing hole*, a drop off of at least nine feet below the platform, or *foot bench* where he stood. While swinging the blowpipe like a pendulum, the blower stretched the balloon (*roller*), to a length of six feet or more. The pull of the iron and the weight of the glass were great, and as a result, the blower usually attached a chain to his belt and around a post to prevent him from falling into the swing hole. When the roller was of proper shape and length, the blower heaved it up to an iron crane with a cradle located in front of the furnace, so it could be reheated. He quickly blew more air into it, trapping it by putting his thumb over the blowpipe's end. As the roller was heated, the air inside expanded and forced an opening at the far end of the roller. The blowpipe was then removed by touching the edge near the glass with a cold wet iron. The roller was now a long cylinder of glass with rounded ends.

After the roller cooled a little, the rounded ends were cracked off by placing a strip of molten glass around the cylinder where it was to be separated and touching it with a wet metal rod, causing them to crack off, leaving the cylinder with open ends. The ends, if they could be saved, were prized as bells or domes. Next a worker threw sawdust onto the cylinder, over its entire length.

Because of the cylinder's shape, the sawdust fell to the bottom. An iron rod was then run along the bottom of the cylinder until it was grooved. This groove was then touched with a wet metal rod causing the cylinder to split along its entire length (some companies preferred to cut the cylinder, while still hot, with shears). This curved sheet was then carried to a flattening oven where it was heated until pliable and then flattened. The resultant sheet, about 6 to 12 feet square, was placed in a barrel-like container filled with boiling water (*dip*) where it was tempered for about an hour. The sheet was then cut into panes. The last handmade cylinder glass made in the

United States was blown in Bridgeton, New Jersey, in 1926 by the LeFevre Glass Company.

In general, the quality of cylinder glass was not good, containing numerous air bubbles, blisters, and marks by tools used for flattening and, its thickness not consistent. During 1903, the American Window Glass Company developed a method for the mechanical blowing of cylinders several times larger than mouth blown cylinders. Cylinders up to 50 feet in length and 40 inches in diameter were made. These were cut into sections, flattened, annealed and cut into stock sizes. This method was used until about 1920 when it was replaced by the more efficient method of drawn glass. See *float glass; broad glass.*

cylinder knop A knop, cylindrical in shape, but often drawn inward slightly at the top and the bottom.

cyma reversa See *ogee.*

Cyprian glass An art glass developed by Frederick Carder at Steuben, made from about 1915 into the 1920s. It was a pale green, iridescent glass with a Celeste blue ring applied at the rim [the only obvious difference between this glass and Aqua Marine; both are frequently mistaken for Verre de Soie (sometimes made a turquoise ring which adds to the confusion)]. It does not resemble *Cypriote glass.*

Cypriote glass An opaque art glass, developed by Arthur J. Nash for Louis Comfort Tiffany. It was made in several colors with an irregular, finely pitted nacreous surface, wholly or partially roughened, to resemble the corroded iridescent surface texture of long buried Roman glass. The roughened surface resulted from the heated body being rolled on a marver covered with powdered glass. The term was applied by Tiffany to some of his other types of glass having an antique finish and *Cypriote glass* was sometimes labeled by Tiffany as *Antique Glass.*

Cyprus glass A colored glassware developed by Fritz Heckert in 1898 and made by him for several years. This Bohemian-styled glassware had a matte finish, embellished with enameling.

Czechoslovakian glassware Glassware made in former Bohemian facilities after 1918 when Czechoslovakia became independent, and in new ones established since then, all of which were nationalized in 1946 under the Communist regime. The 1938 invasion by Hitler and the subsequent Nazi occupation caused tremendous devastation within the industry from which it has never recovered. The 58 facilities which existed at the close of World War II were consolidated into 15 under the Communist regime. The level of glass production in 1946 was approximately 20% of that before the war and the quality was inferior. Czechoslovakia is now two separate countries. Glassware of every type and description has been made in that region since the 14th century. The two most famous names to come out of the 600 years of glassmaking are Moser and Loetz. See *Bohemian glassware.*

Czechoslovakian perfume bottle, stopper, light amber, nude in wreath stopper, 6-1/2" h. Davanna Collection

Czechoslovakian perfume bottles
Between 1928 and 1939, the country's perfume bottles were a tremendous success. From the most basic to the most ornate, they showed exquisite artistic taste and intriguing beauty and were of superior quality, workmanship, and style. They were made in a variety of types of glass in a variety of styles and shapes with a variety of decorative motifs.

The focal point of these was frequently the stopper. Often it was three times the height of the bottle itself and, while hand ground to fit a specific bottle, the stopper had a design which may or may not match that of the accompanying bottle. The stoppers were decorated in a wide variety of designs, including geometric designs, scenery, birds, flowers, fish, nudes, children, hunters, cupids, butterflies, mythological figures, etc. Women were common subjects, in all states of dress and undress. Men, except as part of a couple, were rarely depicted.

Some stoppers were tinted to match the bottle, but most were of colorless glass. Most stoppers came with a glass dauber, usually of clear glass although some were tinted to match the bottle or stopper. The bottles are classified by size in four categories: small, up to 3-1/2 inches; medium, 3-1/2 to 6-1/2 inches; large, 6-1/2 to 8-1/2 inches; and extra large, 8-1/2 inches and over (the rarest). They were made of lead glass (less than 30% lead) or the more expensive lead crystal (40% and above lead). Those with a higher lead content had a slight gray tint, undetectable if the glass was colored. They were popular in the United States during the Depression era because of the variety, superb quality, and moderate price.

They were imitated by the Japanese in the 1930s and again in the late 1940s. Most Czechoslovakian perfume bottles were decorated with hand-cut designs; some with intaglio decoration frosted to better show the detail. Some stoppers were made with designs pressed on both sides of the glass (*double stoppers*), and usually twice as thick as other stoppers. Some stoppers were molded with openings in the glass; these were called *openworked* or *pierced stoppers*. Occasionally jeweled filigree (lace-like ornamental work of delicate or intricate design made of metal set with glass jewels) was used to embellish these bottles.

Other decorative techniques used to embellish perfume bottles and stoppers were frosting, enameling, and hand painting. Frosting was achieved using hydrofluoric acid. Enameling used pigments derived from metallic oxides permanently applied to the bottle by firing at relatively low temperatures in order to fuse the enamel to the glass' surface. Handpainting (Aka *cold painting*) applied lacquer or oil-based colored pigment to the glass without subsequent reheating. The colors of these perfume bottles were extraordinary; but the five most common or basic colors were: clear, blue, pink, yellow, and green.

Since each manufacturer had its own formulations for colored glasses, the range of shades and variations within each color is phenomenal. Each company had its own trade name for various colors; opaque colors being rarer than the transparent ones. Stoppers and bottles were not made in the same colors in equal quantities so it is often quite difficult to match the same color bottle and stopper. Many perfume manufacturers had custom-made perfume bottles produced in quantity by various Czechoslovakian manufacturers.

When the Nazis invaded Czechoslovakia in 1939, they ruthlessly exploited its resources and industries. Supplies of glassware diminished and were no longer available in the United States. The importers turned to other foreign sources, as well as the United States manufacturers, in order to meet the demand and attempt to duplicate the quality of the Czechoslovakian bottles. Soon Czech craftsmen were brought to the United States to refine the manufacturing of such bottles.

As the war continued, the American glass industry, in large part, converted to war-related production and many craftsmen went to war. As a result, production of perfume bottles and other non-essential glassware declined. The items that took their place were simpler and plainer. After the war, ending in 1945, four things hampered the resurgence of the Czechoslovakian glass industry: (1) the steady loss of skilled craftsmen during the war due to death and emigration; (2) the destruction of many facilities during the war; (3) the Communist control and consolidation of the glass industry and the forced selling of its wares for export to a government agency known as Glassexport which tended to discourage both innovation and originality: and (4) the changing taste of the public.

The glassware produced after the war was inferior and the quality was lower. While some of the companies tried to reintroduce Czechoslovakian perfume bottles to the American public in the mid- to late-1940s, they were not successful. The taste of the average consumer had changed. Early American and Danish Modern styles became the fashion of the times. Now Czechoslovakian glassware, including perfume bottles, represents only a small percentage of the world market. Also see: *dram bottle; miniature; atomizer; perfumette.*

dabber See *drop stopper*.

Daccius bottle See *Frontinus bottle*.

dairy bowl A shallow circular bowl for separating cream from raw milk. Specimens in Nailsea glassware are recognized by a hollow everted rim equipped with a pouring lip.

Vaseline glass shoe in Daisy & Button pattern, 4" h.
Davanna Collection

Daisy & Button A pressed glass pattern made to replicate the cut glass pattern called *Russian*.

daisy glassware (Aka *daisy-in-square, daisy-in-diamond, daisy-in-hexagon*) A molded glassware embellished with a stylized daisy enclosed within a square, diamond, or hexagon. Its creation has been attributed to Henry William Stiegel. See *Diamond Daisy*.

dalle-de-verre (Aka *dalles, chunk glass, slab glass*) Thick (about one inch, ranging from about 0.75 inch to 1.6 inches) slabs of colored glass normally fractured with a special hammer and anvil into a desired shape, but which may be used in the slab form as originally made, cast in open molds. European slabs are typically about 8 by 12 inches; those made in the United States are about 8 by 8 inches. It is used in stained glass windows.

Dalzell, Gilmore, Leighton Co.
(1888-1901) A table glass manufacturing facility in Findlay, Ohio. Three Dalzell brothers (Andrew, James, and William) and Pittsburgh banker E.D. Gilmore owned a facility in Wellsburg, West Virginia (Dalzell Brothers & Gilmore), previously located in Brilliant, Ohio. In April 1888, it signed contracts to relocate to Findlay. In 1888, William Leighton Jr., and his son, George, joined the company. The name became Dalzell, Gilmore & Leighton Co. It was nearly finished by August 1888. The Wellsburg facility closed and the equipment moved to Findlay. In early September 1888, workers came to Findlay from Wellsburg; three furnaces were in operation by December 1888.

The products made at Findlay were the same as those made at Wellsburg, which included goblets and tumblers, tableware and some novelties. In August 1889, the company installed a tank furnace, replacing an entire 11-pot furnace. In mid-1891, it began a large-scale production of kerosene lamps. In 1892, the company increased its tableware lines, and, to commemorate Columbus' discovery of America, introduced the Ferdinand and Isabella Lamps and several other lamps, including a night light (a very small kerosene lamp, holding only a few ounces of kerosene, with a milk glass base and a crystal chimney in the shape of a cross)

When the natural gas supplies in the area began to run short in December 1892, the company converted to fuel oil in January 1893. Other tableware lines were introduced. In the fall of 1893, it shut down during labor disputes, but reopened in November 1893. During 1894, one furnace was modified to burn producer's gas, made from coal and less expensive than fuel oil. Over the next few years, more tableware lines were introduced. By 1897, it was among the leading producers of kerosene lamps, having modified the collars. The tin collar had been secured by plaster of Paris, which tended to disintegrate and become loose. The company developed a machine that clenched these collars by forcing them over the glass.

In early 1899, the company invented a new patented lamp-making machine, making lamps in a continuous operation. In the late summer of 1899, company stockholders approved its sale to the National Glass Company (see *National Glass Company*). By mid-1901, it was making lamps exclusively. On November 30, 1901, the furnaces were shut down and most of the machinery and equipment moved to Cambridge. The mold shop remained open until February 1902 and then all activities ceased. See *Findlay glass*.

Dalzell Brothers & Gilmore Glass Company
A glass manufacturing facility established in the fall of 1883, originally in Brilliant, Ohio, in the old Brilliant Glass Works facility. In the fall of 1884, it moved to Wellsburg, West Virginia, operating there until 1888 when it moved to Findlay, Ohio. See *Dalzell, Gilmore & Leighton Company*.

Dalzell-Viking Corporation
See *New Martinsville Glass Manufacturing Company*.

Damascened
See *Tiffany Damascened*.

damasco, vetro
A decorative glassware created in Italy, about 1948, by Ercole Barovier for Barovier & Toso. It is characterized by two wide vertical bands, one translucent, made of clear amethyst color, and the other made of white filigrana threads set in gold glass.

Damascus glassware
A type of Syrian-Islamic glassware made from about 1250 to 1400, identified with, but not necessarily made at, Damascus; quite possibly at Ragga and/or Aleppo until 1402, when Damascus was pillaged by the Tartars. At that time the local glass industry moved to Samarkand. The wares included flasks, beakers, candlesticks, and bowls embellished with figures in bright colors. Wares also included mosque lamps with enameled and gilded designs. The wares are also referred to as being *a la facon de Damas*. See *enameling, Islamic; Syrian glass*.

Danish glassware
Glassware made in Denmark. The earliest recorded was made at a facility in Jutland from about 1550 until about 1650, when it closed because of a scarcity of wood fuel. After years of no production in this area, it was realized that peat was abundant and could be used as fuel. As a result, the Holmegaards Glassvaerk was established in 1825 by Count Christian Danneskiold Samsoe on his estate at Holmegaard on Seeland, where there was a large peat bog. This company made quality glassware for the table. From 1830 on, many small facilities began to appear throughout Denmark, making table and ornamental ware. In 1847, the Kastrup Glassworks was established near Kastrup. This company originally made green glass bottles, then tableware, and, in 1880, pressed glass in German and English styles and forms. In 1965, the two facilities merged and now dominate the production of Danish service and industrial glassware. There are a few craftsmen producing ornamental engraved studio glassware.

Dannehoffer & Brothers
See *Williamsburgh Flint Glass Works*.

Danner machine
See *tubing*.

Danziger texture
See *reamy texture*.

Daphne Ewer
A translucent and opaque white glass ewer, with a ribbed handle attached to the shoulder and rim, claimed to be the most remarkable example of ancient enameling (red and gray) and gilding. It has an inscription in Greek and portrays the myth of Daphne, who turned into a laurel tree so she would not be captured by the pursuing Apollo. The ewer was probably made at Antioch, but the enameling is considered Roman, dating from the late 2nd to early 3rd century AD. It is now in the Corning Museum of Glass.

d'Argental
(1) A signature used on occasion by St. Louis, signing its wares "St. Louis Munzthal" or "d'Argental." (2) One of several cameo-types of glassware made in the late 19th century, named for its creator who lived in France. Comparable to the wares of Emile Galle and Rene Lalique, it is an acid cut, multi-layered, cameo glass embellished with floral and scenic designs.

Dark & Dickson
See *Honesdale Glass Works*.

dark lantern
(Aka *policeman's lantern*) A lantern designed to be held in the hand. With one glass and three solid metal sides, it

was constructed so that a sheet of metal could be slid into channels to cover the glass, preventing its light from being seen.

Darling Glasshouse The name of a potential but non-existent glass manufacturing facility. In 1747, Thomas Darling of New Haven, Connecticut, was awarded a patent by the Connecticut General Assembly, granting him the exclusive privilege to make glass in that state for 20 years. He never utilized the privilege.

Darners, left: red and green splatter on white ground, right: blue iridescent.
Krause Publications

darner (Aka *darning egg*) A round or egg-shaped object, often with a handle, used by homemakers and seamstresses to separate material while being mended or darned. See *hand cooler.*

darning egg See *darner; hand cooler.*

date flask See *grape cluster flask.*

dauber A narrow glass rod about 5/8 to 1-1/4 inch long with a pointed, rounded or ball tip, attached to, or part of, a stopper or top of a perfume bottle. Some reach almost to the bottom of the bottle. Most were plain, but some figural and beaded string ones exist. Because they were extremely slender and made for practical use, many have broken. Some long ones that were broken have been modified and now appear as short daubers. Also see *drop stopper.*

Daugherty Brothers See *Century Cut Glass Company.*

Daum Freres A glass manufacturing facility, for many years known as Daum Freres, but more recently Cristalleries de Nancy, at Nancy, France. The company was under the control of the Daum family since purchased in

1875 by Jean Daum (1825-85). Initially the company made watch and table glass. Subsequently Jean's two sons, Jean-Louis Auguste (1853-1909) and Jean-Antonin (1864-1931) took over. As followers of Emile Galle, they made glassware in the Art Nouveau style, colored glass with enameled floral embellishment, glass etched using hydrofluoric acid, a cameo-type iridescent glass, cased glass, and glass made using numerous diverse methodologies. In 1899, they patented a technique for embellishing the surface of the inner layer of a vase, overlaying it with one or more layers of different colored glass. Among the new forms created was a vase called a *Berluze*, distinguished by its tall thin neck. They created other techniques for embellishing glass, including *Vitrification* and *Verre de Jade* (see *Vitrification* and *Verre de Jade*). Paul Daum (1890-1944) and Henri Daum (1894-1966), sons of Auguste, and Michel Daum (b.1900), son of Antonin, withdrew from the established production styles in 1925 and began making clear crystal glass in free forms as well as cased and acid-etched colored glass in the art deco style. Since 1966, the production of art glass made of *pate-de-verre* has been reinstated, designed by outside artists, including Salvadore Dali. In 1965, Jacques Daum (b 1919), grandson of Auguste, became the company's president. Today the company concentrates on luxury glass. All wares made for consumer sales have the engraved Daum signature used at the time of production or for a specific type of glassware. The signature has varied many times over the years.

Daum Nancy A signature of the Daum Freres of Nancy, France, often affiliated with their cameo-type iridescent glass. The background around the design was eaten away by acid. If a piece has the word "France" as part of the signature, it was made after 1919.

Daumenglas (German) (Aka *Daumen-humpen*) Literally, *thumb glass*: a barrel-shaped beaker tapering slightly inward toward the mouth, with round concave impressions for gripping with the thumb and fingers. It often has loops of trailing, encircling it above and below the impressions, simulating barrel hoops. They were made in Germany and the Netherlands of greenish

Waldglas during the 16th and 17th centuries. Some have a domed cover with a finial.

Davenport's Patent Glass

Glassware embellished to simulate engraving or etching, made by a process patented in 1806 by John Davenport. The process required the outer surface of the glass to be covered with a paste containing powdered glass. When the paste was removed from specific areas, the intended design was left uncovered and then fired at a relatively low temperature to fuse the glass powder to the surface without melting it. The ware is generally inscribed with the word "Patent" on the label, made and affixed using the same method. See *powder decorated glass.*

David & Goliath See *Wier, Don.*

Day, William, & Company See *Franklin Glass Company.*

day tank

A small, direct-fired furnace in which three to ten tons of raw materials (enough to keep workers busy for the entire day shift) could be melted in 12 hours. It was usually charged and fired at night, melting the batch, so it would be ready by the time the day shift arrived. The day tank differs from the pot furnace in which the melting glass is protected from the flame. In day tanks, the fire plays directly on the glass, making it unsuitable for making many types of glass.

decalcomania

The technique of transferring pictures or designs from specially prepared, treated paper to an article of glass and permanently bonding them to the medium.

Wine decanter, Bohemian glass, ruby cut-to-clear, faceted stopper, grapes and grape vines, 13" h.
Davanna Collection

decanter

A bottle used at the table for serving wine after being decanted from the cask, so as not to have the dregs in the serving bottle. When the binning of wine began in England during the mid-18th century, decanters were used for serving wine taken from the bin in the original bottle or the decanter bottle. Some decanters were used for sherry or port (normally served with matching glasses), and later some were used for spirits, cordials, and even ale.

The early English decanters (1725-1750) were comparable in form to the decanter bottles, differing only in that early ones had a projecting string rim for tying the cork. After about 1730, glass stoppers were used. From about 1775, they became more slender than the earlier club-shaped bottles. However, some were barrel- or mallet-shaped with a disk stopper. Toward the end of the 18th century, broader types were made with a bulbous body, glass rings around the neck, and usually a mushroom stopper.

In the second half of the 18th century, decanters with a square cross section came on the market (used today mainly for whiskey). They are generally made of clear uncolored glass; however, some are of colored glass. Many are plain, but some are embellished with faceting, raised diamonds or hobnail cutting. Some made from about 1755 carried a bottle label with the name of the contents. If made of clear glass, the decanter generally had the name of the contents engraved on it. If made of colored glass, the decanter featured the name either enameled or in gilt. A few were furnished with silver mounts. Their capacity varied from half pints to quart sizes, with larger sizes called *magnum decanters.* The most common sizes made today for whiskies are 4/5 quart or liter. See the following types of decanters: *bell; bottle shaped; claret; club shaped; Cluck-Cluck; cruciform; guest; Irish glassware; lipped pan; magnum; mallet; onion shaped; piggy dog; Rodney; shaft & globe; ship's; shouldered; spirit; stirrup; tantalus; tapered; toilet water; three ring;* and *whiskey. Also see bar bottle; decanter bottle; decanter jug; decanter set; decanter rings;* and *wine urn.*

decanter bottle (Aka *serving bottle*) Before the more familiar, modern decanter, the decanter bottle was used for bringing wine from the cask to, and serving it at, the table (see *decanter*). The earliest ones, dating from the mid-17th century, have a bulbous or wide-shouldered body, a long neck, and a kick base. Around 1680 they changed to a shorter neck and broad body. Around 1735, their form changed to a longer body and neck. From about 1750, they looked like a modern wine bottle, having a cylindrical body and straight sides. The earliest were of blackish-green or dark brown glass, made and imported by the Glass Sellers' Company and often bore, on a small glass pad on the shoulder, the date and maker's initials.

decanter jug A jug used as a decanter, usually with a shouldered body sloping inward toward the base, a thin neck with a funnel or a lipped mouth, and a loop handle extending from the rim to the shoulder. Some have a glass stopper; some a metal hinged lid. Often there is a frilled collar at the base of the neck. See *octagonal decanter jug*.

decanter rings The rings encircling the neck of most English and Irish decanters, providing the user with a firmer grip. The number of rings is usually between one and four and their style depends on the period of production and the maker. In cross section, some rings are: (1) triangular, jutting from the body at an acute angle; (2) square, jutting in a square or slightly rectangular form; and (3) rounded, jutting in a semi-circular form. Some are embellished with cutting or a feathered or notched pattern. Some are called *double rings*, which is not two rings but one ring slightly divided or scored to appear as two; there are also similar *triple rings*.

decanter set A set usually consisting of three or four decanters, each often labeled or engraved with the name of the contents. Some were furnished with a leather traveling case or a stand when placed on a sideboard. On occasion, the latter had a central post with a sweetmeat dish mounted atop or an overhead handle, and with rings affixed to the stand to hold the stoppers when removed. See *tantalus decanter*.

decanter stand See *coaster*.

decanter wag(g)on A rectangular stand about a foot in length, with insets on top to hold two decanters. It had four wheels and a small handle for pulling it from person to person at the table. Their origin is credited to King George IV of England, who proposed they be used to avoid having a guest sitting beside the King rise to pass wine to a guest on the other side.

decay (Aka *crisseling*, *sick glass*, or *glass rot*) It is caused by any one or more factors, including: (a) composition of the glass; (b) environment (contact with soil and moisture); (c) mixing and melting practices; (d) time; (e) temperature; and (f) contact with liquids. The symptoms are: (a) crazing; (b) crusts; (c) weeping; and (d) plugs.

deceptive glassware (Aka *disguised glass*) Glassware that normally takes the form of a drinking vessel with a bowl having a thick base and sides, making its contents appear greater than actual.

Deckelpokal (German) A tall covered goblet having thin sides and a stem of the blown hollow inverted baluster or knopped type or combination of both, interspersed with several pairs of flat collars or mereses. It is often engraved and has a finial matching the stem.

decolorizing agent A mineral or substance used in glass making to counteract or neutralize the greenish or brown color resulting from iron particles in the silica component of the batch, or imparted to the batch by iron or other impurities, inherent in the pot or elsewhere, during the production process. It does not remove the color or impurities causing the color, but acts solely as a chromatic neutralizer. The decolorizer and iron each absorb the light the other transmits, if in equal quantity. If both are present in too great a quantity, then little light will be transmitted, and the glass, if relatively thick, will take on a gray or blackish color.

Decolorization using manganese (*glassmaker's soap*) was used by the Romans in the 2nd century. Nickel was used later, and the glass took on a slight bluish tint. At the end of the 18th century, cobalt, in very small quantities, was used as a decolorizer. Too much cobalt caused the batch to turn blue. In general, the purer the sand, the less undesirable color will be present. See *color*.

decorating lehr A tunnel-type oven with a moving belt. After glass is decorated with painting, silk screening, etc., it is placed on the belt, which moves it through the kiln where it is gradually heated, then cooled to set the colors or decoration.

decoration The act of adding something to an object in order to make it more visually pleasing. Glassware is embellished in one of the following ways: (a) applying the decoration (applied decoration, such as threading, chains, or other pieces of molten glass applied to a hot glass object); (b) cutting; (c) engraving; (d) etching with acid; (e) painting; (f) enameling; (g) gilding; (h) casing or flashing; and (i) manipulation while hot. See the following types of decorations: *button; cold glass; combed; Estruscan style; jewel and eye; lily pad; merrythought; mirror; painted; palm leaf; scallop shell; scenic; striated; superimposed;* and *underglaze.*

decorator See *Hausmaler.*

DeCordova, Julian See *Houghton Glass Works.*

deep carving See *Tiefschnitt.*

Deep River Cut Glass Works See *Niland, Thomas A. & Co.*

defect A failing in a piece of glassware that may have originated during, or occurred as a result of, a problem in a method of manufacture. They include cords, stones, seeds and manufacturing problems associated with future decay. See *cord; stone; seeds;* and *decay.*

Degenhart, John and Elizabeth See *Crystal Art Glass.*

DeGoey, C.R. A glass-cutting shop in Providence, Rhode Island, operated by Cornelius R. DeGoey, one of the former owners of the Hope Glass Works who, on leaving, sold his interest to his brother, John R. C.R. operated the Providence shop since the mid-1940s. Later he moved it to Laconia, New Hampshire. See *Hope Glass Works.*

Deidrick Glass Company A glass cutting shop in Monaca, Pennsylvania, which made cut and engraved glassware during the first quarter of the 20th century. Most of its

engraved pieces were further adorned with a silver deposit decoration, retailed as *Silvart* (registered on July 25, 1916).

dejeuner service A small breakfast service that includes a platter, cup and saucer, teapot or coffeepot, sugar bowl, cream jug or milk jug, and jam pot.

DeLaChapelle, Ernest, & Company See *Constitution Flint Glass Works.*

Dell Glass Company A glass manufacturing company in Millville, New Jersey, operating for a short time during the 1930s, making a variety of colored glassware.

DeLong & Company See *Durhamville Glass Works.*

Jeanette Glass Delphite (opaque blue) custard in Cherry Blossom pattern. Davanna Collection

Delphite An opaque light blue color; it is sometimes incorrectly called *blue milk glass.*

Dema Glass Ltd. See *Dennis Glassworks; Webb's Crystal Glass Co. Ltd.; Edinburgh Crystal Glass Co.*

Demer Brothers Company See *Herbeck Demer Company.*

demicrystal A glass having a lead content of 20% to 24%, used by many glassmakers in Europe during the 19th century. It lacked the brilliance and had an inferior ring when compared to glass with a higher lead content (30%) used in England.

demijohn A large bottle (often wrapped with wickerwork) having a bulbous body and thin neck.

demitasse A cup and saucer, both of which are smaller than the normal or traditional size.

DeNehou, Louis Lucas The originator of the technology for making large plates of glass by casting during the 1660s. In 1688 he acquired, under the name of Abraham Thevart, an exclusive right in France to make plate glass using his process. In 1695 he established a glass manufacturing facility at Chateau de Saint Gobain.

Dennis Glassworks An English glass manufacturing facility at Amblecote, near Stourbridge, established in 1855 by Thomas Webb I (1804-69), operating as Thomas Webb & Sons. On Webb's retirement in 1863, his sons, Thomas Webb II (1837-91) and Charles Webb, took over. In 1869, on the death of Thomas Webb I, they were joined by another son, Walter Wilkes Webb. After Thomas Webb II died, the company continued to be managed by Charles and Walter until Walter's death in 1919. It was then purchased by Webb's Crystal Glass Co. Ltd., and it is now part of Dema Glass Ltd., having been acquired by the Crown House Group in 1964.

Dennis Vase See *cameo glass; Pegasus Vase.*

Dennisville Glass Manufacturing Company A window and bottle glass manufacturing facility established by Nathaniel Holmes, Christopher and Richard Ludlam, Morris Beasley, Eleazer Crawford, Amos C. Moore, and Samuel Mathews in 1836 in Dennisville, New Jersey.

Denny & Beelen (1800-1802) A short-lived glass manufacturing facility established in the Manchester part of Allegheny County, Pennsylvania, which closed because of a shortage of fuel. The coal on the south side of the river and the cost of transporting it across the river was too great.

Denson, John Born in 1886 in Cooper's Plains, near Corning, New York, he learned the glass cutting trade at J. Hoare & Co., starting there at age 14. He later was employed as a cutter for Hunt Glass and, for a short time, at O.F. Egginton Company. About 1920 he entered a joint venture, forming Denson &

Cosgrove. From about 1920 to 1925, it operated a cutting shop in Gibson, New York. In 1925 it moved to Corning, where Steuben became the principal customer. They made stoppers for Steuben and also cut pictorial and geometric designs at the request of individuals. The company closed about 1930.

Denson, Roy In 1975, Roy, son of John Denson, retired from Steuben where he worked as a gaffer for over four decades and opened his own cutting shop in Corning, New York. He began repairing cut glass, cutting for individual customers, and making jewelry from glass.

Denson & Cosgrove See *Denson, John.*

Dentil design A design used as trim on the rim of cut glass, consisting of a flat rim with square notches cut at regular intervals.

Federal Glass Co. plate, green, Sharon pattern (Depression Glass).
Davanna Collection

Hazel Atlas tea cup & saucer, green, Florentine #2 pattern (Depression Glass).
Davanna Collection

Depression Glass Depression glass normally refers to colored glassware of the 1920s and 1930s or colored glassware of the Depression Era, the name being relatively modern. When colored glassware made its appearance on the American market in the late 1920s, it received little recognition from the public as something out of the ordinary. Typically it was sold as inexpensive everyday tableware in the "Five & Dime" stores, Sears & Roebuck, Montgomery Ward, etc. It was made in many colors and patterns by numerous facilities. Collectors and writers have provided names to patterns otherwise unnamed by the maker.

Practically all of this ware was made by machine using one of these processes: *chipped-mold; paste-mold; cut-mold; pressed-mold; acid etched;* or *mold etched*. It can be identified in several ways, including date of manufacture, color, pattern, manufacturer, method of manufacture, and "kind" of glass (being collected as *Depression Glass*). The six companies that made the largest quantities were: Anchor Hocking, Federal Glass, Hazel Atlas, Indiana Glass, Jeanette Glass, and Macbeth-Evans.

desart glass See *dessert glass*.

design (1) One or more motifs used to decorate an object. (2) The actual drawing that is the basis for the pattern. See *pattern*.

desk set A set for use on a writing desk, typically including two paperweights and one ink bottle or an inkwell and pen, paperweight, letter opener, and blotter holder. After the advent of the ballpoint and felt tip pens, it was extremely rare for such sets to include any items of glass.

dessert glass (Aka *desart glass*) A large receptacle, often with a scalloped rim, used to hold and serve sweetmeats. During the early 18th century, it superseded the sweetmeat glass, often used for serving fruits. Such glasses with deep bowls were intended for such sweets as ice cream and custard. Those with shallow bowls were used for sweetmeats that could be picked up with the fingers.

Detroit Cut Glass Company A small, short-lived glass cutting shop in Detroit, Michigan, in 1918.

Deutsche Blumen (German) Literally, *German flowers*. Naturalistically painted flowers, either as individual flowers or several flowers tied loosely in bouquets, introduced as embellishments on porcelain by J.G. Horoldt at Meissen about 1740. The

design followed the style called *Indianische Blumen*, and was imitated by numerous facilities between 1750 and 1765. The designs were used on some opaque glassware in Germany during the last half of the 18th century.

DeVez vase, cameo cut, black poppy decoration, three layers: black, green, and red, 9-3/4" h.
Krause Publications

De Vez A glass made at the Cristallerie de Pantin, Pantin, France, comparable in style to that made by Marinot, Rousseau, and others. It was a cameo type, dating from about 1890. Mr. de Varreux, art director of the facility, signed the pieces "De Vez."

DeVilbiss medicinal atomizer.
Heartland Discoveries

De Vilbiss Company Founded in 1888 by Dr. Allen De Vilbiss in Toledo, Ohio, it made air compressors, building its reputation around the mechanical control of air. It became one of the largest and most famous makers of perfume atomizers. It created an atomizer with an adjustable tip for controlling the spray. Atomizers, which were developed for spraying the throat with medication, were adapted to perfume bottles in 1907. The perfume atomizers were originally fitted to ordinary saltcellars and sold as the De Vilbiss Perfumizer, soon outselling the medicinal atomizers. The company is credited with making perfume bottles, but it only made the atomizers.

The bottles were made by other United States makers, including Steuben and Fenton (especially during World War II), as well as others in Europe, from 1925 until 1938. The majority were made in Czechoslovakia, with some from France and Italy. The bottles were commissioned by De Vilbiss and most have acid stamped marks on the glass, stamped metal (brass plated with gold or nickel; rare ones of silver) collars, or paper labels identifying them as De Vilbiss bottles, each being fitted with a patented De Vilbiss atomizer head. The earliest bottles were made in the United States until the company realized they could be made cheaper in Europe. During World War II, most bottles were made in the United States. In 1928 the company introduced the pump top spray bottle; the atomizer was discontinued in 1969. It now makes paint sprayers, humidifiers and medical equipment.

devitrification The process of converting glass into a crystalline substance. By heating the materials of which glass is made to about the temperature needed for vitrification, about 1,300°C to 1,550°C, the glass liquefies. By permitting it to cool very slowly or too long, or if portions of the tank, furnace, or pot are too cool, it devitrifies, becoming crystalline, with a milky appearance. This also occurs in kiln-cast glass where the material in the mold tends to cool too slowly. At that point, the devitrified glass is no longer capable of being used in making glassware and other glass products. The crystals formed are known as devitrification crystals. It may also develop as a result of ineffective annealing or inadvertent heating of the glass to a high temperature. Glass having a high lime content tends to devitrify more readily than other types of glass.

Devonshire cut A cut glass pattern consisting of a large cut star surrounded by smaller cut stars and other cut motifs.

dew drop glass An art glass having an overall surface embellishment of *hobnail* protuberances made by mold pressing, then expanding the object by blowing, and finalizing it by manipulation. It was developed in 1886 by William Leighton Jr. and William F. Russell, at Hobbs, Brockunier & Co. Occasionally the ware was given an opalescent surface, known as *opalescent dew drop*.

dew-like glass See *rugiadoso, vetro.*

Dewar bulb or tube See *Dewar flask.*

Dewar flask (Aka *Dewar bulb, Dewar tube*) A double-walled glass vessel for holding and storing liquid air, liquid oxygen, liquid nitrogen or other liquids having an extremely low temperature of liquefaction. It had a vacuum in the space between its two walls, aiding in the prevention of heat conduction. On occasion, the exterior of the glass was silvered to minimize the absorption of radiation. They were named after British chemist Sir James Dewar (1842-1923).

DeWitt-Gayne Glass Works See *Waterford Glass Works.*

dey cup A milk cup or bowl; from the word *dey*, an old term meaning *dairy.*

De Zeng & Co. See *Redwood Glass Works; Clyde Glass Works.*

diatano, vetro (Italian) An ornamental glass designed by Angelo Barovier, for Barovier & Toso, about 1975. It is a clear, transparent glass embellished with wide engraved festoons, generating a delicately hazy effect.

Diamon Kut A trademark, filed on September 20, 1916, issued on December 26, 1922, of the Pope Cut Glass Company. It was normally affixed to their tableware with a paper label, but on some pieces it was etched on the glass.

diamond (1) A cut glass geometric motif. Lines cut perpendicular to each other formed the square base and tapering sides of a *nailhead* or pointed diamond. The diamond motif was borrowed from English designs, but American cutters developed their own version of the pointed diamond by flattening the point and cutting a cross on it, calling it a *cross cut* or *strawberry diamond*. A large strawberry diamond is often called a *pineapple diamond*.

A *relief diamond* is an enlarged version of a nailhead. A *St. Louis diamond* consists of hollowed out diamonds grouped in a cluster. Some refer to hexagons grouped in the same manner as the *St. Louis diamond*. See *checkered diamond cutting; raised diamond cutting; expanded diamond; strawberry diamond cutting; Venetian diamond*. (2) A form of pure carbon that has crystallized in a cubic lattice under tremendous pressure, considered, at present, to be the hardest substance known to man. Diamonds, both natural and man-made, are used in the embellishment of glass (see *diamond point engraving*) and in various tools, such as saws, drills, cutting wheels, abrasive discs, and belts used in engraving, cutting (with a glasscutter), etc.

diamond air trap A decoration consisting of air bubbles trapped within the glass in a diamond-shaped pattern. The process, patented by W.H., B. & J. Richardson in England in 1857, involves blowing a gather of glass into a mold with projections in the desired design. The gather is removed from the mold and covered with a second gather, trapping pockets of air in the indentations left by the projections.

Diamond Art Glass Company See *Digby Cut Glass Company*.

Diamond Cut Glass Company (1) (1915-1925) A glass cutting facility in Philadelphia, Pennsylvania. (2) See *Digby Cut Glass Company*.

Diamond Cut Glass Works (1900-1915) Established by Abraham Diamond in New York City, it was first listed as Diamond Cut Glass Works in 1910. In 1915, the principal owners were Lawrence I. and Minnie Cohn.

diamond cutter A cutter used to make miters on newer cut glass, coming into use after the Brilliant Period. They create visible striae or lines on the major miters that can be seen with a magnifying glass and cannot be removed by acid polishing. The presence or absence of such lines can aid one in determining the period when the cut glass was made.

diamond daisy (Aka *daisy-in-square, daisy-in-diamond*) A pattern-molded design having a daisy-like flower enclosed in a square, set in a diamond formation.

diamond faceting A style of faceting forming a diaper pattern of vertically positioned diamonds, often used on stems and bowls of drinking glasses, on decanters, etc. See *checkered diamond*.

Diamond Finish A trademark issued to Thatcher Brothers on December 31, 1895. It was used on their cut glass since August 1894, in the form of paper labels printed in red ink.

Diamond Flint Glass Company See *Foster Brothers Glass Works*.

Diamond Glass Company (1) See *Ravenna Glass Company*. (2) The successor to the Dugan Glass Company of Indiana, Pennsylvania. Thomas Dugan withdrew from the Dugan Glass Company in late December 1912/early January 1913, but retained his stock. The company retained the name until July 1, 1913, when it was changed to Diamond Glass Company. It continued to make many of the Dugan lines, some fine lines of blown, light cut, and iridescent wares and many unique candy containers in the shapes of fire engines, locomotives, cash registers, etc.

In mid-1916, it changed its name to the Diamond Glass-Ware Company. In early 1920, it introduced some new iridescent colors under the name *Lustre Line*, such as *Rainbow, Egyptian, Royal*, and *Golden*. In late 1924, it changed to non-iridescent colors, introducing many new lines. The Depression caught up with the company and on December 17, 1930, it ceased operations. In January 1931, it reopened, but on a greatly reduced scale. On June 27, 1931, it was badly damaged by fire and closed. Its signature was a "D" in a diamond. See *Dugan Glass Company*. (3) A glass manufacturing company established in Montreal, Canada, during the late 1880s. In 1890, it purchased the Nova Scotia Glass Company; on August 10, 1891, the Burlington Glass Works, Hamilton, Ontario, Canada; in 1892, the Hamilton Glass Works, also of Hamilton; and, in 1898, the Lamont Glass Company of Trenton, Nova Scotia. It made pattern glassware. See *Foster Brothers Glass Works; Lamont (Diamond) Glass Company*.

Diamond Glass-Ware Company See *Dugan Glass Company.*

diamond molded pattern A molded decorative pattern, mainly on salts, in the form of diamonds of assorted sizes, varying with the mold and the extent of expansion after removal from it. Small diamonds, normally circular or oval, were sometimes called *pearl ornaments* in England. There are three varieties: (a) overall pattern; (b) rows above vertical fluting; and (c) checkered diamonds.

Diamond Poinsettia A trademark of the W.P. Hitchcock Co.

diamond point engraving The technique of embellishing glassware by engraving using a diamond point. Earliest engravings date from Roman times, although it has been reported that it was done with flints rather than diamonds. It was used on Islamic glass. During the 16th century, it was used by decorators in Venice and Hall-in-Tyrol on Venetian glass (cutting not practiced because of its thinness). It was used by German engravers imitating the Venetian style, and by Dutch and English engravers. It was first done in England during the 16th century on glassware made at the facility of Jacopo Verzelini. In Holland, it was used mainly by amateurs embellishing wares with calligraphy during the 17th century. While diamond point engraving declined during the 18th century as wheel engraving and enameling came to the forefront, it was still used for stippling from the 1720s to the late 18th century.

Indiana Glass Co. goblet, ruby top with clear bottom and stem, *Diamond Point* **pattern.**
Davanna Collection

diamond studded A style of decoration in the form of raised diamonds.

diamond thumbprint See *thumbprint.*

diamonding A form of embellishment on beveled mirrors, made by cutting a sequence of intersecting depressions along the beveled edges, creating a diamond pattern formed at the point of intersection. A patent for a mechanical technique was granted in 1678 to John Roberts.

diaper A repetitive pattern wherein the units of design are similar and connected, or nearly so, to each other. See *dot-and-cross diaper.*

diatreta (*Latin***)** Literally, *cut vessels*; singular, *diatretum.* The technique of carving glass in relief and further carving in back of that relief so the design is above the surface and connected to it by tiny struts or bridges. It was first referenced by the Roman poet Martial in his writings during the late 1st century AD.

diatreta, psuedo vasa See *pseudo vasa diatreta.*

diatreta, vasa See *vasa diatreta.*

Diatreta glass A glass created by Frederick Carder, about 1952, at Steuben, to replicate the Roman *vasa diatreta.* The ornamental pieces were made using a modified *cire perdue* process and fastened to the body of the object by tiny glass struts. A similar decoration was made on some Tiffany vases. See *pseudo vasa diatreta.*

diatretarii (*Latin***)** An ancient Roman term for the decorators of glass, not to be confused with the *vitrearii* (the glassmakers and blowers). It was the deep cutting on cage cups by the diatretarii that led them to be called *vasa diatreta.*

dice glass A tumbler, about three inches high, with a double-walled bottom encasing dice.

dichro(mat)ic glass Glass exhibiting different colors depending on the angle or nature of light falling on it, as when observed by reflected or transmitted light. It may be caused by the addition of a very small percentage of colloidial gold or uranium to the batch; the use of copper oxide in a reducing atmosphere; or by coating glass with various chemicals, giving it specific properties with respect to reflected and transmitted light. See *transmutation color; Lycurgis cup; Alexandrit.*

Diders & McGee A glass manufacturing company established about 1895 in Brilliant, Ohio.

Didio Brothers Cut Glass Company A glass cutting shop established in 1914 in Buffalo, New York. It moved several times within the city, but was still operating in 1964.

Didymium glass A form of neodymium glass used for lenses in safety glasses.

die away See *shaded glass.*

die patterned paperweight A paperweight made by placing powdered colored glass, picked up on a molten gather of glass and encased in clear glass, in the pattern grooves of a metal mold. They are inexpensive and generally used for souvenirs or advertising pieces.

die sinker A person who makes metal molds.

Dier Goblet A glass goblet, considered to have been made by Jacopo Verzelini, having three engraved panels with the name "John-Jone" and "Dier 1581" and the Royal (Elizabethan) Arms. It is presumed to be a marriage glass. A stag, unicorn, and two hounds are depicted over the names and around the funnel-shaped bowl. On the stem is a large hollow fluted bulb between two small knops.

diffraction A modification that light undergoes, as in passing by the edges of opaque bodies or through narrow slits, in which the rays appear to be deflected, producing fringes of parallel light and dark or colored bands.

diffusion The reflection or refraction of light from an irregular surface or erratic dispersion through a surface.

Digby Cut Glass Company A glass cutting shop established during 1919 in Seattle, Washington. From 1920 to 1924, it used the name Diamond Cut Glass Company and, in 1923, the Diamond Art Glass Company, as well as the Digby name.

Dillaway, Hiram See *Boston & Sandwich Glass Co.*

Diluvium Similar to Egermann's *Lithyalin,* a glass resembling stone, made by Josef Rindskopf's Sons of Kosten, Germany. Pieces were often cut or carved in intaglio or cameo.

diminishing lens A polished glass concave lens that concentrates light, making the image smaller (the opposite of a magnifying lens). Prior to 1646 they were used to embellish glassware made by George Schwanhardt and later as a single lens or in an overall pattern on German and Bohemian glasses. Occasionally a portrait or other design is positioned directly opposite the lens, appearing through the lens in reduced size.

dinner set Complete table sets, usually marketed as services for four, six, eight, or 12, consisting of dinner plates, fruit plates, soup bowls, dessert plates, and tumblers and cups for beverages. It may also include serving plates, coasters, ashtrays, candleholders, sugars and creamers, salts and peppers, grill plates, candy jars, cookie jars, and butter dishes. Individual pieces of inexpensive sets were often distributed as premiums with various products to entice people to buy it in order to obtain a complete set.

dinnering the men A custom, initiated at the Mather Glass House, whereby boy apprentices would go to the general store at eleven o'clock each morning and pick up enough food for the noon meal for all employees at the facility.

diota (Greek): (Literally, *two eared*) A jar, primarily of Greek pottery, used for storing water, wine or oil, somewhat like an amphora, but with a pointed bottom. It has two side handles from which its name is derived. Some small ones were made of Roman glass during the 2nd century AD, with loop handles attached to an encircling thread and extending from midway up the neck to the shoulder.

dip A barrel-like container filled with boiling water into which are placed sheets of window glass to be tempered. They usually remained there for about an hour.

dip mold (Aka an *open mold*) A one-piece mold open at the top, used to provide the object being made only with its shape or to make pattern-molded glassware, later expanded by blowing. They were originally carved from a block of wood, later from blocks of clay, stone, or metal, and were about one foot deep and a few inches across, often carved on the inside with a series of heavy parallel ribs. The gaffer, while standing over the mold, would lower (dip) the gather of molten glass into the mold and expand it slightly by blowing so that its sides pressed into the ribbing of the mold. The paraison was carefully raised from the mold, imprinted with the design and/or in the desired shape, then blown and reshaped (if necessary) into its final form.

dip-overlay method See *flashing*.

dipper See *kyathos*.

dipstick A rod, made of iron or bronze, used for extracting a small gather of molten glass from the pot and trailing it onto an object. It usually has one end bent at a right angle so the trailing could be applied more easily. See *gathering iron*.

Directoire style See *Neo-classical style*.

diseased glass See *grisselling*.

disguised glassware See *deceptive glassware*.

dish A shallow vessel (a) on which food is dispensed or served at the table or (b) off of which it is eaten. It is generally circular or oval with a ledge and well. The term is reserved primarily for those vessels 12 inches or more in diameter; smaller ones are typically called *plates*. Specimens in Roman glass cast in two-piece molds are embellished with cutting. See the following types of dishes: *ambrosia, jam, pickle, preserve, relish, salad, sauce, shell, vegetable, wafer.* Also see *bowl; ambrosia glassware.*

dish light A chandelier in the form of a broad, circular, slightly concave piece of glass suspended from the ceiling by three chains fastened to the metal rim mounted on the glass.

Above the glass, arms stretch from the rim to a central metal frame that holds a font for fuel. They were made in many sizes for use in a variety of places from narrow vestibules to large rooms, and occasionally were made in pairs. The chains, rim, finial below the glass, and ceiling attachment were often ormolu. They were used in England during the Regency period about 1810. See *lampada pensile*.

disk A small, flat, circular object with a circular hole in the center. Many were made in Egypt about 200 BC and in China. Their exact purpose is unknown.

disk stopper A stopper that came into popular use after the spire stopper. It is flat and circular; the edges are plain, scalloped, or notched.

dispensary container (Aka *pottle, Winchester quart, Corbyn*) A jar made in a variety of sizes, used in a pharmacy for storing various liquids. See *carboy*.

distaff See *spindle*.

Dites & McGranigan See *Ensell & Wilson*.

Dithridge, Duncan A businessman, with showrooms in New York City, specializing in cut glass acquired from small cutting shops in the area. His trademark was *Floral Crystal*.

Dithridge & Company A glass manufacturing facility in Pittsburgh, Pennsylvania, and associated with another in Martins Ferry, Ohio. See *Fort Pitt Glass Works; Dithridge Flint Glass Company; Pittsburgh Lamp, Brass & Glass Company.*

Dithridge Flint Glass Company (1881-1891) Edward D. Dithridge Jr. purchased a building owned by the Union Flint Glass Works in Martins Ferry, Ohio, establishing a glass manufacturing facility. In 1887, the company moved to New Brighton, Pennsylvania, where it made cut and engraved blown lead glass; pressed wares; lighting wares; and lead glass blanks for resale.

Diversarum Artium Schedulae A technical document written by Theophilus of Helmershausen in Paderborn, Germany, during the 11th century, providing one of the earliest descriptions of, and recipes for, making and staining glass.

divided lens A bifocal or trifocal lens.

Dobelmann, J.B., Company See *Greenpoint Flint Glass Works.*

documentary specimen Any piece of glass or glassware which lends credence, or provides factual information, relative to the history of glassware, including those: (a) bearing the signature or mark of the maker or decorator; (b) possessing an unusual mark or enlightening inscription; (c) uncovered during a particular excavation; (d) handed down in a family connected with an early or historic facility; (e) embellished with armorial bearings; or (f) written about in old documents.

doghouse The area at a glass manufacturing facility where the batch is fed into the furnace.

Doerr Glass Company Inc. (1916-1970) A glass manufacturing facility founded by Herman Doerr in Vineland, New Jersey, making hand-blown wares for use in scientific and research laboratories and later adding its own engraving and grinding shops. Doerr died in 1930 and was succeeded by his son, Albert J. In 1932, a brother, Paul, became chief executive officer. During the Depression of the 1930s, it tried importing blanks, but sources were unreliable so it built a furnace for its glassblowing operations. In 1936, Francis O. Doerr became head of the firm. During World War II, when metal was scarce, the company made lamp fonts and bases of glass.

Dolce Relievo glassware (Aka *soft relief glassware*) A glassware made of opaque white or ivory colored glass, flashed with clear glass. After it was covered with an acid resistant substance, a design was cut through it onto the surface of the glass. The glass left exposed was etched away using acid, leaving the design in shallow relief on the ground color. It was made by Stevens & Williams Ltd. in the 1880s.

Dolly Varden hat A piece of glassware resembling a woman's hat with a very wide brim.

dolphin beaker A beaker with two rows of hollow *elephant trunk* prunts around it, similar to those on a claw beaker, except those on the upper row end in a fish-like tail. The prunts in the upper row are of dark blue glass; the upper portion in a shape of a dolphin's head and the lower pincered to look like fins. They were made in Cologne, Germany, in the 4th century. Other similar beakers from the same period have embellishments of different shellfish (e.g., shrimp), snails, and other sea creatures and fall under the general heading of *dolphin beakers.* See *shellfish beaker; dolphin bottle.*

dolphin bottle A small globular receptacle similar to a Greek aryballos. They rest on a flat or rounded bottom and have a disk or funnel mouth and two thick curled handles on the shoulder which, on some, reach to the disk around the mouth. Each handle has a hole in it so a bronze chain or hook could be attached to suspend it from the user's wrist. The bottles were so-named because the shape of the handles on some are suggestive of a dolphin. They are believed to be of Roman origin, probably made during the 1st to the 4th centuries A.D.

Dolphin candlestick, mid-1800s, probably from New England, clear glass, 10" h.

dolphin candlestick Glass candlesticks in the shape of coiled dolphins with a candle holder at the top and base at the bottom. Many were made at Sandwich in vaseline, clear, white, or bicolored glass.

dolphin motif A motif used on or for candlesticks and other wares mainly by glassmakers in the Pittsburgh, Pennsylvania, or New England areas. In the 1860s, McKee Brothers made a *petticoat dolphin compote* having a flared base and an open ribbed coupe top with an opalescent rim, made of light peacock blue or canary yellow glass and measuring about five inches tall.

dome (1) A tall cylindrical glass object, the sides curving inward toward the top, forming a closed hemispherical cover, used during Victorian times to cover displays of imitation fruit, bouquets of artificial flowers, etc. They were made by the same technique used for making broad glass; that is, by blowing a large bubble, forming it into a cylinder, and then shearing the end opposite the dome. (2) (Aka *crown*) The glass in a paperweight above the motif.

dome cover A cover, hemispherical in shape, fitting on the vertical collar of a container. Some are double domed, having a smaller dome resting on the larger one.

domed foot A foot that is domed, high or low, in shape. There are several variations: domed and terraced (solid or hollow); terraced domed; beehive domed (solid or hollow); and double domed, with one dome above the other. Such feet are usually circular, but some have a square base. It was originally made so the pontil mark could be pushed upward to allow the glass to stand and not scratch the surface on which it was placed. They were made and used mainly during the 17th and 18th centuries.

Dominion Glass Company A glass manufacturing concern operating in Montreal and Wallaceburg, Canada, during the late 19th and 20th centuries. In 1913, it merged with, and became known as, the Diamond Flint Glass Company, which purchased other facilities in the region, such as the Hamilton Glass Works, Sydenham Glass Company and the Burlington Glass Works. It made pattern glassware. See *Foster Brothers Glass Works*.

Domino drip tray A tray designed to hold a cream pitcher within a center ring with space for sugar cubes around it, preferably Domino (a brand name) sugar cubes.

Doorknob, approx. 2" d., brass attachments and iron joiner.
Davanna Collection

door knob A knob used to release a door latch. Some were made of glass of various types, such as pressed (most common), cut, etc. A patent for a pressed glass door knob was granted in the United States to John Robinson of the Stourbridge Flint Glass Works, Pittsburgh, Pennsylvania.

door knocker A device attached to a door consisting of a plate with an attached arm. The end of the arm is tapped against the plate to alert those inside of a visitor.

door plate A flat decorative glass piece, usually rectangular in shape, set into the panel of a door, secured by external framing or screws, to prevent marring the door. It is usually placed around the knob or around or under a door knocker.

door porter See *doorstrop*.

doorstrop (Aka *door porter*) A heavy object used to keep a door ajar. They are made of solid glass and usually have an irregular global or ovoid shape with a flat bottom, measuring from three to six inches high and weighing up to six pounds. Many old ones were made of greenish bottle glass, often the dregs in the melting pot at the end of the day that would otherwise be discarded or *dumped* (*dump* being often applied to glass doorstrops). They are normally larger and heavier than paperweights, but there are smaller ones called *bottle green paperweights*.

Some are embellished with interior tiny air bubbles, either in a pattern or at random. The bubbles were made using a spot mold or by pressing the paraison into chalk spread on the marver, adding more molten glass and repeating the process, perhaps several times (the heat caused the chalk to emit gas, forming the bubbles in the pattern of the chalk).

Some are embellished with an internal pot of stylized flowers or several flowers in tiers. The process used involves making a paraison with three or more layers of cased glass, after which a pointed instrument is pushed into the top of the mass to push down the layers and form trumpet-like shapes within the piece, often with a cavity at the top. When another layer of glass is added, an air bubble or tear is trapped in the cavity. Some large ones have pear-shaped bubbles with a silvery thread at the narrow end. Several were made in the United States of many types of glass from the late 19th century into the 20th century. Many were made in the form of humans and animals, especially cats.

Doped Glasses See *Rare-Earth (Doped) Glasses.*

Doped Ware A term used by glassworkers at Fenton Art Glass Company for a patterned iridescent ware, now called *Carnival glass*. It comes from the substance, which the workers called *dope*, sprayed on the glass while very hot, causing the iridescence. The hotter the glass when sprayed, the better the iridescence. The *dope* was usually ferric or stannic chloride, or a combination of the two, dissolved in a liquid solution. Fenton started making its iridized glass in 1907, the first company to do so.

Doppelpokal *(German)* A Pokal having another Pokal as its cover.

Doppelscheuer *(German)* A cup, the bowl of which is in the form of a *Scheuer*, with a flat cover that repeats the form of the bowl (without the handle). Some were made in Venice or southern Germany and were dated 1518. Others were made in northern Europe during the 15th and 16th centuries.

Doppelsturzbecher *(German)* A drinking glass in two parts, each of which is a *Sturzbecher*. One is inverted over the other (rims together). Usually the stems are of different lengths, the top one being shorter, giving the appearance of a finial.

Doppelter Krautstrunk *(German)*

Literally, *double cabbage stem* glass. A type of Krautstrunk, one inverted, resting on the rim of another. They were made in Germany during the 16th century.

Doppelwandglas *(German)* Literally, *double wall glass*. See *Zwischengoldglas*.

Dorflein, Philip A mold maker for perfume, toilet and scent bottles, historical flasks, and other glassware, working in Philadelphia from 1842 to about 1890, supplying molds to several glass houses in the area.

Dorflinger, Christian (1828-1915) Originally spelled Doerflinger. Born in France, he trained as a glassmaker, serving an apprenticeship (completed in 1846) under the supervision of his father's brother, also named Christian, at the Cristalleries de Saint-Louis. His diploma stated that he had mastered every aspect of the glassblowers' craft and was familiar with the techniques of cutting and stone engraving. After receiving his diploma, he, his mother, his younger brother Edward and his sisters came to the United States.

Arriving in Philadelphia, Pennsylvania, Christian and Edward got jobs at a pharmaceutical glass manufacturing facility in Camden, New Jersey, working there until 1852, then moving to Brooklyn, New York, where Christian established his first facility. (See *Dorflinger, C., & Sons* for firms established and operated by him.) In 1863, on his physician's advice, he retired to White Mills, Pennsylvania, where he established a glass manufacturing and decorating business in 1865, when his health improved. See *Dorflinger, C., & Sons; Concord Street Flint Glass Works; Long Island Flint Glass Works; Greenpoint Flint Glass Works; Wayne County Glass Works; Dorflinger Glass Co.*

Dorflinger, C., & Sons Christian Dorflinger's first glass manufacturing facility, the Long Island Flint Glass Works, was established on Concord Street in Brooklyn, New York, in 1852. In 1858, he built another on Plymouth Street in Brooklyn, and, in 1860, the Greenpoint Glassworks on Commercial Street, Brooklyn (here the *Lincoln Service* for the White House was made in 1861). In 1863, on his physician's advice, he retired to White Mills, Pennsylvania. From 1863 to 1866, the operation of the Long Island Flint Glass Works was entrusted to his employees and, in 1866, he sold it to J.S. Hibbler. In 1879, Hibbler changed its name to Hibbler & Rausch, and in 1889, to Hibbler & Company. In 1893 he closed the facility. The Greenpoint Glassworks was also entrusted to his employees, later leasing it to E.P. Gleason and selling it in 1902.

In 1865, Dorflinger's health improved and he constructed a facility at Indian Orchard, Pennsylvania. Later the same year he constructed a larger one in White Mills, Pennsylvania, initially called the Wayne County Glass Works where, in 1867, he opened a glass cutting shop. In 1881, C. Dorflinger & Sons was established when Christian's sons (William, Louis J., and Charles) entered the business, owning and operating the Wayne County Glass Works (White Mills site), Wayne Silver Company, Hawley Glass Company, and Honesdale Glass Company. In 1903, at the peak of operations, the White Mills location had 1,150 acres, 27 production buildings, and almost 100 workers' cottages, employing about 650 people. It made glass blanks for its cutting operations and for 22 other cutting shops. In 1904, Christian retired and his son, William, became president and CEO.

During the next 10 years, the company attempted to reduce costs and still meet the demands for quality dinnerware. From 1907 until it closed, the company was plagued by several fires, and the damaged building was not rebuilt. After Christian died in 1915, the three sons began fighting among themselves. The two unmarried daughters, Nellie and Katherine, became directors in the company. On her death, Nellie left her interest to Katherine, who ended up controlling Christian's estate. The facility closed in 1921 and, in 1925, was sold.

dot-and-cross diaper A diaper pattern consisting of parallel crossing lines embellished with two dots on the lines between each intersection and one dot within each square or diamond.

dotted prunt See *raspberry prunt.*

double balsamarium See *double unguentarium.*

double bottle A bottle divided internally into two compartments, each having its own mouth and spout. See *multiple bottle; double cruet.*

double cabbage stem glass See *Doppelter Krautstrunk.*

double cased glass An object having two gathers of different colored glass over the base glass.

double chip glass See *feather glass.*

double cone bottle A glass container in the shape of an inverted cone with the tip cut

off, forming a flat base, on the rim of which is another upright conical-shaped piece tapering upward to form a narrow neck. The rim of the upper cone overlaps the rim of the lower. They were made in Germany during the 14th and 15th centuries.

double cruet A bottle, used for holding oil and vinegar, with an interior division forming two distinct containers, each having its own neck, mouth and stopper. They are made as separate bottles and fused together. See *double bottle; multiple bottle; gemel flask.*

double cushion knop A variation of the cushioned knop, having the shape of a slightly flattened sphere with a ring above and below.

double dome cover See *dome cover.*

double eagle glass A winged glass having an elaborate stem constructed of threads and the appearance of a double-headed eagle. They were made in the *façon de Venise* in Germany and the Netherlands in the late 16th-early 17th centuries. The twisted rods occasionally had clear or colored pincered cresting along the outer edge. The German term is *Doppeladlerglas.*

double-ended gin glass A drinking glass consisting of two funnel bowls connected at their bases. Occasionally they are in the form of deceptive glasses with thick sides.

double etching A decorative technique. The object to be decorated is covered with an acid-resistant medium and a design is inscribed through it onto the glass. Then the object is dipped in acid, etching a design where the medium has been removed. After removal, the areas etched are coated with the medium and another design is inscribed through it. Again it is dipped in acid and a second design is etched where the medium was removed. By varying the time the object is in the acid, the depth of etching is controlled. This technique was used by Frederick Carder at Steuben on some ware (a layer of Alabaster glass was cased between two layers of different colored glass; the pattern etched on the outer layers appear in three shades of color) .

double flashing Flashing a glass object with two or more layers of glass of different colors. It was common in Germany during the 1830s.

double flint glass See *flint glass.*

double gilding The application of a second layer of gold leaf over the first.

Double Glass A name patented by Benjamin Bakewell Jr. in 1874. It refers to a two-color simulated cut or engraved overlay glassware made entirely by pressing. The two colors of glass are joined only where the surfaces come in contact with each other by using interchangeable plungers, rings, and molds.

double glass (1) See *Zwischengoldglas.* (2) See *overlay glass.*

double gourd shape The shape of a vase or other object where the upper and lower parts are spherical (the upper being slightly smaller), joined by a short narrow waist.

double impression In pattern-molded glassware, there are numerous ribbed patterns, usually designated by the number of ribs in the total pattern, i.e., 12, 18, 20, 32, 36, etc. It has been found that many of the patterns containing higher numbers of ribs were made by dipping the paraison into the ribbed mold, removing it, turning it and dipping it a second time, creating a pattern with twice as many ribs as in the mold.

double lozenge A cut glass miter motif in the form of an elongated diamond divided in the center with an "X."

double magnum See *wine bottle, sizes.*

double ogee A shape or ornamentation in the form of an extended ogee molding resembling two connected "S's."

double ogee bowl A bowl or drinking glass whose sides have a double ogee shape.

double overlay See *overlay glass.*

double rolled A term used to define the manufacture of both commercial and stained glass that is not blown. The glass, mainly cathedral glass, passes between two rollers as it comes from the furnace, forming large sheets of uniform thickness. Both rollers may be smooth or one may be engraved or etched with a design. The surface has a "texture" impressed on it.

double scent bottle A compartmented bottle, small and cylindrical with openings at both ends and divided internally in the center, for holding perfume and smelling salts. They were made in a variety of colors and were usually faceted. The perfume compartment was usually sealed by a ground glass stopper, further protected by a metal screw cap. The side for smelling salts was usually sealed with a spring-fitted hinged lid. The caps or lids were usually made of silver or brass.

double series air twist See *air twist; double series twist.*

double series twist A twist with another (air or opaque) twist encircling it, made by making one twist, then adding molten glass and repeating the process wherein the inner rod is wrenched into an even tighter twist. Occasionally several intertwining outer twists are used, or one or more spiral threads, or a multi-ply band of threads around the inner twist. The two types of double series twists are abbreviated as DSAT (air) and DSOT (opaque).

double shot glass (Aka *bar tumbler*) Typically, a two-ounce glass (a standard shot glass holds one ounce) about three inches tall. Dating to about 1850, they are heavy, with thick bottoms and sides.

double stoppers Stoppers that are flat and pressed on both sides with an intaglio design. They are usually twice as thick as those with a design on one side and are usually found on Czechoslovakian perfume bottles.

double strip bead A bead made by heating two ribbons of glass, placing them on either side of a metal rod, and fusing the edges together. The rod is removed and the hollow tube that is formed is cut into bead-size pieces that are polished with the edges rounded by heating.

double unguentarium (Aka *double balsamarium*) A receptacle in the form of two unguentaria fastened together, having one loop handle on each side and an overhead loop handle extending over both vessels. See *unguentarium*.

double wall glass

See *Zwischengold-glas; Dewar flask.*

double wine glass A wine glass with a bowl at each end of a common stem, resting on the rim of one bowl while the other is upright. One bowl typically is larger than the other, the larger for red wine, the smaller white wine. They are usually of light green glass, often with gilt embellishments and an elaborate connecting stem, occasionally in the form of a figure, normally a woman, so that when the glass rests on the larger bowl, it resembles a woman in a full-length dress bearing a basket on her head.

double X-cut vesica A cut glass motif, a variation of the X-cut vesica where the vesica is crossed by curved miter lines forming two Xs within it. Each section is cut with different patterns.

doubler A large dish, bowl, or plate designed for two people to eat from at the same time.

Douerlein, Fred In 1879, he blew the first bulb for Edison's electric light while employed at the Corning Glass Works.

Douglass & Taylor; Douglass, Rutherford & Co. See *Kentucky Glass Works.*

dove flask A flask of Roman variegated glass shaped in the form of a dove with smooth sides and an elongated tail serving as a spout. Made in the 1st century A.D., it was used to hold perfume. Later ones were made of opaque white glass. They were very detailed and enameled with feather markings in various colors. These were also made in Europe during the 18th century.

dovecote bottle A bottle penetrated with four holes. It had the appearance of a dovecote (a pigeon house) with tiny opaque white and blue doves that appear to be flying in and out of the holes. They were made during the Dark Ages in the Seine-Rhine area.

Dowesborough Glasshouse A window and bottle glass manufacturing facility

established in 1783 in Guilderland Township, near Sand Lake, New York, by John DeNuefville and his son, Leonard. It operated intermittently until 1787, then closed. In 1792, it was purchased by McClallen, M(a)cGregor & Co., naming it the Albany Glass House. See *Albany Glass House.*

Doyle & Company (Aka *Doyle, Sons & Co.*) A glass manufacturing facility established in Pittsburgh, Pennsylvania, in 1866 by William and Joseph A. Doyle and William Beck, that made flint and pressed glass tableware. In 1868, it built a new facility in Pittsburgh, closing the old one. In 1878 a fire caused production to be curtailed. In the early 1880s, its assets were purchased by the Phoenix Glass Company of Philipsburg (Monaca), Pennsylvania, which, in 1891, was purchased by the U.S. Glass Company, becoming *Factory P.*

drageoir See *sweetmeat dish.*

dragged decoration See *combed decoration.*

dragladling The ladling of hot glass from the pot into another container, usually an iron kettle filled with water. This is done when it is advantageous to save the glass. The term is derived from the words "drag ladle."

dragon (stem) glass or goblet A winged glass, the stem of which is made of threads twisted and formed into the shape of a dragon. They were made in the *façon de Venise* in Germany and the Netherlands in the late 16th and early 17th centuries. Occasionally the stem was further embellished by clear or colored cresting along the outer edge.

Drake, George W., & Company

Established about 1900, this glass cutting facility was located in Corning, New York. It did cutting for the Bronson Inkstand Company (which it later purchased) and several other companies on blanks supplied by Dorflinger and Pairpoint.

dram bottle A small perfume bottle with a capacity of 1/8 ounce or a dram of perfume. See *purse bottle; miniature or mini perfume bottle; perfumette.*

dram glass (Aka *dram cup, dram pot, dram dish, joey, ginette*) A small drinking glass intended for spirits with a capacity of about two to three ounces. They had a funnel or conical bowl, an everted rim, and a short or rudimentary stem resting on a heavy foot. Usually the lower half of the bowl was solid. They were occasionally made as *double dram glasses*, having two bowls of different sizes, one acting as the foot while the other was used for drinking. They were made from the latter half of the 17th century.

drapery glass An old type of opalescent sheet glass having extensive rippling on the surface, commonly called a *convulsed surface*, giving it the appearance of folds of drapery or clothing. It was developed in the United States in the late 19th century, machine-made in large quantities, and primarily used for garments on figures in religious pictorial windows.

drawn glass (1) Flat glass made by the drawing process, replacing the cylinder method, being more efficient and much less costly. Since more flat glass could be made by this process, there was a substantial reduction in the number of facilities making flat glass. In the United States, the number was reduced from about 100 in 1899 to 16 in 1929. Drawn glass is of a higher quality but does not have a perfectly flat surface because it has to be ground and polished. The Pilkington Brothers of England invented a process for making flat glass where it was ground and polished on both sides as it emerged from the annealing lehr. (2) Tubes, rods, or strings of glass made by drawing them, by hand or machine, from a furnace while hot. See *tube; rod.*

drawn shank See *drawn stem.*

drawn stem (Aka *drawn shanks, straw stems, shank stem*) The stem of a drinking glass made by drawing the metal from the bottom of the bowl to form a stem "at one" with the bowl, in contrast to a stuck shank. They are simpler to make than twist and other stems attached at both ends, one to the bowl, the other to the foot. The drawn stem glass is made in two distinct parts: the bowl with the stem attached and the foot. When the bubble for the bowl is formed on the blowpipe, a pontil takes up the glass at the top of the bowl, and the thicker blob at the end of the blowpipe is drawn out into a stem. Most drawn stems are solid, but some have a hollow core. Drawn stem glasses generally have simple round or trumpet bowls.

dredging box See *saltshaker.*

Dresden Decorated See *Crown Milano.*

dresser set See *dressing table set.*

dressing Various glass embellishments found on chandeliers or candelabra, including drops, snakes, arms, and pinnacles.

dressing glass or mirror (Aka *shaving mirror*) An adjustable mirror used for shaving, mounted on swivel supports attached to a set of drawers. See *toilet mirror.*

dressing table set A group or set of objects intended for use by women at a dressing table. The usual three-piece set includes a comb, brush, and mirror. Other items that may be included are perfume bottles, powder bowls or boxes, ring stands, jars, hair receivers, trays, etc.

drinking bowl A bowl, generally circular and low, similar to that used from the 5th to the 9th century as a communal drinking vessel. Some were made of Islamic glass, possibly in Persia during the 9th century, and had the appearance of turquoise or another mineral. During the 10th and 11th centuries, they had a gilded rim and mount in the Byzantine style.

drinking glass A hollow glass vessel intended for drinking a beverage. They are almost always symmetrical, with a flat bottom or stemmed foot (exceptions have a rounded or pointed bottom). They have been made in many shapes and sizes, and have varying styles with respect to the bowl, stem, base, and embellishment. They may be divided into two main types: those with stems and those without. Those with stems are normally for wines, ales, cordials, and other alcoholic beverages. Stemmed wine glasses have been fashionable in England for several centuries and have gone through an evolutionary process since the 17th century. The tendency has been from large bowls with short stems to smaller slender bowls with longer and more sophisticated stems. See the following types of glasses: *wine; ale; champagne; whisky; toddy; punch; juice; gin; thistle; English drinking; German drinking.* Also see *beaker; tumbler; stein; goblet; mug; tankard; rummer; drinking horn.*

drinking horn A drinking vessel having the appearance of a crescent-shaped horn; some early ones resemble a cone. Some are of Roman glass, dating from the 1st century A.D. The majority are of Frankish glass dating from about 400 to 700 A.D. Blown as a cone beaker, they were bent while warm and embellished with applied threads spiraling around the horn horizontally, in vertical loops, or in a zigzag pattern (the wolf's tooth pattern); sometimes patterns are combined. On some horns the tip is pointed, some flattened. The mouths of many have a jagged edge, as if broken off. Some, embellished with diamond point engraving and two suspensory rings, were made from a later date until the 17th century in the Netherlands and in Germany. See *rhyton.*

drinking vessel Any cup, bottle, dish, bowl, or other container from which a person can drink.

drip pan (Aka *grease pan*) A permanent or removable tray, beneath and surrounding, the nozzle of a candlestick to catch the wax dripping from a burning candle. The French term is *bobeche.* See *save all; spreader.*

driven glass See *sheared glass.*

dromedary flask A flask in the form of a dromedary (one-humped camel) carrying a globular vase. Some have been attributed to Syria, dating from the 6th to the 8th centuries A.D. The vase on the dromedary is embellished with colored threads of glass in a zigzag pattern.

drop A glass ornament suspended as an adornment from a chandelier, candelabrum, girandole, or candlestick. They may be smooth or faceted and are made in a variety of sizes, shapes, and styles. Some have a small hole near the top for direct suspension or are dangled from an intervening glass button. See the following types of drops: *Albert; button; icicle; mirror; pear; prism; rule; Rupert's; spear; Waterford.*

drop beaker See *Nuppenbecher.*

drop burner A whale oil lamp burner that is dropped into the font and held over the oil by a metal plate larger than the opening in the font.

drop knop A knop that is wider near the bottom than the top and tapering inward at the bottom.

drop molding See *block molding.*

drop stopper (Aka *dabber, applicator*) A stopper with a dauber attached for applying perfume.

dropped bottom A bulge or droop at the bottom of a vessel having a rounded body. Such vessels may include casters, teapots, etc.

dropper flask A flask or bottle having a globular body and a wide, tall neck culminating in a funnel mouth. It has a small, gradually narrowing tube serving as a dropper, projecting from the middle of the body. Some have a loop handle extending from the body perpendicular to the dropper. They were made of Syrian and Roman glass, dating from the 1st to the 4th centuries. They have been called *feeding bottles,* but this is unlikely since the tip of the tube is not finished but broken off, and the position of the handle lends itself more for pouring than for feeding an infant.

drug jar A jar used in a pharmacy for holding wet or dry drugs. These jars are made in the form of an *albarello.*

Apothecary jar, 11-1/2" h.
Davanna Collection

drugstore furniture Glass items used in a drugstore or pharmacy, including show jars, mortars and pestles, retorts, tubing, funnels and bottles for prescriptions, tinctures, extracts, oils, etc.

drum stick A frigger in the form of a straight stick used for striking a drum. It is about eight inches long, with a sphere-like protuberance at one end.

drunkard A stemmed drinking glass with multiple rings and/or knops on the stem, to provide the user with a secure grip.

DSAT The abbreviation for *double series air twist*.

DSOT The abbreviation for *double series opaque twist*.

duck head handle Loop-shaped handles having tails, found on various jugs believed to have been made in the 8th century in Mesopotamia.

ducks-on-a-pond paperweight A hollow paperweight made *at-the-lamp*, having enclosed within it one or three small glass ducks fused to the interior so it appears they are swimming above the ground. Related weights have swimming swans and walking pigs. Most were made by Baccarat or St. Louis.

ductile A substance that exhibits the property of being able to be drawn out, molded, or shaped into a desired form, as in the case of molten glass.

Duff & Campbell See *American Glass Works*.

Duffield & Company See *Excelsior Flint Glass Works*.

Dugan, Thomas See *Northwood, Harry*.

Dugan Glass Company Thomas Dugan came to the United States from England in 1882 and began working for Hobbs, Brockunier, and later Harry Northwood at his various facilities. He appears to have been a partner in Northwood's facility in Indiana, Pennsylvania, when it joined the National Glass Company in 1899. Dugan managed this facility until mid-January 1904, when he purchased it from National Glass, renaming it the Dugan Glass Company. He made substantial quantities of pressed pattern glass. In July 1913, the name became Diamond Glass Company.

The official name after mid-1916 was Diamond Glass-Ware Company. It made several lines of carnival glass as early as 1909, having begun experiments with iridizing as early as 1902. Almost one quarter of the carnival glass found today was made there between 1910 and 1931, the year it was destroyed by fire. Its famous "Diamond-D" mark was introduced on some lines between 1905 and 1907. Some of the lines it made were a continuation of those made by Northwood at the facility, keeping the same name on some of the more popular lines and using new names on some of the less popular.

Dugan also founded another facility in Indiana, Pennsylvania, in 1892, originally known as the Indiana Glass Co. before being changed to the Dugan Glass Company. He was affiliated with the Dugan Glass Company of Loraconing, Pennsylvania, Cambridge Glass Company, and Mound Valley Glass Company, and finally settling down in Lancaster, Pennsylvania, working for Anchor Hocking. See *Diamond Glass Company*.

dumbbell knop A knop in the shape of a dumbbell, positioned vertically and drawn in at the top and the bottom.

dumbwaiter An object with a central stem and three or four circular trays, one above the other, getting progressively smaller toward the top.

Dummer, George, & Co. Born in New Haven, Connecticut, in 1782, he later moved to Albany, New York, where he was a glass cutter at the Hamilton Glass Works. Prior to 1821, he opened a glass retail store in Manhattan, New York. By 1824, he had erected a glass manufacturing facility in Jersey City, New Jersey, making blown, mold-blown, cut and engraved glass, adding pressed glass in 1827. It was known as the Jersey Glass Company, Dummer's Jersey Glass Company and, about 1830, P.C. Dummer & Company (after a brother became an active owner). Adjacent to this facility, he built the Jersey Porcelain & Earthen Ware Company in 1826.

In 1846, the name became Dummer & Lyman; in 1848, George Dummer, Lyman & Co.; and in 1851, George Dummer & Co. (George Dummer Jr.) They remained under the control of the Dummer family until 1862 when they were taken over by Reeds & Moulds, who closed them during the latter years of the Civil War. Later Matthiessen & Wiechers bought it, converting it to a sugar refinery.

Dummer, P.C., & Co. Dummer & Lyman: See *Dummer, George, & Co.*

dump A doorstop made of glass. Popular during the Victorian Era, they were usually cone-shaped with numerous bubbles of air, sometimes arranged in a pattern.

Dunbar (Flint) Glass Corporation
(1918-1953) A glass manufacturing facility established in Dunbar, West Virginia, which made glass chimneys. By the time of the Depression, it was successful with its blown and pressed tableware. The glass was also famous for its colors. Because of the known periods within which the glass was made, it can often be dated by color. During the 1920s, *Rose pink* and *Bermuda green* wares were made. In the early 1930s, Stiegel green, ruby, and cobalt blue were made. In the late 1930s, blue and ruby luster, amethyst and topaz were its prime colors. The company embellished many of its pieces with gilded designs and the Rambler Rose border.

Dunbarton Glass Works A facility constructed specifically for making crown and cylinder window glass in Dunbarton, New York, in 1802. In 1850, Howe, Scofield & Co. was operating it; by 1874, Monroe, Cowarden & Co.; and in 1879, Monroe & Hess. In 1890, it was sold to the United Glass Company. In 1895, the American Window Glass Company bought it and closed it.

Duncan & Dithridge During the early 1900s, this New York City company was an agent for many cut glass manufacturers and other glass companies.

Duncan & Heisey In 1866, Ripley & Company established a glass manufacturing facility to make table and bar goods, mainly pressed wares, in Pittsburgh, Pennsylvania. However, it did cut and engrave some glassware. In 1874, the company was operated by George Duncan & Sons. In 1876, it added novelty wares. In 1886, the operating firm was Duncan & Heisey, which operated it until 1889 when it became part of the U.S. Glass Company, known as *Factory D*. See *Duncan & Miller.*

Duncan & Miller Pall Mall ruby red and crystal swan, 12" l.
Heartland Discoveries

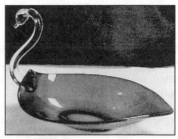

Duncan Miller opalescent hobnail top hat, 4" h.
Tri-State Antiques

Duncan & Miller ad introducing "The New Puritan," Pottery, Glass & Brass Salesman, May 1930.
Krause Publications

Duncan & Miller In 1874, George Duncan, his sons George and James, and his son-in-law, Augustus H. Heisey, established a partnership called George Duncan

& Sons, taking over the Ripley & Company facility (see *Duncan & Heisey*). George Duncan Sr. died in 1877. In 1886, the firm of Duncan & Heisey was formed by James E. Duncan and Augustus H. Heisey, who took over the facility. John Ernest Miller worked there as a designer and is credited with designing the most famous of all Duncan's glassware lines, *Three Face*.

In 1889, it became *Factory D* of the U.S. Glass Company and was destroyed by fire in 1892. At that time, Heisey moved to Newark, Ohio, setting up his own facility. Duncan built a new facility in Washington, Pennsylvania, and, in 1895, went into a partnership with John Ernest Miller, forming Duncan & Miller. In 1900, it reorganized as Duncan Miller Glass Company, continuing to make pressed glassware in such patterns as *Amberette, Duncan Flute, Button Arches, Zippered Slash*, etc., marketed under the name "Genuine Miller." In August 1955, the company's molds and equipment were sold to the U.S. Glass Company. One year later the facility was destroyed by fire.

Duncan & Sloan See *National Glass Factory*.

Duncan, George, & Sons See *Duncan & Miller; Duncan & Heisey*.

Dunmore Glass Company See *Vermont Glass Factory; Lake Dunmore Glass Company*.

Duquesne Glassworks A glass manufacturing facility built sometime after 1800 in Belle Vernon, Pennsylvania (then part of Virginia), by Kindall & Patten. It failed in 1834. In 1836, William Eberhart Sr. took over the inactive facility, making window glass and hollowware. In 1841, he constructed another facility. In 1853 or 1854, he failed and the facility stood idle for a short time before being taken over by George A. Berry & Co. In 1865, under new management, it became the Duquesne Glassworks. In 1876, the operating firm was R.C. Schmertz & Co. It was still operating in 1886.

Durand vase, c. 1920, pale yellow iridescent glass with applied thread decoration. The Corning Museum of Glass

Durand plate with green and white pulled center, unsigned, 8" d. Krause Publications

Durand, Victor Jr. See *Durand Art Glass; Vineland Flint Glass Works*.

Durand, Victor Sr. Born in France, he came to the United States in 1889 and worked for various glass companies, including Tiffany and Whitall-Tatum in Vineland, New Jersey. See *Vineland Flint Glass Works*.

Durand Art Glass An art glass suggestive of Tiffany or Steuben iridescent glass, made by Victor Durand Jr. from about 1912 to 1924 at the Vineland Flint Glass Works in Vineland, New Jersey. Durand was a descendant, on his mother's side, of the Baccarat family. He identified some of his work with paper labels while other pieces were signed "Durand" incised in script ("Durand" sometimes enclosed in a large "V"). Since Kimball was associated with the firm of Kimball & Durand, some glassware attributed to Durand was marked "K" with a loop on the vertical line of the letter and a hook on the lower part of the same line. Durand Art Glass was an iridescent glass with most of the embellishments applied in several designs or motifs, often commingled. Some designs are made by trailing fine threads over the surface or by pulling threads into the glass to form a pattern. Cutting and engraving, often on overlay glass, were also used.

Durhamville Glass Works A window glass manufacturing facility established in 1845 in Durhamville, New York, by DeWitt Stephens. In 1850, Fox & Gregory was operating it; in 1851, Fox Brothers; then Fox & Son; in 1859, Fox & Co.; and in 1876, DeLong & Co. In 1890 the United Glass Company took control. In 1895, the American Window Glass Company acquired it and closed it.

duster See *saltshaker.*

Dutch glass See *Netherlands glass.*

Dutch, Royal, Glassworks A glass manufacturing facility established in 1765 at Leerdam, near Rotterdam, which made ornamental ware and table glass. It is still an actively operating glassworks.

duty by weight A tariff levied on glass (by weight) in England in 1745, 1777, 1781, and 1787, which meant the heavier the ware, the greater the assessment. Therefore, makers tended to make smaller, lighter objects or to migrate to Ireland where a duty was not imposed.

Duval, Isaac, & Co. A flint, green bottle, and window glass manufacturing facility established in 1813 in Wellsburgh, formerly Charlestown, West Virginia, by Isaac Duval and Nathaniel and John Carr (one source spells the name *Carl*). The company also made quality cut lead crystal and green hollowware. In 1828, Duval died and the company closed. It was soon taken over by John and Peter Blankinsop and renamed the Riverside Glass House (Company). About 1838, they took on several partners, all glassmakers from Ireland. About 1842 the operater was Blankinsop, McCarty & Torreyson, and in 1879 it was managed by Charles Brady, John Dornan, J. Flannagan, and A. McGrail. The company joined the National Glass Company in 1901 and was closed the same year. In its final years it made mainly bottles and flasks. Many of its molds were sold to the Cambridge Glass Co.

Duycking, Ever(et)t Also spelled Duijcking, Duyckengk, Duyckinck, and Duyckink. He came from Holland to New Amsterdam (now New York City) about 1638 as an employee of the Dutch West India Company, which gave him a land grant. In 1640 he was stationed in Connecticut, but soon returned to New Amsterdam where he married in 1646, and settled in lower Manhattan. He painted portraits, painted and stained glass, and was a glazier and glassmaker. In 1654 he established a glass manufacturing facility in New Amsterdam (see *New Amsterdam glasshouses*). Here he made window glass and, possibly, some bottles and off-hand articles, later with his son Gerrit. In 1674 he sold it to Jacob Milyer (or Melyer). He died in 1702.

dwarf ale glass A small, short stemmed drinking glass, the bowl of which was usually of inverted conical shape. These glasses were made in England from the early 17th century to the early 19th century. Each has a capacity of about three or four ounces.

Dyott, Thomas and Michael See *Dyottville Glass Works; Kensington Glass Works.*

Dyottville Glass Works Originally called the Philadelphia & Kensington Glass Works, this company was a glass manufacturing facility established by Joseph Leacock and Robert Towers in 1771 in the Kensington district of Philadelphia. It was sold to John and Samuel Elliot, who made mainly bottles. It changed ownership many times over the next few years. About 1825 Thomas W. Dyott (1771-1861) acquired an interest in it and, in 1831, became its sole owner, changing its name to the Dyottville Glass Works about 1833. Dyott sold patent medicines, calling himself "Dr. Dyott," and became an agent for the Olive Glass Works of Glassboro, New Jersey, in 1817.

The Dyottville Glass Works made bottles and historical flasks, including those depicting the presidents of the United States and, from 1831, flint glass. Dyott went bankrupt in 1838 as a result of financial speculation and the facility was taken over by his brother, Michael, followed by many successive owners until after 1926. See *Kensington Glass Works.*

Ee

Eagle Cut Glass Company A glass cutting house established in 1908 in Minneapolis, Minnesota. It was still operating in 1918. See *Olson, Arthur.*

Eagle Glass & Manufacturing Company A glass manufacturing facility established in Wellsburg, West Virginia, in 1894 by the four Paul brothers, making novelty items in milk glass. In 1924, it closed its glass operations, continuing as the Eagle Manufacturing Company, making containers for the petroleum industry.

Eagle Glass Works (1) A window and bottle glass manufacturing facility established in 1799 in Port Elizabeth, New Jersey, by Thomas and James Lee with members of the Stanger family and local businessmen. James Lee left in 1806/07 to establish a facility in Millville, New Jersey, but he and Thomas did not sell their interest in the Port Elizabeth facility until 1810. By 1817, it was called the Eagle Glass Works, operated by Josiah, Harrison & Co.

In 1818, Samuel P. Weatherill purchased it and the Getzinger family operated it from then to 1846 when it was sold to Cooper & Townsend. Over the next few years, its ownership changed several times until sold at sheriff's sale in 1862. Samuel Townsend purchased it, leasing it to Mitchell & Irwin who operated it for several years before closing it. It sat idle for some time until John Focer reopened it, operating it until it was sold in 1881 to Whitney Brothers. They operated it until 1885, closing and abandoning it. (2) (Aka *Eagle Glass Co.*) A glass manufacturing facility established prior to 1821 in Pittsburgh, Pennsylvania. Between 1821 and 1852, it operated intermittently. In 1852, it was operated by Bobe & Albeitz or Bobo & Albeitz, making vials, bottles, and flasks. It was in operation at least through 1857.

ear(ed) cup or ear(ed) dish
See *porringer.*

ear trumpet A hearing aid shaped like a trumpet with a slight bend; some in the form of a tube about 14 inches long, having a rounded upper end with a small orifice and flattened everted rim. The end with the small orifice is placed to the ear while the trumpet end is directed toward the speaker, directing and amplifying the speaker's voice to the listener.

Early American Line A line of glassware made by Phoenix Glass Company from 1938 to 1943, consisting of pieces of milk glass decorated in blue and pink with a pearlized (lightly iridized) or caramel luster (heavily iridized) finish.

early Sandwich glass Glassware made at the Boston & Sandwich Glass Company, between 1825 and 1840, using a mold (rather than blown).

East Indies flowers See *Indianische Blumen.*

East Lake Glass Works A glass manufacturing facility established in 1885 in East Bridgeton, New Jersey, by Kirby & McBride.

East Liverpool Specialty Glass Company Incorporated in 1883 in East Liverpool, Ohio, it packed jelly into glass containers purchased from other companies. After financial problems, it reorganized and incorporated as Specialty Glass in 1888 and moved to Jeanette, Pennsylvania. See *Specialty Glass.*

East Middlebury Glass Company (1813-1817) A cylinder window glass manufacturing facility in East Middlebury, Vermont, by George Chipman and others, but soon sold to the owners of the Vermont Glass Factory.

East River Flint Glass Works See *Lafayette Flint Glass Works.*

East Wheeling Glass Works See *Oesterling, Henderson & Company; Central Glass Company.*

Easter egg An egg-shaped object, usually of blown glass, that was a favorite with children in the mid-1800s. Older ones were hand painted; plain ones of opaque white glass were also used to attract hens to a nest.

Ebeling, Philip A foreman of the mold department at Dalzell, Gilmore & Leighton who invented several processes involving lamps. In 1894, he invented a process by which lamp collars were forced over the glass rather than attached by plaster of Paris. In 1899, he invented a lamp-making machine (U.S. Patent No. 653,412) that made lamps in a continuous operation, reducing the need for skilled laborers and making a uniform product with less breakage. Prior to this the foot and font were made separately and fused while still hot.

Ebenezer Cut Glass Company (1915-1957) A glass cutting facility established in Ebenezer, New York, making only light cut wares.

Eberhart, Isaac P. See *New Geneva Glassworks.*

Eberhart, William, Sr. & Jr. See *Whiting & Eberhart; Duquesne Glassworks.*

ebony The color of glass that is black or appears black under reflected light.

Eclipse Tumbler Company (1912-1918) A glass manufacturing facility established in Lansing, Michigan, moving in 1913 to Findlay, Ohio, changing its name to Findlay Cut Glass Company.

Economy Tumbler Co. See *Morgantown Glass.*

ecuelle (*French*) A covered porringer with two flat pierced ears or handles.

Edelweiss cane A white star-shaped millefiore cane with a core of bundled yellow rods, having the appearance of a flower by that name.

Edenhall A Hawkes line of cut and engraved glassware, less expensive than its *Gravic* line, issued during the 1920s, its name being derived from the Edenhall Goblet.

Edenhall Goblet A goblet engraved for Hawkes by William H. Morse in 1920, depicting a king presenting a goblet to an individual with the words "Presentation of the Goblet" below.

edge (1) The narrow band between upper and lower rims of a plate or the inner and outer rims of a vase, bowl, or other hollow vessel. (2) The thin surface of an object where two plane surfaces meet, such as the edge of a box. See *beaded edge; rolled edge.*

Edison Lamp Company Thomas Edison, after years of experimenting in his laboratory in Menlo Park, New Jersey, discovered that thin fibers were adequate to act as filaments in an incandescent lamp if they were protected by a vacuum within a glass bulb.

The first bulb for the new "electric light" was blown by Frederick Douerlein at the Corning Glass Works in 1879. Over the next few years, light bulbs were made one at a time. It took two men to make each bulb. In 1898, the Edison Lamp Company was established in Menlo Park, New Jersey, to make light bulbs (mold blown) on a commercial basis. From then until 1915, very few improvements were made to the process, resulting in the bulbs being very expensive and their use restricted.

Edmonds, Bingham & Co. See *Zanesville White Flint Glass Manufactory.*

Edwards, Way & Company See *Washington Glass Works.*

Left: gold-decorated egg, ruby glass, 3-1/2" h; right: ruby-flashed on clear glass egg, cut-to-clear, 5" h.
Davanna Collection

egg An ovoid, egg-shaped object, usually blown, serving either as an ornament, a container, or a hand cooler, or had a practical purpose, being used in place of a real egg to attract a hen to a nest. As a container the shape and size of an egg, in towns where alcoholic beverages were banned, they were filled with alcohol, the contents being consumed through an opening in the pointed end. For ornamental purposes, eggs were made of all types of glass and were often elaborately embellished. See *Easter egg; hand cooler.*

egg and star border An ornamental border pattern consisting of repetitive ovals and stars.

Boyd pale green rooster eggcup, 4" h.
Davanna Collection

eggcup A small semi-ovoid cup resting on a stemmed foot, used for serving a soft-boiled egg, in the shell. Those commonly found today are from the 1840s through the 1870s with early pressed flint glass patterns, usually of colored or opaque white glass with a folded rim and occasionally a domed cover. Some were made in matching sets, suspended from a silver stand and, as companion pieces, small silver spoons and, at the top of the stand, a glass saltcellar.

egg frame A small metal, usually silver, silver plate, or gilt wash, stemmed open bowl or holder into which a glass liner (eggcup) was placed. See *eggcup.*

egg furnace A glass furnace developed around the shape of an egg by Heikki Kallio in Finland. It is considered a radical design,

claimed to have several advantages over traditional furnaces (easier to empty and clean, less likely to have cold spots because there are no corners, ability to better reflect radiant heat downward on the molten glass because of the three-dimensional arch at the top which is stronger than the traditional two-dimensional arch over a rectangular furnace).

egg knop A knop, either ovoid or egg-shaped, positioned vertically. It is one of the rarest knops, being one of the most difficult to make, and normally comprises the total stem.

Eggerman technique A copper wheel engraving technique so-named for the man who made it popular in Bohemia during the late 1700s. The glass is brought up from below and placed against the wheel with light pressure, as opposed to cutting where the object is placed against the wheel from the top.

Egginton, O.F., Company
See *Egginton family.*

Egginton & Brewster (1895-1901) Walter Egginton and G.H. Brewster purchased the Addison Mosaic Glass Co., in Addison, New York, adding a cutting department, making its own blanks.

Egginton family Born in 1822, Oliver F. Egginton was employed as a cutter for Thomas Webb & Sons in England before coming to the United States in 1865. His brother, Enoch, was superintendent of the Portland Glass Company, having previously cut glass at J. Hoare & Co. and Dorflinger's Greenpoint facility. Another brother, Joseph, headed the cutting department at Portland Glass Company. In 1867, these brothers plus another, Thomas, established the St. Lawrence Glass Company in Montreal, Canada. In 1873, Oliver became foreman for Hoare, working there until going to Hawkes. From 1893 until 1896, he and his nephew, Walter E., and son, Walter F., were employed there as cutters and designers.

In 1896, after declining an offer from Sinclaire to form a partnership, Oliver established the O.F. Egginton Company in Corning, New York, soon joined by his son Walter F. It was partial to the heavily cut designs popular during the Brilliant Period. Oliver died in 1900, and the company was taken over by Walter F., changing the name to Egginton Rich Cut Glass Company. It used an acid polishing technique that was very difficult to detect, giving a hand-polished appearance. It used the acid-etched signature of a star nearly encircled by a crescent with the word "Egginton" block printed on the crescent.; this trademark was registered on January 23, 1906. It purchased blanks from several companies here and abroad. It failed to go along with the trend toward lighter cutting. As a result, by February 1918, it was bankrupt. See *Egginton & Brewster.*

Egginton Rich Cut Glass Co. See *Egginton family.*

eglomise (French) Embellishing glass by applying gold leaf or, on occasion, silver leaf, or both, to an object and engraving it with a thin needle point. The object was not fired after engraving, and the embellishment was not permanent, so it was usually applied on the surface's reverse to be viewed, protected by a coating of varnish, metal foil, or another sheet of glass. Occasionally, there is supplementary background embellishment in black or color where the foil has been removed by etching. The term, *eglomise*, stems from the 18th-century French writer, artist, and art dealer, Jean Baptiste Glomy (or Glomi) (d. 1786), who used the process extensively. It had been practiced in ancient times by the Egyptians and Romans and later in Bohemia and Italy. See *verre eglomise; gold engraving; Zwischen-goldglas; Medaliionbecher.*

Egyptian blue or (faience) A ware made in Egypt, from before 3000 B.C., of ground quartz melted with an alkali, formed to the desired shape and coated with a glaze of a similar substance (copper calcium tetrasilicate) which was pulverized and colored to a characteristic blue with copper. The term *faience* is inappropriate since the object's body is not pottery and the glaze does not contain tin oxide as is the case with *glazed faience.*

Egyptian glass Not including the vitreous glass on stone and ceramic objects, and the so-called Egyptian faience (all made prior to 3000 B.C.) the earliest glass vessels known to exist are three small ones. They are presumed to be of Egyptian origin and bear the royal cartouche of Tuthmosis (Thothmes) III (1501-1447 B.C.). The vessels were made about 1470 B.C. in what is considered the first glass manufacturing facility of record. This was later than some objects made in Mesopotamia about 2000 B.C. It is believed the earliest glass products were made from fritted glass imported from Asia in the form of blocks, because the Egyptians at this time did not have the ability to make glass and the glassworkers were most likely brought there from Western Asia after combat victories there.

The making of glass objects in any quantity did not occur until the New Kingdom (the first era of the New Kingdom, the Eighteenth Dynasty—1580-1350 B.C.), especially from the reign of Amenophis, about 1390 B.C. The glass making centers were based in the larger urban areas, mainly Thebes, Tel el Amarna, Lisht, Gurob, and Menshiyeh. The shapes of early pieces varied extensively, animals and fish were common.

Many perfume bottles, oil bottles, and tiny jars were made, taking the forms of vessels of other materials. Generally they were small, used to hold cosmetics and toilet materials. Amulets and pendants of glass and colored glass imitating precious stones (used in jewelry) were made. Small-scale sculpture was made by the *cire perdue* process. Glassmakers experimented with the use of bright colors, using copper to produce turquoise, bluish green, and wine red; iron and manganese for deep black; finely divided silver for black; manganese for brownish purple and violet; cobalt for blue; antimony and tin oxide for opaque white; and antimoniate of lead for opaque, glowing yellow. By the mid-Ramesside period (c. 1200 B.C.) the Egyptians had perfected virtually all the glassmaking techniques that were to be used during the remainder of the dynastic period. Core glass was the predominant type of glass made until about 1150 B.C. when glass making began to decline. It wasn't until the founding of Alexandria in 322 B.C. that Egypt again saw the beginnings of a new glassmaking era. Alexandria is credited with making the first cased, flashed, and overlay glass. Almost all pre-blown glass has the appearance of pottery, often opaque or, at best, translucent.

Eichbaum, William Peter Descended from a family of glasscutters in Westphalia, he worked for Louis XVI in Paris and is believed be a founder of the glass village of St. Louis. In 1793, he came to the United States. From then until 1796, he is believed to have been Superintendent of the Schuylkill Glass Works. In 1797, he began work at O'Hara & Craig at their Pittsburgh Glass Works.

In December 1798, he, with partners and employees of the works, leased the facility and operated it as Eichbaum, Wendt & Company. Not being successful, in 1800, he left, opened a tavern and hotel and, as a side line, cut tumblers and decanters. In 1810 he went to work for Bakewell & Page as a glass cutter, introducing to the United States the German *Kugel*; a round concave cutting known as the *bull's-eye*; and the concave, hexagonal diamond motif which, when on the neck of a bottle was called the *St. Louis neck*. He is also credited with cutting the first crystal chandelier in America in 1810.

Eichbaum, Wendt & Co. See *Pittsburgh Glass Works.*

Eick, Peter A. (1875-1935) Born in Brooklyn, New York, his father, Joseph, was a glasscutter for Hoare & Daily. Peter went to work for Hawkes in 1885, working there until he opened his own shop in 1912 in Corning, New York. He used lead glass blanks from Union Glass Co. and Pyrex blanks from Corning. He did rich cuttings, floral cuttings, and monograms.

Eick, William B. A glasscutter in Corning, New York, cutting during the 1910s.

Eight Priests, Goblet of the An Islamic goblet of colorless glass with a bowl having enameled strapwork on a white beaded ground, resting on a European silver gilt foot (believed to have been made in the 13th or 14th centuries). The goblet itself is attributed to Raqqua, made during the late 12th/early 13th century. It was housed at the Douai Museum, destroyed during World War I, together with its French leather case. The coat-of-arms on the leather case suggests it was brought from Palestine by a Crusader in 1251.

A similar goblet is in the Museum at Chartes and another, later one, is in the British

Museum. Fragments of others are at the Victoria & Albert Museum in London.

Eisenrot *(German)* Literally, *iron red*. A stain formulated about 1500, used on stained glass windows.

El Mexicano See *Catalonian.*

electioneering glassware Plates, jugs, and other types of glassware inscribed with names and/or slogans of candidates seeking elective offices. Specimens are found in America, England, and other countries, with the design executed by diamond-point engraving, wheel engraving, enameling, pressing, etc.

Elector's Beaker See *Kurfurstenhumpen.*

Electrical Glass Company It purchased the vacant Boston & Sandwich Glass Company facility in Sandwich, Massachusetts, in October 1889. It held four patents: a glass insulator for telegraph poles, an electric lamp shade, a glass conduit for running electrical wires underground, and a window glass for skylights. It upgraded the facility and began making glassware like that of the Boston & Sandwich Glass Company, but closed after a few months.

electrofloat process See *float glass.*

elegant glass Better quality 20th century glassware of companies such as Heisey, Cambridge, Fostoria, etc., as opposed to the less expensive Depression glass of the same era.

Elgin Jug An egg-shaped claret decanter with a tall neck, a mouth with a pouring lip, one curved handle, and a stopper. Frederick E. Kny, a Bohemian artist working for the Dennis Glassworks of Thomas Webb & Sons, wheel engraved it and exhibited it, unfinished, at the Paris Exhibition of 1878 (it was completed in 1879). Its decoration consists of an encircling frieze in relief portraying an adaptation of a portion of the Elgin Marbles, featuring a contingent of horsemen from the Parthenon Freize, and encircling by bands of acanthus and reeding.

Elgin Vase An urn-shaped vase engraved by John Northwood (began in 1864, completed in 1873). It has an encircling frieze with an adaptation of a section of the Elgin Marbles featuring a contingent of horsemen from the Parthenon Frieze and encircling bands of acanthus, Vitrivian scrolls, and ivy leaves. It was commissioned by Benjamin Stone and made of clear glass at his facility, Stone, Fawdray & Stone, of Birmingham, England.

Elite A trademark of Gowans Kent Co., Canada, used on its cut glass.

Elite Cut Glass Manufacturing Company See *Clinton Cut Glass Company.*

Elixer of Life Bottle A flattened globular wine bottle with a flat bottom and an attenuated neck tapering upward to a narrow mouth. The neck is nearly concealed with thick spiral trailing. They have an inscription, in gilt, which means *Elixer of Life,* and made in Persia, probably at Qum, during the 18th and 19th centuries.

Elizabeth Furnace Glasshouse

(1763-1765) A glass manufacturing facility in Elizabeth Furnace, Pennsylvania, built by Henry William Stiegel. After he began operations at his Mannheim facility, it was closed. Its primary products were window glass, bottles, and hollowware. See *Stiegel, Henry William.*

Ellenville Glass Works (Aka *Ellenville Glass Factory*) A glass manufacturing facility organized and built by employees of the Willington Glass Works. It began operations in 1832 or 1836 (depending on the source) at Wawarsing in Ellenville, New York. It made bottles and some hollow ware. Depending on the source, it closed in 1852 or 1880.

Elliott & Gray See *Kensington Glass Works.*

Elliott, John, & Company See *Kensington Glassworks.*

El(l)wood City Glass Company In late 1898, the buildings, fixtures, and property of the Northwood Glass Company's El(l)wood City, Pennsylvania, facility were sold to the American Lamp & Brass Company of Trenton, New Jersey, operating it as Clark Brothers Glass Company. It reorganized in 1905 as the El(l)wood City Glass Company.

Elmer Glass Works See *Bassett Glass Works.*

Elmer Window Light Company A glass manufacturing company financed by the town of Elmer, New Jersey, in conjunction with the Clark Window Glass Company, Bridgeton, New Jersey. It was built in 1885 and sold in 1888 to Butcher & Waddington, closing in 1893; however, for a brief period in 1895 bottles were blown there. Shortly thereafter, Gibson & Elmer began blowing battery jars, but failed after a short time. In 1900, the Novelty Glass Company operated it, but it too failed (Novelty also operated the Bassett Glass Works in Elmer in 1901). See *Bassett Glass Works.*

Elmira Cut Glass Company (Aka *Elmira Glass Cutting Company, Ferris Brothers, Ferris Cut Glass Company*) A glass cutting facility established shortly before the turn of the 20th century, by John C., Joel, George R., and Frank E. Ferris, in Elmira, New York. It closed about 1911.

Elmira Window Glass Works (1896-1908) A window glass manufacturing facility in Elmira Heights, New York. The employees made canes about six feet long with large knobs on the end and spiraled with different colors, and paperweights. It is these ancillary objects for which it is best known.

Elson Glass Company A glass manufacturing facility established in 1882 in Martin's Ferry, Ohio, by William K. Elson (previously with the Central Glass Company and Belmont Glass Company), on the site of the Sweeney, McCluney & Co. facility, making pattern glass and lighting wares. In 1893, it was operated by workers from the Hobbs Brockunier glassworks (having closed), being renamed the West Virginia Glass Company. After labor problems during the depression of 1893, it closed. In 1896, it reopened as the West Virginia Glass Manufacturing Company. In late 1898, it joined the National Glass Company and, in 1902, severed relations with that combine, and was sold to the Crystal Glass Company. See *Ensell & Wilson.*

Ely, Reed & Co. See *Clyde Glass Works; Southwick & Woods.*

embossed glass Glass with an embossed relief decoration, usually made either by pressing a background pattern onto the surface or by etching it. Flat glass panels and windows used on commercial buildings are most commonly embossed. In its simplest form, the pattern was etched into the glass to a depth of about 1/10 inch and the recessed portion given a matted finish by abrasion. Another type, known as *French embossed glass*, involved a more complicated process creating a multiple shading of the pattern by treating the area to be embossed with acids of various strengths. Sections of the glass and pattern were progressively protected with an acid-resistant substance. French embossing is often combined with other decoration. The embossed side of the glass is placed so it is protected from the weather.

email en resille sur verre *(French)* A type of enameling on glass or rock crystal done during the early 17th century in France and neighboring areas. The designs most often used are flowers, scrolls, arabesques, etc., which are engraved on the glass. The depressions created by the engraving are lined with gold foil and filled with enamel having a low melting temperature. It was not popular, used for only a short time because of problems with fusing the enamel to the glass without having it melt or crack.

Emeralite lamp A lamp with a shade of emerald-green glass on the outside plated with white-opal glass on the inside, patented by Harrison D. McFaddin on May 11, 1909. They became popular because the light produced was reported to be restful on the eyes. They were made from 1909 into the 1940s in many shapes and sizes, most marked with the name. They have been reproduced but these and replacement shades are of lesser quality than the original because the fusion of the layers of green and white glass is poorly done and the edges are rough.

Emmett, Fisher & Flowers See *New England Glass Co.; Boston Porcelain & Glass Manufacturing Company.*

Empire See *Harcourt.*

Empire Cut Glass Company (1) Believed to have been a distributor or sales outlet for many small glass-cutting shops, it shared showrooms with the Rochester Cut Glass Company and Cut Glass Products (both believed to have been sales outlets and distributors) in Chicago, Illinois. (2) A glass cutting company established in the early 1890s in New York, New York. In 1904, it was sold to the H.C. Fry Glass Company, which moved the operations to Flemington, New Jersey. Its trademark, placed in label form on the glassware, consisted of its name surrounding an eagle with spread wings. It operated until 1925. Many of its designs and patterns were created by Louis Iorio. See *Iorio Glass Shop.*

Empire Glass Company (1) A glass manufacturing facility established in 1852, at Bern(h)ard's Bay, New York. It was still operating in 1877. (2) A glass cutting company in Cleveland, New York. (3) A glass manufacturing facility established during 1900 in Jeanette, Pennsylvania, making lighting glassware. In 1910, it was renamed Jeanette Shade and Novelty Company.

Empire State Flint Glass Works (1857-1895) A glass manufacturing facility established by Francis Thill, in Brooklyn, New York. About 1891, it was renamed Francis Thill Sons & Company. It made flint glass tablewares and some cut glass.

Empire style A variation of the Neo-classical style prevalent in France, from about 1800 to 1820, and which followed the *Directoire* style. It is analogous to the Regency style in England, often called the *English Empire* style, and characterized by flowery classical motifs, incorporating Egyptian motifs and others stemming from the Napoleonic campaigns. Mounting objects in gilt bronze continued and new decorative themes initiated.

empontil The use of a pontil for any of a variety of reasons. See *pontil.*

enamel A pigment of a vitreous nature, getting its color by the addition of a metallic oxide or oxides, and applied to glassware as a surface decoration by a firing process (see *enamel firing*). It differs from cold colors in that: (a) it is fused into the surface of the glass and not as readily affected by wear; (b) it results in a relatively smooth surface only slightly discernible to the touch; and (c) its final color is attained only after firing, not necessarily discernible on application. Enamel colors are either opaque or transparent and usually mixed with a flux to facilitate melting at a relatively low temperature (see *muffle kiln*). See *opaque enamel; transparent enamel; enamel colors; enamel firing; enameling; enameling lehr.*

enamel colors Colors applied to glassware by the technique of enameling, and subsequently fused to the object's surface at a relatively low temperature in a muffle kiln. They are metallic oxides blended with a frit of finely powdered glass, suspended in an oily medium to facilitate brush application. The medium is burned off and the actual colors develop during firing at a temperature of about 965-1300°F. In the early years, the colors were normally opacified with tin oxide. Later, about 1810, transparent enamel was formulated. It is extremely important that (a) the enamels fuse at a lower temperature than the glass (see *enamel firing*) or they will not properly fuse to the glass, and (b) the enamel and the glass have about the same ratio of contraction or the enamel will crack or raise from the surface. See *cold colors.*

enamel firing A relatively low-temperature firing of enameled glassware in a muffle kiln, to affix permanently enamel colors to the glassware (during the 16th century, Venetian and German enamels were fixed in an ordinary furnace). The enamels are blended with a flux, generally borax, to lower the fusing point below that of the glass so that its form will not be altered. Sometimes several firings are needed if different colors are applied.

enamel glass A term, sometimes misleading and incorrectly applied to opaque white glass made in the 18th century, because its appearance and composition (containing tin oxide) are similar to that of enameled or tin-glazed pottery. The term *enamel*, when used in conjunction with glassware, should be limited to the vitreous fusible pigment used for surface embellishment. See *enamel; enamel colors; glass cake; Nevers figure: Schmelzglas.*

Enamel Jewels Small objects made by Emile Galle in the mid-1880s in imitation of jewels; made by building up several layers of enamel on a metallic foil base and fusing it to a piece of glass.

enamel twist A twist made by using threads of opaque white or colored glass embedded in clear glass, as in making millefiore canes type, and twisting them.

Cobalt-blue enameled vases, 11" h.
Davanna Collection

enameling The process of embellishing glassware by using surface enamel. It dates to at least the 15th century B.C.; the earliest known being an Egyptian jug bearing the name of the Pharaoh Tuthmosis III. It was known in Roman times and used during the Islamic period in Egypt and Syria, in China in the 18th century, in Venice from the 15th century, and elsewhere from the 16th century. Most enameling, executed on modern wares such as bottles and domestic glassware is mechanized.

enameling lehr A lehr used to set or fix enamel. The primary difference between an annealing lehr and an enameling lehr is that the former has a hot zone where the object enters and is used to gradually cool the object, while the latter has a cold zone where the object enters and is gradually heated to a temperature of about 965° to 1300°F at which the enamel fuses into the glass and then is gradually cooled as in an annealing lehr.

encased glassware Objects of colored or overlay glass covered with a coating of clear glass, such as paperweights. Where overlay glass is involved, the correct term is *encased overlay*.

encased glassware, metal See *metal-encased glassware*.

encased overlay See *encased glassware; overlay glass*.

encased overlay paperweight A type of overlay paperweight cut with windows, printies, or other designs, and encased in clear glass. See *encased glassware*.

encasing process A process used for encasing the design of a paperweight. Once the millefiori canes, sulfides, or lampwork figures have been made, they are arranged on a metal template and heated to just below their melting point. A metal collar is then placed around the arrangement and a worker gathers a ball of molten glass on a pontil rod, rolling and working it into shape on a marver, and lowering it into the collar, picking up the preheated design.

After the design is picked up, it is reheated at the glory hole and another gather of clear molten glass is added, forming the dome of the weight. The worker rolls the pontil rod back and forth across the arms of his chair so the glass, still soft, will not sag and the dome is shaped and smoothed using a wet, concave wooden block or contoured pad made of newspaper. While still pliable, tongs are used to form a slender neck at the base of the weight. When it has cooled sufficiently, the worker gives the rod a sharp tap, causing the weight to break off and fall into a bed of sand. It is then annealed, ground, and polished. When desired, the dome is faceted or cut.

enclosed ornamentation (Aka *enclosure*) An embellishment in the interior of a solid piece of glassware, such as in many paperweights and some door stops.

enclosure See *enclosed ornamentation*.

encrusted cameo (Aka *cameo incrustation* or *crystallo ceramie*) A sulfide.

encrusted glassware Glassware having haphazardly attached to its body, and protruding from the surface, very small glass fragments applied after the piece was marvered and formed. It was frequently used on Roman glass produced from the 1st to the 4th century. See *flecked glassware; blobbed glassware; jewelled glassware*.

End-of-day cased satin glass comport, outer layer deep topaz, inner layer bright slashes of color, c. 1880, 3-3/4" h. x 6-3/4" d.
Tri-State Antiques

end-of-day glass (1) (Aka *off hand* or *off hand blown glass*) An American expression for *friggers*, made from glass left in the pots at the end of the day, after production is finished. Normally such glass would be discarded, later used as cullet. Instead some workers would take it and make various items, frequently one-of-a-kind or out-of-the-ordinary, for themselves or friends, or to be sold. The practice was common and sanctioned by management. (2) An incorrect term often applied to slag glass and spattered glass. While appearing to be made from glass left over at the end of the day, they were planned production glasses, made in quantity and quite popular during the latter part of the 19th century. See *slag glass*.

Englewood Cut Glass Company A glass cutting house established about 1917 in Chicago, Illinois, and operated into the 1920s.

English drinking glass Any of several types of drinking glasses used for specific beverages, such as wine, champagne, ale, toddy, etc., made in numerous shapes and sizes. The styles of the bowls, stems, knops, and feet changed from time to time, making it relatively easy to identify the date of production. Following is a summary of some of the distinguishing characteristics:

Major Stem Groups: Baluster (true and inverted), c.1685-1735; Plain, c.1730-1775; Air-twist, c.1745-1770; Opaque-twist, c.1755-1780; Faceted, c.1760-1810.

Minor Stem Groups: Molded pedestal or Silesian, c.1715-1765; Balustroid, c.1725-1760; Composite, c.1745-1770; Incised-twist, c.1745-1770; Mixed or color twist, c.1755-1775; Rudimentary.

Bowl shapes: Funnel; Bucket; Trumpet; Round funnel; Cup; Bell; Ogee; Double ogee.

Common knop shapes: Drop; Cylinder; Annulated; Bobbin; Acorn; Swelling.

Basic foot shapes: Folded conical; Domed; Plain conical; Terraced; Flat.

English glass and glassware

English glass dates from crude domestic glass made shortly after the Roman withdrawal. It wasn't until the arrival of Jacopo Verzelini and his Venetian workmen in 1571 that England was able to have its own source and supply of good-quality glass tableware. Verzelini obtained Royal authorization in 1575 when Queen Elizabeth I awarded him a license "to make drinking glass in the manner of Murano," with the agreement that he instruct Englishmen in the art. In 1615, an edict was issued forbidding the use of wood as fuel, but by then most furnaces had converted to coal, bringing about an improvement in the quality of glass, causing glasshouses to move from the forests to seaport cities where coal from Newcastle could be delivered.

From 1618 until the arrival of Oliver Cromwell (1599-1658), Sir Robert Mansell had the exclusive right to make glasswares, establishing glass making as an industry in England. About 1676, George Ravencroft introduced his new formula for making lead glass that was much more durable and softer than previous formulae without lead. This permitted deep cutting, having a much greater brilliance and richness, and permitted England to become an exporter. By the end of the 17th century, about 100 facilities were making lead glass. Glassware made from the end of the 17th century onward showed dramatic changes in shapes and styles, enabling a piece to be dated quite accurately. The following chart shows the progression of these shapes and changes with time:

Date	Medium	Bowl	Stem	Knop
1695	uneven, experimental, grayish tint	trumpet shaped	baluster shape, occasional rings and tear, heavy and simple	combination of cushion, pads
1705	improved and color, fewer imperfections, some cutting and engraving	simple funnel, trumpet, etc.	simple baluster, inverted baluster, pedestal	ball, cushion, acorn, egg, cylinder, annulated, angular, etc.
1710	more cutting and engraving, more colored glass, esp. cobalt blue	became thinner	became lighter into longer straighter pieces	often teared or shaped
1715	specialized glasses of all kinds		straight sided molded with decoration, Silesian	
1750	more cutting and engraving; popularity of sets of glassware; variety of colors	became smaller and simpler	straight with interior decoration	

English wine bottles

Glass bottles made solely for holding wine were first made in England about the middle of the 17th century, superceding the previously used earthenware bottles that were absorbent and susceptible to leakage, and even replaced the popular and more secure German 16th-century stoneware bottles. Early ones were made of thin green glass, but Sir Robert Mansell introduced, about 1630, bottles made of dark green or brown bottle glass, making wine bottles fashionable in England. They were initially used to transfer wine from the imported cask and later for binning wine. Their shape evolved over time from the *shaft-and-globe* bottle to one having much straighter sides, a more pronounced shoulder and a shorter neck; then came the *onion-shaped* bottle, followed, from about 1715, by the *slope-and-shoulder* bottle; and, about 1750, the *cylinder* bottle, still popular today. The last type became more advantageous after binning became a common practice with the innovation of the cork during the 16th and 17th centuries. The straight-sided bottles were more easily stored on their sides and the cork kept moist, becoming more popular after the invention of the cork screw about 1681, leading to the use of the *flush cork* as a replacement for the tied-on cork, secured by means of a string rim. See *wine bottle, sealed; Hogarth bottle.*

New England Glass Co. goblet, c. 1860-1870, clear, deep-blue cased glass.
The Corning Museum of Glass

engraved glass Glass embellished with engraving, reaching its pinnacle during the cut glass Middle Period from 1830 to 1876. Unlike the engraved soda-lime glass of the Early Period, the glass used during the Middle Period contained lead oxide, making it easier to engrave and giving it a more brilliant appearance. The designs were mainly mythological or historical scenes delineated in minute detail. See *graffito, vetro.*

engraved motifs Of the large number of engraved motifs, flowers were first in popularity, with the daisy being the preferred engraved motif. Each company seemed to have its own favorite flower; Sinclair preferred laurel; Tuthill the *Rosaceae* pattern with a cut rosette band; Hawkes the *Satin Iris*; and Fry the lily. The copper wheel permitted the engraver to execute more detailed designs in smaller areas. The more enterprising companies did not limit their output to flowers, but included scenes, human figures, portraits, animals, birds, and fish.

engraver's lamp See *water lens.*

engraving The process of embellishing glass involving cutting the design into the surface of the glass. There were various techniques available, such as: (a) diamond-point engraving, using a diamond or steel point in a manner similar to drawing with a pencil; (b) (copper) wheel engraving, using a copper wheel in conjunction with an abrasive such as pumice and linseed oil; and (c) stippling, by penetrating the surface of the glass just enough to make minute dots using an instrument with a steel or diamond point. Etching and sandblasting are other processes related to engraving. Some techniques akin to the work of the lapidary were also used in earlier times on glass in Egypt and Rome, and later in Venice, Germany, Bohemia-Silesia, Holland, France, and England.

Engraving was best done on glass of reasonable thickness producing a good brilliance when cut. As a result, the process developed into a fine art after the introduction, in Bohemia and Silesia, of chalk glass and in England of lead glass, both superceding the brittle, thin, and fragile Venetian soda-lime glass. See the following subjects on engraving: *diamond point; wheel; rock crystal; transfer; steel point; stone; reverse; cold; figured; Italian; Bohemian-Silesian; English; French; German.* Also see *stippling; stained glass, surface treatments; graffito, vetro; cut glass; Mattschnitt; Islamic glassware; high relief; Hochschnitt; incised.*

Ennion A glassmaker who, during the first quarter of the 1st century A.D. on the Syrian coast at Sidon, made some fine specimens of mold blown glass, some using three or four part molds (see *Sidonian glass*). He occasionally marked his name or "Ennion made it" on a pad on the vessels' handles, sometimes adding "Sidon" and sometimes his name, in Greek and Latin letters, is molded on the piece. Some objects inscribed with his name have been found in Italy; it being speculated he moved there at some time. There are 21 known pieces bearing his mark, including cups, jugs, and two-handled bowls, embellished with stylized plant forms and reeding.

Ensell & Cuthbert See *Clinton Glass Works.*

Ensell & Plunkett See *Virginia Green Glass Works.*

Ensell & Wilson A bottle glass manufacturing facility built in 1849 by Ensell & Wilson at Martin's Ferry, West Virginia. In 1852, the operating company became Wallace, Giger & Ensell, followed by Dites & McGranigan, then Hohn & Souner. It was purchased in 1861 by Sweeney & Co., making pressed, blown and cut glass tablewares. In 1863, Sweeney, Bell & Co. operated it, and in 1867/8, the operating company became Sweeney, McCluney & Co., closing it shortly thereafter. In the latter years it made blown, cut, and pressed glass wares, concentrating on bar goods, lamps, and candlesticks. See *Elson Glass Company.*

Ensell, Wendt & Co. See *Pennsylvania Flint Glass Works.*

Enterprise Cut Glass Company (1) Originally established in Honesdale, Pennsylvania, by George E. Gaylord, operating as the Enterprise Glass Company. In 1905, it moved to Elmira Heights, New York, changing its name to Enterprise Cut Glass Company. It got most of its blanks from Belgium, purchasing a few from Union Glass Company, Somerville, Massachusetts. One of its best-known patterns was *Rambler Rose*. It used no marks or signatures. It closed in 1917. (2) See *Figueroa Cut Glass Company.*

Enterprise Glass Company (1) See *Enterprise Cut Glass Company.* (2) See *Ballinger Glass Pail Works.*

Enterprise Glass Works A glass manufacturing facility established in Ravenna, Ohio, in 1878.

entry light A glass lantern, with square sides, placed or mounted near the front door of a house.

Diamond & Lace four-part epergne by Fenton. French opalescent with aqua crest, 12" d. x 11" h.
Tri-State Antiques

epergne *(French)* An elaborate centerpiece for the dinner table, normally including numerous small dishes, cruets, and salt cellars buttressed by branching arms, often furnished with candle nozzles. They became popular in the United States in the early 19th century. Many were made by the Sandwich Glass Company; however, the majority sold in the United States were made in Europe. Only a few specimens are signed.

Erhardt & Schaeffer (1895-1897) A glass cutting house in Syracuse, New York. In 1897, it became known as Schaeffer & Co.

Erickson Glass (1943-1961) A glass manufacturing facility established by Carl Erickson and his son in Bremen, Ohio, making cased lead glass objects, both pattern molded and freeform. Its products were marked with their name in diamond point.

Erlacher Glass Max Roland Erlacher was born in Austria in 1933 where he learned engraving, working for J. & J. Lobmeyr. In 1957, he accepted an offer to work for Steuben, engraving at first examples of the more difficult designs. He completed *The Hull* in 1957 and *Romance of the Rose* in 1977. Since 1952, even in Europe, he has had an engraving shop in his home. In 1975, he and his wife opened Erlacher Glass in Corning, New York. In 1977, he left Steuben to devote full time to his shop where he accepts commissioned work for copper wheel engraving. He has engraved limited edition paperweights for the Paperweight Collectors Association and cut a presentation piece for Baccarat. He made a moderately priced tableware in *Vintage* and *Stars & Stripes* patterns. He got many of his blanks from the West Virginia Glass Specialty Company. On light cut wares, he uses the *Shamrock* label for his signature.

Erskine Glass & Manufacturing Company
A glass manufacturing facility in Wellsburg, West Virginia, affiliated with the Consolidated Lamp & Glass Company, operating about the same time.

Eska Manufacturing Co. A glass cutting house in Baltimore, Maryland, using the trademark *Vestalia*.

essence pots or vases See *cassolette*.

Essex Glass Works A glass manufacturing facility established in 1787 in Boston, Massachusetts, by Robert Hewes, Charles F. Kupfer, Richard Hunnewell, Samuel Whalley, and Edward Payne, the official name being the Boston Crown Glass Manufactory. The General Court of Massachusetts, in that year, granted it the exclusive right to make glass in the State for a period of 15 years. After a series of trials and errors, cylinder glass making in volume got under way in 1793, quite successfully. In 1809, it reorganized under the name Boston Glass Manufactory. See *Boston (Crown) Glass Manufactory*.

Estelle (Estellville) Glass Works
(1825-1877) John H. Scott established a window and bottle glass manufacturing facility in Estellville, New Jersey. In 1834, Daniel Estelle purchased it, and in 1868, it was operated by Getzinger & Rosenbaum. In 1875, Alexander H. Sharp purchased it, closing it in 1877 because of a fuel shortage and competition from the coal-fired glass furnaces in Pennsylvania.

etching (Aka *acid etching, acid engraving*) Embellishment on the surface of glass by hydrofluoric acid, varying from a satin mat finish to a deeper rough effect. The process involves covering glass with an acid resistant wax, etc., (a) removing a portion of it, (b) scratching through it with a sharp tool, creating a design, or (c) printing the pattern on stone or metal, transferring it to paper and pressing the resultant inked pattern against the object to be etched. The object is then exposed to a mixture of hydrofluoric acid, with potassium fluoride and water, etching the exposed design into the body. The depth of the etching varies with the concentration of, and the time of exposure to, the acid. Hydrofluoric acid was not generally used for etching glass until the middle of the 19th century, although it was discovered in 1771. During the 19th century, the process was used to embellish thin tableware, not suitable for wheel engraving. It was later used by Emile Galle and his followers to facilitate engraving in high relief (the process being used to quickly eat away large background areas, leaving the area of relief to be engraved raised). It is also used on modern architectural glass to produce textures and patterns. The process is gradually being replaced by sand blasting because of hazards associated with the use and handling of the acid. See *satin glass; etching, color; etching, satin; double etching*.

etching, color A combination of hydrofluoric and sulfuric acid, in addition to other chemicals, used to do acid cut-back work on cased glass to expose the underlying color.

etching, satin The use of hydrofluoric acid as an etching agent to create a surface on glass with a satin appearance.

etching cream (Aka *Sugar Acid*) A cream used for etching glassware. It is much safer to use than hydrofluoric acid, but still hazardous, usually consisting of a mixture of ammonium bifluoride, barium sulfate, demineralized water, and sugar (to increase the viscosity).

Etna Glass Works See *New Bremen Glass Manufactory; Amelung, John Frederick*.

Etruscan style decoration A style of decoration imitating that on ancient Etruscan pottery, employed by W.H., B. & J. Richardson of Stourbridge, England, about 1850, depicting figures and floral designs in black enameling.

etui *(French)* A small case fitted with miniature implements, such as scissors, needles, a knife, etc. They are of various shapes and daintily embellished and mounted with gilt hinges and collars.

etwee An antiquated way of spelling *etui*.

Eureka Art Glass Company
See *Blenko Glass.*

European "Art" Glass Art glass made in Europe and frequently confused with the works of Tiffany or Steuben. Since many makers of good art glass did not sign their works, this fact only adds further to the confusion, being sold as "unsigned Tiffany," etc.

Evangelists, The Four See *Apostelglas.*

Evans, Thomas A. See *Mastadon Works.*

Evans & Company; Evans, Thomas, & Co. See *Crescent Glass Works.*

Evans, Schreve & Roberts See *Waterford Glass Works.*

Evans, Sell & Company See *Crescent Glass Works; Fahnstock, Fortune & Company.*

Evans, Thorpe & Co. See *Wood, R.D., Glass Works.*

Everhart See *Baltimore Glass Works.*

everted Turned outward in shape, such as the lip of a jug, pitcher, or sauceboat, or the rim of some vessels.

ewer A jug, usually tall with a sphere- or egg-shaped body and long neck, resting on a flaring base, having one large loop handle extending from the shoulder to, or above, the rim with a pouring lip. On occasion they have a spout extending upward from the body's lower part and fastened to the upper part by a bridge. They are sometimes accompanied by a basin *en suite*. Some have been made of glass, especially marbled or opaline glass. See *ampulla; Irish glassware, jugs and ewers; nef ewer.*

ewer and basin A large pitcher with a matching basin.

excavated glass See *scavo, vetro.*

Excelsior Flint Glass Company
See *Excelsior Glass Works.*

Excelsior Glass Company See *Foster Brothers Glass Works.*

Excelsior Glass Works (1) (Aka *Capewell & Brothers, James G. Capewell Works, Bamford Glass Works, Kaighn's Point Glass Works*) A glass manufacturing facility established in 1841, in Camden, New Jersey, by John and James G. Capewell and John Bamford, making flint glass: blown, pressed, plain, cut, and engraved. Between 1841 and 1857, various members of the Capewell family were associated with the facility. In 1857 it was sold at sheriff's auction. From 1859 to 1864 the following operated it: Union Glass Manufacturing Company; Cochran & Company; Bowman & Chisholm: Thomas Burnes; and U.S. Glass Works. In 1865 Duffield & Company took over, making tableware, lamp shades, and drug, confectionery, and perfume bottles. Soon thereafter, it closed.

(2) A glass manufacturing facility established by Francis and James Plunkett in 1856, in Birmingham, Pittsburgh, Pennsylvania, making window glass and glassware. In 1859, the operating firm was Wolfe, Plunkett & Company and, in 1863, Wolfe, Howard & Company, making lamp chimneys and other flint glassware. Also in 1863, the company added a second facility, operating it as Excelsior Flint Glass Company, making silvered glass reflectors. Both facilities were still operating in 1886.

(3) See *South Wheeling Glass Works.*

(4) (1878-1899) A glass manufacturing facility established by Michael Sweeney in Wheeling, West Virginia, in 1878. In 1879, Henry Helling became its principal stockholder and agent, moving it to Martin's Ferry, Ohio, operating as Buckeye Glass Company. It was one of the first to introduce colored pressed tableware about 1884. Harry Northwood was enticed from LaBelle in April 1887 to work here. He left after one week, returning to LaBelle for more money and a promotion. It was destroyed by fire in 1894 and immediately rebuilt. In 1895, George Duncan became its president.

Exeter Flute A flute glass made to commemorate the Coronation of Charles II

(1660) and most likely engraved for a banquet at Dorchester in 1665 to honor his visit. It is diamond point engraved with a likeness of Charles II, the inscription "God Bless King Charles II" and a stump of an oak tree with a sprouting branch (the oak stump representing the beheading of Charles I; the sprout representing the Stuart Restoration under Charles II). The Exeter Museum, the owner, has records indicating it may have been engraved by Christof le Jansz, a Dutch engraver, but no record indicating that it was ever used at Exeter. A comparable flute, but without the sprouting oak stump is in the Toledo Art Museum, Toledo, Ohio, believed to be made in the Netherlands, engraved between 1660 to 1680; and still another, but with only the engraved coat-of-arms of Charles II, exists.

exotic birds A decorative motif portraying various exotic birds, originally used as an embellishment on Meissen porcelain and called *Fantasie Vogel*.

expanded diamond See *ogival; expanded glassware.*

expanded glassware Glassware, which after being shaped in a mold, was enlarged by blowing, before any further enhancement by manipulation. Examples are American specimens with *expanded vertical ribbing* or *expanded diamonds*, especially Stiegel-type glassware.

experimental piece A glass article made as an experiment. Usually these are trial pieces for a new line or new finishes on an existing line.

Exposition Glass Works See *Glass Manufacturers Exhibit Company.*

extrinsic decoration Various styles and types of superfluous embellishment added after a piece has been shaped and annealed.

extrusion The pushing of hot glass through a die to make tubing or rods of a particular shape or dimension. This can be done through automatic pressing and blowing operations.

Eyden & Handel See *Handel & Co.*

eye (1) The grate's center in the siege of the glass furnace; the furnace's hottest part. (2) A hole in the side of a glass furnace used to keep the blowpipe and pontil hot and ready for use. (3) The hole, or *occhio*, in the floor of a lehr through which heat is transmitted. (4) The colored tip or pearl on the prunts of some Nuppenbecher and other 15th and 16th century Antwerp and German glassware. See *glass eye; glass with eyes; Littledon, Harvey K.*

Eye bath, cobalt blue, 2-1/2" h.
Davanna Collection

Boyd eye bath (eye cup), cobalt blue.
Davanna Collection

eye bath (Aka *eye cup*) A small cup-like vessel with a concave rim made to conform to the shape of the eye, usually resting on a stemmed foot. It is similar to an eggcup, only smaller. Some have a sphere-like reservoir between the cup and base.

eye bead A bead (one of several varieties, all looking slightly like an eye) almost always used as a talisman (an object supposed to possess occult powers and worn as an amulet or charm). The major varieties are: (a) spot beads (each with a single piece of glass of one color attached to or pressed into the surface); (b) stratified eye beads (each with a piece of colored glass pressed into the surface and another fastened to it, and so on); (c) ring eye beads (each with a ring or rings of glass of different colors pressed into the surface); and (d) cane eye beads (each with a slice of cane pressed into the surface). The spot and stratified varieties were made as early as 1300 B.C., the ring type about the 9th century B.C. and cane type about the 6th century B.C. and all continued to be prevalent during Roman times. They were also made in China in the 4th and 3rd centuries B.C. and considered to be the earliest form of Chinese manufactured glass.

eye cup See *eye bath.*

eye glasses See *vision aids.*

eye miniature A small painting of a loved one's eye mounted in a ring, locket,

broach, etc. They were popular for a short period during the late 18th century and are often mistaken for Masonic jewelry, the eye being highly symbolic to the Order of Free & Accepted Masons.

eye paint phial A thin vertical tube about 3 inches tall, to hold eye paint (*kohl*), sometimes accompanied by a glass rod used to apply it. They were made in Egypt about 1380 B.C.

Eygabroat-Ryon Company Incorporated (1901-1913) A glass cutting house established in Lawrenceville, Pennsylvania. About 1907, Ryon bought out Eygabroat and changed the name to Ryon Cut Glass Company, purchasing its blanks from Pairpoint and Dorflinger. In 1908, Ryon purchased the former Standard Cut Glass Company in Corning, New York, operating a glass cutting shop there until 1911.

Ff

fable glassware Glassware with enameled decoration depicting animals and figures from various fables, such as *Aesop's Fables*.

Fabric Glass A Tiffany Favrile iridized glassware.

face glass A mirror or looking glass.

facet The level or concave surface formed when the side or top of an object is shaped with a flat or rounded grinding wheel.

faceted bowl A bowl of a drinking glass of any shape embellished with faceting.

faceted glass Glass of any type other than flat glass, embellished by grinding to flatten or nearly flatten a portion of the surface area, considered a type of cut glass. *Soda glass* is not appropriate for such cutting because of its brittleness. However, *potash glass* and *lead glass* are frequently faceted. Many drinking glasses have faceted stems with a series of vertical connected plane surfaces surrounding it, called a *flat cut stem*. It is called a *faceted stem* if it is *scale faceted* or *hexagon faceted*. Some glassware is embellished with shallow circular concavities or *printies*. Not only are stems faceted, but also handles and knops. Some faceting has been noted on Roman glass and on Middle Eastern glass made as early as the 8th century. See *beveled glass.*

facet(ed) paperweight A paperweight having a surface decoratively cut, generally in facets, printies, or flutes. In addition, the bottom often has star cutting, or hobnail or strawberry diamond patterns. Some have cutting over the entire surface, usually in the form of graduated facets of hexagonal, square (called *brick*), or honeycomb shape. Others are faceted only on top or around the lower part. When the dome is cut in facets, it increases the reflections, makes it glisten more, and produces a kaleidoscope effect.

faceted stem A stem embellished by faceting of various types. Some have vertical connected plane surfaces surrounding the stem; others have a diaper style, diamond facets (higher than wide); connecting hexagons; or scale or shell faceting. On occasion, a single knop may occupy the center of the stem with the faceting continuing over it. Faceted stems were fashionable on English glasses from about 1750 to 1810.

faceting A style of embellishment of three predominant types: (a) *circular* in the form of small circular concavities; single, in bands, and overall; (b) *hexagonal* by forming a diaper pattern of vertically placed lengthened hexagons used on the stems of some English drinking glasses; and (c) *scale* in the form of overlapping scales resembling the enameled scale ground used on the stems of some English drinking glasses (see *imbricated*).

facon de Venise, a la Literally, *in the style of Venice*. It applied to high-quality glassware made throughout Europe, often by emigrant Venetian glassworkers, especially to the thin soda glassware embellished in filigrana or with elaborate decorations made from the mid-16th century through the 17th century.

factory mark A mark or inscription placed on glassware indicating the facility that made it. They are generally impressed, scratched, etched, or engraved on the bottom (most often on the outside) of the piece, but have been placed elsewhere on it, such as on the handle, etc. Many U.S. facilities used paper labels for identification, most of which have worn off or been removed over the years. Many chose not to mark their products at all.

Fahnstock, Albree & Co. See *Pittsburgh Glass Works.*

Fahnstock, Fortune & Co. A glass manufacturing facility established during the mid-19th century in Birmingham, Pittsburgh, Pennsylvania, making lamp chimneys, vials, etc. It was eventually sold to Evans, Sell & Company and was still operating in 1868.

faience A mixture of quartz sand and an alkaline substance which, when covered by a vitreous glaze, can be molded, cast, or even thrown on a wheel. It is unrelated to the tin-glazed faience of Europe. Scientifically, glass is similar to faience.

Fairfax Cup A tumbler with sides sloping slightly inward toward the bottom. Made of opaque turquoise glass that appears red when viewed by transmitted light, it was embellished with a scene depicting a fountain and figures from the legend of Pyramus and Thisbe in blue, green, and yellow enameling. Also, two gilt bands encircle the cup, one above and one below the scene. It was made at Murano about 1480, and has been in the Fairfax family since before 1643.

Fairton Glass Works (1892-1905) A glass manufacturing facility founded by Furman R. Willis and Azariah More in Fairton, New Jersey. Known as the Willis-More Company, it made snuff bottles, soda and beer bottles, mineral water bottles, and other containers. In 1896 it was renamed the Jefferson Glass Works.

Fairview Glass Works See *Virginia Green Glass Works.*

Mosser ruby glass fairy lamp, 5-1/2" h. Davanna Collection

Fairy Lamp (Aka *Clarke's Patented Pyramid Night Light, squatty candle, mortar, vigil light, Fairy Night Light*) A lamp of two parts, a special candle and a shade—small, domed shaped, with a vent hole at the top—originally made by Samuel Clarke who, between 1886 and 1892, made candles and tapers. He patented the shade in several countries and licensed glassmakers in England, Europe, and the United States to make them. The prime licensed maker in the United States was the Phoenix Glass Co., Monaca, Pennsylvania. In the late 1880s, Lazarus & Rosenfield of New York City imported them from Bohemia. The shades were made of every type of glass in a variety of colors and styles. Some had a satin or quilted surface and some were made in novelty form, such as animals. The special candles were of wax with a double wick of twisted rush, burning from four to eleven hours. The lamps were used on tables, attached to chandeliers and candelabra, or positioned under food warmers. There are some small kerosene lamps holding a small amount of kerosene also called *Fairy Lamps* (rare). See *Cricklight.*

Fairy Night-Light See *Fairy Lamp.*

fake A piece of genuine old glassware that has had its body or embellishment(s) changed in some way for the sole purpose of deceptively enhancing its value. See *forgery; reproduction.*

Falcon See *Falcon Glassworks.*

Falmouth Glass Works The United States Glass Company, incorporated on February 16, 1849, established the Falmouth Glass Works at Falmouth, Cape Cod, Massachusetts. The company made tableware.

Familienhumpen (*German*) Literally, *family beaker.* A Humpen or Stangenglas embellished with an enameled representation of a couple and their children arranged by ages and, in most cases, inscriptions indicating the name and age of each family member. Sometimes, instead of actual figures, there is a representation of the family tree. They were made during the 17th and 18th centuries, primarily in Franconia.

family beaker See *Familienhumpen.*

fan cutting (Aka *shell border; fan escallop*) A line cut glass motif generally found on the scalloped rim of a bowl, consisting of a series of short mitered lines radiating from a central point, having the appearance of an open fan. Sometimes it is extended from a simple fan to form a semi-circle. See *shell border; flashed fan.*

fan escallop See *fan cutting; shell border.*

Opalescent hobnail fan vase, Fenton's Topaz, c. 1930s.
Heartland Discoveries

Farber Bros. Compote, green glass liner, 5" d., nude stem, overall 8" h., signed. Patent # 87496/ 1924011 on two lines.
Davanna Collection

fan vase A vase generally from about 1-1/2 to eight inches tall with a narrow bowl with two (front and back) parallel sides. From the front or back it is shaped like a triangular fan with a slightly convex rim. The bowl is usually separated from the base by one or more knops. They are usually made of clear or colored glass, sometimes embellished with bubbles or an engraved pattern. The best examples were made by Frederick Carder during the 1920s.

Farber Brothers Louis and Harry (d.1929) Farber, born in Russia and educated in Europe,

came to the United States and worked for their brother's firm, S.W. Farber Company, in Brooklyn, New York. The company made nickel- and silver-plated hollowware and aluminum, brass, and copper goods sold under the trade name "Farberware." In 1915 Louis and Harry established Farber Brothers in New York City to make quality hollowware and brass goods at competitive prices. In the 1920s, the development of chromium plating resulted in the company changing to chromium-plated wares and plated wares (first silver and nickel, then chromium) with glass and ceramic inserts. In 1932 it received a patent for a *clip-on/clip-off* holder for its glass and china inserts, allowing broken or chipped inserts to be replaced easily. This combined with the chromium, which required no polishing, created incredible sales during the mid- to late 1930s. Items sold under the name *Krome-Kraft.* In 1935 it purchased the Sheffield Silver Company of Jersey City, New Jersey, moving operations there. While owned by Farber Brothers, Sheffield remained a separate company, making sterling and silver plate items with glass inserts using the *clip-on/clip-off* design.

World War II was a difficult time for them because metals and other raw materials were needed for the war effort. After the war, production resumed, but America's tastes had changed and sales began to decline. More emphasis was placed on Sheffield as silver began to replace chrome in the giftware market. During the 1950s and early 1960s, sales declined further. Farber Brothers closed in 1965, but Sheffield remained in operation, continuing to make quality silver-plated ware in Jersey City until 1973 when it was sold to the Reed & Barton Silver Company of Taunton, Massachusetts. The primary supplier of the glass inserts used by Farber Brothers was Cambridge Glass Company until it closed in 1958, then Morgantown Glass Works supplied them. Corning Glass made *Pyrex* inserts for serving dishes for heated foods. Some of these inserts were engraved by J. Hoare & Co.; later ones were engraved by Corning.

Farm Yard Assortment Covered dishes made by Challinor, Taylor & Company, *Factory C* of the United States Glass Company, about 1895. They included a duck, rooster, hen, swan, and eagle in the form of covered dishes and a pickle dish in the form of a fish.

Farmer's Glass Manufacturing Co.
(1814-1815) A cylinder glass manufacturing facility in Clarksburgh, Berkshire County, Massachusetts.

Farrell & Bakeoven See *Kensington Glass Works.*

fascis A bundle, as in a bundle of glass rods. See *millefiori.*

fauna paperweight A paperweight in the form of, or has imbedded within, an animal, reptile, insect, etc.

Favrile See *Tiffany Favrile.*

Favrile Fabrique See *Tiffany Favrile Fabrique.*

feather glass A cathedral glass made by sandblasting the surface, then applying hoof and horn animal glue and placing it in a dryer oven or on a rack. As the glue dried, it contracted, pulling tiny slivers of glass away from the surface. The result was a pattern with the appearance of a fern or feather with intermittent and irregular sandblasted areas. Glass to which one application of glue has been applied is called *single chip*; glass with two applications, *double chip*, has a more crystalline surface. It was made extensively during the Victorian era in a moderate range of colors.

feather holder An object designed to hold a feather. Examples were made of glass in China during the Ch'ing Dynasty from about 1662.

feathered decoration An embellishment on ancient core glass similar to combed decoration, making a zigzag pattern. It is also found on some Islamic and Spanish glassware made after the Roman era. See *feathering.*

feathering (1) Small miter cuts used to outline a motif, radiating from its edge. (2) Embellishment in which applied bands of colored glass are pulled from the body with a special bent tool, forming fine pointed hooks. It was frequently used on ancient core glass. See *feathered decoration.*

Federal Glass Company "Soup'n Sandwich" snack set, four plates and four cups, heatproof milk glass.
Davanna Collection

Federal Glass Co. fruit dish, green, Patrician pattern.
Davanna Collection

Federal Glass Company (1901-1979)
A glass manufacturing facility established in Columbus, Ohio. During the late 1920s it began making green restaurant supplies, tumblers, kitchenware, and tableware. Early wares bear the Federal trademark, a capital "F" within a shield. In 1931 it made its first mold etched pattern, *Georgian*, and in 1934 its first chipped mold design, *Mayfair*. In the late 1930s it used the paste mold method to make two other patterns, *Heritage* and *Columbia*.

Federal Hill Works See *Baltimore Glass Works.*

Federal lamp (Aka *feeder lamp*) A lamp invented in 1820 that allows the user to refuel it safely while being used.

Federzeichnung Glassware with brown glass sections and trails of gold on a satin finish, made in Germany during the late 1800s.

feeder A mechanical device used to make and deliver gobs of glass to a glass feeding device. It consists of a channel of refractory materials connected to the front end of a glass melting tank furnace. This channel, or *forehearth*, conditions the glass before it enters the feeding device, ensuring uniformity of temperature and viscosity. After passing through it, the glass enters the feeding device consisting of a round basin with a hole at the bottom, called the *orifice ring*. Above this is a large-diameter, rotating refractory tube that can be raised or lowered. This tube, or *sleeve*, controls the rate of flow (the nearer the orifice ring, the smaller the amount of glass able to flow through). Inside it is a reciprocating, refractory plunger. The stream of glass is allowed to flow down through the orifice ring and, as the plunger moves down, it forces extra glass through it, thickening the stream, resulting in a stream with regular thickenings flowing out. Below the orifice ring is a pair of automatic shears that sever the stream into gobs of glass, dropping them into molds. Dropping two gobs at a time—*double gobbing*—into two waiting molds is a normal practice. *Triple gobbing* is becoming common, and *quadruple gobbing*—four gobs at a time into four—is also being practiced.

feeder lamp See *Federal lamp.*

Grouping of nursing bottles, T.C. Wheaton Glass Company, Millville, NJ, 1880-1920. Museum of American Glass at Wheaton Village, Millville, NJ.

feeding bottle (1) A boat-shaped vessel totally enclosed except for two openings: a hole in the top for filling and controlling the flow from it by use of the thumb, and a small projecting tube for dispensing the contents either directly or through an attached nipple. They were used for feeding infants and invalids from about 1840. Made of clear glass, they are generally plain, although some ornate ones exist. (2) An upright bottle, a forerunner of the modern baby feeding bottle, usually cylindrical or pear-shaped. Some have a glass feeding tube extending through the stopper, down to the bottom of the bottle to prevent the feeding baby from sucking air. See *dropper flask.*

feeding cup A cup with a spout and partially covered to prevent spilling, designed for feeding children and invalids. The spout is normally straight on early examples, curved on later ones, with a loop handle at right angles to the spout. See *Halfdecker glassware.*

Feeney & McKanna (1906-1928) A glass cutting facility in Honesdale, Pennsylvania. In 1914 it became McKanna Cut Glass Company, purchasing blanks for heavy cutting from Fry, Libbey, McKee, Fostoria, U.S. Glass, Westmoreland, Corning, and Williamsburg Flint Glass Company, and for light cutting from Heisey, Mound City, Central Glass, and Duncan & Miller.

feldspars A group of minerals, principally *aluminosilicates* of potassium, sodium, and calcium. They are a cheap, pure, fusible source of aluminum oxide, containing all the necessary glass-forming oxides. The aluminum content serves to lower the melting point of glass and retard devitrification. They have the general formula $R_2O.Al_2O_3.6SiO_2$, where R_2O represents Na_2O (sodium oxide), K_2O (potassium oxide), CaO (calcium oxide), or any mixture of them.

Felix Fecit Bottle See *Frontinus bottle.*

felt wheel A wheel of compressed felt used with a fine abrasive powder to polish glass.

fenici, vetro (Italian) Literally, *phoenix glass.* Glassware with bands of opaque white glass (lattimo) manipulated with a special tool (*maneretta*) to create a pattern of white waves, festoons, feathers, or ferns. It is reminiscent of ancient glassware with combed decoration made with colored bands contrasting with the color of the body (termed *vetro a pettine* or *vetro a piume*).

Fenton animals

Fenton animals Animal forms made in over 100 colors by the Fenton Art Glass Company.

Fenton, Frank Leslie (1880-1948) Born in Indiana, Pennsylvania, he graduated from high school as valedictorian in 1897 and apprenticed at the Indiana Glass Company, becoming a foreman in 1898. In 1900 he began work at the Jefferson Glass Company, then later at the Bastow Glass Company. When it was destroyed by fire, he moved to Northwood Glass in Wheeling, West Virginia. In April 1905 he decided to form his own company with his brother, John, raising cash by selling stock and opening a decorating shop that became the Fenton Art Glass Company.

Fenton ad showing several examples of Fenton Art Glass wares, 1962.
Krause Publications

Fenton Art Glass Company

(FAGCO) Established in 1905 in Martins Ferry, Ohio, by Frank (1880-1948) and John (1869-1934) Fenton as a decorating shop (mainly cut glass) using blanks purchased from others. Another brother, Charles H., who had worked for Northwood, soon joined them. In 1907 the company moved to Williamstown, West Virginia, and began making its own glass. In 1909 John Fenton left over a policy dispute and organized his own company, the Millersburg Glass Company. Another brother, Robert C., joined the company in 1910.

FAGCO was famous for its early carnival glass (called *Iridill*) made between 1907 and 1920 in over 150 different patterns. It also made custard glass, chocolate glass, opalescent glass, stretch glass, and colored depression glass. Free-hand or off-hand pieces made without molds were introduced in 1925, an unprofitable venture that was discontinued in 1927. Between 1910 and 1926, sales increased steadily, except during World War I when raw materials, natural gas, and manpower were in short supply. To help relieve the manpower shortage, boys and women were hired. The first time women were hired to work in the hot metal department. Its peak year was 1922.

From 1927 through 1938, Fenton experienced several years of losses or marginal profits. Two major accounts—A.F. Dormeyer and Allen B. Wrisley, both of Chicago, Illinois—helped it survive. In 1939, with the advent of World War II, business picked up dramatically as imports from Europe fell as companies had to stop exports, shift production to the war effort, or close for lack of raw materials. Even though it lost many of the customers it gained during the war, 1944 through 1948 were Fenton's biggest sales years of the decade. It started 1947 with a year's backlog of orders. However, by the end of the year, as the market changed, the backlog was eliminated.

Charles Fenton died in 1936, James E. in 1947, and Frank L. and Robert C. in 1948. With the passing of the first generation, the next took over. It included Frank L. Fenton's sons, Frank M. and Wilmer C., and Robert C. Fenton's son, Robert C. Jr. Sales increased in the late 1950s-early 1960s and have continued to grow over the years with yet another generation of Fentons in leadership positions.

Various paper labels have been used since the 1920s, but the vast majority of these have disappeared over time. Only since 1967 has the logo been stamped into the glass. See *Fenton animals.*

fern ash Ash obtained by burning ferns (bracken), used extensively in making *verre de fougere.* Being a source of the potash, it contains the necessary alkali ingredient for making such glass. See *soda.*

fern decorated glassware Glassware embellished with engraved representations of ferns, made mainly in Scotland, by John Ford at the Holyrood Glassworks. First exhibited in 1862, the glassware was made until the end of the century.

fern glass See *verre de fougere.*

ferret (1) An iron tool used by a workman to test melted glass to see if it is ready to be worked. (2) An iron tool used to make the ring at the mouth of bottles.

ferret(t)o (1) A substance used to color glass, made from calcining copper by placing layers of thin copper sheets and powdered sulfur (*brimstone*) in a covered crucible over a fire. After several hours it was opened, and the reddish or blackish copper sheets were removed and ground into a fine powder [*ferret(t)o*], added to the batch to make a green-colored glass. (2) An oxide of iron mixed with copper scale, added to a batch to make a green-colored glass. (These definitions are from different sources and may describe the same process even though the first does not reference iron as the term *ferret(t)o* would indicate.)

Ferris Brothers; Ferris Cut Glass Company See *Elmira Cut Glass Company.*

Ferris Glass Company (1910-1913) A glass cutting company established in Corning, New York, by John C. Ferris (associated with the Elmira Cut Glass Company and Arcadia Cut Glass Company) during the period when the Elmira Cut Glass Company was having labor difficulties, causing it to close in 1911.

Ferroline A black pressed glass patented on July 21, 1881, by Enrico Rosenzi and made until 1885 by the West Side Glass Manufacturing Co. and the American Ferroline Company, with limited success. It is said coal dust was used as the coloring agent. The trademark, registered on June 26, 1883, is a spread eagle on a pine branch. Rosenzi claimed it was as indestructible as iron; this claim was proved false.

Ferstler & Christian (1912-1918) A glass cutting company operating in Brooklyn, New York.

festoon A decorative pattern in the form of garlands of flowers, leaves, fruit, ribbons, or drapery, which, because it is suspended from the two ends, hangs in a natural curve. See *swag.*

festooned glassware Glassware made of brownish green bottle glass previously attributed to the Nailsea Glasshouse and presently credited to other unidentified facilities. The entire surface was embellished with white festoons called *quillings.*

fettling The technique of placing handles and spouts on a piece.

Feurhake, Henry A catalog publisher and printing engraver from Pittsburgh, Pennsylvania, who was issued a patent for the "Improvement in Process of Preparing Glass Molds" in 1879. It explains decorating pressed glass in the mold, making it cheaper than if done by decorators after removal. The embellishment involves etching and a unique granular surface that covers the entire or a portion of the exterior and obscures and reflects light to some extent. Feurhake assigned his patent to mold maker Washington Beck. Using these molds, the Fort Pitt Glass Company made a line of glassware called *Crystaloid*; the process used to make it was called *crystalography.*

fialai (*Italian*) A division of the Venetian glassmakers guild specializing in bottle making.

fiber glass (Aka *fibrous glass*) Glass made into fibers as small as 0.00002 inch in diameter by blowing strong jets of steam or air onto molten glass as it emerges from platinum nozzles or by a spinning process where molten glass flows into a rapidly revolving container with numerous small holes near the bottom through which filaments of glass emerge. There are other techniques used on a much smaller scale. Such fibers can be woven into textiles, accumulated into a mat, and made into insulation, tape, air filters, and numerous other products, such as pipe (with plastic bond).

Fiberglas(s) A trademark used for an assortment of commodities made of or with glass fibers or glass flakes, including insulated wools, mats, acoustical products, yarns, electrical insulation, and reinforced plastics.

fibrous glass See *fiber glass.*

fibula An ancient ornament consisting of a bronze pin (for attaching to clothing) with a coiled spring and catch, resembling the modern safety pin. Some have a curved bow encapsulated within a glass leech-shaped tube or a *runner* (if in the form of a half section of such a tube) joined to the pin. The tube is sometimes opaque white, embellished with marvered color trailing combed in a feather pattern. Some have been discovered at Etruscan sites in Italy, credited to the 9th to the 7th centuries B.C. Some were made locally, and others were made in what is present day Yugoslavia. The glass used may have been imported in the form of bars or rods and worked by local craftsmen. Fibulae could have been introduced by the Dorians about 1100 B.C. or made from broken pieces of bracelets of Celtic glass. See *leech glass.*

Figueroa Cut Glass Company (1914-1926) Established by John F. Rothfus and Charles Strunk in Hammonton, New Jersey, making cut glassware. After the company closed, F. Rothfus purchased the Enterprise Cut Glass Company in Hammonton, operating it until 1949. Prior to managing these companies, Rothfus was affiliated with the Miskey-Reynolds-Rothfus Company (1906-1912) and the Rothfus-Nicolai Company (1912-1914), both cutting houses in Hammonton. In 1914 Henry Nicolai established the Henry Nicolai Company.

figure (1) An object representing a human or animal, alone or in a group. (2) An adornment attached to a vessel.

figure candlestick A candlestick having a shaft in the form of a figure supporting the candle nozzle. Some exist in the form of a caryatid—a sculptured female figure used as a column—or a dolphin.

Figure, nude female stem, burnished-gold bowls. Left: 6-3/4" h.; bowl, 1-1/2" d. Right: 7-1/4" h. wine; bowl, 2" d.
Davanna Collection

figure stem A stem in the form of a figure, the most common being a human figure.

figured beaker A beaker embellished with relief figures. A famous group consists of mold blown cylindrical beakers tapering inward toward the bottom, embellished with four standing figures in relief around it. The figures look to the right or in opposite directions, and are isolated by columns having a pediment above or a festooned garland between them. The figures portray individuals from mythology. Most likely they were made in Syria and elsewhere during the 1st and 2nd centuries A.D. Over 20 such beakers are known, ranging in height from about 4 3/4 to five inches.

figured blank A blank to be further decorated by cutting, having a portion of the final design already impressed upon it. They are made by blowing glass into a mold containing part of the design, usually the major and deepest cuts. They reduce cutting costs and the refractive qualities of the glass.

figured engraving Embellishment accomplished by hardstone-point engraving or linear wheel engraving, often depicting mythological scenes and figures around shallow, colorless bowls. Early ones were made in Egypt, later ones in Rhenish workshops. Some have additional faceting and shading created by abrasion. Others were made during the 17th and 18th centuries.

figured flasks (Aka *historical* or *pictorial flasks*) Figured flasks were popular from 1812 to 1870. As time progressed, the quality and design degenerated. They were made mainly of olive green, olive amber, and aquamarine glass in New England, New Jersey, Pennsylvania, and the Midwest.

figured glass During the mid-19th century, figured glass generally was called wheel cut glass. By the start of the 20th century, it also referred to etched and pressed pattern glass.

figured pocket bottle A pictorial flask.

figured pressed glass An older term for *pattern glass*.

figurine (1) A small individual figure. The earliest recorded figurines were made of Egyptian glass during the 14th and 13th centuries B.C. by fusing powdered glass using the casting process. Those having a flat back were made in an open press mold; three-dimensional ones were cast in two-piece molds. (2) A figure; a statuette.

fili, vetro a (Italian) Literally, *threaded glass*. Glass embellished with opaque white or colored threads of glass or both, encased in clear glass in continuous non-intersecting lines (as in *vetro a retorti* or *vetro a reticello*) in a spiral, volute, or helix pattern. It is a form of filigrana embellishment, called *latticino*, when the threads are white.

filigrana (Italian) (Aka *vetro filigranato* (Italian). Literally, *thread grained*. Glassware with various styles of embellishment made of clear glass with opaque white or colored glass threads or occasionally a single white thread. However, the trade prefers the term be used for all styles of embellishment on clear glass with a pattern formed by embedding threads of glass. This includes: (a) *vetro a retorti*—twisted threads fixed in clear glass forming lace-like patterns; (b) *vetro a reticello*—crisscross threads fixed in clear glass forming a fine network, usually with tiny air bubbles trapped between the crossed threads; and (c) *vetro a fili*—embedded threads in a spiral, helix, or volute pattern fixed in clear glass. When used in the broader sense, *filigrana* would include *vetro di trina* (lace glass). The *filigrana*-style was introduced by the Venetians in the 16th century, encouraged by the twisted opaque white

threads in the rope edge of some bowls of Roman glass from 100 B.C. to 100 A.D. (see *filigree*), lasting until the 18th century. It has been used in Bohemia, Silesia, Germany, the Netherlands, Belgium, France, Spain, the United States, and China, and again in Murano in the 20th century. The commonly used term for *filigrana* is *filigree*, but it is also referred to as *threaded glass, lace glass, muslin glass,* and *cotton glass.*

filigree The English term for *filigrana*. As applied to glassware, it is to be differentiated from that used to describe metalwork made with wires. Filigree work began during the 2nd or 1st century B.C. Filigree rods are made by taking two or more opaque colored rods of glass, twisting them together in rope fashion while still plastic, and subjecting them to extreme heat to fuse them together.

In the 1700s the Venetians revolutionized and greatly improved the method of production. In their method, a bulb of plastic glass was blown into a heated mold lined with colored or opaque white glass rods alternated with clear rods. The rods clung to the outer surface of the item when it was removed from the mold. When placed on a body of clear glass, the clear rods lost their individual identity, and only the colored and opaque white rods were visible. By skillfully twisting the inflated paraison while still plastic, the glassmaker obtained the effect of colored and/or opaque white threads spiraling around the body of the finished article. It was not until the 1850s that American manufacturers began use filigree decoration. See *filigrana*.

filigree ground See *muslin ground*.

fill-in A relatively new technique for repairing chips in glassware by using either an ultraviolet curing glue or a clear epoxy/acrylic substance. The portion to be filled requires the gradual buildup of the material, a very slow process. The area filled in may become lusterless and foggy when exposed to bright lights, glass cleaners, or even handling.

fillets The narrow strips of glass used around the border of a mosaic window. In earlier times, when stained glass was cemented into masonry openings, fillets were designed to be broken if the window had to be removed. By breaking these, the window could be removed without being taken apart or broken. During the 19th century, one of the earliest decorative window styles involved the use of wheel cut fillets around the leaded quarries. Such windows were usually glazed into a wooden sash and set into the framed opening.

fin A thin ridge of glass that may appear on pressed or mold blown glassware as a result of molten glass being squeezed between sections of the mold. They may be removed or reduced by fire polishing.

Findlay Cut Glass Company See
Eclipse Tumbler Company.

Findlay Flint Glass Company (1)
(1886-1901) A glass manufacturing company operated by the Dalzell-Gilmore Leighton Company. See *Findlay glassware.* (2) (1889-1891) A glass manufacturing facility in Findlay, Ohio, making tableware, jars, lamp fonts, seed cups, birdbaths, novelties, inkwells and stands, lantern globes, jelly tumblers, etc., and "private mold wares" (see *private mold work*).

Findlay glassware spooner, cinnamon ground, tulip, daisy, and thistle motif, 4-1/4" h.
Krause Publications

Findlay glassware (1) Glassware made
by any one of at least sixteen companies located in or near the town of Findlay, Ohio, during the late 19th through the early 20th centuries. Between 1870 and 1890, the number of facilities in the state of Ohio expanded from nine to sixty-seven, thirty-five new facilities between 1884 and 1890 alone. Some made window glass, bottles, or lamp chimneys, but five made tableware: Columbia Glass Company; Bellaire Goblet Company; Dalzell, Gilmore & Leighton

Company; Model Flint Glass Company; and Findlay Flint Glass Company.

The primary reason they located in Findlay was the presence of an abundant source of inexpensive fuel, natural gas. The first well was drilled in 1884, and by April 1886 there were seventeen wells. Land was often donated for these facilities by land syndicates. The city of Findlay bought the local gas company in 1887, becoming its own supplier. Fearful that the supply of natural gas was running out caused Findlay to increase rates up to 1000%. Over the next few years, many companies switched to fuel oil. During this period, many independent companies considered merging to reduce competition and costs, and to control output and prices. As a result, members of the Western Flint & Lime Glass Protective Association created the United States Glass Company in February 1891. Columbia Glass Company became known as *Factory J* and Bellaire became *Factory M*. The natural gas shortage of December 1892-January 1893 caused both companies to close. Model Glass Company survived because of fuel oil backup. Dalzell, Gilmore & Leighton Company converted entirely to fuel oil. Findlay's five tableware facilities made pressed and mold blown wares in lead and soda-lime glass. In addition to its abundance of natural gas during the late 1880s, Findlay had a good rail transportation system for delivery of raw materials and shipment of finished products.

(2) (Aka *onyx, Findlay onyx*) A rare art glass made about 1889 by Dalzell, Gilmore & Leighton Company. It was a molded ware made in various patterns and numerous colors, usually white or ruby, which was made by layering two or three compatible shades using controlled, repeated firings. Silver, ruby, or black (also called *syrup brown*) patterns were molded into the glass, often with luster trapped between the layers. Heavy bases resulted from the manufacturing process. It was made for a short period. See *Onyx glass.*

Findlay Onyx See *Findlay glassware; Onyx.*

Findlay Window Glass Company A
window glass manufacturing facility established in 1886 in Findlay, Ohio, operating into the 1890s.

fine glass Glass made from the best of the molten glass in the pot, considered the mid-layer located below the *gall* and above the *tale*.

fine line bands A cut glass motif of miter cut parallel lines made with a gang wheel in which the grooves were cut with a diamond point stylus. The gang wheel was introduced in 1913 by the Norton Company of Worcester, Massachusetts.

finger bowl (1) A small bowl used to hold water to cleanse the fingers at the table when eating with the fingers was common. Early English ones were cylindrical, similar to a tumbler (frequently called *water glasses*) and believed to have been used to cleanse the mouth after a meal. Originally, they were called *wash hand glasses*, then *finger cups*, and finally *finger bowls*. As the terms changed so did the shape, changing from the tumbler shape to cup-shaped to widened cylindrical bowl. They were made of colored, clear, or opaque white glass with enameled decoration. Cut or engraved ones, often with a matching underplate, were made during the late 19th-early 20th centuries. Rare ones had a glass cover with a knopped finial and matching underplate. While usually circular, some are three-lobed or other shapes. Presently finger bowls are often used for dips and sauces. *Lipped finger bowls* are cylindrical with a flat bottom and one or two lips in the rim; their original use was probably as a wine glass cooler. (2) A glass bowl used by a manicurist to soak and soften a customer's nails prior to trimming, or by a barber or hair stylist to wet the fingers when setting or grooming a customer's hair. They are about three inches in diameter and about one inch high.

finger cup See *finger bowl*.

finger cut See *printie*.

finger glass See *thumb glass*.

finger vase A fan-shaped vase with five flower holders arranged like the fingers on a hand.

fingered glasses See *thummers*.

Fingernapfen (German) The circular indentations used to obtain a firm grip on a variety of German drinking glasses and beakers.

finial The terminal ornament of an object, specifically that on the cover of any vessel. The finial is not only decorative, but also serves as a handle or lifter. It has frequently been called a *knop*, but that term is best reserved for bulbous embellishments on the stems of glassware. Finials are made in a wide assortment of forms and styles, such as acorns, shells, birds, animals, flowers, fruits, mushrooms, pine cones, etc. Many are engraved or cut, and faceting is common. They tend to have characteristics of the period of production. See *swan finial*.

fining process (1) Skimming and removing impurities from the top of molten glass prior to it being worked. (2) (Aka *refining* or *hot stoking*) A process used to remove unwanted bubbles from melted glass prior to it being worked, usually done by melting the batch to a high temperature as quickly as possible and keeping it there for a period of time.

finish (1) The condition of the outer surface of glassware, i.e., smooth, satin, iridized, etc. (2) The top of the bottle neck. Prior to mechanization, when a bottle was shaped on the blowpipe, it was cut from the pipe at the neck, which was the final part of the bottle to be finished. Today, in modern bottle making, the top of the neck is made first; however, the term *finish* is still used.

finish mold See *ring mold*.

finishing See *glass, manufacturing, finishing*.

finishing mold The second of two molds used to make modern bottles. The first, called a *paraison mold*, forms the bottle, which is then transferred to the finishing mold for the final details.

Finley Glass Company See *Haley, Jonathan*.

finned bowl A bowl having almond-shaped projecting bosses—pointed fins—around it.

Finnish glassware Glassware made in Finland. The first recorded Finnish glass manufacturing facility was established by Gustaf Jung at Nystad in 1681 and closed in 1685. It was succeeded by another at Avik (1748-1833) and at Mariedal (1781-1824). There were also some other short-lived facilities worked primarily by Swedish craftsmen making simple utilitarian glassware and chemist's glass. The leading glass manufacturing facilities now are Riihimaki, Karhula-Iittala, and Notsjo (Nuulajarvii), the latter established in 1793. The initial endeavor to make modern artistic glass in Finland was about 1928. After World War II the Finns emerged as great art glassmakers by integrating utilitarian qualities with artistic styles in the modern Scandinavian mood. Their Savoy vases are some of their most famous artwork.

fioleri or fiolario The guild of window glass and glass vessel makers, working from the 13th century in Venice and then Murano.

fire bottle A small bottle designed to hold phosphorus (completely under water). A splinter of wood was dipped into the phosphorous and then scraped on a dry rough surface, causing a flame. This was a forerunner of the friction match.

fire clay A clay capable of being exposed to a very high temperature without fusing, used in making crucibles or pots in which a batch of glass was fused. It has a high silica content and small amounts of lime, iron, and alkali. English Stourbridge clay has long been considered the best. In the United States, good clay was found in Delaware in 1815. Later better clay, found in Missouri, withstood higher temperatures and was more resistant to the action of the flux. However, between 1790 and 1860, until the Missouri clay became widely available, 60% of the fire clay used in the United States came from Germany.

fire extinguisher A spherical or pear-shaped object of glass filled with water (usually colored red) or a fire retardant, and then sealed. When a fire occurred, a fire extinguisher was thrown at it. On breaking, it released its contents, hopefully putting out or retarding the fire.

Fire-King ad, September 1952.

Fire-King Hostess Delight 8-piece snack set, turquoise blue with gold trim.
Heartland Discoveries

Fire-King Oven-proof dinnerware and tableware made by Anchor Hocking Glass Corporation from 1842 to 1976. The dinnerware was made in a variety of patterns and colors, including white with various rim colors. The company used a molded mark or oval foil paper labels.

Fire extinguisher, "Auto Fry Stop" Model C-37, 11" h.
Davanna Collection

fire over To permit a furnace or melting pot to idle at operating temperature after a batch of melted glass was removed and before the ingredients of a new batch were entered. If a unit is allowed to cool, it is likely to crack or the clay or brick to deteriorate on reheating.

fire polishing (Aka *flame polishing*) The process of reheating a finished glass object in order to obliterate the marks left by tools or molds, and at the same time produce a lustrous smooth surface, duplicating that of fire blown and cut glass. It eliminates the lusterless surface that on occasion is left on the glass by the iron in a mold. It was first used in England on pressed glass about 1834. The object is normally heated at the glory hole. Because of its tiny stipples, lacy glass did not hold up well under fire polishing, tending to obliterate the stipples. It has been superseded in many instances with acid polishing. See *polishing*.

fired gilding See *mercuric gilding; honey gilding*.

fired-on color Color applied, then baked on glassware at a fairly high temperature. It is less likely to wear off than colors applied by other techniques. See *firing*.

fired-on decoration A type of decoration made by first painting or silk screening a design on a glass object and slowly applying heat to the object in a decorating lehr.

Fireglow glass An art glass resembling English Bristol glass, except when the object is held to the light, a reddish brown to red color is observed. It was made during the 1880s by the Boston & Sandwich Glass Company in an opaque tan color (referred to *cafe au lait*—coffee with milk) and other companies in the United States and Europe. Pieces usually have a satin finish and elaborate designs in various colors.

fireman's horn An object in the shape of a fireman's horn, made primarily during the 19th century as presentation pieces.

firing (1) The process of fusing the ingredients of a batch by elevating the temperature of the furnace, pot, or crucible to the appropriate level, maintaining it there for the appropriate period of time. (2) The process of reheating an unfinished glass object to make it somewhat plastic so that further work or manipulation may be done. (3) The process of reheating a glass object in order to fix enameled decoration or gilding, normally in a muffle kiln at temperatures ranging from 700 to 900°C. See *enamel firing*. (4) The period of time a glass company was in continual operation with furnaces in production or fired. This was usually from September 1 to May 1 in the United States, the summer being too hot for workers to be at or near the furnaces without serious health effects. Dates varied depending on the facility's location. In colder climates, many facilities started before September 1 and shut down after May 1.

firing foot A relatively thick and heavy foot, such as on a firing glass, frequently pitching slightly outward and having a rounded edge.

firing glass (Aka *bumping glass*) A short drinking glass about four inches high, generally a dram glass with a short thick stem, thick foot, and bowl in a variety of shapes, usually waisted. It was so named because, when banged on the table, it sounded like a gun discharging. They were used at ceremonial occasions, banged on the table after a toast. Made in England from about 1740 to 1800, they may be unadorned or bear emblems or an insignia.

Fischer Cut Glass Company (1915-1918) A small glass cutting house in Atco, New Jersey.

Deep amber fish bottle with embossed fish on side and scales above. Probably held Cod Liver Oil, 9" h.
Davanna Collection

Fish bottle, purple-brown wine, 10-1/2" h.
Davanna Collection

fish bottle (1) A bottle with the body in the form of the head and front part of a scaly fish (with no tale), extending into a long tapering neck. They were made of mold blown Roman glass in the 1st to 3rd centuries A.D. Earlier ones were made of Egyptian core glass from about 1504 to 1320 B.C. In these, the opening was the mouth of the fish and the body had combed decoration, dragged forward to replicate scales. (2) A bottle in the form of a fish, having a head, full body, and tail, generally made by a molding process. As a result, the details of the fish, such as the scales, are quite explicit. The mouth of the fish is the mouth of the bottle.

Fisher's Factory See *Bloomingdale Flint Glass Works.*

fisherman's float (Aka *seine ball*) A large glass ball used as a float for a fisherman's net; also a duplicate of such a float suspended in the window of his house as a spiritual connection with the fisherman at sea. It was generally of green glass, often etched with a name and number, and on occasion a spiritual inscription or filigrana stripes in anticipation that it would float ashore in the event of a disaster at sea. They differ somewhat, both in appearance and purpose, from a witch ball. See *seine balls.*

Fisler & Bacon; Fisler & Beckett See *Fislerville Glass Works.*

Fisler & Morgan Dr. Charles F. Fisler joined Moore Brothers & Company in 1880, and in the same year, withdrew to organize his own glass manufacturing facility, Fisler & Morgan, in Clayton, New Jersey. His partners were Albert S. Fisler and Henry and Walter Morgan. A few years later it was sold to F.M. Pierce Company.

Fislerville Glass Works A glass manufacturing facility established in 1850 in Fislerville, New Jersey, by Jacob P. Fisler Jr. and Benjamin Beckett. The company made bottles, flasks, and other hollowware, including the *Jenny Lind flask* to commemorate her arrival in the United States. In 1851 Beckett sold out to Edward Bacon, and the name became Fisler & Bacon. In 1856 Bacon was killed. Fisler rented the company to John M. Moore, who purchased it and, in 1859, the name became John M. Moore & Co. In 1863 John's brother, D. Wilson, joined the firm, the name becoming Moore Brothers & Company. When the town's name became Clayton in 1867, the company was called the Clayton Glass Works. It expanded over the years, making fruit jars and pharmaceutical, beverage, and ink bottles. It closed shortly before World War I.

fistula A *blow pipe.* See *blow pipe.*

Five Senses A group of allegorical figures representing the five Aristotelian senses of seeing, hearing, smelling, tasting, and touching. They were portrayed by engraving and enameling in Germany and Bohemia during the 18th century.

fix To make more permanent or stable.

Flaccus Company A glass manufacturing facility in Wheeling, West Virginia, known for its glass animals, some on intricate bases of field and woodland scenes. It may have been affiliated with the Flaccus Brothers Company, a food and condiment business located in the same city.

flack'ed A colloquialism for a flask.

flacket A flask.

flacon *(French)* A small bottle fitted with a stopper. Scent bottles or smelling bottles fall within this category. See *scent bottle.*

flagette A flagon.

flagon (Aka *flagette*) A vessel used at the table for pouring liquids, generally wine or alcoholic beverages, similar to a tankard. The original was similar to a pilgrim bottle with a screw cap while subsequent examples have a loop handle, sometimes a long spout, and usually a hinged metal lid with a thumb rest for opening. The term is cccasionally used for a vessel holding wine at the Eucharist, especially those made of Roman glass from the 1st century. However, at later dates, they were used for drinking beer.

flake A thin layer of glass split from an object, leaving a smoother surface than a chip. See *chip.*

Flambo Ware An opaque glassware of tomato red color made by the Pairpoint Glass Works prior to 1924. Most was made for the Christmas holiday season. Processes associated with production proved to be rather difficult, especially production of a uniform color.

flame polishing See *fire polishing.*

flame working A technique of working with glass where heat is applied to the object in a specific area. Objects made by this process are called *lamp work.*

flammiform A decorative effect in the shape or form of a flame, sometimes as enameling or on the upper edge of wrythen molding. See *wrythen molding.*

flanged foot A foot that is hollow on the bottom, resting on an incurved flanged rim.

flash(ed) A thin covering of translucent colored glass over a base glass, usually clear, most often found on paperweights and hollowware. See *flashed glass; flashed-on color; flashing.*

Flashed Amberina An Amberina made some years after the original by flashing a portion of a piece of amber glassware with an amber glass mix containing gold or selenium. The flashed portion was then heated, causing it to turn ruby. It was cheaper to make since only the flashing contained gold or selenium, unlike Amberina where the entire piece contained gold and selenium. *Flashed Amberina* does not have a pontil mark.

flashed fan Small fans (see *fan cutting*) cut between the prongs, vanes, or miter cuts of other fans.

flashed glass Glass made by coating a base of clear or lightly tinted glass with a thin layer of colored or opaque glass, usually by dipping the gather into the molten colored or opaque glass. See *flashing; Tiffany Reactive Glass.*

flashed-on color Color added on the surface of clear glass, usually a transparent color, such as ruby or amber, in the form of a lacquer. It is a cheap imitation of flashing. The coating is not fired on and, therefore, has the tendency to wear off over time.

flashed single star A cut glass motif. A single star with small miter cuts between the larger radiating vanes.

flashed star See *star.*

flashing (1) (Aka *dip overlay method*) The application of a thin layer of glass, normally colored, on a body usually of clear or lightly tinted glass. The process involves dipping the object into molten glass, a process quite different from that of making cased or overlay glass, which has a thicker layer. If of a contrasting color, the flashing could be easily ground or etched to produce a design. A piece covered with clear glass is referred to as *encased* glass rather than *flashed glass.* Flashing has been imitated by using flashed-on colors or coating an object with powdered glass of a different color fused to the body. See *double flashing.* (2) The process of twirling a paraison on a punty rod to flatten it into a disk when making crown glass. (3) Feathering. (4) Subjecting an object to intense heat after it has been removed from a mold to eliminate mold marks.

flask A small receptacle for holding spirits and other liquids. They are divided into two types: (a) Those for placing on a table, customarily globular or pear-shaped with a short neck, a small mouth, and a stopper. Some made in Germany were "eight-sided" (four-sided with chamfered corners), embellished with *Schwarzlot*, or painted in enamel or cold colors. Some have been made in shapes of animals or other figures.

(b) Those to be carried on the person. They are usually elliptical or oval in cross-section, having flat or slightly convex sides rising to a shoulder or tapering to a short neck. They are usually pint size or smaller. Half-pint size ones are called *pocket bottles* or *pocket flasks*. It is common for flasks to be molded with various forms of embellishment on the sides, especially those made in the United States. Those with pattern molding were made mainly between 1810 and 1835. The glass used in making these was generally a soda or lime glass, usually in greens, ambers, browns, and blues. Midwestern glasshouses did make some in amethyst, but they are quite rare. See the following examples of flasks: *barrel; bellows; Ceredo; date; dromedary; dropper; dove; flower enclosing; flying bird; gemel; grape cluster; head; helmet; historical; holy water; hunting; indented; Janus; lenticular; lentoid; lentil; Lind, Jenny; mallet; molar; monkey; pictorial; Pike's Peak; pilgrim; pistol; Pitkin; pocket; ring; screw (Schraubflasche); scroll; shell; tobacco.*

flask within flask A glass flask or bottle made with a smaller flask on the inside, secured to the bottom. The outer flasks are in a variety of shapes, frequently embellished with snake trailing. They were made in the Rhineland during the 3rd and 4th centuries; their intended use is not known.

flaskin A small flask or pocket flask.

flat A dish with no footed base or stem.

flat bouquet A decorative motif in a bouquet paperweight, of a bouquet of flowers with leaves positioned flat, parallel to the base of the weight. See *standing bouquet*.

flat cut stem A vertical stem connecting plane faceted surfaces. On occasion, the faceting is waisted or bulging, and at times the edges notched where the faceted planes meet.

flat diamond cutting A variation of the raised diamond cutting achieved by leaving an area between the crisscrossed diagonal grooves uncut so a flat unadorned area

remains, instead of an area embellished with pointed diamonds.

flat flutes See *flute cutting*.

flat foot A foot having a flat bottom made during the 19th century after there was no longer a need to have raised feet to prevent the pontil mark from marring a surface.

flat glass Glass formed with two parallel or nearly parallel flat surfaces. Early glassmakers had two techniques for making flat glass: casting or the crown method (see *cast glass; crown glass*). Pieces made by these techniques were relatively small. Over time, as larger panes were needed, new techniques were developed. The cylinder glass method was used to make somewhat larger panes (see *cylinder glass*). In the 1920s the drawn glass method was developed, producing even larger panes (see *drawn glass*). It was much more efficient than the cylinder process, but the glass was not perfectly flat and had to be ground and polished. In 1959 the float process was developed, producing a flat, smooth glass without additional grinding and polishing (see *float glass*).

flat star A cut glass motif made by using a miter wheel to cut a five-pointed star or pentagram, similar to that made with a continual line without raising a pen or pencil from the paper. It became a common cut glass motif after 1900, as a labor saving method. See *star*.

flattened knop A knop having a flattened globular shape.

flattening oven An oven used as an integral part of the cylinder glass process. After the blown glass cylinder was split, it had to be flattened, requiring the reheating of the cylinder in this oven. When the split cylinder became soft, it was flattened into a sheet.

flecked glassware A glassware having a surface mottled with flecks of opaque glass, usually white, of various shapes and sizes and scattered at random over the surface. To make it, broken chips or bits of glass were spread on a marver, adhering to a gather of molten glass as it was rolled over them. When the mass was reheated and blown, the piece was marvered until the surface was smooth with the chips embedded in it. This process was used on Roman glass at Alexandria during the 1st century A.D. and later on French and German glass during the 17th and 18th centuries. A similar process was used in England in the 19th century, using bits of material other than glass or of glass with a composition different from the body. See *encrusted glassware; blobbed glassware.*

fleeting dish (Aka *flit* or *flitter*) A shallow dish or bowl used for skimming; examples include skimming cream from milk and skimming fat from hot broth.

Flemington Cut Glass Company A glass cutting company established in 1908 in Flemington, New Jersey, by Alphons G. Muller. It purchased its blanks from Fry, Fostoria, Heisey, Duncan & Miller, Imperial, Libbey, and Union Glass (Somerville, Massachusetts). Muller originally sold only his own wares at showrooms within the facility, but about 1925 he diversified and became a major distribution outlet for the world's finest china and dinnerware. Until the late 1980s, it was the largest retailer of its kind in the world with the largest selection of china, glass, and gifts in any one location, making light cut wares, especially customized initialed ware. Today it is a much smaller operation, having given up most of its space to antique dealers and eliminating cutting operations. It is operated by the fifth generation of Mullers.

Flemish glass A cathedral glass having an impressed design of many furrows extending in all directions.

flexed funnel bowl A funnel bowl on a drinking glass with a rounded bottom, broadening like a funnel to near the rim and then continuing vertically upward.

flint An impure variety of quartz (SiO_2) which, after being heated to approximately 400°C, can be easily crumbled and powdered. It has been used in making flint glass. See *flint glass.*

Flint & Lime Glass Manufacturers of the United States A loose confederation of several American glassmakers organized during the Civil War, meeting annually from 1862 to 1866. It was divided into three regions: New England; East Coast (primarily companies from Brooklyn and Philadelphia); and West (primarily companies from Pittsburgh, Wheeling, and Ohio). Because of the time frame, there were no representatives from the Confederate states.

flint glass A term applied incorrectly to lead glass; its use is somewhat justified because, during the development of lead glass in England, calcined or ground flint was often substituted as a source of silica in the batch. Later sand was substituted for flint, but the term continued to be used for lead glass. Since 1682, flint glass has been classified as (a) *single flint* or *thin flint* and (b) *double flint* or *thick flint.* Both types of glass had the same composition and lead content, but the *double flint* was made to remedy the lightness and fragility of *single flint.* It was made from a double gather of metal, resulting in a sturdier ware that was popular, though costlier. Today the term *flint glass* has been superseded by *lead crystal.* In the United States, flints were never used to make glass, but the term made its way here and became accepted for referring to any high-quality glass. *Flint glass* is also an optical glass (see *optical glass*).

Flint Glass Factory See *Keene (Marlborough Street) Glass Works.*

Flint Glass Works See *Sweeney, M. & R.H.*

flint iridescent See *Verre de Soie.*

flip (glass) A beaker used for mixing and drinking *flip* made by mixing beer, wine, or hard cider and other spirits and sugar, heated in the glass by inserting a hot iron into it. It is between 5-1/2 and 6-3/4 inches high, somewhat taller than the usual four-inch tumbler. They are usually cylindrical or taper slightly outward from the base to the rim. Larger ones often had a cover with a dome and a hollow, pointed globular finial. They were made during the 18th and 19th centuries.

flip-flaps See *musical glasses.*

flip-flop A toy or unusual glass whimsy made at numerous glasshouses. It was a cross between a hookah pipe and a hand-held oil can in the shape of a funnel or trumpet, with a thin membrane of glass across its end. It was so named because, when one blew down the tube, it caused a membrane to vibrate, producing a flip-flop or beeping sound.

flit or flitter A fleeting dish. See *fleeting dish.*

float glass Sheet glass made by a process developed by Pilkington Brothers Ltd., introduced in 1959 and becoming the world's principle method of making flat glass. In this process, a continuous ribbon of molten glass, up to eleven feet wide, advances from the melting furnace, floating along the surface of a molten tin bath. The changes in atmospheric conditions and temperature, normally causing irregularities in the surface of the glass, are strictly controlled. As a result, irregularities tend to melt out, the glass becoming flat. Control of the feed to the bath determines the thickness of the sheet, ranging in thickness from 1/10 of an inch to one inch. The sheet is then fire polished and annealed, eliminating the need for grinding and polishing. One furnace may produce 1,000 tons of glass a day. A further development of the process in 1967, known as the *electrofloat process,* allows the glass to be tinted as it passes through the bath. See *glass, manufacturing, shaping.*

Floradine (Aka *Findlay Floradine*) A line of glassware made from about 1891 to 1901 by Dalzell, Gilmore & Leighton Glass Company, using the Onyx molds. It is a single layer ware having a rose color and satin finish, decorated with white opal flowers.

Floral Crystal A trademark of Duncan-Dithridge used on its cut glass wares.

Florentia Glass An art glass developed by Frederick Carder at Steuben Glass Works, made in the late 1920s and early 1930s. It is embellished with an overall relief pattern of adjacent leaves with the points projecting upward from the base, usually of pink and green powdered glass fused into the body of the object. After annealing, the surface was often given a mat finish.

Florentine (1) A trade name used by Fenton for its satin iridescent glass. (2) A line of glassware introduced by the Consolidated Lamp & Glass Company in January 1927, with designs acid etched into the surface. Several patterns were used, such as a plum pattern on green glass, a rose pattern on coffee colored vases, and a stippled pattern in crystal vases. It was known as the *2000 Line* in the undecorated or patternless version.

Florentine *Art Cameo* Glass A glassware made in France, England, and Bohemia to look like English cameo glass. Its decorations appear to be acid etched or wheel cut, when in actuality they were made of a heavy paste, usually satiny white, applied to the surface and embellished with enamel. They were made during the late 18th and early 19th centuries. Some are signed *Florentine.* See *cameo glass.*

Florentine glassware Glassware made in Florence, Italy, beginning in the 14th century. Early wares were primarily of bottles and beakers. During the 16th and 17th centuries, objects for medical and scientific purposes were made as well as luxury glassware made *at-the-lamp* by Venetian artisans working under the patronage of the Medicis. In 1567 Luigi Bertolo of Murano bargained unsuccessfully with Cosimo de'Medici in an effort to gain a glassmaking privilege. Several years later, a fourteen-year contract was agreed upon, and a facility was in operation by 1579, making glassware in the Venetian style. A glasshouse was established with the financial assistance of Don Antonio de'Medici in the 17th century. See *Tuscan glassware.*

floret(te) A slice or set-up of a large cane composed of a group of glass rods of various colors arranged, usually concentrically, in a stylized floral pattern. The term is occasionally used for a cane with a cross section resembling a single natural or stylized flower. They are often used in millefiori, circlet, concentric, or garland types of paperweights.

Florian, Ferdinand (*Fred*) Born in 1869, he came to the United States in his teens and began working for George Duncan & Sons. He developed a formula for an amber stain, first used by the company in 1867. He was an engraver, remaining with Duncan most of his career.

Florida (or Tinted) line A line of glassware made by Dorflinger from the *Kalana* patterns. Some was selected and sent to the Honesdale Decorating Company to be hand colored. Some of the patterns are called *Florida* and some rarer patterns are called *Tinted*, with no apparent difference between the two except for the name. See *Kalana Art Glass.*

Floriform Vases A Tiffany product from his Corona glasshouse, made by Thomas Manderson, first gaffer there. The vases were of wine glass shape, free formed curves, or pincered rim. The bowls represented a flower, onion, or bulb set on a long slender stem with one or more swellings and a bombe foot. The entire vase or a portion of it may be decorated.

flower See *deutsche Blumen; Harvard Glass Flowers; Indianische; flat bouquet; standing bouquet.*

flower block A glass receptacle designed to hold standing cut flowers. It consists of a vertical column of glass with glass disks (with holes for the stems) at two levels. Some, patented in 1921 by Frederick Carder at Steuben, are embellished with a glass figure or animal, usually with a mat finish; they have a peg on the base that fits into a hole in the block. A similar block was patented by Arthur Nash in 1917 for Tiffany Furnaces.

flower center (1) A vase specifically designed to set in the center of a table or sideboard. (2) Any short-necked bulbous vase.

Flower City Glass Company A glass manufacturing facility in Rochester, New York, operating during the 1910s. It was affiliated with the Genesee Cut Glass Company.

flower enclosing flask A "Persian" glass flask, jug, or kalian, usually pear-shaped with a tall thin neck, a foot ring, and a floral or fruit embellishment of colored glass within the bowl, secured to the bottom. In the production process the ornament was made *at-the-lamp* and secured within the bowl while being blown. It is believed they were first made in Venice during the 18th and 19th centuries for export to the East and were later

replicated in Persia in the early 19th century. See *vase with enclosed bouquet.*

Flower paperweight, single standing daisy, 4" h.
Davanna Collection

flower paperweight A paperweight having as its predominant motif a single embedded flower, differing from a bouquet paperweight. A variety of flowers, some fantasized or stylized, are represented, but usually all have the same type of leaf. The most often used Baccarat flowers are primrose, pansy, and clematis; the rose is rare and the lily-of-the-valley rarest of all. The most often used St. Louis flowers are dahlia, clematis, chamomile (or pom-pom), and fuchsia. With the exception of the classic Clichy rose, Clichy made few such weights. The principle makers of these paperweights in the United States were New England Glass Company, the Boston & Sandwich Glass Company, and Whitall, Tatum & Company. The embedded flower may be flat and two-dimensional or standing and three-dimensional, some covering the entire piece. The motif is, on occasion, within a basket made of staves of alternating colors. The ground is usually clear but is sometimes colored or a carpet of lattice work.

flower root glass See *hyacinth vase.*

flower stand An ornamental glass receptacle designed to hold cut flowers. It has from three to six vertical tubes for holding the stems of individual flowers. See *bouquetiere.*

flowered glassware A wheel engraved glassware made from about 1735 to 1785 in England. It was engraved with representations of flowers or floral festoons, or grapes and vines on wine glasses or decanters, hops and/or barley on ale glasses, or apple branches on cider glasses.

flue cover A round plate used to cover the hole in the wall where the stove pipe joined the chimney after the stove and attached pipe were removed during spring housecleaning. Many were made in part or entirely of glass. Some had a litho print behind the glass or a reverse painting on glass. Oval and round ones were common; square, rectangular, and diamond shapes are rare.

Flugelglas(er) *(German)* Venetian winged glasses made in the 17th century, replicated by German craftsmen. They are also called *Schlangenpokals*. See *winged glass*.

fluid lamp Any lamp that burns a liquid fuel to produce light.

fluogravure A process developed at Muller Freres involving bonding enamel to a single or double layer glass vessel, then etching it with hydrofluoric acid so that it appears painted.

fluorescence See *ultra-violet radiation*.

Fluorine Liquid A fluid used to etch names or designs on glassware, made by covering ammonium bifluoride crystals with hydrofluoric acid, shaking it, and allowing it to stand for a few days. See *badging*.

flush crumb bead See *crumb bead*.

Flushed Glass An embellishment on glass developed by E. Rousseau and E. Levelle during the Art Nouveau period. It is made by coating an object with a colored glass dust and firing it to fuse the dust to the surface, producing a faint flush of color.

flute cordial glass See *ratafia glass*.

flute cutting A geometric pattern on cut glass consisting of a series of parallel groves, either mitered (V-shaped, called *pillar flutes*) or of concave semi-circular or semi-elliptical sections (called *round* or *hollow flutes*). On occasion the grooves are separated by a common arris (a ridge formed where two surfaces meet at an exterior angle), as on a Doric column. Flute cutting may be in straight lines, curved (spiralling), or decoratively shaped (e.g., petal shaped). On some glasses it extends down and across the bottom of the bowl and part way down the stem, with the upper ends of the flutes terminating in a point (*bridge fluting*). A faceted stem is sometimes said to have *flat flutes* or *hollow flutes*. The ridges created between flutes is sometimes notched (see *pillar cutting*). Frequently flutes are cut on the necks of water carafes, decanters, and cruets, and on the spouts of pitchers and on stems or pedestals. A pattern involving only flutes was called *Plain Flute* by Libbey and *Colonial Flute* by Dorflinger.

flute (glass) A tall, narrow, medium-sized drinking glass with a bowl of inverted conical shape resting on a short stem, often merely a knop or a small baluster with mereses. During the 17th century, Dutch and German ones were used for drinking wine and measured from sixteen to twenty inches tall. Similar ones were made in Venice. Some filigrana ones even have a cover. They normally have engraved embellishment, sometimes commemorative illustrations. Modern flutes, shorter that the originals, stand about five inches high and are used as champagne glasses. See *Exeter Flute; Scudamore Flute; Chesterfield Flute; flute; tulip glass*.

fluted edge A scalloped edge.

Fluted glass toothbrush holder with gold-wash top, 7" h.
Davanna Collection

fluting Relief ornamentation in the form of a series of shallow, generally vertical, parallel grooves of semi-circular cross-section. It is the opposite of reeding or ribbing, and generally associated with cut ornamentation. See *flute cutting; bridge fluting; combed fluting*.

flux (1) A substance added to enamel colors to lower their fusion point during firing, below that of the glass to which they are applied. Some softening of the glass is essential to hold or cement the colors to it. (2) An alkaline or metallic substance added to the batch to facilitate fusing of the silica and, at the same time, stabilize the batch. The most common fluxes are soda (in Venetian glass), potash (in Bohemian glass), wood ash (in forest glass), and lead oxide (in lead crystal). (3) (Aka *fluxing agent*) In stained glass, any substance, such as rosin, applied to surfaces to be joined by soldering to free them of oxide and make the solder adhere to and join together pieces of lead came surrounding or between two pieces of stained glass.

fluxing agent See *flux*.

fly To break or explode into many pieces, caused by cooling a glass object too suddenly.

fly trap (Aka *wasp catcher*) A vessel having a small orifice through which flying insects, attracted by a lure, can enter but not easily escape. They were fashionable in the mid-1800s.

flying bird flask An ornamental flask (Zierglas) having four passageways or orifices in the body. Within each is a representation of a pigeon that appears to be flying. The pigeons were made of white glass with blue glass heads, three facing in one direction, the fourth in the opposite. They were made of Roman glass in the Rhineland during the 3rd or 4th century.

foam glass (Aka *cellular glass*) A lightweight cellular form of glass made by chemical foaming molten glass. Pulverized granules of glass are placed in molds, mixing them with a substance which, when heated, discharges bubbles of gas. The resultant slabs are sawed and used in construction of walls and for insulation. It is less dense than water.

fob seal A seal bearing a monogram or design crafted in intaglio, used for leaving an imprint on sealing wax. It is mounted on a shank, one to two inches long, with a small ring for hanging on a chain or hook. Some were made in England about 1750 and were later made of colored glass. See *letter seal*.

foiling (Aka *foliating*) An old process for silvering mirrors. A flat surface was covered with thin blotting paper and sprinkled with chalk dust. On top was placed a sheet of tin foil on which was spread a layer of mercury using a hare's foot. The foil and mercury formed an amalgam. A sheet of paper was placed over this, and plate glass was placed on top of the paper, which was carefully removed to avoid air bubbles from forming. Weights were placed on the glass and the table tilted to remove the excess mercury.

folded foot (Aka *welted foot*) A foot, sometimes conical or domed, with a base rim slightly turned under to create a double layer of glass, lending stability and reducing the chance of breakage. They are seen on drinking glasses, candlesticks, and other common objects. The width of the fold was from 0.2 inch to over 0.4 inch on larger glasses. On some the fold is not under but over the rim.

folded rim The base rim of a foot or top rim of a bowl that is folded back onto the main body forming an even, rounded edge instead of a sheared-off edge that has to be ground and polished. Normally twice as thick as the body of the piece, it lends stability and strength to the rim or foot, making it less susceptible to chipping or cracking.

foliating See *foiling*.

fondi d'oro (Italian) The gold sandwich glass made during glassmaking's "ancient" times. The earliest known specimens have been reconstructed in part from fragments found in the Roman catacombs. The bottoms of these cups and bowls have a small central medallion of engraved gold leaf, often embellished by painting, secured and protected by a sheet of fused glass. The subjects on the medallions are from Christian and Jewish symbolism, biblical history, classical mythology, and games. Occasionally they have dedications to saints and heroes. The outer layer of the glass is often colored, but mostly both layers are colorless. They are believed to have been made from the 3rd century to the early 5th century when burial in catacombs was discontinued. Forgeries were made in the 18th century. See *gold engraving*.

font (1) A holy water stoup (receptacle for holy water). (2) A fountain. (3) The reservoir for oil in a lamp.

font molding (Aka *investment casting*) A method of pressing glass where all articles pressed are absolutely identical in form and dimension, used for precision instruments.

foot The part of a vessel or other object on which it stands or rests, but it does not include the base. In glassware the term applies either to the part of the object that broadens from the stem or to the lower parts of individual legs attached to the body. The foot may be in a variety of shapes—circular, square, hexagonal, scalloped, or purely decorative—and styles, which is of value in identifying the period of production. Generally, the diameter of the foot is about equal to the diameter of the bowl (often a method of determining if it has been trimmed to remove chips). See the following types of feet: *annulated; ball and claw; beehive; bun; conical; corrugated; domed; firing; flanged; flat; folded; helmet; honeycomb; lemon squeezer; overseam; overstring; pedestal; short stemmed; square; star; stemmed; terraced.*

foot bath (Aka *cistern*) A deep oval basin normally having a handle at each end of its long axis, used for bathing or soaking one's feet. See *cistern.*

foot bench The platform above the swing hole on which the blower stood while elongating the cylinder in making cylinder glass.

foot blower The worker in a shop who attaches feet to various articles. See *foot maker.*

foot clappers Two thin pieces of wood, normally beech, held together with hinges and having an opening or slot cut in one of the pieces within which to insert the leg or stem of a glass being made. When a blob of molten glass attached to the lower end of a stem or leg is inserted into the slot and the clappers squeezed together, the blob is flattened and a foot with a round base is formed. It has no tool marks on it, unlike those caused by the use of steel pucellas. A foot so made may have to be trimmed or require additional manipulation.

foot maker A member of a team, chair, or shop who assists the gaffer in making feet for

glass objects, such as wine glasses. See *foot blower.*

foot rim See *foot ring.*

foot ring (Aka *basal rim*, *foot rim*) A slightly projecting rim on the underside of a vessel or other object on which it rests, serving two purposes: decoration and protection. It may be made by (a) applying a glass coil to the bottom of the object; (b) pinching out a small fold on the bottom; or (c) fusing onto the bottom a thin layer of glass with its rim bent downward. See *base ring.*

footed beaker A beaker resting on a stemmed foot or three bun feet. See *Schaper glass.*

footed bowl A bowl resting on a wide, hollow cylindrical stem attached to a splayed, slightly domed foot. See *standing bowl.*

footed plate See *salver.*

forceps Similar to *pucellas*, often used by lamp workers and generally made from engineers' spring dividers.

Ford, Edward, Plate Glass Co. See *Libbey-Owens-Ford Inc.*

forehearth A trough connected to the front end of a tank furnace. See *feeder; tank furnace.*

forest glass See *Waldglas.*

Forest Spires A unique ornamental glass object designed by Golda Fishbein and made at Steuben in 1973. It is in the shape of a tall prism with its three sides engraved with a group of interlacing fir trees. The branches of the trees overlap so that their reflections appear and disappear as the observer moves around it. It was presented to Emperor Hirohito by President Gerald R. Ford on his visit to Japan in 1975.

forgery With respect to glassware, a very close copy of a piece of valuable old glassware made for the sole objective of deceiving prospective buyers. It is usually offered for sale as authentic at a price close to that of the authentic piece but substantially above its true value. The detection of a forgery is aided by: (a) the presence or absence of a pontil mark (forgeries may have one, but the absence of one is not conclusive evidence); (b) the relationship between weight and resonance (not only lead glass emits a ring, but also barium glass; even heavy lead glass decanters will not ring); (c) weight (some vessels of soda glass are thickened to simulate the weight of lead glass); (d) color; (e) presence of lead; (f) enamel (differences between thick and thin); and (g) most important, faults of form, style, or workmanship. See *fake; reproduction.*

fork A wooden pole about four to five feet long, having two iron or wooden prongs covered with asbestos on one end, used to carry stemware or other pieces to the lehr after being completed.

form (1) A heat-resistant object into which molten glass is poured and from which, after cooling, a glass article is removed in its final shape. (2) A heat-resistant object onto which a softened glass article is placed to give it its final form, used in the *slumping process.* See *slumping.*

former mold A mold having the same shape as the object to be made. A flat glass blank is placed on the mold and made into an object by sagging it over or into the mold.

forming See *glass, manufacturing, shaping.*

Fort Pitt Glass Works A glass manufacturing facility established in 1827 in Pittsburgh, Pennsylvania, by Curling & Price (Robert B. Curling, his sons, William and Alfred B., and William Price). The facility made cut, pressed, and molded flint glassware. In 1828 the operating firm became R.B. Curling & Co.; by 1831, R.B. Curling & Sons; in 1834, Curling, Robertson & Co.; in 1856, Curling, Ringwalt & Co. (dissolved in 1857); and, by 1863, Edward D. Dithridge was the sole proprietor, working there since 1839 as a glassblower and becoming a partner in 1856. He stopped making tableware and began making lamps and lamp globes and chimneys under the name of Dithridge & Co., which was used by his son, Edward D. Jr., after Edward Sr. died in 1873. It operated until about 1900. See *Dithridge Flint Glass Company.*

Fort Trumbull Glass Works (1865-1870?) A glass manufacturing facility in New London, Connecticut, which made small bottles and vials for medicinal products and remedies; large bottles up to the fifteen-gallon carboy usually in light green, aquamarine, and amber; and some offhand pieces, including pitchers and candlesticks with lily pad decorations.

Foster, Jeremiah J. See *Olive Glass Works; Olive & Harmony Glassworks.*

Foster, John S. Associated with the South Boston Crown Glass Co. (est. 1824), Champlain Glass Works (est. 1827), Redford Glass Works (est. 1830), and Redwood Glass Works in 1833.

Foster, Joseph See *Granite Glass Company; Foster's, Joseph, Glasshouse.*

Foster Brothers Glass House A glass manufacturing facility established by George and Henry Foster in 1855 in St. Johns, Quebec, in lower Canada. A third brother, Charles, joined them a short time later. It made blown glass tableware and bottles. In late 1879 it was purchased by William and David Yuile and was called Yuile Bros. Glass Works or the Excelsior Glass Company. In 1880 it moved to Montreal. About 1886 the name became the North American Glass Company; in 1891 the Diamond Glass Company; and in 1902 the Diamond Flint Glass Company. In 1913 it merged with the Dominion Glass Company.

Foster's, Joseph, Glasshouse A glass manufacturing facility built by Joseph Foster in Stoddard, New Hampshire, in 1842, which failed after a short time. He later erected another facility in the area. It operated intermittently, making bottles until it was taken over by the Granite Glass Company in 1850, which operated it in conjunction with its own facility.

Fostoria Chintz bowl, 7" d.
Tri-State Antiques

Fostoria's Jamestown creamer and sugar, amber.
Heartland Discoveries

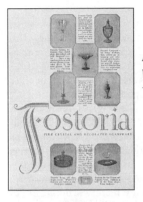

Fostoria glassware ad, March 1926.

Fostoria glassware ad, November 1958.

Fostoria Glass Company

The largest glass manufacturing facility making hand-made glass in the United States today. It was established in 1887 in Fostoria, Ohio, by Lucien B. Martin, but when local gas supplies dwindled in 1891, it moved to Moundsville, West Virginia, making high quality glassware. In 1983 it was sold to the Lancaster Colony Corporation and, in 1986, the former Fostoria facility closed. Some items are still being made from old Fostoria molds.

Fostoria Glass Specialty Co.

A glass manufacturing company established in 1899 in Fostoria, Ohio. It made its first glass in 1907. In 1917 it was purchased by the General Electric Company and moved to Cleveland and then Niles, Ohio.

Fostoria Lamp & Shade Company

A short-lived glass manufacturing facility in Fostoria, Ohio, operating during the late 1880s.

Fotoform A photosensitive glass, essentially a lithium silicate modified by potassium and aluminum oxides with traces of cerium and silver compounds—the photosensitive ingredients.

found A measure of the time required for melting the batch, starting when the ingredients are put in the furnace, stopping when the molten metal is ready to work. See *founding*.

founder See *mixer*.

founding The beginning stage of making glass; the process of charging and melting the batch in the furnace. It is the period during which the ingredients of the batch are heated to about 2450°F to fuse them. This occurs prior to the maturing period requiring about 12 hours during which the molten glass cools down to a working temperature of about 2000°F. See *found*.

fountain ink An ink bottle having side spouts or ports for holding pens as part of its body.

Fourcault Process A process used for vertically drawing a continuous sheet of glass from the furnace, developed by Emile Fourcault between 1902 and 1914 in Belgium. See *glass, shaping*.

Foval glass An opalescent art glass made by the H.C. Fry Company between 1925 and 1929. Gold was used in the batch and embellishing was done with colored glass, normally a combination of two colors in pastel shades of green, pink, and blue.

Fowler, Crampton & Co. See *Concord Street Flint Glass Works*.

Fox & Co.; Fox & Gregory See *Durhamville Glass Works.*

Fox Brothers (A.R. and S.H.) See *Durhamville Glass Works; Rensselaer Glass Factory.*

fox head cup A stirrup cup in the form of a fox's head. Its mouth and ears form the feet on which it stands.

fractional shot glass A tumbler with a capacity of less than one ounce, having a small diameter or thick bottom.

fracture A series of tiny cracks radiating from a central point, caused by the piece being struck by an object. The point of contact is the central point from which the cracks radiate.

fractured piece A piece that has been broken or damaged in some way or has a part or parts missing, and subsequently has been repaired without any attempt to hide the repair or deceive an observer or buyer. See *shelf piece.*

fragment A piece broken from an object. Glass fragments are found less often than ceramic shards (fragments of earthenware) at excavation sites and waste heaps because they tended to be reused as cullet. Shards and fragments usually serve as a fairly reliable method of identifying similar surviving ware, but it is extremely important to distinguish between those found at a facility site, which are likely but not necessarily to be from that facility, and those discovered at dumps, which may be from other facilities not in the vicinity. See *waster.*

fraille A framed apparatus specifically designed for carrying glass.

Francisware A product of Hobbs, Brockunier & Company made during the 1880s; an amber trimmed tableware that is clear or frosted, pressed or blown molded. The most commonly found pattern is *hobnail*, but a swirl design was made. It is not the same as *Francis Ware*, a japanned tinware.

Franconian glassware Glassware made in Franconia located in middle Germany. Its best-known products are the Ochsenkopf beakers made at Bischofsgrun in the Fichtelgebirge (Fir Mountain) region, where glasshouses have existed since 1561. The Kreussen district in upper Franconia was known for its white enameled ware with dotted borders with cresting and interlaced arcs. Generally, lighter colored enamels were used.

Frank, William, & Sons See *Frankstown Glass Works.*

Frankish glassware (Aka *Merovingian* or *Teutonic glassware*) Glassware made between 400 and 700 A.D.—the date that the custom of burying vessels with the deceased was discontinued. While found throughout Central Europe, the heaviest concentrations are in Belgium and the Rhineland, considered to be the place of manufacture. Frankish glassware was made during the Dark Ages, following the decline of the Roman Empire in the West. The wares were of soda-lime glass, made before the use of potash in making Waldglas, about 1000 A.D. The forms and embellishment of the glassware were derived from Roman wares but were of lesser quality and craftsmanship, altered to suit Teutonic taste. Surviving specimens are mainly drinking vessels with no handle, foot, or base, such as the cone beaker, bag beaker, palm cup, and drinking horn. They are usually made of a crude greenish, bluish, or brownish glass with bubbles, striations, and little color control, and without any embellishment except trailed threads.

Franklin Cut Glass & Watch C(h)rystal Manufactory A business in Pittsburgh, Pennsylvania, that made crystals for watches and cut glass from blanks made and supplied by others. It operated during the late 1820s and 1830s.

Franklin Flint Glass Company A glass manufacturing facility established by William T. Gillinder in 1861 in Philadelphia, Pennsylvania, making chimneys for lamps and chemical wares. In 1863 the name became Gillinder & Bennett. In 1867 Bennett sold his interest to Gillinder's sons, James and Frederick, and the name became Gillinder & Sons. In 1871 Gillinder died and his sons took over. In 1863 it had added pressed glass tableware to its output; in 1867 camphor glass and paperweights, and in 1880 cameo glass and cut glass for a short period. In 1883 it established a window glass facility just north of Philadelphia, which closed in 1888. In 1889 it moved its pressing department to Greensburg, Pennsylvania, taking advantage of natural gas supplies. In 1891 it joined the United States Glass Company (*Factory G*), at which time all operations still owned by Gillinder & Sons were returned to Philadelphia. As a condition of joining the combine, Gillinder & Sons agreed not to make tableware for twenty years. In 1912 the sons of James Gillinder (William T., Edwin Bennett, and James), partners in Gillinder & Sons, purchased the Orange Flint Glass Works (aka Brox & Ryal Glass Company) in Port Jervis, New York, operating it as Gillinder Brothers. The Philadephia facility continued to be operated as Gillinder & Sons, and in 1930 it closed. The molds, equipment, and many of the operations were moved to Port Jervis.

Franklin Glass Company (1) A glass manufacturing facility established in 1851 in Kent, Ohio, by Kent, Wells & Company, making bottles and hollowware. In 1864 Day, William & Company took over, operating it as the Rock Glass Works. (2) (1859-1860) A glass manufacturing facility established in South Boston, Massachusetts, making plain, molded colored, and cut flint glass, possibly as an attempt to re-establish glassmaking in the former American Flint Glass Works facility.

Franklin Glass Factory Company or Franklin Glass Works Incorporated in 1812 in Franklin (Warwich), Massachusetts, to make window glass and hollowware. In July 1813 glassmaking began, but the blowing operations were not successful. They were begun again in October 1813, as were the window glass operations. On February 14, 1816, after experiencing hard times, the business was sold to Nickerson, Cobb & Company. In April 1816, the furnace failed and operations ceased. The facility was torn down in 1820.

Franklin Glass Works A green-glass manufacturing facility established by Christian L. Stanger in 1810 in Malaga, New Jersey. It was purchased in 1820 by Daniel H. Miller, who in 1829 sold it to John G.

Rosenbaum. In 1830 Rosenbaum hired the Whitney Brothers to operate it. Rosenbaum died in 1860 and it was closed. In 1861 Rosenbaum's heirs reopened it, adding capacity and making only window glass. In 1873 it was known as the Malaga Glass & Manufacturing Company. See *Harmony Glass Works; Malaga Glass Works.*

Franklin wick lamp Benjamin Franklin is believed to have invented the first double-spout wick found on most whale oil and camphene lamps. Two wicks tend to give a cleaner and brighter light than a single wick since they create a greater air current and consume more oxygen.

Frankstown Glass Works A bottle and flask manufacturing facility established by William Frank & Sons in association with Ephriam Wormser, Frank's brother-in-law. In 1858 the name became the Frankstown Glass Works, and in 1866 Wormser deeded his holdings to Frank. In 1874 it burned and ten weeks later a new facility was in operation on land owned by Wormser. William Frank gave up his interest in the company in 1876. See *Pittsburgh Green Glass Company.*

frater vitrearius (*Latin*) The person associated with a monastery (from the 9th century in Europe), responsible for the monastery's glass windows.

free blown glass Glassware shaped solely by blowing using a blowpipe and manipulating using traditional glassmaker's tools, without the aid of molds. See *free formed glass.*

free formed glass Glassware shaped solely by manual methods in asymmetrical form, often in the art nouveau style. It is occasionally of flashed or cased glass enclosing threads of white glass. It has been made in Venice and by Emile Galle, Daum Freres, and Baccarat. Many pieces were made by Frederick Carder at the Steuben Glass Works. See *Grotesque glassware; handkerchief bowl; free blown glass.*

free time glass Glass items made by workers during their lunch hours or other free time, using the facility's glass (with the owner's knowledge).

Free Will (or Freewill) Glass Manufactory
(Aka *Washington Glass Works*) A glass manufacturing facility established in 1835 in Squankum (now Williamstown), New Jersey, making bottles, vials, and flasks, from half-dram vials to two-gallon demijohns. It failed in 1836 and was purchased by Nicholson, Warrick & Company. Again it failed, went into bankruptcy, and was taken over by Bodine & Black in 1837, followed by Bodine & Coffin (Joel Bodine and William Coffin Jr., operators of the Winslow Glass Works) in 1841.

From 1843 to 1846, Joel Bodine managed the facility, operating it as Bodine & Sons. In 1846 it closed but was reopened by Bodine in early 1856, operated in conjunction with his Washington Glass Works. In 1856, Bodine withdrew and his sons took over, operating as Bodine Brothers. In 1864 one of the sons, John Bodine, and Walker R. Thomas took over, operating as Bodine, Thomas & Company. In 1866 it incorporated as Williamstown Glass Manufacturing Company, continuing to make mold blown bottles until about 1917, under various managements. By 1915 it made beer and liquor bottles almost exclusively, but when the Prohibition Act was passed the output of the works declined.

Freehand Ware
An art glass made by the Imperial Glass Company, Bellaire, Ohio, from 1923 to 1928, using manual methods (no molds). It is an iridescent glass often confused with carnival glass and Imperial's *Imperial Jewel*, an onion skin glass also mistaken for carnival glass.

French, Samuel H., & Company
A distributor of cut glass in Manayunk, Philadelphia, Pennsylvania, operating during the early years of the 20th century.

French cameo glass
A technique developed in France for acid engraving cameo relief designs on blanks of cased colored glass, one aspect of the trend in glassmaking known as *l'art Nouveau*. It became fashionable about 1880 and remained so until just before World War I. It was not the intent of the makers to compete with English cameo glass. Some of the most famous French cameo artists were: Joseph Brocard; M. Leveille; Eugene Rousseau; Maurice Marinot; Auguste and Antonin Daum; Muller Freres; La Gras; Andre De Latte; Williaume; Edward Michel; Alphonse G. Reyen; M. Walter; Tessire du Motay; Mareschal; and Kessler. Most of it was signed. It was subsequently made throughout Europe. French embossed glass: See *embossed glass.*

French glassware
French glassmaking originated at the time when the Roman Empire expanded into what is now France. Early on the Seine-Rhine area made some well-designed and identifiable glassware and some mold blown bottles during the 2nd and 3rd centuries. After the fall of the Empire, the Roman influence began to disappear, but glassmaking survived in Northern Gaul. A different style of glass came into being, spreading from Frankish Gaul and the Rhineland west to England and north to Scandinavia. The Frankish or Merovingian glass was made in a pale amber or greenish *verre de fougere.* The domestic glassware was similar to that made in the utilitarian materials of wood, horn, or metal, such as cone beakers and drinking horns with applied ribs, ribbed drinking bowls, and plain small palm cups.

The most intricate of the Frankish drinking vessels is the *Russelbecher.* Glass from the 5th to the 9th centuries cannot be differentiated with respect to political borders as known today. From the 9th to the 14th centuries (the Dark Ages), the church discouraged making hollowware but encouraged making stained glass windows.

New structural styles developed requiring larger windows, and plain glass was used to a much greater extent. During the 14th and 15th centuries, a naturalistic movement appeared, becoming integrated in the pictorial scenes of the painted windows. French colored glass became extremely fashionable in Europe.

Facilities were established at Nevers and Paris in 1603 by Henry IV. In 1665 Venetian glassmakers were enticed to come to Paris to make mirrors and, by 1669, the French mirror industry was so well established that a prohibition was placed on the importation of Venetian mirrors. In 1688 the exclusive right to make large plates of glass by casting was granted to Abraham Thevart. During the late 16th century, glass enamellers emerged, making miniature models *at-the-lamp.* Many concentrated in Nevers, where they were made in large quantities well into the 19th century. From 1700 to 1750, glassware made from *verre de fougere* with hollow cigar-shaped stems supporting conical bowls was popular. By the middle of the 18th century this light metal was replaced by glass in the English and Bohemian style, made from soda imported from Spain (*verre pivette*).

Lead glass was not made until 1772. From 1750 to 1789, there were about 300 facilities in operation in France. During the 18th century, clear metal came mainly from the north; a pink crizzled metal from central and western France; and a dark green metal from southern France and Spain. There was no real driving force in France to establish a practical glass manufacturing industry until 1764 when the glasshouse of Sainte-Anne at Baccarat was founded by the Bishop of Metz, successfully making window and soda glass tableware until 1789. With the onset of the Revolution, it floundered, closing in 1802. In 1817 it reopened, making lead glass, and was renamed Compagnie des Cristalleries de Baccarat.

By the middle of the 19th century, France was a leader in fashionable and ornamental ware of fine quality. Its facilities began making glass paperweights of the millefiori type in the late 1840s. The three leading makers were Baccarat, St. Louis, and Clichy. By this time France had gained a reputation as one of the most significant makers of fine luxury glassware.

Also during this period a renewed craze for Italian inspired techniques resulted in interesting concepts of bright color contrasts and millefiori, striped, spiral, and latticino patterns. This was followed by the Art Nouveau period, the most brilliant period for French glass. Emile Galle was one of the most distinguished artisans during this period; others included Eugene Rousseau, Dawm Freres, Maurice Marinot, Rene Lalique, Muller Freres Luneville, and Landiers & Fils, Serves. Among the great facilities of the period were St. Louis at Munzthal (today Compagnie des Cristalleries de St. Louis, trademark "Arsale"); Stumpf, Touvier, Viollet & Cie (today Cristallerie de Pantin, trademark "De Vez"); Cristallerie Schneider (trademark "Schneider" or "Le Verre Francais"); Le Gras & Cie at St. Denis (trademark "Le Gras"); and Burgun Schverer & Co. at Meissenthal (trademark "Verrerie d'Art Lorraine BS & CO.). At the beginning of the 20th century the *pate de verre* technique became famous in France. See *French cameo glass; French engraving; French wine bottles.*

French Holophane Company See *Verlys Art Glass.*

French wine bottles Bottles with a kick base to hold wines, varying in shape and color depending on the location of the source (in France) of the contents, facilitating identification. Bordeaux red wines (clarets) are in dark green bottles; white wines in clear bottles. Both have vertical sides and sharp shoulders. Burgundy red wines are in dark green bottles; white wines in light green bottles. Both have vertical sides and a gently tapering shoulder and neck. Alsatian wines are in narrow green bottles having a markedly tapering shoulder and neck. Champagne bottles are green, somewhat wider and heavier, with a tapering shoulder and neck and string rim. Other regional wines are often found in bottles of distinctive shapes. Wine bottles come in a variety of sizes (see *wine bottles, sizes*).

fret See *key fret.*

friendship cane A glass cane in the shape of a walking stick. Customarily a ribbon with a bow was fastened on the cane with which to hang it on the wall of a sitting room or bedroom. Thatcher Brothers made many as novelty items.

Friese, Phillip R.I. & John F. See *Baltimore Glass Works.*

frigate glass A piece of glassware on which a ship and its name are engraved.

friggar See *frigger.*

frigger Also spelled *friggar.* Any small glass object made by a craftsman for his own personal use as an ornament or present or for sale, usually made "after hours" from glass leftover in the pot at the end of the working day (*End-of-Day* glass). It was an established practice in the industry that this glass belonged to the workmen to do with as they chose. Many areas with a concentration of glasshouses reserved specific days for the workmen to exhibit their wares, often with prizes awarded. The word *frigger* is derived from the English *friggle*, meaning *to fuss*. End-of-Day glass was routinely used in England to describe friggers; in Scotland it was *whigmeleeries*; and in the United States it was *off-hand* glass.

fringe The cut glass motif called a *blaze*. See *blaze*.

frit Some of the ingredients used in making glass, such as cullet (first melted to remove impurities), sand, and alkali, preheated in a calcar (but not to such a high temperature to completely melt or fuse them), cooled and ground into a powder, which is added to the batch to be melted into glass.

Fritsche, Hieronimus William (Also spelled Fritchie) (1860-1940) A glass engraver from Bohemia who moved to England in 1873, working at Webb's Dennis Glassworks. There he introduced the style of embellishment known as *Rock Crystal Engraving* with engraving often so deep it had the appearance of glass sculpture. An example of his work is the *Fritsche Ewer* with a mask of Neptune engraved under the lip, waves and fish on the body, and shells on the foot. By 1881 he was engraving in Dublin for T. & R. Pugh. In 1888 he moved to Corning, New York, working for Hawkes. His specialty was engraving hunting scenes. He taught his son, Francis, to engrave in his home shop. In 1902 he went to work for Libbey in Toledo, Ohio, returning to Hawkes in 1904. In 1905 he again opened his shop in his home in Corning. His son, Francis, went to work at Hawkes and, in 1913 and 1914, he worked for Hoare in Wellsboro, Pennsylvania. In 1916, H.W. Fritchie moved to Philadelphia where he opened another engraving shop, later moving it into his home. About 1935 went to work for Strawbridge & Clothier, engraving monograms on glassware while continuing to do some work in his shop at home.

fritting chamber A chamber in some glass furnaces, flanking the main furnace where the ingredients of the batch were first fused into frit. See *frit*.

fritting furnace See *calcar*.

Frizlen Cut Glass Company (1907-1930) A glass cutting company established in Vineland, New Jersey, which moved to Mount Holly, New Jersey in 1918. In 1918 part of the building was rented to William G. McIlvain & Company, a cut glass wholesaler selling his wares.

Frogs, 5" d.; 4" d.
Davanna Collection

frog A flower stem holder of heavy glass with holes to hold the stems. They were set inside a bowl or shallow vase, holding the stems of individual flowers in position.

Frontier Cut Glass Company A glass cutting company established in the early 1900s in Buffalo, New York. Until shortly before World War I, it cut heavy wares and, as styles changed, began cutting the more popular lighter wares. It later changed its name to National Glass Manufacturing Company and was still operating in the 1950s.

Fro(n)tinus bottle A bottle of cylindrical or barrel shape of mold blown green Roman glass with a thin vertical neck, a disk mouth, one or two handles attached at the shoulder and the rim of the mouth, and a series of horizontal bands covering the upper third and lower third of the body. On its base is the molded mark of the maker, e.g., *Frontin O* (hence the name) or *Felix Fecit* or *Daccius F*. Some sources say Frontinus had a facility in Gaul, at either Boulogne or Amiens, operating during the 3rd or 4th century.

frost Finely powdered glass made by pulverizing glass bubbles blown unusually thin. Frost was used by Frederick Carder at Steuben to embellish the surface of his Cintra, Cluthra, and quartz glasses.

frosted glass See *crackle glass.*

frosting (1) A maze of small fissures on the surface of glass due to weathering. (2) A mat effect on the surface of glass using hydrofluoric acid. (3) The effect created by using frost. See *frost.*

fruit An ornament in the form of a piece of fruit, e.g., apple, lemon, etc. See *fruit paperweight.*

fruit bowl A bowl used for serving fruit, generally between eight and twelve inches in diameter and four to six inches tall, with a foot ring or three or four feet. See *fruit server.*

fruit bowl, Venetian A large cylindrical receptacle about as high as it is wide, resting on three small bun feet, with two vertical scroll handles, and/or a domed cover with a high finial. They were made at Murano during the 16th century and used mostly in wealthy households. Some are embellished in reticello style or with diamond point engraving.

fruit cooler An urn-shaped vessel with a deep body to hold ice or cold water and a dish or bowl that fits over it for holding fruit.

"Atlas Whole-fruit Jar" by Hazel Atlas.
Davanna Collection

fruit jar (Aka *canning jar, Mason jar*) A glass jar for "putting up" or preserving fruits, made for use in the home since about 1829. There are over 4,000 varieties. The most famous fruit jar was patented on November 30, 1858, by John Landis Mason, a New York tinsmith. He was twenty-six.

Solid fruit paperweights, peach in frosted peach color and apple in red with green leaf.
Davanna Collection

fruit paperweight (1) A paperweight having embedded within it a central motif, either a single piece of fruit or more than one piece (the same or different type). The fruit may be in a basket or on a cushion, positioned formally or randomly within. (2) A type of paperweight in the form of a piece of fruit, either alone or on a glass base. Some are hollow, others solid. American ones were made at the end of the 19th century.

fruit server A U-shaped dish sometimes on a pedestal, used for serving fruit. Today they are often called *banana boats.* See *fruit bowl.*

Fry, Henry C. (1840-1929) In 1857, Fry moved from Lexington, Kentucky, to Pittsburgh, Pennsylvania, becoming a salesman for the William Phillips Glass Company and later manager of the O'Hara Glass Works. He left to fight in the Civil War. In 1867 he joined with William A. Scott to form Fry & Scott, establishing a glass manufacturing facility in Pittsburgh. Fry left in 1872 to establish the Rochester Tumbler Co., which became the H.C. Fry Glass Company in 1900. See *Fry & Scott; Fry, H.C., Glass Company; Empire Cut Glass Company.*

Fry & Scott A glass manufacturing company established in 1867 in Pittsburgh, Pennsylvania, by Henry C. Fry and William A. Scott. See *Fry, Henry C.*

H.C. Fry bowl, opalescent swirls, cobalt-blue rim, 8-1/2" d.
Krause Publications

Fry, H.C., Glass Company (1872-1934)

In 1872, Henry C. Fry established the Rochester Tumbler Co. in Rochester, Pennsylvania, and became its president. Until 1900 it primarily made glass tumblers—up to 150,000 pressed and cut tumblers daily. In that year the name was changed to H.C. Fry Glass Company and emphasis shifted to fine cut glassware. It made some of the finest lead blanks, some in unusual shapes, with a high lead content, extremely desirable for deep miter cutting. The company never revealed the formula or lead content of the blanks. About 1915 it began using cheaper figured blanks. Fry signed some of the good and bad pieces with "Fry." In 1922 the emphasis changed again to making an art glass known as *Foval* or *Pearl Art Glass*, an opalescent glass often with applied silver mounts made by Rockwell Silver Co. of Meriden, Connecticut. *Foval* was made with gold added to the batch and had a milky white appearance with handles, finials, and other attached parts of colored glass usually in pastel shades of greens, pinks, and blues. It reorganized twice, in 1925 and 1933.

Fuchia A trademark of W.P. Hitchcock Co. used on its cut glass.

fuddling cup A vessel consisting of several cups joined together by hollow handles, forming a circle. In order to empty one cup, it is necessary to empty all since the contents of the cups flow to the lowest cup through the hollow handles. The term is from the verb "to fuddle," an old term meaning "to drink to excess."

fuel Over the centuries many fuels have been used to supply heat for melting the ingredients to make glass. For centuries wood had been the sole fuel. In the beginning of the 17th century, coal began to be used. This was followed by oil and gas (either natural or from coal or oil) in the 19th century. In the 20th century electricity began being used. Peat has been used as a fuel on occasion.

fuel grate See *grate*.

fugitive (1) Colors either hard to form or strike. (2) A change in color of a piece of glass while being worked or while simply at rest, caused by the release of volatiles.

fulgarites Long tubes of silica glass formed when lighting strikes the earth in sandy areas, vitrifying the sand. They have been known to exceed twenty feet in length.

full lead crystal (Aka *crystal superieur*) Lead glass containing at least 30% lead oxide. See *half lead crystal*.

Clear glass castor set, c. 1815-1835.
The Corning Museum of Glass

full-size piece mold A mold having two or more pieces used in making glassware where the object taken from the mold is the approximate size of the finished article. It is different from glassware that is pattern molded and later expanded. See *part size piece mold*.

Fuller, Fred H., Cut Glass Manufacturer (1916-1927)

The only Corning, New York, glass cutting company known to have been founded and operated by a woman—Nell Fuller. She named the firm after her husband because a male name was more acceptable to the public and business community. The company cut and stone engraved glassware for Hunt, using crystal, colored, stained and, on occasion, pressed blanks.

fulminating gold Gold in colloidal suspension in a solution of *aqua regia*, used in making ruby glass.

fuming The process wherein glass is exposed to fumes, such as those of tin oxide or silver nitrate, which affects a thin layer of glass on the surface of a piece, creating iridescence.

Glass funnel fluted on the inside, mouth 5" d. Davanna Collection

funnel An object having a hemispherical or cone-shaped mouth above a thin tube for discharging liquid into a narrow-necked receptacle.

funnel bowl A bowl of a drinking glass in the shape of a funnel with its mouth slightly wider than a conical bowl. There are two variations: rounded bottom and pointed bottom.

funnel mouth A mouth of a receptacle in the shape of a funnel. See *spittoon*.

furnace An enclosed place in which heat is produced for melting the components of a glass batch. See *pot furnace; reverberatory furnace; Siemens furnace; tank furnace; egg furnace*. The earliest known written recording of glassmaking is found in the cuneiform tablets from the reign of King Assurbanipal of Assyria during the 7th century B.C., telling of the invention of the reverberatory furnace.

Furnaces changed over time. The earliest ones were similar to those used for iron melting with one small pot heated with wood from below. Some of the Roman furnaces, instead of being common furnaces, were two-tiered structures with the stoke hole below the melting chamber. In Palestine, from the 4th to the 7th centuries, there were tank furnaces in which the furnace itself served as the receptacle for the melted glass. In southern Europe there were round beehive-shaped furnaces divided into three tiers: the stoke hole at the bottom, a middle chamber with glory holes to access the pots of melted glass, and an upper chamber to anneal the finished products. In Corinth during the 11th and 12th centuries, there were rectangular three-tiered furnaces having chambers similar to the beehive furnaces. In northern Europe, rectangular furnaces had the various compartments adjacent to and on the same level as the main melting chamber, sharing a common fire channel or linnet holes transmitting heat from the main furnace to subsidiary kilns. In England during the 12th and 13th centuries, they were oval or rectangular.

In Venice the *beehive* furnace was developed during the 15th century. In these furnaces the pots were placed on a circular shelf in the middle chamber, and a hole in the center of the shelf provided access to the fire below. The shelf above the pot chamber was the annealing area. In the late 17th century, because of the need to produce greater heat as a result of the pots being closed to protect the glass from discoloration by smoke, the beehive furnace was modified. This was accomplished by removing the leer and placing the remainder of the furnace inside a large cone-shaped structure with a stack. The glassmakers worked in the area between the furnace and the wall of the cone. The greater heat generated was the result of the draft created by underground tunnels, regulated by doors at the base of the chimney. These doors also provided a way for workers to enter the operations area. The 20th century brought the introduction of the large tank furnace, fired by oil, gas, or electricity.

furnace shaped Formed by heat from the furnace rather than by molding, blowing, or pressing.

furniture (1) Pieces of furniture embellished with glass. Some were entirely covered, such as those made in Russia in the 18th and 19th centuries. (2) Furniture made entirely of glass in a variety of sizes from very small to full size, such as a full-size table in the Corning Museum of Glass. Very small pieces are used as novelty or decorative pieces, or as toys such as doll house furniture.

fused glass (1) Stained glass made by placing glass of different colors side by side or in layers, and heating it until the individual pieces are fused into a single mass. Unlike other types of stained glass objects, fused glass has no leading and there are no limitations on the surface or thickness of the pieces. Therefore, individual pieces can have a mat, gloss, or faceted finish for effect, or be of various thicknesses for a three-dimensional effect. (2) A term used erroneously for fused silica.

fused quartz Pure silica melted to yield a glass-like material on cooling. It is used for various apparatus and equipment, such as vacuum tubes where its high melting point, ability to withstand large and rapid temperature changes, chemical inertness, transparency, including ultraviolet light, and electrical resistance are valuable. It is made as fibers for heat resistance, low expansion coefficient, and insulating value.

fused silica (Aka *vitreous silica* and *silica glass*, and erroneously as *fused glass*) It is made by high temperature pyrolysis of silica tetrachloride, and is highly resistant to both chemicals and temperature. The high silica glass, *Vycor*, approaches fused silica in some of its properties and is characterized by low expansion and a high softening point. This imparts high thermal resistance, permitting it to be used beyond the temperature ranges of other glasses. It is highly transparent to ultraviolet radiation, difficult to make in transparent form for transmission of light within the visible spectrum, and has the lowest ultrasonic absorption of any material.

fusiform Shaped like a spindle or a cigar, tapering inward at both ends.

fusing The process of heating pieces of glass until they combine or merge together, forming a single piece.

fusion The creation of a homogeneous liquid mass by melting together diverse substances.

Fustat glass Glass made at or in the vicinity of Fustat, the Islamic capital of Egypt, between 642 and 969 A.D.

Gg

Gabler & Gue See *Brownsville Glass Works.*

Gabler, John C., & Company A window glass manufacturing facility established in 1830 in Brownsville, Pennsylvania. In 1867 it was operated by A.F. Gabler & Co. Note: This is most likely the Brownsville Glass Works because the dates and location coincide, and it was operated at one time by the firm Gabler & Gue. See *Brownsville Glass Works.*

gadget (Aka *snap*) Also spelled *gadjet*. A metal rod used by glassmakers since about 1760. It has a circular spring clip on one end used to grip the foot of a newly formed glass while the gaffer finishes the top by trimming the rim with shears, softening the lip to make it smooth, etc. A simple plunger was pushed to secure the clip holding the glass and pulled to release it. It was designed to take the place of the pontil and prevent leaving a pontil mark, but the spring clip puts pressure on the foot, and so instead of a pontil mark, a less obvious pressure mark remains. After about 1900 the spring clip was covered with asbestos threads, eliminating the pressure mark. Later, when clappers were used, no marks were left on the foot. See *tools, glassmaker's.*

gadjet See *gadget.*

gadroon An embellishment in a continual pattern of short cyclical segments of reeding, either molded, applied, or deep cut, positioned vertically or diagonally, or twisted. Some have points projecting from the upper end of the rows (*spiked gadrooning*). Instead of being in parallel ribs, some radiate from a central point (*radial gadrooning*).

gaffer (Aka *master blower*) The lead glassmaker (or master) of a team, chair, or shop, often considered the most important member of the team. He not only does the most skilled and intricate work, but also governs the practices, procedures, and routines of the entire team until the object is completed and sent to the lehr for annealing.

Gaines Pardessus & Co. See *Waterford Glass Works.*

Gaiter (or Gaither) bottle A small stoppered bottle filled with hot water and placed in a shoe to warm the inside before worn. They were popular from the late 1830s through the 1880s.

galanterie *(French)* A small knickknack or trinket presented by gentlemen to their ladies in the 18th century. It was to be carried on the person, usually in the pocket or in a small purse or bag, or placed on a dressing table or in a cabinet. Included are etuis, snuff bottles, smelling bottles, patch boxes, patch stands, needle cases, etc.

gall (Aka *sandever, sandiver, sandgall* or *glass gall*) The scum that rises to the surface of a batch of glass being melted, which must be skimmed and removed. It is formed by salts in the alkalis that have no attraction for silica, or by having the wrong proportions of ingredients.

Gallatin, Albert (1761-1849) Born in Geneva, Switzerland, Gallatin came to the United States in 1780, establishing a glass manufacturing facility in New Geneva, Pennsylvania, in 1797 (New Geneva Glassworks). It was operated by Albert Gallatin & Co., making mainly window and bottle glass, and closed in 1847. In 1804 he established another facility in Greensboro, Pennsylvania, in operation until about 1840. He served as Secretary of the Treasury of the United States from 1803 until 1813. See *New Geneva Glassworks.*

Gallatin & Nicholson; Gallatin, Albert, & Co.; Gallatin-Kramer Glass See *New Geneva Glass Works.*

Galle, Emile (1846-1904) A leading advocate of the craftsmen and artists who congregated in Nancy, France, during the Art Nouveau movement. His father, Charles Galle-Reinemer, was a designer of luxury faience and furniture at St. Clement-sur-Oise that expanded to make mirrors and table glass. Emile's earliest undertakings were in faience and furniture, then he gradually turned to glass.

After mastering the essentials of glassmaking, he studied art at Weimar and traveled to Paris and London to study glassmaking. In 1867 he established a glass manufacturing facility and, in 1874, he and his father moved to Nancy and began making art glass. Emile began to develop innovative techniques for making and embellishing glass, including cameo glass (see *Galle cameo glass*). Emile is considered to be one of the most proficient glass enamellers of all time, developing a series of translucent enamels called *Emaux-Bijoux* (jeweled enamels), which produced an amazing effect when fired over metallic foil. He was influenced by Japanese styles and designs and retained an active interest in botany. His facility developed intricately cut cased glass and made, from the early 1890s, much "standard Galle" with colored floral relief patterns on opaque white backgrounds.

Galle exhibited some of his works at the Paris Expositions of 1878 and 1884 and the Expositions of 1889 and 1900, and was a founding member and president of the *School of Nancy* (1900-1914). His items, particularly those after 1889, are signed quite visibly, as are some pieces made by his collaborators. In 1897 he instituted complex marquetry techniques used in inlaid glass. He was often called "The Wizard of Nancy." After his death, his wife, Henriette, continued to operate the business until her death in 1914, after which her son-in-law, Paul Pedrizet-Galle, took over until it closed in 1931. See *verrerie parlante; verre de tristesse; marqueterie de verre; Claire-de-Lune.*

Galle cameo glass A cameo glass developed by Emile Galle. Because he had numerous assistants and collaborators, it is impossible to tell which of the pieces he made and which were made by others, since almost all pieces were signed. After his death in 1904, a star was put in front of the *Galle* signature, but only for a short period of time.

galleried rim The rim of a receptacle extending horizontally outward, then vertically upward; the rim always greater in diameter than that of the body. It is found on some sugar bowls made in the United States from the 19th century. The cover rests within the rim unlike the traditional style that is flanged and rests on the rim of the vessel.

gallipot A small jar generally with a handle, used in apothecaries.

Galway crystal See *Wedgwood glassware.*

game pieces Sets of glass objects for playing specific games, such as chess. See *astragal.*

gang A shop or chair.

gang wheel An abrasive wheel used in making cut glass designs having two or more parallel V-shaped cutting edges, made by cutting V-shaped grooves in a flat-edged wheel using a pointed hard steel rod, sometimes tipped with a diamond. It is used to cut two or more parallel grooves into the glass at the same time, resulting in perfectly parallel cuts, significantly reducing time and labor costs. It was introduced in 1913 by the Norton Company of Worchester, Massachusetts, a manufacturer of cutting wheels.

garland paperweight A paperweight in which florets are organized to form a single garland or two entwined garlands. Some have a central motif; others have additional florets interspersed within the curves of the garlands. The best were made at Clichy.

garniture A set of decorated ornamental objects, such as vases or candelabra, for display purposes mainly on mantels or tables. They generally consist of three pieces (i.e., a candleabra with two arms and two other pieces), on occasion five, with the centerpiece slightly larger.

gasolier A chandelier illuminated by gas rather than candles, made of various metals but often with portions and/or embellishments of glass.

Gatchell, Moore & Co. See *Hamilton Glass Works.*

gather(ing) A blob of molten glass attached to the end of a blowpipe, pontil, or gathering iron before it is formed into an object, made by dipping and twirling the pipe or iron into a pot of molten glass. It may be supplemented by adding more molten glass as manipulation of the piece advances. The addition of the same color glass to the original gather does not appear as an additional layer, being merged into a single mass. A thick, heavy glass object is often referred to as being made from a *heavy gather*.

gatherer The assistant to the gaffer and a member of the chair or team whose job is to collect a gather or gob of molten glass of the approximate size needed on the blowpipe, pontil, or gathering iron (by dipping it in the molten glass several times), and take it to the presser or blower.

gathering iron A long thin rod used by the gatherer in making glass objects. It is dipped into a pot or crucible of molten glass and twirled until the desired quantity of molten glass has adhered to it. Sometimes a blowpipe is used to collect the gather when it is intended to shape the glass by blowing. Sometimes a pontil iron is used to collect the gather when additional molten glass was needed for embellishment or casing. See *dipstick; pontil*.

gauze See *gauze twist*

gauze ground See *muslin ground*.

gauze twist A twist made when opaque threads are wound to create a rope-like effect, similar to a cable twist, but the threads are finer and more loosely wound. It is found either alone, in intertwining pairs, in groups of four, or as part of a double series twist.

Gayner Glass Works (Aka *Gayner Glass Company*) John Gayner, a partner in the Waterford Glass Works in Salem, New Jersey, leased the Holz, Clark & Taylor facility in Salem in 1874 and purchased it in 1879. In 1898 he incorporated as the Gayner Glass Works, which remained in the Gayner family until 1956 when it was sold to Universal Glass Products. It made bottles (from very small to fifteen-gallon demijohns) and jars; canning jars were its specialty. See *Craven & Brothers*.

Gazelle bowl with stand, c. 1935-1956, Steuben Glass, Inc.
The Corning Museum of Glass

Gazelle Bowl, The A crystal glass bowl made in 1935 by Steuben. Designed by Sidney Waugh, the original was engraved by Joseph Libisch. It is of blown, clear crystal glass resting on a solid base with four flanges and engraved with twelve leaping gazelles. It has been commissioned more than fifty times, and replicas are in several museums throughout the world.

G.C.Co. This signature inside a shamrock is the trademark of the Gundy-Clapperton Co., a glass cutting house in Canada.

gem, paste See *paste jewelry*.

Gem Manufacturing Company See *Haley Brothers Glass Factory*.

gem-like glass See *gemmato, vetro*.

gemel flask (Aka *gimmel flask*) A flask with an interior partition dividing it into two parts, each having its own neck and mouth. Made as individual bottles, they were blown separately and fused together. The name was derived from the third sign of the Zodiac, Gemini, the Twins. These flasks, often embellished with pincered rigaree trailing as well as other applied ornamentation or of colored or white glass embellished with loopings, were popular in the United States during the first half of the 19th century. Those with a flat base were likely used as a double cruet for holding oil and vinegar.

gemmato, vetro (Italian) Literally, *gem-like glass*. A glass developed by Ercole Barovier about 1937. It had a surface slightly roughened and, to a certain extent, resembling a stone.

gemmaux (French) Glassware made in France by a technique involving fusing small pieces of varicolored glass into a relief pattern.

gemstone glass Glass bowls, necklaces, ornaments, etc., having the appearance of gems and semi-precious stones, first made in Egypt at Alexandria and during Roman times by Alexandrian craftsmen for use by the middle class who could not afford the real gemstones. There are two basic types of multicolored glass from which they are made: streaky (a non-homogeneous blend of two or more different color glasses) and mosaic (made of fragments of glass).

General Glassware Company See *Haley, K. R., Glassware Company.*

Genesee Cut Glass Company A glass cutting company established about 1911 in Rochester, New York, operating until about 1925. It was affiliated with the Flower City Glass Company.

Geneva Glass Manufacturing Company A bottle and hollowware manufacturing facility established in 1810 in Geneva, New York, probably affiliated with the Ontario Glass Manufactory, a window glass facility near Geneva. About 1827 the Geneva facility was purchased by a Mr. Schemerhorn.

Gentile, Peter and John Peter was a glassmaker in Italy before coming to the United States, working for the Morgantown Glass Works. His son, John (born in 1923), began working there with his father. In 1947 they built their own facility making paperweights. In 1963 John began to sign some of his weights with a "G" or a "JG"; all were signed after 1975.

Gentilshommes Verriers Literally, *gentleman glassmakers*. From about 1490, French glassmakers achieved the right to be called *Gentilshommes*, attaining privileges given only to nobility. Lorraine glassmakers referred to themselves as *Chevaliers* and were sanctioned by the government to carry swords.

gentleman glassmakers See *Gentilshommes Verriers.*

George III glassware Glassware with a decorative motif associated with George III or his reign, either by an engraved portrait or cipher. Since George I and successive kings of England were also the electors (later kings) of Hanover, Germany, between the years 1714 and 1837, the portrayal of George III and his consort, Queen Charlotte of Macklenburg-Strelitz, also appears on some glasses made during that period in Germany. The royal cipher was also engraved on a wine glass made by New Bremen Glassworks, Maryland, as late as 1785.

Georgian ale glass An ale glass made from about 1770, having a bowl slightly more globular than conical and a stemmed foot.

Gerlach & Son See *Redwood Glass Works.*

German Cut Glass Company See *Laurel Cut Glass Company.*

German drinking glass Glasses made in many shapes and sizes embellished with enameling or prunts and frequently with long inscriptions. See *Humpen; Pokal; Romer; Berkemeyer; mug; tankard; Stangenglas; Nuppenbecher.*

German enameling The earliest known German enameling was during the second half of the 16th century, copying Venetian enameled armorial glasses previously imported. It is found on the typical German *Humpen* and *Stangenglas*, evolving from basic simple motifs to covering the entire surface. Early motifs were often coats-of-arms, then subject motifs (religious, scenic, allegorical, historical, showing artisan and guild activities, satirical, or family scenes), usually accompanied by a date and/or an inscription. See *Reichsadlerhumpen; Kurfurstenhumpen; Apostelglas; Willkomm(humpen); Familienhumpen; Westphalia Treaty Humpen.*

Their place of manufacture is generally not identifiable except for some such as the *Ochsenkopfglas* made in Franconia, the *Hallorenglas* made in Halle, and the *Hofkellereiglas* made in either Saxony or Thuringia. Enameling became more conservative and of higher quality in the 17th century, and the artists often signed the pieces. A new style of embellishment, *Schwarzlot*, was introduced by Johann Schaper and his proteges. The use of opaque enamels was followed by transparent ones, introduced about 1810 by Samuel Mohn, his son Gottlob Samuel Mohn, and Franz Anton Siebel. By the 1750s only occasional enameling was done on opaque white glass. See *Basdorff glass.*

German engraving Wheel engraving was introduced into central Europe shortly before 1600 by Casper Lehman(n) and became highly developed during the 17th and 18th centuries in German glassmaking centers such as Nuremberg, Potsdam (Berlin), Magdeburg, Frankfort-am-Main, Weimar, and Brunswick. Engraving in the 17th and 18th century was in baroque and rococo styles. Much elaborate wheel engraving was done in Hochschnitt and Tiefschnitt.

German flowers See *Deutsche Blumen.*

German glassware Here *German* covers all German-speaking countries, including Germany, Austria, Bohemia, and Silesia. In the 2nd and 3rd centuries Roman glass was imported in substantial quantities into German lands. As the Roman Empire fell, the glass manufacturing industry in the Rhineland prevailed until its finest craftsmen moved to Altare in the 9th century. Glassmaking became localized with small glasshouses built in the woodland areas, making *Waldglas* (see *Waldglas*). The first objects made were mold blown palm cups of plain, ovoid shape. During the 14th century, prunts were added.

During the 14th and 15th centuries, the Romer, Nuppenbecher, Maigelein, and Kuttrolf were introduced. During the late 15th-early 16th centuries, the cost of fuel rose dramatically, wood being used in the new smelting industry. Many glass facilities moved to Bohemia and Silesia where wood was still plentiful and inexpensive. At this time, production and decoration of thin glassware in Venetian style was widespread.

In the 16th, 17th, and 18th centuries, new forms and styles originated, including the Stangenglas and the Humpen. In the early 17th century diamond point engraving became popular and Bohemian decoration of glass began. About 1700 this decoration was improved and refined with the use of water power, a more

reliable and constant source, to propel the cutter's lathe. At about the same time, potash-lime glass was developed. Silesian and Bohemian glassmakers began using new wheel engraving techniques in Hochschnitt and Tiefschnitt, using thicker glassware.

The art of enameling glassware was introduced in the second half of the 16th century, including Schwarzlot and translucent enamels. In the late 1600s Bohemia became the center of enameling, followed by Bavaria, Franconia, Saxony, Thuringia, and the Tyrol, the finest being made in Saxony. In the mid-17th century a gold ruby glass was developed by Johann Kunckel, and *Bohemian glass* was introduced. Uranium glass—*Annagrun* and *Annagelb*—was made by Joseph Riedel's Dolny Polubny factory and named for his wife, Anna Marie. A true black opaque glass was patented in 1820 as *Hyalith. Lithyalin* was made in 1828. Cased glass was made in great variety and color combinations (some etched, engraved, or enameled) in the mid-19th century. In order to meet the demand for souvenirs, spa glasses, etc., a lot of superior and inferior glass came out of Bohemia. In the last half of the 19th century, art glass played a considerable role in German glassmaking (see *Jugendstil*). Today it is more about color, free form, and combining unrelated materials.

German half-post method The strengthening of flasks by the addition of an extra gather of glass to the lower portion of the body, introduced into the United States by European glassblowers in the early 18th century. See *half-post method; Pitkin flask.*

German jewel star See *star, wheel engraved.*

German Plate & Cut Glass Company See *German Rich Cut Glass Company.*

German Rich Cut Glass Company In 1912 the German Plate & Cut Glass Company was established by Richard German in Brooklyn, New York. It was still operating in 1918 under the name German Rich Cut Glass Company.

German wine bottle Bottles to hold German wines, made in a variety of shapes and colors. A specific shape and color indicates the region where the contents are produced. Rhine red wines are in tall, thin, brown bottles with prominently tapering necks. Rhine white and Moselle wines are in bottles similarly shaped but green in color. Franconian wines (Steinwein) are in a Bocksbeutel.

Germantown Glassworks The first successful glass manufacturing facility in New England built in Germantown (now Braintree) Massachusetts in 1751 by Joseph Crellinsand and financial backers. Very little glass was made before funds ran out, and it was leased to Joseph Palmer and his brother-in-law, Richard Cranch, in early 1752. They made improvements, bringing in German craftsmen. It became such a curiosity that admission was charged to see the operation. The colonial legislature of Massachusetts granted it an exclusive patent to make glass within the state. It made bottles and window glass (using the cylinder process), but found no market for the bottles. In 1755 it was struck by lightning, burned, rebuilt, and reopened by Jonathan Williams and Joseph Palmer, who operated it sporadically over the next few years, making bottles of various sizes for various uses. In 1769 it was destroyed by fire again and never rebuilt.

geschnitzt *(German)* Literally, *chipped.* Embellishment on glassware created by chipping, a technique developed by Wilhelm von Eiff.

Gesu, Al, glassworks A glass manufacturing facility in Murano whose records date from 1537 when it was owned by Nicolo Andrigo. From 1542 it was operated by Antonio Miotti and, after his death, by his descendents until the 18th century. It made opaque white glass decorated with polychrome enameling. Some items have the factory name as a mark, and some are dated between 1731 and 1747. It is said Aventurine glass was first made here.

Getman, Crawford See *Cleveland Glass Works.*

Getsinger & Allen See *Getsinger & Son.*

Getsinger & Son In 1879 Getsinger & Allen opened a window glass manufacturing facility in Bridgeton, New Jersey. In 1882 John E. Getsinger's son, John B., entered the business and erected another furnace nearby. In 1883 Allen left and it became Getsinger & Son, which made a specialty glass called *Newton Brand* of extremely high quality and double thickness. The company also made window glass, hollowware, canning jars, demijohns, druggists' wares, and bottles in a variety of styles and colors. It operated as late as 1895.

Getzinger & Rosenbaum See *Estelle Glass Works.*

Getzinger family See *Eagle Glass Works.*

Gibbs & Kelly or Gibbs, Kelly & Company See *Gunderson (-Pairpoint) Glass Works.*

Gibbs, William H., & Company See *Gibbs, Kelly & Company.*

Gibbs, Kelly & Company A glass cutting shop established by William Henry Gibbs and Michael Kelly in 1895 in Honesdale, Pennsylvania, with sales offices in New York City. Later that year Frank Steinman joined the firm and, in 1905, Kelly and Steinman formed their own company (see *Kelly & Steinman*). Gibbs became the sole owner of the original facility, operating it as William H. Gibbs & Company. In 1909 it moved to Hawley, Pennsylvania, and about 1911 to Stroudsburg, Pennsylvania. In 1928 it was sold to Arbogast & Stackhouse, who continued operations, switching from lead glass to lime glass blanks during the Depression. Shortly thereafter it stopped cutting, going into the wholesale hotel and restaurant supply business. This was sold to Francis Smith in 1950, becoming the Stroudsburg Glass Company. Gibbs also operated another glass cutting shop, the Barryville Cut Glass Shop, in Barryville, New York, from 1910 to 1912 when it was purchased by Krantz & Sell. Libbey supplied this company with blanks.

Gibson & Elmer See *Elmer Window Light Company.*

Gibson, Charles A rare combination of glassmaker and minister who makes hand blown glass lamps, paperweights, and a variety of novelty items in his facility in Milton, West Virginia. It has operated since the 1960s.

gift glasses Glasses given as gifts, usually to ladies by gentlemen, that commemorate a special occasion or simply bear amorous messages using engraving or enameling.

Gilbert, Turner & Co. See *Coventry Glass Works; Willington Glass Co.*

Gilchrist Jar Company See *Bassett Glass Works.*

gilding The process of embellishing glassware, either on the outside or on the reverse of the glass, using gold leaf, gold paint, or gold dust. Gold leaf with engraved designs sandwiched between layers of glass has been used since ancient times. Some Roman glass gilding involved applying gold leaf to a bubble of hot glass and, when the bubble was expanded by blowing, the gold leaf would crack into speckles. Another method used on Roman and later on Venetian glass involved sprinkling granular gold dust on molten glass.

On Islamic glass, from the 12th to the 14th centuries, gold was applied as colloidal gold and fired; it was often combined with enameling. Some Venetian glassware from the 16th century has gilding as the sole form of embellishment, but mostly it is combined with enameling. Some German diamond point engraving has gilding as supplemental embellishment.

By the 17th century, gilding was done using gold leaf, fired on by one of several methods, or by unfired gold painting in Venice, Hall-in-Tyrol, and the Netherlands. English glassware was embellished with gilding during the 18th and 19th centuries. In Spain gilding was applied to wheel engraved glassware at La Granja de San Ildefonso in the 18th century and similarly in Germany. See *gold engraving; gold decoration; Zwischengoldglas.* Also see the following types of gilding: *unfired; double; powder; fired; mercuric; honey; granular; oil; cold.*

Gill, Mitchell & Company See *Acme Glass Works.*

gill glass (or tumbler) A container that holds one-quarter of a pint (four ounces) or *gill.*

Gill's Improvement A modification made to glass furnaces beginning in the late 1770s, which improved air quality by consuming some gases and smoke generated during fuel burning.

Gilliland, John L. A glassmaker employed at the New England Glass Co. who established, with John and Richard Fisher, the Bloomingdale Flint Glass Works in Manhattan, New York in 1820. It closed in 1840. In 1822 Gilliland withdrew and established John L. Gilliland & Co. in Brooklyn, New York, which operated the Brooklyn Flint Glass Works (Aka *South Ferry Glass Works*), making high quality cut glass. In 1864 Amory Houghton Sr. and Jr. acquired controlling interest in the company, moving it to Corning, New York, and establishing the Corning Glass Works.

Gillinder, William T. (1823-1871) An English glassmaker who learned the art of paperweight making at George Bacchus & Sons, coming to the United States in 1853 and working at the New England Glass Company. Leaving after a short time, he moved west, working at various glassworks in Pittsburgh, St. Louis, and elsewhere. He moved to Philadelphia, Pennsylvania, in 1861 and bought a glass manufacturing facility he renamed the Franklin Flint Glass Works. In 1863 he went into partnership with Edwin Bennett, forming Gillinder & Bennett.

During 1867, after Gillinder's two sons, James (b.1844) and Frederick (b.1845), joined the company, it became Gillinder & Sons. Shortly thereafter it acquired the Philadelphia Flint Glass Works, which closed in 1930. After William T. died, his sons managed the facilities. In 1888 the company moved the pressed glass operations of the Franklin facility to Greenburg, Pennsylvania (see *Gillinder & Sons*). In 1912 the three sons of James Gillinder withdrew to establish their own facility, Gillinder Brothers Inc., in Port Jervis, New York. Charles Challinor (1841-1932), employed at the facility from 1867, made many paperweights.

Gillinder & Bennett See *Gillinder, William T.*

Pressed glass lion on mound, signed "Gillinder & Sons, Centennial Exhibition," 1876.
Davanna Collection

Flared bowl, pressed Amberina, Gillinder & sons, Philadelphia, PA, c. 1886. Museum of American Glass at Wheaton Village, Millville, NJ.

Gillinder & Sons Gillinder & Sons owned of the Franklin Flint Glass Works and the Philadelphia Flint Glass Works, both in Philadelphia, Pennsylvania. As proprietors of the Franklin Flint Glass Works, (see *Gillinder, William T.*) it moved the pressed glass operations to Greensburg, Pennsylvania in 1888, operating it as Gillinder & Sons. Later it merged with the U.S. Glass Company (*Factory G*).

Gillinder Brothers Inc. A glass manufacturing facility established in 1912 in Port Jervis, New York, by the three sons of James Gillinder (son of William T. Gillinder) after they withdrew from Gillinder & Sons.

gilt bronze Bronze that is mercurially gilded, used in France as a mount for glass and porcelain ware. It is often loosely referred to as *ormolu*.

gimmel flask See *gemel flask*.

gin glass A glass for serving gin, similar to wine glasses but smaller in size and made in a variety of shapes. They are generally about 3-1/2 to 4-1/3 inches high.

ginette Litterally, *small gin*. A dram glass. See *dram glass*.

Giometti Brothers The Giometti family came to the United States in the 1870s. The father was employed at Hawkes as a cutter. The sons established their own glass cutting shop in Corning, New York. Because of its lack of capital, the company was purchased by a lawyer named Sebring, who continued to operate it for a short time as the Sebring Cut Glass Company.

girandole (*French*) (1) In France, an elaborate sconce having one or more branches for candles, often with a mirrored back plate. (2) (Aka *luster, table luster*) In England, a candelabrum from 1766 to 1792. (3) A sconce—an object that hangs on a wall; it has a convex wall mirror with two branched candlesticks. (4) The nozzle and drip pan of a candlestick.

girasol (*Italian*) Literally, *sunflower*. A milky semi-precious stone reddened in direct sunlight and resembling an opal. The glass resembling it has been made in Italy since the early 18th century.

Glacier Glass A heavily textured line of tableware made by Whitefriars Glass Works.

Gladiola A Tiffany Reactive Glass pattern.

glasperlein (*German*) A technique of embellishing glass by creating an outer "skin" of colored glass beads, creating a picture or scene looking like a mosaic picture.

glass

Origin of Term

The term *glass* is believed to be derived from the Latin *glacies*, meaning "ice," which chucks of natural occurring glass—*obsidian*—strongly resemble, or from the old English term *glas*, meaning "green," the color (caused by impurities) of early glass (see *Waldglas*).

Definition

The American Society of Testing Materials defines glass as "an inorganic product of fusion which has cooled to a rigid condition without crystallizing." Physically, it is a rigid supercooled liquid having no definitive melting point and a sufficiently high viscosity to prevent crystallization (a liquid existing in a solid state). Chemically, it is the joining of non-volatile inorganic oxides resulting from the decomposition and fusing of the alkali and alkaline earth compounds, sand, and other constituents, forming a product having random atomic structure. It is further defined as (a) the end product of the fusion of siliceous matter, such as powdered flint or fine sand, with an alkali, salt, or metallic oxide; and/or (b) a congealed solution of an aggregate of several substances of which silica and alkali are constant. The type and proportion of constituents give the product its properties: color/colorless; transparent/translucent/opaque; clarity/distortion of light; etc. Glass has been called a double silicate because it is composed of a silicate of sodium (or potassium) and a silicate of lime. It is a completely vitrified product or a product containing a relatively small amount of non-vitreous material in suspension. It has almost 100% elastic recovery and all the appearances of a solid. Glass is a generic term applied to any object or item that is made of glass.

Properties

Glass is generally transparent but is often made to be either translucent or opaque. Transparency can be an indication that it is either a single crystal or a liquid. When it is cracked or broken, the fracture has no tendency to travel in one direction any more than in any other, establishing that it is a liquid rather than a single crystal. Its transparency also indicates there are no internal surfaces of a dimension approaching the wavelength of light.

When glass is in its molten state, it is plastic—capable of being molded or receiving form—and ductile—the ability to undergo changes of form without breaking; and capable of being shaped by molding, blowing, pressing, and casting as well as being made into fibers. It exhibits great chemical resistance, being attacked by only a few substances, such as hydrofluoric acid, phosphoric acid, and hot, strong alkaline solutions. It is an excellent electrical insulator, having the lowest electrical conductivity of any common material. When made into hollow building blocks with a dead air space inside, it is a good insulator against both heat and cold, having low thermal conductivity. When cooking utensils are made of glass, foods cook more quickly than in metal cookware because metal reflects heat while glass absorbs it.

Glass is non-toxic, non-combustible and quite durable, being able to withstand constant use and exposure. It is almost opaque to ultraviolet radiation. In the absence of added colorant, glass transmits 95-98% of the light to which it is exposed. Common glass has a continuous upper use temperature of about 250°F, but it may be higher depending on its composition (borosilicate glasses with low coefficients of expansion can withstand extreme temperature changes without cracking). Tempered glass can withstand tremendous physical abuse without cracking.

Glass can be easily cut, engraved, etched, and polished to a smooth, shiny surface. It has a high refractive power, excellent for optical instruments, giving cut glass its luster and sparkle. The hardness of ordinary glass is 5.5 (between feldspar and quartz) on the Mohs scale. While considered fragile, the intrinsic strength of all glass is extremely high (up to three million psi), but common glass has a strength well below that (about 1,000 psi) because of surface imperfections, its strength being a direct function of the surface condition. It is elastic up to the point of fracturing. It will return to its original shape once a force is removed, provided the force is not great enough to fracture it.

Occurrence

Glass is ordinarily a manufactured product. The natural occurrence of glass is rare, but it does exist in the form of *obsidian* in areas of volcanic activity and of lightning and meteor strikes. Excellent sand for making glass is found in the United States in Pennsylvania, Massachusetts, New Jersey, West Virginia, Illinois, Maryland, and the James River area of Virginia. It is also found in southern Germany and Czechoslovakia.

Uses

Its uses are numerous, including windows, bottles, structural building blocks, glass fibers, yarns and fabrics, chemical equipment, pumps and piping, vacuum tubes, lightbulbs, containers, optical equipment, utilitarian wares (tableware, vessels, cookware, etc.), and decorative or ornamental wares. Minute glass spheres with partial vacuum interiors and treated exteriors are available for compounding with resins for use in deep sea floats, potting chemicals, and other composites.

Brief History

(*Obsidian*, naturally occurring glass, is not considered in this discussion.) The oldest theory of the origin of glass is known as Pliney's Theory or the *campfire theory*. It states that glass was first made after the discovery of fire when primitive individuals started a campfire on a sandy beach. The heat from the fire caused the sand to fuse, forming glass. The problem is that a temperature of at least 950°C is needed to fuse sand while that of a campfire rarely exceeds 600°C. The current accepted theory is it was discovered by accident during metal smelting (intense heat probably melted the furnace wall, pouring the molten metal onto sand) in Mesopotamia sometime between 3500 and 3000 B.C., where it was used as a vitreous glass coating on stone and ceramic beads.

It was first used independently about 2500 B.C., mainly for glass beads and amulets. Other glass objects were being made there about 2000 B.C. After conquests in Asia by Egyptian Pharoah Tuthmosis III, a glass industry is reported to have been started in Egypt, operated by Asian workers about 1475 B.C. They used imported fritted glass in large blocks from Asian sources because they did not have the ability to make glass on their own. Core glass was made in Egypt between the mid-15th and the mid-12th centuries B.C., followed by a cessation in glassmaking until the 4th century B.C. Sidonian glassware was made in Syria before 1500 B.C. However, from about 1150 B.C. until the 9th century B.C., little glass, except beads and trinkets, was made. At the end of the period, the glassmaking centers, namely Sidon and Tyre and Mesopotamia, were revived. Phoenician traders spread the products along their trade routes.

By the 7th century B.C., the industry had started in Cyprus and Rhodes, spreading east and north over the next few centuries. The oldest known written account of glassmaking dates from the 7th century, recorded by Assurbanipal, an Assyrian king, on cuneiform tablets, telling of the use of the reverberatory furnace. From the 4th century on, less Mesopotamian glass was made, but the Syrian centers were revived, as was Egyptian glass when Alexandria was founded, its glasshouses established in 322 B.C. In the Hellenistic period (320-100 B.C.), much of the glass made in Syria and Egypt was exported to Greece and Italy.

The industry in Italy came into being about 100 B.C., brought there by the Alexandrians who were followed, in northern Italy, by Syrian craftsmen after glassblowing as an art and craft was mastered about 20 A.D. Cumae and Literum were the glassmaking centers of Italy during the first century A.D.

Glass of the pre-Roman period was made by one of the following methods: (a) core glass process, (b) fusing of colored glass rods to make mosaic glass, (c) cold cutting from a raw block of glass, (d) slumping, or (e) casting using a mold, either fusing powdered glass in a mold or using the *cire perdue* process. (For more information on its history, see the country or region of origin, such as Roman glass, French glass, German glass, etc.)

From Roman times through the 19th century, glass was used for utilitarian, decorative, ornamental, optical, or industrial purposes. It was not until the 20th century that specialty glasses were made, including bullet-resistant glass, laminated glass, photosensitive glass, heat-resistant glass, fiberglass, etc.

The Glassmaker

Throughout the history of glassmaking, the glassmaker has been treated with respect and honor for the most part. In ancient Rome glassmakers were given a favored street in a desirable part of the city to ply their craft. During the Byzantine era, the Theodosian Code of 438 A.D specifically exempted glassmakers from taxation. During the Italian Renaissance period, in Venice and Altare, glassmakers ranked with nobility, while in France and England the only profession that an aristocrat could engage in without losing his title was glassmaking.

In the Lorraine region, the *Charte des Verries* gave glassmakers the right to call themselves gentlemen glassmakers and become peers of noblemen and exempt from certain taxes. Mechanization and subsequently mass production, beginning in the second quarter of the 19th century, brought an end to this special treatment as glass became an ordinary substance used by the common person for everyday use.

Composition of Glass

In spite of the thousands of new formulae for glass, lime, silica, and alkali (soda or potash) have remained the major ingredients in over 90% of all glass made throughout the world since about 3500 B.C. These major ingredients in a typical batch are normally supplemented by other ancillary ingredients that, though minor percentages, may have major effects on the properties of the glass. The most important factors in making glass are the viscosity of the molten oxides and the relationship between the viscosity and composition. For more details and sample compositions, see the listing titled *composition of glass*.

Manufacture of Glass

Typical Manufacturing Sequence:

1. transportation of raw materials to the facility
2. storing of raw materials
3. sizing of some raw materials
4. conveying to, weighing, mixing, and feeding raw materials into the melting device
5. burning of fuel to secure the temperature needed (regenerative or recuperative)
6. reaction of raw materials in furnace to form the glass
7. shaping and forming glass products from molten glass produced in the furnace
8. annealing of glass products
9. finishing of glass products
10. storing, packing, and shipping of finished products

Melting: Of the many ways of classifying glass furnaces, one is to classify them as either pot or tank. Pot furnaces in general have a capacity of two tons or less and were used almost exclusively until fairly recent times. They were used for small production

of special glasses or when crucial to protect the melting batch from the products of combustion. They are used mainly in the making of optical glass, art glass, and plate glass made by the casting process. The pots are really crucibles made of selected clays or platinum (a fairly recent development). It is difficult to melt glass in clay vessels without contaminating the product or partly melting or decomposing the container itself. This is not true of platinum vessels.

In a tank furnace, ingredients making up the batch are charged at one end of a large tank made of refractory blocks (some measure 125 feet by 30 feet by five feet in depth, with a capacity of 1,500 tons). The molten glass forms a pool in the hearth of the furnace, across which the flames play alternately from one side and then the other. The glass is worked out of the end of the tank opposite the charging end, the operation being continuous in nature. In this type of furnace, as in a pot furnace, the walls gradually corrode by the reaction of the hot glass. The quality of the glass and the life of the tank are dependent upon the quality of the building blocks.

Small tank furnaces are often called *day tanks*, supplying the needs of the facility for a day, usually heated by gas or heated electrothermally. The foregoing types of tank furnaces are regenerative furnaces and operate in two cycles with two sets of checkerboard chambers. The flame gases, after giving up their heat in passing across the furnace, go downward through one set of chambers stacked with open brickwork. Much of the heat from the gases is removed, the brickwork reaching temperatures ranging from 2800°F near the furnace to 1200°F on the exit side.

Simultaneously, air is being preheated by passing up the other previously heated regenerative chamber and mixing with the fuel gas burned, the resulting flame temperature greater than if the air had not been preheated. At regular intervals, usually between 20 and 30 minutes, the flow of air is reversed, entering the furnace from the opposite side, through the previously heated brickwork, and passing through the original brickwork, which is now cooler. Much heat is saved by this process and a higher temperature is reached.

The temperature of a new furnace can be raised only certain increments each day, depending on the ability of the refractory to withstand the expansion. Once it has reached 2200°F, it is maintained at that temperature at all times. If such furnaces were allowed to cool and be reheated each day, the refractory bricks would rapidly disintegrate as a result of expansion and contraction. A large part of the heat generated is lost by radiation from the furnace, and a much smaller part is actually expended in the melting. Unless the walls were allowed to cool somewhat by radiation, their temperature would get so high that molten glass would dissolve the walls, which will corrode much more quickly. To reduce the action of the molten glass on the walls, water cooling pipes are frequently placed in them.

Shaping: Glass may be shaped or formed by machine or hand molding. The foremost factor to be considered in machine molding is that the design of the machine should be such that the formation of an article is completed in a very short time, during which the glass changes from a viscous liquid to a solid. Following are descriptions of the processes used to shape or form some common types of machine shaped glass:

A. *Window glass.* For several centuries window glass was made by casting, crown, and later, cylinder processes. These have been superseded by automated continuous mechanical processes, mainly the Fourcault and Colburn processes.

In the Fourcault process, a drawing chamber is filled with glass from the melting tank. It is then drawn vertically from the tank through the *debiteuse* by means of a drawing machine. The debiteuse is a refractory boat with a slot in the center through which glass flows continuously upward when it is partly submerged. A metal "bait" is lowered into the glass through the slot at the same time as the boat is lowered, starting the drawing process as soon as the glass starts flowing.

The glass is continuously drawn upward in ribbon form as fast as it flows up through the slot, its surface chilled by adjacent water coils. This ribbon, still traveling vertically and

supported by steel rollers covered with asbestos or asbestos-like material, passes through a 25-foot long annealing chimney or lehr. On emerging, the ribbon is cut into sheets of desired size and sent for grading and possibly further cutting. The Pittsburgh Plate Glass Company (PPG Industries) has operated a modified Fourcault process for making its *Penvernon* glass. These sheets are drawn 120 inches wide and of varying thicknesses up to 7/32 inch by adjusting the drawing rate from 38 inches per minute for single strength glass to 12 inches per minute for 7/32 inch. It replaces the floating debiteuse with a submerged drawbar for controlling and directing the sheet. After the ribbon is drawn vertically through a distance of 26 feet, mostly an annealing lehr, the glass is cut.

For thicknesses above the standard single and double strength, a second annealing operation is performed in a 120-foot standard horizontal lehr. In 1917, Libbey-Owens-Ford Glass Company began drawing sheet glass by another process, the Colburn process. In this, the drawing of the ribbon is started vertically from the furnace, as in the Fourcault process. After traveling about three feet, the glass is reheated, bent over a horizontal roller and carried forward by grip bars attached to traveling belts, moving over a flattened table through the horizontal annealing lehr with 200 power driven rollers, onto the cutting table.

B. *Plate glass.* Between 1922 and 1924, the Ford Motor Company and the Pittsburgh Plate Glass Company each independently developed a continuous automatic process for rough rolled glass in a continuous ribbon. The processes involves melting the glass in large tank furnaces.

The ingredients of the batch feed into one end and the melted glass, as hot as 2900° F, passes through the refining zone and out of the opposite end in a continuous flow. From the refractory outlet, the molten glass passes between two water-cooled forming rollers, giving the glass a plastic ribbon configuration. The ribbon is drawn down over a series of smaller water-cooled rollers operating at a greater speed than the forming rollers. The differences in the speeds cause a stretching effect on the glass, which, combined with shrinking as it cools, flattens the ribbon as it enters the annealing lehr. After annealing, the ribbon may be cut into sheets for grinding and polishing, or, as in the more recent processes, the ribbon may progress automatically for several hundred feet through annealing, grinding, polishing, and inspection prior to it passing through cutting machines and being reduced to salable plates.

The continuous processes have large capacities and are particularly adapted to making a glass of uniform thickness and composition, well suited to the requirements of the automobile industry. Small runs of plate or special glass cannot be made economically using these machines. They are handled in pots and are mechanically cast by machines designed specifically for this type of operation. Twin grinding was an important technical and cost improvement. The ribbon, after passing through the lehr, is ground simultaneously above and below, followed by twin polishing, then it is cut to size and inspected, producing a more uniform plate.

Float glass is a fundamental improvement in making high-quality flat glass, resulting in a continuous sheet of plate glass having both its upper and lower surfaces fire polished. The ribbon of glass leaves the tank in the conventional continuous hot strip, directed onto and along the surface of a bath of molten tin and, in a non-oxidizing atmosphere and under controlled conditions of temperature, it is perfectly flat with parallel surfaces.

While still on the molten tin, the ribbon is cooled to a temperature low enough so the surfaces of the glass are hard enough to enter the lehr without the rollers blemishing the bottom surface. Float glass is produced in 1/8-, 3/16-, and 1/4-inch thicknesses.

C. Wired & patterned sheet glass. In patterned glassmaking, the molten glass flows over the lip of the furnace and passes between metal rollers on which a pattern has been engraved or machined. The rollers form the glass into sheets and imprint the design on them in a single operation. Such glass diffuses the light and ensures a certain amount of privacy. It may be reinforced with wire during the initial forming operations when special safety needs are required.

D. Bottle glass. Until the last century, glass-blowing has relied solely on human lungs for power to shape and mold molten glass. Modern high demands for blown glass, particularly in the form of bottles and jars, have necessitated the development of high quantity, faster, and cheaper methods of production. Machine making of bottles is in reality nothing more than a casting operation using air pressure to create a hollowed volume within the mold. Several types of machines produce paraisons. One is the *suction-feed* type used, with certain variations, in bulb and tumbler making. Another is the *gob-feed* type, used for making all types of ware made by pressing, blowing, or a combination of the two (*press and blow*).

In the *suction-feed* type, the molten glass, located in a shallow, circular revolving tank, is drawn up into a mold by suction. The mold then swings away from the surface, opens, and drops away, leaving the paraison held by the neck. Next, the bottle mold is elevated into position around the paraison and a discharge of compressed air causes the glass to flow into the mold that remains around the bottle until it becomes rigid and another gathering has been completed. The mold then drops the bottle and rises to close around a fresh paraison. The operations are completely automatic and speeds of 60 units per minute are not uncommon.

The *gob-feeder* represents one of the most important developments in automatic bottle making. In this, the molten glass flows from the furnace through a trough with an orifice at the lower end. It drops through the orifice and is cut into a gob of exact size by mechanical shears. The gob flows through a funnel into a paraison mold, starting the formation of the bottle in an inverted position. A neck pin rises into place and another plunger drops from the top, and compressed air forces the glass to the finished form of the neck. The mold is closed on top (which is actually the bottom of the bottle), the neck pin retracted, and air injected through the newly formed neck, forcing the molten glass against the walls of the mold, forming the inner cavity. The mold opens and the paraison is inverted so the bottle is upright. The blow mold closes around the paraison and is reheated for a brief interval.

Air is injected for the final blow, simultaneously shaping the inner and outer surfaces of the bottle. The blow mold swings away and the bottle moves to the lehr. Automatic blowing machines usually consist of two circular tables (paraison mold or blow tables). Movement of the tables is controlled by compressed air, which operates reciprocating pistons, and the various operations on each table are coordinated with the table movement by a motor-timing mechanism, one of the most vital and expensive parts of the equipment.

E. Lightbulbs. The blowing of a thin bulb differs from the blowing of a bottle in that the shape and size of the bulb are determined initially by the air blast itself and not by a paraison mold. The molten glass flows through an annular opening in the furnace and down between two water-cooled rollers, one with circular depressions causing swellings on the glass ribbon that coincide with circular holes on a horizontal chain conveyor onto which the ribbon moves next. The glass sags under its own weight, through these holes. Below each is a rotating mold.

Air nozzles drop on the surface of the ribbon, one above each of the glass swellings or conveyor holes. As the ribbon moves along, these nozzles eject a puff of air that forms a preliminary blob in the ribbon. The spinning mold now rises and a second puff of air, under considerably less pressure, shapes the blob to the mold and forms the bulb. The mold opens and a small hammer knocks the bulb loose from the ribbon. The bulbs drop onto an asbestos-like belt, carrying them to the lehr rack where they slip neck down between two parallel vertical strips that support them as they are annealed. The total time for the entire process, including annealing, is about eight minutes. Machine speeds as high as 2,000 bulbs per minute have been attained.

F. Television tubes. Television tubes consist of three major parts: the phosphorescent screen on which the picture is produced (face screen), the envelope, and electron gun. The phosphor is applied to the face screen of the envelope either by settling or dusting. Initially there had been difficulty in making the glass envelope until centrifugal casting was invented using a revolving mold that produced an envelope

with a more uniform wall thickness. The glass parts are sealed together using gas flame or a gas flame supplemented by electrically generated heat. For colored television tubes, the phosphor is applied to the inner surface of the screen. A perforated neck is mounted behind the screen to properly direct the electron beams. The usual high temperature needed for sealing the tube cannot be employed since this would cause deterioration of the phosphor.

G. Glass tubing. In the Vello process used in making tubing, molten glass flows into a drawing compartment. From there it drops vertically through an annular shape surrounding a rotating rod or blowpipe in which the proper air pressure is maintained to make tubing of the desired diameter and wall thickness.

H. Glass tower plates, bubble caps, prisms, most other optical glass, most kitchenware, insulators, certain colored glasses, architectural glass, and similar items are hand molded. The process consists in drawing a quantity of glass from the pot or tank and conveying it to the mold. The exact quantity of glass is cut off with shears and the ram of the mold driven home by hand or hydraulic pressure. Certain glass forming is carried out by semi-automatic methods involving a combination of the machine and hand molded processes. Volumetric flasks and cylindrical Pyrex sections for towers are made in this manner.

Annealing: To reduce strains and internal stress, it is imperative that all glass objects be annealed, whether formed by machine or hand molding methods. Annealing involves two basic operations: (1) holding the mass above a certain critical temperature for a period long enough to reduce internal stress and strain by plastic flow to a point less than a predetermined maximum, and (2) cooling the mass to room temperature slowly enough to ensure these stresses and strains remain below the same maximum. The lehr or annealing oven is nothing more than an accurately designed heated chamber in which the rate of cooling can be controlled. See *annealing.*

Finishing: All types of annealed glass must undergo established finishing operations that, though relatively simple, are extremely important. These may include cleaning, grinding, polishing, cutting, sandblasting, enameling, grading, etc. Although all of these are not required for every object, one or more is almost always necessary.

Classification

Glass and glassware may be classified in numerous ways and any one piece may fall within several classifications. Some of these are: by country of origin (French, German, etc.); by region (South Jersey, Midwestern, etc.); by city (Zanesville, Pittsburgh, etc.); by decoration (cut, enameled, etc.); by finish (satin, polished, etc.); by type (Waldglas, green glass, etc.); by use (wine, optical, etc.); by era (pre-Roman, George III, etc.); by style (Empire, Art Nouveau, etc.); by composition (lead, borosilicate, etc.); by color (ruby, cobalt, etc.); by company (Baccarat, Steuben, etc.); by maker (Galle, Dorflinger, etc.); by decorator (Mary Gregory, Boyd, Iorio, etc.); by pattern (ten diamond mold, daisy and button, etc.); by method of manufacture (pressed, blown, etc.); etc.

glass bell See *bell; bell jar.*

glassblowing The art or craft where a blob of glass attached to the end of a blowpipe is expanded by a workman who blows into the opposite end of the pipe, the result being a finished or partially finished object. Blowing may also be accomplished mechanically. It is believed glassblowing was first attempted in the city of Sidon in Phoenicia in the first century B.C. The art spread quickly throughout the Mediterranean Region, becoming the norm within 100 years. It is believed to be the greatest innovation in glassmaking in antiquity, and has not been matched in importance until the development of various power-driven machines for glassmaking, including pressed glass, in the 1820s to 1840s.

Glass-Bottle-Mold Factory A bottle mold making facility established in Bridgeton, New Jersey, about 1880 by Richard Trendard and Charles D. Crickler. By 1889 it was one of the largest such facilities in the nation, supplying molds to most of the glasshouses in South Jersey and many others in the state and country, especially in the southern United States and in Canada.

glass bottomed tankard See *tankard, glass bottomed.*

glass cakes Flat tablets of glass, generally opaque, often called *enamel glass.* Made in a variety of shapes and sizes, they often bear an impressed mark of an 18th century Murano glassmaker and were sold locally and as far away as the Orient for making colored enamels. They were usually made in brilliant colors, such as sealing wax red and turquoise blue, but were often white or transparent. Ingots of similar material made in Egypt were their forerunners. See *smalto.*

glass-ceramic A glass used for *cook-serve-freeze* utensils; range, stove, and laboratory bench tops; architectural panels; and telescope mirrors. Corning Glass makes it under the trade name *Pyroceram,* using a standard glass formulation to which a nucleating agent, such as titania, is added. This is melted, rolled into a sheet, and cooled; then it is reheated to a temperature at which nucleation occurs, causing the formation of crystals. The result is a crystallized or devitrified form of glass with properties varying over a wide range. Its properties are closer to those of ceramics than those of conventional glass. Its high temperature capabilities are between borosilicate glasses and fused silica. It has a thermal shock resistance up to 900°C and an upper continuous use temperature of 700°C. In addition, it has superior rigidity and other mechanical properties. The bodies of the items are usually opaque and glossy, either white or colored, non-porous, and can be made with close dimensional tolerances. Some compositions have outstanding electrical properties. It has a higher flexural (capable of being bent) strength than conventional ceramics.

glass cutter An instrument used for cutting glass into pieces, available in a variety of types and shapes. The most common types are diamond tip, steel wheel, and tungsten wheel.

glass enamel A finely ground flux, basically lead borosilicate, blended with colored ceramic pigments. Different grades give characteristics of acid, alkali, and/or sulfide resistance or low lead release to meet requirements for various uses, such as fired-on labels and glass decoration.

glass eye An artificial, removable facsimile of an eye made of glass and decorated to appear like a human eyeball. They were first made about 1579 by Ambrose Pare (1510-1590) in France. Prior to this they were made of stone and other materials in Egypt about 500 B.C., and later in Venice, Bohemia, England, and France.

In Germany Ludwig Muller-Uri, a glass-blower in Thuringia, made improved glass eyes that were developed further in Germany in 1898 by Snellen (b.1862). The majority of quality ones were made in Germany until World War I and, even after 1918, much of the special glass used to make them came from Germany. In 1932 a suitable glass was developed in Chicago. Due to the fact that they are fragile and in a very sensitive area, substitute materials were sought, developed, and used since the 19th century. The globe of a glass eye was made of blown opaque glass, the cornea of clear glass and the colors of the iris and pupils from glass made by adding metallic oxides to the batch.

glass fiber A generic name for any manufactured fiber made with glass or any fiber drawn as a thread from molten glass, in spite of its form, appearance, method of manufacture, or purpose. It may be a continuously extremely thin filament, about 0.0008 inch thick, that can be drawn and wound on a spool.

Glass fibers were made in ancient Egypt and Rome. Fiber of sufficient thinness to be woven or knitted was made about 1840 and used to make neckties and dresses. In 1893 glass fibers were woven with silk thread to make fabrics, but they were too thick and not flexible enough to be folded. Their demand increased because of their thermal, electrical, and sound insulating properties, as well as their inertness, heat resistance, and strength.

The first truly mechanized process for making glass fibers, the Gossler process, was developed in 1908. In this process, cullet was melted in a small tank and the molten glass allowed to flow through a perforated disk. The fibers were pulled out and wound on a drum. Presently there are three processes for making such fibers for yarn and glass fiber wool: (1) Glass marbles are continually fed into an electrically heated platinum crucible with a perforated base through which the molten glass is allowed to drip; pulled out, spun, and wound on a drum. (2) In the fiber wool-making process, molten glass is allowed to flow in streams from the furnace through perforated platinum disks. The streams are hit with a jet of steam, splintering the glass into fine fibers that are coated with a binding agent, formed into a mat, cut, and assembled into bales. (3) This process depends on centrifugal forces to fragment a stream of molten glass into extremely thin fibers. The stream flows from a forehearth of a melting tank onto a swiftly spinning disk—the principle is identical to that used in making cotton candy. The fibers so made are coated with a binding agent and made into insulating mats.

Glass fibers are also used to reinforce plastics and concrete. Those used to reinforce concrete must be made from glass extremely resistant to alkali. Obsolete terms for glass fiber are *glass silk* and *spun glass*. See *optical fiber*.

glass flowers See *Harvard Glass Flowers*.

glass gall See *gall*.

glass grinder A glassworker whose main function was to grind and shape mirrors as opposed to one who cut ornamental glass. He ground the mirror until the surface was smooth and level, and also, if required, beveled the edges and decorated them with embellishments using diamond faceting (see *diamonding*) and shallow cutting.

Glass House, New Jersey See *Stanger Glass Works*.

Glass House Company of New York A company established by Matthew Earnest, Christian Hertell, and the partnership of Samuel Bayard and Lodewyck Bamper to build and operate glass manufacturing facilities. In 1732 it erected a glasshouse on the Glass House Farm in New York City. In 1752 the partnership of Bayard & Bamper bought the facility, naming it the Bamper-Bayard Glasshouse. It closed in 1766. The Glass House Company of New York also operated a second facility in New Windsor, New York, which closed in 1785. These facilities made mainly bottles and chemical glassware.

Glass House Riffle (or Ripple), The See *Scott & Beelen.*

glass insert See *glass liner.*

glass knobs Knobs of glass used as handles or pulls on furniture. Fashionable from about 1800 to 1860, they were blown, cut, or pressed; plain or decorated.

glass liner (Aka *glass insert*) A glass container fitted inside a metal—gold, silver, pewter, etc.—vessel or container such as a salt, sugar bowl, etc. This was done to safeguard the metal from corrosive contents, such as acids, alkalis, salt, etc. They were popular during the late 18th century.

Glass Manufacturers Exhibit Company A company incorporated by several Pittsburgh, Pennsylvania, glass manufacturers in the 1890s. Its mission was to create an environment where the general public could view and experience all aspects of glass production and buy finished articles. It built a fully operational glasshouse at Exposition Hall along the Allegheny River in Pittsburgh. It had an eight-pot furnace, annealing oven, and molding, pressing, blowing, cutting, engraving, and etching operations, all within full view of the public. The products of all member companies were displayed. Its president was D.C. Ripley. The glasshouse was known as the Exposition Glass Works.

glass manufacturing facility A factory where glass is made; a glassworks or a glasshouse.

Glass of the Golden Star See *aventurine glass.*

glass paste See *pate-de-verre.*

glass picture A picture executed on flat glass by various processes such as painting, engraving, etching, etc. See *panel; mirror painting; back painting; plaque; transfer engraving.*

glass pool An early 1880s term for an association of glass manufacturers that joined together in an effort to defray and share

losses during periods of overproduction and the subsequent shutting down of furnaces.

glass porcelain See *Schopp's glass; Basdorf glass.*

glass pots See *melting pots.*

glass rot See *decay.*

Glass Sellers Company A corporation initially composed of mirror makers, hourglass makers, and merchants that was granted a charter in 1635 by Charles I and reincorporated in 1664 as "The Worshipful Company of Glass Sellers of London." After 1670 one of its primary objectives was to promote research in ways to free English glassmakers of their dependence on European materials. Another was to determine public taste, interpret changes in style and trends, and relay findings to the glassmakers. By 1675 it had 88 members. Initially it imported glassware from Murano. From 1667 to 1673 it sent to Murano designs for glassware in the more simplified styles preferred by the English.

During 1674 it contracted with George Ravenscroft to begin research on a new type of glass, and he became its official glassmaker. He established two glasshouses in London in 1673 and 1674, with funds provided by the company for experimentation. By 1676 he developed a commercial process for making lead glass, solving the problem of crisseling. In recognition for this, he was granted permission to use the raven's head seal on his glassware.

glass silhouette A silhouette painted on the back of plate or convex glass.

glass silk Long but not continuous monofilaments of glass made by several early processes used for the mechanical drawing of glass fibers.

glass stainers colors The *paints* used by traditional stained glass artists; monochromatic vitreous oxides with a range of colors from *tracing black* to *rusty brown*, brushed unto glass and usually worked in some manner such as matting, stippling, picking, shading, etc., before being fired in a kiln and fused to the glass.

glass with eyes See *occhio, vetro.*

glass wool An airy, lightweight mass containing short glass fibers amassed into a thick blanket or lightweight block, usually made by a blowing (forced air) or centrifugal process. The threads have a density considerably less than those of spun glass. It is used for insulation, filtration of acids, etc.

Glassbake A trade name of McKee Glass Company, beginning in the 1920s, for a line of cookware, children's sets, and fish sets.

Glassboro Glassworks The second glass manufacturing facility in New Jersey, established in Glassboro in 1780-'81 by Jacob Stanger and two brothers, former employees of Casper Wistar. It had several changes of ownership until it became the Whitney Glass Co., acquired in 1918 by the Owens Bottle Co. In the 18th century its wares were typical of South Jersey style glassware.

glasses, eye See *vision aids.*

glasshouse A factory where glass is made; a glassworks or glass manufacturing facility.

glassmaker's iron A hollow steel tube, one end of which is rounded to form a mouthpiece while the other has welded to it a hardened steel knob used for gathering molten metal.

glassmaker's mark A mark used by a glassmaker so his work can be positively identified. They have been placed on glassware by glassmakers since early times, and may be in the form of a signature, initials, inscription, or devise made by molding, scratching, etching, or engraving. Not all glassmakers signed their work; in fact most pieces are not signed. Some makers only signed their best works. Some pieces have a signature of an individual, even if not made by him, but by craftsmen in his shop. Some pieces have marks that are forged in an effort to defraud.

glassmaker's soap (Aka *soap of glass*) Black oxide of manganese. A decolorizing agent. When added to the batch in appropriate proportions, it tends to neutralize the metal's natural color caused by impurities in the batch, making it clear.

glassmaker's tools See *tools, glassmaker's.*

glassmaking The art of making glass or glassware.

glassman (1) A person who makes or sells glass. (2) A glazier.

Glasstown Factory A glass manufacturing facility founded by James Lee and others in 1806 in Millville, New Jersey. By 1814 Gideon Scull was owner, making window glass. In 1827 it was owned by Burgin, Wood & Bodine; in 1829 by Burgin & Wood; in 1833 by Wood & Pearsall; in 1836 by Scattergood, Book & Company; then becoming Scattergood & Haverstick. In 1838 John M. Whitall, Haverstick's brother-in-law, joined the firm; it became Scattergood, Haverstick & Whitall but was known as the Phoenix Glass Works. Soon Haverstick retired and it became Scattergood & Whitall. In 1845 Scattergood retired. Franklin, John Whitall's brother, joined it and, in 1848, Edward Tatum (John Whitall's brother-in-law); the firm became Whitall Brothers & Company. In 1857 C.A. Tatum joined it and Franklin Whitall left; the name changed to Whitall Tatum & Company (changed in 1901 to Whitall Tatum Company). It was known for its high-quality mold blown wares. In 1854 Whitall Tatum purchased the South Millville Plant. See *Whitall Tatum Company; South Millville Plant.*

glassware Objects and ware made of glass.

glasswork (1) The making of glass and glassware. (2) The fitting of glass or glazing. (3) Glassware or articles of glass.

glassworks A factory where glass is made; a glasshouse or glass manufacturing facility.

glasswort Any of several chenopodiaceous herbs of the genus *Salicornia*, having succulent leafy stems. These marsh plants were burned to obtain ash, used as a source of alkali (soda) in the glass industry from Renaissance times and earlier. It was known as *barilla* in Spain; as *roquetta* in Egypt.

Glasteel The trademark for an engraving laminate formed by spraying a slurry of powdered glass onto a steel base and firing at high temperature. During the firing, a chemical reaction takes place between the glass and steel, resulting in a chemical bond being formed between them. It is used in making corrosion-resistant process equipment, piping, pumps, valves, and heat exchangers.

Glastenbury Glass Factory Company

A bottle glass manufacturing facility established in Glastenbury, Connecticut, in 1816, remaining in operation until the late 1820s/early 1830s. It also made offhand pieces, including bowls and inkwells.

glaze (1) To furnish or fill an opening with sheets or panes of glass. (2) In ceramics, a coating on a piece that is basically a thin layer of glass.

glaz(i)er A person who fits glass or panes of glass into an opening in windows, doors, etc.

glaz(i)er's pie A phenomenon that occurs as a glassworker is making a stained glass window. As lead came and glass are continually added to the work, the center of the window tends to rise above the bench, forming a hump similar to that which occurs when a pie is baked.

glaz(i)ery (1) The work of a glazier. (2) Glasswork.

glazing (1) The act of fitting sheets or panes of glass in a frame, usually a window or a door; what a glaz(i)er does for a living. (2) Panes or sheets of glass set or made to be set in frames, as in windows and doors. (3) In stained glassmaking, the activity involved in the making of a stained glass window on a bench.

glazing compound See *putty*.

globe cup A covered standing cup with a body and lid forming a sphere, generally resting on a stem (baluster shaped or of a human figure, e.g., Hercules) and engraved with the current details of the earth or the heavens.

glory hole A small hole in the side of a glass furnace, often at right angles to the main working or gathering hole, where glass is reheated quickly for further working or finishing.

Glory Star, Victorian See *star, wheel engraved*.

Gloucester Glass Works See *Clementon Glass Works*.

glue chip decoration An embellishment made by covering the surface of a paraison with a glue that shrinks when it dries, tending to pull flakes of glass from the surface. Then it was placed in an acid bath to remove the sharp edges and provide a satin finished texture. It was used by Frederick Carder at Steuben in the 1920s. See *feather glass*.

glyptic Susceptible to carving, especially as applied to hard stones and gems, but applicable to certain types of glass with incised relief cutting, such as Hochschnitt, and cameo cutting. See *plastic; ductile*.

gob A glob of molten glass cut or severed by shears from a stream of molten glass or gathered from the furnace on a blowing or bit iron. See *feeder*.

gob feeder See *feeder; glass, Manufacture of Glass, shaping*.

Cut glass goblet, hobstar and pinwheel pattern, 10-1/2" h.
Davanna Collection

Goblets, ruby glass cut-to-clear, left goblet: 8-1/2" h., right goblet: 7-1/2" h.
Davanna Collection

goblet A drinking glass with a large bowl resting on a stemmed foot, between eight and ten inches tall; some are known to measure eighteen inches. The stem is in a variety of forms and styles, some very elaborate, and sometimes in the form of a figure or an animal. The German term is *Pokal*.

goblet, covered A goblet with a cover that usually has an ornate finial (see *goblet*), used for festive events and occasionally as a loving cup, with or without handles.

goblet vase A vase in the shape of an unusually large goblet with a large bowl and footed stem. At times the mouth is narrower than the bowl, providing a collar on which to rest a cover.

Goddess's hair (Aka *Pele's hair*) Natural glass fibers made by strong winds blowing across molten basaltic volcanic rock.

godet A drinking cup or jug.

godet lamp A suspended spearbutt (truncated cone) or cup-shaped lamp. See *mosque lamp*.

gold (a) A metallic agent used in imparting color to glass. See *gold ruby glass; purple of Cassius*. (b) The metal used in its various forms to embellish glassware, e.g., as gold leaf (see *Zwischengoldglas; fondi d'oro; gold engraving*), granular gilding, and gilt painting, either fired on or unfired (see *gilding*).

Gold Aurene See *Aurene*.

gold aventurine See *aventurine*.

gold band (mosaic) glassware A ribbon glassware embellished all over with vertical bands of varicolored or colorless glass. Some bands are formed of gold foil laminated between two layers of clear glass. Specimens exist in the form of small *alabastra* made in Egypt and the eastern Mediterranean region during the 2nd and 1st century B.C.

gold decoration Embellishment on glassware by using gold in one of its forms: (a) gold leaf encased between two layers of clear glass; (b) gold leaf or powder mixed with a fixative, painted on as an enamel and fixed by firing; and (c) gold leaf applied to the surface using a semi-permanent fixative without firing. Gilding is most frequently done by (b) above. In this, the gold is mixed with a fixative, such as honey, egg white, mercury, etc.

The resultant thick liquid is painted or brushed on the object, then fired in a low temperature kiln. It may be combined with different enamel colors or used alone. The gold lacks luster when taken from the kiln but may be burnished to a high luster.

Cold gilding is a less permanent method of embellishment requiring the gold leaf to be laid over some sort of oil or gum on the glass and dried at room temperature or very low heat. It is fragile and easily washed or rubbed off. This is used mainly on cheaper objects. "Fancy" Victorian cut glass ware was often gilded in this manner and, even though the gold may have been rubbed or washed off, the pattern may be visible because of the fixative.

gold engraving A style of embellishment on gold leaf applied to the back of glass. The gold leaf is engraved with a pointed object; the design is safeguarded either by the glass itself or an additional layer of glass fused or cemented over it.

gold glass (1) Glass having gold leaf applied to its surface or sandwiched between two layers of glass. It has been made since the Hellenistic period, throughout the Roman period until today. See *Zwischengoldglaser*. (2) Glass in which a small amount of gold (colloidal) has been added to the batch during production, imparting a ruby red color to it. See *gold ruby glass*.

Gold Ruby A ruby glass made with gold by the New England Glass Company.

gold ruby glass Glass with a deep ruby color made as a result of a precipitate of colloidal gold being added to the batch. The procedure for making it was alluded to by Antonio Neri in his book published in 1612. It was later developed by Johann Kunckel, probably before 1679, at the Drewitz glasshouse in Potsdam, near Berlin. He used gold chloride in the batch and reheated (struck) the grayish finished object, producing the ruby color.

Some less expensive Bohemian glass imitations were made by using copper instead of gold, by flashing ruby colored glass over colorless glass, or by adding a ruby stain over colorless glass. These were often cut and engraved showing the design contrasted against the underlayer of clear glass. In the United States, solid gold ruby glass was made by most of the leading glass manufacturers. Being rather expensive to make, it was often used only for parts of objects. *Amberina* was a variation of gold ruby glass.

gold sandwich glass See *Bohemian glass; Zwischengoldglas.*

gold topaz A deep yellow stain developed by Friedrich Egermann.

Golden Agate glass See *Holly Amber glassware.*

Golden Glow A trademark registered on April 22, 1913 by H. C. Fry Glassware Company and used on its glass reflectors.

Golden Novelty Manufacturing Company See *Golden & Jacobson.*

Goldstone glass Gold aventurine glass, brownish with innumerable tiny and closely spaced spangles of gold. The same embellishment has been used on some Chinese snuff bottles and paperweights.

Good Success Plaque See *Bonus Eventus Plaque.*

Goodman, Harry (1883–1961) Born in Latvia, he came to the United States about 1900 and worked as an engraver of jewelry and silverware in Coudersport and Honesdale, Pennsylvania. By 1919 he moved to Corning, New York, and opened a jewelry store. From 1925 to 1931, he cut and engraved bits of fine crystal and art glass, setting them in jewelry.

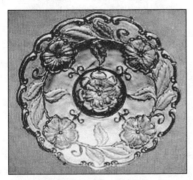

Goofus glass plate in gold with red flowers, 11" d.
Davanna Collection

Goofus glass (Aka *Mexican Ware, Hooligan glass, Pickle glass*) An inexpensive type of luster painted glassware, spray painted prior to firing. Harry Northwood and other American glassmakers made a lot of it during the late 1800s, including Crescent Glass, Imperial Glass, and LaBelle Glass from about 1890 to 1920. It lost its popularity because, as the glass was repeatedly handled and washed, the paint tarnished or scaled off. It was originally painted gold, red, green, bronze, pink, purple, and other bright colors; red and gold combinations were more common than blues and greens. Bowls and trays are the most common items found. The favorite designs involved flowers of all types. It was used as a premium or prize at carnivals, fairs, etc.

Goose Neck Vases A product of Louis Comfort Tiffany, the vases imitated Persian rosewater flasks, having a bulbous base and a tall curving neck or stem.

gorge de pigeon A soft grayish-pink color used extensively in France during the Napoleonic era, primarily in making opaline glass.

Gorham Silver Company A silver ware manufacturing company that also specialized in silver deposit glass.

Gossler Process See *glass fiber.*

Gothic arch A cut glass motif created by curved miters that converge into a sharp point at the top, resembling a Gothic arch. It is often used to separate other motifs.

gottefle (Greek) The Greek equivalent of the *gutraf.* See *gutraf.*

Gould & Hoare See *Hoare, J., & Company.*

gourd A bottle. A hollowed-out gourd was often used for the same purpose as a bottle.

government job Friggers or other offhand items made by a glassworker for himself or his friends using the owner's material and, on occasion, made on the owner's time.

Gowans-Kent Co. A Canadian glass cutting company that used the trademark *Elite.* See *Clapperton & Sons.*

Graal glass An ornamental glassware developed in 1916 by Simon Gate at Orrefors Glasbruk, made by a process that was a variation of that used by Emile Galle in making his cased glass. It involved making an object of cased glass and cutting and etching a pattern through the outer layer to reveal the inner layer. Then the object was subjected to furnace temperatures to impart fluidity and smoothness to the design and was flashed with clear glass.

Originally, the ware used was thin and light, but, after 1930, Vicke Lindstrand and Edward Held revamped the technique. The ware was heavier, more massive, and thickly cased, and sometimes combined with the techniques used to make Ariel glass. The name was inspired by the legend of the Holy Grail. Production techniques have been advanced in recent years by designer Eva Englund, who makes pieces featuring animals and flowers.

grace cup A ceremonial standing cup passed from person to person at the table after grace was said.

graffito, vetro *(Italian)* Literally, *engraved glass.* An ornamental glassware with surface embellishment created by engraving applied gold leaf.

Graham, E.E., Glass Works (Company) A glass manufacturing facility established in 1895 in Brilliant, Ohio.

Granger, C., & Co. See *Mount Vernon Glass Company.*

Granger, O.H., & Company (1844-1890) A bottle and flask manufacturing facility in Mt. Pleasant, New York, formerly known as the Mount (Mt.) Vernon Glass Company [see *Mount (Mt.) Vernon Glass Company*]. It moved from Vernon, New York, because the supply of wood was exhausted. The new operator was O.H. Granger & Company, becoming Granger, James & Co., then Granger, James & Todd. It was commonly known as Granger Company, the Mount (Mt.) Pleasant Glass Works, the Saratoga (Mountain) Glasshouse, Lake Desolation Glass Works, or simply the Mountain (Glass) Works. About 1865 it was acquired by the Congress Spring Company, which became the Congress & Empire Spring Company. It

moved to the Congressville section of Saratoga and was then known as the Congressville Glass Works or the Congress & Empire Spring Company Glass Works. See *Mountain Glass Factory.*

Granger, James & Co.; Granger, James & Todd; Granger Company See *Granger, O.H., & Company.*

Granger, Southworth & Co. See *Mt. Vernon Glass Company.*

granite-backed glass Sheet glass with a rough texture on one side.

Granite Glass Company A black glass bottle manufacturing facility established in (South) Stoddard, New Hampshire, in 1842 by Joseph Foster, failing shortly thereafter. He built another in the area, but the operation was marginal at best, and, in 1850, it was taken over by the Granite Glass Works. See *Granite Glass Works; Foster's, Joseph, Glasshouse.*

Granite Glass Works A bottle glass manufacturing facility established in 1846 in Stoddard (Mill Village), New Hampshire, by Gillman Scripture, Calvin Curtis, and John M. Whiton. It burned that winter and was immediately rebuilt. In 1850 it purchased Joseph Foster's facility in (South) Stoddard (see *Granite Glass Company; Foster's, Joseph, Glasshouse*), operating it in conjunction with its own. In 1856 the works failed and Curtis & Messer (George L. Curtis and B.F. Messer) took over operations. In 1858 the partnership was dissolved and Curtis operated it alone until 1872, when it closed. It made demijohns, black glass bottles, figured flasks, and jars.

granular gilding A style of gilt embellishment used on glassware, giving the surface a granular dust-like appearance. It was used on several pieces of Venetian cristallo, on some wares made in Southern Netherlands during the 16th century, and on some of the goblets attributed to Jacopo Verzelini. See *G S Goblet.*

grape cluster flask A flask (amphoriskos) embellished with a mold blown cluster of grapes on both sides. The sides were made from the same mold and then joined. Some had a short neck and small mouth, but others with a spreading base or flat foot had a tall neck, disk mouth, two vertical side handles and two small loops at the rim for a carrying strap. The seam indicates where the two identical sides were joined. They were made of Roman glass in Syria and probably in Italy and Gaul, in the 1st to 3rd centuries. Similar ones have dates instead of grapes. See *shell flask*.

grape ripener A hollow dome-shaped object about ten inches high with one flattened side and an orifice on the shoulder through which a developing bunch of grapes is inserted to promote growth and ripening. There is a knob at the top to suspend it outdoors, yet prevent animals from feeding on them. They were frequently made of Nailsea glassware.

grapefruit glass A relatively modern piece of glassware with a hemispherical bowl resting on a flat base, used for serving a half of a grapefruit.

grate (Aka *fire grate* or *siege*). The area in a glass furnace between the melting chamber and ash pit where fuel is fed to the furnace and through which ashes fall into the ash pit.

Gravic glass A name used by T.G. Hawkes & Company for its intaglio cut glass. Most pieces bore the acid etched signature "Hawkes Gravic Glass."

Cut glass gravy boat with matching (separate) underplate.
Davanna Collection

gravy boat An oval bowl used for serving gravy. Most have a spout for pouring and a handle at the opposite end. Some have a matching plate either separate or attached to the bowl.

Gray, John T. A company operating in Pittsburgh, Pennsylvania, during the 1870s, manufacturing glass signs.

Gray & Hemingray A glass manufacturing facility established in 1848 in Cincinnati, Ohio, moving in 1851 to Covington, Kentucky and operating until 1865, then moving to Muncie, Indiana. It made tableware, lamp glass, apothecary bottles, chemical apparatus, etc.

Grease Blue A shiny, very deep electric blue glass made by the Boston & Sandwich Glass Company, used often in making dolphin forms.

grease pan See *drip pan*.

great salt (Aka *standing salt*) A large salt cellar used as a communal salt.

Greek glassware Until recently, no glassmaking site on the Greek mainland or its islands, dating from antiquity, had been discovered. Some samples of inferior glass have been attributed to a shop in Crete, probably dating from the 3rd to the 1st centuries B.C. There is some evidence that it was made on Rhodes and Cyprus, and a shop has been discovered on the mainland at Olympia. It was also made at Corinth and a few other locations during the 11th and 12th centuries A.D.

Greek vases See *alabastron, amphora, amphoriskos, aryballos, askos, diota, kylix, kalpis, kantharos, karchesion, krater, kyathos, lagynos, lekthos, oenochoe, olpe, pelike, phiale, pyxis, prochoos, skyphos, stamnos.* For Roman names, see *acetabulum, ampulla, modiolus, poculum, stamnium, trulla.*

Greek wave pattern See *Vitruvian scroll.*

Green, Haughton See *black glass.*

Green Aurene See *Aurene.*

green aventurine See *aventurine.*

Green Bank (or Greenbank) Glasshouse (1842-1858) A glass manufacturing facility established in Green Bank, New Jersey, by William Coffin Sr. and his son, Bodine (some sources state it was his son John). When William Sr. died in 1844, Bodine (or John) operated it until just prior to 1850. From March 1850 until February 1852, E.L. Wells & Company operated it. From March 1852 until July 1853 it was operated by

D.O. Ketchum, making bottles. From August 1853 to 1857 it was closed. In 1857 it was operated for a short time by a group of glass-blowers from Glassboro, New Jersey, making glass on a cooperative plan.

green glass (1) Glass of a natural green or brownish color caused by the presence of iron in the batch. It is considered natural color because it is neither rendered colorless by the use of decolorizing agents nor artificially colored by colorizing agents (see *definition 2* below). It is often called *bottle glass* because it was often used to make some bottles. It is generally made from coarser, less pure materials than from finer wares. See *Waldglas; Nailsea glass.* (2) Glass deliberately colored green by the use of oxides of copper, chromium, iron, and sometimes uranium. See *uranium glass; Annagrun.*

green milk glass See *milk glass.*

Green Opaque glassware An art glass of a yellowish-green solid color, not cased, often with a blue stain used to produce a mottled pattern on the upper part of the object. If the blue stain is used, the object is embellished with a gold border below it. It was developed by the New England Glass Co. about 1887.

green quartz See *quartz glass.*

Greenaway, Kate (1846-1901) A famous illustrator of children's books. Her first book, *Under the Willows*, was published in 1878. Her sketches were published in newspapers and magazines and on greeting cards, and pictures of children and other designs often appear on glassware. The girls are identified by their high-waisted Empire dresses.

Greenpoint Flint Glass Works A glass manufacturing facility founded by Christian Dorflinger in 1860 with assistance from Nathaniel S. Bailey in New York City, New York. Dorflinger used his version of the assembly line, having several workers working on one piece of glass. They made a lot of rich cut and eloquently engraved glassware. President and Mrs. Lincoln placed an order for his cut glass for the White House. When Dorflinger semi-retired in 1862, he entrusted the facility to Nathaniel Bailey and John B. Dobelmann.

After a disagreement with Bailey, Dorflinger bought him out in 1872. Dobelmann then took over and, in 1873, changed the name to J.B. Dobelmann Company, a subsidiary of C. Dorflinger & Sons. In 1875 Dorflinger bought out Dobelmann, who continued to manage the facility until 1882, at which time Dorflinger leased it to Elliot P. Gleason to make lighting fixtures. See *Dorflinger, C., & Sons.*

Greensburg Glass Company A pressed glass manufacturing facility (previously operated as the Brilliant Glass Works) established in 1889 in Greensburg, Pennsylvania. It joined the National Glass Company in 1899 and closed in 1902.

Greentown glass Glass made by the Indiana Tumbler & Goblet Company, Greentown, Indiana, between 1894 and 1903. In 1899 it became part of the National Glass Company. Its patterns were often numbered as well as named and made in clear, milk, and colored glass. The dolphin dish and cover with a fish finial is its most famous piece. Jacob Rosenthal developed his famous chocolate glass there in 1900, and in 1903 he developed the color *Golden Agate* with the Holly Amber pattern expressly designed for its production. See *Indiana Tumbler & Goblet Company.*

greeting card See *window greeting card.*

Gregory, Mary (Alice) (1856-1908) Born in Providence, Rhode Island, Gregory lived most of her life in Sandwich, Cape Cod, Massachusetts, working as a decorator at the Boston & Sandwich Glass Company from 1872 until 1888. She was a follower of Kate Greenaway, an English illustrator of children's books, imitating her style by painting or enameling glassware with figures of young girls and boys. Her sisters also worked for the company as decorators. Contrary to popular belief, it is now believed she and her sisters decorated wares in colors, not just in white. See *Gregory, Mary, glassware.*

Gregory, Mary, glassware (1) Glassware made at the Boston & Sandwich Glass Company embellished by Mary Alice Gregory. The embellishment was believed to have been always in white enamel and never tinted, but now it is believed she decorated many objects in colors. The children she depicted on glassware were always in the five- to twelve-year range and were performing some activity (e.g., holding a butterfly net, looking into a birdhouse, holding or blowing a horn, flying a kite, holding or picking flowers, etc.). (2) Glassware made in the United States during the 1870s and 1880s embellished with figures of young children solely in white enamel, regardless of maker or artist. See *Gregory, Mary, type glassware.*

Mary Gregory-type glassware: green glass vase, 8" h.; blue glass pitcher, 4-1/2" h.
Davanna Collection

Gregory, Mary, -type glassware

Glassware in the Mary Gregory style made in the United States, Europe, and elsewhere. It may be divided into two categories: (a) that made during the 1870s through the 1890s, and (b) that made in recent years. Items made from the 1870s until about 1900 are considered Mary Gregory type glassware even though much was made during the Mary Gregory era from about 1872 to 1888. It is distinguished from Mary Gregory glass by one or more of the following: (1) Mary Gregory glassware is always enameled solely in pure white (see *Gregory, Mary, glassware [2]*) while Mary Gregory type may have tinted enamels (e.g., flesh tones, rouge, etc.); (2) Mary Gregory glassware depicts children from five to twelve years old while Mary Gregory type may depict teenage children; (3) the glass used for Mary Gregory glassware is typically cruder than the more refined and ornamental glassware used for the Mary Gregory type; (4) in Mary Gregory glassware, the enameling is usually lighter and plainer than that on Mary Gregory

type, which is usually heavier and more elaborate; and (5) Mary Gregory glassware was made until about 1888 while the Mary Gregory type was made until about 1900. One type was made by the Mt. Washington Glassworks in the 1890s for Pairpoint Manufacturing Company, which used it with their silver holders. The other Mary Gregory type is that made in more recent years and/or that which is being made today. Much is made in Mexico and is extremely crude. West Germany is making some cheaply designed items with tinted figures (imported by A.A. Import Co. of St. Louis, Missouri). The Westmoreland Glass Co. made some fair reproductions consisting of a series of four plates, all in black glass with reticulated borders, and four vases.

Grenade fire extinguisher, clear liquid, 4-1/2" d.
Davanna Collection

Grenades, left and right have pale red liquid, center contains dark red liquid, 5-1/4" l. x 3-3/4" d. Davanna Collection

grenade A sealed bottle of globular shape with a short neck, serving as a rather primitive form of fire extinguisher. They were filled with water and hurled into the flames. Early ones, about 3.5 inches in diameter, have been discovered in the arsenal at Rhodes. See *bomb.*

grey (or gray) cutting The frosted surface appearing on glassware after it has been decorated by cutting and before any polishing has occurred. Sometimes the frosted surface is combined with polished areas.

grid stopper A vertically flat, pressed glass stopper with vertical grooves on one side and horizontal grooves on the other so that they form a grille when observed together.

Gridel A Baccarat term for a glass cane with a black silhouette. It was named for Emile Gridel, whose silhouettes of animals were observed by his uncle, manager of Baccarat, who used the idea to create canes. Gridel later became a prominent painter.

grille plate A plate divided into sections, introduced during the 1930s. Usually they are divided into three sections, two of 90 degrees and one of 180 degrees, frequently used in restaurants to separate meat, vegetables, and potatoes.

grinder, glass See *glass grinder.*

grinding (1) The process of removing excess glass from an object being embellished using abrasives or abrasive wheels. (2) The process of giving a frosted effect to the surface of a glass object using abrasives.

grisaille (1) Decorative painting in varying shades of gray (*en grisaille*) or in white and muted colors, sometimes to simulate relief sculpture. See *monochrome; camaieu, en.* (2) A brownish paint made from an oxide of iron, fused onto the surface of glass to define details in stained glass windows. See *grisaille window.*

grisaille window A late 13th century development in making stained glass windows, enabling the maker to use plainer glass and reduce costs. Some plain portions of the window were painted in gray or brown enamel with the use of only a few pieces of colored glass, usually in brilliant reds or blues and painted with designs of trellis plants and foliage.

grosses verrerie (French) A maker of window glass as opposed to *petites verrerie*, a maker of hollowware.

grotesque From the Italian *grotteschi*, a decorative motif consisting of imaginary and, in part, half human and animal figures with acanthus foliage. They are used with masks, similar to classical theatrical masks, and mythological figures. Their inspiration was based on murals in the ruins of Nero's Golden House in Rome and adapted by Raphael in embellishing the loggie of the Vatican. As a result, they are often called *Raffaelesche* and should not be confused with arabesques. They continued to be fashionable until the beginning of the rococo period about 1730.

Grotesque glassware Mainly free-formed bowls and vases made of glass, developed and named by Frederick Carder about 1929 at Steuben. Usually they were colorless at the bottom, shading into various transparent colors toward the top. See *shaded glass.*

ground The flat or slightly domed decorative background that becomes the interior motif in a paperweight. On occasion they are simply glass of a single opaque or translucent color. They are often very detailed and quite varied, often made of many canes or of filigrana or latticino glass. See the following types of grounds: *basket; carpet; checker; choux fleur; color; cushion; filigree; gauxe; jasper; lace; latticino; moss; mottled; muslin; pebble; rock; scale; sodden snow; stardust; imbricated.*

ground gold See *ormolu.*

ground stopper A glass stopper having the portion fitting into the neck of the bottle ground, resembling frosted glass. Normally the inside of the neck is also ground to provide a snug fit.

groviglio, vetro (Italian) An ornamental glassware developed by Venini about 1950. It has a mass of irregularly twisted thin copper wires embedded throughout the glass.

grozing (Aka *knocking off*) Any one of a series of activities ranging from gnawing away slivers and pinpoints from the glass edges to doing actual carving on certain pieces. One of the most common methods of grozing is to nip away the glass using a tool that leaves a jagged edge.

grozing iron A notched spanner-like implement used by a glassmaker to snip or gnaw away a raw rim, edge, etc., of a piece of glass, leaving a jagged edge.

Guernsey Glass Company A glass manufacturing facility established in 1967 by Harold Bennett in Cambridge, Ohio, making novelty items as well as designing items made for it by others.

guest decanter A small decanter with no stopper used by a guest at his or her dinner place or bedside.

gug(g)let (Aka *gug(g)ler*) A globular bottle with a tall, thin neck and onion-shaped mouth.

guilloche A pattern of chain trailing with a large space in the midst of the loops between the pincered intersections. See *chain*.

Mosser ruby glass fairy lamp, 5-1/2" h. Davanna Collection

Gundersen (Pairpoint) Glass Works The Pairpoint facility of New Bedford, Massachusetts, was purchased by Isaac N. Babbitt in 1939. It was reopened on a small scale as the Gundersen Glass Works after Robert Martinus Gundersen, who began working at the Mount Washington Glass Works in 1888, became the new company's plant manager. An important part of its business was making replacement pieces to match those broken or lost from sets sold throughout the years. In 1952 the name became Gundersen Pairpoint, a division of National Pairpoint Co. It made some fine crystal ware, both engraved and plain, called *Pairpoint Heirlooms*.

Business slowed and it closed in December 1956. It moved to a smaller location in East Wareham, Massachusetts, beginning production in September 1957. It is sometimes called *Pairpoint of Wareham* or *Bryden's*

Pairpoint after a manager who worked at Gundersen Pairpoint. This facility closed in March 1958. In October 1956, the old facility in New Bedford was destroyed by fire. Several glass manufacturing facilities were founded by Mount Washington/Pairpoint employees. They include: Blackmer (Cut) Glass Company, New Bedford (1894-1916); Crystal Palace, Scotsdale, Arizona; Edward Koch & Company, Chicago, Illinois (1899-1926); Gibbs & Kelley, Honesdale, Pennsylvania and other locations (1895-1928); Keystone Glass Company, Hawley, Pennsylvania (1902-1918); Libbey Glass Company, Toledo, Ohio (1888-); Ohio Glass Company, founded by Pitkins & Brooks, Bowling Green, Ohio (1904-1912); Skinner Glass Company, Philadelphia, Pennsylvania (1895-); Smith Brothers, New Bedford (1874-1899); Thatcher Glass, New Bedford (1886); Thatcher Glass, Fairhaven, Massachusetts (1893-1907); and Whaling City Glass Company, New Bedford. A new Pairpoint facility was built in 1970 in Sagamore, Massachusetts. See *Mount Washington Glass Company; Pairpoint Glass Works.*

Gundersen Peachblow A "new" *Peachblow* made from 1952 to 1956 by Gundersen Pairpoint. It was not as well colored as the original and was much heavier. The original *Peachblow* was made by Mt. Washington.

Gundy-Clapperton Co. (1905-1931) A Canadian glass cutting company that operated in Toronto. See *Clapperton & Sons.*

gutraf (German) A vase with a long twisted or double twisted neck used to hold oil. It is similar to a Persian sprinkler and the Greek *gottefle.*

guttate Any decoration having a spotted appearance.

guttular jar A jar decorated with a series (usually in two parallel rows) of small S-shaped hooks attached to the body by a drop of glass, tending to loop downward and outward. They were usually of clear glass and may have appendages of clear or colored glass. They are believed to be of Russia origin, made in the 3rd and 4th centuries.

haematinum Also spelled *haematinon*. A blood red opaque glass in which cuprous oxide crystals become visible against a colorless background if viewed under a magnifying glass. It was the first glass made using lead oxide as a flux; analysis indicates it contained up to 15% lead with cuprous oxide as a coloring agent. It was made in the early Egyptian period (8th to 6th century B.C.) and the Roman period and was used in enamels and mosaics. It was first called *haematinum* by Pliny the Elder, who indicated it was made in Italy

Hagerty, A.J., & Company See *Hagerty Glass Works.*

Hagerty Glass Works (1856-1895) A glass manufacturing facility established by the Hagerty Brothers in Brooklyn, New York, making carboys, demijohns, green glass hollowware, fruit jars, and other containers. Though it operated under various names, Hagerty family members were always associated with it. It was known as A.J. Hagerty & Company when it closed.

Hahne, Joseph Hahne went to Corning, New York, after World War I to work for Hawkes as a glass cutter. He worked there until he retired in 1943. He operated a home cutting shop in Corning from 1930 until his death in 1944.

Haid, L.E. A Pittsburgh, Pennsylvania, company making ornamental glass signs during the 1870s.

Haines, Jonathan See *Clementon Glass House; Waterford Glass Works; Hammonton Glass Works.*

hair jewelry Designed as a memorial for the dead, hair jewelry was created in the form of brooches and lockets within which was a lock of hair mounted on a silk background or on a gold slide under a faceted crystal medallion. Generally, the initials of the dead are woven on the silk or engraved in the gold. They were popular in England and in Europe from the 17th through the 19th centuries.

hair pin Thin glass pins used to hold hair in place. They were made in varying lengths from about 4-3/4 to 6-1/4 inches and in a variety of decorative styles. They were made in China during the T'ang Dynasty (618-906). Some were hollow with heads in the form of a lotus bud.

hair receiver A part of a dresser or vanity set used for holding hair left on a brush or comb. They were was usually 1-3/16 to 2-3/8 inches high and 3-1/8 to 4-3/4 inches in diameter and had a cover with a 3/4- to 1-1/2-inch hole.

hairline crack A fine line in a glass object brought about by trauma—stress, heat, or age. It may be restricted to the exterior or penetrate the glass. Many are caused by the outer surface of the glass cooling more rapidly than the interior, causing stress. Those in pressed glass are caused by the mold and plunger not being kept at a uniform temperature or because of slight slippage within the mold. Most occur on the plunger side of the object, the side normally not having a pattern.

Hale, Atterbury & Company See *White House Works.*

Haley, Jonathan Born in England in 1841, Haley came to the United States in the late 1860s, settling in Cambridge, Massachusetts, where he was joined by his brother, William. Together they created many glassware designs. Jonathan later worked for the Rochester Tumbler Company where he designed a steam-operated glass press, receiving a patent in 1873. In 1874 when his son, Reuben (see *Haley, Reuben*), was two, he went to Russia where he sold the rights to his press design for $30,000, which he used to establish the Findlay Glass Company. He secured a contract with New York City to provide heavy pressed glass plates used in the "vault lights" in the new subway system. During the financial panic of 1893, the city lacked funds to pay for the glass, and Haley went bankrupt. He was noted for his animal designs that included the monkey, owl, donkey, and stork.

Haley, K. R., Glassware Company

(1905-1987) Kenneth R. Haley was born into a family famous for its glassware designers; his grandfather, Jonathan, and his father, Rueben, both plied the art. While in school, Kenneth worked summers in the model shop of the United States Glass Company, later becoming a member of the sales department. He then went to work for the Old Economy Glass Company, later Morgantown Glass, as assistant sales manager. He worked for his father for a while in 1926 at Consolidated Glass, while working for the United States Glass Company. He learned to carve and chisel molds while designing for other companies. He married Mary Lewis, daughter of the president of Consolidated Glass.

From 1928 to 1934, Haley worked as a design engineer for the Phoenix Glass Company. When his father died in 1933, he inherited some of the molds from the *Martele* line, made by his father for Consolidated Lamp & Glass Company. Since Consolidated had closed in April 1933, Kenneth entered into a contract with Phoenix for a percentage of the sales of glassware made from these molds.

When Consolidated reopened in 1936, it demanded the return of the molds (which were returned in early 1937) and continued to make the line and expanded it. In 1934 Kenneth went to Greensburg, Pennsylvania, to execute molds for the Overmeyer Mold Company of Pennsylvania, becoming vice president of the company in 1937. In 1939, in partnership with Herman Lowerwitz (president of American Glass Company), he established the General Glassware Company, a glassware distributor in Greensburg, designing and making models of glassware.

The American Glass Company of Carney, Kansas, an affiliate of General Glassware, used these designs and models to make molds from which they made wares sold through the General Glassware Company. When Lowerwitz died in 1946, Kenneth dissolved the partnership, incorporating as K. R. Haley Glassware Company, which closed in 1972. In 1967 Kenneth became vice president and sales manager of the Louie Glass Company in Weston, West Virginia. He was never directly involved with making glassware in any of his ventures.

Haley, Reuben (1872-1933) The son of

Jonathan Haley (see *Haley, Jonathan*), who, when young, went to New England, working as a die maker for a silver manufacturing firm. He moved to Pairpoint and, when it closed in 1893, went to work for Hocking Glass Company before returning to the Midwest to work for Fostoria Glass Company. A few years after the National Glass Company was formed, he went to work there as chief designer. He was particularly successful in creating a number of pressed glass imitations of heavy cut glass for various facilities in the National combine. He made some designs for the *Near-Cut* pattern of Cambridge Glass and for the *Prescut* patterns of McKee. He brought out the *Chippendale* line for the Lancaster facility and did some work for Beatty-Brady Glass Co., Ohio Flint Glass, Riverside, and Rochester Tumbler

After the breakup of the National Glass Company, he formed a partnership with Addison Thompson in Rochester, Pennsylvania, designing wares for many glass companies. After this partnership was dissolved, he started his own company, Metal Products Company, in Beaver, Pennsylvania. About 1911 he was employed by United States Glass Company as chief designer, becoming vice president, and remaining there for about fifteen years. He then went to work for the Phoenix Glass Company where he worked until his death.

In his own business, he designed glassware for several companies including Consolidated Lamp & Glass Company (designing the *Martele* line for them), Indiana Tumbler Company, and Morgantown Glass Company, making most of the molds as well. This accounted for the similarities in many of the early lines made by these companies. His son was Kenneth Haley.

Haley, William See *Haley, Jonathan*.

Haley Brothers Glass Factory (1892-1895) A glass manufacturing facility established in Bloomdale, Ohio, making pressed glassware, glass tiles, and glass washboards usually marked "Gem Manufacturing Company."

half decker glassware Glass vessels in the form of an oval sauceboat with the front half mostly covered, leaving only a small orifice for pouring. It is debatable whether they were sauceboats (which they are similar to), cream boats, or baby feeding vessels.

half-hour glass A sand glass used on a ship to measure the time of a watch (the time a sailor was required to stay on deck and keep watch for other ships, shoals, lighthouses, icebergs, etc.). Usually, the time measured was less than a half-hour, often fourteen or twenty-eight minutes.

half lead crystal Lead crystal containing between 24% and 30% lead oxide. If the crystal contains in excess of 30% lead oxide, it is called full lead crystal.

half-post method A process for molding an object in which a gather (or *post*) of molten glass is dipped into the pot a second time so it is covered half way (*half post*) with additional molten glass. The gather is somewhat thicker on the lower half and less susceptible to breakage. It was used in making some Pitkin flasks.

Hall, David & Neal See *Kilgore & Hanna.*

Hall, Pancoast & Craven See *Salem Glass Works.*

Hall & Callahan (1914-1917) A glass cutting shop established in Meridan, Connecticut.

Hall & Grovier (1835-1843) A glass manufacturing facility in Mount Clemens, Michigan, making free-blown wares.

hall lantern A lantern often with a highly decorative frame or case, to be suspended from a hook in the ceiling of a lobby, foyer, hallway, etc.

Hallorenglas *(German)* Made in Saxony from 1679 to 1732, a Humpen or Stangenglas, often with a cover, with colored enameling illustrating the biennial Pentecost observance of the guild of salt workers of the town of Halle-an-der-Saale in Saxony. They were decorated in one of four styles, all of which show a panorama of the town, the guild house, the procession of marchers, and the arms of the guild. It was customary for a marcher to carry such a beaker in the procession.

Hallstatt cups Small cups of Celtic glass discovered in Hallstatt, Austria, made from the 6th to the 5th centuries B.C. and reported to be some of the earliest vessels not made over a core. They taper inward toward a small base and generally are embellished with vertical ribbing.

Halter, J., & Company Joseph Halter is known to have been a glass cutter as early as 1905 in Brooklyn, New York. In 1909 he established J. Halter & Company, a glass cutting facility there. Later he established a second facility there, called Halter Cut Glass Company Incorporated. The company closed in 1921.

Hamilton, William In 1814 he patented the egg-shaped bottle for containing mineral waters. The bottle had to be laid on its side, keeping the cork moist to prevent the carbon dioxide from escaping. They became popular during the 1840s and continued to be made until 1916.

Hamilton & Company A glass manufacturing facility established in Pittsburgh, Pennsylvania, in 1863 by W.H. Hamilton & Company, making flint glass bottles, vials, druggists' ware, and green glass. Another was erected in 1880. In 1886 its name became J.T. & A. Hamilton.

Hamilton (Glass) Manufacturing Society (Company) See *Albany Glass House.*

Hamilton Glass Works (1) A window and bottle glass manufacturing facility established about 1816 in Hamilton County, Ohio, and believed to have closed in the early 1820s. (2) A glass manufacturing facility established in Hamilton, Ontario, Canada, in 1865 by Gatchell, Moore & Co. It was operated by (Geo.) Rutherford & Co. from 1872 to 1892. In 1892 it was purchased by the Diamond Glass Company Limited of Montreal, Canada, which later became the Dominion Glass Company Limited. It closed in 1895. It made bottles and a variety of other glass containers.

Hammonton Cut Glass Company A small, short-lived glass cutting shop operating about 1910 in Hammonton, New Jersey.

Hammonton Glass Works (1817-1857) William Coffin Sr. erected a cylinder glass manufacturing facility in Hammondtown (now Hammonton), New Jersey, named after his son, John Hammond Coffin. Bottles and flasks were added shortly after production started.

About 1819 Jonathan Haines of the Clementon Glassworks became a partner, leaving to establish the Waterford Glass Works in Waterford, New Jersey in 1822. In 1823 Coffin made his son, William Jr., a partner. In 1828 William Jr. became a partner in the firm of Coffin, Pearsall & Company, erecting a facility in Millville, New Jersey. After about two years at the Hammonton Glass Works, William Jr. withdrew to help his father establish a new facility in Winslow, New Jersey. William Sr. continued to manage the Hammonton facility until 1836.

In 1836, Bodine Coffin (another son of William Sr.) and Andrew K. Hay (a son-in-law of William Sr.) took over management of the facility under the name of Coffin & Hay. In 1838, the Coffin & Hay partnership was dissolved. Other Coffin & Hay partnerships arose in the future, i.e., Coffin & Hay in Winslow Township, New Jersey. William Coffin Sr. again managed the facility, which burned in the same year. It was rebuilt and reopened in 1840.

In 1844 William Coffin Sr. died. The company was managed by two of his sons, William Jr. and Edwin Winslow Coffin. In 1851 Edwin sold his interest to William Jr., who continued to operate the facility until it closed. See *Clementon Glass Works.*

Hamon Glass Company A glass manufacturing facility established in 1932 in Scott Depot, West Virginia. Hamon began blowing glass at ten, was a consultant for the Kanawha Glass Company, and taught glassmaking at Pilgrim Glass Company. Hamon Glass made many types of glassware, including paperweights, blown glass, and glass

sculptures and marbles. It began to make crackle glass in the late 1940s. In 1966 it merged with Kanawha Glass Company, each keeping its own name and operations. Some wares identified as Kanawha were possibly Hamon and vice versa.

hanap (Aka *standing cup*) A large drinking cup in the shape of a goblet with feet and no handles, popular in the 17th century.

Ruby glass hand bell, 4-1/4" d. x 7-1/4" h. Davanna Collection

hand bell A bell with a vertical handle, usually seven to eight inches tall. They have been made for centuries and are still being made today.

hand blown Free blown glass; glassware or objects made without a mold.

hand candlestick See *chamber candlestick.*

hand cooler A solid ovoid object used (a) by ladies in ancient Rome to cool their hands, (b) in the 18th and 19th centuries by young ladies attending dances and being wooed, (c) as a darning egg, or (d) on occasion, if egg-shaped, to attract hens to the nest. Some were made by St. Louis with millefiori embellishment. Steuben made molded and polished hand coolers in ovoid animal form, such as a sleeping cat.

hand mirror A small mirror set in a frame with a projecting handle, used most often at a dressing table.

hand molded Hand pressed. See *Glass, Manufacturing, Shaping.*

hand on breast See *Mano sul Seno, La (Italian)*.

hand press A small press similar to a pair of pliers having large jaws with a design or pattern on them. They have been used in Europe since at least 1785, and later in the United States to press stoppers for decanters, parts for chandeliers, and the feet of salts, goblets, and compotes.

hand pressed (Aka *hand molded*) Glass made using a hand-operated press as opposed to machine-operated press.

hand warmer See *pulse glass*.

Handel Glass Co. (1885-1936) Philip J. Handel (1866-1914) was trained as a glass designer and decorator at the Meriden Flint Glass Company. In 1885 he went into a partnership with Adolph Eyden, opening a decorating shop in Meriden, Connecticut, called Eyden & Handel. In 1893 he took control, renaming it Handel & Company, commonly known as the Handel Glass Company. The company made no glassware; it only decorated glassware with etching, enameling, and/or painting. After his death it was managed by his widow, Fanny. In 1919 management was taken over by Philip's cousin William Handel. The business, which became The Handel Company, made primarily decorative gas and electric lamps with glass shades in the Tiffany style. It made leaded, reverse painted, ice(d) glass and other types of shades. Many of these were decorated by *chipping*, often used on overshot glass. The result was a shade commonly called the *chipped ice shade*. The ware was usually marked "Handel."

Handkerchief vase, green,
4" h. x 5-1/2" d.
Davanna Collection

handkerchief vase A vase most often of 20th century Venetian glass. The sides were pulled straight up and randomly pleated, resembling a handkerchief. See *handkerchief bowl; vaso fazzoletto*.

handlapping The process of hand rubbing glass with diamond or Carborundum pads to remove or correct engraving mistakes or eliminate minor defects.

handle A part of a cup, mug, jug, creamer, or other vessel by which it is held when used or carried, usually having a space for the fingers or hand for holding and strong enough to support the object and its contents. A handle is distinguished from a lug, which does not have space for fingers or hand. Although usually single (as on a creamer, gravy boat, cup, etc.), double handles (as on a sugar, some nappies, and some heavier vessels) are not rare. Wares with three or more handles are rare. Handles may be horizontal or vertical, single or interlaced at the side of the vessel, or overhead (bail), in many shapes and styles. See *celery handle; intertwined handle; open handled; handles, knife and fork*.

handle, strap See *strap handle*.

handle gatherer A worker with a team or shop, responsible for gathering the quantity of molten glass needed to form a handle.

handler A highly skilled worker responsible for putting handles on pitchers and other glassware. The work must be done quickly while the handle and body are within the appropriate temperature range—cool enough to maintain shape, not too cool to prevent adherence, and not too great of a temperature difference between them so as to cause heat checks.

handler's marks An identification mark used by some glasshouses to identify the worker who applied the handle to an article. Fenton has used these marks since the late 1930s.

handles, knife and fork Glass handles into which were inserted a steel or silver knife or fork. Cut glass handles were popular at the end of the 19th century. See *knife; cutlery*.

hanging lamp A lamp suspended from the ceiling by chains attached to the rim, mainly used in a church. In its simplest form, it is a shallow bowl with a ball finial at the bottom. The earliest were made of Persian glass. See *mosque lamp; lampada pensile; cesendello; sanctuary lamp.*

hanging unguentarium An unguentarium with loops for attaching to a suspensory cord. Some have a tall overhead loop. Some double unguentaria have two such loops, above which is a third. Still others have a series of small loops along the sides.

Hanna & Wallace See *Union Flint Glass Works (Pittsburgh, Pennsylvania).*

Hannen, Henry, & Co. A glass manufacturing facility established in Birmingham (Pittsburgh), Pennsylvania, prior to 1850, making brown and colored glassware.

Harcum & Co. See *Hope Glass Works (Pennsylvania).*

hard glass Glass with a high melting temperature that has nothing to do with the physical property of hardness.

harmonica glass See *musical glasses.*

Harmony, D., & Co. See *Cookstown Glass Works.*

Harmony Glassworks A glass manufacturing facility established in 1813 in what is now Glassboro, New Jersey. It was founded after Edward Carpenter died and the Olive Glassworks started to decline. At that time some glassblowers from the Olive Glassworks, led by some of the Stanger family and John Rink, built a new furnace near the Olive works. This facility was named the Harmony Glassworks, which operated as Rink, Stanger & Company.

When Rink died in 1823, his interest was purchased by Daniel K. Miller, owner of the Franklin Glass Works of Malaga, New Jersey, founded by Christian L. Stanger in 1810. The Harmony Glassworks merged with the Olive Glassworks in 1824, forming the Olive & Harmony Glassworks. In 1834 the Stanger family, represented by Lewis Stanger, sold its one-third interest in the company to Thomas H. Whitney,

who purchased all other interests in 1837 and changed the name to Whitney & Brothers.

The "brothers" were his two sons, Thomas H. and Samuel A., who took over the company upon the death of their father, changing the name to Whitney Brothers. The name was changed to Whitney Glass Works in 1882. See *Olive Glassworks; Olive & Harmony Glassworks.*

Hartell & Lancaster; Hartell, Letchworth & Co. See *Union Flint Glass Co. (Kensington, Pennsylvania).*

Hartford Glass Manufactory A bottle glass manufacturing facility established in Hartford, Connecticut, in 1827 by Merrow & Bidwell, making bottles, flasks, jars, canisters, inkstands, ink bottles, and other offhand pieces.

Hartley, James An English glassmaker who, in 1847, patented a process for making thin sheets of glass by pouring molten glass directly onto a casting table. The molten glass was rolled to form an inexpensive, rough plate glass. The cathedral glass and figured rolled glass used in making stained glass today is the result of his work.

Hartman, Henry F. A glass cutter from St. Louis, Missouri, who worked at the Missouri Glass Company. He worked for the Findlay Cut Glass Company after he moved to Ohio. He opened his own glass cutting shop in 1922 in Findlay.

Harvard (1) (Aka *chairbottom*) A cut glass motif, a variation of the *cane* motif in which alternate buttons are starred and crosshatched. In some cases alternate rows of buttons are starred and crosshatched; in others alternate buttons in the same row are starred and crosshatched. (2) A Libbey cut glass pattern bearing no resemblance to the *chairbottom* pattern of the same name. It is a *square-on-square* motif—a square cut over a square of the same size (at a 90° angle) inside of a larger set of squares cut in the same manner. The resultant triangles near the edge are crosshatched or diamond cut. Fans are cut between these triangles and the scalloped edge of the piece.

Harvard Glass Flowers (Aka *Ware Collection*) A collection of naturalistic full-size reproductions and anatomical sections of numerous flowers made in glass, all botanically accurate. It consists of 847 life-size models of flowers from America and other countries, plus 3,218 enlarged flower and anatomical sections representing more than 780 species and varieties of 164 families of flowering plants. There are also three special exhibits: lower plant (ferns, fungi, and bryophytes); fungal diseases on fruits; and pollenization with insects. These were made *at-the-lamp* by Leopold Blaschka and his son, Rudolf, near Dresden, Germany, between 1887 and 1939. Leopold died in 1895 and Rudolf continued with the project alone. They were donated to the Botanical Museum of Harvard University in memory of Dr. Charles Eliot Ware by his widow and daughter, Elizabeth C. and Mary Lee Ware, who financed their making.

Haselbauer, Frederick The owner of an engraving shop in Corning, New York, which operated between 1921 and 1938, making engraved and light cut wares. See *Haselbauer, J.F., & Sons.*

Haselbauer, Joseph F. (1852-1949) Born in Bohemia, Haselbauer came to the United States in 1866 to study engraving. He and his brother, Augustus, worked for Hoare & Daily in Brooklyn, then Corning, and then back to Brooklyn. Joseph's training ended in 1875; he became a master cutter. From then he operated his own glass cutting shop where he did work for Hoare, Dorflinger, and others. He became a teacher of the art, his first pupil being his son, Frederick, who began engraving studies about 1900. In 1910 Joseph, Frederick, and another son, George, turned their shop into a business called J.F. Haselbauer & Sons. After the business closed in 1938, Frederick, then sixty-two years old, went to work at Steuben. In October 1947 he left and went to work at Hawkes where he worked until he died. See *Haselbauer, J.F., & Sons.*

Haselbauer, J.F., & Sons A glass cutting house in Corning, New York, established in 1910 by Joseph F. Haselbauer and his sons, Frederick and George. After 1921 until it closed in 1938, it operated under the name Fred Haselbauer, Glass Engraver.

hash dish A usually round or oval covered serving dish with a false bottom or pan beneath to hold water that is heated by a candle or spirit lamp to keep the contents of the dish warm and moist.

Haskins Glass Company In 1902 this company purchased the former Northwood Glass Company facility in Martins Ferry, West Virginia, making glassware and lighting goods. Fire destroyed most of the facility in 1909. See *Beaumont Glass Company.*

hat A bowl in the form of a hat. Some are large, most are small. Molds used for medicine bottles were ideal for blowing the crown of a hat, and many have raised lettering that a bottle would have. While the stove pipe hat was the most common, other types of hats were made and are quite rare. See *pitcher hat; tumbler hat; Dolly Varden hat.*

hat shaped A dish, bowl, vase, toothpick holder, or other small accessory in the shape of an upside-down hat, generally a stovepipe or top hat.

Hatch & Clark (1884-1930) A glass cutting facility (using Dorflinger blanks) established in Seelyville, Pennsylvania, by George E. Hatch and Thomas B. Clark. Within two years the operating firm became Clark & Wood, and then T.B. Clark & Company. Hatch left in 1886 to form his own facility in Brooklyn, New York (see *Hatch & Company*). Wood was Clark's brother-in-law and, though his name was used in the firm's name for a short time, he remained with the firm for several years. Although the cutting operations were in Seelyville, the offices and showrooms were in Honesdale, Pennsylvania. A new facility was built in Hawley, Pennsylvania, about the turn of the century. From about 1920, it stopped making cut glass and made mostly gold decorated glassware.

Hatch & Company (1886-1892) A glass cutting shop established in Brooklyn, New York (at the same address as Hibbler & Rausch) by George E. Hatch. Several cutting shops were at this address so that they could avail themselves of the blanks made by the Dorflinger glass works.

hatched Embellished with fine lines producing the overall visual effect of shading. Sometimes there are two sets of equidistant parallel lines crossing each other at an oblique or right angle (*crosshatching*).

hatpin A large pin used to secure a lady's hat by being inserted through the hat into the hair. They were used primarily from the Victorian days until styles changed about 1940. The head of the pin was sometimes embellished with a small glass ornament, such as a tiny bird or colored bead.

Cobalt-blue hatpin holder with folded-in crimped top in grape pattern, 7" h.
Davanna Collection

hatpin holder A small vessel used to hold hatpins, resembling and often mistaken for a bud vase. They usually have a cylindrical cross section while bud vases usually have a round one and taper toward the base. Hatpin holders may be plain, decorated, or cut. They were made from about 1860 to 1920, coinciding with the period when hatpins were most fashionable. Taller ones for holding longer hatpins were fashionable from about 1890 to 1914. Those made of slag and carnival glass are highly prized.

Haught, Swearer & Co. See *Brownsville Glass Works*.

Haughwout, E.V., & Company
Established in the late 1850s, it was listed in various references as importers and manufacturers of sterling silver, china, glassware, cut glass, etc., with showrooms in New York City and Paris. It may have had its own glass cutting shop known as Brooklyn Cut Glass where John S. O'Conner worked.

Hauptmann & Konigstein Hauptmann and Konigstein were copper wheel engravers from Meisterdorf. Hauptmann came to Corning, New York, in 1908 to work for Sinclaire. He left in 1911 and went to Brooklyn, New York, where he met Konigstein, his nephew, who had just arrived in the United States. They worked together in Brooklyn for a short period, and in 1915, returned to Corning to work for Sinclaire. About 1923 Konigstein left to work as a machinist at Corning's Hood Foundry and then for Ingersoll-Rand. About 1929 Konigstein and Hauptmann moved to a farm on Rose Hill, outside Corning, where they engraved for several years.

Hausmaler (German) Literally, *home painter*. A self-employed decorator of glass, porcelain, enamel objects, or faience during the 17th and 18th centuries in Germany, Austria, and Bohemia. They bought undecorated ware from a glasshouse and decorated it either at their home or studio. The best were often superior to the glasshouse's own decorators, some of which maintained studios employing a number of assistants and apprentices. The English call them *independent* or *outside decorators*. See *Schaper, Johann; Preissler, Daniel; Faber, Johann*.

Hausmalerei (German) The decoration of porcelain, faience, glass, and enamel objects by a Hausmaler.

HaVen, C.D. The United States inventor of insulated window glass in 1930.

Hawkes, Thomas G., & Company
Thomas Gibbon Hawkes (1846-1913) was born in Cork, Ireland. He was a descendent of the Hawkes and Penrose families, glassmakers and cutters in Dudley, England, and Waterford, Ireland, for five generations. He studied civil engineering for two years, coming to the United States in 1863. Employed as a draftsman and salesman at Hoare & Dailey's facility in Brooklyn, New York, he learned the art of cutting glass. In 1870 he moved to Corning, New York, to become superintendent of their cutting shop at the Corning Glass Works. He established his own cutting shop in 1880. In 1890 Henry P. Sinclaire Jr. came to work for Hawkes and was a full partner by 1890. The company was originally called Hawkes Rich Cut Glass Co. but was

changed to Thomas G. Hawkes & Company in 1890. It purchased blanks from the Corning Glass Works until 1903, at which time Hawkes, Frederick Carder, and others established the Steuben Glass Works. After Thomas' death, his son, Samuel, took over, cutting glass until 1962. Many pieces are marked with a trademark—either an "H" or a Trefoil ring (shamrock) enclosing a fleur-de-lis and two hawks.

Small Hazel Atlas bottle with "LAGO" on side, 4-1/4" h.
Davanna Collection

Hawkes Rich Cut Glass Company

See *Hawkes, Thomas G., & Company.*

Hawley Glass Company
A glass manufacturing facility established in Hawley, Pennsylvania, by William Dorflinger, son of Christian Dorflinger, and four partners in the late 1880s. It became a subsidiary of C. Dorflinger & Sons. It was destroyed by fire on May 3, 1907.

Hawley Glass Works
A green glass bottle manufacturing facility established in Hawley, Pennsylvania, about 1872. It was still operating in 1885.

Hay, Andrew K., & Co.
See *Winslow Glass Works.*

Hay & Campbell
See *Union Glass Works (Pittsburgh, Pennsylvania).*

Hay & Hanna
See *Union Flint Glass Works.*

Hay & McCully
See *Union Flint Glass Works.*

Hay, Bowdle & Co.
See *Winslow Glass Works.*

Hay, Coffin & Co.
See *Winslow Glass Works.*

Hazel Atlas teacup and saucer, blue, Moderntone pattern.
Davanna Collection

Hazel Atlas bowl, 4" d. x 1-1/2" h. Embossed "Complements of Hazel Atlas Glass Co. — John W Davis Day— Aug 11-24— Clarksburg, W.VA."
Davanna Collection

Hazel Atlas Glass Company
A glass manufacturing facility established in Clarksville, West Virginia, operating there since 1902. In 1928 it was recorded as the "World's Largest Tumbler Factory." Many popular mold etched patterns were made there during the 1930s. It also made some of the blue *Shirley Temple* glassware. It has had facilities in Washington, Pennsylvania; Zanesville, Ohio; and Wheeling, West Virginia.

Hazelbauer & Lundgren
(1904-1912) A glass cutting facility in Brooklyn, New York. After closing, Hazelbauer became general foreman of Thomas Shotton Cut Glass Works.

HD The trademark of the Honesdale Decorating Co.

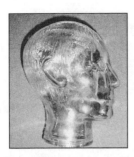

Male head, clear glass, 9-1/2" h. Davanna Collection

head A full relief, three-dimensional representation of a person from the neck up. A head of the Emperor Augustus made from Roman glass during the first century is known to exist. See *bust*.

head flask A flask in the form of a human head, having a tall thin neck (and sometimes a low cup-like mouth) rising above the center of the head. Some have a loop handle extending from the rear of the head to the middle of the neck, and some are janiform (see *Janus flask*). The flasks were mold blown of Roman glass from the 1st to the 4th centuries. Rare examples have a small hole in the bottom and were used as sprinklers. See *Schusterglas*.

Headquarters in America for Art Glass A name used by the Mt. Washington Glass Company.

heart-and-vine pattern A pattern found on some Iris glassware.

heat absorbing glass Glass made so as not to permit transmission of infrared radiation, but to allow transmission of a high percentage of other types of radiation.

heat check A tiny white line appearing at the point of attachment of a handle, caused by the difference in temperature of the handle and the body of the piece. It can be eliminated if both pieces are at the same temperature. Heat checks may or may not develop into cracks.

heat forming The process of forming glass articles by using heat.

Heat-resistant glass (1) (Aka *borosilicates*) A soda lime glass containing about 5% boric oxide, which tends to lower the viscosity of silica without increasing its thermal expansion. It has a low coefficient of expansion and high softening point. Its tensile strength is about 10,000 pounds per square inch; the continuous use temperature is 482°C. It transmits ultraviolet light in the higher wavelengths and, therefore, is used in making "sunlight" lamps and similar equipment. It is being researched as possible storage-disposal media for high level radioactive wastes. Also see *Pyrex*. (2) See *Vycot*.

heat sensitive glass A colored glass that changes color when reheated at the furnace. Examples include *Amberina*, *Peachblow*, and *Burmese*.

heat tempering The gradual cooling, over a period of hours or days, of glass(ware) in order to prevent the object from shattering due to stresses inherent within it. See *annealing*.

Heaton, Maurice Born in 1900, he was a glassmaker from England who came to the United States in 1944. From 1931 he made modern glass murals and lighting fixtures. In 1947 he invented a process for firing and shaping, in the furnace, glassware enameled and decorated with scratched figures. From 1961 he covered his enameled wares with several layers of clear glass. His studio was in Nyack, New York.

heavy baluster A drinking glass, either a wine glass or goblet, with a baluster stem. They were made in England of high quality glass from about 1685 to 1710 and were called *first period baluster*.

heavy gather See *gather*.

hedgehog glass See *Igelglas*.

Hedwig Glasses Thick walled beakers deeply cut with relief decoration in the form of stylized figures of a lion, griffon, and eagle with palm leaf motifs. These glasses were so named because two of the known surviving specimens allegedly were the property to St. Hedwig (1174-1243), patron saint of Silesia, who is reported to have witnessed the miracle of water turning into wine in one of them. They were believed to have been made either in Egypt or in some western country by an Egyptian craftsman or in Persia during the 11th or 12th century. However, in 1966, B.A.

Shelkovnikov of the Hermitage Museum in Leningrad proposed they were the work of a 12th century White Russian glass shop operated by Polish craftsmen under Byzantine influence. The prime reason for this was that fragments of similar articles have been found there. Their origin is still considered unknown. Similar glasses have been used as reliquaries and have 13th century metal mounts.

Heinz Brothers See *Monarch Cut Glass Company.*

Heisey, A.H., & Co., Inc. A glass manufacturing facility established in 1893 or 1895 (depending on the source) in Newark, Ohio, by Major Augustus H. Heisey. He was previously associated with Geo. A. Duncan & Sons (he married Duncan's daughter), which remained in operation until 1954. A.H. Heisey & Co. Inc. was a major supplier of pressed and figured blanks to cutting and decoration shops all over the United States. Its trademark was an "H" in a diamond or a diamond without the "H" (the diamond elongated vertically), first used in November 1900. Sometimes paper labels were used, especially on items to be further decorated by others.

The Imperial Glass Company purchased many of the Heisey molds and reproduced Heisey ware without the trademark. When Imperial closed, the Heisey Collectors of America purchased, in 1985, all Heisey molds Imperial had at the time, with the exception of the *Old Williamsburg* pattern molds because of the high price. After A.H. Heisey's death, the facility was operated by his son, T. Clarence Heisey. See *Heisey glass animals.*

Heisey Orchid pattern basket.
Tri-State Antiques

Heisey glassware ad, May 1930.

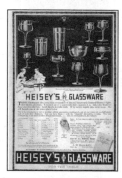

Heisey ad from *Woman's* Magazine, May 1917.

Heisey glassware ad, April 1930.

Heisey glassware ad, September 1930.

Heisey glass animals Glass items in the form of animals made by Heisey. The first, a horse head bookend, was made in 1937. The most famous animals were designed by Royal Hickman, employed previously by the Haeger Pottery Company. All were pressed in a mold. Some were marked with the "H" inside a diamond, some were marked twice, and some weren't marked at all. The majority were made in clear glass, but some were in deep amber, honey amber, and cobalt. Some were frosted all over; some only partially. In 1958 the Imperial Glass Company purchased some of these molds and, in 1962, began reproducing specific animals. Again, some of these have the trademark and some do not. Another method of distinguishing the animals made by different companies from the same molds is by using black light, under which the Heisey animals will have yellow tones while Imperial's will reflect only the color of the light.

Heller Company A glass manufacturing facility making general household tableware during the Depression era. It also made metal attachments for glassware.

Hellmers, Henry T. The superintendent of the Akro-Agate Glass Company from 1922 to 1930 and from 1932 to 1934, where he developed many new colors for use in the company's lines of toy dishes and marbles. He was also superintendent of the Glass Department of the Mantle Lamp Company from 1935 to 1942, where he created new colors used in making its kerosene and electric Aladdin lamps. In 1938 he developed Alacite (see *Alacite*). In 1932 he also developed the pink opaque glass later used in Cambridge Glass Company's *Crown Tuscan*, as well as other colored glasses.

Hellos A Carnival glass color that is green with gold and silver iridescence.

helmet foot An exceptionally high domed foot.

Hemingray insulators, left: 21-59 Hemingray T.S.; right: 3-40 Hemingray 45. Made in the USA.
Davanna Collection

Hemingray Glass Company A glass manufacturing facility established by Ralph and Anthony Gray and Samuel J. and Robert Hemingray in Cincinnati, Ohio, in 1848. It moved to Covington, Kentucky, in 1851, making flint, green, black, and opal glass and many specialty glasses, tumblers, lightning rod balls, insulators, decanters, and fruit jars. In 1864 it became Hemingray Brothers & Company and, in 1882 Hemingray Glass Company. In 1890 it moved to Muncie, Indiana, making insulators, bottles, and fruit jars. In 1933 it became a subsidiary of Owens-Illinois.

Mosser carnival glass hen dish, amber, 5".
Davanna Collection

hen dish A basket-shaped shallow dish with a cover in the shape of a hen, having the appearance of a hen sitting on a nest.

Henderson Cut Glass Company A glass cutting company in Philadelphia, Pennsylvania, operating during the late 1880s and 1890s.

heraldic ware See *armorial glassware*.

Herbeck-Demer Company A glass cutting company operating in Honesdale, Pennsylvania, from about 1904 until 1911.

In that year the Demer brothers, associates in the company, established their own glass cutting company, the Demer Brothers Company, in Hallstead, Pennsylvania, which closed about 1920.

Herbert & Hollis See *Herbert, S., Cut Glass Company.*

Herbert & Neuwirth Company See *Herbert, Max, Company Incorporated.*

Herbert, Max, Company Incorporated (1910-1919) A glass cutting company in New York City, New York. The United Cut Glass Company operated at the same address during the same time period. Max Herbert and Samuel Neuwirth were officers in both companies and together established the Herbert & Neuwirth Company in 1914. In 1919 Herbert died and the companies went out of business (see *Herbert, S., Cut Glass Company*). In 1920 Neuwirth formed his own company in New York City but did not engage in glass cutting.

Herbert, S., Cut Glass Company

A glass cutting company established about 1910 in New York City, closing in 1927. In 1912 it was operating at two locations in the city. It was affiliated with the Max Herbert Company, occupying the same location until 1915. Sigmund Herbert was associated with Herbert & Hollis, glass importers in New York City, from about 1900, and the Rock Crystal Glass Company in Jersey City, New Jersey, from 1918. In 1926 these companies were merged under the name Herbert Glass & Import Corporation, manufacturers of cut glass and importers of glassware.

Herbert Glass & Import Company

See *Herbert, S., Cut Glass Company.*

Hereford Glass Company A glass bottle manufacturing facility founded in 1908 by L.G. Taylor, Julius Way, Charles Vasaman, W.J. Taylor, and several glassblowers in Cape May, New Jersey. While successful, the stockholders voted to liquidate it on October 28, 1909. The Cape May Glass Company took over the facility, making both flint and lime glass in a wide range of colors. It closed in 1924. See *Cape May Glass Company.*

Heritage Series Initiated in 1978—Steuben's 75th anniversary—by Thomas Buechner, president of Steuben Glass. The first item was a limited reissue of Steuben's popular Thomas candlesticks offered to established Steuben customers. This was followed by other reproductions of previously made Steuben pieces.

Herrmann City Glass Works In 1869 Scott & Rapp began to build a glass manufacturing facility and community near Green Bank, New Jersey, in an area it called Herrmann City. It made hollowware, glass buttons, glass fruit, Christmas tree stars and lights, and cut glass. Within six months of startup, Rapp died. The project soon started to decline, and the depression of 1873 caused it to close.

Herrfeldt, J.G., & Company (1910-1923) A glass cutting company in Brooklyn, New York.

Hewes, Robert (1751-1830) From Boston, Massachusetts, he followed in the footsteps of his father, also named Robert, venturing into many professions. Robert, the younger, who inherited a large amount of money when his father died, was a candlemaker, soap manufacturer, butcher, tanner, fencing master, doctor, surgeon, writer, publisher, and teacher of the broad sword. In addition he made *Poland Starch* and *Hewes Liniment*. Sometime before 1780 he became interested in glassmaking. He tried unsuccessfully to establish a facility at Temple, New Hampshire in 1780, selecting the site because of the forests for fuel, the availability of hardwood trees for potash, and good quality sand nearby at Magog Pond. He had plans to make crown and cylinder glass and bottles but had financial difficulties, and his early attempts failed. He erected a facility about 1781, but production lasted about two months, destroyed by a fire started by a drunken fireman. He immediately rebuilt, but on the first firing the structure gave way; severe frost had weakened it. After several attempts to obtain loans and raise money via a lottery, he gave up his attempts to make glass at Temple. In 1787 he became one of the organizers of the Essex Glass Works in Boston and invested in a slaughterhouse as well as in facilities to make

soap and glue. He was associated with many other glass manufacturing facilities in the New England area. Hewes died in 1830 and was interred in Tomb Number 18 in the Common Burying Ground in Boston. See *New England Glass Works; Pitkin Glass Works; Boston Crown Glass Manufactory.*

Hewson Connell & Co. A glass manufacturing facility established in 1816 in Kensington, Philadelphia, Pennsylvania. It was operated by John Connell & Co. from 1817 to 1822.

Hexad of Buttons and Stars A term used by Martha Louise Swan for the cut glass motif known as the *cane variant* or *Russian variant.*

hexagon cutting A decorative pattern on cut glass similar to the hollow diamond pattern, except it has six-sided motifs (honeycomb effect). It is found primarily on the stems of some English drinking glasses made mainly during the third quarter of the 18th century.

hexagonal bottle A mold blown bottle with six sides, many made of colored glass. The body is formed by six vertical or slightly sloping panels leading to a cylindrical neck extending upward from the shoulders. See *square bottle.*

hexagonal bowl A bowl of a drinking glass of hexagonal section, becoming slightly concave as it joins the stem.

hexagonal diamond A cut glass motif having six-sided hobnails.

hexagonal faceting A style of faceting forming a diaper pattern of vertically placed elongated hexagons.

Hibbler, George H., & Company; Hibbler, J.S., & Co. See *Hibbler & Rausch.*

Hibbler & Rausch In 1866, after managing the facility for Christian Dorflinger since 1863, Hibbler purchased the Long Island Flint Glass Works. In 1879 Rausch became his partner, forming Hibbler & Rausch. The facility was called the Concord Street Glass Works, the name used when it was established in 1835. In 1886 Rausch died and the company was dissolved, the new operating firm being George H. Hibbler & Company. In 1892 the operating firm was J.S. Hibbler & Co. It closed in 1893. See *Dorflinger, C., & Sons; Hatch & Company.*

Higbee, J.B., Company A glass manufacturing facility in Bridgeville, Pennsylvania, in operation about 1900. It was formerly Bryce, Higbee & Company (see *Bryce, Higbee & Company*). Some wares were signed with the outline of a bee with an "H" on the left wing, an "I" on the body, and a "G" on the right wing. It closed about 1915.

Higgins & Seiter A retail seller of cut glass, it was an agent for such companies as Libbey as well as numerous others, operating a large catalog house in New York City during the last quarter of the 19th century. It assigned its own names to many patterns even though they were cut and often named by other glass shops and houses.

high engraving See *high relief; Hochschnitt.*

high relief Relief decoration where the portion raised above the background is half or more than half of the natural circumference of the object of the design. The German term *Hochschnitt* embraces all degrees of engraved or cut relief work above the surface of the object. See *low relief; medium relief.*

high silica glass Known as *Vycor*, it approaches fused silica in composition and properties. Finished articles contain approximately 96% silica, 3% boric oxide, and the remainder of alumina and alkali. It may be heated cherry red and then immersed in ice water without shattering and with no other adverse effects. It has high chemical durability and is extremely stable to all acids, except hydrofluoric. In addition, its shrinkage is proportionately even.

highlighting The process in which one or more colors are applied to the raised portion of a glass design to accentuate or *highlight* the design. See *reverse highlighting.*

Hildreth & Co. See *Lockport Glass Works.*

Hinks, Joseph A resident of Birmingham, England, Hinks patented a duplex burner for an oil lamp in 1865. This burner approximately doubled the amount of light a lamp could produce. It consisted of two parallel wicks about 1/8 inch apart. Tiffany used these burners in his oil lamps.

Hinsberger, L., Cut Glass Company A glass cutting facility established about 1895 in New York City, New York. In 1898 it opened a second facility for making beveled glass only. Both facilities were closed in 1913. Its trademark label read "Hinsberger Cut Glass Co., N.Y."

Hinterglasmalerei (German) Painting done on the reverse side of a sheet of glass. See *back painting; mirror painting.*

Hipkins Novelty Mold Shop In 1866 Stephen Hipkins Jr. opened a mold making shop in Bellaire, Ohio, making molds for the Belmont Glass Company and others. In 1876 he closed the shop and went to work for Hobbs, Brockunier & Company, leaving in 1882 to work for the Buckeye Glass Company. In 1884 he and his three sons, Jesse, George, and Howard, opened the Hipkins Novelty Mold Shop in Martins Ferry, Ohio, becoming the largest mold maker in the Midwest. Stephen died in 1920. His sons continued the operations until 1930 when Jesse and Howard sold their interests to George. George continued to operate it until it closed in 1945.

Hirsch & Assoc. See *Suncook Glass Works.*

Grouping of South Jersey historical flasks, c. 1850. Museum of American Glass at Wheaton Village, Millville, NJ.

historical flask (Aka *pictorical flasks*) A whiskey flask made in large quantities in the United States from about 1815 to 1870.

Originally mold blown, some later ones were pressed. The colors ranged from various shades of bottle glass to brilliant hues of amber, blue, green, and purple. They picture a variety of over 400 known subjects in relief, including portraits of early presidents and other famous historical personages— one of the most famous depicted Jenny Lind to honor her visit to the United States— national emblems, contemporary slogans, transportation, fraternal or social emblems, and other decorative subjects. After about 1850 the style gradually shifted with fewer portraits and more scenic motifs and emblematic designs. Historical flasks were made by many facilities in various regions of the country, and some bear their marks.

historical plates Pressed, engraved, or enameled plates that portray a wide variety of historical subjects such as famous persons, places, and things, events, emblems, slogans, scenes, etc., similar to those represented on historical flasks.

Historismus (Aka *historical revival, revivalism*) Objects in the style, fashion, and shape of those made at an earlier date.

Hitchcock, W.P., Co. A glass cutting company in Syracuse, New York.

Kohinoor pattern, clear-glass cut punch-bowl, c. 1900-1910. The Corning Museum of Glass

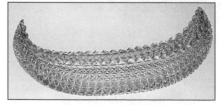

Clear glass canoe-shaped centerpiece, c. 1880-1895. The Corning Museum of Glass

Hoare, J., & Company John Hoare (1822-1896), apprenticed under his father, James, a glassmaker in Cork, Ireland, was employed by various English firms including Thomas Webb & Sons. He operated his own business for five years before coming to Philadelphia, Pennsylvania, in 1848. In 1853 he and five partners established a glass cutting shop in Corning, New York.

In 1855 he bought out all but one and established Hoare & Burns. Then he and another partner bought the cutting shop of the Brooklyn Flint Glass Co., naming it Hoare & Daily. He also operated a cutting shop at the South Ferry Works prior to 1863. In 1868 he became affiliated with Corning Flint Glass, retaining the cut glass department as J. Hoare & Company. His company in Corning operated until 1921. Hoare bought his blanks exclusively from Corning from 1868 to 1896, under a contract barring it from selling blanks to competitors except Hawkes (Hoare brought Hawkes to the United States, employing him as a glass cutter until he established his own facility) and Sinclaire. After that he purchased his blanks from Dorflinger, Union, Steuben, and Baccarat. J. Hoare & Company was the first company to turn glass on a lathe and make cut glass for store display windows.

President Ulysses Grant ordered cut glass for the White House from Hoare. During the 1870s and 1880s, it was one of the largest glass cutting firms in the United States. When John Hoare died, his son, James II, took over, selling it to H.W. Baldwin. In 1906 James II bought it back, operating it until it closed of bankruptcy in 1921. In 1906 James II's son, John S., entered the firm.

In 1914 a branch was opened in Wellsboro, Pennsylvania—John Hoare Inc. or Hoare & Millspaugh—which closed in 1916. The signature used was "J. Hoare & Co." in block letters within concentric circles and the date "1853" (when Hoare opened his first facility in the United States); either "New York" or "Corning" appear below. It was first used in 1895 but was not registered until May 12, 1914. All pieces were signed unless specifically requested by the customer that the signature be omitted. See *Hoare, John, Inc.*

Hoare, John, Inc. (Aka *Hoare & Millspaugh*) A division of J. Hoare & Co. operating in Wellsboro, Pennsylvania, from 1914 to 1916.

Hoare & Burns See *Hoare, J., & Company.*

Hoare & Daily See *Hoare, J., & Company; Dorflinger, C., & Sons.*

Hoare & Millspaugh See *Hoare, John, Inc.*

hobnob Originally, goblets used for hot drinks. Currently "hobnob" means *to associate on friendly terms* or *to drink together.*

Hobbs, Barnes & Co. See *Hobbs, Brockunier & Co.; Virginia (Green Glass) Works.*

Amber shading to red, pressed-glass bowl, c. 1886-1890.
The Corning Museum of Glass

Hobbs, Brockunier & Co. In April 1845, the idle facility of Plunkett & Miller (South Wheeling Glass Works or Excelsior Glass Works) in Wheeling, West Virginia, was purchased by John L. Hobbs and James B. Barnes operating as Hobbs, Barnes & Co., making flint and colored glass that was cut, plain, and molded. The first facility was built on this site in 1818. In 1829, John and Craig Ritchie erected a flint glass facility on the site. This was enlarged by the Sweeney Brothers in 1835 and again by Plunkett & Miller.

In 1854 Hobbs, Barnes & Co. bought another facility across the Ohio River at Martin's Ferry. In 1861 it had to close for a period of six months because many workers enlisted to fight in the Civil War. In 1864 the operating firm became Hobbs, Brockunier & Co., becoming the only major producer of fine lime glass in the region. It made three innovations affecting the entire glass industry: (a) use of benzine in the polishing furnace; (b) chilling of molds using cold air; and

(c) replacing litharge with soda-lime in flint glass, a cost reduction.

By 1879 it was the largest facility in the United States. In 1888 it became the J.H. Hobbs Glass Co., and in 1891 it joined the U.S. Glass Company (*Factory H*). It closed during a union strike in 1893. Ten years later it was refurbished and reopened by Harry Northwood (an engraver there in 1882 before he went to La Belle in 1884). There are very few signed pieces and no pattern names. It made *Peachblow* (see *Wheeling Peachblow*), gold ruby glass, dew-drop glass, spangled glass and *Pressed Amberina*. See *Virginia (Green Glass) Works.*

Hobbs, J.H., Glass Co. See *Hobbs, Brockunier & Co.*

Hobbs' Peachblow See *Wheeling Peachblow.*

hobnail (1) Cut embellishment on some Anglo-Irish glassware (see *hobnail cutting*); (2) small, circular prunts arranged in an overall pattern; (3) a decoration of entrapped air bubbles in a regular pattern made by the object having been shaped in a mold with projecting points leaving indentations that were covered with an overlay (see *airlocks*).

hobnail, opalescent See *opalescent hobnail.*

hobnail chain A cut glass motif consisting of hobnail figures surrounding a figure or design.

hobnail cutting. A flat-topped, raised square, hexagon, or octagon button resembling a hobnail (when six-pointed). As a cut glass motif, the hobnail became popular as a "button" in the Russian, Cane, and Harvard patterns. Some cutters left the top plain while others embellished it. The hexagonal button is called a hexagonal diamond; the octagonal button is called an octagonal diamond.

Fenton milk glass goblet, Hobnail pattern.
Davanna Collection

hobnail glass. A pattern on pressed glass with raised bumps in an overall pattern, popular in the 1880s and later. Dozens of hobnail patterns and variants have been made in a wide range of colors. It was perfected in 1886 by William Leighton Jr. and William F. Russell of Hobbs, Brockunier & Co. The original name for hobnail glass was *dew-drop glass*; if it was opalescent, which the vast majority was, it was called *opalescent dew-drop glass.*

hobstar. (Aka *rosette*) A cut glass motif with numerous variations. It first appeared in the Middle Period of American cut glass, becoming common during the Brilliant period. It consisted of a hob or button, relatively high in relief, the miter cuts surrounding it meeting at the outer edge to form points, each cut giving the hobnail one more facet on its side. The number of points usually ranges from eight to thirty-two; some have up to forty-eight; and at least one has sixty. The button was often decorated with a pyramidal star with its own miter cut system around it. See *star.*

hobstar chain A cut glass motif of hobstars completely surrounding a figure or design.

Hochschnitt (German) Literally, *high engraving.* The German term for all degrees of relief embellishment made on glass objects by wheel engraving (carving); the opposite of Tiefschnitt or intaglio. The process involved executing the design in relief by cutting away the ground, similar to that for cameo relief. It became a prominent style of embellishment in Bohemia and Germany in the late 17th century when potash glass made with lime was developed. Its thickness and hardness created an appropriate medium for deep cutting. Hochschnitt was used by the Romans (see *Portland Vase*) and others (see *Hedwig Glasses*), later in China as decoration on scent bottles, snuff bottles, etc., and, in the 19th century, by Emile Galle and others on Art Nouveau glassware.

hock glass A drinking glass for German white Rhine wine. The term *hock* is from the German *Hochheimer* to describe its white Rhine wines. Hock glasses are tall with a stemmed foot, medium size bowls, and in various shapes (usually globular) and colors, pale green being the most common. Occasionally they are embellished with gilt.

Hocking Glass Co. centerpiece bowl with Mayfair Open Rose pattern, 1930s.
Tri-State Antiques

Hocking Glass Company A glass manufacturing company established in Lancaster, Ohio, in 1904 by Lucien B. Martin, becoming part of the Anchor Hocking Glass Co. in 1938. See *Ohio Flint Glass Co.*

Hofbauer, August V. (1882-1968) Born in Austria, Hofbauer began work at age eleven as a carry-in boy at the Vsetin glassworks, eventually becoming a master blower. In 1913 he came to the United States, working at the Morgantown glassworks, A.H. Heisey Company, and in Chicago, Illinois, and Millville, New Jersey. In 1921 he went to work for Durand in Vineland, New Jersey. After Durand was abolished by the Kimble Glass Company, Hofbauer took up creative glassmaking, and in 1932 organized his own business, the Vineland Glass Works Inc., making laboratory ware and later art glass. Among the first items made were glass heat-proof percolators. He had a great knowledge of glass formulae, especially colored glass. After he closed his facility in 1955, and after his wife and son had died, he accepted an invitation from the Colombian government in 1960 to build a facility and teach glassmaking there. On his return to the United States, he went to work for the Kessler Glass Works of Bethpage, Long Island, New York. In the last two years of his life he made pitchers of opaque white and colored glass, swirled in the South Jersey style.

Hofglasschneider (German) *Court Engraver of Glass.* An exceptionally proficient glass cutter attached to the Court of one of the German states during the 18th century. Many signed their works, but with a few exceptions, they did not establish new artistic styles or techniques like earlier glass engravers did. See *Kiessling, Johann; Sang, Andreas; Sang, Johann; Neumann, Johann; Trumper, Carl; Kunckel, Georges; Kohler, Heinrich; Spiller, Gottfried.*

Hofkellereiglas or Hofkelleren (German) Literally, *court cellar glass.* A Humpen with enameled armorial embellishment depicting the arms and usually the initials and titles of the proprietor of the castle. They were made from about 1610 in Saxony and Thuringia for many of the regional ducal wine cellars in Germany. Some rare specimens were double or triple, having two or three Humpen stacked atop each other.

Hogan Evans & Company See *Pittsburgh Glass Manufacturing Co.*

Hogarth bottle A wine bottle with a globular body and a tapering cylindrical neck, so named because they resemble a bottle depicted in an engraving from the series "The Rake's Progress" by William Hogarth (1697-1764). Similar wine bottles of different sizes and shapes are called *Hogarth type bottles.* They were made in the early 18th century in England and the United States.

Hogarth glass A goblet with a wide, inverted bell-shaped bowl and short, thick stem formed mainly by a large knop resting on a domed foot. They originally had a domed cover and pointed finial. Some were made of Netherlands glass engraved by Jacob Sang about 1762. The name comes from goblets depicted in engravings by William Hogarth (1697-1764).

Hogg, George See *Brownsville Glass Works.*

Hohbalusterpokal (German) A Pokal with a stem having one or more hollow knops. Examples made at Nuremberg in the late 17th century were embellished by a number of distinguished engravers, including Heinrich Schwarnhart, Herman Schwinger, and Hans Wolfgang Schmidt.

Hohn & Souner See *Ensell & Wilson.*

holder See *menu card holder.*

holding tongs An implement used by a glassmaker to hold or grip an object while working or shaping it.

hollow baluster stem A stem composed of one or more hollow knops, each of baluster shape, placed vertically and separated by small cylindrical sections and mereses.

hollow cutting The cutting or grinding of a design on glass using a convex-edged tool or wheel.

hollow diamond cutting (Aka *shallow diamond cutting*) A decorative pattern on cut glass made by sinking four-sided diamond-shaped depressions into the glass using a convex cutting wheel so that the edges contact each other and intersect diagonally, giving the effect of a slightly raised design. It is frequently found on the bowl or stem of some English drinking glasses.

hollow flute See *flute cutting.*

hollow knop A knop that is generally globular, hollow (blown) rather than solid, and on occasion contains a coin.

hollow paperweight A hollow paperweight different from the usual solid weights. Some have a design impressed into the inside of the crown. Some have an inner colored cushion, the entrapped air space creating a silvery appearance. Some feature animal figures. Some feature a winter scene with a liquid and substance resembling snow, which when shaken creates a wintery scene. The various types include: (a) crown; (b) ducks-on-a- pond; (c) swimming swans; (d) walking pigs; (e) marbrie; and (f) snow.

hollow relief See *intaglio.*

Fluted hollow stem champagne glass, 5-1/4" h.
Davanna Collection

hollow stem A stem in the form of a hollow cylinder closed at both ends by connecting the bowl and foot, often found on some English drinking glasses. They should be distinguished from the plain stems with an elongated tear within. Hollow stems have no knops but sometimes have a swelling midway between the bowl and foot. They were popular during the mid-18th century and the mid-19th century, but are now quite rare. On occasion the end joining the bowl was not sealed to allow sediment in the wine or other drink to settle into the stem and less likely be consumed by the drinker. These stems were difficult to clean.

hollow stopper A stopper that is hollow and, when open at the bottom, creates a small drinking vessel, convenient for a quick nip.

hollowware All containers as opposed to flat objects. Drinking glasses, bottles, jars, candy containers, etc., are examples of hollowware.

hollowed A concave surface, such as a hollowed diamond or thumbprint, and some mirrors.

Holly Amber glassware (Aka *Golden Agate*) A rare and expensive pressed glassware in the category of Victorian art glass. It is molded with a band of holly sprigs and amber color shading from dark amber to white (the same molds used for clear glass pieces). The amber colored glass was reheated to appear opalescent. It was made by the Indiana Tumbler & Goblet Co. from January 1, 1903 to June 13, 1903. Reproductions are somewhat browner overall.

Holmes, T.J., Co. The oldest continuously operated atomizer company in the United States, founded in 1870 by Thomas Jefferson Holmes in Massachusetts. The company made only medicinal atomizers for nose and throat sprays. Holmes designed a perfume atomizer and received a patent on March 3, 1876. On May 1, 1876, he filed for a trademark, *Favorite*, used for perfumers and atomizers, but he did not make a sincere attempt to publicize the items until the 1930s. T.J. Holmes Co. made the atomizer tops; the bottles were made by other companies. The atomizers have the trademark *Holmspray* etched on the metal fittings or on a paper label attached to the bottom.

Holophane Co. See *Verlys Art Glass.*

Holophane Lighting Company A glass manufacturing company established in 1896 in Newark, Ohio, originally making glass lamp shades and globes and later adding heat-resistant glass for use in lenses, reflectors, etc. It was affiliated with the Holophane Company, which was famous for its Verlys art glass, and became a division of Manville Corporation.

Holton Glass (Cutting) Co. The name sometimes used by the Corning Cut Glass Co. to avoid confusion with the Corning Glass Works. It was named after a foreman named Holton.

Holtz, Clark & Taylor See *Holtz Glass Works.*

Holtz Glass Works A bottle and window glass manufacturing facility established in Salem, New Jersey, in the early 1860s by William Holtz. It was later operated by Holtz, Clark & Taylor.

Holy Water flask A flask made in Venice during the 17th century and used for the storage of holy water. The flask was sometimes rectangular or hexagonal and was decorated with an enameled or cold painted portrait of a saint.

Holy Water stoup A small stoup, basin, or font usually designed to be hung on a wall to hold holy water. Many were made of glass in France, Spain, and the Netherlands during the late 17th and 18th centuries.

Holz, Clark & Taylor A glass manufacturing facility established in the early 1860s in Salem, New Jersey, making bottles and jars. In 1874 John Gayner leased it, purchasing it in 1879. In 1893 it was incorporated as the Gayner Glass Works. See *Gayner Glass Works.*

Homer, Edward See *Chance, Robert Lucas.*

Homestead Glass Works See *Bryce, Higbee & Company.*

Honesdale Decorating Company (1901-1932) A glass decorating facility established in Honesdale (Seeleyville), Pennsylvania, by C. Dorflinger & Sons and operated by Carl F. Prosch of New York, one of its prime decorators. In 1916 Prosch (d.1937) purchased it from Dorflinger and operated it until closing. After Prosch acquired it, he bought lime glass blanks that he etched and to which he added gold tracing. Between 1914 and 1918 some were embellished with pure gold. Most pieces are marked either "Honesdale" in script with the initials "HDC" or an initial "H" on a shield. He made some poor cameo glass imitations. See *Prosch, Carl F.*

Honesdale Glass Company See *Honesdale Glassworks.*

Honesdale Glassworks A window glass manufacturing facility known as the Honesdale Glass Company established in 1840 in Traceyville, Pennsylvania, by Henry Dark and James Dickson. It experienced numerous changes in ownership over the years. It failed in 1849 and was taken over by Lord & Tracey, succeeded by James Brookfield. It closed in 1861 when it was destroyed by a flood. In 1871 it was rebuilt by Christian Dorflinger, becoming a subsidiary of C. Dorflinger & Sons and operating as the Honesdale Glassworks.

Honesdale Union Cut Glass Company A glass cutting facility operating in Honesdale, Pennsylvania, during the 1910s.

honey dish A small, shallow circular bowl used for serving honey; normally less than four inches in diameter and about one inch deep.

honey gilding The process of applying gold to the outer surface of glass in a manner to ensure reasonable permanency (as distinguished from unfired gilding) using gold leaf pulverized in honey, affixed to the object using low temperature firing. Its appearance is somewhat dull but can be burnished to brightness.

honey jar A small globular or cylindrical jar with a cover, used for serving honey.

Some have a fixed saucer-like stand; some are urn shaped with a square foot.

honey pot A beehive-shaped container used to hold honey. The pot's lid forms the top of the hive with a bee-shaped or ring finial.

honeycomb The *St. Louis diamond* cut glass motif.

honeycomb foot A domed foot embellished with a molded honeycomb pattern.

honeycomb pattern A molded pattern in a diaper design of connected, irregularly shaped hexagons used as an overall pattern on some Roman glass bowls made during the 4th century A.D. The bowls were reported to have been made in Syria or Egypt and likely exported to the places where they have been found. The honeycomb pattern is also found on some glassware made during the 18th and 19th centuries.

hookah base A bottle having attached to it a long, flexible tube and on top a receptacle designed for holding smoking tobacco, used mainly in the Near and Middle East. The smoke, which is drawn from the burning tobacco, is cooled as it is drawn through water before being inhaled by the user. Most are made in one of three styles: (a) globular or chamber style; (b) bell shaped; and (c) small globular with a conical bottom for holding in the hand. All have at least one ring around the middle of the neck for a better grip. They were made of Indian glass during the 17th century, at Shariz from the 17th century to the early 20th century, and in England and Ireland from the 18th century for export to India or Persia. The Indian term is *hugga*; the Persian *kalian*; the Turkish *narghile*; and the English *hubble-bubble*.

Hooligan glass See *Goofus glass.*

Hoosier Cut Glass Company A glass cutting facility established in 1921 at the old Atwood Pickle Factory in Walkerton, Indiana. It operated for about five years.

Hope Beaker A beaker decorated in enameling, depicting the Virgin Mary and Jesus, St. Peter and St. Paul, two attendant angels, and a Latin inscription. It was presumed that it and about 25 related pieces were made by Venetian craftsmen. However, based on later findings, they were made during the second half of the 13th century and are attributed to a Syrian facility at a Frankish Court. The beaker is so named because it is housed in the Hope Collection in the British Museum where it has been since 1968. See *Aldrevandini Beaker; Syro-Frankish glassware; Islamic enameling.*

Hope Glass (Cutting) Works A glass cutting facility established in 1872 in Providence, Rhode Island, by Martin L. Kern. In 1891 his son took over, and in 1899, John R. deGoey and his brother purchased the company, using the name until 1951 when it was liquidated by W. Edmund de Goey (see *deGoey, C.R.*). It relocated frequently within the city.

Hope Glass Works (1850-1855) A green and flint glass bottle manufacturing facility established by Harcum & Co. (Lewis & Samuel Harcum) in East Birmingham, Pittsburgh, Pennsylvania.

Horizon glass A Tiffany iridized Favrile glassware.

horizontal step A prismatic cutting made using a miter cut, which gives the appearance of steps when viewed horizontally.

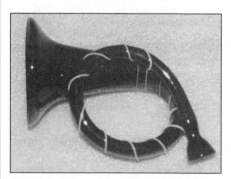

Horn, black glass with white spiral striping.
Krause Publications

horn (1) A facsimile of any of the various types of musical wind instruments. (2) See *drinking horn.* Also see *coach horn; fireman's horn; hunting horn; post horn; powder horn.*

horn-of-plenty pattern A pattern often used on early pressed glass made in the United States, consisting of a series of adjacent cornucopia (horn of plenty). Every other one in the series is embellished with a circle of diagonal raised diamonds in its mouth and a bull's-eye raised pattern on the horn, while the others are conversely decorated with raised diamonds on the horn and a bull's-eye raised ornament in the mouth. See *bull's-eye and diamond point pattern.*

horse dressing glass See *cheval.*

hot cast porcelain A term used in the first patent to describe what is now called white milk glass, which was to be an imitation of china or porcelain. It cost less to make than china or porcelain, yet looked like it.

hot formed (Aka *hot worked*). Glass worked or manipulated while it is hot and pliable.

hot metal man (Aka *color man*) The person who formulates and supervises the mixing of glass batches.

hot plate A glass plate placed between the table and a hot dish or other hot item to protect the table or table cover.

hot printing The technique of transparent printing using tissue paper. It was so-called because a mixture of hot oil and colored matter was added to a heated copper plate prior to the tissue being placed upon it, covered with flannel, and passed through a roller press. Then the printed tissue was placed on a glass object; the back was rubbed with a boss to transfer the design evenly to the object, which was then subjected to low temperature firing in a muffle kiln. See *cold printing.*

hot stoking See *fining.*

hot worked See *hot formed.*

hotel goblet (Aka *No-Nick goblet*) A goblet with a barrel-shaped bowl, the rims slightly curved in at the top so the rims of two goblets would not touch and chip as easily as if they were straight sided. Originally made only for hotels and restaurants, they were later made for the general public. They made their debut after the barrel-shaped goblets.

Hough, Reese & Co. See *Cincinnati Glass Manufacturing Co.*

Houghton, Arthur Amory, Jr. The president and policy director of Steuben Glass Inc. from its incorporation in 1933 (to take over the Steuben Glass Works as a division of the Corning Glass Works) until his retirement in 1972. The great-grandson of Amory Houghton, founder of Corning, he oversaw the changes in policy at Corning from making colored glass with special surface effects—the creations and developments of Frederick Carder—to making the highest quality clear crystal glass of superior design and craftsmanship, regarding all three elements—quality, design, and craftsmanship—of equal importance.

Houghton, Amory, & Son See *Brooklyn Glass Works; Houghton Glass Works; Corning Glass Works.*

Houghton Glass Works A tableware glass manufacturing facility established in 1851 in Sommerville, Massachusetts, by Amory and Francis Houghton. It failed in 1860. In 1864 the Union Glass Company was incorporated. Amory Houghton Sr. and Jr. left in that year, after purchasing controlling interest in the Brooklyn Flint Glass Works. The Union Glass Company (see *Union Glass Works*) operated it until it closed in 1924.

hourglass See *sand glass.*

House & Taylor A glass manufacturing facility established in South Wheeling, West Virginia, in the mid-1800s. The Northwood Glass Company may have had some operations here after the original operators failed.

House of Birks Henry Birks (b.1840) entered the business world at age seventeen, founding Henry Birks & Company, a retail store. He opened a jewelry manufacturing facility in 1887. In 1893 his three sons entered the business, and the name became Henry Birks & Sons. He operated a glass manufacturing facility from 1894 until 1907, selling it to George Phillips & Company and purchasing the Gorham Company of Canada, makers of silver wares. He bought other companies with branches in London and in the major cities of Canada. In 1893 Henry Birks

& Sons of Montreal, Canada, was an agent for Libbey glassware. Roden Brothers made special works for Henry Birks & Sons, which etched the name "BIRKS" on the pieces. Henry Birks & Sons is part of the House of Birks of Montreal.

Houston, James Born in 1921, Houston is a Canadian artist, writer, and glass designer who began working in the design department of Steuben in 1962. Many of his pieces reflect his interest in nature and are influenced by his twelve years in the Arctic. Some combine glass with gold ornament. See *Trout & Fly.*

Houze, L.J., Convex Glass Co. A glass manufacturing facility established in Point Marion, Pennsylvania, in the early 1930s, making all types of glass, including *Chinese Yellow* glassware, glass parts for other companies' products, various lines of tableware, and slag glass products.

Howard, Andrew See *Phoenix Glass Company.*

Howe, Scoffield & Co. See *Dunbarton Glass Works.*

hubble-bubble See *hookah base.*

Huffsey, J. & Co. A glassware distributor in Philadelphia, Pennsylvania. See *Pendleton Glass Works.*

Huffsey, Samuel Huffsey was a glassblower who worked in various facilities in South Jersey and Pennsylvania over a period of 30 years, keeping a detailed journal of his activities and experiences. Many glassmakers moved around as facilities started up, closed, burned, etc., or closed for the summer. Samuel Huffsey was born in Port Elizabeth, New Jersey, on April 5, 1801, went to school until age ten and, in the fall of 1811, went to work at the Union Glass Company there. When it burned in December 1811, he went to work at his father's tannery and went back to school.

When Union Glass reopened in September 1812, he went back. In 1816 he was fired because of sickness, and his apprenticeship was forfeited with a penalty of $500. The Eagle Glass Works opened in 1817 in Port Elizabeth and he went there to work, but it shut down after a couple of months, and he went to work for another facility in the area.

By 1818 the economy of the area was so bad he could not find any work as a glassblower. He then became a helper of a Jonathan Dallas, like his brother and sister before him, in return for food, clothing, and his mother's house rent. He left on his twenty-first birthday, working on a ship for two months and as a team driver. In September 1822 he got a job as a glassblower at the Hammonton Glass Works. When it shut down for the summer in 1813, he went to Philadelphia, doing odd jobs until September when he returned to Hammonton Glass. When it shut down for the summer in 1824, he again went to Philadelphia and, in the fall, started to work for "Dr." Thomas W. Dyott of Dyottsville in Kensington, Pennsylvania.

In June 1826 he married Mary A. Hoffman and left Dyott when he refused to close the facility on Sundays. Two months later he took a silent partnership in a facility in Millville, New Jersey, which went into operation on September 1, 1827. In June 1828 he sold his interest in it, returning as a glassblower in September. In 1830 he went back to Kensington to work for Dyott. He stayed there until Dyott closed in late 1833.

In August 1834 Huffsey began working for William McCully in Pittsburgh, Pennsylvania. He left in 1836, moving back to Kensington and opening a grocery store. When it failed, he bought a team of horses and market wagon and began selling groceries door-to-door. In December 1837 he sold his team and went to work as a glassblower at Green Bank. In October 1838 he was blowing glass in Millville and in 1839 in Bridgeton for Stratton, Buck & Company. He stayed there until it burned on March 1, 1842. He moved back to Philadelphia, working for Dr. Burgin. In the summer of 1842 he did various odd jobs until September, going back to Dr. Burgin as a blower. In April 1846 he gave up blowing because of poor health and became a glass dealer. He was living in Philadelphia in 1867.

Hughes, P.H. Hughes was a glass cutter with a shop in Scranton, Pennsylvania, in the early 1910s. About 1917 he and Howard

Wickham established a glass cutting shop in Scranton. It was short-lived, and in 1920 Wickham and Delbert Branning established the Wickham-Branning Cut Glass Company in Scranton. Branning had been associated with the Keystone Cut Glass Company of Hawley, Pennsylvania, until it closed in 1918.

Hughes Street Works See *Baltimore Glass Works.*

Huguenot A member of the Reformed or Calvinistic Communion of France during the 16th and 17th centuries. After about 1550, due to the persecution of Protestants by Catholics, many left France for other, more sympathetic countries such as England, Belgium, and the Netherlands. Many Huguenots were excellent glassmakers and decorators.

Hull Service A service of over eighty pieces of cut glass decorated with prism cutting, believed to have been made in Ireland. The service was seized from the English frigate *Guerriere* by Captain Isaac Hull after his U.S. frigate *Constitution* captured it on August 19, 1812. It was donated by Hull's descendants to the Wadsworth Athenum in Hartford, Connecticut.

hum glass A small cordial glass or taster.

Clear glass humidor, c. 1896-1906.
The Corning Museum of Glass

Humidor, Imperial Glass Co., Checkerboard pattern, faceted knob finial.
Krause Publications

humidor An "air tight" container in the form of a cylinder or box, used to hold cigars and protect them from drying out.

Humpen (German) A large, wide, nearly cylindrical beaker often tinted Waldglas, having straight sides, a slightly projecting base, and occasionally a cover. They were made in many styles and sizes up to twenty-four inches high and were used for drinking beer or wine. They were usually decorated with enameling (often in cold colors), usually portraying armorial bearings, figures, animals, and local scenes (see *German enameling*). Most were made in Germany, Bohemia, or Silesia, dating from the mid-16th to the 18th centuries, following the earlier taller Stangenglas. Some were made in Venice but were decorated in Germany. See *Reichsadler; Kurfurstenhumpen; Westphalia Treaty Humpen; Hofkellereiglas; Apostelglas; Hallorenglas; Bandwurmglas; Jagdhumpen; Familienhumpen; Stangenglas; Walzenhumpen; Willkomm; Passglas.*

Humphrey(s) Glass Works (1890-1920) A glass manufacturing facility established in Trenton, Nova Scotia, by John M.M. Humphrey(s), making bottles, jars, chimneys and globes for lanterns, and a variety of novelty items. In 1900 it burned and a new one built nearby in 1901, adding soda water bottles, tableware, medicine bottles, and flasks. In 1915 operations were moved to Moncton, New Brunswick, where they remained until closing, making primarily chimneys and globes for lamps and lanterns.

Hungarian glassware Glassware made from the 14th to the 19th centuries in various facilities in Hungary. The earlier wares were made in Venetian style; later ones were made in German and Bohemian styles. The main products were jugs and bottles embellished in enameling in the style of peasant art, and spa glasses from about 1820 for those taking "the cure" at local spas.

Hunnewell & Gore See *Chelmsford Glasshouse.*

hunt glass See *glass hunt.*

Hunt & Bacalles See *Johnson, Aiden.*

Hunt & Sullivan See *Hunt Glass Company.*

Hunt Glass Company Thomas Hunt and his son, Harry, came from England to the United States in 1880 and in 1895 established a glass cutting shop in Corning, New York, with a partner named Sullivan. The shop was named Hunt & Sullivan until 1907. When Thomas Hunt died, Harry took over, operating as Hunt Glass Company. It used blanks from Corning Glass and Hawkes. In 1949 it moved to a modern facility with all new equipment.

Hunter, H. & T. A glass cutting house in Louisville, Kentucky, operating from about 1840 into the 1870s. It purchased its blanks from various Pittsburgh, Pennsylvania, glasshouses.

hunting flask A flask in the form of a pilgrim flask, except for a hole through the center of the body. They were made in Germany or South Netherlands during the 17th century and in France during the 18th century.

hunting glass See *stirrup cup; Jagdglas.*

hunting horn An imitation of a hunting horn—a type of bugle—with a curved tapering form and small mouthpiece. It is often engraved with a hunting motif and the name of the hunt. See *horn.*

Huntington Glass Company A glass manufacturing facility established in 1891 by Addison Thompson and others in what is now Huntington, West Virginia. Originally it was called Central City Glass Company and made tableware.

huqqa (Indian) See *hookah base.*

Hurdals Verk See *Norwegian glassware.*

hurricane shade or glass (Aka *wind glass*) A glass shield usually cylindrical in shape with an everted rim, to be placed around a candle in a candlestick or a luster to protect the flame from being blown out by the wind. See *candle cover.*

Huwer & Dannehoffer See *Long Island Flint Glass Works.*

hyacinth vase (Aka *bulb glass, flower root glass*) A tall glass vase sometimes resting on a stemmed foot and having a cup-shaped bowl, used for growing a flower bulb.

Hyalith glass A dense opaque glass in sealing-wax red (from about 1803) or jet black (from about 1817), developed at various facilities following the development of ruby glass and other strong colors for glass. It was often decorated by fired gilding.

hyaloplastic Derived from the Greek word *hyalos*, meaning *glass*, it describes those activities related to the decoration on glassware made by manipulation, e.g., blowing, threading, trailing, pincering, etc., rather than those made by molding, pressing, cutting, engraving, etc.

hydriske (Greek) A small vessel similar to a Greek hydria. It is urn-shaped with a flat bottom and two horizontal loop handles or one additional vertical handle—the size between a jug and an amphoriskos. They are made of core glass normally embellished with a feathery or zigzag colored pattern in the 4th and 3rd centuries B.C.

hydrofluoric acid A colorless, volatile, highly corrosive acid (HF). It attacks silicates and is used in etching glass. It was discovered by German chemist Karl Wilhelm Scheele (1742-'86), working in Sweden, and its existence was published in 1771. The effect of the acid varies depending on what it is mixed with, e.g., pure acid dissolves the glass, leaving a bright surface (see *acid polishing*). When mixed with sulfuric acid it produces a high gloss on lead glass, and when mixed with ammonia it is neutralized, leaving a frosted effect. See *corroso, vetro.*

ice block An irregularly shaped chunk of greenish tinted glass, appearing like a block of ice, with asymmetrical, jagged edges and a scene or group of individuals carved into the block.

ice blue A very, light crystal blue color.

ice bowl See *ice tub.*

ice bucket See *ice pail; ice tub.*

ice cream dish A small dish, usually 3 to 4 inches in diameter and about two inches deep, used for serving ice cream. On occasion they were in sets accompanied by a matching tray.

Heisey ice-cream tray, Fandango pattern 13" x 8-1/2".
Davanna Collection

ice cream tray Trays, similar to relish dishes; but larger, thicker, heavier, and more complex and elaborate in design. They were originally sold individually or in sets including ice cream dishes. They are relatively rare, made in a variety of shapes and range in size usually from 7 by 12 inches to 12 by 16 inches.

ice(d) glass (Aka *crackle(d) glass, overshot glass*) A decorative glassware with a rough irregular exterior surface, appearing like cracked ice, made by two methods: (a) a partially blown gather of white hot glass is thrust into cold water, removed and immediately reheated so as not to melt entirely the cracks created by the sudden cooling; then carefully blown to enlarge the spaces in the labyrinth of small fissures; or (b) hot glass was rolled on a marver covered with powdered glass or small glass splinters (sometimes colored glass) that adhered to the surface, becoming fused to it when reheated, removing the sharp edges of the splinters. It was first made in Venice in the 16th century; and in Liege and Spain in the 17th century and revived about 1850 in England by Apsley Pellatt who called it *Anglo Venetian Glass*. In France, during the 19th century, the method (a) above was used to make a glassware called *verre craquele*, and method (b) to make *broc a glaces*. A third method was developed more recently by Venici, involving the use of hydrofluoric acid, called *vetro corroso*. It has been made in the United States since the 19th century.

ice lip A guard or fold molded or hand tooled around the lip of a beverage pitcher to catch and hold back ice cubes when pouring a beverage.

Cut glass ice bucket, 5-1/2" d. x 4-1/2" h.
Davanna Collection

ice pail A bucket-shaped receptacle for holding ice for chilling a wine bottle or drinking glass, with or without handles, either open, lug, or bail. See *wine cooler; wine glass cooler.*

ice plate A circular dish, usually 6 to 7 inches in diameter; often with a shallow well; frequently found in pairs, but, because of breakage, singletons are common.

ice tub (Aka *ice buckets, ice bowls*) A container for holding ice, usually about 6 to 8 inches in diameter, and generally one of three types: round with a liner and no handles, round with applied handles, and round with handles as an extension of the blank.

Candlestick with icicle drops. Patterns cut on pressed blank, 9" h. Davanna Collection

icicle drop A long, thin faceted drop that looks like an icicle, cut with three or more sides.

icicle glassware Glassware embellished with icicle drops hanging from its rim; originally believed to be made by the Boston & Sandwich Co.

Ideal Cut Glass Co. A glass cutting house established in 1902 in Corning, New York, moving, in 1904, to Canastoga, New York, where it operated until 1933. From 1905 to 1908, it purchased blanks from Pairpoint, later from Fry, Union, and Libbey.

Igel(glas) (German) Literally, *hedgehog* or *urchin* (*glass*). A drinking glass of inverted baluster or somewhat club-shaped form, with a bulge above the middle (or sometimes of wide cylindrical shape with a bulge) and a spreading kick base on a stemmed foot. Some have drops pulled out into points; others have a smooth exterior. Some are accredited to German craftsmen during the second half of the 17th century. Those with pointed prunts are called *Nuppenbecher.*

Ihmsen, William See *Williamsport Glass Works; Warne, Parkinson & Co.*

Ihmsen & Ulam See *Birmingham Flint Glass Company.*

Ihmsen family A family of glassmakers dating back to the 16th century in Germany. Charles (some refer to him as Christian) Ihmsen was born in Westphalia, Germany, coming to the United States in the mid-1790s. He settled in Frederick, Maryland, working for John Frederick Amelung for a short time.

He moved to Pittsburgh, Pennsylvania, working at various facilities along the way. In Pittsburgh, about 1810, he erected a bottle and vial facility (believed to be the forerunner of Ensell, Wendt & Co.). He was financially involved with several facilities in the area, including Ensell, Wendt & Co.; Ihmsen, Wendt & Co.; Beltzhoover, Wendt & Co.; Sutton, Wendt & Co.

His son, William was involved with the Williamsport Glass Works and Warne, Parkinson & Co. When Charles died in 1828, another son, Christian (b.1804), took over his interests, and expanded the family glass empire, operating various facilities under the name C. Ihmsen; then C. Ihmsen & Company. In 1862, shortly before his death, Christian took two of his sons, Charles and William, into the firm, operating as C. Ihmsen & Sons, going out of business after a few years. Another relative, Dominick, a grandson of Charles, the elder, was associated with Cunningham & Ihmsen. Christian's son, Christian, Jr., was founder of the Ihmsen Glass Co.

Ihmsen Glass Co. A window glass manufacturing facility established in 1814 in Birmingham (Pittsburgh), Pennsylvania. By 1836, it was operated by C. Ihmsen & Co. that had also built a vial and bottle facility. The window glass facility was abandoned sometime before 1840. About 1862, the operating firm became C. Ihmsen & Sons, and in 1885, Christian Ihmsen, Jr., established a glass blowing facility, operating as the Ihmsen Glass Co. In 1895, it closed. See *Pennsylvania Flint Glass Works.*

Ihmsen, Wendt & Co. See *Pennsylvania Flint Glass Works.*

Ikora-Kristall A glassware made from about 1925 by the glass making division of the Wurttemberg Metal Factory, in Goppingen, Germany, of a heavy glass. Some pieces have colored glass inlays and bubbles arranged in a pattern and some have inlaid colored stripes.

Illig, John N. (1879-1948) Born Johann Nicolaux Illig, he learned the art of cutting and engraving at Cristalleries de St. Louis, receiving his Master's certificate in engraving at age 21. In 1902, he was hired by Hawkes, working there until the Sinclair facility opened. He worked there until 1915, then for Egginton a short time. From 1902 to 1915, he operated his own part-time cutting shop in Corning, devoting full time to it after that date. See *Illig Cut Glass Company.*

Illig Cut Glass Company A glass cutting shop established by John N. Illig in 1915 after he left Egginton. It evolved from a part-time business he started in 1902, closing in 1929.

illuminating glassware See *candlestick; candelabrum; sconce; chandelier; luster; lamp; lantern; lanthorn; oil lamp.*

imbricated A design or pattern arranged to overlap like roof tiles or fish scales. It is applied to scale ground patterns and to scale faceting.

Imperial See *wine bottle, sizes.*

Imperial Cut Glass Company (1) (1896-1914) A glass cutting facility in Philadelphia, Pennsylvania. (2) A glass cutting facility in Corning, New York; incorporated in 1903, having the same principals as the Ideal Cut Glass Co.

Imperial Eagle Beaker See *Reichsadlerhumpen.*

Imperial Paneled Grape pattern milk glass plate, 8" d., IG mark.
Davanna Collection

Imperial Glass Corporation ad introducing the new Jefferson pattern.
Krause Publications

Imperial Glass Co. A glass manufacturing facility established in 1901 at Bellaire, Ohio, by Edward Muhleman and some local citizens. Production began in January, 1904; its early products being mainly jelly glasses and hotel tumblers. By 1910, it was pressing large quantities of carnival glass. From 1916 to 1920, it made a line called *Imperial Jewels*, and in the 1930s, introduced opalescent glasswares, stretch glass, and art glass. In 1931, it went bankrupt, but was allowed to operate, reorganizing as Imperial Glass Corporation. In 1939/40, it bought the molds and assets of the Central Glass Works of Wheeling, West Virginia. In May 1958, it purchased the name, molds, and equipment of the A.H. Heisey Glass Company; and in December 1960, it purchased the name, molds, and equipment of the Cambridge Glass Company. From 1964 to 1967, it made glass animals from the Heisey molds. In 1973, it was sold to Lenox, Inc., and, in 1981, to Arthur R. Lorch who made specialty items for Mirror Images. In 1982, it was sold to a Mr. Stahl who made clear and colored glass animals from original Heisey molds. Shortly after, it went into bankruptcy, and in 1984, its assets sold to Lancaster-Colony Corp. and Consolidated Stores International, Inc. The buildings and site were purchased by Anna Maroon of Maroon Enterprises, Bridgeport, Ohio, who developed it as a tourist attraction with sales shops, a glassmaking shop, and a museum. The molds were purchased by other companies, collectors' societies, and individuals. Many of the Cambridge molds were purchased by National Cambridge Collectors, Inc. and all of the Heisey molds, save one line (*Old Williamsburg* pattern), were purchased by Heisey Collectors of America, Inc.

From 1951 through 1973, the trademark of the Imperial Glass Co. was an "I" superimposed over a "G." In 1973, when Lenox purchased it, it was changed to "L.I.G.," and in 1981, when Lorch was owner, it was "A.L.I.G.," and when Stahl took over, it became "N.I.," for "New Imperial." See *Freehand Vase; Nu-Cut; Nu-Art; Imperial Jewel.*

Imperial Glass Factory (1) A glass factory in China, established in 1680, during the reign of Emperor K'ang Hsi (1662-1722). (2) See *St. Petersburg Imperial Glass Factory.*

Imperial Jewel A blue stretch glass made by the Imperial Glass Co. It is an onionskin type glass, being collected currently as carnival glass. Imperial employees called it *Irish eyes.*

impressed decoration A decoration made by either impressing a design (a) on a blob of hot glass, or (b) into the surface of damp sand and dropping a blob of hot glass into it; the impression made using a stamp of wood, graphite, metal, etc. They may be used as an end product or as embellishments on other objects.

incised The action of scratching into the body of an object, either as an embellishment or a means to record a name, date, or inscription. It was done on the molten glass, often with a blunt instrument, making a crude indentation, in contrast to the fine lines cut by engraving on the finished hardened glass.

incised glass See *incised; inciso, vetro.*

incised stem or twist An embellishment on the exterior of a stem in the form of closely spiraled grooving, running its entire length (some having a knop). In earlier pieces the grooving is rather coarse, but later ones have fine-drawn twists. They were popular from about 1850 to 1875.

inciso, vetro (Italian) Literally, *incised glass.* An art glass developed by Venini, the entire surface being covered with closely packed, thin, and shallow grooves or incisings, running in the same general direction, producing a slightly wavy effect.

inclusion flaw A flaw in a piece of glassware that materializes during the making of the piece.

inclusions Minute particles of an extraneous material placed in glass while in the molten state. Examples include the metallic particles found in aventurine glass, the mica particles in Silverina glass, etc. It also includes particles not intentially placed there, such as dirt and dust.

incrusted paperweight See *sulfide paperweight.*

indented flask A flask or beaker of various shapes having, as its prime embellishment, pushed in concavities, either oval or circular. They were made of Roman glass during the 1st to 4th centuries AD; some in the form of ring flasks.

independent decorator See *Hausmaler.*

Independent Glass Company Plunkett & Company established a flint glass manufacturing facility in 1862 in Birmingham (Pittsburgh), Pennsylvania. In 1876, it became the Independent Glass Company. In 1886, it was still in operation, making "crystal glass fruit jars, air tight glass tops."

index of refraction A number indicating the speed of light in a substance, compared to the speed of light in a vacuum or in air. With respect to glassware, it is the measure of the refractive power, or the brilliance, of glass.

India Point Glassworks A glass manufacturing facility established in 1790 by John Brown at India Point, Providence, Rhode Island.

Indiana Glass Co. sugar, custard glass, Flower & Leaf pattern. Davanna Collection

Indiana Glass Company (1) See

Dugan Glass Company. (2) A glass manufacturing facility established in 1893 in Dunkirk, Indiana, going bankrupt the following year. In 1896, the Beatty-Brady Glass Company re-established it using buildings purchased from the Pennsylvania Railroad. On October 28, 1899, it merged with the National Glass Company. In 1908, after the National Glass Company went into receivership, it was sold to the newly formed Indiana Glass Company [See (3) below]. (3) A glass manufacturing facility incorporated in 1907 in Dunkirk, Indiana, taking over the National Glass Company's Dunkirk facility in 1908 [See (2) above], making a general line of hand-pressed wares. In the late 1920s, it made both hand-made and machine-made glassware. Later it became a subsidiary of Lancaster Colony. (4) A glass manufacturing facility established in 1892, in Indiana, Pennsylvania, making decorated lamps, shades, novelties, etc. About a year later, it ceased operations. Thomas Sutton, acting as trustee for Mary C. Lloyd, was awarded title to its land and facilities, leased, in January 1896, for two years to Harry Northwood, who had severed all affiliation with the Northwood Glass Company in Ellwood, Pennsylvania. It operated as the Northwood Glass & Manufacturing Company.

Indiana Glass Works See *Northwood Glass & Manufacturing Company.*

Sauce dish, pressed brown glass with milk-white opalescence, c. 1901-1903.
The Corning Museum of Glass

Indiana Tumbler & Goblet Company In the early 1890s, Greentown, Indiana, offered free land to any business that would locate there. From the late 1800s

through the early 1900s, the eastern central part of Indiana had about 40 glass manufacturing facilities, as a result of readily available, low cost fuel (natural gas); Greentown had such fuel readily available.

D.C. Jenkins, Jr., formerly associated with the United States Glass Company's facility in nearby Gas City, Indiana, accepted Greentown's offer. In February 1894, he formed the Indiana Tumbler & Goblet Company. Later that month an agreement was reached with the town and construction of a facility began; in June of that year, the furnace was fired. It was expanded in 1895, 1896, and 1897, making clear glass tumblers and goblets, other tableware, bar goods, and jelly jars.

In May 1898, Admiral Dewey became a Spanish-American war hero and businesses of all types rushed to commemorate him. Indiana Tumbler & Goblet Company did the same by introducing a new line called *Dewey*. Even though the pattern bore no resemblance to Dewey or anything related to the navy or ships, it was a big success. In November 1898, it installed a 75-ton continuous tank furnace (for tumblers and jelly jars) and automated finishing machines. In 1899, it became part of the National Glass Company, being closed in July 1899, reopening in August. In November 1899, it was again shut down briefly to take inventory.

In January 1900, it closed again. Several weeks later it reopened. A few weeks later Jenkins sold his interest in the National Glass Company (in September 1900, founding the Kokomo Glass Manufacturing Company in Kokomo, Indiana). Jacob Rosenthal became manager and his chocolate glass (see *chocolate glass*) saved the facility from being closed. In 1902, he sold the formula for this glass to the National Glass Company and it was made at other National facilities. In 1902, Pattern No. 450 (*Holly*) went into production as well as a new color called *Golden Agate*. On Saturday, June 13, 1903, the Indiana Tumbler & Goblet Company was virtually destroyed by fire, believed to have been started by a spark from a passing locomotive. Later, it was determined to have been arson; it never reopened.

Indianische Blumen (German) Literally, *(East) Indies Flowers*. A style of enameled

floral embellishment introduced by H.G. Horoldt as a decoration on porcelain at Meissen about 1720. It was copied from the Japanese Kakiemon styles, influenced by the *famille verte* style on Chinese porcelain. The name stems from the fact that large quantities of Oriental export porcelain reached Europe in ships owned by the East India Company. It was also used on opaque glassware (having the appearance of porcelain) in Germany during the second half of the 18th century.

Indies flowers See *Indianische Blumen.*

Ingleson, Forbes & Co. See *Redwood Glass Works.*

initial cane A signature cane. See *signature cane.*

initialed stopper A stopper embellished with an initial identifying its contents. On some, in addition to or in lieu of the initial, the name of the contents may appear (not only on the stopper, but also on the vessel). See *bottle label.*

Wheaton blue "Tuckahoe Country School, 1891" ink bottle.
Davanna Collection

Italian pyramidal inkbottle.
Davanna Collection

ink bottle A small receptacle to hold ink, as a reserve supply for an inkwell. They were made in numerous styles and forms. See *desk set.*

ink glass; inkpot; inkshell See *inkwell.*

ink horn Similar to a drinking horn, but smaller, used to hold ink. They were popular in France during the 9th and 10th centuries.

inkstand (Aka *inkstandishes*) A desk set, usually including an inkwell, pounce pot, and penholder (or drawer for pens).

inkstandish An inkstand.

Cut-glass inkwell with brass fittings, 3-1/4" h.
Davanna Collection

inkwell (Aka *inkpot, inkshell, ink glass*) A small receptacle used to hold ink. Ink in fluid form was developed in 1836; the inkwell following shortly thereafter. Sometimes it is alone, sometimes there are two in one unit and sometimes it is included with trays, pounce pots and penholders as part of a set (see *inkstand*). It is usually a round dish, 1 to 2 inches in diameter and about 3/4 to 1-1/2 inches deep. There is usually a metal cover hinged to it to minimize spilling and evaporation. Sometimes it is merely a glass insert in the inkstand with a frame of metal or wood. A few had associated with them another well or a shaker containing fine sand or steel powder to blot wet ink. See *footed inkwell.*

inkwell paperweight See *footed inkwell.*

inlay A flat piece of decorative glass, usually small, to be embedded in a larger decorative design and made in the form of faces and patterns of many shapes, in polychrome glass. See *cellular technique; hieroglyph.*

Innovation Cut Glass A line of glassware, pressed with light engraving, introduced about 1919 by McKee Glass Company.

Innungsglaser *(German)* A glass or beaker with an engraved decoration depicting the symbol or symbols of a guild, association, or group. If enameled, it is called a *Zunftbecher.*

inscriptions Words, names, and dates, and sometimes marks inscribed on some glassware to record or memorialize the name of its maker or decorator, the date of its making or decoration, information about the circumstances under which it was made or its intended use, or sentimental expression. See *documentary specimens; commemorative glassware; Jacobite glass.*

instruments, musical See *musical instruments.*

insufflated glass See *blown three mold glass.*

Hemingray insulators, green glass; left: No. 12 Patented May 2, 1893, right: No. 40 Patented May 2, 1893.
Davanna Collection

insulator A glass object, 3 to 5 inches high and 2 to 3 inches in diameter, often of beehive shape. It has ribs on the exterior around which wires are wound to secure them, and a hollow base, often threaded, for placing on a peg on the arm of a telegraph or telephone pole. They have been used since 1832 when the telegraph was invented; and usage was increased by the 1876 invention of the telephone. The majority, before the advent of the cable (their death knell), were of pressed glass, mostly green; many with the name of the maker or user in raised letters. Over 300 different types are known. The threadless type were the first made, in general use through the 1870s, when the threaded type

began gaining popularity. The first patent was given to Ezra Cornell in 1844.

intaglio (Pronounced *een-tahl-yee-o,* from the Italian *engraved* or *sculptured*) (Aka *hollow relief, coelanaglyphic*) Embellishment created by carving or cutting below the surface of the glass so the elevations of the designs are hollowed out and an impression made from it creates an image in relief. The background is not cut away, remaining in the plane of the highest areas of design; the opposite of Hochschnitt and cameo. Some was made by wheel engraving in medieval Rome, but its first extensive use was in Germany and Silesia in the 17th century.

The design was left frosted, partially polished, or entirely polished (Hawkes' *Rock Crystal*) for effectiveness. The term generally applies to deeply incised free-form designs, such as figures, flowers, and fruits, rather than geometric designs. Copper wheels used in making intaglio designs range in size from a pinhead to about six inches in diameter, and from as thin as a hair to 1/4-inch thick; up to 50 wheels used on the design on a single piece; the blank kept between the cutter and the wheel. It became fashionable during the latter years of the Brilliant Period, being expensive and requiring thick blanks. Most pieces were ornamental forms, such as vases, cologne bottles, and powder boxes. Fine intaglio was made by Libbey Glass Company, T.G. Hawkes & Co., Tuthill Glass Co. and H.P. Sinclaire & Co.

intaglio (wheel) engraving See *wheel engraving, intaglio.*

Steuben Intersia vase, c. 1920s or early 1930s, transparent amethyst and "French Blue" glasses.
The Corning Museum of Glass

Intarsia glass On May 25, 1850, Edward Pettitt registered his technique for making this glass (see *Pettitt glass*), and on April 6, 1853, William Johnson patented an invention to make it, using the following technique. Two pieces of different colored glass were placed one on top of the other and bonded together by heat. The combined piece was softened slightly in an annealing furnace and a design was impressed on its surface; the upper piece into which the design was pressed was squeezed into, and partially penetrated, the lower piece. The upper surface was ground flat and superfluous glass cut away, leaving only the design embedded in the lower piece. On July 14, 1879, Achille Lemaire of Paris registered his technique for making it, involving etching an applied colored layer of glass prior to applying a second skin of clear glass. On November 8, 1883, Lewis John Murray of Soho & Vesta Glass Works, England, registered his method of making it. It required etching, engraving, or sandblasting a design on a paraison of clear glass plated with colored glass, before blowing it into a cup of glass, entrapping the colored design between two layers of clear glass.

He registered his patent in the United States on December 23, 1884. About 1920, Frederick Carder at Steuben Glass Works developed a type of art glass having a layer of colored glass, usually black, blue, or amethyst, etched with a design and cased between two layers of clear glass, the total thickness of the finished piece being from about 1/16 to slightly less than 1/8 inch. About 1930, Carder developed a commercially acceptable technique for making Intarsia glass requiring three layers of glass; two exterior layers of clear glass enclosed a layer of colored glass etched through with a floral or arabesque design.

All pieces sold were signed with the facsimile signature, "Fred'k Carder," engraved on the lower side of the bowl above the foot or stem, not on the underside of the foot as in the case of Aurene and other pieces. There are a few unsigned pieces, which were experimental or not made for sale. Production was limited, probably only about one hundred pieces, mainly vases and bowls, made for sale, all around 1930. A few goblets and wine glasses were made. Three bowls in the Corning Museum with Pomona Green foliate designs and one French blue vase with amethyst floral pattern have no signatures and may be experimental pieces; the only known Intarsia pieces in those colors.

At the Rockwell Museum in Corning, New York, there is a heavy Intarsia vase about 1/2-inch thick with applied crystal leaves. Carder also used Intarsia decoration on some of his Tyrian and Aurene glasses. Another form of Intarsia, called *New Intarsia Ware*, developed by Carder, consisted of Gold Aurene vases with trailed decorations of leaves and stems in green, marvered into the Aurene matrix. Carder used the term Intarsia as early as 1905 to describe the decoration on some of these pieces; the name derived from the Italian word *intarsiaturo*, a 15th century type of inlaid woodwork.

intercalaire (1) A mottled glass of contrasting colors inspired by French impressionists. (2) A process for applying two layers of decoration to a glass object. The first is applied and covered with a glass skin that acts as a surface on which the second layer is applied.

intercalary A layered glass developed by Emile Galle, having colored crystals and pieces of gold, silver, or platinum trapped between the layers.

interior painted See *Chinese snuff bottles with painted interiors.*

International (Cut) Glass Company (1903-1913) A glass cutting shop in Buffalo, New York. See *Valley Cut Glass Co.*

intertwined handle A handle made of two loops, in plain or strap form, overlapping each other at least twice.

inverted baluster stem A stem or part of one with a pillar-like form, similar to an inverted baluster. See *baluster.*

inverted pyriform See *pear shaped.*

investiture glass A goblet embellished with the arms and insignia of specific European noble orders, used at a banquet following the investiture of a new knight. At the banquet a toast was drunk to him from this goblet and then formally presented to him. They were made during the 17th and 18th centuries in Silesia, Bohemia, Germany, and the Netherlands. During the 19th century they were made for various military orders and awarded for outstanding achievements.

investment casting See *font molding*.

invisible glass An optical glass with a special chemical film bonded to it, which decreases the normal loss of light due to reflection, allowing more light to pass through the lens.

Iorio Glass Shop Louis Iorio, born in Salerno, Italy, in 1878, came to the United States and worked for the Empire Cut Glass Co. After it closed in 1925, he spent his free time cutting for his own amusement and for friends. After the Lindberg Kidnapping trial, his work became widely known because of the influx of people attending the trial in Flemington, New Jersey. Shortly thereafter he and his son opened a glass cutting shop and showroom in Flemington. Louis cut until he died in 1978, sixteen days before his 100th birthday. In 1984, Louis' son and grandson, Richard, were still operating the shop where they cut, engraved, repaired, and sold glassware. They had a large showroom where they exhibited many quality pieces of rare and unique glassware. They also had a small furnace where Richard made his unique art glass. It traded under the name *10-R-10*. It closed and was sold in the late 1980s.

Iowa City Flint Glass Manufacturing Company (1881-1882) A glass manufacturing facility incorporated on April 30, 1880, in Iowa City, Iowa, beginning glass production the next year. It made a carload of glassware per day, but workmanship was crude and most pieces are thick, having visible mold lines. Animal and bird motifs were very popular. Figures were often combined with mottoes, such as "Be Gentle" with a portrayal of a lamb and "Be True" with a portrayal of a dog.

iridescence (Aka *opalescence*) The rainbow-like play of different colors, changing according to the angle from which the object is viewed or with the angle of incidence of the source of light. Natural iridescence on glass is caused by the action of carbonic acid or ammonia salts present in the air or earth which, when combined with moisture, decomposes the glass, forming soluble carbonate of soda or potash. As this material is washed from the surface, there remain small scales of an acid, silicate, alumina, or lead, which break up the rays of light, giving the iridescent effect.

Once the conditions are met, deterioration and decomposition can begin within a short time, as evidenced by the iridescent film on bits of glass exposed to the elements along roadsides. Natural iridescence must be distinguished from that of luster painting and use of acids on glass, and is but one of the changes that may occur on the surface of glass included in the term *weathering*. See *iridescent glass*.

Iridescent Alabaster glass A name used by Stevens & Williams, Brierley Hill, England, for their iridescent glassware.

iridescent glass (a) Glassware that has acquired an iridescence as a result of being interred for a long time in the soil, subject to specific substances (see *iridescence*) and moisture, as in the case of some ancient Roman glass. If immersed in water, the iridescence disappears when the laminations are filled, but returns when the glass dries. (b) Glassware embellished with luster painting. (c) (Aka *luster ware* and *metallized glass*). Modern opalescent glassware where the surface has been exposed to certain metallic oxides and heated in a controlled atmosphere to develop an iridescent effect. It was first made commercially in 1863 by J. & L. Lobmeyr and thereafter by numerous facilities under various patents. On March 9, 1877, Louis Clemandot of Paris registered a process for producing iridescence on glassware by employing, under a pressure, a 15% hydrochloric acid solution. This resulted in nacreous and iridescent effects like those produced by time and atmosphere on ancient glass.

On August 29, 1877, Thomas Wilkes Webb of Thomas Webb & Sons registered a process calling for the use of a closed chamber where fumes from the evaporation of tin or other metallic salts came in direct contact with the surface of the glass. The acid, having an attraction to the surface of the glass, remained permanently bonded thereto, producing rainbow or prismatic colors. On November 29, 1877, Sidney Wittman of London was granted a provisional patent that involved making an iridescent glass by boiling glassware under pressure in a solution of muriatic acid.

On August 13, 1878, Frederick S. Shirley of the Mt. Washington Glass Works received two patents for processes to make iridescent glass: (1) The glass is heated to free it of moisture and expand it so vapors may be absorbed. The gases used are produced by vaporizing mixtures of iodine and bromine or solutions of them or their equivalents in alcohol, petroleum, etc. This resulted in a variety of colors and shades from the palest silver yellow to the deepest wine, dependent on the time of exposure and amount of vapors absorbed. (2) Articles are submitted to the actions of gaseous vapors. On October 12, 1878, Webb's patent of August 29, 1877, was amended to include making crackled iridescent ware. The article, in addition to being exposed to fumes of tin or other metallic salts, was immersed several times in a vat of water, adding a fine crackled effect to the iridescent luster.

On November 29, 1878, Monet, Pere et Fils & Stumpf of Paris was issued two patents for metallizing and iridizing glassware: (1) metallic oxides in the glass were subjected to a reducing flame producing a metallized or bronzed effect on the surface (copper oxide); and (2) cracked effect produced similarly to Webb's.

On October 5, 1879, Franz Emil Grosse of Berlin received a patent to produce an iridescent effect on rolled, blown, or pressed window glass and hollowware. The glass was subjected to fumes of pink salts or the salts were sprinkled on the surface before placing in an annealing oven. The oxidizing salts produced a metallic iridescent sheen on the glass.

On July 4, 1881, T.D. McDermot of England was granted a patent for producing an iridescent effect by using carbonic acid. This was not a true iridescence but had an effect making it appear more like the metallic film on mirror backs. On December 21, 1881, Rice W. Harris of France received a patent on a process similar to that issued to McDermot. On February 27, 1892, John Jacobsen of Boston, Massachusetts, was issued an English patent for an iridizing process in which the glass was pressed in molds (leaving no less than 3,000 lines/inch) to impart a very fine corrugated effect, producing the iridescence. The process was confined to buttons and flat sheets of glass.

The most famous makers of iridescent glass were: Tiffany, Steuben, Quezel, Durand, Loetz (Lotz), the Stourbridge district of England, Fenton art glass (pressed), Imperial Glass Company (pressed), and Northwood Co. (pressed). Less expensive iridescent glass, including Carnival glass, is made by spraying the hot glass object with metallic salts. See *carnival glass; Jade glass; pearl glass; satin glass; Tiffany iridescent glass; Webb's iridescent glass.*

Iridill Fenton art glass' name for its iridescent or carnival glass first produced in 1907.

Iris A trademark registered on August 6, 1912, by the Fostoria Glass Specialty Company, used on its iridescent glass similar to that of Tiffany and Steuben. See *Iris glassware.*

Iris glass (Aka *Rainbow glass, New Bronze glass*) An iridescent glass made by Mt. Washington Glass Company beginning in the fall of 1878, at the time the sole maker of iridescent glass in the United States. On August 13, 1878, Frederick Shirley patented two methods for making it (see *iridescent glass*).

Iris glassware An art glass developed in 1910 by Fostoria Glass Co., trademarked on August 6, 1912, and first made for commercial purposes in November 1910. Usually two or three layers of different colored glass were used with threads of glass pulled into feather-like designs by machine (e.g., *spiderweb, pulled-leafy,* and *heart-and-vine* patterns). Pads of colored glass were sometimes bonded to the surface and tooled to form leaves, flowers, and tendrils; trailings; or drippings of colored glass, which were wound about the object in haphazard fashion.

The main colors used were green, blue, yellow, black, rose, tan, and white. A lot of metallic gold was used, accounting for its high cost. Most was signed "Iris, Fostoria, Ohio" on small, oval-shaped, gummed labels. Without labels it is often sold as "unsigned Tiffany" or "unsigned Aurene."

Iris iridescent glass See *Rainbow iridescent glassware.*

Irish eyes See *Imperial Jewel.*

Irish glassware A term commonly used for glassware made in Ireland at several glass manufacturing facilities from 1780 to about 1835 (with the exception of some early items made about 1585). It was about 1780 when the first Irish glassware was made. The English Parliament eased restrictions on Irish industries, including glass manufacturing, while heavy taxes remained on glass in England (levied by weight, see *duty by weight*).

Irish financiers and English glassmakers saw the opportunity to avoid these taxes levied under the Excise Acts of 1745 and 1777, especially on heavier lead glass. There was an exodus of English glassmakers to Ireland, hence the term Anglo-Irish glass. In Ireland they cut heavier and heavier glass more elaborately.

As time went on, the styles took on an "Irish" form, which included turned-over and turned-in rims, boat or oval-shaped bowls, classic urn forms, plates with wide flat flanges, covers fitted within the rim rather than over it, etc. By the 1800s, cut glass was reaching a high in popularity and prominence. Engraving was still utilized, but only in a few areas. At this time there were many composites and combinations of forms, i.e., pottery and glass, silver and glass.

Most Irish glassware was of heavy lead glass, embellished by wheel cutting and engraving, or made by mold blowing. Most of the wares, except for a few marked pieces, cannot be distinguished by facility, and identification as Irish glassware is made primarily by weight, form, cutting, and absence of color, except for a few bluish pieces made at Cork.

The principal facilities during the period were: Benjamin Edwards of Belfast (1776-1812), Cork Glass Co. (1783-1818), Waterloo Glass Co. (1783-1835), and Waterford Glass House (1783-1851). (See *Belfast glassware; Cork glassware; Dublin glassware; Waterford glassware.*) Free trade for Ireland lasted until 1825 and, in 1835, the Irish glass industry had the first excise tax levied upon it.

iron A metallic element occurring as a natural ingredient in minute quantities in silica (sand), imparting a greenish or brownish color to glass, which can be eliminated using decolorizing agent. In addition to being an undesirable impurity, it is a useful and powerful coloring agent.

In its highest state of oxidation, hexavalent ferrates, it will, in combination with barium, impart a bluish-red color, but these must be melted under high oxygen pressures and cannot be practically made. In its metallic form, iron cannot exist in equilibrium with glass, but its divalent (ferrous) and trivalent (ferric) forms can be. In its reduced state, iron combined with chromium is used to make green bottle glass as found in wine bottles. However, with sulfur and a reducing agent in the form of carbon powder, iron sulfides are formed, imparting a dark amber color. The shade of amber can be manipulated within narrow limits by varying the quantity of carbon powder added in relation to the iron impurity and carbonaceous matter in the raw materials.

As an impurity, iron in its lower oxidation state (ferrous) imparts a bluish-green tint, whereas in the higher (ferric) state it imparts a yellowish-green tint capable of being masked by the addition of complementary colors, such as blue or red. To ensure most of the iron impurity is in the ferric state, oxidizing agents, such as sodium nitrate, are added to the batch in small amounts. In the glass industry, the oxidation of iron is known as *chemical decolorizing* while the masking of the green by blue or red is called *physical decolorizing*, achieved by adding cobalt and selenium.

iron, glassmaker's See *glassmaker's iron.*

Iron City (Window) Glass Works A glass manufacturing facility established about 1865 by O'Hara & Robinson in Pittsburgh, Pennsylvania, making black and green glassware, window glass, bottles, etc. By 1873 the name was changed from the Iron City Glass Works to the Iron City Window

Glass Works. The owners took over the Cookstown Works at about the same time. In 1877 George Wanhoff & Company acquired both facilities. The Iron City Window Glass Works was still operating in 1886, making window glass only.

iron pontil A black discoloration caused when the hot pontil is pressed back into the original pontil mark in an effort to smooth it.

iron red An orange-red color produced from a base of ferric oxide and used in conjunction with embellishment in Schwarzlot.

Irving Cut Glass Company (1900-1933) A glass cutting facility established in Honesdale, Pennsylvania, by six glass cutters, one of whom was William H. Hawken. Its finer brilliant cut wares were on Dorflinger blanks. It later used figured blanks from Fry and Libbey. It did a large export business with South Africa, Spain, China, and Japan. Some pieces were signed "Irving," etched lightly in script.

IS machine A bottle making machine. *IS* identifies the investors, *Ingle and Smith*, and the type of machine, *independent sections*. It can be operated on either the *blow and blow* or *press and blow* process. It may consist of either one section or up to ten sections, each being a separate machine in its own right, synchronized with a feeder mechanism, other sections and any process taking place after the bottles leave the machine(s). Each section can operate using single, double, triple, or quadruple gobs and any may be taken off line for repairs, to change molds, etc., and not effect the operation of any of the others. Nearly any size bottle can be made. Narrow neck bottles are usually made by the *blow and blow* process, wide mouth ones by the *press and blow* process. Currently the *press and blow* process is being used more often for narrow neck bottles.

Isabella Glassworks (Aka *New Brooklyn Glass Works*) (1848-1868) A bottle and flask glass manufacturing facility in New Brooklyn, New Jersey, established by Julius and Thomas Stanger and named for Thomas' daughter. In 1858 Clayton B. Tice acquired it, operating it until it closed.

Islamic enameling Opaque vitreous enameling with gilded embellishment used on glassware made between 1170 and about 1400 when Tamerlane sacked Damascus and the local glass industry moved to Samarkand. It also includes some associated with Fostat (Egypt) from about 1270 to 1340. It is divided into five categories based on style and date rather than the location identified with the categories: Syro-Frankish glassware, Aleppo glassware, Damascus glassware, Chinese-Islamic glassware, and Syrian glassware. See *Islamic glassware.*

Islamic glassware Glassware made during the Islamic period from 622—the year Mohammed was forced to flee Mecca to Medina—until after 1402, including that made in Egypt, Persia, Syria, and Mesopotamia after the Islamic conquest. From the 16th into the 19th centuries, production was sporadic. It may be divided into three periods: the first, from the 7th to the 11th centuries, centers of production in Syria, Egypt, Persia, and Mesopotamia; the second, from the 12th to the 15th centuries, centers in Syria and Egypt; and the third, from the 16th through the 19th centuries, centers in Persia, Turkey, and India.

Since the religion discouraged the portrayal of human figures, Islamic artists and artisans used flora, repetitive geometric patterns, lines, and colors as embellishment called *arabesque* (see *arabesque*). The types of glassware included: (a) wheel engraved wares having linear relief, cameo decoration, and circular faceting made in Persia, Mesopotamia, and Egypt; (b) glass having applied decoration, such as trailing and prunts; (c) luster painted glass; (d) gilded glass; and (e) enameled and gilded glass (see *Islamic enameling*).

Distinctive styles and forms were developed, and were contributed to glass technology, the technique of painting in luster; the perfecting of gold painting and enameling in relief; and near perfection in carving glass in relief. The long neck on flasks is characteristic of Islamic shapes—sometimes plain and straight, sometimes elaborate and curved. During this period, mosque lamps, pilgrim flasks, footed bowls, and rose water sprinklers were made. The glassware was traded within the Muslim countries and throughout the Mediterranean area, Scandinavia, Russia, East Africa, the shores of the Indian Ocean, and even China.

Islamic vase Imitations of mosque lamps made as vases in the 19th and 20th centuries. See *mosque lamp.*

Iszard, Samuel, & Co. See *Pendleton Glass Works.*

Italian Comedy Figures See *Commedia Dell'arte Figures.*

Italian engraving Diamond point engraving was done in Italy between the mid-16th and the 17th centuries, quickly discontinued as other types of embellishment became more fashionable. However, it was used elsewhere on glassware *a la facon de Venise.* Wheel engraving was not suitable because lime soda glass was too thin and fragile for it.

Italian wine bottle The traditional Italian wine bottle is globular (originally often flattened) with a long thin neck. The bottom was rounded, requiring it to be wrapped in straw to provide a flat surface for standing and making binning impossible. Today superior Italian wines are bottled in cylindrical bottles with a kick base, permitting binning.

Ivory cameo glass See *ivory-imitation glassware.*

Ivory Decorated See *Crown Milano.*

Ivory Glass A variation of *Ivrene,* similar but without iridescence. See *Ivrene.*

ivory-imitation glassware (Aka *Ivory cameo glass*). A novelty type cameo glass introduced during the last quarter of the 19th century in imitation of old carved ivory. The process for making it was patented by Thomas Webb & Sons on November 30, 1877, in England and on February 19,1889, in the United States. The ivory-colored or white opaque glass objects were painted or printed upon with an acid-resistant substance and submerged in hydrofluoric acid. The acid ate away the surface not protected, leaving that beneath the resist in relief. On occasion this was complemented by cutting or engraving; sometimes cutting or engraving was the only decoration.

After the acid resist was removed, the object was polished and tinted with brown or other colors in an effort to give an aged appearance and increased prominence to the raised portions. It was fired to fix the color. Often it was embellished with enameling and gilding. George and Thomas Woodall made such wares, generally using Oriental objects as models.

Ivrene An art glass developed by Frederick Carder at Steuben made for commercial purposes in the 1920s. It was a translucent, whitish-colored glassware with a slightly iridescent satin surface, the closest Steuben ever came to making a milk white glass. The batch contained feldspar and cryolite, and the iridescence was produced by spraying stannous fluoride on the object *at-the-fire* in much the same manner as with Aurene and Verre de Soic. A variation called *Ivory* is similar but without iridescence. It was used originally for lighting fixtures, but was used later to make ornamental objects. It was engraved to show the ivory-colored glass under a satin luster. It has erroneously been called *White Aurene.*

J.T. See *Brownsville Glass Works.*

Mary Gregory-type, Jack-in-the-Pulpit vase, 11-1/2" h.
Davanna Collection

Jack-in-the-Pulpit vase A vase resembling the flower, *Jack-in-the-pulpit*, made in a variety of colors, sizes, and glasses. They were very popular during the late 19th-early 20th centuries, having an unconventional trumpet-like shape with a portion of the top rim curled down.

jacks (Aka *pucellas*) A glassmaker's tool used for shaping glass during the blowing process or forming the mouths on open vessels. It has two metal arms joined at one end by a handle.

Jackson & Baggott A cutting house operating in New York City during the early 1800s.

Jackson (Glass) Works (1827-1877) A window glass manufacturing facility established by Thomas H. Richards near Waterford, New Jersey, where his family owned thousands of acres in the Batso/Atsion area and iron smelters and forges (the facility and the area around it named for President Jackson). Richards' sons, Samuel and Thomas, Jr., entered the business, the firm became Richards & Brothers.

In the 1850s, it began making blue glass and table, hollow, and other wares. In October 1851, it won National First Prize for the best surface quality in window glass by the American Institute of New York and given the honor of furnishing 15,000 panes of glass for the walls and dome of the Crystal Palace at the 1853 New York's World Fair. The village that sprang up around the facility, spurred by the railroad built by Samuel Richards in the 1850s, was named Atco in 1866. When Thomas Richards, Sr., died in 1860, Thomas, Jr., devoted his efforts to planning the town and Samuel operated the glassworks, known simply as "Samuel Richards." In 1877, available wood for fuel began to dwindle and a fire partially destroyed the facility.

Jacob's ladder A frigger in the form of a vertical rod resting on a flat circular base; the rod standing between two intertwining spirals of glass threads, each of a different color.

Jacobite glassware English glassware, often wine glasses, for drinking toasts to faithfulness or aspirations of victory prior to the defeat of Prince Charles Edward Stuart (Bonnie Prince Charlie) in 1746. See *Williamite glassware; Charles Edward Stuart glassware; Amen glass.*

jacony A small circular bowl with a flared rim, looped handle, and a foot.

jade glass A popular and fashionable art glass made to resemble jade. Records indicate that it was used as early as the 4th century B.C., especially in China. The Egyptians were experts in making it look like the stone, even with naturally occurring embellishments. Venetians also made it, preferring to imitate marked and striated stones. The Chinese, in the 18th century, used it to make bowls and bottles with elaborate ornamentation. In the 19th century, American and English craftsmen began making an array of pieces.

Stevens & Williams in England and Frederick Carder in the United States began making a variety of objects. Carder frequently cased the body of the piece with a translucent white alabaster layer, engraved a design, letting the jade glass show through. To make it, various oxides were added to the basic white glass batch to make the many colors of natural jade; often applied stems or handles are of colorless glass. The ware is usually a pale green color, but often blue, rose, yellow, or other color. A pink toned version was marketed as *Rosaline* (see *Rosaline*). Plum Jade glass is opaque and was made mainly from 1922 to 1935.

Jade Iridescent glass Opaque jade glass with iridescent crizzle applied. It is very rare.

Fire-King Jade-ite five compartment dinner plate, 9-5/8" d. Heartland Discoveries

Jade-ite A commercial tableware of "heat-resistant" glass. A brochure from a distributor describes it as "the new and only heat-proof glass dinnerware in the delicate beauty of jade green."

Jadite A glassware made by the Jeanette Glass Company; a heavy pressed opaque glassware with a dull pastel jade green color.

Jagdglas (German) Literally, *hunting glass*. Drinking glasses having an enameled or engraved embellishment portraying various game being pursued by hunters and hounds. They are of various types, including Humpen, Stangenglas, goblets, Romer, etc., made in Bohemia, Thuringia, and elsewhere in Germany from the 16th through the 19th centuries.

jam dish A small dish that looks like the bottom of a butter dish, except there is no indentation for the domed lid.

Fenton milk glass jam jar, Hobnail pattern. Davanna Collection

jam jar A small covered jar to hold jam or preserves.

James, Richard A glass cutter and engraver operating a shop in Pittsburgh, Pennsylvania, during the early 1800s.

James & Gatchell; James Glass Works-see *Lancaster Glass Works.*

Jamestown glass houses Jamestown, Virginia, was the site of the first permanent settlement in America in 1607. The first glass manufacturing facility (the *first* industry in America) was established there in 1608 or 1609 by the London Company of Glassmakers, manned by eight Dutch and Polish (or German depending on the source) glass blowers.

The site of the first glasshouse, in the woods near Jamestown, was an ideal location: unlimited supply of fuel, good supplies of sand, and river and sea transportation to ship wares back to England. Its products are unknown because it survived only a short time; the workers turning to agriculture to survive.

In June of 1621, a second facility was built on the mainland near Jamestown Island by the Virginia Company on a profit sharing basis. Its primary objectives were to make window glass, drinking vessels, beads for trading with the Indians (believed to be its only product), and products to send back to England (none were). It was managed by Captain William Norton and operated by six glass workers from Venice (possibly Bohemia) coming under signed contracts.

After a severe storm, an Indian massacre (March 22, 1622), a major fire, much sickness and death, labor problems (in 1624, a worker destroyed the furnace and glass on hand), and delaying tactics by workers in search of good sand, operations finally started, but troubles continued, and on June 15, 1625, they were discontinued. There is no evidence to indicate that either of these reached the stage of continuous production and nothing has been discovered in the area, with the exception of a few fragments of green bottle glass and beads, possibly attributed to one of them. Other glass and fragments found in the area appear to have been of English origin and date from about 1650.

Jansen & Wells Jansen and Wells were glass cutters living in Brooklyn, New York, in the 1890s, operating a glass cutting shop there, as partners, from about 1905 to 1918.

Janus flask A head flask that is janiform (two faces, one each on the obverse and the reverse). Janus was an ancient Roman god of doorways, of beginnings (January, the first month), and of the rising and setting of the sun. He is usually personified as having one head with two bearded faces back to back, looking in opposite directions. Some flasks have dissimilar faces. They are mold blown of Roman glass, dating from the 1st to the 4th centuries.

Janvier Glass Works See *Walsh Brothers.*

Japanese glassware Little is known of the early history of Japanese glassmaking, apparently other than beads; very little, if any, glass was made (in fact, the Japanese term for glass, *bidoro*, is derived from either the Spanish, *vidrio*, or the Portuguese, *vidro*, their terms for *glass*). These beads were made during the Yanoi period (200 B.C.-300 A.D.). Some Matagama beads dating from the 3rd to the 6th centuries have been discovered, and some vessels dating from the Asuka/Nara periods (552-793). Glassmakers of the Nara period made *shari-tsubo* (see *shari-tsubo*).

This was followed by a period of unrest and glass making deteriorated over the next few centuries and finally ceased altogether in the 13th century; however, prior to cessation, some beads, bottles, and mirrors were made. Most of the glass used in Japan during this period was imported from China and Western Asia. During the 17th century, Portuguese, Spanish, and Dutch traders began to bring glassware into Japan, encouraging the Japanese to develop their own industry. This happened slowly during the 18th century, but the vast majority was still imported. Few glassmakers were in business and they were very secretive in making their wares, consisting primarily of beads, ornaments, and other smaller items.

During the late 18th and early 19th centuries, glassmaking began to evolve rapidly as they learned techniques from the West. By the mid-19th century, they were making many items in traditional European styles: bottles (cut and molded), ground glass shades, lamp chimneys, etc. Nagasaki was one of the main glass making centers. Japan made many unique glass items, such as the *pokok-pokon*, hair and comb ornaments, pipes, shiny balls (designed to scare off flies), goldfish bowls, *biidori-e,* etc. Osaka was known for its mirrors and beads; Kyoto for its beads and small pieces of inlay work; and Edo for its lanterns, *biidori-e*, lamps, mirrors, eye glass and, by the end of the 19th century, a variety of cut-glass bowls, vases, and tableware.

Satsuma province was another important center, making cut glass bowls in a light red color; cased and cut glass in a variety of colors, particularly red and blue; platters with gold decoration; bottles and plate glass. This area was destroyed by the British in 1863 and the industry never recovered. After World War II, two facilities in Tokyo began making glassware in the contemporary style. In addition, studio glassware is now being made.

Japonica A rarely used trademark of Cambridge Glass Co. (1937).

Jardelle, Alex A glass cutter, working in the 1810s to 1830s, having his own cutting and engraving shop in Pittsburgh, Pennsylvania, before working at the Bakewell facility. He is most famous for cutting and engraving the Monroe Service in 1817; the Franklin Institute Decanters in 1825; and two vases presented to Lafayette in 1825.

jar A deep, wide-mouthed receptacle used to hold a variety of substances. They normally are cylindrical (with no handles), although some are of baluster or other shapes, and vary greatly in size and style. Many are strictly utilitarian and undecorated, but some smaller ones used for toilet preparations, etc., and are often artistically decorated. See the following types of jars: *guttular; honey; jam; leech; mustard; ointment; pickle; preserve; syrup; specie; fruit.*

jar mill (Aka *ball mill*) A mill used for grinding colors and powdered glass, generally to make enamels. It consists of a jar into which appropriate substances are placed together with some pebbles or ceramic balls and water. It is then rotated to grind the substance.

jarrita (Spanish) A beaker with a rounded body, flat solid base or pedestal foot, and a slender neck with a large funnel mouth. On some there are a row of vertical loop handles extending from the body to the neck, embellished either with pincered trailing or a serrated edge. Some have two rows of such handles, four large ones alternating with four smaller ones. They were made in southern Spain in the 16th and 17th centuries.

Jarves, Deming (1790/1-1869) Born in Scotland, coming to Boston, Massachusetts, as an infant, living there most of his life. His first business venture was selling dry goods until he became a partner in 1815 in the firm of Henshaw & Jarves, an importer of crockery and glassware. In 1815, he married Anna Stutson (Stetson) and they had nine children, two died in infancy.

While with Henshaw & Jarves (selling his share in 1818), his interest in glass was aroused. In 1817, he (and others) purchased, at auction, the Boston Porcelain & Glass Company in the name of their newly formed corporation, the New England Glass Company, and managed it from 1818 until 1825. He received his first patent, in 1821, for a machine that opened molds, followed in 1822 with a patent for improvements in chimneys for lamps.

In 1825, he withdrew to establish the Boston & Sandwich Glass Co. (originally Sandwich Manufacturing Company). In April of that year ground was broken for the facility and, on July 4, the first glass was blown. In 1858, he withdrew from this company to establish the Cape Cod Glass Co., which closed at the time of his death. In 1837, while managing Boston & Sandwich Glass Co., he founded the Mt. Washington Glass Company, turning it over to his son George to operate. Deming Jarves and associate, Hiram Dillaway (from

1828), perfected the process of making mold-pressed glass, and Jarves obtained several patents from 1828 onward; the first dated December 1, 1828. His 1830 patent was one that allowed pressing handles on objects in one operation, the first of its kind (handles having previously been made separately, then attached). This patent was in effect for fourteen years so no other facility was permitted to press objects with handles as an integral part of the body until 1844.

Jarves' companies made mold-pressed wares using mass production techniques, lessening the overall cost. He also obtained, in 1829, a patent for making pressed glass door knobs secured to the turning rod by a glass screw instead of the traditional metal screw. Jarves developed the style of mold pressed glass, known as *lacy glass*. He made improvements and refinements on Bakewell's pressed glass machinery. The original products of the Bakewell machine were rather poor imitations of Anglo-Irish cut glass, but with the Jarves modifications, the products had unique and individual patterns characteristic of pressed glass at its best.

Under his management, the Boston & Sandwich Glass Co. became one of the most successful facilities of all times, winning a number of awards for pressed, cut, and colored glassware. It exported a fifth of its production to South America and the East and West Indies. The New England Glass Company and the Boston & Sandwich Glass Company both closed in 1888 due to the high cost of coal, combined with labor disputes. See *New England Glass Bottle Company; New England Glass Company; Boston & Sandwich Glass Co.; Cape Cod Glass Company; Mt. Washington Glass Company.*

Jarves, J.W., & Co. See *Cape Cod Glass Company.*

Jarves & Cormerais See *Mount Washington Glass Works.*

jaspe See *agate glass.*

jasper (1) See *jasper ground.* (2) A 17th century term for agate glass.

jasper ground A ground that is speckled with small particles of glass, generally of two colors, made to imitate jasperstone.

Salt- and peppershakers, Cubist pattern, transparent green glass, Jeanette Glass Company.
The Corning Museum of Glass

Jeanette Ultramarine (green) plate, Doric & Pansy pattern.
Davanna Collection

Iris & Herringbone candelabra by Jeanette Glass Co.
Tri-State Antiques

Jeanette Glass Company (1900-1983)

A glass manufacturing facility established in Jeanette, Pennsylvania, operating in the old McKee facility, making large quantities of what is now called Depression glass, the first colored wares being pink and green and the first pressed pattern *Cubist* in pink. It made children's sets (and the only company to make cone-shaped pitchers) in Depression glass.

Jeanette Shade & Novelty Company See *Empire Glass Company.*

Jefferis Glass Works See *Fairton Glass Works.*

Jefferson Glass Company (1) A glass

manufacturing facility established in Steubenville, Ohio, in 1900, by workers from Northwood's Indiana, Pennsylvania, facility. Each had broad glassmaking experience, including Harry Bastow and D.J. Sinclair (by 1910, Sinclair was the sole owner). In 1906 it reorganized and, in 1907, built a new facility in Follansbee, West Virginia, moving all operations there, closing the Steubenville facility. It made pressed glass wares, specializing in opalescent wares from 1901 through 1907. In 1910, it was sold; the new owners discontinued tablewares and began making lighting wares. In 1933, it went bankrupt.

In 1913, a relative of D.J. Sinclair, Frank D. Sinclair, purchased the Millersburg Glass Co. and began making glass in December 1916, making lighting specialties as an affiliate of the Jefferson Glass Company. This facility was sold in 1919. See *Bastow Glass Company.* (2) A glass manufacturing facility established in 1912 in Montreal, Canada, an affiliate of the Jefferson Glass Company of Follansbee, West Virginia, making pressed glassware.

jelly dish See *nappie.*

jelly glass A small receptacle with a bowl,

generally of inverted conical shape, but some have a waisted, double ogee or pan topped bowl. Many have no handle, but some have one or two single or double loop (B-shaped) handles. They are about 4 to 5 inches high, having either a rudimentary stem or no stem, in which case the bowl rests directly on the foot (plain, domed, or folded). On some there is a knop between the bowl and the foot. After about 1710, glasses with bell-shaped bowls were made. Jelly glasses were without applied decoration but, after about 1745, various types of cut decoration began to appear. They differ from dwarf ale glasses which generally have a narrower conical bowl and never embellished with cutting. They were used, at the table at the end of a meal, to serve jelly or other similar desserts. See *custard glass; syllabub glass.*

Jena glass The glass used for making

lenses designed to correct astigmatism. It was made as the results of numerous experiments made by Abbe and Schott in Jena,

Germany, bringing about the desired glass in 1884. It included barium, boron, and phosphorus as supplemental ingredients.

Jenkins Glass Company A glass manufacturing facility established in Greentown, Indiana, in 1894, by David C. Jenkins; Greentown having offered him a land grant and $25,000 to build it. It made cut, pressed, and etched glassware, in clear and colored glass, and bar wares and containers. In 1900, he built another facility in Kokomo, Indiana. See *Kokomo Glass Company.*

Jenkins, D.C., Glass Company See *Kokomo Glass Company.*

Jenny Lind flask See *Lind, Jenny, flask.*

Jeroboam See *wine bottle, sizes.*

Jersey City Flint Glass Works (1861-1884) A glass manufacturing facility established in Jersey City, New Jersey, by H. O'Neill, making plain, pressed, molded, and cut flint and colored glassware. Two of its specialty items were headlights for railroad engines and chimneys for railroad lanterns.

Jersey (City) Glass Company See *Dummer, George, & Co.*

Jersey Green The most common color of glass made in New Jersey during the 18th and the first half of the 19th century. It is a rich aquamarine obtained from the unusually pure South Jersey sand with few impurities and contained no hint of yellow.

Jersey Rose A glass rose in some paperweights made by Ralph Barber between 1905 and 1918, and others (see *Millville paperweight*). It is not compact and the tips of its petals are opalescent. It is pink, made from ruby glass, or yellow (rare) and often accompanied by a bud and three realistic green rose leaves. The weights were usually made on a footed base with a cup-like socket in which rests a ball enclosing a rose. A comparable rose is found in some paperweights made about 1934/5 by Emil J. Larsen at the Vineland Flint Glass Works. These were made in deep red and yellow glass and have four leaves.

Jersey turtle paperweight A turtle-shaped paperweight made of green glass by shaping the head and all four legs from a rounded piece of glass. They were first made during the Civil War in Pennsylvania, New York, and Massachusetts.

Jersey Window Glass Works A window glass manufacturing facility established in 1862 in Jersey City, New Jersey.

jeu d'esprit Small items of glass made *at-the-lamp* by softening and working the glass with traditional glassmaker's tools. They may take the shape or form of human and animal figures, miniature household items, etc.

Jew's glass A term formerly used in England for lead glass made in Birmingham for use in making artificial jewelry. See *paste jewelry.*

jewel (1) A small diamond-shaped piece of glass, either clear or colored, and generally faceted, used to decorate the borders of some Irish mirrors (see *Irish glassware*). Some, instead of being faceted, are cut with two or three parallel flutes and, on occasion, are gilded (see *jeweled glassware*).

(2) Small novelty-stained glass forms made to imitate precious stones and used decoratively either singly or as part of a composition. Hand-cut jewels of this type are quite rare. Machine-made jewels are common, still being made. They are made using a solid glass rod; one end heated to a molten state in a furnace and inserted into a mold. A plunger is used to form the jewel. If the plunger has a design on it, the jewel has designs on both sides, called *two-sided.* If not, the mold has the only design and the jewel has a design only on one side, called *one-sided.* The jewels are pressed and placed in a lehr to cool slowly.

After cooling, the flat sides of one-sided jewels are machine polished. The faceted side of the jewel does not normally require polishing. Most are translucent, in all shapes and sizes. Some have chemically etched designs, some hand painted, and some cast in figural forms. Jewels may be integrated into window designs and stained glass lamps for highlighting purposes, frequently set in clusters or strung out as festoons. See *Tiffany jewels; molded jewels; chunk jewels.*

jewel-and-eye decoration Jeweled glassware with *eyes* (tiny glass drops) applied in the center of large drops, made of Frankish glass between 400 and 800 AD. See *jewelled glassware.*

Jewel Cut Glass Company (1906-1928) A glass cutting company established in Newark, New Jersey, originally operating as C.H. Taylor Glass Company. After closing, it went into the greeting card business.

jewel stand with post See *stick dish.*

Jewel star A cut glass design, a variation of the Brunswick star, but differs in being cut with the lines connecting the points running to every sixth star rather than every fifth. It was popular from about 1880 to 1890. See *star foot; star, wheel engraved.*

Jewell glassware A threaded glassware patented on September 6, 1886, by Stevens & Williams. In the manufacturing process, a gather of glass, either clear or colored, was used to create threads that were wound around the ware by machine. The resultant paraison was blown into a cup of glass and then into a ribbed mold, forcing the air traps formed between the threads and the outer casing into vertical rows of air blebs.

Jewelled Enamels See *Galle, Emile.*

jewelled glassware Glass objects with drops of colored glass applied to the surface by touching the object with a heated glass rod. The drops may be marvered into the surface or may protrude slightly, presumably in imitation of cabochon jewels (precious stones of convex hemispherical or oval form). The drops are polished but not cut into facets. Early specimens were from Egypt, Cyprus, Gaul, and the Rhineland, made during the 4th and 5th centuries. Some Frankish glass, made between 400 and 800 A.D., has small colored glass *eyes* applied to larger drops (see *jewel-and-eye decoration*). It was the forerunner of the Nuppenbecher of the 14th century. It was also made at Antwerp during the 16th and 17th centuries and in Germany during the 18th century.

jewelry Various ornaments, including brooches (fibulae), rings, hair rings, ear rings, necklaces, and pendants, worn for individual adornment. Jewelry of pieces of glass has been made from the earliest times in Egypt and Rome, and in Venice probably before the 11th century. Often the pieces of glass used in making the jewelry were shaped *at-the-lamp.* See *bangle; bead.*

jewelry, paste See *paste jewelry.*

Jewish glassware Glass objects decorated with religious motifs of significance to the Jewish faith. Early specimens in the form of hexagonal bottles and small jugs having molded relief embellishment were made in the eastern Mediterranean region about 200 A.D., and in Palestine, between 200 and 400 A.D. So-called *sandwich glass* (two layers of clear glass sandwiching gold leaf engraved with Jewish symbols) was made in the Roman Empire between about 100 and 200 A.D. Amulets embellished with Jewish symbols were made in Palestine during the 3rd and 4th centuries. Such glassware was not necessarily the effort of Jewish glass workers.

jigger A small measuring glass used to measure alcoholic beverages at bars and other public places serving alcohol beverages.

jobber A middleman who would buy assortments of items from a manufacturer at a discount, mark up the prices and resell the merchandise to his customers.

jockey (pot) (Aka *monkey pot*) A small earthenware piling pot or crucible used to make small batches of glass. They are generally placed on top of a larger melting pot in the furnace or on top of the main furnace. See *piling pot.*

joey See *dram glass.*

Johns-Manville Fiber Glass, Inc.
A glass manufacturing company in Toledo, Ohio, now a subsidiary of Johns-Manville Corp., established in 1958 after Johns-Manville Corp. purchased L-O-F Glass Fibers Co., created in 1955 by the merger of Glass Fibers, Inc. (established in Toledo, Ohio, in 1944) with the fiber glass division of Libbey-Owens, Ford, Inc. (established in 1951).

Johnson, Aiden Born in Corning, New York, he learned the glass cutting and engraving trade at Hawkes, then moved to the Ideal Cut Glass Co. During World War I, he worked for the Hunt Glass Works in addition to being a mailman. He returned to Hawkes where he worked until it closed in 1962, a total of 50 years. In addition to his full-time jobs, he operated a home shop in Corning, between 1930 and 1968, the year he sold it to Hunt & Bacalles. He died in 1969.

Johnson-Carlson Cut Glass Company (1906-1922) A glass cutting company in Chicago, Illinois, established by Oscar W. Johnson and John Carlson who also established the Twin City Cut Glass Company, Minneapolis, Minnesota, in 1908, and the Warsaw Cut Glass Company, Warsaw, Indiana, in 1911.

Johnson('s) Glass Works (Aka *Aetna Glass Works*) (1791-1825) A window and bottle glass manufacturing facility established in Frederick, Frederick County, Maryland.

Johnson, King & Company See *Cascade Glass Works; King Glass Co.*

joke glass (Aka *trick glass*) A drinking glass of unusual form designed to make it difficult to use and amuse onlookers. They have been made in the form of a shoe, boot, pistol flask, barrel flask, post horn, phallus, or any of a variety of animals. The siphon glass is a joke glass. See *puzzle jug; mill glass.*

Jonas, George, Glass Company See *Minotola Glass Company.*

Jones, Harry (1881-1934) He was employed by T.G. Hawkes & Co. about the turn of the century and, in 1903, foreman of G.W. Drake & Co., becoming, in late 1907/early 1908, its superintendent. It closed shortly thereafter and he returned to Hawkes as a cutter. About 1915, he opened his own shop, with a small retail store, in Corning, New York. He generally used quality blanks and some pressed blanks purchased from Heisey. He cut mostly geometric designs that were hand polished. He closed his shop in 1930.

Jones, Henry W., & Co. See *British American Glass Works.*

Jones, Thomas G. (1910-1936) A glass cutter living in East Orange, New Jersey, with a cutting shop in New York City.

Jones & Towndsend See *Wood, R.D., Glass Works.*

Jones, Cavitt & Company See *Shepherd Company.*

Jones, Philip, & Co. See *Schuylkill Glass Works.*

jordan Also spelled *jorden.* (1) A vessel, once used by alchemists and physicians, in the form of a glass soda bottle, except with a larger neck, about as large as the vessel itself. (2) A chamber pot.

Josiah, Harrison & Co. See *Eagle Glass Works* (New Jersey location).

jubbe A vessel for holding ale and wine.

jug A wide-mouthed vessel used to hold and pour liquids. They are usually globular, ovoid, or cylindrical in shape with a pouring lip or spout and a loop handle on the opposite side. Some have a hinged lid; however, most having thumb pieces are drinking vessels and should be called a tankard or a mug. In the United States, a jug is often called a *pitcher.* See *ewer; flagon; aiguiere; cantaro.* Also see the following types of jugs. *claret; cooler; cream; Elgin; decanter; helmet; Irish glassware; milk; puzzle; relief; syrup; water.*

Jugendstil (German) The Art Nouveau movement. See *Art Nouveau*

juice glass A small drinking glass in the form of a narrow tumbler; usually, the height twice the diameter.

jumbo shot glass A glass with a capacity of 16 ounces and over four inches tall. While not really a shot glass, it is a replica of the standard-size shot glass. They are rare.

Jung, Melchior & Gustaf See *Swedish glass.*

junk bottle An ale or beer bottle made of thick, sturdy black or green glass, used by home brewers and retailers.

juste A tall jug or flask with a wide body and an elongated straight neck.

Kaighn's Point Glass Works See *Excelsior Flint Glass Works*.

Kalana Art Glass A line of art glass developed at the Dorflinger Glass Works by Charles H. Dorflinger, Charles O. Northwood, and Eugene Dorflinger, Jr. It evolved over a period of years beginning in 1907, eventually included 38 patterns, most named after flowers. The patterns were etched and/or engraved on just about every form of glassware; most etched, requiring up to five separate immersions in an acid bath.

Some, such as *Kalana Forget-me-not* combined etching with engraving, while *Kalana Chrysanthemums* was stone wheel engraved. The most popular pattern was *Lily* and the least (and most expensive) *Egyptian*. The undecorated blanks used were blown at the White Mills facility from the best metal. When the facility closed in 1921, Kalana patterns were made on lesser quality blanks by the Honesdale Decorating Company.

Although it was not signed, an occasional piece may be found with the Dorflinger name in script on the bottom, placed there by John Dorflinger at a later date, only on pieces he was able to authenticate. Normally Dorflinger used paper labels on its wares, with the company name and a picture of a decanter flanked by stemmed glasses (based on the registered trademark of the company).

kaleidoscope (Aka *polyoptrum, polyscope*) An optical instrument consisting of a rotating tube having at one end bits of glass, beads, or other small objects. As the tube was rotated these small objects are shown in continually changing symmetrical forms by reflection in two or more mirrors or reflecting surfaces set at angles to each other. It was patented in 1817 by Sir David Brewster.

kalpis (Greek) A Greek vase of the hydria (see *hydria*) type, for storing and carrying oil and water. It is large and urn-shaped with a flat bottom and rounded shoulder, the neck forming a continuous line with the body. It has two horizontal loop handles attached to the upper part of the body. On some there is also a vertical handle used as an aid when pouring; some without the vertical handle were used as cineary urns. Some date from the 1st century A.D.

Kanawha Glass Company (1957-1987) A glass manufacturing facility established by the Meritt family in Dunbar, West Virginia, making large quantities of crackle glass (all pieces having smooth bottoms). See *Hamon Glass Company*.

Kanne (German) A cylindrical glass, sometimes in the shape of a barrel or truncated cone, similar to a *Humpen*, but smaller.

kantharos (Greek) A drinking cup with a wide mouth, stemmed foot, and two large vertical loop handles usually starting from the bottom of the bowl, extending upward to a loop stretching to or above the rim. The stem may be short or tall; the bowl hemispherical or cylindrical with concave sides. The bodies of some are in the shape of a human head or with a face on the front or back. Some have applied embellishment (see *Brockchen*). Some were made of Roman glass during the 1st or 3rd centuries. They are often erroneously called a *karchesion*, somewhat similar, except it has no stem. Both types are associated with the Greek god, Bacchus. See *head flask*.

karaba (Persian) A large Persian glass flask, made at Shiraz, with a globular shape and jacketed with rushwork.

karchesion (Greek) A drinking cup of Roman glass with a cylindrical bowl, on occasion, with concave sides and wide mouth. Originally made with two handles, but later examples, made in the 2nd and 3rd centuries, are without handles.

Karlsbad Crystal Glassworks See *Myer's Neffe.*

Kastrup & Holmegaards Glassworks

A Danish glass manufacturing company making, since the 1920s, tableware and ornamental glassware in modern styles, in addition to bottles and other ware. Making glass in this area was the idea of Count Christian Danneskiold-Samsoe (d.1823) to take advantage of the peat found in the Holmegaards' Moor on the Island of Zealand. The Count died before the facility was complete and his widow, Henriette, oversaw the project and its opening in 1825 as the Holmgaards Glasvaerk. At first, it made green glass beer bottles.

A second facility, Kastrup Glasvaerk, was built by the Holmegaards Glasvaerk, beginning operations in 1847, at Kastrup, near Copenhagen. It made bottles while Holmegaards diverted its production solely to service glassware. Both facilities were under the control of the same management until 1873, when the Kastrup facility was sold. Another facility was established in 1852 near Aalborg, in Jutland, and it and some other small glasshouses in Aarhus and Odense merged in 1907 with Kastrup. This merger created a company that controlled the manufacture of all Danish industrial glass, except window panes. In 1954, Holmegaards and Kastrup merged to become the present *Kastrup og Holmegaards Glasvaerker A/S.* See *Danish glass.*

Kaulfuss, Ernest (1878-1948) Born in Meistersdorf where he learned engraving, he came to Corning, New York, in 1903 and was employed by Sinclaire where he remained as a cutter until it closed, moving to Hawkes where he worked until his death. From 1908 until 1948, he operated a home engraving shop, cutting for Hunt, Steuben, and Hawkes. He had two brothers, Emil and Louis, who were also engravers.

Kaulfuss, Peter (1841-1927) Born in Europe, he came to the United States as a trained engraver, and settled in Saratoga, New York. He operated an engraving shop,

engraving for Hawkes in the late 1880s. He moved to Corning, New York, in 1913, where he worked for Sinclaire until 1915. From 1919 to 1927, he operated his own shop, cutting for Corning Glass Works and Tiffany & Co.

Kayser Glassware Company A short-lived glass cutting company operating in Milwaukee, Wisconsin, about 1918.

Grouping of paperweights, Charles Kaziun, Brockton, MA, c. 1960. Museum of American Glass at Wheaton Village, Millville, NJ.

Kaziun, Charles Born in 1918, in Brockton, Massachusetts, he was a contemporary American maker of paperweights. He began working with glass from an early age, and by 1942, made his first weights, now known as the *Kaziun Rose.* In the years to follow, he made a variety of weights (mostly of the *millefiore* type), including those with three colors of overlay and a variety of flower patterns. Most of his products, including buttons, earrings, perfume bottles, and weights, are signed with a "K" worked into the design.

Kearns & Co. In 1848, it sold the Zanesville Glass Manufacturing Co., which it acquired in 1842, and constructed a new one. In 1852, it acquired the Putnam Flint Glass Works and, in 1863, built another, converting the old one into a warehouse. In subsequent years, ownership changed numerous times. Both new facilities were in Zanesville, Ohio, operating into the early 1900s. See *Putnam Flint Glass Works; Zanesville Glass Manufacturing Co.*

Kearns, Burns & Carter In 1849, George W. Kearns, Joseph Burns, and John W. Carter, established a bottle glass manufacturing facility in Putnam, across the Muskingum River from Zanesville, Ohio. In 1852, it purchased the Cassell & Gallagher facility. See *Cassell & Gallagher.*

Kearns, Herdman & Gorsuch See *Zanesville City Glass Works.*

Keene (Marlborough Street) Glass Works The earliest New Hampshire bottle manufacturing facility, established in Keene in 1815, operating under various managements until about 1850. It was founded by Henry Rowe Schoolcraft, former manager of the Vermont Glass Factory, and Timothy Twitchell, one of the organizers of the New Hampshire Glass Factory. Soon Twitchell withdrew and, on March 20, 1816, Nathaniel Sprague from the Keene Window Glass Factory joined Schoolcraft. In addition to bottles, it made flint glass wares, including tumblers, wine glasses, decanters, pitchers, and other wares.

In 1817, it failed, taken over by Justus Perry, who specialized in demijohns and black bottles. Even though flint glass products were made there only from late 1815 until August 23, 1817, prior to the take over by Perry, it was called the *Flint Glass Factory.* On September 12, 1822, John B. Wood became a partner, the name changed to Perry & Wood. In 1828, Perry's half-brother, Sumner Wheeler, became a partner and Wood left; the name becoming Perry & Wheeler. In 1832, Quincy Wheeler joined the company and it became Perry, Wheeler & Co., making bottles, figural flasks, pitchers, bowls, inkstands, decanters, and off-hand pieces. See *New England glass manufacturers; Twitchell & Schoolcraft.*

Keene Window Glass Factory See *New Hampshire Glass Factory.*

Keller, Anthony F. & Anthony J. Anthony F. was born in Meisterdorf in 1870 where he learned cutting and engraving, coming to Houston, Texas, before moving, in 1902, to Corning, New York, the year his son, Anthony J., was born. Anthony F. was employed by Hawkes as a cutter in 1902, leaving in 1906 to work for Sinclaire. Over the years, he trained Anthony J. and they worked together from 1922 to 1926 at Hawkes. From 1905, Anthony F. operated a cutting shop in his home, later opening it full time (1920-1932). From 1936 to 1940, they operated a shop in Gibson, New York. In 1938, Anthony J. went to work for Steuben,

engraving there until 1960 when given other employment at the company. A few years later he retired. See *Keller, Henry.*

Keller, Henry (1878-1950) Born in Meisterdorf, the younger brother of Anthony F. Keller, he came to Corning, New York, about 1906, working as a cutter and engraver for Hawkes. About 1909, he moved to Sinclaire, working there until it closed. From about 1909 until his death, he engraved in his home shop, often cutting and engraving for Steuben.

Kellner & Munro Rich Cut Glass (1908-1918) A glass cutting shop in Brooklyn, New York. Its products, cut on blanks from Belgium, were of high quality and sold at Tiffany & Company and other quality retail outlets.

Kelly & Steinman A glass cutting shop established about 1905 in Honesdale, Pennsylvania. Shortly thereafter, it opened another, called the Peerless Glass Company, in Deposit, New York. Both operated until about 1913.

kelp A type of seaweed which when calcined produced ashes once used as a source of soda in the glass industry.

Kelva A pale, pastel painted glass embellished with flowers, designs and scenes made by the C.F. Monroe Company, from about 1904 to about 1910. See *Wavecrest; Nakara.*

Kemple glass Glassware made by John E. Kemple between 1945 and 1960 in East Palestine, Ohio, and from 1957 through 1970 in Kenova, West Virginia. It was made using old molds from defunct manufacturers. The ware is marked with a "K" on the bottom.

Kempston beaker A cone beaker, named for the place it was found in Bedfordshire, England, in 1863. It is in the form of a tall, slender inverted cone of thin blown, light greenish glass, with a slightly everted rim and flattened tip. About 20 similar beakers have been found throughout England; all considered to be made of Teutonic glass during the 5th century A.D. Their average height is between 8-3/4 and 10-1/2 inches, the diameter of the mouth being about 3-3/4 inches;

other beakers have thicker walls and trailing. The Kempston beaker is 10-5/16 inches tall with symmetrical embellishment; trailing wound horizontally just below the rim. There is similar trailing, making continuous vertical loops, on the lower part near the rounded and flattened tip. It is housed in the British Museum.

Kendall & Patten See *Duquesne Glassworks.*

kendi (Chinese) Similar to the Spanish *porro*, having a long neck and a side spout.

Kenner, J. & B., Inc. See *Pairpoint (Manufacturing) Corporation; Mount Washington Glass Company.*

Kensington Glass Works, flask, c. 1826, light-green glass.
The Corning Museum of Glass

Kensington Glassworks A window, crystal, and green glass manufacturing facility established in 1771 by (Robert) Towars & (James) Leacock (or Leacock & Towars) in Kensington, Philadelphia, Pennsylvania. In November 1772, it was sold to John and Samuel Elliott. Isaac Gray became a partner, the firm becoming Elliott & Gray; officially the Philadelphia Glass Works. The Elliotts were pharmacists and merchants, trading as John Elliott & Company, a name associated with the works.

In 1777, Farrell & Bakeover took over, adding plain and cut decanters. In May 1780, Thomas Leiper purchased it and, in 1789, rented it to Phillip Stimel. He was not successful and it closed after a short time, being idle until about 1797 when it was rented to Christopher Trippel & Co. to make bottles.

Some time in 1799 Tripple went out of business and it remained idle until March 6, 1800, when James Butland & Co. purchased it, the principals being Joseph Roberts, Jr., James Butland, and James Rowland. In February 1804, Rowland bought out Roberts, the firm renamed Butland & Rowland. In September 1815, Rowland bought out Butland, it renamed James Rowland & Co., also the Kensington Glass Works, making bottles.

By 1824, Thomas W. Dyott had leased the works, making vials, bottles, and flasks. A self-proclaimed "doctor," he was the patent medicine titan of the time, and the facility was called the Philadelphia & Kensington Glass Factory. In 1831, flint glassware was added. In July 1833, Dyott bought it, changing its name to the Dyottville Glass Works, the first such facility to initiate a twelve-month operating schedule. In 1838, Dyott failed and the facility closed. Dyott died in 1861 at age 90. It sat idle until 1844 when Henry B. Rapp took over. In 1845, Henry Seybert took over and began making flint and colored glass. In 1846, Benners, Smith & Campbell operated it. By 1853, it was being operated by H.B. & J.M. Benners, making bottles of all types. In 1874, it was being operated by H.B. Benners alone, and from 1893 to 1900, by his estate. See *Dyottville Glass Works.*

Kent, Wells & Company See *Franklin Glass Company.*

Kent Glass Works A window and bottle (cylinder) glass manufacturing facility established in 1823 in Kent, Ohio, by David Ladd and Benjamin F. Hopkins (one source claims it was James Edmunds, Henry Pauk and Henry's brother). From 1826, when Hopkins withdrew, Zenas Kent was Ladd's partner. In 1833, Ladd disposed of his holdings, primarily to Kent. Little is known of the future of this works. See *Mantua Glassworks; Park(e), Edmunds & Park(e).*

Kentucky Glass Works A glass manufacturing facility established in Louisville, Kentucky, in 1849, by Taylor, Stanger, Ramsey & Co., making vials, demijohns, and other bottles. In November 1850, Douglass & Taylor (George L. Douglass/James Taylor) purchased it, naming it the Louisville Glass

Works which, in turn, was operated by Douglass, Rutherford & Co. In 1856, Krack, Stanger & Co. managed it. In 1859, lamps, tumblers, and business goods were added. In 1865, the operating firm became J.A. Krack & Co., in 1868, Krack, Reed & Co., and in 1871, L.S. Reed & Brother. In 1875 Captain J.B. Ford took over, closing shortly thereafter.

Kern, Martin L. See *Hope Glass Works (Rhode Island location)*.

Kerr Glass Co. A glass manufacturing facility in Millville, New Jersey, that took over the Whitall-Tatum Co. operations. See *Whitall-Tatum Co.*

Kerzenbecher (German) Literally, *candle beaker*. See *Warzenbecher.*

Ketchum, D.O., & Company See *Green Bank Glasshouse.*

ketchup jug A cruet used to hold ketchup.

kettle drum bowl A large bowl of hemispherical or double ogee shape, mounted on a knopped or plain stem, resting on a molded foot. Its looks like a kettle drum.

Keulenglas (German) Literally, *club glass*. A tall, thin beaker, a type of Stangenglas, slightly club shaped, having a pedestal foot or high kick base. Some are embellished with encircling trailing, not in equidistant circles as on a Passglas, nor a long spiral as on a Bandwurmglas. Some very tall ones are embellished nearly all over with numerous small drops of glass, smaller than prunts. They are made of brownish or greenish Waldglas and are up to 42 inches tall. They were made in Germany and Bohemia during the 15th and 16th centuries.

Kew Blas glassware An iridescent art glass made in limited quantities by the Union Glass Co. in Somerville, Massachusetts, from about 1895 to 1915, comparable with that of Tiffany, Durand, Quezel, and Steuben. Much was signed with the engraved mark *Kew Blas*, (an anagram of W.S. Blake, manager of the facility). The iridescent, mainly golden glass, features primarily shades of tan, green, and brown in feathery and leafy patterns. Some was made of opal glass with a gold luster lining. Some forgeries were made, but these can be distinguished by the fact that the mark is etched rather than engraved.

key A geometric cut-glass motif. In the transition period between the Brilliant and Flower periods, a number of manufacturers and cutting houses used the Greek or Roman key as a decorative border.

key-fret (Aka *fret, Greek fret, meander pattern*) A border pattern in the form of lines meeting at right angles in a continuous repetitive design, suggestive of the wards (notches) of a key.

Keystone Cut Glass Company (1902-1918) A glass cutting facility established in Hawley, Pennsylvania. On closing, the owners, Theodore Wall and George Murphy (Wall & Murphy), established another that operated only a short period. See *Gunderson (Pairpoint) Glass Works.*

Keystone Flint Glass Manufactory A glass manufacturing facility established in 1872 in Pittsburgh, Pennsylvania, specializing in lead glass lamp chimneys and silvered glass ware. In 1879, the G.A. MacBeth Company took over. It was still operating in 1886.

Keystone Tumbler Company (1897-1905) A glass manufacturing facility established in Rochester, Pennsylvania, making mainly pressed tumblers, jelly glasses, beer mugs, and fine blown lead crystal tumblers; the latter often embellished with engraving, sand blasting, gilding, etc.

kick A conical indentation (shallow or deep) in the bottom or base of an object. When in the bottom of a glass or bottle, it adds stability and strength to the piece. It is used, in some cases, to push up the pontil mark to prevent damage to the table's surface. A deep kick was valuable to the person filling the bottle because it held less. See *spiked kick; kick base.*

Kiefer Brothers Cut Glass Company (1908?-1924?) A glass cutting company established in Brooklyn, New York. In later years, it may have operated as Kiefer Products Company.

Kiefer Products Company See *Kiefer Brothers Cut Glass Company.*

Kilgore & Hanna A glass manufacturing facility established in 1830 in Steubenville, Ohio, making bottles and hollowware, closing after a short time. In 1845, Beatty & Stillman (Joseph Beatty & Edward Stillman) purchased it, constructing a second one nearby. In 1847, David and Neal Hall (Hull) took over. Shortly thereafter, Knowles & Taylor purchased it. In 1852, Alexander J. Beatty & Sons took it over, operating as the Steubenville Flint Glass Works. In 1880, operations were moved to Findlay, Ohio. See *Beatty-Brady Glass Company.*

kiln A furnace or oven to melt the various constituents of glass, to fuse enamels, or for kiln forming. See *continuous firing triple kiln; muffle kiln; reverberatory furnace.*

kiln forming The fusing or shaping of glass, usually in or over a mold (i.e., slumping), by heating it in a kiln.

Kimber, A. & B.; Kimber & Co. See *Bridgeport Glass Works.*

Kimber, Benedick See *Bridgeport Glass Works; Brownsville Glass Works.*

Kimble & Durand See *Kimble Glass Company.*

Kimble Glass Company A glass manufacturing facility established by Colonel Evan F. Kimble during the late 1800s in Vineland, New Jersey. In 1931, it took over the Vineland Flint Glass Works after the death of Victor Durand, Jr., moving Durand's operations to its facility, operating as Kimble & Durand. It discontinued making art glass, with the exception of some colored pieces with embedded air bubbles, in the style of Cluthra glass with fewer bubbles. It also made bubble balls in the Tiffany style. See *Vineland Flint Glass Company.*

King, Son & Co. See *Cascade Glass Works; King Glass Co.*

King Glass Co. A glass manufacturing facility established in 1859 as the Cascade Glass Company (see *Cascade Glass Company*), in Pittsburgh, Pennsylvania, making bar goods, confectionary jars, and apothecary wares. In 1864, it was taken over by Johnson, King & Co., in 1869, King, Son & Co. (William S., and Alexander, the son) and, in 1880, King Glass Co. In 1879, it was nearly destroyed by fire and rebuilt. In 1891, it was absorbed by the United States Glass Co. (*Factory K*), making a wide variety of pressed table wares.

King of Prussia glassware Glassware with a decorative motif (frequently engraved) with a portrait or symbol of Frederick the Great of Prussia (1740-86), allied to England during the Seven Years War (1756-63), and popular in England from 1756 to 1757.

King Tut glassware Glassware with an overall pattern of pulled threads, developed by Victor Durand, Jr., at the Vineland Flint Glass Works.

King's Lynn Glass, Ltd. See *Wedgwood glassware.*

Kings County (Rich Cut) Glassworks (1905-1924) A glass cutting house established in Brooklyn, New York.

Kirby & McBride See *East Lake Glass Works.*

Kit-Cat (or Kit-Kat) glass A wine glass so-named because it resembles two glasses pictured in a painting of two members of the Kit Cat Club, done about 1721 by Sir Godfrey Kneller. They have a rounded funnel bowl, conical folded foot, and true baluster stem with compressed knops at the top and bottom.

kite A cut-glass motif of quadrilateral configuration with two equal angles opposite each other as well as two adjacent sides of equal length, shorter than the other two equal adjacent sides, resembling an old-fashioned kite.

Kling, Louis The operator of a cutting shop established about 1920 in Corning, New York, at the same location of the Corning Cut Glass Company.

Klinghoff, S.H. The operator of a glass cutting shop in Scranton, Pennsylvania, in business for a short time around 1918.

Klondike (Aka *Amberette, Amber Satin*) A line of glassware by Dalzell, Gilmore & Leighton of Findlay, Ohio. It consisted of 40 pieces, first marketed in January 1898. The main body is uncolored satin glass with bands, vertical and horizontal, forming a cross, stained old gold. On each side of the bands are deep miters of clear glass.

Klondyke A line of glassware made by the Northwood Co., Indiana, Pennsylvania, first marketed in 1897. It was a pattern, generally on a gold colored glass, with opalescent overtones. Also in this line, but in smaller quantities, were pearl blue, pearl flint, and crystal. Some pieces had raised enameling and gold decorations.

knapping Chipping away flakes of glass from a larger piece of *raw* glass, as in sculpting.

Knickerbocker Cut Glass Company A glass cutting house in Corning, New York, operating from 1902 to 1903, then purchased by Almy & Thomas.

knife A table knife, on occasion, made entirely of glass. Venetian ones having solid twisted handles were made in the 16th and 17th centuries. They were routinely made in clear and colored glass in the United States from about 1920 to 1950, with production peaking in the late 1930s-early 1940s. Many were hand painted with fruit and flower motifs or personally engraved with names and dates for gift giving. Their lengths varied slightly because tips were often broken during manufacture and shortened during the grinding (sharpening) process. Over the years many were reground or nicked during usage. See *handles, knife and fork; cutlery.*

knife rest A small, low implement, many looking like an athlete's dumb-bell. They were used to rest or support a knife at the dinner table to prevent soiling the tablecloth. They are usually of cut or pressed glass about 3-1/2 inches long and 1-1/2 inches high.

knitted glass Reticulated glass.

knob (1) (Aka *knop*) A piece of glass added to an object to form a leg. It may be solid or hollow blown and/or embellished in a variety of ways. See *knop.* (2) Pressed, cut, swirled, silvered, and blown glass objects used as handles or pulls on furniture, doors, etc., popular from about 1810 to 1860. They have been used to hold mirrors in place.

knocker (off) A worker at a facility, usually a young apprentice, who, by tapping the gathering rod or blowing iron with a sharp crack, removed the object from, and any surplus glass on, the rod. He may have the added job, if molds were used, of holding the mold while glass is blown into it and then removing it after blowing is complete.

knocker-upper A person hired by a glass manufacturing facility to walk the streets knocking on the windows and doors of workers to wake them so that they could get to work on time.

knocking off See *grozing.*

knocking up The straightening or repairing of the end of a blowpipe, bit iron, or punty rod. While many blowpipes are made of stainless steel with chromite ends, older ones had softer ends or noses, easily damaged and repaired (or *knocked up*) by a blacksmith who also repaired the bit irons and punty rods.

knop An antiquated form of the word *knob*, originally meaning a small tub or anything round. (1) A component of a drinking glass stem, usually spherical or oblate and having numerous styles. They are either hollow or solid and used singly or in clusters of the same or different types, and may be adjacent to each other or spaced intermittently. Some solid ones have enclosed tears; some hollow ones have a coin enclosed. On early Venetian *tazze*, the body was joined to the stem or foot by a glass ring, or *nodus*, which gradually became a globular knop, or when flattened, a *collar* or *merese*. (2) A finial. See the following types of knops: *acorn; angular; annular; ball; beaded; bladed; bobbin; button; cone; cushion(ed); cylinder; double cushioned; drop; dumb-bell; egg; flattened; hollow; melon; mushroom; proper; shoulder; swelling; wide angular; winged.*

Knopfbecher (German) Literally, *button beaker.* A beaker with part or all of its surface covered with irregular, fairly flat, button-like prunts. They were made in Germany and the Netherlands during the 16th century.

knopped stem A stem on a drinking glass embellished with one or more knops. See *knop*.

Knowles, R., & Company See *Union Glass Works (West Virginia)*.

Knowles & Taylor See *Kilgore & Hanna*.

Knox & McKee: See *Virginia Green Glass Works.*

Knox, Kim & Company A window glass manufacturing facility established in 1867 in Pittsburgh, Pennsylvania. About 1886, it was operated by Abel Smith & Company.

Kny, Frederick Engelbert A Bohemian glass engraver who went to England and was employed at Whitefriars Glass Works and, from the 1860s, at the Dennis Glassworks of Thomas Webb & Sons where he engraved his best known work, the Elgin Jug, completed in 1879. He specialized in rock crystal engraving and in intaglio, signing his work "FEK."

Koch, Edward J., & Company See *Koch & Parsche; Gunderson (-Pairpoint) Glass Works.*

Koch & Parsche Edward Koch, a former employee of the Mt. Washington Glass Co., established on January 1, 1899, a glass cutting shop, Edward J. Koch & Company, in Chicago, Illinois. In the same year, he was president of another cutting firm, Koch & Parsche, in Chicago, which operated until 1907. From 1912 to 1914, another of his companies, Koch Cut Glass Company, was in operation at two locations, Elgin and Chicago, Illinois. From 1914 to 1917, it operated only at the Chicago address, closing in 1936. Its trademark was *Koch-Kut*. In 1917, Koch was president of the Midland Cut Glass Company, Chicago.

Koch Cut Glass Company See *Koch & Parsche.*

Koch-Kut A trademark used by the Koch Cut Glass Company, placed on its cut glass wares on either pressed or figured blanks. See *Koch & Parsche.*

Koh-I-Noor A trademark used on cut glass made by Richard Murr at his studios in San Francisco, California, and Chicago, Illinois.

Kohinur Cut Glass Company See *Laurel Cut Glass Company.*

kohl tube A small receptacle used to hold dark powdery substances, such as antimony sulfide, referred to as *kohl* (used in the East to darken the eyelids or eyebrows). Some include a small bronze application stick. They are generally square, cylindrical, or flattened-pear shaped, but the interior is always cylindrical, about 1/4 to 1/3 inch in diameter. They were made by coiling molten glass around a metal rod and usually embellished with applied threads pulled in a feathery or chevron pattern. They were made in Iran between the 9th and 4th centuries B.C.

Kohlenberg Glass Works A window and bottle glass manufacturing facility established about 1795, near Frederick, Maryland, by Adam Kohlenberg, a former employee of Frederick Amelung. It is believed to have been part of the Amelung enterprise, Kohlenberg having purchased 1,000 acres of land with a glasshouse directly from Amelung or the bankruptcy court. It operated for a few years, into the early 19th century.

Kokesh, William J. In 1939, William Kokesh, after working for the Washington Cut Glass Company since 1915, opened a glass cutting shop in Seattle, Washington. In 1960, it was called Washington Cut Glass Company (see *Washington Cut Glass Company*).

Kokomo Glass (Manufacturing) Company A glass manufacturing facility established in September 1900 in Kokomo, Indiana, by David C. Jenkins, founder of the Indiana Tumbler & Goblet Company and Jenkins Glass Company, both in Greentown, Indiana, after leaving the National Glass Company's facility (formerly Indiana Tumbler & Goblet Company). The Kokomo facility began making pressed glassware in

February 1901. It was destroyed by fire in 1905, rebuilt in 1906, renamed D.C. Jenkins Glass Company, making large quantities of glassware during the Depression era, mainly heavy wares used primarily in hotels and soda fountains. Its trademark was a "J" in a triangle. See *Indiana Tumbler & Goblet Company.*

Kopp Lamp & Glass Co. Founded by Nicholas Kopp, formerly of the Consolidated Lamp & Glass Company, in 1902 in Swissvale, Pennsylvania. See *Pittsburgh Lamp, Brass & Glass Company.*

Kosta Boda perfume bottle, 14" h.; colors on stopper and bottle: blue (inner), ruby (center), clear (outer). Davanna Collection

Kosta glassware The Kosta Glassworks was established in 1742 in Smaland, Sweden (the oldest such facility in Sweden still in operation), by Anders Koskull and Georg Bogislaus Stael von Holstein, first making crown window glass, then chandeliers and wine and beer glasses. In the 19th century, it was the largest, most modern, contemporary glass manufacturing facility in Sweden. In 1864, the Boda Glassworks was established. Boda, Kosta and two other facilities, Afors and Johansfors, merged, forming the Afors Group which makes many varieties of glass, but is famous for its ornamental cut glass and tableware. See *Swedish glassware.*

Koula Beaker, The A Bohemian beaker of conical shape, wheel engraved with allegorical figures by an unidentified engraver known only as the *Master of the Koula Beaker* and named after its original owner living in Prague. Two similar ones are attributed to the same artist; one embellished with allegorical figures and the other, made about 1690, with engraved portraits of Leopold I (d.1705), Holy Roman Emperor, his wife Eleonora Magdalen, and their son Joseph (1678-1711), later King of Hungary, then Emperor. They are decorated in Tiefschnitt with stylized flowers and feathery foliage.

Krack, J.A., & Co.; Krack, Reed & Co.; Krack, Stanger & Co. See *Kentucky Glass Works.*

Kraka glass A glass with a network design developed at the Orrefors Glasbruk by Swen Palmqvist about 1944. Early ones have an opal white glass network between two layers of glass. Later ones have a network of dark blue and golden shades. *Kraka* is a woman in the "Saga of the Vikings," who approached her boyfriend dressed only in a fishing net.

Kralik, Wilhelm, Sohn In 1831, Johann Meyr (1775-1841) inherited a glass manufacturing facility at Eleonorenhain established by his grandfather Joseph Meyr. By 1834, Johann had created one of the major facilities in Bohemia. When he died in 1841, his nephews William Kralik (1806-1877) and Joseph Taschek (d.1862) operated three glassworks at Kaltenbach, Adolf, and Eleonorenhain, as Myer's Neffe (see *Myer's Neffe*). In 1854, they bought facilities at Ernstbrunn and Franzensthal, later adding those of Idathal and Louisenhutte. From 1862, Wilhelm Kralik had complete control of Myer's Neffe. In 1881, his properties were divided among his four sons. Karl and Hugo took over the facilities at Idathal, Adolf and Louisenhutte, operating as Myer's Neffe. Heinrich and Johann took over the Eleonorenhain and Ernstbrunn ones, operating as Wilhelm Kralik Sohn, making large amounts of iridescent glass with both metallic and mother-of-pearl luster that often took organic shapes (having no pontil mark). Colored glass was made in fanciful shapes, often with applied glass in the form of snakes; some glass overlaid in silver. It also made cameo vases of floral design, often with gilding in beige/pink/brown colors. The pieces made by Wilhelm Kralik

Sohn are usually signed. Both facilities closed during World War II.

Kramer, Johann Baltasar A German glassmaker who, with his brothers (Adam, George, and Martin), came to Philadelphia, Pennsylvania, in September 1773, employed at the Manheim facility of Henry William Stiegel from October 1773 to March 1774, then at several other local facilities, and later at the New Bremen Glass Manufactory. When it closed, he, his wife, and children moved west, but was persuaded by Albert Gallatin to return to Pennsylvania in 1794 and help him start the New Geneva Glass Works. He, also known as Baltzer Kramer, died in 1813.

Kramer-Eberhart Glassworks (1817-1845) A glass manufacturing facility established in Greensboro, Pennsylvania, making hollowwares.

Kramer & Reitz; Kramer Family glass See *New Geneva Glass Works.*

Krantz & Sell Company See *Krantz-Smith & Company.*

Krantz-Smith & Company John E. Krantz and John H. Smith established a glass cutting shop in Honesdale, Pennsylvania, in 1893, with showrooms in Chicago and New York City. In 1899 George W. Sell joined the company and Smith left later. From 1908 to 1920, it operated as the Krantz & Sell Company. In 1920, Krantz sold his interest to Sell and it was renamed G. Sell & Company. In 1932, fire destroyed the facility and operations ceased. The Krantz-Smith & Company's trademark was *K.S.Co.* See *Barryville Cut Glass Shop.*

krater (Greek) A vase to mix wine and water. It has a wide body and mouth, two side handles, and a small circular base. There are several variations, including Corinthian, calyx, bell, volute; most glass ones being the calyx type (shaped like the cup-like part of a flower). These have two horizontal uplifted loop handles attached to the lower part of the body. Some small ones were made of Egyptian glass, using the core method, between 1500 and 970 B.C.

krateriskos (Greek) Literally, *small mixing bowl.* A small bowl with a wide mouth and body, and a foot, specifically core-formed bowls made in Egypt between 2000 and 1000 B.C.

Krautstrunk (German) Literally, *cabbage stalk.* A Nuppenbecher with cabbage stalk-shaped prunts and a cup-shaped mouth curving outward from above an encircling thread. It was the forerunner of the Romer. See *Doppelter Krautstrunk.*

Kresson Glass Works See *Pendleton Glass Works.*

Kreta An iridescent glassware made during the late 1800s at the Loetz glassworks.

Kretschmann, Adolf (1871-1955) Born in Meistersdorf, Kretschmann learned the art of engraving in Bohemia. In 1893, he was employed as an engraver at Webb in England, and on learning of the need for engravers in the United States from his brother Fridoli who lived in Corning, New York, he, with Joseph Nitsche, left England.

Adolf went to Chicago where he demonstrated engraving for Libbey at the World's Columbian Exposition. He then went to Corning to work for Hawkes; next for Sinclaire until it closed, returning to Hawkes (Fridoli his brother worked for J. Hoare & Co.). In 1936, he was laid off from Hawkes and worked for a year or two as an engraver in Middletown, New York. From 1918, he operated his own part-time cutting shop in Corning, doing work for Dorflinger, Hunt, Hoare, Hasebauer, and individuals. From 1938 until 1951, he operated his shop full-time.

Krome-Kraft A trade name used by Farber Brothers for its chromium-plated wares with glass and china inserts, made from about 1932 to 1965. The inserts were in the form of hollowware items and attached to the metal base by patented clips so they would not fall out, but could be removed easily for cleaning or replacement if broken.

Krystal Krafters See *Borden, George I., & Company.*

Krys(-) Tol A mark used, with or without the hyphen, by several glass manufacturing facilities. The first to use it with the hyphen was the Ohio Flint Glass Company about 1900 and without, the Jefferson Glass Company (West Virginia) and the Central Glass Company (Indiana) about 1906. It seems to have spread through companies that joined the National Glass Company

K.S. Co. The trademark that was used by Krantz-Smith & Co. and Krantz & Sell Co.

ku *(Chinese)* A Chinese vase, beaker shaped, cylindrical with a bulge midway and a trumpet mouth, based on an ancient bronze form. Some were made of opaque colored glass; the most common colors being yellow and turquoise.

Kuan Liao *(Chinese)* Glass made for the Imperial Court of China by various methods, including opaque monochrome (e.g., yellow) glass, cased and carved glass, and opaque white glass with translucent enameled colors.

Kubiikki ware A series of glass bowls and vases made by the Riihimaki Glassworks. They are square or rectangular, but vary in size and height. They are blown in wooden molds and generally for household use.

Kufic script A kind of angular formal Arabic calligraphy used to decorate Islamic pottery and glassware. Occasionally a "mock" script was used. While giving the appearance of Arabic writing, it consists of indecipherable linear figures. See *neskhi; mosque lamp.*

Kugel (1) Glass (Christmas) ornaments, rather heavy, made from about 1820 to 1890. Ball-shaped ones are more common than fruit and vegetable shapes. They range in size from one to 14 inches in diameter, and are made of thick glass in cobalt, green, gold, silver and, rarely, amethyst. They have heavy brass caps for hanging. (2) A bull's-eye motif. The plural of Kugel is *Kugeln.*

Kugelgravuren *(German)* Engraving in circular or oval motifs, by German craftsmen, known as *Kugler*, using a vertical wheel, in the 18th and early 19th centuries. The curved motif is called in *Kugelschliff.*

Kugler color Glass rods of a concentrated color, originally made by Klaus Kugler of Augsburg, Germany, and today made by many manufacturers.

Kumme *(German)* An ancient German drinking and serving bowl, from which the *Humpen* derives its shape.

Kunckel red Glass-colored ruby red by adding gold chloride to the batch. It was created by Johann Kunckel prior to 1679.

Kungsholm Glasbruk See *Swedish glass.*

Kunzler, Peter, & Co. See *Penn Glass Works.*

Kupfer, Emil F., Incorporated (1911-1930?) A glass cutting company established in Brooklyn, New York. Kupfer, the founder, was also an agent for other manufacturers and cutters.

Kupfer Glass Company A glass cutting shop in Honesdale, Pennsylvania.

Kurfurstenhumpen *(German)* Literally, *Electors Beaker.* Also spelled *Churfurstenhumpen.* A tall Humpen embellished with the enameled portrayal of the Holy Roman Emperor, with the seven Electors of the Empire. On early ones, the Electors are standing at the side of the Emperor; on later ones, they are on horseback in two horizontal rows. The earliest recorded dates from 1511. The same motif appears on some enameled goblets with a stemmed foot and on some diamond engraved Humpen. See *German enameling.*

Kusak Cut Glass Company Antone Kusak, after leaving the Washington Cut Glass Company in 1916, established a cutting shop in Seattle, Washington. He imported blanks, up to 40,000 dozen per year, from Bohemia. It was still operating in the 1960s.

Kuttrolf *(German)* A vessel for containing liquids with a cup-like wide pinched mouth or upper container joined to a globular body by a neck of 3 to 5 intertwining thin tubes. When liquid is poured from it, it flows from the tubes very slowly, a drop at a time, making a bubbling sound. Most have the tubes at an angle to the body, the mouth sloping diagonally; some early ones, of Frankish glass, have tubes in a vertical position. They were used for slow pouring or dripping and sometimes for drinking.

The name is from the German *kuttering* (gurgling) or the Latin *gutta* (drop) or *gutturnium* (a slow pouring dropper for perfume). They were fashionable in the 16th and 17th centuries and derived from 4th century Syrian glass sprinklers, the body made from four tubes connected to form a tall neck. A variation is a tall single tube flask with a thin curving neck, made in Persia in the 18th and 19th centuries, known as *rose-water sprinklers*. The Kuttrolf is also called an *Angster*, from the Latin *angustus*, meaning *narrow*. See *cluck-cluck decanter*.

Ku-yueh Hsuan A style of embellishment on Chinese glassware (and porcelain), broken into several groups: (a) Peking Imperial Palace glassware; (b) glassware probably made at Peking, bearing the mark Ku-yueh Hsuan (Ancient Moon Pavilion) of the legendary artist who embellished it; and (c) glassware made later at various facilities imitative of such wares. The embellishment illustrates scenes of the changing seasons, *European* landscapes, flowers, and figures. The style was developed about 1720 and used for groups (b) and (c) above at later dates, mainly from about 1750 to 1850, and on glassware and porcelain by the same artists.

kyathos *(Greek)* A dipper in the form of a small shallow bowl with one long upright handle often in the form of a loop, originally used to transfer wine from a krater into a cup. Some later ones were made of Roman glass (see *simpulum*). Similar forms, called a *piggin*, were made about 1800 of Anglo-Irish glassware.

kylix *(Greek)* A drinking cup with a calyx-shaped bowl (like a chalice or calyx of a flower) resting on a stemmed foot. Some were made of Roman glass.

LaBastie Works See *Constitution Flint Glass Works*.

label See *bottle ticket*.

label(ed) decanter A decanter engraved with the name of the beverage contained therein, generally alcoholic. In addition, there were often engraved items related to the contents such as apples (cider), hops (beer), grapes and vines (wine).

LaBelle Glass Works A glass manufacturing facility established in 1872 in Bridgeport, Ohio, making pressed glass and flint wares. In February 1884, Harry Northwood was employed by the company as an engraver and later as a designer and mold maker. In late 1884 the company was shut down as the result of a strike. At this time, Northwood left and went to work for Phoenix Glass.

LaBelle soon reopened and, in early 1886, began making a line of opalescent glass. Harry Northwood returned, managing the design and mold department. In April 1887 he again left and went to the Buckeye Glass Company. He returned to LaBelle a week later with a promotion.

In September 1887 LaBelle burned. The company leased a facility in Brilliant, Ohio, while a new facility was being built. The costs of the new facility caused a financial drain on the company, forcing it into bankruptcy. It was sold in late 1888 to the Crystal Glass Company (Works), which operated it successfully for the next 20 years as the Muhleman Glass Company.

Labino, Dominick (1910-1987) A leading American glass technician and consultant. A ceramic engineer, he held over 60 patents related to glass and was instrumental in the development of the heat resistant tiles used in space flights. He had a studio in Grand Rapids, Ohio, where he designed and made glassware

since 1963. He conducted experiments making replicas of ancient core glass using trailed decoration and applied handles and feet. He made some glassware in the style of *vetro a reticello*, and embellished some using colloidal gold. He was a leader in establishing seminars on glassmaking sponsored by the Toledo (Ohio) Museum of Glass. His protege, E. Baker O'Brien, continued with the studio, designing her own wares and continuing to use colors Labino developed. She signs her wares "Labino Studios, Baker."

Labree & Jarves See *Mount Washington Glass Company*.

lace See *filigree*.

Lace-de-Boheme glassware Glassware with white enameled embellishment, often on a clouded or satin ground, made in Bohemia from about 1880 to 1890 as a cheap imitation of quality cameo glass. Another contemporary Bohemian imitation was colored glassware with a thin opal flashing on which a design was drawn, covered with acid resisting ink, and placed in hydrofluoric acid to remove the uncovered areas, leaving a shallow relief design.

lace glass (1) A term applied to *vetro a retorti* and, by some, to *vetro a reticello*. See also *vetro di trina; filigrana*. (2) Glass with delicate patterns sandblasted on it, a common item in entrance areas and on kitchen cabinet doors in the homes of the well-to-do from about 1870 to 1920.

Lace glass (1) A Tiffany Favrile glassware. (2) Glassware similar to Cintra but slightly thinner. It is a cased glass with more bubbles than Cintra, made for a short time about 1930 by a variation of the striped technique used for Cintra glass. It is extremely rare. About sixteen shapes were made, usually with blue and white, pink and white, or black and white stripes.

lace ground See *muslin ground.*

lace maker's lamp A misnomer for an oil lamp said to have been used by lace makers. It has a globular font about two to three inches in diameter, a drop burner, round drip catcher, stem resting on a saucer base, and usually a loop handle on one side. It is believed to be too fragile, too expensive, and impractical for use by a lace maker. In addition, the font is too small to serve as a water lens. Lace makers used any sort of lamp available, or even a candle, with light condensed by a water lens, which was often centered to serve the lamps of several workers. Similar sources of light used with a water lens were also called *cobbler's lamps.*

lace twist A twist made from numerous fine opaque threads arranged in a loose corkscrew fashion to give a lace-like effect.

laced diamond The strawberry diamond cut glass motif.

lacework mosaic glass A mosaic glass made of canes of twisted spiral threads of colorless and opaque white glass, first made in the Mediterranean area in the late 1st century B.C./1st century A.D.

lachrymatory See *tear bottle; unguentarium.*

Lackawanna Cut Glass Company (1903-1905) A glass cutting company in Scranton, Pennsylvania, that cut and sold cut glass by mail on a money back guarantee if not satisfied. Pieces with a signature, an "L" within a diamond, are very rare.

lacquered glass Crystal glassware with a colored lacquer painting fired on in a muffle furnace to make it more permanent. Some Bohemian red and amber lacquer paintings were further engraved with various designs.

lacy (pattern) glass An American mold pressed glassware with its entire surface covered with stippling and motifs slightly raised against a diaper background pattern made by small dots in the mold, producing a stippled appearance—an overall lacy effect. The style was developed about 1830 when designs, not influenced by cut glass, began making their appearance.

Because mechanical pressing of glass was in its infancy, the glass was dull and cloudy, resulting from the relatively cold plunger and mold coming in contact with the molten glass. This could be corrected by reheating, resulting in loss of sharpness and shape, defeating the purpose.

The solution was *lacy glass* where motifs and stippling cover the entire surface to increase the refractive qualities of the glass, giving it a silvery sheen. Lacy glass was developed by Deming Jarves at the Boston & Sandwich Co., the first company to make it, followed by the New England Glass Co., Phoenix Glass Works, Union Glass Co., Fort Pitt Glass Works, Ritchie & Wheat, glasshouses in the Philadelphia and Pittsburgh (Pennsylvania) areas, etc. Similar wares were made in France beginning in the 1840s, and in England, Belgium, Denmark, and Norway. In these countries and in the rest of Europe it was called *sable glass.* Objects made included mainly plates and cup plates, also bowls, trays, creamers, etc., in a variety of patterns with certain themes repeated. It was made extensively between the late 1830s and early 1840s.

Since the largest single producer was the Boston & Sandwich Co., it was commonly called *Sandwich glass* even though it made only a small percentage of the total. The bulk was made in the Pittsburgh area. The early lacy glass made in the New England area was generally of a finer quality, clearer and more brilliant glass and the stippling more detailed and designs more refined than that from the Pittsburgh area. Pieces from New England always rest on a bottom rim band while those from the Pittsburgh area tend to have rims with bands of dots or buttons as part of a scalloped edge.

Foreign-made lacy glass differs from that made in the United States in that: (a) more large pieces were made; (b) designs were heavier looking; and (c) glass tumblers and footed goblets were made. Some of the more common motifs used in the United States were: (a) classic (acanthus leaf, scrolled leaf, cornucopia, oak leaves, shields, etc.); (b) romantic (rose and thistle, flowers, hearts, tulip, etc.); (c) Gothic (Gothic arches, quatrefoils, Roman rosette, etc.); (d) geometric (diamonds, circles, etc.); and (e) historical (commemorative designs related to current events). The most common pieces found today are cup plates, salt and small rectangular dishes, sugar bowls, small bowls, and toddy plates.

Less common items are the creamers, large bowls and plates, and miniature dishes. The rarest include covered round and rectangular dishes, lamps with lacy bases, candlesticks, chamber sticks and compotes—generally the larger the piece, the rarer. Since the 1840s many reproductions have been made, most of cup plates.

lacy glass windowpane A window-pane with stippling and motifs covering the entire surface. There are few patterns known, all the same size (5 by 6-7/8 inches), except one that is five by seven inches. The larger pane, a steamboat as its central motif, is imprinted "J. & C. Ritchie," indicating it was made in 1833 or early 1834 (see *Ritchie Glass Company*). An 1836 advertisement indicates that Bakewell, Page & Bakewell offered them for sale, but one pane bears the Curling & Robertson (Fort Pitt Glassworks) mark. Because of the relationship between the principals of the companies, it is believed they were made by Curling & Robertson and distributed in part by Bakewell, Page & Bakewell.

Originally it was thought that they were cast or rolled, but because of the tail found on the plain side of some, it is now known they were pressed with the design on the plunger. Originally advertised as panes for steamboats, they have been found in door panels, side lights for doorways, and in cupboards. It is believed they were made between 1835 and 1840.

ladder A cut glass motif formed by two vertical miter cuts crossed by several horizontal ones.

laddered stem A stem of inverted baluster shape on which there are four vertical columns of small cut squares, each a ladder-like pattern. Between each column there is a cut decoration.

ladle (1) A cup-like spoon usually with a long, sometimes curved handle used for transferring liquids from one vessel to another. Other types are in the form of a Greek kyathos and the Roman simputum. See *punch ladle*. (2) Similar in shape to that mentioned above except the handle is longer

and the bowl is larger (four to nine inches) and made of steel. It is used to remove molten glass from a furnace prior to recharging.

LaFarge, John (1835-1906) A mural painter who turned to stained glass after a visit to Europe in 1872-'73. He made his first pieces in New York in 1876 and worked with various architects in New England. He invented *opal* glass about 1890.

Lafayette Flint Glass Works (1865?-1895) A glass manufacturing facility established in Brooklyn, New York, possibly by A. Stenger & Company, making flint tableware. It passed through several changes of ownership and, by 1880, was called the East River Flint Glass Works operated by P. Schneider's Sons. From 1882 until it closed it was operated by Francis Storm, making all kinds of flint and colored glassware, including some cut glass.

Lafayette Vases In 1825, at the age of 68, the Marquis de Lafayette toured the United States, visiting the Bakewell facility, which presented him a pair of vases cut by Alex Jardelle. One has an American eagle cut and engraved on it and the other the Marquis's chateau at La Grange.

La-Flo Cut Glass Company (1954-1983) A glass etching and cutting facility established by former employees of the Cambridge Glass Company.

lagynos (Greek) An oenochoe with a low, wide body, an angular shoulder, high thin vertical neck, circular mouth, and angular handle extending from the top of the neck to the shoulder.

Lake Desolation Glass Works See *Granger, O.H., & Co.*

Lake Dunmore Glass Company (Aka *Dunsmore Glass Co., Salisbury Glass Co.*) (1832-1842) The Vermont Glass Factory, which failed in 1817, was reopened in 1832 as the Lake Dunsmore Glass Company incorporated by William Nash, Paris Fletcher, William Y. Ripley, George Chipman, Ebenezer Briggs, and George C. Loomis. It made window glass. See *Vermont Glass Factory.*

Lakefield (Cut) Glass Company

(1915-1920) A glass cutting house in Ontario, Canada.

Lalique, Rene Jules (1860-1945) Born

in Ay, Champagne, France, Lalique's family moved to the outskirts of Paris when he was two. At the age of sixteen, he was apprenticed to Parisian goldsmith Louis Aucoc and attended the Ecole des Arts Decoratifs in Paris. In 1878 he moved to England, attending the School of Art held in the Crystal Palace. In 1880 he returned to France, studying sculpture under Justin Lequien at the Ecole Bernard Palissy. In 1881 he began designing jewelry, mainly elite jewelry in the Art Nouveau style, and making objects of enamel and inlaid glass paste, opening a shop in 1885. In the 1890s he developed an interest in glass and, by 1893, was experimenting with the lost wax method (*cire perdue*).

In 1902 Lalique employed four glassmakers and opened a shop in Paris, making perfume bottles for the commercial trade and a variety of decorative wares. His first commercial success came from the perfume bottles and flasks designed for Coty. About 1909 he rented a facility at Combs-la-ville, near Paris, making molded, pressed, and engraved glassware and some thick engraved window panels. His use of the refractory properties and tensile strength of glass made him one of the first artisans to apply glass to the field of architecture. He was interested in the surface treatment of glass using acid or sandblasting, which resulted in a frosty opalescence. He was a follower of Emil Galle, using the Art Nouveau style as he developed his own unique style.

In the field of architecture, Lalique made chandeliers, fountains, and glass doors for public buildings and private homes. His facility closed during World War I but reopened in 1918 (it closed permanently in 1937), the same year he acquired a facility at Wingin-Sur-Moder (Bas-Rhin). This second facility was shut down in 1940 because of World War II, but reopened in May 1945. Lalique died in that year and his son, Marc, took over. Marc's daughter, Marie-Claude, joined the company in 1956, assuming control after her brother Marc's death in 1977. It operates under the name Cristallerie Lalique et Cie. See *Lalique glassware.*

Vaseline glass perfume bottle, 11" h. x 5-1/2" w., signed "R. Lalique, France." Davanna Collection

Lalique glassware Glassware made by Rene Lalique and, after his death, by Cristallerie Lalique et Cie. Lalique's production, most in the Art Nouveau and art deco styles, covers a wide range including tableware, boudoir accessories, household accoutrements (figurines, vases, lamps, clocks, ashtrays, etc.), and interior and exterior architectural glass. For color, Lalique depended on translucent glass, opaline, or colored glass (black, smoke, jade green, sapphire, blue, or red). On occasion iridescent effects were produced by subjecting the glass to gaseous fumes in a muffle. Colored enamels, translucent and opaque, were also used. A combination of blowing, pressing, frosting, and cutting was often used to achieve the final products. *New* Lalique is being made today. There is also a type of glass made by Rene Lalique that is colorless with a pale blue opalescent mat finish consisting mainly, at first, of small bottles and ornaments and later of large molded vases, bowls, and figures. The motifs often portray plants, animals, and the female body. Signatures found on almost all pieces have been molded, engraved, and sandblasted using a method that caused the letters to be raised. Before Lalique's death in 1945, the ware was marked *R. Lalique*. After 1945 "*R.*" was omitted and the signature was simply *Lalique* or *Lalique France* in script or block letters.

Lalique (unmarked) See *Louver glassware.*

Lamb Glass Company (1921-1963)

A glass manufacturing facility established in

Mount Gilead, Ohio, making milk bottles and preserving jars.

lamekin See *lathekin.*

laminated glass (1) A glass covered with scales like that buried in damp earth for centuries, having acquired an iridescence. (2) Glass made shatterproof as a result of an interlayer of material between two panes of glass and sealed, first made by John Wood in England in 1905. Originally the interlayer required the edges be sealed with pitch, which tended to discolor the glass, so new materials for the inner layer have been developed, requiring no sealing.

The most common material is a sheet of non-brittle plastic. It and the glass have the same physical properties as ordinary glass. In making it, the glass and the plastic are cleaned thoroughly and an adhesive applied to the glass. It and plastic are pressed together to remove all air and bubbles.

Moderate heat is then applied to seal the edges, and it is subjected to high temperatures and hydraulic pressures in an autoclave, bringing the entire interlayer into intimate contact with the outer layers. After this the edges may be further sealed with a water-resistant compound. The plastic used as an interlayer was originally cellulose nitrate; then cellulose acetate; and now a polyvinyl butyral resin that remains clear and colorless, not requiring adhesives or water-resistant compounds in manufacture. The glass, when struck by an object, cracks radially (outward from the point of impact). The splinters of glass tend to adhere to the interlayer. (3) A term used incorrectly to refer to cased glass.

Laminated glass A Tiffany Favrile product in the Art Nouveau style, made to simulate striated stones. This difficult-to-make, multicolored opaque glass was also made in the early 1900s by Quezal. See *agate glass.*

Lamont (Diamond) Glass Company (1890-1902) A glass manufacturing facility established by David and Donald Lamont in Trenton, Nova Scotia, making blown and cut glassware and bottles. In 1898 it was leased to the Diamond Glass Company, which operated the North American Glass Works of Montreal.

Art glass lamp with (new) Santa clip-on shade and pink swirled body on black octagon base.
Tri-State Antiques

lamp A device to produce artificial light. The first lamps produced illumination by means of a light that floated on oil or projected from a small spout, i.e., Roman terra-cotta lamps. Most lamps made prior to the late 1820s were free blown, usually with an applied knop stem and a circular foot or base. A few lamps had a saucer or high hollow pedestal base, the fonts normally plain and free blown. Those that are pattern molded and expanded in ribbing and fluting are extremely rare. A few small lamps were patterned in a dip mold and later, a few were patterned in full size, three-piece molds.

Whale or sperm oil lamps were fitted with burners—usually a thin tin cap with one or two wick holders passing through a short cork into the font. While some were table size (six to ten inches tall), most were smaller, with or without handles (*sparking lamps*). Early pressed lamps, from 1827 to 1835, are distinctive—the pressed base is often attached to the font by a thin wafer of glass or a ringed or ribbed knop.

Height was generally given to a lamp by the stem or shaft formed by a combination of solid or hollow blown knops; a few have fonts and stems with wheel cut decorations.

Pressed lamp bases are made in several shapes and mainly of three distinct types: stepped, cup plate, and lacy. The stepped type is generally hollow and fluted on the inside, giving it a metallic sheen characteristic of most pressed glass. Some have a short shank or stem at the top; others a long stem or shaft. Cup plate bases are so named because they were pressed in molds originally used to make cup plates, but are usually thicker and inverted so the patterned underside becomes the top of the base. Only free blown plain fonts were used with cup plate bases, joined by a wafer of glass.

Three general shapes of these bases predominate: circular, square, and octagonal. The circular base is usually dome shaped, the square is of flaring or pedestal form, with or without steps; and the octagonal slopes to a galleried rim. Some bases, not truly lacy, are placed in this category because they were made during this period. Lamp bases are generally clear, but some are amethyst, blue, emerald, green, and amber (rare and found only on stippled bases).

Lamps made between 1835 and 1860 are also distinctive—heavy and simple. During this period, the dolphin, in a sportive position, was often used to form the shaft. The decorative effect of most standards lies almost entirely in their shapes made in clear or colored glass. They were fitted with either whale oil or fluid burners of pewter or brass. The whale oil burner has a short tube for a wick holder whereas those using camphene and other fuels are more than twice as long and set at a slight angle. Because of the flammability it was necessary to keep the flame farther from the fuel source.

The majority of fonts are hexagonal, cylindrical, or conical with a plain domed top above the pattern. The embellishment on fonts consists largely of plain panels (not bounded by a molding) and simple motifs, such as loops, circles, and ellipses. Some had cut or engraved embellishments. Lamps bearing no traces of mold marks on the plain top above the pattern can usually be attributed to New England Glass Co., made after 1847 in accordance with the Joseph Magown patent for a mold leaving no mold mark. Purples, amethyst, deep green, and jade green are the rarest colors.

Cut glass lamps are rare, especially the *Gone with the Wind* type having a round cut glass bowl. More common are lamps with a mushroom-shaped top (shaped like an inverted bowl). See *lantern; lanthorn; water lens; cesendello; carriage lights; lampada pensile.* Also see the following types of lamps: *agitable; Carcel; Tiffany; lace maker's; godet; mechanical; mosque; miniature; night; oil; peg; sinumbra; sanctuary; solar; sparking; wine glass; Argand; astral; betty; camphene; canal; fluid; nutmeg; Phoebe; Soho; hanging.*

lamp-blown glass Novelty glass items made from easily fusible glass tubes or rods heated in the flame of a lamp and manipulated into toys, figures, ships, jewelry, etc. They have been made in France and Spain since the 16th century. Demonstrations of this technique were popular in the United States during the 19th century and are still being practiced today.

lampada pensile *(Italian)* Literally, *hanging lamp.* A hanging lamp in the form of a wide, shallow glass bowl with a small oil lamp in the center. The bowl is in the shape of a balance pan of a scale and suspended by chains attached to the rim. Some were made in Murano and in Byzantium during the 10th and 11th centuries. See *dish light.*

Lampell & Coutrie A glass manufacturing facility in Pittsburgh, Pennsylvania, making blown wares during the 1870s.

lampwork The technique used to assemble and manipulate glass objects *at-the-lamp* or by using a small flame, such as a Bunsen burner or torch. Miniatures of all kinds, too small to be made *at-the-fire*, are made by lampwork from rods or thin canes prepared in advance. Paperweight patterns are generally assembled on a mold *at-the-lamp* from prepared chips and cane slices before being incorporated into the whole *at-the-fire.*

lampwork paperweight A paperweight made using a process involving assembling and manipulating small components into the final product using a small flame. The components are arranged on a template, reheated, and encased in glass. Most studio artists make such weights. The major difference between weights made by studio artists and those made in facilities is the origin of the encased glass. With few exceptions, studio artists tend to work with commercially purchased solid glass slugs melted and shaped by heat over a gas burner or torch. Facilities make their glass by melting raw materials in furnaces and gather melted glass when encasing the design.

Lancaster Cooperative Glass Works Ltd. See *Lancaster Glass Works.*

Lancaster Glass Co. water goblet, yellow, Jubilee pattern.
Davanna Collection

Lancaster Glass Company A glass
manufacturing facility established in Lancaster, Ohio, in 1908 (1915 by one source) by Lucien B. Martin, making table glassware and clear and colored decorative glassware. In 1924 it was purchased by the Hocking Glass Company, operating under the Lancaster name until 1937. It still operates as Plant No. 2 of Anchor-Hocking.

Lancaster Glass Works A bottle and
flask glass manufacturing facility established in Lancaster, New York, in 1849 by Reed, Allen, Cox & Company. In 1859 it burned and was rebuilt. In 1861 the operating company was Reed, Shinn & Company; in 1863 James, Gatchell & Company; in 1866 James & Gatchell; and later James Glass Works. In 1881 James retired and the company was purchased by employees and named the Lancaster Cooperative Glass Works Ltd. Some sources claim it ceased operations in 1890 while others claim it was 1908.

lanceolate A cut glass motif shaped like a spearhead, except it is tapered at each end. It is found in deep cutting on some crystal glass drinking glasses made at the Baccarat Glass Factory.

Lando, Elena de The first woman glass decorator of record in Venice, who worked in the 1440s.

Lane, Matthew & Company See *Redford Crown Glass Works.*

Lansburgh & Brothers Incorporated Located in Washington, D.C., it registered its trademark, Lansburgh & Bro., for "cut glass of all kinds" on May 20, 1924. It had used the trademark since September 25, 1922. It did not make cut wares but was an agent for other cut glass shops.

Lansing Cut Glass Works (Company) See *Bush Glass Company.*

lantern A portable or hanging enclosure containing an illuminating source with glass or metal around the flame to protect it from drafts. It is usually found in the following forms: (a) a metal support framing a globular-, cylindrical-, or baluster-shaped chimney with a suspensory hook or handle, or (b) a square- or polygonal-section metal frame with four or more panels. Each has a means for providing the source of light, such as a candle nozzle or combustible fuel and a wick. See *mosque lamp; cesendello; entry light; staircase light; lanthorn; barn lantern; bowit; canalboat lantern; dark lantern; hall lantern; barrel lantern.*

lantern-leet The material at the side(s) of a lantern transmitting light, the most common being horn and glass. *Leet,* an old English term for light, was eventually used to describe this material.

lanthalum crown glass An optical glass. See *optical glass.*

lanthorn An early lantern with a metal framework of square or rectangular cross-section with a glass panel in each of the four sides and a candle nozzle within. It is designed to be carried, indoors and out. The flame is protected by the framework and panels. Some have a suspensory hook. Early ones made in the mid-17th century had green window glass panels; later ones had polished plate glass panels sometimes with wheel engraving. The term is a combined form of *lantern* and *horn* from which the translucent panels of earliest lanterns were made.

lap line A mark or blemish in glass caused when a gather cools too much while being carried from the furnace to the mold.

lapidary cutting A decorative technique of cutting facets on glass, similar to the way gemstones are cut. It is frequently used on knife rests and stoppers of decanters and perfume bottles.

lapidary stopper A stopper in the form of a circular knob with faceting over the entire surface, most often found on a square decanter.

large shallow relief diamond A cut glass motif wherein large diamonds are cut in shallow relief. It was commonly used in the early and middle periods of American cut glass.

Larson (sometimes spelled Larsen), Emil J. Born in 1879 in Sweden, Larson became a leading American glassmaker after coming to the United States in 1887. His father was a glassblower at Kosta Glassworks, working for Bacchus & Son in England. He came to the United States with his son to work for Dorflinger. Over the years, Emil was employed at a number of facilities, including Dorflinger until it closed, Pairpoint, Durand, Quezal until about 1926, Vineland Flint Glass as manager until about 1931, Doerr as foreman, and Wheaton as a glassblower. In 1935 he built a facility in Vineland, New Jersey, making pattern molded and free blown ornamental glassware and paperweights. His most famous creation was a rose paperweight known as the *Larson Rose* or *Jersey Rose*. He called his products "Larson glass." He made some reproductions of Stiegel glassware and other forms of glass.

Larson Glass Works A glassblowing facility in Bath, New York, named after its manager, Ivan Larson, but owned by H.P. Sinclaire & Co.

Larson Rose A magnum paperweight made by Emil Larson, similar to the Millville Rose weight by Barber. The story is that Larson once borrowed a weight of Barber's, returning it a couple of weeks later. Within a year, Larson made a similar weight, but larger. Barber never forgave him and their friendship ended. Larson's weight has an upright rose with eleven to fifteen petals and four leaves made in yellow, white, rose, pink, orange, and a few in blue. Larson believes that about 100 of his weights survived the annealing process.

lathe cutting Changing the shape of a glass object using a lathe. The lathe as a glassworking tool dates to ancient times when powered by a handled wheel or bow. A blank in the rough shape of the finished object is mounted on the lathe and a tool with abrasives and lubricant is held against it. The abrasives polish, change the profile, or cut the blank until the desired shape is formed.

lathekin Any piece of wood or bone used to manipulate lead came around pieces of stained glass.

lat(t)esino *(Italian)* A 16th century term for a type of opaque white glass similar to *lattimo*, except it has a bluish cast and slight opalescence.

lattice work glass See *traliccio, vetro.*

Latticino bud vase, 6-1/2" h.
Tri-State Antiques

latticino *(Italian)* Also spelled *latticinio*. A term often misused by being applied synonymously with *lattimo* (opaque white glass) without regard to its true Venetian meaning. While *lattimo* designated only solid opaque white glass, *latticino* applies only to clear glass embellished with embedded threads of colored glass, generally white.

latticino core swirls An inner lattice of colored swirls radiating from the center of a glass marble.

latticino ground A ground composed of threads of white filigrana (latticino) glass in a double swirl pattern, one layer superimposed over the other, rotating in the opposite direction.

lattimo (Italian) Derived from *latte*, meaning *milk*. Opaque white glass. Usually the entire body of the object is made of such glass, but on occasion it is made with broad or sometimes narrow marvered bands or festoons (see *combed glass*). It is distinguished from glass embellished with embedded threads of opaque white glass, e.g., filigrana glass (latticino). *Lattimo* glassware has been made from the mid-14th century and from the mid-15th century in Venice, and later Bohemia, Germany, France, the Netherlands, Spain, England, and the United States. In an effort to imitate enameled porcelain, poly or monochrome enameling was done in many countries. See *latesino; milk glass; opaque white glass.*

lattisuol (Italian) A opaque white glass.

laub- und bandelwerk (German) Literally, *leaf and strapwork*. A late baroque ornamentation that included strapwork with intricate foliage interlacings, often with *chinoiseries* or other figures. It was often used to frame an ornamental painting on glass, either in gold silhouette or with enamel colors. It was frequently used in Germany and Bohemia in the first half of the 18th century. It was used by the wheel engravers and by the *Hausmaler* of Nuremberg, Bohemia, and Silesia.

Laurel The trademark of S.F. Myers Co., used on its cut glass.

Laurel Cut Glass Company (1903-1920) A glass cutting company originally established as the German Cut Glass Company in Jermyn, Pennsylvania, soon renamed Laurel Cut Glass Company. In 1906 it was renamed Kohinur Cut Glass Company, but in 1907 assumed the Laurel name again. Shortly before it closed, it became allied with the Cut Glass Corporation of America. It was one of the pioneers in employing women as polishers and cutters of simple designs.

Lauscha glassware Glassware made at Lauscha in Thuringia, Germany, from 1595. Especially well known are those pieces made *at-the-lamp* since the 18th century. Many facilities are still in this area and make tableware, toys, beads, and Christmas tree ornaments.

Lava vase, Mt. Washington Glass Company, New Bedford, MA, c. 1878. Museum of American Glass at Wheaton Village, Millville, NJ.

Lava glass (1) (Aka *Volcanic glass*) An art glass developed by Louis Comfort Tiffany, usually asymmetrical in form with a rough surface created by mixing pieces of basalt in the batch and a gold iridescence producing a gold pattern in stripes or abstract designs, creating the effect of molten lava. (2) On May 23, 1878, Frederick S. Shirley, general manager of the Mt. Washington Glass Works, applied for a patent based on a "new and useful improvement in the Ornamentation of Glassware," stating that he preferred "to use glass having lava mixed with it, so as to have a dark, perfectly black, or a colored background, so as to make a stronger contrast with the inserted pieces." Often made into pieces resembling ancient articles, it can be blown, pressed, or otherwise fashioned. The formulation for the glass consisted of seven parts of clear flint, one part carbonate of potash, and two parts of lava or volcanic slag.

On September 30, 1879, Shirley applied for another patent for embellishing Lava glass, which he called *Sicilian Ware,* involving the insertion of a design in the glass or on its surface by rolling it, while hot and plastic, over the design pieces, or by pressing them into it.

La Verre Francais(e) cameo glass

One of the many cameo types of glass exported in bulk from France around the turn of the century (19th-20th), losing its popularity about the start of World War I. Later, between 1920 and 1933, it was again made in France by the C. Schneider factory. It is mottled ware usually embellished with various floral designs. Most pieces bear the incised signature *La Verre Francais*.

Layard vase A small barrel-shaped vase of Assyrian origin found by Sir Henry Layard in the ruins of Kouyunjik and housed in the British Museum. Carved from a solid piece of rock crystal, it is nearly transparent and measures 3-1/4 inches tall. It is believed to be the earliest example of Assyrian glass made in the late 7th century B.C. It bears an engraved figure of a lion and an inscription in cuneiform characters including the name of Sargon and his titles as king of Assyria.

layered flash antique See *antique method*.

layered glass A term sometimes applied to various types of glassware made of two or more layers of glass. The terms *cased glass* and *flashed glass* are more desirable for those specific types of fused glass, and the term *laminated glass* for glass rendered shatterproof by an interlayer of plastic. *Layered glass* has been used when referring to (a) glass embellished by a second gather over a portion of the surface, such as in lily pad decoration, (b) Chinese snuff bottles that have designs in glass of various colors applied to areas of the surface, and (c) Victorian glassware made in the first half of the 19th century of layers of white or colored glass in the style of cameo glass, to reveal different colors.

Lazarus & Rosenfeld An importer of Bohemian and other glass with showrooms in New York City during the last quarter of the 19th century and first quarter of the 20th century.

Lazerville Bottle Works A bottle and flask manufacturing facility established in Wellsburg, West Virginia, in the 1840s. It was destroyed by fire in 1857/8 and was never rebuilt.

Jeanette Glass Co. lazy Susan, Dew Drop pattern, 13" d.
Davanna Collection

lazy Susan A revolving tray or server for holding or storing food or condiments. These space-saving devices are usually placed on a sideboard or in the center of a dining room table. The ability to revolve made it easier for the server or guests to reach the items.

Leacock & Towars See *Kensington Glassworks*.

lead A heavy, comparatively soft, malleable, bluish-gray metal, the source of lead oxide used in the making of lead glass. Before the use of lead oxide by George Ravenscroft in glassmaking, lead was used in the form of *litharge*, made by blowing air over the surface of molten lead. When litharge is further oxidized, it becomes *red lead*. The use of red lead in glassmaking requires special furnace conditions since its conversion back to metallic lead would discolor the glass and damage the pot or crucible. Lead is also used in the form of *came* in the construction of stained glass windows. Because of its softness, it can be easily shaped around pieces of colored glass to form various patterns.

lead crystal A colorless, transparent glass made with lead in the form of lead oxide. See *flint glass; full lead crystal; half lead crystal; lead glass*.

lead glass (Aka *glass of lead, flint glass*) Glass made with lead oxide. Lead oxide in small amounts was used in Mesopotamia to enhance the brilliance of glass—mainly in making artificial gems—since before the 11th century. However, its real importance in glassmaking came about 1676 when George Ravenscroft used it in fairly high percentages in the first practical production of glassware. Initially, the lead glass he made was subject to crisseling, but further experiments and formula adjustments created a glass that was strong and clear, rang like a bell when tapped, and was not subject to crisseling. It is relatively soft, has a light dispersing quality creating a brilliance (especially when, from the 18th century on, it was embellished with faceting), is less fragile than the Venetian soda glass, and is more suitable for engraving and cutting. It has a longer working range (its viscosity remains fairly constant over a wider temperature range than other glasses) and is more versatile than other glass.

There are three main types of lead glass: the highest quality has 30% or more of lead; a lower quality has about 24%; and an even lesser quality has about 10%. Glasses with lead contents as high as 92% (density 8.0, refractive index 2.2) have been made. Normally lead glass is melted in closed pots holding between 1,100 and 1,650 pounds. They are closed to keep the molten glass from coming into contact with combustion gases that reduce the lead oxide to black metallic lead. If a large tank furnace is used, only oxidizing flames must come in contact with the melting glass. Electricity is a favored means of supplying heat because of its cleanness.

Large quantities of lead glass are used in making electric light bulbs, neon sign tubing, and radio tubes because of the high electrical resistance of the glass. It is suitable for shielding from nucleonic rays. The ultraviolet light test may be used with some success to determine if an object is made of lead glass; the glass fluoresces with a bluish color under ultraviolet light. If no lead is present, it will fluoresce greenish-yellow or not at all. See *litharge*.

lead mirrors Early mirrors made by pouring melted lead onto heated sheets of glass.

lead monoxide See *litharge*.

lead test A test used as an aid in the identification of lead glass by applying a drop of hydrofluoric acid mixed with a drop of ammonium sulphide to a small area of the object. (Note: Select a site not normally visible, usually on the base or foot ring.) The result is a black area if lead is present, due to the creation of lead sulphide. Soda glass or barium glass show no reaction.

leaded glass A piece of glass made of several smaller pieces of glass held together in a web of lead cames. In general, simple mosaic patterns glazed only with clear glass.

leaf and strapwork See *laub- und bandelwerk*.

lear See *lehr*.

Leavy, Robert J. The production manager at Steuben who, in 1932, developed a *new glass* that was transparent, heavy, yet soft toned with a quality all of its own, being easy to work at the furnace, and very suitable for engraving. It set a higher standard for American clear glass and became the staple for the new art glass production at Steuben.

Lebanon Glass Works A bottle and later window glass manufacturing facility established by Thomas Richards Sr. and his son, Samuel, in 1851 in Woodland Township, New Jersey. In 1866 it was abandoned because of depletion of the wood supply.

LeBlanc, Nicholas The Frenchman credited in 1792 with using soda ash or carbonate of soda to replace the impure sodas previously used in glassmaking. The impure sodas were in limited supply while the new soda ash could be made from common table salt, sodium chloride, thus making the supply readily available and at a lower cost.

Lechmere Glass Co. A glass manufacturing facility in Cambridge, Massachusetts, incorporated on March 28, 1834.

ledge (Aka *marli*) The flattened, raised portion of a plate or dish surrounding the well. See *rim*.

Ledlie(r) & Ulam See *Birmingham Flint Glass Company*.

Lee, James See *Whitall Tatum & Co.*; *Eagle Glass Works (New Jersey)*.

leech bead A bead in the form of a slightly curved, hollow cylinder resembling a leech. They (or the lengthwise section of them known as *runners*) were used to cover the bow of a fibula on occasion. Some were made of Etruscan glass in the 7th century B.C., having a mavered combed decoration in a feather pattern.

leech glass A glass tube containing a leech, used in early medicine for application to a human body in bleeding a patient. An *artificial leech* is a small glass tube with a scarifier (something that scratches or cuts the skin) used to draw blood by suction. The tube was heated, the open end applied to the skin, which was scratched or cut by the scarifier, and, as the heated air in the tube cooled and contracted, blood was drawn into the tube.

leech jar A receptacle found in pharmacies for holding leeches used in early medicine for bleeding a patient. Most were cylindrical and all have ways of letting in air, i.e., a mesh cover.

Leeds Cut Glass Company A glass cutting company in Bridgeton, New Jersey, operating during the first quarter of the 20th century. It used the *Cut Rose* and *Cut Thistle* designs extensively as decoration.

leer See *lehr.*

Leerdam glassware Glassware made at the Royal Dutch Glass Works at Leerdam in the Netherlands, established in 1765, and, since 1937, a unit of the (Dutch) United Glassworks with facilities in Maastricht and Schiedam. Its products include tableware, bottles, ornamental crystal, and other types of glassware. Under the direction of P.M. Cochuis from about 1912, production of modern glassware was introduced. The Glass Form Center was established in 1968 to conduct experimental and developmental work in glassmaking.

leet An old English term for materials that transmit light, such as horn or glass, used in the sides of lanterns or the panes of windows. See *lantern-leet.*

leftover A covered dish used to hold and store leftover foods in the refrigerator.

leg glass A drinking glass in the form of a woman's leg. It had to be drained before setting down, inverted on its rim.

Lehman(n), Casper (1570-1622) Reputedly the first glassmaker in modern times to use (from about 1590) and receive a patent for (1609) wheel engraving to embellish glass, in spite of the contention that it was resumed at Munich under Duke Wilhelm V during the 1580s. Born near Luneburg, Germany, he left in 1586, living in Munich where he learned the art of engraving. In 1588 he moved to Prague and was employed at the Court of Emperor Rudolf II as a carver of precious stones. In 1601 he was appointed as Imperial Gem Engraver to the court, and in 1608, Imperial Gem Engraver & Glass Engraver. In 1609 he was appointed Royal Lapidary and was granted the hereditary privilege of glass engraving. In 1618 he was joined by his son who, in 1622, succeeded to the privilege on his death. (See *Perseus-Andromeda Plaque.*)

lehr The oven used for annealing glassware. Early ones were connected directly to the furnace by flues. The main problem was that heat and smoke could not be controlled effectively, and their use was impractical. Later they were isolated from the furnace, becoming a separate structure in the form of a long, brick-lined, separately heated steel tunnel through which objects placed in iron pans (see *lehr pan*) being annealed were pushed or pulled. Wares remained in the lehr for several hours while being gradually reheated and then slowly cooled. This type of lehr is reported to have been invented by George Ensell at Stourbridge about 1780. Later mechanical conveyors were introduced to move the glassware, and today they are heated and operated electrically. It is also spelled *lear* and *leer.*

lehr pans Iron pans in which finished glass articles are placed while being annealed; they were preceded by earthenware containers.

New England Glass Company pitcher, c. 1860, ruby over clear glass.
The Corning Museum of Glass

Leighton family Thomas H. Leighton (1776-1849) was an English glassmaker who, after gaining experience in England, Dublin, and Edinburgh, came to the United States. In 1826 he became superintendent of the New England Glass Company, a position he held for almost twenty years. He then founded the Boston Flint Glass Works at Cambridge, Massachusetts. Of his seven sons, two worked at New England Glass. John H. succeeded him as superintendent, and William, skilled in formulating glass metals and colors, developed a new formula for ruby glass about 1858. Prior to that, in 1855 he patented a process for making silvered glass, specifically for door knobs. These appeared to be made of silver, yet they never needed polishing and were cheaper. In 1864 William left New England Glass and went to work for Hobbs, Brockunier & Co. There he made peachblow glass and developed dew drop glass and, about 1883, spangled glass. Henry, a grandson of Thomas H., became an expert engraver at New England Glass.

Leith Flint Glass Co. See *Ysart, Paul.*

lekythos (Greek) A small jug to hold perfume, oil, or ointment. It is tall and slender, generally with a small loop handle attached to the neck and shoulder, a narrow neck for slow, controlled pouring, a cup-like mouth, and a flat base. Some were made of Roman glass from about 300 to 100 B.C. and were used as tomb offerings.

Pressed glass lemon squeezer, 5" d. x 3" h.
Davanna Collection

lemon squeezer A device used to squeeze juice from citrus fruit, usually in the shape of a shallow bowl with a dome in the center. The fruit is cut in half, pushed onto the dome, which is often ribbed, and rotated. The juice collects in the shallow bowl. Many have a loop handle opposite a pouring lip.

lemon squeezer foot A foot frequently found on an Irish fruit bowl or candelabrum. It is molded with deep radial ribs on the underside of a dome and normally set above a solid square foot.

Lemonade & Ox-blood Akro Agate's yellow and red marbleized children's ware.

Boston & Sandwich Glass Company lemonade glass, c. 1870-1888, clear and red glass.
The Corning Museum of Glass

lemonade glass A tall, cylindrical glass taller than a standard tumbler, sometimes with a handle, for serving lemonade. They are often in the shape of a short-stemmed wine glass with a handle.

Lemonescent glass A pale yellow opalescent ware made by Thomas Webb & Sons, England, using uranium salts and arsenic. It is often mistakenly referred to as *Vaseline glass.*

Lenox Glass Works The glass manufacturing facility established in 1853/4 in Lenox Furnace, Massachusetts, by the Lenox Iron Company, in operation since 1848. Soon after it was built, it burned and was rebuilt. It made window glass and other items such as paperweights. After heavy losses, it closed in 1855. Later that year it was leased by James A. (or N.) Richmond. In 1856 he went bankrupt and it closed. In 1858 the original owners resumed operations, making a poor grade of plate glass. In 1862 one source indicates it closed while another indicates it was destroyed by fire and rebuilt, eventually failing and closing in 1872.

Lenox Crystal Located in Mt. Pleasant, Pennsylvania, it is a subsidiary of the Lenox China Company of Trenton, New Jersey, established in 1965 when Lenox took over the Bryce Brothers facility. Lenox Crystal's goal was to make a high quality stemware to complement the china. In 1970 a new, modern facility was built. In 1973 it took over Imperial Glass Company, selling it in 1981.

lens A piece of transparent material, usually glass or plastic, having one or more curved surfaces used to change the convergence of light rays. Two prime uses of lenses are magnifying and vision correction. Glass was first ground into lenses during the late Middle Ages. While it is uncertain who made this discovery, an English monk, philosopher, and scientist named Roger Bacon (1214?-1294?) experimented in this area. See *diminishing lens; magnifying lens; water lens; optical glass; spectacles; bifocal lens.*

lenticular flask See *lentoid flask.*

lentil flask A flask with a narrowed, circular, *lentil*-shaped (flattened globular, or nearly so, both sides convex, a bit like a pilgrim flask) body resting on a flat bottom and having a tall thin neck. They were made in the *façon de Venice.* See *lentoid flask*

lentoid flask (Aka *lenticular flask*) Made of Roman core glass with a lentil-shaped body (see *lentil flask*). It has a cylindrical neck, a disk mouth, and two small vertical loop handles extending from the shoulder to midway up the neck. Early Egyptian ones have a footless, rounded bottom. See *aryballos; lentil flask.*

"let it down easy" process A process developed at Steuben in which the molten stream of glass is sheared off in "seconds" of pouring time. Prior to this it was sheared based on quantity, not time. It was kept a closely guarded secret, but once known, quickly became an industry-wide practice. Since a particular formulation of glass flows at a constant rate at a constant temperature, the size of the gather can be measured by cutting the stream in specific, consistent time intervals.

letter seal A seal (see *fob seal*) mounted on a shank about six inches long, used to leave an identifying imprint on wax when sealing letters or documents.

letter weight A large paperweight usually with an oval or rectangular flat base and a central vertical metal ring or glass finial as a handle. Some were made of Hyalith glass; some by Apsley Pellatt have cameo incrustations portraying prominent persons; and some have a cut base.

Leune A decorating shop established about 1900. Paul Daum became its managing director in the 1920s. Blanks were supplied by Daum Freres and decorated there in polychrome enamels. It later made a series of mold pressed industrial glasses. It was an unsuccessful venture, closing in the early 1930s. All products were signed "Leune."

LeVerre Francais(e) A commercial art glass in cameo style made by Schneider at Epinay-sur-Seine in France. It is a mottled glass formed in layers with the design engraved with acid. Favored motifs were stylized leaves and flowers and geometric patterns. It is marked with the name in script or with inlaid filigree.

Levien Cut Glass Company See *Levine, Louis, Cut Glass Company.*

Levin, Charles A wholesale distributor of cut glass in New York City in the early 1900s.

Levine, Louis, Cut Glass Company (Aka *M. J. Levine Glass Company*) (1910-1922) A glass cutting facility operating in New York City, New York. In later years it was listed as a distributor and jobber of cut glass wares. It was, on occasion, spelled "Levien."

Levine, M.J., Glass Company See *Levine, Louis, Cut Glass Company.*

Libbey, W.L., & Co. See *Mount Washington Glass Works.*

Libbey, W.L., & Sons See *Libbey Glass Company; New England Glass Company.*

Libbey vase, Amberina, lily shape, tricorn.
Krause Publications

Libbey cut and engraved glass ad from **Atlantic Monthly, November 1911.**

Libbey Silex teapot with composite handle, 4" h.
Davanna Collection

Small crystal bowl, 4-1/2" d. x 2-1/2" h., acid etched, Libbey mark on base.
Davanna Collection

Libbey Cut Glass ad from **Century magazine, November 1901.**

Libbey Glass Company A glass manufacturing facility in Toledo, Ohio, resulting from the leasing of the New England Glass Co. in 1874 by William L. Libbey (1827-83) and relocating it to Toledo in 1888, as a result of labor problems. The move was planned by William L. Libbey's son, Edward Drummond Libbey (1854-1925). From its relocation until 1892, the company was known as W.L. Libbey & Sons. From 1892 on, it was known as the Libbey Glass Company. During the so-called *Brilliant Period*, it was the largest cut glassmaker in the world. In 1892, at the Columbian Exposition, it built a 150 by 200-foot Crystal Palace to display its wares. In 1893 it operated the Glass Pavilion at the Chicago World's Fair where 130 craftsmen were blowing and cutting glass; much of it sold as souvenirs, marked *Libbey Glass Co. World's Fair 1893*. From 1883 to 1940, Libbey made colored ornamental glassware using techniques developed by Joseph Locke, examples being *Amberina, Agata, Pomona, Maize,* and *Peachblow.* When Libbey died, control passed to his associates, mainly J.D. Robinson. On Robinson's death in 1929, control passed to his sons, Joseph W. and Jefferson D., who became, respectively, president and vice president. In 1931 the company hired A. Douglas Nash who, in 1933, introduced the high quality *Libbey Nash glassware.* In 1936 the company was taken over by Owens-Illinois Inc., operating first as a subsidiary and then as the Libbey Glass Division, making table glass in contemporary styles and ornamental lead crystal from 1940 to 1945. Currently it makes only tableware using automated mass production techniques, having made no handcrafted glassware since its 1940 *Modern American Series*. See *Gunderson (-Pairpoint) Glass Works*.

Libbey Nash glassware The *Libbey Nash Series* of luxury stemware and ornamental glassware was created by A. Douglas Nash for the Libbey Glass Co. after 1931. Stemware included eighty-two patterns, some in a choice of four colors, and ornamental ware of clear or colored glass in limited quantities. The wares were of superior craftsmanship in cutting and engraving and were generally signed with the Libbey name in script in a circle. Due to the Depression and the decline in sales, the line was discontinued when Libbey was taken over by Owens-Illinois Inc. in 1936.

Libbey-Owens-Ford Inc. A Toledo, Ohio, company resulting from the merger of the Libbey-Owens Sheet Glass Co.—organized by Edward Drummond Libbey and Michael J. Owens who, in 1926, developed a method to mass produce safety glass—with Edward Ford Plate Glass Company formed by Edward Ford in 1898 in Toledo, Ohio. Until 1968 it was known as Libbey-Owens-Ford Glass Company. Its safety glass is used in automobile windshields and marked *L-O-F*. See *Olive & Harmon Glassworks; Toledo Glass Company*.

Libbey-Owens process A process patented in 1905 for drawing a continuous flat sheet of glass vertically for a short distance, bending it over a roller, then directing it horizontally over flattening rollers before moving into the cutting and annealing area. It had advantages over other processes, such as the Fourcault process, which drew glass vertically. By drawing it horizontally, a continuous operation was possible, and the cutting operations were easier to accomplish.

Libbey-Owens Sheet Glass Co. See *Libbey-Owens-Ford Inc.*

Libbey Silex A light blown engraved stemware made by Libbey Glass Co. and sold at lower prices than its rock crystal.

Liberty Cut Glass Works (Aka *Liberty Glass Company*) (1902-1931) A glass cutting facility established in Egg Harbor City, New Jersey, by Thomas P. Strittmatter. It was one of the largest cutting houses in the nation. From 1905 it had facilities in Brooklyn and Manhattan, New York.

Liberty Glass Company (1) A glass manufacturing company with facilities in Sapulpa, Oklahoma, and Coffeyville, Kansas, making pressed glass in the early 1900s. (2) See *Liberty Cut Glass Works*.

Libisch, Joseph Born in Hungary in 1886, Libisch began work at the age of twelve for J. & L. Lobmeyr, then worked in Vienna and Prague. In 1904 he received his master engraver's certificate. In 1911 he came to the United States and began working for H.P. Sinclaire & Co. From 1911 to 1924, he operated a cutting shop in Corning, New York. In 1921 he left Sinclaire, devoting full time to his shop. In 1924 he began working for Steuben (Frederick Carder considered him his best engraver), still operating his shop on a part-time basis until 1937.

The *Gazelle Bowl*, the first engraved piece designed for Steuben by Sidney Waugh, was first engraved by Libisch (1935), as was the *Zodiac Bowl* (1935) designed by Waugh, the *Acrobats Goblet* (1940) designed by Russian artist Pavel Tchelitchev, the *Orchids Bowl* (1954) designed by Sir Jacob Epstein, the *Valor Cup* (1940) designed by John Monteith Gates, and the *Merry-Go-Round* (1947) designed by Waugh. Libisch retired in 1956 at age seventy.

lid A covering designed to close or cover the mouth of a mug, tankard, or other object. They are usually attached to the body of the object by a metal hinge or are mounted in a metal frame.

light (1) An opening in a structure through which daylight can enter. (2) A specific window or window fill, such as a leaded light. (3) A pane of glass.

Light and Darkness A glass wall made from about 200 blocks of Ravenna glass, created by Sven Palmquist and erected in Geneva, Switzerland.

light baluster A stemmed drinking glass popular in England between 1710 and 1735.

It is smaller in size than a heavy baluster, and the stem is composed of a series of small knops of different form, incorporating collars or flattened knops. They are occasionally called *Newcastle glasses* because many were made there. See *Newcastle glass.*

lightbulbs An incandescent bulb; a bulb with a shell made of glass, emitting light due to the glowing of heated material, such as a filament. Originally, they were made one at a time by a laborious process requiring two men to make a single bulb. The gatherer got the molten glass on the end of a blowpipe, then gave it to the gaffer who blew the paraison, being rotated on the arms of the bench and shaped by hand. Next they were mold blown and then made by a suction machine, but the rate of production was very slow.

Lighbulbs now are made by a ribbon machine at a rate in excess of over 1,000 per minute. In this machine, a ribbon of glass about one inch wide flows from the forehearth of a tank furnace, passing between two cooled rollers; one plain and the other with indentations in the shape of discs. A ribbon of glass discs, about four inches apart and connected by a thin strip of glass, is made and placed over a metal belt with holes about one inch in diameter spaced at four inch intervals. The machine is synchronized so that each disc is placed above a hole.

As the belt travels forward, the hot glass commences to sag through the holes, and the automatic production of the paraison begins. As the glass sags, a blowhead comes above it and low pressure blowing begins. As the ribbon moves on, the paraison is formed and enclosed by a rotating wet mold on the belt below. Blowing continues in the mold, then stops. The mold opens and the completed bulb is cut from the ribbon, dropped on a conveyor belt, and carried off to be annealed. The annealing process takes only a short time because of the thinness and uniformity of the glass. See *Deuerlein, Frederick; Edison Lamp Company.*

light cut The same as gray cutting. The light cutting of glassware using copper wheels.

light sensitive glass See *photochromic glass.*

lighter, methylated spirit See *methylated spirit lighter.*

lightning rod balls A glass ball at the center of the rod attached to the roof of a structure so the rod would attract lightning, diverting it from the structure itself and avoiding lightning damage. They were used primarily for decorative purposes.

lightweight glass bottles Such bottles are not made from a lighter glass. The same glass is used for lightweight and standard weight bottles, but because of research and improvements in production methods, a more uniform glass thickness throughout can be maintained, and bottle designs are now made with lightness in mind. Bottles half the weight of their predecessors can be made without any loss in strength. A recent development involving coating containers with tin chloride prior to annealing and organic compounds after annealing has given their surface a lubricity, protecting them from scratching and bruising. They reduce the cost of handling, because they are more resistant to cracking and breaking, and shipping because of the lighter weight.

Lilliputian bottle See *perfumette.*

lily pad decoration An applied embellishment used on glassware in the United States from about 1835 to 1860, especially by Casper Wistar. It is suggestive of a water lily pad on a stem and most often applied to the lower part of a bowl or a jug. Molten glass was applied to the body of a piece using trailing techniques and was tooled upward to form the design. There are three varieties of lily pad decoration: (a) slender, vertical stems ending in a bead-like pad; (b) broader stems ending in oval or circular pads; and (c) curved stems ending in a flat ovoid pad. The following objects were most often decorated with it: (a) pitchers, most with a stemmed foot, some with threading around the rim; (b) plates; (c) covered sugar bowls; (d) compotes; (e) fine tableware; and (f) covered bowls, some with chicken finials on set-in covers.

lime Lime or *calcium oxide, CaO*, is used in making certain types of glass. It is made in several ways, the most common being calcining limestone. It is also found in the sea plant ash used as an alkali in Egyptian glass, and as a natural impurity in the soda and potash used in glassmaking up until about 1660. It was added to the batch in various forms, such as chalk (carbonate of lime) in making a crystal-like glass in Germany, Bohemia, and Silesia in the late 17th and 18th centuries. It adds stability and, at the same time, produces a lighter and cheaper glass that cools quickly, making it useful in making bottles, window panes, and electric lightbulbs.

lime glass A type of glass developed in 1864 by William Leighton at the Hobbs, Brockunier facility (one source indicates John Adams of Adams, Macklin & Co. developed it in the early 1850s). It was used as a substitute for lead glass in making inexpensive glass bottles because it was cheaper, cooled more quickly, and was lighter and less resonant. It is made using bicarbonate of soda (ordinary baking soda, which is cheaper that carbonate of soda) and lime as a flux. See *lime; soda-lime glass; lime-soda glass.*

lime-soda glass Glass made since the Roman era using lime, soda, and sand as the primary raw materials. See *soda-lime glass; lime glass.*

Lind, Jenny, Flask A historical flask made in the United States during the 1850s, embellished with a relief portrait of Jenny Lind (1820-1887), the famous Swedish singer brought to the United States by P.T. Barnum in 1850. This flask had a flattened body and tall neck embellished with a relief wreath and her name. The lower half widened and was embellished with a relief lyre. They were made by numerous glasshouses. A forgery was made in various sizes and colors by the Fislerville Glass Works in South Jersey in 1925.

Lindsay & Company A glass manufacturing facility operating during the 1870s and 1880s in Chartiers, Pennsylvania.

Lindstrand, Vicke (1903-1983) A Swedish designer of modern glass employed at Orrefors Glasbruk between 1928 and 1941. For the next nine years he designed ceramics, and in 1950 began working for the Kosta Glassworks as head designer. He is best known for his glass sculptures and ice blocks. See *Ariel technique.*

linen smoother A glass object used as a pressing iron for pleating starched ruffles. Some from Spain, made in the 18th century, have a heavy bottom, flat or rounded, and a vertical circular solid handle. Similar ones were made in Stourbridge, possibly as friggers, in the 18th century. In England they are called *slickers, slick stones,* or *smoothing irons.*

Linenfold glass See *Tiffany Favrile Fabrique.*

liner A glass object made to fit closely to the walls or interior of a vessel of silver or other metal so that the contents would not come in contact with the metal, causing it to pit, discolor, etc. Often they are used in conjunction with metal openwork patterns that aided in showing off the color of the glass, cobalt being the most popular. They are often used with salt cellars, butter dishes, sweetmeat dishes, and wine coolers. See *sand molding.*

Linford Cut Glass Company (1905-1913) A glass cutting company established in Jamestown, New York, by William H. Linford (b.1842 in England). Upon coming to the United States, he and his son, William H. Linford Jr., worked as glass cutters in Corning, New York, leaving in 1905 to establish their own company.

Linke Colored Glass Shop A glass cutting shop located in Seelyville, Pennsylvania.

linnet holes Small holes in the sides of a furnace connecting the flues with the chambers or the holes in the sides of the main chamber of the furnace connecting it to the various sections. Their main function is to transmit heat to the areas where glass is melted or worked.

lion/lion mask A molded decorative motif used on some hollow blown stems and prunts. It is found on some glassware made in the 4th century B.C. and Venetian glassware (and elsewhere in *facon de Venice*) beginning in the 16th century. The lion was the attribute of St. Mark, being symbolic of Venice.

lip The everted pouring projection (like the lower part of a bird's beak) on the rim of a jug, pitcher, sauce boat, etc. They are made in a variety of styles, some of pinched (trefoil) shape. They are usually directly opposite the handle, but on some pieces, such as ladles, items with two handles, etc., they are at right angles to the handle. See *beak; ice lip; pinched lip.*

lipped bowl (1) A bowl, ogee, or bucket on a drinking glass with a slightly everted rim. (2) A cylindrical bowl with a flat bottom and pouring lip (sometimes with two lips opposite each other). The bowls are used for four different purposes: (a) a bowl for water used after rinsing the mouth at a meal; (b) a finger bowl; (c) a wine glass cooler; and (d) a bowl used to rinse wine glasses when a different wine is to be drunk or when sediment from port is to be rinsed from the glass.

lipped pan decanter A decanter on which the portion above the neck is wider than the neck and shaped like a shallow pan with a pouring lip. See *pan topped.*

lipper A glassmaker's tool made of wood and shaped like a truncated cone attached to a handle, used to form the lip on a jug, pitcher, etc.

liqueur bottle (1) A bottle to hold a liqueur. (2) A large bottle with a bulbous body divided internally into two, three, or four compartments, each holding a different liqueur and having its own neck, mouth, and stopper. See *multiple bottle.*

liqueur glass See *cordial glass; wine glass.*

litharge *Lead monoxide (PbO).* It exists in two forms: (a) red to reddish-yellow tetragonal crystals and (b) yellow orthorhombic crystals. It is also known as *lead oxide, lead protoxide, lead (II) oxide, plumbous oxide, red lead, yellow lead ocher,* and *massicot.* It is used in making lead glass. It was first made commercially in the United States about 1817 by Deming Jarves of the New England Glass Company. He supplied not only New England Glass Company but other local glasshouses as well as some in the Pittsburgh, Pennsylvania, area.

Lithyalin glass A marbled, polished opaque glassware, mostly red but also in other strong colors, to simulate semi-precious (striated) stones. It was developed and patented in 1828 by Frederick Egermann in Bohemia, who made it until about 1840. Early Lithyalin glass may be semi-transparent or in combination with a transparent red or green lining or casing. It was used for a variety of items and combined with many styles of decoration, including gilding. One type, named *Chamaleon-glas,* was introduced in 1835. Imitations were made at many facilities until 1855.

Little Harry Night-Light A very small toy night-light advertised as "one firefly power." It was only 1-1/2 inches tall, giving little light.

Littleton, Harvey K. Born in 1922, Littleton was a glass technician, designer, and glassmaker residing in Verona, Wisconsin. From 1951 he was affiliated with the University of Wisconsin as a teacher and studio glassmaker, initiating the first university glass training program in North America. He developed a formula for a glass with a low melting temperature and a furnace small enough for an individual to melt and blow glass in his own studio. His works include free blown and wrought pieces in his own creative style, in both crystal and colored glass. See *studio glass.*

Livingston Glass Works A glass manufacturing facility operating for a short time in the 1880s in the New Jersey Pine Barrens, near the Lebanon Glass Works.

lizard paperweight A paperweight whose primary motif is a glass lizard. They are of three types: (a) those with it embedded within the crown; (b) those with it gilded and coiled on top of the crown, as made at St. Louis; and (c) those in the form of a lizard, either on a base or alone.

Llewellyn, Gorner (1873-1937) Born in Wales, Llewellyn came to the United States in 1896 and was mold shop foreman at Consolidated Glass, having learned the trade at McKee Glass Company. He worked for several companies before settling at the Phoenix

Glass Company, working there for 20 years. From Phoenix he went to Overmeyer Mould Company in Greensburg, Pennsylvania, and finally ended his career at the reopened Consolidated facility.

lobing Gadrooning.

Lobmeyr, J. & L. A Viennese glass manufacturing facility established in 1823 by Joseph Lobmeyr (1792-1853). The operations were managed after his death by his sons, Joseph (1828-1864) and Ludwig (1827-1917), and were registered in 1860 as J. & L. Lobmeyr. In 1918 Stefan Rath (1876-1960), the son of Lobmeyr's sister, Mathilde, and August Rath, established a subsidiary at Steinschonau, Bohemia, called J. & L. Lobmeyr Neffe Stefan Rath, operating until 1945 when it was nationalized by the new government in Czechoslovakia and no longer connected with the Vienna facility or the company. The Vienna owners, after Stefan Rath, were his son, Hans Harald Rath (1904-68), and then the latter's sons, Harald C. (b.1938), Peter (b.1939), and Hans Stefan (b.1943). The facility has done work in Hochschnitt and Tiefschnitt, as well as made enameled glassware and iridescent glass. It has also produced large crystal glass chandeliers and quality tableware.

Punch cup, Agata, New England Glass Company, Cambridge, MA, c. 1887. Museum of American Glass at Wheaton Village, Millville, NJ.

Locke, Joseph (1846-1936) An engraver, enameller, and glassmaker who formulated many new types of, and created many new designs for, art glass. Born in Worcester, England, he won a prize for an original glass design at age nineteen and moved to Stourbridge to work for Guest Brothers and later Hodgetts, Richardson & Company. He studied cameo glassmaking and, in 1876, made a copy of the Portland Vase. Leaving Hodgetts, Richardson & Company, he worked for Phillip Pargeter at the Red House Glassworks and at Webb & Corbetts.

In 1882 he came to the United States and worked at the New England Glass Company and later the Libbey Glass Company, where he created *Amberina*, *plated Amberina*, *Pomona*, *Wild Rose* (*Peachblow*), *Agata*, and *Maise* glassware and made a few pieces of cameo glass. In 1891 he moved to Pittsburgh, Pennsylvania, becoming the lead designer for the United States Glass Company. In 1900 he opened a workshop, Locke Art Glass Co., in Mt. Olive, Pennsylvania, continuing to make glassware until his death. Some pieces are signed *Locke*, *Locke Art*, or *Joe Locke*.

Locke Art Glass Co. See *Locke, Joseph.*

Lockport Glass Works A bottle and flask manufacturing facility established in 1840 by Hildreth & Co. (Hildreth, Marks, Keep, and Hitchens) in Lockport, New York. By 1869 S.B. Rowley owned it, selling it in 1872 to Alonzo J. Mansfield. In 1878 it was destroyed by fire and rebuilt. In 1900 it was taken over by some local Lockport businessmen.

Loder, Daniel A glass manufacturer who operated a facility in Bridgeton, New Jersey, for a short period of time about 1889-'90.

Loetz deep green iridescent vase with metal work in Art Noveau style; metal work: 18-1/4" h., vase: 14" h.
Tri-State Antiques

Loetz glassware Also spelled *Lotz*. A glassware made at a facility established in 1836 in Bohemia (now Austria) by Johann B. Eisner von Eisenstein and acquired about 1840 by Johann Loetz (1778-1848). After his death it was operated by his widow, Suzanne, as *Johann Loetz Witwe*; *witwe* is German for *widow*. Johann's grandson, Max Ritter von Spaun, managed it from about 1870 (purchasing it in 1879) and was primarily responsible for an increase in the quality and quantity of its wares. In the 1880s it was known for its marbled glass.

During the 1890s it made art glass imitating semi-precious stones, such as agate and aventurine, and in 1897 it began making iridescent glass similar to later Tiffany *Favrile*, for which it received a patent. Much of its Art Nouveau style glass was exported to the United States. After about 1900 it made black and white glassware. In 1908 von Spaun turned it over to his son, also named Max. The elder Max died in 1909. In 1911 the company became insolvent, reorganizing in 1913. Operations were suspended about 1914 at the start of World War I and began again in 1918, after the war. The company was destroyed by fire in 1932, was rebuilt, and continued to operate until 1947. Some pieces made for export after 1891 are signed *Lotz Austria*; some for domestic sale are signed *Lotz Klostermihle*. There may be a symbol—two crossed arrows within a circle and four stars, with or without a signature.

The company made a few cameo pieces in cased glass. Its unsigned iridescent ware is often confused with that of Tiffany. It won grand prizes at Universal Expositions in Chicago (1893), Paris (1889 and 1900), and St. Louis (1904). See the following types of Loetz glass: *Papillon glass; Phenomenon glass; Silberiris glass.*

Log Cabin Night-Light A night-light in the shape of a log cabin made by Atterbury & Company (see *White House Works*) during the 1860s and 1870s. It was of clear and transparent amber, blue, and milk glass.

log glass A sand glass used on ships for timing intervals of fourteen or twenty-eight seconds to determine the sailing speed of the vessel by the length of line paid out while the sand ran through the glass.

Lomax oil lamp An oil lamp with a mold blown drip catcher around the collar, patented by George Henry Lomax in 1870 and made by the Union Glass Company in Somerville, Massachusetts.

Long Cut Glass Company A glass cutting shop established by James F. Long in Toledo, Ohio, during the late 1910s. He was a glassworker and blower, employed by Libbey in the 1890s.

long glass See *yard-of-ale.*

Long Island Flint Glass Works (1) (1874-1893) A glass manufacturing facility established in Brooklyn, New York, by Huwer & Dannehoffer. (2) Founded in 1853 by Christian Dorflinger, it was an outgrowth of his Concord Street Flint Glass Works, remaining under his control until he retired in 1862. Another facility associated with the Long Island Flint Glass Works was built on Plymouth Street, starting operations in 1858. On retirement, Christian turned the management of the Plymouth Street site over to his brother, Edward. See *Dorflinger, C., & Sons.*

look-alike patterns See *pattern glass, look-alike.*

looking glass See *mirrors.*

looped edge bowl A type of molded decoration applied around the top of a bowl consisting of a series of open loops resembling the hoops in the game of croquet. See *croquet hoop* design.

looped trailing Embellishment in the form of a series of vertical looped threads extending above the rim of a vessel. Since the loops are not applied to the surface, *threading* is the preferred term.

looping The technique of applying loops of molten glass, different from the color of the body, to an object and pressing them onto the surface, giving the appearance that they are imprinted. Often they are tooled, pulling them up or down at regular intervals, making a wavy pattern before impressing them into the surface.

L'ora A line of glassware made by Consolidated Lamp & Glass Company, introduced in the late 1920s. It used the same blanks as the *Florentine* line except the *L'ora* line blanks were etched and decorated over the entire surface with a gold colored finish. *L'ora* is written on the base. It is extremely rare, believed to have been a special order for a customer.

Lord & Tracey See *Honesdale Glassworks.*

Lorenz, Frederick (Rudolph Joacim) Sr. See *Pittsburgh Glass Works; Phoenix Glass Works; Sligo Works; Trevor & Ensell.*

Lorenz & Buchanan See *Pittsburgh Glass Works.*

Lorenz & Wightman See *Pittsburgh Glass Works; Phoenix Glass Works.*

Lorraine Method A method used to make broad glass. See *broad glass.*

lost wax process See *cire perdue.*

Lotharingian glassware Glassware made in the Rhineland, especially that made at Cologne. It includes early Roman glass and later Waldglas. It is the older name for Lorraine and originally included what is now Alsace-Lorraine, the low countries, and part of northwest Germany.

lottery glass A drinking glass engraved with a scene associated with a lottery, normally including an inscription offering good wishes. Lotteries were used in the mid-18th century as a means of selling the wares of the smaller German porcelain facilities. Lottery glasses, many made at Newcastle-upon-Tyne, England, were shipped to the Netherlands to be engraved.

Lotton paperweight vase, blue flowers, green leaves, 4-1/2" h. Made by David Lotton, signed 1996.
Davanna Collection

Lotton-style vase.
Davanna Collection

Lotton, Charles Gerald Born in 1935 near Elizabethtown, Illinois, Lotton graduated from high school in 1954 and enlisted in the U.S. Air Force. He left in 1957 and began working for Lockhead Aircraft Corporation. He returned to Chicago, Illinois, entered cosmetology school and, in 1960, became a licensed cosmetologist. Lotton's interest in glass developed in 1965 after a customer brought in a collection of carnival glass. After that he and his wife began collecting glassware and selling all types of glass while continuing to collect carnival glass.

In the summer of 1970, he built a fully equipped glass studio behind his house in Sauk Village, Illinois. Determined to make iridescent glass, he found the appropriate formulations in his research and experimented until he found the formulae and procedures he required. His first item was a crude, lumpy ornament made from the glass of melted soda bottles.

In June 1971 he made his first sale to a retail establishment, C.D. Peacock, Jeweler. He contacted Ms. Lillian Nassau, an art glass dealer who was impressed with his work and ordered twelve of his King Tut paperweights. Soon Lotton and Ms. Nassau's son, Paul, signed a contract giving Paul the exclusive right to sell all the articles Lotton made for a period of five years.

On January 1, 1973, Lotton went into glassmaking full time, making paperweights, perfume bottles, and jewelry. He made a few sets of glasses and windows. One of Lotton's most famous designs was the *Multi Flora*, which underwent continuous changes and refinements over the years. He developed a series of reactive opaque glasses in various colors (red, yellow, green, gray, and plum) called *Mandarin colors*, and made Lily lamp shades in the Tiffany style. He originally bought his cullet from Fenton Art Glass through a broker, adding his own ingredients for color and special effects. He later began making his batches from scratch except for the Fenton cullet used in his milk glass.

When his contract with Nassau expired, he did not renew it, deciding instead to sell to several retail outlets and at major antique shows. Lotton's wife, three sons, and daughter are all in the business. Each operates his/her own business under the umbrella Lotton Art Glass. Each concentrates on a specialty, with some overlapping. Charles, with the aid of his wife, makes larger pieces such as vases, bowls, and lamps. His son, David, makes paperweights, jewelry, and ruby veiled sculptures and blows blanks for other engravers. Son, Daniel, makes miniature lamps and perfume atomizers. Son, John, makes magnum paperweights, sculptures, perfume bottles, and Lily lamp shades. All make vases. Lotton's daughter, Rachel, organizes events. Charles' nephew, Jerry Heer, works as an assistant to the others, does grinding and polishing, and makes some jewelry.

lotus bud bossed beaker See *almond bossed beaker.*

lotus bud cup A cup in the form of a lotus bud or inverted bell made in the latter part of the XVIIIth Dynasty (c. 1400-1320 B.C.) in Egypt; one of the first artistic objects of Egyptian glass.

Lotus Glass Co. Gold and Silver Brocade ad, October 1967. Krause Publications

Lotus (Cut) Glass Company A glass cutting facility established in Barnesville, Ohio, in 1911. The company did only light cutting, often combined with silver mountings and other decorations, and closed in the early 1930s. On April 13, 1920, it registered its trademark, *Lotus* in script, which it had used since July 1, 1911.

Lotz glassware See *Loetz glassware.*

Louie Glass Company A subsidiary of Princess House Inc., owned by Colgate-Palmolive Company in Weston, West Virginia, making hand-blown crystal.

Louisville Glass Works See *Kentucky Glass Works.*

Louvre glassware A line of sculptured glassware with a satin finish designed for commercial use, made by McKee Glass Co. from 1937 to 1942. It is unsigned with no identifying trademark. It is sometimes called *unsigned Verlys* or *unmarked Lalique.* It was molded in a semi or high relief with a sandblasted satin finish. Pieces were finished in two styles: (a) crystal satin on the outside and fire polished on the inside, or (b) in an all-over frosted satin finish, inside and out. There were three design groupings: *Bird of Paradise*, *Tulip*, and *Flamingo*, each in a variety of articles.

loving cup (1) A relatively large (eight-ounce capacity or greater) ornamental drinking vessel with two or more handles and usually a stemmed foot. They were to be passed around to guests who drank from them in twin (two at a time). (2) A large cup with two or more handles presented as a prize, award, or token of esteem or affection.

Low Countries The lowland region near the North Sea, forming the lower basin of the Rhine, Meuse, and Scheldt Rivers. It includes Belgium, Luxembourg, and the Netherlands.

low relief Relief embellishment with the projecting portion only slightly raised. The French term is *bas relief*; the Italian term is *basso rilievo*. The German term *Hochschnitt* encompasses all degrees of decorative relief work above the surface, executed entirely by the use of a wheel. See *high relief; medium relief.*

Lowell Cut Glass Company A glass cutting facility in Lowell, Massachusetts, operating for a short time in the early 1900s.

Lower Factory See *Hereford Glass Company.*

lozenge A cut glass motif consisting of a quadrilateral figure with four equal sides and equal opposing angles (two acute and two obtuse).

lozenge stopper A stopper that succeeded the disk stopper for use on decanters. It is similar to the disk stopper, except it is more elongated in the shape of a lozenge. Some are embellished with faceting near the edge, some scalloped along the perimeter, and some of decorative shape. They were used primarily on decanters with long sloping shoulders.

Lubbers process A process used for making sheet glass involving drawing an extremely large cylinder of molten glass, up to fifty feet long and three feet in diameter, from a tank of molten glass using an iron ring to which the glass adhered. It was developed in the United States, superceding the initial stage of making broad glass.

lucern A *lamp* from the Anglo-Norman word, *lucense*, meaning *light*.

luck An object on which the prosperity or fortune of a person, family, etc., is presumed to depend. The best known example in glass is *Luck of Edenhall*.

Luck of Edenhall A flared beaker of Islamic glass, made and decorated in Syria in the 13th century. It is of clear glass with red, white, and blue embellishment consisting of finely drawn and stylized foliage and geometric forms in Islamic style. It is accompanied by an English leather case dating from the 14th century.

Sources indicate the beaker and case were brought to England from Palestine by a Crusader late in the 14th century. It was in the possession of the Musgrave family of Edenhall in Cumberland, England. Legend has it the beaker was left by fairies on St. Cuthbert's Well, a spring at Edenhall. The family's luck was to continue as long as the beaker was kept safe.

When a member of the family seized it from the fairy king, he informed him, "When the cup shall break and fall/Farewell to the Luck of Edenhall." It has been in the Victoria & Albert Museum since 1958. A beaker, similarly shaped and enameled (with a leather case), is in the Kunstgewerbemuseum, Cologne. See *luck; enameling, Islamic; Aleppo glassware.*

Ludlow bottle See *chestnut flask.*

Ludlow Manufacturing Company A glass manufacturing facility incorporated in 1815 near Ludlow, Massachusetts. It produced green glass bottles for a few years before going bankrupt.

lug An ear, knob, solid scroll, or other attachment affixed to an object and used for lifting or holding it. A handle with space for fingers or a hand to be passed through is not considered a lug. Some lugs have a small opening for a suspensory strap.

Lum, William H., & Son See *Lum & Ogden.*

Lum & Ogden Beginning in 1869, William H. Lum represented various glassmakers at his shop in New York City, New York. In 1875 it was known as Lum & Ogden; later as William H. Lum & Son (Elmer R. Lum). From 1920 to 1929 it may have made some cut glass.

luminaria Light fixtures. Over the years, many have been made almost entirely of glass, especially cut and pressed glass.

luminor A night-light of clear glass in the form of an ornament concealing an electric light, transmitting light from below. Many were designed by Frederick Carder at Steuben in the 1920s. A frequently used Steuben form was a bird of molded glass with feathers and other details added by cutting. See *bubble ball.*

Luna An alabaster/pearly-like, opaque white glass developed by Harry Northwood in 1911-'12 and perfected in 1913, used specifically in electric light shades and globes. The glass could be easily drilled so that chains for hanging could be attached. It was advertised as "no glare," "restful to the eyes," "soft as moonlight," "restful vision," "no fire color," "smooth as satin," etc. There was also an iridized *Luna*, known as *Pearl*, having the appearance of white Carnival glass.

luncheon plate A plate somewhat smaller than a dinner plate, usually eight to nine inches in diameter.

luncheon set A table service in which the plates are smaller than traditional dinner plates, their diameter not exceeding nine inches. A luncheon set usually has fewer pieces than a dinner set.

Lundberg, James After studying glass-working and techniques at San Jose State University during the late 1960s and throughout Europe during the early 1970s, Lundberg began making paperweights in 1972, establishing Lundberg Studios in 1973 in Davenport, California. Several artists work at the studio making lamps, paperweights, glassware, and jewelry in the Art Nouveau style. Lundberg makes clear weights with motifs that include flowers, birds, butterflies, and seascapes. Some are made by inserting the motif into the hot glass rather than encasing it in crystal. They are signed with the studio name, artist's name, date, and number. Since 1980 all pieces are accompanied by a certificate of authenticity.

luster (1) A glass girandole, candelabrum, or candlestick embellished with prismatic pendant drops of glass or crystal, to be placed on the mantle or tabletop. (2) A pendant drop of glass or crystal, smooth or faceted, made in various forms. (3) The original name for a chandelier. Also spelled *lustre*.

luster painting Painting on the surface of glass using metallic oxide pigments, producing a metallic iridescent effect. It has been used as a ground, covering the entire piece, or as a design or pattern. Oxides of gold, copper, or silver, and, more recently, platinum and bismuth, are dissolved in acid and mixed with an oily medium. It is then painted on the glass, fired in a reducing atmosphere, smoky and rich in carbon monoxide. This causes the metal to fuse into a thin film, producing an evenly distributed metallic flashing, unable to be detected by touch. The use of gold yields a ruby color, platinum a silver color, and silver a straw color. It appears on Islamic glass dating from the 9th to the 11th centuries. Most examples have been found in and are attributed to Egypt. In modern times, luster painting has been used on Tiffany Favrile, some Loetz glass, and some glass made by Frederick Carder at Steuben. See *staining; luster stained glass*.

luster stained glass A luster stain applied in much the same way as varnish on the inside or outside of the glass. After applying, the glass is heated to fix the color. Copper luster stains the outside of the article red; other colors are green, blue, yellow, or purple. It is an inexpensive imitation of cased glass. See *cased glass*.

luster ware See *iridescent glass*.

Lusterware, Textured See *Tiffany Iridescent Glass; Textured Lusterware*.

Lustre Art Glass Company A glass manufacturing facility established in Long Island, New York, in 1920 by Conrad Vohlsing and Paul Frank. The company made lampshades and globes similar to those of Quezel. Vohlsing was a son-in-law of Martin Bach Sr., who made Quezel glass. Most of Lustre Art Glass Company's products are unmarked.

lustre glass A shiny, mineral-finished glass somewhat slick to the touch.

lustred glass A glass from the Art Nouveau period, the surface made to simulate the nacreous surface deterioration found on much ancient glass. This was further enhanced by lustered effects, sometimes covering the entire surface or used as a portion of the overall design in the form of threads and patches pulled into imaginative forms. Tiffany's *Cypriote* is one of the better examples of the reproduction of iridescent effects on ancient glass. Much was made by Quezal, Union Glass Company, Tiffany, Steuben, and Durand's Vineland Flint Glass Works. In addition to *Cypriote,* Tiffany also made *Laminated Glass* and *Agate*.

Lutz, Nicholas A skilled glassblower born at St. Louis, France, where he was employed as an apprentice at the St. Louis facility at the age of ten. Later he came to the United States and began working for Dorflinger at White Mills, Pennsylvania. In 1869 he left to work for the Boston & Sandwich Glass Company, working there until it closed in 1888. He then worked at the Mt. Washington Glass Co. and later at Union Glass Co. He made glassware in the Venetian filigrana style as well as paperweights. His favorite motifs were fruits and flowers (see *striped glassware*). Since it is impossible to differentiate his works from those of others, similar wares—regardless of maker—are referred to as *Lutz glass.*

Luzerne Cut Glass Company A glass
cutting company in West Pittstown, Pennsylvania, operating from about 1915 until about 1930.

Lycurgus Cup A glass cup tapering
slightly inward toward the base, depicting in *vasa diatreta* and high relief a frieze of five figures representing personages from the myth of the punishment of Lycurgus by Bacchus (Dionysis). The glass is a soda-lime type, primarily dull pea green in color with an area of yellow green. However, it appears wine red when viewed by transmitted light and exhibits a red tinge when viewed in direct light. This change of color is attributed to the presence of a small percentage (0.003-0.005%) of colloidal gold in the batch. Recent analyses found traces of silver and other minerals that may contribute to the dichromic effect. It is of Roman glass from the 4th century, probably mold blown. It is 6-1/3 inches tall (but may have been taller) with a metal rim affixed at a later date to conceal chips. Before it was purchased in 1958 by the British Museum, it was attached to a modern metal base. This has since been removed, revealing a remnant of the original foot in open work, forming a small base ring. See *vasa cup; dichromatic glass; transmutation glass.*

Lyman, George Dummer, & Co.
See *Jersey Glass Company.*

Lyndeboro Glass Company (Aka
South Lyndeboro Glass Company) A bottle glass manufacturing facility incorporated in 1866 in South Lyndeboro, New Hampshire, by Luther Roby, John Hartshorn, Charles F. Eaton, George H. Sanborn, and Timothy Putnam, beginning operations in 1867. In June 1868 it was destroyed by fire and rebuilt. In 1886 operations ceased. It made bottles of all types from carboys and demijohns (up to fourteen gallon capacity) to small medicine bottles (one ounce capacity), including the first Moxie bottle for "Moxie Nerve Food," as well as lamp chimneys, rolling pins, vases, and some off-hand pieces.

Lynn glassware Drinking glasses, usu-
ally wine glasses or tumblers, and decanters characterized by several (two to eight) contiguous bands of shallow horizontal ribbing. The bands on decanters are wider and fewer than on glasses and probably were made by pucellas during their making. They are accredited to King's Lynn, but have, on occasion, been accredited to nearby Norwich and, as a result, are sometimes referred to as *Norwich glassware.* There is no record of a glasshouse being there, but there was a warehouse in Norwich owned by a King's Lynn glasshouse. It has also been said that Lynn glassware may have been made at Yarmouth, near King's Lynn, between 1728 and 1758.

Lyon, James B., & Co. Born on April 21,
1821, in Pennsylvania Furnace, Pennsylvania. After his formal education was complete, he entered the banking business, and, on January 1, 1849, organized a flint glass company and began construction of the facility in Pittsburgh. In March 1849, the partially completed buildings burned and were rebuilt. In 1851 Lyon purchased the abandoned Hay & McCully glassworks and began production. His facility is the first in the United States to use pressed glass as its main method of production and the first to use natural gas as a fuel. He is noted for giving his findings and discoveries to others for the good of the industry as a whole. See *Union Glass Works; O'Hara Glass Works; Union Flint Glass Works.*

Lyons Cut Glass Company A glass
cutting facility, incorporated on March 7, 1903, in Lyons, New York. Blanks were purchased from Union Glass Works (Somerville, Massachusetts), H.C. Fry, Baccarat, and others. It closed in December 1903, reopened in February 1904, and closed again in 1905. Its trademark was two lions standing on their hind legs, supporting a small banner between them, all within a pentagon-shaped shield, with the name *Lyons.* Few pieces were signed.

Lyons Glass Manufacturing
Company A glass manufacturing facility incorporated in Lyons, New York, on April 17, 1867. It or another facility so named may have been in operation as early as 1846. It made window glass and hollowware.

MacBeth, G.A., Company See *Keystone Flint Glass Manufactory.*

MacBeth-Evans Glass Company See *Pittsburgh Glass Manufacturing Co.*

MacGregor & Company See *Albany Glass House.*

McClallen, MacGregor & Co. See *Albany Glass House; Dowesborough Glass Works.*

McCarty & Torreyson See *Duval, Isaac & Co.*

McCord & Shiner A glass cutting house in Philadelphia, Pennsylvania, operating in the mid-1800s, buying many of its blanks from the Brooklyn Flint Glass Works.

McCue, James H.; McCue, John, J. See *McCue & Earl.*

McCue & Earl (1887-1907) A glass cutting facility established in Brooklyn, New York. From 1905 to 1907 James H. and John J. McCue operated another facility in Brooklyn. From 1907 to 1918, James McCue operated it alone. John J. McCue was the president of the Co-Operative Glass Company of Brooklyn.

McCully, Wm., & Co. See *Williamsport Glass Works; Temperanceville Glass Works; Pittsburgh Glass Works; Phoenix Glass Works; Sligo Glass Works; Mastadon Works.*

McFadden, Harrison G. See *Emeralite.*

McGee-Deiters Glass Company (1904-1909) A glass decorating facility established in Brilliant, Ohio, decorating blanks purchased from other companies.

McIlvain, William G., & Company Established in 1918, a wholesaler of cut glass in Mt. Holly, New Jersey, which leased part of the Frizlen Cut Glass Company building. McIlvain purchased blanks, sending them to Frizlen to be cut. Both closed about 1930.

McK The Trademark of the McKanna Cut Glass Company.

McKanna Cut Glass Company See *Feeney & McKanna.*

McKee The name has been associated with numerous glass enterprises in the United States since 1834, including S. McKee & Co., 1834; J. & F. McKee (McKee Brothers), 1850; Bryce, McKee, 1850; National Glass, 1899; etc. In 1903 McKee Glass Company was established, operating a facility in Jeanette, Pennsylvania, which became the McKee Division of Thatcher Glass Co. in 1951 and was purchased by the Jeanette Corporation in 1961.

McKee, S., & Co. A window and bottle glass manufacturing facility established by James and Samuel (1808-1877) McKee in 1834 in Pittsburgh, Pennsylvania. In 1836 a third brother, Thomas, joined the firm.

McKee Glass Co. wren house, gray body, red roof.
Krause Publications

Reverse Amberina vase, 7-1/2" h.

Bohemian glass decanter.

Cameo glass bowl.

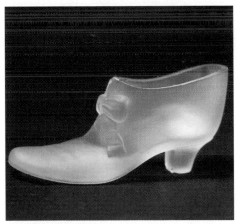

Camphor glass shoe.

All photos courtesy Krause Publications

Carnival glass pitcher in Blackberry pattern.

Carnival glass stemmed rose bowl.

Coin spot glass syrup jug with tin top.

Vase with coralene decoration.

Pair of cloisonné covered ginger jars.

Cosmos glass butter dish.

Findlay onyx vase.

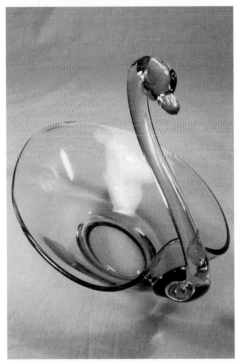

Duncan & Miller swan, blue cast, 11-1/2" l. x 9-1/2" h.

Cranberry glass pickle caster.

Cut velvet vase.

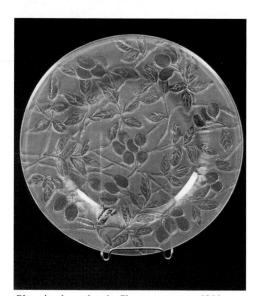

Phoenix glass plate in Cherry pattern, c. 1900.

Lalique signed ashtray, 6" d.

Milk glass covered dish with chicken on basket.

Custard glass footed bowl.

Spatter glass basket, 3-1/2" x 5".

Opalescent glass cruet.

Millefiori handled vase.

Moser glass vase.

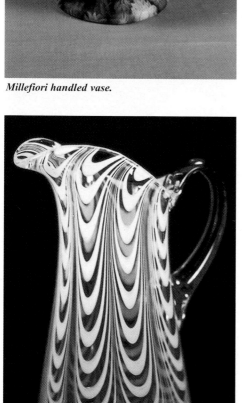

Nailsea pitcher, 9-1/2" h.

Northwood Glass pitcher, 7-7/8" h., and tumbler.

Cut glass cologne with sterling enamel stopper, marked France, 4-1/2" h.

Peachblow bowl, New England, 8" d.

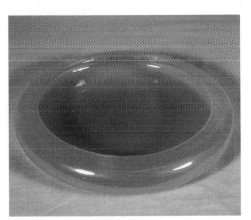

Opaline bowl, 1-1/2" h. x10" d.

Pigeon's blood butter dish and creamer, metal plated base and handle on dome, c. 1890.

Cut velvet rose bowl.

Roman glass from the ruins of Pompeii.

Peking glass bowl, 7" d.

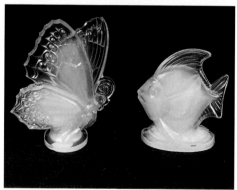

Sabino glass butterfly and fish figures made in France.

Silver deposit glass stoppered bottle.

Purple slag glass celery vase.

Satin glass cracker jar.

Sinclaire Glass vase, 10-1/2" h.

Stretch glass vase with iridescent pinched base, 8" h.

Stevens & Williams vase, late Victorian era, c. 1890.

Spanish lace pitcher and five tumblers.

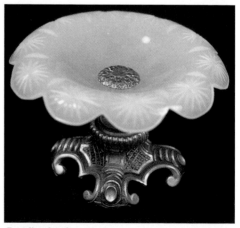

Rosaline bowl.

Opalescent lattice syrup, 6-1/2".

Threaded glass sugar bowl.

Tiffany vase.

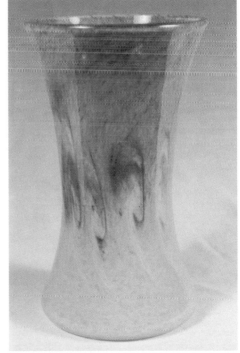

Signed Vasart Glass vase.

Vallery Stahl glass.

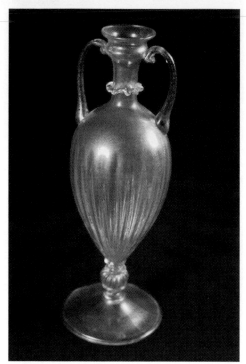

Venetian glass handled vase.

Heisey Glass Co. advertising item.

Art glass overlay vase.

Kimball glass vase with pink mottling, 3-3/4" h.

Pomona glass tumbler with enameled fern and daisies.

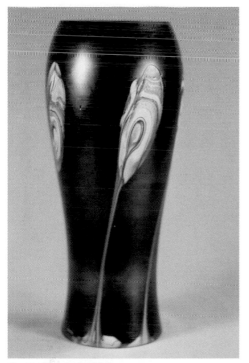

Loetz glass vase, 12" h.

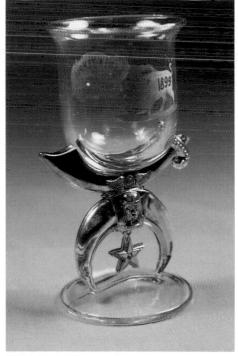

Masonic wineglass.

Mercury glass vases, 12" h.

Lutz glass dish with sterling base and handle.

Nash glass vase.

American caramel slag glass sugar bowl.

Miniature satin glass lamp with petal-shaped shade.

Steuben cranberry cruet with clear faceted stopper, 6-1/2" h.

Crackle glass pitcher.

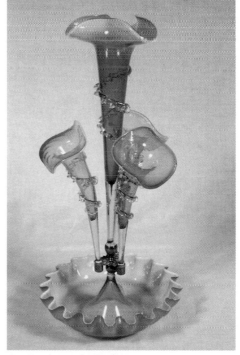

Epergne in cranberry glass.

Cut glass knife rest.

Flashed glass tumbler.

Early Stiegel-type engraved glassware.

Galle cameo glass covered dish.

McKee Brothers Frederick and James McKee established a flint glass manufacturing facility in East Birmingham (Pittsburgh), Pennsylvania in 1850. Over the years it operated as J. & F. McKee, McKee Brothers, McKee & Brother, and McKee & Brothers (when a brother, Stewart, entered the firm). It made cut, molded, and plain clear and colored tableware, bar ware, jugs, and chimneys. In 1889, it moved to Jeanette, Pennsylvania, and in 1899, joined the National Glass Company. In 1903 the McKees left the combine, forming the McKee Glass Company, which became a division of Thatcher Glass Company. In 1850 the McKee brothers joined forces with James Bryce to form Bryce, McKee & Company. See *Bryce, McKee & Company.*

McKinley Act, 1894 An act requiring the name of the country of origin or manufacture to appear on all goods and wares imported into the United States.

McLaughlin Glass Company (1920-1935) A glass manufacturing company in California, which made insulators.

McNamee & Adams A cylinder glass manufacturing facility in South Wheeling, West Virginia, operating during the 1830s.

Macedoine paperweight See *scrambled paperweight.*

Mackey Cut Glass Works A glass cutting facility operating for a short time in New Bedford, Massachusetts, in 1918.

macuahuitl An Aztec sword with obsidian edges, usually with five slicing blades on each side.

madrepore A design on millefiori bowls of the Greco-Roman era, resembling the pattern on a polished slab of limestone with a deep translucent green ground or a subdued purplish tone.

magic lantern A picture projector invented in Italy in the late 16th century, refined in Germany in the early 17th century, and introduced into England in 1665. Glass is used for the various lenses as well as the painted slides.

magnifying lens A polished glass convex lens that diffuses light, enlarging the image; the opposite of a diminishing lens. They are used in visual aids, magnifying glasses, microscopes, binoculars, telescopes, etc.

magnifying mirror A boudoir accessory consisting of a magnifying lens, usually with a crystal handle attached to the mirror back with a metal swivel. The handle was frequently embellished with cut or intaglio designs, in clear or pastel colors to match perfume bottles or other boudoir accessories. On the reverse of the mirror were usually flowers, Watteau prints, cloisonné, or glass medallions (matching one on the handle). Occasionally mirrors were on both sides. They were first marketed in the United States in 1932 by Irice (Irving W. Rice), imported from Czechoslovakia. Because of their popularity other companies began adding them to their lines.

Magnolia Glass Works A window glass manufacturing facility established in 1899 on the border between Magnolia and Somerdale, New Jersey. After a few years it burned and was not rebuilt.

magnum See *wine bottle, sizes.*

magnum decanter A decanter having a general capacity of about two quarts.

magnum paperweight A paperweight larger in diameter than the average three to 3-1/4 inches, being about four inches in diameter.

Magoun, Joseph Born in 1811, he began working at the New England Glass Company as a young man. In the early 1840s he was appointed foreman of the pressing department. He received several patents for inventions allowing molds to be adjusted in a pressing machine (issued on December 6, 1845, allowing, through a series of springs and rods, several molds to be used in one machine, reducing the number needed for making a variety of patterns, and time and labor costs by quick substitution of molds instead of setting up a new machine) and eliminating mold marks on pressed wares. Two patents related to eliminating mold marks were issued on September 25, 1847—one for a fluted goblet mold, the other for a lamp body. He continued patenting molds without joints or placing the joints in inconspicuous places. The New England Glass Company made a lot of money from these patents, even though issued in Magoun's name. In the late 1860s he sued it for part of the earnings resulting from his patents. He was unsuccessful, and he left it shortly thereafter.

mahlstick A short piece of wooden dowel with a soft rubber tip on the end. With the rubber tip placed on the glass, an artist rests his arm on the dowel while painting.

Mahon & Wilson See *Becker & Wilson.*

Maigelein (German) A small, shallow hemispherical cup evolving from the palm cup, resting on a base with a high kick; later ones have lower kicks. Some are plain; others have vertical or spiraling ribs running in opposite directions forming a network pattern of thick or fine ribbing. They were mold blown, blowing molten glass into a ribbed mold and twisting it. For network patterns, glass was blown into a second mold and twisted again, only in the opposite direction. They were made of Waldglas during the 15th and 16th centuries.

maize glassware Glassware developed by Joseph Locke (patented in 1889), made by the New England Glass Co. When it became the Libbey Glass Co., the company continued making maize glassware. The body is of opaque white or cream-colored glass with an overall molded pattern of vertical rows of kernels of maize (sweet corn), further embellished with some wavy tips of husks in green or brown (at times red or blue) rising from the bottom. It was reproduced in the 1960s by L.G. Wright.

Majestic Cut Glass Company (1900-1916) A glass cutting company established by Wolf M. Spiegel and his son, Saul S., in Elmira, New York, moving to Corning, New York, in 1908. It obtained its blanks from Belgium and Pairpoint Corp. Its trademark was the letter "M"; signed pieces are rare.

maker The glassworker or technician who finishes off a piece of glass.

making mark An indentation around a paperweight where the halves of the mold come together.

Malachite perfume bottle, 6-1/2" h., probably Czechoslovakian. Davanna Collection

Malachite An art glass with strata-like layers in shades of green, having the appearance of the mineral (in its natural form). Some pieces are acid etched and signed "Moser/Carlsbad" on the base. Reproductions with paper labels are being made in Czechoslovakia.

Malaga Glass & Manufacturing Company See *Franklin Glass Works; Malaga Glass Works.*

Malaga Glass Works A bottle glass manufacturing facility established by Christian L. Stanger in 1810, in Malaga, New Jersey. It was bought in 1820 by Daniel H. Miller and renamed the Franklin Glass Works. In 1829 he sold it to John G. Rosenbaum, taking the Whitney brothers as partners in 1830, but they left a short time later. In 1857 Rosenbaum offered it for sale; with no takers, he kept it operating. When he died in 1859, it closed. In 1860 it was leased by Whitney Brothers & Warrick. In 1861 Rosenbaum's heirs rebuilt it, making window glass. In 1873 it was incorporated as the Malaga Glass & Manufacturing Company and was still in operation in 1883.

malfin glass Coarse, impure glass caused by the improper or incomplete mixing of raw materials during the melting process. As a result there are bubbles and imperfections in the glass, which tends to become porous quickly.

mallet decanter A cylindrical or hexagonal shaped decanter having the appearance of a stone mason's mallet with nearly vertical sides and a shouldered body. They were made of English glass from about 1740 to 1780.

mallet flask A flask in the shape of a stone mason's mallet, usually with a hexagonal body and long, thin vertical neck. The earliest specimens were found at Pompeii.

Mallory Glass House A glass manufacturing facility established in Mallorytown, Ontario, Canada, by Nathan(iel) Mallory in 1825 or 1839. The facility made free blown containers and whimsies of poor quality.

Maltese cross bottle A bottle of square or hexagonal cross section with sides embellished in relief. On occasion, a Maltese cross was placed above a relief column or altar on one side. They and similar ones with Christian or Jewish symbols were thought to have been made in Syria in the 4th and 5th centuries; now it is believed they were made in Jerusalem in the 6th and 7th centuries. See *Christian glassware.*

Mamburg Glass Company A short-lived glass manufacturing facility operating in Fostoria, Ohio, during the late 1880s.

manchon In cylinder glass manufacturing, a blown glass paraison with the ends opened, forming a cylinder that is reheated, slit lengthwise, opened into a flat sheet, and cut into window panes.

mandarin glass See *Peking glass.*

Mandarin Yellow An art glass developed about 1916 by Frederick Carder at Steuben; a translucent ware colored a monochrome yellow, inspired by the yellow Chinese porcelain from the Ming Dynasty (1368-1644). It was fragile due to inherent internal stresses produced during its making, so only a small quantity was made. Less than a dozen pieces have survived, nearly all cracked due to internal stresses, or broken and repaired. Other hues of yellow used by Carder for translucent glass included amber and topaz.

maneretta A tool used to manipulate molten glass, creating a pattern of waves, festoons, feathers, and fans.

manganese The term refers to manganese compounds used in making glass. In its lower state of oxidation, it is colorless and is a strong oxidizing agent used to make colorless glass. It counteracts the greenish or brownish color imparted by traces of iron in the silica, oxidizing the iron and functioning as a chromatic (color) neutralizer. In its higher state of oxidation, as the oxide *pyrolusite*, it acts as a coloring agent, producing colors ranging from pale rose red to pink to amethyst or purple hues (caused by trivalent manganese). In its divalent state, which cannot be totally eliminated, it imparts weak yellow or brown colors, responsible for the green or orange fluorescence of manganese glasses. When used as a decolorizer, it is called *glassmaker's soap.*

Manheim Glasshouse Henry William Stiegel began constructing a glass manufacturing facility in October 1764 in Manheim, Pennsylvania. The first glass was blown on October 29, 1765. His second and larger facility was completed in 1769. Both failed and, in the fall of 1774, he was placed in debtors' prison and the facilities sold. His first glasshouse made mainly bottles, hollowware, and some tableware; his second made clear and colored glass and enameled, engraved, and pattern molded tableware. See *Stiegel, Henry William.*

mano sul seno, la (Italian): Literally, *hand on breast.* An ornamental object in such a form, designed and executed by Alfredo Barbini in 1948 for the Cenedese Glassworks in Murano.

Mansell, Sir Robert (1573-1656) An English admiral who, after retiring from the Royal Navy, acquired an interest in glass manufacturing in 1615. In 1615 the use of wood as a fuel for furnaces and kilns at glasshouses was prohibited by royal proclamation and he foresaw the potential of coal. He and his partners built a new facility in 1617. In 1618 he bought them out and, in 1623, was granted a monopoly to make all types of glassware using coal as fuel. He held this monopoly, against numerous attacks, until 1642. He hired clay workers to work on replacements for normal kettles unable to withstand the heat generated by the coal, reshaping them to minimize contamination from fallout of coal ash. He made flat glass for mirrors, and spectacles, bottles, lenses, etc. He procured facilities throughout England and Wales and, eventually, Scotland. He even attempted to establish one in Ireland. During the Civil War in 1642, he lost his monopoly; the glass industry in England was disrupted for 20 years.

Alladin lamp, parchment shade, custard glass base, 24" h. Tri-State Antiques

Mantle Lamp Company (of America)

Founded in 1908 in Chicago, Illinois, it began making *Aladdin* lamps in 1909. In 1926 it acquired the Lippincott Glass Company of Alexandria, Indiana, and in 1929 became Aladdin Industries Inc. In 1932 it began making electric lamps.

mantle luster Glass vases with cut glass prisms attached to them, popular in the 19th century and made in a variety of different glasses.

mantle mirror A *chimney (looking) glass.* See *chimney (looking) glass.*

Mantua Glass Company See *Mantua Glassworks.*

Mantua Glassworks

(1822-1829) A bottle glass manufacturing facility established in Mantua Township, Ohio, by David Ladd and Jonathan Tinker (a glassblower from the Mount Vernon Glass Works) in a tannery owned by Ladd's father, Daniel. In 1823 it was sold to the Mantua Glass Company established by Joseph and William Skinner. It made bottles and standard and flint glassware. It

changed ownership several times before closing. A short time after selling it, both Ladd and Tinker each established a facility nearby to make bottle and cylinder glass; both were short-lived. See *Kent Glass Works.*

manufacturer's representative A company employee who sold its wares on a commission basis.

Manwarren, Floyd "Jack" He began his glass cutting career in 1912 at the Ideal Cut Glass Co., Canastota, New York. After World War I he worked for the Robertson Cut Glass Co. for four months, moving to Tuthill, then T.B. Clark, and back to Ideal as a foreman in 1921, working there until it closed in 1933. He then went to Steuben. From 1939 to 1945, he and his wife operated a cutting shop in Beaver Dams, New York, cutting mostly for Hunt Glass and N.O. Phelps Co. During World War II, he worked for Corning Glass Works, and after the war he moved to Newark, New York, to cut for the Phelps Co. He then returned to Corning to work for Hawkes, again opening his own shop and cutting for Hunt. In 1957 he became Hunt's manager. In 1960, after a heart attack, he worked only at his shop. In 1962 he was called to Hawkes and requested to move to Tiffin Glass as a cutting instructor. His son, David, was also a cutter.

Manwarren, David The son of Floyd Manwarren, who taught him the art of cutting glass, beginning about 1940. He was also an expert repairman. He also cut for Vesta Glass and Erlacher Glass. His shop in Corning began operation in 1946.

Maple City Glass Company

A glass company specializing in cut glass established in 1901 by John S. O'Conner. It published ten illustrated catalogs. Very few of its pieces were signed. It was taken over in 1904 by T.B. Clark. See *O'Conner, J.S.*

Maple Leaf Burmese

A Fenton Burmese glass with a maple leaf decal.

maquette A three-dimensional rendering of a work to be made.

marble (1) A marver. (2) A small handmade ball in opaque white or black used by fraternal organizations for voting on potential members. Each voter secretly took a marble from one side of the ballot box, placing it in the other side, which was hidden from the voters' view until opened before the entire voting body. A white marble indicated a favorable vote; a black indicated a negative vote, hence the term *blackballed*. (3) A small ball (average size between 1/2 to one inch) made of glass or other material. Today they are made industrially of colorless glass for further processing into glass fibers or embellished with colored twists; or of plain or embellished colored glass. Both types are used for playing "marbles." The process for making marbles, used since the early 16th century, is to break a solid glass rod into short sections, placing them in a mixture of sand and charcoal that, in turn, is placed in an iron vessel, constantly heated and rotated. This softens the edges of the pieces, wearing them away, making perfect spheres that are further smoothed and polished. While made since the 16th century, the game did not become popular until the mid-1800s.

Following are the various types of marbles

(a) *agates*—stone marbles in a variety of colors, generally having bands of color alternating with white; most are translucent.

(a) *ballot box*— handmade marbles often with pontils, usually opaque white or black; see *(2)* above.

(a) *bloodstone*—green chalcedony with red spots, a type of quartz.

(a) *China*—not made in China, most made in Germany, with or without glaze, generally white with hand-painted designs. Five basic types are lines, bull's-eye, star, leaves and flowers, lines and bull's-eye. They measure 5/16 to 1-1/2 inches in diameter. They're also called *Chinese*.

(a) *clambroth*—opaque glass with evenly spaced outer swirls of one or more alternating colors.

(a) *clay*—one of the most common of the antique types, some hand painted, some plain.

(a) *comic strip*—a series of twelve machine-made marbles embellished with the faces of comic strip characters. Made by Peltier Glass Company of Illinois in the late 1920s, they have a white strip as a background for the line drawings of a cartoon character stamped on them using a special oil. The design was covered with powdered graphite, the excess removed. They were placed in a tray in an oven, and the graphite fused to the marble's surface.

(a) *Crockery*—sometimes called *Benningtons*; most are blue or brown, some are speckled. The clay is shaped into a sphere and coated with a glaze and fired. They range from 5/16 to 2 inches in diameter.

(a) *End-of-Day*—single pontil glass marbles made individually and usually quite large in size. The colored part often appears as a multi-colored blob or mushroom cloud. They are often called *cloud marbles* and are quite rare.

(a) *goldstone*—clear glass spheres filled with copper flakes that turn gold from the heat of the manufacturing process.

(a) *Indian swirls*—usually black glass with a colored swirl appearing near the surface; often irregularly shaped.

(a) *latticinio core swirls*—double pontil marble with an inner area having net-like swirls coming up around the centers.

(a) *Lutz type*—glass with colored or clear bands alternating with bands having copper flecks.

(a) *mib*—a fairly new marble of two or more colors.

(a) *micas*—double pontil marble, relatively small in size. It is made of clear or colored glass with mica flecks reflecting as silver dots when turned. Bright red and Irish green are rare.

(a) *modern*—machine made marbles dating from 1915.

(a) *onionskin*—a spiral type, solidly colored instead of having individual ribbons or threads. They are multicolored.

(a) *peppermint swirls*—made of white opaque glass with alternating blue and red outer swirls.

(a) *ribbon core swirls*—a double pontil marble with a center shaped like a ribbon with swirls coming up around the middle.

(a) *rose quartz*—a stone marble that is usually pink, frequently with fractures inside or on the outer surface.

(a) *solid core swirls*—double pontil marble; the middle is solid with swirls coming up around the core.

(a) *steelies*—hollow steel spheres with a cross where the steel was bent to form a ball.

(a) *stone*—most imported from Germany. They were made from various types of calcite. They were a relatively poor grade of marble. Some were made from agate, bloodstone, rose quartz, or onyx. They usually range from 5/16 to 1-1/2 inches in diameter.

(a) *sulfides*—often called *Queen of Marbles*, they are usually of clear glass with a figure inside. The rarest are those with colored figures inside, with more than one figure inside and of colored glass. The figures are either molded or carved from sulfide salts with a higher melting point than the surrounding glass. They generally have a silvery appearance caused by a layer of air between the figure and surrounding glass. Animal figures are most common, domestic animals more common than wild. The rarest are inanimate objects such as trains, watches, cannons, etc. The next rarest are religious figures and people. Sizes range from one to three inches in diameter. The most common range is 1-3/8 to 1-3/4 inches.

(a) *tiger eye*—stone marbles of golden quartz with inclusions of asbestos. They are dark brown with gold highlights.

(a) *vaseline*—machine-made marbles of yellowish-green glass with small bubbles within.

The various *swirl* types are sometimes called *spirals* or *threaded marbles*, ranging in size from 5/16 to 2-1/2 inches in diameter.

marble bottle Bottles having as a stopper an object that looks like a marble. They date from about 1875.

marble scissors A special tool in the form of a pair of scissors, used to cut a glass rod into "marble"-size pieces.

marble(d) glass (1) Glass embellished with haphazard streaking of two or more colors, resembling marble stone, made mainly in Venice from the 15th through the 17th centuries. See *agate glass; onyx glass; lithyalin glass; Calcedonio.* (2) (Aka *calico glass, mosaic glass, slag glass*) A pressed glass with a marble-like covering made in the 1880s and 1890s by melting opaque white and colored glass in the same pot, not letting the mixture become homogeneous. (3) An addled or opaque glass patented on April 25, 1892 by C.F.E. Grosse in England. It is usually worked on a blower's pipe, sprinkled with pulverized, colored glass, and finished in the usual fashion. It was made in the 1890s by various facilities in England, often in purple and white and white with brown, red, blue, or green. See *mosaic glass; purple slag.*

marbling A process that involves floating and stirring a small amount of bitumen on water and picking it up by placing a glass object against it. After it dries, the glass is subjected to hydrofluoric acid, etching the areas not covered by it.

marbrie paperweights A St. Louis overlay paperweight. It is hollow (blown) with an opaque white overlay embellished with trailed loops curving inward toward the center or outward from the center (the loops are of one or more colors—blue, red, and/or green) and a central motif of concentric canes. Some have a molded lizard resting on the crown. The term is derived from the French *mabre*, meaning *marble*.

marie See *collar base*.

Marie Jeanne See *wine bottle, sizes*.

Marion Glass Manufacturing Company
A glass cutting company established in 1917 in Marion, Ohio, which was still operating in 1960. Its early designs were floral while later ones were light cut. In later years it also made many other decorated products.

mark (1) An identifying mark used by glass manufacturing facilities, glassmakers, and decorators. Only used on a very small percentage of glass made, identification is typically done through analysis of the metal, the style of the piece, and its embellishment. Such marks have been used since ancient times. See the following types of marks: *factory; glassmakers; Chinese reign; Tiffany; registry*. (2) A line, indentation, or rough spot made and left on a piece of glass by a tool, implement, or mold used in making the piece. See the following types of marks: *mold; pad pontil; pontil; shear; seam; waffle pontil*.

Mark, Thomas See *Zanesville Glass Manufacturing Company*.

Marlborough (or Marlboro) Street Glass Works
See *Keene (Marlborough Street) Glass Works*.

marquetry An embellishing technique where fragments of hot glass are applied to molten glass and marvered into the surface, creating an inlaid effect. After cooling, the inlays may be further embellished by carving and engraving.

Marrett, T. A., Glass Factory

A short-lived glass manufacturing facility established in 1849 in New York City, New York.

marriage glass (Aka *betrothal glass*) A drinking glass made and embellished to commemorate a marriage. English ones made from the 16th century are often in goblet or flute form. Bohemian and German ones are often in Humpen or Stangenglas form, sometimes in pairs. Some French *verres de mariage* are embellished with traditional engraved inscriptions: the names and coats-of-arms of the couple. Some rare Venetian ones are in goblet form with enameling depicting biblical subjects and portrait heads of the betrothed or their coats-of-arms. See *wedding cup*.

Marriage Lamp (Aka *wedding lamp*) A double font oil lamp, the fonts branching from the base, which may be of any shape. Between these is a round concave bridge or web of glass, often used to hold matches. They were made in a variety of color combinations of opaque or semi-opaque glass. The base could be of one color, the connecting web another, and the fonts of yet another. It was patented by Daniel C. Ripley & Company on June 4, 1870.

Mars The trademark of the Kings County Rich Cut Glass Co.

Marshall & Stanger (Aka *Brooklyn Glass Works*) (1831 - 1846) John Marshall and Frederick Stanger established a green glass manufacturing facility in Old (or New) Brooklyn, New Jersey. See *Marshallville Glass Works; Brooklyn Glass Works*.

Marshall & Stille See *Marshallville Glass Works*.

Marshall, S.S., & Brother A company in Pittsburgh, Pennsylvania, operating in the 1870s, making stained glass windows.

Marshall, Stille & Company See *Marshallville Glass Works*.

Marshallville Glass Works
(Aka *Cumberland Works*) A glass manufacturing facility established by Randall Marshall and his son-in-law, Frederick Stanger, in 1814, in Marshallville, New Jersey. When the affairs of the Union Glass Co. of Port Elizabeth were settled in 1814, one of its facilities was moved to Marshallville. Marshallville Glass Works originally made hollowware and later only window glass. When Stanger's wife died, he

married the daughter of John Marshall, Randall's brother. In 1830 Stanger left to build a facility in Brooklyn, New Jersey, with John Marshall. At this time Randall took on a new partner, Samuel Stille. The firm became Marshall & Stille, then Marshall, Stille & Company. In 1863 it was incorporated as the Ocean Manufacturing Co. See *Marshall & Stanger; Brooklyn Glass Works.*

martele Literally, *hammered.* A decorative technique producing a multi-faceted surface. It was used often by the Daum Brothers and Galle as a background texture for their designs.

Martele (pronounced mar-te-lay) (French) A line of sculptured glassware designed by Reuben Haley (who also made the molds) and made by the Consolidated Lamp & Glass Company beginning in 1926. The molds were contracted to Phoenix Glass Company in 1933 by Kenneth Haley after his father, Reuben's, death and after Consolidated closed (1932). When it reopened in 1936, it demanded the return of the molds; they were returned in early 1937. Phoenix marketed the line under the name *Sculptured Artware, Reuben* (after Reuben Haley), or *Selden* (after Howard G. Selden, the New York representative for Phoenix). The molds were used in 1948 by the K.R. Haley Glassware Company. In 1970 Anchor Hocking acquired the Phoenix facility, and the *Sculptured Artware* line was made again in 1974. Erskine Glass & Manufacturing Company made wares using these same molds. When Consolidated closed, Sinclaire Glass, Hartford City, Indiana, bought some of the molds, making some wares. *Martele* is a semi-transparent ware with a hand-wrought appearance, often advertised as appearing like Lalique glass. It had several patterns used on various items, such as *La Fleur, Bird of Paradise*, and *Katydid* on vases, *Fish* on trays, *Iris* on candlesticks and jugs, etc. Other items included bonbon boxes, cigarette boxes, plates in various sizes, puff boxes, mayonnaise bowls in two shapes, footed tumblers, etc.

Martin, Lucien B. Beginning his career in the industry with Hobbs, Brockunier & Company as a salesman, he left in 1887,

establishing the Fostoria Glass Company. In 1901 he went to work for the National Glass Company as its sales manager, and when it was dissolved, he established the Hocking Glass Company. When that was sold, he established the Lancaster Glass Company. He died in 1923.

Martin & Baker (1831-1846) A bottle and window glass manufacturing facility in Cookstown, Pennsylvania. In 1837 the operating company was Martin & Church. See *New Boston Glass Works.*

Martin & Church See *Martin & Baker.*

marver A polished iron or marble table upon which molten glass, gathered on the end of a blow pipe or pontil, was rolled into a symmetrical mass. It was also used to embed trailings or other applied glass ornamentation into the surface of the object or as a pick-up surface for pieces of colored glass or a paperweight set up. The molten glass does not adhere to the marver since it is at a much lower temperature than when originally taken from the furnace.

Mary Gregory See *Gregory, Mary.*

Maryland Glass Corporation A glass manufacturing facility that made glassware during the Depression era. Its trademark was the letter "M" within a circle, impressed in the glass.

Maryland Glass Works A bottle and flask glass manufacturing facility established by John Lee Chapman in 1849 in Baltimore, Maryland, perhaps on the site of the former Baltimore Flint Glass Co., also erected by Chapman. It was still operating in 1864.

Maryland Window Glass Works A window glass manufacturing facility established about 1869 in Baltimore, Maryland, by Seim, Emory & Swindell. It was still operating in 1887.

mascaron A decorative motif in the form of a mask (i.e., lion's head mask), occasionally found on glassware made in Venice or elsewhere in the *facon de Venise.*

mascaroons See *blobs.*

Lalique "Tete de Coq" mascot. Clear and frosted glass; 7" h. Molded signature "Lalique France."
Davanna Collection

Fish mascot, Sabino type, 3-1/2" h. x 7" l.
Davanna Collection

mascot (Aka *hood ornament*) A decorative object placed on the hood (*bonnet*) of an automobile. It is usually an emblem or object identifying the car as to its make or model, but often for purely decorative purposes. Of particular note are those made by Lalique during the mid-1920s. These included birds or figures mounted on a base or raised above a light, some fitted with colored filters that revolved.

masello, a (Italian) A technique developed by Alfredo Barbini, involving sculpting or fashioning a block of molten glass without molding or blowing. See *sculptured glassware.*

mask A representation of a face as a decorative ornament. They are often grotesque, depicting human beings, satyrs, and animals and occur in two basic forms: (a) three-dimensional objects used as ornamental ware, and (b) in relief used as decorative ornament. The earliest known glass ones are of *pate-de-verre*, made in Egypt. In Roman times they were often found as ornamentation on the front of vases or the lower end of handles. They were sometimes used later as decorations on a prunt on some Venetian glassware. See *mascaron.*

Mason, J.L. See *Tansboro Glass House.*

Mason jar A jar with an airtight screw-on top used for preserving foods (canning), first patented in 1857 by John L. Mason. It has become a generic term applied to all preserving jars and bottles, whether or not they have a screw-on top.

Masonic glassware Various glass objects decorated with Masonic emblems, insignia, and inscriptions. In the United States, many flasks were decorated with Masonic devices and emblems. Most were made between 1893 and 1917.

Massachusetts Glass Company (1) A glass manufacturing facility established about 1858 in Charlestown (Boston), Massachusetts, making green, black, and amber glassware, fruit jars, carboys, demijohns, druggists wares, and molded wares. It was still operating in 1869. (2) (Aka *Cheshire Glass Co.)* (1849-1855) A window glass manufacturing facility established in Cheshire, Massachusetts. It made several unsuccessful attempts to produce polished plate glass about 1852. In 1855 the equipment was moved to Lenox Furnace.

massicot See *litharge.*

Masson & Company See *Ottawa Glass Works.*

Mastadon Works A glass manufacturing facility established by Thomas A. Evans in 1855 in Pittsburgh, Pennsylvania, which made vials, bottles, and druggists' wares. Later it was sold to Wm. McCully & Co., which was still operating it in 1886.

master cutter (Aka *smoother*) The person at a cut glass facility who took the work of the rougher and refined it, creating a freehand design on the glass, normally designing the pattern.

master glass See *captain's glass.*

masterpiece See *Meisterstuck.*

Masterworks Series

A series initiated in 1966 by Steuben, consisting of one-of-a-kind pieces that combined crystal with precious metals. On average, each piece requires two to three years of planning and execution.

mastos *(Greek)* Literally, *breast*. A hemispherical drinking cup in the form of a woman's breast which, because of its shape, can be rested only on its rim.

mat A glass surface having a dull finish, not glossy, made using one of several methods such as treatment with hydrofluoric acid, shallow engraving, sandblasting, etc. It has been spelled *matt* or *matte*.

mat engraving See *Mattschnitt*.

matagama bead A bead found only in Japan, presumed to be made there from the 3rd to 6th centuries. Shaped like a comma, it was probably used for necklaces.

Amethyst cut-glass match holder and ashtray.
Tri-State Antiques

Pressed glass match safe, 1-3/4" h.
Davanna Collection

match holder Before the invention of the safety match in 1853, matches had wooden stems and were kept in *matchboxes* or pocket size *match safes* because they ignited easily. Both are included in the term *match holders,* which were made in many shapes and forms.

The most common glass ones were cylindrical shaped. They are similar to toothpick holders and were made by numerous facilities through the 1920s.

match safe See *match holder.*

Mather Glass House A glass manufacturing facility established in 1805 (or 1808, depending on the source) by John Mather in East Hartford, Connecticut, making glass bottles and figured pocket bottles. It closed in the 1820s.

matrass A glass vessel used in an apothecary shop.

matrix An intaglio engraved seal with a handle, located on a ring or other contrivance, for impressing on wax. It was normally used for sealing official documents and letters.

Matsu-no-ke A style of embellishment developed by Frederick Carder at Stevens & Williams Ltd. in the 1880s (patented in 1884) and used by him from 1922 at Steuben. It depicts gnarled branches of an ornamental pine tree (*matzu* in Japanese) on which are applied rosettes or daisy-like flowers. It was used on clear crystal, applied to the interior of some ornamental objects with handles of transparent colors, or as an iridescent surface decoration. Often the registry number "15353" is engraved or etched on its body.

matt(e) See *mat.*

Mattschnitt *(German)* Literally, *mat engraving*. Wheel engraved embellishment in intaglio (Tiefschnitt), not polished; having a mat finish, in whole or in part.

Maul, Hebrew & Co. See *Bridgeton Glass Works; Bodine, Joel, & Sons.*

May, Charles The operator of a glass cutting shop in Corning, New York, from 1924 to 1926.

Mayer, Edward W., Glass Cutters

About 1910, Michael Mayer established a glass cutting shop in Port Jervis, New York (next to the Gillinder Brothers' facility), having previously operated a shop in Brooklyn, New York. His son, Edward W. Mayer, took over when his father died and renamed it Edward W. Mayer, Glass Cutters. In 1933

Edward died, and Gillinder Brothers operated it for his widow until 1935 when they bought it, moving the equipment to their facility.

Mayer, Michael See *Mayer, Edward W., Glass Cutters.*

Cut-glass mayonnaise with matching underplate.
Davanna Collection

Base detailing of mayonnaise (right) and underplate (left).
Davanna Collection

mayonnaise set A set consisting of a bowl, underplate, and sometimes a matching spoon for serving mayonnaise. The bowl is similar to a finger bowl in size.

Mays Landing Cut Glass Company A short-lived glass cutting shop in Mays Landing, New Jersey, operating in the late 1910s.

Maysville Glass Manufacturing Co. (1813-1816) A glass manufacturing facility established in Maysville, Kentucky, by Major Isaac Craig, making flasks, window glass, hollowware, druggist supplies, and chemical apparatus.

Maywood Cut A trademark used on glass cut by the Paul Richter Company, Maywood, Illinois.

mazarin See *mazer (bowl).*

mazer (bowl) (Aka *maeser* and *mazarin*). A drinking bowl or large goblet without a footed base. Originally applied to those of wood, it is now applied to those made of any substance.

mead glass An English drinking glass used for drinking mead (a fermented beverage, popular in the 17th and 18th centuries and later, made of honey and water, with yeast and sometimes sherry or other flavoring). They have a shallow spherical bowl with a slightly inverted rim, set on a stemmed foot. The stem is baluster type on early examples; on later ones it is the air twist variety. Another type of mead glass was shaped like a tumbler with a kick base.

meader See *medder.*

meander pattern See *key fret.*

Measuring bottle or jug, 4-cup capacity, 7" h. Fired-on lettering with "Made in the USA" on base.
Heartland Discoveries

measuring bottle A bottle having a specific capacity, originally for measuring oil or wine.

measuring cup See *measuring glass.*

Vaseline measuring glass with lid. One-cup capacity marked in 1/4-cup increments. Lid measures teaspoon, dessert, and tablespoon.
Davanna Collection

measuring glass A graduated glass for measuring liquids, found in a variety of shapes and sizes but usually in tumbler or conical form. Some have a stemmed foot and pouring lip.

measuring spoon A spoon marked with graduations for holding a specified quantity, used to measure medicine (see *medical spoon*) and other liquids. Some older ones have a short, curved handle so the spoon rests in a level position to free the hands for pouring. Those holding a specific quantity often are in nested sets, each sized for a specific measurement.

mechanical or mechanized lamp See *Carcel lamp.*

Medaillonbecher (German) Literally, *medallion beaker.* A Bohemian cylindrical drinking glass embellished in a style related to *Zwischengoldglas* and ancient Roman *fondi d'oro.* The technique was developed in Bohemia and perfected by Johann Joseph Mildner in the 1780s. Signed ones exist from 1787 to 1808.

Mildner made a double-walled beaker of colorless or opaque white glass, then cut a circular recess into the outer wall and inserted, flush with the surface, a medallion. These medallions were embellished on the reverse with engraved gold or silver leaf or red lacquer, depicting a figure of a saint, monogram, portrait, scenic view, or still life. Often parchment was decorated and enclosed in the glass recess. Mildner frequently signed the reverse of the medallion, often adding the name of the sitter of the portrait and date. He sometimes added a motto, verse, or dedication on the other side of the glass and another medallion in the base. See *eglomise; gold engraving.*

medal paperweight A paperweight having as its central motif a replica of a medal, made of thick gold leaf appearing to dangle from enameled ribbons. They were made mainly by Baccarat.

medallion (1) A thin flat tablet, usually circular or oval, bearing a portrait, design, or inscription that is wheel engraved, painted, of gold leaf, or in relief, mainly for personal wear or display. They should be distinguished from a plaque used primarily for wall or furniture decoration. See *sulfide; tassie medallion; phalera; Medaillonbecher.* (2) A glass object used since Roman times as a form of certification by being stamped as a weight for measuring money or goods, or applied to a vessel as a guarantee of capacity. They were used as bottle seals from the 17th through the 19th centuries.

medallion beaker See *Medaillonbecher.*

medallion window A decorative window normally of leaded glass, in the center of which is a circular panel painted with a scene, figure, or symbol.

medder Also spelled *meader* or *mether.* A cup similar to a loving cup, used for drinking mead.

Medford Glass House A glass manufacturing facility established in the early 1840s by William Porter in Medford, New Jersey. It became a farmers cooperative that made window glass. It passed through many ownerships. In 1860 it was known as Cockran's Glass Factory, making tableware. Yarnell & Samuels bought it in 1863, spending so much money on improvements there was none for operating the facility. By 1873 Yarnell & Trimble was the owner. The property and building were sold in November 1887.

Medford Glass Works (Aka *Star Glass Works*) (1894-1923) A bottle glass manufacturing facility operating in Medford, New Jersey. It had several owners over the years, the last owner being John B. Mingin.

Medford Window Glass Factory A window glass manufacturing facility in operation prior to 1836 in Medford, New Jersey.

medical glassware Various objects used by infants and sick people, or for formulating, holding, or dispensing medicines in pharmacies and hospitals. See *pharmacy glassware; albarello; feeding bottle; feeding cup; drug jar; measuring glass; measuring spoon; medical spoon; medicine bottle.*

medical spoon A spoon with a loop handle that bends back under the bowl and serves as a foot, so the spoon rests horizontally, leaving the user's hands free to pour medicines. See *measuring spoon.*

medicine bottle A small bottle used by an apothecary to hold and dispense medicines.

medium relief Relief embellishment raised above the surface, between high and low relief. The French term is *demi-relief*; the Italian *mezzo relievo*. The German term *Hochschnitt* incorporates all wheel engraved relief work.

Meisterstuck (German) Literally, *masterpiece*. A footed pilgrim flask embellished with snake trailing, made in Cologne during the 3rd or 4th century A.D. They were so named because of the quality of their workmanship. Its flat sides were embellished with trailed leaf motifs with gilt and garlands in multicolored glass; the edges and handles featured pincered cresting. Other pilgrim flasks of similar form but with somewhat different embellishments are sometimes called *Meister stuck*, being the designation of a category.

mele A cup or bowl.

mell A warming pan.

Melling, Estep & Company See *Pittsburgh Union Glass Company*

melon knop A knop with several raised segments, similar to those found on some melons.

melt The fluid glass made by melting a batch of raw materials.

melting of glass The temperature at which the raw materials fuse to make glass is normally between 1300 to 1500°C. Achieving such high temperatures was a challenge for the pre-19th century glassmaker whose major source of fuel was wood and occasionally coal. Most older glass is softer than that made today because of a higher portion of alkali, which resulted in a lower melting temperature and resistance to atmospheric attack, often causing it to be covered with a white film or a flaking surface, symptomatic of glass sickness. Heat regeneration and recuperation permitted higher temperatures, and today all furnaces operate using one or two heat recovery systems. Solid fuels have been replaced by fuels such as gas, oil, or electricity. See *pot melting; tank melting; pot furnace; tank furnace; glass, manufacturing, melting.*

melting pot A large clay pot, open topped or hooded, into which the raw materials of the batch are placed and melted.

membrano, vetro (Italian) An ornamental glassware developed by Venini about 1970. The object, usually a large bowl or vase, is divided internally part way into two or four sections by a thin glass partition.

memento mori (Italian) Literally, *remember you must die*. A motif that is a reminder of mortality, i.e., a death's head, or a specific shape, such as a coffin.

Menagerie Set A functional set of items for the dinner table in the shape of various animals made by Bryce, Higbee & Company, including a *Bear Sugar, Bear Horseradish (Mustard), Fish Spooner, Owl Cream Pitcher* and *Turtle Butter Dish.*

menu card holder A small decorative object with a slot for holding a menu or place card.

Meramac Company See *St. Louis Glass & Queensware Company.*

Mercer (Cut) Glass Company (1915-1920) A glass cutting company in Trenton, New Jersey.

Merchant's Cut Glass Company A glass cutting company established prior to 1896 in Philadelphia, Pennsylvania, by a man named Merchant and his two sons, Samuel J. and Jubal J. Merchant. In August 1896 it moved to Woodbury, New Jersey, supplying the John Wanamaker store in Philadelphia with fine cut and engraved glassware before closing prior to 1918.

mercuric gilding Applying gold to the outer surface of glass so it is affixed with a degree of permanency (as compared with unfired gilding). This is accomplished by painting a design on glass with an amalgam of gold and mercury and firing at a low temperature, causing the mercury to vaporize and leaving the gold, which can be burnished to brightness. Mercuric gold has a thin, metallic, brassy appearance, different from the dull rich color of honey gilding, and is cheaper and easier to apply and fix.

mercury band A thin air thread with a silvery appearance surrounding some paperweights near the rim and usually on both sides of a torsade (an ornamental twist). They are usually found on mushroom paperweights made by Baccarat or St. Louis.

Mercury bottle or flask A square, mold blown, colored glass bottle with a high thin neck and flat disk-shaped mouth. The bottom of some have a depiction of the Roman god Mercury in relief. Some also bear the mark or initials of the glassmaker and symbols or initials indicating the contents. They were made between the 1st and the 3rd century A.D. in Gaul and the Rhineland.

Mercury glass vase with white enameling, 5-1/2" h. Davanna Collection

mercury glass (Aka *silvered glass*) A double-walled glass vessel having the appearance of silver. To make it, silver nitrate was put between the walls through a small hole in one of the walls and later sealed. With time, air often seeped in and the "mercury" tended to flake off. It was first made in the 1850s. In the 1880s large quantities were produced in England and the United States by such companies as the New England Glass Company, Boston & Sandwich, and Mt. Washington. Items such as door knobs, tableware, vases, and ornaments were made. It lost favor in the 1890s, becoming popular again about 1910. See *silvered glass*.

mercury mosaic windows A "stained glass" window developed in the United States during the 1880s. To make them, hun-

dreds of small pieces of colored glass (*tesserae*) were mounted in a bed of solid metal with non-uniform amounts between each piece. It was less labor intensive than making stained glass windows.

mercury twist An air twist of clear, high lead content glass affording extra brilliance by using two flat pins to pierce the top of a glass rod so, when drawn out, it gave the appearance of a corkscrew being filled with mercury. The corkscrews are sometimes tight and almost round in cross section. However, the true mercury twist is less tightly wound and more open. Sometimes one or more corkscrews are alternated with each other, encircling an inner twist. See *corkscrew twist; air twist stem.*

merese A flattened ring or collar (button of glass), usually with a sharp edge, placed between the stem and bowl, stem and foot, or different parts of the stem. It is used mainly on wine glasses, goblets, etc., found along the stem in several pairs or sometimes in groups up to ten.

Meriden Cut Glass Company (1895-1923) A glass cutting company established by the Meriden Silver Plate Company (est. 1869) in Meriden, Connecticut. It initially purchased blanks from the Meriden Flint Glass Company, which closed in 1896, then from Mt. Washington/Pairpoint. Meriden Silver Plate Company joined with several others in 1898, forming the International Silver Company. It used paper labels to identify its products.

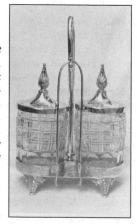

Meriden flint glass, double, pressed Block and Star patterned insert, Viking feet, c. 1884. Krause Publications

Meriden Flint Glass Company

(1874-1896) A glass manufacturing facility established in West Meriden, Connecticut, which made flint glass, opal wares, tableware, rich cut glass, and blanks sold to various glass cutting shops.

mermaid bottle A glass flask shaped and embellished in the form of a sea horse or mermaid. Many were made during the 18th and 19th centuries.

Merovingian glassware See *Frankish glassware.*

Merrow & Bidwell See *Hartford Glass Manufactory.*

Merry-Go-Round, The A covered bowl, ten inches in diameter, resting on scrolls on a heavy base, with an engraved merry-go-round around its exterior. It was designed in 1947 by Sidney Waugh, engraved by Joseph Libisch at Steuben, and presented by President and Mrs. Harry S. Truman to Queen Elizabeth II (then Princess Elizabeth) at the time of her marriage to Prince Phillip in November 1947.

Amber Merry Widow bowl with gold border, 15" d.
Davanna Collection

Merry Widow bowl A bowl normally used as a centerpiece, its height about one half of the overall diameter and its lip extending outward and downward almost to the base.

merrythought decoration A style of embellishment where trailed glass is formed in the shape of a merrythought or wishbone.

Mesopotamian glassware Glass made in the region northeast of Syria and west of Persia, between the Tigris and Euphrates Rivers. It is considered the birthplace of glassmaking because evidence indicates glass was made there before 2000 B.C. Fragments of vessels, most core-formed, discovered at sites near Nineveh are most likely of Mesopotamian origin made from 1525 to 1475 B.C. This was prior to the earliest vessels attributed to Egypt, believed to have been made about 1470 B.C. It is alleged that glassmaking continued there until about 1150 B.C. and was revived during the 9th century B.C. under the influence of Phoenician traders. It again declined in the 4th century B.C. and was not revived until several centuries later. Mosaic glass was made in Mesopotamia beginning in the 15th century B.C. See *pre-Roman history glass.*

messa forma Literally, *half molding.* (Aka *messa stampatura*) A technique for making ribs on the lower portion of a blown glass vessel.

messa stampatura See *messa forma.*

Messina Cut Glass & Decorating Company

Established by Thomas (son of Michael Messina) and Irene Messina in Elwood, New Jersey, this company did mainly light cutting and engraving. See *Zanes-Messina Glass Company.*

metal In glassmaking, the fused material, either in the molten or hard state. It produces glass having a variety of characteristics depending on the quality and proportions of the ingredients making up the batch. It distinguishes the fused materials from the finished object. See *pot metal.*

Metal-encased salt and pepper shakers. Cobalt-blue glass inserts in sterling silver openwork frame.
Davanna Collection

metal-encased glassware A glass object encased within a metal covering, in whole or in part. The covering is often gold or silver, but other metals such as pewter, lead, brass, chrome, and copper have been used. Some such drinking vessels were made in the 6th century B.C.

A glass alabastron, dating from the 1st century B.C., was encased in silver with *repousse* (raised in relief by hammering on the reverse side) embellishment. The worn off silver reveals glass in the lower portion.

On August 18, 1884, Frist Heckert of Petersdorf, Germany, patented a process for encasing glassware in metals. Prior to this, the glass object was made and the metal fixture or mount was fashioned around it. In Heckert's method, open metalwork ornaments were formed by stamping, casting, pressing, or galvanic deposit, placed in a mold fitting tightly against its sides and a gather of glass was blown into it. After release from the mold, the *blow-over* was removed and the rim fire polished.

When ornaments consisting of separate pieces of metal, porcelain, glass, mosaic beads, precious stones, etc., were used, they were cemented, faces to the mold, to a material that would be destroyed by the hot glass, presenting the reverse surfaces of the ornaments to the glass blown into the mold. After the items were formed, it was a simple task to plate the base metal (copper, lead, brass, etc.) with gold or silver deposit.

On June 28, 1901, the Faulkner Bronze Company of England patented another process. It largely duplicated Heckert's method, but the glass was blown into a perforated metal shell with no mold; the molten glass projected through the openings in the shell. See *silver cased glassware.*

metal leaf Precious metals, primarily gold and silver, physically reduced to a very thin sheet. It is often used to decorate glassware.

Metal Products Company See *Haley, Reuben.*

metallic glass (1) Metal alloys having an amorphous atomic structure similar to silica glass, made by cooling the molten alloy very rapidly so that no crystalline structure is formed (glass has no crystalline structure). They are harder than their crystalline counterparts and resistant to corrosion. Those containing iron usually have ferromagnetic properties making them suitable for use as transformer coils. Also see *Metglas.* (2) See *agate glass.*

metallic oxide The oxide of a metal (a) used as a raw material in preparing the batch and as a pigment in imparting color to it, and (b) used in the making of enamel colors to embellish glass. Those used for surface embellishment were suspended in an oily medium so they could more easily be applied with a brush. The colors on the final product developed during firing and were not necessarily the color applied.

The oxides commonly used in making enamels are antimony, cobalt, copper, iron, and manganese; to a lesser extent are chromium, gold, nickel, tin, selenium, silver, titanium, and uranium. Tin oxide was used as an opacifying agent. The final color produced by a metal oxide depends on the nature of the glass, the purity of its ingredients, and the furnace conditions, mainly temperature and the existence of a reducing atmosphere.

metallized glass See *iridescent glass.*

Metallized Glass Aurora Glass Company of London's name for its spangled wares in which flakes of gold, silver, or mica are encased within the glass during its making, scattered throughout its body. It is not plated and items are usually heavier than similar ones made in the United States.

Metglas A registered trademark for an amorphous metal alloy used for transformer coils.

mether See *medder.*

Methuselah See *wine bottle, sizes.*

methylated spirit lighter A bottle having attached to its stopper an iron plunger, forked at the lower end to hold a wad of cotton wool soaked in methylated spirits in the bottle. The wad was touched to a flame using the plunger as a handle and used as a taper to light a cigar or a pipe. They were made in England between 1870 and 1890.

Metropolitan Cut Glass Company See *Metropolitan Glass Works.*

Metropolitan Glass Works (1912-1930) A glass manufacturing and cutting company with two facilities, one in Brooklyn and the other on Long Island, New York. About 1918 its name was changed to the Metropolitan Cut Glass Company. By 1927 it diversified, shifting its prime interest to pottery and changing its name to Metropolitan Pottery Company with locations on Long Island, New York, and in Meriden, Connecticut.

Metropolitan Pottery Company See *Metropolitan Glass Works.*

Mexican Ware See *Goofus glass.*

Meyers, S.F., Company A jewelry store with two locations in New York City, listed in the early 1900s as a cut glass maker. It probably did not make cut glass as it was a retailer of other companies' wares.

Meyr's Neffe In 1814 Josef Meyr took over the Adolfshutte Glassworks named after its first owner, Prince Adolf von Schwarzenberg, and established another at Eleanorenhain. These were inherited by his grandson, Johann, in 1831. In 1841, when Johann died, his nephews Wilhelm Kralik (1806-1877) and Josef Taschek (d.1862) united the facilities of Adolf, Eleonorenhain, and Kaltenbach (dating from 1798) as Meyr's Neffe. In 1854 it expanded, purchasing facilities in Ernstbrunn and Franzensthal, later adding those in Idathal and Louisenhutte.

After Taschek's death in 1862, Kralik gained sole control. In 1881, four years after Kralik's death, they were divided among his four sons. Sons Heinrich and Johann took over the Eleonorenhain and Ernstbrunn facilities, known as Wilhelm Kralik Sohn. The other sons, Karl and Hugo, took over the Adolf, Idathal, and Louisenhutte facilities, retaining the name Meyr's Neffe. The facilities at Kaltenbach and Franzenthal were sold. Meyr's Neffe supplied J. & L. Lobmeyr, using almost all the glass made by the Adolf facility, as well as running an engraving and decorating workshop, making copies of old Bohemian glass and enameled and gilt vases in Moorish style. In 1922 it was taken over by Ludwig Moser & Sohne and renamed the Karlsbad Crystal Works.

mezza forma or mezza stampatura See *messa forma.*

mica flecked decoration Embellishment on glassware using flakes of mica picked up from the marver on a hot gather of glass and covering them with a second gather, often colored, before it is worked into the desired form. The flakes vary in size and concentration. The silvery color usually associated with mica flecks changes, assuming tints of the color of the covering layer. Much was made by Carder at Steuben where he also made *Silverina* (see *Silverina*), which has the mica flecks combined with air trap embellishment. This *Silverina* is not to be confused with that made by Stevens & Williams.

Michcut The trademark of the Michigan Cut Glass Company.

Michigan Cut Glass Company (1906-1911) A glass cutting shop in Lansing, Michigan. Edgar J. Bush was managing it when it was dissolved; then he established the Bush Glass Company. Michigan Cut Glass Company made a fine line of heavy miter cut glassware using imported lead crystal blanks. Cheaper lime glass blanks used by others forced the company to close.

middle-boy The person who reheated a glass object at the glory hole when it became too cool and rigid to be worked by the gaffer. He reheated the object until it became plastic enough to be worked and returned it to the gaffer. To finish an object may require more than one reheating.

Midland Cut Glass Company See *Koch & Parsche.*

Mid-Western type glass Various glassware made by facilities within the Ohio, western Virginia, and Pennsylvania areas (Pittsburgh being the center) during the late 18th-early 19th centuries. Some wares had special features, i.e., the shape of sugar bowls, jam jars, honey jars, etc., generally allow for the continual presence of a spoon by having a small opening in the edge of the lid where it rests on the container. Embellishments such as ribbing, swirling, and various diamond motifs were achieved by forming the object in a pattern mold prior to final shaping and finishing. It was thin blown; other types of early glass were somewhat thicker. The principal colors were blue, purple, amethyst, and yellow-green (made primarily by Ohio facilities).

Midwest Pomona Glass The same as
Pomona Glass (blown), except it was a pressed ware (not blown) in which the mold marks can be seen. See *Pomona Glass*.

Milchglas See *milk glass; opaque white glass; lattimo*.

Milford Glass Works See *Pendleton Glass Works*.

milk-and-water glass A glass similar to opaque white glass except that it is semi-opaque, appearing white in reflected light. It was normally opacified by the inclusion of ashes from calcined bones in the batch. It must be distinguished from opaque white glass having its appearance because not enough opacifier was added during production or the process was not continued long enough to become truly opaque. It was made and traditionally embellished with enamel in Bohemia and Germany from the late 17th through the early 19th century, and in England during the early 19th century.

milk bottles Harvey Thatcher is considered the father of the glass milk bottle, even though A.V. Whiteman had a patent for one in 1880. By the early 1880s they began to appear in New York and New Jersey. Early ones often had bubbles in the glass, but in 1903 machine-made bottles were made without bubbles.

In 1933 the first decorated milk bottles appeared. Embossed bottles followed (pyro-glazing on silk screen colored labels). They were round until 1944 when the square bottle was introduced. The golden age of the glass milk bottle was from 1910 to 1950. The finest were made prior to the 1940s, before homogenized milk became popular, often with odd-shaped necks to contain the cream that separated as the milk sat in the bottle.

The leading makers include Lamb Glass Co. (Mt. Vernon, Ohio), Liberty Glass Co. (Sapulpa, Oklahoma), Owens-Illinois Glass Co. (Toledo, Ohio), and Thatcher Glass Co. (New York). They were made in the following sizes: gill (quarter pint); half pint; ten-ounce (one-third quart); pint; quart; half gallon; and gallon. Paper cartons first appeared in the early 1920s, then disappeared, made another appearance in 1939, but were not popular until after 1950. The plastic milk bottle arrived in the late 1950s, bringing the end of the glass bottle.

milk bowl A bowl in which milk was allowed to separate (the cream rose and was skimmed off), used prior to homogenization. They usually have a cylindrical body with a wide flaring folded rim.

Milk glass vases, Paneled Grape pattern, 10" h.
Davanna Collection

milk glass (Aka *opaque white glass*) First made in England in the 18th century as a low-cost imitation of porcelain or china. In the United States the earliest articles included lacy salts, cup plates, and similar items made in the 1840s by Boston & Sandwich and others. It reached its peak of popularity between 1870 and 1880.

Milk glass objects were made in numerous forms in a variety of patterns with pressed and/or hand painted motifs, including birds, flowers, and historical subjects. Covered animal dishes were popular, especially those with hens, ducks, cats, squirrels, etc., on the cover. Tableware patterns in sets are found less frequently in milk glass than in clear or colored glass. *Sawtooth* was the first pattern to be made in milk glass.

The major makers of milk glass were: Challinor, Taylor & Co., Richardson Hartley Co.,

Atterbury Glass Co. (known for its ducks), and McKee Bros. Many pieces were signed. Westmoreland Glass Company has made many reproductions (some signed "WG") of older milk glass articles. Many old milk glass pieces have a C-shaped rough spot on the foot, formed in the molding process. This spot is not found on the new pieces. Old milk glass is heavier, has less blue, and the texture is less oily.

milk jug A jug or pitcher about seven inches high used for serving milk. Made in a multitude of shapes and styles, it is usually larger than a cream jug but smaller than a water jug.

mill A large iron or steel wheel used by the rougher to put the first deep incisions in a glass blank when making a piece of cut glass.

mill glass A drinking glass having a bowl on the bottom of which is attached a small silver windmill; an empty glass rests on the rim. They include tall flutes and short glasses with rounded funnel bowls made in the low countries in the 16th and 17th centuries.

milled (Aka *milled ring*) Embellished with close-spaced parallel grooves similar to those on the edge of a coin, often found around the foot of some glasses and on some trailing and collars.

milled ring See *milled.*

millefiori *(Italian)* Literally, *thousand flowers.* Embellishing glass with slices of colored canes embedded in clear glass, often arranged in flower-like designs. It was used in Alexandria in the 1st century B.C. and later in Rome in the 1st century A.D. (see *madrepore*). However, it was not called *millefiori* until after its revival and modification in Venice in the 16th century.The Roman method (fusing, in a mold, slices within transparent or opaque glass) was similar to that used prior in making glass mosaic.

The Venetian process involved placing slices in a mold in a closely packed, predetermined pattern and embedding them in a clear molten glass matrix. Venice, or possibly Bohemia, was the first to use the process in making paperweights. The same process was used in the mid-19th century in France at Baccarat, Clichy, and St. Louis, in England at Whitefriars, and in the United States to make such weights.

Millefiori glass, while used mainly in paperweights, is also used in the heavy glass bases of some drinking glasses, vases, ink bottles, scent bottles, jugs, shot glasses, hand coolers, the bases and bowls of some Tazze, stoppers, and the shanks of seals (see *millefiori mosaic, millefiori paperweight; mushroom paperweight*). The making of the earliest millefiori articles was done in the following manner: Rods were sliced either obliquely or at right angles and the miniature cross sectional disks placed side by side in a terra-cotta mold. Subjected to heat, the disks fused together at the edges. The mass, usually quite thick, was drawn out by two workmen walking away from each other, forming a rod several feet long and no greater than one-quarter inch in diameter. After cooling and hardening some, it was sliced into thin pieces.

Later millefiori objects were made in the following way: A heated mold was lined with cross-section disks and a partially blown bulb of plastic glass was inserted and expanded, by further blowing, causing the little cross section disks to be embedded in the plastic metal, which could be handled as any other blown glass. In 1848-1850, Jacopo Franchini of Murano, Italy, made rods whose cross sections portrayed delicate miniatures of elegantly gowned ladies and gentlemen wearing elaborate uniforms with military sashes and medals. The millefiori technique was used by Frederick Carder from about 1909 until the mid-1920s at Steuben, not to make traditional multicolored scattered *thousand flower* patterns but to make a single flower pattern as embellishment on some Aurene vases and geometric designs on plates using regularly placed colored canes and random patterns on bowls using two or more basic colors. The style is still being used at Murano, and it is rather difficult to differentiate the old from the new pieces.

The glasses used in making millefiori glass must have the same coefficient of expansion, contracting and expanding as one with temperature changes. The technique depends on the physical property of ductility, which allows a gather of molten glass to be "drawn out" into a rod or cane. At the beginning of the rod drawing process, the worker took a gather of glass of the desired color. The size depended on the size of the rod to be formed, but normally averaged about six to eight inches long by two to three inches in diameter if rods of one-half inch or less were being made. The gather was made into the selected rod shape either by rolling on a marver if a round rod was desired or by molding to form a square, hexagon, or other cross-section. It was then reheated, if necessary, and a pontil iron attached to one end. One worker held this iron with its glass gather; the second worker, usually a boy, attached a pontil iron to the other end and walked or ran with it along wooden racks where it rested and cooled. Considerable skill was required by the runner; his speed and control determined the size and evenness of the emergent rod. An even pull was important or the rod would vary in thickness.

Mechanical processes introduced at Corning Glass Works and other facilities provide greater control of the size and quality of drawn rods and tubing. After the rods were drawn, they were cut in lengths of about six inches, arranged in a bundle to form the desired design, held together with iron wires and heated until fused into a mass. The iron wire was removed and the molten bundle "stuck up" on a pontil iron and marvered until smooth. Then the bundle was dipped in molten glass to enclose the fused rods in a layer of clear or colored glass; more layers of various colors of glass could be added at this point. Now the mass, design intact, was drawn into a new rod by repeating the process previously described.

The rod retained the same shape and design in miniature as in the original, and the sections of color remained in the same relative positions regardless of how far the molten piece was drawn. After the rod cooled, it was cut into sections or disks. The cold sections were then positioned in a shallow mold in a mosaic type design, along with sections cut from other millefiori or single color rods. The filled mold was heated until the sections fused together.

While the mass was still molten, it was polished by rubbing it with a wood polisher to remove unevenness and make it more uniform in thickness. A pontil iron was then fastened to the center so that the molten mass could be raised from the mold and again heated in the glory hole and shaped with a wooden paddle. Finally, excess fragments were sheared off and the mass fashioned into its permanent form. A ring of colored glass was frequently applied to the edge for embellishment and added strength.

A variation of the technique in which the millefiori object had a crystal glass inside casing was made by placing a previously blown ball of transparent glass, still molten, upon the mosaic pattern after being smoothed with a wooden polisher but before removing it from the mold. This ball was pushed down by the blowpipe until it enveloped the entire mosaic pattern, which was then taken from the mold on the ball, marvered down, and blown out, forming the desired shape.

millefiori mosaic A type of mosaic glass made with canes like those used in making millefiori glassware, except the canes were cut lengthwise or diagonally instead of crosswise. The appearance of the slices is of mingled stripes of various colors. Sometimes such mosaic glass is included under the broad definition of *millefiori*, but since it lacks the characteristic floral appearance of objects made with canes cut crosswise, many designate it as a special type of mosaic glass. It was made in Alexandria in the 1st century, later in Murano.

millefiori paperweight A paperweight embellished with slices, or set ups, of many canes, frequently in the form of a pattern. The canes within the weight are closely packed (close millefiori); scattered haphazardly with intervening clear filigrana glass (scattered millefiori); or arranged in rows or circles with fairly even intervals of clear glass (spaced millefiori). The canes are usually florets, but, on occasion, have a silhouette or shape in the form of a star, hexagon, geometric figure, arrowhead, or pie crust. Some are faceted; some covered by one or more overlays of glass with a window on top and more around the side.

milleocchi, vetro (Italian) Literally, *thousand eyes glass*. A glass developed in 1954 by Vinicio Vianello at the Fabbrica

Salir in Murano. The main feature is an incised embellishment of many adjacent small circles arranged in haphazard patterns. It is used for some tall conical vases.

Miller, Daniel K. See *Olive & Harmony Glassworks.*

Miller, Rowell & Co. See *Clyde Glass Works.*

Millersburg Art Glass Factory
See *Millersburg Glass Company.*

Millersburg Glass Company
(Aka *Millersburg Art Glass Factory*) A glass manufacturing company incorporated in 1909 in Marietta, Ohio, with John W. and Frank L. Fenton as two of its organizers. The facility was built in Millersburg, Ohio, and produced large amounts of Carnival glass. Many molds were made by the Hipkins Novelty Mold Company. Hipkins sued for payment for mold work, resulting in it going bankrupt and reorganizing as the Radium Glass Company in 1911. In 1913 it was sold to Frank D. Sinclair, who operated it as a branch of the Jefferson Glass Company.

Mills, Peter, & Co. (1816-1852) A bottle and flask glass manufacturing facility established in Zanesville, Ohio. In 1832 it was operated by Murdock & Casell. In 1849, after a series of owners, it was operated by Cochran & Brothers.

Mills, Gardner & Co. It leased and managed the operations of the Heinz Brothers cut glass facility in St. Charles, Illinois, from 1913 until it closed in 1915. The glass cutting operations were resumed a short time later by the Heinz Brothers.

Millville Art Glass Company
See *Wheaton Industries.*

Millville Glass & Manufacturing Company
A glass manufacturing facility established in 1871 in Millville, New Jersey.

Millville Glassworks A glass manufacturing facility established in Port Elizabeth, New Jersey, by James Lee and others about 1800. Another facility was established about 1806 by the same group at Millville. After numerous changes in ownership, the Millville facility was acquired by the Whitall brothers in 1844 and became known as Whitall Brothers & Co. in 1849. In 1857 it became Whitall, Tatum & Co. It was later acquired by the Armstrong Cork Co. Its principle products were window glass and glass insulators, and it also made paperweights from about 1863. See *Jersey rose; Millville paperweight.*

Millville paperweight A paperweight made first in 1863 by Whitall, Tatum & Co., named for its location in Millville, New Jersey. The best known is the pedestal type enclosing one of the following: (a) an upright rose motif, made from about 1905 to 1918 by Ralph Barber; (b) a lily motif made by Emil Stanger or Marcus Kuntz; and (c) a scenic motif made by Michael Kane.

Millville Rose (Aka *Barber Rose*) A paperweight in the form of an upright lifelike rose encased in a sphere of crystal, created by Ralph Barber at Whitall Tatum. Barber made the petals, Alex Quernes the leaves. The roses, made from 1905 to 1918, were sold to gift shops for $1.50 each. The petals, three per rose, were made with a special crimping iron Barber developed. All these weights were footed, having a collar between the foot and the sphere containing the rose. The rarest has a rosebud set on a baluster pedestal. The roses were pale pink, white, yellow, and deep ruby.

Millville Rose (modern) A miniature glass paperweight with a rose as the central motif in the style of Charles Kaziun and Francis Whittemore, created by John Allen Choko Jr. and Albert Morgan Lewis Jr., both employed by the Wheaton Glass Company. The best were made in the 1970s. They are not to be confused with the *Millville Rose.*

Milton Vase, The A cameo glass vase with a blue glass base overlaid with opaque white glass, of truncated conical shape having two scroll handles, and embellished with a carved scene of the avenging angel, Raphael, on one side and Adam and Eve on the other. These scenes were inspired by Milton's *Paradise Lost.* It was designed by Peter Pargeter and embellished by both Pargeter and John Northwood. Northwood engraved it, signing and dating it 1878. It was on loan to the British Museum from 1957 to 1975, then sold at

Sotheby's (Belgravia), London, for £26,000 (British). It is currently housed at the Chrysler Museum of Art in Norfolk, Virginia.

Milwaukee Glass Company A glass manufacturing facility operating in Milwaukee, Wisconsin, during the late 1800s-early 1900s, making glassware for home use.

Boyd miniature cars; left: iridescent blue Tucker, 3-3/4" l.; right: Corvette, Vaseline, 3-5/8" l.
Davanna Collection

miniature A representation of an object on a reduced scale. Numerous objects have been made as miniatures, including jugs, baskets, decanters, flasks, tea services, animal figures, plates of fruit, and many other small objects made *at-the-lamp*. Some were made as toys or salesmen's samples, e.g., tiny decanters, bowls, etc. See *toy; frigger; novelty; miniature paperweight*.

Cobalt cut-to-clear miniature lamp, 7" h.
Davanna Collection

miniature lamp Originally referred to as a *night lamp*, it has become a generic term for any kerosene lamp less than sixteen inches tall (including the chimney), made between about 1860 and 1900. Just about every glass manufacturing facility made them in pressed, blown, and/or blown-molded glass, in just about every color and price range. They are classified by (1) size: (a) small—up to six inches tall; (b) mid-size—six to nine inches; (c) junior—nine to thirteen inches; (d) mini-banquet—thirteen to sixteen inches; (2) composition: glass; metal; or a combination of both; (3) description: figural; stem; miniature student; etc.; (4) style: fairy; peg; finger; hand; etc.; or (5) burner type: Olmsted burner (patented in 1877 by Leverett H. Olmsted); American (Acorn, Nutmeg, Hornet and P. & A. Victor); Tom Thumb; or tin burner with reflector.

A stem lamp represents the truest form in miniature of a larger lamp. They have a flaring base, a stem, reservoir, font, and a clear glass chimney or matching shade. A hand lamp and finger lamp are two similar forms of miniature lamps that have a handle. They were designed to be carried from room to room; the kerosene reservoir was at the bottom, and the burner assembly and a shade or chimney was above it. The primary difference is that the handle on a finger lamp accommodates one finger while on a hand lamp the handle accommodates two or more fingers.

miniature paperweight A paperweight ranging in size from about 1-1/3 to two inches in diameter. They are generally similar in their patterns to the standard size. Many are of the millefiori style, and, on occasion, the crown type. Most were made at Clichy, some at Baccarat and St. Louis.

mini(ature) perfume bottles Small cut crystal dram bottles, copies of standard size boudoir perfume bottles, with ground stoppers and daubers, made in a variety of colors and measuring about 2-1/4 to four inches tall. They were made in Czechoslovakia about 1924 and retailed from fifty to seventy-five cents.

Minotola Glass Company
(Aka *George Jonas Glass Company*) A glass manufacturing facility established in the early 1890s by George Jonas near Vineland, New Jersey, which made bottles. After suffering two fires and a major violent strike, Jonas sold it to the Cumberland Glass Manufacturing Company, which changed its name to the Minotola Glass Company in 1903. Subsequently, the Illinois Glass Company bought both it and the Cumberland facility. The Illinois Glass Company merged with the Owens Glass Company, becoming Owens-Illinois. In March 1921 the Minotola Glass Company closed.

mirror Any reflecting surface; in particular, a looking glass with a metallic or amalgam backing used to reflect an image, made for decorative and functional purposes and in many forms and styles over the years. Some are attached to or hung framed on a wall, some for couches and some as hand mirrors (see *chimney glass; pier glass; cheval glass; sconce; Irish glassware*). Some are embellished on the surface or reverse of the glass (see *mirror decoration; mirror painting*). In ancient China and classical antiquity, mirrors were made of polished metal. In Egypt in the 1st century B.C., they were made of a silvered glass, polished metal, and lead-backed glass, lead metal being a reflecting surface.

For centuries, imperfections and distortions due to imperfect melting conditions and impurities in the glass made adequate reflection nearly impossible. Venetian glassmakers maintained they had perfected glass mirrors in 1507. The Dal Gallo brothers of Murano were granted approval to make glass mirrors by a "secret process." Soon mirrors of broad glass were made by Murano glassmakers (*specchiai*) who, by 1569, had their own guild. By the early 17th century many of these craftsmen were teaching the English mirror making.

From the 17th century, mirrors were in great demand throughout Europe for decorating cabinets and couches. Large mirrors were in high demand for wall decoration. In France, various companies were established to make glass solely for mirrors; many later merged into the present St. Gobain company. In England from 1621, Sir Robert Mansell made large quantities of hand and hanging mirrors. By 1663, the Duke of Buckingham was making mirrors. In France about 1687, the casting process for making glass was "discovered" and, in 1691, improved by the British Cast Plate Glass Co. During the early years mirrors were made by the cylinder glass process and the backs silvered with tin and/or mercury. However, about 1840, J. von Liebig, a German chemist, discovered a method of chemically depositing silver onto glass; shortly thereafter the Venetians used a deposit of silver and platinum.

In Spain, the Royal Factory at La Granja de San Ildefonso made large mirrors of exceptionally good quality during the last quarter of the 18th century. Those made during this period were mainly for palaces and wealthy homes. By the late 17th-early 18th century, England was making the finest mirrors at relatively low costs.

Most mirrors were square or *squarish* until the end of the 17th century. The demand for *over-the-mantel* mirrors of ever increasing size continued to grow. The pier glass (a tall narrow mirror placed between windows) came into existence at the beginning of the 18th century. The architectural style of mirrors dates back to about 1725, remaining in vogue until the straight line gave way to the curve in the 1740s. The circular convex mirror became fashionable in England about 1800. See *convex mirror; framed mirror; hand mirror; bull's-eye mirror; Irish glassware, mirror; dressing mirror; overmantel mirror; courting mirror; lead mirror; toilet mirror.*

During the art deco period, almost every room in a house was reflected in peach and smokey mirror panels. Today, mirrors with special decorative treatments are ever increasing in variety, exhibiting such treatments so they appear to be marbled, smoked, colored or plain, painted or even printed.

mirror decoration Embellishment usually on the surface of a mirror in a variety of styles and accomplished by a number of methods: painted, wheel engraved, gilt decoration, transfer printing, molded portrait, etc. See *mirror painting.*

mirror drop A drop having two facets on its back, cut at such an angle that no light is permitted to penetrate, being reflected back toward the viewer in the same manner as from a mirror.

Mirror Images An outlet in Lansing, Michigan, for traditional and other glass products, owned by O. J. Scherschlight and G. Sionakides. Using molds of defunct companies, it has had various manufacturers make limited editions. For example, in the early 1980s, the company, working with the Imperial Glass Company, had a series of animals pressed in cobalt blue glass (known as *Ultra Blue*) from original Heisey molds owned by Imperial at the time. The series was limited to 1,000 pieces/animals, most made in cobalt blue glass, mostly plain, some frosted. It also reissued a series of five animals made by Viking Glass from old New Martinsville molds, in ruby, satin ruby, and/or ruby carnival finishes and other items made by Viking using Cambridge molds.

mirror monogram A monogram executed in reverse so its reflection in a mirror makes it appear normal. They are found on wine glasses made during the 18th century.

mirror painting (Aka *back painting*) Painted embellishment on the reverse (opposite the side being viewed) of the glass of a mirror, most likely originating in England in the late 17th century. The silver was scraped off the back of the mirror where the painting was to go. Then it was painted in reverse—the details first and the background last—primarily in oils. See *panel; Chinese mirror painting.*

Miskey-Reynolds-Rothfus Company See *Figueroa Cut Glass Company.*

Missouri Glass Company (Aka *St. Louis Glass Works*) (1850-1911) A window glass manufacturing facility established in St. Louis, Missouri. In 1854, after a change in ownership, it became the Mound City Glass Works, and in 1857, the Missouri Glass Company. During the mid-1850s, it began making green glass for bottles and a high grade flint glass for blown glassware, and by 1860, cut and pressed tableware. In 1863 it was purchased by Cote, LaSalle & Company, which failed in 1866, reorganized, and remained viable as the Missouri Glass Company. See *Art Manufacturing Company.*

miter (cut) (Aka *miter split, miter corner*) A cut glass line motif, simply a deep V-shaped incision made with a V-shaped cutting stone, usually outlining and unifying the design. Early miters were straight, but with the advent of gas and electricity to power the cutting wheel, giving the cutter uniform wheel speed and more control, the curved miter became prominent. This innovation is credited to Dorflinger. The motif created when curved miters intersect to form a pointed oval is called a *vesica*. A miter may be used as both a major and a minor motif. A popular miter motif consisted of a double lozenge, an oblong diamond divided in the center with an "X." Others include the blaze or fringe, silver thread, fine line bands, horizontal step, fan, flashed fan, various stars, splits, ladders, lozenges, etc.

mixed twist A twist made by combining one or more air twists with one or more opaque white twists, or sometimes one or more opaque white threads. On occasion a colored twist is combined with an air twist (*colored mixed twist*).

mixer (Aka *founder*) The workman in the glass manufacturing facility responsible for mixing the batch and charging the pots.

mixing glass A glass such as a tumbler or goblet used for mixing ingredients for a particular drink. A characteristic feature is a pouring lip, though some recent examples do not have one.

mixing room See *batch room.*

mixture See *batch.*

mock china Opaque white glassware made in imitation of white porcelain imported from China, embellished in the same style and manner.

Model Flint Glass Company (1888-1902) A glass manufacturing facility established in Findlay, Ohio, that made pressed glass tableware in a variety of patterns. Because of shortages of natural gas during the latter part of 1892, it installed oil-fired furnaces, using natural gas in the lehrs. In 1893 it built a new facility, the Albany Glass Company, in Albany, Indiana, and equipment was moved from the Findlay facility for making pressed tableware in clear glass. In 1899 it became the nineteenth company to join the National Glass Company, making a variety of blown glass items.

modeling A technique first used by ancient Syrian glassworkers involving modeling an object, such as an animal, in glass.

Modern American Series The last handcrafted glassware made by Libbey Glass Co. in 1940.

Modern style glass A style of glassware begun about 1900 with a design based on baroque cut glass styles, stressing the architectural quality of glass shapes, their function, and optical properties of the base metal.

Modernistic A line of glassware introduced by Kopp Glass Inc., Swissvale, Pennsylvania, in 1928. It strongly resembled Consolidated's Ruba Rombic.

modiolus (Latin) A drinking cup in a cylindrical shape or with the sides sloping outward slightly toward the rim, with one small loop handle or a pair together, attached just below the rim. Some rest on a foot ring, some on small ball feet. Some were of Roman glass in the 1st century A.D.

Mogul glassware (Aka *Mughal glassware*) Glassware made in India from the 16th century, primarily under Persian influence with respect to style. See *Indian glassware*.

Mohammedan Blue (Aka *butterfly blue*) A Tiffany iridescent color produced on a deep cobalt blue body of glass.

Mohs' scale A scale devised by German mineralogist Fredrich Mohs (1773-1839) as a method for measuring the hardness (resistance to abrasion) of a mineral or other substance. It ranks a series of ten minerals based on hardness, as follows: talc (1); gypsum (2); calcite (3); fluorite (4); apatite (5); feldspar (6); quartz (7); topaz (8); sapphire (9); and diamond (10). The intervals between the listed minerals against which a specimen is rated are not equal. Glass is rated 5.5, making it slightly harder than steel but somewhat softer than rubies.

moil (Aka *overblow, blacks, black moil*) The unused waste glass left on a blowpipe or pontil after the paraison or the object being made is removed. After every making, it is knocked off into a collecting bin, eventually mixed with other broken glass to make cullet.

molar flask A glass flask having a square section, angled shoulder, and a wide vertical neck ending with a slightly everted mouth. The body is extended to form four vertical feet, resembling an extracted molar tooth, and embellished with cutting in a variety of geometric patterns. They were made in Persia, possibly Mesopotamia, and Egypt during the 9th and 10th centuries.

molasses can A syrup jug.

mold A form used in various processes of shaping glassware; mold blown and later mold pressed ware. Some were used to give the glass object its final form, others to give the object a patterning to be worked or modified by further blowing, sometimes almost eliminated. Many open-shaped pieces made before the development of glass blowing are believed to have been molded, some perhaps by the *cire perdue* process.

Originally molds were made from fired clay, then wood, carved stone, and later metal. They have been used from earliest times. The earliest molds were made in one part and, in more recent times, in two hinged parts, followed by three- and four-part molds used for the more complicated forms. Some parts of objects, such as handles and feet, were made in separate molds and later joined to the body of the piece. After about 1825, iron molds were the main type used for mold pressed glassware.

If a company introduced a line of glassware that became popular, other companies were quick to introduce similar lines from similar molds, made in-house or purchased from private mold makers. Some molds were patented. Some manufacturers employed mold designers who had worked for other companies, and they frequently made designs similar to those made for previous employers. If the pattern was unsuccessful, the molds were often sold to another company or renovated and reworked to create different patterns since the expense of renovation was less than the cost of making a new mold. If the pattern was popular, the mold would be worked to its physical limit and eventually the pattern details would become worn and smooth. At this point special maintenance retooling was required, and new pattern details could be instituted at that time or a base plate could be changed. See *sand molding; core forming; mold blown glass; mold pressed glass; dip mold; piece mold; blown three mold glass; full size piece mold; part size mold; paste mold; plate mold; spot mold; waste mold; crimp mold.*

mold blown glass Glassware made by blowing a molten glass paraison (bubble) into a mold. The interior wall of the mold is in the shape of the outer form of the mold blown object, so that the blown object could be reheated and further blown to enlarge its size. In the process of expanding, the pattern imprinted by the mold became diffused. The first mold blown glassware is believed to have been made about 25 A.D. in the Levant region—the area around the eastern Mediterranean Sea between Greece and Egypt. By the middle of the 1st century A.D., production of mold blown glass had spread to Cyprus, and by the third quarter of the 1st century A.D. it had spread to Italy. It was made in Egypt from the 2nd to the 4th centuries, and later universally.

In the United States, production of mold blown glass on a fairly large scale began near the end of the 19th century, becoming the prime method of making glassware, especially of free blown glass. The process was quickly adapted to machines for making bottles and electric light bulbs and was used extensively in the Midwest. It had low relief embellishment in imitation of English cut glass of the early 19th century. To a great extent the method was superceded in 1827 by the process of pressing, leading to mass-produced mold pressed glass. When used to imitate cut glass, the molds were full size, and additional blowing was not needed. The outlines were not as sharp as hand cut originals, but designs could be complex.

mold boy An unskilled laborer at a glass manufacturing facility who moves and opens or closes molds used by skilled laborers, such as blockers or blowers.

mold cast glass Glass items made by pouring molten glass into a shaped mold. It was used in Roman times to make panes for windows and continued to be used in limited applications until the process for making plate glass was developed.

mold chipper See *chipper.*

mold etched process In this process, patterns are "cut" into a mold by a progression of wax tranfers and acid baths, producing glassware that appears etched or incised but with a raised pattern with an etched surface. Most Depression glass is embellished by this process.

mold mark (Aka *seam mark*) Vertical, rarely horizontal, equidistant marks found on pieces of glassware pressed or blown in molds of two or more pieces. They result from molten glass getting into the seam where the pieces of the mold join. While it appears two sections fit together tightly, pressure from blowing or pressing separates them slightly, no matter how securely fastened. They are removed from better quality glassware by hand finishing or fire polishing. See *seam mark.*

mold pressed glass (1) Glass objects made by pressing a mold into glass (while plastic) poured on a flat surface, resulting in the objects having a flat back. (2) Glassware made by the process of pressing molten glass in a mold as distinguished from the process of blowing a paraison in a mold (mold blown glass). Originally made in the United States during the revived rococo period from about 1827 on in an attempt to copy elaborate cut glass, it was made by the Boston & Sandwich Glass Co. and rivals. Early American mold pressed glass sometimes shows mold marks since it was not normally hand finished.

molded glass Glassware made by blowing or pressing a mass of molten glass into a mold. The object derives its shape and pattern, in all or in part, from the mold. See *mold blown glass; mold pressed glass; blown three mold glass.*

molded jewel Pieces of colored glass molded in a variety of shapes, such as leaves, teardrops, and various geometric figures, used in the construction of stained glass articles and windows.

molded pedestal stem See *Silesian stem.*

molding See *font molding; sand molding; split molding.*

molten glass Glass in its melted state after (a) the ingredients have been fused at a high temperature until they become liquid (allowing gases to be driven off and impurities removed) and (b) allowing this liquid to cool until it is plastic and ductile. It is sticky and viscous, and adheres readily to an iron blow pipe and other glass objects previously heat softened.

Monair process A process for engraving linear two-dimensional works with lettering, calligraphy, monograms, etc. Unlike copper wheel engraving, which gives a rounded edge and subtle variations in depth, this produces a sharp precise edge and uniform depth. It was developed in 1949 by Corning and Eastman Kodak to ensure exact duplication of designers' two-dimensional drawings on glass, using an air-propelled abrasive.

Monarch Cut Glass Company
A glass cutting house established in 1901 by Herman and Frank Kotwitz and Richard, Emil, and Otto Heinz in Chicago, Illinois. The Heinz brothers worked for Pitkin & Brooks and the American Cut Glass Company. In 1902 the Heinz brothers bought out the Kotwitz brothers, renaming it Heinz Brothers. In 1905 operations were moved to St. Charles, Illinois, becoming one of the largest makers of cut glass in the Midwest with showrooms in St. Charles and Chicago, Illinois; Spokane, Washington; Helena, Montana; Memphis, Tennessee; San Francisco, California; Berlin, Germany; and St. Petersburg, Russia. C.E. Wheelock & Co. was the distributor for Heinz Brothers, and some articles carry Wheelock's trademark *Radiant Crystal*. Heinz Brothers used no trademark or labels. It closed in 1927.

Monart Glass An art glass developed in the 1920s by Salvador Ysart (1887-1956) at the Moncrieff Glassworks. Objects are heavy, embellished with streaks and splashes of various colors. Some were designed by the wife of John Moncrieff and made only by Salvadore Ysart and his son, Paul.

Macbeth Evans Monax pedestal bowl, American Sweetheart pattern.
Davanna Collection

Monax MacBeth-Evans' name for its milky white glassware first made in the late 1920s.

Moncrieff Glassworks A glass manufacturing facility in Perth, Scotland. Originally the North British Glassworks, it was purchased in 1864 by John Moncrieff. The official name was John Moncrieff Ltd. In 1922 it engaged Salvador Ysart (1887-1956), a glassmaker who came from Barcelona with his three sons in 1904. One of its products was an art glass known as *Monart Glass* that went into production in 1924. Salvador was succeeded at the facility by his son, Paul, in 1948 and he remained until 1961. Salvador and his other sons established Vasart Glass Ltd.

monkey flask A flask in the form of a monkey seated on a wicker chair playing a panpipe. Extending above the monkey's head is a vertical neck terminating in a trumpet mouth. Monkey flasks were made of Roman glass in the Rhineland during the 3rd and 4th centuries.

monkey pot A small clay pot into which the ingredients for making glass were placed and melted, forming molten glass. See *jockey pot; piling pot*.

monochrome Embellishment employing the use of only one color. See *polychrome; grisaille; camaieu, en*.

Monoghan Brothers See *Wangum Cut Glass Company*.

monogram (Aka *cipher*) A character composed of two or more letters, usually the initials of a person, group, or organization, combined or interlaced and used as an identifying ornamentation.

monogram, mirror See *mirror monogram*.

monogrammist "HI" See *Jager, Heinrich*.

Monongahela Glass Company
A glass manufacturing facility established in 1903 in Fairmont, West Virginia. By the late 1920s it was one of the largest makers of pressed and blown glass tumblers in the United States. Some tumblers were trimmed

with gold and platinum. It became part of the Hocking Glass Company in the early 1930s.

Monroe, Edmund See *New England Glass Bottle Company; New England Glass Company.*

Monroe, C.F., Company (1880-1916) Charles F. Monroe operated a glass shop in Meriden, Connecticut, where he sold primarily imported glassware. In 1882 he added a glass decorating shop and, in 1903, a glass cutting shop. The trademark was "C.F.M." See *Wavecrest.*

Monroe & Hess See *Dunbarton Glass Works.*

Monroe, Cowarden & Co. See *Dunbarton Glass Works.*

Monroe Service In 1817, after President James Monroe visited the Bakewell facility in Pittsburgh, Pennsylvania, he ordered a service of decanters, wine glasses, tumblers, oval dishes, and salts. The service was cut by Alex Jardelle in the Colonial-Ashburton pattern modified to include the arms of the United States.

monstrance (Aka *ostensory*) A glass cylinder placed into a gold, silver, or silver gilt configuration, used in some religious services to display the Host (consecrated bread or wafer). There are various types: in the form of a cross; with the cylinder in a vertical position with metal mounts often representing angels, scrolls, etc.; architectural or sculptural in form. They were first made during the 13th century, achieving their final form during the 15th century. The *sun* type has the glass cylinder in a horizontal position surrounded by projecting pieces of metal resembling the rays of the sun, resting on a decorative stem and foot. Some monstrances are very large; one in the cathedral in Toledo, Spain, is fourteen feet tall. The earliest surviving examples are from the 16th century.

Mont Joy(e) Acid cut cameo and enameled glass made by Cristallerie de Pantin (also called *DeVez*) in France, and by Saint-Hilaire Touvoir de Varraux & Co. during the late 19th-early 20th century. Most pieces were not signed.

Mont Joye & Cie See *LeGras & Cie.*

monteith (Aka *chilling bowl*) A large circular or oval bowl used to hold iced water for cooling wine glasses. The rim has a series of scallops, sometimes alternately bent outward to hang wine glasses by the foot and the bowl immersed in iced water prior to serving wine. The earliest known bears the date 1684; the earliest reference in documents is 1683. The name is reported to come from a Scotsman named Monteith who wore a cloak scalloped at the bottom while at Oxford during the reign of Charles II (1660-85). Only two specimens in glass are recorded, both identical in shape and one engraved. See *wine glass cooler.*

Months, The See *Callot figures.*

Montreal Glass Company See *British American Glass Works.*

Moon & Star pattern See *Palace pattern.*

moonlight glass A generic term for semi-opaque glass with a pearly finish made in fairly large quantities in the 19th century.

Moore, John M., & Co.; Moore Brothers & Company See *Fislerville Glass Works.*

mordant An adhesive used to apply gold leaf decoration to glass.

More, Jonas & More A glass bottle manufacturing company founded in 1882 in Bridgeton, New Jersey, by Robert More Jr., George Jonas, and Richard More. About 1885 Robert More Sr. and William Allen joined the firm, which was renamed More, Jonas, More & Co., and a window glass facility was built. In 1889 the Cumberland Glass Company purchased the facilities, becoming known as Cumberland's "B" Factory. In 1920 they were purchased by the Illinois Glass Co. and automated. Today the facility is owned by Owens-Illinois.

Moresques Decorative motifs similar to arabesques, especially those from Spain and Sicily since both were, at one time, under Saracen (Muslims associated with the Crusades) rule. Similar motifs based on Roman decorative motifs are frequently called *grotesques.*

Morgan Cup A semi-globular drinking bowl cast in blue glass and covered with white glass, considered to be the earliest example of cameo glass surviving intact. It is embellished with a white relief frieze, wheel cut and engraved to reveal the blue background, depicting figures in a Dionysiac rite (Dionysus was the classical mythological god of fertility, wine, and drama). On the bottom of the cup is an eight-pointed rosette. It was made of Roman glass in the first half of the 1st century B.C. It was formerly in the collection of J. Pierpont Morgan.

Morgan Vase A Chinese porcelain vase with peach bloom glaze made during the reign of Kang Hsi (1662-1722, Ch'ing dynasty), sold in 1886 from the collection of Mrs. Mary Morgan. A glass vase in imitation of it was made of Peach Blow glass by Hobbs, Brockunier & Co. in the late 19th century. Others have made imitative versions of the color and also the vase.

Morgantown ad, March 1933. Krause Publications

Morgantown Glass Works (Aka *Old Economy Glass, Economy Tumbler Company*) A glass manufacturing facility incorporated in 1899 which, over the years, experienced many changes in ownership and product line. The term *Morgantown glass* has become a generic term for all glass made there. It was purchased by Fostoria in 1965 and closed in 1971.

Morningglory A Tiffany Reactive Glass pattern.

Morris, William The spearhead of the Arts & Crafts movement. His company, Morris & Company, was primarily responsible for rejuvenating interest in stained glass, which had been at a lull since the Middle Ages.

Morris & Nicholson See *Schuylkill Glass Works.*

Mortar and pestle. Davanna Collection

mortar A circular beaker-like vessel in which various materials can be pulverized with a pestle. Many were made of heavy glass in Germany during the 16th century and in England during the 18th century and later.

mortar beaker A beaker having waisted sides, tapering toward the bottom. They were made in the South Tyrol about 1500.

morter See *fairy lamp.*

mosaic (*As applied to portable glass objects rather than architectural mosaics embedded in floors, walls, and ceilings of churches and other structures.*) A plaque, bowl, bead, or other object composed of or embellished with numerous small pieces of varied colored glass. The process for making them, dating to the 15th century B.C. in Mesopotamia, involved placing blobs of molten glass of different colors next to each other and reheating them to a temperature high enough to fuse them together but not blend them. Next the hot plastic mass was drawn into a long thin cane and cut horizontally or diagonally into thin slices. These, of various colors, shapes, and sizes, were positioned contiguously on a core in the shape of the desired vessel and covered by an outer mold, which helped retain the shape. Then it was reheated to a temperature high enough to fuse the edges of the slices. After cooling somewhat, the mold was removed, the object gradually cooled to ambient temperature, and the surface ground smooth. Some are formed on a flat clay surface and made ductile by reheating. At this point the softened glass mosaic could be blown or shaped into various objects, including jewelry, showing a mottled multicolored (not necessarily flower-like) pattern (sometimes called *millefiori* but is not; see *millefiori mosaic*).

The architectural process of embedding tesserae in cement was originally developed by the Greeks and used during the Roman and Byzantine period; however, portable mosaic objects have recently been discovered in Mesopotamia and Iran, dating from the 15th century B.C. Early specimens include rare Byzantine icons made during the 1st century A.D. Some were made by the Romans during the 1st century B.C., and in Venice, mosaic jewelry was made from the mid-18th century. Mosaics were made by the Aztecs or Miztecs during the 14th century. See *opus sectile; slumping; tesserae; Lomonosov, M.V.; Tiffany mosaic; lacework mosaic glass; mosaic bead; mosaic glass.*

mosaic bead It is believed they originated in Alexandria, Egypt, made by cutting thin slices from canes (see *mosaic*) of various designs, placed close together on a flat bed of fireproof clay, put in an oven, and brought to the melting point. Then a heated glass bead was rolled over the bed, the slices adhering to it; the result was ground and polished. At times they were made by cutting off sections of a mosaic cane, grinding and polishing it, and boring a hole in the center. They were made in China (beginning in the late Chou period, 1122-225 B.C.) and in Venice (in the 17th and 18th centuries).

mosaic glass (1) A glassware made in imitation of stone; the process patented by David Challinor of Challinor, Taylor & Company on June 1, 1886. It was made by preparing various colored opaque glasses in different pots; some of each taken and placed together in a single pot, stirred and intermixed, but not so it becomes homogeneous. See *marble (d) glass*. (2) (Aka *purple marble glass*) Dark purple and white opaque ware having a swirled appearance. (3) Sheet glass made up of predetermined regular square patterns resembling mosaic tiles. See *mosaic; lacework mosaic glass; mosaic.*

Mosaic Glass Company A short-lived glass manufacturing facility established in 1887 in Fostoria, Ohio, making mainly window glass and glass tiles. It did make one pattern, No. 51, called "The Mosaic."

mosaic rod A rod made by taking different colored rods, fusing them into a single rod which, while still in the plastic state, could be pulled to any length, still retaining its original pattern.

mosaic windows Decorative windows comprised of numerous pieces of glass, each cut separately and normally held together by and within a network of metal, usually lead cames. They are of leaded glass, mercury mosaics, beveled glass, or any of a multitude of complex designs of figures, scenes, symbols, etc., set within wooden mullions.

Moscow Glass Works A short-lived window glass manufacturing facility established in 1815/16 in Moscow, later part of the city of Cincinnati, Ohio. In 1817 or 1822 (depending on the source), Pugh & Teeter took over the vacant facility and began making glass. In 1820 or 1824 (depending on the source), Pepperd & Teeter leased it. It was still operating in 1832, making cylinder glass.

Moser, L. Kolo(man) (1868-1918) A glassworker and designer in Vienna, who studied at the Vienna Academy (1886-1892) and School of Arts & Crafts (1892-1895). In 1897 he joined other young painters, sculptors, and architects to found the Vienna Secession (Wiener Werkstatte), a movement that rejected the traditional academic "official" art for a style inspired by Art Nouveau. In 1899 he joined the staff of the Vienna School of Arts & Crafts and was appointed a professor a year later.

He was commissioned by E. Bakalowitz & Sohne to design decorative vases, table glass and stained glass windows to be executed by Johann Loetz Witwe, Meyr's Neffe, and Rhineische Glasshutten. The vases were mainly of *Papillon* glass with a metallic iridescence or large luster circles trailing over the surface. He established a studio at Karlsbad (now Karlovy Vary) in Bohemia in the early 1900s, making art glass, cameo glass with enameling, and a form of embellishment using many pieces of applied colored glass. He designed iridescent glass for Johann Lotz Witwe in about 1902. He also made a type of monochrome glass called *Alexandrit*.

Moser ruby glass cruet with gold enameling and beading, 5" h. Davanna Collection

Moser, Ludwig (1833-1916)

Born in Karlsbad (now Karlovy Vary), Bohemia in 1847, he apprenticed to an engraver and studied painting. He engraved in Karlsbad and Germany, setting up a shop in Karlsbad in 1855. During the summer months when the spas were crowded with tourists, he did custom engraving. In the late 1850s he married and became the father of six children. Only his three sons, Rudolf (1860-1908), Friedrich (b.1863), and Oskar (b.1864), lived long enough to become involved in the facility their father would establish.

In 1857 Moser established an engraving studio in Karlsbad after being granted a license to decorate and sell glass made in the region. Demand for his work caused him to open three additional shops and showrooms maintained by talented designers, enamellers, and engravers between 1857 and 1865. However, he was not permitted to make his own glass so he purchased his blanks from Bohemian glassblowers.

In 1870 he opened a new decorating facility in Meistersdorf, and by 1873, had sales outlets in St. Petersburg, New York, Paris, and London. Initially he sold not only his own products, but those of other decorators in the Karlsbad area who, because of Moser's dominance in the marketplace, needed to secure an outlet for their wares. The glassware from the Karlsbad region distributed by Moser had unique artistic characteristics not produced by other European glasshouses.

Moser closed his New York showroom in 1887 because of high operational costs and appraisal values by customs agents. In 1891 he set up another showroom in New York that closed in 1896, the wares sold at public auction. After the death of his first wife, he remarried in 1875. They had four sons: Carl, Gustav, Leo, and Richard. Carl became a doctor, Gustav managed the Paris operations, and Leo and Richard worked in various positions in their father's company. In 1892 Ludwig was granted permission to construct glass furnaces in the Karlsbad area, and in 1893, he opened a new manufacturing and decorating facility in Meierhofen. Melting did not begin until 1895.

Company management soon moved to Meierhofen, which was staffed by the finest craftsmen, artists, and designers Moser lured there by offering free housing and heat. It made chalk glass but not lead glass until 1919, and only in limited quantities. At first it marketed wine sets, tableware, vases, bowls, jardinieres, jewel and ash trays, spa cups, and other decorative glass that was plain, engraved, enameled, and gilded. Custom work for important clientele remained a primary aspect of his business. In 1897 a new shop and showroom were opened in Paris. In 1910 the company had 400 employees, making 6,000 metric tons of glass. In 1903 it opened a retail outlet in Marionbad, followed by another in Franzenbad, Milano, and later in Teplitz and Prague, and another in Paris and one in Bombay.

Ludwig left in 1900, turning management over to his sons, but maintained controlling interest in the company and was its technical consultant until his death. As World War I began in the summer of 1914, production was reduced, but by 1916 it started to increase because of the management of Leo Moser, who continually sought new markets. After the war the market for artistic glass rose dramatically. However, with the collapse of the monetary system, the Mosers sought aid from the Bohemian Union Bank, which gained controlling interest in the company. The Mosers maintained control of the artistic and production management.

In 1922 the Moser firm merged with Meyr's Neffe Adolf Glassworks in Winterberg, forming "The Karlsbad Factory for Crystal Glass Ltd. Co.-Ludwig Moser & Sons and Meyr's Nephews." After the merger, production expanded, being recognized as the foremost Bohemian producer of artist glass and luxury tableware, supplying blanks for the Wiener Werkstatte. In the early 1920s, Moser was the first to introduce a new line of colored glasses based entirely on rare earth oxide colorants. In 1923 it presented a 218-piece crystal drinking tableware set for 24 to Pope Pius XI, creating tremendous publicity for the company, followed by a substantial number of orders. To meet the demand and lower costs of these expensive wares, an assembly line operation was established; several engravers were each given a specific tool designed for a specific task, the production rate increasing threefold with no appreciable loss of quality. His ware soon was given the name "Glass of Kings."

In 1933, with the worldwide depression and the rise of the Nazi regime, the Wisterberg facility was sold and the Mosers sold their interest in the company to the Bohemian Union Bank. From 1933 to 1938 (the year of the Nazi takeover of Czechoslovakia), the artistic output of the facility was primarily influenced by the designs the Mosers made prior to their withdrawal.

The worldwide market for artistic glass began to decline. Under Nazi occupation, all stock in the company was transferred to the German government. It was renamed Staatliche Glasmanfacture Karlsbad, and production shifted to items essential to the Nazi war effort. The workers were sent to concentration camps or kept on as slave labor, but aided the war effort by altering ingredients in the batch so windows and filter glasses often cracked or shattered before the tanks arrived at the front. In early 1945, on Nazi orders, the factory was closed. In May 1945 some workers joined to rebuild the ovens and, by September 1945, were able to make some wares in limited quantities.

After World War II a total rebuilding effort was mounted and the Moser facility began full production under the name Karlovaske Sklo. The artistic wares were based on designs of contemporary artists and those executed prior to 1933. In 1938 at age 59, Leo fled the Nazi invasion, settling in Corning, New York, where he died in November 1974 at the age of 95.

Moses, Swan & McLewee Company
A glass cutting house in Trenton, New Jersey, operating during the late 19th century.

Mosly & Little
In 1779 Elijah Hubbard of Middletown, Isaac Mosly of Glastenbury, William Little Jr. of Lebanon, and Picket Latimer of New London, all from Connecticut, were granted the privilege of manufacturing glass. In 1780 Hubbard and Latimer withdrew. Mosly and Little were then granted a monopoly for fifteen years beginning on July 1, 1780, provided they establish a facility no later than November 1, 1781. Apparently they failed to do so.

mosque lamp
A lantern made of Islamic glass in an inverted bell shape with an oil receptacle inside. They have side loop handles (three on earlier ones, and six on later ones) from which they were suspended by chains from the ceiling. Occasionally the chain passed through the lamp globe. They were usually ornamental, having gilding and vivid enamel colors and often featuring the name of the Sultan, armorial blazons, Neskhi script with quotations from the Koran, dedicatory inscriptions, and floral designs of Chinese derivation. Some smaller ones are plain, said to have been made in Syria in the 11th century. Decorated ones date after 1820. Some were made of Venetian glass for export to the Near East during the 15th and 16th centuries. Those made during the late 13th through the mid-14th centuries exhibit the greatest craftsmanship. Copies have been made in the 19th and 20th centuries and are often called *Islamic Vases.*

Moss Agate glass
An art glass made to emulate the ancient Roman and later Venetian marblized glasses, but made by different techniques. It was developed in the late 1880s by John Northwood in collaboration with Frederick Carder for Stevens & Williams Ltd., at the Brierly Hill Glass Works.

It was later made by Carder at Steuben from about 1910 to 1920. It was made by first casing a paraison of clear soda glass with a layer of clear lead glass and covering it with powdered glass of variegated colors, casing that with another layer of clear lead glass, then shaping and heating it. Cold water was injected into it, causing the inner layer of the soft soda glass to crackle. The water was quickly removed and the object reheated to fuse the interior cracks, but leaving a crackled network appearance. Steuben pieces are usually red, brown, or yellow, and some rare ones are blue. All have variegated color shading as the result of the powdered glass, so no two pieces were identical.

Similar ware was made in France by Eugene Rousseau and E. Leveille and poorly copied by other facilities. Some companies added the crushed powdered glass to the surface while it was still hot and did not add a cover layer, giving a texture to the glass. The original concept was to produce the natural color of moss agate.

moss backed glass A modification of the granite backed design on sheet glass in which the backing is not as rough.

moss ground A ground made of green canes, creating a moss-like appearance. It occasionally has included within it tiny white stars. It was used only at Clichy.

Mosser Glass Retail Store and Offices, factory to the right.
Anna Shotwell

Display of Mosser glassware inside the Mosser Store.
Anna Shotwell

Mosser Glass Company A glass manufacturing facility established by Thomas Mosser in 1964 in Cambridge, Ohio. It manufactures pressed tableware and novelty pieces. Most pieces are signed with an "M" or an "M" in a circle.

Mosserine A cased glass used in the manufacture of shades for Handle lamps, made primarily in green, gold, and brown—colors chosen for their "masculine" appearance.

Mother-of-Pearl glassware (Aka *pearl satin glass*) An art glass having a double flashing. An opaque glass paraison is blown into a patterned mold and covered with a flashing of clear or colored glass, trapping air bubbles in the molded spaces. The original patent for it was given to Benjamin Richardson of England in 1857. The object is covered again with a clear glass flashing. After cooling, it is finished by dipping it in acid to provide a satin surface. Among the patterns for the opaque inner layer (white or colored) are *Herringbone, Swirl, Diamond Quilted, Feather, Moire, Zipper* (close vertical notched ribbing), and *Peacock Eye*, showing through the outer flashing. Some have additional enameled and applied embellishment. The *Rainbow* type has several blended colors. Mother-of-Pearl glassware was made by the Phoenix Glass Co., Mt. Washington Glass Co., and others.

In 1889 Thomas Webb & Sons, England, patented a process for making cameo relief designs on articles of Mother-of-Pearl glass. In this process, a design was painted on the surface of the glass in acid resistant inks and the casing on the rest eroded by acid, leaving a design in shallow relief. The article was removed from the acid before it laid open the air traps. Another technique for achieving this result was to position the molded piece in a glass cup specifically blown to receive it and have a worker blow and shape the entire mass into the article desired. The several layers of glass in each case could be of the same or different colors.

In 1881 William B. Dean and Alphonse Peltier received a patent for making Mother-of-Pearl glassware using a controlled pattern of air traps within the walls of the glass body; the principle being the same as used by Richardson. In 1885 Joseph Webb of Stourbridge, England, who came to the United States and lived in Beaver Falls, Pennsylvania, perfected this glass. He was associated with the Phoenix Glass Co., a large producer of this ware—a plated or cased glass with an opaque white lining.

The primary difference between Mother-of-Pearl and plain satin glass is that Mother-of-Pearl displays a design and has a different surface finish from which it derives its name. Several patterns were used. The air bubbles give it a pearlized appearance and color.

A patent was granted to Mt. Washington Glass Company for a *pearl satin ware*. To produce it, a gather was blown into a mold with projecting points, bands, or other designs forming ornamental depressions in the object. The interior body was covered with a layer of glass sealing and protecting the air in the cavities, and the surface was given a satin finish.

Another method was to line a heated mold with clear or colored glass tubes and blow a gather into the mold, the hollow tubes becoming fused to the surface. Next the paraison was rolled on a marver to embed the tubes into the surface by twisting the paraison while still in the plastic state; articles having pearly swirled stripes on the outer surface.

Ornamental features used to embellish Mother-of-Pearl glass are: (a) silver deposit; (b) enamels; (c) gold and silver leaf; (d) applied glass leaves and flowers; (e) silver, gold, ormolu, or pewter mountings sometimes used for decorative as well as functional purposes; and (f) mica flecks or bits of variegated colored glassware picked up on the gather, becoming an integral part of the embellishment. See *pearl satin glass.*

motif (*As applied to cut glass*) A single or separate figure on a piece of glass. It may indicate the period of production, the intrinsic quality of the article, and occasionally the glasshouse or shop where made. The three basic motifs are: (a) line, the simplest motifs developed from straight lines; (b) geometric, developed into highly ornate motifs during the Brilliant Period of cut glass; and (c) those from nature, developed when interest in ornate designs began to decline as production

costs began to rise. Because of these two factors, many companies producing high quality products during the Brilliant Period turned to copper wheel and stone engraving, inspired by nature, particularly flowers, characterizing the cut glass period just prior to World War I.

mottled glass A collector's term for any multicolored glass. See *slag glass.*

mottled ground A ground made of fused chips of varicolored glass.

motto cup Any small cup or mug painted or etched with a name or phrase.

moullu See *ormolu.*

Mound City Glass Works See *Missouri Glass Company.*

mount A decorative metal attachment, functional (e.g., as a base) or ornamental, placed on an object of generally good quality. In the 18th century mounts were made of gilt, bronze, ormolu, pewter, or silver. See *mounted glass.*

Mount (Mt.) Pleasant Glass Works See *Granger, O.H., & Company.*

Mount (Mt.) Vernon Glass Company A glass manufacturing facility in Mt. Vernon, New York, incorporated in 1810, when the New York State Legislature granted it a charter to make glass. It made bottles, vials, flasks, and flint glass tableware. By 1833 the operating firm was Granger, Southworth & Co. and, about 1842, C. Granger & Co. In 1844, because the fuel supply was exhausted, it moved to Mt. Pleasant, near Saratoga, New York, operating as O.H. Granger & Company. See *Granger, O.H., & Company.*

Vase, Burmese, Mt. Washington Glass Works, New Bedford, Massachusetts, c. 1885. Museum of American Glass at Wheaton Village, Millville, NJ.

Mount (Mt.) Washington Glass

Works A glass manufacturing facility established in 1837 by Deming Jarves of the Boston & Sandwich Co., operated by Luther Russell in South Boston, Massachusetts. In 1839 it was operated by Labree & Jarves (John D. Labree and George D. Jarves, fourteen-year-old son of Deming), the primary products being lamps and chandeliers. From 1840 to 1860, it operated as Jarves & Cormerais, even though George died of consumption in 1850. In 1851 Wm. L. Libbey went there as its bookkeeper, and in 1856, Timothy Howe went as a clerk. In 1861 it closed but, later the same year, was reopened by Howe & Libbey. In 1866 Howe died and Libbey became the sole owner.

The facility was deteriorating, so in 1869, operations were moved to New Bedford, Massachusetts, into the New Bedford Glass Company's premises, which Libbey purchased in 1870. It kept the Mt. Washington Glass Works name, the operating firm being W.L. Libbey & Co. In 1872 W.L. Libbey left to accept a position as agent for New England Glass Co. The management of the Mt. Washington facility passed to Captain Henry Libbey. Mt. Washington was successful, but after the depression in 1873 the company closed in 1874.

Later that year operations were resumed under the management of Frederick S. Shirley, using the name Mount Washington Glass Company. He was innovative in the art glass area, producing White Lusterless, Lava Glass, Burmese, Peachblow, Rose Amber, Amberina, Acid Etched Cameo, Royal Flemish, Albertine, Crown Milano, Napoli, Mother-of-Pearl, Satin, and Iridescent glass. No facility made a greater variety of fine glassware—electric globes, Edison lamp bulbs, door knobs, shades, blown glass, cut glass, chandeliers, etc.—referring to itself as "Headquarters in America for Art Glass." It was responsible for helping to change the trend of American glass from the pressed and patterned pieces to the free blown and sometimes sensationally colored designs of art glass.

In 1894 Mt. Washington became part of the Pairpoint Manufacturing Co. In 1900, as a result of financial difficulties, it reorganized, the name becoming Pairpoint Corporation. In 1938 it sold the glass facility to J. & B. Kenner Inc., a salvage company. Later that year Robert M. Gundersen, a master glassblower who had worked for Pairpoint, organized the Gundersen Glass Works and, in association with I.N. Babbitt, purchased it from Kenner. Once again it flourished.

In 1952, after Gundersen's death, it became part of the National Pairpoint Corporation, the name changed to Gundersen-Pairpoint Glass Works. The chimneys at the works were condemned by insurance underwriters in 1957 and it closed.

Mount (Mt.) Washington

Peachblow A ware made at the Mount Washington Glass Works. On July 20, 1886, it filed trade name papers for *Peachblow*, a ware made of homogeneous glass in shades ranging from a dusty rose at the top fading to a bluish white at the base. Most pieces have a satin finish, but a few are glossy. Like *New England Peachblow* and unlike *Wheeling Peachblow*, it is unlined. It is one of the rarest American shaded glasses, not popular when introduced and made for a short time. It was often embellished with floral designs or verses in old English lettering. There have been many reproductions. See *Gundersen Peachblow*.

Mountain Glass Factory A glass manufacturing facility established in 1801 at Mount (Mt.) Pleasant, New York. It is believed to have made utilitarian glassware. It closed after a short time because of its inaccessible location.

Mountain (Glass) Works A glass manufacturing facility established in 1844 by Oscar Granger in Saratoga, New York. See *Granger, O.H., & Company.*

mounted glass Glass on which metal mounts were incorporated (see *mount*). It was not uncommon for the fragile edges of better glassware to be protected with metal mounts. Pewter was occasionally used, but during the 18th and 19th centuries the use of silver was more common. Damaged pieces or fragments that would otherwise be worthless are often mounted in order to display them. Gold was also used to mount glass, especially small boxes and *objets d'art*. Hallmarks on the mounts help establish the date, but one must be careful in dating the glass by the date on the mount since the glass may be considerably older than the marked mount, which may have been added later to cover a chip or to prevent future damage.

Mousseline glass See *muslin (glass)*.

mouth (1) The opening of a bottle, jug, jar, pitcher, etc., from which the contents is poured. It may or may not have a lip. Some are of special shape or design, i.e., a flared mouth. See *funnel mouth*. (2) The side opening of a crown pot from which molten glass is removed for working.

move The specified number of items or objects of a particular type of glassware a worker was required to make during a turn (usually 4-1/2 hours of actual working time). The number is reached by an agreement between the local union and facility manager. See *turn*.

MSAT The abbreviation for *multiple series air twist*. See *multiple series twist*.

MSMcL Co. The trademark of Moses, Swan and McLewee Co., which manufactured cut glass.

MSOT The abbreviation for *multiple series opaque twist*. See *multiple series twist*.

MT.W.G.Co. The trademark used by Mt. Washington Glass Co.

Mueller Glass Staining Company
A glass decorating company operated by Mrs. Anna E. Mueller in Pittsburgh, Pennsylvania, during the late 1800s. It specialized in staining glassware, the blanks being supplied primarily by McKee Brothers, and made a lot of ruby- and amber-stained wares. About 1900 she sold her patents and equipment to the National Glass Company.

muff A cylinder of glass made by cutting the hemispherical ends off of a long bottle made by blowing a large glass bubble and swinging it on the end of a blowpipe. It was made as part of the process of making broad glass, sometimes called *muff glass*.

muffineer A container or castor having a perforated cover or cap, sometimes of silver, for sifting sugar, cinnamon, etc., on muffins, etc. They are considerably larger than a salt-shaker and were popular in England and the United States during the late 1800s.

muffle A fire clay box in which glass or porcelain objects were enclosed when placed in a muffle kiln. It is designed to protect the objects from the flames and smoke while being subjected to low temperature firing. After enamels or gilding were applied, low temperature firing was necessary to fix them, yet protect the brilliance of the article.

muffle kiln A relatively low temperature (700-900° C) kiln for refiring glass or porcelain objects to fuse enameling, fix gilding, and generate luster.

mug A drinking vessel with a handle and circular rim that rests on a flat base without a stem. Some have a lid with a thumb rest, usually of metal, often silver or pewter. Made in a variety of forms, they are normally cylindrical, although sometimes they are waisted, barrel shaped, inverted bell shaped, double ogee shaped, and occasionally *square* (cylindrical, having equal diameter and height—a square silhouette). *A mug is occasionally, yet erroneously, called a tankard.* See *beaker; stein; scuttle mug; penny mug; shaving mug.*

Muhleman Glass Company In 1888 the Crystal Glass Company took over the LaBelle Glass Company, operating it as the Muhleman Glass Company.

Mulberry A cased glass combining a cranberry and light blue glass made by Fenton Art Glass Company beginning in 1942.

Mulford, Ernest Beginning as a cutter for Hoare & Daly in 1880, he opened a shop in Corning, New York, in 1901, subcontracting originally for Hoare & Daly, then T.G. Hawkes & Co., cutting their simpler designs for their fast-selling items. His shop closed in 1912.

Mulford, Coffin & Hay See *South Millville Plant*.

Mulford, Hay & Co. See *Schetter Glass Works*.

muller A solid piece of glass having a flat, thick base and a handle, used to pulverize enamels with an intermediary into a fine, compatible material appropriate for painting.

Muller Freres (Brothers) They began their career working for Emile Galle. About 1897 Henri Muller left to establish a glass manufacturing facility in Croismare, France. About 1900 Henri and his brother, Desire, established another facility near Luneville (Lorraine), France, called Muller Freres. Soon they were joined by their remaining seven brothers and one sister. Later the facilities were combined, both making an art glass with an overlay of two or three colors and etched embellishments, made by a process using hydrofluoric acid, called *fluogravure* (see *fluogravure*). Its marks were *Muller, Muller Luneville, Muller Freres Luneville, Luneville, Muller Crois Mare,* and *Crois Mare.* Its most active period was from 1905 to 1930. The Depression forced it to stop production in 1933, and in 1936 it ceased operations.

mullion Vertical supporting members separating the openings of a multi-light window.

multifocal lens See *spectacles; bifocal lens.*

multiform glass Intricate shapes not readily made by conventional glass fabrication methods. They are formed by pulverizing or powdering glass, pressing and slip casting the particles into the desired shape, and firing the piece at a high temperature. The particles are consolidated or sintered by fusion into a vacuum-type structure. The products display properties similar to those of the parent glass. It is used to make chemical apparatus, mechanical and electrical parts, and glass to metal seals. It is normally translucent but can be made transparent. Corning calls its transparent multiform glass *Clearform.*

multi-layered cased glass A type of cased glass composed of three or more layers of different colors, carved in the manner of cameo glass, revealing the various colors in different areas of the decoration. Some vases and Chinese snuff bottles were made of this glass and are so embellished.

Multiple bottle, four compartment Marie Brizard, France; contents: triple sec, crème de cacao, crème de menthe, and apricot liqueur. Davanna Collection

multiple bottle A bottle divided internally into separate compartments, each having its own mouth or spout. The earliest known specimens having three or four sections date from early Roman times. Others made in Crete during the late 2nd or 3rd century A.D., are in the form of a globular jug with a handle and three sections. Later cruets were made in two sections with spouts facing in opposite directions. Relatively modern ones, some made in the early 19th century, have four compartments and are usually globular in form. See *double bottle; triple bottle; double cruet; liqueur bottle.*

multiple series twist A combination of twists; one twist with another (air or opaque) encircling it, and a third encircling the second. They were made by making a pattern of holes in the top of a rod and covering them with molten glass. The rod was then drawn and twisted and more molten glass added. The process was repeated at least two and possibly three or more times, using an air twist or an opaque twist. See *double series twist; single series twist.*

Mulvaney & Ledlie(r) See *Birmingham Flint Glass Company.*

Munster Glass identified as being made in Ireland, but not attributed to a particular facility.

muntin A bar separating the panels in a door or the glasses in a multi-paned light.

Munzegewicht *(German)* A disk-shaped weight of colored glass embellished with molded decoration or inscription, made of late Roman glass, Egyptian glass during the 10th and 11th centuries, and later Islamic glass.

mural looking glass Any large mirror to be fastened to a wall, as opposed to a hand mirror or sconce mirror.

Muranese See *New Martinsville Peachblow.*

Murano A group of small islands about five miles from Venice where glassmakers settled before the 11th century. In 1292, an ordinance forbade glass manufacturing facilities to remain in Venice (less than fifteen paces from the nearest structure) because of the danger to buildings and inhabitants from fires long associated with the glass industry. This caused the entire glassmaking guild to move to the islands of Murano in the Venetian lagoon. Another reason for relocating was an attempt to preserve and protect the secrets of Venetian glassmaking by restrictive laws, rigorously though not always successfully enforced, to protect the successful and prosperous monopoly of glassmaking. It was an excellent location since imports and exports could be easily controlled and monitored. It was on pain of death that a craftsman could leave Murano or instruct a resident foreigner in trade secrets without the express permission of the government (continued until the 18th century).

As the 15th century progressed, *cristallo*, an almost transparent glass, the clearest to date and considered the finest in the Western world, was developed. The formula was kept secret in Murano. Murano became one of the most important industrial centers and *the* most important glass center because of the nature of cristallo and the loss of popularity of cut glass. Since the edict of 1469, opening a new furnace in Murano required the approval of the authorities. Glassmakers developed the process for making millefiori canes, *lattimo* or milk glass, and a variety of intricate and delicate stems. They were also traders, making specific wares for specific markets.

In the late 16th and 17th centuries they used the soft, ductile quality of their glass to make many fabulous designs and shapes. Many pieces were made more delicate and fragile, on thinly blown slender stems with cup bowls or a rounded base, often with a wide lip. Larger vases and baskets had a central flared stem and flat-bottomed bowl. There was little other embellishment, except for occasional lattimo spirals or reticello network over the surface. Finishes similar to *ice glass* were used. Diamond point engraving was a popular form of embellishment. As lead glass was perfected during the late 17th century, and cut and wheel engraved glass again became fashionable, the soda glass, which could not be made thick enough for cutting, became less popular and its importance diminished.

Business in Murano fell but was revived as the glassmakers adapted and modified their methods and technology to follow current trends. When their drinking glass business fell with the introduction of lead glass, they shifted to novelties, massive centerpieces, elaborate tabletop settings, large presentation pieces, etc.

From the 16th century on they made mirrors, which became highly regarded by the 18th century because they were blown (not cast), ground flat, and silvered and framed. This method prohibited making large mirrors of one piece of glass. During the 19th century, they made paperweights and developed the *portrait millefiori*. From the late 18th through the early 20th century, originality gave way to imitation, but they made some attractive scent bottles, carved rosaries, simulated pearls, elaborate epergnes, cake stands, and glass fruit and animals.

The renewal of the its glass industry began in the 1920s as ingenuity, innovation, and quality made a comeback. There are numerous glasshouses on Murano; the best known are Barovier & Toso, Salviati (from 1859), Venini (from 1921), Cenedese (from 1945), and Alfredo Barbini (from 1950).

Murano vase with red and blue swirls, 5-3/4" h.
Tri-State Antiques

Murano black and gold dust striped turtle, blown glass bottle, 5-1/4" l.
Tri-State Antiques

Murano glassware Glassware made in Murano, but often referred to as *Venetian glassware*. Early ware consisted mainly of beads, canes, and glass cakes, followed by window panes, mirrors, and utilitarian glassware. During the 13th century artistic glassware was introduced, leading to the development of new varieties of glass (e.g., Aventurine, Calcedono, agate glass, ice glass, cristallo, and millefiori glass) with emphasis on colored glass and manipulated embellishment rather than engraving or enameling.

In the 20th century new techniques were invented, especially for surface treatment, and new styles introduced, including massive overlay glass and hand modeled molten glass blocks. Gaudy tableware and ornamental figures for the tourist trade were produced in great quantities. Chandeliers and other lighting fixtures have long been a specialty.

Murdock & Casell See *Mills, Peter, & Co.; New Granite Glass Co.*

Murphy furnace A furnace developed by M.L. Murphy in the early 1890s for use at glass manufacturing facilities not having a reliable supply of natural gas. It involved burning coal to produce a gas burned in the furnaces.

Murr, Richard A glass cutter who began cutting in 1905 in San Francisco, California. In 1906 he was issued the trademark *Koh-i-noor* (the name of the famous diamond in the British Crown Jewel Collection). In 1907 he moved to Chicago, Illinois. He gradually gave up cutting to become an agent and distributor for other cutting houses. By 1928 he was listed only as a "mercantile consultant."

Murray & Olyphant (1841-1848) A glass manufacturing facility in Mount Morris, New York.

murrhine Glass objects, usually bowls or vases, of mosaic glass made at Alexandria from about 200 B.C. to 100 A.D., highly treasured in ancient times. They were inspired by the ancient murrhine pottery bowls. They were made in the manner of mosaic, from horizontal slices of rods or canes of colored glass fused together over a mold. The technique differs from that used later by the Venetians in making *millefiori glass*, which involved embedding slices of cane in a glass matrix

murrina/murrino A modern mosaic glassware with numerous inserts of varicolored glass embedded as large pieces or as long and wide streaks, differing from the embedded horizontal slices of canes in millefiori glassware. It was made in Murano from the 19th century in imitation of the murrhine glassware made at Alexandria. The name is derived either from ancient murrhine bowls or from the Italian/Latin word *murra* (the material of which the bowls were once made). *Murrina* refers to a slice of a cane; *murrino* the insert of multi-colored glass embedded in a glass object. See *millefiori; mosaic.*

mushroom knop A knop with a domed top in the shape of a mushroom.

mushroom paperweight (Aka *tuft* and *pom-pom paperweight*) A paperweight having as its principle embellishment a central bundle of canes spread out in the form of a mushroom with a domed top supported by a mushroom stem. Normally the canes are multi-colored millefiori, but they are sometimes entirely opaque white and, in rare examples, star dust canes, usually arranged in five concentric rings. Some specimens, usually made by Baccarat, have the canes in haphazard pattern. On occasion the mushroom is standing in a plain or striped basket. St. Louis and some Baccarat weights have a rope (torsade) of entwining white and colored spirals around the central motif. Some St. Louis weights have a white filigrana ribbon and colored ribbon around the mushroom. Many have mercury bands and some overlay glass, with symmetrically cut windows.

mushroom stopper A mushroom-shaped stopper with a flat or domed top and usually molded ribbing radiating from the center to the rim. Some have cut embellishment, but most are molded. They were made after the disk and lozenge types, from about 1780 to 1825, and mostly of Anglo-Irish glass. On some, the mushroom rests on a rather plain, short shank or a globular knop.

musical glasses Glasses used as musical instruments due to their resonant quality. In Germany during the 18th century, tumblers and wine glasses of different sizes, numbering up to thirty-seven and later to 120, were filled with varying amounts of water and occasionally mounted on a spindle. The rims of the glasses were rubbed by the fingers of the player (later pads or leather hammers) to make varying sounds or pitches. Later glasses were custom ground to produce the right pitch when rubbed with wet fingers. An array of such glasses was often called *flip-flaps*. Around 1760 Benjamin Franklin (1706-90) adapted this into an *Armonica* consisting of the rim portions of various sized glasses mounted horizontally on a metal rod, separated from the rod and each other by cork. As the rod was turned, a wetted finger was rubbed over these narrow cylindrical pieces of glass, producing different tones.

musical instruments Various objects made of glass and used to produce musical sounds, such as musical glasses, bells, horns, dulcimers, etc. Some were copied in form only, serving merely as ornaments, such as a violin, bugle, trombone, and others as drinking glasses, e.g., post horn.

muslin (glass) (1) A pattern glass made by overlapping the object with a wax soaked lace material and submersing it in an acid bath, giving it the appearance of muslin cloth. (2) (Aka *Mousseline glass*) A very fragile blown British art glass made from the 1830s. The major producer was A. Jenkinson of Edinburgh. (3) See *filigree; filigrana.*

muslin ground (Aka *gauze, lace,* or *filigree ground*) A ground constructed of lengths of white filigrana (latticino) glass rods laid side by side. When observed from above it gives the appearance of floating gauze or muslin. At times there is an upper layer, haphazardly placed, giving the appearance of twisted floating gauze (*upset muslin*). It was used mainly at Clichy (see *millefiori paperweight; flower paperweight*).

Cut glass mustard with spoon, 3-3/4″ h.
Davanna Collection

mustard jar A small jar used for serving prepared mustard, with a cover or lid with an indentation for a spoon. Those intended for dry mustard have a cover without an indentation.

Mutzer glassware Blown three-mold glass vessels, at one time considered to have been made by Frederick Mutzer or his son Gottlieb. Frederick, born in Germany in the early 19th century, arrived in the United States and began working in the Philadelphia, Pennsylvania, area. There is a theory that the wares attributed to the Mutzers were actually made in secret in limited quantities during the 1920s and 1930s at the Clevenger facility in Clayton, New Jersey. This was done to intentionally deceive Henry Francis duPont (his collection of American decorative arts was housed at Winterthur) and other collectors and experts. The glassware was planted for sale as rare early 19th century glass.

Mycenaean glass paste beads

Beads of glass paste made at Mycenae about 1300 B.C., in the form of small thin tablets with ribbed ends and perforated for threading. They were circular, rectangular, or triangular in shape, and mainly of blue or pale yellow glass embellished with relief Mycenaean motifs, such as rosettes, ivy, and spirals. They were probably used for necklaces, to embellish garments, or to grace diadems (a crown or cloth headband worn as a symbol of power) and skulls of skeletons.

Myers, Joel P. Born in 1934, Myers was a former designer (1963-70) at Blenko Glass Co. He became a teacher and studio glassmaker at Illinois State University. He developed a style of bottle with chrome oxide marvered into a paraison, covered with crystal glass and further blown to make a cased bottle. He also made a series of thin tall drinking glasses, called *Tallest Form*, having bowls of various forms and textures and usually a domed foot.

Myers, S.F., Co. A glass cutting company in New York City, using the trademark *Laurel*.

Myra-Kristall An art glass developed in 1925 by Karl Wiedmann (b.1905) at the Wurttembergische Metallwarenfabrik (W.M.F.). It is similar to the glassware made by Tiffany.

Myth of Adonis, The A unique oval casket made by Steuben in 1966, with engraved glass panels mounted in an ornamental frame of 18 karat white gold. The panels depict the Myth of Adonis, a youth whom Aphrodite, ancient Greek goddess of love and beauty, loved for his beauty. There are eight main panels showing life, death, and rebirth, and eight smaller ones symbolizing the seasons. The upper panels relate to the earth and the heavens; the lower ones the underworld. The cover, which is ornamental with green-gold leaves, has an emerald cut crystal finial. It was designed by Donald Pollard. The engraving was designed by Jerry Pfohl and executed by Roland Erlacher. The gold work on the frame was by Cartier Inc.

mythological subjects Embellishment on glassware, normally wheel engraved, depicting persons or events of Greek or Roman mythology or legend, such as Perseus and Andromeda, Thetis and Peleus (Portland Vase), Lycurgus, Adonis, Pyramus and Thisbe (Fairfax Cup), Apollo and Athena, Bellerophon and Pegasus, Actaeon & Artemus, etc. See *allegorical subjects*.

Nn

nail-shaped bottle A bottle, square in cross-section and pointed toward the base, believed to have been made at Hebron, a city in western Jordan.

nailhead diamond (Aka *sharp diamond*, *relief diamond*, or *sharp relief diamond*.) A cut glass motif consisting of a sharp, pointed diamond with three or four pyramidal sides. See *diamond*.

Nailsea Glass House A glass manufacturing facility in Nailsea, near Bristol, England. It was established in 1788 as Nailsea Crown Glass & Bottle Manufacturers by John Robert Lucas and William Chance with Edward Homer later becoming a partner. In 1790 a second facility was built nearby by William Chance and other partners. In 1810 they were combined and placed under the unified management of Robert Lucas Chance, son of William Chance and nephew of John Robert Lucas. Robert Lucas Chance later purchased the British Crown Glass Co. in Smithwick, England. He then established Chance Brothers, which took over the management of Smithwick and the two Nailsea facilities in 1870. Originally the Nailsea facilities made mainly crown window glass, adding sheet glass and bottles and later household wares, flasks, and friggers. A subsidiary in nearby Stanton Drew made bottles. Large amounts of glassware have been credited to the Nailsea facilities and are called *Nailsea type* because the majority, especially the colorless flint glass, was made in Bristol, Stourbridge, and other English cities, not Nailsea. Glassware made at Nailsea facilities has readily recognizable characteristics. See *Nailsea glassware.*

Nailsea glassware Glassware once believed to have been made and decorated in Nailsea, England. It is now believed that the majority was made at other facilities in England (about 80% at Stourbridge), and should be called *Nailsea type* glassware. The term Nailsea glassware or Nailsea-type glassware is used to describe a type of embellished glassware rather than glassware made in Nailsea. In the early 1800s, Nailsea glassware was a splashed ware, very different from what is considered Nailsea today.

Evolution of Nailsea Glassware. Shortly before 1800, bottles were embellished with a haphazard design consisting of colored stripes. About 1830 articles made of clear glass with colored stripes were associated with the name. From about 1840 to 1845, Nailsea glassware consisted mainly of cased glass objects with *Nailsea type* embellishments, stripes, and colors placed on the ware while still on the pontil, cased in crystal and removed from the pontil. After 1851 pinched decorations were attached around the neck or to the sides of some articles. The *pull-up pattern* was introduced about 1885—the colors and patterns applied to an opaque body in the usual fashion and cased with crystal. About 1890 John Northwood of Stevens & Williams developed the threading pull-up machine; thus the entire operation of casing and manipulating the striped embellishment was completely mechanized. With Nailsea type embellishments in place, many other manufacturers began building on them, making more complex and ornate articles. On some the threading was not cased and was applied to the outside in a variety of colors. Some articles were further embellished with additional applied or enameled decorations. As the trend to further embellish Nailsea wares continued, they were made with another pattern applied, over the encased pattern, using stain, mainly during the last years of the 19th century. Some Nailsea glassware was made in Bohemia during the early years of the 20th century. The three basic groupings of Nailsea glass are: flecked glassware; festooned glassware; and colored (pale green) or clear glass with a simple white filigrana decoration. Items such as witch balls, walking sticks, rolling pins, pole heads, etc., are often credited to Nailsea, as are some bells of multicolored glass, which experts now believe they were made at other locations. The most frequently found color combinations in Nailsea glassware are red and white and green and white.

Nakara A trade name used for a line of decorated opaque glassware made around 1900 by C.F. Monroe Company of Meriden, Connecticut. See *Wavecrest; Kelva*. It is similar to Wavecrest, differing in some aspects. Nakara was also made in pastel colors that are deeper, covering more surface area than on Wavecrest. Also on Nakara, more beading was present; the flowers were larger; large transfer prints of figures, Victorian ladies, cherubs, etc., were present; the shapes were more modest; and ormolu and brass collars were present. Most items were signed, and reproductions abound.

Nancy glassware See *carnival glassware*.

Napanee Glass House (1881-1883) A glass manufacturing facility established in 1881 in Napanee, Ontario, Canada, by John Herring (1818-1898). The company made window glass that proved to be a failure; then made specialty items, such as globes for street lamps and pharmacy glassware, based on orders taken by traveling salesmen.

napkin ring A ring, about 1-1/4 to 2 inches in diameter and an inch wide, for holding a rolled-up napkin at a place setting. They were in vogue less than fifty years, beginning in the late 1870s.

Napoleon's hat. Top cut in Russian pattern, lower portion cut flowers with stems pressed in blank, 15" l. x 4-1/2" h.
Davanna Collection

Napoleon's hat An oblong bowl shaped to resemble Napoleon's hat turned upside down.

Napoli glass An art glass patented in 1894 by Albert Steffen, then supervisor of Mt. Washington Glass Company's decorating department. It is made by forming an outline of a figure or design on one side of the ware and forming the actual figure or design on the opposite. When viewed from the side with the outline, the outline will appear to combine with the main body of the figure or design on the opposite side. When colored glass and metallic bits are used in the decorating process, a single firing is needed to fix the design or figure. When painted on one side, it has to be fired separately from the metallic decoration because, if applied and fired together, they would absorb or run into each other.

Single handle, cut glass nappie, 6" d.
Davanna Collection

nappie (Aka *jelly* or *bonbon dish*) Also spelled *nappy*. An old term meaning *bowl*, but used from the 1870s to the 1930s for small round or oval dishes with flat bottoms and gently sloping sides. Made in a variety of shapes and sizes, they usually measured four to eight inches across. They were a larger form of a sauce dish. Nappies were used for candy, soup, cereal, salad, etc. They often have a single loop handle; some have two loop handles, usually round and measuring from eight to twelve inches across. They were made to hold a single item. Some nappies that were divided into two to four sections could hold multiple items. There are also *covered nappies* (butter dish) and *footed nappies* (small compote).

Nash, A. Douglas, footed vase, iridescent gold, mkd. "544 Nash," 4-1/8" h.
Krause Publications

Nash, A. Douglas

A son of Arthur J. Nash, who worked with his father at Tiffany's Corona facility, until Tiffany withdrew from active participation in 1919. Nash purchased its assets, operating as A. Douglas Nash Associates until 1920 when Louis C. Tiffany Furnaces Inc. was formed. When Tiffany withdrew his financial support of the operations in 1928, Nash with his father and others formed the A. Douglas Nash Corporation. They continued to make art glass in the style of Tiffany as well as some new types developed by Nash, including some tinted glass, lustered glass, a ware similar to Clutha glass, *Chintz* glassware, and *Silhouette* glassware. He used the marks *Corona*, *ADNA*, and *Nash*. After his company failed in 1931, he moved to Toledo, Ohio, working for Libbey as designer and technician in an effort to help the company regain its position in the luxury glass field. One line he designed being *Libbey-Nash* glassware. He quit Libbey in 1935 and was employed by various firms until his death in 1940.

Nash, Arthur J.

(1849-1934) An English glassmaker and technician who worked at White House Glass Works in Stourbridge, England, and became superintendent. Tiffany brought him to the United States about 1895, at first doing experimental work in Boston, Massachusetts. Later he and his sons, A. Douglas and Leslie, worked at Tiffany's Corona facility. While there, Arthur developed *Cypriote* glass and other forms of art glass, contributing much to Tiffany's success.

Nash, Leslie

A son of Arthur J. Nash and brother of A. Douglas Nash, who worked for various companies of Louis Comfort Tiffany. After leaving Tiffany, he started his own glass decorating facility at Woodside, Long Island, New York.

National Cut Glass Company

A glass cutting facility established in 1908 in Minneapolis, Minnesota. It closed about 1920.

National Glass Company

(1) A glass manufacturing facility that made pressed glass tableware. Located in Bellaire, Ohio, it was established in the early 1870s by John Fink and others. In 1877 it was sold to the Rodefer Brothers, who operated it as the National Glass Company until 1891. See *Rodefer Brothers*. (2) A glass cutting and engraving facility operating in Belmont County, Ohio, in the late 1890s, later becoming Rodefer-Gleason & Company. (3) A combination of several (nineteen at its peak) major tableware manufacturers. In the 1890s there was much unrest among tableware manufacturers. Workers' wages and the pricing of similar or identical wares varied among companies; innovations and improvements were postponed to maintain competitive prices; and the public trend was turning away from crystal glassware toward more expensive colored and decorative wares. Representatives of the larger companies met to discuss combining their assets to lessen competition and stabilize prices. After much negotiation, the National Glass Company was founded in July 1899. The primary purpose was to eliminate price competition by controlling prices. On November 1, 1899, it took control of the merged companies from its headquarters in Pittsburgh, Pennsylvania; its first president was Henry C. Fry. Immediately it began closing facilities. Some would reopen, others would not. The earliest to close were those in Zanesville, Ohio, and Summitville, Indiana. In February 1900, one of its most efficient and modern facilities, the Rochester Tumbler Company, burned to the ground and was never rebuilt. Many of its executives left. In 1902 only twelve of the original companies remained, and by March 1903 only ten remained. At this time it reorganized, building three new facilities: one in Cambridge (Cambridge Glass Company); one in Lancaster, Ohio; and one in Jeanette (Jeanette Glass Company). By 1904 the facilities remaining were leased to others, and by 1908 it was in bankruptcy and dissolved. The original nineteen companies were:

The Rochester Tumbler Company, Rochester, Pennsylvania

McKee & Brothers, Pittsburgh, Pennsylvania

Northwood Company, Indiana, Pennsylvania

Greensburg Glass Company, Greensburg, Pennsylvania

Keystone Tumbler Company, Rochester, Pennsylvania

Dalzell, Gilmore & Leighton Company, Findlay, Ohio

Ohio Flint Glass Company, Lancaster, Ohio

Crystal Glass Company, Bridgeport, Ohio

West Virginia Glass Company, Martins Ferry, Ohio

Royal Glass Company, Marietta, Ohio

Robinson Glass Company, Zanesville, Ohio

Indiana Tumbler & Goblet Company, Greentown, Indiana

Canton Glass Company, Marian, Indiana

Beatty-Brady Glass Company, Dunkirk, Indiana

Model Flint Glass Company, Albany, Indiana

Central Glass Company, Summitville, Indiana

Riverside Glass Works, Wellsburg, West Virginia

Fairmont Glass Company, Fairmont, West Virginia

Cumberland Glass Company, Cumberland, Maryland.

National Glass Factory A glass manufacturing facility established in 1893 in Fairmont, West Virginia, by Matthew Duncan and Alexander Sloan (Duncan & Sloan), soon becoming Sloan Brothers Glass Factory, which made flint glass tableware. It closed in 1903 and, in 1904, was taken over by the Monongahela Glass Company.

National Glass Manufacturing Company See *Frontier Cut Glass Company.*

National Pairpoint Corporation See *Mount Washington Glass Company.*

natron Sodium carbonate or sodium sesquicarbonate. Pliny, in the 1st century A.D., told a story about Syrian merchants who placed cakes of natron on the sands by the River Bellus to support their cooking pots. The heat generated by the fire caused the natron and sand to fuse, making the first glass. This account has no basis in fact. Natron was used as the soda or alkali component in making Roman or Egyptian glass, procured from the Wadi el-Natrun, northwest of Cairo, Egypt.

natural glass See *obsidian; tektites; fulgarites; pumice; radiolaria; Pele's hair* or *goddess's hair.*

naval subjects Embellishment on glassware engraved or enameled with designs or motifs illustrating naval engagements. See *ship subjects; privateer glassware.*

navettes Individual detailed glass jewels as opposed to globs. All glass jewels are stamped from molds. Globs are allowed to *crawl* together haphazardly, forming their own shapes. Navettes are in the shape of a marquise (a low, pointed oval with many facets).

NDW An abbreviation for *nipt diamond waies.*

Near Cut A trademark used by the Cambridge Glass Company on their line of pressed glass in imitation of cut glass. The mark and ware were first made about 1906.

Nebuchadnezzar See *wine bottle, sizes.*

necessaire *(French)* A small traveling case containing a drinking glass and a glass knife, fork, and spoon. Some, which also had the case made of glass, were made in Germany and at Murano during the early 18th century. Most were embellished with enameling.

neck That part of a bottle, vase, or other vessel located between the mouth and shoulder or body. It may be long or short and have parallel or sloping sides. Some have interior threading to secure a screw stopper. See *contracted neck; trumpet neck.*

necklace A string of beads, round, oblate, or flat small pierced plaques, or disks of multicolored glass or glass paste (see *pate-de-verre*) made in many places almost throughout the history of glass. Early ones of glass paste were made at Mycenae about 1300 B.C. and others in Egypt in the 4th and 3rd centuries B.C. Some were made of Roman glass in the 1st century A.D.

needle A small pointed instrument generally used for sewing. In most cases, each has an eye at one end and a point at the other. Early examples of colored glass needles were made throughout various parts of the Roman Empire. Believed to be used to adorn hair, they were occasionally embellished with opaque threads wound around one end.

needle case A small receptacle used to hold sewing needles. Most are cylindrical and composed of two parts: a cover fits over a narrower protruding extension of the lower section. Some needle cases of enameled opaque white glass were made in Bohemia. See *galanterie*.

needle etching Acid etching in which, after the object was coated with an acid resistant wax, a design was etched through the coating—often with a needle—and the object submersed in acid. The glass was removed, cleaned, and the remainder of the wax removed. This could be done several times, resulting in a picture having the appearance of a photograph.

nef A table ornament in the form of a fancy rigged sailing ship made in Belgium in the 16th century, the Netherlands in the 17th century, and England in the early 18th century. Occasionally spun glass (glass fiber) is used as an integral part of the overall design, particularly when portraying a ship at sea. Some parts may be of colored glass. See *boat; ship*.

NEGC An abbreviation for the New England Glass Company.

negus A cup from which negus—a punch made from water, wine, sugar, nutmeg, and lemon—was drunk.

Nellie Bly Novelties, particularly small lamps and other gadgets, named after Nellie Bly, who bettered Jules Verne's 80-day schedule around the world.

Nelson, John A. A glass cutter who operated a cutting shop from about 1910 to about 1920 in Brooklyn, New York.

Neoclassical style The resurrection of classical decoration that took place during the second half of the 18th century, replacing the rococo style, and based on that of ancient Greece and Rome. The neoclassical style was brought about chiefly by publicity generated by the excavation of Pompeii in the 1750s. In the initial phases of its resurgence, it is interchangeable with *Adam style* of England and *Louis Seize style* in France. It is noted for the use of swags, ram's heads, and similar motifs considered classical in form. Following the revolution in France in 1789, it developed gradually into the *Directoire style*, mainly a furniture style, and then the *Empire style*. The Empire style was contemporary with the *English Regency style* derived from it. In glassware, the baroque and rococo styles of glass engraving were superceded by faceting and engraving in the neoclassical style. Cylindrical tumblers and straight-sided goblets of simple form superseded the earlier graceful but lavishly embellished forms, especially in Germany. In England slender forms were preferred, the stems of wine glasses becoming somewhat shorter and cutting much less.

Neptune jug An *oinochoe*-shaped jug intricately engraved by the firm of J.G. Green of London and exhibited at the 1851 Exhibition in London.

Neri, Antonio (1576-1614) A writer, chemist, and priest; the author of *L'Arte Vetraria* (*The Art of Glassmaking*) published in Florence in 1612. It was the first printed book on the subject of the glassmaker and glassmaking, providing many formulae for making colored glass and other types of glass. It was translated into various languages: into English by Christopher Merret(t) in 1662, Latin (published in Holland) in 1669, French (1752); and German (1679). Neri noted the attractiveness of lead glass. Neri worked in Florence under the patronage of Don Antonio de'Medici about 1601, in Risa about 1603, and Antwerp in 1604, returning to Florence by 1611.

Nero's cup See *Trivulzio bowl.*

Neskhi A type of cursive Arabic script used as embellishment on some Islamic glassware.

nestoris (Aka *torzella*) A sphere-like jar with two vertical handles attached at the shoulder and rim of the mouth and extending upward above the rim. Each handle has two knobs, one at the juncture of the handle with the body and the other at the top of the handle. A third knob sometimes is located midway between the shoulder and the apex.

net glass See *reticello, vetro a.*

Netherlands glassware Glassware was made at Middelburg in the Netherlands from 1581 (the separation of the Netherlands from the southern part of the Low Countries, now Belgium—see *South Netherlands glassware*) until 1609 (Dutch independence from Spain). From 1609, many facilities were founded in North Netherlands, at Leiden, The Hague, Dordrecht, Rotterdam, Amsterdam, Delft, and elsewhere. At first they relied heavily on Venetian and Altarist craftsmen, and its products were influenced by German and English styles and techniques. During the 17th and 18th centuries, the Dutch prospered by developing three styles of embellishment, mainly the work of amateur engravers: (a) diamond point engraving, predominant from about 1575 to 1690, executed on thin Dutch glasses before English glasses were imported; (b) wheel engraving in German and Bohemian styles predominated from about 1690 to 1750, featuring commemorative glassware and designs of ships and heraldic devices; and (c) stippling predominated from about 1750 to 1800. Modern glassware is being made at the Royal Dutch Glass Works (a unit of the United Glass Works) at Leerdam.

netted glassware Beakers, tumblers, vases, or other glass objects enveloped in a network of delicate wire. Several *Reichsadlerhumpen* with the date "1616," enameled and covered with wire mesh, should be differentiated from the netted glass vessels blown into a wire mesh. Both types were made in Bohemia in the 19th century. See *reticulated glassware.*

network beaker See *vasa diatreta.*

network glass See *reticello, vetro a.*

Nevers figure Small glass figures of an opaque fusible glass, erroneously called *enamel glass* and mistaken for porcelain or faience, made in the late 16th and 17th centuries at Nevers, France, and other places within the country. Specimens range from one to six inches in height, superbly detailed with respect to features and fabrics. Single figures are on stands made of trailed glass threads; those that are not are presumed to be broken from a *Grotto.* Some animal figures are mold blown with applied thin glass threads. Occasionally large assemblages of such figures were made. The figures were made of fragments of opaque glass rods, softened *at-the-lamp*, worked and manipulated with pincers or other tools, often secured on a skeletal framework of copper wire. Most exhibit colored details. Similar figures were made in Venice, Germany, Spain, and England in the 17th century and thereafter. See *Nevers glassware; Four Seasons, The.*

Nevers glassware Glassware made in Nevers, France, dating from the 16th century when Ludovico Gonzaga, as a result of his marriage to Henrietta of Cleves, became Duke of Nevers. Gonzaga brought several Italian glassworkers to Nevers to make glass of various types in Italian style until the 18th century. See *Nevers figure.*

Neville, Asa G., Glass Company A glass manufacturing facility founded by Asa G. Neville in late 1891 in Blairsville, Pennsylvania. The company made gas, electric light, and kerosene globes in lime, lead, and opal glass that was cut, etched, or plain. It also produced battery jars, wine sets, decanters, lamps, founts, and novelties in both blown and pressed glass.

New Albany Glass Works (1) (1812-1891) A glass manufacturing facility established in New Albany, Pennsylvania, which made window glass and bottles. About 1820 it was operated by S.C. Bever & Co. as the Redstone Glass Works, and about 1836 by J.L. Bowman & Co. (2) (1864-1872) A glass manufacturing facility established by Captain John B. Ford, located across the river from Louisville, Kentucky. It made window glass, bottles, and mirrors. In 1869 it purchased three rolling and polishing machines from England to make plate glass. It had limited use at the time, and this caused it to go out of business.

New Amsterdam glasshouses Two glass manufacturing facilities were established in New Amsterdam (now New York City), New York, during the mid-17th century. One was established about 1645 by Everett Duijcking (Evert Duycking) (see *Duycking, Evert*), succeeded by Jacob Milyer (or Melyer) in 1674. The other was established in 1654 by Johannes (Jan) Smedes (Smee) on South William Street, between Wall and Pearl Streets, then called Glassmakers Street or Glass House Street, changed to Smee Street, then Smith Street and finally William Street. The second establishment was sold in 1664. Smedes is believed to have made window glass, bottles, house wares, and possibly some chemical wares. Operations were possibly carried on after that date by the Jansen family.

Clear glass vase, c. 1894-1916.
The Corning Museum of Glass

New Bedford Glass Company (1866/7-1868/9). A glass manufacturing facility established by Theodore Kern and other workers of the Sandwich Glass Factory (after disagreements with management), financed by some New Bedford merchants. It was purchased in 1869/70 by William L. Libbey. See *Mount Washington Glass Works.*

New Boston Glass Works (Aka *Perryopolis Glass factory*) A hollowware and window glass manufacturing facility established in 1816 in Perryopolis, Pennsylvania. In 1832 it was operated by Martin & Baker and, by 1937, Baker, Stewart & Co.

New Bremen Glass Manufactory
(Aka *New Bremen Glass Works, American Glass Manufactory, Amelung Glassworks, Etna Glass Works*) A tableware and window glass manufacturing facility established by John Frederick Amelung & Co. in 1784 in New Bremen, near Frederick, Maryland. A large amount of excellent wheel engraved glassware was made there. Between 1787 and 1790, another facility was built on adjacent land. Due to the small demand for the products, both facilities were offered for sale in 1795. An employee, Adam Kohlenberg, purchased the newer one, operating it for a few years (See *Kohlenberg Glass Works*). These were the only American facilities of the period from which inscribed and dated pieces are known to exist. They are often presentation pieces. However, a number of unsigned pieces have been positively identified as being made at these facilities; identification is based on the quality of the glass and engraving. Its best known piece is the *Bremen Pokal*, made and engraved in 1788 and sent to Germany as an example of its skill. See *Amelung, John Frederick.*

New Brighton Glass Company
Enrico Rosenzi claimed to have developed a perfectly opaque black glass, the formula developed in Venice hundreds of years ago and lost in time. He convinced several businessmen in New Brighton, Pennsylvania, to back him in making it. A facility called the American Ferroline Co. was built in 1884 to make *Ferroline*. Sales were slow, production costs high, and ordinary black glass cheaper, meeting the needs of the public. In 1886 the backers decided to make crystal tableware, changing the name to the New Brighton Glass Company. This also failed. The stockholders decided to make steel, changing the name to the New Brighton Steel Co. After years of success it became the Damascus Steel Company.

New Bronze glass (Aka *Rainbow glassware, Iris glassware*) An iridescent glassware made by Mt. Washington Glass Co. See *Iris glass.*

New Brooklyn Glass Works
See *Isabella Glass Works.*

New Brunswick Cut Glass Company

(1916-1920) A glass cutting facility operating in New Brunswick, New Jersey.

New Columbia Glass Works

A window glass manufacturing facility established in New Columbia (now Nesco), New Jersey, in 1845 by Jesse Richards and James Brookdale. It made high quality window glass and won top prize at the New York Institute for the best color of window glass. In 1848 Richards & Brookdale dissolved their partnership, and William Wescoat, longtime employee, carried on the business until at least 1858.

New England Crown Glass Co.

A crown window glass manufacturing facility incorporated in 1824 by the founders of the New England Glass Company. The company acquired land in East Cambridge, Massachusetts, built a facility, and began making glass. In 1838 it became insolvent.

New England Glass Bottle Company

A glass manufacturing facility incorporated in 1826 by Deming Jarves and Edmund Monroe of the New England Glass Company and the Boston & Sandwich Glass Co. Production began in East Cambridge, Massachusetts (next to the New England Glass Company) in 1827, making all types of bottles, including carboys, gallons, quarts, pints, wines, potter bottles, ink, preserve, mustard, mead, soda, and acid bottles, selling them in Massachusetts, Rhode Island, New York, Maryland, Virginia, Kentucky, Ohio, Louisiana, and the West Indies. It closed in 1845.

Clear glass creamer and sugar, c. 1837, New England Glass Company.
The Corning Museum of Glass

New England Glass Company

The Boston Porcelain & Glass Manufacturing Company was incorporated in 1814 in (East) Cambridge, Massachusetts, making earthenware and glassware. In 1815 Emmett, Fisher & Flowers leased it and began making solely glassware. In 1817 the New England Glass Company, formed by Amos Binney, Edmund Monroe, Daniel Hastings, Deming Jarves, etc., purchased it at public sale. Jarves was named sales and general manager. It originally made plain, cut, engraved, blown, and molded glassware. In 1825 Jarves left to establish the Boston & Sandwich Glass Co. In 1826 Thomas H. Leighton became superintendent, a position he held for about seventeen years. Six of his seven sons were glassmakers, working for the company. All became heads of various departments, and two, William and John, became assistant superintendents. From 1843 to 1865, Captain Joseph N. Howe was superintendent, followed by Henry Whitney Jr. from 1865 to 1870.

By 1827 the company had added pressed glass, paperweights, Lacy glass, an extensive variety of cut and engraved lead glass in both Venetian and English styles, and new colored glasses developed by Joseph Locke. Prior to 1850, silvered (mercury) glass was added.

In the early 1870s, New England Glass Company was offered for sale because of financial problems caused by the higher costs of importing fuel, competition from others using less costly lime glass, the depression of 1873, and labor problems. In 1874 William L. Libbey, who became agent for the company in 1870, leased it after production and sales began to suffer. In 1880 it was known as the New England Glass Company (Works), William L. Libbey & Son, Proprietors. It was a break-even operation at best and, in 1887, the workers unionized and issued new demands. Unable to meet the demands, the workers struck. As a result, the company closed on January 2, 1888. Edward Drummond Libbey, son of William (d. 1883), moved operations to Toledo, Ohio, and the New England Glass Company surrendered its charter on September 18, 1890. Much of its wares were signed; there were eighteen different authenticated signatures and three others that are questionable. Some were used at different times during its history, but many were used at the same time, applied in one of the following ways: cutting, engraving, metal stamping, etching, molding, or printed labels. See *Amberina; New England Peachblow; Pomona; Agata; Maize glassware; Jarves, Deming; Libbey, W.L., & Son; New England Glass Manufacturers.*

New England Glass Works

A glass manufacturing facility established in Temple, New Hampshire, in 1780 by Robert Hewes. It burned shortly after being completed before any glass was made. It was rebuilt, but the furnaces, which he tried to salvage after being exposed to cold weather, could not take the heat and collapsed after a small amount of glass was made. He petitioned the government for concessions and permission to establish a lottery to raise money for rebuilding. Some concessions were granted, but the lottery failed. In spite of this, he rebuilt it in the summer of 1781 and began making glass. Production was short-lived and little glass was made (some crown glass and bottles). The plant closed in late 1781-early 1782. Hewes never exercised the patent granted him on March 1, 1783, giving him the exclusive right to make glass in Boston for seven years. In 1787, Hewes' petition and privilege was rescinded in favor of the Boston Crown Glass Manufactory with which he was associated for a short time. In 1788, Hewes was associated with the Pitkins, who had been granted a 25-year monopoly to establish a facility in East Hartford, Connecticut in 1783. This too was unsuccessful, causing financial loss to the Pitkins.

Peachblow vase, New England Glass Company, Cambridge, Massachusetts, c. 1886. Museum of American Glass at Wheaton Village, Millville, NJ.

New England Peachblow

New England Glass Company's version of *Peachblow* (the creation of Edward Libbey) was on the market in 1885 but not patented until March 2, 1886, as *Wild Rose*. It was not cased like *Wheeling Peachblow*, but of one homogeneous composition throughout. It was partially white or had creamy or ivory tints in the portion not reheated, shading to deep rose (raspberry) in the reheated areas. Some pieces have a glossy finish, but the vast majority are satin.

New Geneva Glasshouse

A window glass manufacturing facility established by Andrew, Baltasar (the Younger), and Theophilus Kramer and Philip Reitz in New Geneva, Pennsylvania in 1837. It was located on the original site of the New Geneva Glassworks, which had been idle for several years. The New Geneva Glasshouse operated successfully for two decades. The last owner was Isaac P. Eberhart, who had the facility torn down in 1857. See *New Geneva Glassworks.*

New Geneva Glassworks

A window and bottle glass manufacturing facility, the first west of the Allegheny Mountains, established by Albert Gallatin & Co. in New Geneva, Pennsylvania. The first glass was blown in January 1798. (Gallatin, 1761-1849, was not a glassmaker by trade, but a statesman—he was U.S. Secretary of the Treasury from 1801 to 1813.)

The New Geneva Glassworks was also known as Gallatin & Nicholson; James W. Nicholson was Gallatin's brother-in-law and a financial backer. He employed the Kramer family, including George and Christian Kramer (1773-1858), all of whom had left the New Bremen Glass Manufactory. There was a partnership between the owners and workers, effective for six years. The workers were to receive regular wages and pay for their share of the investment from their share of the profits. This partnership lasted only until 1799, when many of the financial backers withdrew. In 1803 Nicholson left and it became the Albert Gallatin Company. Eventually, molded and blown household wares were added.

In 1804 coal was discovered across the Monongahela River in Greensboro. In 1807 Gallatin and new financial backers, including Baltasar

Kramer, built a new glasshouse near the coal supply. They operated both for a while, closing the old one after a few years. In 1813 Nicholson returned and it became Messrs. Nicholson & Company, and in 1830, B.F. Black & Co. purchased it. In 1847 it was destroyed by fire. The better products made there are called *Gallatin-Kramer glass* or *Kramer family glass*. See *New Geneva Glasshouse*.

New Granite Glass Company

Peter Mills & Company established a bottle and window glass manufacturing facility in Zanesville, Ohio, in 1816. It was unsuccessful and reorganized as the New Granite Glass Company under James Taylor and Alexander Culbertson. In 1823 both died and Murdock & Casell (Thomas Murdock and Joseph Cassell) took over, making bottles and flasks. In the 1840s, Arnold Lippit purchased it. In 1848 it failed while Lippit was trying single-handedly to operate it and the White Glass Works (Zanesville Glass Manufacturing Company). About 1849, Cockran & Brother took over the facility, failing in 1852.

New Granite Glass Works

(1865-1871) A bottle glass manufacturing facility established in Stoddard Mill Village, New Hampshire, by the four sons of Joseph Foster (George, Charles, Wallace, and Joseph Jr.). In 1868 Charles B. Barrett purchased it, operating it until 1871 when it was destroyed by fire and never rebuilt.

New Hampshire Glass Factory

A cylinder window glass manufacturing facility established in Keene, New Hampshire, by the New Hampshire Glass Company (incorporated in 1814 by John Elliott, D. Bradford, David Watson, John Hatch, Nathaniel Sprague, Aaron Appleton, and Timothy Twitchell). Captain Lawrence Schoolcraft was manager, and his son, Henry, also worked there. Known locally as the *North Works*, it began making window glass in early 1815 and was one of the most successful window glass facilities. In 1817 it failed and was taken over by another firm. In 1825 the name was changed to the Keene Window Glass Factory. In 1832 it was operated by Adams & Co. and in 1847 was purchased by Henry, Timothy, and J.D. Colony, who added bottles. In 1855 it was destroyed by fire and never rebuilt.

New Haven Glass Works

Mark Leavenworth (1852-1912) graduated from Yale in 1771 and practiced law in New Haven, Connecticut. He and his half-brother engaged in the West India trade and several other enterprises. He served in the Army of the Revolution. He later spent much time in England before he settled in Paris in 1799 because of financial problems. His various business ventures failed and by 1805 he was in financial ruin. One of his enterprises in the United States involved glassmaking. In 1789 he built a glass manufacturing facility, the New Haven Glass Works, but no glass was made. He applied to the General Assembly of Connecticut for financial assistance in the form of a lottery in 1790, wanting to expand the facility to make window glass, flint glass, and bottles. While his petition was granted, no glass was made.

New Intarsia Ware

See *Intarsia Ware*.

New Irish glass

See *Gray-Stan glass*.

New Jersey Window Glass Company

A window, and possible bottle, glass manufacturing facility believed to have existed in Brown Pines, New Jersey, sometime prior to 1776.

New Lebanon Glass Company

(1873-1876) A bottle glass manufacturing facility established in New Lebanon, New York.

New Liberties Glass Facture

A glass manufacturing facility in Philadelphia, Pennsylvania, operating from 1771 until 1820. It was then purchased by a group of employees from the New England Glass Company, who also established the Union Glass Company.

New London Glass Company

(1856-1874) A green glass manufacturing facility established in New London, Connecticut, which made bottles and demijohns in dark bottle glass and other items in light aquamarine glass, some almost colorless. In 1859 it was owned by Warren & Co., operating as the Union Glass Works. By 1865 it was leased by N.S. Fish, operating as the Thames (River) Glass Company. Later Fish and William Batty purchased it, selling it to a syndicate in Ellenville, New York, which made only bottles.

New Martinsville Crystal Eagle #18 ruby sugar and creamer, 1936.
Tri-State Antiques

Viking glass ad, December 1970. Krause Publications

New Martinsville Glass (Manufacturing) Co.

New Martinsville Glass (Manufacturing) Co. A glass manufacturing facility (New Martinsville Glass Manufacturing Co.) established in New Martinsville, West Virginia, by Mark Douglass and George Mathehy, former employees of the Speciality Glass Company and the West Virginia Glass Company. Manufacturing operations began in mid-1901, initially making pressed tableware in crystal, colored, and opalescent glass. It was damaged by a flood in early March 1907, and on March 17, 1907, it was destroyed by fire. By October 1907, a newly rebuilt facility was in operation. It is best known for its lamps, vanity sets, figural decanters, and novelty figures.

The company's operations can be divided into three periods: (a) the art and opaque glass era (1901 to 1907); (b) the pattern glass era (1907 to 1937); and (c) the crystal ware era—animals and figurines (1937 to 1944). From 1908 to 1916, David Fisher was manager, bringing it great success in the tableware industry. Between late 1916 and mid-1919, management changed twice before Ira M. Clarke became manager, remaining until September 1926. Clarke had worked at the J.B. Higbee Glass Company, securing several patents for glass banks, candy containers, ashtrays, and matchbox holders. He revived its status and

patented a variety of glassware items. It made a wide range of stationers' glassware (inkwells, sponge cups, pen trays, etc.) and soda fountain and utilitarian household glassware (salt and pepper shakers, cruets, vases, candy jars, etc.). He introduced an extensive line of lightly cut wares and two new pattern lines each year; revived several older patterns and patterns with new names, previously issued by Higbee which had closed; and added new and expensive household items. When Clarke left, Robert E. McEldowney, a longtime employee, became general manager, remaining until Clarke returned in August 1932. In 1933, McEldowney left to work for the Paden City Glassworks founded by David Fisher in 1916. The McEldowney years are characterized by glassware in unusual shapes (triangles a favorite) and intriguing color combinations, in addition to the more traditional articles.

New Martinsville Glass Manufacturing Co. made glassware for other companies, in the form of blanks or from molds provided by them to fill orders or meet deadlines. In the late 1920s-early 1930s, it increased the production of black glass, adding transparent ruby and opaque jade green to its broad color selection. Hand-painted decorations, cutting, and acid etching continued, and vanity sets—normally a powder or puff box with two perfume bottles on a tray or mirror—were an essential part of its production.

During the late 1920s, labor problems and the onset of the Depression caused it to operate for intermittent periods on half-time schedules, and workers were paid in cash and scrip. Facing bankruptcy, Clarke was hired back as general manager on August 1, 1932. At the time the company was shut down, but it reopened on September 19, 1932. Clarke became court appointed receiver on January 3, 1933. In December 1932 it came out with two new lines. With repeal of the 18th Amendment (Prohibition), new sales were generated in beverage sets and glasses. Clarke died suddenly on April 27, 1937, and the facility closed for five weeks. On June 23, 1937, John F. Martin, the company's treasurer, died. The courts sought bids on the facility in July and September 1937, but received none. In July 1938, R.M. Rice and Carl Schultz submitted a bid, and with David Barth formed the New Martinsville Glass Company. Barth started with the company as a packer, rising to assistant general manager under Clarke. He left in June 1938, returning a month later as general manager, and leaving in August 1940 to join the Crystal Division of the War Production Board in Washington, D.C. About a decade later, he established Barth Art Glass.

Very few New Martinsville pieces are signed; those that were had an incised "NM." In 1944 there was a change in management. The company was renamed the Viking Glass Company; the Rainbow Art Glass Company was its subsidiary. Viking made ruby glass animals for Mirror Images (signed with a raised "V"). Viking closed in 1986. In 1987 Kenneth Dalzell (formerly with the Fostoria Glass Company) purchased its assets, reopening it as the Dalzell-Viking Glass Company. Its current wares are marked *Viking* or *Rainbow Cut*. See *Rainbow Art Glass Company*.

New Martinsville Peachblow A

glassware named *Muranese* made at New Martinsville, West Virginia, from the late 1800s to 1907. It got the name *Peachblow* in the early 1940s when large amounts were dumped on the market, as the result of the success of *Wheeling Peachblow*. It isn't comparable to the *Mt. Washington, New England* and *Wheeling Peachblows*.

New Stourbridge Glass Works See
Sowerby's Ellison Glass Works.

New Windsor Glass House (1752-
1785) A window and bottle glass manufacturing facility established in New Windsor, New York, by Samuel Bayard & Company of New York City.

New York City Plate Glass Works
See *Pittsburgh Plate Glass Company.*

New York Glass Works A short-lived
glass manufacturing facility established by Stephen Long in 1820 in New York City, New York. See *Bloomingdale Flint Glass Works; Bloomingdale Glass Works.*

Newark Cut Glass Company (1906-
1918) A cut glass manufacturing facility established in Newark, New Jersey.

Newcastle glass (1) Glass in numerous
varieties and styles made by any one of the several facilities in Newcastle-upon-Tyne from the 17th century until the present. It is noted for its softness, weight and color, making it highly desirable for engraving. In the 18th century large quantities were exported to Holland where it was embellished with wheel engraving and stippling. Newcastle was an important center of window glassmaking and ornamental engraved wares, including stemmed wine glasses, Jacobite and Williamite glassware, and, during the 19th century, cased, pressed, and country market glass. (2) Light baluster glasses embellished by the Dutch. See *baluster, light; balustroid.*

newel ornament An ornament used to
embellish the top of a newel post (a post at the top or bottom of a stairway supporting a banister). Those of glass were solid, spherical in shape, and generally three to four inches in diameter with an integral glass peg by which it was dowelled into the post. They are rare since most have long since broken off.

Newman, C., & Company A bottle
glass manufacturing facility established by Carlton Newman in San Francisco, California, sometime after 1860. On May 7, 1867, he obtained a patent for a "pot for melting glass." It specialized in making wicker-covered demijohns. It was still operating in 1890, most likely the only glass facility in California at this time.

Newton brand window glass A spe-
cialty glass made by Getsinger & Sons in the late 1870s. It was an exceptionally high quality, double thick window glass.

Niagara Cut Glass Company (1905-
1915) A glass cutting shop established in Buffalo, New York.

Nicholson, Messrs., & Company See
New Geneva Glassworks.

nick A defect in a piece of glass usually
caused by bumping it against another piece or other object. They are very small, about the size of a pinhead, smaller than a chip or flake.

nickel A metallic agent used as both a color-
ing and decolorizing agent, and in making

smoky colored glasses. In the making of lead or potash glass, it produces a deep violet to purple color; in soda-lime glass, a yellow color. It was first used as a decolorizing agent in the second half of the 18th century. When used in conjunction with cobalt, the combination decolorizes lead crystal by reducing or neutralizing the yellowish tints produced by other constituents.

Nickel Plate Glass Company (1888-1898)
A plate glass manufacturing facility established in Fostoria, Ohio. In 1889 it moved to a new facility in Findlay, Ohio, where recently discovered gas fields gave the promise of inexpensive fuel. In 1891 it joined the U.S. Glass Company (*Factory N*).

Nickerson, Cobb & Company See
Franklin Glass Factory Company.

Nickolson, Warrick & Company See
Freewill Glass Manufactory.

Nicolai, Henry, Company
A glass cutting shop established in Hammonton, New Jersey, operating from 1906 to 1909. From 1912 until 1914, Nicholai was in business with John W. Rothfus (Rothfus-Nicolai Company) in Hammonton. When Rothfus left in 1914, Nicolai operated it under his own name. In 1916 he worked for the Figueroa Cut Glass Company.

night lamp See *miniature lamp.*

night set See *nite set.*

Niland, J.J., Company
James J. Niland was apprenticed as a glass cutter for six years in England and Scotland, coming to the United States in 1882 to work for Bergen & Niland (Thomas A. Niland, his brother). In 1902 James established a glass cutting shop in Meriden, Connecticut—J.J. Niland Company. Thomas, formerly of Bergen & Niland, left J.D. Bergen Company in 1902 to join his brother. In its early years, it made heavy cut glass. In 1905 Thomas became manager, and in 1918 it was named Niland Cut Glass Company. By 1929 rock crystal was its specialty. After 1935 it was operated on a small scale. It closed in 1959.

Niland, Thomas A., & Company
Thomas A. Niland was employed at the Boston & Sandwich Glass Co., the New England Glass Co., and the Meriden Flint Glass Company before he entered the glass cutting business with J.D. Bergen, forming Bergen & Niland. Niland sold his interest to Bergen and the firm became J.D. Bergen Company. Niland continued to work there until 1896, when he established Thomas A. Niland & Company in Deep River, Connecticut, with partners Jones and Burgess. Shortly thereafter he sold his interest to James and Ansel Jones. Even though he had no interest in it, it was known as Niland Cut Glass Company, sometimes called the Deep River Cut Glass Works, which closed in 1902. In 1897 Niland went back to J.D. Bergen and, in 1902 left to work for his brother at the J.J. Niland Company.

Niland Cut Glass Company See
Niland, J.J., Company; Niland, Thomas A., & Company.

Ninety Six percent silica glass
A glass made by removing all compounds except silica from borosilicate glass after being formed by conventional techniques. It has extraordinary thermal endurance and chemical resistance, and excellent electrical characteristics. It is used for sight glasses, Vycor brand chemical glassware, and windows and antenna shields for space vehicles.

nip
A half-pint and the name of the mug from which it was drunk.

niperkin
A mug, larger than a *nip*, that holds more than a half-pint, most often a pint.

nipple shield
A small conically shaped object with a center hole, placed over a woman's breast to protect her during breast feeding.

nipt diamond waies
A style of network embellishment mainly in the shape of diamonds and lozenges made from applied or mold blown glass threads pincered together at regular yet alternate intervals (hence, *nipped diamond waies*). The term was first recorded by George Ravenscroft in his product price list in 1677. They were made in London and elsewhere into the 1700s and again in Newcastle-upon-Tyne during the late 18th century. Similar embellishment is found on some ancient Roman glass from the 2nd to 4th centuries and on many types of glassware made at later dates. The term is often abbreviated "NDW."

nite set (Aka *tumble up*) A set consisting of a handleless jug with a tall neck and a tumbler, inverted and placed over the neck, serving as a cover. It was usually placed on a nightstand to quench nighttime thirst.

nitrum The same as natron—naturally occurring soda. See *natron.*

Nitsche family Joseph Nitsche (1855-1923), born in Bohemia, learned the art of glass cutting before going to England in 1882 as an engraver for Thomas Webb. About 1892 he came to Corning, New York, first employed by J. Hoare & Co. He started his own home cutting shop in 1894 where his sons, Clement and Ernest, learned to engrave. About 1900 Joseph began working at Hawkes, still working in the home shop doing both copper wheel and stone engraving until his death. Clement also worked for Hawkes, but in 1904 left to work at Sinclair. After it closed, he worked in the family shop and for a period for Westmoreland, also doing some engraving for Hunt. After 1928 most of his work was for Steuben. In 1937, after closing the shop, he taught engraving at Steuben until he retired in 1950 at age seventy.

Nixon & Cook See *Vermont Glass Factory.*

No-Nick goblet See *hotel goblet.*

nodus (Latin) Literally, *knot.* A glass ring used on early Venetian *tazze* to join the body to the stem or foot. Over time it evolved into a globular knop, or when flattened, a collar or merese.

noggin A small mug with a round body and a small mouth.

Norcross, S., & Company; Norcross, Samuel & Urich See *Tansboro Glass Works.*

Norman slab glass A type of stained glass made by blowing molten glass into a long square or rectangular- shaped mold, then cut to yield five rectangular pieces—the four sides and the base—having a slightly uneven surface and texture and containing all of the "flaws" associated with medieval stained glass. The name has no apparent connection with Normandy or the Normans.

Normandy method A name used for the process used for making crown glass. See *crown glass.*

North American Glass Company See *Foster Brothers Glass Works.*

North British Glassworks See *Moncrieff Glassworks.*

North Wheeling (Flint) Glass Works See *Sweeney Brothers.*

North Works See *New Hampshire Glass Factory.*

Northwestern-Ohio Cut Glass Company A distributor of cut glass for many small cutting shops in Chicago, Illinois.

Northwood, H., (&) Co. A glass manufacturing facility established by Harry Northwood and his cousin, Thomas Dugan, in 1902 in the old Hobbs, Brockunier facility in Wheeling, West Virginia, after it had been purchased and closed by the United States Glass Company (*Factory H*). It was repaired and modified, and production began in September 1902, making vast quantities of tableware from unique blown ware to pressed ware, and numerous novelty items. Northwood revived glassmaking designs and techniques from the past, developing many new innovative patterns and decorative treatments, and experimented with many new colors. Many of its wares were similar to those made during his earlier ventures, but it continually made new lines, breaking tradition by issuing them in mid-year as well as the traditional January issuance (in 1906 a new *Intaglio* line was issued in mid-year). In late 1905 it began putting its new trademark—*N-in-a-circle*—on its wares, also using the "*underlined-N-in-a-circle*" mark. Not all pieces were marked.

In 1902 it introduced lighting ware (as the United States was shifting from kerosene illumination to electricity), making kerosene lamps, shades for gas lighting and electric fixtures, and in 1908, iridescent ware. In 1911-1912, Northwood made many experimental batches of an alabaster-like opaque white glass called *Luna* developed for use in electric light shades and globes. An iridized version was called *Pearl*, which had the basic characteristics of Carnival glass. *Luna* was believed to infringe upon the patent rights of Mac Beth-Evan's *Alba*, so Northwood agreed to pay royalty payments. After a few payments, he stopped because Mac Beth-Evans was suing numerous other companies, including General Electric, for patent infringement. When the final judgment was issued, Northwood had to pay about $42,500, but *Luna* sales resulted in high profits through 1920 since he expanded its use to household articles. He held several patents for lighting goods and fixtures and continued to make several lines of pattern glass during the 1900s and 1910s, and numerous colored and decorated wares between 1915 and 1919.

On February 4, 1919, Northwood died at age 58, after which the company reorganized. It was renovated during 1921-1922, and accrued substantial debts. In September 1925 it went into receivership and closed in December 1925. On June 14, 1926, it was sold at auction to Dollar Savings & Trust, which resold it to P.J. Gast & Sons Inc.

Northwood, Harry The son of John Northwood I, Harry was born in Stourbridge, England, in 1860. He apprenticed in the glass-making industry at age fourteen and attended a provincial art school. His brothers, Carl and John II, also entered the trade. In November 1881 Harry came to the United States and secured work with his cousin, Thomas Dugan—who came to the United States at about the same time— as glass etchers at Hobbs, Brockunier & Co. In 1882 Harry married Clara Elizabeth Beaumont and had two children, Harry Clarence (H.C., b.1883) and Mabel Virginia (b.1884). In early 1884, Harry left Hobbs, going to the LaBelle Glass Works. While LaBelle was shut down during much of 1884 and 1885, because of labor problems and the flooding of the Ohio River, he worked at Phoenix Glass, returning to LaBelle in 1886. In April 1887 he left LaBelle for the Buckeye Glass Company, where he stayed for about two weeks, returning to LaBelle for a significant pay increase. He became manager with the official title of Metal Maker & Designer. The LaBelle facility burned in September 1887 and, in October 1887, Harry resigned in a dispute over rebuilding it. Harry then worked for Elson Glass for a short time before establishing his own facility, Northwood Glass Company (for activities between 1887 and 1899, see *Northwood Glass Company; Northwood Glass & Manufacturing Company*). After his Indiana, Pennsylvania, company became part of the National Glass Company, he became its sales agent in London. He tried unsuccessfully to become a member of its board of directors. In late 1901 Harry returned from England, but went back in February 1902 when his father died. He returned to the United States in March 1902, and in April purchased (with his cousin Thomas Dugan) the old Hobbs, Brockunier facility, operating it as H. Northwood (&) Co. See *Northwood, H., (&) Co.* Northwood died on February 4, 1919.

Northwood, John, I (1836-1902) An English glassmaker whose specialty was cameo glass. At the age of twelve he began working for W.H., B. & J. Richardson at Stourbridge, and later for Benjamin Richardson I. In 1860 at nearby Wordsley, he established J. & J. Northwood with his brother, Joseph, as business manager. About 1881 he became technical advisor to Stevens & Williams Ltd. In 1873, after nine years of work, he completed the Elgin Vase. In 1876, after 20 years of experimentation, he won a prize for making a copy of the Portland Vase. In 1878 he completed the Milton Vase and, in 1882, the Pegasus Vase (for Thomas Webb & Sons). About 1880 he invented a machine for making herringbone embellishment in glassware by pulling glass threads embedded in molten glass, and a template machine for making precise geometric patterns, enabling etched glass to rival engraved glass. In 1885 and afterwards, he invented tools enabling the glassworker to impress raised flower prunts on the body of a vessel. He also invented a glass crimping device; a glass expansion testing machine facilitating research into the physical characteristics of cased glass necessary for making commercial cameo pieces; perfected processes using various acids for etching glass; and developed designs and colors that allowed cameo-like effects to be made rapidly. His work was perpetuated by his son, John Northwood II, and by his followers, including George and Thomas Woodall, who established the Northwood School at Stourbridge where designing was done for several companies until about 1890. At that time less costly methods of embellishment were introduced. John I had two other sons, Carl and Harry. See *Northwood, John, II; Northwood, Harry.*

Northwood, John, II (1870-1960) The son of John Northwood I, he made cameo glass inspired by the work of his father. In 1906 he finished a cameo plaque measuring fifteen inches in diameter, depicting the *Birth of Aphrodite*. See *Silveria glassware.*

Northwood Company See *Northwood Glass & Manufacturing Company.*

Northwood cream pitcher, amethyst, Cable & Grape pattern.
Davanna Collection

Northwood Glass Company A glass manufacturing facility established in December 1887 by Harry Northwood. Occupying the facility of the former Union Glass Company and Dithridge Glass Company, it began making glass in January 1888. After four years, operations were moved to a new facility in Ellwood City, Pennsylvania because of: (a) small furnace capacity; (b) it was in the flood zone of the Ohio River; (c) labor problems; and (d) incentives from Ellwood City. The Martins Ferry facility was closed in July 1892. The Columbus Glass Company took over the facility, anticipating opening in the spring of 1894, but financial difficulties prevented it. In early 1895, some glassworkers made plans to reopen it, but nothing materialized. In late 1895 it was leased to the Beaumont Glass Company, founded by Percy Beaumont, Northwood's brother-in-law. (See *Beaumont Glass Company*).

The Ellwood City facility opened in October 1892, making mold blown glassware in distinctive colors. In general, the wares were less expensive than those made in Martins Ferry, even though many patterns were made in both locations, and greater attention was paid to the decorating department for etching, engraving, and cutting. Because it had its own gas well, it

did not have to depend on a public utility with uncertain supplies and rates, or outside sources of fuel. In May 1894, operations ceased when the crown on the furnace collapsed. However, the decorating department continued to operate until the inventory was exhausted. A new Murphy furnace was installed, going into operation in July 1894. In January 1896, Northwood purchased a facility in Indiana, Pennsylvania, leaving the Ellwood City operations to associates, and became immersed in the operations of the Indiana facility. As soon as he left the Ellwood City facility, law suits and financial difficulties caused Northwood to leave the company and the facility to close. In late 1898, it was purchased by the American Lamp & Brass Company, operating as Clark Brothers Glass Company. In 1905 it reorganized as the Ellwood City Glass Company. See *Northwood Glass & Manufacturing Company.*

Northwood Glass & Manufacturing Company (Aka *Northwood Company, Indiana Glass Works*). A glass manufacturing facility founded by Harry Northwood in Indiana, Pennsylvania, in February 1896, after he severed ties with the Northwood Glass Company in Ellwood City in January 1896. Samuel Dugan Sr. (his wife's brother) and his three sons came with Northwood. For two years he leased the Indiana Glass Company facility (closed in late 1893) and began making glass in March 1896. Its first advertisements list fine crystal, fancy art glass in colors, tableware, lamps, and novelties. Initially many articles were made in patterns and shapes identical or similar to those made at Ellwood City, but soon new styles, shapes, and patterns began to appear.

In 1897 Frank Leslie Fenton came to work in the decorating department, was made its foreman within a year, but left with Harry Bastow, Northwood's plant manager, to work for the newly established Jefferson Glass Company in 1900. In 1897 Northwood introduced two new lines, *Klondyke* and *Alaska*, both highly successful. In January 1898, Northwood's lease expired and Steubenville, Ohio, made him an offer to move operations there. The town of Indiana countered and Northwood stayed, but he purchased and expanded the facility. In 1898 the *Louis XV* line was introduced; in early 1899, *Intaglio, Opaline Brocade* (now called *Spanish Lace*), and *Venetian* lines; and in June 1899, the *Pagoda* line.

On September 4, 1899, it became part of the National Glass Company, known as the Northwood (Glass) Works or Factory 13. In October 1899, Northwood and his wife sailed for England, being named the London sales agent of the National Glass Company. Factory 13 issued the *Nautilus* line (now called *Argonaut Shell*) in January 1900. Northwood attempted, unsuccessfully, to obtain a seat on the board of directors of National Glass. After he returned from England in 1902, he founded the H. Northwood Company. In the meantime, National appointed Harry Bastow superintendent and Thomas E.A. Dugan manager of Factory 13, and several new lines were introduced. In 1903 National was in a bad financial shape, and several key individuals who had placed their companies in National's hands left. These men established new companies and facilities and competed with National, which sold Factory 13 to Thomas Dugan in December 1903, and by mid-January 1904, Dugan Glass Company was formed. See *Dugan Glass Company.*

Northwood (Glass) Works See *Northwood Glass & Manufacturing Company.*

Norton Park Works See *Edinburgh Crystal Glass Co.*

Norwegian glassware Plans for establishing a glass industry in Norway were conceptualized in Copenhagen, Denmark, in 1739, and the first facility was built at Nostetangen in 1741. It operated until 1777, making primarily tableware and chandeliers. From 1754 to 1766, the industry was under the direction of Casper Herman von Storm who, in 1760, received a monopoly for Norway (and Denmark) until 1803, after which several privately owned glassworks were established. Von Storm founded the Hurdals Verk (which made crown glass from 1755 and added tableware and chandeliers) and the Hadelands Glasverk (which made bottles from 1765). Both were staffed by Germans. He tried to replicate English wares, imitating the Anglo and Anglo-Venetian styles, hiring James Keith from England in 1775.

In the late 1770s, crystal production of tableware was moved from Nostetangen to Hurdals

Verk, and, in 1809, to Gjovik Verk. Production at Gjovik Verk declined over the years, closing in 1843. In 1852 the Hadeland facility underwent a reorganization and was renovated, making tableware and ornamental glass in modern styles and forms using modern methods of production. Currently this facility is Norway's chief producer of fine wares. Pressed glass has been made there since 1855, while engraving, acid etching, and cutting have been exercised with great skill. From 1855 to 1860, a series of cased tankards were made, embellished with geometric cuttings cut in the Bohemian manner. In the 20th century, Hadeland became the dominant maker of tableware and embellished wares in Norway. A more recently established facility is Norsk Glasverk at Magnor, which has made decorative glassware and tableware since 1950.

Norwich glassware See *Lynn glassware.*

nose The end of a blowpipe dipped into a pot of, and onto which was gathered, molten glass.

nose holes See *bye holes.*

nosegay A motif consisting of a flat bouquet with millefiori canes as flowers.

notched A V-shaped cut or folded edge, especially in cut glass.

notched prism (Aka *beading*) A cut glass motif made of two miter cuts close together, either parallel or slightly divergent, then cutting or notching the prism between the two. It resembles a string of beads, and may be horizontal or vertical. See *prism.*

notched prism flares A cut glass motif that is a variation of the notched prism, made by spreading the miter cuts and inserting fans at one or both ends.

Nova Scotia Glass Company A glass manufacturing facility established in May 1881 in Trenton, New Glasgow, Nova Scotia, located close to a good supply of coal, sand, and shipping facilities. The company made pressed mold blown and cut glassware, including goblets, tumblers, lamps, and lamp shades. It was purchased in 1890 by the Diamond Glass Company of Montreal and closed in 1892.

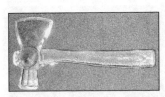

*Hatchet,
8" l.
Davanna
Collection*

novelty (1) A generic term used to describe small glass items made using manual and/or mechanical techniques. Handmade ones were made by lamp workers and blowers, but pressed glass ones predominated the market during the late 19th century. Miniature ones have been made in the form of animals, ships, books, hats, anvils, baby carriages, etc., even complete sets of water glasses and pitchers for doll houses or as salesmen's samples. Some, such as paperweights, had a utilitarian as well as ornamental purposes; some were used as match and toothpick holders and small dresser boxes. (2) Pieces that were not part of a standard set (i.e., a covered dish in the form of a chicken) but were added to a previously made pattern (i.e., a gravy boat, not part of the original set) or made with modifications in design were also called *novelties*.

Novelty Glass Company (1) A glass manufacturing facility established in 1880 in Fostoria, Ohio, later becoming U.S. Glass Company's *Factory T.* (2) See *Brilliant Glass Works.* (3) See *Elmer Window Light Company; Bassett Glass Works.*

Novogrudok glassware Glassware and fragments excavated between 1958 and 1962 at Novogrudok, in southern Russia, are attributed to a facility operating there as early as the 12th century. They consist mainly of fragments of (a) beakers (*Stopka*); (b) long, thin blue bottles with narrow necks, small mouths and rounded bottoms, some with a painted dove; and (c) pieces of a beaker now called a *Hedwig glass*. The glass is varicolored, colorless, or opaque white with occasional pieces of double layered glass. Some are painted with gilt and white and red enamel.

nozzle See *candle nozzle.*

nozzle, tulip See *tulip nozzle.*

NUART A trademark registered by the Imperial Glass Company about 1920.

NUCUT A trademark of the Imperial Glass Company used on its wares in imitation of cut glass.

Nuppenbecher *(German)* Literally, *drop beaker.* A beaker of Waldglas, either cylindrical or slightly conical, tall or short, the main feature being an overall pattern of large drops of glass on the lower part of the body. These were fused on by first touching the body of the vessel with heated glass on the tip of an iron rod and drawing them upward or outward to a point. On some of colorless glass the drops are embellished by a small opaque drop (eye). They were made in Germany, Bohemia, and likely the Netherlands, and date from the 14th century. Early ones have the drops in a random arrangement. Later ones, from the 15th and 16th centuries, are arranged in diagonal or vertical rows. Smaller ones vary in height from 2-1/3 to 4 inches, having one or more horizontal rows of drops. Larger ones may be up to 10 inches tall while Bohemian ones exist up to 18 inches, with five to nine rows of drops and an applied crinkled or toothed foot rim. A few have a footed stem with threading or engraving, some have a kick base, and some have a cover. Similar beakers have, instead of straight sides, a cup-shaped mouth curving outward from above an encircling thread; these are called *Krautstrunk.* See *Warzenbecher.*

Nuremberg glassware Glassware embellished in Nuremberg since the 16th century, consisting primarily of shallow wheel engraving and enameling in Schwarzlot. Shallow engraving, often accompanied by diamond point engraving, was done at Nuremberg from 1622 until about 1725. However, from about 1700, it was gradually superseded by deeper cutting as soda glass glassware was gradually replaced by Bohemian glassware, a potash glass, more suitable for deep cutting. Shallow engraving was in the style known as *Blankschnitt.* The glasses typically had a hollow knopped stem with mereses. Some enameling (some in translucent colors) was also done at Nuremberg, especially in Schwarzlot after about 1655.

Nutmeg Lamp A trademark for a small night lamp made by Gausler, Hoffman & Co., about 1875.

O.C. The trademark used by A.E. O'Conner and J.S. O'Conner.

O.W. The abbreviation used by glassmakers for *openwork*. Since many objects with openwork or latticework were made of white milk glass, often called *opal ware*, many have incorrectly misinterpreted it as "opal ware" instead of "openwork."

oatmeal glass Sandwich or other patterned glass used as premiums in containers of merchandise in an effort to entice buyers. It was originally used as premiums in boxes of oatmeal.

objets d'art (a) Small, valuable objects that cannot be easily categorized under a traditional heading. (b) A term used by auctioneers and others for an object that is worthless or nearly so.

objects of vertu (Aka *objets de vitrine, bibelots*) The generic term used for painstakingly handcrafted valuable items including fob seals, scent bottles, buttons, chatelains, wine labels, etc.

oblate A globular shape somewhat flattened at the poles.

obsian A glass in imitation of the naturally occurring glass called *obsidian*, recorded by Pliny, the Elder, a Roman naturalist and writer (27-79 A.D.).

obsidian (Aka *volcanic glass*) A volcanic mineral considered to be the earliest form of natural glass, sharing all the basic physical properties of ordinary glass. It is normally black, very dark green, or gray in color; splinters transparent or translucent, exhibiting a lustrous brilliance. It was an article of commerce by 3,000 B.C. It was used by the Egyptians during pre-dynastic times and by Aztecs, Mayas, and other North American and South American civilizations in pre-Columbian times. It reached its ultimate usage during the peak of the Aztec civilization, for blades for hunting and warfare, such as the points of spears and arrows, and knives, swords (*macuahuitl*), and tools. After the Aztecs were conquered by the Spanish, the Spanish used it for many of their own tools, including blades for shaving. It was not until the late 1700s that steel totally supplanted obsidian in Mexican technology.

Obsidian is considered a semi-precious stone that can be burnished. The Aztecs used it in jewelry, bowls, ceremonial masks, and mirrors. It can be found in quantity in many areas of the former Aztec empire, there being in excess of fifty spots identified in Mexico and Guatemala. In the 1970s it was discovered that the edge of a freshly chipped flake of obsidian is considerably sharper than surgical steel, being used in eye surgery because the evenness of the cut allows the wound to heal more quickly. Some black glass, because of its physical resemblance to obsidian, is often referred to by that name.

occhio See *eye*.

occhi (o), vetro (Italian) Literally, *glass with eyes*. A decorative glassware developed by Venini. The main feature is the colored or white opaque body embellished with a mosaic pattern of fragments of clear glass of irregular shapes and sizes, arranged more or less in rows.

Ocean Manufacturing Co. See *Marshallville Glass Works*.

Ochsenkopf (German) Literally, *ox head*. (Aka *fichtelgebirgsglas*) A beaker or occasionally a goblet or miniature tumbler embellished with an enameled representation of an ox head above a symbolic fir- covered mountain. There are four rivers flowing from the mountain: the Main, Naab, Saale and Eger. The ox head is represented in many variations. The mountain, *Ochsenkopf*, is in the Fichtelgebirge region of upper Franconia, Bavaria. A church or house is often depicted on top of the mountain, usually encircled by a painted chain with a padlock to protect its wealth. An inscription explaining the associated legend is on the reverse. Some also have a coat-of-arms, symbolic motif, flowers, or figures. They were made mainly in Upper Franconia, from about 1656 through the late 18th century. See *German enamelling*.

O'Conner, John Sarsfield Born in Ireland in 1831, he was employed by Turner & Lane glass cutters in New York City from 1841 to 1864. He also worked for Haughwout, then served in the Union Army, returning to Haughwout as superintendent, working there until it closed in 1870. He then went to work for Dorflinger, where his many innovations revolutionized glass cutting. He invented a hardwood polisher; a machine to vacuum ground glass, reducing the mortality rate from inhalation of small glass particles by cutters; and a special cutting wheel enabling glass to be decorated using a curved miter cut, patenting several designs using it. He left Dorflinger in 1890, established a shop in Hawley, Pennsylvania, sold it in 1900 to Maple City Glass Company, and opened another in Goshen, New York, the same year, operating it until 1919. In 1902, he opened another, the American Cut Glass Company, in Port Jervis, New York, operating it until the end of 1903; his son Arthur was manager. He purchased blanks for his Hawley facility from Dorflinger and for his Goshen facility from France. He operated both shops under the name *J.S. C'Conner - American Rich Cut Glass*. He used a trademark label, "O.C.", Hawley, Penna.

O'Conner, Arthur E. The son of John S. O'Conner, Arthur worked in his father's Goshen, New York, facility from 1900 until his father started the American Cut Glass Company in 1902. He managed this facility from its opening until it closed in late 1903.

octagonal bowl A bowl on some drinking glasses having an octagonal horizontal

section and being slightly concave where it joined the stem.

octagonal decanter jug A decanter jug, the lower part of the body of octagonal horizontal section, sloping shoulder, long thin neck, loop handle, and stopper.

octagonal diamond A cut glass motif—an eight-sided hobnail. See *hobnail*.

oeil-de-perdrix *(French)* Literally, *partridge eye*. A diaper pattern of dotted circles used as a ground on some opaque blue glass made in Bristol about 1840 to simulate Sevres porcelain.

oenochoe *(Greek)* A jug having an ovoid body, vertical loop handle, flat base, and usually a trefoil lip, made in numerous shapes and sizes. Some have a circular mouth, some a beaked lip, and some a spout. There are two types: (a) ones with the neck set off from the shoulder, and (b) ones with a continuous curve from the neck to the body, such as the *olpe*. Glass ones are small (1-1/2 to 3-1/2 inches), used to hold toilet preparations. They were made in the eastern Mediterranean region in the 15th and 14th centuries B.C.; others in the 5th and 4th centuries B.C.; and some of Roman glass from the 1st century B.C. to the 1st century A.D. (core glass vessels with a pinched lip and normally combed embellishment).

Oesterling, Henderson & Company (1863-1939) (Aka *East Wheeling Glass Works*) A glass manufacturing facility established by glassworkers in Wheeling, West Virginia, making flint glassware. In 1869 its name was changed to the Central Glass Company.

off-hand (blown) glass (Aka *end-of-day-glass*) Pieces of glass blown or hand fabricated by workers to satisfy their individual desires and not part of the normal facility production, usually made from melted glass left in the pots at the end of the normal work day. Quite often they were functional or utilitarian pieces. See *end-of-day glass; frigger; free blown*.

ogee (Aka *Cyma Reversa*) A shape in the form of a double curve; a convex and concave curve joined together, as in the letter "S," and often perpetuated to form a double ogee.

ogee bowl A bowl on some drinking glasses that initially curves out from the stem, goes in a little and out again, in the form of an elongated "S." It was popular in the second half of the 18th century.

ogival (Aka *expanded diamond, reticulated*) A molded pattern in a diamond-like formation.

ogling glasses Opera glasses. See *polemoscope.*

O'Hara & Craig See *Pittsburgh Glass Works.*

O'Hara & Robinson See *Iron City (Window) Glass Works; Cookstown Works.*

O'Hara Glassworks A glass manufacturing facility established in 1853 by James B. Lyon & Co. (which succeeded Wallace, Lyon & Co. in the management of the Union Glass Works established by Hay & Campbell in 1831) in Pittsburgh, Pennsylvania. It was named for James O'Hara, who established the first glass manufacturing facility in the area. It was on or adjacent to the abandoned works of Hay & McCully, which was established in 1829 and destroyed in the flood of 1832. The O'Hara facility made flint glass tableware in blown, cut, pressed, engraved, and gilded glass, later switching from flint to lime glass. It was incorporated as the O'Hara Glass Company Ltd. in 1875, and in 1891 joined the U.S. Glass Company (*Factory L*). See *Union Flint Glass Works (Pittsburgh).*

Ohio Cut Glass Company A glass cutting company established in the early 1900s in Bowling Green, Ohio, by Pitkin & Brooks, making heavy- and light-cut glassware. In 1904 it burned, was rebuilt, burned again in 1912, and closed. See *Gunderson (Pairpoint) Glass Works.*

Ohio Flint Glass Company A glass manufacturing facility established in 1899 in Lancaster, Ohio, after its Dunkirk facility was destroyed by fire. It soon merged with the National Glass Company, and in 1938, with the Anchor Hocking Company. It was

one of the prime makers of machine-made mold etched glassware and the largest maker of Depression glass.

Ohio Glass Co. A glass manufacturing facility established in Pittsburgh, Pennsylvania, by General James Wilkinson, Anthony Beelen, Hugh Scott, Ebenezer Denny, etc. It was unsuccessful and, in 1802, the equipment was sold to O'Hara & Craig.

Ohio-Stiegel See *Stiegel type glassware.*

oil A cruet.

oil gilding See *unfired gilding.*

Oil lamp, 29-1/2" h.
Tri-State Antiques

Oil lamp, Torpedo, plain font, pattern on base.
Krause Publications

oil lamp Any lamp having a wick and using oil as a fuel. They were made in Murano in the 16th and 17th centuries in extraordinary shapes. Those made during the early 18th century had a font for oil in the shape of a flattened globe with a hole in the top for a wick. It rested on a stand with a high-stemmed foot. A loop handle was normally attached to the stem. Some had a drip pan to catch any spilled oil. Some later ones had a font in the form of a globe and usually two or three projecting spouts to hold wicks. They were made in a variety of shapes and sizes in the United States. See *wine glass lamp; sparking lamp; whale oil lamp; peg lamp; sinumbra lamp.*

oinochoe Singular is *oinochoai*. Small pitchers made by the Etruscans in central Italy in the 7th to the 5th centuries B.C. They were core formed in blue, yellow, or brown glass, embellished with pincered spikes pulled outward from the body in irregular rows. While the Greek term means *wine pourer*, they were usually made for perfumes and oils.

ointment jar A small shallow bowl with a cover, used mainly for ointments, unguents (a liquid or semi-liquid salve for treating sores or wounds), cosmetics, and dentifrices. There are circular ones about 1-1/2 inches in diameter made of Roman Glass in the 1st century A.D. See *pyxis.*

Ointment Jar A specialty product of Parker Brothers Glass Factory in the 1890s. It had a nickel-plated screw top and was made in a variety of sizes, from 1/4 ounce to 16 ounces.

O'Keefe, Michael A glass artist working in Seattle, Washington, specializing in paperweights that are three-dimensional translucent forms made in a variety of soft, subtle colors, the exterior shape specifically fashioned to complement the interior motif. He uses the silver veiling technique extensively in creating them. Certain elements in the formulation cause the silver to change color from brown to yellow or from yellow to blue. Each weight has the artist's name and date of completion engraved on its bottom.

Old Colony Cut Glass Company (1914-1925) A glass cutting company incorporated on June 20, 1917, in Fall River, Massachusetts.

Old Economy Glass See *Morgantown Glass.*

Old Glass House See *Washington Glassworks.*

Old Roman glass A glass made by Thomas Webb & Sons starting in 1888, similar to and often mistaken for *Clutha glass* but without speckles of aventurine. See *West Lothian Glassworks.*

Olean Glass Company A glass manufacturing facility in Olean, New York, which made bottles and flasks in the late 1800s.

O'Leary, Baily & Smith See *Franklin Cut Glass and Watch Crystal Manufactory.*

O'Leary, Mulvaney & Co. See *Birmingham Flint Glass Company.*

Olin, Delos V. A glass cutter who worked for Hawkes for about a year beginning in 1905. Later, in addition to working for his father in his grocery store, he cut glass in his shop in Corning, New York, selling his wares to the public and other glasshouses, including Hawkes.

olive An elliptical cut or printie made with an appropriate shaped wheel on a glass lathe.

olive dish See *pickle dish.*

Olive Glassworks A bottle glass manufacturing facility established in 1781 in Glassboro, New Jersey, by five Stanger brothers, former employees of the Wister Glassworks. In 1784, after a series of buyouts, Carpenter & Heston became owners, adding window and flint glass. In 1808 it was taken over by Edward Carpenter & Co. (Carpenter, son of Col. Thomas Carpenter of the Stanger Glassworks, acquired his father's share.) After his death in 1813, it fell into disrepair. By 1816 it was reopened by David Wolf. In 1817 Thomas W. Dyott was an agent for it. In 1821 it was bought by Isaac Thorne, a relative of the Stangers. In 1824 Jeremiah J. Foster purchased it and merged it with the nearby Harmony Glassworks. See *Olive & Harmony Glassworks.*

Olive & Harmony Glassworks A glass manufacturing facility known as the Harmony Glassworks, which made bottles, flasks, druggists wares, and other hollowware. It was established by Rink, Stanger &

Co. in 1813 in Glassboro, New Jersey, about 400 yards south of the Olive Glassworks. In 1823 Rink died, his interests purchased by Daniel K. Miller of the Franklin Glassworks. In 1824 Jeremiah J. Foster purchased both the Olive Glassworks and the Harmony Glassworks, merging them into the Olive & Harmony Glassworks. In 1835 Thomas H. Whitney invested in it and, in 1837, he, with his brother Samuel, became sole owners, operating as Whitney Brothers. They were grandsons of Colonel Heston, previously associated with the Olive Glassworks. In 1887 the company was incorporated as the Whitney Glass Works. In 1918 it became a division of Owens Bottle Company, and then of Libbey-Owens-Ford Co.

Oliver's skull A *chamber pot. Oliver* refers to Oliver Cromwell.

olpe *(Greek)* A wine jug resembling the oenochoe, having a pear-shaped body, vertical loop handle extending from the shoulder to the rim, and large circular mouth sometimes adorned with a trefoil lip. Some were made in the eastern Mediterranean region about 400 B.C.

Olson, Arthur R. A glass cutter associated with the following Minneapolis, Minnesota, companies: Eagle Cut Glass Company, Standard Cut Glass Company, Queen City Cut Glass Company, and Olson Cut Glass Company. See *Queen City Cut Glass Company.*

Olson Cut Glass Company See *Queen City Cut Glass Company.*

omnium A whatnot or miscellaneous item.

omnium gatherum A collection of miscellaneous items.

omom A perfume sprinkler made of Syrian glass in the 13th century. It had an oblate spherical body, kick base, and tall, narrow, tapering vertical neck. At the base of the neck where it joins the body, there may be an ornament attached. Some have combed or enameled embellishment with motifs of mixed Islamic and Chinese origin. They are normally five to eight inches in height.

Omom is believed to be a crude transliteration of *qumqum* (Syrian origin).

omphalos A shallow bowl having a low rim and flat bottom with a central concavity; the interior has a corresponding bulge. *Omphalos* means *navel* but has other meanings: (a) the boss of a shield and (b) a conical stone in the temple of Apollo in Delphi believed to be the center of the earth. They are similar to the Greek *phiale mesomphalos* and the Roman *phalera* and were made from the 8th century B.C.

one-off piece Handmade, one-of-a-kind pieces.

Oneida Glass & Iron Company Incorporated in 1809 in Taberg (now part of Annsville Township), New York, it made charcoal pig iron and metal hollowware (skillets, pots, kettles, etc.). It was granted a charter by the New York State Legislature to make glass but never did.

Oneida Glass Factory Company (Aka *Shearman's Works*) A cylinder window glass manufacturing facility in Vernon, New York, granted a charter to make glass in 1809 by the New York State Legislature. Its first directors were Watts Sherman, Abraham Varick, John Steward, Jr., Alexander B. Johnson, Lawrence Schoolcraft, and Richard Sanger. Its first manager was Willett H. Shearman and its products were marketed in Utica by E.B. Shearman. In 1822 it leased the Utica Glass Company (see *Utica Glass Company*), operating both facilities until 1836 when the directors decided to close the works and sell the real estate.

onion shaped bottles See *wine bottles, shapes.*

onion shaped decanter A decanter having a body more or less globular in shape, except for a sloping shoulder.

Ontario Glass Manufacturing Company A window glass manufacturing facility established in 1810 in Geneva, New York. It was possibly affiliated with the Geneva Glass Manufacturing Company. See *Geneva Glass Manufacturing Company.*

Onyx A line of glassware made of two layers of glass and having a pattern, usually floral, decorated with a metal luster between the layers. The glassware was made by Dalzell, Gilmore & Leighton from 1889 to about 1891. It is generally white, but occasionally is amber, lavender, and rose.

onyx glass (1) A glass opacified by crystallization by either physical or chemical means. Glass is a non-crystalline, supercooled liquid, and crystallization or devitrification causes it to lose its transparency. Using these facts, it is possible to induce a controlled amount of crystallization in order to make the glass opaque or *opal*. By slowly cooling glass from its low viscosity state (or not supercooling it), crystallization takes place without the help of opalizing agents. However, if fluorides are added, they form the nucleii for crystal formation even with a normal cooling cycle. Varying amounts of sodium or potassium fluorides are added to the batch for varying degrees of opacity.

(2) A glass, clear when molten, becoming opalescent when manipulated or worked into a shape or form because of the dispersion of light caused by particles in the glass. This opalescence occurs as a result of the separation and suspension of minute particles of various types, sizes, and densities, dispersing light as it passes through them. This opal glass often arises from the growth of non-metallic crystals of nucleated silver particles developed from an original clear glass containing the silver.

(3) A translucent white glass that becomes partially opacified because of oxides of tin added to the batch. When observed by transmitted light, the glass seems to produce brownish and reddish tones (*sunset glow*). It was used to make glassware in Venice in the 17th and 18th centuries, and in Germany and Bohemia in the late 17th through the 19th centuries where the opacifying agent was the ashes of calcined bones. It was made in England during the 19th century for *Country Market glass*. Although often attributed to Bristol, onyx glass was made in numerous facilities throughout England. Some is made of milk-and-water glass rather than pure white glass. See *cranberry glass; silver onyx; opaline; opaque white glass; opalescent glass.*

opacifier A substance that produces an opacity in glass, from a milky translucence to a dense white. Those commonly used to make a milky translucent glass are arsenic, antimony, and various phosphates and fluorides, while those used to make a dense white are tin oxide, titania, and zirconia. There are numerous other opacifiers, including niobium pentoxide, bone ash, fluorspar (calcium fluoride), cryolite, and zinc sulfide.

opal ware Pronounced *o-pal*. A solid white glass, now commonly called *milk glass* (*milk white glass* or *opaque white glass*).

opal glass (1) Any glass with a milky white appearance. (2) A glass having a color that can be seen through, and reflects back from, the surface of the glass. It was developed in 1890 by John LaFarge.

opalescent Reflecting an iridescent light; having a milky iridescence; exhibiting a play of colors like that of an opal. See *iridescent.*

opalescent dew drop glass See *dew drop glass; hobnail glass; opalescent hobnail.*

opalescent glass (1) The same as iridescent glass. See *iridescent glass.*

(2) An iridescent glass developed by Frederick Carder at Steuben, having the appearance of the opal gemstone. The opalescence was produced *at-the-fire* and dependent on the bone ash (calcium phosphate) added to the batch. Its four basic colors were made by adding metallic oxides to the batch; chromium for green (*Green Opal*), gold for pink (*Pink Opal*), uranium for yellow (*Yellow Opal*), and copper for blue (*Blue Opal*). He created a variation of the *Yellow Opal*—a glass shading from opal to yellow, called *Straw Opal*. The opalescence was developed by quickly cooling the partially formed object with a jet of compressed air while on the blowing iron and reheating it in the glory hole. If the entire piece was quickly cooled and reheated, the whole object became opalescent. If only a portion was quickly cooled, a shaded effect resulted. An opalescent pattern could be obtained by shoving the molten gather into an iron mold and directing a jet of cool air onto the surface as it was rotated by the workman, causing the raised portions of the design to be

chilled while the lower areas remained hot. After reheating, the object displayed an opalescent design on a plain background.

(3) A type of glass, popular during the late 19th century, having a raised opalescent white design. The process involved covering a paraison of colored glass with a layer of clear glass containing bone ash and arsenic and blowing it into a pattern mold, creating a raised design on the surface. The article was reheated, causing the raised portion to become opalescent against the original ground. The hobnails, thumbprints, or other raised designs tended to cool more quickly than the rest of the article, becoming opaque on reheating. A comparable version with raised white or colored designs was patented in England in 1889 by Thomas Davidson of Gateshead-on-Tyne. The principal patterns of this translucent ware with a raised opaque white design on a translucent background were: *Dew Drop, Inverted Thumbprint (Coin Spot* or *Polka Dot),* and *Swirl.* Common shades are clear white, bluish white, and amber; the clear is known as *Spanish Lace,* the amber in the hobnail pattern is sometimes erroneously called *Franciscan Ware.* It was also made in pressed pattern wares. There are many reproductions. See *English opalescent glass.*

(4) (Aka *opal glass*) When applied to stained glass, it refers to machine-made, semi-opaque glass used extensively in making stained glass windows and lampshades. Sheets of it, usually double- or hand-rolled, are typically multicolored. There are several degrees of translucency as follows: light (very translucent), medium light (medium translucent), medium (hard to see through), and dark (cannot be seen through). It is often associated with Tiffany's stained glass works, although there are vast differences between the machine rolled opalescent glass of today and the Tiffany product.

Fenton cranberry opalescent hobnail vase with crimped rim, 5" h. Tri-State Antiques

opalescent hobnail A shaded opalescent glassware; an attempt to emulate cut or engraved overlay glass.

Opalescent Optic A Tiffany Reactive Glass pattern.

opaline A slightly translucent glass made by adding to the batch the ashes of calcined bones to opacify it, and metallic oxides to produce color, usually pastel hues. On occasion, instead of pastel hues, a whitish (but less dense than) opaque white glass or glass exhibiting strong colors (e.g., dark blue) or black was made. The name was derived from *opalin,* first used by Baccarat about 1823. It is believed the first opaline glass was made at Murano in the 17th century, being inspired by Bohemian colored glass, and later in France. It has been made again at Murano since about 1932. The early French specimens look like traditional opaque white glass, but later pieces are closer to *milk-and-water glass (Beinglas).* The best French specimens were made between about 1840 and 1870 at Baccarat, St. Louis, and Choisy-Le-Roi. It is made in many colors—pale green, turquoise, deep blue, pink, coral, ruby red, yellow (rare), *bulle de savon (savonneuse*-soap bubble, rainbow hue) and *gorge-de-pigeon* (pigeon's blood). In 1612 Antonio Neri suggested in his books a formula for a similar glass for carafes, vases, candlesticks, and boxes, some having gilt bronze mounts. Opaline has been mold blown or mold pressed and occasionally, before about 1835, embellished with cold colors and enameling later. It was made in the United States by the Boston & Sandwich Glass Co. beginning after 1830. See *opal glass; pate-de-riz.*

opaline paperweight A paperweight made by Clichy in the form of a rectangular opaline glass plaque measuring about 2-1/3 by 3-1/5 inches; some were shaped like a book. Generally enclosed within it is a single flower or small flat bouquet. Because they are made of opaline glass, they cannot act as magnifiers.

Opalique The trade name of an opalescent glass made by James A. Jobling & Co. in the 1930s, in imitation of that made by Lalique and Sabino. It was a poor seller, and production ceased in 1940.

opaque Not capable of transmitting light. Some glass designated as *opaque* is slightly translucent, especially that made into articles with thin walls.

opaque enamel An non-transparent enamel normally made by adding tin oxide to the pigment. When used to embellish glassware, it is applied thickly and is perceptible to the touch. It was the main medium for embellishing glass by enameling until the development of transparent enamel about 1810.

opaque glass With reference to stained glass, opaque glass is any glass that is not transparent, including not only truly opaque glass but translucent glass.

opaque opal A flashed opal glass having a muted (milky) finish made by Fisher, Lamber, and Wheaton Industries.

opaque twist White or colored opaque rods twisted into lacy patterns and pulled into thin rods for decorative stems or worked into the body of glassware. They were popular in England on stemware between about 1745 and 1780. They are often called *cotton twists* in the United States.

opaque twist stem A stem having as its primary embellishment any of a variety of twists of opaque white glass in the form of threads or tapes. They followed air twist stems as a trend and continued to be fashionable until about 1877 when cut stems came into fashion. To make them, first a steel cylinder is lined with several rods of opaque white or colored glass and glass is forced into the cylinder, the rods adhering to the side of it. This cylindrical glob of molten glass, about four inches wide and four to five inches long, is then rolled back and forth on a marver until the white or colored rods become embedded in it. To get the rods deeper inside the mass, it is coated on the outside with another layer of glass. By rolling this back and forth across the marver, it is formed in a shape of a carrot. The carrot is then knocked off the pontil and placed in an annealing oven, after which it is placed in storage. Later, when needed, it is taken from storage and heated slowly inside a layer of fireclay. When hot, the fireclay falls apart, the hot carrot is picked up on a pontil, its narrow end further heated and drawn out slowly. When the appropriate length is reached, the end is cut, forming a new rod. The carrot is taken back to the pot to keep hot. The servitor, meanwhile, will form or shape the rod, twisting it to the desired form.

opaque white glass Glass having the appearance of white porcelain, opacified usually with tin oxide. Experiments to make it were done in Venice. Glassmakers succeeded in developing practical methods of production in the latter part of the 15th century. Some rare specimens dating to the 16th century survive. It became fashionable, and in great demand, during the 17th and 18th centuries as a replacement for porcelain from China. Later European facilities began making it with enameled embellishment, similar to that on porcelain. It was made and embellished in Venice, France, Germany, Bohemia, and China in the late 17th-early 18th centuries. The Venetian glass was occasionally embellished with iron red enameling *encamaieu* or with gilt motifs in Rococo style, typically Chinoiseries, Watteau subjects, and mythological subjects, on plates, tumblers, candlesticks, vases, etc. Opaque white glass was included in the wares purchased in 1667 from Venice by John Greene. Relatively small items were initially made later in England at several facilities from the late 17th century. It was also made in Spain, and in Bohemia or Germany for shipment to Spain and Portugal. In Venice it was not only used to make tradiional wares, but also filigrana decoration. It is often called *milk glass*. The Italian term is *lattimo*, the German *Milchglas*, *Porzellanglas* and *Porcellein-Glas*; the French *blanc-de-lait*. See *opal glass; milk-and-water glass; milk glass; opaline; Basdorf glass; latesino.*

open handled Handles having an opening for the finger or hand to reach through to better hold and stabilize the object (as opposed to lug handles, which have no hole).

open mold See *dip mold.*

openwork Lattice work. Work that is perforated. It may be made by contriving a network of channels, either by casting (see *diatreta*) or by cutting (see *cage cup*).

openwork border A border formed of lattice work (openings in the glass) used on some glassware. It became popular in the early 1800s. It often consisted of a stately and naturalistic form of flowers and scrolls and was often combined with clear and stippled backgrounds. Most are made in clear glass, but some are made of colored glass.

openwork stopper A stopper molded to show openings in the glass, most often found on Czechoslovakian perfume bottles.

opera glasses See *polemoscope*.

optic blown See *optical glass*.

optic mold An open mold having a patterned interior. A paraison of glass is introduced into it and inflated to embellish its surface.

optical fiber An extremely fine-drawn glass fiber of exceptional purity having the capability of transmitting laser light impulses with high fidelity. They are made from high purity quartz and coated with germanium-doped silica using a technique called *vapor deposition*. After pulling these fibers to a microscopically small diameter, they are fabricated into cables containing 144 filaments each to be used in telephone systems as replacements for copper cables. Other uses are in the medical profession as diagnostic aids, for inspections of engines, nuclear reactors, etc., and in the military in the area of communications.

optical glass (1) (Aka *optic blown*) Glass that has been mold blown and additionally blown to increase the size, or lessen or modify the lines of the pattern by blowing into a plain mold. (2) High quality glass used in making lenses, prisms, etc. Hundreds of different optical glasses are currently being made. Each has its own characteristic composition, adjusted to give the glass a particular property for a specific purpose (color, light absorption, refractive index, photochromic properties, etc.).

The raw materials used in making it have to be exceptionally pure. The sand must have an extremely low iron content. Usually a relatively low iron content quartz rock is ground and crushed into sand; the iron present is further reduced by chemical means to 0.001 % to eliminate the green tint. The glass must be of exceptional homogeneity or uniformity. This is achieved by mechanical stirring or passing an electrical current through it, and air bubbles are eliminated by a refiring process. Forming is done by pressing the glass in molds made of cast iron or heat-resistant steel; the shape of the blank, either concave or convex, is determined by the plungers. The lenses are then passed through an annealing lehr and may be toughened using a method similar to that used for flat glass. However, chemical toughening using ion exchange technology is more widely practiced. It involves dipping of hot lenses into a bath of molten potassium nitrate where larger potassium ions replace some of the smaller sodium ions on the glass surface, a layer of compression being created. Occasionally lithium is used to replace the sodium ions.

In general, the requirements of optical glass (used in scientific instruments, not spectacle or ordinary glass) are: (a) the composition of the glass ensures the required optical properties; (b) the batch is of sufficiently low viscosity; (c) the glass will not devitrify (loose its properties as a glass, such as transparency, hardness, brittleness), even upon long annealing; (d) it must be as colorless as possible without using decolorizing agents that may impart unwanted properties to the glass; (e) it must be free from bubbles and striae, which may distort clarity; (f) it must be capable of being ground and polished easily; and (g) it must be able to withstand diverse atmospheric conditions.

The finishing of lenses requires three phases: roughing, smoothing, and polishing. There are several categories of optical glass: (a) flint (*extra dense* with a high lead content and refractive index; *dense* with high lead content and refractive index, but not as high as in *extra dense*; *light* with moderate lead content and refractive index; and *extra light* with low lead content and refractive index); and (b) crown (*soda potash crown* with low lead content and refractive index; *crown flint*; *light barium crown* with some barium content; *dense barium crown* with high barium content; *extra dense barium crown* with a very high barium content; *lithium crown*; and *borosilicate crown* with a relatively low refractive index. See *photochromic glass*; *spectacles*; *bifocal lenses*.

opus interrasile (Latin) Literally, *work in low relief* or *bossed.* See *silver cased glassware.*

opus sectile (Latin) A mosaic panel or decoration on a wall or floor made with pieces of glass embedded—not fused—in cement, molten glass, or another medium. See *veneer (glass).*

Or Verre A glass, probably a variety of striped Cintra glass, recorded in the diaries of Frederick Carder of Steuben about 1921.

orange glass See *sweetmeat glass.*

orcel A small vase.

Orient & Flume A glass blowing studio established in 1972 in Chico, California, by Douglas Boyd and David Hopper. It synthesizes different glass styles and techniques from many different time periods and parts of the world, adding its own artistic interpretations. It developed its reputation by making brilliant iridescent glass paperweights with Art Nouveau motifs and intricate surface embellishments often combined with traditional paperweight designs and production techniques. Most were clear cased rather than with surface designs. They are signed, dated, and numbered on the base, each issued with a certificate of authenticity.

Oriental Glass Company A glass decorating facility established in Pittsburgh, Pennsylvania, during the early 1890s, operating until 1905. It decorated pressed glass tableware and made a large amount of ruby-and amber-stained glassware.

orifice ring In a glass furnace, in the automatic feeder mechanism (see *feeder*), the orifice ring is the hole at the bottom of the round basin through which molten glass flows.

origin The *place of production* as opposed to its source. See *provenance.*

ormolu From the French *or moulu.* Literally, *ground* or *pulverized gold.* Ormolu is an alloy of copper, zinc, and tin, is the color of gold, and is often used to imitate gold. It has the appearance of gilded brass, an alloy of copper and zinc, and gilded bronze, an alloy of copper and tin. Ormolu originally referred to gilded bronze; however, it is now used loosely to describe brass or bronze, fire gilded, mercuric gilded, or even copper gilded (a cheap soft imitation of the other types). It has been used as a mount or embellishment on glass, as has gilded bronze. See *gilt bronze.*

ornamental glass See *Zierglas.*

Orpheus beaker An engraved covered beaker reported to be the most prestigious piece crafted by Gottfried Spiller. It portrays Orpheus wearing a laurel wreath and playing his lyre to a group of beasts at the foot of a tree trunk. Although unsigned, it is attributed (since 1786) to Spiller and assists in the identification of his other works. A vase embellished with the same subject was designed by Victor Prouve for Emile Galle.

Orr, L.A., Company (1909-1917) A glass cutting house established by L.A. Orr (treasurer of the Queen City Cut Glass Company) in Rochester, Minnesota.

Orrefors perfume bottle, etched swan design, 4-1/4" h., signed and dated, 1965.
Davanna Collection

Orrefors vase with etched girl with flowers, 7" h.
Davanna Collection

Orrefors Glassworks A glass manufacturing facility in Orrefors, Smaland, Sweden, established in 1726 as an ironworks. It was later abandoned and converted in 1898 to a glass manufacturing facility, making utilitarian glass such as ink and medicine bottles, window panes, and cheap domestic glassware. In 1913 it was bought by Johan Ekman who, with his manager, Albert Aklin, decided to make decorative glassware. They brought in Simon Gate (1883-1945) in 1916 as designer, and Edward Hald (b.1883) in 1917 (see *Graal glass; Orrefors Graal glass; Ariel glass; Kraka glass; Ravenna glass*). In 1946 it was bought by Henning Beyer. It has an affiliated glassworks at Sandvik, making utilitarian glassware. It is known for its tableware and ornamental cased glass. The company also made and exported large chandeliers, stemware, and engraved ware.

Orrefors Graal glass A glass designed for Orrefors by Simon Gate and Edward Held in 1917. Galle's standard cased glass vases with clinging flower patterns played an important role in its development. Graal glass received its final form while still subject to the heat of the furnace, giving the motifs a delicate mobility. The Graal technique was modified during the 1920s and, during the 1930s, the related technique, *Ariel*, was created.

Osborne, H.F., Company See *Osborne, Boynton & Osborne*.

Osborne, Boynton & Osborne A wholesaler of crockery and glass in Detroit, Michigan. It was periodically listed in directories as a cut glass manufacturer, but it never made it. Established about 1907, its name was changed to Osborne-Boynton Company in 1914 and to H. F. Osborne Company in 1918.

Osborne-Boynton Company See *Osborne, Boynton & Osborne*.

osculatory A pax; an early Catholic ecclesiastical tablet bearing a religious representation, kissed first by the priest and then the congregation. Some were made of Italian glass, embellished with diamond point engraving. The glass pax was especially popular in the 15th and 16th centuries.

osier glassware Press molded glassware having an overall pattern in the form of interlaced willow twigs (basketwork). It was made of opaque white glass during the late 19th century. The leading manufacturer was Sowerby's Ellison Glassworks.

ostensory See *monstrance*.

Ottawa (Cut) Glass Co. A glass cutting house in Ontario, Canada, established in 1913 and operating for a short time.

Ottawa Flint & Bottle Glass Company A glass and bottle glass manufacturing facility in Ottawa, Illinois, operating in the 1880s.

Ottawa Glass Works A glass manufacturing facility in the Point Cavagnol district of Como, Quebec, Canada, established in 1845 by Masson & Company. Over the next few years, ownership changed frequently and shareholders came and went. Business expanded until about 1875, then started to decline because of cheaper imports from the United States. Shortly thereafter it closed. It made bottles, containers, lighting equipment, and possibly window glass. It was known in its later years as the Canada Glass Works Co. Ltd.

Ottawa Novelty Glass Company See *Peltier Glass Company*.

Otto of Roses perfume bottle A bottle shaped like a throwaway scent bottle holding *Otto of Roses* perfume, a popular fragrance from the mid-1800s through the early 1900s. From about 1900, it had a diamond motif, cut glass stopper, and measured about 5-1/2 inches long. See *scent bottles (throwaway)*.

outlined twist A twist with an outside thread of a different color than the inner white opaque twist.

Output Company of America A distributor of cut glass made by various glass cutters in Chicago, Illinois. One of its directors was Herman T. Roseen, associated with Roseen Cut Glass Company, Central Cut Glass Company, and Roseen & Collins.

outside decorator See *Hausmaler*.

oval chamber pot See *bourdalou*.

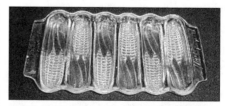

Cornbread baking tray marked "Miracle Maize-Design Patent Applied For," 12" l. x 6-1/4" w. Davanna Collection

ovenware Glassware generally of borosilicate glass, resistant to thermal shock likely to occur during cooking or baking processes.

over blow (Aka *moil*) The excess portion of the paraison attached to the blowpipe or pontil, removed after the object has been cracked off the blowpipe.

overlay (1) The outer layer of glass on an article of cased glass. Some paperweights and other articles with two or more layers of glass of different colors over a base layer are referred to as *encased overlays*. Some Chinese snuff bottles are made of overlay glass, having two to four layers of different colored glass, cameo cut to produce a design, motif, or pattern against the ground color. Others have a single overlay consisting of several colors applied to different areas of the same ground. In the United States, *overlay* is often used as a synonym for *cased* glass. (2) A type of embellishment, sometimes called *overlay type*, made by fusing to the body of an object ornamentation in the form of glass flowers, fruit, leaves, etc. It was made during the 19th century by several glasshouses in England and the United States.

overlay paperweight A paperweight made with one or more layers of colored glass covering the dome, typically a thin underlay of opaque white glass as the first layer, then one or more overlays of colored glass, which are ground away to provide windows to view the central motif. There is normally one window at the top so the motif may be viewed from above and one or two rows of four to six windows surrounding the sides through which the motif can be seen in the round. Specimens made at the St. Louis facility are encased with another layer of clear glass after the windows have been ground. The traditional colors of the outer overlay are: (a) at Baccarat, turquoise, bright blue, and emerald green; (b) at Clichy, turquoise and deep pink; and (c) at St. Louis, dark blue, emerald green, and apple green. At each of the windows the opaque white underlay (first overlay) produces a thin white line framing the window.

overmantle (mirror) A mirror to be placed above a mantelpiece. These ornamental, normally rectangular mirrors date from the 18th century. From about the middle of the 19th century, they often had shelves on each side.

overseam foot A foot found on some drinking glasses made with applied glass threads radiating outward from the base of the stem to just over the edge of the foot. They were made in England during the mid-18th century, often in the form of a dram glass.

overshot glass Glass with a rough surface created by tiny bits of glass impressed on the gather during its making. It was made with both clear and colored glass by the Boston & Sandwich Glass Company from 1860 to the 1880s. It has no design or pattern and should not be confused with the *Tree of Life* pattern glass. *Crackle glass* is occasionally called *overshot glass*.

overstring foot A foot on a drinking glass similar to an overseam foot, except the radial trails are thicker. They were often made in the form of a dram glass in England during the 18th century.

Overstrom, Henning A Swedish glassblower who, at various times during his career, was employed at: the Mosaic Glass Company, Dorflinger, and Steuben, where he was the first workman to sign on with this new company in 1903.

Oveszny, Joseph (1884-1955) Born in Hungary, Oveszny learned the art of engraving in Bohemia. He came to Corning, New York, about 1914, working for Sinclaire and Corning Glass. From 1933 to 1935, he worked at Westmoreland, then returned to Corning and opened a home glass cutting shop. In 1939 he became an engraver at Steuben, remaining until 1949, except for a few months in 1943 when he worked for Corning Glass Works. Then he worked at his shop until his death.

oviform Ovoid, in the shape of an egg. See *ovoid*.

Ovington Brothers A New York glass distribution company distributing Schneider Art Glass.

ovoid In the shape of an egg; having the solid form of an egg. See *oviform*.

ovoid bowl A bowl on some drinking glasses that is vertically ovoid.

Owanda Glass Company A short-lived glass cutting shop in Honesdale, Pennsylvania, which burned in 1908.

Owens, Michael J. A glass technician from Toledo, Ohio. In 1901, while he was superintendent of production at Libbey Glass Co., he invented the automatic bottle blowing machine that gathered molten glass by suction, forming the bottle in a single operation. See *Libbey, W.L., & Son; Toledo Glass Company.*

Owens Bottle Co. See *Olive & Harmony Glass Works; Whitney Glass Works.*

Owens Bottle Machine Co. See *Owens-Illinois, Inc.*

Owens-Corning Fiberglass Corp. This company, which specialized in fibrous glass products, was established in 1938 in Toledo, Ohio, by Owens-Illinois Inc. and Corning Glass Works.

Owens-Illinois Inc. A leading glass producer in the United States. Owens Bottle Machine Company was established in 1903 at Toledo, Ohio, by Michael J. Owens, with financing provided by his associate, Edward Drummond Libbey. While superintendent of production at Libbey Glass Co., Owens invented the automatic bottle blowing machine in 1901. In 1929 the company merged with the Illinois Glass Co., becoming Owens-Illinois Glass Co., later Owens-Illinois Inc. In 1931 the company developed fiberglass working with Corning Glass Works. In 1955 it developed lightweight glass solder. See *Libbey, W.L., & Son; Toledo Glass Company; Whitney Glass Works.*

OX Collection The name given by Steuben to crystal items set aside for official government gifts. The "O" stands for official and the "X" is the usual designation for formative designs. It consists of about twenty pieces, ten blown and cut and ten engraved. Some, such as the Audubon Plates, are considered both "OX" and stock items. Others are strictly "OX" items.

ox head See *Ochsenkopf.*

Oxford Lavenders Tall, narrow, faceted scent bottles imported into England during the early and mid-19th century and sold at fairs. The bottles usually contained *attar of roses.*

oxidizing agent Any substance capable of affecting the chemical change known as oxidation and, in the process, is itself reduced.

oxidizing atmosphere A condition within a glass furnace in which there is an excess of oxygen. It is the opposite of a *reducing atmosphere.*

oyster A pattern of concentric swirls or arcs often found on the base of some milk glass items.

P & B A trademark of Pitkin & Brooks.

P Diamond Finish A trademark of F.K. Parsche & Son, Glass Cutters.

Packwood, N., & Company (Aka *Packwood-Northwood Cutting Shop*) Nehemiah Packwood and his son were glass cutters at Boston & Sandwich, opening a glass cutting shop about the time Boston & Sandwich closed in 1888. The business remained in operation until shortly after 1920.

pad base A base of a vessel formed by applying a small gathering of molten glass spread out to form a base.

pad pontil mark A pontil mark made by applying a gather of glass to the bottom of an object before removal from the blow pipe and placed on the pontil, intended to reinforce a thin base.

paddle A tool used by a glassmaker. A slab of wood with a handle used to marver and shape glass being worked. More recently a paddle is made from a slab of carbon and fitted with a handle.

Paden City comport, Peacock & Wild Rose pattern, 6-1/2" h.
Tri-State Antiques

Paden City, Orchid etched compote, 6-5/8" h. x 7" w.
Krause Publications

Paden City Glass (Manufacturing) Company (1916-1951) A glass manufacturing facility established in Paden City, West Virginia, initially making tableware. In the 1920s it expanded to include colored wares in crystal and opaque glass in a variety of patterns and styles. It maintained its high standards of handmade wares until 1949 when, under new management, it was automated to reduce production costs. It closed due to financial problems. It bought many molds from the Barth Art Company.

Painesville Glass Works A glass manufacturing facility established in Painesville, Ohio, by Samuel Pollack in 1825.

Painted Amberina A glass in imitation of Amberina developed by Joseph Locke at the New England Glass Company in 1883. The process for making it was patented in 1895 by Andrew Stock and Emil Mueller of Pittsburgh, Pennsylvania. The glass was initially painted, in part, with a blend of copper oxide and yellow ochre that was "set" by bringing it to a temperature slightly below the melting point. After cooling, it was again painted and reheated. A ruby color was struck in the first coat and the second coat changed to a yellow, amber or green. It has an unusual iridescence.

painted decoration Embellishment by painting on glassware using cold colors or enameling.

painted enamel ware Any of several small objects crafted for the table and desk, including small boxes, toys, knobs, souvenirs, etc., enameled with a scene, picture or motto, such as "A trifle from...." On occasion, transfer print patterns were used in addition to enameling.

painted glass (1) Chinese painted wares of glass, usually using an opaque white glass background. Typically enamel painting on glassware was similar to that on porcelain. It is known as *Ku-Yueh Hsuan*. See *pennelato, vetro*. (2) Windows embellished with either monochromatic oxides (glass staining colors) or with colored enamel paints. They could be of mosaic construction or a single pane.

Painter Glass Cutting Shop A glass cutting shop established by Robert Painter in 1904 in Corning, New York. His brother, Ernest, was one of his cutters. It closed in 1906. Robert became a plumber and Ernest a carpenter, both cutting, part time, until about 1915.

painting (1) The embellishment of glass mirrors by painting on the surface, fashionable in England in the 18th century. Many Dutch artists specialized in this (see *mirror painting*). (2) Painting done on the front or reverse of glass. See *panel; scenic decoration; Venetian scenic plates; luster painting; mirror painting; reverse painting on glass; unfired painting; cold colors.*

painting on glass See *mirror painting; Chinese mirror painting.*

pair Two objects of the same nature and form, such as figures, salt and pepper shakers, and oil and vinegar cruets, which harmonize with or are suited to each other. They are intended to be used as a unit or stand together. It is not necessary that they be identical, only related.

Pairpoint Corporation See *Mount Washington Glass Company.*

Pairpoint jar, apricot with white daisies, silver-plated fittings, 3″ h., signed.
Krause Publications

Pairpoint Glass Works The Pairpoint Manufacturing Company (Corporation) of New Bedford, Massachusetts, was organized in 1880, named after its first superintendent, T.J. Pairpoint. It made a variety of useful and ornamental household goods, including holders for pickle castors, flatware, handles for brushes, wine coolers, jewelry and cigar cases, casket hardware, candlesticks, etc. Britannia, an alloy of tin, copper, antimony and zinc, was the base metal used in making most of their wares. German silver was also used (most of its silverware was signed). Many pieces were made of a combination of glass made by the Mt. Washington Glass Company and Pairpoint's own silver between 1880 and 1894. On July 14, 1894, they merged. In 1900 the Pairpoint Manufacturing Corporation became Pairpoint Corporation.

The first quarter of the 20th century was one of great prosperity for Pairpoint, introducing quantities of glass and silver products. In the late 1880s it bought the New Bedford Paper Company, the largest maker of paper tubes for the textile industry in the United States. It also embellished Limoges china blanks and made cut and engraved glass, overlay glass, paperweights, and many other products. From the 1920s to 1938, it made some fine colored wares.

The Depression of 1929 nearly caused glassware production to be discontinued. In the 1930s it established the Pairpoint School of Glassmaking to persuade young artisans to learn the art of glassblowing and engraving, but young Americans were reluctant to serve a four-year apprenticeship at low wages, and the school failed. In 1934 production in the silver and glass departments was severely curtailed by the Depression and the influx of inexpensive wares from Japan, and in 1937, they ceased operations. In May 1938, these departments and buildings were purchased by J. & B. Kenner Inc. In 1939 it sold the glassmaking portion to Isaac N. Babbitt, who announced the resumption of the glass division. Robert Gundersen, in charge of the company for several years under Pairpoint and considered to be one of the foremost glassmakers in the world, would be affiliated with the new operation. See *Gundersen*

(Pairpoint) Glass Works; Mount Washington Glass Company.

Pairpoint Heirlooms See *Gundersen Pairpoint Glass Works.*

Pairpoint Manufacturing Company

See *Mount Washington Glass Company.*

Pairpoint paperweight A paperweight made shortly after 1910 by the Pairpoint Manufacturing Company. It was a solid glass sphere (mounted on a flat bottom base) containing spirals of glass threads of two colors (white and cobalt blue or ruby red), in a vertical ovoid shape, surrounded by evenly spaced air bubbles. The base of some bear the engraved name of Carl Banks.

Pairpoint of Wareham See *Gundersen Pairpoint Glass Works.*

paisley A teardrop shaped design in which the curving line folds back upon itself. It was a common motif in Renaissance-style stained glass and is often found in fancy beveled glass.

Paisley Shawl Monart glass with crushed colored enamels worked into swirls on the surface and given a glossy finish by exposing it to fumes at the glory hole.

L.E. Smith water goblet, blue, Palace (Moon & Star) pattern.
Davanna Collection

Palace pattern A pattern in clear glass introduced during the 1880s by Adams & Company. The name subsequently changed to *Moon & Star* pattern. It was collected by singer Kate Smith when her song, "When the Moon Comes over the Mountain" became popular. This, in turn, started a collecting craze. It has been reproduced over the years

by several companies, the latest being L.E. Smith Company. Many reproductions were made in color.

pall A ceremonial covering for a coffin. Some made in China in the late Chou dynasty (about 400-240 B.C.), perhaps at Ch'in-ts'un, consisted of several small rectangles of glass, originally with inlaid gilt ornamentation, stitched together vertically and horizontally by small loops of wire.

Palladian window (Aka *Venetian window*, *Serlian motif*-first appearing in Serlio's "Architettura" in 1537) A three "light" opening with a round-headed center section flanked by square-headed sidelights, found often in American buildings constructed during the 18th century. In the late 19th century it was reworked into numerous variations, frequently using colored or stained glass, and can still be found in a variety of variations, usually including decorative glazing. It was named after Andrea Palladio (1508-1580), an Italian Renaissance architect who used the form extensively, though never as a window. Its use as a window did not emerge until the mid-1700s when English *palladianism* became popular.

pallet A glassmaker's tool similar to a wide spatula. A square piece of metal or wood attached to a handle, used to make the flattened base on a jug, decanter, or other vessel, or for forming molten glass on the end of the blowpipe. See *tools, glassmaker's.*

palm column vase A thin, vertically cylindrical "vase" of core glass with combed decoration and, at the top, spreading palm fronds. They were often used to hold makeup for the eyes, sometimes with a thin wooden stick for applying it (see *kohl tube*). They were made in Egypt during the late XVIIIth and XIXth dynasties (c. 1400-1250 B.C.).

palm cup A small cup of hemispherical shape with no handle and often a kick base, to be held in the user's palm. Unembellished ones exist, made during the 6th century of Frankish glass. Some later ones of Frankish glass were decorated with mold blown ribs. Similar shaped ones were made later of Islamic glass

and, during the 16th century, in the Rhineland of Waldglas (often embellished with molded rosettes in raised slots). They were also made in England during the mid-19th century (marked *Elfin* with gilt on the interior).

palm leaf decoration (pattern) An embellishment of threads of glass combed alternately upward and downward. See *combed decoration.*

Palme, Edward, Jr. (1893-1968) Born in Serbia, Palme came to New York with his father, Edward Sr., in 1905, leaving shortly for Charleroi, Pennsylvania. In 1907 he moved to Corning, New York, where he studied engraving under his father. His first employer was Sinclaire. He worked there until he joined the armed services in World War I. After the war he worked for Hawkes as a cutter and engraver, also working in his father's cutting and engraving shop. About 1932 he established a cutting and engraving shop in Corning. He left Hawkes in 1936, then worked at Steuben, retiring in 1960 and continuing to work in his home shop until 1966.

Palme, Edward, Sr. (1867-1951) Born in Bohemia, he learned cutting and engraving in Meistersdorf, receiving his master's certificate in Vienna and becoming an engraving instructor and supervisor at Lobmeyr in Vienna. He and his family came to New York in 1905, moving to Charleroi, Pennsylvania, and, in 1907, to Corning, New York, where he worked for Hawkes as a cutter and engraver. He opened a cutting and engraving shop, which he operated until 1947.

Palmer & Clark A bottle and hollowware glass manufacturing facility established in 1821 in New Portage, Ohio (now a part of Barberton). It operated only a few years.

pan An antiquated term for a bowl.

pan topped bowl A bowl on some drinking glasses and other hollow glassware with the curved upper portion wider than the curved lower part—somewhat pan-shaped, the upper portion like a shallow pan, with a deep round funnel below. In depth, the *pan topped bowl* falls between the *saucer topped bowl* (shallower) and *cupped topped bowl* (deeper).

Panama A cut-glass trademark of the W.P. Hitchcock Co.

Pandora glass A patented name for a glassware reminiscent of Roman Glass excavated at ancient burial sites. All kinds of Roman vessels were copied in Pandora glass. Very few of the articles made of Pandora glass could be finished at the furnace. Staining and special embellishments were desirable in order to achieve the required result. The article was subjected to various mineral vapors in a muffle, giving it an azure blue surface, slight sheen, and aged appearance. The variegated enamel embellishment is representative of the Roman epoch, even to the point of having breaks in the outline to simulate age, and a pontil mark is on all specimens. Compared to Roman glass originals, Pandora pieces are slightly heavier. It was a Czech-Baroque glass made during the 1890s but not made in great quantities.

pane glass Glass in flat sheet form as most glass used for glazing windows. It was first made using the casting process. Later different techniques and methods were employed to make crown glass, broad glass, and plate glass. A more recent method is used to make float glass. Flat sections cut from all types of glass are termed panes. See *rulli.*

panel A flat tablet generally used as a fixed decoration set into a wall or suspended from above in front of a wall. It is decorated in relief, normally with enameled scenes or mosaic designs. Some decorated in relief may have been used as plaques. Mosaic ones were made at Alexandria from 100 B.C. to 100 A.D.; see *opus sectile.* Some made at Murano were of opaque white glass enameled with biblical subjects or scenic views. See *scenic decoration; sunken panel; paneling.*

panel cut A cut-glass motif made using the flat edge of a grinding wheel. It is similar to the flute motif except the flute cut is concave and the panel flat.

paneled paperweight A paperweight with a number of similar or identical millefiori canes organized in triangular groups or panels radiating outward from a

central motif, with canes of adjacent panels of contrasting colors and motifs. Sometimes the panels are separated by other types of embellishments such as a row of canes or a ribbon twist.

paneling A decorative pattern consisting of a sequence of adjacent or close parallel vertical depressions in the form of arches with a rounded or oval top. The panels were made using the flat edge of a grinding wheel or by blowing the paraison into a dip mold with the design. They were deeper in a piece formed with two gathers of molten glass. It was commonly used in the 18th century on vases, some possibly made at the Stiegel glassworks.

Pantin Glassworks A glass manufacturing facility established in 1851 by E.S. Monot at La Villette, near (now in) Paris, moving in 1855 to Pantin (Seine), outside of Paris. After several name changes, it became the Cristallarie de Pantin about 1900, operated by Sainte Hilaire, Touvier, de Varreux et Cie. Some paperweights with flowers, lizards, etc., are believed to have been made here. After World War I the company merged with DeGras & Cie, operating as Verreries et Cristalleries de St. Denis et Pantin Reunies, using the marks *Pantin*, *DeVez* (the pseudonym of its art director) and *Degue* (the name of one of its master glassmakers).

pap boat (Aka *sucking bottles*) An ovoid or pear-shaped container with a tube-shaped spout for feeding infants and the infirm. *Pap* is a diluted gruel made of bread boiled in water.

One of a pair of paperweights, c. 1900, clear, white, blue, and red glass.
The Corning Museum of Glass

Lalique "Chrysis" paperweight, clear satin glass, 5-1/2" h., signed "Lalique France."
Davanna Collection

Murano millefiori paperweight, 5-1/4" d. x 3-1/4" h.
Heartland Discoveries

paperweight A small, heavy object placed on papers to keep them in place on a desk. Originally, they were quite plain and purely functional. In more recent times a paperweight is better defined as a small, heavy decorative or ornamental object.

Weights, as they are called, are usually spherical and about three inches in diameter, but some are pentagonal, scalloped, polyhedral, etc. Modern ones may be created in unusual shapes. They are often high domed to magnify the interior motif; some rare ones are flat domed. The most prized ones are of the overlay type with windows that reveal and tend to reduce the apparent size of the interior motif. Some are embellished with slices (set ups) of millefiori canes or subject motifs often superimposed on an intricate ground or cushion or with a diamond or star cut bottom. The art of paperweight production reached its pinnacle of development in France.

History of Paperweight Making. The earliest glass weights, called sulfides, were sculpted ceramic cameos encased in crystal. First developed in the 1750s in France, they were later enhanced and perfected in England by Apsley Pellatt, who received a patent on his technique in 1819. Glass encrustations, often memorializing important individuals or historic events, were popular throughout the 19th century. In addition to paperweights, they were used to ornament a variety of articles including decanters, perfume bottles, seals, candlesticks, buttons, and jewelry. The earliest were made in Murano and Bohemia about 1843. The earliest recorded signed and dated specimens are those marked "S.L.1845". Pietro Bigaglia of Venice is believed to be the first to display millefiori weights at the Exhibition of Austrian Industry in Vienna in 1845. It is generally accepted that this was the beginning of France's interest in making weights even though some may have been made prior to the Exhibition. The classic period of millefiori and lamp work weight making occurred from about 1845 to 1860. During this period, three outstanding facilities in France set the pace in style and production for weights of excellent quality: Compagnie des Cristalleries de Baccarat, Cristalleries de Saint Louis and Clichy-la-Garenne. English facilities swiftly imitated the French companies and, about 1848, millefiori weights were being made in London and Birmingham. The most prominent of English makers during the 19th century were Bacchus, Whitefriars, and Islington.

In the United States, weight making in considerable numbers did not begin until after the New York Exhibition of the *Industry of All Nations* in New York City in 1853. Many of the early American weights were imitative of the French style. American makers later developed their own distinctive styles and techniques of manufacture, specifically *lamp work* weights. After about 1860 interest in paperweights declined in Britain and Europe but continued to flourish in the United States, intermittently into the early years of the 20th century. The best known American makers were New England Glass, Boston & Sandwich, Gillinder, Mt. Washington and Millville.

Since about 1930 China and Japan have been part of the weight market. Theirs are easily identifiable because they are made of soda glass, high in alkali content and not as clear as crystal or lead glass weights.

Weight making was becoming a lost art in the 1950s when Paul Jokelson, an importer and avid weight collector, approached Baccarat and Saint Louis with a proposal to revive the classic art since they had not been made in any significant numbers for more than eighty years. Artists and craftsmen spent nearly 20 years in research and experimentation rediscovering the techniques used in making sulfide, millefiori and lamp work weights. Once they succeeded and production began, interest in contemporary weights blossomed. Since then several facilities and studio artists have joined Baccarat and St. Louis in making modern weights of excellent quality.

French Paperweights. Clichy: Many weights are signed with a "C" in black, green or red in the center of a cane within the weight. Some rare ones have Clichy spelled out on canes. It is known for the use of a pink or white rose in the pattern. *St. Louis*: Famous for its tiny dancing figures or animals in the center of a cane. *Baccarat*: Many weights are signed with a "B" or "B" with a date. Famous for its tiny figures of animals in the center of a cane. *Monot Pere et Fils et Stumpf* (Pantin, France): Many weights include natural objects, such as flowers and animals, especially reptiles; many have air bubbles throughout the mass, looking like pearl drops; and many have millefiori of roses, leaves, and fruit embedded in lumps of clear glass. Many French weights were further enhanced by cutting and faceting. Some are of the overlay or cased glass type that may be cut. A colored opaque or clear glass base was often used as a ground on which an encrusted sulfide or cameo was superimposed. The subject of the majority of these were busts, full length portraits, seals, religious or allegorical medallions, hunting scenes, etc.

Other European Paperweights. Various English facilities made weights. *Letter weights*, a specific type of weight, were a small portion of George Bacchus & Sons' production. Most Bacchus weights are relatively large, generally over three inches in diameter, and all contain millefiori. Whitefriars began making weights about 1848. Antique Whitefriars weights use concentric millefiori spacing schemes. *Pinchbeck weights* are made of a bas-relief metal insert held in place by a base of copper, tin or other substance. This was covered, rather than encased, by a glass dome. Some excellent weights were made in Venice, Belgium, and Germany. The Belgian facility of Val St. Lambert made mainly patterned millefiori weights. Although rare, it made some lamp work pieces, sulfides, and overlays. A few Bohemian cameo-type weights are known, and Scotland made some weights. Some weights with large floral motifs in bright colors were made in Czechoslovakia. Orrefors and Kosta made some weights in Sweden.

American Paperweights. American weights were made extensively by some facilities, but generally speaking they do not equal the finest of the French in quality and technical perfection. Some of America's best weights were made by New England Glass, Boston & Sandwich, and by John Gilliland in his Brooklyn, New York, facility. At Sandwich *candy* and millefiori type weights were made in fairly large quantities, as were fruit and floral designs (*Poinsettia* is one of the most widely known, but there was also *Dalhia, Pansy, Fuchsia,* and *Strawberry*).

Many of the finest made at Sandwich were the creation of Nicholas Lutz from St. Louis, France, who specialized in floral and fruit weights with tiny colored pears, apples, or cherries with green leaves and stems on a latticinio background. Tiny glass buttons having the general appearance of very small paperweights were also made there. Weights made at New England Glass were similar in design and equal in quality and workmanship to those made at Sandwich; both used the finest quality flint glass.

The best of New England Glass' weights were made by Francois Pierre from Baccarat. New England Glass made some exceptionally good cameo weights; its blown apple and pear weights were the finest of their type. John L. Gilliland excelled in making weights of the millefiori type. Mt. Washington Glass Works also made some excellent weights. In 1894 it became part of the Pairpoint Manufacturing Co., which made some beautiful weights.

From 1863 to 1912, Whitall, Tatum & Co., Millville, New Jersey, made numerous weights, but was not influenced by the French or English styles. In 1863 it established a wooden mold department and made footed inkwells, or *inkwell paperweights*, with lily and fountain designs in the globular body with a matching stopper. By 1880 many unusual weights were being made at Millville when Ralph Barber, Emil Stanger, Marcus Kuntz, John Rhulander, and Michael Kane were the leading glass craftsmen, where the outstanding achievement in weight making was the *Millville Rose*. Ralph Barber is generally given credit for making these weights, but all facilities in Millville made them. The roses were made in deep rose, pink, white, and yellow, with and without stems. They are usually upright, but a few are tilted and others are suspended on their side. Most rest on a heavy circular foot. Some have a standard circular foot with a plain cylindrical stem, and a few have a baluster stem. Barber made them from 1905 to about 1912.

A popular type of weight, inferior in design and craftsmanship and made in many variations, consisted of a large semi-spherical form with a flat ground base and an inscription accompanied by leaf and floral sprays and various insignia usually on a milk white background. Sometimes there is an inscription with a design in milk white in a colored glass weight.

Weights were also made in Pittsburgh, Pennsylvania; at the Dorflinger facility at White Mills; at the Ravenna Glass Works; and in other Midwestern facilities. At the Redford Glass Works and Redwood Glass Works, crude weights from aquamarine glass were made. Modern United States weights have been made by Charles Kaziun and Paul J. Stankard.

Paperweight Manufacture. Certain aspects of the manufacturing process, such as encasing a design in crystal, faceting, and finishing a piece, are identical for millefiori and lamp work style weights. Once the millefiori canes or lamp work figures have been made, they are positioned on a metal template and heated to just below the melting point, and a metal collar is placed around the arrangement. A glassworker gathers a ball of molten glass on the end of a pontil rod, which he then rolls and works into shape on a marver. The hot molten glass is placed in the collar and the preheated design is picked up. This first gather makes up the ground of the weight. After being picked up, it is reheated in the glory hole and another gather of clear molten glass is added as the worker begins to form the dome. Successive layers are added until the dome is formed. The layers do not appear as separate layers, but as a homogenous mass.

The worker continually rolls the pontil rod back and forth across the arms of his chair so the still soft glass will not sag or become misshaped. During this part of the process the dome is shaped and smoothed with a wet wooden block or contoured pad of tissue or newspaper. While the glass is still pliable, tongs are used to form a slender neck at the base of the weight. When the piece has cooled sufficiently, the worker gives a sharp tap to the pontil rod, causing the weight to break off and fall into a bed of sand. It is then annealed, an extremely critical process. Occasionally the gathers of glass and design elements within the weight tend to cool at different rates, causing it to crack or shatter. The final stage of the process is grinding and polishing. During this stage the pontil mark is ground down and, if desired, the dome is faceted or cut with a grinding wheel.

Even if numerous weights of the same design are made, each has its own individual character. Making weights is a process of building, not blowing. The term *blown paperweight* is descriptive but frequently incorrectly used; such weights have a hollow dome. The primary techniques of production are millefiori, lamp work and enclosures (sulfides).

Sizes of Paperweights. Miniature: 1.5 to 2 inches in diameter. *Standard*: 2.5 to 3.25 inches in diameter. *Magnum*: larger than 3.25 inches in diameter. See the following types of paperweights: *American; animal; Baccarat; barber's pole; basket; Bohemian; bottle green; bouquet; British*—antique, modern, Victorian; *butterfly; Caithness; candy; carpet; checker; circlet; Clichy; closed millefiori; cluster; concentric; cross; crown; cut base; die patterned; door stop; ducks-on-a-pond; encased overlay; faceted; fauna; flower; fruit; garland; hollow; incrusted; inkwell; Kaziun; lamp work; lizard; Macedoine; magnum; marbrie; medal; millefiori; Millville; miniature; mushroom; opaline; overlay; Pairpoint; panelled; patterned; pedestal; pell-mell; Perthshire; picture; piedouche; Pinchbeck; pom pom; posy; reptile; St. Louis; salamander; scattered millefiori; scrambled; sentimental; spray; snake; snow; spaced millefiori; spoke; strathearn; subject; sulfide; swimming swans; swirl; Tiffany; tricolor; triple; tuft; vegetable; walking pigs; Whitefriars; window; zodiac.*

paperweight glass, Tiffany
See *Tiffany paperweight glass.*

Papillon glass
Literally, *butterfly glass.* An opaque glass in a variety of colors flecked with multiple, closely grouped iridescent spots in the shape of raindrops, similar to a section of a butterfly's wing. It was introduced in 1899 by Max Ritter von Spaun of the Loetz glassworks.

Parabelle Glass
A studio glass shop established in Portland, Oregon, by Gary and Doris Scrutton, specializing in millefiori paperweights. They make their own glass, developing their own colors. Their weights are in the classic style, encompassing a wide range of designs, including close packed millefiori, garlands, and stave basket weights. In 1972 Gary set up a studio, specializing in stained glass and crystal and glass repair. In 1983 he sold it to his sons and established, with his wife, Parabelle Glass. Their weights always include a cane with the initials "PG" and the year of manufacture.

parabolico, vetro *(Italian)*
A glass developed by Ercole Barovier in 1957,

appearing as a patchwork of pieces in a checkerboard pattern; pieces having alternating vertical and horizontal stripes.

paraison See *parison.*

parfait A tall, somewhat conically or cylindrically shaped ice cream dish with a short , broad foot, used for sundaes in soda fountains of the past and gaining in popularity as desserts are becoming more popular and extravagant.

Pargeter, Philip (b. 1826) A glassmaker from a Stourbridge glassmaking family. His paternal uncle was Benjamin Richardson of W.H., B. & J. Richardson, who offered a reward of 1,000 pounds (English) to anyone who could make an accurate replica of the Portland Vase after the original was destroyed in 1845. Pargeter, the lessee of the Red House Glassworks at Wordsley, England, persuaded his cousin, John Northwood, to work with him to make a copy, and, at a later date, reproduced the Milton Vase (1878) and three portrait tazze. Pargeter made cased glass in blanks to be embellished with cameo engraving by others, and designed glassware and cameo decoration. See *Portland Vase: Reproductions; Pargeter-Northwood tazze.*

Pargeter-Northwood tazze A group of three tazze made of blue cameo glass by Philip Pargeter, engraved by John Northwood. The central portraits on them depicted Isaac Newton (symbolic of science), John Flaxman (art), and William Shakespeare (literature), each signed by Northwood and dated 1878, 1880, and 1882, respectively. Their rims are embellished with a wreath of ivy on the Newton tazze, hawthorn leaves and acorns on the Flaxman tazze, and oak leaves on the Shakespeare tazze. Each has a domed foot embellished with acanthus leaves, detachable so the shallow cups may be displayed as plaques. The portraits are taken from jasper medallions made by Joseph Wedgwood. They were on loan to the British Museum from 1959 until they were sold in 1975 in London by Sotheby's (Belgravia).

Parks, Edmunds & Parks A glass manufacturing facility established in 1824 in Kent, Ohio, making tableware using the blown three-mold technique. It operated only for a few years.

parison Also spelled *paraison* (French). (1) The rounded mass into which the molten glass is first gathered on a blowpipe or pontil and rolled when first taken from the furnace (old definition). (2) A gather on the end of a blowpipe after it has been blown into a bubble. Sometimes a parison is called a *bubble*— an inflated gather of metal. (3) Any piece of glass in its molten state.

Park(e) & Hanna; Park(e) & Campbell; Park(e), Campbell & Hanna See *Union Flint Glass Works (Pittsburgh, Pennsylvania).*

Park(e), Edmunds & Park(e) (1824-1934) A glass manufacturing facility established in Kent, Ohio, making bottles, flasks, and some blown three-mold glassware. *Kent Glass Works.*

Parker & Casper (1867-1869) A glass cutting shop established by Charles Parker and Charles Casper in Meriden, Connecticut. When it closed, Casper established the Meriden Silver Plate Company, and, about 1895, the Meriden Cut Glass Co. About 1892 Parker established a short-lived glass cutting shop known as the Charles Parker Company.

Parker Brothers Glass Factory A glass bottle manufacturing facility established in 1885 in West Bridgeton, New Jersey by Clayton Parker of Crowleytown, New Jersey, and his four brothers. This factory made the Mason "Improved" canning jar, patented in 1858 by John Mason. It made some pressed ware and a specialty known as "The Ointment Jar."

Parr pot A jug with a hinged lid, embellished with wide vertical bands of opaque white (lattimo) glass with narrow lines of clear glass between them. It has silver gilt mounts hallmarked "1546-47" and bears the enameled arms of William, Lord Parr of Horton, uncle of Henry VIII's sixth wife. It was previously in the collection of Horace Walpole at Strawberry Hill. Another lidded jug of identical glass and similar shape, except for slightly different mounts, is in the British

Museum and is believed to have been made in the Netherlands in the first half of the 16th century. Its mounts are hallmarked "London 1548-49." It has been reported that a similar jug is listed in the 1559 and 1574 possessions of Queen Elizabeth I.

parrot nose shears Shears not only used for shearing but also, because of the specially shaped nose, used for holding punty rods when being attached to a piece of glass.

Parsche, F.X., & Son Co. Frank X. Parsche (b.1847) was born in Meistersdorf, Austria, coming to the United States in 1873. He worked for Burley & Tyrell in Chicago, Illinois, as an engraver. In 1874 he established this glass cutting company in Chicago. His son, Frank C. (1876), was his partner. In 1893 Edward J. Koch joined the company, which became Koch & Parsche. In 1907 they split and Parsche formed his own company, using the original name. During the Brilliant Period of cut glass, it obtained blanks from Pairpoint, Union, Steuben, Fry, Baccarat, St. Louis, and Val St. Lambert. In 1964 it was operating as Parsche Studios with family members still cutting. In 1981 it was operated by Russel and Donald Parsche.

part size mold A dip or small piece mold used to impress a design on a piece of glassware, later expanded by blowing.

partridge eye See *oeil-de-perdrix.*

parts of a glass object See *base; body; bowl; cover; finial; flange; foot; knob; knop; lip; rim; stem.*

Passglas *(German)* A tall, cylindrical or club-shaped beaker having a pedestal or kick base; a type of Stangenglas embellished with three to seven equidistant horizontal bands of colored enamel or trailed rings of glass, serving as measuring indicators for the contents (the volume between any two adjacent bands is equal to that between any other two adjacent bands). They were passed among beer drinkers and each was expected to drink the amount indicated by the next horizontal band on the glass. However, if the drinker did not stop when the remainder of the beer filled the beaker exactly to the band, he was required to continue to the next band. Often between the bands there is enameling depicting pictorial subjects or small prunts. Those made in Thuringia (a former state in central Germany) often have a playing card painted between the bands (Spielkartenhumpen). These glasses were made in Germany, Bohemia, and the Netherlands from the 16th through 18th centuries. Sometimes a Bandwurmglas is called a Passglas, but that is inaccurate since the spiral threads of the Bandwurmglas do not make equal divisions.

paste jewelry (Aka *paste gem*) Imitation gems usually made of *strass*, a glass with a very high lead content. They have been made since the 12th century from a primitive form of lead glass with good refractive qualities, rivaling the brilliance of natural gems. The lead glass used for artificial gems made at Birmingham, England, as late as 1836 was called *Jew's glass.* The use of the term *paste*, often used for glass imitative of precious stones, dates from the translation by Christopher Merret in 1662 of Antonio Neri's book. The term *strass* dates from the 18th century.

paste mold An iron mold covered with a paste of resinous beeswax or a wooden mold charred on the inside, used in making blown molded wares because the object being made could be rotated within the mold, tending to leave it with a polished surface.

paste mold process A process used to make certain glass articles with a polished surface. Because it is expensive, it was seldom used on Depression glass or other inexpensive glassware. It involves expanding the paraison and simultaneously rotating it within the mold. Any patterns within the mold must be in very low relief. Objects made by this process are relatively free of seams and mold marks.

paste roller A rolling pin. See *rolling pin.*

Pastel Tiffany See *Tiffany Reactive Glass.*

Pasternoster-Kugel(chen) The German term for *prayer beads*, as opposed to *Perlen* or *Glas-Perlen*, beads for personal adornment or export.

pastry mold cane A cane having a central rod surrounded by other rods flaring out at the base and often used as a central motif, used in making some paperweights. Sometimes they were just scattered within a millefiori pattern. See *pie crust cane*.

Patapsco River Glass House
See *Baltimore Glass Works*.

patch box A small shallow ornamental box to hold black patches, fashionable cosmetic accessories for a time during the 18th century.

patch stand A small, circular, low stand about 2-1/2 inches in diameter and one inch high, having a flat top and pedestal base or footed stem, used on a dressing table in place of a patch box.

patched glass See *pezzato, vetro*.

pate-de-cristal A type of *pate-de-verre* made of high quality glass, resulting in the article having a greater translucency (almost transparent) and greater resonance.

pate-de-riz (Aka *alabaster glass, clam water glass*) An opaline glass having a grayish color resembling gypsum. It was named by the St. Louis facility about 1843. It was a cheap substitute for white opaline glass, having a slightly rough, sticky, coarse or matted surface, often used as a base for embellishment.

pate-de-verre *(French)* Literally, *glass paste*. A ware made by grinding glass into a powder, adding a fluxing medium so it would melt readily, coloring it (if colored glass was not pulverized originally), and forming it in a mold. Some items are suggestive of semi-precious stones, formed by positioning different powdered ingredients in the mold. Some were made into polychrome high relief or busts by building up incremental layers in the mold, and if needed, further refined by carving after being fired. The process originated in ancient Egypt and was revitalized in France during the 19th century. Most wares made by this process were signed. Some of the major exponents of this technique were: (a) Henri Cros (1840-1907) and his son, Jean, making plaques with mythological themes; (b) Albert Dammouse (1848-1926) worked at Sevres and made a fragile *pate-de-verre* or *pate d'email*, comparable to porcelain, and embellished with delicate plant forms in pastel shades; (c) George Despret (1862-1952) worked in heavier, more massive types of pate-de verre, sugary in color; (d) Almeric Walter (1859-1942) began working at Daum in 1904 and in 1919 on his own, using a pate-de-verre mass much thicker and more robust in a wide variety of colors; (e) Jules Paul Brateau (1844-1923); (f) Gabriel Argy-Rousseau (b.1885) began by making thin wares, later thicker wares, including bowls, dishes, and fruit, plant, and insect forms in high relief; (g) Francois Decorchement (1880-1971), using his own furnace at Conches, made plaques and windows, first thin items and, commencing in 1910, thicker, more transparent (pate-de-cristal) items. Sometimes they were highly polished and/or had plain cutting. Daum made window plaques of pate-de-verre in clear colors. *Pate-de-verre* was often called *pate-de-riz*. See *tasse medallion*.

patella cup A Roman drinking cup, dating to the 1st century A.D., with a double convex silhouette and a ring foot. *Patella* is Latin for *kneecap*.

paten A plate used to hold the bread in the Eucharist (the sacrament of Holy Communion), having a shallow well and a wide rim. Some have a long projecting handle.

patent lamp See *carcel lamp*.

patera *(Latin)* A Roman vessel similar to a Greek *phiale*, with a small, often shallow bowl from which to pour libations. It differs from the *phiale* in that it has one flat horizontal handle and a foot ring or stemmed foot. They were made of Syrian glass from the 1st to 3rd centuries in forms and shapes derived from silverware. Similar vessels were made at Cologne, in the Rhineland, in the 3rd century, embellished on the bottom with snake trailing in a variety of colored glasses. See *trulla*.

patination The controlled use of a chemical dust, powder, or vapor to produce a textured effect, giving the appearance of a textile, snow, leather, etc. The chemical may be applied to the surface or between two layers of glass.

pattern A design in some way imparted on glass objects, usually consisting of one or more motifs. See the following patterns: *bull's-eye and diamond point; cut glass, patterns; heart-and-vine; honeycomb; horn-of-plenty; pigeon eye; public domain (see cut glass, patterns); pulled leady; quincunx; rim; spider web; sunburst.*

Pattern glass tumbler, 3-3/4" h.
Davanna Collection

Pattern glass bowl, Heart with Thumbprint, gold trim, scalloped, 10" d.
Krause Publications

pattern glass Pressed glass made in table settings is often called pattern glass. The discovery of a mechanical means of making press-molded glass articles was the most significant contribution made by American craftsmen to the development of the glass industry during the 19th century. A fire on December 17, 1836, destroyed much of the U.S. Patent Office, leaving patent records before this date incomplete. Therefore, controversy exists about who was first to develop pattern glass and with what devices. However, it is known that on December 6, 1845, Joseph Magouun received a patent for

a manually operated glass press. On March 29, 1864, Frederich McGee and Charles Ballinger received one for a steam-operated glass press. And on March 5, 1872, William King received one for a revolving block type press and Henry Learures received one for an air-cooled glass press.

There are three basic methods for pressing glass: (a) block molding, the simplest; (b) split molding where the mold is in two or more parts; and (c) font molding where each article is identical in form and dimension to every other article made from the same mold. This was an inexpensive method of making glassware for the average person and revolutionized the glass industry. Shortly after 1840, pattern glass eclipsed the popularity of lacy glass, becoming fashionable toward the middle of the 19th century. It was made in large quantities over the next 50 years, its designs differing sharply from those of Lacy glass. During the depression from 1836 to 1840, manufacturers were looking for ways to reduce costs and find new patterns to stimulate purchases. It was at this time that fire polishing was introduced, but lacy glass did not hold up well to it. The new designs, composed largely of geometric motifs, took on the appearance of cut glass after fire polishing. Pattern glass was made from a good quality flint glass and had a pleasant bell tone. Most articles were of clear rather than colored glass; handles were applied.

After the Civil War, lime glass was used in making it. This enabled an even less expensive ware to be made, activating the industry since more people could now afford it. The simple early designs of loops and ribs were replaced by more ornate designs of geometric patterns in imitation of cut-glass patterns and stylized flowers. There were many variants of patterns as glassmakers adapted the more popular designs of their competitors, often making only minor changes. New shapes and forms appeared. Colors were used more widely, many pieces made of a solid color or flashed. Frosting, etching, and gilding were common forms of embellishment. The center of the industry during this period moved from New England to the Midwest. The 1870s brought more elaborate naturalistic patterns (patterns now commonly called *pattern glass*) and clear and frosted patterns with figures. Overall patterns, partly geometric, were in fashion during the 1880s.

pattern glass, look-alikes Various objects with patterns very similar in design but not made from an identical mold. Such patterns usually involve different shaped objects, handles, and finials. There is often great confusion when attempting to determine the maker.

pattern glass, copy Patterns very similar in design with only the most minute variations, generally considered forgeries, causing much litigation during the 1880s. There is often great confusion when attempting to determine the maker. Many U.S. patterns were copied, made by Canadian companies under different pattern names, and often shipped back to the United States and sold, thus adding more confusion.

pattern molded glass Glassware blown in a mold. The interior of the mold has a raised pattern so the object being made has the pattern with a convexity on the inside underlying the concavity on the outside, as distinguished from (a) blown three-mold glass having outside convexities opposite the inside concavities, and (b) mold pressed glass that shows the pattern only on the exterior with a smooth interior. It is made using a part size dip mold or part size piece mold and expanded by blowing. It is differentiated from glass so patterned in a full size piece mold. Pattern molding has been used since the earliest days of American glassmaking by Amelung, Stiegel, etc. Ribbing is very common—the article often identified by the number of ribs (sixteen, twenty-four, etc.). Diamond and honeycomb patterns were also common. A daisy shape within a diamond is rare and believed to have been made by Stiegel.

patterned paperweight Several types of paperweights with the canes within the dome arranged in a definite pattern rather than a haphazard fashion.

Patterson Frey Specialty Company A glass decorating firm operating for a short period in the late 1800s in Uniontown,

Pennsylvania, making ruby- and amber-stained glass and other decorated ware fashionable during the Victorian era.

pax The same as *osculatory*.

Peach Bloom A peachblow ware made by Stevens & Williams, similar to the peachblow made by Thomas Webb & Sons, called *Peach Glass*. See *Peachblow*.

peach bloom See *Peachblow*.

Peach Glass A cased peachblow glass made by Thomas Webb & Sons, in shades from pink to deep red. The surface is either mat or glossy and occasionally embellished with gold.

Peach Quartz See *quartz glass*.

Peach Skin A trademark received by Frederick S. Shirley of the Mt. Washington Glass Co. in 1886 for a velvet-like finish on various wares, created by sandblasting or using acid.

Peachblow vase with crimped rim, cased white interior, 12" h. Tri-State Antiques

Peachblow (A descriptive term used generically to describe a type of glass made by numerous companies over the years and often written in the lower case, *peachblow*.) An art glass made by several U.S. facilities as well as several in Europe in imitation of the peach bloom glaze found on some Chinese porcelain made during the reign of K'ang Hsi (1662-1722); see *Morgan Vase*. One version, made from 1885 by New England Glass Company, was a cased glass in shades from an opaque white or cream color to deep rose or bright pink (polished pontil). Another, made by the Mt. Washington Glass Co., was opaque, shaded in pastel tones from pale grayish white to rose or purplish pink (the pontil mark often covered with a raspberry-like blob of glass). When Mt. Washington sued for patent infringement, it kept the name *Peachblow,* and New England Glass changed the name of its ware to *Wild Rose.*

Another type of cased glass by Hobbs, Brockunier & Co., called *Wheeling Peach-blow,* was shaded in darker colors (yellow to red) and had a silky or glossy surface. It was used for tableware and decorative objects and was the earliest version of *Peachblow,* made from about 1883. It often has a molded drapery pattern on the inner layer (*Wheeling Drape*). *Peach Glass,* by Thomas Webb & Sons, was a cased glass shaded from pink to deep red with a mat or glossy surface, at times adorned with gold embellishment. A similar ware called *Peach Bloom* was made by Stevens & Williams. An uncased version was made by the Boston & Sandwich Glass Co., often with a molded swirl pattern and colored pink. Some pieces had a bail handle resembling a thorny branch.

There was also a *Gundersen-Pairpoint Peachblow,* heavy and thick compared to other types, in shades from opaque white to various rose tones, ranging from a delicate pink to deep crimson. Imitations of all these were made in Bohemia and reproductions have been made elsewhere. Generally all are of poor quality and easily detected as such. In the early 1920s, Frederick Carder made a *Peachblow* similar to *Wheeling Peachblow,* the lining being of alabaster glass.

peacock Carnival glass with a smoky gray-blue color.

Peacock colors See *Tiffany Peacock colors; Peacock Feather glassware; Tiffany Peacock Feather glassware.*

Peacock Feather glassware (1) An art glass made by Victor Durand Jr. at Vineland Flint Glass Works; a flashed ware with a feather pattern. (2) See *Tiffany Peacock Feather glassware.*

pear drop A drop that is pyriform (pear shaped) and usually faceted. Some are long and tapered while others are flat.

pear shaped Pyriform in shape; made in the form of a pear. The most common items made in this shape are pitchers, vases, and teapots. *Inverted pyriform* is used when the article has the greatest diameter in the upper portion. See *baluster.*

pearl (1) A decorative motif in the form of a small attached glass bead as applied as an eye on the tip of prunts on some Romer, Nuppenbecher and goblets. They are also found on some items made in the southern Netherlands, likely at Antwerp, from the second half of the 16th century and in Germany from the 17th century. They were often turquoise blue set on clear glass. (2) A gather of glass attached to the end of the paraison and pushed up over the paraison to form a second layer of glass in an even band. This is tooled or molded into a decorative design, generally swirled, looking like drapery. When molded, the paraison with the band was generally expanded in a fluted dip mold. It is also called *purl.* (3) A glass bead in imitation of a pearl, common with Venetian glassmakers. They were made from tubes of glass of varying size. The tube is heated on the end and a small bubble blown, in which is made two holes for stringing. It is further shaped if desired. After removal from the tube, the inside of the bead is sprayed with glue and a powder made from fish scales is added to give the bead a *pearly* look. Color is added to the inside of the bead if desired.

Pearl See *Luna.*

Pearl Art Glass See *Foval Glass.*

pearl ash or pearlash (Aka *potash*) Refined commercial potassium carbonate (K_2CO_3), a common flux (alkali) used in glassmaking. See *potash.*

Pearl Iridescent glass A ware made with opaline or alabaster glass by the Richardsons of Stourbridge, England. It was blown in a dip mold and coated with a crystal overlay before iridizing.

pearl ornaments An all-over molded pattern of small diamonds or ogivals.

Pearl Satin glass An art glass made by several different processes and, as a result, with many different appearances, all similar in that they had a pearly lustered surface or lustered stripes. Patents were issued to several companies in the United States and France during the 1880s for various processes and methods of manufacture. Items made by Stevens & Williams Ltd. were named *Verre de Soie,* but they were also called *Mother of Pearl Satin Glass* and *Pearl Ware.* Pearl Satin Glass is an opaque glass, normally patterned, with a white lining. Unlike other satin finished glass, it has a pearl finish sometimes achieved by air bubbles or air locks trapped in indentations made by the mold or by acid etching the outer surface. Some of the most common patterns are diamond quilted, raindrop, and hobnail. It was often made in various combinations of colors, at times with one merging into the other. Some pieces had the coloring of a rainbow. Embellishments include gold and silver, enamels, applied glass, and coraline. See mother-of-pearl glass.

Pearl Ware See *Pearl Satin glass.*

pearl ware See *mother-of-pearl glass.*

pearlash See *pearl ash.*

Pearline Glass A specialty glass of Davidson's of Gateshead, patented in 1889. A transparent glass shading to opaque made in various colors, the most common being blue and yellow. Some pieces have a raised design, often in a color different from the base.

peeble ground A ground similar to a jasper ground, except the canes are larger and coarser.

pebbled glass Glass embellished with numerous small, irregularly shaped, haphazardly placed spots of glass in bright colors on a different colored (typically light blue) background. It was made in France, Venice, Germany, and elsewhere in the 17th century.

pectoral A small ornamental tablet, some with inlaid glass, worn on the breast or suspended around the neck by a cord or a string of beads, often counterbalanced by a smaller one on the back. They were originally used as jewelry in Egypt, but by the XVIIIth Dynasty (about 1540 BC) they had become amulets and are often found buried in tombs.

pedestal (1) An object or part of one raised above a surface on a tall stem, such as a pedestal vase. (2) A type of stem known as a *Silesian* stem in England. See *piedouche.*

pedestal foot (1) A foot of a drinking glass, solid or hollow, tall and slightly wider toward the bottom, having a concave sloping exterior. They are often found on the *Passglas* or *Stangenglas.* Sometimes it has a kick or a pontil mark. (2) See *pedestal paperweight.*

pedestal paperweight (Aka *piedouche*) A type of paperweight resting on a small pedestal or a rim at the base, slightly wider than the body. They were made at Clichy, St. Louis, Baccarat, and Stourbridge.

pedestal stem See *Silesian stem.*

Peerless A trademark of Kelly & Steinman, Glass Cutters.

Peerless Cut Glass Company A cut glass company in Brooklyn, New York, operating during the 1910s. See *Kelly & Steinman.*

peg lamp (Aka *stand lamps, socket lamps*) A small whale oil lamp having a glass peg extending from the base of the font. An integral part of the lamp, the peg fit into the socket of a candlestick or other holder. Some made in the United States were highly decorated. The overall height of the lamp, from the bottom of the peg to the top of the shade, is normally between eight and 9-1/2 inches.

Pegasus Vase A cameo glass vase with a blue body and white overlay with motifs depicting Amphitrite and Aurora and the finial, Pegasus, made by John Northwood (signed and dated 1882 on the body and cover) at the Dennis Glassworks of Thomas Webb & Sons (also called the *Dennis Vase*). The handles are representations of sea horses carved from solid glass by Edwin Grice and finished by Northwood. It was exhibited before completion at the Paris Exposition in

1878 and is now in the Smithsonian Institute in Washington, D.C.

pegging Pricking an object of molten glass with a special tool to leave a tiny depression that is covered with molten glass, trapping air inside and forming a tear as the trapped air expands from the heat of the added glass.

Peking glassware (1) (Aka *Mandarin glass*) A general type of Chinese glassware likely made at Po Shan in Shantang Province for the Imperial Court during the 18th and 19th centuries. The glassware was usually in the form of small items such as animals or vegetables made in dark blue, azure, or various shades of yellow. (2) (Aka *Beijing glass*) A Chinese cameo glass made to imitate porcelain, which became popular in the 18th century. By 1725 multi-layered carving resulted in a cameo effect, leading to a wider range of shapes and colors. It was originally made at the first facility founded in Peking in 1680, which was closed from 1736 to 1795. During this period it was made in Poshan and shipped to Peking for finishing. In spite of this it was still called Peking glass and continued to be made using the old methods and techniques. Replicas are currently on the market.

Peking Imperial Palace glassware Glassware made at the workshop established in 1680 in the Peking Imperial Palace during the Ch'ing Dynasty, by the Emperor K'ang Hsi (1662-1722). It was the first facility in China to make glass in large quantities. It made blown wares in the style of Venice and the Netherlands, under the guidance of Jesuits. Much of this early glass exhibits crisselling. As time passed, the works expanded, making snuff bottles (see *Chinese snuff bottles*) embellished with cameo cutting, Ku beakers of clear and monochrome glass, enameled glassware in Ku-Yuen Hsuan style, and pendants and other objects of colored glass imitating jade. Some pieces bear a Chinese reign mark.

Pele's hair See *Goddesses' hair.*

pell mell paperweight See *scrambled paperweight.*

pellets Small pellets of glass about the size of a pill, made commercially for studio glassworkers. Because of the shortage of good quality and reliable cullet, they are commercially prepared, often to the glassmaker's specifications. The advantages to using pellets are: (a) no exposure to toxic dusts; (b) no mixing of raw materials; (c) consistent quality of the glass; (d) regular supply; (e) founding is easier; (f) refractories last longer; (g) less storage area required; and (h) less housekeeping.

Peloton glass (Aka *spaghetti glass, shredded coconut glass*) An art glass embellished with applied short filaments of glass, patented in Bohemia in 1880 by Wilhelm Kralik of Neuwalk. The process involved: (a) dipping of a gather or partially shaped piece of glass into a container holding filaments or threads of colored glass; (b) throwing of filaments onto the body; or (c) rolling the paraison on a surface on which filaments were scattered. The object was then pressed, tooled, or manipulated into the desired form. The body was normally of clear, colored, or opaque white glass, often acid treated to produce a satin surface. Reproductions are being made.

Peltier Glass Company A glass manufacturing facility established in 1886 in Ottawa, Illinois, by Victor J. Peltier. He was born in France in 1833 and worked in the glass industry there before coming to the United States in 1859. He worked for various facilities before going to Ottawa to become superintendent of the Ottawa Flint Glass & Bottle Company. In the early years at his facility, which was originally the Ottawa Novelty Glass Company, he made marbles and specialty and novelty items. In 1919 the facility burned and Peltier's sons, Sellers and Joseph, rebuilt it, renaming it Peltier Glass Company. It continued to make marbles—the most famous being the twelve Comic Strip marbles made in the late 1920s—and many other items. It was sold in 1984. The new management makes industrial marbles and many other products. In 1985 it purchased some molds from the Westmoreland Glass Company. It is still in business, operated by heirs, doing mostly contract work and making novelty items.

pen A pointed instrument used for writing or drawing with ink or similar fluid medium. Specimens in various styles have been made of glass, especially the so-called Nailsea glass.

pen stand A stand on which to rest a pen, often in ornamental form, made from the mid-18th through the 19th centuries.

pendant (1) An ornament suspended around the neck. Some were made of colored glass in Greece from about 1400 and 100 B.C.; in a variety of shapes in Rome during the 1st century A.D.; and in square or rectangular form with metal suspensory mounts in Germany during the 15th century. Some were made in China of opaque glass imitating jade. They were often made in sets, accompanied by necklaces, rings, buckles, and other similar objects. (2) A small glass object suspended as an ornament from a chandelier, candelabra, etc.

Pendleton Glass Works (Aka *Milford Glass Works, Kresson Glass Works*) (1838-1859) A glass manufacturing facility established by Matthias Simmerman in Pendleton (later Milford, then Kresson), New Jersey, making bottles and hollowware. Lippincott, Wisham & Co. operated it about 1849, selling its wares through J. Huffsey & Co. of Philadelphia. In 1856 it was sold at sheriff's sale to Joseph Iszard. Samuel Iszard & Co. was formed shortly thereafter, with Joseph, his son, Ira, and his brother, Samuel, as principals.

Penn Cut Glass Company A glass cutting company in Prompton, Pennsylvania. It burned about 1930 and was never rebuilt.

Penn Glass Works (1) See *Sligo Glass Works*. (2) (1874-1877) A glass manufacturing facility making lamp chimneys, tumblers, and other glassware, established by Peter Kungler & Co. in Birmingham (Pittsburgh), Pennsylvania.

pennelato, vetro (Italian) Literally, *painted glass*. An ornamental glass developed by Venini. The prime feature is numerous irregular swirling streaks of various colors covering its surface and embedded in it. The haphazard design is created when the articles are heated, blown, and twisted.

Pennsylvania Flint Glass Works (1813-1895) A bottle and window glass manufacturing facility established in Birmingham (Pittsburgh), Pennsylvania by Ensell, Wendt & Co., originally called the Birmingham Glass Works. Shortly thereafter the operating company became Ihmsen, Wendt & Co.; in 1821, Beltzhoover, Wendt & Co.; and about 1831, Sutton, Wendt & Co. About 1835 it added cut, plain, engraved, and pressed flint glassware. By 1836 the operating company was Whitehead, Ihmsen & Phillips, changing the name to the Pennsylvania Flint Glass Works. Later it was operated by Young, Ihmsen & Plunkett, and from 1850 to 1867 by C. Ihmsen & Sons. In 1855 it made only window glass. It was later operated by Ihmsen Glass Co.

Pennvernon glass A glass made by Pittsburgh Plate Glass Co., using a modified Fourcault process. See *glass manufacturing, shaping*.

penny mug A small drinking cup or mug.

pentagon A cut-glass motif in the form of a pentagon with five sides and five equal angles.

Pepper, Charles (1868-1960) A glassblower, gaffer, and paperweight maker employed at Whitall Tatum in Millville, New Jersey, starting as a tending boy at age nine. He was later an assistant to John Ruhlander, making many paperweights, most of which he gave away during his final illness.

pepper bottle A small receptacle to hold ground pepper. It has a cover with an attached small spoon that fits into the bottle instead of a pierced cover as a castor.

Pepperd & Teeter See *Moscow Glass Works*.

Peppermint Stick Bowl A bowl believed to have been made at the Mt. Washington Glass Works, measuring 8-5/8 inches in diameter by 2-5/8 inches tall and having a clear crystal satin exterior with an overlay lip of rosaria cut in the picket fence design. The bottom is cut with a twenty-four-point star. The cuttings are smoothed and polished, as is the interior.

Percival, Sir Thomas The inventor of the first successful coal-fired glass furnace, which replaced wood as fuel (See *Proclamation of 1615*) prior to 1611. Percival made modifications to the furnace at Winchester House in Southwark, which was operated by Edward Salter and later leased to Edward Zouch. In 1611 Percival, Zouch, and others received a patent for a period of 21 years to make glass (supposedly only window glass) using coal as fuel. In 1615 Percival joined with Sir Robert Mansell in establishing a facility to take advantage of it, but by 1618 Percival had sold his interest to Mansell.

Perfection Funnel Works A company founded by Augustus Gersdorff in the late 1880s in Bridgeton, New Jersey, believed to have been the only facility in the United States devoted solely to making funnels (copper, tin, and *glass*). It made over a million a year.

Perfection Glass Company (1902-1906) A glass manufacturing facility noted for what it called *separating glassware*. Syrups, cruets, carafes, jugs, decanters, sugar shakers, etc., were made in two sections for easy filling. The tops of the pieces were fastened to the bottoms by a locking ring with a gummed washer separating them. The company also made a *separating* butter dish—designed to hold ice in the bottom—and berry sets, tumblers, iced tea glasses with drip trays, and preserve jars with glass tops and threaded rubber locking and packing rings combined.

perforated decoration See *traforato*.

perfume atomizer A perfume bottle having a pump and mister—an apparatus that takes a drop of perfume and transforms it into a mist by mechanical means using air and a nozzle—rather than a cap or stopper. One of the largest and most famous makers was the DeVilbiss Company, which, in 1936, patented and marketed a line of cut crystal atomizers designed by F. A. Vuillemenot and made in Czechoslovakia. They achieved their greatest popularity during the 1920s. See *atomizer; DeVilbiss Company*.

perfume bottle (Aka *scent bottle, cologne bottle*) A bottle used to hold perfume.

Perfume is Latin meaning "through smoke," indicating the oldest perfumes were most likely incense. The first known use of glass bottles to hold perfumes, oils, and/or cosmetics was in Egypt during the 18th Dynasty, circa 1500 B.C. They were made by attaching a sand core to a metal rod dipped into molten glass or with a strip of softened glass wrapped around it, forming a bottle. It was smoothed by reheating and rolling on a marver. They were brightly colored in opaque shades, usually a dark or light blue in imitation of semiprecious stones, and decorated with zigzag or wavy threads of glass of contrasting colors. The majority were about four inches tall, primarily used by the nobility and the wealthy.

The discovery of glassblowing in two- or three-piece molds about the 1st century A.D. greatly facilitated their making, especially those that were primarily transparent browns, greens, and purples. Some perfume bottles made of mosaic glass or in imitation of precious stones were made for the wealthy. Some were multi-sided and some were molded with various designs, such as shells, mythological figures, grapes, and human heads, a fashion revived during the 19th century. The Venetians made small glass bottles for holding costly fragrances from the 13th century. Perfume did not come into general use in Europe until the 15th century, although it was imported into London beginning in 1179. France, famous for its perfumes, had its first perfume makers in Paris about 1190. The making of scent bottles in England was well established by 1630. In the 17th century, glassblowers in Murano made their finest scent bottles or *flacons* of ornately styled colored glass with millefiori or latticino decorations. They were made of *milchglas* in Germany. During the 17th century the French made *flacons* in colored and opaline glass, often in imaginative shapes. In England, those bottles of colored lead glass are usually associated with Bristol because they were made there from 1760 to 1825. They were among the earliest items made by the American colonial glassmakers, Stiegel and Amelung being the most famous. During the 19th century in England, Apsley Pellatt made some of the finest. Cologne was introduced into the United States about 1830, and since more cologne is required to produce the same effect as perfume, cologne bottles tended to be larger. The Boston & Sandwich Glass Company made heavy flint glass cologne bottles from the 1840s to the 1870s. These were usually free or mold blown, the majority hexagonal in shape.

The Victorian era brought a tremendous increase of exotic and varied styles, forms, and colors for perfume bottles. Some were inlaid with precious stones. One of the most unusual items associated with glass perfume bottles is the stopper. Many stoppers were unique and decorative, some larger than the bottle. See *Czechoslovakian perfume bottles.*

perfume lamps Small lamps, usually less than six inches tall, with a small indentation in the top of the shade for perfume. The heat from the bulb causes the perfume to evaporate, scenting the room. They were often advertised as night-lights made of cut crystal, polished glass, or frosted glass with hand-painted decorations. They were popular during the 1930s. At the time the polished and frosted lamps retailed for about $1; cut crystal ones and those with hanging pendants retailed from $2 to $6.50.

perfume sprinkler See *sprinkler.*

perfumettes (Aka *Lilliputian bottles*) Dram perfume bottles that were introduced in the United States about 1932. Made of hand-cut and polished crystal with ground glass stopper applicators, ranging from 2-1/8 to 2-1/2 inches tall, they originally sold for about 50 cents each.

perlai (*Italian***)** A division of the Venetian glassmakers guild that made beads, canes, and paste for beads. It was further divided later into the *conterie* (makers of beads for the commercial trade) and the *canne* (makers of large beads and prepared enamels for exportation).

Perlen or Glas Perlen (*German***)**
Beads for personal adornment or for export, as opposed to *Pasternoster Kugel(chen)* (prayer beads).

Perry & Co. (1824-1827) A green glass manufacturing facility operating in Cumberland, Maryland.

Perry & Wheeler See *Twichell & Schoolcraft.*

Perry & Wood See *Twichell & Schoolcraft; Keene (Marlboro Street) Glass Works.*

Perryopolis Glass Factory See *New Boston Glass Works.*

Perseus-Andromeda plaque A glass plaque wheel engraved by Casper Lehmann about 1606, illustrating the myth of Perseus rescuing Andromeda from the dragon. Above the portrayal, cartouches (rounded convex surfaces usually surrounded by ornamental scrollwork) bear the crowned initials of the Elector Christian II of Saxony (d.1611) and of Hedwig, the daughter of Frederick II of Denmark, who became his wife in 1602.

Persian The Russian cut glass pattern where the button is cut with a small hobstar.

Persian glassware Glassware made in Persia (now Iran) between the 3rd and the 19th centuries, including some made earlier during the Achaemenid dynasty (550 to 330 BC). Much glassware from the medieval period found in Persia is believed to have been made in what is now Iraq, Egypt, or Syria. Some was made during the 18th and 19th centuries in Bohemia. However, there are many specimens made during earlier and later periods in the Persian style, believed to have been made there.

The first creative period of Persian glassware was during the Sassanian period from about 226 to 642 A.D. Blown glass was made during the 3rd and 4th centuries while wheel engraved, facet, and linear cut pieces were prevalent during the 5th and 6th centuries. Many of these latter items, which were embellished with shallow concavities in a honeycomb or quincunx pattern, were exported. The Islamic period followed, resulting from the conquest of Islam by the Arabs in the 7th century. The glass industry was revived in the 9th and 10th centuries under the Samanids (819-1004) at Nishapur and Afrasiyab (Samarkand). During this time thin glassware was embellished with grinding, cameo cutting, applied trailing, enameling, and gilding, often inspired by the art of China. After the conquest by the Mongols under Tamerlane in 1402, little glassware was made until the industry was revived under Shah Abbas I (1587-1628). It was made at Isfahan during the Safavid dynasty and later, but the major area of production was at Shiraz until the 19th century. It was here the best Persian glassware was made because of the availability of the finest raw materials. During the 16th century a lot of glassware was made in the Venetian style when Italian craftsmen taught the art to local artisans. The major products were tall ewers and perfume sprinklers, mainly in deep blue. Due to the demand for Persian glassware, much was exported to the Far East during the 17th century. However, during the mid-19th century, Bohemian glassware, particularly cut cased glasses having enameling and gilding, was imported into Persia.

Persian Pearl Fenton Art Glass Company's name for its white Carnival glass made in 1911, 1927, and 1933.

perspective (glass) A term used for a mirror, spy glass, and telescope.

pestle A somewhat club-shaped object used for pulverizing a substance in a mortar.

Peter Mills & Company See *New Granite Glass Company.*

Peterboro(ugh) glasshouses A series of glass manufacturing facilities in Peterboro (originally *Peterborough*), New York. The first, established about 1783 (operating for a short time) by David Goff (b. 1757), made window glass. The second, established about 1805, made cylinder window glass. In 1810 another glasshouse was erected by Peter Smith, for whom Peterboro was named. In 1811 the second and third facilities were operated by Smith & Solon. There are two versions regarding the final years of these facilities: (1) In 1818 Backus & Fenn purchased the facilities, operating them until 1830. (2) In 1819 Gerrit Smith (son of Peter Smith of Smith & Solon) operated them until 1830.

petites verrerie (*French*) A maker of glass hollowware, as opposed to a *grosses verrerie,* who made window glass.

petroti A process for making almost transparent glassware that was developed in ancient Rome at the time of Nero.

Pettitt glass A type of Intarsia glass. On May 25, 1850, Edward Pettitt of Birmingham, England, registered a technique for rolling plates of window glass with ornamental designs between two layers of glass. In the process, pieces of colored glass previously stamped, cast, or cut into ornamental forms were applied to a sheet of glass. Next, another sheet was either cast or rolled over the design, sandwiching the forms between two layers.

pezzato, vetro (*Italian*) (Aka *patched glass*) An ornamental glass developed by Venini about 1951. It was made of pieces of glass, roughly square shaped and of many colors, fused into a patchwork quilt mosaic effect. The process involved laying the pieces of glass side by side and heating them, fusing them into a flat piece, and then forming it into a free formed object.

phalera (*Italian*) A medallion placed in a holder, suspended on the breast of a horse, or worn by a soldier as a mark of rank. Some were made of Roman glass during the 1st century A.D.

phallus glass (1) A drinking glass in the form of a penis and testicles with an up-curved funnel-shaped drinking spout above the testicles. Some were made of greenish clear glass in Germany during the 16th and 17th centuries. Some were made of free formed glass with no embellishment except for a small applied glass ornament. (2) A German drinking glass made in a variety of shapes with phallic motifs, generally in the form of relief embellishment, during the 1st century A.D. at Cologne and the 15th century at Siegburg. See *joke glass.*

phantasmagoria A device similar to a *magic lantern,* except that its figures are painted in transparent colors on an opaque glass background instead of on transparent glass.

pharmacy glassware Various objects found and/or used in a pharmacy, including vials, bottles, Albarellos, carboys, jars, leach jars, phials, poison bottles, mortars, pestles, retorts, species jars, medicine bottles, etc.

Phelps, D.J., Inc. See *Phelps, N.O., & Son.*

Phelps, Nathaniel O. Born in Grouveneur, New York, in 1890, Phelps learned the art of engraving at Hawkes beginning in 1905. From 1910 to 1916 he cut for Sinclaire and, after service in World War I, returned there, working until it closed in 1928. He then moved to Rochester, New York, and established a glass cutting company (see *Phelps, N.O., & Son*). From 1921 to 1927, he operated a home shop in Corning, New York, cutting for Hunt and Steuben. From 1928 until 1942 he cut only as a hobby, working full time at various other jobs.

Phelps, N.O., & Son A glass cutting shop established in Rochester, New York, in 1928 by Nathaniel O. Phelps, who worked there only part time from when it was established until 1942. In 1942 the name was changed to that of his son, D.J. Phelps Inc., operating until after 1961.

Phenomenon glass An iridescent glass introduced in 1899 by Max Ritter von Spaun of the Loetz glassworks. It was in a variety of colors embellished with glass threads pulled at random across its surface.

phial (1) A small glass bottle to contain ointments, medicines, etc. Some were made of Roman glass with trailed decoration around the body about 100 B.C. (2) Any small glass bottle made during modern times for use in a pharmacy. See *vial.*

phial, eye paint See *eye paint phial.*

phiale *(Greek)* A shallow bowl with a flat bottom or a foot ring and without handles, used either as a wall ornament or to pour libations. Those having a crystal boss (forming a hollow on the underside) are called *phiale mesomphalos.*

Philadelphia & Kensington Glassworks See *Dyottville Glass Works; Kensington Glass Works.*

Philadelphia Cut Glass Company A small cutting shop in Philadelphia, Pennsylvania, operating from about 1912 into the early 1920s.

Philadelphia Flint Glass Works See *Gillinder, William T.*

Philadelphia Glasshouse A glass manufacturing facility established in 1683 in Philadelphia, Pennsylvania. Little if any glass was made there.

Philadelphia Glassworks See *Kensington Glass Works.*

Philadelphia Works See *Schuylkill Glass Works.*

Phillips & Best A glass manufacturing facility established in 1840 in Pittsburgh, Pennsylvania, making cylinder and bottle glass for a short time.

Phillips & Company See *Beck, Phillips & Company.*

Phillips, George, & Co. See *House of Birks.*

Phillips, Joseph, & Company See *Sterling (Cut) Glass Company.*

Phillips, William See *Phillips, Best & Co.*

Phillips, Best & Co. In 1840, William Phillips established a flint glass manufacturing facility in Pittsburgh, Pennsylvania, making cut, pressed, and plain glassware. By 1850 it was operated by W. & R.B. Phillips; by 1857, Phillips, Best & Co.; and by 1867, John Best alone.

Phillips Glass Company See *Sterling (Cut) Glass Company.*

Phoebe lamp A lamp similar to a *Betty lamp* except it often has two wicks. The name is derived from the Greek word *phoebe*, meaning "bright."

Phoenician glass Glassware made in Phoenicia, an ancient kingdom on the Mediterranean in the region of modern Syria, Lebanon, and Israel, dating from the 8th century B.C. Its early wares were inlays in ivory plaques and a variety of vessels made by casting and slumping.

Phoenix The English trade name for *Pyrex*.

Phoenix glass See *fenici, vetro.*

Phoenix Glass Co. bowl, peach and white,
11-1/2" d.
Davanna Collection

Phoenix Glass Company The Phoenix
Glass Company was a glass manufacturing
facility established in 1880 in Water Cure
(later Phillipsburgh, then Monaca, in 1892),
Pennsylvania. Andrew Howard was the
founder and president and William I. Miller
was secretary/treasurer. Originally it made
glass tubing to insulate electrical wires, an
unsuccessful project. It then negotiated with
Dithridge Glass, a lamp chimney and glass
reflector maker, whereby Dithridge closed and
the owner, E.D. Dithridge, became manager of
the Phoenix facility. For the next two years the
company made chimneys and reflectors.

On July 1, 1882, Phoenix entered into an
agreement with Charles Challinor to purchase his decorating shop, J.A. Bergen &
Company. As part of the agreement, Challinor would supervise Phoenix's new decorating department. In 1883 it added lamp globes
and gas shades. It burned in January 1884.
Soon thereafter it took over the Doyle, Sons
& Co. facility. The original facility (Plant
No.1) was rebuilt and enlarged. The Doyle
facility was called Plant No. 3. Plant No. 2,
located in Washington, Pennsylvania, made
lighting wares until it closed in 1902. Plant
No. 3 made incandescent bulbs, operating in
Monaca until 1946. In 1891 the company
underwent a major reorganization. On February 3, 1895, Plant No. 1 was again destroyed
by fire. The company then took over the old
Dithridge facility at New Bridgeton, Pennsylvania, while Plant No. 1, which made lighting wares since 1890, was rebuilt.

In 1883 the company started making some
Victorian art glass, contracting on September
17, 1883, with Joseph Webb, nephew of Thomas Webb, to become the company's superintendent of operations. Webb was an expert
in etching glass, and his glass formulae came
from his family's trade secrets. Webb stayed
there until 1894, when he moved to Dithridge
& Co. Phoenix then hired Julius Teets of
Germany, an expert in the deep etching, who
helped the company become a leader in the
area. Joe Duffner was hired as a hand decorating artist. On October 6, 1885, the company entered an agreement with George W.
Fry and Rochester Tumbler Company
whereby they would serve as its sales agents
in the northeastern United States. It made art
glass, including a variety of art glass lighting
shades, until about 1890. It then shifted production to decorated, etched, and cut glass
(making large quantities of colored cut
glass), and subsequently shifted back to
lighting ware. At the 1892 Columbian Exposition in Chicago, it joined with The General
Electric Company in an exhibit to show the
new invention of electric illuminators. For
the event, Phoenix provided 5,000 colored
incandescent bulbs.

Andrew Howard died in 1904 and his son,
Thomas H., became president, a position he
held through 1964. After lightbulb production
became mechanized in the early 1900s, the
company discontinued production in 1906. It
continued to make globes at an increased rate
by upgrading its equipment. In 1930 it celebrated its 50th anniversary by issuing a golden
anniversary cigarette box in green glass with
an acid etched design on the lid.

Though it made a lot of decorative glassware,
the company's main emphasis was always
lighting glassware until the mid-1930s. Over
the next few years, Phoenix introduced several new lines. The *Reuben line* (see *Reuben*
line) was made from late 1933 until early
1936. The *Sculptured line* (see *Sculptured*
line), introduced in 1933, was made until
1958 with limited quantities made in 1976
and 1978 (this strictly for its employees). In
1938 it made some milk glassware after purchasing some molds, in 1937, from the bankrupt Co-Operative Flint Glass Co.; the line

was called the *Early American line* (see *Early American line*). It also made colored, iridescent, and Venetian style wares of flint glass. In the late 1880s it was exporting many of its products to Canada, British Columbia, Mexico, and South America. It advertised itself as "sole manufacturers of celebrated Webb Cameo Glass." In the late 1800s, Plant No. 1 developed a *Pearl Satin glass*, often confused with Lalique wares. It made many commercial products in addition to lighting wares, such as bottles, tableware, etc.

In 1964, Plant No. 1 suffered its third major fire. In the same year Thomas H. Howard retired and W.H. Goff became president. In 1970 it was acquired by the Anchor Hocking Corporation. In 1971 Paul B. Schmunk succeeded Goff as president of Phoenix. On June 15, 1978, the company suffered its fourth major fire, leveling about 80% of the facility. In September 1978, Anchor Hocking began a $25 million reconstruction program. It dedicated the new facility on September 6, 1980, issuing a commemorative vase and ashtray to celebrate its 100th anniversary. In 1987 Newell Corporation acquired Anchor Hocking, and Phoenix became part of Anchor Hocking Industrial Glass. See *Doyle & Company*.

Phoenix Glass Works (1) A glass manufacturing facility erected in the early 1820s and in operation by 1824 by Thomas Caines, located across from the South Boston Crown Glass Works in South Boston, Massachusetts, where he previously worked. In 1852 Caines retired and the company was operated by Caines & Johnston (William Caines, Thomas' son, and William Johnston, Thomas' son-in-law). When Johnston died in 1855, Thomas returned, managing it until his death in 1865. In 1859 the operating company became Thomas H. Caines & Son (son William), and in 1867, Wm. Caines & Brother. Financial problems developed and, in late 1869, it was placed in receivership and closed on May 1, 1870. It made cut, pressed, lacy, and blown three-mold flint glass tableware. (2) (1832-1880) A vial and bottle glass manufacturing facility established in Pittsburgh, Pennsylvania, by William McCully. It traded as Phoenix Glass Works, operated by William McCully & Co. until after 1841.

About 1855 the following companies, in addition to the Phoenix Glass Works, were operated by a single management firm: the Sligo Glass Works (established by Frederick Lorenze), the Pittsburgh Glass Works (established in 1841), and the Empire Glass Works (established in 1855). This firm was still operating the four plants in 1868. (3) A glass manufacturing facility in Bristol, England, beginning operations in 1789, and owned by Wadham, Ricketts & Co. It specialized in cutting and engraving glassware during the early 19th century. It later became Powell & Ricketts. (4) See *Glasstown Factory*.

phoenix nursing bottle A nursing bottle originally made in the 1880s, so named because of the likeness of a phoenix bird on the side of the bottle. Its stopper consisted of a cork through which ran a long tube with a nipple at the end. The tube bent so the bottle could be placed in an upright position in the crib while the baby drank. At the time, mothers did not hold the bottle while their baby drank.

photochemical glass A photosensitive glass having a distinctive composition that can be cut by acid, allowing a design to be made on it from a photographic film. When the glass is dipped in acid, the exposed areas are eaten away, leaving the design on the film on the glass in three dimensions. See *photosensitive glass*.

photochromic glass A glass invented in 1964 by the Corning Glass Works, used in lenses for eye glasses and sunglasses. It is light sensitive, darkening on exposure to ultraviolet light. Its composition differs from that of photochemical glass in that the process of darkening is reversible—the glass reverts to its original color when removed from the influence of ultraviolet light. One type is a silicate glass containing dispersed crystals of colloidal silver halide precipitated within the melt during cooling and subsequent heat treatment at a temperature between the strain point and the softening temperature. Alkali borosilicates are the most suitable glasses for this purpose. Photochromic glasses are frequently used in variable-tint prescription lenses, darkening in sunlight and returning to original clearness indoors—

85% light transmission when clear; 45% in sunlight. They are unique in that they can be made light sensitive to different portions of the spectrum. The typical composition of such glass is:

SiO_2	(silica)	52.4%-51.0%
Al_2O_3	(alumina)	6.9%-6.8%
Li_2O	(lithium oxide)	2.6%-2.5%
BaO	(barium oxide)	8.2%-8.0%
Br	(bromine)	0.23%-0.11%
CuO	(copper oxide)	0.016%-0.016%
Na_2O	(sodium oxide)	1.8%-1.7%
B_2O_3	(boric oxide)	20.0%-19.5%
PbO	(lead oxide)	4.8%-4.7%
Ag	(silver)	0.31%-0.30%
Cl	(chlorine)	0.66%-0.69%
ZO_2	(zirconium oxide)	2.1%-4.6%

photosensitive glass A glass containing a small amount of a photosensitive substance, i.e., gold, silver, or copper compound. When ultraviolet light is passed through a photographic negative onto its surface, a latent image is formed within the glass, which is converted, as the glass is heated, to a visible image made up of tiny metal particles. In a special type of this glass, *photosensitive opal*, the metal particles of the photographic image within the glass serve as nuclei for the growth of non-metallic crystals that are confined to the area of the image. These areas are dissolved by hydrofluoric acid more rapidly than the adjacent glass. As a result, the glass can be formed into intricate shapes without using mechanical tools. See *photochemical glass*.

pi (Chinese) A circular disk with a hole in the center—in Chinese lore, a symbol of heaven. Some pi in imitation of similar jade objects were made in China during the late Chou and Han dynasties.

piano feet Solid glass supports placed under the feet of a piano to prevent marring the floor. John Davenport, an English glassmaker, made piano feet by press molding. They were patented in 1874.

piatto (Italian) A plate, usually circular, made in a variety of sizes. The Italian terms for the various sizes are: *piatto imperiale* (imperial plate), about 25 inches in diameter; *piatto reale* (royal plate), about 20 inches; *piatto de cappone* (plate for capon), about 16 inches; *piatto da tavagliola* (napkin plate), about 10 inches.

piatto da pompa (Italian) Literally, *ceremonial plate*. A plate lavishly embellished and usually for display on a buffet or suspended from a wall. Some have a deep center well (*cavetto*).

pick-up decoration A process whereby a hot paraison is rolled in chips of glass that adhere to it and are marvered in, before being inflated to the desired shape.

Pickle castor, 11" h., clear pressed glass insert.
Davanna Collection

pickle castor A glass jar, about six inches in height, usually held in a silver plated frame and used to hold pickles. A cover and tongs are normally with the jar. It was in the form of a fancy clear pressed glass insert. Those not having a frame were usually made of decorated colored art glass. They were extremely popular in affluent Victorian households, becoming popular in the United States after the Civil War. They reached their peak about 1885. By 1900 they had all but vanished from maker's catalogs. They are being reproduced today in large numbers. See *pickler*.

Boyd blue stag glass pickle dish, "Love's Request is Pickles," 9-1/4" x 5-1/4". Boyd mark and signed by Bernard Boyd.
Davanna Collection

Canoe-shaped pickle dish, blue insert, 9-1/2"l. x 7-1/2" h.
Davanna Collection

pickle dish (Aka *olive dish, pickle glass*) An oblong dish for serving pickles, similar to but smaller than a celery dish.

pickle glass See *pickle dish.*

Pickle glass See *Goofus glass.*

pickle jar See *pickler.*

pickler (Aka *pickle jar*) A receptacle for serving pickles. They are usually cylindrical with a flat bottom and flat-topped stopper or cover. See *pickle castor.*

pictorial flask See *historical flask.*

picture cane A silhouette cane employing more than one color within the silhouette.

picture paperweight A rare type of paperweight, the motif of which is a painted picture. Many have a window at the top.

pie crust cane (Aka *pastry mold cane*) A type of millefiori cane with a scalloped border similar to the edge of a pie crust. It often has a tiny central raised round rod, which is many times included in the motif of Clichy paperweights.

piece mold A mold of two or more parts hinged together, used in making glassware in either *part size* or *full size*. They are used to shape an article or make pattern molded glassware. See the following types of molds: *dip; part size piece; full size piece.*

piedouche (French) Literally, *pedestal*. A base or foot attached to an object in the form of a supporting pedestal or sometimes a saucer-like stand, such as found under a sauce boat, jam pot, etc. Some paperweights have a supporting pedestal-like base or plinth—square block at the base of a column—instead of the typical flat bottom. See *pedestal paperweight.*

pier glass A tall, narrow mirror to be placed in a pier—a portion of a wall between a door and window, two doors, or two windows. The width of the mirror varied to suit the size of the pier, which changed with the style of different periods. In early specimens, the mirror was divided into two or more vertical sections due to constraints of size resulting from manufacturing techniques. Some were embellished with branches having candle nozzles. Their frames conformed with the style of the period. See *chimney glass; sconce.*

Pierce, F.M., Company See *Fisler & Morgan.*

pierced stopper See *openwork stopper.*

pig (1) An object in the form of a pig, usually standing, made in a variety of types of glass and sizes. Some are embellished with wings as in the motto "....until pigs fly." Some were made of solid glass; others hollow. Some were made in the form of flasks, some as friggers. (2) (Aka *tower*) A block of iron about eight inches square at the base tapering to about one inch square at the top with semi-circular notches at various depths used to support, and prevent from moving horizontally, the blowing or pontil iron as the worker is rotating the object when reheating it at the glory hole or furnace. (3) The struts holding the pattern to the main body of a piece of *vasa diatreta*.

pig iron A slang term used by glassmakers for figured blanks commonly used in the cut glass industry (after the Brilliant Period) as a method of reducing costs. It is believed to have originated among workers at the Irving Cut Glass Co.

pigeon-eye pattern A style of decoration on some Islamic glassware in the form of a mold-blown overall pattern of continuous hexagons, diamonds, etc., enclosing raised circles. In the center of each raised circle is a depression, giving the appearance of an eye. Most items with this pattern have been attributed to various periods ranging from the 7th to the 13th centuries.

pigeon's blood glass A red-orange glass made in the late 19th century. Later glasses referred to by this name are deep red. See *ruby glass*.

piggen or piggin A small glass receptacle in the shape of a small half barrel with a vertical handle in the form of a tall stave, used to dip milk or cream. The form is similar to a Greek kyathos.

piggy-dog decanter A decanter in the form of a hollow standing dog or pig. The tail curved upward to form a handle and the snout formed the spout. Often there is a glass stopper to seal the mouth, preventing spillage. They were made during the 19th century.

Pilchuck School See *Chihuly, Dale*.

pilgrim bottle See *pilgrim flask*.

pilgrim flask (Aka *pilgrim bottles, costrel*) A flattened gourd-shaped bottle with one or two pairs of lugs at each side; some lugs had holes for suspension. They were of Roman origin, but glass ones date from the 15th century. They were originally used by pilgrims to carry drinking water. Some have a metal screw cap. See *flask; lentoid flask; hunting flask; Meisterstruck*.

Pilgrim Glass pitcher, blue crackle glass with clear handle, 4-1/4" h.
Davanna Collection

Pilgrim Glass Co. ad, February 1962.
Krause Publications

Pilgrim Glass Company In the late 1940s Walter Bailey operated a small glass manufacturing facility, Tri-State Glass Manufacturing, in Huntington, West Virginia. He sold it to Alfred E. Knobler, who moved it to Ceredo, West Virginia in 1956. From 1949 to 1970, its main product was crackle glass in ruby, tangerine, amethyst, smoke, sapphire, amber, green, and crystal. The company made many hand-blown colored glasswares and paperweights in the 1970s. Robert Moretti, chief designer, was solely responsible for paperweight designs. It had two trademarks, one a strawberry mark on the base. It changed the colors of its labels: first yellow, then black, then white and silver, then black, blue and white, and then black and white.

piling pot (Aka *jockey pot, monkey pot*) A pot or crucible used to melt small batches of artificially colored glass. It was normally placed on top of a large covered melting pot in the furnace, first used prior to 1662—the year first mentioned by Christopher Merret.

Pilkington Brothers Ltd. A British glass manufacturing company established in 1826 as St. Helens Crown Glass Company by John William Bell. It was one of the world's largest makers of flat glass and also made many other types of industrial glass. The company was operated by Greenall & Pilkington in 1829 and Pilkington Brothers Ltd. in 1849. In 1773 the British Cast Plate Glass Co. was established at Ravenshead, making plate glass. In 1901 it was purchased by Pilkington Brothers Ltd. In 1945 Chance Brothers Ltd. of Birmingham became a subsidiary. Pilkington has several subsidiaries and facilities throughout the world, making industrial glasses, including plate glass—made since 1959 by the float glass process—laminated and safety glass, optical glass, fiberglass, pressed glass, etc. See *drawn glass; float glass.*

Pilkington Glass Limited A glass manufacturing facility that made sheet glass. It was established in 1913 in Toronto, Canada, by Pilkington Brothers Ltd.

pillar A type of ribbing where the rib is broad and rounded at the top.

pillar cutting A decorative pattern on cut glass, in the form of a series of parallel vertical convex ribs, used often in England on glassware in the Regency style. It is the reverse of flute, which has concave ribs.

pillar flutes Flute cutting.

pillar molded bowl (Aka *ribbed bowl*) A bowl of hemispherical shape with no foot, having 15 to 30 closely placed vertical ribs, sometimes slanting, extending from the bottom to slightly below the rim. The ribs were formed by the process of pillar molding and were modified over time. The bowls, which range from five to eight inches in diameter, were made in several colors of Roman glass about 100 A.D.

pillar molding A style of angular ribbing characteristic of pillar molded bowls. The process of making early Roman ones, about 100 A.D., was different from that used for later Venetian ones. Roman ones were mold pressed, had interior depressions behind the exterior

ridges, and were finished by grinding and sometimes by wheel or fire polishing. The ribs were made by working up the plastic glass with pincers and other tools while the article was on the mold. Sometimes the ribs were irregularly spaced. Later Roman specimens were mold-blown on a second gather. Venetian ones have additional embellishment made by horizontal trailing of threads of glass, melting them in.

Pilsner glass A glass of conical shape tapering either to a flat base or a short stem with a flat base, used for drinking beer or ale.

pincered trailing See *quilling.*

pincering A method of embellishing glassware by using pincers to squeeze various pieces of ornamentation, such as threading or wings or flame-like protuberances on the stems of some Venetian goblets, especially winged glasses, and on the walls of some Islamic bowls.

pincers A tool used for embellishing glassware by squeezing pieces of ornamentation, such as threading, while still in the molten state. Some pincers have decorative patterns on them to impress a design. Pincers may be used to remove foreign matter, such as stones, that are picked up with the gather. See *pincering.*

Pinchbeck, Christopher (1670-1732) A London clockmaker who developed a copper-zinc alloy closely resembling gold. "Pinchbeck" became synonymous for cheap or counterfeit. See *Pinchbeck paperweight.*

Pinchbeck paperweight A paperweight in which an ornament, molded in high relief, is covered by a dome in the form of a magnifying lens. The ornament is made of Pinchbeck—an alloy of copper and zinc used to imitate gold and sometimes silver in inexpensive jewelry. The paperweights were popular about 1850; their makers are unknown. The design is often set in a pewter or marble base or on occasion in copper, tin, alabaster, or cardboard. This base is screwed or cemented to the dome, which extends beyond the base.

pinched lip A lip of a vessel of trefoil shape, such as a jug or pitcher, first used on the Greek *oenochoe.* It was later on jugs, pitchers, and ewers whose designs were based on classical prototypes.

pinched trailing A decorative pattern made by applying or trailing threads of glass to an article in parallel lines and pincering adjacent threads together at regular intervals, producing wavy lines. It is similar to *nipt-diamond-waies*. See *quilling*.

pineapple cup (Aka *ananaspokal*) A covered cup resembling a pineapple, standing on a pedestal. They were made in Germany during the 1500s and 1600s. Some are up to 30 inches tall.

pineapple diamond See *diamond*.

pine cone glass A glass vessel with ovoid body, stemmed foot, short neck, and overall relief imbricated embellishment in imitation of a pine cone. They were made during the 16th and 17th centuries in Germany in *facon de Venise* style. Their use is uncertain, possibly as containers for smelling salts.

pink glass See *Purple of Cassius; cranberry glass; selenium; opaline*. Sometimes there is accidental pink coloring in crisselled glass, especially glass made in France.

pink slag glassware (1) An art glass molded in ornate patterns in various shades of pink made by the Indiana Tumbler & Goblet Co. (2) A glass made by Cambridge Glass Co. in only two patterns: inverted fan and feather.

pinnacle A tall and thin ornamental glass object that tapers upward, to be affixed to a chandelier as embellishment. Many were faceted or ornamentally cut.

pinnacle stopper A spire stopper.

pint See *wine bottle, sizes*.

pinwheel A cut glass motif known also as *buzz* or *buzz star*. See *buzz*.

Pioneer Cut Glass Company (1905-1920) A glass cutting house in Carbondale, Pennsylvania.

Pioneer Glass Company A glass decorating shop established 1891 in Pittsburgh, Pennsylvania. During the short time it operated, mainly as a decorating shop, it made

some ruby- and amber-stained glassware and other decorated ware popular during the Victorian era, as well as some older, more popular patterns previously made by other facilities.

pipe See *church warden's pipe; tobacco pipe*.

pipe stopper or pipe stopple A stopper or tamper used to pack tobacco in the bowl of a pipe, made from the mid-17th century through the mid-19th century. Many were decorated, some carved or pressed into human or animal figures.

pipette A narrow graduated glass tube, sometimes with a slight bulge in the middle, used for measuring and transferring liquids from one container to another.

pipette-shaped bottle A small, slender bottle with a slight bulge in the center, usually holding perfume or oil. They were first made of Roman glass in the late 3rd century in the eastern Mediterranean area.

pistol flask A flask in the form of a pistol. Those of colored glass with enameled decoration were made in Bohemia and Germany (Saxony). Those of plain glass were made in Murano. Those of colored or colorless glass with various decorations were made in several other facilities. They usually have a metal stopper to close the end of the barrel, which served as the mouth of the flask.

Cut glass pitcher, Brilliant Period, 12-1/2" h.
Davanna Collection

pitcher A jug used most often to hold water as evidenced by the fact that it often came in matching sets with six or twelve water tumblers. They were made by several companies in a variety of shapes and sizes. The three most common shapes are conventional, squat, or tankard. See *pitcher, side pocket.*

pitcher, side pocket A pitcher with an opening and compartment below the handle—separated from the main body and its contents—to hold ice to keep the contents cold. They were popular during the 1870s and 1880s.

pitcher hat A glass pitcher in the shape of a helmet or London bobby's hat, mounted on a silver base or contained in a silver liner.

Pitkin flask A small, half- to one-pint mold-blown flask attributed in general to the Pitkin Glass Works. Pitkin flask became a generic term because it was made at several other New England and Midwestern facilities. It has a double thick lower half made by the *half post method.* Some have vertical or swirled ribbing or both, made by inserting the paraison in a ribbed mold, then removing it, twisting it, and reinserting it in a mold. They were generally of amber and green glass, but some were blue or amethyst. The overall shape is ovoid, somewhat flattened, tapering slightly to a short cylindrical neck. The Pitkin Glass Works listed them in their wares from 1788 through 1830.

Pitkin Glass Works A glass manufacturing company established in 1783 by William and Elisha (or Joseph, depending on the source) Pitkin and Samuel Bishop in East Manchester, formerly East Hartford, Connecticut. It operated under a grant by the General Assembly in Hartford. This allowed the company a 25-year monopoly to make all kinds of glass in the state of Connecticut, beginning when the first glass was made, no later than three years after being granted. It did not meet this requirement and was not able to retain its monopoly. By 1788 a facility was built and operational, with Robert Hewes as its first superintendent. He left after about a year, being blamed for all operational and financial problems. Originally established to make crown glass (there were several unsuccessful attempts at this venture), its principle products were green and black glass bottles and free-blown, pattern-molded, historical, chestnut and *Pitkin* flasks (see *Pitkin flask*). After Hewes left, the General Assembly granted the owners the right to raise money by means of a lottery, which was unsuccessful. Another lottery was requested of the General Assembly in May 1791 and was again approved. Pitkin Glass Works remained in operation until 1830, closing because of lack of wood.

Pitkin & Brooks In 1872 Edward Hand Pitkin went into the glass and china business in Chicago, Illinois. He was soon joined by Jonathan Williams Brooks, Jr., forming Pitkin & Brooks, a wholesale china and glassware distributor (incorporated in 1891). They established a glass cutting facility in Chicago, followed by another called the Ohio Cut Glass Company in Bowling Green, Ohio about 1900. This facility burned in 1911 and another was built in Valparaiso, Indiana, closing in 1918. All its operations closed in 1920. Its mark was "P & B." At one time it was the largest wholesale distributor of glassware and crockery in the Midwest.

Pittman, R.H., Cut Glass Co. (1914-1916) A glass cutting facility in Lawrenceville, Pennsylvania.

Pittsburgh City Glass Works See *Cunningham & Company.*

Pittsburgh Cut Glass Company (1) A glass manufacturing and cutting facility established in Pittsburgh, Pennsylvania, in 1809, operating until the late 1870s (?) (1909-1921) A glass cutting facility in Pittsburgh, Pennsylvania.

Pittsburgh Flint Glass Manufactory See *Bakewell & Company.*

Pittsburgh Glass Co.: See *Pittsburgh Glass Works* (2).

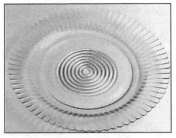

MacBeth Evans plate, Petalware pattern.
Davanna Collection

Pittsburgh Glass ad, 1933.
Krause Publications

Pittsburgh Glass Manufacturing

Company A glass manufacturing facility that originally made blown and pressed tableware and lamps, established in 1866 by Atterbury, Challoner & Hogan (soon after Challoner, Hogan & Company) in Pittsburgh, Pennsylvania. It later became Challoner & Taylor; in 1889, Hogan, Evans & Co.; and in 1890, MacBeth Evans Glass Company. In 1884 Challoner & Taylor opened another facility in Tarentum, Pennsylvania, which joined the U.S. Glass Company (*Factory C*) in 1891. Shortly thereafter it burned and was never rebuilt. The Pittsburgh Glass Manufacturing Company, operated by MacBeth Evans, had facilities in Marion, Elwood, and Bethavan, Indiana. It made a large amount of kitchen ware and tableware, introducing its first mold-etched pattern in 1930. In the late 1930s it introduced three patterns, *Chinex*, *Cremex*, and *Monax*, to compete with tableware made by the china and pottery industry. In 1937 it was purchased by the Corning Glass Works. The MacBeth Evans name was used into the 1940s. The Pittsburgh facility currently makes *Corningware* and is often called "The Bush."

Pittsburgh Glass Works (1) (1797-

1883) A glass window, bottle, and hollowware manufacturing facility established in Pittsburgh, Pennsylvania, by Craig & O'Hara. Major Isaac Craig (1742-1826) and General James O'Hara (1754-1819) were officers in the Revolutionary War. Pittsburgh Glass Works was the first glass manufacturing facility in the area. William Peter Eichbaum was hired to oversee the erection of the glasshouse and supervise its operations.

The first glass was blown in June 1797; one source indicates early 1798. It was the first of its kind to use coal as a fuel instead of wood. In December 1798 it was leased to Eichbaum, Wendt & Co. (Frederick Wendt and Charles Ihmsen). In 1800 Craig & O'Hara again took over management. Wendt stayed on as foreman, and William Price of Stourbridge, England, became superintendent. In 1802 the company added a flint glass furnace, buying equipment from the closed Ohio Glass Company (some sources state no flint glass was made). At the same time it hired Ohio's superintendent, J.B. LaFleur. One source states Price remained superintendent until 1805, then was replaced by Frederick Magnus Amelung, son of John Frederick Amelung, who was superintendent until 1809.

In 1804 Craig withdrew and O'Hara continued as its sole owner through 1818. On his death in 1819, Frederick Lorenz Sr., age 25, bought and managed it. In the same year, he took over the Trevor & Ensell facility. In 1841 he became one of the organizers of Wm. McCully & Co., managing its operations. In 1851 Wm. McCully & Co. was dissolved, taken over by Lorenz & Buchanan, which soon became Lorenze & Wightman (Frederick Lorenze Jr.). In 1860 it was leased to Fahnstock, Albree & Co. In 1863 Lorenz & Wightman (Moses Lorenze) assumed control and, in 1871, Thomas Wightman & Co. operated it as the Point Bridge Works until it closed.

(2) A green and black vial and bottle glass manufacturing facility established by Alexander (1819-1875) and David H. Chambers (d.1862) in 1843 in Pittsburgh, Pennsylvania. In 1852/3, a new, larger facility was built, adding a better grade of bottle glass and window glass. It was the first U.S. glass manufacturer to increase the size of window panes from the small ones then in use. When David died in 1862, Alexander managed operations alone until his death in 1875. The operations were then taken over by his son,

James Alexander, and H.B. Hutton. It was still operating in 1886 under the names Pittsburgh Glass Works and Pittsburgh Glass Co.

Pittsburgh Green Glass Company A bottle, flask, and green glass manufacturing facility established by Wormser, Burgraff & Company in 1854 in Pittsburgh, Pennsylvania. In 1857 the operating firm became E. Wormser & Company and, in 1875, Wormser Glass Company. In 1886 it was still operating. See *Frankstown Glass Works*.

Pittsburgh Lamp & Brass Company See *Pittsburgh Lamp, Brass & Glass Company*.

Pittsburgh Lamp, Brass & Glass Company A company formed in Pittsburgh, Pennsylvania in 1901 as a result of a merger between the Dithridge & Co., Kopp Lamp & Glass Company, and Pittsburgh Lamp & Brass Company.

Pittsburgh Plate Glass Company The former name of a glass manufacturing company presently operating as PPG Industries. Founded in 1880 by John B. Ford at Creighton, Pennsylvania, it was originally called the New York City Plate Glass Works. It soon became the Pittsburgh Plate Glass Company. New facilities were soon built in Ford City and Tarentum, Pennsylvania, to meet the rapidly expanding need for plate glass. By 1886 it had over 6,000 workers and made over 50% of the glass used in the United States. By 1891 it had seven facilities. In 1926 it developed a machine to draw sheet glass directly from the furnace.

Pittsburgh process A method of making continuous sheets of glass in which the glass is pulled directly from the furnace and held at the edges so it may be drawn as a long vertical sheet into a high tower. See *plate glass; sheet glass*.

Pittsburgh Union Glass Works A window and bottle glass manufacturing facility established by Melling, Estep & Company in 1866 in Pittsburgh, Pennsylvania. In 1874 the operating firm was Stuart, Estep & Company. It was still operating in 1886.

Pittston Cut Glass Co. A glass cutting facility established in 1902 in Pittston, Pennsylvania.

pizzo, vetro (Italian) Literally, *lace glass*. An ornamental glassware developed by Venini about 1970. It has irregularly shaped pieces of opaque glass embedded within clear glass in a pattern resembling lace with small connected loops and projecting ends of *threads*.

place card holder See *menu card holder.*

Placidia, Galla, cross An ancient Byzantine jeweled cross (known as *di Desiderio*) believed to have been made during the 3rd or 4th century. At its center is an attached *Fondo D'oro* with portraits of a family group. The glass plaque on it is inscribed in Greek characters, believed to be the artist's name, the father in the picture, or the person to whom the plaque was dedicated.

plain flute See *flute cuttings.*

plain stem A stem having no embellishment, but, on occasion, does contain a *tear*.

plancher A plate.

plaque A flat, thin tablet often attached to a wall as a decoration or inlaid in furniture. Some are embellished with relief, mosaic, engraving, painting, and enameling. (a) *Decorative molded relief plaques:* some have figures of persons, *amorini* (infant cupids), mythological or religious motifs. They were made of Roman glass in the 1st and 2nd centuries; some were used as panels. (b) *Mosaic plaques:* some made in Egypt and possibly Italy in the 1st and 2nd centuries. (c) *Engraved plaques:* some made in Bohemia, Spain, and Germany in the 17th century. (d) *Enameled plaques:* some made of opaque white glass in Germany and Italy in the 18th century. (e) *Painted plaques:* some are painted on the reverse of the glass to provide protection when displayed. See *medallion; roundel.*

plastic A medium capable of being modeled, molded, or shaped when soft and then hardened. Examples include wax or natural clay before being fired, or glass in the molten state.

plat See *dish.*

plate A shallow table utensil from which food is served or eaten. They are usually circular (occasionally oval or square) with a ledge and well or, in some modern patterns, an upcurved rim. They range in size from about six to eleven inches in diameter. They are usually of clear, opaque white (resembling porcelain), colored transparent, or opaque colored glass. Some of clear or transparent glass are embellished with engraved, filigrana or enameled designs, sometimes with gilding or platinum trim around the rim. Some plates of white or colored opaque glass are embellished with molded designs, enameling and other embellishments often found on porcelain or pottery plates of the specific period. See *dish; platter; piatto.* Also see the following types of plates: *hot; bread and butter; cup; grill; historical; ice; luncheon; salad; bread; sherbet; toddy; Venetian scenic.*

plate glass Originally the term referred to a type of glass cast or rolled while molten into "plates" or sheets and hand polished to make mirrors. Later it referred to any glass ground and polished, regardless of the method of manufacture (see *Bicheroux process; coulage; Fourcault process; Pittsburgh process; Libbey Owens process*). Those in the trade still use this definition. It has the same composition as window glass (soda-lime-silica) with these differences: (a) longer time needed for annealing, usually three or four days, to eliminate the distortion and strain caused by more rapid cooling, and (b) the intensive grinding and polishing needed to remove inherent imperfections, producing a bright, highly reflective finish. These relatively thick sheets of glass are often used for large windows, mirrors, tabletops, etc. The general public has broadened the definition, considering plate glass to be any thick glass.

plate mold A mold used to put an identification on bottles, usually in the form of a name, monogram, trademark, picture, etc., appearing in raised letters on the side of the bottle. A mold was made of the identification and placed in an appropriately sized slot inside the bottle mold.

plate protector A circular glass disk designed to fit into the well of an enameled porcelain plate, serving to protect the decoration during use.

plateau A stand resting on a plinth (short base) or short legs, serving as a centerpiece for a dining table. They were in vogue during the late 18th/early 19th centuries. Some are merely a mirror set in a metallic frame, which may have a low decorative gallery.

Plated Amberina (1) A cased art glass made in limited quantities, patented by Joseph Locke in 1886, and made solely at the New England Glass Co. It has a cream colored lining bordering on chartreuse, with a fiery opalescence caused by the Amberina coloring on the outer surface shining through the inner. A piece of opal or opalescent glass plated with a gold ruby mixture was reheated at the glory hole to develop a deeper color in certain areas, blending into the lighter part not sufficiently reheated to develop color. It is similar to the *Peachblow* made by Hobbs, Brockunier & Co. All known pieces of true *Plated Amberina* were vertically ribbed. The interior lining was never white as was Wheeling *Peachblow*. It, as well as *Peachblow*, are being reproduced. (2) A line of glassware made by the Fenton Art Glass Company in 1962/63. It was a blown cased glass with an outer layer of selenium ruby glass over an inner layer of milk white glass.

plated ware See *cased glass.*

plating (1) A 19th century term used in the United States to describe what is now called *casing*, i.e., *plated glass* is not *plate glass* but *cased glass.*(2) To the stained glass worker, it is placing two pieces of glass into one cane. (3) Placing a metallic layer onto the surface of glass, i.e., silvering and electroplating.

platinum Aurene See *Aurene.*

platinum band Platinum trim having the appearance of silver, applied to the rims of some glassware, especially tableware.

Platonite A trade name for white opal (with fired-on color), heat-resistant glassware used by Hazel Atlas beginning in the 1930s.

platter A large shallow dish, plate, or tray used for serving food. It is usually oval and has a ledge and sometimes a well. See *plate*.

Platts Glasshouse See *Webb family; Webb, Thomas, & Sons.*

plinth A base, foundation, stand, support, or pedestal on which a glass sculpture is placed.

Pliny, The Elder (23AD-79AD) His Latin name was Gaius Plinius Secundus, a Roman writer, naturalist, and encyclopedist. In his book, *Natural History*, written in the second half of the first century A.D., he provides the following account of the discovery of glass: A ship belonging to traders in nitrum was anchored along the coast of what is today modern Lebanon. The sailors went ashore to prepare a meal. Since they could find no rocks to support their cauldron, they rested it on lumps of nitrum from the cargo. When these lumps became heated and combined with the sand on the beach, a fluid flowed in rivlets from the fire which, on cooling, hardened into a solid. This, he stated, was the "origin of glass." This account has no basis in reality since the temperatures produced could not be hot enough to melt the components. It is now believed glass was first made in Mesopotamia, now Iraq and northern Syria, between the Tigris and Euphrates Rivers, about 2,500 years before Pliny's time. He was the uncle of Gaius Plinius Caccilius Secundusor Pliny, The Younger (69? AD-113?AD), a Roman writer, orator, and statesman.

Plum Jade An art glass developed by Frederick Carder at Steuben, made using a complex process involving three layers of glass with an acid etched design. Two layers of amethyst glass were cased around a layer of alabaster glass. The desired design was created in wax ink on the outer layer, and the object was dipped into an acid bath until it ate away about one-half of the outer layer. Then the background was similarly wax inked, and the object again dipped into the bath until a thin layer of amethyst remained. The final design appeared in three shades of amethyst, enhanced by the middle layer of alabaster and inner layer of amethyst. See *jade glass.*

plunger A metal component on a pressing machine, which forces the glass into the contours of a mold or forms a preliminary hollow space for subsequent blowing operations.

Plunger Cut A trademark registered on January 30, 1906, by the A.H. Heisey & Company, applied to its pressed and figured blanks shipped to other glass cutting facilities. Sometimes they bore its trademark—an "H" within a diamond-shaped figure. Numerous design patents were issued to the firm for these blanks.

Plunkett & Company See *Independent Glass Company.*

Plunkett & Miller See *Hobbs, Brockunier & Co.; South Wheeling Glass Works.*

Plunkett, Francis and James See *Excelsior Glass Works.*

plush glass Satin glass.

ply The number of strands or threads of opaque glass used in making a particular type of twist, e.g., up to 20-ply.

Plymouth Rocks Glass novelty items made by the Ink Stand Co. after 1876, dated 1620, as centennial souvenirs. Some were in the form of paperweights. See *Plymouth Rock paperweight.*

Plymouth Rock paperweight A clear, solid glass replica of Plymouth Rock with the date "1620" on one side and a poem about the rock on the other. These were made shortly after 1876 by the Ink Stand Co. See *Plymouth Rocks.*

Plymouth Street Glass Works See *Concord Street Flint Glass Works.*

pocket flask or bottle A flat flask (about half-pint capacity) generally used to hold alcoholic beverages. It is carried on a person's body, usually in the hip pocket. It is similar to a pilgrim flask except there are no lugs. It usually has a screw cap, hinged lid, or other form of stopper. Early ones were protected against breakage by being made of thick glass, sometimes reinforced with added strips of glass; later ones were often encased in leather or metal. Some were embellished with engraving, trailing, or prunts. Many were made in Spain during the 17th and 18th centuries.

pocket glass A small mirror carried in one's pocket or purse.

pocket lantern A small lantern, usually made of tin with one or two glass or mica sides and a reflector for transmitting light. They measured three to four inches on a side. They could be folded on all sides because the top and bottom had hinges.

pocket tumbler A tumbler that is blown and flattened to an oval shape to better fit in a person's pocket. Many tumblers embellished with trailed threading were made in Spain during the early 17th century. Some of transparent cobalt blue or amethyst glass, often with combed opaque white stripes, fired gilding, or white opaque speckling, were made during the 18th century at La Granja de San Ildefonso.

poculum *(Latin)* A drinking cup usually of globular or cylindrical shape, having a low, funnel mouth, rounded bottom resting on a ringed foot and one or two vertical loops, and angled handles extending from the rim down to the body. The earliest were made of Roman glass. See *skyphos; pterotos cup.*

Podesta The group in Venice (Murano) given the power to determine who would, or would not, be allowed to make glass.

podger A platter, dish, or shallow porringer, from the word *podge*, a contraction of *porridge.*

poet technique The addition of a foot to a glass object made by taking a portion of molten glass from a cylinder formed on another paraison or glass bubble and attaching it to the base of the object while it is in the plastic state.

Poetry in Crystal A series of crystal pieces made by Steuben, designed to interpret visually and convey the feeling of specific poems commissioned from major living poets. It was conceived in 1961 by the Poetry Society of America, which sent letters to 40 poets, offering $240, on behalf of Steuben, for each original unpublished poem submitted for

consideration. Thirty-one poems were received and interpreted into crystal. Steuben originally displayed the works at its New York shop on April 18, 1963.

Point Bridge Works See *Pittsburgh Glass Works.*

point cut (Aka *writing diamond*) A type of diamond cutting where the cutting stone is tapered to a point so sharp it can be used to write on glass.

pointed diamond See *diamond.*

pointed loops A cut glass motif consisting of curved miters converging at the top and bottom, forming a pointed oval, often embellished with a minor motif within it.

poison bottle A bottle used in a pharmacy to hold poison. These bottles were made in a variety of shapes and sizes but normally have a distinctive form and external ridges to be readily recognized by touch (some have a raised skull and crossbones). Generally their necks are narrow and the tops have two tiny holes (in a removable or fixed stopper) to regulate the flow of the contents. Bottles with a removable stopper allow it to be filled easily from the top while those with a fixed stopper usually have a corked hole in the bottom for filling. A small distinctive label, mainly the traditional skull and crossbones, is usually affixed to the bottle. Smaller ones are for home use. These are similarly ridged as a safety precaution and used for medicines containing poisonous components.

poison tankard A tankard with a crystal body and silver mounts, made in Germany during the 16th century. According to superstition, crystal was able to disclose the existence of poison in a drink.

Pokal *(German)* A goblet with a stemmed foot and cover (often missing) with a finial, made in Germany from about 1680 to 1850. It was passed among guests for drinking a toast, similar to a modern loving cup. Often called a *Gesundheitglas*, it ranged in height from ten to twenty-four inches. It is often embellished in baroque style with Hochschnitt and Tiefschnitt engraving, and the stems had balusters, mereses, and knops.

Some were engraved with elaborate motifs, but most had simple portraits or scenes and inscriptions. The style of embellishment was characteristic of the region where the glass was engraved. See *Doppelpokal.*

pokon-pokon A glass toy resembling a flexible funnel, thin and somewhat pliable, that made a ringing sound when blown. They were made in Japan of clear or colored glass, often embellished in bright enamel patterns.

Polar Star The Russian cut glass pattern where a large pyramidal star is combined with a small hobnail.

polariscope An instrument using polarized light to show stress in glass.

pole glass See *Stangenglas.*

pole head A decorative ornament made in a variety of symbolic designs affixed to the top of a pole such as those carried in and near Bristol, England, by various clubs and guilds. A few are made of so-called Nailsea glass— opaque white streaked with pink and blue glass. The poles were generally about 6-1/2 feet in height and embellished with colored ribbon.

polemoscope (Aka *ogling glass*) A device using lenses and mirrors to view objects not in the direct line of vision of the observer. Invented by a man named Henelius in 1637, it allows one to observe a person or object while appearing to be looking in another direction.

p'o-li The Chinese term meaning *clear glass. P'o-li-chuan* were bricks of colored glass, measuring two inches by four inches by twelve inches, sold to glassworkers and enamelers. See *pomana.*

policeman's lantern See *dark lantern.*

polished cut See *Blankschnitt.*

polisher In a cutting house or shop, a polisher was the person who, after the cutting was complete, polished to a brilliant luster the object, which was smoky or whitish as a result of the cutting. The polisher used wooden wheels to polish the deepest cuts, and cork and felt wheels shaped like cutting wheels to polish the shallow cuts.

polishing The process of giving glass objects a smooth brilliant surface after being cut or engraved. Originally it was accomplished by hand methods involving first using a fine-grained stone rotating wheel, then a finer wheel of lead, wood, cork, or felt in conjunction with putty powder. Some cut or engraved glass is left partially unpolished to give a contrasting effect. Later, to reduce expenses, acid polishing and fire polishing were used. See *fire polishing; polisher.*

polissoir A polishing pad used to polish plate glass.

polka dot glass (1) The name of Fenton Art Glass's cranberry glass with raised opalescent circular spots, originally made in 1955. (2) See *coin spot glass; opalescent glass.*

Pollard, Donald Born in 1924, Donald Pollard was a glass designer and painter who became a staff designer at Steuben in 1950, making original designs for many important ornamental pieces during the Houghton era. Though he designed the pieces, the engraving design and engraving were executed by others. He conceived the idea of combining glass with precious metal embellishments. See *Myth of Adonis.*

polverina Potash obtained from plants in the Levant (the area of Syria, Israel and Lebanon bordering the eastern shores of the Mediterranean and Aegean seas), used as an alkali in making glass. It was imported into England for use in making crystal glass.

polycandelon A hanging light fixture consisting of a flat metal ring hung from the ceiling by three chains with apertures to hold usually three to six point-tipped cone beakers serving as oil lamps, cups with a projecting stem, or cups in the shape of a human female breast.

polychrome Strictly, embellishment using more than two colors. However, with respect to glass, they are wares of two or more colors as distinguished from wares of one color (*monochrome*). Wares of two colors should technically be called *bichrome.*

polyoptrum (Aka *polyscope*) An object similar to a kaliedoscope, which creates multiple images of an object being observed.

polyscope See *polyoptrum.*

pomana Glass bricks made in Bohemia in imitation of the Chinese *p'o-li-chuan*, for export to supply the Chinese market. See *p'o-li.*

pomander A receptacle used to contain aromatic substances, popular in Europe during the 16th and 17th centuries. They were usually spherical in shape and about one to two inches in diameter. They were often engraved and worn on a chain around the neck. It was a forerunner of the *vinaigrette.*

pomegranate bottle A core glass bottle in the shape of a pomegranate, embellished with colored trailing combed in a festoon or feather pattern. They were made in Egypt from the XIXth through the XXIst Dynasties (14th to the 10th centuries B.C.).

Pomona glass An art glass developed by Joseph Locke in 1884, patented on April 28, 1885, and made at the New England Glass Co. from 1884 to 1888. Sometimes referred to as *Cremona*, it was expensive, fragile, and difficult to make. It was made of clear glass, enlarged by repeated mold blowing, and its surface was partially stained in amber, blue, and rose. It was always bordered at the top by a pale honey amber band about an inch wide. Each piece was composed of two distinct surfaces and may or may not have had an added motif, either etched, tinted, or stained. The most common added motifs were daisy, pansy, rose, butterfly, blueberry, and cornflower. Gold was sometimes used as an added embellishment. A few pieces were pattern molded.

There are two versions: (a) *First Grind* was made by covering the object with an acid-resistant substance into which were scratched fine lines, then dipping it in acid, leaving etched lines on the surface, often described as an uneven feather-like frost effect; and (b) *Second Grind*, made by rolling the object in particles of an acid-resistant substance, then dipping it in acid, leaving a mottled surface but an even frosting. The *Second Grind* was

favored because it was cheaper to make. When this design was combined with the honey amber banded top and frosted white stippled background, it was further etched and colored by staining. Firing completed the process, making the coloring permanent. The tops of bowls, vases, and pitchers were frequently crimped or fluted, and many had delicate, applied legs. Wares include stemware, bowls, trays, vases, and pitchers—mainly ornamental rather than functional wares. In the late 1880s, a Midwestern type of pressed (not blown) glass with a light amber band and frosted body, sometimes embellished with flowers and leaves or similar patterns in relief, was made and sold as Pomona. See *Midwest Pomona glass.*

pompadour style See *rococo.*

Pompeian glass A bubbly glassware produced by John Walsh during the 1920s.

Pompeian Blue Vase See *Vendange Vase.*

pom-pom paperweight See *mushroom paperweight.*

pontil (Aka *puntee* or *punty*) An iron rod to which a partly formed molten glass object is transferred from the blow pipe. The final shaping of an object, the finishing of the neck (if a bottle, vase, etc.), the attaching of handles, the applying of ornamentation, etc., are usually done while the object is on the pontil. It is also used to draw out plastic glass to almost any length in the form of a rod or tubing. In order to make the plastic glass object adhere to the pontil, a small gathering of molten glass (punty wad) must be attached to it. When the object is *finished off*, it is knocked off the pontil, leaving a pontil mark. See *pontil mark; glassmaker's tools.*

pontil mark A scar or rough mark found in the center of the bottom of a piece of glass where the pontil was attached. On early wares it was often pushed up into the base, making a *kick*. On later wares it was usually smoothed by grinding and, by about 1850, eliminated altogether (see *gadget*). It was pushed up or ground smooth to prevent scratching the surface on which the object was placed. Many old glass objects show a pontil mark (and almost all forgeries do). Smooth globs of glass are often placed on the bottoms on new articles so they appear old or blown. See *pad pontil mark; waffle pontil mark.*

pony See *whisky glass.*

Pope Cut Glass Company (1916-1924)
A glass cutting company located at various addresses in New York City. Its trademark was Diamon Kut (see *Diamon Kut*).

Populonia bottles Nine bottles found in a grave in Populonia, Tuscany, Italy. These blown bottles are pale green in color, nearly round in shape with a short tapering neck. All are decorated with wheel-abraded waterfront scenes and inscriptions.

porcelaine en verre An opaque white glass made by a process for which Bernard Perrot was granted a patent about 1670.

porcelain glass See *Porcelleinglas.*

Porcelleinglas (German) Literally, *porcelain glass.* An opaque white glass; milk glass. It was the subject of experiments by Johann Kunckel; a few of his pieces have been positively identified. A facility at Basdorf in Prussia made this glass from 1750 on, embellishing it with painted flowers. It was to be in imitation of porcelain. Another facility in Potsdam made glass. See *Basfdorf glass.*

porringer (Aka *pottager, pottinger, ear cup, ear dish*) A shallow or deep bowl with one (most common) or two flat horizontal handles or ears. Its design was based on silver and pewter prototypes. It was intended to hold porridge or broth, not hot drinks. Unlike the posset pot, it rarely has a cover. Smaller ones are often mistaken for bleeding cups.

porro (Spanish) (Aka *porron*) A tavern drinking vessel derived from the wine skin, having a globular or conical body, tapering upward to a narrow neck, funnel or trefoil mouth, long attenuated spout extending from the body at an upward angle, and no handle. They are used for drinking wine by pouring it directly into the drinker's mouth. They are similar to a Spanish cruet (setrill), the difference being the spout of a porro tapers to the mouth, while that of a setrill widens toward the mouth. See *cantir.*

port Any of the many openings in a glass furnace through which flames or fuel enter or exhaust gases escape.

port glass A small drinking glass with a stemmed foot and bowl in a variety of shapes and styles. It is smaller than a sherry glass and is used to drink port wine.

Porter, Joseph, & Sons; Porter, Shreve & Co.
See *Waterford Glass Works.*

Portland Glass Company
See *Portland Glass Works.*

Portland Glass Works (1864-1873)
A glass manufacturing facility established in Portland, Maine, as the Portland Glass Company, making lamp chimneys and pressed tableware in clear and colored glass. It prospered until September 17/18, 1867, when it was destroyed by fire. It was rebuilt and in operation by April 1868, but it never regained its former prosperity. In 1870 it reorganized, changing its name to the Portland Glass Works. It closed, unable to compete economically with other facilities in the area. Some wares are signed "P.G.Co."

Portland Vase A vase of Greek amphora type made of blue translucent cased glass (molded), so dark it appears as black glass except when seen by transmitted light. It is embellished with a casing of white opaque glass carved in cameo relief. Below each of the two vertical handles is a carved head of Pan, the Greek god of forests, flocks, and shepherds, portrayed with the head, chest, and arms of a man and the legs and sometimes horns and ears of a goat. The heads separate the encircling frieze into two groups of figures. The bottom of the vase is missing (see *Portland Vase Disk*).

Although its origin is unknown, it has been attributed to Roman glassmakers and is believed to have been made between the 1st century B.C. and 1st century A.D. or 138 and 161 A.D., depending on the source. Because of a sea dragon in the design, one frieze is believed to depict the myth of the marriage of Peleus, king of the Myrmidons and father of

Achilles, and Thetis, a sea nymph, the daughter of Nereus and the mother of Achilles. It is 9-1/2 inches tall and, when illuminated from the front, appears to be made of agate or jade, but when lit from behind, it glows with an amber red tint.

History. Now known as the *Portland Vase*, it was originally called the *Barberini Vase* because it was in the Palazzo Barberini in Rome in 1642. It was considered to be a cinerary urn of Alexander Severus (Emperor 222-235), depicting a scene related to his birth. The figures are thought to depict him and his mother, Julia Mam(m)aea. This is now considered untrue. The first known record of the vase indicates it was in the possession of Cardinal del Monte (1549-1627) at the Palazzo Madama near Rome, discovered in 1582 in the Monte del Grasso sarcophagus. The Cardinal's heirs sold it, about 1600, to Cardinal Fransesco Barberbini, nephew of Matteo Barberini (Pope Urban VIII, 1623-44). About 1780 it was sold by Donna Cornelia Barberini Colonna, Princess of Palestrina, to James Byres, a Scottish antiquary resident in Rome. In 1783, he sold it to William Hamilton, British Ambassador to the Court of Naples. He took it to London and, before 1785, sold it to the Dowager Duchess of Portland, hence its name. After her death in 1785, it was sold at auction to a Mr. Tomlinson, acting for the Duchess' son, the third Duke of Portland. In 1810, it was loaned to the British Museum by the fourth Duke of Portland. The Museum purchased it in 1945. It was reported that it was cracked by the Duchess of Gordon in 1786. It was smashed into over 200 fragments in 1845 by William Lloyd, but professionally restored and yet again in 1948. See *Vendange Vase; Auldjo Jug.*

Reproductions. (1) A copy was made of cased glass by Philip Pargeter and engraved by John Northwood between 1873 and 1876. It has a base in the form of the Portland Vase Disk. It was signed and dated 1876. It was on loan to the British Museum from 1959 until 1975 when it was sold at auction for £ 30,000 English. (2) An earlier copy, probably a test model, in colorless glass with wheel engraving was made by Pargeter and Northwood about 1865. (3) A glass replica was made in 1878 by John Locke. (4) Pottery copies were made in Jasperware in 1790 by Josiah Wedgwood; one example is in the British Museum. Other copies were made by the Wedgwood facility, the most recent being a series measuring six inches high, made in 1976 in a new Wedgwood color known as *Portland Blue.* (5) Less accurate copies have been made over the years by Staffordshire potters. (6) James Tassie cast sixty plaster copies from a mold by Giovanni Pichler before the original vase was delivered in 1783 by James Byres to Hamilton. (7) The earliest attempt to make a glass copy was by Edward Thomason and a Mr. Biddle at Birmingham Heath Glassworks in 1818; however, they failed to complete the white casing.

Portland Vase Disk A flat circular disk of blue glass cased with opaque white glass carved in cameo relief with a figure in profile. At one time it constituted the base of the Portland Vase, believed to have been affixed to it prior to 1642. It is not the original base for the following reasons: (a) the blue color of the disk is paler than that of the vase; (b) the carving on the disk was not done by the same person who carved the vase; and (c) the disk was cut from a larger piece of glass. It depicts a Grecian youth, possibly Paris, wearing a cap, a symbol of freedom.

portrait glassware Glassware in many forms, embellished in various styles with a miniature portrait. The earliest known are medallion portraits engraved through gold leaf on the reverse side of the glass. They were made of Roman glass between the 2nd to the 4th centuries. Later ones include (a) portraits enameled on Humpen in Germany, Bohemia, and Silesia from the 16th through the 18th centuries; (b) portraits made by stippling in the Netherlands in the 18th century; drinking glasses with portraits of contemporary clients engraved in gold behind glass at the Spa in Franzensbad during the late 18th and early 19th centuries; (c) glass panels with a portrait in relief or enameling; some of heavy glass in Venice during the 16th century; (d) medallions with relief portraits, such as Tassie medallions and sulfides; (e) commemorative glassware with a portrait, such as Jacobite glassware, King of Prussia glassware, etc.; (f) engraved marriage glasses and wedding cups, or enameled portraits made at Murano and elsewhere.

Portugese glass See *Spanish and Portugese glass.*

posset glass See *posset pot.*

posset pot (Aka *posset glass, spout glass, spout cup*) A vessel used for drinking posset (a hot beverage made of milk curdled with wine or ale, with bread crumbs and spices). They have vertical or curved sides, two vertical loop handles, sometimes a cover, and a thin curved spout extending from near the bottom. The spout is placed so the drinker can avoid the curdled milk on the surface. Some have a slightly flairing base or a low stemmed foot. They may also have been used for caudle (see *caudle cup*) or syllabub (see *syllabub glass*). They were made in England by George Ravenscroft and others during the 17th century, and in Venice for the English.

post A flat disc of hot or molten glass. See *post technique.*

post horn A drinking glass in the form of a post horn, having a funnel-shaped mouth on which it rests when empty and a looped (or double looped) stem. They were made in Germany during the 17th and 18th centuries. See *bugle; coach horn.*

post technique A flat disc of hot glass, called a *post,* is formed, attached to a pontil, and then attached to the base or base ring of the object being worked. It is used instead of a wad of glass to attach the pontil to it. It is often used when making glass cylinders for sheets of stained glass.

posy paperweight A paperweight having a posy or nose gay as its central motif, somewhat smaller than the motif of the bouquet type. They usually have no ground but a cut base.

pot A crucible of fire-resistant clay in which the ingredients for a batch of glass are heated and fused. There are three types: (a) the *skittle pot* having the appearance of an open barrel; (b) the *crown pot* having a domed top and a side opening (*mouth*); and (c) somewhat smaller pots used to make colored glass. The larger pots are generally about four feet high

and three feet in diameter. They are made by hand from clay capable of withstanding intense heat without cracking and from which iron particles have been removed magnetically. During the early years of glassmaking in the United States, the best clays were imported from Holland, Germany, and England. However, suitable clays were found in the state of Delaware, the Bordentown and Burlington areas of New Jersey, and later in Missouri.

The clay received at the facility was taken to the pot house, ground, exposed to the elements to age or ripen (up to a year), and screened, and about 20-25% of clean and ground old broken pots (*potsherds*) was added to it. Water was added, creating a thick paste that was worked into a putty-like paste by kneading with bare feet (*pugging*). This was put away to age, or ripen, for another three to six months (pots could not be made during cold weather). The bottom of these pots is about five inches thick, made in a mold. The sides are built up from the base in a slow, manual process, taking several weeks of continual building alternated with slow drying.

The completed pot was allowed to harden, or season, at ambient temperatures from four months to a year, then placed in a warm room where any moisture in the clay was removed. It was then placed in the annealing arch or auxiliary furnace (see *pot arch*), where it was slowly subjected to intense heat—almost the temperature of the melting furnace—and then transferred to a vacant arch in the main furnace (see *pot settling*) while extremely hot. The transfer from the auxiliary to the main furnace was a tedious and dangerous task, one not liked by workers because of the fragile nature of the pot and high temperatures involved. Many companies resorted to incentives or punishment to ensure workers showed up for the transfer.

Once the pot is in the main furnace, a lump of clay, slag or coal was thrown against it to test its soundness; a clear ring meant it was good. The ingredients for making glass were shoveled into it, some containing about a ton of materials. The first batch made in a new pot was not used for regular production since it rids the pot of foreign matter and loose materials and coats the interior with a protective layer of glass. A pot used for making bottle glass usually lasted on an average of seven weeks before starting to break up. An unusually good covered pot used for making flint glass could last up to a year, the average being eight to ten weeks. See the following kinds of pots: *corner; crown; glass; jockey; piling; rouge; skittle; spill.* Also see *pot furnace.*

pot antique See *antique method.*

pot arch A furnace or kiln in which the pot (see *pot*) is subjected to intense heat and from which it is transferred to the glass melting furnace by the process of pot settling. See *pot or pot settling.*

pot furnace A furnace in which pots are placed so ingredients of a batch may be fused, forming molten glass. Until relatively modern times, it was heated by wood or peat; great quantities of fuel were used. Fuel was the primary reason glassmakers frequently moved from place to place in forested areas as supplies became exhausted. In England, from about 1615, pit coal became the primary fuel, replacing wood, which was banned to glassmakers since the invention of coal burning furnaces (see *crown pot*). The use of coal spread to other countries and remained the prime fuel until relatively recently, replaced by oil, gas, and electricity.

A pot furnace normally had a capacity from six to twenty pots, arranged in a circle above the heat source. The direct application of heat to the pot was superceded by a process using the hot gases generated, passing them through recuperators. Recuperative furnaces are constructed of refractory brick and have refractory and metal tubes through which air, required for the combustion of fuel, is led into the furnace. On the outward journey, the hot gases preheat the air in the tubes, producing higher temperatures using less fuel, reducing overall costs. The melting of the batch may take up to 48 hours, requiring temperatures of 1300 to 1500º C. For small volume production, the pot furnace has the advantage that glass can be melted in a number of pots, and several types or kinds of glass can be melted and worked at the same time. The circular arrangement of pots with the mouths facing outward for gathering molten glass was established so there was relatively easy access to the molten glass. See *tank furnace; reverberatory furnace.*

pot glass (1) (Aka *pot metal*) Glass melted in open or covered pots in a furnace never used for machine production of glassware. It was primarily used in batch operation of handmade glassware (all hand blown glass is pot glass). When there are several pots in a furnace, each may contain a different color. (2) Current usage of the term indicates glass of a single homogeneous color.

pot melting The melting of glass in relatively small quantities in a pot, used to make small quantities of handmade glass, including much lead crystal.

pot metal (1) Full-antique (mouth blown) colored glass. (2) Pot glass. See *pot glass.*

pot ring A fire clay ring that floats on the surface of molten glass in an open pot. Molten glass may be moving in the pot because of turbulence caused by the heat. The ring keeps the glass within it comparatively motionless. The gatherer always puts his pipe within the ring to gather glass as free of bubbles and impurities as possible.

pot setting or pot settling The process of transferring a pot from an auxiliary furnace (*pot arch*), via a cart consisting of two long rods on wheels, to a vacant arch in the main melting furnace. It must be done while the pot is extremely hot and the glass melting furnace is in operation, with no sudden changes in temperature. This is an extremely dangerous process for the workers since the temperatures of the pot arch, the pot, and the furnace are extremely high. Generally fire bricks must be removed from the furnace wall while hot, the old pot removed, the new pot installed, the furnace rebricked and sealed— all while the furnace is in operation. See *pot.*

potash (Aka *Potassium carbonate* [$K_2O.CO_3$], *pearl ash*). As the alternative to soda, an alkali ingredient used in making glass. It was obtained in early Germany and Bohemia by burning beechwood, oak, or other timber (see *Waldglas*), and in France by burning fern and bracken (see *verre de fougere*). Retrieving it from the ashes was done by leaching them, evaporating the lye and calcining the residue. Other sources were salt peter (nitrate of potash), refined commercial potassium carbonate (pearl ash), and burnt sediment of wine. Today most potash is made commercially from potassium chloride. Glass made with potash becomes rigid more quickly after heating than glass made with soda as the alkali. Potash glass is harder, more brilliant in clarity and tone, and more suitable for cutting and engraving. It is used in making lead glass, and, on occasion, combined with lime to prevent crisselling.

potash glass Glass made using potash as the alkali. See *potash.*

potassium-lime glass A glass having as its three major components: silica (60-65%); potash (12-18%); and lime (5-12%). Forest glass or *Waldglas* is a type of this glass.

potato ring A circular silver stand to hold a glass bowl or dish. They were made in Ireland during the second quarter of the 18th century.

potichomania The process of imitating painted porcelain by painting or otherwise embellishing the interior of glass vessels. One process involves gluing pictures to the interior, varnishing them, and sealing them in place with caulk or plaster that also served as a background.

Potomac Glass Company (1904-1929) A glass manufacturing facility operating in Cumberland, Maryland.

Potsdam Glass Factory A glass manufacturing facility established in 1679 at Potsdam (Berlin), by Elector Friedrich Wilhelm of Brandenberg (d. 1688), in addition to one established in 1674 at nearby Drewitz. From their establishment until 1693, the two facilities were under the direction of Johann Kunckel, the prime motivator in the development of gold ruby glass and responsible for introducing chalk into a batch to obviate crisselling. The Potsdam facility burned in 1688, was rebuilt, and, in 1736, operations were moved by Kunckel's successors to Zechlin, remaining under government control until 1890.

potsherds Old glass melting pots, broken, cleaned, and ground for use in making new pots. About 20-25% of potsherds is added to new or virgin clay when making new pots.

Potter & Bodine See *Bodine, Joel, & Sons.*

Potters, Barbara, goblet A goblet having a bell-shaped bowl on a tall stem with a hollow urn-shaped knop with four lion's head masks, inscribed "Barbara Potters, 1602." The bowl and foot are embellished with floral designs in diamond point engraving. It was thought to have been made by Jacopo Verzelini but, since it was made after his retirement in 1592, it is now considered to have been made by one of his former Italian glassmakers at the Blackfriar's Glasshouse of Sir Jerome Bowes. See *Verzelini glassware.*

pottager or pottinger See *porringer.*

pottle A pitcher, pot, or tankard from which glasses are filled. It has a capacity of two quarts. See *dispensary container.*

pouch bottle A drinking vessel of a somewhat globular or ovoid shape, having a waisted neck and wide mouth, and a rounded or pointed bottom. It is shorter and squatter than a bag beaker. The embellishment on the bottle is (a) on the neck, a horizontal spiral in an uninterrupted trail and, on the body, a zigzag or merrythought (wishbone) trail; (b) a spiral on the neck only; or (c) corrugations on the body. The majority have been found in Kent, England, made there during the 7th and 8th centuries. A few have been found in Scandinavia.

Poultry Glassworks A glass manufacturing facility in Detroit, Michigan, specializing in paperweights. The company used silver veiling among other techniques (see *silver veiling technique*).

pounce pot A container to hold pounce (a fine powder used to prevent ink from spreading when writing on unsized paper or over an erasure) or to prepare parchment for writing. They were often included as part of an inkstand.

pourer A press operator at a facility that "poured" molten glass into a mold under the press.

powder decorated glass An art glass having a design made by applying to the surface a coating of powdered glass of various colors. The process was patented in 1806 by John Davenport of Longport, Stoke-on-Trent, England, and involved applying a paste of powdered glass, making the design by scraping the paste away with a pointed tool and heating it to lightly fuse the design to the glass. The patent referred to the results imitating engraving or etching, but it resembles neither. The designs were frequently heraldic insignia or sporting scenes. See *Davenport's patent glass*.

powder gilding The application of small particles of gold to glassware as a form of decoration. (1) Gold was chemically precipitated and large grains removed. The smaller particles were mixed with an adhesive and applied to the glass in usually three coats. (2) Gold particles were mixed with powdered glass and borax and applied to glass; the area of application stood out in relief from the surface, much like enameling.

powder glass A time recorder, similar to a sand glass, consisting of a set of four such glasses in a compartmentalized case. The set was designed to record quarter hours by starting the glasses at fifteen-minute intervals and was used for timing sermons during the mid-18th century.

powder horn A flask in the form of an ox or cow horn used by soldiers and hunters to hold gunpowder for priming purposes. They were made of glass in Germany during the 17th century, and have a metal screw cap or hinged lid.

Powell & Volkaier A glass manufacturing facility established in Elmer, New Jersey, in the early 1920. It closed in 1925.

Powelton Cut Glass Company (1910-1953) A glass cutting house established in Philadelphia, Pennsylvania, moving within the city several times over the years. In its early years it made brilliant patterns on heavy blanks. However, after 1918, it made only light cut wares and painted designs on glass.

pre-blown glass Ancient glass; glass(ware) made prior to the technique of blowing, developed in Syria during the 1st century B.C. It tended to take the form and appearance of pottery of the era.

pre-blown-three-mold-glass Blown-three-mold-glass characterized by its thickness and ground rims, necessary to finish the piece where it was blown over the top of the mold.

Premier Glass Company See *Consumers Glass Company Limited.*

premiums Glassware used as promotional items for *giveaways* by various businesses. One common method of distribution was inserting it, normally in the form of various dishes, in cereal boxes. It aided in selling the product as purchasers attempted to collect complete sets.

Prescut A trademark used by McKee Glass Company since the early 1890s and finally registered on November 29, 1904. It was used on an imitation cut glass it made by pressing.

presentation glassware Glassware in various forms, such as a tumbler, goblet, bowl, etc., embellished to commemorate its presentation to an individual or group on some auspicious occasion. See *commemorative glassware*.

preserve dish A tall, footed dish for serving preserves—fruits, vegetables, etc., prepared by cooking them in sugar. They have often been used as candy dishes.

Preserving jar, marked "Trademark – Lightning – Reg. U.S. Patent Office." Base marked "Putnam 888." Davanna Collection

preserve jar A small jar made in various shapes and styles, usually with a cover, for serving preserves and jams. Many are elaborately embellished with cut patterns. They are called *sealers* in parts of Canada. See *preserve dish.*

preserving jar A mass-produced jar used by a homemaker for "putting up" (or preserving for future use) various fruits and vegetables. See *Mason jar.*

press An automatic or hand-operated machine used to press glass into molds.

press-and-blow process A process developed in the 19th century for making bottles, in which the paraison was pressed out within the mold by means of a large plunger and then transferred by hand to another and final mold, where it was blown by compressed air into the required shape.

pressed amberina A type of amberina made by Hobbs, Brockunier & Co.

Pressed glass salt and pepper on pegged base with center toothpick holder.
Davanna Collection

Grouping of pressed glass, United States, c. 1860-1900. Museum of American Glass at Wheaton Village, Millville, NJ.

pressed glassware Pressing glass by hand dates to the 1st century A.D., but mechanical pressing dates to the 1820s. It is this glass that *pressed glassware* is used to describe. The process of pressing glass by machine is considered the greatest technological advancement and economically significant manufacturing technique since the invention of glassblowing, making possible infinite diversification of plain and patterned glass. In the early 1830s, motifs were of two basic types: designs from cut-glass patterns and designs that could not be done by a cutter. It allowed skilled workers to be replaced with cheap, unskilled labor, permitting more and a greater variety of glassware to be available to a larger segment of the public at lower prices.

Pressed glassware is defined as glassware made by the process of shaping an object by first placing a gather of molten glass into a metal mold and pressing it with a metal *plunger (follower)* to form the shape of the inside surface. The resultant piece, termed *mold pressed,* has an interior shape independent of the exterior—in contrast to mold blown ware where the interior shape corresponds to the exterior—and the edges of its pattern and rim are sharp, unlike the edges on mold blown wares. Mold blown glassware usually has a smooth texture—an almost polished appearance. However, early pressed wares, made from 1827 to 1840, normally pressed one piece at a time, have a granular texture, giving the surface a mat appearance. Since hand finishing an article is not a component of the pressing process, the edges of rims and bases are rough.

Early pressed glass patterns are on the interior of the piece and any brilliance achieved is caused by the refraction of light from the facets of the pattern through the plain surface. While the unpatterned surfaces appear smooth, they are slightly uneven, rarely as smooth as polished glass. A majority of articles have concentric ripple marks showing an uneven swirl action on the inner or upper surface. These were caused by the molds not being heated adequately; the number and degree of ripples vary with the degree of coolness of the mold. The mat surfaces between the facets pressed into the article contribute to the metallic luster of the glass when viewed from the inside. The smoother the unpatterned portion of the surface and the more facets in the pattern, the more sparkle in the glass. Those articles having a stippled background or stippling in the motif reflect to the greatest degree the silvery metallic luster found only in pressed glass.

The main criteria for obtaining a perfectly pressed and patterned article were: (a) accurate alignment of the mechanism (the mold stationary, the plunger in straight vertical alignment with it, and both close fitting, yet providing for air vents); (b) the appropriate heating of the mold (the mold must be heated to the correct temperature; if the metal was too cool, blemishes were caused on the surface of the piece, usually appearing as swirled ripple marks, slightly rough hairline fissures, check marks, or fairly deep scratch-like fissures with rough edges; if too hot, the glass would adhere to the plunger and mold); and (c) the use of the exact amount of molten glass (too much or too little glass cause problems with the plunger, creating an incomplete or too thick piece, and may cause the glass to cool too quickly or slowly, cracking before annealed). The fissures were sometimes called *shear marks*, *seams*, or *scratches* and were created when the shears used for cutting the glass from the punty rod were unclean, causing a chilling effect.

Originally pressing was a two-man operation, requiring a gatherer to gather the molten glass and a presser to shear off the gather with one hand so the correct amount would drop into the mold. With his other hand, he operated the lever that lowered the plunger into the mold, pressing the glass. The molds used were composed of at least two pieces: (a) the *receiving die* into which the metal dropped from the pontil and (b) the *plunger*. Later a *cap ring* or *rim* made of cast iron or brass was introduced as an integral part of the mold. Stippling on early pressed glass was created by using drills to create dimples in a cast iron mold or by punches used for smaller holes to create a stippling effect in brass molds. Early molds could be *chipped* (*engraved*) or *cast* (cheaper) to make a pattern. If the molds were too hot, the glass might adhere to them, remaining in the depressions, and the next piece pressed would lack

that portion of the pattern. One of the advantages of pressed glass was being able to mix designs and patterns, offering a great variety.

While New England Glass and Boston & Sandwich are often credited with initially making pressed glass, there were other companies working in this area. On September 9, 1825, a patent was issued to J.P. Bakewell of Bakewell & Company for improvements in making glass furniture knobs by a pressing operation. On November 4, 1826, a patent for improvements in making glass furniture knobs was issued to Henry Whitney and Enoch Robinson of New England Glass. On October 16, 1827, a patent for using molds for pressing glass, called *Dummer's Scallop* or *Coverplate,* was issued to Phineas C. Dummer of Jersey City, New Jersey. On the same date a patent was issued to George Dummer, Phineas C. Dummer, and James Maxwell for forming glass using mechanical molds. At the time George Dummer & Company operated the Jersey City Glass Works in Jersey City. On December 1, 1828, Deming Jarves obtained a patent for pressing melted glass into molds. In 1829, he was granted a patent for a pressed glass furniture knob with a glass screw rather than a metal one, and, in 1830, for a mold for pressing a handled article in a single pressing operation. New England Glass was the first, followed by Deming Jarves of Boston & Sandwich, to make pressed glass on a large commercial scale. Other early U.S. producers from 1827 to 1840 were: Providence Flint Glass Manufactory; John L. Gilliland & Co. (Brooklyn Flint Glass Works); R.B. Curling & Sons (Curling, Robertson & Co.); Fort Pitt Glass Works; Bakewell & Co.(Pittsburgh Flint Glass Manufactory); O'Leary, Mulvaney & Co.; Parke, Campbell & Hanna (Union Flint Glass Works); Whitehead, Ihmsen & Phillips (Pennsylvania Glass Works); Ritchie & Wheat (Ritchie & Wilson); M. & R.H. Sweeney & Co; Jersey Glass Co.; J. & T. Robinson; Stourbridge Flint Glass Works; and Dyottville Glass Works.

The pressing process became a standard method of making many wares during the 1830s and used for making the majority of American glassware by the late 1850s. The presses used were hand operated until 1864 when a patent was issued for a steam press. While attribution of early pressed glass to a particular facility can be made in only a small number of cases, there are definite distinctions between *Eastern* and *Midwestern* pressed glass, with exceptions in both areas. Stippling on Midwestern lacy glass is coarse compared to that made in Eastern facilities. When glass with distinctive design characteristics is concentrated in a particular area where there were possible glass manufacturing facilities and does not turn up at all or infrequently in the vicinity of others, it is presumed to be made in the area of greatest concentration. Cloth-like stippling has been found so far only on Midwestern lacy.

In many instances individual pieces have been accompanied by tradition and family history that often bears out the area of production. The use of fine diagonal ribs as a border or background is an Eastern design. Fine concentric rings were used more often in the East than in the Midwest; this is also true of the sawtooth termination of the stippled background. The use of a halo of blazes running into shoulder stippling is exclusively Midwestern. Edge design is also a clue to the manufacturing area. There are several serration edges typical of Midwestern glass, such as the large rounded, alternating large rounded and pointed, and bull's-eye serration. Rope edging was used in both the East and Midwest. Eastern plates and dishes of various sizes usually rest on a flat base or rim, often on a rope ring rim. Many Midwestern articles have small ball feet that, when observed through the interior of the vessel, appear to be bead motifs in the patterns, or they have motifs in high relief at the edge of the center forming *table rests*. The dome shoulder is found only on Sandwich glass; the serrated rim slightly below a sharp convex curve formed at the top of the shoulder or border of the plate. Midwestern designs tend to be somewhat bolder in scale and accent.

Non-mechanical pressed glass has been made in England since shortly before 1827 and since then, made as a cheap reproduction of cut glass. It was often made in colored glass and sometimes with pressed faceting and ridges in low relief. Although the pressing process was originally used to imitate cut glass, its later use led to the development of new forms for which the technique was especially suitable, e.g., lacy glass, cup plates, etc. The mechanical method of pressing glass is considered to be an American invention, attaining its greatest popularity from 1850 to 1900. Hundreds of patterns were made in complete table settings. Up until 1864, most American pressed glass contained lead. In that year, William Leighton of Hobbs, Brockunier & Co. developed a soda lime glass where bicarbonate of soda replaced soda ash. It cost less than half as much as lead glass to make and could be worked and cooled more rapidly. Its optical clarity was good, and it could be pressed thinner than lead glass.

pressed mold process A process in which a mold shaped around a wooden model is used to form a glass object. Glass so made was without embellishment and not polished.

presser The skilled person in a shop whose job it is to ensure the proper amount of molten glass is allowed to flow from the end of the punty rod into a mold, cutting its flow with scissor-like shears. He also ensures the plunger is inserted into the mold and held there for the proper amount of time to prevent the glass from sticking if held in place for too long or to prevent an incompletely formed piece from being produced if released too quickly.

pressing The process for making pressed glass. Molten glass is poured into a mold, forming the outer surface of an article. A plunger is then lowered, with pressure, onto the mass, forming an article with a smooth interior and patterned exterior. Flat plates and dishes are formed in a base mold where the upper section folds down to mold the top, not unlike a waffle iron. Fine pressed glass pieces are often finished by hand to remove mold marks, and, when finished properly, are sometimes difficult to distinguish from cut glass. There are three methods of pressing glass: block molding, split molding, and font molding.

prickly glass See *Stachelglas.*

prig A small pitcher.

primavera, vetro (Italian) Literally, *springtime glass.* An ornamental glass developed by Ercole Barovier for Barovier & Toso about 1927. The characteristic feature is a crackled, translucent effect. Articles are embellished with black glass handles and narrow bands on the base and mouth.

Primrose glass A pale yellow glass patented by G. Davidson & Co. in the 1890s in England. It is molded or free form, plain or shaded, undecorated or embellished with pseudo-cut decoration.

Prince of Wales service A service of glassware housed in the Royal Collection at Windsor Castle, bearing the engraved insignia—three feathers—of the Prince of Wales. It includes numerous decanters and wine glasses. The glasses have a wide cushion pad and ornamental foot. It was made between 1810 and 1820 for the future George IV while he was Prince Regent.

Prince Rupert's ball, drop, or tear See *Rupert's drop.*

Cut glass syrup with pewter top and handle. Encircling the body are cut overlapping printies (clover cut). Davanna Collection

printie (1) (Aka *puntee, punty, printy*) The opposite of a prunt. It is a decorative pattern on cut glass consisting of a shallow concavity, circular or oval, made with a slightly convex cutting wheel. They are generally made in a pattern—sometimes V-shaped rows—surrounding the article. They are often found on various vessels and some overlay paperweights. Circular ones are called *ball cut,* oval ones are called *thumb marks* or *finger cuts,* and overlapping ones are called *clover cut.* Articles with the clover cut pattern were made by the New England Glass Company. (2) A bull's-eye motif (Irish). See *curved cutting; punt.*

printy See *printie.*

prism (1) A drop of triangular section (see *prism drop*). (2) Embellishment on cut glass (see *prism cutting*). (3) A transparent body used for refracting or dispersing light into a spectrum, usually having a rectangular base and equilateral triangular section.

prism cutting A decorative pattern (see *cut glass, patterns*) consisting of long, straight mitered grooves, cut horizontally in parallel lines so the top edges touch. It is typically found on the neck of a jug or decanter in rings of diminishing size, extending upward from the body to the rim. A variation is the *alternate prism,* cut vertically or horizontally with small sections of ridges alternating with small sections of grooves.

prism drop A small glass drop triangular in section with plane surfaces acting as a prism and, by the reflection of light, revealing the colors of the spectrum. They are often found on a chandelier.

privateer glassware Glassware, usually wine glasses, engraved with the representation of a commissioned private sailing vessel in full sail and usually an inscription bearing the names of the captain and ship. They were mainly made of glass in England during the 18th century. See *naval subjects; ship subjects.*

private mold work Making a quantity of wares to meet a customer's order. Perfume companies, large department stores, liquor companies, etc., would place orders with various companies to make specific quantities of specific type(s) of glassware to their specifications, using their molds. It provided a steady source of income for many companies and eliminated risks associated with placing a new pattern line on the market. This was a common practice as was making glassware for other companies, using their molds, to fill orders. The products made were not advertised by the maker but by the mold owner. The actual maker is usually not known to the public.

procession cup A standing cup or bowl of cylindrical form resting on a hollow or knopped stem above a spreading foot, embellished with an enameled frieze portraying a procession of people surrounding the object. They, as well as similarly embellished tazze, have been ascribed to Venice, made from about 1450 to 1500. They are among the earliest specimens of enameled decoration done at Murano. See *wedding cup.*

prochoos *(Greek)* A slender form of an oenochoe. A small jug with a tapering globular body, thin neck, small mouth, high arched handle, and stemmed foot for pouring wine or holding water for washing hands before eating. They were also made in lower, more compressed forms. Some were made of Roman glass in the 3rd and 4th centuries.

Proclamation of 1615 The forests in many areas of England were diminishing rapidly because trees were being cleared for agricultural purposes and for use as fuel for iron smelters and the glass industry. Finally, on May 23, 1615—because of the scarcity of wood for building ships and houses—the "Proclamation Touching Glasses" (Proclamation of 1615) was issued, barring the glass industry from using wood. Coal was eventually used, but new technology was necessary because coal burned hotter. This caused the rapid destruction of melting pots and created much carbon, which got into the open pots, causing seeds in the molten glass. Kettles could not withstand the greater heat. Eventually clay pots made of Stourbridge clay were developed in an unusual shape, designed to withstand the heat and reduce the carbon that fell into them. The proclamation also banned the import of glass and immigration of glassworkers from other countries.

Proclamation Touching Glasses
See *Proclamation of 1615.*

profession glass See *Standehumpen.*

prongs A tool, normally made of steel, used by glassmakers to direct the pontil into position on the piece of hot glass to be worked.

proof phial A small glass phial (vial) with a sting around its waisted neck. This was lowered through the bung of a barrel of wine or alcoholic beverage to extract a sample of the contents to test for the percentage of alcohol.

proper knop A knop in the shape of an oblate sphere.

Prosch, Carl F. (1866-1937) Born in Austria, he worked as a sales representative and designer for Bawo & Dolter, an American importer of china and glass. In May 1900, Dorflinger brought him to his White Mills facility as supervisor of his soon-to-be created subsidiary, the Honesdale Decorating Co. In 1915, the year of Dorflinger's death, Prosch bought the subsidiary. See *Honesdale Decorating Co.*

provenance Also spelled *provenience.* The source of a specimen of glass or other art object, referring to its prior ownership or place of discovery, not its place of production (the origin).

provenience See *provenance.*

Providence Flint Glass Company (1831-1833) A glass manufacturing facility established in Providence, Rhode Island, making all kinds of table glass, pressed glass, apothecaries, and chemical wares, generally of high quality.

Providence Glass House (1) In 1752, Isaac C. Winslow was granted the sole privilege of making glass in Rhode Island by the General Court of Rhode Island. He named his potential facility the Providence Glass House, but, based on historical records, it is unlikely that he ever constructed it or even exercised the privilege. (2) A glass manufacturing facility established about 1790 by John Brown in Providence, Rhode Island. It is believed to have closed after the first melt.

prunt A blob of glass applied to an object, usually a type of a drinking vessel. They served two purposes: (1) an embellishment and (2) a surface affording a firm grip in the absence of a handle. They are made in a variety of forms and sizes; sometimes globular, pointed (called *thorned boss*) or irregularly shaped, and occasionally impressed with a mask (see *lion's head prunt*) or diaper pattern of droplets (see *raspberry prunt*). Usually a large number of prunts were applied to an object, either haphazardly or in the form of a pattern. They were often used on Roman and Frankish glass, on glass in the *façon de Venise* in the 16th and 17th centuries, and on 16th and

17th century German glass as found on a *Nuppenbecher*, *Warzenbecher*, *Romer*, etc. Some German glasses have prunts on the interior as well as the exterior (see *Stangenglas*). They should be distinguished from the small drops of glass applied in an overall surface pattern. See *blobs; dotted prunt; strawberry prunt.*

pseudo-faceted stem A glass stem made in a mold by a pressing operation, resembling cut faceting. They were made in Hesse, Thuringia, and England in the first half of the 18th century. See *Silesian stem.*

pseudo vasa diatreta Various objects characterized by a surrounding network, or other reticulated ornamentation, of glass not cut from the original mass but applied later when the object was reheated. See *scallop shell chalice; cage cup; diatreta glass.*

pterotos cup A type of skyphos characterized by two vertical loop handles (*wing shaped*), the upper edge having a flat thumb piece level with the rim, and a carved finger piece attached midway down the bowl, near their bottom. They are of Roman glass resembling contemporary silver cups. Some made from the late 3rd century B.C. to the 1st century A.D. have handles cut from solid mold blown glass. Some made in Sidon have an impression on the body made from a coin. Others, made from about 100 B.C. to about 100 A.D., have attached mold-blown handles; some have bowls similarly shaped but larger, with a pedestal foot. *Pterotos* is derived from the Greek word *pteron* meaning *wing.*

public domain patterns See *cut glass, patterns.*

pucellas (Aka *tool, tongs*) A glassmaker's tool made of two metal spring arms joined at one end by a curved metal handle. It was used to form the size and shape, both inside and out, of the bowl of a drinking glass or other circular shaped hollow article while being rotated on the pontil. Later they were made of steel (*steel jacks*). They left striation marks on the inside of the bowl where they touched it. They were superceded by a wooden ended tool, giving a softer effect with fewer striation marks. Pucellas were used until about 1830. See *woods; tools, glassmaker's.*

puff-patter Sold in the United States in the 1930s, a puff-patter was a high quality French swansdown powder puff attached to a cut crystal handle, in clear and pastel colored glass. It was often designed to match perfume bottles and magnifying mirrors. Most were made in Czechoslovakia and are quite rare.

puffer See *sofietta.*

pugging In the manufacturing of pots, a mixture of clean, ground, used broken pots is mixed with screened, unused, virgin clay and water, forming a thick paste that is kneaded by workers with their bare feet to form a putty-like mixture. This kneading process is called *pugging.*

Pugh & Teeter See *Cincinnati Glass Manufacturing Co.; Moscow Glass Works.*

pulegoso, vetro (Italian) Literally, *bubbled glass*. An ornamental opaque glass developed by Venini about 1928, having many irregularly spaced air bubbles within the glass, some bursting on the surface, giving the ware a blistered and pitted effect. Sometimes it is covered with a flashing of smooth clear glass; this flashed ware is called *vetro pulegoso sommerso.*

pull test A test to ascertain whether or not two batches of glass to be used in making a cased glass object or other ware, where two or more glasses are used, have a compatible coefficient of expansion. If they do not, the finished object will crack or shatter when subjected to any sudden change in temperature. The test used by Frederick Carder at Steuben involved making a rod of glass from each of the batches, fusing them together, and pulling the resultant molten mass into a thread. If it remained reasonably straight on cooling, the batches were considered compatible. If the thread curled beyond a certain tolerance (one batch contracted more rapidly than the other), the batches were incompatible.

pulled leafy pattern A pattern on Iris glass.

pulley salt See *capstan salt.*

pull-up vase A vase embellished by inserting colored or white glass threads in the base and drawing them up into the body with a pointed iron hook. The method was developed by John Northwood at Stevens & Williams Ltd. Later he invented a machine to do this, making intricate patterns.

pulse glass A hand warmer consisting of a small vial partly filled with water. The air is removed from the vial and the vial sealed, creating a partial vacuum. The water, now under low pressure, boils from just the heat of the hand. Benjamin Franklin is credited with bringing it to the United States after discovering it in common use in Germany.

pumice A form of natural glass created by volcanic action. The molten materials that would ordinarily cool to a crystalline state are vitrified into a glassy form by quick cooling. The gasses released from the volcanic action are captured within to form a foamed material, known for centuries as an excellent polishing substance.

Cut glass, two-part punch bowl, 12" d. x 15" h. Davanna Collection

punch bowl A large circular bowl used for serving hot or cold punch, made from the 17th century. Early ones may have a short knopped stem with a domed foot; later ones are embellished with cutting and engraving or pressed motif. They are often accompanied by a matching glass ladle and a set of glasses. See *toddy lifter.*

punch cup A small cup for serving punch with bowls in many shapes and sometimes a short stem. It may be part of a matching set accompanying a matching punch bowl. See *punch glass.*

punch filler See *toddy lifter; punch ladle.*

punch glass A drinking glass for serving punch. It may be part of a matching set accompanying a matching punch bowl. Some

early ones had a conical bowl with a baluster stem. Since the third quarter of the 18th century, when glassware made specifically for serving punch was introduced, they have been formed with a handle but no stemmed foot. Hot punch became popular about 1763; punch glasses with handles were made from that time. At one time glass tankards were used for drinking punch.

punch ladle A long-handled ladle used for serving punch, often made to match a punch bowl. They have been made since the mid-18th century and were superceded by the toddy lifter.

punt A small printie. Examples of it are located in a pattern encircling the vessel just below the rim.

punt mark A manufacturer's mark on the bottom or base of a bottle, widely used after 1850.

puntee; puntee rod; punty rod See *pontil; printie.*

puntee mark See *pontil mark.*

punty See *thumbprint; pontil; printie.*

punty wad A small gathering of glass attached to the pontil to make the glass object being made adhere to it.

Purdah glass Transparent, tinted glass sandblasted to varying depths to cause transmitted light to produce different effects, either a design or picture.

purl See *pearl.*

purled glass A vessel with ribbing around the base.

purlee glassware A type of glassware so designated in a list, dated 1677, of pieces being sold by the Glass Sellers' Company. It is presumed *purlee* referred to a pearl-like surface, or a glass trail or thread applied in a circuit (encircling the object or a portion of it and having no end), derived from the word *purl*, meaning *embroider.*

purling See *gadrooning.*

purple glass Glass colored purple using an oxide of manganese or nickel in the batch.

purple marble glass See *mosaic glass.*

Purple of Cassius (Aka *rouge d'or, rose pink*) A crimson-purple pigment sometimes used to color glass. It is prepared by adding a chloride of tin and colloidal gold (finely divided particles of gold suspended in a liquid) to the batch. The glassware produced became ruby red when reheated. The process was named after Andreas Cassius (d.1673), though it was first published by German chemist Johann Rudolf Glauber (1604-68) in 1659. It was often used by German Hausmaler during the 17th century to color enamel used for embellishing faience and glass and in China for painting *famille rose* porcelain.

purple slag glass A *slag glass* colored purple and white, made by several companies in the United States and England. The largest maker in the 1870s and 1880s was Challinor, Taylor & Co. It is still being made today.

purpurin An opaque glass made in Bohemia, purplish in color, with a slightly clearer shade marbled in. It was often painted, cut, gilded, or engraved. It was popular in the 19th century. Karl Faberge used it to carve small animals.

purpurine A deep red color popular in the late 1860s and the 1870s, used to embellish porcelain, furniture, and glass.

purse bottle A small bottle to hold perfume, carried in a woman's purse. They were usually 1.5 to 3 inches in length, had screw-on tops with a dauber attached, and had a capacity of a dram (1/8 ounce) of perfume. They were popular in the 1930s, originally retailing for $0.25 to $0.59 empty and $1 to $1.50 filled with perfume (it was common then for merchants to purchase perfume in bulk, dispensing it in these bottles). Millions were made in Czechoslovakia.

Putnam, Wilmot (1881-1969) Born in Dix, New York, he learned engraving at Hawkes, working there from 1901 to 1915; then for J. Hoare & Co. from 1915 to 1920; and H.P. Sinclair & Co. from 1920 to 1928. He also cut for the Bacalles Glass Shop and the Fuller Cut Glass Co. After Sinclair closed in 1928, he returned to Hawkes, remaining there until it closed in 1962. From 1920 until his death, he operated a shop in Corning, New York, where he cut for his former employers, the Hunt Co., and individuals.

Putnam Flint Glass Works A flint hollowware and bottle glass manufacturing facility established in 1852 in Putnam, Ohio. Shortly after it began operations, it was taken over by Carter & Woodruff and later sold to Kearns & Company. In 1881 it made the Haines patent fruit jar.

putto *(Italian)* The form of a small boy, usually naked or almost so. Since the word *putto* (pl., *putti*) is Italian for a young male child, it is often used loosely and interchangeably with *amorino* (a winged, naked infant boy, i.e., Cupid), but should be ascribed only to a wingless male figure. It has been used often as an embellishment on glassware.

putty (Aka *glazing compound*) A substance used by glaziers to fix glass sheets into a frame.

putty knife A knife used by glaziers and other glass workers to apply putty. The blade is available (or modified to suit the worker's needs) in various widths.

puzzle jug A drinking glass made in the same manner as pottery puzzle jugs. It has an openwork upper half through which the drink spills unless the consumer sucks the liquid up through a concealed tube extending from the bottom of the glass to an aperture in its rim, while the consumer's fingers close other apertures in the rim. See *joke glass; siphon glass.*

pyramid An arrangement of sweetmeat glasses and/or jelly glasses on a salver. It has as its center piece a tall sweetmeat glass (often called a *captain glass*) surrounded by smaller glasses placed on a salver which, in turn, rests on glasses placed on a larger salver. There were often three such tiers. They were common at formal dinners in England during the 18th century.

pyramid night light See *fairy lamp.*

pyramid star or pyramidal star A cut glass motif made by cutting triangular prisms radiating from a central focal point. It is frequently used in the center of the button of a hobstar and is one of the principal motifs of the Russian pattern. See *star.*

Pyramus & Thisbe See *Fairfax Cup.*

Pyrex mixing bowl, red, 1-1/2 qt., #402.
Davanna Collection

Pyrex ad from the Ladies' Home Journal, September 1916.

Pyrex ad, December 1932.

Pyrex The trade name for heat-resistant oven glassware made by the Corning Glass Works and its licensees. It is made with borax and is technically a *borosilicate glass.* It was developed in 1912 to resist the heat shock that caused railway brakemen's lanterns to brake on exposure to the elements. The term is often used generically for all heat-resistant glassware used in the home. The English equivalent of *Pyrex* was called *Phoenix.*

pyriform Shaped like a pear. See *pear shaped.*

Pyroceram A trademarked glass ceramic crystalline material developed in 1957 by S.D. Stookey at Corning Glass Works. The process involved melting and forming ordinary glass; then, by further reheating, transforming it into closely grained crystalline ceramics having special strength and heat-resistant qualities. See *glass ceramic.*

Pyroceram Brand Cement A trademark used for certain powdered glasses that are thermosetting and used for sealing inorganic material in vacuum tubes. The resultant seals are crystalline and have service temperatures in excess of the sealing temperatures.

Pyroceram Brand 9608 A trademark for a crystalline ceramic material made from glass by a controlled nucleation process. It is used in telescope mirrors and special purpose ceramic products.

pyrolusite See *manganese.*

pyrometer A metering device used to measure the temperature of a furnace or kiln.

pyros A term used for milk bottles with colored labels affixed by silk screening or pyro-glazing.

pyx In the Christian church, a pyx is a vessel in which the Host—the consecrated wafer of the Eucharist (the sacrament of Holy Communion, the sacrifice of the Mass, the Lord's Supper)—is preserved. See *church glassware.*

pyxides or pyxis (Greek) A covered, box-like receptacle, usually cylindrical in shape, used on the dressing table to hold jewels and trinkets. Later, during the 1st century B.C., some were made of blown Roman glass. Quite a few have been excavated in Crete, a Greek island in the Mediterranean. They appear to have been made in three-part molds from fused crushed glass.

Qq

qarabah *(Persian)* See *carboy*.

quaffing cup A drinking cup, especially one for intoxicating beverages.

quaich or quaigh *(Scottish)* A shallow, circular drinking vessel; a deep saucer with two or three lugs or flat handles, similar to a small porringer.

Quaker City Cut Glass Company (1902-1927) (Aka *Cut Glass Corporation of America*) A glass cutting company established in Philadelphia, Pennsylvania. In 1924 it moved to Jermyn (now Germantown), Pennsylvania. After World War I it became affiliated with the Laurel Cut Glass Company, but separated a short time later. Quaker City moved back to Philadelphia. It used gum labels depicting a bust of William Penn.

quarrel (Aka *quarry*) A small pane of glass that is square, diamond, or rectangular in shape. Windows made with them are called *quarried windows*. They were often embellished with paints and enamels depicting flora and fauna and made throughout Europe from medieval times to the 17th century.

quarried window See *quarrel*.

Quarrier, Ott & Co. See *Union Glass Works (West Virginia)*.

quarry See *quarrel*.

quart See *wine bottle, sizes*.

quartz Silica, silicon dioxide (SiO_2). Here referring to the most common form of the mineral silica, sand.

quartz glass (1) A name occasionally (though erroneously) applied to fused silica. (2) An art glass developed by Frederick Carder at Steuben, made using a process similar to that used to make Cintra glass. However, it was given a crackled effect by briefly plunging a gather of molten glass into cold water, causing only the surface to shatter. It was then reheated so the cracks were thoroughly fused and heated again and rolled over powdered colored glass that was pulled or manipulated into a pattern. Finally it was covered with another layer of colored or clear glass and sometimes given a satin surface using acid. Depending on the color of the outer layer, it was called *Rose Quartz, Alabaster Quartz, Amethyst Quartz, Blue Quartz, Green Quartz, Peach Quartz, or Yellow Quartz*. Sometimes embellishment was added in the form of applied glass decoration in relief, then acid etched.

quatrefoil A decorative motif formed of four lobes or leaves radiating from a common center, set at right angles to one another.

quatrefoil stem A stem on a drinking glass of inverted baluster shape, usually hollow, though sometimes solid, having the wider part pinched into four vertical lobes. On occasion the sides of the lobes are impressed with hatching.

quattro-cento glasses A stemmed, wide-footed goblet or wine glass of Venetian origin, the bowl having a double curve tapering slightly inward at the top. They are often transparent cobalt blue (other colors do exist) and are embellished with opaque solid enamels, often depicting mythological scenes. The grass and trees are in a bright green enamel.

Queen City Cut Glass Company A glass cutting company established in 1913 in Rochester, Minnesota. It closed during World War I, but in 1918 it reopened as the Olson Cut Glass Company. See *Olson, Arthur*.

Queen's Burmese Frederick Shirley of the Mt. Washington Glass Company sent pieces of his *Burmese glass* to Queen Victoria and Princess Beatrice in 1886. Several were embellished with a floral design, flowers executed in a raised enamel. Much was done in pure gold and reduced with acids. The queen and princess so admired them that the design became known as the *Queen's Design*. Thomas Webb & Sons purchased a license from Shirley to make this ware in England, where it was known as *Queen's Burmese*. Colors were generally from lemon yellow to pink, and the items were embellished with painted flowers and birds. See *Burmese glass*.

Queen's Design See *Queen's Burmese*.

Queen's Ivory Ware A type of opaque whitish glass with a creamy, ivory color inspired by articles of old Japanese carved ivory. It was patented by Sowerby's Ellison Glassworks in 1879, where it was made in the late 1870s and early 1880s.

Quezal Art Glass & Decorating Company (1901-1925) A glass manufacturing facility established in Brooklyn, New York, by two former employees of Louis Comfort Tiffany, Martin Bach (d.1924) and Thomas Johnson. It made opalescent glassware and other forms of art glass similar to Tiffany's Favrile and Steuben's Aurene. The name was trademarked in 1902, a second trademark was issued in 1907. The latter shows the *quetzal* or *quezal* (a Central American bird with brilliant and colorful plumage). *Quezal* is often engraved in block letters on the bottom of the piece. Vases and lamps were the primary objects made in rather simple rounded or fluted shapes, sometimes with wavy rims. The embellishment was in the glass itself in the form of various metallic luster colors, almost always based on flora designs. After a change in ownership, the company closed. Martin Bach Jr., son of the founder, and others from the company went to work at the Vineland Flint Glass Works. Conrad Vohlsing, son-in-law of Martin Bach Sr., continued to make a Quezal type glass called *Luster Art Glass* at his facility in Elmhurst, New York.

quill holder See *spill holder*.

quilling (1) A style of embellishment in the form of closely spaced festoons of white

opaque glass. It is found on some so-called Nailsea glass and on some glass made at Alloa, Scotland. (2) (Aka *pinched or pincered trailing*) A style of decoration consisting of applied bands of glass pinched into a wavy formation. See *festooned glassware*.

quilt molding A decorative molded style surface embellishment on the bowls of some Venetian wine glasses. The exteriors have the appearance of quilting—diagonal crisscross ridges enclosing slightly oblique diamond forms.

quilted cushion glass An art glass with the appearance of quilting, made as a cased glass with an opaque inner layer, mold blown in a diamond pattern and covered with a thin layer of transparent glass. The nature of the process traps an air bubble within each diamond. The surface is given a satin finish using hydrofluoric acid. It was made by Thomas Webb & Sons and Stevens & Williams Ltd. about 1880.

quincunx pattern A style of embellishment with motifs placed in an overall diaper pattern, resulting in groups of five—one in the center and one on each corner. It was used during the 2nd to the 6th centuries and the 9th to 11th centuries on Persian glassware embellished with contiguous (but not overlapping) shallow wheel engraved circular concavities so arranged. It was used later in Bohemia and elsewhere. *Quincunx* is Latin for "five-twelfths."

Quinte-Clapperton Amalgamated See *Clapperton & Sons*.

Quinton Glass Works A window glass manufacturing facility established in 1863 in Quinton, New Jersey, by George and Charles Hires, John Lambert, and a former store owner named Smith, operating as Smith, Lambert & Hires. In 1864 Smith retired, and in 1866 Charles Hires returned to farming, selling his interest to George R. Morrison. In 1867 Lambert withdrew, and the operating firm became Hires & Morrison. In 1870 Morrison left and George Hires became the sole owner. In 1872 Charles Hires returned, and the operating firm became Hires Brothers. Then they took in three partners, and the operating firm became Hires, Halthaus, Prentice & Ward. William Plummer, George Hires' brother-in-law, was made a partner at age 21 and the name changed to Hires & Company. In addition to window glass, it made many kinds of specialty glass, such as silvered glass for mirrors, plate glass, and enameled glass. In 1878 the Hires Turner Glass Company was formed. John Turner came from England, working for John Lucas & Company's glass division. Then he went to manage Hires & Company's Philadelphia office and warehouse. In 1911 he succeeded George Hires as president. Samuel Gilmore was president from 1926 to 1936, at which time William Plummer Jr. took over from 1936 to 1963. The company's main offices are in Wilmington, Delaware, and it is one of the nation's leading distributors of architectural glass.

quirk A pane of glass in the shape of an equilateral parallelogram with oblique angles.

quoniam A drinking cup.

R The trademark placed on cut glass made by Roden Bros. Ltd.

radial gadroon See *gadroon.*

radiant Design lines or figures extending outward from a central point.

Hurricane lamps, silver-plated fonts, Radiant Crystal etched shades, 24" h. Tri-State Antiques

Radiant Crystal A trademark placed on cut glass distributed by C.E. Wheelock & Company of Peoria, Illinois.

radiant star A cut-glass single-star motif in which the vanes radiating from the focus are of different lengths.

radiation controlled glass Two types of glass fall within this category: (1) *nuclear radiation absorbing glasses*—both soda-lime and lead glasses with added stabilizers so they will not darken under radioactive bombardment, used for shielding windows in hospitals, atomic laboratories, and atomic vessels); and (2) *radiation-sensitive glasses*—glasses that either glow when exposed to ultraviolet light after exposure to radiation or discolor when exposed to radiation, used as radiation indicating dosimeters.

radiolaria Microscopic single-celled organisms living alone or in colonies forming a jelly-like mass found near the surface in warm waters. They construct their skeletons of natural glass from oxidized silicon in seawater that, over time, descend to the bottom of the ocean, forming a siliceous mud (*Barbados earth*). This is used by jewelers as an abrasive for grinding and polishing precious stones. They are likely the oldest group of animal represented by fossils.

radio premium An item such as a cup or plate given away usually in exchange for a proof-of-purchase from a radio sponsor's product. Most items feature the hero of the program such as Dick Tracy, Buck Rogers, Amos & Andy, etc.

radium finish A shiny iridescent finish on Carnival glass, as opposed to the mat iridescence. A mat iridescent finish is made by spraying the glass with an iridizing agent while extremely hot. The shiny finish is made by spraying the glass while somewhat cooler.

Radium glass A line of iridescent glassware made by the Millersburg Glass Co., introduced in 1911 and having the appearance of metal. It consisted of novelty and specialty items.

Radium Glass Co. See *Millersburg Glass Co.*

Radnt A pressed, heat-resistant glassware for use in the kitchen, made by H.P. Sinclaire & Co. in the mid-1920s.

Raffaelesche See *grotesques.*

rafraichissoir (1) A receptacle for cooling foods or beverages, usually consisting of a large goblet-like vessel into which a smaller one is suspended in a metal mount. Ice is placed in the large vessel, surrounding the inner one, cooling its contents. See *caviar bowl.* (2) A monteith or large punch bowl. See *monteith.* (3) A cylindrical bowl used for cooling a single wine glass.

railroad flask A flask made in the United States in the 19th century picturing a horse-drawn or steam-powered railway coach or engine. Some have the slogan "Success to the Railroad" in raised letters on the side. They were made mainly of green or amber glass in full-size two-piece molds.

Rainbow A Tiffany *Reactive Glass* pattern.

Rainbow Art A trademark used by the Viking Glass Co.

Rainbow Art Glass Company A
glass manufacturing facility established in 1942 in Huntington, West Virginia, by Henry Manus, making small, hand-fashioned and decorative ware of opal, spatter, cased, and crackle glass. Crackle glass was made until the company burned in the 1960s; none was made since it was rebuilt. It decorated glassware for other companies. In the early 1970s, Viking Glass acquired it, continuing to make small animals. When it went out of business, the "Rainbow" name was purchased by an employee and is now operated as Rainbow Glass Inc., Proctorville, Ohio. See *New Martinsville Glass (Manufacturing) Co.*

Rainbow (iridescent) glassware
(Aka *Iris iridescent glassware, New Bronze glassware*) An iridescent glassware with rainbow hues, patented by Frederick Shirley in 1878 and made by the Mt. Washington Glass Co. See *Iris glass.*

Rainbow Lustre See *stretch glass.*

raised diamond cutting A decorative cut-glass pattern made with a mitered wheel to cut parallel diagonal grooves close together, the top edges being common to two adjacent grooves. These grooves were crossed at right angles with a similar series of parallel adjacent grooves, resulting in an overall surface pattern of raised four-sided diamonds in pyramidal form, each having a sharp pinnacle. Although the pattern is usually cut diagonally, it is sometimes cut in a horizontal-vertical grid. The pattern is often found on Anglo-Irish glassware made between 1780 and 1825. See *hollow diamond cutting; strawberry diamond cutting; hobnail cutting; cross-cut diamonds.*

Rakka glassware See *Raqqa glassware.*

ramarro, vetro (Italian) Literally, *lizard glass.* A glass with a green mottled surface designed by Ercole Barovier for Barovier & Toso.

Ranftbecher (German) A low beaker with a tapering or waisted body on a thick-cut cogwheel base, typically embellished with transparent enameling and gilding. They were made in Vienna about 1815 to 1828, in Biedermeier style, often embellished with enameling. Some were wheel engraved in Bohemia and elsewhere.

range A narrow piece of glass remaining after cutting sheet glass stock.

range set A group of items specifically for use in the kitchen, usually consisting of a covered grease or dripping jar and oversize salt and pepper shakers.

ranter A large beer jug.

Rapp, Henry B. See *Kensington Glass Works.*

Raqqa glassware A Sryrian-Islamic glassware identified with, but not necessarily made at, Raqqa (Rakka), a city in modern Iraq. Many items identified as Raqqa glassware were probably made at Aleppo or Damascus. It was made during the Islamic period, from about 1170 to 1270, and included beakers of clear glass embellished with gilding and enameling, often with inscriptions in various colors. A characteristic feature is a diaper pattern of dots in white and/or turquoise blue. See *Eight Priests, Goblet of the; Islamic enameling; Syrian glass.*

Rare-Earth (Doped) Glasses A German chemist named Auer experimented with placing rare earth elements in the glass batch. In the early 1920s, rare earth oxides became commercially available, but because they were comparatively weak colorants, high concentrations are required to produce moderately weak shading. This, plus their high costs, limited their use to moderately expensive art glass. The Moser firm was the first to make Rare-Earth Glasses in quantities of any magnitude. The rare earths used were neodymium (Nd) to produce a red violet color or brownish-red color; prasedymium (Pr) to produce a greenish yellow; lanthanum (La); and combinations of these to produce other colors. The glasses change their apparent color depending on the background illumination and thickness of the glass and generally found in art deco or modern styles.

raspberry prunt (Aka *dotted prunt*) A flat circular prunt with a relief design, having the appearance of a raspberry, impressed on it using a special tool. They were used as embellishment on several types of German glasses, including the *Romer*, *Stangenglas* or *Warzenbecher*, and on some hollow stems of drinking glasses made by George Ravenscroft and others. The German term is *Beerennuppen*. See *strawberry prunt*.

ratafia glass (Aka *flute cordials*) A drinking glass used for drinking *ratafia* (a liqueur flavored with almonds and fruit kernels), popular during the second half of the 18th century. It is a flute glass made in two styles: (a) with a narrow, tall funnel shaped bowl and (b) with a thin cylindrical-shaped bowl with a rounded bottom, both having a stemmed foot. The stem is sometimes embellished with an opaque twist; the bowl sometimes with light fluting and/or engraved floral designs or border. The capacity of the bowl is between one to 1-1/2 fluid ounces.

Rautenglas German glassware having simple cutting made in the 1930s.

Ravenna Flint Glass Company A glass manufacturing facility established in 1822 in Ravenna, Ohio, making lamp chimneys, hollowware, and other glassware. In 1885 it was purchased by the Crown Flint Glass Co.

Ravenna glass An ornamental glass made by Orrefors Glasbruk, developed about 1947 by Sven Palmqvist, tinted in transparent colors and used for making heavy objects. The glass is inlaid with abstract patterns in brilliant hues, giving a mosaic effect. See *Ravenna technique*.

Ravenna Glass Company A window and bottle glass manufacturing facility established in 1857 or 1864, depending on the source, in Ravenna, Ohio, and incorporated in 1867 by George Robinson, D.C. Coolman, J.D. Horton, F.W. Coffin, and H.H. Stevens. It traded as the Diamond Glass Company. It was still operating in 1885.

Raven's Head A seal bearing a raven's head in relief. George Ravenscroft was first permitted to use this in 1677 on glass he made for the Glass Sellers' Company, in recognition of his contributions in the development of lead glass (offering assurances as to the quality of the new glass).

Ravenscroft, George (1632-1683) An English glass technician who perfected the process for making lead glass. He was a merchant dealing in glass in London and Venice. In 1673 he established a glass manufacturing facility at the Savoy in London where, after eight months of experimentation, he successfully made a *crystalline glass*. In 1674 he obtained a patent permitting him to make it for seven years. He made an arrangement with the Glass Sellers' Company to set up a second facility at Henley-on-Thames and sell his entire production of *crystalline glass* to it. Due to an overabundance of potash in the batch, originally introduced in excess to assist fusing, the new glass developed the defect called *crisselling*. To counteract this, he introduced a lead oxide in lieu of additional silica, and, by 1676, succeeded in making lead glass on a commercial basis. To acknowledge his achievement, in 1677 the company agreed that the new glass be impressed with the Raven's Head seal. He retired from the Henley facility in 1678. He was succeeded by his brother, Francis, and his associate, Hawley Bishopp, who succeeded him at the Savoy in 1682. Lead glass was finally perfected for mass commercial production in 1681.

raw Materials that have not been processed.

rayed Arrows or spoke-like designs often found on the bottoms of glasses, i.e., rays emanating in all directions from a central point.

rayed base A single star motif when placed on the bottom of a vase, pitcher, or other article.

razor hone (sharpener) A contrivance used to sharpen razor blades. They usually consist of a flat base on which a glass arc is mounted. The blade is placed within the arc—

with the edges to be sharpened toward the glass—and honed by moving it back and forth with light pressure, then gently stroking each of the edges against the glass, restoring the blade and prolonging its life. They were popular during the 1920s and 1930s. Fenton made some.

Reactive Glass See *Tiffany Reactive Glass.*

Reading Artistic Glass Works (1884-1886) A glass manufacturing facility established by Lewis Kremp in Reading County, Pennsylvania, which made many items, including spittoons and whimsical canes, in several opalescent colors and traditional flint colors. Some glassware had either mottled, overshot, or craquille finishes.

realgar glass A glass made in imitation of *realgar*, an almost pure form of arsenic disulfide—an orange-red mineral, poisonous to the touch, used in China to make figures of Taoist deities in the belief it contained the germ of gold. Realgar glass was made in China in the 18th century It was used to make figures, snuff bottles, cups, and vases.

Vertical-ribbed reamer, 5" d.
Davanna Collection

Orange reamer, c. 1930-1940, opaque white glass.
The Corning Museum of Glass

reamer A juicer; an object used to squeeze juice from citrus fruits; a dish or shallow bowl with a ridged or fluted dome in the center. Reamers are footed or flat bottomed, all with handles opposite or at right angles to a pouring lip. They were made in numerous styles and colors by many manufacturers. One of the largest was McKee, pressing them from many types of glass. Other major makers were Fry, Hazel Atlas, and Hocking.

reamy texture (Aka *Danziger texture*) A textured design on glass, mainly stained glass, consisting of a swirling surface undulation.

Recessed ware, clear glass stoppered bottle, gold label with black lettering, signed "W.T. & Co."
Davanna Collection

recessed ware The most decorative of all medicine containers designed to hold tinctures and other medicinal products, patented by Whitall Tatum on April 2, 1889, but made prior to then. Previously, the edged-in-gold lettered glass labels on medicine bottles were subject to chipping, being raised above the glass surface of the bottle. Recessed ware had a recessed rectangular space for a glass label in the bottle. A thin piece of glass, the size of the recess, was bent and annealed. Then the pharmaceutical name was etched backward on the concave (inner side) of the label, the letters edged in gold leaf. The label was affixed in the recess with resin and beeswax, leaving the bottles with a smooth, flush surface. In 1902 Whitall Tatum was making them in blue and clear glass. Because their making was a labor-intensive hand process, production ceased once less expensive machine blowing became an established practice. In the 1930s, when George M. Scattergood joined Whitall Tatum, he revived making them. They were lettered in Lancaster, Pennsylvania. The U.S. was a major customer. When used on ships during World War II, they proved to be a hazard to the personnel in sickbays. The Navy cancelled their contract and manufacturing ceased.

rectangular bottle A four-sided bottle of rectangular horizontal section. Some have one or two angular flat-reeded handles extending from the sloping shoulder to just below the mouth.

recuperation The technique used to introduce preheated air into a combustion chamber. The air is heated by passing it near or around ducts carrying the exhaust gases, improving the efficiency of combustion and reducing fuel consumption since the air does not have to be raised from ambient to the desired temperature. See *regeneration*.

Red Aurene A name erroneously used for *Rouge Flambe* glass. See *Aurene*.

red glass Glass that has developed a red color as the result of adding an oxide of gold, iron, or copper to the batch. See *gold ruby glass; ruby glass*.

red lead Lead oxide, red; *minium*; lead tetroxide; Pb_3O_4. The essential ingredient used in making lead glass. See *litharge*.

red staining Techniques developed by Friedrich Egermann using a red stain made from copper.

Red-Cliff Company (1950-1980) A Chicago, Illinois, firm distributing quality reproductions of old flint glass patterns and old decorated china. In the late 1960s-early 1970s, it contracted with Fenton Art Glass to make goblets based on five early glass designs from molds it owned. Each piece was clearly marked "Red-Cliff," together with the company logo, on the bottom of the foot. When Red-Cliff closed, Fenton kept the goblet molds as a part of the debt settlement.

Reddick, McKee & Company See *Acme Glass Works*.

Redford (Crown) Glass Works A company established in 1830 in Redford, New York, which built a crown glass manufacturing facility in March 1831. It was incorporated in April 1832 by Charles W. and Gurdon Corning, Gershom Cook, and John S. Foster, who left the Champlain Glass Works to supervise it. He left at the end of 1832 to form the Redwood Glass Works. In 1836 the name became Cook, Lane & Corning. It was closed from 1843 to 1846. In 1846 Matthew, Lane & Company reopened it, operating it until late 1851/early 1852.

Redstone Glass Works See *New Albany Glass Works*.

reducing atmosphere A non-oxidizing condition existing in a glass furnace. The atmosphere in the furnace is rich in carbon monoxide, made as a result of insufficient oxygen available for complete combustion, affecting the glass in a crucible. A reducing atmosphere is needed for a red color to be produced by the introduction of copper, as cuprous oxide, into the batch. It is in contrast to an oxidizing (smokeless) atmosphere. The effect of a reducing atmosphere was known in the 7th century BC by glassmakers in Mesopotamia. Various methods have been used to attain such an atmosphere. The Chinese commonly used wet wood in the furnace.

Redwood Glass Manufacturing Co. See *Redwood Glass Works*.

Redwood Glass Works A window glass manufacturing facility established in Alexandria, New York in 1833 by John S. Foster, formerly with the South Boston Crown Glass Co.,1824; Champlain Glass Works, 1827; and Redford Glass Works, 1830. Schmauss & Co. was the first to operate the company after Foster's death in 1834. Between 1835 and 1844, the following companies operated it: Gerlach & Son; Ingleson, Forbes & Co.; and H.S. White. In 1844 DeZeng & Co. took over and, in 1853, the Redwood Glass Manufacturing Co. was formed, operating until after 1877.

Reed, L.S., & Brother See *Kentucky Glass Works*.

Reed & Barton A silver company specializing in silver deposit glass and china.

Reed & Moulds See *Jersey (City) Glass Company.*

Reed, Allen, Cox & Company; Reed, Shinn & Company
See *Lancaster Glass Works.*

reeding (Aka *ribbing*) Relief ornamentation in the form of a series of parallel convex reeds or ribs; the converse of fluting.

refined glass An exceptionally fine, smooth, pure glass in which impurities have been removed to the greatest extent possible in preparing the batch, and bubbles and imperfections eliminated while preparing the product. See *malfin glass.*

refining See *fining.*

refining agent A substance added to the batch, acting as an accelerator and/or decolorizing agent; increasing homogeneity by providing a mixing action in the melting operation; and reducing inherent seeds by producing large bubbles to which small bubbles adhere as they rise to the surface. In the past, one of the main refining agents was arsenic oxide, now replaced largely by antimony oxide. Others are calumite, sodium sulfate, and barium sulfate.

Reformation beaker A Humpen with a cover, commemorating the beginning of the Reformation in 1517. Embellishment depicts the seated figures of Martin Luther, Phillip Melanchthon, and two Dukes of Saxony. It was made in Germany in the mid-17th century.

refraction The change in direction of light when rays pass from one medium to another.

refractive index See *index of refraction.*

refractory blocks Special construction blocks used for lining glass furnaces, developed specifically for the industry because of the unusually severe conditions encountered in the furnace. Sintered zircon, alumina, mullite, mullite-alumina, electrocast zirconia-alumina-silica, and chrome-alumina are typical blocks. The latest practice in regenerative furnaces uses basic refractories because of

alkali dust and vapors. Furnace operating temperatures are limited mainly by silica brick crowns, which are economical to use.

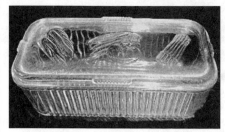

Refrigerator dish with molded vegetables on lid, 8-1/2" w. x 3-1/4" l. x 4" d.
Davanna Collection

refrigerator ware Dishes, often with a cover, used for storing food in the refrigerator. They were often made in bright colors and in stackable sets. They were popular during the 1930s through the 1950s. At present most are plastic, but glass and metal ones are still available.

Regency style An English decorative style—a variation of the French Empire style—evident in chandeliers and other glassware. They prevailed between 1811 and 1830, during part of the reign of George III when the affairs of the Crown were in the hands of the Prince Regent, later George IV. In everyday usage, the dates extend before and after these dates. Generally during this period, the rendering of classical subjects lacked the lightness of the earlier neoclassical and Adam styles and tended to be pompous and heavy. Egyptian motifs belong mainly to this period and tend to mark the renewal of interest in ancient Egypt following Napoleon's campaign there in 1798.

regeneration A process using waste heat from the furnace to preheat the air used as a source of combustion. It differs from recuperation, which takes the heat from the exhaust gases and transfers it to the burner air on a continuous basis. The regeneration process does the same on a cyclic basis. It involves passing the hot gases over refractory blocks. Once hot, the exhaust gases are passed through another regenerator and ambient air passes over the hot blocks to the burner. This is reversed every few minutes to ensure a constant supply of preheated air to the burners.

regenerative furnace See *Wanne.*

Rehoboam See *wine bottle, Sizes.*

Reichsadler *(German)* The Imperial double-headed eagle picturing the coats of arms of dukes, electors, etc., a frequently used motif used during the 17th and 18th centuries on German glassware.

Reichsadlerhumpen *(German)* Literally, *Imperial Eagle beaker.* A tall Humpen embellished with an enameled black double-headed Imperial Eagle of the Holy Roman Empire, with its wings outspread. There are 56 shields, in groups of four, representing the constituents of the Empire. On early ones (about 1751 to 1599), a crucifix is superimposed on the neck of the eagle. On later ones (about 1585), an orb (about 1670 to 1676) or portraits of Emperor Leopold I with his sons or the seven or eight Electors and an inscription, "The Holy Roman Empire and its Member States." On the reverse of some from the 16th century, there is an enameled *Brazen Serpent.* Some later ones have floral designs. The same designs appear on some goblets, mugs, Stangenglas, and bottles. Some have a cover that is often missing or is broken. Similar ones were made in Bohemia and Franconia in the late 16th century and elsewhere in the 17th century. See *German enameling.*

Reid, J.E., & Company A glass cutting house in Rochester, Minnesota, operating for a short period around 1909/1910.

Reighard, Jacob Reighard invented and patented the first glass font for lamps with a separate orifice for adding fuel without unscrewing and raising the burner and wick. He assigned his patent to Hale, Atterbury & Company, the first to make glass fonts with a separate fill opening.

Reisinger, Wells & Co. A glass manufacturing facility beginning operations prior to 1850, in Birmingham (Pittsburgh), Pennsylvania. Owned by E.C. Schmertz, it was still operating in 1886.

re-issue An article or pattern made at a later date from the mold used in the original production.

Reitz & Everhart See *Baltimore Glass Works.*

release agent A substance used on the inside of a mold to ensure the object being cast will separate from the mold without causing damage.

relic (1) An object, custom, etc., that has survived, wholly or partially, from the past. (2) An object of historic interest because of its age and association with the past, or that serves as a keepsake or souvenir. (3) Remaining fragments, surviving parts, or ruins of something from the past. (4) Some personal memorial of a saint, martyr, or other sacred person.

relief An embellishment protruding, in varying heights, above the main body of the object. The degree to which it protrudes is given one of three general classifications: high, medium, and low relief. It is made by cutting, wheel engraving, etching, sandblasting, and molding. Wheel engraving in relief is called *cameo engraving* or *carving* when executed on cased glass. See *cameo glass; Hochschnitt; Tiefschnitt; wheel engraving, relief; high relief; low relief; medium relief; intaglio; dolce relievo glassware.*

relief, hollow See *intaglio.*

relief, soft See *dolce relievo glassware.*

relief diamond The cut glass motif known as *nailhead diamond.* See *diamond.*

relief jug A small jug or phial (vial) made in the form of an animal or fruit by Syrian glassblowers in the 2nd and 3rd centuries A.D.

relief wheel engraving See *wheel engraving, Relief.*

reliquary A small box, casket, goblet-like receptacle, etc., for keeping or displaying a religious relic. Some were designed and made for a specific purpose. Some are tall and cylindrical, having a cover with a finial in the form of a cross. Others adapted for this purpose were made in Germany, France, and the Netherlands in the 15th and 16th centuries in the form of a beaker or *Krautstrunk*. Many were made at Murano and Hall-in-Tyrol, from the 16th century. See *sealed reliquary*.

Four compartment relish dish, green, 7-1/4" d.
Davanna Collection

relish dish (Aka *pickle dish*) An oblong or elongated dish to serve relishes, made in many shapes and sizes—three by six inches to seven by fifteen inches.

Rensselaer Glass Factory (1806-1853) A crown and cylinder window-glass manufacturing facility established by Jeremiah Van Rensselaer, Elkanah Watson, George Pearson, and James Kane (of the Hamilton Manufacturing Society), operators of the Albany Glass Works (House) at Glass Lake (Rensselear Village, now Sand Lake), New York. In late 1812, the crown glass part burned, was rebuilt and in operation in January 1913. In February 1816, after the cylinder part burned, it was auctioned. The buyer operated it until 1819, selling it to Crandell, Fox & Co., which failed in 1824. In 1825 Richard J. Knowlson purchased it; in late 1826 it began making window glass. In April 1830 it was incorporated as Rensselear Glass Manufacturing Company by Knowlson, Daniel M. Gregory, and Isaac B. Fox and was leased to some South Jersey glassblowers. John B. Schmauss & Co. operated it for a short period in 1834. Soon thereafter William and John Gabler bought it, selling it in 1835 to Stadler, Rush & Co. In 1838 it failed and sold to Albert R. and Samuel H. Fox, who

operated it until 1853 when it burned and was not rebuilt. (There are a variety of histories associated with this facility. The time frames the various owners operated it vary, as well as the order of ownership. However, the names of the various owners are consistent, and the above order seems to be the most realistic with respect to the dates.)

Reppert, George & Jacob
See *Baltimore Glass Works*.

reproduction A close copy of a genuine old glass object, made without any intent to deceive. There is usually some distinctly identifiable differences between the original and copy. Some have been made where the original is unique and known to be a museum piece, such as the Portland Vase. See *fake; forgery*.

reptile paperweight A large group of paperweights that represent, or have as a central motif, various reptiles, such as salamanders, snakes, and lizards. The reptile was sometimes enclosed within a dome; molded or hand worked and affixed to the weight, either on the dome or on a flat base; or molded in the shape of a reptile.

resist A preparation used to protect glass from acid during the etching process. The surface of the glass not covered with the resist is etched by the acid, forming the sunken parts of the design. Resists include beeswax and resin, paraffin wax and motor oil, bitumin and a solvent, etc.

resonance The quality of returning sound, such as the ring produced when certain glass, particularly lead glass, is struck. It is sometimes considered a test for forgery but is not the ultimate indicator, since glass other than lead glass, such as barium glass, is also resonant. Resonance in glassware depends not only on the type of glass but also on whether the shape of the object permits free vibrations when struck, i.e., a drinking glass as distinguished from a decanter. Some forms of drinking glass do not resonate.

reticella bowl A bowl made from the 3rd century B.C. to the 1st century A.D. While many theories have been proposed regarding their method of manufacture, they consist of fine threads of twisted glass fused together and molded in the shape of a bowl. The threads are placed around the circumference of the bowl or arranged in parallel lines across the bowl and fitted with a rim.

reticelli glassware Mosaic glassware having a lace-like appearance.

reticello, vetro a Literally, *glass with small network*. A glass embellished with opaque white or colored threads of glass or both, embedded in clear glass in a crisscrossed diagonal design giving the appearance of a diamond lattice network, originally made in Murano. The embellishment is a type of filigrana (sometimes called *latticino*) decoration. Some of the terms formerly used at Murano for this glass are *a redexalo* and *a redexin*.

There are three varieties: (a) that made with fine threads; (b) that with coarse threads; and (c) that with both, running in opposite directions. It has been used on vases, jugs, etc., and on plates where the network becomes distorted toward the center or edge. A descriptive term is *network glass* as distinguished from *lace glass*. See *retorti, vetro a; trina, vetro di.*

Several processes for making this glass have been described, and several methods have been used over the years in Murano. Following are the most common methods of production: (1) A bulb or cylinder of glass blown in a mold on which parallel threads of glass (almost always opaque white threads) are running diagonally in one direction, having been picked up on a gather. This is then blown into another bulb or cylinder with threads running diagonally in the opposite direction. The two bulbs or cylinders become fused together. The threads on each bulb must be equidistant so that, when fused, they will form equal and similar diamond shapes, except for distortions tending to form toward the extremities of the glass. (2) A bulb of glass is made with diagonal threads and folded in half, and the two halves are fused together, making the crisscrossed threads. This method assures equal spacing of the threads but is difficult to make. (3) A bulb of glass is made with diagonal threads, and the glassblower sucks on the tube to remove the air from the bulb, collapsing it to a flat disk, making a double wall of crisscrossed threads.

(4) A bulb of glass is made with diagonal threads; it is then cut and twirled to make, by centrifugal force, a flat plate. Another plate is made with diagonal threads in the opposite direction and the two are fused together. In all these methods there tends to develop, within the spaces made by the crossed threads, small, sometimes microscopic, air bubbles, which occasionally become elongated, forming thin wavy lines. Sometimes the enclosed areas have unequal sides. After the piece is made it is reheated, blown, and manipulated into various forms (vases, jugs, plates, etc.).

reticulated (1) Manipulated trails of glass appearing as an open network or *knitting*, originally a 16th to 18th century Venetian technique used in friggers and Nailsea type novelties. See *filigrana; reticello, vetro a.* (2) A diamond or ogival pattern-molded design. See *ogival.*

reticulated glassware Glassware on which embellishment has the appearance of, or is in the form of, networking. There are several varieties: (a) objects embellished with embedded glass threads forming an overall network or lattice pattern, such as *vetro a reticello*, or a similar pattern made by wheel engraving or cutting; (b) objects having an openwork net that is undercut, such as the cage cup (*vasa diatreta*) or *situla pagana*; (c) objects made of glass strands pincered together to form a mesh (see *traforato*); and (d) objects covered with or blown into wire netting (see *netted glassware*). This includes ware made by Tiffany, where glass (often opaque jade-green glass) was blown into a network of heavy *Tiffany Green* bronzed wire with wide apertures so the glass protruded slightly in spaces formed between the wires.

retort An apparatus for distilling liquids, of ovoid or globular shape with a long thin attenuated spout extending from the upper part of the body, downward to a receptacle placed at its end to catch the distilled liquid. Sometimes there is a stoppered orifice near the top of the body, used for filling. Its rounded bottom rests on a circular metal stand, under which is a heat source. As the liquid in the retort is heated, the vapors rise, entering the spout, cooling and running down to the container below. Impurities or higher boiling liquids remain in the retort. Many have a place to insert a thermometer. By knowing the boiling point of the liquids in a mixture, one can tell which liquid is being distilled at a particular temperature.

retorti, vetro a (Aka *vetro a retortoli*) Literally, *glass with twists*. Clear glass in which is embedded twisted threads of glass, originally made at Murano where it is usually called *zanfirico* or *sanfirico*. It has parallel adjacent canes (vertical or spiral) made by flattening and fusing them together. It includes embellishments made with opaque white or colored threads or both, embedded in the fused canes. It is included in the general terms *filigrana* (*filigree*) and *latticino* when only white threads are used. See *reticello, vetro a; vetro di trina; striped glass.*

retortoli, vetro a See *retorti, vetro a.*

Reuben line A line of glassware designed by Reuben Haley for Consolidated Lamp & Glass. The molds were owned by Haley and, when Consolidated closed in 1932, Haley's son, Kenneth, took them to Phoenix Glass where he worked from 1928 to 1934. He and his father (d.1933) received a commission on sales from Phoenix. Glassware made from these molds, called the *Reuben line,* from late 1933 to early 1936. Phoenix had difficulties achieving the finishes produced at Consolidated—Phoenix pieces have single-color highlighting over a crystal base—and the line was only moderately successful. Today pieces are difficult to find, as is identification, because the paper labels reading "Phoenix—Reuben Line" have mostly disappeared. The line is considered to be the genesis of its *Sculptured Glass.* When Consolidated Lamp & Glass reopened in 1936, Haley returned the molds for their use. See *Martele.*

reverberatory furnace (Aka *reverberatory kiln* or *oven*) An early glass melting furnace dating to the 7th century B.C. It is somewhat paraboloid in shape, made so the heat created by the burning fuel was reflected downward toward the pots arranged around the inside. Above the pots were openings (*bocche*; see *bocca*) through which the workmen inserted rods to extract the molten glass. Some had a small hole, called a *glory hole*, used for reheating a partially made glass object for further manipulation or for fire polishing.

reverse amberina A piece of amberina where the ruby color is on the lower part of the piece, shading to amber at the top; the reverse of amberina. To create this, the bottom of the piece had to be held in the flame.

reverse engraving See *transfer engraving.*

reverse foil engraving Embellishment of glass in which gold or silver leaf is applied to the reverse of a piece, engraved, and covered with varnish, another type of metal foil, or piece of glass.

reverse glass painting See *reverse painting on glass.*

reverse painting on glass Painting on glass in reverse so the front of the glass remains clear and smooth and the painting is on the back. Details are painted first, progressing to the background, which is always painted first in traditional paintings. They date to the early 1700s and were popular during the early and mid-1800s. They were made by German immigrants. At the turn of the 20h century, reverse painting on glass was often used on advertising mirrors. On early ones, tinsel was often used as the background, combined with particles of butterfly wings, floss of milkweed, mother-of-pearl, or textured materials and were called *tinsel paintings* or *crystal paintings.*

revolving server (Aka *Lazy Susan*) A server with one or two flat trays that revolve around a central post and on which may be placed several serving bowls, making it easier for guests to see and partake of the offerings on it, eliminating passing bowls.

Reyen & Schaning (1912-1918) A glass cutting company established in 1912 in Brooklyn, New York.

Rhodes glassware Glassware made on Rhodes, an island in the Aegean Sea off the coast of Turkey, as early as the 7th century B.C. by migrant Mesopotamian glassworkers. The vessels made were core-formed flasks of typical Greek shapes of the period.

The facilities closed in the late 5th century B.C. About the middle of the 4th century B.C. new facilities were built and core-formed vessels were again made. By the late 3rd century B.C., Rhodes had the only remaining glasshouses in the area, making beads, pendants, and a few gold sandwich-glass vessels.

rhyton *(Greek)* A drinking cup usually in the form of a head of a person or animal, tapering to a rounded or pointed bottom, so it could stand only when inverted. Some were made in the form of a drinking horn. Some were made of Persian glass during the Achae-menid dynasty and also of Roman glass.

rib mold A pattern mold for bottles, bowls, etc., scored in heavy vertical ribbing.

ribbed bowl See *pillar molded bowl.*

ribbing See *reeding; pillar molding.*

ribbon glassware (1) Glassware embellished with alternating narrow or wide bands of opaque white glass (lattimo). It may be vertical, horizontal, or spiral. It is found on some Venetian glass made in the 16th and 17th centuries. (2) Glassware consisting of rolled clear glass, having parallel ribs on one surface. (3) Glassware made by fusing strips and/or rods of glass together and slumping the resultant mass over a form.

ribbon machine See *lightbulb.*

Rice & Johnson (1841-1843) A glass manufacturing facility established in Harrisburg, New York, making tableware with lily pad embellishment and some bottles.

Rice Harris & Son See *Islington Glass Works.*

Richard & Hartley Flint Glass Company A glass manufacturing facility making window glass, lighting fixtures and, later, specializing in pressed glassware. The company was established in 1866 or 1869 (depending on source) by Joseph Richards and William T. Hartley in Pittsburgh, Pennsylvania. In 1884 it moved to Tarentum, Pennsylvania, and was renamed the Tarentum Glass Company. See *Tarentum Glass Company.*

Richards, Jesse See *Batsto Glass Works; New Columbia Glass Works.*

Richards, Thomas, Samuel and Thomas Jr. See *Jackson Glass Works; Lebanon Glass Works.*

Richards & Brookdale See *New Columbia Glass Works.*

Richards & Brothers See *Jackson Glass Works.*

Richter, Paul, Company (1914-1940) A glass cutting house established by Paul Richter in 1914 in Maywood, Illinois. In 1920 it expanded to include pottery and general merchandise in addition to glass cutting. It purchased its blanks from Libbey-Owens. Richter perfected an acid bath formula that remained his closely guarded secret. The company's trademark was *Maywood Cut.*

Ricketts, Henry In 1821 in England, Ricketts patented (patent no. 4623) a mold blowing method for making glass bottles. It used a foot-operated *open-and-shut* metal mold that shaped the entire bottle, including the string rim, in one operation. The process has not changed over time but is now mechanized. Ricketts was also, in all probability, the first modern manufacturer to mark his bottles. On the bottom was molded "H. Ricketts & Co. Glass Works Bristol."

Ridgway & Co. See *Rockville Glass Works.*

Ridley Goblet A goblet of clear purple glass with a flaring mouth and three equidistant rings of trailed glass around the bowl, resting on a silver-footed stem. It is believed to have been associated with Bishop Ridley of Oxford (d. 1555).

rigaree An applied decoration of trailing where a ribbon of glass is impressed by a wheel into parallel notches in the body of an object. The ribbons are tooled in parallel lines forming tiny continuous ribs or ruffled collars. It was used on some Victorian art glass.

rim The narrow area on the edge of a vessel, found on such objects as plates, vases, cups, etc. Rims may be embellished with enameling, gilding, engraving, cutting, applied wrought decoration, etc. See the following types of rims: *folded; basal; foot; string; galleried; turn over; Van Dyke; arcaded.*

rim pattern A pattern encircling the rim of an object. It may be cut, engraved, gilded, enameled, etc.; some of the most popular are bull's-eye, rope, serrated, or scalloped.

ring (1) An ornamental circlet to be worn on the finger. Some were made of glass since ancient times. Larger rings were made as bangles and armlets. See *thumb ring.* (2) The sound made when certain glass objects are struck gently by another object. The type of glass and shape of the object are important to the nature of the ring. The highest quality ring will be made by a wide mouth object or a flat object, such as a bowl or plate, made from lead or barium glass. See *resonance.*

ring beaker A German beaker embellished with attached glass loops from which are suspended glass rings.

ring casing A process for providing a border ring casing of gold ruby or other clear transparent colors for engraving or etched decoration. It was developed by Frederick Carder and consisted of blowing a cylinder of colored glass about two inches in diameter and 12 to 18 inches long. After annealing, the cylinder was cut into rings of desired width, usually from one to 1-1/4 inches. They were reheated and applied to the paraison, which was completed by offhand blowing. It was then usually cut or engraved.

ring flask A circular flask, often embellished with prunts and a molded pattern, with a small hole through the center. They were made in France and Germany during the 17th and 18th centuries.

ring holder See *stick dish.*

ring mold (Aka *finish mold*) A mold used in making bottles to form a *finish*, in conjunction with a paraison mold. It formed a completed *finish*, permitting the paraison to be placed in a final mold and blown into a completed bottle. See *bottles, 19th century.*

ring-necked decanter Decanters with long necks encircled by two or more rings of applied glass. They were common in England and made the decanter easier to hold.

ring tray See *stick dish.*

Ring trees; left: 2" x 3" single pole with tray; right: 8-1/2" h. multi-limb tree in cobalt blue.
Davanna Collection

ring tree Small tree-like objects to hold rings for safekeeping, popular during the mid-Victorian era. They have a trunk, resting in a small dish, from which protrude several leafless branches to hold the rings. See *stick dish.*

Rink, Stanger & Co. See *Olive & Harmony Glassworks; Harmony Glassworks.*

Ripley (Daniel C.) & Company A glass manufacturing facility established as Ripley & Company in 1866 by Daniel C. Ripley, George Duncan, John and Jacob Strickel, Nicholas Kunzler, and Thomas Coffin in Pittsburgh, Pennsylvania. It made bar goods, flint glass tableware, lamps, and chimneys. In 1874 Ripley left and the company was renamed George Duncan & Sons. Ripley established another facility nearby, named Ripley & Company, making the same wares. In 1891 his company joined the U.S. Glass Company (*Factory "F"*). Also see *Duncan & Heisey.*

Rippenglas *(German)* A type of German glassware made in the 15th and 16th centuries in one of several forms, such as a flask, bowl, or beaker, with vertical or diagonal ribbing and sometimes a stemmed foot.

riser A channel cut or formed-in-a-mold, which allows air to escape when glass is melted or when molten glass is poured into it.

Ritchie, J. & C. See *Ritchie Glass Company.*

Ritchie Glass Company (Aka *Wheeling Flint Glass Works*) A glass manufacturing facility established in early 1829 in Wheeling, West Virginia, making cut, plain, and pressed glassware of high quality. It was the first flint glass facility to operate in the Wheeling area, established by John Ritchie and Jesse Wheat. In 1831, Wheat left to form his own company, Wheat, Price & Company. John Ritchie operated it alone for a time before selling half interest to his brother, Craig. The firm became J. & C. Ritchie. In 1834 George Wilson bought into it and the name changed to Ritchie & Wilson. At that time it added crown glass. It operated until 1837 or 1850, depending on the source, closing for financial reasons.

Ritchie & Wheat; Ritchie & Wilson See *Ritchie Glass Company.*

riverboat glasses See *steamship glasses.*

Riverside Glass House See *Duval, Isaac & Co.*

Robertson Cut Glass Co. A glass cutting company established in Catskill, New York, operating for a short period in the early 1900s.

Robi(n)son, John; Robi(n)son, J. & T.; Robi(n)son, Anderson & Co. See *Stourbridge Flint Glass Works.*

Robinson & Ensell The first glass manufacturing facility in the United States to make flint glass. It was established in 1807 in Pittsburgh, Pennsylvania, by George Robinson and Edward Ensell. In 1808 it was sold to Bakewell & Page, which later became Bakewell, Pears & Co. Edward Ensell remained with Bakewell & Page as superintendent. See *Bakewell & Company.*

Robinson Glass Company A glass manufacturing facility making pattern glass, established by John Robinson in 1893 in Zanesville, Ohio. In 1900 it joined the National Glass Company and was dismantled the same year.

Robinson Salt Cellar A salt cellar in the form of a bireme galley (one with two banks of oars). They were made of opalescent glass by John Robinson at the Stourbridge Flint Glass Works from about 1830 to 1836.

Robj bottles Figural bottles made in earthenware, glass, or porcelain from about 1925 to 1931 for the Robj retail store in Paris. These art deco bottles were very popular in the United States.

rocaille *(French)* Literally, *rockwork.* Ornamentation developed in France in the 18th century, characterized by forms derived from the artificial rockwork and pierced shellwork popular at the time. *Rocaille*—together with the Louis Quinze and Pompadour styles—is called *rococo* in England and the United States.

rocchetta *(Italian)* (Aka *polverina*) Soda or salts made by calcining plants that grew along the Eastern Mediterranean seaboard.

Rochester Cut Glass Company A cut glass company with showrooms in Chicago, Illinois, in 1912. The Empire Cut Glass Company and the Cut Glass Products Company also had showrooms at the same location. The location of the facility, if one existed, is unknown. It may have been only an agent or distributor for manufacturers of cut glass.

Rochester Tumbler Company (1872-1901) A glass tumbler manufacturing facility established in Rochester, Pennsylvania. In 1886 it was the largest tumbler manufacturer in the world. In 1897 it acquired exclusive rights to a new machine developed by the Toledo Glass Company for making tumblers. In 1898 it joined the National Glass Company, which assumed the rights to the machine. Also see *Fry & Scott.*

rock crystal *Natural quartz.* Usually colorless (or nearly so), mainly translucent, almost chemically pure silica (SiO_2) quartz. Its atoms are arranged in an orderly pattern, making its structure crystalline, as opposed to glass where the atoms are in a random pattern. As a result, it is generally harder than glass, depending on its composition. Glassmakers from the earliest times have sought to imitate it. It was carved in medieval Egypt, Iraq, and Persia, and somewhat later in Bohemia. It was not until Casper

Lehman(n) introduced wheel engraving on hard stones and glass that carved rock crystal diminished in popularity. A patent was granted to George Ravenscroft in England in 1674 for making a crystalline glass "resembling rock crystal."

Rock Crystal

(1) A term adopted in 1908 by the McKee Glass Company for its *imitation* cut glass. (2) A specialty of Hawkes. Intaglio cut glass where the cut areas have been polished to the original clarity of the main body rather than left silvery. See *rock crystal engraving*.

rock crystal engraving

A style of deep intaglio wheel engraving in which all parts of the engraving are polished to the same degree as the main body. This is in contrast to ordinary wheel engraving where the engraved areas were left unpolished, appearing gray or dull. It was developed in England during the 1880s and 1890s and was used extensively by Thomas Webb & Sons. Hawkes used it in the United States, calling the ware *Rock Crystal*.

Rock Crystal Glass Company

(1916-1923) A glass cutting company established in Jersey City, New Jersey.

rock crystal watch

Rock crystal was used for watch cases, popular in Europe between about 1600 and 1675. The smokey variety was rarer than the clear. The case was usually formed from two pieces of rock crystal, one hollowed for the movement. The pieces had metal frames to hold the hinges and clasp. Most outer surfaces were cut with facets or patterns; they were rarely smooth.

Rock Glass Works

See *Franklin Glass Works*.

rock ground

A ground of a paperweight having the appearance of quartz-like rockwork made of various elements—bits of glass or sulfides, mica, sand, etc. It is sometimes the sole embellishment, but often it is the ground for *snake* weights made by Baccarat. See *snake paperweight*.

Rockville Factory

(1836-1849) A bottle glass manufacturing facility established in Steubenville, Ohio, by Wells, Henry & Co. In 1846 it was taken over by Hunter, Morris & Foster.

Rockville Glass Works

A glass manufacturing facility established about 1815 by Ridgway & Co. in Rockville, north of Milford, Pennsylvania. It operated for only a short time.

rockwork

See *rocaille*.

rococo

A style of decoration that followed the baroque style in France. Its characteristic features are asymmetry of ornamentation and a litany of motifs such as rockwork, shells, flowers, foliage, and various types scroll work (often termed *C- and S- scroll*). It started in France under Louis XV (1715-74), and was simulated in Italy, Germany, Austria, and to a lesser extent in England. It was followed by the neoclassical style (aka *Adam style* or *Louis Seize style*). In France it is called *rocaille*, *style Boucher*, *style Louise Quinze*, and *style Pompadour*. It is quite apparent on wares made in Silesia (see *Silesian glassware*) from about 1725. In England the change to *rococo* was hastened by the Glass Excise Act of 1745, which imposed a tax on glass based on weight. As a result, lighter, thinner glass was used, and engraving, enameling, and gilding gained in popularity. A resurrection of rococo (*revived rococo*) took place in the 19th century under Louis-Phillipe in France. Its influence was felt in England during the 2nd quarter of the 19th century. Glassware exhibiting extravagant cutting and heavy fluting, often with cut radial stars under the bases.

rod

A solid, thin, cylindrical shaft of glass that is clear, opaque white, or monochrome colored. A cane is made from a number of rods. A rod may also be used to make filigree embellishment. The process for making a rod involves first gathering molten glass from a pot and marvering into a thin cylinder. A pontil is attached to the end opposite the gathering iron. Next the iron and pontil are pulled in opposite directions. The cylinder is drawn out into a rod, its thickness determined by two factors: the thickness of the cylinder and the distance the glass is drawn. Once formed, it is cut into usable sections. Usually it is retained for use as formed, but on occasion it is shaped in a mold to give a cross-section of a star, hexagon, silhouette, lobed figure, etc. See *mosaic rod*.

rod- and core-forming A method of making the earliest glass vessels. It involved building up a solid core of sand and clay around a rod. The core was covered with molten glass and marvered into shape. When the glass cooled, the rod was removed and the core material scraped out, leaving a hollow object. The rod by itself was frequently used to make small solid objects. See *core glass; core forming.*

Rodefer Brothers (1877-1952) Albert D., John F., and Thornton A. Rodefer purchased the National Glass Company of Bellaire, Ohio, operating under that name until 1891 when John sold his interest to his brothers. It was renamed Rodefer Brothers. In 1892 it burned and was immediately rebuilt. In 1898 Albert sold his interest to Thornton. When Thornton died in 1910, his son, C.W. Rodefer, became sole owner. The company made glass balls used on lightning rods, globes for lanterns, other parts for lights and lamps, and advertising paperweights.

Rodefer-Gleason & Company See *National Glass Company.*

Roden Bros., Ltd. A silver plate ware manufacturer in Toronto, Canada. From 1891 it made cut wares of lead glass in geometric and floral patterns.

rolled edge Glassware having an edge curved toward or away from the center.

rolled glass Sheet glass made by passing the hot metal between rollers. It is frequently patterned.

roll(er) (Aka *cocoon*) The cylinder of glass made by the blower in the cylinder glass process.

rolling pin A toy, frigger, or utilitarian object in the form of a rolling pin. They were made of so-called Nailsea glass, originally called *Bristol rollers,* during the late 18th and early 19th centuries by numerous English facilities in Nailsea and Bristol. Glass ones for shaping dough were derived from a container to hold salt.

In England from the 17th century, salt was heavily taxed because it was essential to life. It was kept in sealed containers, usually wide-mouthed cork bottles. About 1790 the first salt rollers appeared in the Bristol area. Made of dark olive-green glass tapering toward the ends, they were open at one end with a ground glass stopper to keep out dampness and prevent pilfering. The stopper and the closed end of the cylinder had glass knobs around which a cord was tied to suspend or hang it near the hearth where it was cleaned daily for good health or good luck.

As time passed, the salt disappeared and housewives used the containers to shape pastry. The sides became parallel and one of the knobs had a stoppered hole so it could be filled with hot or cold water for rolling the dough. Some were used to store flour, tea, sugar, candy, or salt. Many were made of opaque white glass, embellished with unfired painted mottoes, poetry, flowers, etc. They were popular as gifts, love tokens, and as containers for smuggling. In the United States they were generally of clear (some engraved) or painted opaque white glass and were for practical use. Most decorated ones were used for decorative purposes.

roll-on enamels A powdered color made from ground glass and placed on a marver to be picked up on a gather of hot glass.

Roman glass A broad term embracing glass made from about the 1st century B.C. to the 5th century A.D. throughout the Roman Empire, including glass made by Syrians or Alexandrians in what is now Italy, and in Gaul, the Rhineland, and possibly in England. Its wide-ranging production was largely the result of glassblowing created by the Syrians about the 1st century B.C., which became the standard within 100 years. The earliest known specimens of true blown glass are perfume bottles found in excavated sites in Sicily and southern Switzerland. Also during this period, bowls, medallions, panels, and other objects were molded from molds cut with decorative designs, and narratives were developed at about the same time as glassblowing. Mosaic glass also was made, as was some cameo glass and vases. The glass was generally colored and embellishments included trailing, blobs, threading, cold painting, gold leaf (often sandwiched between two layers of glass), enameling, cutting, and engraving.

The period of Roman glass began to deteriorate about 400 A.D. at about the same time as the Empire, tied to moving the Imperial Court from Rome to Constantinople (now Istanbul). It was under Augustus Caesar (Gaius Julius Caesar Octavianus, 63 B.C.-14 A.D.), who ruled from 27 B.C. to 14 A.D., and his successors that glassmaking became an empire-wide industry; the peak period from the 2nd to the 4th centuries A.D. The Romans, while primarily making luxury items for the wealthier in the early years of the empire, were using mold-blown techniques to create utilitarian products for the average citizen in increasing quantities by the 2nd century A.D. (see *Daphne ewer; gemstone glass; Lycurgus cup; Portland vase*). Glass had a variety of other uses, such as mosaics, pavements and exterior wall coverings. The Romans were quick to use the glassmaking techniques of others, such as blowing and molding glass for dishes, commercial storage jars, etc.

As the Empire expanded, glassmakers moved into newly acquired areas or were absorbed into the Empire by the acquisition of new territories. The products made were indicative of the needs of the peoples and the times. Styles and products changed or were adapted to meet these needs. By the 1st century A.D., window glass made by casting was being used in homes, primarily to keep out rain and cold rather than let in light.

The first glass marketers took advantage of their trade. Square jars were developed to replace the round bottom versions that wasted space and required more packing. As the Empire and the glass industry began to deteriorate in the West at the beginning of the 5th century A.D., the Roman glassmaking traditions in the eastern part of the empire continued for several hundred years. In the western part the products of the Roman glassmakers in Italy, the Rhineland, Gaul, and Belgium created the basis for glassmaking in those areas for hundreds of years.

Rome Glass Works A cylinder-glass manufacturing facility established by Oscar and Henry Granger, operating a short time in the early 1840s in Rome, New York. After abandoning this project, the Grangers moved to Saratoga Springs to establish the Mountain Glass Works. See *Granger, O.H., & Company.*

Romer (German) Developed from the Nuppenbecher, the most important of the Rhenish vessel forms. Specimens made of Waldglas in the 15th century were short beakers in the shape of an inverted cone with applied glass drops on the lower part. From the late 15th through the early 16th centuries, the flared mouth gradually developed into a hemispherical bowl, resting on a wide hollow stem with a foot formed by a glass thread wound on a glass cone. Later the foot was hollow blown with a thread of glass wound around it during the 18th century. Over the years the applied drops on the stem developed into prunts or lion's head masks. Still later the drops were sometimes drawn out into points or loops. Some bowls were embellished with enameling or diamond-point engraving. Seventeenth century Dutch specimens were large (up to 15 inches high); the bowl was made of engraved soda glass and the foot was plain and folded. They continued to be made of Waldglas into the 17th century. Later colorless glass was used. A version of the Romer was made in England by George Ravenscroft, its stem embellished with raspberry prunts. Romers are still being made, but the trailing on the foot has been replaced by close-horizontal raised mold-blown rings. It was the traditional glass for drinking white Rhine wine. The name possibly was derived from the Lower Rhenish word *roemen,* meaning *to boast.*

romkin See *rummer* (3).

rondel See *roundel.*

rope edge An edge on some glass bowls or dishes and some mosaic ware made in ancient Rome from about 100 B.C. to 100 A.D. It was made by applying a cable of patterned cane, often with a white thread along the rim. A similar type appears on the foot rim of some Chinese bowls made during the K'ang Hsi period (1662-1722); the rope is a twisted single thread crudely joined to form a complete circle.

roquetta A marine plant native to Egypt and the Near East. The ash of this plant was used as a source of soda, the alkali needed to make early glass. See *barilla; glasswort.*

Rosaline glass (1) A pink or rose-colored type of Jade glass made by Steuben. Some pieces were embellished with engraved designs. See *Jade glass.* (2) A pink slag glass made by Fenton Art Glass in 1977 and 1978. Production was stopped because the batch tended to erode the pots.

rose (1) A decorative motif used in some canes in millefiori glassware and in some paperweights. See *Jersey rose; Kaziun rose.* (2) A replica of the flower made in glass, sometimes enclosed within a dome to form a paperweight.

Rose, Augustus Born in Gibson, New York, he finished his cutting training in the late 1890s and was employed at T.G. Hawkes & Co. before leaving in late 1906 to establish a cutting shop (combined with a grocery store) in Gibson. His brother, Frank, assisted him.

Rose Amber A shaded ware made from 1884 to 1958 by the Mt. Washington Glass Co. and its later owners, Pairpoint and Gundersen. New England Glass had patented the ware as *Amberina* prior to Mt. Washington using the same name. New England Glass sued Mt. Washington and a settlement was reached when Mt. Washington agreed to call their ware *Rose Amber.* The name was first used in 1884, and trademark papers were granted on May 25, 1886. Gold was used in the batch to produce the ruby color. After the metal was formed into an article, it was partially reheated at the glory hole. The reheated portion turned from amber to red, and if reheated further, the red turned to fushia-red. The portion not reheated remained amber. The ware was plain blown or pattern molded in the expanded diamond or inverted thumbprint patterns; some pieces were acid etched and engraved. The newer *Rose Amber* by Pairpoint and Gundersen has color very much like the original, from transparent amber to ruby and engraved with initials, names, and dates. Some pieces are signed "Libby," purposely misspelled to avoid legal action by the Libbey Glass Company.

Cased (white interior) cranberry rose bowl, 4" h.
Davanna Collection

Rose bowl, opalescent swirl, blue ground.
Krause Publications

rose bowl Spherical bowls having a somewhat flattened top and bottom and small circular opening in the top, the edge of which is often crimped or pinched. They are usually filled with water to just above the mid point and a rose or rose petals floated on top. On occasion the bowl was simply filled with rose petals. Some were for ornamental purposes only. The rose scent emanating from the bowl helped freshen the air in the parlor or dining room. Originals are rare, made in a variety of glasses during the mid-1800s. Modern examples are being made in large quantities. The original bowls were normally four to twelve inches in diameter and usually tri-footed.

rose petal finish Peachblow glass articles with a satin finish.

rose pink See *Purple of Cassius.*

rose quartz See *quartz glass.*

Rose Teinte (Aka *Baccarat's Amberina*)
An art glass similar to Amberina with tinting
from pale amber to rose, made by Baccarat
for a short time commencing in 1916 and
later in 1940. It was made with less gold than
Amberina, making it more delicately colored.

rose water dish A dish associated with a
ewer or pitcher, used by guests at a dinner
between courses or at the end of the meal to
catch the water used to cleanse their hands.
The pitcher was filled with rose water that
was poured over the guests hands held over
the dish.

rose water sprinkler See *sprinkler.*

Roseen & Collins See *Roseen Brothers
Cut Glass Company.*

**Roseen Brothers Cut Glass
Company** A glass cutting house established
by Herman T. and Joseph Roseen in 1904 in
Chicago, Illinois. Its assets were sold to the
United States Cut Glass Company in 1905. In
1906 Herman T. Roseen and Andrew Swanson established the Central Cut Glass Company in Chicago. On August 17, 1915, Roseen
patented a dipping device for polishing several
pieces of cut glass at one time. In 1925 when
Swanson sold his interest to a man named Collins, the firm became Roseen & Collins. Until
this time it had made only heavy-cut glass, but
thereafter it made light-cut and rock-crystal
glassware. It closed in 1932.

Rosenbaum, John G. See *Bridgeton
Glass Works; Stratton, Buck & Company.*

Rosenfeld, Ken A paperweight artist
from Los Angeles, California, who creates
detailed lamp-work designs in the traditional
French style, including a variety of single
flowers, bouquets, fruit arrangements, and
the *Vegetable Garden.* His paperweights are
signed with an "R" cane, and his name and
the date are engraved on the base.

Rosenthal, Jacob Born in Pittsburgh,
Pennsylvania, in 1855, he began his career in
glassmaking at the age of eleven as a carrying-in boy at Campbell, Jones & Company.
During the next 20 years he worked at several
facilities in Pittsburgh and Upper Ohio Valley. In 1889 he went to work for the American Glass Company in Anderson, Indiana,
leaving in 1898 to work for the Royal Glass
Company. When Royal was absorbed by the
National Glass Company in 1899, Rosenthal
was sent to Lancaster, Ohio, as plant manager
of the Ohio Flint Glass Works. A few months
later he was sent to the Indiana Tumbler &
Goblet Company as plant manager. In 1906
he went to work for the Fenton Art Glass
Company. When Fenton moved to Williamstown, he supervised construction of the new
facility and became its manager, a position he
held until he retired in 1929. His sons, Paul
and Clarence, worked at Fenton; Paul becoming manager when his father retired, holding
that position until he retired in 1949. Clarence was in charge of the mold shop when
first established in 1907. One of Jacob's most
famous creations was *chocolate glass* (now
called *caramel slag*), which he developed in
late 1900 shortly after he started at the Indiana Tumbler & Goblet Company. He also
created Pattern No. 450 (*Holly*) and a new
color, *Golden Agate.*

rosette (1) A decorative ornament with its
components arranged in a circular pattern.
An example is a stylized rose in full bloom
where equally spaced petals often alternate
with stylized leaves. (2) A small glass ornament in this form attached to, or secured
with, a metal screw, used to hold a mirror to
its frame or the wall. (3) A glass ornament in
this form, larger than a mirror holder,
attached to a hook-like device and used to
hold back a curtain on a window. Also see
star. (4) A *hobstar.* See *hobstar.*

Ross & Co. This company fitted a large flat
boat with a furnace and tempering oven in
1842 and launched it on the Ohio River at
Pittsburgh, Pennsylvania, making glassware
that it sold at farms and settlements along the
shore. It was in operation for only a short
time.

rotary polishing The process of polishing a glass object being turned on a lathe,
using various tools and an abrasive.

Rothfus-Nicolai Company See
Figueroa Cut Glass Company.

rotting (1) Very deep etching of a piece of glassware using a strong hydrofluoric acid solution. See *acid etching*. (2) A form of glass decay often caused by the use of inadequate stabilizers in the batch and exacerbated by damp conditions. See *crisselling; decay*.

rouge box A small box used to hold rouge. Most have a removable lid; some have a mirror and separate compartment for holding kohl—eye makeup—on the underside.

Rouge des Anciens A red-colored glass. A patent was granted to Bernard Perrot about 1670.

Rouge Flambe An art glass developed by Frederick Carder at Steuben, made about 1916-17. Its color was inspired by Chinese *famille rose* porcelain and made in shapes similar to Chinese ceramic articles. The color was produced by the addition of selenium and cadmium sulfides to the batch and it ranged from a deep, rich red (the color Carder was seeking) to orange or coral pink. It has a glossy finish and is sometimes erroneously called *Red Aurene*. It was difficult to make and particularly vulnerable to breakage caused primarily by strains in the glass.

rouge pot (1) A small container to hold rouge. Some were made of Roman glass during the 1st century A.D. They were ball shaped with a tiny opening at the top. See *globular ungentarium*. (2) A small container to hold rouge. They are usually square, though some are round, and often of cut glass. Most were made in Czechoslovakia, introduced into the United States about 1936.

rougher In cutting glass, the rougher is an apprentice with the task of rough cutting deep miter lines in the pattern, leaving the details and finer cuts to another (the smoother). The rougher sometimes has the additional task of marking the blanks by putting crude pattern lines on them prior to cutting.

round (1) A pharmacy bottle or jar, cylindrically shaped, ranging usually from six to ten inches in height. Early ones from the late 18th century were of clear glass with variously shaped stoppers, while later ones were often of usually blue or green colored glass. They were used for holding pills or medicinal syrups, had a capacity between five and sixty fluid ounces, and generally were labeled with the contents. (2) A tall cylindrical, covered jar used by confectioners to hold sweets.

round flutes See *flute cutting*.

round thumbprint A bull's-eye motif, oval in shape.

roundel (1) A circular plaque embellished with a painting in enamel or gilt within a circular border or cartouche. (2) An ornamental medallion. (3) (Aka *bull's-eye glass*) Round disks made of antique glass: (a) by a glassblower first blowing a bubble and twirling it on the end of the blowing iron to flatten it by centrifugal force; or (b) by machine, where circles of glass were made either by pressing (sometimes enhanced with surface designs or raised textures) or spinning. They are usually made of translucent, sometimes opalescent, glass in many colors and range in size from about one to twelve inches. Characteristic of the hand-made roundel (also spelled *rondel*) is the knobby mark in its center where the blowing iron was *cracked off*. Machine pressed roundels have similar marks, but they are not as sharply pointed. (4) Bottle glass used in early windows and door lights.

roundelet A bull's-eye motif.

roundheaded A window or door that forms an arched opening. It is traditionally used for the center light of a Palladian window.

roundlet See *thumbprint*.

Rouse, Hiram (1883-1970) Born in Corning, New York, and trained in engraving at Hawkes, Rouse went to work for Sinclaire in 1905. In 1915 he gave up engraving for other jobs. In 1919 he returned to the glass business, working for the Corning Glass Works, but after a few years left, only to return as a smoother in 1935. From about 1910 to 1967 he had a cutting shop in Corning where he originally cut mainly for Hunt and Fuller.

Rowland, James, & Co. See *Kensington Glass Works*.

Rowley, S.B. See *Lockport Glass Works*.

Royal Flemish ewer, alternating blue and tan panels with raised gold separation lines, chrysanthemum blossoms and foliage.
Krause Publications

Royal Flemish glassware

Glassware created and made, first about 1890, by the Mt. Washington Glass Company; the name was patented in 1894. It is semi-transparent in earthy colors with an acid finish, embellished with gold relief and enameling. Some patterns are reminiscent of those on Chinese cloisonne. Raised gold enamel lines separate the various elements of the design. The various patterns include Asian scenes, ducks in flight, and abstract subjects. Some pieces were quite showy, having brick red or green backgrounds heavily outlined in gold. Others were delicately executed in gentler shades, often gold, beige, and brown, and smartly embellished. It is similar to Crown Milano, except Royal Flemish is semi-transparent and the designs are in dark shades of brown or rust. Some pieces were identified with paper labels with a double-headed eagle with a crown in the center and the initials "Mt.W.G.Co." Others bear a diamond outline in red with the initials "RF" (the stem of the "R" forms the stem of the "F" with the bars facing left) and the number under the diamond. It was not a financial success and only a small amount was made.

Royal Glass Company

(1898-1903) A glass manufacturing facility established in Marietta, Ohio, by M.F. Noll, A.D. Follett, H.G. Chamberlain, D.B. Torpy, and A. Thompson, making household glassware. It burned in 1903 and was never rebuilt.

Royal Oak Goblet

A marriage glass in the form of a goblet with a cylindrical bowl resting on a knop stem, made in 1663 to commemorate the marriage of Charles II and Catherine of Braganza. It is embellished with a portrait of the couple in diamond point engraving. Between their portraits is a picture of Charles II surrounded by a wreath of oak leaves on a formal tree and the inscription "Royal Oak." The Royal Arms of England and the date—1663—appear on the reverse. Its origin is uncertain, being attributed to both the Netherlands and/or the facility of the Duke of Buckingham. It has been reproduced several times but with no intent to deceive.

Royal Ruby

A dark red-colored glassware made by Anchor Hocking Glass Corporation, introduced in 1939. The color was made by adding copper to the batch. It was a pressed ware made with automated machinery. World War II created shortages of copper for non-military uses, and production was discontinued in 1943. The glass was made again from 1950 to 1967, and again in 1977.

Royalit

A rare-earth glass, very costly to make, made by the Moser firm. Brownish-red in color, it was made by combining neodymium oxide with selenium in the batch.

"Ruba Rombic" liquor bottle, six whiskey glasses, and tray, c. 1928-1932, topaz-colored glass.
The Corning Museum of Glass

Ruba Rombic

A line of glassware introduced in February 1928 by the Consolidated Lamp & Glass Company. It was designed by Reuben Haley in the Art Moderne style, a cubist creation. The pieces had strong, severe triangular and romboidal planes. The line included tumblers, flasks, bowls, and numerous other pieces, all having a satin finish. *Ruba* is derived from "Reuben" and *Rombic* from the word romboid, even though one advertisement states *Ruba* means epic or poem and *Rombic* means irregular in shape. Three patents were issued for Haley's design of a Ruba Rombic plate, vase and bottle on April 10, 1928. These were assigned to Consolidated.

Ruba Rombic was made in the following colors: common—*Jungle green, Jade, Smokey Topaz, ???Lilae???, Sunshine (Honey)*, and *Silver (Silver Gray* or *Silver Cloud)*; rare— *Clear Opal, Black, Red, Crystal, French Crystal, Florentine Acid Etched and Smokey Topaz* with silver highlighting.

Rubena Crystal A transparent glassware shading from red to clear, made by Hobbs, Brockunier & Co. See *Rubena glass.*

Rubena glass A transparent glassware in shades from red to clear, first made by George Duncan & Sons about 1885. Hobbs, Brockunier & Co. also made Rubena, calling it *Rubena Crystal.*

Rubena Verde A Victorian glassware made about 1890 by Hobbs, Brockunier & Co. and later by several others. Hobbs called its ware *Ruby Amber Ware*, made often in the inverted thumbprint pattern. Rubena Verde is a transparent ware in shades from red to cranberry to green or yellowish-green or amber. It was made to gain some of the market of the more expensive *Amberina.*

Rubigold A name used by both Imperial Glass Company and Fenton Art Glass Company to describe their Carnival glass having a marigold color with a red iridescence.

Ruby Amber Ware Hobbs, Brockunier & Co.'s name for its version of *Amberina*, made about 1890. It was a form of Rubena Verde. See *Rubena Verde.*

ruby glass (1) A *flushed* glass, deep red in color, sometimes confused with red carnival glass. It was made from the late 1800s until World War II.

(2) A deep red ruby-colored glass made by several companies during the late 1800s when it reached its peak of popularity. It was made by adding colloidal gold to a batch. When the glassware was reheated at the glory hole (or *struck*), it turned from a yellow amber color to a ruby red. In the 1890s the American Flint Glass Workers Union had special provisions applying to all workers involved in making ruby glass. They were required to produce only 90% of the items required of other workers making crystal or other colored glass because of the time needed to strike the desired color. Over the years gold has been replaced by selenium and/or copper as the colorant in the batch.

(3) A red-colored glass shaded from pale-rose pink through cranberry shades to intense red shades, known as Bohemian red and pigeon blood. Many shades have been produced since Roman times through the present. Some have been made by plating—the thicker the plating, usually the deeper the color. Over the years several coloring agents have been used to produce red glass. They include copper oxide, gold, chrome salts, selenium, arsenic, and lignite.

(4) A term applied by Frederick Carder to a ruby-colored glass he developed at Steuben, but still related to earlier gold ruby glass. It was of two types: (a) Glass of a pink color, called *Gold Ruby*, made by adding 22 karat gold in colloidal form to the batch. Sometimes various other metallic oxides were added to the batch. The glass was usually made in solid lumps (*sausages*), each about one inch in diameter and two to three inches long. They were yellow until reheated in the lehr under a reducing flame, at which time they turned ruby. The sausages were put in secure areas, because of their high gold content, until needed, then they were brought out, reheated, worked into a *cup* and used to case the object being made. (b) *Selenium Ruby*, sometimes wrongly called *Cadmium Ruby*, was made by the inclusion of cadmium selenide and zinc sulfide in the batch, resulting in a brilliant red glass, sometimes shading to orange. Both types were usually used as a thin flashing over clear or alabaster glass. Other *Gold Ruby* colors were made at Steuben by adding coloring oxides to the basic ruby glass batch. These include *Purple Gold Ruby* (gold and cobalt), *Amethyst Gold Ruby* (gold and manganese), *Brownish Yellow Gold Ruby* (gold and iron), and *Cinnamon Gold Ruby* (gold and uranium). See *cranberry glass; gold ruby glass.*

ruby luster A copper- or gold-based luster giving an intense ruby iridescence to the glass.

Ruby Mother-of-Pearl Westmoreland Glass Company's name for its red iridized glass.

Ruby Onyx An object formed of onyx glass and cased in an outer layer of transparent ruby glass. It was patented in 1889 and resembles a natural gemstone.

Ruby-stained pitcher, *Button Arches,* frosted center band with gold trim, applied colorless handle. *Krause Publications*

ruby stained/flashed souvenirs

Ruby stained or flashed glass made by applying a thin layer of ruby-colored glass or stain over clear glass. During the late 19th-early 20h centuries, many personalized souvenirs were made of this type of glass. They were often engraved with the location of an attraction, date, and sometimes the buyer's name.

rudimentary stem A stem that is extremely plain and quite short, generally no more than a knop between the bowl and the foot, or a short, plain stem with a small knop, merese, or collar.

rugiadoso, vetro *(Italian)*: Literally, *dew-like glass.* An ornamental glass developed by Ercole Barovier for Barovier & Toso about 1940. It has an overall surface texture and appearance similar to fine dew, made irregular by fusing small glass splinters to it.

Ruhlander, John (1860-1935) Born in Hamburg, Germany, he worked at various glass facilities along the Rhine River and as a glassblower in Havana, Cuba, before coming to Philadelphia, Pennsylvania. From there, he went to Glassboro, New Jersey, employed by the Whitney Glass Works. Then he went to Millville, New Jersey, remaining there until his death. One of his best works is a rare sixteen-part decanter made in 1907 with the assistance of A. Woodruff Harris. It is twenty-eight inches tall and has a base with eight compartments and a removable top with eight smaller compartments. He made some pitchers, inkwells, and rose magnum, umbrella and mushroom paperweights.

rule drop A long drop with perpendicular sides.

ruler A straight glass rod for ruling lines on paper, about 10 inches long and 1/2 inch thick. Some were made by the Falcon Glassworks, embellished with twisted millefiori canes laid lengthwise.

rullo *(Italian)* The plural is *rulli.* A small, circular pane of glass made in the same manner as crown glass with a bull's-eye at the center and a folded rim. When placed in horizontal and vertical rows, they were used for windows prior to the technical ability to make larger panes. They were made of colored glass or multi-colored filigrana (reticello) glass in the 19th century.

rumkin See *rummer* (3).

rummer (1) An English drinking glass, the result of the gradual evolution of the German *Romer.* The most common form is the 19th century form—a low goblet with a stemmed foot, usually domed or square. Early ones made about 1690 have a knopped stem, sometimes of baluster shape, and a folded foot. In the late 18th century the bowls were made in various shapes and were often engraved, and the foot often had cut designs. The name is a corruption of the German word *Romer* because early ones were used for white Rhine wine, having no connection with rum. (2) A glass made about 1677 by George Ravenscroft. It had a cup-shaped bowl with a spreading foot and hollow stem and was embellished with prunts. (3) A term used in England for the German *Romer,* also called a *romkin* or *rumkin.* (4) An 18th century green goblet with a globular bowl, stem, and domed foot, sometimes with gilt embellishment on the bowl. (5) A large cup or drinking glass with a short stem, oval bowl, and small foot, made in the late 18th to early 19th centuries. See *toddy rummer.*

runner (1) A channel in a mold that directs the flow of the molten glass to ensure proper filling of the mold. (2) See *leech bead.*

Rupert's drop [Aka *(Prince) Rupert's ball or tear*] An odd tadpole-shaped, solid soda-lime glass object about two inches long with a bulbous end tapering to a thin curved tail, normally made of green or yellow-brown glass. They were made by dropping a small blob of fairly hot molten glass into cold water, letting it remain there until it cooled. They were not affected by a blow on the bulbous end. However, if the tail was broken or the surface scratched, the drop shattered with the noise of a small explosion, due to differential internal stresses. The internal stresses were caused by the cold water shrinking and hardening the surface more quickly than the core. These were introduced to England from Germany by Prince Rupert (1619-82), a nephew of Charles II.

Russelbecher Literally, *trunk* or *proboscis beaker.* The same as a claw beaker, considered the most elaborate of Frankish drinking vessels, made from the late 5th century onward. The claw is applied to the cool glass beaker in the form of a hot glass blob causing the surface of the beaker to soften at the point of contact. As it is applied, the gaffer continues blowing the vessel, making a hole at the softened point of contact and inflating the blob, which is pulled outward and downward with the tip being pressed back to the glass surface one or two inches below.

Russell Flower Pot A glass flower pot with an attached saucer made in a single operation, patented by William F. Russell on November 6, 1877. At the time Russell was working for Hobbs, Brockunier & Company. Later he was the manager of Model Flint Glass Company.

Russian Crystal A trademark registered by Frederick Shirley and used on Mt. Washington Glass Company's cut glassware for several years. Registered on January 30, 1883, it was usually affixed to cut-glass articles on a paper label.

Russian cut pattern One of the most intricate of the cut-glass patterns and possibly the best known, designed by Philip McDonald and assigned to Hawkes on June 20, 1882. It obtained its name when the Russian Embassy in Washington, D.C., and the United States Embassy in St. Petersburg, Russia, ordered banquet services in this pattern. In 1886 Grover Cleveland chose it for the White House service used at State dinners. It was unique in that Cleveland requested and received it with the addition of an engraved crest with an eagle. It was enlarged by Presidents Benjamin Harrison, William McKinley, and Theodore Roosevelt, used in the White House until 1938 when Franklin Roosevelt changed to a less expensive ware.

Originally, Hawkes cut it in a pyramidal star and the hobnail, covering the entire surface. The original patent stated the hexagonal button formed could be clear or decorated. Variations were made and later different names were given, though *Russian* is used for all. Variations include: *Ambassador; Canterbury; Cleveland, Persian*, and *Polar Star.* In *Ambassador* hobnails were crosshatched. In *Canterbury* a pyramidal star was placed on each hobnail. In *Cleveland* hobnails were unadorned. In *Persian* hobnails were covered with a hobstar. And in *Polar Star* there was a large pyramidal star and very small hobnail. Few pieces are signed.

Some companies made further changes in the original design. Dorflinger reduced the amount of cutting by using a twenty-four-point star on the base. New England Glass (later Libbey) placed a corner fan on a square item to reduce the cutting. Pairpoint divided the pattern with clear vertical flutes. Hawkes also varied it with ribs and pillars.

Russian glassware Relatively recent archeological excavations at Novogrudok have turned up fragments of glass objects dating to the 3rd or 4th centuries A.D. They are of many shapes and sizes and embellished with painting, gilding, etc. Since the 11th century, glassware has been made by many facilities in Russia, including Novogrudok. The early wares included beads, jewelry, goblets, pilgrim flasks, and a type of beaker known as a *Stopka*, made at Kiev, Kostroma and other sites.

In the 17th century there were two well-known facilities near Moscow: (a) The facility at Dukhanin made mediocre greenish flasks and panes. It received a license in 1634, issued to Julius Koiet of Sweden, and was opened after his death by his son, Anton. (b) The Izmailovskii Glassworks, established in 1669, made tableware. It closed between 1706 and 1725. In the 1710s, state-owned facilities were opened at Jamburg (now King-isepp) and Zhabino, both closed in the 1730s. During the 18th century several privately owned facilities were established, including the Mal'tsev Glass Factory, Bachmetov Glass Factory, Minter Glass Factory, St. Petersburg Imperial Glass Factory, and the H.V. Lomonosov facility. By 1812 there were over 140 private facilities, but only a few made quality glassware. From 1850 to 1870, more facilities opened and older ones expanded.

Many varieties of glassware were made, including colorless, colorless crystal, opaque white, and cased glass embellished with engraving, enameling, and transfer printing. A lot was made in the Art Nouveau style of Emile Galle after about 1900.

Russian variant The cut-glass motif known as *cane variant*.

Rusticana A glass with serpent designs developed at Loetz by Max von Spaun about 1900.

Rutherford (Geo.) & Co. See *Hamilton Glass Works*.

Ryon Cut Glass Company See *Eygabroat-Ryon Company Incorporated*.

S A trademark used by H.P. Sinclaire Co.

saber A tool used by glassmakers to skim glass gall or sandever off the surface of melted glass.

Perfume bottle, "Gaite," draped nude, 6" h., signed "Sabino, Paris."
Davanna Collection

Sabino, Marius Ernest (1878-1971) Born in Acireale, Italy about 1900, he went to Paris, designing lamps and light fittings in wood and metal. After serving in World War I, he set up a business making light fittings. His earliest efforts included copies of old oil and gas lamps adapted for electricity. He began to experiment with glass, using it architecturally. He created illuminated glass pilasters and cornerstones, massive glass doors, columns, tables, and room dividers, as well as huge chandeliers made of molded glass sections assembled in a variety of models with wrought iron fittings. He also made a full range of decorative glass, including electroliers, wall appliques, floor and table lamps, vases, bowls, figurines, and other sculptures (see *Sabino Art Glass*) using clear, colored, stained, enameled and opalescent glass, and frosted glass polished with cork, by blow molding and press molding. He designed all of the *objets d'art* and several molded frosted glass shades. Vases and bowls were made in a full range of clear, opalescent and colored glass, frequently molded with geometric patterns; some had a continuous frieze of human figures (faces, busts, or full bodies). He made a full line of glass figures, including nudes, animals, fish, etc. With the onset of the Great Depression, he introduced two inexpensive types of opalescent glassware sold under the trademarks *Verart* and *Vernox*. In 1939, at the beginning of World War II, he ceased production. Several years later, in the 1960s, he began again to make glass, at first small opalescent glass animals, birds, butterflies, nude figurines, etc. After his death, his son operated the facility until the mid-1970s. The molds were sold to an American company that continued to make items in France.

Sabino Art Glass An art glass made by Marius Ernest Sabino in his studio in France during the 1920s and 1930s, using opalescent frosted and colored glass in the art deco style. In 1960, using molds modeled by hand in wood and then cast in iron, he once again began making art glass using a special formula. The glassware was characterized by a golden opalescence caused by the addition of gold to the batch. In the same year he introduced a line of figurines ranging from one to eight inches in height. Although his family continued to make glassware for export after his death in 1971, they were not able to duplicate his formula. Sabino wares are marked with a molded name, an etched signature, or both.

sable glass A European term for lacy glass or stippled glass.

sack glass A drinking glass formerly used for drinking sack, originally any strong dry white wine, but, in the 17th century in England, any wine imported from Southern Europe, especially sherry from Spain. The name is derived from the French *vin sec* meaning *dry wine*. A sack glass is comparable to a sherry glass used during the 19th century when the term *sack* ceased to be used. Some ordered from Venice by Alessio Morelli and specifically designated as such, had a cylindrical bowl with straight sides and a short stem of inverted baluster form between two mereses.

Pale green glass saddle bottle, 8-1/2" h. Davanna Collection

saddle bottle Gourd-shaped bottles with round bottoms for easy carrying in slings on saddles. However, the majority were placed in beds of sand in wine cellars or were hung on walls.

sadness glass See *verre de tristesse*.

Safe Glass Company (1880-1898) A glass manufacturing facility established in 1880 in Bowling Green, Ohio, moving to Ford Key, Indiana in 1892 and to Upland, Indiana in 1896. It made various types of canning jars.

Safety fruit jar A fruit jar of clear amber glass, having the word "Safety" in raised letters on the side, made by the Salem Glass Works from 1895 to 1910.

safety glass (Aka *shatterproof glass*) A composite or laminate of two or more sheets of plate glass separated by an inner layer of plastic, usually polyvinyl butyral, bonded to the glass to minimize shattering on impact. Instead of breaking like a normal sheet of glass, it shatters into small fragments which, for the most part, adhere to the plastic. It is now required for automobile windows. See *laminated glass; tempered glass; wired glass.*

saggers Boxes of refractory brick used in a kiln to protect glass being melted into molds or slumped from the direct action of flames or flame borne particles. See *sagging; slumping*.

sagging The process of reheating a glass blank, usually a sheet of glass, so it gradually flows by gravity over or into a former mold, taking on the shape of the mold. See *slumping*.

Saint See listings normally spelled with the abbreviation *St.*, such as St. Louis, St. Petersburg, etc., under that spelling as it would normally appear alphabetically.

salad bowl A large circular or, on occasion, boat-shaped bowl for holding and serving salad.

salad dish *or* **salad plate** A plate used for an individual serving of salad. They are usually 7 to 7-1/2 inches in diameter.

salad set A set normally consisting of a large serving bowl and six or more smaller bowls or nappies (for individual servings), which often have underplates.

Salade, Frederick See *Columbia Glass Works*.

salamander paperweight A paperweight having a salamander as its primary interior decorative motif. Some have a salamander coiled on top of the crown.

Salazar, David In 1972 Salazar began working with glass at Lundberg Studios, primarily interested in the design and production of paperweights. He later established a studio in Santa Cruz, California. His weights have colorful as well as classic motifs. He makes miniature weights with superbly executed surface designs, and a marbrie weight fashioned in the classic St. Louis design. All his weights are signed and dated on the base.

Salem Glass Works A glass manufacturing facility established in Salem, New Jersey, in 1862 by Henry D. Hall, Joseph Pancoast, and John V. Caven (Hall, Pancoast & Caven), making a variety of jars and bottles in various sizes and types. In 1870 the operating company became Craven & Brothers and, in

1895, it was incorporated as the Salem Glass Works. In 1934 it was sold to Anchor Cap & Closure Company, which merged with the Hocking Glass Corporation, becoming Anchor Hocking Corporation.

Salem Glasshouse A glass manufacturing facility near Salem, Massachusetts (the first in New England and the second in what would later be the United States) established by Obadiah Holmes and Lawrence Southwick (a year later, Ananias Concklin) in 1641. Glass was blown occasionally. Operations ceased in 1643 but reopened a short time later, operating off and on until 1661. It made some window glass, bottles, and lamps.

saler A salt or salt cellar.

salesmen's sample See *samples-in-little.*

saliva A defect in glassware in the form of a group of small air bubbles, usually the result of the inadequate discharge of air from the gather or premature cooling of the gather.

salmanasar See *wine bottle, sizes.*

Salopain ware A blue and white opaque glass decorated with colored motifs, made during the 18th century by the Caughley Glassworks in England.

salsola soda See *barilla.*

salt (1) A term applied to the alkali used in making glass. (2) A container for *salt* or salt cellar, originally called *salers.* Adding the word *cellar* to the older term *salt* came about as the result of the corruption of the French word for salt, *saliere* and/or the Italian, *saliera.* See *great salt; Robinson salt cellar; salt cellar; small salt; standing salt; trencher salt; capstan salt.*

salt cake An impure form of sodium sulfate (Na_2SO_4), long accepted as a minor ingredient in making glass as have other sulfates, such as ammonium and barium sulfates, said to remove scum forming in tank furnaces. Carbon should be used with sulfates, reducing them to sulfites. Arsenic trioxide may be added to the batch to facilitate the removal of bubbles. Nitrates of sodium or potassium are added to oxidize iron, making

it less evident in the finished glass. Potassium nitrate or carbonate is used when making many of the better grades of table, decorative, and optical glass.

salt cellar A small, shallow bowl to hold salt for the table. They are usually circular, oval or boat-shaped but were made in a multitude of unusual shapes and designs. Most have a flat base or rest on a stemmed foot. Early English ones were large, up to 12 inches tall, for common use at the table, commonly called *standing salts* or *great salts.* In the 17th century smaller, individual salts were called *small salts* or *trencher salts.* From 1780, English and Irish ones were embellished with cutting. Some French ones are square or rectangular, often with two wells to accommodate adjacent diners. Many Italian salts are large; some have a figure mounted on the rim at each end. Some from Bohemia are embellished in *Zwischengold glas. Open salts* (called *salt dips* or *dishes*) were popular in America from the 18th century until the shaker type appeared in the 1860s (see *saltshaker*). Pressed salts were made as early as 1827—among the first items made by pressing—by New England Glass, Boston & Sandwich, and Jersey Glass. These and later ones were made in a variety of patterns, shapes, and colors, many of lacy glass. Some salts in the shapes of birds or animals are considered novelty items. Steigel was the first American glassmaker to make salts commercially. Covered salts, while rare, are usually found with a lacy pattern. Historical salts—salts with a likeness of a person or object or scene of historical significance—were made during the early pressed glass period. See *salt* (2); *Irish glassware.*

salt cup A term for a salt.

salt dip See *salt cellar.* A large salt cellar so named because guests would often dip celery or other condiments in it.

salt dish See *salt cellar.*

salt roller See *rolling pin.*

saltshaker A shaker used to contain and sprinkle salt. Its development was not considered until salt was made fine enough to pour through holes, and the screw top was developed in 1858 by John Mason. Bottom-filled shakers with corks were used prior to the screw-top, top-filled shakers. They became popular in the 1860s. In 1871 a method was found that kept the salt free-flowing even in damp weather. The open salt became a thing of the past. A salt shaker is also called a *shaker salt, spice box, condiment box, dredging bow, sifter or duster.*

Cut-glass salt and pepper shakers.
Davanna Collection

Salt and pepper sets; left: set in auto; right: set in hat.
Davanna Collection

salt & pepper sets Generally of the *shaker* type and made as a matched pair—one for salt, one for pepper. Some sets are not matched but are designed so one compliments or contrasts with the other. Sets are made in a tremendous variety of shapes, sizes, and styles. Some have a pedestal base, glass tops, sterling silver tops, and mother-of-pearl tops. Occasionally the salt is a bowl and the pepper is a small bottle, usually covered with a hinged lid with an opening for a small spoon or with a shaker top with small holes.

salver (Aka *waiters, foot plates*) A large circular glass dish or shallow bowl, normally with a pedestal foot. Some have a baluster or Silesian stem. Glass salvers should be distinguished from those made of silver—simple flat trays used for presenting letters or visiting cards. On occasion, jelly or sweetmeat glasses were placed in a circle on a glass salver. Occasionally another smaller, similarly laden salver was placed on these glasses, forming a centerpiece, with a large sweetmeat glass in the center; the arrangement was called a *pyramid*. The salver was also used as a *presentoir* for offering a glass of wine. Salvers were made in England in the late 18th century, and also in Murano. See *alzata; cake plate.*

samples-in-little Miniatures of actual products carried by salesmen so they could show samples and display their wares without carrying full-size products. They were usually as detailed as the full-size product. Many old *samples-in-little* are considered items for doll houses or children's toys.

sanctuary lamp An oil lamp of cylindrical form made in Spain during the 16th century. It is slightly taller than it is wide and has a horizontal disk rim. They are often embellished with enameled insignia of various religious orders. See *hanging lamp.*

sand The most common form of silica (SiO_2) used in making glass. It is an impure form of silica usually taken from the seashore, but preferably from inland beds where it is more easily ground and freer from impurities. Sand used in making glass should have a low content of iron (less than 0.045% for tableware and 0.015% for optical glass) and other impurities. It must be well cleaned, heated amply to remove carbonaceous matter, and screened to obtain fairly uniform small grains.

sandblasting The process of embellishing glassware by projecting fine grains of sand, crushed flint or powdered iron at high velocity onto its surface. A stencil, with the design cut into it, is used to cover the object being embellished. The open portion is the design and is subjected to the blast. A wide range of effects can be obtained by varying the quality of sand and the force and duration of the blast. The design is left in a grayish mat finish. Sandblasting was invented by Benjamin Tilghman, a Philadelphia chemist, in 1870. It was first used to embellish large glass panels but soon was used on smaller objects for decorative effects by modern glassmakers.

G.F. Morse devised a smaller sandblaster to be used by studio glassmakers. It is often combined with other decorative processes. See *stained glass, Surface Treatment.*

sand box A container with a perforated lid to hold a fine sand for spreading on ink to dry it.

sand casting see *sand molding.*

sand core glass A frequently used but incorrect term for core glass. It is now the opinion of many experts that sand was not used as the core in making articles by this method, but probably mud with straw as a binder. See *core glass.*

sand glass An instrument used for measuring time in the form of a reversible device made of two connected vertical glass vials mounted in a frame. From the upper vial a quantity of sand runs through a small neck into the lower vial, which is identically shaped and sized but inverted. The time required for the upper vial to empty is usually a specific amount. When all the sand has passed from the upper to the lower vial, it is turned over and the process repeated. The most common measure of time is one hour, i.e., *hour glass.* Smaller ones measure shorter periods, such as a half-hour glass or an egg timer; larger ones measure longer periods (see *powder glass*). In early ones, a metal disk or diaphragm with a tiny hole was placed where the necks of the vials meet, joined by an applied glass thread. Later, in the 18th century, they were joined with a sealed metal bead. When the metal was eliminated, the entire device was made of one piece of glass with a small passage through which sand would flow. After the short throat was made, the large end of one of the vials was sealed and, after sand was inserted, the other sealed. They were first imported into England from Germany, the Low Countries, and Venice in the early 16th century.

sand molding (Aka *sand casting*) The process involved carving a wooden block of the desired shape and embellishment, forcing it into a bed of damp sand, carefully withdrawing it to leave an exact impression, and blowing a paraison into the depression. After cooling, it is removed from the mold. Marks left by the sand are eliminated by polishing.

sandever, sandgall, sandiver See *gall; glass gall.*

Clear glass salt, c. 1830-1840.
The Corning Museum of Glass

Sandwich glass: (1) Any of the numerous types of glass made by the Boston & Sandwich Glass Co. between 1825 and 1888. Molded glass made there from 1825 to 1840 is often called *early Sandwich glass.* (2) A term used in the United States for pressed glass made by the Boston & Sandwich Glass Co. as well as other facilities in the area. (3) Double-wall glass having sandwiched between the walls an inner layer of engraved gold or silver leaf. See *Zwischengoldglas.* (4) A generic term for *lacy glass,* regardless of origin; much was made by the Boston & Sandwich Glass Co.

Sandwich Manufactory The original name of the Boston & Sandwich Glass Company.

Sandwich Manufacturing Company See *Boston & Sandwich Glass Co.; Jarves, Deming.*

sandwich plate See *cake plate; sandwich server.*

sandwich server A round or hexagonal plate or salver, sometimes with a handle or center loop handle, used to hold the plate as it is passed around the table to serve sandwiches to guests.

sandwiching The process of making glassware in which a thin layer of gold or silver leaf is *sandwiched* between two layers of glass, as in *Zwischensilberglas(er)* or *Zwischengoldglas(er)*. It was used in ancient times and revived in Bohemia during the 1600s.

sandy glass Lacy glass or stippled glassware.

Santa Maria A rare line of glassware inspired by Christopher Columbus' flagship, introduced by the Consolidated Lamp & Glass Company in January 1926. The item made in greatest quantity was a rectangular, covered cigarette box. Other items include console bowls, covered cigar jars, ship candlesticks, and trays. The candlesticks are called *Santa Maria Dolphins* and were reproduced by the Imperial Glass Company and the K.R. Haley Glassware Company.

Saranac Crown Glass Co. A crown window glass manufacturing facility established in Jefferson County, New York, prior to 1834, operating until at least 1855. It was probably associated with the Redford Crown Glass Works.

Saracens A member of the nomadic tribes on the Syrian borders of the Roman Empire. The term was used in Europe during the Middle Ages for the adherents of Islam and for glassmakers and decorators in the region who were known for their soda lime glass (which often had numerous minute bubbles, varying in color from bottle green to amber) and for their manipulation of glass and its decoration, especially enameling.

Saratoga (Mountain) Glasshouse See *Granger, O. & H., & Company.*

sarcophagus See *cellaret.*

Sargon alabastron A three-inch tall alabastron of thick, green transparent glass, embellished with an engraved lion and, in cuneiform characters, the name of Sargon II of Assyria (722-705 B.C.). It is believed to be the earliest surviving glass vessel not made over a core. It was made either from a raw piece of glass or a cast blank. In either case it was formed by cutting and grinding, and finished by polishing (the interior shows spiral grooving). Some experts believe it was made in a mold, and the interior markings came from grinding after it cooled. The surface is

weathered, appearing whitish with a greenish iridescence. It was excavated at Nimrud, near Nineveh, and was believed to be made in Mesopotamia during the late 8th century. See *cold cutting.*

sash The wood or metal framing that holds window glass. A double hung sash slides up and down. A casement sash is either fixed in position or hinged to swing open.

Sassanian glassware Pre-Islamic glassware made in Persia and Mesopotamia under Sassanian Emperors from about 226 to 642. During this period, glassmaking was revived after a cessation following the Achaemenid dynasty (550 to 330 B.C.). Roman techniques were brought to the area by craftsmen from conquered territories. Some glassware was colored and mold blown. The finest specimens were cut glass with faceted decoration; some had overall decoration in the quincunx pattern. More elaborate types of cutting are on Islamic rock crystal and probably glassware, although none have been uncovered to date. See *Persian glassware; Mesopotamian glassware.*

Satin Engraved Glass A T.G. Hawkes trade name, dating from about 1903, used on a finely engraved line of wares where the design was left in a mat finish.

satin etching See *etching, satin.*

satin finish A cloudy or frosted translucence with a velvet-like finish on glass resulting from acid etching, sandblasting, etc. It may be found on any glass but mainly on transparent glass. It may appear as a design or pattern, may cover the entire surface, or may cover all portions except the design or pattern. See *mat finish.*

satin glass Any article of glassware with a velvety or satin finish that may cover the entire surface, or the entire surface with the exception of the design. If a design is intended for the article, an acid-resistant material is used to make the design, and the article is dipped in hydrofluoric acid (the reverse of etching). The etching process involves covering the entire article, except for the design, with an acid-resistant material, and then dipping it in hydrofluoric acid so that only the design has a satin finish. The dull satiny surface develops after the article has been subjected to a hydrofluoric acid bath. Nearly all satin glass was cased, having a white lining, but there were numerous exceptions. Many companies made satin glass, each having its own individual method or process. While most plain satin glass is in varicolored or shaded tones of rose, yellow or blue, some is of one color or clear glass. A patent for making satin glass was issued to Frederick Shirley of the Mt. Washington Glass Works on June 29, 1886, and to Joseph Webb of Phoenix Glass Company on July 6, 1886. Both got their ideas from Benjamin Richardson, who outlined the method in 1858. These early processes required a paraison be blown in a mold and then treated in various ways (most often in an acid bath) to achieve the satin finish. It has been reproduced in relatively large quantities since World War II. See *Mother-of-Pearl glass; verre de soie.*

satin iridescent glass A satin-stretched, somewhat rough-surfaced (never smooth or shiny), iridescent glass. Sometimes the finish is called *satin* or *crackle mineral finish.* Fenton called its wares *Florentine*; Imperial called it *Satin Iridescents*; and U.S. Glass called it *Aurora.*

Satin Iridescents Imperial Glass Co.'s name for their satin iridescent glass.

Satin Tone Duncan & Miller's name for one of its frosted lines of glassware.

satirical glassware Beakers and other glassware embellished with subjects of a satirical nature.

sauce boat A boat-shaped vessel usually with a handle at one end and pouring lip at the other, used to serve sauce or gravy. It normally rests on a spreading base or short legs, sometimes with a cover and a saucer attached to the base. Some have a lip on both ends and two side handles. They must be distinguished from a *bourdalou.* See *cream boat.*

sauce bottle A small bottle shaped like a decanter, often with a pouring lip, used for serving sauces and condiments. Some are inscribed with the name of the contents.

sauce dish A circular dish about 4-1/2 inches in diameter, with a flat bottom and slightly curved sides, used for serving sauces and preserves. Often of lacy glass, they were made in the United States by the Boston & Sandwich Glass Co. See *nappie.*

saucer A small, round shallow dish, especially one designed to hold a matching cup. It has a small well in the center to secure the base of a cup.

saucer champagne glass See *champagne glass.*

saucer dish See *strawberry dish.*

saucer topped bowl A bowl found on some drinking glasses, the upper part shaped like a shallow saucer with a deep round funnel below it.

Saunders reamer See *reamer.*

sausage A solid lump of glass, generally made from leftover parts of a batch, and set aside for future use.

save-all A hollow, cylindrical object that slips over or into the nozzle of a candlestick, spreading out at the bottom or top to form a disk for catching the wax drippings from the candle. It allowed the dripped wax to be cleaned off quickly and simply by removing it without disturbing the candlestick, or especially a chandelier or sconce.

savon, boule de (French) Literally, *soap bubble.* (Aka *savonneuse*) A color found on some opaline glass, having an iridescent soap bubble hue.

Savoy vase (1) A thick, blue glass vase with signs of grisselling, formerly attributed to the Savoy glasshouse of George Ravenscroft, believed to be made there about 1674. It is housed in the Toledo (Ohio) Museum of Arts. (2) A vase designed in 1937 by architect Alvar Aalto, made since then by the Kahula-Iittala Glassworks in Finland. Made of clear green glass, it has a unique style with freely undulating lines (curling vertical sides) and asymmetrical form.

sawing The process of cutting and/or shaping glass using a diamond-bladed hand or power saw.

Saxon glassware Glassware made in the forest regions of Saxony (a former state in southeastern Germany) from the Middle Ages, embellished primarily with enameling in the style of neighboring Bohemia and Franconia. Clear glass was embellished with polychrome motifs with borders of white enamel dots on a gold ground. Later the main production centers were Dresden and Weissenfels. From 1606 to 1608, Casper Lehman(n) was employed in Dresden and, from 1610, Casper and Wolfgang Schindler were glass engravers. A number of facilities were established by Freiherr Walther von Tschirnhaus (on orders from Augustus the Strong) and operated by Bohemian craftsmen. From 1717 to 1744, Johann Christoph Kiessling was court engraver at Dresden. From 1680 to 1697, Johann Neumann was court engraver at Weissenfels. Later Johann Georg Muller was court engraver until 1783. Much enameled glassware was made there starting about 1610.

scabbard fitting A small, decorative glass attachment placed on a scabbard, made in China during the Han dynasty (206 B.C.- 220 A.D.).

scale Bits of metal, usually in the form of its oxide, that become detached from metal implements used to stir the batch or shape the object and become imbedded in the glass object.

scale cutting A decorative pattern, sometimes on cut glass (especially on the stems of some English drinking glasses) in the form of overlapping scales (imbricated design). See *scale faceting.*

scale (scaling) dish A shallow, saucer-like dish used to skim the cream off of milk.

scale faceting A style of imbricated decoration on glassware—faceting in the form of overlapping scales. It was used on the stems of some drinking glasses. See *scale cutting.*

scale ground An imbricated diaper pattern composed of overlapping scales found on enameled glassware made in Murano dating from the late 15th and early 16th centuries. See *scale faceting; cesendello; standing cup; imbricated.*

scallop shell chalice A chalice of Roman or Rhenish glass with a tall cylindrical bowl resting on a stemmed foot, dating from the 4th century. The bowl is embellished in pseudo-vasa diatreta style, having attached vertical columns decorated with three scallop shells. Similar ones have the attached columns without the shells.

scallop shell decoration A decorative relief motif often on glassware, such as shell flasks of Roman and Venetian glass, and a scallop shell chalice made in Cologne in the 4th century.

scalloped A border consisting of a series of circle segments with an undulating (serrated) edge. On cut glass the circle segments are customarily ribbed with a fan.

Scandinavian glassware The earliest glassmaking in Scandinavia dates from the 16th, and 17th centuries. In Jutland (the peninsula comprising the continental portion of Denmark) and in southern Sweden, the remains of primitive glass furnaces and fragments of their products have been dated from about 1550 to 1650. The early forest glasshouses were staffed by Germans and financed by royalty and nobility, making mainly window glass and drinking glasses. It was believed to have operated on a seasonal basis. See *Swedish glassware; Norwegian glassware; Finnish glassware; Danish glassware.*

scattered millefiori paperweight See *millefiori paperweight.*

Scattergood & Haverstick; Scattergood & Whitall; Scattergood, Booth & Co.; Scattergood, Haverstick & Co. See *Glasstown Factory.*

Scattergood, Haverstick & Co. See *Whitall, Tatum & Co.; Glasstown Factory.*

scavo, vetro (Italian) Literally, *excavated glass.* Ornamental glassware developed by Cenedese, having an overall rough mat finish, predominately gray with splashes of various colors. It is made by fusing applied powdered minerals into the surface of the glass, which is formed into bowls, animal figures, etc.

scenic decoration Embellishment depicting scenic views normally of well-known buildings and localities usually enameled, etched or engraved on the surface of a glass object.

scent barrel A scent bottle made in the form of a barrel, resting horizontally on its side with a bung hole in the center of the top.

scent bottle (Aka *perfume bottle*) A small bottle to hold perfume, made in a wide variety of forms. They have a tiny orifice at the mouth to retard the flow and usually a ground glass stopper (sometimes a metal screw cap). They have been made since the 6th century B.C. They were originally made in Egypt. Shortly thereafter they were made of Islamic and Roman glass, and later in many European countries and in China. Some have millefiori embellishments, and some Bohemian ones are made of cased glass. Some English ones are of opaque white glass or blue or green glass; some have embedded sulfides; and some are enameled. Some are double bottles to hold two perfumes. In the early 20th century, attractive scent bottles for the commercial market were made by Rene Lalique for Coty and by Emile Galle for Guerlain. Some are provided with silver or gold mounts. See *smelling bottle; perfume bottle; cologne bottle, scent barrel; springel glass.*

scent bottles (throwaway) Scent bottles made for the average person to use the contents and then be thrown away. Most were crudely made, but some were well made. They were normally made of clear glass, hand blown, and embellished. The majority were made in the Germanic areas of Europe. They were long and narrow, cylindrical in form, measuring usually seven to eight inches with a ground stopper with a round, flat top. They were often referred to by the name of the contents, such as *Attar of Roses* or *Otto of Roses*, and sold at numerous spas, fairs, and shops. See *Otto of Roses.*

scepter (1) A rod about seven inches long of opaque gray glass (its intended purpose unknown), usually embellished with a combed feather pattern and, embedded lengthwise in the rod, a bronze wire to prevent or minimize breakage. This suggests the pieces preceded Egyptian glass, which was not very fragile. They may have been made in Palestine about 1000 B.C., where they were found. (2) A rod or wand held in the hand as a symbol of regal power, usually extravagantly embellished, made with settings of precious metals and jewels. Some were made of glass, and many replicas of those made with precious metals and jewels were made of glass.

Schaeffer & Company The firm that continued the operation of the Erhardt & Schaeffer glass cutting house of Syracuse, New York, making cut glass from 1897 until it closed.

Schaeffer & Erhardt See *Erhardt & Schaeffer; Schaeffer & Company.*

Schaffer, Max, Company (1910-1928) A glass cutting company in New York, New York, operating at various locations within the city until closing.

Scharling, John H. A craftsman working in Newark, New Jersey, who, in 1893, received a patent for laminating metal to glass, including a process for etching through the finished layer. The metals were mainly silver and gold.

Schaum, Frederick & Lewis; Shaum & Everhart See *Baltimore Glass Works.*

Scheck, M.E., & Company A glass cutting shop established in 1907 in Chicago, Illinois. In 1908, M.E. Scheck became affiliated with Gustav Erickson.

Schelling, Peter Born in Neustadt, Germany (now Prudnik, Poland) in 1933, he began studying engraving at age 16, receiving a certificate from the *Staatliche Fachschule fur Glasindustrie* in Zwiesel, Germany. He stayed an additional year to study complex engraving methods. He came to the United States in 1953, employed as a copper wheel engraver for Steuben, working there until he retired. In

1970 he began teaching engraving at Corning Community College. Since he came to the United States, he has engraved at his home shop in Corning, New York. He signs his work "P.Schelling" in diamond point script. He works alone making engraved vases, bowls, pendants, and paperweights.

Schetter(ville) Glassworks A window and green glass manufacturing facility established by Frederick Schetter in 1832 in South Millville, New Jersey. It failed in 1844 and was purchased by Mulford, Hay & Co. In 1854 it was taken over by Whitall Brothers & Co. and combined with their Millville Glass Works (established by James Lee & Associates). See *South Millville Plant.*

Scheuer (German) A short drinking glass. The bottom half is hemispherical. The upper half is in the form of a short cylindrical neck with a wide mouth, usually embellished with prunts, one lengthened, serving as a handle. They were made in Germany during the 15th century.

Schiesshausglas (German) Literally, *shooting lodge glass.* A drinking glass made during the 17th century in Saxony, used by members of a shooting lodge and embellished with its emblem. They were of conical shape with a pedestal foot and a cover with a finial.

Schangenfadenglas (German) Glassware embellished with applied threads of glass trailed on its body in serpentine patterns, then pressed flat and notched. It was made in the 2nd and 3rd centuries in the Rhineland (part of Germany, west of the Rhine River). See *snake trailing.*

Schangenpokal (German) Literally, *snake goblet.* (Aka *Flugelglaser*) A winged glass in the form of a pokal with a snake stem. They were made in the *facon de Venise* in Germany and the Netherlands during the 17th century. See *snake glass.*

Schmauss, John B., & Co. See *Rensselaer Glass Factory.*

Schmelzglas (German) Literally, *enamel glass.* In the 17th and 18th centuries, *Schmelz* was a term applied to opaque glass. In Germany it was later incorrectly applied to agate glass, a solid opaque glass with several colors blended together in imitation of natural stones. See *enamel glass; agate glass; calcedonio.*

Schmertz, E.C. See *Reisinger, Wells & Co.*

Schmertz, R.C., & Co. See *Duquesne Glassworks.*

Schmertz & Quinby See *Brownsville Glass Works.*

Schneider (Art) Glassworks A glass manufacturing facility known in France as *Schneider, Cristallerie,* established in Epinay-sur-Seine in 1903 by Charles (1881-1953) and Ernest (1877-1937) Schneider (Charles studied under Emile Galle and Daum Freres). The original commercial production of glassware was replaced in the 1920s with the production of decorative glassware in the Art Nouveau style. Its main wares were cased glass of two or three colors, some embellished using hydrofluoric acid. Pieces were signed *Schneider* in block letters or script, occasionally filled with red or gold; *Le Verre Francaise*; or with a filigree design. The rarest were those signed *Charder* (a contraction of *Char*les Schnei*der*). The artistic direction changed in 1948 when the lead passed to Robert Schneider, Charles' son. In 1962 it moved to Lorris (Loiret). There have been four distinct periods in its history: 1903 to 1923, making only commercial glassware; 1923 to 1930, art glass; 1930 to 1945, glassware of very light and transparent colors, such as smoked and amber shades in addition to clear; and since 1945, only clear crystal glass. Sometimes a piece of its ware was signed *Ovington* or *Ovington, New York*—Ovington Brothers being its New York distributor. One of Schneider's most popular colors was an orange shade called *Tango*, a color very difficult to produce. It made a mottled glass with a cloudy effect, often mistaken for *Cluthra*, however, it had fewer bubbles.

Schneider, George, Cut Glass Company (1905-1913) A glass cutting company operating in Brooklyn, New York.

Schneider's Sons, P. See *Lafayette Flint Glass Works.*

Schopp's glass A glassware made in Stennewitz, Germany, to imitate porcelain. The facility making it had been denied permission to make porcelain because those in power believed another maker of porcelain would be too much competition for a Berlin manufacturer. Originally called *glass porcelain*, it was later renamed *Schopp's glass* after a workman who originally made it between about 1750 and 1783.

Schraubflasche *(German)* Literally, *screw flask.* A flask with a threaded neck designed for use with a screw-on top.

Schraubmacher A German term for a specialized craftsman whose primary function is to cut threads on glassware for covers or to join two pieces together. See *screw-joined glassware.*

Schuller, C.P., Cut Glass Company A glass cutting company operating during the late 1910s in New York, New York. It also operated as Charles P. Schuller Cut Glass & Lamp Company.

Schuller, Charles P., Cut Glass & Lamp Company See *Schuller, C.P., Cut Glass Company.*

Schusterglas *(German)* Literally, *shoe maker glass.* A term applied to various forms of caricature head flasks, so named because one well-known example depicts a misshapen head reported to be that of Nero's fool, a shoemaker. They are of Roman glass made during the 1st/3rd centuries A.D.

Schuylkill Glass Works (1) (1780-1796) A glass manufacturing facility established on the Schuylkill River north of Philadelphia, Pennsylvania, by Robert Morris and John Nicholson. The company made hand-blown decanters and wine glasses of soda-potash glass and wheel engraved them. William Peter Eichbaum was its superintendent from the time he arrived in the United States (1793) until the company closed. (2) A glass manufacturing facility established in 1807 near the Schuylkill River, Philadelphia, Pennsylvania, making green and flint glass. After 1810, it was known as Phillip Jones & Co., and in 1813, the Schuylkill Glass Works, making bottles and adding window glass in 1819. In 1822 it was advertised for rent. In 1823 it began making glass again. It was also called the Philadelphia Works.

Schwarzlot *(German)* Literally, *black lead.* (1) A low viscosity enamel that is black or has a sepia (brown, grayish-brown or olive-brown pigment) effect. It is prepared from powdered glass and copper oxide. (2) Embellishment in transparent enamel in black linear style, inspired by engraving and used by German Hausmaler from about 1650 to 1750. Pieces executed in Schwarzlot often have additional embellishment using iron red and, on occasion, gilding. The use of Schwarzlot on glassware was introduced in Nuremburg by Johann Schaper and his disciples, and was practiced by Hausmaler during the early 18th century in Bohemia and Silesia. The motifs used were primarily landscapes, battle scenes and mythological subjects. However, at the beginning of the 18th century the motifs included *laub-und-banblework* and chinoiseries. Sometimes details were scratched out with a needle. Reproductions were made during the 19th century.

Schwenksville Glassworks A glass manufacturing facility located in Schwenksville, Pennsylvania.

scissile glass A glass in which there are crystals that separate as a result of imperfect fusion of the metal or the metal cooling too quickly. It is a type of *sick* glass (see *cut glass, Damages*). When the glass is held against a strong light, a web of minute fissures can be seen.

scissors A tool used to pick up and cut away surplus molten glass during the formation of all handmade articles.

scole A cup used for toasting, derived from the Celtic word for *skull* (originally vessels for toasting were made from skulls of enemies). Variations include *skail, skalle, skayle,* and *skole.*

sconce (Aka *wall sconce*) A wall bracket with one or more projecting arms supporting candle sockets. Some are made with a mirror or plaque as the central feature. On some there are figures serving as candle holders. The candle nozzles usually have drip pans.

They were made in Venice during the early 17th century and reproduced in England before the 18th century. Some are quite large, about a yard high. Pier or chimney glasses with attached glass sockets for candles are not classified as sconces. The term sconce was used as early as 1715 for a bracketed candlestick but is now occasionally used to refer to a detachable nozzle of a candlestick, especially one with a drip pan attached. See *thousand eye sconce.*

Scott, John H. See *Estelle Glass Works.*

Scott & Beelen (Aka *Scott's Glass-house; The Glass House Riffle* or *Ripple*) A glass manufacturing facility operating during the late 18th and early 19th centuries in the Manchester district of Pittsburgh, Pennsylvania. It may have been the first glasshouse west of the Allegheny Mountains, in operation before the Pittsburgh Glass House of O'Hara & Craig. Its timeframe of operation is uncertain, as is its exact location.

Scott & Rapp See *Hermann City Glass Works.*

Scott's Glasshouse See *Scott & Beelen.*

Scottish glassware Glassware made in Scotland commencing about 1610 and continuing to the present day. The first facility was established by Sir George Hay in 1610 at Wemyss and transferred to Sir Robert Mansell in 1627. Two rival facilities were established in 1617. After the use of wood as a fuel was banned in 1615, facilities using coal were established in 1628 at Leith, making primarily green glass bottles. About 1664 the glass industry got a boost when the government forbade the general public from purchasing bottles not made in Scotland. In 1682 Charles Hay, a relative of George Hay, established a facility at Leith, as did others soon after. By 1777 there were seven facilities operating in the area, making bottles and drinking glasses as well as friggers. In 1750 a facility was established at Alloa making bottles with quilling and friggers. In the second half of the 17th century, the Prestonpans Glasshouse was established, with another established at Leith in 1864 (later Webb's Crystal Glass Co.) to make tableware. The North British Glassworks was established at Perth in 1864, later becoming the Moncrieff Glassworks, makers of Monart glass.

scrambled paperweight (Aka *Macedoine, Pell Mell, and candy weights*) A paperweight having as its primary embellishment a mass of different millefiori canes (some have interspersed pieces of white filigrana) in a scrambled formation. They were made at St. Louis, Clichy, and Murano.

scratching The act of diamond point engraving.

screen printing The process of pressing enamels through a screen to produce a design on a piece of glass. Screens may be made of nylon, polyester, silk, stainless steel, etc.

screw cap A type of cover normally made of metal but occasionally made of glass, having interior threading designed to screw on and fit securely over the mouth of a vessel, such as a castor, saltshaker, etc.

screw flask See *Schraubflasche.*

screw-joined glassware Objects of glass with a stem made in two separate parts. One part, usually the upper part, is threaded on the outside so it will screw into a knop on the lower part, which is threaded on the interior. Made in Bohemia and Germany. The threads are cut by a *Schraubmacher.*

scroll flask An American creation, the scroll flask is a flattened flask of mold-blown glass usually shaped like a heart with the point upward. It has a flat base, a short cylindrical neck, and is embellished with several elaborate relief scrolls following the outline of the flask. There is often further embellishment or inscriptions within the scrolls.

scroll salt See *capstan salt.*

Scudamore flute (Aka *Chesterfield flute*) A flute glass in the form of the Exeter flute, engraved with the Royal Arms of England and the arms of the Scudamore family, each enclosed within a wreath below which is an engraved festoon of fruit. Owned by the Earl of Chesterfield and attributed to the facility of the Duke of Buckingham, it is believed to have made and engraved in the Netherlands.

sculptured glassware Studio glassware formed and shaped by the artist from a solid block of glass, carved into the final form without blowing or molding.

Sculptured Line A Phoenix Glass Company-owned design and its most famous line of molded and hand-blown wares, in production by 1934. Some pieces were designed by Kenneth Haley and are often confused with the *Reuben Line*, made with Rueben Haley molds previously used by the Consolidated Lamp & Glass Company. However, the *Sculptured Line* was made from new molds of different designs and had different finishes. It is often called the *Selden Line* because Howard Selden played a vital role in its sales as he had with many Consolidated lines. He controlled this line, having great influence within the company. The *Sculptured Line* consisted of vases, bowls, covered boxes, platters, and a few other items, each in a variety of patterns. They continued to be made by Phoenix until 1958, when they became uneconomical to make. Phoenix did, however, make a few pieces in solid colors in very limited quantities in 1976, and strictly for its employees at Christmas in 1978—200 Thistle and 300 Wild Geese vases in milk glass, and 40 Dancing Girl vases in maroon glass. In 1948 Kenneth Haley had Phoenix make an assortment of pieces for K.R. Haley Glassware Company Inc. In the late 1960s, the Davis-Lynch Company, Star City, West Virginia, made some of the line's blown vases in conjunction with Phoenix. In 1976 Jeanette Shade & Novelty Company made some pieces of the line for Phoenix.

scuttle A shallow trencher or platter. The word is derived from the Latin *scutella*, meaning a dish or platter.

scuttle mugs See *shaving mugs*.

Sea Chase, The An ornamental crystal glass luminor depicting a crescent-shaped cluster of five dolphins emerging from a crescent wave. The flat base made in the form of a wave rests above a concealed light that illuminates it, traveling through to illuminate the dolphins. It was designed by Lloyd Atkins for Steuben in 1969 and engraved by Peter Schelling.

Sea Foam Colors Imperial Glass Company's name for its transparent ware with an opaque edge.

sea horse (scent) bottle A small smelling bottle with a flattened body, its lower portion curled to one side in a snail-like form. They are free blown, usually embellished with applied trailing. Some were made of colorless glass with colored trailing. They were made mainly in the late 18th-early 19th centuries in South Jersey, Pennsylvania (mainly at the Manheim Glass Works) and New England (mainly at the Boston & Sandwich Glass Works), but some were probably made in England and Scotland.

sea plants, ashes of See *kelp; roquetta; barilla; glasswort; fern ash*.

seal An engraved stamp used to make an impression on sealing wax. See *blob seal; bottle seal; fob seal; letter seal*.

sealed glassware (1) Glassware bearing a seal identifying the manufacturer. (2) Bottles having an affixed bottle seal. See *bottle seal*.

sealed reliquary A reliquary originally made as a drinking glass, but adapted by a church or religious order to preserve a religious relic or document. The mouth of the glass is closed with a cover and sealed with wax by a high-ranking member of the church or religious order. In some cases it was made from a bottle, the neck being broken off and the opening sealed with wax (a common practice in Spain).

sealed wine bottles See *wine bottles, sealed*.

sealer A Canadian term for a *preserve jar*. See *preserve jar*.

sealing A thermal finishing process wherein several pieces of glass are partially melted and joined together after they are formed. Glass may also be sealed successfully to a metal if both have similar coefficients of expansion.

seam mark A slight, narrow ridge on a glass object indicating it has been made in a mold. The seam appears where the joints of two adjacent parts of a mold meet but separate slightly during production, allowing molten glass to seep into this space. It is created by the applied pressure on the mold during the pressing or blowing process or the result of a poorly fitted or worn mold, which may also cause relief patterns to be less sharp. On higher quality pieces they are usually smoothed away by grinding or fire polishing.

Seasons, The Four See *Four Seasons, The.*

Seattle Cut Glass Company (1917-1923/4) A glass cutting company operating in Seattle, Washington.

Sebring, James See *Corning Cut Glass Co.*

Sebring Cut Glass Company See *Giometti Brothers.*

Secession The Austrian term for the Art Nouveau movement.

second glass block A small dipper-shaped iron block, one of two used in making cylinder glass. The *second glass block* was actually the first of the two used. When the gatherer picked up a blob of glass on the end of the blowpipe, he used this block to give the blob a rough form before an additional blob was gathered. See *blow block.*

section The outline of an object as it would appear if bisected by a plane, either horizontally or vertically.

seeds (1) Undissolved tiny bubbles of gas or air that do not rise to the surface during the melting process. They were common in inadequately heated old furnaces but less common in modern furnaces. If not removed or eliminated, they appear as tiny specks in finished articles. Large bubbles tend to rise quickly to the surface while smaller ones rise slowly—the smaller the bubble, the slower it rises. The creation of large bubbles is necessary for they tend to rise quickly, taking many small bubbles with them. (A common practice for creating large bubbles is to place a raw potato into the batch, which makes steam in the form of large bubbles.) Also, if the temperature of the batch is reduced about 180°F for about one hour, after the ingredients are completely melted, most of the smaller bubbles will be absorbed in the molten glass. Seeds do not usually occur in modern furnaces having thermostatic controls, but when or if they do, they must be skimmed off, especially if the product is a high quality crystal glass. (2) Impurities in molten glass or a finished article, the result of flecks of dust or dirt from tools entering the molten glass, or from the environment during the making or finishing processes.

seedy glass Any glass containing seeds. It may be older glass containing seeds that could not be or were not removed during production or newer glass in which seeds are intentionally integrated in the glass.

seedy texture A texture having minute bubbles throughout its entirety.

Seim, Emory & Swindell See *Maryland Window Glass Works.*

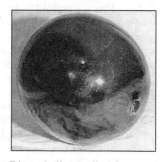

Green glass seine ball, 5" d., probably Japanese. Davanna Collection

seine balls Blown balls usually of green, blue or amber glass used to keep fishermen's nets (*seines*) afloat. See *fisherman's float.*

Selden Glass See *Consolidated Lamp & Glass Company.*

Selden line See *Martele; Sculptured Line.*

selenium An agent used in modern times to colorize or decolorize glass. Being a non-metallic element, it forms selenites, selenates, and selenides with various metallic elements. Most are colorless, but free selenium ions give the pink color to soda glass. This is vital for decolorizing glass in making bottles because it neutralizes the natural green caused by iron impurities. Selenides produce a deep red color in glass. When combined with cadmium sulfide, it produces a brilliant sealing wax red color, which was used by Frederick Carder at Steuben to make a ruby glass. Depending on the composition of the base glass and the furnace atmosphere, ruby glasses can develop their color during the melting process or during the final stages of production when the color is *struck* on reheating. If increasing amounts of selenium are added to a cadmium sulfide glass, the color of the batch will change from pure yellow to orange and finally to a brilliant red, known as *selenium ruby.*

selenium ruby glass See *selenium; ruby glass.*

Sell, G., & Company See *Krantz-Smith & Company.*

semi d'or Glass objects that have gold dust within them.

Seneca Glass Company A glass manufacturing facility established in 1891 in Fostoria, Ohio, at the former site of the Fostoria Glass Company, by immigrants from the Black Forest region of Germany. In 1896 it moved to Morgantown, West Virginia, and began making fine blown and cut crystal. During the Depression era, it introduced a wide variety of colored glass but remained famous for its rock crystal wares. Seneca now makes plain and cut goblets, sherbets, wine glasses and other tableware, and inexpensive colored glassware, specialty Christmas items, and several series of glass bells.

sentimental paperweight A paperweight, popular in the late 19th century, containing such inscriptions as *Home Sweet Home, Remember Me, From a Friend*, etc.

separator A material used in the casting or slumping process that allows glass to be removed from the mold or kiln without sticking. Magnesium oxide, silica, and plaster of paris are a few of the separators used at usual kiln temperatures. Boron nitride is often used at higher temperatures.

serass A crystal flint glass of the finest quality. See *brilliant lead glass; fine crystal; flint glass.*

Serlian motif See *Palladian window.*

serpent stemmed glass See *snake glass.*

serrated An edge or rim of an object that is notched or resembles the teeth of a saw.

server A tray used to serve food to guests.

service A set of glass tableware that includes both hollowware and flatware, made *en suite.* During the 18th century, drinking glasses were made in varying shapes— depending on the specific wines or other beverages served—and sizes. Soon it became popular among the upper classes to have sets of the various glasses to serve guests. After this it became fashionable for the sets to match or be embellished in similar motifs or designs. The next step was to have other table objects and wares matching the glasses, including bowls, decanters, dishes, etc. The range of items of the same design made by a particular factory was often so great the buyer would select only a few items. Likewise, the range of shapes, sizes, and decorative patterns was so great, the buyer could choose from an extremely wide selection. See *setting; tea service.*

serving bottle See *decanter bottle.*

serving rummer See *constable glass.*

servitor The worker who assisted the blower, at times forming the lesser parts of a piece such as stems or feet. The latter typically was done by another team member, the *bit gatherer.* When glass was blown into a mold, it was generally the servitor who attached it to the pontil rod and finished it.

set (1) More than two objects of the same or similar form, compatible with each other and used together as a unit; it is not necessary the objects be identical. A set is an extension of a pair. (2) A term used to describe the act of quickly and carefully placing a new pot, brought up to temperature in a pot arch, into a vacant space in the furnace (see *pot setting*).

Setrill (*Spanish*) An *oil cruet.* Those made in Catalonia during the 15th century have a globular body, tall, thin neck, loop handle, and long, thin curved spout. See *porro*.

setting (1) A group containing all of the articles required for *setting* a table or a single place at the table. Settings of glassware for the single place may include a goblet, wine glass, finger bowl, and salad dish. See *service*. (2) A shortened form of *pot setting*—the placing of a pot into a furnace. See *pot setting*.

set up A section sliced from a cane, such as that used in making mosaic and millefiori glass.

Sevres type vase Vases made of English colored glass decorated by an unidentified painter, believed to have worked in a porcelain factory because they are decorated in the style of some Sevres porcelain vases. They were made most likely in Bristol about 1840. Similar ones were made at Stourbridge at about the same time, with embellishment similar to that on some Derby porcelain vases. See *enameling, English*.

Seybert, Henry See *Kensington Glass Works*.

sgraffito Embellishment in which there is one thick layer of glass onto which is bonded a thinner layer, or to which a stain, enamel, etc., is applied. The top layer is then scratched to reveal the lower layer.

shabt. See *ushabti*.

shade (1) A protective glass cover used to protect a clock or ornament. They are usually large and cylindrical in shape (with a dome top and decorated finial). Some conical ones are known. They were made in France from the 18th century to protect Nevers figures and were made later in England, becoming popular during the Victorian period. See *dome*. (2) A glass object used to surround a light source and diffuse it, or to protect the flame from drafts in the case of oil and gas lamps. Banquet lamps (*Gone with the Wind*-type lamps) were the first to have attractive shades. With the advent of the use of kerosene and then electricity, glass shades came into their own. Some of the firms specializing in them were Dietz (1874), Dithridge (1896), Douglas (1871), and Bartlett (1871). (3) The degree of darkness or brightness of a color.

shaded glass Glass that has a variation of colors blending into one another, found normally on the interior layer of an object of cased glass. The process involved taking a gather of glass of one color and blowing it slightly so as to make the end away from the blowing iron thinner. The bubble is then dipped into a batch of glass of another color so that only the thin lower part is covered. The paraison is then blown to develop a glass object of even thickness with blended colors. Other methods for making a shaded glass are *striking* and *die away*. It was used by Frederick Carder at Steuben to make his *Grotesque glassware*.

shaded opalescent Pressed or pattern molded pieces of glassware on which the raised sections have an opalescent white color. It is made by coating the initial paraison with a heat-sensitive glass, then blowing or pressing it into a mold. After cooling somewhat, it is reheated at the glory hole until the raised portions of the pattern take on the opalescent white color.

shaft The column of a candlestick located between the nozzle and the base. They are in many styles, solid or hollow, and have many types of embellishment. Some on a figure candlestick were made in ornamental form, such as the shape of a woman or dolphin.

shaft & globe bottle See *wine bottle, Shapes; shaft & globe decanter*.

shaft & globe decanter An early English decanter of soda glass made since about 1725, prior to the development of lead glass. It has a globular body with sloping shoulders and tall cylindrical neck. Some are embellished with gadroon ribbing on the lower half while others are embellished with *nipt-diamond waies*. See *wine bottle, Shapes*.

shallow diamond cutting See *hollow diamond cutting*.

sham bottom See *sham dram*.

sham dram An inexpensive drinking glass with a deceptive bowl, holding less than the established measure of whiskey, Scotch, etc.

It was used by the bartender for toasts or when a customer wished to buy him a drink. It is considered a poor relative of the toast-master's glass. If it has a thick, heavy base, it is sometimes called a *sham bottom*.

Shamrock (1) A trademark used by Erlacher Glass on its light, cut designed wares executed by Floyd Manwarren and Max Erlacher. (2) A trademark used on glass-ware embellished at Corning.

shamrock cane A usually green cane with a silhouette of a shamrock within it, used in making a paperweight. They were used often by Baccarat. See *concentric paperweight.*

shank glass (Aka *stuck shank glass, shank stem glass, three part glass*) A drinking glass made in three separate parts—the bowl, stem, and foot—and attached together. See *drawn shank; stuck shank.*

shank stem glass (1) A glass made with a drawn shank. (2) A shank glass.

shaping The three basic methods used for shaping glass are *free blowing, mold blowing,* and *pressing.* See *glass, Manufacturing, Shaping, for details.*

shard (Aka *sherd, potsherd*) A broken piece or fragment of an object. With respect to glassware, it is usually a fragment of a glass object generally unearthed at an excavation site.

shard glass Embellishment in which colored glass is blown into a thin bubble and broken into fragments or *shards*. These are spread on a marver, picked up on a paraison, and marvered into it, then blown into the desired form.

shari-tsubo Glass vessels of religious significance ceremoniously buried beneath Buddhist shrines but able to be filled from above with offerings from monks or worshippers. They were first made during the Nara period about the 7th century A.D.

Sharp, Alexander H. See *Estelle Glass Works.*

Sharp & Westcott See *Wood, R.D., Glass Works.*

sharp (relief) diamond The cut-glass motif known as *nailhead diamond.*

shatterproof glass See *safety glass.*

shaving box A small jar or box with a cover to hold soap used to make lather for shaving.

shaving mirror An adjustable mirror used for shaving. See *dressing glass or mirror.*

shaving mug A mug designed to hold shaving soap. It is used by men for mixing shaving lather by adding a small amount of water to soap generally shaped to fit into the mug. They were popular about the time of the Civil War but came into their own when a rash, called *Barber's Itch,* swept the country in the late 1800s. Barber's Itch—ringworm—developed in the bearded areas of the face and neck. It was caused by fungi and characterized by reddish patches. Until then a barber used a common mug and brush for all customers, causing the rash to spread quickly. It was then men wanted their own mugs (with their names and/or occupations on them), which were kept at the barbershop, usually on shelves in orderly rows. Most were ceramic, but many were glass. A *scuttle mug* is any shaving mug shaped differently from the standard mug.

shaving paper vase A vase used in barber shops to hold small neck strips (paper strips placed around the neck to protect the collar from the oils of the hair and shaving lather and to minimize the amount of hair going down a person's back) or small strips of paper used by the barber to wipe his razors while shaving his customers. The larger vases for neck strips are about eight to ten inches tall and five inches in diameter. The small vases for wiping strips, called *waste bowls,* are about four inches tall.

shear mark (1) A scratch-like fissure normally found at the center of the bottom of pieces. It has rough edges and is relatively deep, caused by unclean shears cutting the gather from the punty rod. The shears had to be very sharp and the cutting done quickly. If the gather was cut from the punty rod with unclean shears, a chilling effect resulted, causing at the point of contact a fissure in the glass that was not obliterated nor healed in the process of forcing the metal into the mold and remaining as a blemish. (2) A blemish formed when the cutting was not done quickly enough, leaving a small "tail" of glass stringing behind the blob as it went in the mold. This "tail" cooled quickly and, when the pressing began, it caused a distinctive blemish, often in the form of a swirl, as it melted back into the body. If the gather turned while dropping into the mold, the shear mark would appear in a location other than the center. It is also called a *straw mark*.

sheared glass (Aka *driven glass*) An object such as the bowl of a goblet that, after being blown, is sheared from the blowpipe while still hot. The rim is then made round and smooth by reheating. See *cracking off*.

shearer A person who watched over and cared for a furnace at a glass manufacturing facility.

shearing the furnace Tending to the furnace at a glass manufacturing facility.

shearings (Aka *cuttings, clippings*) Slivers or pieces of waste glass cut or sheared from an object while being formed and still in its plastic shape. See *shears*.

Shearman's Works See *Oneida Glass Factory Company*.

shears A tool used by glassmakers to trim a piece of glassware in the course of its making, such as the rim of a drinking glass attached to the pontil by the base or held by a gadget. See *tools, glassmaker's; parrot nose shears*.

sheet glass Large flat sheets of glass having parallel plane sides made by various methods that have changed and improved over time, allowing ever larger sheets to be made. Sheet glass has been made by the following methods: casting, broad glass process, crown or Normandy process, cylinder glass process, Bicheroux process, Lubbers process, Pittsburgh process, Fourcault process, and, since 1959, float glass process. See *plate glass*.

Sheets & Duffy (1856-1859) A bottle glass manufacturing facility operating in Kensington (Philadelphia), Pennsylvania.

shelf piece (1) An object that has been broken and sometimes repaired. Though not suitable to use as intended, it is displayed because of its beauty or uniqueness. See *fractured piece*. (2) An object which, because of its beauty, uniqueness, worth, intrinsic value or heirloom quality, is not used as intended but is displayed.

shell border (Aka *fan scallop*) A fan (see *fan cutting*) cut within a scallop motif on the rim of a bowl, radiating to the upper edge of the scallop. The extremity of each mitered groove in the fan is usually notched.

shell dish A dish in the form of a scallop shell. The earliest known were made of Roman glass during the 3rd century A.D. Later ones with the shell positioned on a stemmed foot were made in Bohemia of rock crystal in the 17th century and of glass in the 18th century. See *ambrosia dish*.

shell flask A flask (amphoriskos) with a blown mold replica of a scallop shell on both sides. Each side is made separately and fused together, the seam indicating where the sides were joined. Some have a short neck and small mouth. Others with a stemmed foot have a tall neck, a disk mouth, two vertical side handles and two small loops at or below the rim for a carrying strap. They were made of Roman glass in the Rhineland from the 1st to the 3rd centuries, and copied in Murano in the 16th and 17th centuries. For the same technique, see *grape cluster flask*.

shellfish beaker A beaker of ovoid form normally with four small feet, embellished with two or more rows of applied hollow glass figures (shrimp or shellfish) around the body. They were made in Cologne during the 4th century. See *dolphin beaker*.

Shepard, J., & Co. See *Zanesville Glass Manufacturing Company*.

Shepard Company See *Shepherd Company*.

Shepherd & Webb See *Webb family; White House Glassworks*.

Shepherd Company (1863-1895) (Aka *Shepard Company*) A glass manufacturing facility that made pressed glass tableware in Birmingham (Pittsburgh), Pennsylvania. In 1865 Campbell, Jones & Company took over operations. In 1880 James Dalzell was hired as agent and, in 1883, became president. Soon after he left to form a glassworks (Dalzell Brothers & Gilmore). In 1886, Jones, Cavitt & Company took over operations, operating it until it closed.

shepherd's crook A tall staff with a curved handle used by a shepherd while tending his flock. Examples have been made of glass, strictly for ornamental purposes. See *walking stick*.

Pink Depression glass sherbet, 3-1/2" h.
Davanna Collection

Sherbet, Patrician, green.
Krause Publications

sherbet A small dish, usually footed, to serve sherbet, ice cream or dessert to guests.

sherbet plate See *bread & butter plate*.

sherd A shard or a potsherd. An archaeological term for broken pieces of pottery or glass.

sherry glass A small drinking glass for sherry, with a stemmed foot and a bowl of

various shapes and sizes. It is slightly larger than a port glass. See *sack glass*.

Shields & Knapp A glass cutting shop in Hawley, Pennsylvania.

ship A small model of a rigged sailing vessel made by craftsmen *at-the-lamp* in the Bristol area of England during the 19th century. They are usually of clear glass with details such as riggings of colored glass resting on a sea of glass fiber. They are now made by artisans at craft shows.

ship candlestick A candlestick with an unusually wide circular base to ensure stability on a ship. England was a major producer during the early 19th century. See *ship's decanter.*

ship glass An English drinking glass with a wide, thick foot and short stem to ensure stability on a ship. Ship glasses were made with a wide variety of bowl shapes and stems.

ship-in-bottle A miniature replica of a sailing ship enclosed within a glass bottle. The traditional process of making one was to make a small wooden hull with masts hinged to it and push this into the bottle through the neck. Strings were attached to the masts so that, when the masts were pulled upright in the bottle, the strings remained as part of the rigging. The surplus string was burnt off or attached to the bottle with wax, and the bottle was sealed with wax. Modern ones are made with a glass ship inserted in the bottle by secret processes. On occasion the ship is completed in its entirety, placed in one half on the bottle and the other half fused to it with the seams at the top and bottom when it is displayed horizontally.

ship subjects Engraved or enameled embellishment on glassware depicting various types of ships. During the 18th century such engraving was done in various countries, including Holland and Russia. See *privateer glassware; naval subjects*.

ship's decanter (Aka *Rodney decanter*) A decanter used in the cabin of a ship's officer. It is of circular section with an unusually broad bottom to ensure stability on a ship at sea. Its sides sometimes extend downward and outward in a straight line from the neck to the base while others form a fluid concave curve. Most are highly ornamented with faceting and cutting, and some have applied rings around the neck, spaced to fit the fingers for a firmer grip. The rings must be applied with great skill so they appear uniform with no visible overlap or joint.

Shirley, Frederick S. A glass technician and manager of the Mt. Washington Glass Co. In the 1880s he acquired patents for numerous types of art glass, including Crown Milano and Burmese. In 1886 he received licenses to use the names Peachblow and Peach Skin on company products.

Shirley Temple glassware Usually blue transparent glassware with a picture of Shirley Temple on the outside surface. It was often given as a premium with cereal. Drinking glasses and small cream pitchers were most common.

Shizuku A product of Awashima Glass Co., Tokyo, Japan. Mold blown glass with a roughened surface texture resembling raindrops. *Shizuku*, in Japanese, means *raindrop*.

shoe A decorative object made in the form of a lady's shoe or slipper. Many were made in Nailsea and Murano (with lattimo stripes), and in Spain and France. In the United States they were frequently made in the *Daisy & Button* pattern. See *boot glass; slipper.*

shoemaker glass See *Schusterglas.*

shoo-fly flask A flask made in the late 1800s to hold a mixture of molasses and brown sugar used for baking, i.e., shoo-fly pie.

shooting lodge glass
See *Schiesshausglas.*

shooting star See *star.*

shop (Aka *chair*) A shop consists of a *gaffer* (the master blower and head of the shop) and his assistants: *blower* (second assistant), *servitor* (first assistant), *sticker-up,* a boy usually called a *taker-in,* and sometimes others if the nature of the work required more. This team has both skilled and unskilled workers, each having a specific, well-defined task. It was normally required to make a specific number

of items (a *move*) during a shift (a *turn*) in accordance with an agreement between the local union and the facility manager.

short stemmed foot A foot made in the following manner: In shaping the foot of an object, a gather applied to the base of a bowl was tooled into straight sides for about 1/4 to 3/8 inch, then smoothed out into a flaring foot with a slanting upper surface.

shot glass (1) A glass vessel filled with lead shot to support and clean quill or lead pens. (2) A small drinking glass similar to a whiskey glass. They were so named, mainly in the United States, because they are used to serve a single measure or *shot* of whiskey. Their capacity is one or 1-1/2 ounces, and they normally measure from 1-3/4 to 3 inches high. They have no foot, stem or handle, and have a flat, convex or pointed base and thick bottom. Whiskey glasses held slightly more. See *fractional shot glass; double shot glass; jumbo shot glass.*

Shotton, Thomas, Cut Glass Company Coming to the United States from England in 1884, Shotton began working for T.G. Hawkes. He left in 1893, moving to Brooklyn, New York, where he established a glass cutting facility. He had additional but short-lived facilities in New York City and Corning. All operations ceased in 1923.

shoulder The bulge below the neck but above the body of a vase, bottle, or similar vessel.

shoulder knop A knop, basically cylindrical but bulging at the top and drawn inward to meet the stem. Sometimes it has molded embellishments and/or enclosed air bubbles.

shouldered decanter A decanter with sides sloping slightly inward toward the bottom and a shoulder that slopes inward, narrowing to form the neck.

shouldered stem See *Silesian stem.*

show furniture Medicinal bottles (decorative, professional-looking containers) with Latin labels, generally found on pharmacist's shelves and in doctor's offices. They were made of clear glass and in a limited number of color, the primary color being green.

show globes Glass globes used to enclose hanging lights in apothecary windows. Many were cut or engraved. They were made from the 1870s to the 1900s in the United States. Plain ones are generally more recent.

show objects of glass Quality bottles, jars, and urns that are cut, engraved, or hand decorated for display in drug stores and doctor's offices, creating a more professional atmosphere and appearance. They were usually quite large, ranging to 32 inches tall with a capacity of 10 gallons.

shredded coconut glass See *Peloton glass.*

Shreve, Evans & Roberts See *Waterford Glass Works.*

shrimp bowl See *caviar bowl.*

shtoff (Russian) A special beaker used for drinking vodka.

Shull-Goodwin Glass Co. See *Wheaton, T.C., Company.*

Sicilian ware See *Lava glassware.*

sick glass (1) A piece of glass not properly tempered or annealed. *Sickness* often shows as tiny random cracks or flaking, followed by gradual disintegration. Some early glasses were so badly affected that they would *weep*, feeling damp to the touch. (2) Chemical disintegration of glass due to a faulty formula, often because of too much alkali in the mixture. The glass may appear damp and give off an odor of ammonia, and pieces may flake off. The term *crizzling* was used in England during the 1670s for *sick* glass that gradually devitrified because of excess borax in the batch. (3) A piece of glass that exhibits cloudiness or haziness, mainly the result of a liquid leaving a deposit on its inner surface that cannot be removed by any cleaner or chemical. It also may be the result of impurities in the batch from which the piece was made. The haziness or cloudiness usually disappears when the glass is wet. See *decay; crisseling.*

Sidone, Vetro (Italian) An ornamental glass developed by Ercole Barovier for Barovier & Toso about 1957. It has a checkerboard pattern made by fusing square and rectangular pieces of opalescent glass with a narrow, colored center stripe going in the opposite direction from that of the adjacent pieces. See *murrina.*

Sidonian glassware (1) Glassware possibly made from before the 15th century B.C. at Sidon (and Tyre) on the Syrian coast. These sites, as well as sites in Mesopotamia, are considered the earliest glassmaking centers. The glass is said to have been made from sand on the banks of the River Belus (see *natron*). Some mold-blown vessels with "*Sidon*" stamped on a pad near the handle provide grounds for believing the first glassware was blown there, probably during the 1st century B.C. On some signed pieces there is also a name stamped near "*Sidon*," most likely that of the maker. The glass was thin and colorless but not transparent. Early glass was often pale bluish green, later glass was yellowish, and some was deliberately colored white, purple, blue, opaque, etc. The main vessels were mold-blown flasks, jugs, beakers, bowls, and mercury bottles distributed widely by Phoenician traders. Sidon (now Saida, near Lebanon) was the capital of Phoenicia until it ceased being a nation by the 1st century B.C. At that time Syrian glassmakers migrated to Italy and elsewhere, establishing new facilities. See *Syrian glassware.* (2) (Aka *Allasantes*) A glassware patented by Thomas Wilkes Webb of Thomas Webb & Sons on June 9, 1876. Colored threads were attached to the articles, and expansion by heat caused them to form odd patterns.

siege (1) The floor or bed of a glass furnace on which the pots rest. (2) The floor of a glass tank. (3) See *grate.*

Siemens furnace See *Wanne.*

sifter See *castor; saltshaker.*

sight size With respect to windows, the actual size of the glass letting in the light.

signature cane A millefiori cane bearing the name or initial(s) of the factory of origin or the artist creating the paperweight.

signed glass The identification on glassware, usually a small trademark, identifying it with the manufacturing facility in most cases. Occasionally, though, the decorator or distributor signed it with his mark. Signing, except for a few older pieces, started in the 19th century. Some companies used it only on certain pieces (usually the better ones) and/or for certain years. Some had several signatures. Not all pieces were consistently marked; sometimes only one item in a set is marked. Signatures can be mold impressed. Cut-glass signatures are generally acid impressed (stamped with an acid solution), usually on the center of the base inside the top surface but sometimes off center, on or just below the handle, or in an inconspicuous place where it does not affect the refractory qualities of the piece. Overall, relatively few pieces are signed.

Signet Glass Company (1913-1916) A glass cutting facility in Corning, New York, purchasing its blanks from and shipping its wares to Hawkes. This led to the belief that its operations were within the Hawkes facility. Its trademark was a stamped script *Signet*.

Silberiris glass A glass with a pitted surface, introduced in 1900 by Max Ritter von Spaun of the Loetz glassworks. It was often undecorated but occasionally was given a chain design or other surface decoration.

Silesian glass Glassware made in Silesia, which became part of Poland during the 11th century and a part of Bohemia beginning in 1526. In 1742 the various Bohemian provinces, one of which was Silesia, came under Austrian, Prussian, and Polish rule, later being divided between Poland and Czechoslovakia. The principal glass manufacturing centers were in the Riesengebirge, a mountainous area adjoining Bohemia, and in the Hirschberger Tal. Included in these regions were the facilities of the Counts Schaffgotsch at Petersdorf, and those at Schreiberhau (from the mid-14th to the 19th century) and Friedrichsgrund. Silesian glassware was embellished by engravers at Warmbrunn. See *engraving, Bohemian-Silesian*.

Silesian stem (Aka *pseudo-faceted stem, pedestal stem, shouldered stem, molded pedestal stem*) A ribbed and shouldered molded stem made in England and Germany. Early ones dating from about 1715 were four-sided, became six-sided and, from about 1725, eight-sided and smaller with rounded shoulders. They were seldom used on wine glasses after about 1740, but were used often on heavier tazze, candlesticks, and sweetmeat glasses. After about 1725 some stems on wine glasses were accompanied by one or two knops, but only on specific pieces. Knops are not found on sweetmeat glasses.

Silex See *Libbey Silex*.

silhouette An outline of an object, figure or portrait filled with a monochrome color, normally black. There are two distinct types associated with glassware:(1) Enameled embellishment used during the Empire period. Miniature medallions with silhouettes in black were often inserted within the body of the goblet on the reverse of the glass. (2) Made of glass in a mold and inserted in some canes used in making millefiori glass. The process of making these involved first carving the desired silhouette on the inside of the iron mold and pouring in molten, dark-colored glass. Once formed it was removed on a pontil and covered with clear or opaque glass, then drawn to make a long thin cane, eventually sliced, and set in molten glass. They represented animals, butterflies, dancing figures, etc., as well as profiles of famous persons, or were custom made for specific customers. Several different silhouettes are often found in a paperweight, each surrounded by florets. See *silhouette cane*. (3) A stemmed glassware where the stem is of black glass in the form of one of a variety of animals. They were developed by A. Douglas Nash and made by his company, but not while he was there.

silhouette cane A cane having inserted within it a silhouette of an animal, insect, flower, dancing person, devil, famous person, etc., normally of black, white or solid color glass. Modern ones have included the signs of the Zodiac. Baccarat was famous for these. See *silhouette*.

silhouette glassware Stemmed tableware where the stem was of black glass in the form of various animals. It was developed by A. Douglas Nash at the A. Douglas Nash Corp., but was not made until after he left to join the Libbey Glass Co. in Toledo, Ohio. See *figure, stem*.

silica Silicon dioxide, SiO_2. A compound occurring widely in nature as sand, quartz, flint, and diatomite, and one of the essential ingredients in making glass. The most common form used in making glass is sand (an impure silica) obtained from seashores or inland beds. The Venetians used white pebbles from the rivers, grinding them into sand-like consistency. In England, at least as early as about 1650, calcined and powdered flints were used (see *flint glass*). Pure silica can be used to form glass, but its fusion requires such high temperatures it is commercially impracticable; it is used in making certain laboratory glassware that is subjected to high temperatures. Silica is either in the form of an odorless and tasteless white powder or clear crystals. It is insoluble in water and most acids, except hydrofluoric acid. It is soluble in molten alkali and combines chemically with most metallic oxides. It melts at 1710ºC, forming a glass with the lowest known coefficient of expansion (*fused silica*) and a thermal conductivity about half that of ordinary glass.

silica glass See *fused silica*.

silk glass See *verre de soie*.

silk screening See *stained glass, Surface Treatments*.

sillabub glass See *syllabub glass*.

Silvart A trademark registered on July 25, 1916, by the Deidrick Glass Company. It was used on its engraved pieces with silver deposit embellishment.

silver A metallic agent used in the glass industry as a coloring agent when added to the batch, as an embellishment when decorating glass, and as a reflective medium when backing mirrors. Following are some of the ways in which silver is used: (1) silver leaf used with or instead of gold leaf in embellishing Zwischengoldglas; (2) silver nitrate used in backing mirrors and in making silvered glass; (3)

silver sulfide used to produce staining with the deep yellow color and to develop a straw yellow color used in luster painting; (4) elemental metallic silver used to make silver electroplated glass; and (5) silver foil used in making Silveria glassware. A small amount of silver in the glass of the Lycurgus Cup may have helped to produce the dichroic effect.

silver cased glassware A glass vessel blown as a lining into a silver shell with openings in it, forming a decorative pattern as the glass bulged through the openings. It was called *opus interrasile* and made of Roman glass during the 1st century A.D., becoming popular at various times throughout history. See *metal cased glassware*.

Silver City (Cut) Glass Company A
glass cutting facility established in 1905 in Meriden, Connecticut.

Black glass vase, c. 1925-1949.
The Corning Museum of Glass

Silver deposit jar, clear glass, 5" h., ground stopper, molded signature "H" in diamond (A.H. Heisey & Co.).
Davanna Collection

silver decorated glass Mounting glass objects in metals has always been a method of ensuring glass was somewhat protected, especially at its weakest points. This was popular in the 1890s. Tiffany often mounted or decorated some of his pieces in silver. As an extension of this, many companies specialized in decorating glass with silver. In the 1920s silver mounted or decorated glass again became fashionable. An additional form of silver or metal mounted glass was the making of a metal case into which glass was blown (see *silver cased glassware*). Many companies put silver rims on bowls, pitchers, and compotes to beautify as well as to minimize chipping. Vases and urns were often given a silver base to add weight to beautify and minimize tipping. Many items were embellished with silver, including lids on dresser jars, stoppers on decanters, handles on syrup jugs, tops on salt and pepper shakers, etc. Sterling silver was used on finer pieces, and silver plating on less expensive ones. See *silver deposit glass*.

silver deposit glass Silver deposited on glass usually by an electrodepositing process (see *silver electroplated glass)*. A patent for electrodepositing silver on glassware was issued in England in 1877. This was quicker and less expensive than blowing double wall vessels. Since the silver was only a thin coating on the glass, it tended to discolor and was susceptible to chipping, flaking, and wear. A variation in the plating process produces a layer not silver colored, but metallic red, blue, or green.

In the United States the first processes for silver decoration on glass were developed in the 1880s, and by the 1890s many companies were making it. It is still being made today; the modern process involves using potassium and ammonium hydroxides. Alvin Manufacturing, Reed & Barton, and Gorham were silver companies specializing in silver deposit glass. Designs included fruit, floral, abstract, curving linear, etc. H.C. Fry Glass made many opalescent art glass pieces with silver deposit decoration. John H. Scharling of Newark patented his method of laminating metal to glass in 1893. It included etching through the finished layer of metal or through metal and glass together. The resulting slightly raised metal pattern was embellished further with engraving. In another process, solid sterling silver with a cut-out design was applied to glass using a chemical method so the cut-out of the design appeared against clear or colored glass. These wares were often called *silver overlay*. During the Depression era, much silver deposit glass was made by the Cape Cod Silver Deposit Art Glass Company and Century Metalcraft Corp.

silver diamond Dorflinger's term for the English version of the cut-glass motif called *strawberry diamond*. See *strawberry diamond*.

silver electroplated glass An art glass with electrodeposited silver on the surface (see *silver deposit glass*). One process was patented in 1889 by Oscar Pierre Erard and John Benjamin Round for Stevens & Williams Ltd. It involved using a special flux containing silver mixed with turpentine to form a wash that was painted on the glass to make a design. The piece was fired and placed in a solution of silver through which an electric current was passed, causing the silver to deposit where the flux was painted. It was popular from about 1890 until 1920.

silver onyx glass A glass object having the appearance of being plated or cased with silver. A piece of creamy opaque to pale orange opaline glass is painted with a platinum luster, then fired to fix the coating.

silver overlay glass See *silver deposit glass*.

silver shape The form given to some glassware, copied or adapted from a silver prototype.

silver staining The silver yellow color obtained by surface staining using various silver compounds, mainly silver nitrate. It involves an approach different from making colored glasses. It is based on a property of the silver ions (also the basis of the term *stained glass*) being able to replace some of the alkali ions in the glass when heated to just below its softening point. The silver ions diffuse into the glass and are reduced to elemental silver when they come in contact and react with other ions associated with impurities or with a decolorizing agent such as iron or arsenic.

silver thread Fine line miter cutting used to fill in the background on a cut-glass object, adding brilliance to the piece.

silver veiling technique A technique used in making a specific type of paperweight involving the melting of silver and glass together. On reheating the mixture, the silver is drawn to the surface where a design is developed. As the design is made, the glass is drawn and twisted, the silver causing it to change colors (brown to yellow, yellow to blue, etc.) depending on its formula. The color is controlled to an extent by the rate of heating and cooling of the glass. Once the design is formed, an additional layer of glass encases the design and the exterior is fire polished.

silvered glass (Aka *mercury glass*) An ornamental glassware having an overall silver appearance like a vacuum bottle. It is made by placing a solution of silver nitrate in the space between the walls of a blown double-walled vessel, pouring it through a hole in the base. After filling, the hole is sealed tightly with papier-mâché, glass disk, plaster plug, small cork, lead plug, or even, on better pieces, silver (sometimes signed with the maker's name). This forms an air-tight seal to prevent the silver from discoloring through oxidation. If the seal is not air tight, the silver nitrate will gradually turn black. Elemental mercury was often used to produce the silver appearance instead of silver nitrate. Sometimes such ware was engraved or flashed with a colored glass, cut to show the silver inner layer.

A patent for the silvering process was issued in 1849 to F. Hale Thomson of London. Some disks used as seals are impressed with his name as patentee or with the name of E. Varnish & Co., a licensee. The first U.S. patent was granted on January 16, 1855, to William Leighton of New England Glass for a silvered door knob. His mark appears below the seal on some pieces. Another patent was issued on April 4, 1865, to John W. Haines of the Boston Silver Glass Company for improvements in silvering glass pitchers. Substantial amounts of silvered glass were made by Brooklyn Flint Glass and companies in England, France, and Belgium between 1855 and 1885. It is much less expensive to make than silver or silver-plated articles. It

should not to be confused with silver deposit glass.

Silveria glassware A type of art glass with a silvery appearance created by silver foil being embedded between two layers of clear colorless or colored glass. To make it, a primary bulb was blown to almost full size before it picked up the silver foil from the marver. A protective layer of glass was then placed over the foil by immersing the bulb into a pot of fluid glass. Trailings of colored glass, usually green, were trickled haphazardly on its surface or deliberately to create a design. In addition, a few articles have small leafy attachments. On some pieces the silver foil has become oxidized over time, becoming dark brown or black, usually if crisselling or cracks have occurred in the outer layer or if air has penetrated the space between the layers.

The process was developed about 1900 by John Northwood II and made initially by Stevens & Williams. Some specimens are marked "S & W" with the word *England* or a small *fleur-de-lis*. On February 13, 1878, Paul d'Humy of Soho, Middlesex County, England, patented a comparable means of embellishing glass. His method differed in that the primary bulb was only partially blown before picking up the gold or silver foil from the marver. As a result, when the paraison was expanded, the foil trapped between the layers tore apart, giving a different effect than Silveria. On November 29, 1878, a patent was registered in England by Monot, Pere et Fils & Stumpf of Paris for another process of applying a layer of gold or other metal foil either between two layers of glass or on the exterior for the purpose of producing the ornamental effect known in France as *Chine Metallique*. The patent indicated the outer shell, rather than the inner, was to be completed first. Others, such as Galle, Daum Brothers, and Rousseau, used these processes to various extents in making some of their art glass. This ware should not be confused with *Silverina* glass.

Silverina glassware An art glass developed by Frederick Carder in the 1920s at Steuben. The techniques for making it had been in existence for several years. It was made by picking up flakes of mica on the paraison and covering them with a layer of clear colored glass. The flakes vary in size and density (the silvery color from the mica is influenced by the color of the outer layer), and are combined with trapped air bubbles. It should not be confused with Silveria glass.

silvering Any number of methods of decorating glassware with silver, including a method used as an alternative to or combined with gilding (which is rarely used because of the tendency to tarnish); making mirrors; used instead of gold leaf in the *Zwischgold-glas* technique; etc. See *silver cased glassware; silver decorated glassware; silver deposit glass; silver electroplated glass; silver staining; silver veiling technique; silvered glass; mirror.*

Simms Modern Cut Glass

Company Beginning his career as a glass cutter in Detroit, Michigan about 1903, Joseph A. Simms established a company there in 1918. In 1927 the name was changed to Crystal Mirror & Glass Company, which closed about 1935.

Simpson & Co. See *Simpson, Leake & Stenger.*

Simpson, Lake & Stanger

See *Simpson, Leake & Stenger.*

Simpson, Leake & Stenger A short-lived glass manufacturing facility established in 1848 in Pittsburgh, Pennsylvania, specializing in colored glasses used for lanterns and amber color patent medicine bottles. One source refers to the company as Simpson, Lake & Stenger.

simpulum (Latin) A small (4 to 4-1/2 inches high) Roman ladle with a circular bowl and a short, flat handle extending vertically, for dipping wine to honor a god. Specimens were found in 1961 in the ruins of Herculaneum, dating shortly before 79 A.D.—the year Vesuvius erupted. They were related to the Greek *kyathos.*

simulated cameo An inexpensive glassware made in Bohemia. Its design in white enameling was made to simulate true cameo glass with a carved white overlay.

Clear glass vase, Sinclaire & Company, c. 1910-1928. The Corning Museum of Glass

Sinclaire, H.P., & Company H.P. (Henry Purdon) Sinclaire's father, H.P. Sr., worked for the Brooklyn Flint Glass Works. H.P. was four years old in 1868 when the company moved to Corning, New York. The Sinclaire family moved with it. H.P. Sr.'s brother-in-law, Amory Houghton, was president of the company, which later became the Corning Glass Works.

In his early years, H.P. Jr. developed a talent for drawing natural objects. He later worked one summer for J. Hoare & Co., but he did not like it, so he entered the Rochester Business University. After receiving training, he accepted a position as bookkeeper with Hawkes Rich Cut Glass Works. While there he studied the glass cutters, did some designs from nature on glass, and learned all phases of the industry. At the age of 27 he became a partner, director, and secretary for Hawkes (Hawkes' trademark includes a *fleur-de-lis* for the French name of *Sinclaire*).

Hawkes was famous for its brilliant cut glass, but Sinclaire continued to engrave objects of nature. His distaste for brilliant cut glass increased, leading him to establish H.P. Sinclaire & Company in Corning in 1904. He obtained his blanks from Dorflinger and Hawkes and attempted to shift America's taste from brilliant cut to engraved glassware. He marked his glass with an "S" in a wreath, but only after it had passed a rigid inspection. In later years he used the block printed *Sinclaire* as the signature (usually found on the rim or foot edge of stemware). Some pieces have both signatures. Pieces were made of clear, blue, amber, green, and ruby glass. Only a small percentage of his total production was marked.

During World War I and thereafter, good quality blanks were difficult to find, so he began making his own (using the Dorflinger formula) at a facility he built in 1921 in Bath, New York, where some cutting operations were conducted. In 1923, Sinclaire's son, Murray, joined the company, but by then competition from Europe had cut into business. In an effort to remain viable, the company started to make new lines of glassware, including lines of colored glass, undecorated glass, institutional glassware, and a heat-resistant pressed glassware called *Radnt*, for kitchen use. Sinclaire died in 1927, and in 1928 the Corning facility closed. The Bath facility closed in 1929.

single cable See *cable twist.*

single chip glass See *feather glass.*

single flint series See *flint glass.*

single series twist A twist with one column of spiral decoration, either an air or an opaque twist surrounded by clear glass. It is sometimes abbreviated for reference as *SSAT* (single series air twist) and *SSOT* (single series opaque twist). See *double series twist.*

single star A cut-glass motif made with a miter cut, in which there are equal length vanes radiating from a central point. It is often found on the bottom of vases, pitchers, etc., and is the least expensive of the star motifs to cut. It is often called a *rayed base* when the motif is on the base. See *star.*

sintering Heating a mixture of materials so they become a coherent mass without being melted. See *frit.*

sinumbra lamp Literally, *without shadow lamp.* An oil lamp that does not cast a shadow because of its design. It was patented in France in 1820 by George Phillips of London. It was made of metal, had a globular reservoir (font) for oil, and rested on a metal stand.

siphon glass A joke glass with a tube extending vertically upward in the center of the bowl. Placed over this tube is a larger one that continues downward from a hollow stag-like figure whose mouth extends beyond the rim of the glass and from which the user sucks the contents. They were made in Germany and Russia from the 16th through the 18th centuries.

site A flat plate of *cristallo* glass that is ground, polished, and silvered, used in making mirrors. It was made in Venice and, by 1570, was exported to mirror makers in Antwerp, Rouen, and England.

situla (Latin) A bucket-shaped receptacle, normally used to hold holy water, with a flat base and two small loops or lugs near the rim for attaching an overhead handle. Roman and Byzantine ones were made during the 3rd to the 5th centuries, and were about eight inches deep. See *situla pagana; aspersorium; bucket.*

situla pagana (Latin) (1) (Aka *Situla di San Marco*) A situla of greenish Roman glass with an overhead handle, embellished using the vasa diatreta technique. The upper half has a hunting frieze, and the lower half has a network-type embellishment of tangential arches in cage style. It was likely made by Italian craftsmen during the 3rd and 4th century A.D., and brought into the Treasury of St. Mark's Cathedral, Venice, when Venice conquered Byzantium. (2) A similar situla but of violet colored glass, likely made in Byzantine during the 5th century, and also housed at St. Mark's. It is embellished with wheel engraved Bacchanalian scenes executed in intaglio.

size In the glass manufacturing industry, size refers to glutinous substances such as glues, resins, etc., used to bond colors or precious metal leaf to glassware.

skail; skalle; skayle See *scole.*

Skinner, William, & Son The Skinner family has a history of over 300 years as stone cutters, engravers, and glass cutters. William Skinner worked in Stourbridge, England, before coming to the United States to work for Pairpoint, then Dorflinger. In 1895 he established a glass cutting shop in Philadelphia, Pennsylvania, making brilliant cutware on heavy blanks. In 1899 he moved to Hammonton, New Jersey. William's son, Thomas, born that year, managed the company in later years. In 1901 the company erected its own glass manufacturing facility in Hammonton. By 1915 it was using pressed blanks in its cutting frames. By 1920 its production was at its lowest, but it continued making stemware and black plate glass desk sets until about 1930. From 1930 to 1940 it made mirrored picture frames, table plateaus, and ashtrays. As of 1964 it was making holders for desk pens, and has since gone out of business.

Skinner Glass Company See *Gunderson (-Pairpoint) Glass Works.*

skittle (pot) A tall, cylindrical, yet relatively small, clay pot or crucible (shaped like a *skittle*—a pin in ninepins) in which the ingredients for making glass were fused. The skittle was used until the invention of the crown pot. It was used later for making colored glass and for melting colors or enamels.

skole See *scole.*

Skull of Doom A life-size skull carved from a solid piece of pure crystal, believed to be of Aztec origin, made in the 1400s during the colonial period. It was obtained from Mexico during the mid-1800s and was later owned by Tiffany's, which sold it to the British Museum in 1898. The museum cleaning staff refused to work unless the skull was covered.

skyphos *(Greek)* A drinking cup, hemispherical or semi-ovoid in shape, with a low-to-medium-height bowl, and sides curving inward toward a flat base or foot ring. Two loop side handles, one horizontal and one vertical, are attached at or just below the rim. The form was adapted from the Greek *skyphoi. Skyphos* has been used to include the type of cup with wing handles (sometimes called a *pterotos cup*). See *poculum.*

slab glass (Aka *Dalle-de-Verre, Dalles*) Extra thick colored antique glass cast in thick slabs, usually 8 by 12 inches or 12 inches square and from 1/2 to 1 inch thick.

slag glass An opaque multicolored pressed glass, streaky like marble. The streakiness was caused by the inclusion in the glass of some waste slag, usually from a local iron works, such as the silicate skimmed off molten steel. This is similar to the process used in making *ironstone china*, a type of opaque stoneware.

Slag glass has been mistakenly called *end-of-day glass*, which is made from the odds and ends of glass left over at the end of a normal day's production. Articles were usually made by press molding molten glass (some was mold blown), making inexpensive wares in various colors. Because it was multicolored, it was often called *calico, spatter* or *mottled* glass. It was made from about 1875 to 1890 by several facilities in northeastern England near some ironworks. Some true slag glass, though never called such when first made, was produced in the United States by a few manufacturers, including Challinor and Northwood. Both called it *Mosaic* (Ruth Webb Lee called it *marble glass*).

The most common color of slag glass was purple. The largest maker was Challinor (patenting its process for making this "variegated" glass in June 1886), followed by Atterbury & Company and Northwood. More recently, purple slag glassware were made by Imperial, Fenton, Westmoreland, Boyd, and L.G. Wright.

There are three types of slag glass: (a) *fuse mix*, colors well blended, flowing gradually from one to the other; (b) *open mix*, having a clear line of demarcation between colors; and (c) *over mix*, having no white although it does have areas of clear glass. Slag glass was difficult to make because the white did not always adhere to the purple, caused by different annealing requirements; it sometimes appeared cracked or unconnected. There are some pieces of true slag glass dating from about 1840, considered to be of American origin. France and Czechoslovakia made some in the late 1800s. Besides purple, it has been made in blue, green, deep amber (called butterscotch or caramel), red or orange-red, and black or gray-black. See *marble glass; Tyneside glassware.*

Slane & Burrell See *South Boston Crown Glass Co.*

sleeve (1) A *save-all*. (2) A large-diameter refractory rotating tube capable of being raised or lowered, suspended vertically just above the orifice ring. It controls the flow rate of molten glass. The nearer the sleeve is to the orifice ring, the smaller the amount of molten glass flows through. The farther the sleeve is from the orifice ring, the greater the amount of flowing glass. Inside it is a reciprocating refractory plunger. While there are various ways of controlling the shape and weight of the gather, the most important is being able to raise or lower the sleeve. See *feeder.*

slice cutting Vertical flute cutting.

slick stone; slicker See *linen smoother.*

slider A coaster. See *coaster.*

Sligo Glass Works (Aka *Penn Glass Works*) A window glass manufacturing facility established in 1824 by Frederick Lorenze Sr. in Pittsburgh, Pennsylvania. In 1851, Wm. McCully & Co. took over operations. It was still being operated in 1886 by McCully. See *Pittsburgh Glass Works.*

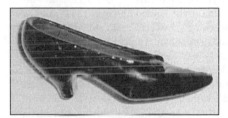

Cobalt-blue lady's glass slipper, 5-1/2" l.
Davanna Collection

slipper An object in the form of a lady's flat slipper, generally made by flattening a glass bottle lengthwise and embellishing the upper part with snake threading. They were made in the Rhineland during the 3rd century A.D. See *shoe; bourdalou.*

Sloan Brothers Glass Factory See *National Glass Factory.*

sloar The book of records or accounts of a glass manufacturing facility.

slop basin A small bowl to hold *slops* (tea rinsings/used tea leaves), originating in Britain in the early 18th century.

slope & shoulder bottle See *wine bottles, Shapes.*

slumping The process of heating glass until gravity forces it to conform to the contours of the form on which it rests. The process dates to the 8th century B.C. in the Levant. The original objects made were hemispherical-shaped mosaic bowls. A round mosaic disc was made by fusing pieces together, draping it over a mold, placing it in the furnace and reheating it until it softened and formed around the mold. It was removed from the mold after cooling slightly but while still hot.

small salt A small salt cellar introduced in England during the 17th century, when it became common to provide each diner with an individual salt in lieu of the large communal salt cellars (*great* or *standing salt*). They were usually about one inch high and two to three inches long; smaller ones have been made over the years. Some early ones have a hemispherical bowl resting on a pedestal base. Later ones tended to follow contemporary silver patterns.

smalt A deep blue pigment for coloring glass, prepared by fusing together zaffer, potassium carbonate, and silica, grinding the resultant product into a powder. It was imported into England from Saxony until native deposits of cobalt were found.

smalto (Italian) (plural is *smalti*) Literally, *enamel.* A piece of opaque colored glass in a thin slab (called *smalto in pan*) used in large quantities to make mosaics and embellish glassware, mirror frames, tables, and consoles, and, in Russia, to inlay floors. On occasion it was embellished with gilding. It was made in Russia at the St. Petersburg Imperial Glass Factory and the studio of M.V. Lomonosov. It was also used as a source of jeweler's enameling colors. See *glass cakes.*

Smear Glass See *Catalonian.*

Smeedes, Jan The first glassmaker on the island of Manhattan, New York. The street where he operated (later South William Street) was then called *Glass-maker's Street.*

smelling (salts) bottle (1) A small glass bottle or vial with a ground stopper, used to hold an aromatic volatile salt known as smelling salts, usually *spirits of ammonia.* Smelling salts were inhaled by ladies to avoid faintness—the "vapors"—or prevent headaches often brought on by the fashionable but restrictive clothing of the 1800s. Smelling salts usually were purchased at a pharmacy in large, plain bottles and transferred to smaller bottles or vials to be carried by the lady on her person or in her purse. It was related to the scent bottle but not intended for perfume. (2) A type of scent bottle, free blown or molded in a variety of shapes and colors; many of Stiegel-type glassware and made by the Boston & Sandwich Glass Co. and other facilities. See *cologne bottle; sea horse bottle.*

Smith, Frederick See *Champlain Glass Company.*

Smith, Gordon E. A paperweight artist from New Jersey whose interest in glass began at the age of 14 when his father bought him a melting torch and some scrap glass. After graduation from high school, he studied glassmaking at Salem County Community College and began work in the scientific glassblowing industry. He was introduced to paperweight making while working at Kontes Scientific Glass. The Kontes encouraged him, and he became a weekend volunteer at the Wheaton Museum of American Glass. Here he learned about paperweights and their making and soon began developing his own distinctive techniques. His weights reflect an intricate knowledge and understanding of the classic lamp work techniques as well as a creative design approach. He signs his weights on the side with etched initials "GES" and the year of production.

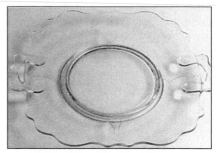

L.E. Smith tray, clear, Mt. Pleasant pattern.
Davanna Collection

Smith, L.E., Company A glass manufacturing facility established in Mt. Pleasant, Pennsylvania, by Lewis E. Smith (d.1931) in 1907. The facility, which was housed in the old Anchor Glass Factory, made utilitarian glassware. In 1911 Smith sold his business but allowed his name to be retained. In 1979 the company was purchased by Libbey-Owens-Ford. It was famous for its black glass introduced in the late 1920s, at which time it also marketed its line of glass animals.

Smith, William A glass decorator who came to the United States in 1851, after working for twelve years at various facilities in Birmingham, England, and was hired by Boston & Sandwich. Soon he established a decorating company, the Boston China Decorating Works, where he gilded and enameled glass lamps and china. His sons, Harry and Alfred, were trained by him and operated the design department of the Mt. Washington Glass Company from 1871 until 1885, when they established their own decorating company. See *Smith Brothers.*

Black amethyst two-handled vase, L.E. Smith, c. 1930s.
Heartland Discoveries

Smith Bros. vase, melon body, white body, Royal decoration, gold enamel floral decoration, gold-beaded rim, rampant

lion in shield mark, 3-1/4" d. x 2-1/4" h.
Krause Publications

Smith Brothers Harry A. and Alfred E. Smith, sons of William Smith, went to New Bedford, Massachusetts, in the spring of 1871 under an agreement with William L. Libbey to operate the decorating department at the Mt. Washington Glass Company. In 1874 they leased the shop, bought stock, and began conducting the decorating phase of its business. In 1876 they occupied their own building, decorating blanks purchased from Mt. Washington and others in the United States and abroad. They ranked first in their specialty by the glass industry. In 1885 they established an independent business, Smith Brothers, in New Bedford. Many of their decorators stayed with Mt. Washington. As a result, many products of the two are of similar design, making it almost impossible to determine which decorated certain objects. One of the Smith Brothers' most famous products was the *Smith vase*, made in the late 1800s until it was copied and cheaply reproduced by several others. Their mark was a lion on a rampart within a shield or the words *Smith Bros*. After many successful years, business began to decline and, in 1899, the company filed bankruptcy. Alfred returned to the Mt. Washington decorating department and Harry went to Meriden, Connecticut, to work. See *Smith, William; Gundersen (-Pairpoint) Glass Works.*

Smith & Solon; Smith, Peter & Gerrit See *Peterboro Glasshouse.*

Smith, Abel & Company See *Knox, Kim & Company.*

Smith, Lambert & Hires See *Quinton Glass Works.*

Smoke bell, probably New England, c. 1880. Museum of American Glass at Wheaton Village, Millville, NJ.

smoke bell A bell-shaped shade with a ring handle designed to hang over an oil lamp or candle to catch the soot and protect the ceiling.

smoother A member of a glass cutting team who took over where the rougher left off, using stone wheels instead of steel, and water as a lubricant rather than liquid sand. The wheels ranged from two to four inches in diameter and were of many types, such as concave, convex, flat, shallow point, deep point, etc. Holding the blank previously worked by the rougher, he looked through the glass following the pattern outline, filling in details. The cutting had a gray or mat finish, which could be left as is or polished. On engraved glass, the smoother or engraver used a diamond stylus, scratching away the surface. He later used copper wheels from a fraction of an inch to four inches in diameter, lubricated with oil and emery powder or fine-grained impure corundum (the object brought up from beneath the wheel). Roughing is usually not necessary on engraved pieces. While most engraving is left unfinished to provide a contrast, some is polished. See *master cutter.*

smoothing iron See *linen smoother.*

snake A decorative object on English glass found attached on the central shaft of lusters and candelabra, in the form of a curved, tapering, faceted ornament that points upward.

snake glass A winged glass, the stem of which was made by manipulating glass rods (having enclosed twisted colored opaque threads) into a convoluted pattern resembling a snake. The rods were so intricately entwined they provided enough support, and no independent stem was needed. Sometimes the finial on the cover was similarly made. They were made in the *facon de Venise* in Germany and in the Netherlands in the late 16th and 17th centuries, copied in the late 19th century at Ehrenfeld, near Cologne, Germany. Sometimes the rods were further embellished with clear or colored pincered cresting along the outer edge and, at the top, a stylized eagle's head. See *threading.*

snake goblet See *Schlangenpokel.*

snake paperweight A paperweight whose principal motif is a snake embedded within the dome or resting on top of it. Those embedded within are normally coiled with their head across their body, resting on a muslin ground (St. Louis) or on a rock ground (Baccarat), and have mottled colored markings in green or red. Only a few were made at Baccarat and St. Louis. A related weight has a glass worm, lizard or Gila monster embedded within it.

snake threading See *snake trailing.*

snake trailing A type of embellishment made of applied trailed glass threads in a twisting, haphazard, serpentine pattern. Some bottles, bowls, and jugs so embellished were found in the Near East, considered to be Syrian glassware. Others found in the Rhineland were probably made at Cologne during the 2nd and 3rd centuries A.D. The trailing is usually a different color than the body, but some Near Eastern ones have trailing of the same color. On some specimens from Cyprus, the *snake* is given a triangular head and the trailing somewhat flattened. When such embellishment is fundamental to an object, as on a winged glass, it is preferably called *snake threading.*

snap (case) A special tool developed about 1850 and used by glassmakers, often the warming-in boy, for grasping in its jaws a hot glass object—just released from the mold or being heated in the glory hole—by its collar base. The jaws are of the specific size and shape of the collar base so as not to damage the hot object when handled, manipulated, or finished. It eliminated the need to use a pontil rod, which left a scar on the piece. See *gadget.*

snapper-up boy The person who used the snap to grasp the collar base after an object was removed from the mold. They were usually 12- to 15-year-old boys who were often responsible for spraying on an iridizing agent.

snapping up The process of grasping a hot glass object, removed from the mold, by its collar base with a *snap.*

sneaker Any large vessel or container for liquid refreshments, used to serve, such as a punch bowl, or to drink from directly, such as a brandy snifter.

Sneath Glass Company See *Canton Glass Company.*

snow(storm) paperweight A paperweight different from the usual paperweights in that its dome is hollow and filled with a liquid in which there are tiny pieces of a white substance. When shaken, the white pieces become scattered throughout the liquid and slowly float to the bottom like snowflakes. There is usually a winter scene inside the dome.

Snowball A product of Dalzell, Gilmore & Leighton, first made in late 1888. A grotesque black human figure in a costume, equipped with a brass tray with a decanter, glasses, and other items. A "Mrs. Snowball" with two children was soon added; she was eventually called Daisy.

snowflake glass Made in China during the 18th century, this was a colorless glass with white inclusions and bubbles producing what appears, unintentionally, to be a snowstorm. Covered by an overlay, it was used to make some Chinese snuff bottles of cameo glass.

snuff bottle A small vial used to contain snuff, a prepared powdered tobacco inhaled through the nose. It is similar to a scent bottle but has a larger mouth and is fitted with a tiny spoon attached to the cover. Snuff bottles, made mainly in China, are usually intricately carved on the surface, usually by women during the 18th century. Their use spread to Europe in the 19th century. Instead of being carved, many were painted (all on clear glass), often in reverse on the interior of the bottle with tiny brushes inserted through the neck. See *Chinese snuff bottles.*

snuff box A container to hold snuff (see *snuff bottle*), popular from the 17th through the 19th centuries. There were two varieties: a small one to be carried in the pocket, usually holding a half-ounce or less of snuff; and one for the table, in a variety of sizes. Originally, larger ones came with rasps to grate the tobacco into small particles suitable for inhaling, but later in the 19th century snuff could be purchased in the powdered form, making the rasp obsolete.

soap, glassmaker's; soap of glass

See *glassmaker's soap; manganese.*

soap bubble glass See *bulle de savon.*

socket lamp See *peg lamp.*

soda (ash) Sodium carbonate (Na_2CO_3) is the principal compound used to supply what is called "soda" in making glass. Other sources are sodium bicarbonate ($NaHCO_3$), salt cake (an impure form of sodium sulfate, Na_2SO_4), and sodium nitrate ($NaNO_3$). The latter is useful in oxidizing iron and accelerating the melting process. It is used instead of potash (potassium carbonate) as the alkali ingredient of glass, a flux to reduce the fusion point of silica. In early Egypt, it was derived from naturally occurring *natron* (a mineral, hydrated sodium carbonate, $Na_2CO_3 \cdot 10 H_2O$). It was later derived from the calcined ashes of marine plants, such as glasswort (prepared salt called *barilla* when from Spain and *roquetta* when from Egypt) and kelp (used in Norway, other Scandinavian countries and England). When supplies of soda became scarce, Germany, Bohemia, and France substituted potash (see *Waldglas; verre de fougere*), made by burning woods of certain trees or ferns and bracken. Venetian and Venetian-style glass continued to be made with soda. Today both soda (made chemically) and potash are used in glassmaking. See *soda glass; water glass.*

soda glass Glass of which the alkali constituent used in the batch is soda, such as in Egyptian, Roman, Venetian, and Spanish glass, as contrasted with Waldglas in which potash was used. In England it was made until making lead glass became commercially feasible in 1676. Much was made in *facon de Venise* and is often difficult to distinguish as to origin. It is slightly brownish, yellowish, or greenish-gray and, unlike lead glass, lacks resonance, even though a very thin soda glass vessel will often ring when struck. It is fairly light in weight, remains plastic longer than potash glass and is easier to manipulate. It contains no lead and is harder and more brittle. Since it contains lime, it is often called *soda lime glass.* It represents the largest tonnage of glass made today, having wide applications, including windows, transparent fixtures, containers of all kinds, flat glass, automobile glass, tableware, etc. Its general composition is: 70% to 74% SiO_2; 10% to 13% CaO; 13% to 16% Na_2O. Such glasses do not melt at too high a temperature and are sufficiently viscous so as not to divitrify, but not too viscous to be workable at reasonable temperatures.

soda lime glass See *soda glass.*

soda potash glass See *optical glass.*

sodden snow ground A ground consisting of textured opaque white glass.

sodium carbonate See *soda; natron.*

sodium silicate (Aka *water glass* or *soluble glass.* Any of several compounds with formulae in ratio from $Na_2O3.75SiO_2$ to $2Na_2OSiO_2$.)It is the simplest form of glass made by fusing sand and soda ash. It is used in soaps, detergents, adhesives, water treatments, bleaching, dyeing, sizing, and fireproofing of textiles, paper pulp, ore treatment, soil solidification, glass foam, pigments, drilling fluids, binders for abrasive wheels, foundry cores, and molds, waterproofing mortars and cements, and flame retardants. See *water glass.*

sof(f) ietta (*Italian*) A tool used as a *puffer* by the glassblower to inflate further a vessel after separation from the blowpipe, but while it is still attached to the pontil. It is a curved metal tube attached to a conical nozzle. After the object is reheated, the glassblower inserts the nozzle into the mouth of the object, sealing it, and blowing through it to inflate the paraison.

softening temperature The temperature at which glass can be molded. See *transition temperature.*

soft relief See *dolce relievo glassware.*

Soho lamp In 1830 Crosse & Blackwell, grocers and suppliers, designed this lamp to burn a special candle that slipped free in the base and could be raised or lowered by a small thumbscrew. It was fitted with a globe, shade, and base, and was made in numerous styles.

solar control glass Window glass coated or made with substances that control the amount of infrared and sometimes ultraviolet radiation.

solar lamp A lamp closely related to the astral lamp, patented by Cornelius & Company in 1843. It had a modified Argand burner, designed to burn lard, and had a reservoir immediately below the flame. An internal mechanism screened the flame so it became a column of light. They were efficient and economical. Solar chandeliers were also prevalent.

solder glass Glasses, usually lead borate glasses, which melt at low temperatures (as low as 700°F) used to seal glass to glass or glass to metal, without distortion. It is applied to the surfaces to be joined as a powder suspended in a volatile liquid, then heated.

solid iron See *pontil.*

soluble glass See *water glass.*

Solvay, Ernest (1838-1922) The creator of a process developed in Belgium in 1866, bearing his name, that reduced the cost of making sodium carbonate used in the glass industry. It involves saturating a concentrated solution of sodium chloride with ammonia and passing carbon dioxide through it. After calcining, the sodium carbonate was ready for use. Prior to this, sodium carbonate was made primarily from the ashes of plants.

Solvay process See *Solvay, Ernest.*

somersault glass See *Sturzbecher.*

Sommerso, Vetro (Italian) A decorative glassware developed by Venini about 1934, similar to cased or flashed glass in that it has a layer of varying thickness over an ornamental under layer, often with a design in *murrina* or *vetro pulegoso.* The outer layer of glass is colorless or of a different color.

South Boston Crown Glass Co. The Boston (Crown) Glass Company built a facility in (South) Boston, Massachusetts, in 1811, operating it in conjunction with its own. It made crown glass. It experienced problems during the War of 1812, due to the British blockade of American shipping,

cutting off supplies of sand from Demerara, British Guiana.

Thomas Cain(e)s began working there at the end of 1812 and persuaded the owners to build a small furnace to make flint glass, leasing it to him. The wares were sold through the parent company as were those wares of the main facility.

The primary products were tableware, chemical apparatus, apothecary supplies, lighting goods, bottles, and flasks, many of them made of window glass rather than flint glass. It also made some cut glass. In 1824, the Boston (Crown) Glass Company was reorganized and, on February 4, 1824, the South Boston Crown Glass Co. was incorporated by the members of the Boston (Crown) Glass Company. They leased the facility, operating as the South Boston Glass Co. and the South Boston Flint Glass Works. On June 23, 1927, glassmaking was discontinued at all facilities associated with the Boston (Crown) Glass Company. It is believed the facility was used between 1827 and 1843 by others to make various types of glassware.

In 1843, the American Flint Glass Works was established by Patrick F. Slane, who took over the idle facility. It made a wide variety of fine quality glass, including pressed, blown, and cut glassware. About 1848 it was operated by Slane & Burrell. On April 28, 1854, it was incorporated as the American Glass Company, which went out of business in 1858.

South Boston Flint Glass Works See *South Boston Crown Glass Company.*

South Boston Glass Bottle Manufactory A glass bottle manufacturing facility operating during 1926 and 1927 in South Boston, Massachusetts, making bottles of all sizes.

South Boston Glass Co. See *South Boston Crown Glass Co.*

South Ferry Glass Works See *Gilliland, John L.*

South Jersey Glass Works See *Swedesboro Glass Works.*

South Jersey glass manufacturing facilities (early)

New Jersey has a long history of glassmaking, dating back to Casper Wistar's facility established in 1739 in Alloway. During the Colonial period, numerous facilities were established in the state, primarily in the southern part where two large deposits of sand well-suited for glassmaking were located. One deposit was four miles south of Millville, and the other was near Williamstown, each supplying several facilities far and wide over the years. While many operated for only a few months, two operated for two years, one for three, two for five, two for ten, four for twenty, two for thirty, one for thirty-five, and one for forty years. As with early glasshouses, ownership changed frequently, and workers were almost migrant in nature. The fuel used by these early furnaces was wood. Coal did not become the main fuel until the 1850s. The *Census Report of 1840* indicates there were 28 facilities and four glass cutting houses in the state, employing 1,075 workers. In 1869 there were 42 facilities, ten located in or near Millville, and four each at Glassboro and Winslow.

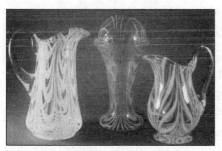

Grouping of South Jersey looped glass. Museum of American Glass at Wheaton Village, Millville, NJ.

South Jersey (type) glassware

Glassware made in the style and tradition of Casper Wistar and others in southern New Jersey (South Jersey), using the same techniques and embellishment. The articles are free blown, shaped, and decorated by manipulation, designed and made by individual workmen. Having a charm and style of its own, it cannot be attributed, with any degree of certainty, to any particular facility or area or even to the region. Some articles were made in New England, New York or even the Midwest.

The ware was similar to northern European *Waldglas* with a few unique designs. The most common forms were: (a) large bowls with straight slanting sides, some with foldover rims and crimped circular bases, rarely footed; (b) barrel shaped pitchers, often with a thumb rest handle, usually small with a tiny pouring lip; narrow waisted pitchers with globular bodies and applied circular feet, plain or crimped, some with foldover rims; and ear- or semi-ear shaped handles, usually flat and ending in a curl ("strap handles").

Glassware was made from about 1740 to the mid-19th century. Glassware made until about 1825 is often called *early South Jersey glass*. It was made of bottle glass, often naturally colored. Typical colors were aqua, aquamarine, aquamarine with opaque white, amber, olive amber, blue, or a combination of colors. Most colored glass was made between 1820 and 1850, often ornamented by manipulation. The most prominent embellishment was the lily pad, very common on bowls, jugs, and goblets. This embellishment was created after the article was blown, by dipping it partway into molten glass and picking up a second gather on the lower portion, which was then tooled up into points around the original form. There are three types of lily-pad decoration: (a) slim vertical stems ending in a bead (18th-early 19th century); (b) wider stem and spherical or oviform pads (about 1830 and later); (c) arced stem culminating in a leaf-like pad (later 19th century). Other typical embellishments include blobs, seals, striating or whorling, leaf-shaped prunts, quilling, threading, rigeree, trailing, gadrooning, applied ribbons, crimps on feet or under handles, looping (mainly red, white, and blue), superimposed and swaggered design tooled decoration, and swan finial.

South Lyndeboro Glass Company

See *Lyndeboro Glass Company.*

South Millville Plant

(Aka *Bottletown* or *Schetter(ville) Glassworks*) A window glass manufacturing facility established in 1832 by Frederich and Phillip Schetter, south of

Millville, New Jersey, in an area that became known as Schetterville, later South Millville. It was bought in 1844 by Lewis Mulford, William Coffin Jr., and Andrew K. Hay. In 1845 it began making green glass bottles and vials. In 1854 Whitall Tatum purchased it, and in 1865 it became the first in the industry to set up a chemical laboratory for the analytical control of the formula for batches. In 1863 a second furnace was added to make flint glass, with only limited success. During the same year, the formula for making lime glass became known to the industry, but it still used flint glass to make its pharmaceutical bottles. In 1897 it became the first to make flint glass using gas as a fuel in both its day and continuous tanks. After trying numerous flint glass formulae, it finally found one easily controlled in the blowing process, allowing the gaffers free time to make art glass objects and paperweights (not on a commercial scale). A fire in 1890 resulted in rebuilding and enlarging the facility.

Beginning in the mid-1860s, the company made a variety of bottles for druggists, physicians, perfumers, and food purveyors. In 1868 it began making lettered plate ware and decorative containers for medicines (*shop furniture*). Perfume bottles and chemical ware were introduced in 1878. The company initiated catalogs in 1876, advertising its various wares and colored glasses. In the late 1880s it made borosilicate glass for a short time. In 1902 black glass, completely light proof, was made for use in small, 1/4- to 4-ounce prescription bottles. It also made *recessed ware*, a highly decorative medicinal container.

South Netherlands glassware

Glassware made in the southern portion of the Low Countries (now Belgium), including that made in Antwerp from 1549 to 1629, in Liege from about 1569 to 1611, and from about 1626 to 1700, and in Brussels from about 1623 to 1700. See *Belgian glassware; Val Saint Lambert Glass Co.*

South Stoddard Glass Company

A bottle and flask glass manufacturing facility established in (South) Stoddard, New Hampshire, in 1842 by Joseph Foster. It failed after a short time and was taken over in 1850 by the Granite Glass Works. Of its many founders, only two remained by 1853, Lumen Weeks and Frederick A. Gilson, operating as Weeks & Gilson. In 1873 operations ceased, caused by the increasing trend for clear glass bottles. The company made colored ones because of the impurities in the available sand. To import purer sand was too costly to compete.

South Wheeling Glass Works

(Aka *Excelsior Glass Works*) A flint glass manufacturing facility established by Plunkett & Miller about 1836 in Wheeling, West Virginia (believed to be a continuation of the Carothers facility). They vacated it in 1839 after completing a new facility across the river in Martins Ferry. In 1845 the idle buildings were bought by Hobbs, Barnes & Co. See *Hobbs, Brockunier & Co.; Virginia Green Glass Works.*

Southwick & Woods

A bottle glass manufacturing facility established in 1864 in Clyde, New York. In 1868 it was operated by Southwick, Reed & Co., which took over the Clyde Window Glass Works established in 1827 by DeZeng & Co. Later the operations were taken over by Ely, Reed & Co. Both facilities closed in 1880.

Southwick, D.H., & Company

A flint glass manufacturing facility operating in Wheeling, West Virginia, during the mid-1800s.

Southwick, Reed & Co.

See *Southwick & Woods; Clyde Window Glass Works.*

spa glass

A tumbler embellished and sold during the 18th and 19th centuries at fashionable spas and resorts in Silesia and elsewhere. They were often embellished with an engraved illustration taken from an incident from the life of a visitor or a local scene and an engraved inscription.

space lamp

An *Argand* or *Astral lamp*. See *Argand lamp; Astral lamp.*

spaced millefiori paperweight

A paperweight in which each individual millefiori cane is surrounded by clear glass; a geometrically arranged millefiori paperweight. See *millefiori paperweight.*

spaghetti glass

See *peloton glass.*

spall A shallow, rounded flake, chip, or splinter on a glass object, generally near the rim.

spandrels In Gothic stained glass windows, representational figures are surrounded by medallions, and the spaces between them are called *spandrels*.

Spangled glass tumbler, Inverted Thumbprint pattern, colorless shading to orange ground, white, and silver spangles, 3-3/4" h. Krause Publications

spangle(d) glass An art glass developed by William Leighton Jr. at Hobbs, Brockunier & Co. in 1883, used for various items, mainly glass baskets, and often further embellished with applied glass flowers. Spangled glass was eventually made by several companies during the Victorian era using the following method: A glob of opaque glass, white or colored, was gathered from the melting pot and rolled while still hot on a marver spread with flakes of a substance (mainly mica but also silver; gold, nickel, copper, etc.). The glob, with its adhered flakes, was covered with an additional layer of glass of desired color, then blown and finished in the usual manner. The colorless mica flakes, subjected to heat during the gathering, blowing, and finishing operations, had considerable opacity, tending to reflect the tint of the outer layer of glass. If the superimposed layer was clear, the mica flakes or spangles, as they are called, took on a silvery hue. Sometimes the outer layer was multicolored, created by using odds and ends of colored glass rods. Layers of white or colored glass were added to make the spangles show up more brightly. Some spangled glass is unlined, the surface sprinkled with gold or silver dust. It is often confused with spatter

glass and frequently has a frilled or ruffled design, or is molded with ribs or patterns on the body. Sometimes the rim and foot have hand-shaped ornamentation. See *spangled glass* by Sandwich.

spangled glass by Sandwich This was made in a different way than other spangled glass, and was made somewhat earlier than that by Hobbs, Brockunier & Co. in 1883. Its body was thick and of solid color glass, often dark blue or deep green. It was plated with a thin layer of glass containing a mixture of fine particles of various colored substances, not coarse particles, as in Hobb's product. Gold or silver dust was at times added to this mix. Sandwich also made a mottled mixture of colors, often sprinkled with gold. This glass was not cased, but the varicolored particles were fused into the surface in such a way that the final product appeared enameled.

Spanish and Portugese glass The glass industry here began about 100 B.C. as the Roman Empire's influence began to be felt. The glass from this era was identical to other Roman glass except it was made with a different flux—barilla—from the ashes of salt marsh plants found along the Spanish coast. During the centuries of Roman rule, Hispano-Roman glass was made in all the usual forms: molded bottles, drinking cups, plates, mosaics, bowls, jars, etc., in shades of green, cobalt blue, topaz, brown, amethysts, and purples. As the Empire declined and the Visigoths moved in, glass making continued but at an inferior level during the 5th to 8th centuries.

After the Visigoths, the Moors invaded, bringing the Eastern influence that persisted through the following centuries. In the 11th century, the Christian armies defeated the Moors and reestablished Western control over Spain, but the Eastern influence over glassmaking remained. In the 13th century, many Islamic craftsmen settled on the Iberian peninsula, mainly in the areas of Almeida (Portugal) and Catalonia (Barcelona, Spain). In 1324, the glassmaking facilities in Barcelona were closed because of risk of fire, but toward the end of the 15th century glassmaking began there again. During the 16th century, the Iberian peninsula was relatively peaceful. The Court supported the glass industry, and Venetian influence began to replace the Eastern and Moorish influence. The principal centers of glassmaking were in Catalonia (Barcelona), Castile (Cadalso), and Andalucia (Seville and Granada), and at the Royal Factory at La Granja de San Ildefonso.

During the 18th century, the Catalan style and tradition began to die away, and the shapes of the wares became more pedestrian. The quality of the glass began to decline, having a grayish uneven tone. Local styles began to develop in the forms and decorations of the wares, such as with the cantir (cantarro), porro, botijo, almorratxa, etc. In 1809, the King withdrew his support of the glass industry, and the final period of Spanish craftsmanship ended.

Stained glass windows for churches were made from the 13th to the 16th centuries. Later significant production of glass articles included mirrors, chandeliers, and a variety of jugs, vases, and drinking glasses, and pieces made and embellished at the lamp. Colored, colorless, and opaque glass was made with embellishment primarily in white filigrana, and pincered work and trailing. Some early Barcelona pieces were embellished with enameling, as was some later glassware from San Ildefonso.

Spanish Knobs A line of glassware introduced in 1929 by Consolidated Lamp & Glass, closely related to its *Catalonian* line (see *Catalonian*), except for a series of knobs built into the design.

Spanish lace glass A shaded, opalescent glassware made in the United States and England after 1885, fashionable in the late 1800s, in imitation of cut or engraved overlay glass with opalescent flowers and foliage. The Victorian glass pattern gave the appearance of white lace on a colored background. Blue, yellow, cranberry, and clear glass were made with this distinctive white pattern. See *opalescent glass.*

sparking lamp A small, low oil lamp with an opening at the top of the font for a wick, inserted through a metal collar which, in turn, is inserted in or screwed to the rim of the font, or held in place by a wire. They

were called *sparking lamps* because, in the early 1800s, courting (referred to as *sparking*) males were to measure the length of their visit with lady friends by the duration of the light. (The father or mother controlled the length of the stay by controlling the amount of oil in the lamp.) They were made in the United States in many forms and sizes and with numerous styles of embellishment. The principal types were the *wine glass* lamps with a stemmed foot and those with an attached loop handle. See *lamp.*

spatter glass (Aka *splash[ed] glass, splash ware*) To make it, various colored fragments were spread out on a marver; and the gather rolled over them, and the gather blown to the desired form. It was then reheated and finished. The *spatter* could be controlled by choosing the color or colors of the fragments and their design or lack thereof. It contained no mica and was unlined, unlike spangle glass. On occasion it was dipped into a pot of clear glass, locking in the pattern before finishing. Several companies made spatter glass (Hobbs, Brockunier the largest), but varied their product by using different colors to avoid patent suits. During the Victorian era it was usually highly embellished, often frilled and ruffled, molded with ribs or patterns on the body. The rim and foot often have hand-shaped ornamentation. It has been mistakenly called *End-of-Day* glass. Legend has it that the fragments used to make the colors were made from the glass left in the pots at the end of the work day. This is doubtful since there is so much of it available the fragments had to be commercially made. See *End-of-Day glass; slag glass.*

speaking glassware See *verrerie parlante.*

spearbutt Truncated cone shape.

spear drop A long drop with a pointed shape, similar to the head of a spear.

spearhead The point attached to the head of a spear, at times of solid glass, often obsidian, chipped to form an edge leading to the point. They were used by some Native Americans and aborigines of central Australia. Arrowheads were similarly made of glass.

specchiai *(Italian)* A division of the Venetian glassmakers guild specializing in making mirrors.

Specialty Glass Company A company incorporated in 1888 in East Liverpool, Ohio, as a result of the bankruptcy and reorganization of the East Liverpool Specialty Glass Company. It did not make glass, merely packed jelly in glass containers. It moved to Jeanette, Pennsylvania, buying a large tract of land and selling off lots to workers with the enticement of free natural gas. In mid-1889 it began erecting buildings, but ran out of money. Charles and George West purchased 53% of its stock for $40,000; George became president, and Charles became secretary/treasurer. The name changed to Westmoreland Specialty Company. See *Westmoreland (Specialty) Glass Company.*

specie glass See *specie jar.*

specie jar (Aka *specie glass*) A large cylindrical though often globular glass jar used in a pharmacy to hold drugs and medicines. However, in the second half of the 18th century, they were used for window displays, filled with colored water or, on occasion, made of colored glass. The top openings were fitted with a hollow ground stopper, similarly filled or colored. Still later they were used for storage. Some had a narrow neck or mouth while others, usually cylindrical ones, had a wide mouth. After about 1830 they were made larger in size, usually in three sizes, and normally embellished with a painted coat-of-arms. Sometimes a light was placed behind them so they would serve as a condensing lens (see *water lens*).

spectacles (Aka *eyeglasses*) Sheet glass is usually the starting raw material for a spectacle lens. It is marked out, cut into pieces, placed in a rotary heating furnace, heated to the softening point, and pressed to the required surface curvature using dies and plungers. It is then annealed, emerging for further processing. Spectacles fall into two main groups: single vision and multifocal, both cut in accordance with a prescription. Multifocal lenses are normally either the one-piece or fused construction type. Most multifocal vision lenses have one spherical surface

and another that's either spherical or toroidal. They are finished by grinding and polishing. See *vision aids; bifocal lens.*

Spencer Cut Glass Company A short-lived glass cutting facility established in May 1910 by Arthur J. Spencer (formerly of the Arcadia Cut Glass Company) in Newark, New York, leasing space from the Arcadia Cut Glass Company.

spice box See *saltshaker.*

spice plate A small dish or saucer to hold sweetmeats, gingerbread, cake, or dried fruit—all at one time—called *spices*. It was once common practice to take wine with *spice*, served on a *spice plate*.

Spider Web pattern A pattern used on Iris glassware.

Spider Webbing glassware Glassware with a trailing of fine glass threads over its entire body, simulating a spider web. It was made by Victor Durand Jr. at the Vineland Flint Glass Works.

Spielkartenhumpen *(German)* (Aka *Altenburg Passglas*) A *Humpen*, usually a *Passglas*, embellished with one or more enamel depictions of contemporary playing cards, usually in complete sets of 52 playing cards. They were made in the 17th and 18th centuries in Thuringia, a former state in central Germany. Inspiration for them most likely came from the playing card industry at nearby Altenburg. Some specimens are probably of Saxon origin.

spiked gadroon See *gadroon.*

spiked kick A kick in the form of a spike projecting up into a bowl or vessel.

spill, spill box See *spill holder.*

spill holder (Aka *spill, spill vase, spill box, spill pot, quill holder*) A vase, usually cylindrical in shape, used to hold spills. Spills were originally rolled pieces of paper, unrolled and placed under a lamp to catch any spillage of oil while filling. Later they referred to a wooden splinter or paper taper used to obtain a light from a fire to light a pipe, candle or lamp. Spill holders made in the United States usually have a heavy bowl resting on a short footed stem and measure normally five to six inches in diameter. They were sometimes used to hold cigars and are often confused with *spoon holders*. They were made only during the mid-19th century. See *spoon holder.*

spill pot, spill vase See *spill holder.*

spindle A round stick tapered toward each end with a notch at one end to attach the yarn, used in hand spinning. Some spindles were made of glass in Spain in the 18th and 19th centuries, sometimes in the form of a tapering rod with an ornate handle.

spindle whorl A pierced weight, usually thicker at the center than at the top and bottom, attached to a primitive spindle (prior to the invention of the spinning wheel). Some were made of glass in China and elsewhere.

spinning process See *crown glass.*

spirit decanter A decanter used to hold spirits, such as whiskey, as opposed to wine. They usually bore the name of the contents, such as gin, brandy, rum, etc., painted in gilt or enamel. Some featured an initial on the stopper.

spire stopper (Aka *pinnacle stopper*) A stopper in the form of a spire, extending upward to a pinnacle. Early ones were cone-shaped and uncut; later ones were almost entirely cut with faceting or hollows forming a shallow diamond pattern. They are often found on whiskey decanters, and are an early form of stopper, made about 1750, shortly after stoppers first came into use on decanters.

spittoon (Aka *cuspidor*). A receptacle into which a person would spit, or expectorate. They are usually globular in shape with a wide flaring rim, normally wider than the bowl. Some have a high, large funnel mouth or, on occasion, a short neck, and small funnel mouth. Some were made of glass in India by Persian craftsmen in the 16th century; in Persia during the medieval period and the 18th and 19th centuries; in Venice during the 19th century for export to Persia; and in China at the Peking Imperial Palace workshops during the Ch'ien Lung period (1736-95).

spittoon, lady's An inappropriate term used to describe a flower holder having a shape similar to a spittoon; a small deep bowl with an out-turned rim or collar.

Spitzbecher *(German)* A beaker of Frankish glass in the form of a tall, thin, inverted cone, embellished on the lower part with diagonal trailing during the 5th to the 7th centuries, and with vertical trailing during the 5th and early 6th centuries. The upper part was embellished with horizontal trailing. It had to be inverted to be put down when empty to "ward off the evil eye."

splash(ed) glass or ware See *spatter glass.*

splayed base (Aka *spreading base*) The base of a vessel flaring outward toward the bottom.

split (1) A decorative pattern on cut glass in the form of a deep miter cut often used to separate the elements of a pattern. Often several splits in the form of ovals (see *vesica*) were arranged in an encircling band, common during the Adam period. On occasion, they form star patterns or other designs. They are of several types: vesica, split vesica, split square, X-cut vesica, and double X-cut vesica. See *combed fluting.* (2) See *wine bottles, Sizes.*

split mold(ing) A method of pressing glass where the mold is made up of two or more parts.

split square A cut-glass motif consisting of a vesica crossed by other curved miters to form "squares."

split vesica A cut-glass motif consisting of a vesica cut down the middle by a straight miter cut.

splosh Colored glass that is crushed and pulverized. The resultant powder is sprinkled on glass objects while being worked at the furnace.

spoke paperweight A paperweight with a design suggestive of the spokes of a wheel. It is similar to the swirl type but with the radiating lines straighter and less twisted. They were made by Clichy and St. Louis.

Spon Lane Glassworks A glass manufacturing facility at Smethwick, near Birmingham, England, owned from 1824 by Robert Lucas Chance. From 1830, Chance developed improvements to the methods for making broad glass. In 1851 the company made 300,000 panes of glass for the Crystal Palace in London.

spool salt See *capstan salt*.

spool stem See *capstan stem*.

spoon An implement for serving, stirring, or eating foods. It has an ordinarily oval or circular shallow bowl attached to a horizontal handle, the length and style of which is variable. Some of the earliest were made of Roman glass; some later ones were made of Venetian glass during the 16th century (usually with *reticello* embellishment).

Spooner, cutting on pressed blank, 6" h. Davanna Collection

spoon holder (Aka *spooner*) A glass receptacle in the form of a goblet with a large, deep ovoid bowl resting on a stemmed foot with a scalloped rim. The stem is usually longer than that of a spill holder with which they are often confused. Spoon holders were used to hold spoons at the table (knives and forks were placed at each setting), and were fashionable from the mid-19th century until the late 1910s.

spooner See *spoon holder*.

sport cup A Roman drinking vessel made in the 1st century A.D., mold blown and decorated with fighting gladiators or chariot races.

sporting glassware Various glass vessels, mainly drinking vessels such as beakers, rummers, or goblets decorated with engraved or enameled scenes depicting sporting activities, such as horse racing, hunting, shooting, etc. English specimens date from about 1760. Some enameled Humpen are embellished with sporting scenes.

spot mold A sectional mold used to make a paperweight or other solid glass object, embellished with a pattern of regularly spaced air bubbles made by small spike-like protuberances on the inside of the mold. When the paraison, which may have been embellished with an interior motif, is placed in the mold, the sectional portions of the wall tighten around it, and the spikes are forced into the glass, creating small cavities. When the piece is cased, air bubbles are trapped, forming a pattern made by the spikes.

spot resist A shaded opalescent glassware; an attempt to emulate cut or engraved overlay glass.

spout The tubular protuberance on a vessel through which its liquid contents are poured. A pinched or beaked shaped pouring lip is often called a spout. They appear in many shapes and styles. After about 1850 they were usually molded and attached to the body. See *beak*.

spout cup or glass See *posset pot*.

Spraque & Schoolcraft See *Twichell & Schoolcraft*.

spray paperweight See *bouquet paperweight*.

spreader An ornamental dish with a central hole that slips over the nozzle of a candlestick. Some serve to catch the wax drippings and are removable for cleaning (see *drip pan*). When a candlestick also has a *save-all* above the spreader, especially on a sconce or chandelier, the spreader serves as the piece to which drops are attached.

spreading base See *splayed base*.

spring clip A metal device attached to a pontil to hold the foot of a vessel while the bowl is being finished. They are used to avoid making pontil marks.

Spring Garden Works See *Baltimore Glass Works.*

Spring Garden Glass Works A bottle glass manufacturing facility established in 1850 in Baltimore, Maryland, by a group associated with the Baltimore Glass Works and operated on a cooperative plan. After 1855 it failed and was taken over by Baker Brothers & Company, the owners of the Baltimore Glass Works. It was still operating in 1880.

springel glass (Aka *casting bottle*) A scent bottle used to scatter scent about a room.

springtime glass See *primavera, vetro.*

springtool The simplest style of metal tongs used for pincer work and applying handles. It was simply two pieces of wood fastened together by a piece of leather at one end and a spring between them.

sprinkler (Aka *rose water or perfume sprinklers*) A glass vessel made in a variety of forms, all characterized by a shape that causes the contents to pour slowly or in drops.

sprinkler top perfume bottle Small perfume bottles with tops that would screw or pull up to allow perfume to be sprinkled a drop at a time. When the top was screwed or pushed down, the opening was blocked and contents sealed within.

sprue In a pressing operation that allows for more than one object to be pressed in the same mold, the individual pieces are joined together by a thin piece of glass known as a connecting fin or *sprue*. It is easily broken from the main piece.

spun glass An obsolete term for *glass fiber.* Recently the term has been used loosely for any type of glass fiber drawn from molten glass by a centrifugal process.

spy glass A lens used to see distant objects. It evolved into opera glasses and binoculars in the mid-19th century.

spy hole A small, narrow opening in the covering of the *bocca* or the center of the temporary clay screen placed in the working hole during the melting process. Through this hole the melting could be observed, impurities could be skimmed from the top of the molten glass, or samples of the metal could be withdrawn for testing. See *bye hole; glory hole.*

square bottle A four-sided bottle, probably first made of thick green or blue Roman glass during the 1st and 2nd centuries A.D., usually with a cylindrical neck topped with an extended rim. Many have a handle, reeded (see *celery handle*) and angular, extending from just below the mouth to the sloping shoulder but not beyond its perimeter so as not to interfere with packing and storing them close together. They were mold or free blown and flattened on the sides, sometimes embellished with relief decorations and, on the bottom, with Greek or Latin inscriptions. The size varies depending on the thickness of the glass and shape of the shoulder. The proportion of width to height also varies. A square bottle is a variation of the rectangular bottle but should not to be confused with the square jar having a wide mouth, or with the Mercury flask. See *Maltese Cross bottle.*

square foot A foot, square in shape, commonly used in England and elsewhere during the early 19th century. It is found mainly on rummers, bonnet glasses, bowls, candelabra, etc. Some were crowned by a circular dome shape or lemon squeezer foot.

square headed A door or window opening that is square or rectangular.

squares See *whiskey decanter.*

squatty candles See *fairy lamp.*

SSAT The abbreviation for *single series air twist.*

SSOT The abbreviation for *single series opaque twist.*

St. Clair Glass Company A glass manufacturing facility established in 1941 in Elmwood, Indiana, by John B. St. Clair and his sons, John Jr. and Edward, former employees of the MacBeth-Evans Company. It made numerous small items of carnival, pink, and caramel slag. It also made custard glass and, later, paperweights. It is most famous for its lamps.

St. Gobain Glass Company The

French national glass company established in 1693 to make plate glass and mirrors. In 1653 a glass manufacturing facility was established by Richard Lucas de Nehou at Tourlaville in Normandy. In 1667 it merged with another facility established in 1665 by Jean Baptiste Colbert in Paris. Colbert's facility had a monopoly to make mirrors. Another facility was established by Abraham Thevart at Tourlaville in 1688. This facility was managed by Nehou's nephew, Louis-Lucas de Nehou, operating under the sponsorship of Louis XIV. Another was built in 1693 at St. Gobain in Picardy (*Manufacture Royale des Grand Glaces*). The Tourlaville, St. Gobain, and Paris companies were combined in 1695 as *Manufacture Royale des Glaces de France*. The Tourlaville facility closed in 1787. The Picardy facility thrived, becoming the French national glass company, known since 1830 as the *St. Gobain Glass Co.* Its monopoly for making cast plate mirrors lasted more than 100 years but ceased when a plate glass facility, now owned by Pilkington Brothers Ltd., was established in England in 1773. It has gone into other product lines including fiberglass, and has facilities in the United States.

St. Lawrence Glass Company (1)

(1867-1875) A glass manufacturing facility operating in Montreal, Canada, originally making telegraph insulators and bottles, then pressed pattern glass and cut-glass wares, and a variety of oil lamps, lamp chimneys, shades for gas and oil lamps, and pharmaceutical glassware. (2) See *Egginton family*.

St. Louis diamond (Aka *honeycomb*) A

cut-glass motif consisting of concave hexagons or quadrilateral diamonds cut into the glass, usually used to cover an area such as the neck of a carafe or pitcher. See *diamond*.

St. Louis Flint Glass Works A flint

glass manufacturing facility believed to be the first west of the Mississippi River, established in St. Louis, Missouri, in 1842 by James B. Eads. In 1849 it closed, but after a short period it opened under new ownership, making only green glassware until 1854, when cut and pressed flint glassmaking was resumed.

Shortly before the Civil War it was bought by Bayot & Cummings, making only flint glass bottles. It was still operating in 1880.

St. Louis Glass Factory A glass manu-

facturing facility, one of the most famous companies in France, established in 1767 at St. Louis on the site of a facility in existence since 1586. In 1767 the name *Verrerie Royal de St. Louis* was conferred upon the facility by Louis XV. Its early wares were comparable to Bohemian glassware, but in 1781 it independently discovered a process of making an equivalent to English lead glass. Several changes of ownership followed and, in 1829, under new ownership, its name was changed to *Campagnie des Verreries et Cristalleries de St. Louis*. Being in Alsace-Lorraine (part of Germany from 1871 to 1918), some wares were signed *St. Louis-Munzthal, d'Argental* (see *Argental*), or *Arsale* or *Arsal*. It has collaborated with Baccarat from 1825 to the present. In 1932 they jointly acquired the Le Creusot Glass Factory (formerly St. Cloud Glassworks). After surviving the War of 1870 and the two World Wars, when it was closed, it has become one of the leading makers of both traditional and modern crystal tableware. It is also known for its paperweights made during the 18th century (see *St. Louis paperweights*). The company revived paperweights in 1953, making classic, sulfide, and overlay weights.

St. Louis Glass & Queensware

Company A glass manufacturing facility established in St. Louis, Missouri, in the mid-1930s. In 1939 it changed its name to the Meramac Company, Manufacturers of Glassware.

St. Louis Glass Works See *Missouri Glass Company*.

St. Louis-Munzthal See *St. Louis Glass Factory*.

St. Louis neck A motif located on the

neck of a bottle or decanter consisting of cut concave, hexagonal diamonds. Beginning at the shoulder, the diamonds tend to get smaller as the shoulder narrows into the neck.

St. Louis paperweight Paperweights

made by the St. Louis Glass Factory, the first

of the glass manufacturing facilities in France to begin making paperweights. One of its earliest millefiori weights is dated 1845, and, by 1848, it was making a wide range of lamp work pieces as well. It displayed paperweights in many Paris exhibitions. The last recorded showing was at the Paris Exhibition in 1867, when interest was on the decline. Rare specimens are signed and dated. When present, the date appears on canes constructed with the numerals (all one color, either red, blue, or black) appearing in separate rods fused together with the "SL" cane above the date. Signature canes appear only with the date canes, but not vise-versa. Many of the weights made between 1845 and 1867 are of the millefiori type, either patterned or scrambled. Some have canes showing a silhouette, particularly of animals and dancing figures. There were also some of the flower, fruit, or subject type, or crown or overlay. Reptile weights were very popular. The overlay specimens are encased in clear glass and generally have a star cut or strawberry diamond base. There are a few magnum and miniature types. A characteristic of its weights was a slightly flattened dome.

In 1953, after a lapse of 86 years, it began to make weights again. Workers and craftsmen at the facility were consulted and numerous experiments conducted in an attempt to rediscover the forgotten millefiori, lamp work, and sulfide paperweight making techniques. As a result, some weights were made during the next few years, but it was not until 1970 that it began making quality weights on a regular basis. Each year it creates a collection of limited edition weights, many fashioned after 19th century designs. It specialized in a variety of styles and techniques, including mushroom weights, piedouches, upright bouquets, and magnum-encased double overlays. It also makes a number of paperweight related items, i.e., hand coolers, candlesticks, newel post tops, and pen holders. Modern St. Louis weights contain a cane with a date and the initials "SL," each made in a limited edition, accompanied by a certificate of authenticity.

St. Paul Glass Company (1900-1943)

A glass manufacturing facility established in St. Paul, Minnesota. Only cutting and beveling of flat plate glass was done.

St. Petersburg Imperial Glass Factory

The Russian state glass manufacturing facility originally established by Peter I—Peter the Great, tsar from 1682 to 1725—during the early years of the 18th century in St. Petersburg. Shortly after his death, many of the state facilities were closed. About 1743 a new state glass facility was established in St. Petersburg, operating until the 1770s. In the mid-18th century another one was built and, in 1777, leased to Prince Potemkin, who moved it to Ozerki, near St. Petersburg. In 1792, after Potemkin's death, it reverted to the state, becoming known as the St. Petersburg Imperial Glass Factory. These facilities, under Peter II (tsar from 1727 to 1730), Anna Ivanovna (tsarina from 1730 to 1740), Elizabeth Petrovna (tsarina from 1741 to 1762), and Catherine the Great (tsarina from 1762 to 1796), made articles mainly for the Court and aristocracy. Its primary products were crystal goblets and large chandeliers and girandoles, all made at Ozerki. During the 19th century, the St. Petersburg facility made drinking vessels of clear glass with engraved and enameled embellishments. The most common motifs were the heraldic eagle and the Imperial monogram. In 1862, there were several unsuccessful attempts to sell the St. Petersburg facility because of economic conditions. Operations were eventually moved to the site of, and combined with, the Imperial Porcelain Factory until operations ceased during the 1917 Revolution. See *Russian glassware.*

stabilizer

A substance added to the batch to make the resultant glass more impervious to decay and devitrification. The primary substance was calcium oxide (CaO), generally from calcium carbonate ($CaCO_3$).

stacking glasses

Drinking glasses designed in shape and size to be placed safely and effectively in a vertical stack with the foot and stem of an upper glass resting in the bowl of the next lower glass. The height of the foot and stem is approximately the height of the bowl.

Stadler, Rush & Co. See *Rensselaer Glass Factory.*

staff head A knob that embellishes the upper end of a staff.

Stag Head, The A 44-pound glass ornament in the form of a stag's head designed by George Chevalier for Baccarat in 1952. Individual ones were presented to French President de Gaulle, Russian General Secretary Leonid Brezhnev, and other heads of state.

Stage Brothers Cut Glass Company
A glass cutting company established in 1911 (incorporated on November 24, 1914) in Lawrenceville, Pennsylvania, operating until the early 1920s. At first it made heavy, brilliant cut glassware, switching to cutting figured blanks and then to light cut wares in mat finish and rock crystal. See *Stage-Kaskins Cut Glass Company.*

Stage-Kaskins Cut Glass Company
A glass cutting company in Lawrenceville, Pennsylvania (incorporated on December 22, 1914). Kaskins stayed for less than a year. Stage remained, operating it until his death in 1949. See *Stage Brothers Cut Glass Company.*

stained glass There are many different types of *stained glass*. The differences in the manufacturing processes provide the particular characteristics of each type. Stained glass, like all glass, is composed primarily of silica obtained from sand with varying small amounts of iron, limestone, soda ash, and borax. The relative percentage of iron is one of the important variables in the process.

The different colors of stained glass are obtained by the addition of various metal oxides to the basic materials. Microscopic examination of 12th century red and blue glasses shows very thin alternate-colored and clear layers, indicating the batch was not homogeneous. From the 13th century, a more intensive color was made that could be layered or flashed over a paraison of clear glass by dipping it in a separate pot of molten glass of the desired color. A portion of the surface was then rubbed away with sand or a grinding agent to reveal the bottom layer, now done using a masking agent and hydrofluoric acid. Any lines or slight imperfections in the sheets are usually considered a bonus because they catch the light, making the glass sparkle. The process of making sheet glass by hand is known as the *antique method*. See *antique method.*

Colors. Simple, single color glass is known as *pot glass*. The pot contains molten glass from which the blower extracts it to be blown. Blue is made by introducing cobalt oxide or a combination of cobalt and chromium oxides into the batch. Red uses selenium in combination with cadmium and copper salts. Red-pink or gold-pink uses manganese oxide and gold oxide (this color can vary between deep cherry red and light camellia pink and is expensive to make). Purple uses manganese oxide in conjunction with cobalt oxide. Yellow uses selenium and chromium in conjunction with cadmium salts (in the 14th century yellow-stained glass was made by applying a thin film of silver nitrate onto the surface of the glass and fixing it by firing; the colors ranged from pale yellow to dark ochre). Green uses copper and chromium salts (in the 14th century emerald green was made by applying silver nitrate to blue panes). Sulfur yellow uses sodium. Black uses concentrated copper salts.

Antique (Handmade). The term *antique* used to describe stained glass refers to the 19th century method of making glass that, with some modifications, is still used. It does not mean the glass is old but that the method of manufacture is old. It is usually blown in elongated cylindrical bubbles about fourteen inches in diameter and five feet long. As the glass is being blown, the bubble is rotated with an up and down motion in a cylindrical trough to achieve even shaping. At the same time it is intentionally scratched by metal protrusions—spikes—in the trough's inner walls. These protrusions differ with each maker, becoming an identifying characteristic, creating the *action* within the glass. The process ingrains the crystalline surface texture characteristic of antique glass. Next the ends are cut off of the cylindrical bubble, and the remaining cylinder split lengthwise with a hot knife or diamond cutter, flattened, and passed through an annealing oven to remove strains and brittleness. The glass has random streaks, ripples, undulations, bubbles and/or other irregularities that catch transmitted light in areas of preferred thickness, which provide the best scattering of light. These areas are cut from larger sheets and are subsequently sold at higher prices. This creates considerable waste, called *curious* glass, sometimes sold by glass supply houses at a discount.

Antique (machine made). Machine-made antique stained glass is made with an even thickness and a consistent color and high brilliance. It is made in clear and light tints of gray, blue, amber, green, and flesh tone. It is less expensive than handmade glass and often is used for backgrounds in stained glass windows.

Craquel Antique. This glass, when in its molten state and still on the blowpipe, is quickly immersed in water prior to blowing. Only the outside surface is cooled, resulting in the crackled effect. Sheets may have a large- or fine- craqueled effect depending on the maker (another identifying characteristic).

Flashed. This consists of a light-colored glass base coated with a thin skin of a deeply, contrasting colored glass. It should not be used on projects requiring firing because the thin layer has a tendency to pull back from the edges. Flashed glass should be cut on the unflashed side and etched on the flashed side.

Flashed Antique. This glass is made by dipping a large bubble of a base-colored glass (usually the lighter of two colors) into a pot of darker colored glass, blown, and made in the same manner as other antique stained glass. The resultant glass has a thin layer of the deeper colored glass on a thicker layer of base glass. Reds, greens, and blues are often flashed. Flashed glass is often used when engraving, sandblasting, or acid etching is needed.

Full Antique. In making this glass, the hand blown cylindrical bubble is pierced at one end and the edges are fluted into a cylinder. The pierced end is grasped by a metal cage, attached to a pole, and the blowpipe removed from the other end. The glass is reheated and the other end pierced and fluted. The next steps are similar to the general glassmaking technique for sheet antique. Because full antique is made from smaller bubbles than sheet antique, it has a more uneven thickness that tends to produce a color shading in the glass that ranges from dark to light. It is available in a wide range of colors.

Painted. Most stained glass windows have painted details over the colored and plain pieces. The paint is a mixture of very soft glass ground with various metallic oxides to make a black or brown powder. (The red color on the back of some Venetian windows is iron oxide that shows black against the light.) The powders are mixed with oil or gum and water, although an older formula recommends honey, to render the paint thick enough to stay on the brush as well as to prevent flaking. Silver chloride or nitrate mixed into a paste with pipe clay is also used as enamel, staining the glass yellow. The painted pieces are reheated to a temperature at which the surface of the glass starts to melt—but not to flow and distort—causing the paints and enamels to sink into the surface.

Reamy Antique. This glass is a variant of streaky antique, lighter in tone and color, permitting a greater amount of light to pass. It has heavy cords and mottled areas that have extra surface materials, which lends it a primitive, handmade appearance. It is available in clear, light amber, various browns, off whites, greens, and light blues. It may contain seeds (air bubbles).

Streaky Antique. This is made in a similar fashion to flashed glass except the base bubble is not completely coated by the overlay(s). Instead the color(s) used in coating is (are) intertwined and swirled about the base color, so the surface color is not homogeneous.

Surface treatments. Sandblasting: This is done by pitting the top surface of the glass using various grades of sand directed under pressure at the glass. A stencil is used, exposing the areas of the glass to be blasted. Various depths and textures can be achieved by using different grades of sand. The portion sandblasted appears *frosted*.

Carving: A treatment used to deeply etch glass done by sandblasting in order to produce shadings within the design, in effect creating a textured *bas-relief*.

Wheel Engraving: Engraving glass is more expensive than sandblasting. The design is generally engraved in the transparent glass by scratching the bottom surface, usually with a stone lathe using wheels of various sizes and shapes. The wheels are made of sandstone, aluminum oxide, or silicon carbide. The engraved area appears *frosted*. If the design is to be transparent, the engraver will use a cork polishing wheel with jewelers rouge and pumice powder.

Silk Screening: A process by which a design is etched on the glass surface using an etching cream or hydrofluoric acid, which passes through the design made on a silk screen or nylon mesh to the surface of the glass below. The cream is safer and easier to use than acid. In this process, the design is first transferred photographically to the silk screen. Then the areas of the design not to be etched are masked. The warm cream is then applied to the silk screen and passes through to the nonmasked areas onto the glass. The silk screen is removed and, after a three- to four-minute wait, the cream rinsed away. Silk screening can be used on nearly any type of glass. See *curious glass, cathedral glass; slab glass; roundels; jewels; opalescent glass; cat's paw opals; feather glass; beveled glass; mercury mosaic window; Tiffany stained glass; stained glass window; staining.*

stained glass window A decorative window, often found in churches, made of pieces of colored, flashed, or enameled glass fitted into channeled lead strips and set in an iron framework. The oldest windows, made about 1065, are believed to be in the Angsburg Cathedral. The most well-known windows are in the cathedrals at Chartes and Le Mans, and in the Sainte-Chapelle in Paris. Medieval ones were made of small pieces of glass. The size increased over the years. The process for making them involves: (a) making of a full-scale plan of the design, known as a *cartoon*; (b) cutting pieces of colored glass to the required shapes; (c) painting pieces, if necessary; (d) laying out the pieces in the desired pattern; (e) leading, soldering or cementing them in place; and (f) securing panels to the iron crossbars of the window with copper ties. The finest windows of colored glass were made in the 13th

and 14th centuries. From the 16th century on, most were made by painting with enamels on colorless glass panels. After a decline of almost three centuries, the art was revived in the 19th century. A modern development is the use of *slab glass*, where the pieces are cemented together instead of being leaded, and the surface is embellished by chipping.

staining The process of coloring the surface of annealed glassware using brushed-on colored pigments that sink into the surface where applied, leaving it almost smooth. The technique was used on early Islamic glassware by an unknown process, and in medieval Europe using a silver stain. A method of staining was later developed by Friedrich Egermann, using silver chloride to produce a yellow stain (about 1820) and a red stain (about 1840) as a cheap substitute for flashed glass. The articles made were usually embellished with engraving or etching. The normal colors of glass made by staining are brownish yellow (amber) and deep ruby, ruby red being the most common. The stains were lightly fired and the wares embellished by engraving, revealing the thinness of the staining. The process was used only rarely in the United States.

staircase light A lantern or encased candleholder to light a hall or stairway. Generally they were quite ornate, the framework sometimes gilded or japanned. The glass panels were square, rectangular, hexagonal, octagonal, or circular in shape.

stamnium (Latin) A bottle with a cylindrical body, tall, thin neck, and disk mouth. It has two characteristic handles extending from the shoulder vertically upward and curving inward, attached to the neck below the mouth. They were made of Roman glass in the 3rd and 4th centuries.

stamnos (Greek) A ovoid storage jar used in ancient Greece with a high shoulder, short neck, wide mouth, two horizontal loop handles attached at the shoulder, and sometimes a cover. Similar to the *neck-type* amphora, it was made of Roman glass.

stamp plates Plates having an open edge or latticework around the rim that owners often covered with cancelled postage stamps. They are sometimes found today decorated with oil painting of flora or fauna.

stand lamp See *peg lamp.*

standard The stem of a glass.

Standard Cut Glass Company (1) A glass cutting facility established in the early 1890s in New York, New York. Its trademark label was its name with an American flag. (2) (1905-1908) A glass cutting facility established in Corning, New York, a Hawkes subcontractor. (3) (Aka *Standard Engraving & Cut Glass Company*) (1911-1915) A glass cutting facility established in Minneapolis, Minnesota. It cut floral patterns. Many patents were assigned to it as late as 1914. See *Olson, Arthur.*

Standard Engraving & Cut Glass Company See *Standard Cut Glass Company.*

Standard Lamp & Glass Company A company in Trenton, New Jersey, making cut-glass shades and lamp globes in the early years of the 20th century.

Standard Window Glass Works See *Woodbury Glass-Works Company.*

Standehumpen (German) Literally, *profession glass.* A Humpen embellished with enameling depicting individuals in various professions, made in Franconia in the 17th century.

standing bouquet A decorative motif within the dome of a paperweight (see *bouquet paperweight*), consisting of a bouquet of glass flowers with their leaves. It is three-dimensional and vertical in relation to the base. See *flat bouquet.*

standing bowl (Aka *footed bowl*) A glass bowl usually about 4-3/4 to 6-1/4 inches high on a wide hollow spreading foot, often having a slightly everted rim, for serving fruits or sweetmeats. See *standing cup.*

standing cup A large glass cup (usually 6-1/4 to 8 inches high) with a cylindrical bowl resting on a wide, hollow, sometimes ribbed spreading foot. Sometimes there is a

knop in the stem, and occasionally there is a domed cover. They are of Venetian origin, dating from the 15th or early 16th centuries. See *procession cup; Bologna goblet; Barovier cup.*

standing salt See *great salt.*

standish See *inkstand.*

Stangenglas (German) Literally, *pole glass.* A tall, narrow, cylindrical beaker usually resting on a pedestal base in a number of different forms with a variety of embellishments and measuring about eight to twelve inches high (some are up to 16-1/2 inches). Early ones of Frankish glass, from the 5th and early 6th centuries, are embellished with applied drops of glass. Later ones made in Germany in the 15th to 17th centuries are either (a) smooth with spiral trailing or enameling, or (b) the entire surface is covered with prunts (some raspberry, some pointed), sometimes on the inside and outside. Many are of greenish or brownish Waldglas, probably from Germany or the Netherlands. Some nearly colorless items were made in Saxony and Venice in the 16th century for the German market, or in Germany and Bohemia in the *facon de Venise* with enameling. See *Knopfbecher; Spechter; Passglas; Bandwurmglas.*

Stanger, Christian See *Franklin Glass Works.*

Stanger, Lewis, & Son See *Temperanceville Glassworks.*

Stanger, Thomas & Julius See *Isabella Glassworks.*

Stanger, William See *Clementon Glassworks.*

Stanger & Dotterer See *Brooklyn Glass Works.*

Stanger Brothers See *Olive Glassworks.*

Stanger Glass Works Jacob Stanger (born *Stenger*) and his family owned a glass manufacturing facility in Dornhagen, Germany, but because of unsettled conditions there in the 1760s, the government would not allow its sale. The family, which included at least seven sons (Jacob, Solomon, Daniel, Peter, Christian, Adam, and Philip, and possibly John and Francis, although they may have been grandchildren), walked away from the works, coming to the United States in 1768 with only a few personal belongings.

Once here, Jacob and his oldest sons began to work for Wistar in South Jersey. When it closed, Soloman, who became the head of the family when Jacob died, went to work at Stiegel's Manhiem facility shortly before it went bankrupt. At this time the Stangers decided to erect a facility, choosing a site in southern New Jersey later known as Glass House, then Glassboro. Soloman purchased land there in 1779 and established a successful furnace on the site. Because of the devaluation of currency, the family went into debt, mortgaging their land, equipment, and facility. Between 1783 and 1786, they sold most of their possessions.

In 1783 Colonel Thomas Carpenter and his brother-in-law, Samuel Tonkin, purchased the interests of Peter, Philip, and Francis, becoming partners with Solomon and Daniel. In September 1784 Colonel Thomas Heston purchased a quarter interest from Solomon, and Samuel Tonkin purchased the same from Daniel. No members of the Stanger family had a financial interest in the facility. At this time it was operated by Heston & Carpenter, making bottles, window glass, and flintware.

Some of the family members left to establish their own facilities in Port Elizabeth, New Brooklyn, and Marshallville. Many, extended by marriages, remained at the Glass House facility. From 1808, when Thomas Carpenter's son, Edward, took over ownership, it was called Edward Carpenter & Co., the Olive Glassworks. Various members of the Stanger family were involved in the ownership or management of at least seven facilities in southern New Jersey.

Stankard, Paul J. Born in 1942, Paul J. Stankard was an American maker of paperweights working in Mantua, New Jersey. After having worked as a scientific glassblower for 10 years, he became interested in antique French paperweights, especially floral ones because of his interest in botany. His weights may be largely described as *botanical*

or *environmental*, and the design, color, and construction of each is carefully planned, executed, botanically accurate and naturalistic. His earlier weights bear an etched signature on the base or side, or include an "S" or "PS" signature cane as part of the motif. His more recent works contain an "S" signature cane.

stannic acid See *tin oxide.*

staple fiber Short lengths of glass fiber.

star A cut-glass geometric motif in the form of a *star.* In many instances the type is indicative of the period of production and quality of the cutting. The *single star* consists of an indefinite number of single miter cuts of equal length extending from a central focal point; the ends of the cuts not connected. There were several varieties. Hawkes and Dorflinger varied the length of the rays in an eight-point star, placing it in the center of the base of an object. Hawkes adapted it as a border. The *shooting star* had deeper miter cuts than the *single star.* The total points were maintained at eight, and fans were positioned between them. This was a dominant motif between the Brilliant and Flower periods. A *pyramidal star* is a *single star* with deep miter cuts so the area between each pair became a raised, elongated triangle. Hawkes popularized this in its *Russian* pattern. The *flat star* was developed from lines that crisscrossed to create an eight pointed star. In some versions the two rays at midpoint extend farther than the others. J. Hoare & Co. elongated the four midpoint rays; this came into fashion after 1900. Hoare often built a border of elongated stars. Modern imported cut glass relies heavily on this motif, leaving it intentionally unpolished for decorative effect and to reduce costs. The *hobstar* is so-called because of its raised center, serving as a dominant motif in the Brilliant and Flower periods, however, its structure changed with time. Relatively deep cuts intersecting lines formed the points of the hobstar as well as the facet center. The number of points on the star corresponded to the number of facets on the center. The points varied from eight to thirty-two, depending on the size and shape of the object and the period of cutting. A *pyramidal star* with a *hobstar* often embellished the raised center. Dorflinger, Hawke, Hoare, and Clark were the earliest to popularize the eight-point *hobstar.* The embellishment on the top of the facet center varied with the cutter—it could be unadorned or have crosshatching, a single star, a flat star, or a hobnail. As the Brilliant period moved toward overall cutting of the surface, the points on this type of star increased to the maximum of 32 with the characteristic facet center. Hoare and Egginton were noted for arranging tiny hobstars in clusters; others made a border of them. With the increased costs of production toward the end of the Brilliant period, the number of points on the hobstar diminished, and the center was so shallowly cut that it looked like a flat star. The more ornate hobstar was called a *rosette* because the deep and intricate cutting so raised the hob center that it resembled a rosette. Mt. Washington, Hawkes, Egginton, and Sinclaire created several patterns in the *rosette* motif at the height of the Brilliant period. The *flashed star* contained eight, ten, or twelve points with fans between the points. Sometimes the pattern crosshatched the points; the embellishment of the center varied with the company. See *star, wheel engraved.*

Star, German Jewel See *star, wheel engraved.*

Star, Jewel See *star, wheel engraved; Jewel star; star foot.*

Star, Victorian Glory See *star wheel engraved; star foot.*

star, wheel engraved An engraved motif in the form of a star. Early English stars had eight, twelve or sixteen points. From about 1830 to 1840, the number increased to twenty-four; from about 1840 to 1850, to thirty-two. From about 1850 to 1860, the points are of different lengths (*Victorian Glory Star*). From about 1880 to 1900, the number decreased to sixteen, rounded somewhat with crosshatching (*Jewel Star*). See *star.*

star cut base The base of a paperweight, plate or other glass object embellished with a star, usually a *single star,* cut into the base.

star dust cane A type of cane used in making a paperweight. It is made of a central rod surrounded by six white rods to form a star-shaped section or corrugated shape. Occasionally there is a colored star or dot in the center, sometimes cased with colored glass. They were used at Baccarat to make a ground or sometimes with other canes as a center motif.

star dust ground A carpet ground composed of many white canes that are star shaped or corrugated, sometimes with a colored dot or star in the center. There are larger canes with floret or silhouette patterns usually within the motif.

star foot A foot of a drinking glass or other piece of glassware with a base, the bottom of which is embellished with a wheel engraved star. See *star, wheel engraved, for details.*

Star Glass Works See *Medford Glass House.*

Star Holly glassware An art glass made to simulate the jasperware made by Wedgwood. About 1951 the Imperial Glass Company made a pressed milk glass with a border of holly leaves and a center medallion on a shield shaped like a star with seven holly leaves. It was made with blue, green, and rust colors brushed on around the design and a mat surface with white leaves against the colored background. The Imperial Glass Company mark, an entwined "IG," appears in raised letters on the bottom of each piece. Because the coloring proved difficult and the process expensive, it was made for only a short time.

star opal See *opalescent glass.*

Statt Brothers John W., James, and Fred Statt established a cut glass shop in 1905 in Manayunk, Philadelphia, Pennsylvania. It went out of business. One brother, Fred, continued. The Fred Statt Company was in Philadelphia from 1930 to 1936.

Statt, Fred, Company See *Statt Brothers.*

stave A flat narrow strip of glass, colored or opaque white, used to embellish some paperweights. In one type (see *swirl paperweight*), long strips are used in a swirling pattern. In others (see *millefiori paperweight*), such as the concentric and flower, short pieces are placed near the design, positioned vertically to form a basket enclosing the central motif.

steamship glasses Pillar molded glasses, made mainly in the Midwest, with heavy ribs sometimes edged with a layer of trailed white or contrasting color. They are so named because the wide base and weight gave them great stability.

Stebbins, Thomas; Stebbins & Chamberlain; Stebbins & Stebbins See *Coventry Glass Factory Company.*

Stechelglas (*German*) Literally, *prickly glass.* A bottle made in the Rhineland, embellished with randomly scattered small prunts, not as densely placed as those found on other ware of the period.

steel jack See *pucellas.*

steel point engraving Engraving somewhat coarser than diamond point, generally associated with the decoration of bottles and inexpensive soda glass souvenirs during the mid-19th century, primarily in Newcastle, England, and Alloa, Scotland.

stein A thick, heavy drinking glass similar to a mug with a looped handle and hinged lid. The capacity is usually about a pint, but it may hold up to a quart. They have long been popular in Germany and elsewhere in Europe for drinking beer.

Steiner Glass Company A glass manufacturing facility established in Buckhannon, West Virginia, in the 1870s.

Steinfeld Brothers A highly diversified company in New York, New York, having cut glass as one of its lines between the late 1910s and the early 1920s.

stem The part of a vessel, particularly a drinking glass, connecting the bowl to the base or foot. It may be long or short and one of several styles. The styles of stems of English wine glasses changed from about 1680 to after 1777, the features serving to identify the period of production. Many of the changes were the result of the taxation on glass under the Glass Excise Acts of 1745 & 1777. Following is a listing of the various types of stems and their period of popularity:

Period of Popularity	Type of Stem
1680 - 1725	true and inverted baluster stems, often with an enclosed tear and many variations, and combinations of the knop
Late 1730s	development of air twist stems
Early 1740s	opaque twist stems
Late 1740s	color twist stems
About 1745 on	cut and faceted stems
Up until 1770	hollow diamond patterns
Up until 1800	fluted patterns
About 1800	raised diamond patterns and prismatic patterns

Also see the following types of stems: *air twist; applied; baluster (true baluster); balustroid; bobbin; capstan (spool); cigar shaped; collared; color twist; composite cut; drawn (drawn shank); faceted; pseudo-faceted (Silesian); flat cut; hollow; incised twist; inverted baluster; knopped; laddered; opaque twist; pedestal (Silesian); plain; quatrefoil; rudimentary; shouldered (Silesian); Silesian; straw; stuck shank; tear (teardrop); wire; figure; hollow baluster; spool (drawn shank); molded pedestal (Silesian).*

stem gatherer A member of a team, chair, or shop assisting the gaffer in making objects such as wine glasses by gathering a small amount of glass—enough to make a stem—and giving it to the stem maker for completion.

stem maker A member of the team, chair, or shop assisting the gaffer in making objects such as wine glasses. The stem maker takes the gather of glass from the stem gatherer and works it into the desired shape for the stem of a particular piece of glassware.

stem work Intricate patterns of glass threading that constitute the entire stem of some drinking glasses, i.e., without any vertical supporting column.

Stemless Daisy See *Cosmos.*

stemmed foot The foot of a vessel attached to the body by a stem, particularly on drinking glasses. It may be circular, square, ornamental shaped, or any of various other styles.

stemware Any drinking vessel having a stem, in a variety of shapes, sizes, types, and kinds of glass and generally marketed in sets of four, six, eight, or twelve pieces.

Stenger The original spelling of the last name of members of the family of Jacob Stanger.

Stenger, A., & Company
See *Lafayette Flint Glass Works*.

step cutting A cut-glass line motif consisting of adjacent horizontal lines in a parallel fashion. Visually it suggests a stairway.

stepped stem goblet A goblet characterized by a stem consisting of a series of about six thick, graduated rings, becoming smaller as they approach the foot. They were made in Bohemia about 1850.

Stephens, DeWitt See *Durhamville Glass Works*.

Sterling (Cut) Glass Company
The Sterling Glass Company was established in Cincinnati, Ohio, prior to 1904. Joseph Phillips was its president until 1910 and, from 1910 to 1913, a salesman. After this he entered the cut glass business with Joseph Landenwitsch, forming Joseph Phillips & Company. In 1918 Phillips left and Landenwitsch became president of what was then the Phillips Glass Company. The Sterling Glass Company closed in 1950 but was reorganized by some employees as the Sterling Cut Glass Company.

Steuben Glass ad, December 1925.

Steuben Glass ad, June 1926.

Steuben Glass ad from **The House Beautiful** *magazine, November 1926.*

Steuben Glass ad from **The House Beautiful** *magazine, April 1925.*

Steuben Glass Works
Now known as Steuben Glass Inc., the leading American manufacturer of ornamental glassware. It was established as the Steuben Glass Works in Corning, New York in 1903 by Frederick Carder, Thomas G. Hawkes and Mr. and Mrs. Willard Reed. Carder was its manager.

Because of the materials needed for the war effort during World War I, many of the raw materials, especially lead, were in short supply for products not essential to the war effort. Steuben fell in this category and was forced to curtail production. Corning Glass was making insulating, optical, and laboratory glassware for the military and remained in full production. As a result, on January 7, 1918, Steuben was acquired by Corning, becoming its Art Glass Division.

Steuben lost money every year from 1918 through 1932, except for a brief period in 1926. In 1932 the production manager, Robert J. Leavy, created a new transparent metal of great brilliance. It became the crystal glass the company used in later products and for which it has become famous.

During the 30-year management of Frederick Carder, he created new types of glass in numerous colors with numerous surface effects, making various wares in innumerable forms. The Depression and years of financial loss led to a reorganization in October 1933, under Arthur Amory Houghton Jr. Houghton was a great grandson of the founder of the Corning Glass Works, who became president in 1936 and had sole control over the direction and policies of the company. The name of the company was changed to Steuben Glass Incorporated, wholly owned by the Corning Glass Works.

As part of the reorganization, the company's intent was to gradually phase out the production and use of all colored glass and exploit the new crystal glass (known as *10-M*) developed by Leavy by creating new forms and styles, using engraved embellishments. In 1933 Houghton appointed John Montcith Gates as chief designer, sculptor Sidney B. Waugh as first designer, and in 1936, George Thompson as head of the newly created design department. Until that time the only decorating done at Steuben was acid etching. All cutting and engraving was done off premises by independent contractors working at home shops. The designing had been totally separated from production—designing done in New York City, production in Corning.

From 1934 through 1937 the company launched a nationwide advertising campaign. In addition to its New York retail store, in began opening others: Chicago (1935), Boston (1935), and Palm Beach (1937). In 1937 Steuben encouraged independent engravers to work for Steuben at the facility, and by 1938 all decorating was done on site. International recognition

soon followed. However, with the advent of World War II, raw materials again became scarce, and its products were not considered a necessity. Production dropped dramatically, and the stores in Chicago and Palm Beach closed. The New York store remained open because of the business created by its Antique Room (see *Steuben's Antique Room*). It retailed its wares through leading department stores throughout the Northeast and Midwest.

Steuben geared up again after the war. In 1950, the *snowflake* became its symbol because the snowflake is nature's most perfect form of crystal and Steuben was mankind's most perfect form of crystal. It opened a new facility in May 1951, switching from pot to tank melting (the molten glass agitated with a non-reactive platinum rod) to improve clarity, purity, and uniformity. It was designed to permit access to visitors to watch the various operations, including blowing, polishing, and decorating.

Beginning after the reorganization of 1933, tableware was made with emphasis on elegance, with some services designed and made for individual customers. However, ornamental pieces of imaginative designs and with skillfully engraved embellishments came to be Steuben's forte. In 1937 it made a series of pieces designed by 27 contemporary artists (*Twenty Seven Artists in Crystal*). In 1954 it made a series designed by 20 British artists (*British Artists in Crystal*), and in 1956, another by Asian artists (*Asian Artists in Crystal*). In spite of these, it has generally relied on ideas from its own designers, including Gates, Waugh, and Thompson, and later Lloyd Atkins, Donald Pollard, Paul Schulze, James Houston, and Don Wier.

In 1963 Steuben created a series inspired by 31 commissioned works of poetry (*Poetry in Crystal*). A more recent development is the use of gold ornamentation made by leading jewelers to accent the crystal glass article, such as that used on the Myth of Adonis. Among outstanding pieces made in the Houghton period are *The Gazelle Bowl, The Valor Cup, The Trout & Fly, The Great Ring of Canada,* and *The Sea Chase*. Unique pieces have been made for presidential presentation from the Truman administration, such as *Merry-Go-Round* and

Forest Spires. In March 1975, Steuben introduced its first piece of jewelry. In April 1977, for the first time in its history, early examples of newly introduced pieces were numbered and signed with the designer's mark, in addition to the Steuben signature. In 1972 Houghton retired, succeeded by Thomas S. Buechner, who was succeeded in 1985 by Kirtland C. Gardner III. The trend at Steuben has been to design and create simple but sophisticated pieces because of the expense involved in making more complex works.

Steuben's Antique Room
In 1941, as World War II expanded, Cecil Davis, a London glass dealer acting as Steuben's agent, began buying antique glass from the hard-pressed English gentry. He exported it to New York where Steuben had converted the mezzanine floor of its New York retail store into the Antique Room. Douglas Carson, an antiques expert working for the antiques dealer Stair & Company, was asked to manage Steuben's Antique Glass Department. The volume of sales generated by this room helped carry it through the war. Because the raw materials for making glass were in short supply and Steuben's products were not considered essential, its production fell and it was forced to close its Palm Beach and Chicago stores. In 1952 the Antique Room was closed. The best of the remaining pieces were consigned to the Corning Museum of Glass and the rest sold to antiques dealers or consigned to auction at Parke-Bennet.

Steubenville Flint Glass Works
See *Kilgore & Hanna*.

Stevens & Miller
See *Clyde Glass Works*.

Cased glass bowl, opal outside with pink inside, vaseline glass ribbon rim, Stevens & Williams, c. 1890s.
Tri-State Antiques

Hurricane lamps, silver-plated fonts, Radiant Crystal etched shades, 24" h.
Tri-State Antiques

Stevens & Williams Ltd.
A glass manufacturing facility in Brierley Hill, near Stourbridge, England, originally known as the Moor Lane Glass House, leased to Joseph Silvers (his daughter married Wm. Stevens) and Samuel Cox Williams. They purchased the firm in 1847. When Stevens purchased Silvers' interest, the firm became Stevens & Williams. It made much decorative glassware including *Tapestry Ware, Jewell Ware, Threaded Ware, Intaglio Ware, Matsu No Ke, and Moss Agate*. See *Alexandrite; Silveria glassware*.

Stevens, Crandall & Company
See *Empire Glass Company*.

Stevens, Miller & Co.
See *Clyde Glass Works*.

stick dish
(Aka *butter receiver, butter ball holder, bonbon, confection dish, ring tree, ring holder, ring tray, jewel stand with post*) A small dish with a round, upright cylinder or post rising from its center; the post having a round or cut *and* polished knob at the top. A miniature stick dish is identical to a stick dish except the center post has no knob.

stick lighting
Also known as *stickwork*. The process of using a sharp, pointed object to scratch details in painted or enameled decoration.

stick up
Affixing a pontil rod to a partly finished object.

sticker up
An assistant to the blower, who affixed the pontil iron to a partly finished object.

sticking the pot A process used by Frederick Carder when producing random bubbles in glassware. Just before the wares were to be made, a freshly cut willow pole about two inches in diameter *and* four to five feet in length was thrust into the pot of molten glass, then quickly withdrawn, causing the glass to bubble as a result of gasses released from the wood. Gathers of glass taken from the pot for the next half hour or so would contain bubbles of various sizes. This was repeated as often as necessary. It was also used to change the color of the glass in the pots. A batch of molten glass normally had a greenish tint as a result of iron impurities in the sand. The right amount of manganese would eliminate the greenish tint, producing a clear, colorless product. If too much manganese was added, the glass acquired a pinkish tint. If the pot was stuck by a willow pole one or more times, it eliminated the pinkish tint.

stickwork See *stick lighting.*

Stiegel, Henry William Born on May 13, 1729, in Cologne, Germany, Heinrich Wilhelm Stiegel was the oldest of the six children of John Frederick and Dorothea Elizabeth Stiegel. He, his mother, and younger brother, Anthony, came to Philadelphia, Pennsylvania, on August 3, 1750. After staying in Philadelphia for a year, he moved his family to Lancaster County, Pennsylvania, and worked for Jacob Huber, a wealthy iron master, at his Elizabeth Furnace near Shaefferstown, Pennsylvania. On November 7, 1752, he married Huber's daughter, Elizabeth, becoming Huber's assistant. In February 1758 his wife died and he, with financial backers, purchased Huber's furnace. He married Elizabeth Holz in October. He retained the name Elizabeth Furnace.

On April 10, 1760, he became a naturalized citizen, changing his name to *Henry William Stiegel.* He then acquired another furnace, known as Charming Forge. In 1762 he built a glass manufacturing facility at Elizabeth Furnace, near the iron foundry at Manheim. He imported craftsmen from his home area of Mannheim, Germany, and the first glass was blown on September 18, 1763. It was then that he assumed the self-proclaimed title of "Baron." In October 1764 he began building a second glass facility known as the Mannheim Glassworks. The first glass—a fairly high quality tableware—was blown on October 29, 1765. Then the Elizabeth Furnace glassworks was closed.

In 1769, Stiegel opened another facility nearby—the American Flint Glass Works. In 1772 he renamed it the American Flint Glass Factory. It was intended to be the first American facility specializing in high quality flint tableware, both clear and colored. He expanded the facility each year for the next three years in spite of the country's depression.

Economics (the depression, wasteful management and competition from abroad) caused all of his facilities to close and be sold in 1774. The original facility was purchased by Paul Zantzinger, who kept it in operation until at least 1780. At first Stiegel made bottles and window glass but later added soda lime glass, lead glass, and colored glass, especially blue and amethyst with some greens and browns. The wares were usually mold blown, often with a daisy pattern (see *daisy glassware*) or with sophisticated diamond designs. He also embellished glassware with enameling and wheel engraving. It was of reasonably good quality comparable to that of Europe, and the designs were, for the most part, copies and adaptations of European ones.

It is stated by some sources that Stiegel died an impoverished man in 1785. However, the Census of 1790 indicated that he was living in Warwick Township, Lancaster County, working at the Mt. Hope Furnace. There are very few documented pieces of his work. Glassware made at other facilities in the style and tradition of glassware made at his facilities is called Stiegel-type. See *Elizabeth Furnace Glasshouse; Manheim Glasshouse; Stiegel-type glassware.*

Stiegel-type glassware Glassware made at various facilities in the tradition of glassware made at the facilities of Henry William Stiegel, using his techniques and having a similar style and decoration. It is not assignable to any particular facility or area, nor is it even indigenous to the region (some was made as far away as Ohio). The ware was made of clear or colored glass, especially blue or amethyst, and some lead glass with embellishments executed in various styles, including: (a) wheel engraving (only in clear glass); especially tiny leaves and flowers; (b) enameling in vivid colors, especially hearts, birds, and flowers; (c) cutting; (d) gilding; and (e) pattern molding, which included such patterns as diamond, diamond daisy, daisy in hexagon (most pattern molded pieces were made in colors). The designs used in embellishing this ware were castles, birds, flowers, etc. Styles were predominantly English and European, including daisy and sunken panel glassware. Some imported glassware is indistinguishable from American. Glassware of the Stiegel-type made at Zanesville, Ohio, by craftsman from Manheim, Pennsylvania, has been called *Ohio Stiegel*. Many Stiegel-type pieces were made by Amelung. See *blown three mold glass*.

Stimel, Philip See *Kensington Glassworks*.

stippling The process of embellishing glass by striking a diamond or hardened steel point against the glass so that the image or likeness desired is made by many shallow dots called *stipples*. Sometimes the image is made by short lines or tiny scratches in the surface of the glass instead of dots. The way in which the dots are clustered provides the highlights or details of the image—its intensity varies with their closeness. Shadows and background result from leaving the polished glass untouched. The technique was introduced about 1621 in Holland by Anna Roemers Visscher, but it was not until 1720 that it was used as an exclusive means of embellishing glass. Only Dutch engravers, mainly amateur artists, used stippling in the 18th century. Much of the glass came from Newcastle, England. In England the art of stippling has been revived since about 1935 by Laurence Whistler and is now practiced by his three children and others. Pressing glass with a stippling effect was developed about 1830, for decorative purposes, and to help compensate for the loss of brilliance caused by the cold molds and to mask shear marks. The tiny dots added a refractory quality, lending a silvery sheen to the glass. The largest maker of pressed stippled glass was Boston & Sandwich, but it was not the only one. In England it was called *sable (sandy)* glass while Americans called it *lacy glass*.

stirring rod A thin rod of glass used for stirring liquids, frequently used in laboratories because of its resistance to chemicals, and in bars to stir drinks. They are of varying lengths from six to ten inches. They are sometimes twisted with the ends flattened; on occasion one end is pointed. The first recorded stirring rods were made of Roman glass during the 1st and 2nd centuries A.D.

stirrup cup (1) (Aka *hunting glass, fox head cup, coaching glass*) A drinking cup that was an adaptation of the ancient *rhyton*, without a handle or foot. Because of its irregularly shaped bottom, it must rest inverted on its rim when not in use. They were made in numerous forms, often animals. (2) Any type of glass used to consume the final drink taken by a mounted rider or huntsman before departing. See *stirrup decanter; fox head cup*.

stirrup decanter A decanter with a pointed bottom and, on occasion, a pouring lip and handle, carried by an attendant to a horseman. It was often part of a set that may include a tray, stirrup cups, and glasses. It was placed into a hole in a tray.

Stockton, Bankard & Co. A window glass manufacturing facility operating in the early 1850s in Wheeling, West Virginia.

Stoddard glass Glass made at any of the four facilities in and near Stoddard, New Hampshire between 1842 and the 1880s. The wares generally consisted of window glass and dark amber-green bottles and decanters. See *blown three mold glass*.

Stoehr, Keech & Co. A glass manufacturing facility established in Massillion, Ohio, in 1882. In 1885 it moved to Canton, Ohio, and in 1890 to Marion, Indiana. It made wares for the table in clear and colored glass.

stoke hole See *tease hole*.

Stokely & Campbell A bottle glass manufacturing facility established in 1831 in Wheeling, West Virginia. It was still operating in 1837.

stoker See *teaser.*

Stokes & Ely See *Clyde Glass Works.*

stone A speck of foreign matter sometimes found in a batch of molten glass that must be removed, especially if a high quality crystal glass is being made. In early flint glass, the specs were red and black, caused by poor fusion of the lead oxide and silica. They are generally formed: (a) by using materials whose particle size is too coarse; (b) by poor batch mixing; (c) by not providing a high enough temperature to completely melt the materials; (d) by keeping the melted glass at too low a temperature while working it; (e) by not melting the batch for enough time; (f) by the inclusion of foreign materials in the batch; and (g) by inadequate stirring of the molten glass.

stone engraving A process used in making *nature* motifs. The stone wheel was used to cut the deep intaglio motifs that were popular in the late 19th to early 20th centuries, carrying over, in a limited way, from the *Brilliant period* to the *Flower period* of cut glass. Tuthill, Sinclaire, and Hawkes made the greatest quantities of intaglio glass. Tuthill favored clusters of fruit, flowers, and butterflies. Hawkes called his intaglio wares *Gravic glass*, using both fruit and floral patterns. Rarities include Libbey's *Lovebirds* in the *Wisteria* pattern, Hawkes' *Ear of Corn,* and Tuthill's *Fruit Cluster.* Several patterns combined intaglio with celestial cut motifs.

stone glass Glass made in imitation of various stones since Egyptian times. See *Lithyalin; Hyalith; Diluvium; Moss Agate; mosaic glassware; marble glass.*

Stookey, S.D. An employee of the Corning Glass Works who developed photosensitive glass (1947), glass ceramic crystalline materials (pyroceram, 1957), and photochromic glass (1964).

stoop See *stoup.*

stopka (Russian) A beaker, tall and cylindrical, tapering slightly toward the bottom, resting on a thin foot ring, and having a flaring mouth. They were made at several Russian facilities during the 11th and 12th centuries.

stop(pe) See *stoup.*

stopper An object that fits in the mouth of a vessel, such as a decanter or cruet, closing and sealing it, preventing the contents from evaporating and becoming contaminated. They were made in various shapes, sizes, and styles, usually matching the vessel's style. Some made about 1750 are ground to fit securely in a specific vessel, and a few screw into the neck of the vessel. On more expensive decanters, the stopper was matched specifically to the bottle, each numbered to ensure they left the facility as a pair. The stopper was quite fragile and, because of its function, was often lost or broken. Replacements are frequent, some being good reproductions of the original. See the following types of stoppers: *bulbous; bull's-eye; conical; conical faceted; disk; grid; hollow; initialed; lapidary; lozenge; mushroom; pinnacle; spire; target.*

stopper rounds Wide mouth containers with stoppers fitted with great precision.

stopping knife A tool made from an ordinary table knife with the blade shortened and shaped to a half round, used by stained glassworkers.

Storm, Francis See *Lafayette Flint Glass Works.*

story lamp A lamp whose shade had around it a series of pictures telling a story.

stouk See *stoup.*

stoup (Aka *stop(pe), stoop* or *stouk*) Any small bucket, pail, pitcher, or drinking cup with a handle.

stoup, holy water See *holy water stoup.*

Stourbridge (Flint) Glass Works (1823-1845) A glass manufacturing facility established by John Robi(n)son in Pittsburgh, Pennsylvania. About 1830 its operating firm was J. & T. Robi(n)son, and, in 1836, Robi(n)son, Anderson & Co. John Robi(n)son died in 1835/6, and his sons, Thomas and John Jr., were the "Robi(n)son" in the new firm, and Alexander M. Anderson was formerly associated with Bakewell's. It made plain and cut flint glassware. Pressed, green, and opalescent glass were added later.

stouter A lathe used to make intaglio glass, invented in the late 19th century and attributed to John Northwood at Stourbridge.

Stouvenal, Joseph, & Co. (1837-1871) A glass manufacturing facility originally specializing in cut glass and later pressed glass, established in New York, New York. Stouvenal was the first glass cutter of record in New York. During its history, either Joseph or one of his two brothers, Francis or Nicholas, were in charge of production.

strain The force that develops between the surface and interior of glass as a result of flaws in the annealing process, differences in coefficients of expansion between two joined pieces of glass, or minute objects that may have formed or been included in the glass.

strain cracking Deterioration in a glass object. Strain cracking looks like tiny cracks in the wall of the glass, occurring at regular intervals and caused by stresses and strains due to faulty annealing.

strain point temperature The temperature at which the flow of glass begins.

Strand A trademark used by the Kings County Rich Cut Glass Company.

strap handle An early form of applied handle consisting of a thick ribbon of glass usually ending at the base with a decorative squiggle or curlicue. Later applied handles were round.

strass A brilliant lead glass used in making artificial gems; a borosilicate of potassium and lead, with small quantities of alumina and arsenic. When uncolored, it is used in making imitation diamonds because it is transparent and very refractive but much softer. The addition of various metallic oxides and salts to a batch of uncolored strass produces colored strass, used to make imitations of most precious stones such as emeralds, garnets, etc. The term is derived from the name of a jeweler, George Frederic Strass (1701-73), born at Wolfisheim, near Strasbourg, where he learned to make jewelry and artificial gems. He moved to Paris in 1724 and developed, between 1730 and 1734, new techniques to make imitation precious stones even though imitation diamonds were made in Paris in the 17th century. He relinquished their production in 1752 to Georges-Michel Bapst (1718-70), his niece's husband. Artificial gems are now made primarily in Czechoslovakia, Austria, and France. Many sources have attributed their creation to Joseph Stras(s) (er) of Venice, but there is no record of his existence. See *paste jewelry.*

Strathearn Glass Ltd. A glass manufacturing facility established in 1963 to take over the business of Vasart Glass Ltd. after a major interest in it had been acquired by the Scotch whisky distillers, Wm. Teacher & Sons Ltd. The operation and personnel were moved from Perth in 1964 to the new facility at Crieff. It continued to make paperweights, some in entirely new designs, bearing its initial and date. It also made colored glass items as well as the *Glenasty* range of heavy clear glassware. In 1968 Stuart Drysdale, who had organized Vasart Glass Ltd., left together with some personnel and, in 1970, established a new facility called Perthshire Paperweights Ltd., which made only paperweights.

Stratton, Buck & Co. See *Bridgeton Glass Works.*

Straus, L., & Sons In 1852 Lazarus Straus came from Bavaria to Georgia where he imported and sold fine china and glassware. In 1865 he moved to New York City where he established an import and selling house for fine china and glassware, named Straus & Company. This company became L. Straus & Sons in 1872. In 1888 it started a glass cutting facility. It won six awards at the World's Fair in Chicago, Illinois, in 1893, more than any other company. Straus cut much fine glass to order and sold a lot in Europe. Its trademark was a representation of a round diamond and the words "Straus, Cut Glass" or a star in a circle, affixed using paper labels. The cutting operations were discontinued in 1925 as the market declined. One of Straus' sons was a partner in the firm of Abraham & Straus. In 1964 L. Straus & Sons became Straus-Duparquet.

Straus-Duparquet See *Straus, L., & Sons.*

straw marks (1) An annealing mark. A flaw caused by waste material left in the mold that burns when molten glass is put in, leaving a scar on the glass. The term is derived from the belief that, after an object was made, it was dropped into a bed of straw to minimize breakage. The straw supposedly left a mark on the glass on impact. (2) See *shear mark* (2).

Straw Opal An opalescent glassware, pale milky yellow in color, developed at Whitefrairs glassworks by Harry Powell. It was made between 1877 and 1879.

straw stem See *drawn shank.*

strawberry dish (Aka *saucer dish*) A shallow dish with fluted sides and a scalloped rim for holding individual servings of fruit. They often come in sets accompanied by a serving bowl.

strawberry diamond cutting (Aka *American version, crosscut diamond*) A variation of raised diamond cutting made by leaving an uncut space between the diagonal grooves so that a flat area results instead of pointed diamonds. The flat areas are cut with crosshatched grooves to make them into a group of low relief diamonds. In England it is called *laced diamond*, and sometimes, erroneously, a *hobnail pattern*. A further, more complicated pattern is made by making the original grooves in pairs or threes so that a new ridge is made between the rows of strawberry diamonds. This is known as the *English version* of the strawberry diamond. Dorflinger called his version the *silver diamond.* A simplified version of the strawberry diamond, the *checkered diamond*, has a flat area cut in groups of four small diamonds instead of larger numbers (usually sixteen). See *flat diamond cutting; diamond; cross hatching.*

strawberry prunt A slightly convex prunt with relief embellishment impressed on it with a tool with markings resembling a strawberry. See *raspberry prunt.*

streaky glass Glass with a blending of two or more colors.

streaky cathedral glass Cathedral glass of more than one color, exhibiting swirls of various colors as well as all the other attributes of cathedral glass.

strengthened glass See *tempered glass.*

stress The force per unit area on a body, which causes it to distort, being perpendicular to the area.

Blue Satin iridescent stretch glass bowl. Top 8" d., bottom 4-1/2" d., 3-1/2" h.
Davanna Collection

stretch glass An iridescent glass whose surface looks similar to onionskin, originally made as an inexpensive copy of glassware made by Tiffany, Carder, and others. It was later made as a type of glass in itself. It is any iridescent glass with no pattern, in a variety of colors and often confused with art glass. The iridizing fluid used was usually a metallic oxide which, when added to hot glass, caused it to crizzle. When its form was changed, the iridizing fluid broke up and made an *onion skin* or stretched finish as the glass cooled. One of the major producers in the 1930s was Imperial Glass Company, which called the glass *Rainbow Lustre.* It was also made by other companies, including Northwood in Indiana, Pennsylvania, and Wheeling, West Virginia during the early years of its popularity, and by Fenton during the later years. See *satin iridescent.*

striae Undulating or cord-like markings on glassware caused by variations of temperature within the furnace or by the unequal density of the materials used. See *striated decoration; striation marks.*

striated decoration (1) An intentional embellishment in the form of a series of parallel lines, often curved, in the metal. It was used on some English ware during the 18th and early 19th centuries. See *striae; striation marks*. (2) Colored loops intrinsic with the body of the piece.

striation marks Tool marks usually visible on most early handmade glassware. They appear as lines from the top to the bottom of the piece and around the circumference of the body, caused by the tool when it is applied to the glass when it is being formed. Those on the feet of glasses appear when the steel tool was used (up to 1830). After this date, they no longer appear because wooden tools were used.

strigil *(Latin)* Literally, *scraper*. A scraper used by ancient Romans to scrap the skin after bathing.

striking The process of raising the temperature of already melted and cooled glass to a point at which color appears or glass opacifies. It is a well-known phenomena used for making gold ruby glass and some sulfide or sulfur bearing glasses. See *shaded glass*.

String holders, c. 1890-1900, amber and cobalt-blue glass.
The Corning Museum of Glass

string holder (Aka *twine holder*) A holder for balls of string. They were made in a variety of shapes, such as a hanging bell or beehive, with a hole through which the string is fed. They were used in grocery stores and homes during the 1800s and early 1900s. Many were made in blown or pressed glass between the 1860s and the 1920s.

string rim (or ring) A ring of trailed glass or lip encircling the neck of a wine bottle or decanter just below the mouth. It is often added to facilitate the attaching of a string or wire to secure the cork in the bottle, used prior to the introduction of the close fitting *flush cork*.

stringing Trailing.

striped glassware (1) Hollow glassware embellished with parallel stripes of opaque white or colored glass sometimes spiraling around the piece as a result of being twisted after the white or colored glass rods had been embedded in the body. It was made during the 19th century. A patent for a special process was registered in England in 1885 to William Webb Boulton of Boulton & Mills. (2) In the United States it applies to glass known as *vetro a retorti*, which may be divided into three classes of blown glass: (a) *Venetian*—fragile, very light in weight, and very ornate; (b) *Lutz*—named after Nicholas Lutz, fairly light in weight, not very fragile, mostly utilitarian, made by Lutz in the 1870s for Boston & Sandwich; and (c) *modern*—imported from Italy, heavier, and more brilliantly colored than earlier pieces.

striped silvering An embellishment on mirrors where portions of the silvering, in the form of stripes, have been removed.

Stroudsburg Glass Company A wholesale hotel and restaurant supply facility in Stroudsburg, Pennsylvania. See *Gibbs, Kelly & Company*.

strut (Aka *pig*) A small rod holding the pattern to the main body of the piece of *vasa diatreta*.

Stuart, Estep & Company See *Pittsburgh Union Glass Works*.

stuck shank The stem of a drinking glass made separately from the bowl and attached to it, in contrast to a drawn shank. A stuck shank glass is made in three parts: bowl, stem, and foot. See *applied stem; shank stem glass*.

stuck up A base that is ground and polished.

student glass In the late 1920s, the countrywide Depression greatly reduced the demand for Pairpoint products. However, in the early 1930s, a few workmen were again making glassware and silverware, and the company established the Pairpoint School of Glassmaking. Glass made by the young apprentices is called *student glass*. The school was not successful because the students were unwilling to accept the low wages paid during the long and tedious apprenticeship.

Studies in Crystal An ongoing series of works of art in glass, in excess of 200 pieces, initiated in 1955 and made by Steuben. They have no functional purpose and include both engravings on prismatic forms and free sculptured abstractions.

studio glassware Glassware made by artist craftsmen rather than glassmakers in a manufacturing facility. It is made and embellished by them under the immediate supervision of the designer who usually signs it.

Until the end of the 19th century, most glass manufacturing had settled down to the stage where it was a highly specialized, industrialized craft. The most original, individual results were obtained only in embellishing objects finished or completed by a large or fairly large facility. This embellishing was often carried out away from the facility. Toward the end of the 19th century, many talented artists and designers became interested in the medium but were used to working for individual clients rather than mass manufacturers. A search began to simplify the process of glassmaking.

In 1962 Dominick Labino, a scientist and artist, succeeded in developing a new formula for glass that could be melted in a small kiln holding enough material for an individual or a small team. In the same year Harvey K. Littleton built, at the University of Wisconsin, a small kiln designed for Labino's glass. He also developed his own formula for low melting point glass. Today many major companies make "studio glass" for use by individuals, some of the largest being Steuben, Rosenthal, and Orrefors.

Over the years studio glass has had obvious changes in design and subject. Originally most pieces were functional, but have changed to abstract images, even on practical objects such as bowls and jugs. Every type of object is made in glass now by the studio artists, including paperweights, stained glass panels, etc. Many glasshouses have now set up *studios* for use by individual artists and designers. In 1962 the Toledo (Ohio) Art Museum sponsored a group to work in this manner. Over 100 universities now offer courses in studio glassmaking.

Sturzbecher *(German)* Literally, *somersault glass*. A drinking glass with a stem but no foot so when emptied it must be inverted on its rim (the same as a rython or English stirrup cup). Early examples of Frankish glass were made from about 400 to 700. See *dopplesturzbecher; Spitzbecher; whistle goblet*.

stylized Modifying the appearance of an object from its natural appearance to a more abstract pattern or conventionalized style of expression.

subject paperweight A large class of paperweights that includes various types. The embellishment is an embedded motif, usually made *at-the-lamp* or handmade, and must be distinguished from embellishment of millefiori canes. The process used involves first making the central motif, embedding it in a blob of molten glass, and then gathering more molten glass on top until the desired size dome was obtained. If an overlay is desired, the clear glass dome is covered with a thin layer of colored glass and windows ground.

sucket glass A shallow bowl with a highly decorative, fluted rim used for holding candies or dried fruit.

sucking bottle See *pap boat*.

suction feeder See *glass, Manufacturing, Shaping*.

Suffolk Glass Works A glass manufacturing facility established in 1852 in (South) Boston, Massachusetts, by Joshua Jenkins who managed it until 1880. At one point it occupied two locations in South Boston. In 1862 Jenkins & Laselle was the owner. From 1880 until it closed in 1885, S.B. Lowland managed it. After it closed, the buildings remained vacant and burned in 1900. On September 18, 1860, Jenkins received a patent for a *tubilated fount* for lamps. It involved blowing a lamp reservoir with two openings, one for the wick and one for filling the oil, in one operation. A large part of the facility's production was devoted to it and other types of kerosene lamps. In addition it made blown, pressed, and cut flint glassware and lamp chimneys, and druggists' and chemists' ware.

Cut-glass sugar and creamer on high knopped teardrop stems, approx. 6" h.
Davanna Collection

sugar & creamer A small pitcher and a matching sugar bowl used for serving sugar and cream at the table. They were made in all types and kinds of glass, in standard and unusual shapes.

sugar acid See *etching cream.*

sugar basin See *sugar bowl.*

sugar bowl A bowl, sometimes with a cover, for serving sugar at the table. They are often cylindrical, globular, or pear shaped and rest on a flat bottom, sometimes with a spreading base, a knop-stemmed foot, or small bun feet. They may or may not have two side handles. They were sometimes made *en suite* with a dinner service, tea service, or creamer. Early ones had no lids, but lids were standard on later ones. They were once called *sugar basins.*

sugar box A small covered container used to hold sugar, generally in the form of a box or chest. Prior to the 18th century, sugar was

an expensive, imported commodity, used only by the wealthy. Sugar boxes, therefore, were quite rare, generally brought out when tea was served and then put away. They are not to be confused with sugar bowls or modern day sugar canisters.

sugar castor (Aka *sugar dredger*) A castor usually of baluster or cylindrical shape with a domed cover (sometimes screwed to the container) for sprinkling sugar. See *sugar shaker.*

sugar crusher (Aka *toddy stick*) An ornamental rod similar to a pestle, about five inches long with a large flattened end, used for crushing sugar in a glass of toddy.

sugar dredger See *sugar castor.*

Sugar shaker, Diamond Side pattern, original top.
Krause Publications

Consolidated Lamp & Glass Co. Pine Cone sugar sifter, approx. 1895, salmon color, 5" h.
Davanna Collection

sugar shaker A shaker usually with a screw-on top with holes, used to dispense sugar by shaking. It is somewhat larger than a salt shaker. They are scarce because the dampness and coarseness of the sugar created problems with dispensing through the shaker top, limiting the market. They were pressed or blown in every type of glass and are currently being reproduced. See *sugar castor.*

suite, en *(French)* Two or more pieces shaped and embellished in a like manner or fashion so they form a set, such as a dinner service or tea service.

sulfur An alternate spelling for *sulphur.* See *sulphur.*

sulfur(e)s A type of paperweight that has a motif of bouquets, flowers, fruits, animals, or insects enclosed within the dome.

sulphide A silvery-looking, opaque medallion enclosed in transparent glass. The process was first attempted about 1750 in Bohemia but was not successfully accomplished until later in France by Barthelemy Desprez. In the last quarter of the 18th century, he made fine cameos and medallions of prominent people in a white porcellanous material. In the early 19th century, he enclosed these in transparent glass. Because of the thin layer of air between the medallion and the glass, these items had a silvery appearance. They were, on occasion, set into plaques of glass, framed for hanging on the wall; or in the sides or bottoms of goblets, beakers, bottles, paperweights, and other objects.

In England Apsley Pellatt made similar wares, calling them *cameo incrustations* or *crystallo ceramie.* He obtained a patent for the process in 1819. They were also made at Baccarat and Clichy and other French facilities and copied in Bohemia and Germany about 1830. They were also made about 1814 at Bakewell's in Pittsburgh, Pennsylvania, in the form of profile portraits of prominent citizens. Ones depicting prominent persons of the past and present are being made at Baccarat.

The creation of the modern sulphide is a complex process. The artist first prepares numerous drawings and detailed plans for the piece. A model, much larger than the size of the finished cameo, is made of molding clay. Because of the subsequent reduction in size, special attention is paid to pertinent details.

The model is then cast in plaster, the surface further refined and minute details enhanced. From this a bronze model is made, polished, and mounted on a reduction plate where an undistorted reproduction of a much smaller size is cut into steel. Then a carefully prepared mixture of clay, sand, and soapstone is poured into a plaster cast made from the steel mold. The cameo is hydraulically pressed and heat treated, placed on a circular steel plate, and carefully covered with a gather of clear or colored molten glass. See *encrusted paperweight; sulphide paperweight.*

Sulphide paperweight of Pope Pius XII, ruby ground, signed. Corning Museum of Glass

sulphide paperweight A paperweight having as its principal embellishment an embedded sulphide (cameo incrustation) and made using the same methods as sulphides except additional glass is added to form the ground of the weight and the dome. Then it is annealed, polished and, if desired, faceted, but it is rarely of the overlay type. Specimens made at Baccarat and Clichy feature portraits of prominent persons and depictions of mythological characters and hunting scenes.

sulphur A non-metallic element used in the glass industry as a colorant in combination with iron and carbon for the large scale production of amber glass—colors ranging from light straw to deep reddish brown and even black. Sulphur may be used to produce a pure blue color in boro-silicate glasses containing a high percent of boric oxides. In combination with calcium in almost any glass, sulphur produces a deep yellow color. Cadmium sulfides, which have a deep yellow color, are often used in making enamels and glasses. In some sulphide glasses, the color does not develop in the molten glass but has to be *struck* by raising the temperature until the color appears.

summer stop An annual practice among pre-modern glass manufacturing facilities where the facility was shut down for about six weeks during the summer, from about mid-July through the first of September. This was done because the heat of the summer combined with the heat of the furnaces made it almost impossible to work. The summer stop also provided time to conduct general repairs, rebuild furnaces, modernize, etc., without disrupting the process or the workers.

sunburst A cut-glass motif made by encircling a *bull's-eye* with prism flares.

sunburst pattern A decorative pattern in the form of a disc—representing the sun—surrounded by radiating rays, found on some flasks of mold blown glass made in the United States. The points of the rays are often within a plain or scalloped oval border. Sometimes the rays almost meet at the center, which is sometimes a plain oval, concentric rings, or other decorative device.

Suncook Glass Works (1839-1850) A continuation of the Chelmsford Glass Works after it moved to Suncook Village, New Hampshire, in 1839. The company moved because of the scarcity of fuel and the high cost of production and living. William E. Hirsch & Assoc. operated it, making window glass using the cylinder process. The glass initially was fairly good, having an aquamarine or light green color. The company made other glassware including pitchers, jars, and other utilitarian tableware. The sand near the facility, at Massabesic Pond, was soon found to contain a high iron content, and the glass became dark in color and was not salable. The glassworks began importing sand from the Morris River area, increasing costs. In 1845 the duty on imported glass was lowered, making it cheaper.

sunflower glass See *girasol.*

sunglow glass Glass colored by exposing it to the sun's rays, dry areas being best. In most cases the glass will turn purple, resulting from manganese used in the batch.

Today's glass is made with an inhibitor that slows such discoloration.

sunken panel A decorative style in the form of adjacent or close vertical depressions, in the shape of arches, made by mold blowing a single gather of metal and sometimes a second gather. It is found on American glassware, some probably made by Henry William Stiegel. See *panelling.*

Sunset Glass An iridized Tiffany Favrile glassware.

Sunset Glow See *opal glass.*

Sunshine Cut Glass Company A company established sometime prior to 1916 in Cleveland, Ohio, making cut-glass novelty wares of inferior quality. In 1917 Theodore R. Vetter was the firm's vice president and, in 1928, department manager. In 1916 he organized the Vetter Cut Glass Manufacturing Company in Cleveland (associated with both at the same time), which made a superior grade, later switching to pressed and other glassware such as mirrors and plate glass. In 1954 Vetter sold it to Milton Glass. In 1964 it was owned and operated by Robert M. Yates and Peter C. Sanelli.

supercooled liquid A liquid that has been cooled to below its freezing point without changing to a crystalline state. Glass is the most common and best known.

superimposed decoration Embellishments on glassware, such as swagging and lily pads, formed by tooling a second layer of glass on the body of a formed piece.

support bars Iron bars fastened to the inside of mosaic window and door panels to aid in supporting the weight of the glass and canes.

supreme A tall glass used to serve sherbet during the early 19th century.

surface engraving The most shallow of all types of engraving done on glassware too thin for cutting or deep engraving. Monograms and coats-of-arms are usually of this type. See *wheel engraving, Surface.*

surface wheel engraving See *wheel engraving, Surface.*

Surfeit water glass A delicate, flute-shaped drinking glass, the top being less than one inch in diameter, fashionable during the mid-Georgian period (1714-1830). Surfeit water was an extremely strong brandy.

Susquehanna Cut Glass Company
A glass cutting facility established in 1910 by Albert Roye (previously employed at the Val Bergen Cut Glass Company) in Columbia, Pennsylvania. It was still operating in the 1960s as the Susquehanna Glass Company.

Sutton, Wendt & Co.
See *Pennsylvania Flint Glass Works.*

swag A decorative pattern in the form of a festoon, often in relief.

swagged design A design made by adding a cusp at the base of a motif, pulling it into a point.

swan finial A finial so-called "swan" even though it more closely resembles a duck or a chicken, often found on the covers of sugar bowls.

Swankyswigs kiddie cup, squirrel and deer, brown, 4-1/2" h.
Krause Publications

Swankyswigs Embellished glass containers filled with Kraft Cheese Spread dating from the early 1930s. Production was discontinued during World War II (the paints were needed for the war effort) and resumed after the war ended. They were popular during the Depression, being used as tumblers and juice glasses when empty. The first designs were hand applied. When popularity increased, new, additional, and more intricate machine-made patterns and designs were introduced, test marketed prior

to large scale production. As a result of limited distribution of the unpopular test marketed designs, they are hard to identify. The last colored pattern was *Bi-Centennial Tulip* made in 1975. The spread is still available but in a crystal type glass.

Swarovski frogs, clear crown; left: clear eyes; right: black eyes.
Krause Publications

Swarovski, D., & Co. A glass cutting facility established in Tirol, Austria, by Daniel Swarovski in 1895. It once was the largest maker of cut crystal in the world and a leader in the development of automated precision cutting methods using water power. It cuts industrial stones for fine grinding, optical products for binoculars, crystal for use in costume jewelry and traffic reflector signals, as well as standard glassware. It has two jewelry divisions and is famous for its chandelier ornaments. Giftware lines include candleholders, boxes, paperweights, desk items, animal figures, and other figurines. All figurines have a lead content of 30% or greater. In 1987 the International Swarovski Collectors Society was founded. The company makes one figurine each year for the society, introducing a new theme every three years. Initially its figurines were signed "SC" in block letters. Beginning in 1989, a figure of a swan became part of the signature. Items made for the society are signed with "SCS," the initials of the designer, and year made. Its name is now Daniel Swarovski Corporation, headquartered in Zurich, Switzerland, with design facilities in Wattens, Austria, and manufacturing facilities in eleven other countries, including one in Cranston, Rhode Island.

Swearer, N. & P. See *Bridgeport Glass Works.*

Swedes' Glass A glass manufacturing facility constructed in what is now Pennsylvania by Swedish immigrants in the late 1630s.

Swedesboro Glass Works (1896-1920) (Aka *South Jersey Glass Works*) A glass manufacturing facility established in Swedesboro, New Jersey, by eleven glassblowers from Royer's Ford, Pennsylvania. The company made soda and beer bottles, ink bottles, whiskey bottles, carboys, and *Castoria* bottles.

Swedish glassware Continuous production of glass in Sweden began about 1580 when a facility was built in Stockholm, staffed by German craftsmen and financed by royalty. It operated until about 1640, when the patent was taken over by Melchior and Gustaf Jung, father and son. With the help of Italian glassmakers, they operated several facilities in and around Stockholm and in Finland (then a Swedish province) until 1695.

The Kungsholm Glasbruk in Stockholm was established in 1676 by Giacomo Scapitta, making glass in the Venetian style until closing in 1815. Skanska Glasbruket, at Henrikstorp in Scania, operated from 1691 to 1760, making engraved glass in rustic style. Goteborg Glasbruk in Gothenburg operated from 1761 to 1808 and is best known for its stylish neoclassical models, many in deep blue or opaque white glass and embellished with cutting, engraving, or gilding. In 1742 the Kosta facility in Smaland was established and is still in operation. During the 19th century, it became the largest, most modern facility, becoming affiliated with the Kosta-Boda glassworks (the Boda Glassworks was established in 1864). In 1810 a facility was established at Reijmyre on Ostergotland, which soon equaled Kosta in both size and efficiency.

Pressed glass was made in Sweden from the 1840s, initially using molds from abroad. Cutting in a complex Brilliant style was stressed in the late 19th century. From 1890 some art glass in the Galle style was made. In the 20th century, during World War I, the Swedes encouraged facilities to engage artists as designers. In 1916 Orrefors, established in 1898 to make utilitarian glass, began making art glass. During this period Kosta paralleled Orrefors. After the war, a new generation of young designers began to rebel against the stylishness and restraint of Swedish art glass, attracting many foreign studio glassmakers.

Sweden is noted for glassware called *Swedish Modern,* made from about 1917. It is famous for pieces of original design and artistic ornamental styles, as well as its superior tableware. Over 100 small facilities have operated in the glassmaking district near Vaxjo in Smaland. More than 30 are still operating.

Swedish Modern See *Swedish glassware.*

Sweeney & Co.; Sweeney, Bell & Co. See *Ensell & Wilson; Sweeney Brothers; Sweeney, M. & R.H.*

Sweeney & Sweeney Glass Co. See *Sweeney, M. & R.H.*

Sweeney, M. & R.H. A flint glass manufacturing and glass cutting facility established in 1831 in Wheeling, West Virginia. In 1845 it was operated by M. & T. Sweeney; in 1848 by Sweeney(s) & Bell; and in 1852 by T. Sweeney & Son. In 1863 it purchased the Ensell & Wilson facility It operated both for a short time as Sweeney & Co., later in 1863 as Sweeney, Bell & Co., adding chemical glassware. In 1867 the operating company became Sweeney, McCluney & Co., closing the Wheeling facility (also called Sweeney & Sweeney Glass Co.) and the Flint Glass Works. See *Sweeney Brothers.*

Sweeney, M. & T.; Sweeney, T., & Son See *Sweeney Brothers; Sweeney, M. & R.H.*

Sweeney, McCluney & Co. See *Ensell & Wilson; Sweeney Brothers; Sweeney, M. & R.H., & Co.*

Sweeney Brothers A flint glass manufacturing facility established in 1835 in Wheeling, West Virginia, operating as North Wheeling Glass Works, making a good quality cut glass. It closed in 1868 when the company moved to Martins Ferry, Ohio (closing during the financial crisis of 1873). The operating companies were: M. & R.H. Sweeney (1835-1845); M. & T. Sweeney (1845-1848); Sweeney(s) & Bell (1848-1851); T. Sweeney & Son (1852-1863); Sweeney, Bell & Co. (1863-1867); Sweeney, McCluney & Co. (1867-1868). See *Sweeney, M. & R.H.*

sweet stand A sweetmeat bottle or covered vase.

sweetmeat Highly sweetened food, such as preserves, candy, cakes, pastry, or any sweet delicacy, such as candied fruit or bonbons.

sweetmeat bottle A wide mouth bottle made specifically to hold certain sweetmeats, namely preserves (fruits preserved with sugar).

sweetmeat dish (Aka *frageoir*) A bowl with low feet used for holding sweetmeats.

sweetmeat glass A stemmed receptacle with a shallow bowl for serving sweetmeats, likely *dry sweetmeats*, such as nuts, chocolates, dried fruits, etc. (*Wet sweetmeats*, such as jam, fruit or the like, are eaten with a spoon.) If the central sweetmeat glass held an orange, it was called an *orange glass*. Sweetmeat glasses were made in a variety of forms and styles with low, wide bowls (often of double ogee shape), sloped or domed feet, and stems (often Silesian or, rarely, an opaque twist stem). They were often embellished with cut decoration. The rim of the bowl was at times flanged or ornamental, often scalloped or serrated, or with looped trailing. Those with a plain level rim were often used as drinking glasses, erroneously called *champagne glasses*. From the mid-18th century, sweetmeats were often served in a larger dessert glass or in small bowls suspended from an epergne. A small sweetmeat glass is called a *comfit glass*.

sweetmeat stand A large composite piece used as a centerpiece for a table. It has a stand or epergne from which are suspended several small dishes for sweetmeats.

swelling knop A knop, somewhat cylindrical in form, bulging slightly in the center.

swimming swans paperweight See *ducks-on-a-pond paperweight*.

Swindell Brothers See *Crystal Window Glass Works*.

swing hole A drop off or hole at least nine feet below the platform or foot bench on which a blower stood while swinging the blowpipe back and forth to stretch the cylinder of glass while blowing it to the desired length, usually six feet or more; a step in making cylinder glass.

swing mirror or swing(ing) glass See *cheval (glass)*.

swirl paperweight A geometrically arranged paperweight with ribbons of glass swirling out from a central cane, enclosed in a glass dome. The embedded swirls were usually of two alternating colors, one of which was often opaque white glass. Sometimes it had a small central motif. Almost all were made at Clichy.

swirled ribbing An embellishment on mold blown glass made by expanding and twisting a ribbed paraison after removal from the mold.

swirls A cut-glass motif having a series of miter cuts curved to produce a whirling or spinning effect.

Swizzle sticks of various colors and strengths. One at top hollow with paper advertisement for "Old Methusalem" whiskey.
Davanna Collection

swizzle stick A thin glass rod with an enlarged end, used to stir a drink to remove effervescence. It was originally used to stir swizzle, a sweetened alcoholic drink made with rum. In more recent times it is used to stir champagne, although this is disapproved of by those who appreciate wines. See *toddy stick*.

sword A full size replica of a saber or other type of sword, usually made of clear glass, with an ornamental guard and grip. They were made as friggers in England from the late 18th to the mid-19th century, often used in glassmaker's processions in Bristol and Newcastle.

sword guard or slide A small, slitted device to be fitted over the blade of a sword. Some were made of glass, in imitation of jade, in China during the Han Dynasty (206 B.C.-220 A.D.).

Sydenham Glass Company Limited
A glass manufacturing facility established in 1894 in Wallaceburg, Canada, in 1913. It became part of the Diamond Glass Company, then later part of the Dominion Glass Company, then known as its Wallaceburg Works. In 1900 it burned and was immediately rebuilt. It made a wide variety of blown and pressed glassware.

syllabub glass Also spelled *sillabub*. A vessel used for drinking syllabub, a beverage once popular in England. It was made from fresh cream whipped to a froth, with sherry, ratafia, and spices added. From about 1677 the practice was to drink it from a posset pot. From about 1725 special glasses were made—often called *whips* from *whipt sylla-bub*—similar to the posset pot without the spout, and either one or no handle. Then, about 1770, their design changed and they looked similar to jelly glasses, some engraved with an "S" to distinguish them from jelly glasses.

Syrian glassware Glassware made in Syria, encompassing all from early Sidonian glassware (about 1700 B.C.) through the end of the period of Islamic glassware in 1402. The art of glassblowing was discovered in Syria about 100 B.C. and, possibly after a period of free blown glass, the process of mold blown glass was developed. The Romans were quick to exploit these techniques. Syrian glass includes glassware attributed to Raqqa, Aleppo, and Damascus.

Syrian temple shrine glassware Made between 1893 and 1917, it pictures various shrine symbols. In most cases the pieces were dated.

Syro-Frankish glassware A type of Islamic glassware of uncertain origin, at one time attributed to Venice but more recently to Syrian craftsmen working at an unidentified Frankish Court from 1260 to 1290 during the period of the Crusades. It includes a group of twenty-five enameled beakers, such as the Aldrevandin beaker.

Milk glass syrup with hand-painted flowers and robin's egg blue applied handle, 6-1/2" h., c. 1880.
Tri-State Antiques

Clear glass syrup pitcher, c. 1898-1910, U.S. Glass Co.
The Corning Museum of Glass

syrup jar or jug A jar or jug for holding and serving syrup. Some are blown or pressed and some have pewter or silver lids and/or bases. The handles are usually pewter, silver, or glass.

10-M A glass of extremely high refractive quality that permits the entire spectrum of a light wave, including the ultraviolet range, to pass through. This is accomplished by removing from the batch most of the iron impurities responsible for trapping ultraviolet light. Minute traces of iron caused a greenish tint that had to be removed by a decolorizing agent, such as manganese dioxide, which, while neutralizing the greenish tint, imparted a slight pinkish tint of its own. 10-M required no decolorizing agent. It was created between 1929 and 1932 when two experimental lines were made. This glass resulted in all colored glass being phased out at Steuben.

10-R-10 See *Iorio Glass Shop*.

table bell A bell with an ornamental finial rather than a vertical handle as on ordinary hand bells.

table bottle Any bottle, such as a decanter or carafe, used to serve water or beverages.

table luster See *luster*.

table of crown glass A crown of glass made from a flattened blow of glass, usually between 38 and 50 inches in diameter, subsequently cut into window panes. It weighed from 15 to 32 pounds, 25 pounds being average, and the blowpipe weighed 18 to 20 pounds.

table ornament See *centerpiece*.

table set A group of table articles consisting of a matching sugar bowl, creamer, spoon holder and butter dish.

tableware Articles used at the table for eating, drinking, etc. Here it refers to glassware used at the table for drinking.

Methods of Manufacture. Blown Handmade Tableware. A *blower* dips a preheated blowing iron into molten glass and, by rotating it, gathers just enough to produce the bowl. He then blows a bubble and shapes it by rolling it, still on the end of a blowing iron, on a *marver*. He then blows his paraison to the final shape, continually rotating the blowing iron. The blowing iron with bowl attached is passed to the *servitor*, who adds the stem and foot, made from small amounts of glass brought to him by the *bit gatherer*. The completed article is then broken off the blowing iron and taken by the *taker in*, who is responsible for the annealing process. The article can then be hand decorated.

Pressed Handmade Tableware. The *gatherer* gathers the glass on the end of an iron rod from a pot or forehearth of a tank furnace and runs it into a mold. When the *press operator* feels enough glass has entered the mold, he cuts it with a pair of shears, launching a plunger into the mold, applying pressure using a lever attached to the plunger. After the glass has set in the mold, the article is pushed out by a small plunger at the bottom and taken away for annealing. Multi-piece molds may be used. The marks left by the mold are often concealed within the pattern or removed by fire polishing.

Blown, Automatic Machine-Made Tableware. From the melting tank furnace protrudes the forehearth, where the glass is conditioned (maintained at the appropriate temperature and consistency). A ram with two cavities connected to a vacuum line at each end rotates to the forehearth, dipping into the molten glass, which is sucked into the cavities. It is lifted off and, on its way back to the machine, a knife cuts off the ribbon of glass trailing from it, leaving the required amount of glass in the cavities. The two lumps of molten glass are placed on top of waiting rotating spindles and a puff of air starts a bubble. As this is occurring, the spindles with the bubble at the top turn through a semi-circle from an up to a down position, enabling the glass to become elongated to a correct paraison shape. The paraisons are then enclosed in the blow molds and the spindles continue to rotate while the final blowing is done. The molds then open and the article is released. The tops of the articles are then burnt off and the article annealed. This process is used for making hollowware. Stemware bowls are made by the same process as other hollowware with one difference; the stem with the foot is pressed out on another machine. The bowl and stemmed foot are brought together and fused. Machines now make the entire unit (bowl, stem and foot) in one piece.

Pressed, Automatic Machine-Made Tableware. Made in the same manner as manual pressed, except the gathering operation is replaced by an automatic feeding device and the single mold is replaced by a number of molds on a large rotating table. The table rotates, stopping intermittently, as each mold stops beneath the feeding machine to receive its charge of glass. After this it moves on to the next stage where a hydraulic plunger presses it. After the glass has set, it is removed and taken away for annealing.

Tacoma A trademark used by the W.P. Hitchcock Co.

taffeta glassware The original name for carnival glass. See *carnival glassware.*

tail When molted glass is sheared after the proper amount falls into a mold, a thin sting of glass follows the blob into the mold. Because it cools quicker than the bulkier mass, it often does not melt fully into the mass, leaving an imprint like a coiled snake that is called a *tail*. Conversely, if a mold is not properly heated, the first bit of glass falling into the mold, again in the form of a string, cools quicker than the blob that follows, and a similar design may be left. Such tails are more apparent on the plain side, which depends on whether the mold design is on the base of the mold or on the plunger.

taker-in The first job in learning the glassmaker's trade; the apprentice of the team, chair or shop who assists the gaffer. The taker-in is responsible of taking the finished article to the lehr (annealing oven).

talcum shakers Containers for holding and dispensing (by shaking) talcum powder, introduced into the United States about 1936. Resembling extra large salt shakers, they are generally made in assorted colors of cut crystal. Czechoslovakia was their largest exporter.

tale The top layer of molten glass in a melting pot, just below the scum (gall), caused by impurities in the raw materials. It contains some impurities that have not reached the surface.

tale goods Glass objects made from the molten glass at the top of the pot (tale), and considered inferior to those made from the molten glass in the middle of the pot, considered the finest.

tall boy Any tall cup, glass, bottle or pottle (a serving vessel with a two-quart capacity).

Tallest Form A series of tall, slender drinking glasses with a bowl of various forms and textures and usually a domed foot, made by Joel P. Myers.

Tanagra style figures Replicas or adaptations of Tanagra figures, made of *pate-de-verre* by several French glassmakers, including Gabriel Argy-Rousseau, Georges Despret and Almeric-V. Walter. The originals were made of terracotta and molded in Greece and at colonies in Italy and Asia Minor. Those of the highest quality were found in 1874 in ancient tombs in the Tanagra district in Greece, dating from the late 4th century B.C. on. They represent men and women and gods and goddesses and are between seven and eight inches tall.

tango An orange-colored glass made by the Schneider Glass Works.

tank furnace A furnace used for making glass articles such as bottles and window glass, the ingredients of which are melted in a shallow tank. They are used exclusively for large-scale automated production, capable of producing over 450 tons of bottle glass or 1,000 tons of flat glass a day.

A tank furnace consists of a large rectangular bath, known as the *melting end*, connected by a narrow channel at the bottom to a smaller semi-circular bath, called the *refining* or *working end*. Usually there are a series of oil or gas burners on each side of the furnace, heating alternately. It is a regenerative type furnace. When the firing is from the left side, the flame sweeps across the top of the glass from left to right, and waste gases are exhausted through a large refractory chamber called the *regenerator* (packed with refractory brick, located on the right and left sides). As the waste gases channel their way through the brickwork, they give up a large portion of their heat, which is held until the process is reversed and the firing done from the opposite side. The combustion air is drawn into the furnace over the preheated brickwork. Heat is extracted by the air and returned to the furnace, creating high temperatures and substantial fuel savings. The entire tank is covered by a refractory brick arch, called the *crown*.

Forehearths protrude from the working end of the furnace. Molten glass flows into them, prepared for entry into the feeding mechanisms. Raw materials are fed automatically at the back of the furnace and melted as they move toward the front. Only well melted glass from the bottom of the tank can pass through the narrow channel, called a *throat*, into the working end of the furnace, where it is conditioned and made into the final product. See *pot furnace, day tank.*

tank glass Glass made by melting the ingredients of the batch in a tank. It is of only one color. Raw materials are continually fed into the furnace at the melting end, and the melting is continuous. The operations at the front or working end of the furnace may be continuous or batch. Generally they are continuous, such as in making bottles or window glass. Molten glass is drawn from the forehearth on a continuous basis.

tankard A drinking vessel with a handle on one side, an unembellished circular rim and usually a hinged metal lid. The usual capacity of a vintage tankard was about one quart; anything smaller is called a *mug*.

tankard, covered A tankard with a separate glass cover instead of a hinged metal lid. Many were made in England during the early 18th century.

tankard, glass bottomed A tankard, usually of pewter, with a bottom made of glass.

Tansboro Glass House A hollowware and bottle glass manufacturing facility established in 1848 in Tansboro, New Jersey, which closed after a short time. About 1850 it was reopened by Samuel and Urich Norcross, who operated it until 1856 when John Landis Mason took over operations to make his famous fruit jars. Having many problems, he hired Joel Bodine and Charles Adams to manage production. Bodine & Adams operated it until at least 1872, making bottles and flasks. After that, the Bodine family continued to operate it until it closed in July 1885. Frank Bodine was its last operator.

Tantalus decanter A set of three or four decanters enclosed within a locked rack. They were square in cross section and embellished with cutting (usually the alternate panel pattern). The name stemmed from the mythical Phrygian King, Tantalus. Condemned for his crimes, Tantalus had to remain in Tartarus (the underworld), standing chin deep in water and unable to drink or eat, with fruit-laden branches hanging just above his head. See *decanter set.*

tape twist A twist made of a strip of opaque glass rather than threads. Occasionally tapes of different widths are combined in a spiral twist and sometimes part of a double series twist.

tapered decanter A decanter, the sides of which are almost vertical from the base to the shoulder, tapering into a neck.

taperstick A holder used to grasp a taper or a thin candle, usually with a molded pedestal shaft with knops, tears or mereses; a flat, terraced or domed foot; a candle socket or nozzle, shallow and of small diameter; and, on occasion, a snuffer. A taper was used mainly for lighting candles or pipes, but some were used as a small tea candlestick on a tea table. They were made from the late 17th century, were popular during the second half of the 18th and early 19th centuries, and were usually in the style of contemporary candlesticks.

tapestry ware Glassware threaded and painted with enamels made by Stevens & Williams about 1892.

tapeworm glass See *Bandwurmglas.*

Tarentum Glass Company (1884-1918) A glass manufacturing facility established by the Richards & Hartley Flint Glass Company (moving from Pittsburgh, Pennsylvania) in Tarentum, Pennsylvania. It became part of the United States Glass Company in 1891 (*Factory E*). It operated until April 1918 when it was destroyed by fire and never rebuilt. It made cut, engraved and pressed glassware. See *Richards & Hartley Flint Glass Company.*

target balls Prior to 1880, when the clay pigeon was invented, blown-glass balls were used extensively for target and shooting competitions. They were hand blown in a three-piece mold and were about 2-3/4 inches in diameter, having a ragged hole where the blowpipe was twisted free. They were introduced about 1840 in England and used until World War I, most popular from 1870 to 1880. The most common ones are unmarked with the exception of the blower's code, consisting of dots, numbers, etc., identifying the maker. Some are embellished with a dot or diamond pattern, being more likely to shatter when stuck by a pellet. Some have names and/or patent dates on them.

target stopper A bull's-eye stopper.

Tarsitano, Delmo & Debbie A father and daughter team that began making paperweights in 1976, creating their own designs and what they refer to as *earth-life weights* showing various animals and insects in their natural environment, enclosing rocks, flowers and plants on a realistic earth ground. Debbie lives in Massachusetts and has a studio in her home. Delmo's studio is in Long Island, New York. While each makes the designs and setup in their studios, the weights are all encased within the dome at the Long Island studio. Debbie has made a number of weights in affiliation with glass engraver Max Erlacher—Debbie's flowers and plants set

against Erlacher's engraved background scenes. All weights are made in small editions. Until 1980 they were signed with the initial "T" cane, then changed to a "DT" cane for Debbie and an "AT" cane for (A) Delmo.

tartan twist A twist in the form of several interlaced spirals, each of a different color, frequently enclosing a white spiral core.

tassaker A variation of *tasse*. A cup or goblet. See *cup.*

Tassie medallion A medallion made by James William Tassie, his nephew, William, or their successor, John Wilson. Tassie first made reproductions of ancient engraved gems and later, from about 1766, medallions in white and colored glass paste of a finely powdered potash lead glass. This was softened by heating and pressed into a plaster of Paris mold (made from their own original wax relief portraits in profile), using an opaque white glass paste. Some were made in relief mounted on glass or other materials. They are from 3/4 inch to 4-1/3 inches in height and 3/4 inch to 3-1/2 inches in width. The reliefs are somewhat larger. The subjects are royalty and famous persons, usually contemporaries. Some bear an impressed signature or a "T". See *pate-de-verre; sulfide.*

taster or tastour A small cup or dram glass or a very small wine or brandy glass.

tavern glassware Glassware for use in taverns and kitchens. Heavy and thick, it was made to take hard use and wear.

Taylor, C.H., Glass Co. See *Jewel Cut Glass Company.*

Taylor, John, & Co. See *Brownsville Glass Works.*

Taylor & Stites See *Cape May Glass Company.*

Taylor, Stanger, Ramsey & Co. See *Kentucky Glass Works.*

Taylor Brothers (1902-1912) Albert and Lafayette Taylor and John H. Williams formed a glass cutting company, Taylor Brothers & Williams, in Philadelphia, Pennsylvania. In 1904 it became Taylor Brothers.

tazza (Italian) (1) An ornamental "cup" or serving plate, usually with a wide, flat, shallow bowl on a stemmed foot, often with handles. See *tiered tazza; standing bowl*. (2) A compote. (3) An Italian term for a cup.

tea bottle See *tea caddy*.

tea bowl A small cup with no handle, made and used in the Far East for drinking tea. Specimens in enameled opaque white glass were made in China, sometimes with a saucer *en suite*. Many were made in Europe, mainly in Bohemia and southern Germany. These were usually made of enameled opaque white glass speckled with blue or manganese and occasionally green specks.

tea caddy (Aka *tea jar; tea canister; tea bottle; teapot*) A covered or stoppered container used to hold dry tea at the table, often with a tea pot or kettle. It is often rectangular with sloping curved shoulders and a short cylindrical neck; some have a metal hinged lid. Glass ones were of clear and opaque white glass, often in pairs inscribed *Bohea*, *Green* or *Hyson*. The term *caddy* is derived from the Malasian word *kati* (a weight of 1.2 pounds). See *tea canister; tea vase*.

tea candlestick A candlestick (shorter than the usual 10 inch height), usually from 4-3/4 to 7 inches tall with a thin nozzle. Their real purpose is uncertain; either placed on a tea table where the candle would burn for a short time, serve as a taperstick for holding a lighted taper to light candles or pipes, or melt sealing wax. Their style paralleled that of candlesticks.

tea canister (1) A container to hold tea. Tea was contained within a tea caddy which was, in turn, placed within a tea canister; the tea caddy being a liner. (2) A *tea caddy*.

teacup A cup, usually of hemispherical form, used for drinking tea. It has one handle and is accompanied by a matching saucer (teacups made prior to the early 1800s did not have handles). Its capacity is about four fluid ounces. See *cup plate; tea bowl; tea plate*.

tea jar See *tea caddy*.

tea plate A plate, about six to seven inches in diameter, somewhat larger than a *cup plate* but with the same function. Teacups, prior to the early 1800s, did not have handles and it was customary to pour hot tea in a saucer (wider and deeper than today's), where it would cool more quickly, drinking it directly from the saucer. The cup was placed on a tea plate to prevent the cup from soiling the tablecloth. See *cup plate*.

teapot A covered vessel made in a variety of shapes, styles and sizes, many whimsical, used to brew and serve tea. It usually has one spout and, opposite it, one handle. The spout is usually attached near the bottom to drain the tea without disturbing the floating tea leaves. It has a strainer where the spout joins the body to prevent tea leaves from being poured into the cup.

tea service A service, normally for more than one person, for serving tea. It usually consists of a teapot, tea caddy, milk jug, cream jug, sugar bowl, cups, and saucers.

tea tray A tray large enough to hold a teapot, creamer, and sugar, or larger so as to hold teacups and saucers, spoons, and other items for serving tea.

tea vase A covered tea caddy or tea jar, ovoid in shape, with a small mouth for pouring out dry tea leaves rather than spooning them.

teaming To reduce transportation costs, rural glass manufacturing facilities would often build spurs or sidings to connect their operations to a railroad, enabling them to get raw materials and ship products more quickly and at less cost. This connection was called "teaming."

teal A medium to dark greenish-blue color.

tear An air bubble in the shape of a teardrop often encased, singly or in multiples, in the stem of some drinking glasses or other glassware or in a finial or a solid knop. It was originally made accidentally, but later was made deliberately. The process used to make them is called *pegging*, which involves pricking a small depression in the stem, knop, finial, etc., with a metal tool and covering it with molten glass to entrap air, forming a bubble. When the object is drawn out, the bubble becomes tear-shaped. Sometimes the object was twisted slightly while being drawn so the bubble became twisted. See *air twist; Rupert's drop.*

tear bottle (Aka *lachrymatory*) An unguentarium for holding perfumes and unguents (ointment or salve); many consider them *scent bottles*. It was once believed their purpose was to collect tears of mourners or of pining ladies whose knights were off fighting. They have been depicted on ancient wall paintings and found in Roman tombs. They are made in many shapes, but most have a small body and tall narrow neck. Sometimes the neck is three to four times the diameter of the body. Others have no bowl or body, but merely a tall cylindrical neck about six to 12 inches high resting on a small flat circular base. Most are purple in color. See *candlestick unguentarium.*

tear stem (Aka a *teardrop stem*) A stem that has embedded within it an air bubble in the form of a tear, sometimes elongated or twisted. See *tear.*

tease hole (Aka *stoke hole*) A hole in the lower portion of a glass furnace through which fuel was introduced.

teaser (Aka *stoker*) A worker who regulates the fires in a glass furnace and is responsible for loading raw materials into a furnace.

Teeter, Henry See *Cincinnati Glass Manufacturing Co.*

tektites Any of several kinds of small, glassy bodies in various shapes, such as rods, teardrops, spheres, dumbbells, etc. While most are black, some are green, a few are yellow. They usually weigh from less than an ounce to a pound. Their exact origins are unknown. It is believed some are formed when a meteorite or lightning hits the earth in sandy areas, such as beaches. In Australia, tektites are known as *australites*, and in Texas, they were once called *black diamonds*.

Tel El Amarna Vases A product of Tiffany; vases in lavish shapes in a variety of colors with a plain mat finish and linear zigzag frieze of glass (in another color), often near the rim, on an iridescent ground. They were inspired by objects found at the tomb of Amenhotep IV in Egypt.

Temperanceville Glassworks (1) A window and hollowware manufacturing facility established in Lewisville (*Temperanceville*), New Jersey, in 1834, just south of the Harmony Glass Works. The owners were some of the original founders of the Harmony Glass Works and Franklin Glass Works. Two were Jacob and Lewis Stanger (after he left the Harmony Glass Works); the third was Daniel Miller. Later more of the Stanger family entered the business, which eventually became Lewis Stanger & Son. It got its name because they employed only "temperance" (non-alcohol drinking) men. In 1841 it failed and Whitney Brothers, owners of the Olive & Harmony Glassworks, took over operations. They were followed shortly by Eben Whitney and Woodward Warrick, who stopped making window glass and concentrated on bottles, marketing their wares through Whitney Brothers. In 1849, Warrick sold his interest to Eben Whitney. In 1859 Thomas W. Stanger (nephew of Lewis) and Woodward Warrick purchased it, enlarging it in 1864 to make cylinder glass. In 1883, Stanger died and Warrick turned operations over to his three sons (J. Price, T.D., and H.S.) and it was called Warrick Glass Works. It closed sometime after that. In its later years it made hollowware and cylinder flasks. (Note: This Thomas Stanger is not the Thomas Stanger who operated the Isabella Works in New Brooklyn.) (2) A window glass manufacturing facility established in 1824 in Temperanceville (Pittsburgh), Pennsylvania. From 1840 to 1851, it was operated by Wm. McCully & Co. and, in 1871, by Thomas Wightman.

temperature The measurement of heat. The two familiar scales are Celsius (centigrade—freezing point of water 0ºC; boiling point 100ºC) and Fahrenheit (freezing point of water 32ºF; boiling point 212ºF). The conversion formulae between the two scales are:

$$Celsius = (F - 32) \times 5/9$$
$$Fahrenheit = (C \times 9/5) + 32$$

tempered glass (Aka *strengthened glass*) A sturdy, durable glass used for doors and windows in automobiles and for piping. It has high internal stresses and, if the surface is broken, it shatters into many pieces without sharp edges. In the first stage of making it, a controlled heat annealing process is used, resulting in the uniform stresses found in ordinary glass, being replaced by a controlled, very low stress level. It is very high in compression and very weak in tension. In the second stage, physical tempering is done by taking the already tempered glass, reheating it to just below the softening point, and quenching it in air, molten salt or oil so the exterior cools more quickly than the interior. As a result, the interior pulls on the outside surface, putting it into compression whereas the interior develops compensating tension, providing a three-fold increase in strength. *Chemcor* is a chemically strengthened glass, having up to three to five times the strength of evenly tempered products. The stress is made by an ion exchange process (chemical tempering). In this process, a sodium glass is immersed in a molten lithium salt bath where the sodium ions in the surface layers are replaced by lithium ions, resulting in a glass with a lithium glass surface and sodium glass interior. Since lithium glass has a lower coefficient of expansion, it shrinks less on cooling than the interior sodium glass. *Chemcor* can be bent or twisted and does not fracture as easily as ordinary glass. A commercial tableware called *Centura* is made using this chemical tempering process. It is lighter but three times stronger than ordinary tableware. See *tempering*.

tempering   A process wherein a formed glass article is made more sturdy and durable by physical or chemical processes. See *tempered glass*.

Temple Glasshouse   (1780-1782) A crown window glass manufacturing facility established in Temple, New Hampshire, by Robert Hewes of Boston in 1780. The company probably made bottles.

ten diamond mold glass   A glassware made in Zanesville, Ohio (see *Zanesville glassware*) and other locations in the United States, using a mold with a pattern having ten roughly formed diamonds in a lateral chain around the object, and a row of ten vertical ribs near the bottom.

tender   A worker responsible for overseeing the tempering of glass objects in the ovens or lehrs.

tension   The effect of stretching in an effort to increase area or volume.

teroma   Glass decorated with a pebbly paint.

terraced foot   A foot with a series of steps, one extending beyond the other. Variations are *domed & terraced* with a domed section above the terracing; and *terrace-domed* with the terracing in the domed section.

terrarium   See *Wardian case*.

tesserae   Small pieces of colored glass, usually square, used to make mosaics. The term is derived from the Greek word *tesseres*, meaning *four sided*. The earliest source of tesserae is uncertain; however, fragments found at Torcelli, near Venice, indicate some were made in the 7th century. Many were made from the 9th to the 14th centuries at Murano for decorating churches in Venice. The process for making mosaics using tesserae involved cutting cakes of glass into pieces and embedding them in cement rather than fusing them together.

tessuto, vetro *(Italian)*   An ornamental glass developed by Venini, with numerous narrow vertical stripes of white opaque glass similar to *filigrana* glass, except the threads are flattened, making stripes or narrow bands, often twisted and manipulated, creating a watery or wavelike look.

test tube unguentarium   A type of unguentarium in a thin, tall, cylindrical form with a rounded bottom, made of Roman glass during the 4th century A.D..

Teutonic glassware   See *Frankish glassware*.

textured lusterware   A multicolored ware made by Tiffany with inlaid embellishments; the most famous is the *Peacock Feather*. See *Tiffany Iridescent Glass*.

Thames (River) Glass Company   See *New London Glass Company*.

Thatcher Brothers   In 1886 George Thatcher bought the cutting department of Smith Brothers, starting his own glass cutting shop in New Bedford, Massachusetts. He had previously worked at Boston & Sandwich, Mt. Washington, Vasa Murrhina Art Glass and Smith Brothers. In 1891 his brother, Richard, who was working at Corning, joined him, forming Thatcher Brothers. In 1894 it built a new facility in Fairhaven, Massachusetts. Crystal canes, called *friendship canes*, were made as novelty items. In 1907 it closed, burning in 1918. Its trademark, *Diamond Finish*, was issued in 1895; labels printed in red ink were affixed to the glassware.

Thatcher Glass See *Gunderson (-Pairpoint) Glass Works.*

thermal shock The effect on a substance resulting from a rapid temperature change which, in ordinary glass, causes stress within it because the surface expands and contracts more rapidly than the interior, causing it to crack and/or break.

thermometer An instrument for measuring temperature. It is customarily a closed tube with a bulb at one end containing a liquid, such as mercury or alcohol, that expands or contracts with changes of temperature. These temperature changes are indicated by the rising or falling of the liquid in the tube, marked in appropriate graduations depending on its planned use, such as for body, baking, refrigeration, etc. Early ones were made of Florentine glass during the late 16th-early to 17th centuries.

Thier(r)y, Augustine, & Company See *Constitution Flint Glass Works.*

Thill, Francis See *Empire State Flint Glass Works.*

thimble A small cup-shaped sewing tool used on the finger to enable the user to more easily push a needle through fabric.

thistle bowl (1) A bowl of a drinking glass shaped like a thistle, with the mouth formed as a thistle head. There are two variations: one with a solid bottom portion; the other hollow. (2) A large bowl, similarly shaped, with an everted rim, the lower portion bulging appreciably. They are usually embellished with cutting, normally with diamonds in diagonal rows, or cut miters. Between the upper and lower parts there is usually a band with cut fluting or swirls. See *thistle glassware.*

thistle cup A cup with a body in the shape of a thistle, with a bulging lower portion, slightly waisted above, an everted rim and applied handle.

thistle glassware A drinking or celery glass made in the form of a thistle. They are made in many sizes, each with a stemmed foot and waisted bowl. The lower portion is hemispherical, usually embellished with diamond cutting or molded pattern. Above the bowl is a funnel-shaped mouth representing the flower head.

Thompson, Andrew Born in Ireland in 1818, he came to the United States, buying the A.J. Miller & Company machine shop (est.1847) in Pittsburgh, Pennsylvania in 1849. He made molds, glass pressing equipment and other machinery and appliances for the industry. By 1880 it was one of the largest of its kind in the United States.

Thompson, George Born in 1913, an American glass designer who joined Steuben's newly established design department as a senior staff designer in 1936. His signature appears on many important pieces of ornamental colorless glassware as well as vases, bowls, candlesticks, and tableware made throughout the Houghton era at Steuben.

Thompson Glass Company (1889-1891/2) A glass manufacturing facility established in Uniontown, Pennsylvania, making pressed glass tableware and novelties.

Thompson Glassworks A short-lived window and green glass manufacturing facility established by Thomas Thompson about 1830 in Pittsburgh, Pennsylvania.

thorned boss A pointed prunt. See *prunt.*

thousand eye glass See *milleocchi, vetro.*

thousand eye sconce A tin or iron sconce with a reflector made of a mosaic of mirror glass.

thousand flowers See *millefiori.*

thread A thin strand or trail of glass, circular in cross section, used as an embellishment on glassware, such as in making some twist stems, filigrana decoration, etc. A small amount of molten glass is gathered on an iron and allowed to drop on to a glass object being rotated, allowing the trail to spiral around the object, forming the desired pattern. See *trailing; threading*.

thread circuit   A very thin band of applied glass encircling the rim or neck of a glass vessel.

thread grained glass   See *filigrana*.

thread testing   A fast, simple method of testing the compatibility of two different glasses. Two small pieces of glass are heated, pressed together and reheated until soft. Then the combined mass is pulled apart, forming a thread. If the thread remains relatively straight on cooling, the glasses are likely compatible. If it bends, they are not.

thread twist   A twist made of a thread of opaque glass, sometimes forming a vertical column or spiral. It is often found in conjunction with another type of twist, forming a double series twist.

thread wound bottle   A bottle embellished with a spiraling opaque glass thread over the entire body, from the base to the neck. Care is taken to ensure even spacing between the spirals. The pattern is not made by one continuous thread, but by a number of threads joined to each other, which is quite apparent from the several points of thickening where one thread ends and the next begins. They were made of Roman glass during the 1st century A.D.

Threaded glassware pitcher, pink and yellow swirl.
Krause Publications

threaded glassware   Glassware embellished with applied glass threads, attributed to early glassworkers of the Nile Valley. The glassworkers embellished the glass objects by winding them with threads of glass of several colors, *combed* into feather-like patterns using a tool similar to a buttonhook. The designs made were subjected to heat to become an integral part of the body, then smoothed by rolling the object on a marver. After the advent of blown glass during the 1st century A.D., threads of glass were wound around objects so the user could gain a better grip. Until the mid-19th century, glass threads were applied by hand (see *thread*).

On May 6, 1876, William Hodgetts of Hodgetts, Richardson & Sons of England, patented a mechanical device capable of applying glass threads to articles. On June 9, 1876, *Allassantes* or *Sidonean glass* was patented by Thomas Wilkes Webb. It had colored threads of glass attached to the article and the expansion created by heat caused them to form into intriguing designs. On November 26, 1878, another patent was issued to William Hodgetts. On September 10, 1880, William Henry Stuart, Stafford, England, was issued one for a threading process. In this, a paraison was rolled in pulverized glass or enamel prior to threading. After the threading was completed, the article was reheated, causing the pulverized glass or enamel to melt and run while the threading remained intact.

On February 20, 1885, a machine was patented for making threaded glassware, eliminating even more of the handwork and making the threading more uniform. Marvering and *warming in* (the heating of the threaded glass article to make the threads sink into the body, giving it a smooth surface except for the threaded portions, which were slightly raised) became an important part of the process. Stevens & Williams embellished some of their threaded ware by painting the body with enamels. Nicholas Lutz made a lot of threaded glass while employed at Boston & Sandwich before going to Mt. Washington Glass Co., which also made some threaded ware (grinding and polishing the pontil mark—Boston & Sandwich left it rough).

Many facilities made threaded glass to keep up with the demands of the mid-1800s. Later threaded glassware was usually thinner as were the threads, then restricted to narrow areas of the body. See *fili, vetro a; filigrana.*

threading (1) The process of attaching glass threads as a form of independent embellishment as opposed to trailing, where the threads are applied to the surface of the object. Sometimes the terms threading and trailing are used interchangeably, especially when threads are used as incidental surface decoration rather than being an essential part of it. See *stem work.* (2) The process of drawing glass threads through molten glass as a method of embellishing an article.

Three Face A glass pattern where the stem or occasionally the knob on the lid or cover has three faces of frosted glass in relief, 120° apart. It was originally the exclusive product of George Duncan & Sons. In its catalog, it is called *Pattern No. 400.* Workmen at the Duncan facility called it *Three Sisters*, and others called it *Three Graces*. Several different items were made in this pattern during the 1870s, including sugars, creamers, spooners, butter dishes, salvers, compotes, lamps, celeries, biscuit jars, pitchers, etc. Beware of reproductions.

Three Graces See *Three Face.*

three mold glass See *blown three mold glass; three section mold blown glass.*

three part (or piece) glass See *shank stem glass.*

three ring decanter A decanter with three glass rings encircling its neck, made in many sizes and styles. They were first made about 1780 and still are today. Early ones were of relatively light metal, but the later ones were of heavier metal. See *Irish glassware, Decanters.*

three section mold blown glass (Aka *three mold glass, blown three mold glass*, and *contact-three-section-mold-glass*). Glass blown to full size in a three-part (hinged) mold. The design was cut on the inside of the mold and, when blown in the mold, it was impressed on the glass. It was

made to compete with cut glass and a lot was made at Sandwich (see *blown three mold glass*). The principal designs were: *Baroque* or *shell; arched* or *Gothic;* and *geometric* (vertical ribbing, bands-diamond diapering, diamond-in-the-square, oblique ribbing, herringbone motifs, horizontal ribbing, sunburst, spiral ribbing). It has three perceptible mold marks where the sections of the mold join, sometimes eliminated by intense heat (*flashing*). The principal colors were: clear; shades of blue; emerald green (rare); amethyst (rare); light yellowish green; and shades of olive amber. It was made from about 1810 to 1850, peaking in popularity in the late 1820s. Little was made after 1840.

To make an object, the blower held the gather of glass on the blowpipe within the mold and blew until it took on the design of the mold. The mold was opened and the object, still on the blowpipe, was removed. An assistant, called a *sticker up*, attached a pontil iron to the base, and the blowpipe was broken from the mouth, then finished using a variety of tools. If a heavier object was being made, a one-part mold was used. The gather was dropped and pushed into the mold, and the blower blew, ensuring the gather came into contact with the entire design only on the lower part. After this, the object was removed from the mold and the excess glass near the blowpipe expanded quickly by a quick burst of air by the blower. When this *overblow* burst, the object fell into a pit of sand. After cooling, the mouth of the object was finished.

Three section mold blown glass is differentiated from mechanically pressed glass in a three section mold. First, the mold marks are different. On pressed glass they are clearly defined, caused by the high pressure and sudden striking of the metal plunger. This forces the molten glass into all the crevices of the mold, widening it slightly at the hinges, allowing some molten glass to seep in, and because of exposure to the cooler air, harden quickly. The blowing process does not create much pressure, and the mold separates only slightly, allowing less seepage. Generally, immediately after the removal of the blown article from the mold, it was reheated quickly to eliminate mold marks. Second, the mold marks on pressed glass are in different positions than on three section mold blown glass. On pressed glass articles having a stem or foot, the mold mark runs from the rim to the foot because the article is usually pressed in one piece. With blown articles, the stem and/or foot may be drawn out from the body or molded separately and applied to the body. Thus the foot or stem will have no mold marks or the marks will not be in the same line as those with the body. Third, the surfaces of the objects differ. Blown-glass articles have a convexity on the inside corresponding to a concavity on the outside, and vice versa. The only exception is on unusually thick glass where only slight undulations may be felt. Pressed glass always has a smooth inside surface. Fourth, in blown glass articles there is never a decisive break between the motifs of the design, while in pressed articles the pattern is sharp and the motifs are decidedly separate. Fifth, pressed glass patterns have an unmistakable resemblance to cut-glass patterns, while those of blown glass do not. Sixth, the glass used in the pressing operation is usually not of the quality used in the blowing process (there are many exceptions). See *blown three mold glass.*

three sisters See *three face.*

three-two-one batch A batch consisting of three parts sand, two parts soda and one part lead.

throat See *tank furnace.*

Thum & Bitters A short-lived bottle glass manufacturing facility established in Philadelphia, Pennsylvania, in 1808.

thumb glass A drinking glass with circular indentations on its sides, permitting it to be held firmly between the thumb and fingers to prevent slipping. Some tall ones, up to 14 inches, were provided with three indentations on each side for both left- and right-handed persons.

thumb print (1) An embellishment on some pressed glass made in the United States, in the form of an overall diamond pattern of oval-shaped shallow depressions arranged in rows encircling the object. It is used on plates, flips, pitchers, mugs, bowls, compotes, etc. Variations include the *almond thumb print* (slightly pointed at the upper end) and *diamond thumb print* (enclosed in diamonds made by diagonal stripes). When used on a tumbler, the depressions served as diminishing lenses through which to see those on the opposite side the glass. (2) A geometric form of a cut glass motif, merely a concave circle or oval, originating in Europe where it was called *bull's-eye* or *punty.*

thumb ring A broad ring originally worn by an Oriental archer to protect his thumb when drawing the bow string; later strictly ornamental. They were made in China during the K'ang Hsi period (1662-1722).

thumbmarks See *printie.*

thummers (Aka *fingered glass*) Tumblers with deep depressions in the lower part, pushed in while the glass was still plastic, serving as a grip for holding.

Thuringian glassware Glassware made at several facilities in Thuringia, a former state in central Germany; the earliest was made at Lausnitz, Arnstadt and Gotha. A facility at Tambach, in Franconia, was owned by Duke Bernhard von Sachen-Weimar (1604-39), a patron of glass manufacturing. At Weimar, Andreas Friedrich Sang was the court engraver from 1738 to 1744. At Arnstadt, Alexander Seifferd (1660-1714)—son of Anton Seifferd, court engraver from about 1650 to 1660 to Carl XI Gustavus at Stolkholm—was glass engraver from 1685 to 1714. Heinrich Jager engraved from about 1715 to 1720, and Samuel Schwartz from 1731 to 1737. At Gotha, Casper Creutzburg engraved Passglas, later enameled with pictures of playing cards, which became a local industry (see *Spielkartenhumpen*). At Lauscha, a facility has been in existence from 1595 where enameling was done and articles were made *at-the-lamp*, as well as beads, toys, etc. Technical pharmaceutical glassware was made during the 19th century at Ilmenau.

Tibby Brothers Glassworks On June 19, 1866, the Tibby brothers (William, Matthew and John) established a glass manufacturing facility in Pittsburgh, Pennsylvania. They later constructed another in Sharpsburgh, Westmoreland County. It made flint glass, vials, bottles and druggists' wares. Both facilities were still operating in 1893.

Tice, Clayton B. See *Isabella Glassworks.*

Tice, C.B., Company A glass manufacturing facility operating in Medford, New Jersey, in 1864, making hollowware and tableware.

tid bit A two- or three-tiered serving dish of progressively smaller plates (advancing upward), connected by a central metal pole and measuring about 12 to 15 inches tall.

tieback A contrivance to hold a curtain back from the window, normally consisting of a U-shaped bracket, one side fastened to the frame of the window and the other facing the room with a decorative disk, boss, emblem, etc. The curtain held within the U-shaped bracket.

Tiefschnitt (German) Literally, *deep carving.* The German term for *intaglio.* Wheel-engraved embellishment on glass in which the design is cut below the surface of the glass, the reverse of relief and opposite of *Hochschnitt.* The technique was developed by Casper Lehmann at Dresden and Prague about 1605 and shortly after at Nuremburg by Georg Schwanhardt and his followers. Sometimes the engraved areas were polished; sometimes only partially polished to provide a more dynamic effect. See *Mattschnitt.*

tiered goblet A double goblet where the cover of the lower, larger goblet becomes the base for the upper, smaller one. Some were made in Bohemia during the late 17th century.

tiered tazza A double tazza; a smaller tazza setting on top of a larger one.

Tierhumpen (German) Literally, *animal beaker.* A tall humpen enameled with scenes depicting various animals doing human activities. They were made in Germany and Bohemia during the late 16th and 17th centuries. See *German enameling.*

tiff glass or mug Any drinking vessel of fair size used for serving *tiff* (an alcoholic beverage or drink, like syllabub). See *syllabub glass.*

Tiffany, Louis Comfort (1848-1933) The leading exponent of the Art Nouveau style of glassware in the United States. Tiffany was inspired by the work of Emile Galle and made a great variety and quantity of art glass using techniques and styles of embellishment he developed, such as colored cased and iridescent glass. His success was mainly due to his own artistic capabilities, combined with the technical skill of his associate, Arthur J. Nash.

Tiffany was not a glassmaker; however, he designed glassware, closely supervising its making at his facility. The son of Charles L. Tiffany, the prominent New York jeweler, Louis graduated from the Flushing Academy on Long Island, New York, studied painting in New York in 1866 and in Paris in 1869. In Paris he became acquainted with the Art Nouveau movement and later with Siegfried (Samuel) Bing (1838-1905), whose shop— *Le Salon d'Art Nouveau*—became the European retail outlet for his works and those of other Art Nouveau artists. He traveled to Spain, Italy and North Africa, including Egypt.

After his return to New York in 1870, Tiffany showed his works done in Europe, and he became an associate member of the National Academy of Design (becoming a full member in 1880), and a founding member of the Society of American Artists. He won numerous awards for his paintings in the United States and Europe. In 1879, he founded Louis C. Tiffany & Associated Artists, an interior decorating firm.

When he began buying colored panes from glasshouses for his stained glass windows, he was disenchanted by the quality and colors available. He entered the glass field, hiring chemists to develop colors and surface effects, using Louis Heidt's glassworks in Brooklyn, New York, where he developed *Favrile Glass.* At first he designed and decorated windows for churches and aristocratic homes, and lighting fixtures and lamps.

Associated Artists separated from Tiffany & Co. in 1882.

In 1884 Tiffany's wife died and he had no his interest in working, so his father commissioned him to redecorate his town house in New York City, inspiring him to go back in business. In 1885 he established Tiffany Glass Company in Brooklyn and remarried. This facility made mainly decorative glass windows and interior decorations. He again visited Europe in 1889, and saw the works of Galle, Loetz and others. In 1892, he established the Tiffany Glass & Decorating Company and a glass manufacturing facility at Corona, Long Island, New York, which continued to make glassware until 1928. In addition to these locations, Tiffany Art Glass was blown at both Jersey City and Hoboken in New Jersey. The Jersey City site was in operation by 1894 and the Hoboken facility, known as Tiffany Furnaces, was in operation by 1904.

Tiffany's success was established at the Chicago World's Fair in 1893 and at the Paris Exposition in 1900. After several company name changes, he withdrew from active involvement, retiring in 1919. In addition to glassware, he made other products in Art Nouveau style which he distributed, from 1900, through his Tiffany Studios in New York City. In 1902, he took over his father's jewelry business, using it as an outlet for his glass jewels and glassware.

In 1898, he, with Nash and others, established the Stourbridge Glass Company at Corona. Its name changed in 1902 to Tiffany Furnaces Inc., operated by Arthur J. Nash, working under the direct supervision of Tiffany, making blown and decorative glassware. Tiffany Studios decorated many theaters, resort hotels and railroad stations. In 1920, Tiffany divided the company into Tiffany Studios and the Louis C. Tiffany Furnaces Inc. He kept one share of stock in Tiffany Furnaces and gave 110 shares to a foundation (set up a few years before to aid young artists), five shares to his son, Charles, 55 shares to the Nash family, one share to George Heidt (a relative of Louis Heidt and a member of the Board of Trustees of the foundation and a director of Tiffany & Co.) and

eight shares to Joseph Briggs, the manager of Tiffany Studios until its liquidation upon his death in 1938.

Tiffany Furnaces continued to be run by A. Douglas Nash. However, Tiffany became increasingly irritated by the commercial use of his name, so in 1928 he withdrew financial support and use of his name from Tiffany Furnaces, giving all stock on hand to Briggs, who made lamps with it until his death. At this time, A. Douglas Nash formed his own company, A. Douglas Nash Corporation, which operated until failing in 1931.

Lamps were one of Tiffany's greatest achievements. They usually had bronze bases in various naturalistic forms, such as tree trunks, and shades of stained glass in floral and insect patterns. Best known is his wisteria lamp based on a design by Curtis Freskel. He also made jars, humidors, glass tiles, carved cameo vases, etc. He was also famous for his paintings, stained glass windows, stone mosaic work, glazes on pottery, enamels on copper, handmade jewelry, architecture, etc. See *Tiffany* items that follow.

Tiffany Aquamarine A glassware made by Tiffany beginning in 1913—light green glass to simulate sea water, with embedded representations of aquatic plants and marine life. The articles (bowls, vases, door stops, paperweights, etc.) were generally heavy and thick, normally with a slight depression in the top, giving the appearance of being filled with water. Only a few specimens were made.

Tiffany Cameo Glass While Tiffany's exact method of making of cameo glass is unknown, the results achieved were unique. Through the use of acid he was able to remove the surface around the motif, usually flowers and leaves, so it stood out in high relief. Most were made with his *Favrile* glass as a base. They are superior to the acid cut backs made by Steuben and the acid-etched wares of the French cameo glass artists. They were handworked, the simplest taking about five to six weeks to complete.

Tiffany Carved Glass A term applied by Tiffany to any of his glassware (colorless, colored or lustered) embellished by cutting or engraving, including relief and intaglio.

Tiffany Cypriote See *Cypriote Glass.*

Tiffany Chapel A chapel interior designed by Tiffany. This Byzantine-inspired interior was constructed from classical forms, columns and arches and furnished with mosaics and leaded glass windows. He exhibited it at the 1893 Columbian Exhibition in Chicago, Illinois, winning numerous medals. It was dismantled after the exhibition. In 1898 it was purchased by Mrs. Celia Whipple Wallace, who gave it to The Episcopal Cathedral Church of St. John the Divine. It was installed in the cathedral's basement, modified to fit under the ceiling, used as a chapel for about 10 years, then closed and forgotten. Over the years it suffered water damage.

In 1916 Tiffany expressed his concern to the church, which allowed him to remove it at his own expense. After substantial repairs, he had it installed in a building at his Long Island estate, Laurelton Hall. In 1949, 16 years after Tiffany's death, the Tiffany Foundation sold portions of it to various institutions.

In 1957 a large portion of Laurelton Hall was destroyed by fire. Hugh and Jeannette McLean purchased the stained glass windows and architectural fragments that survived the fire. Hugh was a young artist-in-residence there in 1930, under a program established by Tiffany; Jeannette later established The Charles Hosmer Morse Museum of American Art, named in honor of her grandfather, on the Rollins College campus in Winter Park, Florida. In 1959, they purchased some previously sold parts. Over the next few years, they researched the locations of the various parts of the chapel sold in 1949. As these became available they purchased them, storing them in packing crates. Jeannette died in 1989 and Hugh in 1995. In 1997 the Board of Trustees of the Museum endorsed the restoration of the chapel, which was completed in 1999 and, in mid-April of that year, was again opened to the public.

Tiffany Damascened A *Favrile* glass developed by Tiffany about 1910, with stripes of gold and colored luster arranged in a wavy pattern. It simulated the watery

appearance of *damascened steel* (also called *watered steel*—a hand-wrought steel repeatedly folded over and welded, then etched to reveal the resulting grain, giving the appearance of waves). It was later made by A. Douglas Nash.

Tiffany Fabric Glass A *Tiffany Favrile* iridized glassware. See *Tiffany Favrile.*

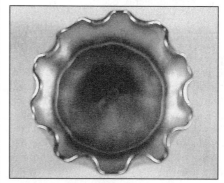

Tiffany Favrile salt, signed "L.C.T. Favrile," bluish golden iridescence, 2-1/2" d.
Davanna Collection

Tiffany Favrile After conducting numerous experiments with glass for use in his stained glass windows, Tiffany had accumulated a significant quantity of pot metal in splendid colors, but it could not be used for windows. Rather than consider it waste, he used it to make small glass objects and for experiments resulting in the development, about 1892, of his *Favrile* in the Art Nouveau style. This glass had an iridescent surface simulating that of ancient Roman glass, excavated after being buried for centuries in humid soil. The bluish green, golden and other surface colors were given a mother-of-pearl effect by spraying the surface, while hot, with various metallic salts that were absorbed into the glass. The luster depended on the color and density of the metal. The multicolored embellishment featuring naturalistic motifs was embedded or applied. The glass was used to make a variety of objects; mainly vases of various shapes and sizes, trays, cigarette boxes, toilet boxes, bonbonniers, lamp shades, etc., signed with Tiffany's name or initials. The name *Favrile*, registered in 1894, was also etched on the glass or printed on a label. It is derived from the German *Faber* meaning *color*, and/or *fabrile*, Old English meaning *belonging to a craftsman or his craft* (hand-made). *Fabrile* was first used as a trade name before *Favrile*, a name that could be registered. It was imitated by Loetz and other Bohemian glassmakers. Some of the trade-marks used for *Tiffany Favrile* glass were: *Tiffany Favrile Fabric Glass, Tiffany Favrile Horizon Glass, Tiffany Favrile Lace Glass and Tiffany Favrile Twig Glass.*

Tiffany Favrile Fabrique A pressed glass with the appearance of fabric, having numerous vertically or horizontally arranged folds, used exclusively for panels in lamp shades. However, a circular one-piece shade was invented by Leslie Nash in 1913. A design was made on them by coating a copper mesh screen with glass. The trademark was registered in June 1914.

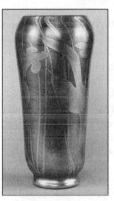

Tiffany vase, c. 1900-1928, transparent iridescent gold and blue lead glass.
The Corning Museum of Glass

Tiffany Flashed Glass See *Tiffany Reactive Glass.*

Tiffany Floriform Vases See *Floriform Vases.*

Tiffany Furnaces See *Tiffany, Louis Comfort.*

Tiffany Glass & Decorating Company See *Tiffany, Louis Comfort.*

Tiffany glassware (general) Glassware made in a variety of forms and styles by the successive companies of Tiffany. It was mainly in Art Nouveau style and made of colored cased and iridescent glass. The most famous was his *Favrile* glass. Tiffany did not use enamels. Embellishments were solely in the shape, texture and color of the glassware itself, the embedded or applied glass enhancements, and the luster finish. At times engraving and cutting were used for further enhancement. Beware of forged signatures. See *Tiffany* items; *agate glass; Cypriote glass; diatreta glass; lava glass; textured luster glass; laminated glass.*

Tiffany Goose Neck Vases See *Goose Neck Vases.*

Tiffany Horizon Glass A *Tiffany Favrile iridized glass.* See *Tiffany Favrile.*

Tiffany Jack-in-the-pulpit vase, c. 1912, dark blue glass.
The Corning Museum of Glass

Tiffany Iridescent Glass An iridescent glassware made by Tiffany. The form is usually quite simple. Many items are in classic shapes like gourds, balusters, urns, etc. Others are considered precursors of modern art, being irregular and asymmetrical in form. Many vases were fashioned in the form of flowers. Embellishment is done mostly with glass, either incorporated into or applied to the surface. Some pieces of embellished transparent glass, usually those with motifs of fish or flowers, had a luster applied to their inner surfaces, creating an *under-the-water* effect. The glassware giving this effect is often called *paperweight glass* (see *Tiffany Paperweight Glass*). The other main forms of embellishment were cutting and engraving executed in a manner resembling cameo or intaglio glass, most often in plain gold or blue, but also in a multicolored ware with inlaid embellishments (called *Textured Luster Ware*). Also see *Cypriote Glass.*

Tiffany Jewels Glass objects made to be worn as jewelry or as additional embellishment on other glass objects. They included glass *scarabs* in the form of a beetle, made in several sizes and colors, some iridescent.

Tiffany Lace Glass A *Tiffany Favrile* iridized glass. See *Tiffany Favrile.*

Tiffany Laminated Glass
See *laminated glass.*

Louis C. Tiffany lamp, c. 1900, bronze base and finial with lead glass shade. The Corning Museum of Glass

Tiffany lamp A table or hanging lamp made by Tiffany, the highlight being the shade. They were constructed from a large number of variably shaped pieces of multicolored glass, placed in an arrangement often imitating floral or other natural forms. The table lamps have a bronze base in the form of a tree trunk. The most famous Tiffany lamp is the *Wisteria Lamp*, based on a design, in 1904, by Curtis Freskel. The design simulates a wisteria vine with a bronze tree-like base and shade resembling realistically trailing wisteria with an irregular bottom line. Many types of lamps were made, including *Apple Blossom, Lotus Blossom, Dragon Fly, Spider Web*, etc. Related, but of different form, is the *Lily Lamp* with individual lily-shaped shades hanging from separate branches.

Tiffany marks Few, if any, of Tiffany's earliest pieces were signed. Some were simply inscribed with an "X" or an "O" followed by a number with a letter in front or after. Some paper labels were used. His signed pieces bear the following signature marks: *Louis C. Tiffany*; *L.C. Tiffany*; *L.C. Tiffany, Inc.-Favrile*; and *L.C.T.*

Tiffany mosaic plaque, c. 1900-1910, multicolored iridescent glass, metal.
The Corning Museum of Glass

Tiffany mosaic A mosaic composed of glass tesserae, embedded as embellishment in a wall or copper ornamental disk, or on lampshades and other objects. Some tesserae were made of iridescent glass.

Tiffany Paperweight Glass A type of art glass developed by Tiffany that was made in many forms, colors and styles of embellishment, usually with floral patterns. These patterns were made by embedding multicolored glass, creating the design, within an inner layer of glass. This was covered with another layer, which was usually given an iridescent surface. The term *Paperweight* has been applied in the United States to similar glass objects made by Steuben and others because of the similarity of the embellishment to Tiffany Paperweight glass or his paperweights, not because it is designed to be used as a paperweight. In addition to floral motifs, fish or aquatic motifs were used, creating an *under-the-water* effect.

Tiffany Pastel See *Tiffany Reactive Glass.*

Tiffany Peacock Colors Iridescent colors made by Tiffany on translucent glasses of dark blue, green or red; also a light golden iridescent color with a body of translucent pale amber color glass. See *Tiffany Peacock Feather glassware; Peacock Feather glassware.*

Tiffany Peacock Feather glassware An iridescent glassware developed by Arthur J. Nash for Tiffany. It has a variety of colored areas in the body of the piece, formed in a combed feather pattern, and often inlaid within it is a piece of dark glass resembling the *eye* of a peacock feather. The process involved making a paraison, then adding to it, at intervals, small amounts of molten glass of various colors or textures. This was reheated, enlarged and manipulated to achieve the desired form and pattern. Prime examples are the various vases and bowls in a variety of shapes. See *Peacock Feather glassware.*

Tiffany Reactive glass (Aka *Pastel Tiffany, Tiffany Pastel, Tiffany Flashed Glass*) An art glass made by Tiffany, so named because of the color change occurring when the glass is reheated. Some pieces are made with inlaid pieces of glass of many colors; some are internally lustered, creating an *under-the-water* effect. The decorative patterns varied greatly and included some called *Rainbow, Gladiola, Morning Glory* and *Opalescent Optic.* See *gold ruby glass.*

Tiffany Reticulated Glass An art glass by Tiffany, made of opaque jade green glass blown into a network of green bronzed wire mesh and protruding slightly through the wire.

Tiffany stained glass Tiffany did not like the stained glass windows in cathedrals in Europe because they seemed gloomy (too much lead; colors generally dark). As a result, he experimented extensively, and in 1878, established his own facility, which burned shortly after operations started. From 1880 to 1893, he continued his experiments at the Heidt facility in Brooklyn, then built a facility at Corona on Long Island, New York, with Arthur J. Nash in charge. Here Tiffany created new types of stained glass more suited to his tastes, which added a lightness and color to the windows he designed and constructed.

Tiffany Studios See *Tiffany, Louis Comfort.*

Tiffany Sunset glass An iridized *Tiffany Favrile* glassware.

Tiffany Tel El Amarna Vases See *Tel El Amarna Vases.*

Tiffany tiles Squares of glass, from one to four inches wide and a half-inch deep, made by Tiffany to be embedded in screens and to embellish mantelpieces and walls. They were made by pouring molten glass into open molds and pressing it to form different patterns. Some were iridescent. Some rare ones, called *Turtleback*, have a convex surface with a central depression, used to embellish shades of some of his lighting fixtures. They were made by Louis Comfort Tiffany & Associated Artists from 1879.

Tiffany Twig glass An iridized *Tiffany Favrile* glassware.

Tiffany Vetro di Trina An extremely rare glassware made about 1910 by Tiffany, so named because it simulated Venetian *vetro di reticello.* However it differed from it, having crisscrossed opaque white threads farther apart, leaving large interstices but no embedded air bubbles. This was the result of marvering after the threads were applied. It was sometimes given a lustered surface.

Tiffany leaded glass window, c. 1905. The Corning Museum of Glass

Tiffany window A decorated window made by Tiffany with colored glass designs depicting floral subjects, landscapes, biblical stories, copies of paintings or abstract motifs. In making these, the colored glass was first cut to conform to the intended design, and the leading was afterward shaped to fit the glass.

Tiffany & Kimble Glass Company A glass company noted for making glass ornaments, known as *bubble balls*, during the 1930s and 1940s.

Tiffin Cut Glass Company A glass cutting company in Tiffin, Ohio, making cut glassware from about 1910 to 1915.

Tiffin Copen blue vase with open rose embellishment, c. 1940s, 12-3/4" h.
Tri-State Antiques

Tiffin ad from **Good Housekeeping,** *December 1927.*
Krause Publications

Tiffin (Art) Glass Company A glass manufacturing facility established in 1887 in Tiffin, Ohio, by A.J. Beatty & Sons, making tableware and decorative items, such as lamps and globes, in its early years. On January 1, 1892, it became a subsidiary of United States Glass Co. (*Factory R*). From 1923 to 1926, its most popular ware was black satin glass. In 1962, United States Glass Co. filed for bankruptcy and the Tiffin plant was purchased by the employees who continued to operate it until 1966 as the Tiffin Art Glass Company. Then it was sold to Continental Can Company and, in 1969, to Interpace and subsequently to Towle Sterling, Inc. In 1980, it closed.

tiles Small glass panels used for paneling walls and occasionally floors, made at least since the first century A.D. in the Roman Empire. See *Tiffany tiles.*

Tilghman, Benjamin A chemist from Philadelphia, Pennsylvania, who invented a machine for decorating glass by sandblasting. The patent was received in 1870 for a machine capable of directing a fine stream of sand, at high velocity with compressed air, onto glass. It first used to decorate large glass panels.

Tillyer Brothers See *Winslow Glass Works.*

Tilson, Thomas In 1663, he was granted a patent for the "invention" of lead glass, thirteen years prior to Ravenscroft first making it on a commercial basis. However, Tilson's product, being a true lead glass and of better quality than his predecessors, was not commercially viable, being too brittle to make common wares.

tin luster An iridescent layer on glass by treating it (a) with a solution of tin salts in resin, then fired, or (b) with a spray of tin chloride or tin nitrate suspended in water or alcohol on a hot glass.

tin oxide (Aka *stannic oxide*) A chemical used to opacify glass in making opaque white glass and tin glaze for pottery.

tinsel painting See *reverse painting on glass.*

tint A color tinge given to glass by an ingredient or impurity inherent in the raw materials, as distinguished from a color resulting from the deliberate addition of a mineral oxide or other coloring agent to the batch.

Tinted line See *Florida (or Tinted) line.*

tintor de mojolis A term used in Venice beginning in the 13th century for painters or enamelers of glassware.

tissue box A box to hold tissues, introduced into the United States about 1937. Many were made in Czechoslovakia.

titanium A metallic agent recently used as a coloring agent, producing hues of yellow-brown.

toast master's glass A glass sometimes tall and thin but usually with a bowl having a thick wall and bottom, giving a deceptive impression of its contents. Its capacity is usually between 1/2 and 3/4 ounce, designed so a toastmaster may make several toasts without consuming much alcohol.

toasting glass (1) A tall, thin wine glass with a conical bowl and extremely slender stem that could be snapped effortlessly between the thumb and finger. As a result few have survived. It was considered a type of firing glass with a capacity often between two and four ounces. Many were made in England during the second quarter of the 18th century, specifically for drinking a toast. (2) See *toast master's glass*.

tobacco flask Snuff bottle. Some were made of cased glass, embellished with cameo cutting, in China during the 19th century and Japan during the 18th century. Others were of colored glass and not embellished.

Mosser Large Cherry Thumbprint, tobacco jar, green opal, 9-1/2" h.
Davanna Collection

tobacco jar A jar for holding tobacco, usually in three sizes, ranging in height from six to eight inches. They are often mistaken for cracker jars, which have a flat lid, while tobacco jars have a domed lid, which provides space for the placement of a sponge, moistened with water, to keep the tobacco fresh (moist).

tobacco pipe An ornamental object in the form of a smoking pipe. Some colored ones were made in the Nailsea, Bristol and Stourbridge areas of England, probably as trade ornaments for tobacconists or for display in their shop window. Some were made in extremely unusual shapes. A pipe with a very long stem and a small bowl is called a *church warden's pipe*. Some that were ornately embellished with a long twisted stem were made in Spain during the 18th century.

toddy glass (Aka *flip*) A drinking glass for drinking hot toddy. It is tall, thick-walled and has no stem, often embellished with wheel engraving and an inscription. See *toddy plate*.

toddy lifter (Aka *punch fillers*) A hollow vessel, often embellished with cutting, about six inches long, for transferring punch from a bowl to a glass. It is in the shape of a tube with openings at both ends and a bulb near one end. The bulbous end is dipped into the punch bowl until the bulb is filled with punch (capacity of about a wine glass). A thumb is placed over the hole at the opposite end, creating a vacuum and holding the punch in the bulb. It is removed from the bowl and placed over a glass and the thumb removed, releasing the punch into the glass. Some have a collar serving as a finger grip at the middle of the neck. Believed to have been invented in Scotland, they were made in England and Ireland during the 18th and early 19th centuries. See *wine siphon*.

toddy plate A circular plate about four to 5-3/4 inches in diameter (somewhat larger than a cup plate), made in the United States and used in conjunction with a glass of hot toddy, as a rest for the hot glass or spoon. Some were made of lacy and pattern molded glass. See *toddy glass*.

toddy rummer A large, sturdily built glass vessel in which hot toddy was prepared. They were made from the 1780s, often with engraved bowls.

toddy stick (1) A small spatula for stirring hot toddy. (2) A *sugar crusher*.

toilet bottle (Aka *camphor bottle, vinegar bottle*) A bottle holding about eight ounces of a liquid to be used in the dressing room.

toilet glass See *toilet mirror*.

toilet mirror (Aka *toilet glass*) A mirror used on a dressing table, first made in England about the time of (and included in toilet sets after) the Restoration (1660-1688), fashionable in France earlier. These were usually square in shape, normally embellished with stump work, and supported by a hinged strut at the back. Later they were framed, swiveling between uprights, mounted on a stand fitted with drawers and compartments for toilet articles.

toilet set (Aka *bathroom sets*) A group of articles for use on a lady's toilet table, usually consisting of three or more pieces including: a powder bowl or box with a cover, perfume or toilet water bottle(s), lotion bottle, peroxide bottle, boric acid bottle, bath salts jar, cold cream jar, cotton dispenser, water goblet, hair receiver, etc. Usually of pressed glass or cut crystal and accompanied by a tray, many were imported from Czechoslovakia during the 1930s.

toilet water bottle A small bottle with a stopper or cap for holding toilet water; an accessory found on the toilet table and normally part of a toilet set. See *cologne bottle.*

toilet water decanter A small decanter to hold toilet waters, often with a label designating the contents. They usually are made in sets of three. See *cologne bottle; toilet water bottle.*

Toledo, Ohio, glass companies
There were four leading glass manufacturers in Toledo, Ohio, making a variety of industrial glass: Owens-Illinois Inc.; Libbey-Owens-Ford; Owens-Corning Fiberglass Corp.; and Johns-Manville Fiber Glass Inc.

Toledo Glass Company
A glass manufacturing facility established by Edward Drummond Libbey, Michael J. Owens and others to make lamp chimneys and tumblers using Owens' semi-automatic machine originally used to make light bulbs. Under Libbey's leadership, his backing of Owens' bottle making machine and his perfecting of the Colburn process, it became Owens-Illinois Inc., and a new company, Libbey-Owens-Ford (L-O-F), was formed.

tongs (1) Metal tools with two long arms, pivoted or hinged together, used to handle hot glass objects. (2) As described in (1) above, except one side (occasionally both sides) has a design that could be impressed on a piece of glassware by grabbing it and applying light pressure (called *stamped decoration*). It is used mainly on open vessels such as bowls and beakers.

tool (1) Any of the numerous instruments used by glassmakers to form and shape an object, including the crimper, block, gathering iron, pontil, shears, blowpipe, pallet, pincers, lipper, scissors, jacks, pucellas, compass, measuring sticks, battledor, clapper, etc. (2) To modify the shape or form of an object with a tool.

tool, the See *pucellas.*

tooling The process of shaping molten glass after the bubble is formed using pincers, paddle, shears, etc., to make such features as the handle, rim, foot, stem, knop and applied decorations.

White cut-to-cranberry toothpick with gold trim, 3" h.
Tri-State Antiques

Westmoreland milk glass toothpick, hobnail design, 2-1/2" tall.
Davanna Collection

toothpick (holder) In the 1800s, it was considered polite etiquette to pick one's teeth after eating, and toothpicks were kept on the table in a small container. They were made in a variety of novelty shapes, such as a hat, lady's shoe, barrel, etc., often of pressed glass, occasionally with a matching tray. Other pieces often confused with, or mistaken for, toothpick holders include master salts, toy or salesmen's sample spooners, shot glasses, match holders, mustard pots, tiny vases and small rose bowls. To determine if the piece is a toothpick holder: (a) a small bundle of toothpicks should rest easily in the piece with ample space at the top to allow the extraction of a single toothpick; and (b) they should stand erect or nearly so and not fall out or down.

Topaz A bright yellow color.

topographical glassware Glassware embellished with scenes of buildings, views of cities, or other landmarks, usually depicted by engraving or enameling. They are still popular today. The most common embellishments are transfer prints.

Toronto Glass Company (or Works) (1894-1900) A glass manufacturing facility established in Toronto, Canada, by glassblowers from the Burlington Glass Works in Hamilton, originally making bottles and containers, later adding flint wares and cast glass paperweights. Internal friction among the owners is blamed for its closing.

torsade A twisted ring of opaque white or colored glass, or a combination of both, which is part of the embellishment of some paperweights. It often encircles the motif (see *mushroom paperweight; upright bouquet*), especially ones made at St. Louis. Some consist of a gauze twist within a spiral twist (see *twist*).

tortoise shell glass An art glass having the appearance of a tortoise shell; a brown mottled glass between two layers of glass with a glossy finish. A process for making it was developed by Francis Pohl of Silesia, registered in 1880. It involved breaking into small pieces several bubbles of blown glass of different shades of brown. Then a paraison of clear glass was blown into a globular shape and cut almost in half. Into this was inserted another semi-globular piece earlier rolled onto the pieces of brown glass and marvered. The inserted paraison was blown until it contacted the outer halves, sandwiching the brown glass, and formed into the desired shape. Another process involves gathering bits of brown glass on a paraison, forming an article and coating it with silver chloride and yellow ocher or other pigment. It was made by Boston & Sandwich Glass Co. and other U.S. and European facilities.

torzella See *nestoris*.

tot (1) A small drinking glass with a capacity of about eight ounces. (2) A small cordial glass or taster.

toughening glass Glass has exceptional compressive strength because, being non-crystalline, it has no lattice or crystalline structure. In its pure state—molten glass untouched and unexposed to the atmosphere—it has an very high tensile strength (resistance of a material to longitudinal stress). In reality, it does not exist in this state because, when exposed to the atmosphere or formed into an article, its tensile strength is reduced to about 10,000 pounds per square inch, about one-hundredth of that expected in the pristine state, due to the existence of minute submicroscopic flaws. After the article has been handled, the tensile strength is reduced to about 5,000 pounds per square inch. Because the compressive strength is extremely high, glass will only break in tension (under load or subjected to impact). If the surface of the glass could be put in a state of compression before the article were to break, the compression would have to be overcome and sufficient tension applied for fracture to occur. This principle is used in making toughened plate glass for car windshields, shop windows or domestic glassware.

If a piece of glass is uniformly heated on both sides, the outer surface tends to expand, but is prevented from doing so by the cold inner layer and a state of temporary compression on the outside is created, while the inside is in tension. Under these conditions the glass will not break. As long as the temperature does not reach that at which flow occurs, it will not revert to its original state on cooling. If this stress pattern can be induced permanently, the glass would be ten times stronger (toughened) than that annealed in the customary manner. In the toughening process, a well-annealed, stress-free glass is heated to just above the annealing point and the surfaces rapidly chilled and frozen. At this stage there are no stresses since the inside of the glass, which is still plastic, can accommodate the linear contraction of the surfaces. On further cooling, the inside becomes rigid, continuing its linear contraction while the previously frozen surfaces do not contract further, and are placed in a state of compression. The chilling of the surfaces is done with air jets arranged in a predetermined pattern, which can be seen on a car windshield when light falls on it from a certain angle. The glass is in the state of disturbed stress balance and, when the outer surface is penetrated, the glass shatters into small fragments.

Most car windshields are now made of laminated glass rather than toughened glass in order to prevent glass fragments from flying about. Chemical toughening of glass by ion exchange is now widely used on lenses. In this, the hot lenses are dipped in a bath of molten potassium nitrate and the larger potassium ions replace some of the smaller sodium ions from the glass surface, thus creating a layer of compression. Occasionally lithium is used instead of potassium to replace the sodium ions.

Towers & Leacock See *Kensington Glass Works.*

tower See *pig.*

Towle Sterling Inc. See *Tiffin (Art) Glass Company.*

Townshend Acts of 1767 The English considered the Colonies a source of income and tried to keep them from making any product that the English could make a profit on through exportation. In 1767, to capitalize on this, the Townshend Acts were enacted by the English Parliament. It selected five groups of products on which it placed a Colonial import tax. Since the glass industry in the colonies

was almost nonexistent and the few products produced were crude, it was included as one of the groups. Parliament hoped to obtain the equivalent of $100,000 from the duty on glass alone. In 1768, the Colonies adopted the Non-Importation Agreement, agreeing, in theory, not to import these items.

toy An English term used during the 18th century for small objects or trifles made for amusement or as souvenirs, such as scent bottles, thimbles, miniature animals and small figures. In the United States it is used to describe traditional toys made of glass as well as miniature tableware items, such as cups and saucers, punch bowls, etc. Many items, which are miniature versions of standard size items, are in reality salesmen's samples.

toy set With respect to glassware, a miniature pressed set of tableware, usually having a matching sugar bowl, creamer, spoon holder and butter dish.

Trabucco, Victor A glass sculptor since 1974; creator of classic style lampwork paperweights since 1977. Working in his studio in Buffalo, New York, he makes magnum size weights and was the first American studio artist to eliminate the seam usually visible on lampwork weights. His primary subjects are flowers, bouquets, fruit and animals. His flowers are full, three-dimensional and botanically correct. His weights usually include a "T" or "VT" cane, and his signature and date of manufacture are engraved on the side of each.

trademark As defined by the Trademark Act of 1946, "any word, name, symbol or device, or any combination thereof, adopted and used by a manufacturer or merchant to identify his goods and to distinguish them from those manufactured or sold by others." The use of trademarks as signatures on glassware began to a limited extent during the early 1860s. The first one registered was the word "CENTENNIAL" used by Thomas G. Cook of Philadelphia in 1873. In the 1870s they were used mainly by lamp makers. Under the Act of 1881, new registrations were valid for 30 years. Since 1905, continual protection can be had by renewal every 20 years and may be transferred and/or renewed as long as it is used in interstate or foreign commerce. Some were never registered or only registered after being used for many years. Those pressed in glass have an advantage over etched or engraved trademarks, and especially over one on a paper label. The etched or engraved trademarks may be worn away, and paper labels typically come off over time. Some companies had no trademarks. A trademark used by a retailer, wholesaler or dealer who is not the manufacturer is called a *private brand mark*. See *signature*.

traforato *(Italian)* Literally, *perforated*. (Aka *a traforo*) Embellishment in an openwork pattern as in wicker basketry, used mainly on glass baskets. It is made by pincering together, at regular intervals, parallel horizontal strands of glass.

trailed curcuit (1) A chain or guilloche-type embellishment. (2) An embellishment with several closely spaced applied glass threads forming a continuous pattern.

trailed ornament A decorating technique where a glassblower attaches looped threads of glass to the surface of a vessel, allowing them to melt into its body.

trailing The process of applying threads of glass on the body, handle or foot of a vessel, or on the neck for easier gripping. It involves simply laying or winding threads of glass, still in the plastic state, onto a glass object. They may be laid into a pattern. However, it is not necessary they remain as placed or wound. They may be drawn into a pattern, impressed with a patterned wheel or formed into chains, or pincered or notched. The process is believed to have been first used on Roman glass. It is to be distinguished from threading.

trailing, pincered or pinched See *quilling*.

transfer engraving (Aka *glass picture, transfer print, reverse engraving*) A polychrome picture on the back of usually flat glass. They have been made in England from about 1670 until the Victorian era. The glass used was generally very thin crown glass with slight visible ripples, and the process used is very difficult. First the back of the glass was coated with Venetian turpentine and allowed to dry and harden. Then a black and white mezzotint was soaked in water, drained and

spread carefully on the prepared glass, eliminating any air bubbles trapped between the mezzotint and the glass. After being allowed to dry, the area was again soaked with water and the paper carefully rubbed off with the fingers, removing the pulp and leaving the ink. Once done, the ink picture remaining was painted with transparent oil colors, usually flat washes, leaving a shading to the mezzotint. The pictures were mainly portraits, commemoratives, motifs, rural and indoor scenes and allegorical subjects, rarely signed. They were never coated with varnish, which would detract from the translucency.

transfer print *Transfer engraving*, but not associated with transfer printing.

transfer printing A process of embellishing by first inking an engraved copper plate with a special ink prepared from metallic oxides, transferring the design to paper and, while the pigment was still wet, pressing onto the surface of the ware, leaving an imprint, subsequently fixed by firing. The process was likely invented about 1753, was used on ceramics, and about 1809 used on glass. Sometimes the design was printed in monochrome on opaque white glass; on occasion it was printed in outline and filled in by polychrome painting. See *transfer engraving*.

transition temperature The temperature at which an amorphous material, such as glass, changes from a brittle, vitreous state to a plastic state. It is dependent on its composition and extent of annealing.

translucent (Aka *semi-transparent*) Permitting the passage of light, but in a diffused manner so objects beyond cannot be clearly seen. See *transparent; opaque; opal glass*.

transmutation color A color that changes hue when seen by transmitted light (light passing through the glass). Glass colored turquoise blue (as a result of copper oxide in the batch and melting in a reducing atmosphere) shows as red when so viewed. The Lycurgus Cup in reflected light appears pea green but wine red when viewed by transmitted light.

transom (1) The horizontal cross member above a door or window opening. (2) The small window above a door or large window [directly below that defined in (1)].

transparent Having the property of transmitting light without diffusion so objects beyond can be distinctly seen. See *translucent; opaque.*

transparent enamel An enamel that is transparent, as distinguished from earlier, usually opaque enamel, used mainly for embellishing stained glass windows.

Transparentmalerei (*German*) A style of painting developed in the early years of the 19th century, presumably by Samuel Mohn (1762-1815), using transparent enamels.

Travaise glass In 1907, the Boston & Sandwich facility was reopened by Alton Manufacturing Co. and began making Travaise glass, a quality glassware designed to compete with that of Tiffany.

traveling flints A nickname for skilled glassworkers who, because of their demand, moved from company to company with great frequency.

Fan-shaped snack tray with section for cup, Daisy & Button pattern, 10" at widest part. Davanna Collection

tray A flat receptacle in an enormous variety of sizes and shapes with a low vertical sloping or curved rim, a flat bottom, and sometimes with a low stemmed foot. See *ice cream tray; battleship tray.*

tree bark bottle A glass bottle with a *gutta-percha* (made from the solidified milky juice of some Malaysian trees) covering resembling tree bark with small wooden pieces partially implanted under the bark,

appearing as if the limbs were sawed off. Most were used as barber bottles.

trefoil A form or ornamentation with three equal foils or lobes. See *pinched lip.*

trellis A cut-glass motif consisting of a fan crossed by parallel miter cuts.

trellis pattern A molded pattern of crossed diagonal raised lines forming small diamond-shaped depressions.

trellis-work basket A glass basket with a molded overall pattern resembling a garden trellis.

trembleuse (*French*) A cup combined with a special saucer with a vertical projecting ring into which the cup fits. The ring may be fairly high and pierced with ornamental designs. Sometimes a deep well replaces the ring. They are so made to prevent spillage caused by a shaky hand.

Tremont Glass Works A short-lived glass manufacturing facility established about 1860 in South Boston, Massachusetts, by J.M. Cook. The company made plain, cut, pressed and colored flint glass; gas, kerosene and solar shades; chimneys; and chemical glassware.

trencher A rectangular or circular flat tray on which meat or other food is served or carved. The name is derived from the trench or channel carved, molded, pressed, etc., into the base around the inside edge, designed to catch the juices from the meat, preventing it from flowing onto the table.

trencher salt A salt cellar with no feet, resting flat on the table. They are circular, oval or rectangular, with one to three wells, made to be placed alongside the diner's trencher plate.

Trevor & Ensell A window and bottle glass manufacturing facility making flint glassware, established in 1812 by John B. Trevor and John Ensell in Pittsburgh, Pennsylvania. In May 1816, Trevor sold his interest to a man named Bolton. It was taken over by Frederick Rudolph Joacim Lorenz in 1819. See *Pittsburgh Glass Works.*

Trichterpokal *(German)* A pokal with a funnel-shaped bowl.

trick glass See *joke glass; puzzle jug; siphon glass; yard-of-ale.*

tricolor paperweight A bouquet paperweight in which the central motif—a bouquet set within green foliage—has red, white and blue flowers resting on a clear glass ground. They were created to commemorate the French Revolution of February 1848.

trifle dish A bowl for serving trifle, a light dessert made of cornstarch and eggs.

trina, vetro di *(Italian)* Literally, *lace glass.* A term loosely used to designate various types of filigrana glass; applied by some to *vetro a reticello* and by others to *latticimo glass* with intricate patterns, without distinguishing which type of filigrana was intended. It has been replaced by *vetro a reticello* and *vetro a retorti.* Also see *Tiffany vetro de trina.*

trionfo *(Italian)* Literally, *triumph.* An elaborate centerpiece made of many different pieces, arranged as a grouping, to adorn a large ceremonial dining table. They were made in Venice during the 18th century, often representing a formal garden scene. Especially ornate ones were called *grande trionfo da tavolo.*

triple bottle A bottle divided internally into three compartments, each with its own mouth or spout. The earliest recorded were made of Roman glass in the Rhineland during the 3rd and 4th centuries. They were free blown, consisting of three globular bottles connected together or a single blown bottle with vertical partitions made by running a wooden tool up and down the length of the body. Some had an angled handle on one section. See *multiple bottle.*

triple cutting Fine line cutting consisting of two fine crosshatched cuttings and a third that created a design on the crosshatching.

triple paperweight A paperweight consisting of three superimposed paperweights of graduated sizes, the smallest at the top, each made separately and fused together.

triple series air twist See *air twist.*

triple twist The next logical extension of a double series twist.

Trippel, Christopher, & Co. See *Kensington Glassworks.*

triptych Three mirrors, usually taller than wide, hinged together to stand upright without bracing.

Tri-State Glass Manufacturing See *Pilgrim Glass Corporation.*

Triumph of Venus cup A goblet-shaped vessel of sapphire blue glass. The base and stem have the appearance of a tree trunk, and the bowl is in the form of a barrel cut in half. Around the bowl are enameled scenes of Venus riding on a throne atop an alligator-shaped wheeled cart with attendants before and aft. It was made in Venice in the mid-15th century.

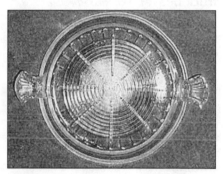

Fire-King 7" d. trivet.
Davanna Collection

trivet A three-footed hot plate normally about seven inches in diameter. The term has now come to refer to any item (regardless of shape) with short feet (regardless of number) on which hot items are placed so as not to damage another surface. Those designed for irons are made most often in the shape of an iron.

Trivulzio Bowl (Aka *Nero's Cup*) A cage cup of *vasa diatreta* type, the network made of blue glass with an inscription in emerald green. It came from the Trivulzio Collection in Milan.

trombone A glass ornament in the form of a trombone. See *musical instruments; horn.*

trophies A decorative motif depicting trophies of various types. A trophy was originally the arms of a beaten enemy hung by the Greeks on an oak tree to celebrate victory. This led to the motif of military trophies, including helmets, shields, axes and drums. Later other motifs were used in ornamental form, including love trophies with doves, bows and arrows, and quivers; musical trophies with flutes, violins, etc.; horticultural trophies with beehives, watering pails, and wheelbarrows; etc.

Trout & Fly, The An ornamental piece made of crystal by Steuben in 1966. It depicts a trout (cased) leaping from the water, grasping in the corner of its mouth a Royal Coachman fly of 18 karat gold. There are bubbles within the body, trapped by indentations in the inner glass before casing. It was designed by James Houston.

truck beaker See *Russelbecher.*

trulla (Latin) A ladle or dipper in the form of a bowl with a solid horizontal handle; the bowl is usually shallow, about 1-1/2 inches deep (some were deeper). They were made of Roman glass during the 1st century A.D. See *patera.*

trumpet bowl A bowl of a drinking glass that is tall, conical, and slender, with slightly concave sides, flaring at the mouth.

trumpet neck The neck of a vase or other vessel flaring outward toward the mouth.

trunk beaker See *claw beaker.*

tub A bucket such as an ice or butter *tub.* See *Wanne.*

tube (Aka *tubing*) A thin, hollow, usually cylindrical stick of glass, as opposed to a solid rod or cane, for conveying or containing liquids or gases. They were originally made as follows: first the glassmaker gathers molten glass from the pot or tank on the end of a blowing iron, rolling it on a metal plate into a thick cylinder, then reheating and enlarging it by repeating the operation. He blows a bubble in this and rolls it again. His assistant attaches an iron rod to the bottom of the cylinder and the blower draws the thick cylinder into a tube, blowing into it while drawing. The outside diameter, wall thickness and length are all determined by the maker's skill. Glass rods are made in the same manner except that no blowing is required. In the automatic process, using the Danner machine, glass flows from the tank over a rotating hollow mandrel, called a *tube.* As it is drawn mechanically, air is blown into it to maintain the correct bore. The outside diameter, bore and wall thickness are all governed by the size of the orifice through which the molten glass flows, the air pressure and the rate at which the glass is drawn.

tubular receptacle A tall, thin, cylindrical glass receptacle—its exact use uncertain—with overall wheel cutting of a network of diamond or oval facets, made of Persian or Mesopotamian glass during the 5th and 6th centuries.

tuft paperweight See *mushroom paperweight.*

tulip glass (1) A medium-size drinking glass with a tulip-shaped bowl, rounded toward the bottom and resting on a stemmed foot. The rim of the bowl is sometimes curved slightly outward (open tulip), but more often curved slightly inward (closed tulip). (2) A modern champagne glass with a tall, thin bowl, almost cylindrical.

tulip nozzle A decorative candle nozzle in the shape of an open tulip.

Tumble up, red cut-to-clear Bohemian glass.
Davanna Collection

Tumble up, red cut-to clear Bohemian glass
Davanna Collection

tumble up A two-piece set consisting of a glass bottle and small tumbler, which, when not in use, is seated upside down over the bottle neck, serving as a cover. It is usually used on a nightstand to quench nighttime thirst. See *nite set.*

Tumbler, 19th century, bluish-green glass.
The Corning Museum of Glass

tumbler A drinking glass with no stem, foot, or handle, and a flat base, usually of circular cross section and cylindrical, waisted, or barrel-shaped form or with sides tapering slightly inward toward the base. The cylindrical form is often called a *water glass.* They are of various styles and sizes depending on the intended use (to hold whisky, soda, water, iced tea, lemonade, etc.). Early ones made of Frankish glass from the 4th through the 7th centuries had a convex or pointed base so they could not stand erect—hence the name *tumbler*—and were placed in sand to keep it upright, or the contents was consumed at one time and returned to the table upside down—hence the expression "bottoms up." See *beaker; pocket glass; pocket tumbler.*

tumbler hat A glass object in the form of a hat, made normally from molds used to

make water tumblers. After the tumbler was made and the glass was still in the plastic stage, the top was folded down to form a brim. The final product was finished by hand.

Tunkahannock Glass Company A glass cutting shop in Tunkahannock, Pennsylvania, operating between 1894 and 1906, though some sources indicate it operated until 1915.

tureen Derived from the French *terrine*, meaning "flat-bottomed dish." A circular or oval serving bowl, usually with a cover, to serve soup or vegetables. Many were made of enameled opaque white glass in a variety of shapes and sizes, some elegantly embellished. They sometimes are accompanied by a matching stand and/or ladle.

turn A glassworker's shift, usually considered 4-1/2 hours or one-half day. Production rates were often stated in terms of a turn, such as the shop or crew was to make x-number of bowls per turn.

Turner, Gilbert & Co. See *Coventry Glass Works.*

Turner & Lane A glass cutting house established in the early 1840s in New York City, New York, closing about 1864. John S. O'Conner worked there before the Civil War.

turn-over rim A rim on some bowls and salt cellars of Irish glass and drinking glasses that is curved outward and downward.

Turtleback Tiles See *Tiffany Tiles.*

Tuscan A trademark used by the Cambridge Glass Company between 1936 and 1954.

Tuscan glassware Glassware made in several towns in Tuscany where the glass industry was well developed by the 16th century. The industry declined near the end of the 18th century after the last of the Medicis, a family sponsoring much of the industry. The wares were primarily bottles, flasks and stained glass windows. See *Florentine glassware.*

Tuthill, C.G., & Co. See *Tuthill Cut Glass Company.*

Tuthill Cut Glass Company (1900-1923)

A glass cutting house established in Middletown, New York, by Charles Guernsey Tuthill (pronounced Tuttle) as C.G. Tuthill & Co. In 1902 the name became Tuthill Cut Glass Company when Charles was joined by his brother, James F., and sister-in-law, Susan C. Tuthill. Charles, trained by Hawkes, created most of the designs and did some cutting and engraving. He was famous for his intaglio cut wares. James developed improved acid polishing techniques. Susan managed the facility and was quality control manager. Ninety-five percent of its blanks were purchased from Corning Glass Co., made using a special formula provided by Tuthill for its exclusive use. At times special blanks were purchased from Dorflinger and Pairpoint. Most wares were unsigned until about 1913, at which time it began signing them using three different signatures. All three signatures were in script with underlying emphasis: one line under the signature (1913 to 1918), a double line (1919 to 1923) or stylized fish under the signature. Prior to the Middletown operations, the Tuthills had operated a cutting shop in Corning, New York, between 1895 and 1900.

Tuthmosis glass

Three known core glass vessels bearing the cartouche of Tuthmosis III (c.1504-1450 B.C.), to honor the pharaoh said to be the founder of the glass industry in Egypt. One, a jug of opaque light blue glass embellished with colored trailing and powdered colored glass fired on but not fused into the body, is in the British Museum. The second, a cup of inverted bell shape of light blue glass with yellow and dark blue combed decoration, is in the Agyptische Staatssammlung in Munich. The third, a jug of inverted bell shape of undecorated turquoise blue glass, is in the Metropolitan Museum in New York City. They are all of Egyptian glass and among the earliest known glass vessels believed to have been made shortly after 1500 B.C.

Twelve Apostles See *Apostelglas.*

Twelve Cardinal Virtues See *Virtues, Twelve Cardinal.*

Twelve Months, The

A decorative allegorical subject depicting twelve enameled figures, each dressed with the appropriate attributes for the month that he or she represents. The month is usually inscribed near the proper figure. It appears on some Bohemian glassware made between about 1680 and 1770.

Steuben Glass vase from "Twenty-seven Contemporary Artists," c. 1939, clear glass. The Corning Museum of Glass

Twenty-seven Artists in Crystal

A collection of works conceived by John Gates, managing director and director of design of Steuben in 1937, after painter Henri Matisse offered to provide the company with a sketch to be engraved on glass. Gates then sought 26 other renowned painters, sculptors and printmakers to commission designs to be engraved on glass. The works were then engraved on vases, plates, bowls and urns and exhibited at Steuben's New York shop beginning on January 10, 1940, closing on February 14, 1940.

Twichell & Schoolcraft

A flint glass bottle and tableware glass manufacturing facility established in 1815 in Keene, New Hampshire, by Timothy Twi(t)chell and Henry Rowe Schoolcraft. In 1816 Nathaniel Spraque joined the firm after Twichell left, and the name changed to Spraque & Schoolcraft. It failed in 1817 and was taken over by Justus Perry. At this time the main products were green and flint glass bottles and flasks. In 1822 the operating company became Perry & Wood; 1828, Perry & Wheeler; 1830, Perry, Wheeler & Co; and 1835, S. & Q. Wheeler. In 1850 it closed because of lack of fuel. See *Keene (Marlboro Street) Glass Works.*

Twig Glass See *Tiffany Twig Glass.*

Twin City Glass Company (1908-1918)

A glass cutting company established by Oscar W. Johnson (of Johnson-Carlson Cut Glass Company, Chicago, Illinois) in

Minneapolis, Minnesota. In 1910 operations were moved to St. Paul, Minnesota.

twin grinding See *glass manufacturing, Shaping.*

twine holder See *string holder.*

twists Embellishment in the stems of English drinking glasses made by twisting the rod of glass in which were embedded air bubbles, or threads or tapes of opaque white or colored glass. The making and use of twists dates from about 1735; they were fashionable from the 1740s to the 1760s. There are over 150 varieties of twists in different forms and combinations. See the following twists: *air; cable; color; color mixed; corkscrew; cotton; double series; enamel; gauze; incised; lace; mercury; mixed; multiple series; outlined; single series; tape; tartan; thread; triple.* Also see *retorti, vetro a.*

two-and-three part glasses Two-part glasses are made with drawn stems—the bowl and stem are made of one piece, with an added foot. When the stem is made separately, it is a three-part glass, often more elaborate than drawn or two-part glasses since the process allows more easily for decorative bowls and complicated stems and stem shapes. There are simple, plain stem shapes occasionally made in three parts to give a wider set to the bowl, and if the design requires a slender stem that does not swell toward the top, as a drawn stem will do.

two-eared jar See *diota.*

two-tiered goblet A double goblet where one rests on top the other. Most were made in Bohemia.

Tygert Valley Glass Company See *Beaumont Glass Company.*

Tyneside glassware Glassware (apart from that made at Newcastle-upon-Tyne during the 17th and 18th centuries), mainly inexpensive pressed glass, made during the 1880s in large quantities at several facilities in northeast England. These facilities included Sowerby's Ellison Glassworks, Greener & Co. at Ware Glass Works in Sunderland (its mark was a lion with a halberd—a shafted weapon with an ax-like cutting blade, beak and spike) and George Davidson & Co. at the Teams Glass Works at Gateshead-on-Tyne (its mark was a lion on a battlement parapet). Other small facilities made like wares. See *Newcastle glassware.*

types of glassware (identification)
(a) *Free blown* (rough or polished pontil mark beneath the font or base; pontil mark on cover or outside of top). (b) *Blown in part size pattern mold* (feel contours of pattern on inside of piece; see or feel mold marks; pattern is sharper and smaller near the base, fainter and larger near the top; rough or polished pontil mark). (c) *Blown in full size mold* (pattern is the same everywhere on the piece; feel contours of pattern on inside of piece; pontil mark rough, polished, or covered by a pattern). (d) *Pressed* (pattern can be felt only on the outside; the inside is smooth; pressed edges are blunt, not sharp like the edges of cut glass; see or feel mold marks). (e) *Cut* (edges are sharp; polished pontil mark or cut design on base or foot; pieces can be free blown or mold blown). (f) *Engraved* (engraving usually gray but sometimes polished and clear; the edges of the design curve or angle into the main body of the piece). (g) *Etched* (edge of design cuts vertically into glass; usually grayish or mat finish).

Tyrian glass A rare art glass developed by Frederick Carder at Steuben about 1916-17. An opaque glass showing two colors: a pale blue-green when the piece is first fired but which, after reheating the partially formed object at the glory hole in a controlled atmosphere (oxidizing conditions), changes to a bluish-purple. The longer it was heated the deeper the purple. Some pieces show both colors with a blend from greenish-turquoise at the top to a shade of purple at the bottom. Some have added embellishment of applied leaves and trailed threads of gold Aurene glass, smoothed into the surface. On occasion the Aurene glass was sprayed at-the-fire with stannous chloride to give it an iridescent sheen. A few vases have a hooked decoration of Aurene glass around the neck, superimposed on white glass and smoothed into the surface. The trailed threading is in relief on a few pieces. The name Tyrian, given by Carder, was suggested by the imperial purple fabrics of ancient Tyre. All pieces, except a few experimental ones, are signed.

Uu

Ulster Glass Factory A window glass manufacturing facility established about 1812 in Ulster County, New York. It was still operating in 1855.

Ultra Marine A blue-green glassware made by the Jeanette Glass Manufacturing Co.

ultraviolet light See *ultraviolet test*.

ultraviolet test A test using ultraviolet radiation (long wave black light) to identify certain glassware, producing a fluorescence of a characteristic color if there are fluorescent elements present. The test is used to distinguish paperweights made by Baccarat, Clichy, and St. Louis, but the result is not conclusive. It is used to determine if the glass contains lead. Clear glass containing lead will fluoresce with a bluish color while glass containing no lead will fluoresce with a greenish-yellow color or not at all; glass containing uranium will also fluoresce with a greenish-yellow color. A recent reproduction or copy of an old piece will often fluoresce with a pink or purplish color. Many tests produce inconclusive results. It can also be used to detect repairs or defects in glass, fluorescing black or purple. Ultraviolet light is also called *black light*.

umbrella stand A cylindrical container about one foot in diameter and two feet high, used to hold umbrellas.

unbreakable glass See *Warzenbecher*.

undercutting The process of embellishing glassware in high relief by cutting away some of the glass between the body and its decoration, leaving an intervening open space. See *vasa diatreta*.

underdish (Aka *underplate*) Any small plate made to accompany and be placed under another article, such as a salad bowl, mayonnaise, handled saucer, finger bowl, etc.

underglaze decoration A rare embellishment on glassware, involving the use of applied colored threads beneath, and fused to, an outer layer of clear glass.

Underiner, Nicolas (1862-1932) Originally spelled *Undreiner*. Born in Limberg, Lothringen, he came to Corning, New York, in 1903, working at Hawkes, and in 1906 went to work at Sinclair. He also worked for Hoare and, from 1920 into the 1930s, he cut and engraved for Hunt. He operated a cutting shop in Corning from 1906 until 1932.

underplate See *underdish*.

undine A glass vessel used by a physician to irrigate a body part, such as an eye or nasal passage. It is globular in shape with an opening near the top for filling, opposite of which is a projecting thin, curved tube for irrigating.

unfired gilding (Aka *cold gilding, oil gilding*) The process by which gold is applied to the outer surface of glass without firing. Since it is applied without firing, it lacks permanency. It was a primitive method by which a preparation of linseed oil was applied with a brush, after which gold leaf was affixed and allowed to dry without firing. It was easily rubbed off and could not be burnished. Where the gilding has rubbed off, the design may still be seen because, generally, the pattern remains visible as a result of the remains of the fixative. The process is similar to that of applying cold colors. See *cold colors*.

unfired painting See *cold colors*.

Unger Brothers (1901-1918) A glass cutting house in Newark, New Jersey. It cut heavy glass at first, but as costs increased and styles changed, it resorted to cheaper pressed blanks. Some wares were signed; some had the name etched in script; and some had *Unger* block-printed as the top part of an oval and *Bros.* as the bottom half.

unguentarium (plural *unguentaria*) (Aka *balsamarine*). A small receptacle to hold toilet preparations (e.g., oil, scent, kohl), in numerous shapes and sizes (usually from one to six inches high). Early ones made in Egypt were of two forms: (a) columnar-shaped kohl pots, flaring at the top in the form of a lotus capital, and (b) globular jars, sometimes flattened on the sides, with a pair of small handles. Some later ones of core glass are in the form of various types of Greek vases (e.g., aryballos, alabastron, lakythos, ampulla), having combed decoration. Others made in the Roman period were of colored or colorless glass and of spherical or conical shape, generally with a slender neck. Sometimes two were joined and some made in unusual shapes, such as fish, pigs, etc. Many have an overhead loop handle or loops at the side (see *hanging unguentarium*). Some were made of Roman glass from the 1st century A.D. and of Islamic glass from the 5th to the 8th centuries. Many were placed in Roman tombs, mistakenly thought to have been used to hold the tears of mourners, and erroneously called *tear bottles* or *lachrymatories*. See *candlestick unguentarium; double unguentarium; globular unguentarium; test tube unguentarium*.

Uniak, J.M. A glass cutter who operated in New York City, New York, during the 1910s.

Union Cut Glass Company A glass cutting company in Honesdale, Pennsylvania. It later became the Irving Cut Glass Company.

Union Flint Glass Company (Aka *Union Glass Company*) A flint glass manufacturing facility established in 1826 in Kensington (Philadelphia), Pennsylvania, by craftsmen from New England Glass (William Granville, William Swindell, William Bennett and William Emmett). The company made plain and cut tableware. Late in 1826, Granville and Swindell left and Charles Baldren Austin entered, and its name changed to Charles B. Austin & Co. In 1840 Austin died and Bennett assumed control, adding colored glassware. He was a poor manager and in 1844 it closed. Hartell & Lancaster reopened it in 1847. In 1858, Hartell, Letchworth & Co. operated it, and it was still operating in 1874.

Union Flint Glass Works A flint glass manufacturing facility established in 1829 in Pittsburgh, Pennsylvania, by Hay & McCully (Capt. John Hay and William McCully). In 1831, the operating firm became Hay & Hanna. In 1832, it was destroyed by a flood, then by fire, and was rebuilt. In 1839 it was operated by Park & Hanna; 1848, by Hanna & Wallace; 1849, by Wallace, Lyon & Co.; 1852, by James B. Lyon & Co.; and 1875, by O'Hara Glass Co. See *O'Hara Glass Works*.

Union Glass Company (1) (1851-1924) A glass manufacturing facility established in Somerville, Massachusetts, by Amory and Francis Houghton. They left in 1864 and acquired the Brooklyn Flint Glass Co. In 1854, the Union Glass Company was incorporated with the Houghtons and J.P. Gregory as the original officers. After 1864, it continued under the direction of a Thomas Dana and became prosperous, making vast amounts of pressed, blown, and blown-molded glass, silvered glass, cut-glass blanks, and cut glass. It made tableware, lighting devices (mainly kerosene lamps), lamp chimneys, gas globes, and shades. After Dana's death about 1891, operations were continued by his son-in-law, Julian de Cordova, who became the sole owner, and thereafter made art glass in the Art Nouveau style until the company closed. It is best known for its *Kew Blas* ware. See *Houghton Glass Works*. (2) (1851-1899) A window glass manufacturing facility established in Cleveland, New York, owned and operated by various firms over the years. In 1877, it was acquired by the Cleveland Glass Company; in 1889, by the United Glass Company; and in 1899, by the American Window Glass Company of Pittsburgh, Pennsylvania, which quickly closed it. See *Cleveland Glass Company*. (3) See *Union Flint Glass Co.* (4) See *Union Glass Works*.

Union Glass Factory (or Works) A window and bottle glass manufacturing facility established by Frederick and Jacob Stanger and William Shough between 1806 and 1811 in Port Elizabeth, New Jersey. In June 1811, Randall Marshall bought a quarter interest in it. In December 1811 it burned, was rebuilt and fired up in March 1812. In 1814 many of the workers left upon learning it might be dissolved. In November 1814, Joshua Brick, Isaac Townsend, and Stephen Willis were appointed by the court to divide the property into four equal shares. For a time it operated as two separate and distinct businesses under one roof, each operating one furnace. One business was operated by Randall Marshall and one by Jacob Stanger and William Slough, who took a partner, Abraham Reeves, Marshall's father-in-law. Marshall moved to Marshallville, New Jersey, and constructed a facility there. By 1818, the remainder of operations of the Union Glass Factory were closed, and later it was destroyed by fire.

Union Glass Manufacturing Company See *Excelsior Flint Glass Works.*

Union Glass Works (1) See *New London Glass Company.* (2) A facility of the Northwood Glass Company established in 1887 in Martins Ferry, Ohio. (3) A flint glass manufacturing facility established by Captain John Hay and Henry Campbell (Hay & Campbell) at Etna, near Pittsburgh, Pennsylvania, in 1831. In 1834 it was operated by Park(e) & Campbell, and in 1837 by Park(e), Campbell & Hanna. Various firms operated it from 1846 to 1850. In 1848 or 1850 (depending on the source), it was operated by Wallace, Lyon & Co., followed, in

1853, by James B. Lyon & Co. (4) (Aka *Union Glass Company*) A window glass manufacturing facility established about 1830 in North Wheeling, West Virginia, by S.G. Robinson. In 1835, R. Knowles & Company operated it, making bottles and flasks. In 1851, it was operated by Quarrier, Ott & Co.

union set (Aka *dressing mirror, shaving mirror*) A framed swivel mirror mounted between two uprights attached to a base with one or more small drawers.

Union Stopper Co. A glass manufacturing facility in Morgantown, West Virginia, which made glassware for the Sengbusch Self-Cleaning Inkstand Co. of Milwaukee, Wisconsin.

United Cut Glass Company See *Herbert, Max, Company, Incorporated.*

United Glass Company See *Durhamville Glass Works; Dunbarton Glass Works; Cleveland Glass Works; New London Glass Company; Union Glass Co.; Wistar Glass Works.*

United States in Crystal
See *Americana Series.*

United States Glass Company

Company Name Designation	Location	Company Name Designation	Location
Adams & Co. Factory A	Pittsburgh, Pennsylvania	King Glass Company Factory K	Pittsburgh, Pennsylvania
Bryce Brothers Factory B	Pittsburgh, Pennsylvania	O'Hara Glass Co. Factory L	Pittsburgh, Pennsylvania
Challinor, Taylor & Co. Factory C	Tarentum, Pennsylvania	Bellaire Glass Company Factory M	Findlay, Ohio
Geo. Duncan & Sons Factory D	Pittsburgh, Pennsylvania	Nickel Plate Glass Co. Factory N	Fostoria, Ohio
Richards & Hartley Factory E	Tarentum, Pennsylvania	Central Glass Company Factory O	Wheeling, West Virginia
Ripley & Company Factory F	Pittsburgh, Pennsylvania	Doyle & Co. Factory P	Pittsburgh, Pennsylvania
Gillinder & Sons Factory G	Greensburg, Pennsylvania	A.J. Beatty & Sons Factory R	Tiffin, Ohio
Hobbs Glass Company Factory H	Wheeling, West Virginia	A.J. Beatty & Sons Factory S	Steubenville, Ohio
Columbia Glass Co. Factory J	Findlay, Ohio	Novelty Glass Co. Factory T	Fostoria, Ohio

United States Cut Glass Company

In 1905, it purchased the Roseen Brothers Cut Glass Company of Chicago, Illinois. In 1912, it was under the direction of Herman Kotwitz (see *Monarch Cut Glass Company*) who, in 1914, operated it as the Western Cut Glass Company (see *Western Cut Glass Company*).

United States Glass Company (1) A

company resulting from a merger of several tableware manufacturing facilities. The goal was to regulate production, maintain prices, and expand the scope of its operations. In February 1891 it applied for a corporate charter in Pennsylvania, as a holding company for several affiliated companies. The combine became effective in July 1891, with Daniel C. Ripley of Ripley & Company as its president. The identities of the many patterns made by the various facilities were lost in volume production. It was very economically minded and tended to use a variety of shortcuts and labor-saving methods. The affiliated companies were often identified only by letter. A listing of its companies is on the previous page.

After a major strike from 1893 to 1896, many facilities were closed, never reopening. In 1904, only the following companies were affiliated with the combine:

Adams & Company	Factory A
Bryce Brothers	Factory B
Ripley & Company	Factory F
King Sons & Company	Factory K
Doyle & Company	Factory P
A.J. Beatty & Sons	Factory R

The combine also added the following new facilities to its operations before 1904:

Factory D	a gold decorating facility
Factory H	a plate etching facility
Factory U	a tank operation (Gas City, Indiana)

In 1910, the following facilities were built in Glassport:

Factory O	a tank operation
Factory N	a decorating facility

During the Great Depression of the early 1930s, many facilities were closed and never reopened. There were other companies affiliated with the United States Glass Company. It did not use a trademark until 1914, it was simply "U.S." It had showrooms in Pittsburgh, Pennsylvania (the main offices); New York, New York; Philadelphia, Pennsylvania; Baltimore, Maryland; and San Francisco, California. In 1962, it filed for bankruptcy. (2) See *Falmouth Glass Works*.

United States Glass Works See *Excelsior Flint Glass Works*.

Universal Glass Products See *Gayner Glass Works*.

Unlimited Piece Work A practice of paying glassworkers only for the good pieces made with no guarantee of payment for hours worked. See *Unlimited Turn Work*.

Unlimited Turn Work A practice of paying glassworkers by the piece, but with a guarantee of payment of his regular hourly rate for each hour worked. See *Unlimited Piece Work*.

Upper Factory See *Cape May Glass Company*.

upright bouquet A floral design positioned vertically as it would normally appear in a vase.

upset muslin See *muslin ground*.

uranium A metallic agent used in coloring glass, giving rise to a prominent fluorescent yellowish green or greenish yellow color. When mixed with antimony, topaz and amber colors result. In very high lead glass (71% lead oxide), adding uranium results in a deep red color.

uranium glass A type of glass made using uranium in the batch, producing a yellowish green (*Annagrun*) or greenish yellow (*Annagelb*) glass. It was developed by Joseph Riedel. See *uranium; Vaseline glass*.

urchin glass See *Igelglas.*

urinal A receptacle to hold urine. They are appropriately shaped for either male or female use. In the past, a urinal was used for uroscopy (inspection and analysis of urine by means of diagnosis). Early ones, dating from about 1500, were shaped like a pouch. Later ones for women were globular with a vertical neck, and those for men were globular with a horizontal neck at the top. The more modern shape is hemi-ovoid with a flat bottom and uptilted neck. While it is not known with certainty where and when they were first made, they are mentioned in literature as early as 1300. Glass ones have been made in England since the 16th century.

Clear-glass covered urn, c. 1880. The Corning Museum of Glass

urn A classical form made in various shapes and styles. However, the traditional shape of the body is globular or ovoid, curving inward toward a stemmed foot, the mouth smaller in diameter than the body. It often has two side handles. In classical times it had many uses: for holding fluids, for ornamental purposes, for holding lots to be drawn, for containing the ashes of the dead (these should not be classified as urns, in spite of popular usage), etc.

ushabti (Aka *shabti* or *shawabti*) An ancient Egyptian mummiform figure deposited in a tomb with the mummy of the deceased, serving his spirit in the afterworld. Most bear inscriptions in hicroglyphs and are generally about four inches high, but range in height from one to 35 inches; early glass ones range from seven to 15 inches.

U-shaped bowl A bowl of a drinking glass (used only to serve ale), cylindrical in shape with a rounded bottom, resembling the letter "U." They were sometimes wrythen or embellished with thumbprints and generally rest on a knopped stem.

Utica (Crown) Glass Company A crown window glass manufacturing facility established north of Utica, New York, in 1809 by Peter Bours, John Stewart, Seth Dwight, Hugh Cunningham, and Benjamin Walker. They received a special charter from the New York State Legislature because the legislature had already issued a charter for making cylinder window glass to Oneida Glass Factory Company. Crown glass was only made by one other facility in the country and was considered superior to cylinder glass. The operation was not too successful, and it struggled along until 1822, when it was leased to the Oneida Glass Factory Company. On August 18, 1836, both facilities closed. See *Oneida Glass Factory Company.*

vacuum gather process A bottle making process in which molten glass is sucked into the paraison mold by vacuum. The mold, under partial vacuum, is dipped into molten glass, which rushes into it to fill the vacuum. The major problem is when the mold is dipped, it makes the molten glass too cold and stiff to be *vacuumed* by the next set of molds. This is overcome by having a large rotating pot, insuring hot glass is always available while the chilled glass is taken away to be reheated. This process is seldom used now in making bottles. It is used more often in making tumblers, wine glasses and other domestic blown glassware.

vacuum tube A sealed glass tube having most of the contained gas removed prior to sealing. The gas is removed to a pressure low enough to permit the passage of electrical discharges between metallic electrodes projecting into the tube from the outside.

Val Saint Lambert, Cristalleries du The largest maker of cut and engraved crystal glass in Belgium, established in 1825 near Liege, on the site of the former Val Saint Lambert Cistercian monastery (established in 1202, abandoned in 1797). The company was purchased in 1825 by Francois Kemlin (1784-1855), formerly a glassmaker at the Voneche Glassworks. He, with Auguste Lelievre (1796-1879), also formerly at Voneche, built a new glass furnace. This furnace was in operation in 1826 and was operated by English craftsmen. Initally it made crystal glassware in contemporary English styles, later adding art glass in the Art Nouveau and art deco styles. It also made some paperweights in the mid-19th century and cameo glass featuring cased glass bodies lavishly cut with a lapidary wheel and acid engraved. Between 1879 and 1883, it acquired three subsidiaries near Liege and

Namur, and in 1972, a facility in Canada. It is under the control of the Societe Generale de Belgique.

Vallely Cut Glass Co. A glass cutting shop in Buffalo, New York, which began operations in 1903 and in 1904 merged with the International Cut Glass Company.

Vallely Glass & Mirror Company (1924-1954) A glass manufacturing facility operating in Toledo, Ohio, making artistically engraved and embellished mirrors.

Vallerysthal glass vase, amberina ground with gold daffodils, 12" h.
Krause
Publications

Vallerysthal Glassworks A glass manufacturing facility founded in 1836 by Baron de Klenglin in Lorraine, France (on the site of a centuries-old glassworks), a subsidiary of Plaine de Walsch glassworks founded in 1707. The two facilities were united under the name United Glass Works of Plaine de Walsch & Vallerysthal in 1854. In 1855, the venture was dissolved. The Vallerysthal facility became Klenglin & Cie., making fancy colored glass in large quantities. After the Franco-Prussian War in 1870, it ended up in Germany and, as a result was cut off from its sales outlets. In 1872, it purchased the nearby Portieux Glassworks in France, and the name changed to the United Glassworks of Vallerysthal & Portieux.

It made large amounts of art glass, even though the main product was tableware, usually etched. It also made a small amount of Art Nouveau glass. After World War I, Alsace-Lorraine was returned to France and again it became solely a French firm.

Valley Glass Company See *Whitla Glass Company.*

Steuben Glass covered valor cup, c. 1940, clear, engraved glass.
The Corning Museum of Glass

Valor Cup, The A large two-handled, covered urn designed in 1940 by John Monteith Gates. It was made by Steuben for the British War Relief Society to commemorate the Battle of Britain and bears the Royal Coat-of-Arms. It was made by John Jansson and engraved by Joseph Libisch. A replica was presented to Gates on his retirement.

V.A.M.S.A. See *Barbini, Alfredo.*

Van de(r) Mark, Brace & Hall Successor to the Enterprise Cut Glass Co. (closed in 1917), in Elmira Heights, New York, it took over Enterprise's assets in 1918, purchasing blanks from Libbey Glass.

Van Dyke rim A rim on the bowls of some vessels and the foot of some drinking glasses. When on the bowl, it is scalloped (usually in trefoil pattern). When on the foot, it is in the form of a series of sharply pointed motifs, either cut or engraved. The term is derived from the pointed lace collars and/or beards of men found in many of the portraits painted by Sir Anthony Van Dyke (Dyck) (1549-1641).

Van Etten, Ambrose (1884-1953) Born in Gibson, New York, he and his twin, Eugene, started in 1898 working for Hawkes (older brother, Archie, already working there). In 1911, Ambrose took a position as cutting foreman at the Ideal Cut Glass Company. From 1917 to 1920 he piloted a New York excursion boat. He then returned to cutting, working for Hunt, and from 1933 to 1936, working in New York City. From 1920 to about 1950, except from 1933 to 1936, he operated a cutting shop in Gibson, New York, later moving to Horseheads, New York. He cut on inexpensive blanks and Pyrex glass, primarily floral cuttings, names and initials, mostly for individuals. During World War II he did some work for the Corning Glass Works.

Van Heusen & Charles A wholesale china and glass business established in Albany, New York, in 1843. While pieces of cut glassware with its name have been found, it did not make any. It merely acted as agent and distributor for Libbey and other makers, generally small cutting shops. In 1964 it changed its name to Van Heusen, Charles & Company.

Van Houten, E.J.S. See *Williamsburgh Flint Glass Company.*

Van Houten Cut Glass Co. A glass cutting company in New York City, New York.

Van Rensselaer Glass Works A glass manufacturing facility in Albany, New York, about 1807.

Hand-painted Bristol glass vanity powder with bud vase on cover, 9" h.
Tri-State Antiques

vanity set A set of items used on a dressing table, usually of three pieces (two bottles and a powder box), occasionally with a plateau mirror. Many pressed glass sets were made in Czechoslovakia during the 1930s, retailing in the United States for about $1. Those made in the United States, many of cut glass, were more expensive, retailing from $25 to $30.

vari-baluster stem A stem with two or more balusters, each of a different size.

variegate To diversify or vary the external appearance, especially by using different colors in the form of spots, patches or streaks, usually in a random pattern.

vasa diatreta *(Latin)* (singular is *vasa diatretum*) Glass vessels, the body encircled by a network or other openwork pattern, attached to the main body by glass struts (*pigs*), producing a three-dimensional effect. The Latin name was given to it by J.J. Winckelmann, based on his theory that the *diatretari* in Roman times did only such reticulated work, whereas they were glass cutters, as distinguished from the *vitrearii* (glassblowers and glassmakers) (see *cage cup; Lycurgus Cup*).

The process for making cage cups and other examples of it has been disputed. Following are three processes that could be used to make it: (1) The inner receptacle and the outer network were made independently, then fused together. This theory has been abandoned. (2) The double walled vessel was made by inserting the separately made inner glass into the outer glass without fusing them together. Then tiny glass struts were pushed through the heated outer wall to the wall of the inner glass in order to connect, yet separate, the walls. After this, the outer wall was ground to form the cage or design. This theory has been rejected. (3) The outer wall was cut and/or undercut from a single cold mass, most likely mold blown. This left the cage, or outer relief embellished portion, standing free from the inner receptacle except for small glass struts. This theory of lapidary work was conceived by W.B. Honey. It is now considered to be the process used, confirmed by grinding marks on the outer wall of the inner receptacle and air bubbles in adjacent parts of the inner receptacle and the outer relief work being in the same direction.

vasa murrhina (1) A Latin term for *murrhine glassware*. (2) An art glass made in the United States. In 1884, Dr. Flower took over the inactive Cape Cod Glass Works in Sandwich, Massachusetts. Here he and John Charles DeVoy experimented with making variegated colored glass they called *vasa murrhina*. DeVoy was issued a patent in 1884. It is believed the Sandwich Glass Works may have made it also. Generally it is a heavy, blown ware, some patterned in molds, made as follows: The first gather of molten glass, usually a solid color, formed the lining. This was coated with particles of metal, mica or glass in variegated colors (sometimes pulverized to dust), subjected to intense heat to fuse the particles to it and covered with a gather of glass. Some of the so-called *vasa murrhina* is clear glass with the variegated colors rolled in on the marver. It is often confused with *aventurine* and *spatter* or *spangle glass*. Dr. Flower also had a company in Hartford, Connecticut, the Vasa Murrhina Art Glass Company. (3) A glass, similar to (2) above, made in recent years by the Fenton Art Glass Company.

Vasa Murrhina Art Glass Company See *vasa murrhina*.

Vasaline glass See *Vaseline glass*.

Vasart Glass Ltd. A glass manufacturing facility established in 1948 at Perth, Scotland, by the father and brothers of Paul Ysart after leaving the Moncrieff Glassworks. It made vases, sold as "Vasart Glass," and paperweights (primarily the millefiori type, often forming a part of various utilitarian objects). In 1960, it was reorganized by Stuart Drysdale, a lawyer, and, in 1963, a major interest was bought by Scotch whiskey distiller, Wm. Teacher & Sons Ltd. The business and personnel formerly associated with Vasart were transferred, in 1963, to Strathearn Glass Ltd., which moved to a new facility at nearby Crieff in 1964.

vase A vessel in many forms, styles and shapes, but usually round and taller than it is wide, normally for ornamental or flower display purposes; some have an ornamental cover. Molds for lamp fonts were often used to pattern the bowls for vases. The bowls were drawn out to increase their depth and expanded after removal from the mold. The majority have trumpet-shaped bowls with a flaring pleated, fluted or scalloped rim. *Center vases* are bulbous, short necked vases (Aka *flower centers*); *bud vases* are small, tall, narrow vases to hold a single bud. Many vases have become discolored over time because of hard water leaving calcium deposits. Vases usually range from six to twenty-four inches high. The smaller vases are bud vases, the larger ones are center vases or presentation pieces. See the following vases: *auldjo; candlestick; columnar; cornucopia; Elgin; fan; goblet; Greek; handkerchief; hyacinth; Islamic; Jack-in-the-pulpit; Morgan; palm column; Pegasus; Pompeian blue; Portland; pull up; savoy; Sevres type; spill; tea; vendange; Milton.* Also see *handkerchief bowl; vaso fassoletto; mosque lamp; spill holder; vase luster.*

vase a oreilles *(French)* Literally, *vase with ears*. A vase, introduced at Sevres in the 1750s, having a baluster shape. It is supported by a stemmed and spreading base, a short neck and two scroll handles emanating upward from the sides of the mouth, curving down to the shoulder. The handles, in profile, resemble human ears.

vase candlestick A candlestick having, instead of a columnar stem, a glass urn-shaped bowl supported on metal legs. From the rim of the bowl are suspended pendant lusters or chain festoons. They were made from about 1777 to the late 19th century. See *candlestick vase.*

vase luster A colored glass vase embellished with lusters for decorating a mantelpiece, usually in pairs, in the form of a tall goblet or chalice and normally have a scalloped rim, around which hang icicles. They were made in Bohemia during the Victorian period and often had opaque-colored flashing, cut to reveal the transparent glass beneath. Many were embellished with oil gilding.

vase with ears See *vase a oreilles.*

vase with enclosed bouquet A large vase that has within the bowl a glass floral bouquet attached to its bottom. They were made in Murano during the 17th and 18th centuries, and in Shiraz (in Iran) during the 19th century. See *flower enclosing flask.*

vase with enclosed figure A vase which has a figure inside.

vase with flower stalk A vase that has a tall flower stalk complete with leaves and flowers projecting upward through its mouth. These vases were made in Murano during the 17th and 18th centuries and in South Germany during the 18th century.

Vaseline glass A transparent yellowish-green or greenish-yellow glass, so named in the early 1950s because the color and appearance is similar to Vaseline petroleum jelly. No manufacturer ever used the term to describe it. When first made, it was called *yellow* or *canary* glass, another misnomer. Some true vaseline glass was made by adding uranium oxide (usually 2%) to the lead glass formula and will flash two colors in sunlight and fluoresce under ultraviolet light, creating a yellow-green glow. Other yellow-green glass will not fluoresce or glow under ultraviolet light and neither will other antique glass, except Burmese, custard and other wares with uranium oxide.

The earliest known uranium glass is a mosaic excavated from a Roman villa on the Bay of Naples, dating to about 79 A.D., containing a little over 1% of an oxide of uranium. The Chinese used some uranium in their glass jewelry made in the 17th and 18th centuries. The process of isolating uranium dioxide from pitchblende in 1841, and the development of methods for pressing glass in the 1830s gave rise to the first commercial use of uranium in glass making in the 1850s. The Boston & Sandwich Glass Company made some *canary* glass items in the 1840s. Lloyd & Summerfield of England began the first large scale production of uranium glass beginning in 1857.

In vaseline glass, the most popular pattern was the Daisy & Button, first introduced by Gillinder & Sons for the centennial in 1876. Other companies followed suit. About 55 patterns were made in canary and vaseline glass; about 30 are still considered common. Other patterns, not originally made in vaseline glass, were made later. Its height of popularity was from 1860 to 1890. It was popular because yellow-green is the last color to see in diminishing light before total darkness and the first seen when going from dark to light. It was a sharp contrast to the usual dark and drab Victorian settings.

Vaseline glass was often blown and/or cut in small quantities on special order. The glass in its product form emits radiation, but not above normal environmental background levels. However, in its molten state, it was highly radioactive, emitting radon gas as well as alpha, beta and gamma radiation. Therefore, the blower was subjected to high levels of radiation. By the 1890s it was becoming unpopular. Some opalescent vaseline glass was made, but in very small quantities.

The glassmaker given credit for first using uranium oxide as a coloring agent is a Czech named Frantisek Riedl, who noted the uranium salts obtained from pitchblende often caused glass to have a yellowish or greenish tint. He named the two colors *Annagelb* (Anna yellow) and *Lenoragrun* (Lorena green) after his two daughters. He only made the glass in small quantities. His nephew, Joseph, Anna's husband, started production on a larger scale, changing the name *Lorenagrun* to *Annagrun*, in honor of his wife. Before 1840, the Czechs made some uranium glass rods, called *chameleon*, used as a raw material for some costume jewelry. Eventually they added other ingredients to the uranium-containing batch to create new colors: selenium to make pink, sulfur to make orange, and cadmium to make amber, making it until the start of World War II. They started making it again in the 1970s. In the United States, production of uranium glass was suspended by the Atomic Energy Commission from 1942 until 1951.

When under the varying light frequencies of the sun, candlelight, and gaslight, vaseline glass changes color from the yellow to green range and back again. Incandescent light has low fluctuating frequencies, so Vaseline glass's color never varies from the yellow range—hence its decrease in popularity with the increased use of the electric light. From 1900 to 1941, several attempts were made to revive the popularity of Vaseline glass. After 1951, when some uranium oxide was allowed to be used in the private sector, it was very expensive and only small quantities of vaseline glass were made. Since the 1960s some small companies have been making a small range of items in Vaseline glass. It is sometimes spelled *Vasaline*. See *Annagrun; Annagelb; lemonescent glass.*

Vaupel, Louis F. (1824-1903) Born Ludwig Heinrich Friedrich Vaupal in Schildhorst, Germany, he worked with his father in a local glass manufacturing facility. In 1836, his family established a facility in Breitenstein, where he became a glass blower and engraver. In 1850, he came to the United States and, in 1853, became an engraver at the New England Glass Co. He later supervised the engraving department, remaining there until he retired in 1885. From then until about 1890, he did some Bohemian-style wheel engraving at home, often commemorative or presentation pieces. His early work was on clear glass, but later appeared on colored flashed glass, mainly ruby colored. A few pieces were signed.

VDS The common abbreviation for *verre de soie.*

vegetable dish A dish usually oval with a wide rim, accompanied by a flat or slightly domed cover similarly shaped. Some covers were made with a detachable handle, removed so the cover could be used as a second matching dish. Many were made of lacy glass in the United States.

vegetable paperweight A paperweight with a central motif consisting of embedded glass vegetables, often turnips, placed in a white filigrana basket. A few were made in St. Louis.

veined onyx A two-toned color effect consisting of black and white veins.

Vello process A process used to make glass tubing. See *glass, Manufacturing, Shaping.*

velvet finish Satin finish.

Vendange Vase (Aka *Pompeian Blue Vase*) A large amphoriahos of blue glass with white cameo embellishment, executed in a manner similar to the Portland Vase, except the relief is deeper. The white cameo embellishment depicts scenes with Bacchanalian putti beneath the handles, with vines and doves and a scene with sheep surrounding the vase. Beneath the flat bottom there is a knot, unlike the Portland Vase. It was found at Pompeii and is believed to have been made in Rome. See *Auldjo vase.*

veneer (glass) The decorative covering on walls (and sometimes floors) using slabs, plaques or tiles of glass, often used in ancient Egypt and Rome. The smaller pieces were fused together or pressed into molten glass to form larger pieces. See *opus sectile.*

Venetian ball An object, normally globular in shape, composed of fragments of canes of various patterns and colors. These are compressed into a mass with no intended design and pressed into a transparent glass bubble which, in turn, is fused to a glass ball by sucking out the trapped air. They were made from about 1840. They are not considered paperweights even though some have been made using such fragments (*scrambled, macedoine* or *pell-mel* weights).

Venetian diamond See *ogival.*

Venetian enameling Enameling executed at Venice and Murano on clear colored glass and opaque white glass. It is believed enameling was done on glassware as early as the end of the 13th century, but no firm proof exists. From the late 15th century enameling was done in Venice, similar to that on Islamic glassware during the 13th and 14th centuries. Angolo Barovier is thought to have reinvented the technique. Enameling was first used on sapphire blue (see *Barovier cup*) and other colored transparent glassware. However, near the end of the 15th century, the use of colored glass tended to diminish and colorless tended to increase. By the end of the 16th century, enameling was not used to any great extent in Venice, except on opaque white glass (see *lattimo*); becoming popular

again during the 18th century. See *Venetian Scenic Plates.*

Venetian glass parrot, 11" h., crystal pedestal and base, mottled green body, red beak and red and yellow eyes.
Davanna Collection

Venetian glassware Glassware made in Venice from about 450 A.D. (glassmakers from Aquileia fled to escape barbarian invasions, going to Venice, and were joined by others from Byzantium and other areas of the Middle East) and in Murano from before 1292 (the year in which an ordinance forbade glasshouses in Venice, except for a few small furnaces that were at least 15 paces from the nearest structure) to the present. By 1268, a guild of Venetian glassmakers had been formed, divided into separate guilds based on specialty: *fialai* (bottle makers); *cristallai* (hollowware or crystal makers); specchiai (mirror makers); *perlai* (makers of beads, canes and pastes for beads) and *stazioneri* (retail sellers of glass). Later the *perlai* were divided into two guilds: the *conterie* (makers of traditional beads for sale commercially) and the *canne* (makers of large beads and enamels in the form of cakes for exportation).

In 1271, the Glassmakers *Capitolare* was approved. The guild laid down strict rules and regulations for the conduct of, and a privileged position for, its members and prohibited both the import of glass into Venice and the making of glass there by foreign makers. One rule was a ban on divulging trade secrets outside Venice. If a workman left the city without permission, he was ordered to return and, if he didn't, his relatives were sent to prison. If he still didn't return, an assassin was sent to kill him. Other rules, established then and later, required a minimum of three working holes per furnace, a restriction on fuel (only willow or alder could be used, allocated by senior judges), the prohibition of the export of potash, cullet and sand, the maintenance of two watches overnight (because of the risk of fire), the prohibition of the use of alum from Alexandria (it lowered the quality of the glass), and the annual export of wares to occur once a year only after the furnaces had closed down in August. Wares were exported to northern European areas, including Germany, and the Mediterranean area by the Venetian mercantile fleet. The primary purposes of the rules and regulations were the creation of a finer product and protection of its methods of manufacture. These rules remained in effect until the middle of the 18th century. In spite of them several workmen left, becoming well known craftsmen in other countries, but many were attracted to Venice from other countries.

By 1290, the making of Venetian glassware was well established and highly regarded. However, because of an increasing fear of fire, an edict was issued by the Grand Council of Venice in 1292 ordering many facilities to move from Venice to the nearby island of Murano where most Venetian glass continues to be made today.

The earliest glassware made in Venice consisted mainly of beads, jewelry, mirrors and window glass. Early composition of Venetian glass was affected by the terms of the 1277 treaty between the Doge of Venice and the Prince of Antioch in which there was a provision for cullet to be brought from the Near East for use in Venice. Enamellers from the former Byzantine Empire came to Venice to work in the late 1200s through the mid-1300s. Venetian merchants exported glass from about 1300. However, the city's importance as a glass manufacturing center and as an exporter of glass followed the development of *cristallo*, using manganese, during the 15th century. This soda glass (made using an alkali-*barilla*-imported from Alicante, Spain) was thin and fragile, not suitable for engraving, prompting its embellishment during production using methods such as trailing and threading.

Venetian glassmaking was at its peak during the 16th and 17th centuries, its products and techniques copied throughout Europe. The industry deteriorated dramatically during the 18th and 19th centuries, and Venice lost its dominant commercial position as more durable potash glass and lead glass made in England and northern Europe gained in popularity and gradually superceded the fragile soda glass. Venice surpassed other countries in making colored (especially blue, green, and purple) glass and agate glass, and in the development of filigrana, millefiori, mosaic and ice glass. Only a small amount of engraving was done while a great deal of enameling and gilding was done during the 15th and 16th centuries.

The Venetian reputation was revived somewhat during the late 19th and early 20th century as a result of the efforts, at Murano, of Salviati, Barovier, Venini, Cenedese, Alfred Barbini, and others, in addition to making a large quantity of beads and souvenir wares for tourists. Because of the iridescence of some of the wares made there, it is frequently confused with carnival glass. See *Venetian enameling; Murano; Torcello glassware.*

Venetian Threaded See *Verre Moire.*

Venetian window See *Palladian window.*

Venice glass An article of glass, such as a cup, mirror, vase, compote, etc., made of fine crystal.

Venini figure with white latticino design in pants and emerald green sash and shoe buckles, 10-1/2" h.
Tri-State Antiques

Venini & Co. A glass manufacturing facility in Murano, originally established in 1921 by Paolo Venini (1895-1959) of Milan, and

Giacomo Cappellin (b.1887) of Venice, as Vetri Soffiati, Muranesi Cappellin-Venini & C. (Cappellin & Venini). Prior to the company's founding, Cappellin had ordered, for his shop in Milan, glassware to be made in Murano by Andrea Rioda (d.1921) in the forms and styles of Venetian glass made in the 16th century. In 1921, just before Rioda died, Venini & Cappellin took over his facility, engaging Vittorio Zecchin (1887-1947) as designer. It continued to make glassware inspired by old paintings. In 1926, the company was dissolved when Cappellin withdrew and Venini & Co. was formed. Venini began reviving the making of millefiori and filigrana glassware and introduced many new techniques, especially those involving original surface treatments. Although Venini was its chief designer, he engaged famous outside designers, such as Salvador Dali. On Venini's death in 1959, the company passed to his daughter and her husband, Ludovico Diaz de Santillana. Among the new styles developed by Venini are: *vetro battute, vetro composto, vetru corroso, vetro groviglio, vetro membrano, vetro pennelato, vetro pulegoso, vetro sommerso, vetro tessuto, vetro pezzato,* etc. In the 1950s, Venini introduced his well-known handkerchief bowl (*vaso fazzoletto*) made of *vetro a retorti* (*zanfirico glass*).

ventose See *cupping glass.*

Verart An inexpensive line of opalescent glassware developed by Sabino at the onset of the Great Depression to bolster sales and compete with the cheaper wares of others.

Verlys Art Glass A handcrafted, blown (some molded), satin finish glassware with a high relief design in the art deco style made by the Holophane Company of Verlys, France, beginning after 1931. In 1935, an American branch was opened by the A.H. Heisey Co. as an affiliate of the existing Holophane Lighting Company. The wares made by these were very similar, but the American version was less expensive. Both signed their wares *Verlys* (the French ware had a molded signature; the American ware was diamond point etched). It was not made in the United States after 1957. See *Louvre glassware.*

vermicelli collar See *vermicular.*

vermicular (1) A decorative pattern in the form of innumerable painted lines with tiny curves suggesting the appearance of being eaten by worms or being made by their tracks. It was created at Sevres for use on porcelain during the late 1750s and adapted as enameled or gilt embellishment on Bohemian glassware during the 19th century. (2) A wavy, clear glass thread trailed on a glass object around a collar on a stem, the bottom of a bowl of a glass, or the neck of a bottle or jug.

vermicular collar See *vermicular.*

vermiform collar See *vermicular collar.*

Vermont Glass Factory (Aka *Salisbury Glass Company*) A cylinder glass manufacturing facility established in Salisbury, Vermont, by Epapheas Jones, who was granted a charter by the Vermont State Legislature in 1811. Construction began in 1812; glassmaking began in 1813. Its first superintendent was Henry Rowe Schoolcraft, who left in late 1814 to establish the Keene Glass Works. In 1814 it was leased by Nixon & Cook. In early 1915 it burned and was rebuilt. It closed between 1816 and 1818, laying idle until 1832, when it was renovated by the (Lake) Dunmore Glass Company. In 1842 it closed. The Vermont Glass Factory also had a branch facility making bottles and hollowware in East Middlebury, Connecticut (see *East Middlebury Glass Co.*). It operated under the same ownership as the Salisbury facility from 1813 until it failed about 1817. See *Lake Dunmore Glass Company.*

Vernox An inexpensive line of opalescent glassware developed by Sabino at the onset of the Great Depression to bolster sales and compete with the cheaper wares from others.

Verona glass An art glass with a clear body and an overall decoration made by covering the design with wax and spraying it with hydrofluoric acid, which etches the background, leaving the design untouched when the wax is removed. It was made by the Mt. Washington Glass Co.

verre (French) Originally, any cup from which wine was drunk; presently, any glass.

verre blanc massif *(French)*
Extremely fine crystal.

verre coule (*French*) Plate glass or any large piece of flat slab glass made by pouring molten glass into a form on a flat even surface.

verre de fougere *(French)* Literally, *fern glass*, *forge glass* or *glass of bracken* (depending on the source), also called *chambourin*. A primitive greenish glass made in France after the Roman era, and so named because the alkali in the batch was provided by potash made from burnt bracken (fern). During the same period potash derived from burnt beech wood was used as the alkali for making *Waldglas*, to which it is analogous. It was made in the forest areas where this source of potash was readily available. The Dauphine in southeastern France was such an area, and a large quantity of such glass was made there during the 14th century. The term is used interchangeably with Waldglas. Both were made in forest areas and were similar in composition.

Verre de Jade Literally, *Jade Glass*. A technique developed at Daum Freres for decorating the surface of glass. The object is subjected to the *Vitrification* process (see *Vitrification*) and a layer of clear glass blown over it.

Verre de Soie *(French)* Literally, *silk glass*. (1) (Aka *VDS*, *Flint Iridescent*) An art glass developed by Frederick Carder at Steuben shortly after 1903 and made until 1918. It has a flint glass body with a smooth silky surface, iridized by a stannous chloride spray *at-the-fire* while the glass is nearly molten. It is often camphor colored, but many pieces range in color from camphor to rainbow hued. Its surface has thin radiating lines resulting from the glass expanding when reheated after being sprayed. It is further embellished with trailing, prunts or engraving and, on occasion, a turquoise-colored glass ring applied around the rim. It was used to make many wares, including vases, stemware, cologne bottles, etc. See *Aqua Marine glass*. (2) *Mother-of-Pearl glass* (*pearl satin glass*) made by Stevens & Williams Ltd., England, in 1885/86.

Verre de Tristesse *(French)* Literally, *glass of sadness*. A glass vase made by Emile Galle, from about 1892, to be buried with the dead, even though the practice was not sanctioned by the church. Several of a dark brown/blackish glass embellished with carving are known to exist.

Verre Double *(French)* (1) When in lower case letters, an object with two layers of glass of different colors, usually used in making cameo glass. (2) When in upper case letters, used by Emile Galle to describe his flashed and cased glassware.

verre eglomise *(French)* (1) Glass embellished on the reverse side, usually with a red, blue or black ground, backed with gold or silver metallic foil and cut or engraved in the desired pattern. The process for making it is very old—older than the French mirror and picture frames made by Glomy (d.1786) from whom the name is derived. The glass borders on some mirrors were embellished by this process in the late 17th century and later. (2) A type of *Zwischengold* embellishment used on various jewelry and medallions.

verre frise *(French)* An embellishment consisting of very thin applied glass threads. See *Nevers Figure*.

verre moire *(French)* A threaded glassware made by the Phoenix Glass Co. of Beaver, Pennsylvania. *Venetian Threaded* was the trade name under which it was offered for sale in 1886.

verre pivette *(French)* A heavier glass made in France from the 1750s. The glass was made from soda from Alicante, a seaport on the Mediterranean in southeastern Spain. It replaced the previously used lighter glass used in France prior to this time. The wares were in the English and Bohemian styles.

verre plat *(French)* See *glassware*.

verre triple A glass developed by Emile Galle using three separate layers of glass superimposed to give the enclosed design a sense of depth.

verrerie *(French)* (1) A French term that applies to specific types of glassware and to glassmakers: (a) *grosses verreries* were window glassmakers, and (b) *petites verreries* were makers of hollowware. (2) See *glassware.*

verrerie parlante *(French)* Literally, *speaking* glassware. A glassware made by Emile Galle from 1884. Each piece bore a quotation from a writer of poetry or prose, which was used as inspiration for the form or decoration of that particular piece.

verrier A maker of hollowware as opposed to a *vitrier*, a maker of window glass.

verriere *(French)* See *monteith.*

Verrerie de Sevres Founded during the reign of Louis XV, this glass manufacturing facility was purchased by Landier in 1870. Landier changed the name to Cristellerie de Sevres. He also changed production primarily to cut lead crystal vases. In 1855 Landier took over the Maes & Clemandot facility at Clichy, which had developed a bright crystal made with zinc oxide in the batch and new techniques for engraving on thick-walled glass vessels, specializing in colored crystal. The new company was called United Crystal Works of Sevres & Clichy. In the 1890s it made a wide range of decorative glass, including tortise shell, aventurine and marbled, and colored glass animals and fish. Around 1900 it made items in the Art Nouveau style with floral designs in cameo relief, using hydrofluoric acid on the transparent or opaque colored glass. Vases, bottles, bowls and decanters were made in this style; decanters had floral designs often with floral-shaped stoppers in various colors. It made cameo vases with opaque overlay and silver mounts. Most of the finer wares were signed using one of its several signatures.

Verzelini, Jacopo (Giacomo) (1522-1616) A Venetian glassmaker, who, after being employed as such for twenty years in Antwerp, was brought to England in 1571 by Jean Carre to manage his Crutched Friars Glasshouse. When Carre died in 1572, Verzelini took over. In 1574 he was granted, by Queen Elizabeth I, a monopoly for a period of twenty-one years to make *cristallo* in the Venetian style on the condition he teach his craft to the English. The facility was destroyed by fire in 1575 and rebuilt, thriving for 17 years. His facility was the first in England to use diamond point engraving, making commemorative glasses. He retired in 1592 and, during the remaining years of his monopoly, the facility was operated by Sir Jerome Bowes. After the monopoly expired, its future was contested by Verzelini's sons, Francis and Jacob, who became involved in litigation with Bowes and his assignees and went to prison in 1598.

Verzelini glassware Glass goblets generally attributed to the Crutched Friars Glasshouse of Jacopo Verzelini. There are only nine pieces known to exist. Eight are dated between 1577 and 1586 and are embellished with diamond point engraving (one has additional gilding). The ninth, dated 1590, is embellished only with gilding. The engraving is considered to have been executed by Anthony DeLysle or, in the case of the *Barbara Potters goblet*, by decorators working for Sir Jerome Bowes, who took over the Verzelini monopoly in 1592.

vesica pattern A pointed oval formed by two intersecting curved miters. It is a popular pattern on American cut glass, used as a simple motif.

vesicle A pariason.

Vesta Glass (1) A range of lighting glass, in art deco style, designed by Walter Gilbert and made by John Walsh in the late 1920s. (2) In 1965, Richard Pope left the Corning Glass Works and established Vesta Glass in Corning, New York, making paperweights, carved glass objects (using sand blasting), reproductions of hand-pressed early American glass, stained glass, glass animals, and cut and engraved glass. In 1977 it took over the distribution of a major line of glass Christmas ornaments. It has a showroom called *The Glass Menagerie* in Corning.

Vestalia A trademark used by the Eska Manufacturing Co.

vetri a serpenti *(Italian)* Glassware made with canes of spiral and twisted colored glass.

verti intagliate (*Italian*) Glassware engraved by diamond point.

vetro The Italian term for *glass*. Numerous types of ornamental glass have been made at Murano, especially during the 20th century with locally adapted names and often include the word *vetro*. In addition, the term has been used in conjunction with other descriptive words (usually of Italian origin), which generally describe the object. See *aborigene, vetro; fili, vetro a; ghiaccio, vetro a; pettine, vetro a; piume, vetro a; redexalo, vetro a; redexin, vetro a; reticello, vetro a; retorti, vetro a; retortoli, vetro a; astrale, vetro; barbario, vetro; battute, vetro; bollocine, vetro; composto, vetro; corroso, vetro; Damasco, vetro; diafano, vetro; trina, vetro a; Tiffany vetro di trina; fenici, vetro; filigranato, vetro; gemmata, vetro; graffito, vetro; groviglio, vetro; inciso, vetro; membrano, vetro; milleocchio, vetro; occhio, vetro; parobolico, vetro; pennelato, vetro; pezzato, vetro; pizzo, vetro; pressato, vetro; primavera, vetro; pulegoso, vetro; pulugoso sommerso, vetro; rammurro, vetro; rugiadoso, vetro; scavo, vetro; sidone, vetro; sommerso, vetro; tessuto, vetro; traliccio, vetro.*

Vetter Cut Glass Manufacturing Company See *Sunshine Cut Glass Company.*

vial (Aka *phial*) Originally, any small vessel that held liquids. More recently, a small glass bottle to hold liquids, usually medicines. In Ireland the term designates a scent bottle that is oval and flat with a small glass stopper or screw-on silver cap.

Victoria A trademark used by the W.P. Hitchcock Co.

Victorian Glory Star See *star, wheel engraved; star foot.*

Victory beaker A drinking vessel of Roman mold blown glass with the words "Take the Victory" (in Greek) inscribed on the side.

victory cup A broad cylindrical cup, dating from early Imperial Rome, molded with laurels and inscriptions commemorative of a particular victory. It is the forerunner of the circus bowl.

Vienna Secession Founded in 1897 by several young Viennese painters, sculptors and architects, who rejected the traditional academic "official" art in favor of a more adventurous style inspired by the Art Nouveau movement.

Vienna Workshops See *Wiener Werkstatte.*

vigil light See *fairy lamp.*

Viking Glass See *New Martinsville Glass (Manufacturing) Co.*

vinaigrette (1) A glass cruet to hold vinegar. (2) A small glass bottle to hold smelling salts or scented vinegar, formerly carried by ladies. The contents was used to avoid faintness or eliminate foul odors. They are from 1/4 by 3/4 inches to three by four inches in size. Some were blown or cut with detailed designs or patterns. Some were in the form of animals, watches, etc. Often they had tiny rings attached to one end to hang them from a chatelaine hook or watch chain. They had a cap, underneath which was a grille or pierced cover that fitted in or over the mouth to restrict the flow of the contents. Some had a sponge under the cap to apply scent to the body.

vinegar bottle See *toilet bottle.*

vinegar glass See *carnival glass.*

Grouping of Durand Art Glass, Vineland Flint Glass Works, Vineland, NJ, 1924-1931. Museum of American Glass at Wheaton Village, Millville, NJ.

Vineland Flint Glass Works

A glass manufacturing facility established in 1897 in Vineland, New Jersey, by Victor Durand Jr. (1870-1931), born in Baccarat, France. His father (Victor Sr.) and grandfather had worked at Baccarat, and he worked there briefly before coming to the United States at age 14, joining his father who worked at Whitall-Tatum in Millville, New Jersey. He left home and took jobs at various facilities in West Virginia, Ohio and Pennsylvania, and Canada over the next nine years, returning to New Jersey in 1895. In the same year, he and his father leased the Vineland Glass Manufacturing Co. (established in 1892 to make green glass). Durand converted the furnace to make flint glass and began making lamp chimneys and bottles, expanding to laboratory glass and tubing, changing the name to Vineland Flint Glass Company.

The company merged with Kimble Glass Co. in 1911, only to separate in 1918. About 1915 it began making towel rods and other bathroom fixtures from colored opaque and opal glass. Its specialty was the inner core of vacuum bottles. By 1920, Victor Jr. was the sole owner and it was the largest individually owned glass manufacturing facility in the nation making glass tubing. In 1924, Martin Bach Jr., former owner of the Quezal Art Glass & Decorating Co., and others from his company, which recently closed, came to work at Vineland and began making art glass. Bach was manager of the art glass production, copying much from Quezal's line, made in opaque and transparent glass. Opaque was reserved for vases, rose bowls, perfume atomizers, lamp shades and vases; transparent was reserved primarily for tableware. The opaque art glass wares were expensive to make and required several stages of decoration. It soon began creating new colors and designs. After Durand died in 1931, the company was purchased by the Kimble Glass Co. and art glass was, for the most part, discontinued.

The Vineland Flint Glass Works made many varieties of lustered glassware, including *Ambergris, Spider Webbing, Peacock Feather, King Tut*, etc. Under Bach, it made many lamps with glass shades of various shapes and colors. Originally the lamps were made from "seconds" of vases, using shades left from Quezal's inventory. Because of demand, Durand began making entire lamps, some with hand-painted parchment shades and antiquated metal bases. Globes that looked like bubble paperweights were made as nightlights. Its early wares were unsigned. Signing began after Bach arrived, and the sale of art glass increased dramatically. It was signed *Durand* in script, often with a superimposed "*V*," made with a dental drill. Durand also had a cutting shop supervised by Charles D. Link, who had previously owned a cutting shop with his brother in Bridgeton, New Jersey (see *Aetna Cut Glass Company*).

Vineland Glass Manufacturing Co.

See *Vineland Flint Glass Works*.

Vineland Glass Works Inc.

See *Hofbauer, August V.*

Violin flask, cobalt blue color, "2" on base, 7" h. Davanna Collection

violin flask

A bottle in the shape of a violin, made in the United States during the 19th century. The flask was made of mold-blown glass in a number of sizes and colors (blue, purple, yellow and opaque white), often embellished with emblems and inscriptions.

virgin

See *bed warmer*.

Virginia (Green Glass) Works

(Aka *Virginia Works*) In 1818 or 1820 (depending on the source), George Carothers constructed a glass manufacturing facility to make flint glass wares in Wheeling, Virginia (now West Virginia). The demographics of the area did not warrant its size so, after a short time, he downsized it, converting it to make green bottle glass. Soon thereafter he sold it to Knox & McKee of Pittsburgh, retaining him as superintendent. In 1822 it added (cylinder) window glass; the name changed to the Virginia Green Glass Works. In 1830 Ensell & Plunkett took over operations, making bottles and clear flint glass wares. In 1832, Wheat, Price & Company took over, renaming it the Fairview Glass Works. About 1839 its name was changed to the South Wheeling Glass Works and, in 1845, it was taken over by Hobbs, Barnes & Co. (John L. Hobbs and James B. Barnes, both formerly of the New England Glass Company). In the same year they took over the Excelsior Glass Works of Plunkett & Miller, moving its equipment to the Fairview facility. The sons of these two entered the firm. In 1849, the elder Barnes died and his son died in 1863. In 1864 Charles W. Brockunier, its bookkeeper and office manager, was made a partner, renaming it Hobbs, Brockunier & Company. See *Hobbs, Brockunier & Company.*

Virtues, Twelve Cardinal A decorative allegorical motif depicting the virtues (e.g., *Faith, Hope, Charity, Humility*, etc.), used as an enameled embellishment on German Humpen. Sometimes the opposite motif was used—a motif depicting vices, such as laziness, greed, etc. Such Humpen were made during the 16th and 17th centuries, most likely in Franconia.

viscosity The property of a fluid, or, in this case, glass, that resists the force tending to cause it to flow. It is measured in *poises.*

Vision aids; top: pince-nez (j); bottom: spectacles (i).
Davanna Collection

vision aids Various devices having one or more glass lenses used to assist an individual's vision. They were first made in Italy by Salvino d'Amato, about 1286, and were improved afterward by Allessandro Spina. Their use increased rapidly after the invention of printing in 1436. The lenses were then made mainly in Germany and the Low Countries (the area now within the borders of Belgium, Luxembourg and the Netherlands). They were not imported into England until about the mid-1620s.

Sir Robert Mansell soon realized the market for lenses and began making and exporting them as well as selling them in England to spectacle makers. They were made in many forms and styles, indicative of the different periods of manufacture, including: (a) *nose spectacles* (two lenses, no side arms, and a bridge to rest on the nose); (b) *temple spectacles* (two lenses and tight fitting side arms with attached rings which pressed against the temples); (c) *wig spectacles* (two lenses and long or hinged double-length side arms at the end of which were rings used tying a ribbon at the back of a wig); (d) *quizzer* (single lens on a short frame suspended by a ribbon); (e) *pivoted eye glasses* (two lenses that fold over each other on a frame); (f) *lorgnette* (two lenses that fold alongside, or into, a long ornamental handle); (g) *fan spectacle* (one lens set at the pivot of a lady's fan); (h) *monocle* (single lens held in place by the bones around the eye); (i) *spectacles* (two lenses with a nose bridge and two arms placed over the ears; early ones had straight arms; later ones curved arms that bent around the ears); (j) *pince-nez* (two lenses with no side arms clipped to the nose by a spring); (k) *spy glass* (a short telescopic lens for use with one eye); (l) *opera glass* (two medium-length convex lenses set in an adjustable frame); (m) *bifocals* (spectacles where each glass has two different lenses, for close and distant vision); (n) *trifocals* (spectacles where each glass has three different lenses, for close, intermediate and distant vision); and (o) *contact glass or lens* (single lens with no frame designed for fitting snuggly over the eye ball). Long distance and scientific vision aids include such instruments as binoculars, microscopes and telescopes. See *diminishing lens; magnifying lens; water lens.*

Visscher, Anna Roemers (1583-1651)
A scholar and poet in Amsterdam, and talented amateur decorator of glassware. During the second quarter of the 17th century, she introduced a distinct style of calligraphic (diamond point) engraving with which she embellished beakers and Romers. She also embellished a few pieces with stippling, outlining the design in linear fashion and using stippled dots to produce the impression of light and shade. The inscriptions were accompanied by representations of naturalistic flowers, foliage, fruit and insects copied from contemporary prints. Some pieces are signed. She was the first woman to work in the medium of glass whose name is recorded in documents. Her sister, Marie Tesselschade Roemers Visscher, was also an artist.

Visscher, Marie Tesselschade
Roemers (1594-1649) The younger sister of Anna Roemers Visscher, who embellished glassware with calligraphy.

vitrail See *glassware.*

vitrearii (Latin) The glassmakers and glassblowers of ancient Rome, to be distinguished from the *diatretarii,* who were cutters of glass.

Vitrearius, Laurence
A glassmaker, probably from Normandy, who came to England in 1225 and established a glass manufacturing facility at Dyers Cross, near Chiddingfold, prior to 1240. The surname, *Vitrearius,* means *glassmaker.* He was the supplier of window glass used in King Henry III's Chapel in Westminster Abbey. It is believed that he obtained his colored glass from facilities on the European continent. His son, William le Verrir (which also means *glassmaker*) and possibly his grandson are reported to have continued the business, making window glass, small bottles and flasks. About 1300, either his son or grandson was granted a Royal Charter for the town of Chiddingfold. See *Wealden glassware.*

vitreous (1) Of the nature of or resembling glass, or having properties similar to glass, such as transparency, brittleness, hardness, glossiness, etc. (2) Of or pretaining to glass. (3) Obtained from or containing glass.

vitreous enamel Enamel made from powdered glass and/or materials that will transform into glass when fired.

vitreous silica See *fused silica.*

vitrescent Becoming or tending to become glass, or capable of being formed into glass.

vitri- (Latin) Glass. It is used in the formation of compound words to mean *glass.*

vitric (1) Of or pertaining to glass. (2) Of the nature of or resembling glass.

vitric panel A term used for a sheet of glass.

vitrier A maker of window glass, as opposed to a *verrier,* who is a maker of hollowware.

vitrification The process of changing certain materials into glass or a glassy substance by heat and fusion, such as happens when silica and an alkali are heated to the appropriate temperature.

Vitrification A process for embellishing the surface of glass developed at Daum Freres. In it, a paraison is rolled over powdered colored glass on a marver and reheated until it vitrified on the surface, remaining rough. The surface could then be etched, polished, left rough or treated in another manner to achieve various effects. See *Verre de Jade.*

vitrify To convert to or to be converted into glass.

vitrine (1) A glass or glass fronted cabinet, either free standing or resting on a base; sometimes the sides are also glass. They were used to display any of a variety of small objects and were first made during the mid-18th century. (2) A glass cover for anything.

vitro An alternate spelling of *vetro* found in some literature.

Vitrock Hocking's term and trademark for its white opal glassware not having a glazed overlay.

Vitrolite The trade name of sheets of opal glass in a variety of shades and degrees of translucency.

vitro-porcelain See *cast porcelain.*

Vitruvian scroll (Aka *Greek Wave Pattern*) A classical style of embellishment in the form of a repetitive series of convoluted scrolls, the overall form resembling stylized waves.

Vogelsong Glass Company (1949-1951) A glass manufacturing facility established in Huntington, West Virginia, known for its crackle glass, one of the many types of glass it made.

Vohlsing, Conrad The son-in-law of Martin Bach Sr., who, after Bach's death in 1920, continued to make a Quezal type glass marked *Luster Art Glass* in Elmhurst, New York.

voider A large tray to remove dishes, plates, flatware, etc., and waste and leftover foods from the table.

volcanic glass See *obsidian.*

Volcanic glass See *Lava glass.*

volunteer glass A drinking glass, normally a rummer, engraved with inscriptions inspired by the British and Irish volunteers who served in the war with France in 1793. They were made during the late 18th-early 19th centuries.

volute A spiral or whorl, as often found on Ionic or Corinthian capitals. It was popular with 19th century American glass artists and craftsmen, often ending their scrolling lead lines with a jewel.

von Liebig, J. A German chemist who, about 1840, discovered a method of chemically depositing silver on glass in making mirrors.

von Spaun, Max The manager of the Johann Loetz facility for Loetz's widow from about 1870, purchasing it in 1879. He procured the secrets of making iridescent glass from a former employee of Tiffany. He modified these secrets to suit his purposes. He subsequently obtained a patent in 1898. Von Spaun died in 1909. See *Loetz glassware.*

voyder A large dish or tray.

Vycor A glass with a high silica content, approaching fused silica in some of its properties. It softens at about 1482° C. See *high silica glass; fused silica.*

Ww

wafer dish A small flat dish resting on a stemmed foot, used to hold wafers (small, thin, flat adhesive disks, about the size of a dime, used as a seal on letters).

wafer box A small box to hold wafers. See *wafer dish.*

wafer stamp A small columnar object similar to a letter seal. The end of the shank of a letter seal has an intaglio design while that of a wafer shank is smooth to press down on and secure a glued wafer to seal a letter or document. The shank of the wafer stamp was about one to 3.5 inches long. It was sometimes rectangular and occasionally enclosed a single or double sulfide embedded in a colored ground.

waffle (pontil mark) A pontil mark made by attaching to the pontil a small gather of molten glass with a crisscross pattern impressed upon it prior to it being attached to a paraison. It allows the pontil to be separated from the object more easily because the area of contact is reduced (rather than a large area of contact, the waffle allows contact with several small, separated areas) and remains on the object. They appear on some Steuben glass.

waisted An object, usually a vessel, having a smaller diameter at the middle than at the top or bottom and sides, forming a continuous inward curve. See *waisted bowl.*

waisted bowl A bowl of a drinking glass having sides that are waisted. Variations are *waisted bucket, bell,* and *ogee.*

waiter A salver. See *salver.*

Waldglas (German) (Aka *natural forest glass, green glass*) Literally, *forest glass.* A primitive glass (greenish, yellowish, or brownish) made in facilities in the forests of Germany during the Middle Ages. The alkali ingredient was provided by potash made from the ashes of burnt beech wood and other woods, similar to the bracken used in France during the same period to make potash used in *verre de fougere* (the terms often interchanged because the types of glass were similar). The glassware was thick, robust, and primitive in form, usually mold blown and embellished with prunts and trailing. Its natural coloring was once thought to be the result of crude production methods and lack of skill when compared to the clear glass later developed. However, the color has become popular and fashionable, commercially imitated in modern glass. It survived into the 17th century when supplies of wood began to dwindle.

Waldglashutte (German) A forest glass manufacturing facility such as the ones that existed in central Europe during the early Middle Ages. During this period, they were moved as local wood supplies were exhausted. The term no longer applied once glassmakers settled at a particular site, especially when granted patents or authorization by a local or regional ruler, and alternate fuels, such as coal and peat, became available. The word Hutte (hut) is believed to have been used because of the peaked roof normally found on such temporary facilities. Each year craftsmen, organized into guilds, worked from Easter until St. Martin's Day (November 11), while their families lived in the villages that tended to grow up around them.

walking pigs paperweight See *ducks-on-a-pond paperweight.*

walking stick A glass replica of a walking stick made in a variety of styles and usually about 48 to 55 inches tall (related pieces are in the form of a shepherd's crook). They were sometimes made with an overlay of clear glass encased in a colored inner glass; more often they were hollow. They were made in England during the first half of the 19th century. Some were used in glassmaker guild's processions in the towns of Bristol and Newcastle or hung in the home as an ornament believed to ward off disease or evil spirits They were cleaned daily, and it was a bad omen if it was broken. They are usually attributed to Nailsea and the surrounding area, but some were made in the United States.

Wall & Murphey See *Keystone Cut Glass Company.*

wall pocket (Aka *wall vase*) A flower vase, made in England and the United States, designed to be attached to a wall. They are often called *cornucopia* because most tend to be of that shape.

wall sconce See *sconce.*

wall vase See *wall pocket.*

Wallace & McAfee Co. See *Consolidated Lamp & Glass Company.*

Wallace, Giger & Ensell See *Ensell & Wilson.*

Wallace, Lyon & Co. See *Union Flint Glass Works.*

Wallaceburg Cut Glass Co. A Canadian glass cutting company.

Wallaceburg Works See *Sydenham Glass Company Limited.*

Walsh, David (1885-1927) The operator of a cutting shop connected with the Union Glass Company's facility in Somerville, Massachusetts. Most of his business was wholesale to five stores, including Tiffany's. He had a retail showroom in Somerville.

Walsh Brothers Glassworks (Aka *Janvier Glass Works*) (1897-1910) A glass manufacturing facility founded in Janvier, near Franklinville, New Jersey, by the Walsh brothers who obtained a patent in 1899 for a type of Aventurine glass. It is believed a functioning glass manufacturing facility was operating on this site as early as 1890.

Walter, Emile (1865-1949) Born in Alsace-Lorraine, he learned to cut and engrave glassware at the St. Louis glassworks. In 1902, he came to Corning, New York, employed by Hawkes. In 1904, he began cutting at his home shop in Corning, continuing to work for Hawkes until he retired in 1936. He continued operating his home shop until 1942.

Walzenhumpen *(German)* Literally, *cylinder beaker.* A Humpen embellished with the coat of arms of a member of the nobility.

Wangum Cut Glass Company (Aka *Monoghan Brothers*) A glass cutting company in Hawley, Pennsylvania, operating for a short time during the late 1910s.

Wanhoff, George, & Company See *Iron City (Window) Glass Works; Cookstown Works.*

Wanne *(German)* Literally, *tub.* (Aka *Siemens furnace*) A regenerative tank furnace developed in 1856 by Frederick and Karl Wilhelm Siemens, designed for making steel. In 1860 it was modified for making glass by their brother, Hans, in Dresden. To make glass, the ingredients of the batch were placed in a large tank and, after heating with gas and fusing, the molten glass flowed out where it was later remelted in pots. During the 1870s and 1880s, it was used worldwide for the mass production of flat glass and bottles. It was seldom used to make tableware and luxury glass where smaller quantities were needed.

Wardian case A metal-framed, glass-enclosed container within which house plants were grown. Popular in the mid-19th century, they were named for their creator, Dr. Nathaniel B. Ward (1791-1868), a London doctor and naturalist. An early exponent of cultivating flora under glass, he made his first case in 1838. Today they are called *terraria.*

Ware Collection See *Harvard Glass Flowers.*

warming-in The reheating of pressed items to make the glass workable during the finishing process. The job falls to the carrying-over and warming-in boys. The carrying-over boy takes the glass from the mold with pincers and conveys it to the warming-in boy who, in turn, attaches it to a *snap* and inserts it into the glory hole in the reheating oven where it is heated to 2300°F-2500°F. The warming-in boy must not let it get too hot and begin to melt or the form and molded pattern will be lost; if not heated enough, it will not be pliant. After the item is reheated, he takes it to the finisher, who uses wooden or metal tools to shape, crimp, or flare the article.

warming-in boy An unskilled laborer at a glass manufacturing facility responsible for reheating an object at the glory hole, after the object has been molded or while it's being finished by skilled members.

Warne, Parkinson & Co. A glass manufacturing facility established in 1816 in Williamsport, Pennsylvania. It soon failed and was purchased and rebuilt by Black & McGrew. It was leased to William Ihmsen about 1830.

Warren & Co. See *New London Glass Company.*

Warrick Glass Works See *Temperanceville Glassworks.*

Warsaw Cut Glass Company Oscar Johnson and John Carlson of the Johnson-Carlson Cut Glass Company established the Warsaw Cut Glass Company in Warsaw, Indiana, in 1911. The official name was Johnson-Carlson Cut Glass Company Incorporated. In the early 1920s, it shifted from heavy to light cut wares. It closed in 1930 but reopened in 1933 on a small scale. In 1957 it was sold to, and operated by, Jackson T. and Mildred Dobbins.

Washington Glassworks A glass manufacturing facility established in 1809 in Washington, D.C., operating under several different ownerships until 1852. The company made window glass but was noted for the whimsies and glassware made by employees.

wart beaker See *Warzenbecher (German).*

Warzenbecher (German) Literally, *wart beaker.* (Aka *Kerzenbecher*) A heavy, thick, cylindrical glass vessel shaped like a tumbler with a flat bottom and rounded at the top. The lower two-thirds of the exterior may feature scattered prunts, irregular in shape and size, or diagonal rows of raspberry prunts, above which is often an engraved inscription in German: "*Fill me up and drain*

me / Throw me down / Pick me up / And fill me up again." Because of their durable quality, they are often called *unbreakable glasses.* They were made of German Waldglas during the 16th and 17th centuries.

wash hand glass See *finger bowl.*

Washington City Glass Works See *Washington Glass Works.*

Washington Cut Glass Company A glass cutting shop established in 1914 in Seattle, Washington, by Antone Kusak (see *Kusak Cut Glass Company*) and Edward Zelasky, both from central Europe and formerly employed at the Fostoria Glass Company. In 1916, Kusak left, establishing his own company, while Zelasky continued as sole owner. The company closed in 1955 after Zelasky died. In 1960, Wm. J. Kokesh used the original name for his company (see *Kokesh, Wm. J.*) since he married Zelasky's daughter. Zelasky's son left the company before World War II and opened his own shop (see *Zelasky, Edward, Jr.*).

Washington Glass Works (1) A window glass manufacturing facility established in the District of Columbia by Andrew Way Jr., Jacob Curtis, Horace H. Edwards, and Solomon Stanger (or Stinger) in 1807. In 1809, the operating firm became Edwards, Way & Company. It closed in 1818 but reopened in 1820, operating as the Washington City Glass Works into the early 1840s, being put up for sale in 1843. In addition to window glass, it made a variety of blown wares and did some engraving. (2) (1839-1917) A bottle and hollowware glass manufacturing facility established in Williamstown, New Jersey, by Joel Bodine & Sons. In 1856, it purchased the idle Freewill Glass Manufactory across the road, combining operations. In 1864, Walter R. Thomas entered the firm, which then became Bodine, Thomas & Co. In 1866, it incorporated as the Williamstown Glass Manufacturing Co. See *Freewill Glass Manufactory.*

wasp catcher See *fly trap.*

wassail bowl A large, deep, two-handled vessel traditionally passed counterclockwise by partyers sharing a drink.

waste bowl A bowl, usually larger than a finger bowl, included with some water sets. It was used to discard water left in the glass before being refilled. See *shaving paper vase.*

waste mold A mold designed to be used only once and destroyed after a single use.

waster Glassware, defective in manufacture or *out-of-fashion*, that is unsalable. It was discarded in an area called a *waster heap*. There are fewer glass wasters than ceramic because the majority was reused as cullet. When found on the site of a glass manufacturing facility, wasters are quite valuable and often are conclusive evidence for identification and dating of wares made there. It is important to be cautious when dealing with wasters because cullet was often brought in from other facilities. See *documentary specimen; fragment.*

waster heap See *waster.*

watch glass (1) The glass covering a watch dial, first used about 1630. Prior to this, watch dials were uncovered or the entire watch was enclosed in a case of rock crystal. From about 1630 to 1700, rock crystal, as well as glass, was used as a cover. The earliest samples were dome-shaped or formed from sections cut from blown-glass spheres. (2) A *half-hour glass.* See *half-hour glass.*

water craft or croft See *carafe.*

water glass (1) A drinking glass of cylindrical form with an expanded foot, made from about 1680 to 1770. The term was applied in England during the 18th century to a glass different from a tumbler (a tumbler was considered to be a glass with sides slanting slightly inward to the base). (2) Formerly, a finger bowl. (3) (soluble glass) Silicate of sodium solution. A glassy substance containing a high content of soda, sometimes made unintentionally when molten glass contained too much silica, becoming thick and viscous, and more soda was added in an effort to remedy it. It can be dissolved in water as a viscous, syrupy fluid used for fireproofing, as an adhesive for paper in making corrugated paper boxes, as a sealant (for preserving eggs), etc. See *alkali silicates.* (4) A glass tube used to indicate water level. (5) A glass container for holding water for growing bulbs, plants, etc. (6) A device used to observe objects beneath the surface of water, generally an open tube or box with a glass bottom. (7) A method of measuring time, similar to an hour or sand glass, except water was the medium used instead of sand. See *clepsydra.*

water jug (1) A jug with a globular body, flaring neck, lipped rim, and loop handle opposite the pouring lip. (2) A jug made as part of a water set.

water lamp A lamp in the form of a large ovoid glass vase, with a flat base and constricted neck widening into an everted mouth, serving as a vase and lamp base. It was converted into a lamp by filling the vase with water and inserting into its mouth an electric fixture and shade mounted on an insulated metal unit. The water enhances the optical effect (as with a water lens) and provides greater stability. Some were designed by Frederick Carder at Steuben during the 1920s.

water lens (Aka *condenser lens*) A globular receptacle often with a vertical neck and spreading base. When filled with water, it was used as a condensing lens, concentrating light from a nearby source, such as a candle or oil lamp. They were used by lace makers, engravers, and others needing good light for close work. Sometimes several were placed around a single light source to accommodate several workers. They are sometimes erroneously called a *lace maker's lamp.*

water pot A small Chinese pot for holding water into which ink in solid form (powder or pulverized) was dissolved, then used for writing or painting. Some were made of glass during the reign of Ch'ien Lung (1736-95). These were embellished with enameling.

water set A set of vessels for serving drinking water, normally consisting of a large jug or pitcher and one to 12 goblets or tumblers, and sometimes a tray and waste bowl. All pieces are decorated *en suite.* Cut and engraved pitchers, jugs, goblets, and tumblers were made at many facilities, most with classic patterns and in classic designs; many had frosted surfaces or floral engravings. The lily pad pitcher continued to be made in South Jersey well into the second half of the

19th century. Many pitchers have a stemmed foot and are embellished with threading around the rim.

Waterford drop A unique oval-shaped drop made by the Waterford Glass Company.

Waterford Glass Company See *Waterford Glass Works.*

Waterford Glass House; Waterford Glass Ltd. See *Waterford glassware.*

Waterford Glass Works The glass manufacturing facility and village in Waterford, New Jersey, were established by Jonathan Haines about 1822. Haines was associated with the Clementon Glass Works, also known as the Gloucester Glass Works, leaving it to join with William Coffin Sr. to create the Hammonton Glass Works. In 1828, he died at age 37 and the facility was purchased by Shreve, Evans & Roberts. Later its operator was Porter, Shreve & Co. and still later Porter & Sons. John Porter paid his workers higher than average wages and closed his operations on Sundays (see *Waterford wages*). After his death, it operated for about a year and closed in 1862. In 1863 it was sold to Maurice Raleigh, closing during the Civil War. Prior to closing, it made window glass, hollowware, tableware, and bottles. In 1870, several molds were sold at sheriff's sale to R.H. Tice for use by his son, C.B., operator of the Isabelle Glass Works. In the same year, it was reopened as three separate and distinct operations under a single management, the DeWitt-Gayne Glass Works and later by Gaines Pardessus & Co., making lamp shades and stained glass. In 1874, Maurice Raleigh and John Gaynor operated it as the Waterford Glass Company. See *Gaynor Glass Works.*

Waterford pitcher, ribbed applied handle, 10-1/2" h.
Krause Publications

Waterford glassware Glass made at Waterford, Ireland, commencing in 1729. It was not until 1783 that activities became significantly important. In England, the Glass Excise Act of 1745 taxed flint glass by weight, tending to discourage making heavy glass items. In 1780, the Irish glass industry was allowed complete freedom to export its wares. In 1783, George and William Penrose established the Waterford Glass House, employing John Hill, a Stourbridge glassmaker, as manager. In 1786 Hill left, and Jonathan Gatchell, his protégé, succeeded him, becoming a partner in 1799 when the Penroses retired. Gatchell managed it until his death in 1823 and was succeeded by George Gatchell, who managed it until 1851 when it closed due to the newly imposed Irish tax on glass.

This was the only glass manufacturing facility in Waterford during this period, and its products account for the fame of the Waterford name. The wide variety of wares made there were, in general, heavy, deeply cut, and clear in color (no blue tint), free from striae, specks, and other blemishes. The only styles cut between 1783 and 1851 were prismatic cuttings with graceful swags, multi-ray stars, and sharp medium and tiny diamonds in wide and single bands. Unless there is a stamped seal indicating the maker's name, identification is difficult. No so-called *Waterford chandelier* has ever been validated as a product of the facility. A few decanters marked on the bottom *Penrose Waterford* were quite possibly made there before 1799. They have three neck rings, a wide pouring lip, an ovoid body and bases usually encircled with molded combed fluting. In 1951 a new company, Waterford Glass Ltd., was established. Its modern facility makes excellent wares and has a worldwide export business in its cut glass.

Waterford wages A standard of pay established during the 1850s by John Porter of the Waterford Glass Works, which was higher than the norm. Traditionally, glassworkers were underpaid, considering the conditions and hazards under which they worked. Porter upped the wages of his employees and soon other glasshouses had to follow suit. He was the first employer to close his facility on Sunday by making process innovations, allowing for such closing. This too became an industry standard.

Waterloo Glass House See *Cork glassware.*

Watson, Benjamin R. (1880-1942) Born in Birmingham, England, Watson came to the United States with his father in 1884. (Watson's father, Joseph, worked for Hawkes in Corning, New York.) He learned the art of cutting glass at Hawkes, where he worked the rest of his life. He also operated a cutting shop at his home in Corning, beginning in the early 1920s, cutting primarily floral and geometric designs. During the Depression when Hawkes' employees worked part-time, he engraved used liquor bottles to which he added stoppers, selling them for $1 apiece. He continued operating the shop until shortly before his death.

Watteau subjects Pastoral scenes taken from, or inspired by, French engravings of paintings by Antoine Watteau (1684-1721), used as enameled embellishment on glassware, particularly on opaque white glass during the Rococo period.

Waugh, Sidney B. (1904-1963) An American sculptor who was appointed by Arthur A. Houghton Jr. in 1933, as first designer at Steuben. He graduated from Amherst College before studying architecture at Massachusetts Institute of Technology. He became fascinated with glass after visiting Orrefors in Sweden in 1930. From 1929 to 1932, he worked as a Fellow in Sculpture at the American Academy in Rome. His agreement with Steuben required him to work one-third of his time at the company; the remainder of the time he was free to do his own sculpting. He specialized in designing forms for molded and cut-glass pieces and making designs for engraved pieces. Some of the most famous works he designed were: the *Mariner's Bowl*; *Europa Bowl*; *Zodiac Bowl* (all three completed in 1935); *Gazelle Bowl*; *Narcissus Vase*; *Atlantica*; *Wine, Women & Song Bowl* (1939); *American Ballad Series* (1943);

Merry-Go-Round Bowl (1947); and the *Americana Series* (1948-1959).

wave pattern, Greek See *Vitruvian scroll.*

Wavecrest satin glass saltshaker, Erie Twist pattern, hand-painted floral decoration, signed "C.F. Monroe Co." Krause Publications

Wavecrest ware A ware, suggestive of *Crown Milano*, made by the C.F. Monroe Company, on blanks purchased from others. All pieces were formed from opaque white glass and blown in full-size molds, then painted in pastel colors and embellished with flowers at the Monroe facility. Production began during the late 1890s and the wares were made until Monroe closed in 1916. After 1898, the name *Wavecrest* was used; items were marked *Wavecrest* and included the company's initials. Two of its other marks were *Kelva* and *Nakara*.

Way Brothers Glass House (1806-1835) A cylinder glass manufacturing facility established in Washington, D.C., by the Way Brothers with the aid of financial supporters. By 1809, the Way Brothers had become the sole owners.

Wayne County Glass Works A glass manufacturing facility established by Christian Dorflinger on the east side of the Lackawaxen River, paralleling the Delaware & Hudson Canal connecting Honesdale and Hawley, Pennsylvania. The site was selected for its cheap supply of coal and nearness to good transportation. From 1865 to 1867, it made commercial glass and blanks for cutting and engraving. A cutting shop was added in 1867. All operations expanded rapidly. It eventually became part of C. Dorflinger & Sons. In 1874 it made a large service of glassware for President & Mrs.

Grant for their daughter's wedding. See *Dorflinger, C., & Sons.*

Wayne Cut Glass Company A glass cutting company established in 1904, incorporated on January 1, 1905, in Honesdale, Pennsylvania. In the summer of 1910 it opened a second site in Towanda, Pennsylvania. Both facilities closed about 1919.

Wealden glassware Glassware made in England near Chiddingfold (in the Weald of Kent, Surrey and Sussex) by glassmakers who emigrated from France from the 13th through the 15th centuries, settling in this wooded region. They were soon joined by some English craftsmen, and about 1567, by other glassmakers from Lorraine, France, who came with Jean Carre. From 1580, they began dispersing to Hampshire and western England, and then to Stourbridge, Newcastle-upon-Tyne, and to other parts of England. Their glass was similar to the late Roman glass. At first it was light green, then later a darker green, much like Waldglas. The wares were mold blown and embellished with trailing, some were wrythen. When the Proclamation of 1615 prohibited the use of wood as fuel for industrial purposes, the Wealden glass industry ceased.

wear marks Tiny, normally nearly invisible markings on the base or foot of a plate, vase, bowl, drinking glass, etc., indicating normal wear occurring over the years. They are most often scratches running randomly in all directions. They can be made artificially to deceive a buyer into believing the item is old. This is done by rubbing the item over a rough surface or with an abrasive. These tend to give themselves away by being too regular, evenly spaced, and running in one direction. On the other hand, glassware used for ceremonial or religious purposes may have been kept in a cabinet or special container most of its life and would show few signs of wear, even if genuinely old. Examination by loupe is an excellent method of determining wear. See *bruise.*

weatherglass See *barometer.*

weathering Chemical changes on the surface of glass caused by exposure to adverse conditions of the atmosphere or soil; water leaching alkali from the glass, leaving siliceous products that appear as dulling, iridescence, frosting, scaling, or decomposition. Weathering is distinguished from crisselling.

Webb, Corbett, Ltd. The owner of glass manufacturing facilities making high-quality household and ornamental wares. Its original facility was the White House Glassworks at Wordsley, near Stourbridge, England, conveyed by W.H., B. & J. Richardson in 1897 to Thomas Webb & Corbitt Ltd., which changed its name, in the 1930s, to Webb, Corbett, Ltd. The original facility burned in 1913 and its operations moved to a new one at Coalbournhill, near Stourbridge. In 1906, it took over the operations of another facility at Tutbury, Staffordshire. In 1969 it became a unit of the Royal Doulton Group.

Webb, Joseph (1852-1905) Born in England, he came to the United States about 1883 with his younger brother, Hugh Fitzroy Webb (1855-1939). They were sons of Joseph Webb (1813-1869), a British glass maker and cousin of Thomas Webb. After coming to the United States, Joseph was employed at the Phoenix Glass Company from 1883 to 1893 as superintendent; then at Libbey for a short period, in charge of its exhibit at the World's Fair of 1893. In early 1894, he went to work for Dithridge's Fort Pitt Glass Works, and then for Tarentum Glass. By late 1900, Joseph and Hugh had established their own company, Webb Decorative Glass Company, in Coudersport, Pennsylvania. It was short-lived and Joseph started work at New Martinsville Glass in December 1901, replacing Mark Douglass (who moved to the Cooperative Flint Glass). Within two months of starting there, it placed the *Muranese* line on the market. He left New Martinsville in 1904 and took a position at the Haskins Glass Company. From there he went to Byesville Glass, where he was the general manager, a position he held until his death.

Webb, Thomas, & Sons vase, bulbous lobes, diamond-quilted pattern, satin body with mother-of-pearl interior, shaded blue ground, 5-7/8" h.
Krause Publications

Webb, Thomas, & Sons

A glass manufacturing facility near Stourbridge, England, making high-quality household and ornamental glassware. Its establishment began when John Webb (1774-1835) became affiliated with the White House Glassworks in the early 1830s. In 1835, Thomas Webb I (1804-69) inherited it and, to devote full attention to its operations, withdrew in 1836 from Webb & Richardson, which operated the Wordsley Flint Glassworks. Soon thereafter he withdrew from Thomas Webb & Co., which operated the White House Glassworks, to form Thomas Webb & Sons. This company began operating the Platts Glasshouse in 1837, continuing until 1856 (Platts Glasshouse had been making glass at Amblecote, near Stourbridge, for over 100 years). In 1856, Thomas Webb & Sons opened a new facility at Dennis Hall, the Dennis Glassworks. When Thomas Webb I retired in 1863, he was succeeded by his sons, Thomas Wilkes Webb and Charles Webb, who were joined in 1869 by another son, Walter Wilkes Webb. In 1919, the Dennis Glassworks was purchased by Webb's Crystal Glass Co. Ltd. This, together with Thomas Webb & Sons (no longer having a member of the Webb family in the firm), became, in 1964, a part of Crown House Ltd. Thomas Webb & Sons had acquired a license in 1886 to make Burmese Glass, and began making cameo glass, known as *Webb's cameo glass*. It also made, during the 1880s, *Alexandrite, Peachblow, Iridescent Glass*, satin glass, and numerous other types of art glass.

Webb Art Glass

See *Phoenix Glass Company.*

Webb Decorative Glass Works

See *Webb, Joseph.*

Webb glass

Glassware made by Thomas Webb & Sons at Stourbridge, England. During the Victorian Era, this company made many types of art and cameo glass, all considered Webb glass.

Webb's Bronze Glass

A glassware made by Thomas Webb & Sons, similar to Webb's Iridescent Glass, except it is heavier, has a rough pontil mark and a mold embellished surface. It has the same color as the Iridescent Glass.

Webb's Crystal Glass Co. Ltd.

A company established in 1919 to take over the operations of the Dennis Glassworks from Thomas Webb & Sons. Soon thereafter it acquired the Edinburgh & Leith Glass Co. The facility at Norton Park was closed in 1974 when operations were moved to Peniciuk. In the 1930s, it acquired the Wordsley Flint Glassworks. These facilities were acquired in 1964, along with the Dema Glass Co., Chesterfield, by Crown House Ltd.

Webb's Iridescent Glass

An iridescent glassware made by Thomas Webb & Sons, similar to Webb's Bronze Glass, except it is lighter, has a ground pontil mark, and rarely a mold embellished surface. Both lines were made in the same color.

Webster & Briggman

A glass cutting company established about 1910 in Waterbury-Naugatuck, Connecticut, moving to Meriden, Connecticut, in 1917. It closed in 1923.

wedding cup

A large standing cup or bowl made and embellished to commemorate a marriage. Venetian ones, dating from the 15th century, often have portraits of the couple, embellished with an encircling procession or allegorical scenes, all enameled. They are usually in the form of a bowl, about 4-3/4 to 6-1/3 inches high with a slightly everted rim and resting on a tall, hollow spreading foot. They were generally of transparent blue or green, or opaque white glass.

wedding glass

See *marriage glass; wedding cup.*

wedding lamp See *marriage lamp.*

Wedgwood glassware Cut glass wares made by two subsidiaries of Josiah Wedgwood & Sons Ltd.: (a) Wedgwood Glass, King's Lynn, Norfolk, England, which acquired, in 1969, the King's Lynn Glass Ltd., established in 1967; and (b) Galway Crystal, Galway, Ireland, established in 1967 and acquired in 1974. The wares made include drinking glasses, decanters and ornamental objects of full-lead crystal glass (clear and colored), solid glass zoomorphics (ascribing to animal forms or attributes to beings or things not animal), and fruit paperweights.

Weeks & Gilson See *South Stoddard Glass Company.*

weeping A condition of glassware where the surface attracts moisture mainly because of a high alkaline content in the glass.

weight See *paperweight.*

welcome (beaker) See *Willkomm(humpen).*

welded rim See *folded rim.*

well (1) The depressed central portion of a plate or dish within the ledge or *marli.* (2) A container designed to hold a fluid, such as ink (inkwell).

Well Spring Carafe A carafe of ovoid form resting on an extended base with a high neck and undulating mouth. It is of clear glass, with thin, green enameled leaves surrounding the body, extending upward from the base, with a circle of flowers around the shoulder. It was designed by Richard Redgrave (1804-1888) for Henry Cole's Summerly's Art Manufacturers and was made by John Fell Christy at the Stangate Glass Works in Lambeth, London, in 1847.

Wells, E.L., & Company See *Green Bank Glasshouse.*

Wells, Henry & Co. See *Rockville Factory.*

Wellsboro Glass Co. A facility in Corning, New York, making cut glass using inexpensive blanks in 1916 and 1917. It was originally in Wellsboro, Pennsylvania, but little is known of its history at that location.

Wellsburg Glassworks (1815-1854) A glass manufacturing facility established about 1815 in Wellsburg, Virginia, maker of tableware.

welt A small strip of glass at the edge of a folded foot (often on stemmed drinking glasses), usually turned under, but sometimes turned over. Its purpose is to strengthen the foot, reducing the risk of chipping.

welted foot See *folded foot.*

went flinty When milk white glass turned to a delicate opalescent (a shading somewhere between opal and crystal) without deliberate action and through no fault of the glassmaker, it was because the body of the glass burned out, or *went flinty,* causing it to revert, more or less, to its crystal or clear stage.

Wescoat, William See *New Columbia Glass Works.*

West, George R., & Sons See *West Brothers.*

West Brothers (Aka *George R. West & Sons*) (1921-1929) A glass manufacturing facility established in Jeanette, Pennsylvania, by George West and his two sons (Charles & George Jr.), making candy and mustard containers. It closed when George died. See *Specialty Glass; Westmoreland (Specialty) Glass Company.* It was located near the Westmoreland Specialty Glass Company, which George managed with his brother Charles. George sold his interest to Charles after management disagreements.

West Side Glass Manufacturing Company (1879-1885) A glass manufacturing facility established near Bridgeton, New Jersey, by Benjamin Lupton and several partners who were experienced glassmakers. It made Mason jars, ink bottles, and other containers. It also made large amounts of a black pressed glass called *Ferroline,* created by Enrico Rosenzi, who claimed it was as indestructible as iron. In 1885, the facility burned and never rebuilt.

West Virginia Glass Company See *Elson Glass Co.*

West Virginia Glass Manufacturing Company See *Elson Glass Co.*

West Virginia Glass Specialty Company Located in Weston, West Virginia, it is currently operating, making stemware of various types and other wares with fired-on ceramic decorations.

Western Cut Glass Company About 1914, Herman and Frank Kotwitz organized the Western Cut Glass Company, Chicago, Illinois (formerly the United States Cut Glass Company), making heavy and light cut wares, much of its products sold to the Marshall Field & Co. retail chain in Chicago. It closed in 1918. Herman was affiliated with Monarch Cut Glass Company and the United States Cut Glass Company.

Western Flint & Lime Glass Protective Association See *American Flint & Lime Glass Manufacturers.*

Western Glass Company (1904-1905) A glass manufacturing facility, operating out of the old Boston & Sandwich facility.

Westford Glass Company (1857-1873) A glass manufacturing facility in Westford, Connecticut, making mainly bottles, from small ink bottles to five-gallon demijohns, flasks, and some offhand wares such as candleholders, rolling pins, and preserve jars. In 1865, it declared bankruptcy, reorganizing as the E.A. Buck & Company, making only bottles.

Westite Glass with a marble-like appearance used mainly for bathroom fixtures. It was made by the Brilliant Glass Company in West Virginia during the 1920s and 1930s.

Westite Glass Company See *Brilliant Glass Company.*

Westlake Ruby Glass Works A glass manufacturing facility established in 1887 in Columbus, Ohio, by Milton W. Westlake, originally named the Milton W. Westlake Glass Works. It made clear glass and flashed ruby glass articles in old patterns as well as

some engraved glass. Its wares are marked with paper labels.

Westmoreland milk glass bowl, 9" d., Line 1881 Paneled Grape pattern, molded signature: "W" under "G."
Davanna Collection

Westmoreland Glass Company covered dish, c. 1960-1963, opaque white glass.
The Corning Museum of Glass

Westmoreland Glass ad, February 1962. Krause Publications

Westmoreland (Specialty) (Glass) Company The Westmoreland Specialty Glass Company was founded in 1889, in Grapeville (later Jeanette), Westmoreland County, Pennsylvania. Charles Howard West and George Robinson West purchased 53 percent of the stock in Specialty Glass (recently built near a railroad and gas well, but never operated) for $40,000. The rest was purchased by George M. Irwin. In January 1891, Irwin withdrew, having served as president since its creation. George became president and Charles became secretary/treasurer. In late 1889, production of glass began.

In 1921, George became dissatisfied with the direction the company was taking. He sold his interest to Charles, left and formed West Brothers (see *West Brothers*) with his two sons. In 1925, it changed its name to the Westmoreland Glass Company, making handcrafted, high-quality glassware. Several reorganizations took place over the years. In the early years, it also made condiments to fill many of the containers it made, such as candy jars. It also made cut glass, the largest producer in the United States during the 1920s and 1930s; engraved and etched glass; cut colored and stained glass; milk glass, considered the best in the world; and carnival glass.

In the early 1930s it made much colored ware, going back to clear glass about 1935. In the 1940s through the 1960s, it produced black, ruby, and amber glass. Among its other products were cased glass, enameled ware, crackled glass, gold and silver decorated glass, opaque glass, and many specialty glasses. In May 1982 it closed, reopening in July. It closed for the last time on January 8, 1984.

Its molds were sold to other companies, such as Dalzell/Viking Glass Co.; Russo Wholesale Glass Dealers; Summit Art Glass; Plum Glass; Treasured Editions Limited; and Fenton Glass. Westmoreland's trademark was a keystone with a "W" inside (*Keystone W*, since 1910); a keystone with the overlaid initials "W G Co" inside; and later, beginning in 1949/1950, a "W" or "WG" without the keystone. These were stamped on a limited number of lines or wares. Paper labels were used on many of its wares. See *Specialty Glass.*

Westphalia Treaty Humpen A
Humpen embellished with enameling to commemorate the Peace of Westphalia in 1649, depicting the Holy Roman Emperor joining the hands of the King of France and Queen of Sweden, surrounded by members of the clergy and laymen, all below a stellar cluster. It also bears inscribed biblical quotations and a prayer of thanks. The scene is based on an engraving by Mathaus Rembold, executed in Ulm about 1648. It has a domed cover with a high finial. It was made in Franconia between 1649 and 1655.

Westville Flint Glass Works A glass
manufacturing facility established in 1865 in Camden, New Jersey, by J.B. Capewell & Company with James G. Capewell as manager. It specialized in lamp chimneys but made other wares, including casters for which J.B. received a patent in 1864.

wetter-off The worker, as part of a chair
or team, responsible for detaching a blown object from the blowpipe. This is accomplished by moistening a piece of iron and touching it to the object near the blowpipe and tapping the glass with the iron near that point.

wetting off See *cracking off.*

Wetzel, Robert, Glass Company A
glass manufacturing facility established by Robert Wetzel in 1975 in Zanesville, Ohio, making handcrafted glass items, each marked with an "RW."

Weyburn, E.D. A glass manufacturer and
dealer in Pittsburgh, Pennsylvania, during the 1870s, which made only a token amount of the wide variety of products it dealt in, buying the bulk from other manufacturers and decorators. In 1878, Weyburn patented a stopper designed to fit any bottle.

Whale oil lamp, 9" h.
Davanna Collection

whale oil lamp An oil lamp using whale or sperm oil as fuel. It is tall with a large font resting on a base or pedestal and topped by a *burner* of tin or cork, sitting in an orifice atop the font and fitted with a tin cap through which the wick passed into the font. Above the *burner* was mounted a glass shade to protect the flame. The shade was sometimes ornamental and embellished with a decorative pattern. See *lamp*.

Whaling City Glass Company See *Gunderson (-Pairpoint) Glass Works*.

Wheat, Price & Co. See *Virginia Green Glass Works*.

Wheaton, T.C., (&) Company See *Wheaton Industries*.

Left: Cory filter rod, U.S. patent 1927287. Right: Wheaton bottle, marked on bottom "M.B.W. – Millville." Side: Holling & Smith Co. Manufacturing Chemists, Orangeburg, New York, USA. Davanna Collection

Wheaton Industries In 1883, Dr. Theodore Corson Wheaton (b.1852), both a pharmacist who received his degree in pharmacology in 1876 and a physician who received his M.D. from the University of Pennsylvania in 1879, moved to Millville, New Jersey, where he practiced medicine and opened a pharmacy and general store. In 1888 he purchased an interest in, and later acquired, the Shull-Goodwin Glass Company in Millville and began making bottles and glass tubing. In 1926 he purchased the Millville Bottle Works. He did not begin to install automated machinery until 1938, maintaining a "hand" shop to make specialty electronics and laboratory ware. In 1888 it

was renamed T.C. Wheaton & Company. In 1901 it was incorporated as the T.C. Wheaton Company which, in 1966, became Wheaton Glass Company and now Wheaton Industries.

The company initially made pharmaceutical bottles and scientific ware, which it has continued to make throughout its history. It also made numerous other items such as flasks, and specialty glass objects such as paperweights. Commemorative bottles, flasks, and decanters were introduced in 1967.

The initial bottle of its presidential series, with John F. Kennedy's likeness, was the first to appear on a canteen-type flask. Is production was suspended in 1974. From 1975 to 1982, the Wheaton Historical Association resumed the Presidential and Christmas series (two of several series previously made that included Great Americans, Movie Stars, Political Campaigns, and Space), making only 5,000 each by hand on a semi-manual bottle machine. From 1982, they have been made by the Millville Art Glass Company under a licensing arrangement.

Wheaton Village An 88-acre park in Millville, New Jersey, featuring an 1880s village. Its primary theme is the history of American glassmaking. Within the village is a 20,000-square-foot museum where more than 7,000 glass objects are displayed. In the village are craftsmen of all types, but the emphasis is on glass. Glassmakers demonstrate old techniques for making various types of glass objects, such as pitchers, bottles, paperweights, vases, plates, etc. Exhibits trace American glassmaking history from the first glassworks in the colonies to the automated glassworks of today. One exhibit shows a cutaway model of T.C. Wheaton's glasshouse as it appeared in 1893.

wheel engraved star See *star, wheel engraved*.

wheel engraving The process of embellishing the surface of glass with pictorial decorations, formal decorations, and/or inscriptions by the grinding action of a rotating wheel, using abrasive disks of various materials and sizes. These discs or wheels are continually wetted with a lubricated abrasive during use. The wetting agent, usually pumice in grease, is applied to the wheel as the engraver holds the object against the underside or behind it. The process was developed from the use of the lapidary's wheel to grind precious stones and cameos. The technique used is similar to that used for cutting glass but involves more skillful and artistic workmanship. After the glass is engraved, it is usually polished with cork wheels or acid. Some areas are, or the entire article is, often left unpolished. The art of engraving was used in Egypt, Syria, Persia, and medieval Rome.

The modern use of wheel engraving for embellishing glass was developed by Casper Lehman(n) at Prague about 1600. Engraved wares became popular after the thin Venetian glass, unsuitable for relief engraving, was replaced mainly by the thicker, more durable Bohemian potash lime glass and English flint glass.

Intaglio Wheel Engraving. The technique of embellishing the surface of glass in intaglio by wheel engraving where the wheel incises and carves the design below the surface; also called *Tiefschnitt. Relief Wheel Engraving.* The technique of embellishing the surface of glass in relief by wheel engraving. The ground is cut away, leaving a raised design in the manner of cameo relief. The result is polished, partially polished, or left mat; also called *cameo relief, carving,* or *Hochschnitt. Surface Wheel Engraving.* The technique of embellishing glass by wheel engraving, but only to a very shallow depth, just slightly below the surface. Examples include inscriptions and some usually sketchy ornamental designs.

Wheeler, S. & Q. See *Twichell & Schoolcraft.*

Wheeler & Davis See *Davis, Greathead & Green.*

Wheeling Drape A piece of glassware in *Peachblow* made by Hobbs, Brockunier & Co., having a molded drape pattern on the inner layer.

Wheeling Flint Glass Works See *Ritchie Glass Company.*

Wheeling Peachblow This glass is often called the *original Peachblow*, created by Hobbs, Brockunier & Co., Wheeling, West Virginia, shortly after 1883. It was designed to simulate the coloring of the original Morgan (Peachblow) Vase, which sold for $18,000 in the late 1800s. It is a cased glass made by plating a gold ruby glass over an opaque white base. The technique is similar to that used in making Amberina. It shades from a vivid rose red at the top to a bright deep yellow at the base. All objects have a white lining and either a satin or gloss finish. The rare vases, with either a satin or gloss finish, on a gargoyle stand are priceless. It is often confused with plated Amberina; however, it is never ribbed and its lining is opaque white.

Wheelock, C.E., & Company Located in Peoria, Illinois, a wholesale and retail distributor of china, glass, and pottery. In the 1890s, it was an agent for Libbey's cut glass. In May 1915 it was issued a trademark: a representation of a padlock on which its name and the legend *Radiant Crystal-Rich Cut Glass Since 1898* were shown. Paper labels with this trademark were pasted on each piece of cut glass sold since August 1, 1898.

Wheelock companies The following Wheelock companies were distributors and agents for Libbey Glass Company: (a) C.E. Wheelock & Company, Peoria, Illinois; (b) George H. Wheelock & Company, Elkhart & Wheelock, South Bend, Indiana; (c) W.G. Wheelock, Janesville, Wisconsin; and (d) A.W. Wheelock, Rockville, Illinois.

wherry cup A large cup or glass used for drinking *wherry*, an alcoholic beverage made from the pulp of crab apples after the juice has been pressed from them.

whiffing cup A brandy snifter. See *brandy glass.*

whigmeleeries The Scottish term for a *frigger*. See *frigger.*

whimsies These are not production items but novelty items made mainly during the Victorian era by workers at glass manufacturing facilities as a special gift for family and friends. They were made from the part of the

batch left over at the end of the day. They were usually miniature, free-blown or blown-in-the-mold objects, normally serving no practical purpose, except to please the maker and/or delight the receiver.

whipped cream bowl A small bowl six to seven inches in diameter and about 2-1/2 inches deep, used to hold whipped cream. They were sometimes considered small berry bowls.

whips See *syllabub glass.*

whipt-syllabub See *syllabub glass.*

whisky decanter (Aka *square, case bottle*) A decanter for serving whisky, originally of square section, introduced in England during the second half of the 18th century. They are often of elaborate cut glass and made in many facilities in the United States, England, and elsewhere. Some are engraved with the name of the distillery. The shape was convenient for keeping a set of three or four in a fitted box which, on occasion, also contained glasses *en suite*. In the 1950s, many whisky makers in the United States began bottling their product in inexpensive decanters of square, round, oval, and rectangular cross section during the Christmas holiday season. Also see *Tantalus decanter.*

whisky glass (Aka *pony, shot glass*) A small drinking glass without a stem, in the form of a small tumbler having a capacity usually from one to three ounces (though one to one and one-half ounce sizes are most common). They are intended for drinking neat (straight) whisky or as a measurer for whisky when preparing a mixed drink.

whisky sample glasses Little shot glasses carried by salesmen during the late 1800s-early 1900s to impress customers. They were promotional or advertising pieces, often with an advertisement of the whiskey on the side, used to give free samples. Sometimes businesses used them for advertising, which was usually a message or a logo etched into the glass or painted with white enamel.

whisky set A decanter, matching small tumblers or whisky glasses, and often a matching tray.

whisky taster A very small tumbler, so small it was doubtful it ever held alcohol. It was probably a toy, salesmen's sample, or even a communion glass. Its exact function is not known.

whisky tot A small, conical decanter-type receptacle for serving a dram of whisky (some are double size). It is either plain or engraved with a silver lid with thumb rest. They were made during the early 20th century by John Grinsell & Sons Ltd. of Birmingham. The mount was made by Barker Elis Silver Co. Ltd., also of Birmingham, England.

whistle goblet A goblet having attached to it a glass whistle, metal whistle, or dragon-shaped whistle, used to summon a waiter or waitress when a refill was desired. Some were so cleverly made they had a dial that registered the number of times it was blown (or the goblet filled). They were not considered true goblets because they had no foot or flat base, only a stem, and they had to be inverted and placed on the rim when empty. The whistle was attached to the end of the stem and, in some cases, may have been added at a date later than the goblet was made. They were made in Venice, Germany, and the Netherlands during the 17th century. A related object is a goblet with a metal rattle attached to the stem.

Whitall Brothers & Co. See *Schetter Glassworks; Whitall, Tatum & Co.; Glasstown Factory.*

Whitall, Tatum & Co. A glass manufacturing facility established in Millville, New Jersey, in 1806 by James Lee of Port Elizabeth and his associates, making window glass and bottles. Prior to 1828, it was acquired by Burgin, Wood & Pearsall of Philadelphia, and shortly thereafter, by Scattergood, Haverstick & Co., making green and clear glass wares. In 1844, Whitall Brothers & Co. acquired it, and in 1857 it became Whitall, Tatum & Co., which also purchased the facility in South Millville, New Jersey, established by Frederick Schetter in 1832. It later became part of the Armstrong Cork Company. See *Glasstown Factory; South Millville Plant.*

White, H.S. See *Redwood Glass Works.*

white acid etching A type of acid etching that totally obscures the glass.

White Aurene See *Ivrene glass; Aurene.*

White Burmese Glass A name incorrectly applied to Mt. Washington's *White Lusterless Glass.* See *White Lusterless Glass.*

white glass (1) Crystal or clear colorless glass. (2) Any white glass, such as milk glass.

White Glass Company or Works See *Zanesville Glass Manufacturing Company.*

White House Glassworks A glass manufacturing facility in Wordsley, near Stourbridge, England, built in 1825 and leased in the 1830s to John Webb (1774-1835) and John Shepherd (Shepherd & Webb). After Thomas Webb I (1804-69) inherited his father's portion in 1835 and Shepherd retired, Webb decided to devote himself to it full-time. In 1836 he withdrew from the firm of Webb & Richardson, which operated the Wordsley Flint Glassworks. When Shepherd died in 1842, the operating firm became Thomas Webb & Co. Thomas Webb I conveyed it to W.H., B. & J. Richardson. In 1897 it was transferred to Thomas Webb & Corbett Ltd. (this Thomas Webb was Thomas Webb III, son of Thomas Webb II). The name changed in the 1930s to Webb, Corbett, Ltd. Its operations, after a fire in 1913, were moved to Coalbourhill, near Stourbridge.

White House Works A glass manufacturing facility established in Birmingham (Pittsburgh), Pennsylvania, in 1858/9 by Hale, Atterbury & Company, making blown and pressed tableware. About 1861, it obtained a patent for "a new manufacture consisting of glassware with open illuminated relief work on the surface." By 1867, it was operated by Atterbury & Company, which advertised "flint glassware and every variety of plain and colored glass." James Seaman and Thomas Bakewell Atterbury of the founding firm were principals, as well as grandsons of Sarah Bakewell Atterbury of the famed Bakewell glass family. In 1889, it

obtained a patent for relief work on the surface of glass. The marver was tooled with a design, pulverized glass or enamel was placed in the depressions, and a hot paraison of glass was rolled over it, picking up the medium and imparting the design to the glass object; reheating set the design on the glass. The facility closed in late 1893/early 1894.

White Lusterless glass In 1881, Frederick Shirley was making ornamental items of pure white glass which, after its surface had been dulled with hydrofluoric acid, looked like alabaster. It was the first Art Glass made at the Mt. Washington Glass Co. and officially named *White Lusterless glass.* Albert Steffin, superintendent of the facility, designed the maidenhair fern embellishment used on it. Many different articles were made of this glass. In addition to the maidenhair design, it was embellished with pink and blue cornflowers, pansies, wild roses, scenes, etc. Many antique dealers, incorrectly, call it *White Burmese.*

White Mills Glassworks (1862-1921) A glass manufacturing facility established by Christian Dorflinger in Honesdale, Pennsylvania. See *Dorflinger Glassworks.*

Whitefriars Glass Works A glass manufacturing facility established in London prior to 1680, in a former Carmelite monastery, hence the name. In 1834 it was acquired, after several ownership changes, by James Powell, operating as James Powell & Sons. From 1860 it made glassware commissioned by William Morris and designed by Phillip Webb, forerunner of English glass in the Art Nouveau style. From the 1850s, it made colored flat glass used in stained glass windows and tesserae used in mosaics. From about 1874, hand-blown glass was made in the style of ancient Roman glass and Waldglas, under the direction of Harry J. Powell (1835-1922), manager, chief chemist, and glass designer. Powell retired in 1919. In 1923 it moved to Wealdstone in Middlesex. In 1962 it assumed its former name, Whitefriars Glass Ltd. It was known for its cut lead glass in several colors, as well as clear, including bowls, decanters, and a heavily textured line of tableware known as *Glacier Glass.* It has made paperweights since 1848 and continues to make millefiori ones in which a single cane displays its signature and date of manufacture. It previously made stained glass windows for many well-known buildings such as St. Paul's Cathedral. More recently, it has made glassware with engraved figures copied from the windows of Coventry Cathedral by John Hutton, who previously engraved the window panels.

Whitefriars paperweight A paperweight by Whitefriars Glass Ltd., which made them from 1848 until present; most often in traditional forms made by the major French paperweight manufacturers. Some more recent ones are more fancifully shaped with innovative motifs. Some, especially those of the millefiori type, have canes which display a signature and date of manufacture.

Whitehead, Ihmsen & Phillips See *Pennsylvania Flint Glass Works.*

Whiting & Eberhart (1833-1859) A window glass manufacturing facility established in Cookstown, Pennsylvania, by George Whiting and William Eberhart Sr. In 1836 Eberhart left; the new firm became Whiting & Hough, later Whiting & Emery, which failed in 1850. Then William Eberhart Jr. acquired it for a short period. In 1857 George Kendall became owner.

Whiting & Emery; Whiting & Hough See *Whiting & Eberhart.*

Whitla Glass Company (1887-1892) A glass manufacturing facility established in Beaver Falls, Pennsylvania. In April 1890 it reorganized as Valley Glass Company, making pressed glassware. It burned on April 9, 1892.

Whitney & Brothers See *Harmony Glass Works*

Whitney Brothers See *Olive & Harmony Glassworks; Harmony Glass Works; Eagle Glass Works; Crystal Glass Manufacturing Company.*

Whitney Glass Co. See *Glassboro Glassworks.*

Whitney Glass Works As a boy, Thomas Heston Whitney went to work at the Harmony Glass Works for $1 per week, and,

at age 18, became a clerk there. When he was 22, he purchased a third interest in it and by 1838 became sole owner. His brother, Samuel, went to work there, learning all phases of the business, intending to drive out the competition. A third brother became a copartner with a brother-in-law, Woodward Warrick, in the Temperanceville Glass Works.

While other glassworks were closing due to the lack of cheap fuel, the Whitneys had previously secured their fuel supply, buying hundreds of acres of woodland in the vicinity. In 1853, they began experimenting with anthracite coal as fuel. As Thomas dabbled in politics, Samuel took over more management responsibilities. The Civil War had a disastrous effect on many glasshouses but had little effect on Whitney's operations. In the late 1870s, Samuel and Thomas retired and Thomas' son, John Perkins Whitney, and nephew, Thomas Whitney Synnoth, took over. In 1887, the name became the Whitney Glass Works.

In the early 1900s the company was growing so rapidly, workers could not be found locally and were sought from other states and countries. The automatic bottle blowing machine by Michael J. Owens went into experimental use in April 1904, and glassblowers were rapidly replaced. In 1918, a new automated facility was opened as the Owens Bottle Works. This company prospered until the Depression caused financial problems, forcing it to merge with the Illinois Glass Corporation to form the Owens-Illinois Glass Corporation, and the Glassboro facility was closed. Later, Owens-Illinois opened a container division in Glassboro. See *Olive & Harmony Glassworks; Temperanceville (New Jersey) Glassworks; Harmony Glass Works.*

Whitney & Warrick See *Temperanceville (New Jersey) Glassworks.*

whorl rod A millefiori cane component with a spiral cross section, frequently used at the center of a cluster of star rods.

Wickham & Hughes; Wickham-Branning Cut Glass Company See *Hughes, P.H.*

wide angular knop A knop similar to an angular knop, except wider at the central bulge.

Wiederkomm(humpen) *(German)* Literally, *come again (beaker)*. A term used by A. Nesbit in a book published in 1871, referring to *Willkomm(humpen)* and other types of enameled Humpen housed in the British Museum. It has not been used elsewhere.

Wiener Stil *(German)* Literally, *Vienna style*. A style of glassware developed in Vienna during the early 20th century, the majority made in Bohemia. Its leading exponent was Josef Hoffman, an architect, designer, and founder of the Wiener Werkstatte. It featured female figures and geometric patterns.

Wiener Werkstatte Literally, *Vienna Workshops*. A system of crafts workshops in Vienna, founded by Koloman Moser and Josef Hoffman (artistic director), and financed by Fritz Warndorfer (commercial director), making a variety of objects in gold, silver, and the baser metals, as well as bookbindings, leather ware, glassware, furniture, and fittings.

Wier, Don Born in 1903, Wier was an American glass designer on the staff of the design department of Steuben, designing some major pieces of ornamental glassware, such as *David and Goliath*.

wig A head covering, usually of human hair, but a few are made of very fine glass fiber threads attached to a network in the traditional manner.

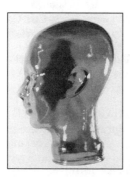

Wig stand, female head, green glass, 11" h.
Davanna Collection

wig stand A globular stand to hold a wig, the globular portion resting on a stemmed foot. Some have been made by the Falcon Glassworks, embellished with millefiori decoration. The bases of some are made of metal, embellished with enameled or cloisonne decoration and often surmounted by a silvered glass globe. Many are in the form of a human head resting on a neck.

wig stand vase A vase with the characteristic feature being a globular cover that fits into the mouth of the vase, serving as a wig stand. They are sometimes bulbous with a stemmed foot, high neck and everted rim into which the globular cover fits. The cover often has a tube extending downward, midway into the vase to provide some stability. Some have been made of enameled opaque white glass. They were made in France from about 1715 to 1720 and in the United States in the early 19th century.

Wightman, Thomas, & Co. See *Pittsburgh Glass Works; Temperanceville (Pennsylvania) Glassworks; Phoenix Glass Works (Pennsylvania).*

New England Glass Works pitcher, Wild Rose pattern, c. 1886-1888, opaque pink, white glass.
The Corning Museum of Glass

Wild Rose glass An art glass developed at the New England Glass Company by Edward Drummond Libbey, probably assisted by Joseph Locke, and patented by Libbey in 1886. It was shaded from a creamy white to a rose color and had a mat or gloss finish. The name was adopted and used after Mt. Washington Glass Co. sued for infringement of its patent for *Peach Blow glass*. See *New England Peachblow*.

Williamite or William III glassware English glassware expressing compassion and support for William III (1650-1702), the hereditary prince of Orange who came to the throne in 1689; his struggle with James II (1633-1701); and/or celebrating his victory at the Battle of the Boyne in 1690. It is engraved with mottoes, portraits, horses, and objects symbolizing or reminiscent of William III, his victories, or memory. Most were engraved in Ireland where affection was strong for William III. His political opponents were the Jacobites. See *Jacobite glassware.*

Willington Glass Company A glass manufacturing facility established in West Willington, Connecticut, by Abiel Johnson and financial backers in 1814, beginning operations in 1815. By 1831, Gilbert Turner & Co. was operating it and the Conventry Glass Factory Company. In April 1847 it was sold to a partnership that operated it until closing in 1872. It made bottle and window glass, figural and standard flasks, snuff bottles, inkwells, jars and candleholders, and offhand pieces, many of black glass. Most wares were marketed in the New England states, New York and Pennsylvania. The Lorillard Tobacco Company purchased many of its snuff bottles, and Edmund G. Booz its house-shaped bottles. See *Coventry Glass Factory Company.*

Williamsburgh Flint Glass Works A glass manufacturing facility established in Williamsburgh (Brooklyn), New York, about 1845 by Berger & Walter, making cut, plain, and colored glassware. By 1879 Dannehoffer & Brothers were the operators. About 1887 E.J.S. Van Houten became affiliated with the firm, remaining a principal until it closed in 1919. It was frequently called Van Houten's Williamsburgh Flint Glass Works. Its trademark was a representation of the American flag surrounded by the words "Van Houten, Cut Glass, New York," used from 1896 to 1919.

Williamsport Glass Works A window glass manufacturing facility established in Williamsport (Pittsburgh), Pennsylvania, about 1820 by William & Ihmsen. About 1830 it began operating another one, previously constructed in 1816 and operated by Warne, Parkinson & Co. In 1840, William McCully & Co. took over both facilities, operating them until 1850.

Williamstown Glass Manufacturing Co. See *Washington Glass Works; Freewill Glass Manufactory.*

Willington Glass Co. A glass manufacturing facility established in 1814/1815 in West Willington, Connecticut, making bottles, flasks, and other hollowware. By 1831, Gilbert Turner & Co., owner of the Coventry Glass Works, took over operations. In 1847, ownership changed again, and in1848 it closed (lack of wood), reopening in 1849 and operating until 1872.

Willis & More Company See *Fairton Glass Works.*

Willkomm(humpen) *(German)* Literally, *welcome (beaker).* A salutation-type drinking glass used to greet guests, embellished with an enameled salutatory inscription and at times a portrait of the host. They were large, some with a capacity of over a gallon. They were made in Germany and Lorraine between the 16th and 18th centuries. It is the converse of the Wiederkomm(humpen), used to say *come again* to departing guests. See *Wiederkomm(humpen).*

Wilson & Sons See *West Lothian Glassworks.*

Wilson, Frank, & Sons (1894-1897) A glass cutting house established in Corning, New York, by Frank Wilson, who came from England in 1872. Prior to this, he and his sons, Joseph and Robert, were employed by several glass cutting firms. It purchased its blanks from Baccarat.

Wilson, W.S., Cut Glass Co. A glass cutting facility in Lawrenceville, Pennsylvania.

Winchester quarts See *dispensary container.*

wind glass See *hurricane shade.*

window (1) An opening in the wall of a building designed to admit air and light. They are customarily furnished with casements and sashes surrounding panes of transparent glass, usually capable of being opened and closed, except those that are fixed in modern climate-controlled buildings. Apart from fixed stained glass windows in churches, the earliest glass windows were probably made by casting, as those in Pompeii. Windows with panes of glass were made in France and elsewhere during the Middle Ages. These were leaded windows of two types: (a) Windows with rows of small glass roundels, having a bull's-eye pontil mark (*boudin*) in the center. These were made from crown glass with the spaces filled with small glass triangles (*coins*), common in Italy and the Netherlands; (b) Windows with flat panes, cut from broad or crown glass, mounted in lead within a wooden frame. Window panes for homes and carriages were often embellished by glaziers with a coat-of-arms; some were embellished with wheel engraving. They were sometimes colored: some stained yellow during the Middle Ages; some flashed with ruby glass; and others colored throughout. After the invention of cast glass about 1687, windows became more widely used because of the ability to make large quantities at a low cost. Today plate glass windows and panels, usually tinted glass, cover the entire exterior of some buildings and skyscrapers. (2) A facet (clear to reveal the interior) on an overlay paperweight. See *window paperweight*.

window glass By definition, the *bubbly* glass found in old homes, tending to turn lavender by the action of the sun. See *windowpane*. It was one of the two main products of early American glasshouses; the other was bottles. Oiled parchment, animal skins, and/or wooden shutters were used to cover windows prior to making window glass when it was scarce and costly.

window greeting card Oblong glass sheets, about four by six inches, etched with holiday greetings (primarily Christmas, some Easter) and suspended in a window. They were made during the early 20th century in Millville, New Jersey.

window paperweight (Aka *overlay paperweight*) A traditional paperweight with a colored glass overlay having generally circular openings ground into the overlay to reveal the motif within. There is usually a top window

and four to six windows surrounding it. On some weights, there are numerous windows covering the whole weight or just the lower half. Sometimes the windows are separated by flutes. These weights often have two layers of glass forming the overlay. The first, called the underlay, is a thin layer of (usually) opaque white glass, and the second is of a darker colored (usually) transparent glass. When the windows are ground, the opaque underlay forms a thin border around the edge of each window.

windowpane A plate of glass used for filling a window sash within a frame. The first were made during the Roman period in the 1st century A.D.. The earliest in the United States were made prior to 1700 and measured generally 4-1/2 by 5-3/4 inches. About 1725, double hung windows came into being and the size of the panes increased to six by eight inches. By 1750 the size had increased to seven by nine inches, and by 1800 to nine by 12 inches. Over the years the size of panes continued to increase and, in 1883, the Pittsburgh Plate Glass Company advertised them up to 12 by 15 feet. The increases in size have led to the question of supply and demand: Was the increase in size over time due to technological advances (creating the supply) or was it due to changes in architectural design (creating the demand)? See *window glass*.

windowpane, lacy glass See *lacy glass windowpane*.

Windsor Glass Company (1887-1895) A glass manufacturing facility established in Pittsburgh, Pennsylvania, making pressed glass tableware and novelties.

wine bottle A bottle for storing and/or serving wine, made of brown, green or black glass in various shapes, sizes and styles, in numerous facilities throughout the world. See *English wine bottle; Italian wine bottle; German wine bottle; French wine bottle.*

Shapes—*Shaft-and-globe bottle* (bulbous body and tall tapering neck); *onion-shaped bottle* (squat and short-necked, to be binned up-side down); *slope-and-shoulder bottle* (straight sides); *cylinder bottle* (commonly used today). *Sizes*—*Bottle* (normally 2/3 to 7/10 quart-capacity); *magnum* (two-bottle capacity); *Marie Jeanne* (three-bottle capacity); *double magnum* (four-bottle capacity); *Jeroboam* (five-bottle capacity); *Rehoboam* (six-bottle capacity); *Methuselah* or *Imperial* (eight-bottle capacity); *Salmanasar* (12-bottle capacity); *split* (quarter bottle or 6-1/2- to 8-ounce capacity); *pint* (half bottle or 13- to 16-ounce capacity); *quart* (1/4 to 1/5 gallon or 26 ounces/32 ounces U.S.).

wine bottle, sealed Wine bottles made in England from the 17th century on, bearing a seal in the form of a glass medallion affixed to the bottle on the body or shoulder. The lettering impressed upon the seal normally indicated the name of the owner, wine merchant or brand of the contents; many bore a year date (the earliest recorded was 1652). See *English wine bottle.*

wine chair A team who made wine glasses, usually a maker, servitor, foot blower, and gatherer.

wine cooler A bucket-shaped receptacle, with or without handles and/or a cover, for holding ice to chill a single bottle of wine or champagne. They are nothing more than large ice pails.

wine cup A small cup (smaller than a tea bowl) with no handle, used in the Far East for drinking wine. Some were made of glass in China during the Ch'ien Lung period (1736-95).

Wine glass, c. 1870, clear glass.
The Corning Museum of Glass

wine glass A drinking glass for wine, made in various shapes, sizes, and styles, and usually stemmed. Those made in more recent times are often classified by type, such as port, champagne, sherry, etc., each type most suitable, in terms of shape and size, for that particular wine. See the following types of wine glasses: *brandy; champagne; hock; port; tulip; doublewine; toast master's; toasting; burgundy; claret; cordial; sherry; flute.*

wine glass, ale An ale glass in the form of a stemmed wine glass, embellished with engraved motifs of hops and barley.

wine glass, double See *double wine glass.*

wine glass cooler (Aka *wine rinser*) A shallow or cylindrical receptacle containing ice water for cooling the bowl of an immersed wine glass. The glass is usually suspended by its stemmed foot from one or two notches or lips on the rim of the cooler. They were first used in the late 17th century, gaining popularity in the 18th century. It is believed coolers with two lips on opposite sides (instead of the more common single lipped or cylindrical containers) were used to rinse and cool an empty glass before serving one wine while another glass was being used for a different wine. Sometimes they are called *finger bowls* and may have served both purposes.

wine glass lamp A 19th century type of *sparking lamp* in the form of a contemporary wine glass (made in various shapes), with a stemmed foot and font. It is enclosed by having the glass curve inward from what would be the rim to a central orifice where a metal collar was inserted, or screwed on, to hold the wick. They were made by several companies.

wine label See *bottle ticket.*

wine rinser See *wine glass cooler.*

wine set A decanter with matching wine glasses and, on occasion, a matching tray.

wine siphon A 16-inch long, thin glass tube with a hole at each end, and, near one end, a small bulb or a curved trumpet-shaped mouth. It was used to transfer wine from a container to a drinking glass by dipping the bottom of the tube into the wine, stoppering the top with the thumb, lifting the tube from the wine, moving it over a wine glass, and removing the thumb, draining the wine into the glass. See *toddy lifter.*

wine urn A receptacle for serving wine by means of a spigot at its base. Some were in the shape of a decanter with a stemmed foot.

wines Small pucellas, used primarily for making goblets. See *pucellas.*

winetaster A very small wine or brandy glass, often used for wine tasting. See *taster.*

wing handled cup; wing shaped cup See *Pterotos cup; skyphos.*

winged glass or goblet A goblet with a stem elaborately embellished with applied threading in wing-like designs extending from both sides of the stem in the form of loops, twisted rope or snake-like patterns, occasionally in the form of sea horses, dragons or a double eagle, and so intricate there was no need for an independent stem. The *wings* were often fashioned from colored glass with additional pincered trailing or cresting of clear glass. The goblets were made of clear soda glass in Venice during the 16th and 17th centuries and copied in Germany and the Netherlands during the same period. See *snake glass; double eagle glass; dragon glass; Ehrenfeld.*

winged knop A knop with embellishment in the form of two or more pincered vertical projections, suggestive of wings.

Winslow Glass Manufacturing Company See *Winslow Glass Works.*

Winslow Glass Works In 1829, William Coffin Sr. of Hammonton, New Jersey, purchased tracts of timber in Camden County and there, in 1831, he and his son-in-law, Thomas Jefferson Perce, and his son, William Coffin Jr., built a glass manufacturing facility. William Sr. named the area Winslow after his youngest son, Edward Winslow Coffin. The company was officially named William Coffin Jr. & Company. In 1833 William Sr. retired and William Jr. and T.J. Perce took over, renaming it Coffin & Perce. In 1935, Perce died and William Coffin Jr. operated it alone. In 1938, he sold half interest to Andrew Hay. Soon a third partner, Tristan Bowdle, was admitted and it became Coffin, Hay & Bowdle. In 1847 Coffin sold his interest to his brother, Edward, and John B. Hay, Andrew's nephew. In 1850, Bowdle retired, and the firm became Hay, Coffin & Company. In 1851, Edward sold his interest to Andrew who, with his nephew John, became sole owners, becoming Andrew K. Hay & Company. In 1866 it was incorporated as Winslow Glass Manufacturing Company. Andrew Hay died on February 17, 1881. John Hay and his heirs operated the company until 1884 when Tillyer Brothers of Philadelphia, Pennsylvania, leased it from William Coffin Hay, Andrew's son. The company originally made window glass, added bottles in 1838, and expanded over the years until it had two window and one hollowware operations in close proximity. In 1892 all three operations were destroyed by fire. In the 1840s Christian Stanger Jr. was a supervisor at the facility.

wire stem A stem, tall and extremely thin (about 1/4 inch in diameter), made by being drawn from a trumpet-shaped bowl of a drinking glass. They are found mainly on toasting glasses. This is quite appropriate since it was an 18th century custom to snap the stem after offering a toast. As a result, few specimens have survived.

wired glass Sheets of glass having a wire mesh fused between them, preventing the glass from *flying* when broken. It is a form of safety glass.

wishbone decoration Trailed embellishment in the form of a wishbone or merry-thought.

Wistar mug, c. 1760-1820, gray-green glass.
The Corning Museum of Glass

Wistar, Casper Born Casper Wurster in 1696, son of Johannes Casper Wurster, he was a glassmaker who came to Philadelphia, Pennsylvania, from the Palatine region of Germany in 1717. He pursued menial jobs in and around Philadelphia and eventually bought land in what is now Northampton County, Pennsylvania, later subdividing and selling it to German immigrants. With the money he made, he became a partner in the Colebrookdale iron furnace in Berks County, Pennsylvania, and established a brass button factory in Philadelphia. He offered a multi-year guarantee on each button, and it made him rich. By 1726 he was able to invest in a second iron furnace, Pool Forge, also in Berks County, and married Catherine Jansen (or Johnson). A son, Richard, was born in 1727.

In 1738 Wistar bought approximately 2,000 acres of land in Alloway (originally Allowaystown, later Wistarberg), near Salem, New Jersey. The land had good sand, a lot of wood, good clay and a stream with access to the Delaware River. He found four skilled German glassmakers—Casper Halter, Johan Martin Halter, Johannes Wilhelm Wentzel, and Simeon Kreismayer—and brought them to the United States. They were to be provided with all materials, tools, food, shelter, and servants, as well as one-third of the profits from a glassworks that Wistar was to build. In 1739 a furnace was built and made ready for the autumn blast. The works was known by various names: Wistar Glass Works, Wistarberg Glass Works, and United Glass Company. It made green glass for window lights and hollowware, bottle glass of an olive-amber color for spirits, and "white" or clear glass.

Wistar died in 1752, and his son, Richard, took over. For about two years after Casper's death, the business continued to grow; then the quality of the wares began to deteriorate. Many workers were indentured servants, glassworkers and blowers from Rotterdam, Poland and Germany, whose passage to the United States was paid for by Casper Wistar. They began to leave after Richard took over. The cheap labor was one of the prime reasons the operation prospered. It operated only sporadically beginning in late 1775/early 1776, and finally was offered for sale in 1780. In 1781 Richard Wistar died in Rahway, New Jersey, before the facility was sold. His widow, Sarah, and son, John, tried to operate it but failed, and it was closed and abandoned.

The jugs and free-blown vessels were made in both clear and colored glass and were usually embellished with spiral trailing, lily pad decoration and opaque white stripes and loops. As other facilities were established in the area, and in other areas, they tended to make similar wares. These wares, no matter where they were made, became known collectively as *South Jersey glass* (see *South Jersey type glassware*).

Wistar(berg) Glass Company; Wistarberg glass See *Wistar, Casper.*

Wisteria lamp Based on a design by Curtis Freshnel and created by Louis Comfort Tiffany, the lamp's base is in the form of a vine and the shade was patterned after hanging lilac wisteria blossoms in a wavy, irregular shape. It is considered simply a *Tiffany lamp.*

witch ball (Aka *witch bottles*) A glass globe three to seven inches in diameter to be hung in a window or placed on a stand to ward off evil spirits or prevent disease, wiped clean daily to remove evil lurking in the area. They had their origin in England in the 17th century: small spherical bottles made in response to requests from people who wanted a container for holy water. These, over time, gradually became spherical glass balls, the water forgotten. They were very popular from the early 1820s to late 1890s; many made in Nailsea. In the 1850s it moved from the window to become a mantle ornament. They should *not* be confused with heavier glass *seine balls* or small lamp globes. Witch balls were usually of colored glass, mainly blue, green, or red. They were often silvered on the inside or daubed with various colors that sparkled when hung. Some were embellished with decalcomania (transferring a tracing of a decal onto the glass body) or potichromania (water coloring) process. Some had loops of multicolored glass marvered into the surface. Some had a small hole at the top for a peg and string for suspension (sometimes several were hung vertically on a single string), and some had a small neck at the top. They were also made in Catalonia, Spain. Modern imitations have been made with a silvery lining. See *witch bottle.*

witch bottle A bottle filled with pins, human hair, fingernails, bones, and similar items, so named because these bizarre relics would supposedly ward off evil spirits. See *witch ball.*

witch canes Small, decorated, fragile glass canes, usually five to six inches long, used as a substitute for and serving the same purpose as *witch balls.*

Wolfe, Hard & Company A short-lived glass manufacturing facility established in Pittsburgh, Pennsylvania, in 1836, which made cylinder and bottle glass.

Wolfe, Howard & Co.; Wolfe, Plunkett & Co. See *Excelsior Glass Works (Pennsylvania).*

Wolf's tooth An embellishment on Frankish glassware—mainly cone beakers and drinking horns—in the form of zigzag trailing or a continuous series of long vertical loops.

Wood & Pearsall See *Glasstown Factory.*

Wood, R.D., Glass Works A window glass manufacturing facility established in Millville, New Jersey, about 1863. It was later leased to Sharp & Westcott, then Evans, Thorpe & Co. The Wood family operated it again later. In 1881 Jones & Townsend leased it. It is not known when it closed.

wood ash The usual source of alkaline fluxes used by glassmakers. It is the primary source of potash in the batch, as opposed to the ashes of vegetable matter and seaweed, which are sources of soda.

Woodall, George & Thomas George (1850-1925) and Thomas (1849-1926) were English glass engravers and cutters, working as apprentices of John Northwood until 1874. They worked in partnership with Thomas Webb & Sons, later making glassware influenced by the Art Nouveau style, especially cameo glass.

woodblock A heavy block of wood with a quarter sphere depression, used to give a gather of hot glass a symmetrical spherical form during the early stages of shaping it.

Woodbury Glass Manufacturing Company: In March 1820, it petitioned the Assembly to buy land and build a window and bottle glass manufacturing facility in Woodbury, Connecticut. The petition was granted, but there was no indication that the facility materialized.

Woodbury Glass Works jar. Museum of American Glass, Wheaton Village, Millville, NJ

Woodbury Glass-Works Company
Lewis M. Green began making syrups and elixirs in Woodbury, New Jersey in the 1850s. After the Civil War, his son, George, joined him, moving the business to Athens, Ohio, then moving it back to Woodbury. Soon George took over the business and began to advertise heavily. By 1883, Green's Laboratories was mailing out five million free almanacs on two continents, many printed in Spanish, French, and German. Nine presses ran continuously to print calendars, almanacs, labels, cartons, posters, and signs. His syrups and elixirs contained no alcohol and were prepared under amazingly sanitary conditions (rare at the time). His patent medicines were in plain, aqua-colored bottles, purchased from nearby facilities. Green, feeling it was more efficient to make his own bottles, established the Woodbury Glass-Works Company for this purpose in 1881. Because of his many construction ventures, he needed large quantities of window glass. So in 1882 he established the Standard Window Glass Works, and in 1883, built a second facility in North Woodbury.

Woodbury Standard Window Glass Works See *Woodbury Glass-Works Company.*

woodjack See *woods*.

woods A glassmaker's tool with two wooden arms connected at one end by a metal spring handle, used in shaping blown glass, especially the bowl. It is similar to the metal pucellas that it superceded about 1830. Woods minimize striation marks more so than metal pucellas.

Woodstock Glass Manufactory

(1810-1835) A glass manufacturing facility established in Woodstock Township, New York, by the Madison & Woodstock Glass Manufacturing Association, making window glass. It is believed that it later added bottles.

Wordsley Flint Glassworks A glass

manufacturing facility established in Wordsley, England, in 1720 by a Mr. Bradley who established a partnership, Bradley & Ensell, to operate it. It was later taken over by Wainwright Bros., who operated it until it closed in 1825. In 1829, Thomas Webb I (1804-1869), in partnership with W.H. and B. Richardson, took over, operating it as Webb & Richardson. After Webb inherited the White House Glassworks in 1835, the partnership was dissolved in 1836. It was succeeded by W.H., B. & J. Richardson, and by Henry Richardson & Sons Ltd. In the 1930s, it was acquired by Webb's Crystal Glass Co. Ltd. Glassmaking had already stopped at the time of purchase, but some glassware with the Richardson label, made at the Dennis Glassworks, was made and sold until the late 1960s by Thomas Webb & Sons.

working furnace Usually of a circular or rectangular form made of fire brick with a domed top leading to a chimney (a single chimney may be used as a common flue for two or more furnaces). Within this, placed around the wall and equally spaced, were the pots. These pots were made by hand of the purest clay, normally mixed with powder from pulverized old pots. The new pot was allowed to dry for about a year and gradually exposed to heat until it reached the temperature of an active furnace. A hole was knocked into the side of the furnace, the pot inserted and the hole rebricked, leaving an opening to reach the pot (an opening was provided for each pot so several teams could work at the same time).

Additional openings, called glory holes, were also placed in the side of the furnace for inserting a glass vessel to reheat it, making it plastic enough to form, shape, or rework.

working holes See *bocca*.

working year Before modernization of glass manufacturing facilities and continuous year-round operations, facilities shut down during the summer because of the warm weather, compounded by the heat from the furnaces, making working conditions unbearable. During the shutdown, furnaces were repaired and rebuilt. The working year was considered the period during which the furnaces were continuously fired. Depending on the location and the owner, it was from 39 to 44 weeks long. The shutdown period always included July and August; the latest start up date was October 1.

wormed glasses Wine glasses with an air twist or cotton stem.

Wormser, Burgraff & Company; Wormser Glass Company See *Pittsburgh Green Glass Company*.

woven glass See *tessuto, vetro*.

Wright, Frank Lloyd (1867-1959) One

of America's foremost architectural designers. Wright's use of glass within his designs was as revolutionary as the designs themselves. He used glass to open up living spaces, both between living areas within the structure and living areas and the landscape outside. He moved from elaborate art glass windows early in his career, to pioneering applications in mid-career, to more extensive components in his later years. His interior lighting fixtures made extensive use of glass, designed to enhance the overall unity of the structure.

L.G. Wright green auto ashtray, early
American, 3" l.
Davanna Collection

Wright, L.G., Glass Company A company established in the late 1930s by L.G. Wright, a former salesman for the New Martinsville Glass Company. He purchased old molds from the Northwood, Dugan and Diamond glass companies and had Fenton, Fostoria, Westmoreland, Viking and Imperial use them to make tableware that he resold to numerous retail outlets.

Wright Rich Cut Glass Company A glass cutting house established in 1904 by Thomas W. Wright in Anderson, Indiana. By 1914, it was out of the cut-glass business, reestablished as the Wright Metal Manufacturing Company. Most cut pieces are signed *Wright* in script.

writing diamond See *point cut.*

wrought button knop A spherical, ribbed knop found on short stems of some English wine glasses. Its use came into prominence after the hollow baluster stems of the mid-17th century and before the subsequent plainer stems.

wrythen Embellished with spiral or swirling reeding, ribbing and/or fluting. Sometimes it is *mistakenly* called *flammiform*, but wrythen embellishment is vertical ribbing, softened and swirled to encircle the rising shape of the glass. It is most often seen on small, low-stemmed ale glasses, extending upward to the top of the glass or stopping just below the rim. When there is a clear edge to the glass, it is referred to as *flammiform*, since the swirls end irregularly in a flame-shaped pattern. Where the pattern ends determines the correct term to be used, but generally creates confusion.

wrythen molding or ornamentation See *wrythen.*

Wurzburg flask A Syrian Islamic pilgrim flask embellished with gilded scrolls and enameled in eight colors with scenes depicting hunting and feasting events. It was made of Aleppo glass about 1250 and so named because it was in the possession of a family in Wurzburg for a long time.

Xx-Yy

X-cut vesica A cut-glass motif. Curved miter splits passing through the vesicas in the process of forming ovals or other configurations; separate parts of the vesica cut with different patterns. The curved miters cross the vesica to form an "X" within. See *vesica; double X-cut vesica.*

yacht jug A cream jug with an inverted rim to prevent slopping caused by the motion of a ship.

Yall, Clark & Cowan A glass cutting shop in St. Louis, Missouri, on the same site as the Missouri Glass Company and the Art Manufacturing Company.

yao-ping (*Chinese*) A small flask or bottle to hold or contain drugs, medicines, or snuff.

yard-of-ale A type of ale glass, varying in height from about 30 inches to over 40 inches and having a capacity of about a pint. They are long, thin, tubular vessels of clear, plain glass with a trumpet mouth. Early ones, dating from about 1685, had a foot. Later ones had a globular receptacle at the bottom, making them trick glasses. When nearly empty and tilted high to get out the remainder of the ale, air rushed into the globe, causing the ale to squirt out on the drinker. They were made in England during the 19th century. If made in smaller sizes, they were frequently referred to as *half-a-yard-of-ale* or *quarter-of-a-yard-of-ale.* Modern versions have been made since about 1955.

Yarnall & Samuels; Yarnell & Trimble See *Medford Glass Works.*

yellow glass Glass with a yellow coloring. Lead glass was so colored by the inclusion of antimony oxide in the batch. Early Egyptian glass included yellow trailing, and Roman glass was given a yellow color, using iron in the ferric state. Lead chromate was used in the early 19th century to produce a yellow color, replacing an earlier mixture of silver, lead, and antimony. A silver compound was used to stain the surface of the glass a deep yellow as found in some stained glass windows. Uranium was sometimes used to make glass because it had various greenish-yellow and yellowish-green shades. The Chinese made yellow monochrome opaque glassware called *Imperial yellow.* See *Vaseline glass.*

yellow quartz See *quartz glass.*

yoke A Y-shaped piece of metal, generally brass or bronze, fitted with two steel balls that can rotate at the base of the V. It is used by glass blowers to hold the blowing iron or punty iron when pieces are being reheated at the glory hole.

Young, A.; Young, Haines & Dyer
See *Boston Silver Glass Co.*

Young, Ihmsen & Plunkett
See *Pennsylvania Flint Glass Works.*

Ysart, Salvador & Paul Paul was a glassmaker, born in 1904 in Barcelona, Spain, to a family of glassmakers. His father, Salvador (1877-1955), grandfather and brothers, Augustus (d.1957) and Vincent (d.1971), were glassblowers. Salvador was a Catalan glassmaker in Barcelona, moving to Marseilles in 1909. He worked for Schneider Brothers and, in 1915, moved to Scotland. In 1922 he began working for Moncrieff with his son Paul; his other sons soon began working there. Paul worked as an apprentice at St. Louis, moving to Scotland in 1915. He was employed by the Leith Flint Glass Company of Edinburgh and later moved to Glasgow. In 1922 he moved with his family to Perth and worked for the Moncrieff Glassworks; in

1938 he was creating quality paperweights. His father and brother left in 1948 to form the Ysart Bros. Glassworks, later Vasart Glass Ltd. near Perth. Paul remained at Moncrieff until 1963, making Monart glass and weights. From 1963 to 1971 he worked for the Caithness Glassworks at Wick, making weights. In 1971 he established his own facility, Paul Ysart Ltd., at Wick. Here he made quality weights, signed on a cane with the initials "PY." Paul retired in 1979.

Ysart Bros. Glassworks See *Ysart, Paul; Vasart Glass Ltd.*

Yuile Bros. Glass Works See *Foster Brothers Glass Works.*

Zz

zaffer Also spelled *zaffre*. An impure oxide of cobalt obtained by fusing cobaltite with sand, used in making smalt and blue glass.

zaffre See *zaffer*.

Zanes-Messina Glass Company A glass cutting shop established in Hammonton, New Jersey, about 1944 by Michael Messina. The company did only light cutting, mostly for individual customers. Messina was employed by William Skinner & Son in 1911. See *Messina Cut Glass & Decorating Company*.

Zanesville City Glass Works A window glass manufacturing facility established in 1864 in Zanesville, Ohio, by Noah and George Kearns. In 1876, the operating firm was Kearns, Herdman & Gorsuch.

Zanesville Glass Manufacturing Company (Aka *White Glass Company or Works*) A glass manufacturing facility established in 1815 in Zanesville, Ohio, by Ebenezer Buckingham, Samuel Sullivan, Davis Marpole, John Hanne, Rees Cadmalader, Samuel J. Herrick and Isaac Van Horn, after being granted a privilege by the Ohio legislature. It made pattern glass, clear hollowware and physicians' and apothecaries' ware. In 1816 it added window glass, bottles and historical flasks. In 1817 the company was offered for sale. Thomas Mark leased it in 1820, but it failed after a short time. In 1823 J. Shepard & Co. (Joseph Shepard, Charles Bostwick, and James Crosby) took over. Shepard withdrew in 1838 and it closed. In 1842, Kearns & Co. (George W. Kearns, W.F. Spence, Samuel Turner, George Wendt, Joseph Burns, and Thomas Reynolds) reopened it. Spence and Turner sold to Arnold Lippet in 1840. In 1848, Lippit bought out the remaining stockholders and attempted to operate it in conjunction with the New Granite Glass Company. In 1851, he too failed, and the facility closed.

Zanesville glassware Glassware made in Zanesville, Ohio, at several glass manufacturing facilities from about 1815 to about 1845. Zanesville glassware is also called *Ohio glass* since none was signed or attributed with any certainty to any particular glasshouse. Some ware had distinctive styles, such as covered bowls with double domed tops, a fat round ball as a finial, applied handles with pincered decoration, winged stems, ten-diamond-mold embellishment, etc. See *Zanesville Glass Manufacturing Company; Mills, Peter, & Co.; Zanesville White Flint Glass Manufactory*.

Zanesville White Flint Glass Manufactory A short-lived glass manufacturing facility established in 1820 in Zanesville, Ohio, by Edmonds, Bingham & Co.

zanfirico *(Italian)* A term used in Venice and Murano for *vetro a retorti*.

Zechuchoth A term found in some versions of the Bible (Job 23:17) translated as rock crystal or any other hard, transparent substance.

Zelasky, Edward, Jr. The son of Edward Zelasky (see *Washington Cut Glass Company*). He left his father's business prior to World War II to establish a cutting shop in Seattle, Washington. He specialized in engraving and initialing glassware until World War II.

Zierglas *(German)* Literally, *ornament glass*. Glassware made primarily for ornamental purposes intended for display rather than for practical use.

zigzag star A term used by Martha Louise Swan for a *flat star* cut-glass motif. It is similar to the five-pointed star made using a continual line without raising the pen from the paper.

zipper A cut-glass motif consisting of parallel lines at right or acute angles to a split, cutting them in two.

Zirat Fladske A product of the Gjovik Verk in Norway, made during the 1830s. A long-necked decanter with a globular or rectangular body, with strips and blobs of glass; on occasion, of colored glass, sometimes in the form of letters or dates.

zodiac paperweight A paperweight having one of the signs of the zodiac as its primary motif displayed against a colored background.

zuccarin(o) *(Italian)* Literally, *basin for sweets*. (1) A glass vessel similar to the Kuttrolf, but made in Venice during the late 17th and 18th centuries. (2) Any covered bowl or dish.

Zunftbecher *(German)* Literally, *guild beaker*. Glass beakers, made from the late 17th century, embellished with enameling with symbols associated with a particular group, guild or association. These, when engraved, are called *Innungsglaser*.

Zwischengoldglas(er) *(German)* Literally, *gold between glass*. (Aka *double glass*) A Bohemian drinking glass embellished with gold leaf. This was created using a process in which the outer surface of one glass was embellished with engraved gold leaf and a bottomless glass was sealed over it, using colorless resin to bind the glasses, protecting the design. The inner glass was ground with great exactness for almost its entire height to permit the outer glass to be fitted precisely over it. Silver leaf was often used instead of gold leaf. The technique is old. Greek specimens date to 300 B.C.; Persian date from the 2nd to 4th centuries A.D.; Islamic date from the 9th and 10th centuries (these differ; the gold was applied in suspension); and Egyptian and Syrian date from the 12th century A.D.. Another fairly modern method involves enameling glassware on its reverse, using gold or silver foil, fusing to it a layer of transparent glass. The best date is from 1730 to 1755. Also see *Zwischensilberglas(er); Bohemian glass*.

Zwischensilberglas(er) The same as *Zwischengoldglas(er)*, except silver foil is used, sandwiched between two layers of glass.

Manufacturers' Marks

All marks depicted appear courtesy of Krause Publications unless otherwise noted at the end of the listings.

1932–48

Akro Agates

1883

Amberina

Anchor Hocking

AURENE

Aurene

Ball

After 1929

Blenko

Blenko

Cambridge Glass

NEAR CUT

Cambridge Glass

T.B. Clark

T.B. Clark

BURGLAR'S HORROR

Trademark of Clark's patented pyramid night-light.

Consolidated Martelé label

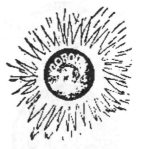

Corona Cut Glass Co.

CRICKLITE

Cricklite

Crown Milano

Dd

d'Argental

1895–1942
Daum

DeVez

Diamond Finish

Dithridge & Co.

Dithridge Flint Glass

Dorflinger

Dugan's "Diamond-D"

Ee

Eggington

Fostoria

Ff

Federal Glass Co.

Fire-King

Fire-King oven ware

Gg

Gallé

Gallé

1900–58

Heisey

GILLINDER

Gillinder & Sons

Gravic

Handel

1903–1920
Post–1920

Hawkes

Hazel Atlas

A.H. Heisey

1895–1920

J. Hoare & Co.

Hocking Glass

Hope Glass Works

Imperial Nucut Mark

Later Imperial marks

Early Imperial cross mark

Iorio

Jeanette Glass Co.

Jefferson Glass

Kk

Kelva

Kew-Blas

Ll

LALIQUE
R.LALIQUE

Lalique

Lalique

Laurel Cut Glass Co.

Le Verre Francais

Libbey

1896–1906

Libbey Cut Glass

Loetz

Lotus

Mm

c1852–1950

McKee

Moser *Moser Karlsbad*

Moser

Muller Fréres

Muller Fréres

KOH-I-NOOR

Murr trademark

Nn

Northwood

Northwood signature mark

Northwood "N" in circle mark

Nuart/Nucut

Oo

Orrefors

Orrefors

OVINGTON'S

Ovington's

Owens Illinois

Pilkington Brothers

1904–30s

Prescut

Pp

*Pittsburgh Glass
Manufacturing Co.*

Qq

Quezal

1901–25

Quezal

Pairpoint

*Pittsburgh Glass
Manufacturing Co.*

Rr

Royal Flemish

Phoenix

*Pittsburgh Glass
Manufacturing Co.*

Ss

St. Gobain

VOLLENDEN
• PHOENIX •
WARE
Phoenix

Plunger

Pilgrim

*Sabino
France*

Sabino

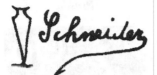

Schneider

Schneider

**Frederick Shirley Peach
Blow and Peach Skin**

L.E. Smith

Smith Bros.

1903–32

Steuben

Straus Cut Glass

Stevens & Williams

Tiffany

Tiffany Favrikfabrique

Tiffany Favrile

**Tiffany Favrile Glass
trademark**

Tiffany Studios

c1960

Tiffin Glass

Val St. Lambert

Val St. Lambert

Vallerysthal

Vasart

Vasart

Verlys

Ww

Waterford

**WAVE CREST
WARE**

c1892

Wave Crest

c1910

Westmoreland

Westmoreland

Wheelock

Woodbury Glass Works

The following marks appear courtesy of Heartland Discoveries,
www. heartland-discoveries.com:

Aurene

Ball

T. B. Clark

Clark's pyramid
night-light

Corona Cut Glass Co.

Cricklite

Crown Milano

Clarke

Diamond Finish

Dithridge & Co.

Dithridge Flint Glass

Dorflinger

Egginton

Gillinder & Sons

Gravic

A.H. Heisey

Hope Glass Works

Iorio

Jefferson Glass

Kelva

Laurel Cut Glass Co.

Libbey Cut Glass

Lotus

Murr

Ovington's

Pairpoint

Phoenix

Pilkington Brothers

Pittsburgh Glass Manufacturing Co.

Plunger

St. Gobain

Frederick Shirley

L.E. Smith

Straus Cut Glass

Tiffany Favrikfabrique

Tiffany Favrile Glass trademark

Tiffany Studios

Westmoreland Hand Made Glass

Wheelock

The following marks appear courtesy of Davanna, Inc.:

Fire King oven ware

Pilgrim

BIBLIOGRAPHY

Allen, Denise. *Roman Glass in Britain*. Buckinghamshire, United Kingdom: Shire Publications Ltd., 1998.

Appleton, Dr. Budd. *Akro Agate*. Self-published, 1972.

Art-Journal Special Issue, The. *The Crystal Palace Exhibition Illustrated Catalogue: London, (1851)*. New York, N.Y.: Dover Publications Inc., 1970.

Arwas, Victor. *Glass: Art Nouveau to Art Deco*. New York: Harry N. Abrams Inc., 1987.

————. *The Art of Glass: Art Nouveau to Art Deco*. Windsor, Berks, England: Andreas Papadakis, 1996.

Asharina, Nina, Tamara Malinina, and Liudmila Kazakova. *Russian Glass of the 17th-20th Centuries*. Corning, N.Y.: The Corning Museum of Glass, 1990.

Atterbury, Paul, ed. *Popular Antiques*. Norwalk, Conn.: Longmeadow Press, 1977.

Atterbury, Paul, and Lars Tharp, consulting eds. *The Bulfinch Illustrated Encyclopedia of Antiques*. New York, N.Y.: Little, Brown & Company, 1998.

Avila, George C. *The Pairpoint Story*. New Bedford, Mass.: Reynolds-DeWalt Printing Inc., 1968.

Baldwin, Gary, and Lee Carno. *Moser—Artistry in Glass (1857-1938)*. Marietta, Ohio: Antique Publications, 1988.

Barr, Sheldon. *Venetian Glass: Confections in Glass 1855-1914*. New York, N.Y.: Harry N. Abrams Inc.,1998

Barret, Richard Carter. *Blown & Pressed American Glass*. Bennington, Vt.: Bennington Museum, 1966.

Barta, Dale & Diane, and Helen M. Rose. *Czechoslovakian Glass & Collectibles, Book II*. Paducah, Ky.: Collector Books, 1997.

Bassett, Sara Ware. *The Story of Glass*. Philadelphia, Pa.: The Penn Publishing Company, 1917.

Bayer, Patricia, and Mark Waller. *The Art of Rene Lalique*. Secaucus, N.J.: Wellfleet Press, 1988.

Beard, Frances Rogers and Alice. *5000 Years of Glass*. New York, N.Y.: Frederick A. Stokes Company, 1937.

Bedford, John. *Bristol and Other Coloured Glass*. New York, N.Y.: Walker & Company, 1966.

————. *English Crystal Glass*. New York, N.Y.: Walker & Company, 1966.

Bennett, Harold and Judy. *The Cambridge Glass Book*. Des Moines, Iowa: Wallace-Homestead Co., 1970.

Bennett, Ian. *Book of American Antiques*. London, England: The Hamlyn Publishing Group Limited, 1973.

Boggess, Bill and Louise. *American Brilliant Cut Glass*. New York, N.Y.: Crown Publishers Inc., 1977.

————. *Identifying American Brilliant Cut Glass*. West Chester, Pa.: Schiffer Publishing Ltd., 1990.

Bosker, Gideon, and Lena Lencek. *Salt & Pepper Shakers, Identification & Price Guide*. New York, N.Y.: Avon Books, 1994.

Bray, Charles. *Dictionary of Glass: Materials & Techniques*. Philadelphia, Pa.: University of Pennsylvania Press, 1995.

Bredehoft, Neila and Tom. *Fifty Years of Collectible Glass: 1920 - 1970; Easy Identification & Price Guide, Volume I*. Dubuque, Iowa: Antique Trader Books, 1997.

————. *Hobbs, Brockunier & Co.: Identification and Value Guide*. Paducah, Ky.: Collector Books, 1997.

Brooks, John A. *Glass*. London, England: Purnell & Sons, --.

Burkholder, John R., and D. Thomas O'Connor. *Kemple Glass: 1945-1970*. Marietta, Ohio: The Glass Press Inc., 1997.

Burton, John. *Glass: Philosophy & Method: Hand-Blown, Sculptured, Colored*. New York, N.Y.: Bonanza Books, a Division of Crown Publishers Inc., 1967.

Butler, Joseph T. *American Antiques: 1800-1900: A Collector's History and Guide*. New York, N.Y.: The Odyssey Press, 1965.

Cambridge University. *Glass at the Fitzwilliam Museum*. Cambridge, England: Cambridge University Press, 1978.

Cameron, Ian, and Elizabeth Kingsley Rowe, eds. *The Encyclopedia of Antiques*. Greenwich House, N.Y.: William Collins Sons & Co. Ltd., 1973.

Chervenka, Mark. *The Black Light Book for Antiques & Collectible, 4th Edition*. Des Moines, Iowa: Antique & Collectors Reproduction News, 1998.

Chihuly, Dale. *Chihuly: Bellagio*. Seattle, Wash.: Portland Press, 1999.

————. *Chihuly Projects*. Seattle, Wash.: Portland Press, 2000.

————. *Chihuly: Form from Fire*. Daytona Beach, Fla.: The Museum of Arts & Sciences Inc., in association with University of Washington Press.

Corning Museum of Glass. *A Decade of Glass Collecting, Selections from the Melvin Billups Collection*. Corning, N.Y.: Corning Museum of Glass, 1962

————. *Glass Drinking Vessels from the Strauss Collections*. Corning, N.Y.: Corning Museum of Glass, 1955.

————. *Tools of the Glassmaker*. Corning, N.Y.: Corning Museum of Glass, 1980.

Corning Museum of Glass, Toledo Museum of Art, Lillian Nassau Ltd. *Masterpieces of American Glass*. New York, N.Y.: Crown Publishers Inc., 1990.

Corning Museum of Glass & The American National Committee of the International Association of the History of Glass.

Glass Collections in Museums in the United States & Canada. Corning, N.Y.: Corning Museum of Glass, 1982.

Couldrey, Vivienne. *The Art of Louis Comfort Tiffany.* Secaucus, N..J: Wellfleet Press, 1989.

Cousins, Mark. *20th Century Glass.* Secaucus, N.J.: Chartwell Books, 1989.

Davidson, Marshall B., auth. and ed. *Three Centuries of American Antiques.* New York, N.Y.: Bonanza Books, 1979.

Davis, Frank. *Antique Glass & Glass Collecting.* New York: Hamlyn Publishing Group Limited, 1973.

Davis, Frank. *The Country Life Book of Glass.* Feltham, Middlesex, England: Country Life Books, 1966.

Drepperd, Carl W. *A B C's of Old Glass.* Garden City, N.Y.: Doubleday & Company, 1949.

DiBartolomeo, Robert E., ed. *American Glass, Pressed & Cut.* Vol. II. New York, N.Y.: Weathervane Books, 1974.

Dillon, Edward, M.A. *Glass.* New York, N.Y.: G.P. Putnam's Sons, 1907.

Dorn, Sylvia O'Neill. *The Insider's Guide to Antiques, Art & Collectibles.* New York: Doubleday & Company Inc., 1974.

Drepperd, Carl W. *The Primer of American Antiques.* Garden City, N.Y.: Doubleday, Doran & Co. Inc., 1944.

Drury, Elizabeth, ed. *Antiques.* Garden City, N.Y.: Doubleday & Company Inc., 1986.

Duncan, Alastair, Martin Eidelberg, and Neil Harris. *The Masterworks of Lewis Comfort Tiffany.* New York: Harry N. Abrams, 1993.

Ehrlich, Doreen. *Frank Lloyd Wright Glass.* London, England: PRC Publishing Ltd.,2000.

Eige, Eason, & Wilson, Rick. *Blenko Glass: 1930-1953.* Marietta, Ohio: Antique Publications, 1987.

Elville, E.M. *Paperweights & Other Glass Curiosities.* London, England: Spring Books, 1967.

Ezell, Elaine, & George Newhouse. *Cruets Cruets Cruets, Vol. I.* Marietta, Ohio: Antique Publications, 1991.

———. *Cruets Cruets Cruets, Vol. II.* Marietta, Ohio: Antique Publications, 1993.

Farber Brothers. *Krome-Kraft by Farber Brothers.* New York: Farber Brothers, 1941.

Farrar, Estelle Sinclaire, and Jane Shadel Spillman. *The Complete Cut & Engraved Glass of Corning.* New York, N.Y.: Crown Publishers Inc., 1979.

Feller, John Quentin. *Dorflinger: America's Finest Glass, 1852-1921.* Marietta, Ohio: Antique Publications, 1988.

———. *Dorflinger Kalana Art Glass.* Marietta, Ohio: Antique Publications, 1988.

Florence, Gene. *Collectible Glassware from the 40's, 50's, 60's.* 3rd ed. Paducah, Ky.: Collector Books, 1996.

———. *The Collector's Encyclopedia of Depression Glass.* 3rd ed. Paducah, Kentucky: Collector Books, 1977.

———. *The Collector's Encyclopedia of Depression Glass.* 13th ed. Paducah, Kentucky: Collector Books, 1998.

———. *Florence's Glassware Pattern Identification Guide: Easy identification of Glassware from the 1920s through the 1960s.* Paducah, Kentucky: Collector's Books, 1998.

———. *Pocket Guide to Depression Glass.* Paducah, Kentucky: Collector Books, 1979.

———. *Very Rare Glassware of the Depression Years: Third Series.* Paducah, Kentucky: Collector Books, 1993.

Forsythe, Ruth A. *Made in Czechoslovakia.* Galena, Ohio: Ruth A. Forsythe, 1982.

———. *Made in Czechoslovakia, Book 2.* Marietta, Ohio: Antique Publications, 1993.

Foulds, Diane E. *A Guide to Czech & Slovak Glass.* Praque, Chech Republic: Libertas a.s., 1995.

Freeman, Larry. *Iridescent Glass—Aurene, Carnival, Tiffany.* Watkins Glen, N.Y.: Century House, 1964.

Fry, Plantagenet Somerset. *The World of Antiques.* New York, New York: The Hamlyn Publishing Group Limited, 1971.

Fyson, Nance. *Decorative Glass of the 19th and Early 20th Centuries.* Devon, England: David & Charles, 1996.

Gardner, Paul Vickers. *Frederick Carder: Portrait of a Glassmaker.* Corning, New York: The Corning Museum of Glass, 1985.

———. *The Smithsonian Illustrated Library of Antiques: Glass.* (Prepared by the Cooper-Hewitt Museum). Washington, D.C.: The Smithsonian Institution.

———. *The Glass of Frederick Carder.* New York, N.Y.: Crown Publishers Inc., 1971.

Garmon, Lee, and Spencer, Dick. *Glass Animals of the Depression Era.* Paducah, Kentucky: Collector Books, 1993.

Garner, Philippe, Editor. *The Encyclopedia of Decorative Arts, 1890-1940.* London, England: Grange Books, 1996.

Garner, Philippe. *Emile Galle.* New York, N.Y.: Rizzoli International Publications Inc., 1979.

Glickman, Jay L. *Yellow - Green Vaseline! A Guide to the Magic Glass.* Marietta, Ohio: Antique Publications, 1991.

Goldstein, Sidney M.; Rakow, Leonard S.; & Rakow, Juliette K. *Cameo Glass: Masterpieces from 2000 years of Glassmaking.* Corning, N.Y.: The Corning Museum of Glass.

Hanna, Paul, Guest Editor. *A Touch of Glass: Contemporary Views of Art Glass and Its Origins.* Lubbock, Texas: West Texas Museum Association, 1983.

Hardy, Roger & Claudia. *The Complete Line of the Akro Agate Co.* Clarksburg, WV: Clarksburg Publishing Company, 1992.

Harrington, J.C. *A Tryal of Glasse: A Story of Glassmaking at Jamestown.* Richmond, VA: The Dietz Press, Incorporated, 1972.

Hartley, Julia Magee, and Cobb, Mary Magee. *The States' Series, Early American Pattern Glass.* Lubbock, Texas: Craftsman Printers Inc., 1976.

Haslam, Malcolm. *Collector's Style Guide, Art Nouveau.* New York, N.Y.: Ballantine Books., 1988.

Hawley, Gessner G., rev. *Condensed Chemical Dictionary.* 10th ed. New York, N.Y.: Van Nostrand Reinhold Company, 1981.

Haworth-Maden, Clare, ed. *Centuries of Style: Tiffany Glass.* Edison, N.J.: Chartwell Books, 1998.

Heacock, William. *1000 Toothpick Holders: A Collector's Guide.* Marietta, Ohio: Antique Publications, 1977.

———. *Collecting Glass: Research, Reprints & Reviews; Vol. I, II & III.* Marietta, Ohio: Richardson Printing Corporation, Vol. I, 1984; Vol. II, 1985; Vol. III, 1986.

————. *Encyclopedia of Victorian Colored Pattern Glass*. Books I, II, III, IV, V, VI, VII and IX. Marietta, Ohio: Antique Publications, 1974 through 1987.

————. *Fenton Glass: The First Twenty-Five Years*. Marietta, Ohio: O-Val Advertising Corp., 1978.

————. *Fenton Glass: The Second Twenty-Five Years*. Marietta, Ohio: O-Val Advertising Corp., 1980.

————. *Fenton Glass: The Third Twenty-Five Years*. Marietta, Ohio: O-Val Advertising Corp., 1989.

————. *Old Pattern Glass: According to Heacock*. Marietta, Ohio: Antique Publications, 1981.

————. *Rare & Unlisted Toothpick Holders*. Marietta, Ohio: Antique Publications, 1984.

Heacock, William, and Patricia Johnson. *5,000 Open Salts: A Collector's Guide*. Marietta, Ohio: The Glass Press Inc., 1982 (Reprint, 1995)

Heacock, William, James Measell, and Berry Wiggins. *Harry Northwood: The Early Years; 1881-1900*. Marietta, Ohio: Antique Publications, 1990.

————. *Harry Northwood: The Wheeling Years; 1901-1925*. Marietta, Ohio: Antique Publications, 1990.

————. *Dugan/Diamond: The Story of Indiana, Pennsylvania Glass*. Marietta, Ohio: Antique Publications, 1993.

Herman, Lloyd E. *American Glass: Masters of the Art*. Washington, D.C.: Smithsonian Institution Traveling Exhibition Service in association with University of Washington Press (Seattle, Wash., and London, England), 2000.

Heiges, George L. *Henry William Steigel*. Manheim, Pa.: George L Heiges, 1937.

Heisey Collectors of America Inc. *Heisey's Glassware Manufactured by A.H. Heisey & Co., Newark, Ohio, U.S.A., Catalogue No. 76, Supplement to Catalogue No. 75*. Heisey Collectors of America, 1982.

Hodge, Jessica. *Lalique*. San Diego, California: Thunder Bay Press, 1999.

Honey, H.B. *English Glass*. London, England: Collins, 1946.

Hornung, Clarence P. *Treasury of American Design & Antiques*. New York, N.Y.: Harry N. Abrams Inc., 1950.

Hotchkiss, John, F. *Cut Glass Handbook & Price Guide*.____: Hotchkiss House Inc., 1970.

Huether, Anne. *Glass and Man*. Philadelphia, Pa.: J.B. Lippincott Company, 1963

Hume, Ivor Noel. "Glass in Colonial Williamsburg's Archaeological Collections." *Colonial Williamsburg Archaeological Series No.1*. Williamsburg, Va.: The Colonial Williamsburg Foundation, 1969.

Hunter, Frederick William. *Stiegel Glass*. New York, N.Y.: Dover Publications Inc., 1950.

Jones-North, Jacquelyne Y. *Czechoslovakian Perfume Bottles & Boudoir Accessories*. Marietta, Ohio: Antique Publications, 1990.

Ingram, Clara. *The Collector's Encyclopedia of Antique Marbles*. Paducah, Ky.: Collector Books, 1972.

Innes, Lowell. *Pittsburgh Glass 1797-1891: A History & Guide for Collectors*. Boston, Mass.: Houghton Mifflin Company, 1976.

Jenkins, Dorothy H. *The Woman's Day Book on Antique Collectibles*. Secaucus, N.J.: Citadel Press, 1981

Jenkins, Emyl. *Emyl Jenkins' Appraisal Book*. New York: Crown Publishers Inc., 1989.

Jones-North, Jacquelyne Y. *Perfume, Cologne & Scent Bottles*. West Chester, Pa.: Schiffer Publishing Ltd., 1986

Ketchum, William C., Jr. *The Catalog of American Collectibles*. New York, N.Y.: Mayflower Books Inc., 1979.

Klamkin, Marian. *The Collector's Guide to Depression Glass*. New York, N.Y.: Hawthorne Books Inc., 1973.

Klein, Dan. *Glass: A Contempory Art*. New York, N.Y.: Rizzoli International Publications, 1989.

Klein, Dan, and Ward Lloyd. *The History of Glass*. New York, N.Y.: Cresent Books, 1984.

Knittle, Rhea Mansfield. *Early American Glass*. New York, N.Y.: The Century Company, 1927.

Koch, Robert. *Louis C. Tiffany's Glass—Bronzes—Lamps*. New York, N.Y.: Crown Publishers Inc., 1971.

————. *Louis C. Tiffany, Rebel in Glass*. New York, N.Y.: Crown Publishers Inc., 1964.

————. *Louis C. Tiffany's Art Glass*. New York, N.Y.: Crown Publishers Inc., 1977.

Kohler, Lucartha. *Glass: An Artist's Medium*. Iola, Wis.: Krause Publications, 1998.

Kovar, Lorraine. *Westmoreland Glass: 1950-1984, Vol. I & II*. Marietta, Ohio. Antique Publications, 1991.

Kuspit, Donald Burton. *Chihuly*, 2nd ed.. Seattle, Wash.: Portland Press, 1998.

Lalique, Rene, et Cie. *Lalique Glass: The Complete Illustrated Catalogue for 1932*. Corning, N.Y.: The Corning Museum of Glass, in association with Dover Publications Inc. (Mineola, N.Y.), 1981.

Lechler, Doris Anderson. *Toy Glass*. Marietta, Ohio: Antique Publications, 1989.

Lee, Lawrence, George Seddon, and Francis Stephens. *Stained Glass*. New York: Crown Publishers Inc., 1968.

Lee, Robert W. *Boston & Sandwich Glass Co.* Wellesley Hills, Mass.: Lee Publications, 1968.

Lee, Ruth Webb. *Early American Pressed Glass*. New York: Ruth Webb Lee (Ferris Printing Co.), 1933.

————. *Nineteenth Century Art Glass*. New York: M. Barrows & Company Inc., 1952.

————. *The Revised Price Guide to Pattern Glass, Third Edition*. New York: M. Barrows & Company Inc., 1963.

————. *Sandwich Glass Handbook*. Wellesley Hills, Mass.: Lee Publications, 1947.

————. *Sandwich Glass*. Wellesley Hills, Mass.: Lee Publications, 1966.

————. *Victorian Glass*. Wellesley Hills, Mass.: Lee Publications, 1944.

————. *Victorian Glass Handbook*. Wellesley Hills, Mass.: Lee Publications, 1946.

Lesieutre, Alain. *The Spirit and Splendour of Art Deco*. Secaucus, N.J.: Castle Books, 1978.

Lewis, J. Sydney. *Old Glass & How to Collect It*. New York, N.Y.: Dodd, Mead & Company, 1925.

Lind, Carla. *Frank Lloyd Wright's Glass Designs*. Rohnert Park, Calif.: Pomegranate Artbooks, 1995.

Lindsley, Bessie M. *American Historical Glass*. Rutland, Vermont: Charles E. Tuttle Company, 1980.

Luckey, Carl F. *An Identification & Value Guide to Depression Era Glassware*, Third Edition. Florence, Alabama: Books Americana Inc., 1994.

Madigan, Mary Jean. *Steuben Glass: An American Tradition in Crystal*. New York: Harry N. Abrams Inc., 1982

Magee, Arthur K. *How to Find and Identify Early Flint Pattern Glass*. Denver, Colo.: Egan Printing Company, 1964.

Mallalieu, Huon, gen. ed. *The Illustrated History of Antiques*. Philadelphia, Pa.: Courage Books, An Imprint of Running Press, 1993.

Mariacher, Giovanni. *Glass from Antiquity to the Renaissance*. Feltham, Middlesex, England: Hamlin House, 1970.

Marshall, Jo. *Glass Source Book*. London: Quarto Publishing plc, 1990.

McCain, Mollie Helen. *The Standard Pattern Glass Price Guide*. Paducah, Kentucky: Mollie Helen McCain (Image Graphics), 1980.

McClinton, Katherine Morrison. *Collecting American Glass*. New York, N.Y.: Gramercy Publishing Company, 1950.

———— *A Handbook of Popular Antiques*. New York, N.Y.: Bonanza Books, 1946.

————. *American Glass*. Cleveland, Ohio: The World Publishing Company, 1950.

McGee, Marie. *Millersburg Glass*. Marietta, Ohio: The Glass Press Inc., 1995.

McKearin, George S. & Helen. *American Glass*. New York: Crown Publishers Inc., 1941.

————. *Two Hundred Years of American Blown Glass*. New York, New York: Crown Publishers Inc., 1966.

Measell, James. *Greentown Glass: The Indiana Tumbler & Goblet Company*. Grand Rapids, Michigan: Grand Rapids Public Museum, 1979.

————. *New Martinsville Glass, 1900-1944*. Marietta, Ohio: Antique Publications, 1994.

Measell, James, ed. *Fenton Glass: The 1980s Decade*. Marietta, Ohio: The Glass Press Inc., 1996.

Measell, James, and Don E. Smith, *Findlay Glass: The Glass Tableware Manufacturers, 1886-1902*. Marietta, Ohio: Antique Publications, 1986.

Mehlman, Felice. *Phaidon Guide to Glass*. Englewood Cliffs, New Jersey: Prentice-Hall Inc., 1983.

Metz, Alice Hulett, *Early American Pattern Glass*. Paducah, Ky.: Collectors Books, 1999.

————. *Early American Pattern Glass*, Book II. Paducah, Ky.: Collectors Books, 1978.

Michael, George. *Basic Book of Antiques & Collectibles*. Radnor, PA: Wallace-Homestead Book Company, 1992.

Middlemas, Keith. *Antique Glass In Color*. Garden City, N.Y.: Doubleday & Company Inc., 1971.

Miller, Judith. *Miller's Antiques & Collectibles: The Facts at Your Fingertips*. London, England: Reed International Books Ltd., 1994.

Miller, Judith and Martin, ed. *Miller's Pocket Dictionary of Antiques*. New York, N.Y.: Penguin Books USA Inc., 1990.

————. *Miller's Pocket Antique Fact File*. London, England: Reed International Books Ltd., 1988.

————. *Miller's Antique Checklist: Glass*. London, England: Reed International Books Ltd., 1994.

————. *Miller's Antique Checklist: Art Deco*. London, England: Reed International Books Ltd., 1991.

————. *Miller's Antique Checklist: Victoriana*. London, England: Reed International Books Ltd., 1991.

Miller, Robert W. *Mary Gregory and Her Glass*. Des Moines, Iowa: Wallace-Homestead Co., 1972.

Moore, N. Hudson. *The Collector's Manual*. New York: Tudor Publishing Co., 1906.

————. *Old Glass: European and American*. New York, N.Y.: Tudor Publishing Company, 1935.

Mortimer, Tony L. *Lalique*. Secaucus, N.J.: Chartwell Books Inc., 1989.

Mordock, John B., and Walter L. Adams, *Pattern Glass Mugs*. Marietta, Ohio: The Glass Press Inc., 1995.

Murray, Melvin L. *Fostoria, Ohio, Glass II*. Fostoria, Ohio: Melvin L. Murray, 1992.

National Cambridge Collectors Inc. *The Cambridge Glass Co*. Paducah, Ky.: Collector Books, 1976.

National Committee to Save America's Cultural Collections. *Caring for Your Collections*. New York, N.Y.: Harry N. Abrams Inc., 1992

Neptune, William G. *Ye Olde Anteek*. Lagro, Ind.: Commercial Printing, 1970.

Newark, Tim. *The Art of Emile Galle*. Secaucus, N.J.: Chartwell Books Inc., 1989.

Newbound, Betty. *The Glass Collector's Almanac*. Union Lake, Mich.: Betty & Bill Newbound, 1987.

Newell, Clarence A. *Old Glass Paperweights of Southern New Jersey*. Phoenix, Ariz.: Papier Presse, 1989.

Newman, Harold. *An Illustrated Dictionary of Glass*. London: Thames & Hudson Ltd., 1977.

Nicholson, Paul T. *Egyptian Faience & Glass*. Buckinghamshire, United Kingdom: Shire Publications Ltd., 1993.

Norman, Barbara. *Engraving & Decorating Glass*. New York, N.Y.: McGraw-Hill Book Company, 1972.

————. *Glass Engraving*. Rutland, Vt.: Charles E. Tuttle Company, 1987.

Northend, Mary Harrod. *American Glass*. New York, N.Y.: Tudor Publishing Co., 1944.

O'Connor, D. Thomas, and Charles G. Lotton, *Lotton Art Glass*. Marietta, Ohio: Antique Publications, 1990.

Old Dartmouth Historical Society—New Bedford Whaling Museum. *(Reprint of the 1894) Pairpoint Manufacturing Company Catalogue*. Marietta, Ohio: The Glass Press Inc., 1997.

Oliver, Elizabeth. *American Antique Glass*. New York: Golden Press, 1977.

Over, Naomi. *Ruby Glass of the 20th Century*. Marietta, Ohio: Antique Publications, 1990.

Padgett, Leonard E. *Mt. Washington Glass Co*. Clinton, Maryland: Leonard E. Padgett, 1976.

Palmer, Arlene. *Glass in Early America*: Selections from the Henry Francis du Pont Winterthur Museum. Winterthur, Delaware: Henry Francis du Pont Winterthur Museum, 1993.

Papert, Emma. *The Illustrated Guide to American Glass*. New York, N.Y.: Hawthorn Books Inc.,1972.

Paul, Tessa. *The Art of Louis Comfort Tiffany*. London: Quintet Publishing Limited, 1987.

Pavia, Fabienne. *The World of Perfume*. New York, N.Y.: Knickerbocker Press, 1996.

Pearson, J. Michael. *Encyclopedia of American Cut & Engraved Glass (1880-1917), Vol. 1, Geometric Conceptions*. Miami Beach: J. Michael Pearson, 1975.

———. *Encyclopedia of American Cut & Engraved Glass (1880-1917), Vol. 2, Realistic Patterns*. Miami Beach: J. Michael Pearson, 1976.

———. *Encyclopedia of American Cut & Engraved Glass (1880-1917), Vol. 3, Geometric Motifs*. Miami Beach: J. Michael Pearson, 1978.

Pearson, J. Michael and Dorothy T. *American Cut Glass for the Discriminating Collector*. New York: Vantage Press Inc., 1971.

———. *A Study of American Cut Glass Collections*. Miami Beach: J. Michael & Dorothy T. Pearson, 1969.

Pepper, Adeline. *The Glass Gaffers of New Jersey*. New York: Charles Scribner's Sons, 1971.

Percy, Christopher Vane. *Lalique: A Collector's Guide*. New York, N.Y.: Cresent Books, 1989.

Peterson, Arthur G., Ph.D. *400 Trademarks on Glass (with alphabetical index)*. Gas City, Ind.: L-W Book Sales, 1992.

———. *Glass Salt Shakers*. Des Moines, Iowa: Wallace-Homestead Book Co., 1970.

Petrova, Sylvia, & Jean-Luc, Olivie. *Bohemian Glass: 1400-1989*. New York: Harry N. Abrams Inc., 1989.

Phillips, Phoebe (ed.). *The Encyclopedia of Glass*. New York: Crown Publishers, 1981.

———. *The Collectors' Encyclopedia of Antiques*. N. Dighton, Mass.: World Publications, 1993.

Phipps, Frances. *The Collector's Complete Dictionary of American Antiques*. Garden City, N.Y.: Doubleday & Company Inc., 1974.

Pickvet, Mark. *Shot Glasses: An American Tradition*. Marietta, Ohio: Antique Publications, 1989.

Plaut, James S. *Steuben Glass*. 3rd edition. New York: Dover Publications Inc., 1972.

Polak, Ada. *Glass: Its Tradition and Its Makers*. New York, N.Y.: G.P. Putnam's Sons, 1975.

Prescott-Walter, Robert. *Collecting Lalique Glass*. London, England: Francis Joseph Publications, 1996.

Pullin, Anne Geffken. *Glass Signatures, Trademarks & Trade Names from the Seventeenth to the Twentieth Centuries*. Des Moines, Iowa: Wallace-Homestead Book Company, 1986.

Reilly, Gerald, ed. *Wheeling Glass, 1829-1939: Collection of the Oglebay Institute Glass Museum*. Olgebay Institute, ———.

Reno, Dawn. *The Official Identification and Price Guide to American Country Collectibles, First Edition*. New York, N.Y.: House of Collectibles, 1990.

Revi, Albert Christian. *American Cut & Engraved Glass*. New York: Thomas Nelson Inc., 1965.

———. *American Pressed Glass & Figure Bottles*. New York: Thomas Nelson Inc., 1964

———. *Nineteenth Century Glass: Its Genesis & Development*. New York: Galahad Books, 1967.

Rice, Ferill J., ed. *Caught in the Butterfly Net*. Williamstown, W.Va.: Fenton Art Glass Collectors of America Inc., 1991.

Righter, Miriam. *Iowa City Glass*. Des Moines, Iowa: Wallace Homestead Co., 1966.

Rinker, Harry L. *Stemware of the 20th Century: The Top 200 Patterns*. New York: House of Collectibles, 1997.

Robertson, R.A. *Chats on Old Glass*. New York: Dover Publications Inc., 1969.

Rockmore, Cynthia & Julian. *The Room by Room Book of American Antiques*. New York: Hawthorne Books Inc., 1970.

Rockwell, Robert F. *Frederick Carder and his Steuben Glass, 1903-1933*. West Nyack, N.Y.: Dexter Press Inc., 1968.

Rogove, Susan Tobier, and Marcia Buan Steinhauer. *Pyrex by Corning: A Collector's Guide*. Marietta, Ohio: Antique Publications, 1993.

Rose, James H. *The Story of American Pressed Glass of the Lacy Period (1825-1850)*. Corning, N.Y.: The Corning Museum of Glass, reprint 1967.

Rossi, Sara. *A Collector's Guide to Paperweights*. Secaucus, N.J.: Wellfleet Books, 1990.

Rothenberg, Polly. *The Complete Book of Creative Glass Art*. New York, N.Y.: Crown Publishers Inc., 1974.

Sanford, Bob. *The Bonita Glass Co.* Delaware, Ohio: Researched Glass Facts, 1997.

Sandwich Historical Society. *Sandwich Glass*. Sandwich, Mass.: Sandwich Historical Society, R.L. Gerling, Pres., 1981.

Savage, George. *Glass*. London, England: Octopus Books Limited, 1972.

———. *Glass & Glassware*. London, England: Hennerwood Publications Limited, 1973.

Schrijver, Elka. *Glass & Crystal I, From Earliest Times to 1850*. London, England: The Merlin Press Limited, 1963.

———. *Glass & Crystal II, From 1850 to Present*. New York: Universe Books Inc., 1964.

Schroy, Ellen Tischbein. *Warman's Glass (Encyclopedia of Antiques and Collectibles)*. Radnor, Pa.: Wallace-Homestead Book Company, 1992, 1995.

Schultes, Richard Evans, and William A. Davis. *The Glass Flowers at Harvard*. New York: E. P. Dutton Inc., 1982.

Schwartz, Marvin D. *Collectors' Guide to Antique American Glass*. Garden City, N.Y.: Doubleday & Company Inc., 1969.

Schwartz, Marvin D., ed. *American Glass, Vol 1, Blown & Molded*. New York: Weathervane Books, 1974.

Selman, Lawrence H. *Collectors' Paperweights: Price Guide & Catalogue*. Santa Cruz, Calif.: Paperweight Press, 1986.

Sferrazza, Julie. *Farber Brothers Krome Kraft*. Marietta, Ohio: Antique Publications, 1988.

Shuman, John A., III. *The Collector's Encyclopedia of American Art Glass*. Paducah, Ky., 1988.

Sinclaire, Estelle F., and Jane Shadel Spillman. *The Complete Cut & Engraved Glass of Corning*. Syracuse, N.Y.: Syracuse University Press, 1997.

Sloan, Jean. *Perfume & Scent Bottle Collecting*. 2nd Edition. Radnor, Pa.: Wallace-Homestead Book Company, 1989.

Solverson, John F. *Those Fascinating Little Lamps*. Marietta, Ohio: Antique Publications, 1988.

Spillman, Jane Shadel. *Glass from World's Fairs, 1851-1904*. Corning, N.Y.: The Corning Museum of Glass, 1986.

———. *Knopf Collectors' Guide to American Antiques, Glass: Tableware, Bowls and Vases*. New York: Alfred A Knopf Inc., 1982.

———. *Knopf Collectors' Guide to American Antiques, Glass: Bottles, Lamps and Other Objects*. New York: Alfred A Knopf Inc., 1983.

———. *White House Glassware: Two Centuries of Presidential Entertaining*. Washington, D.C.: White House Historical Association, 1989.

Spillman, Jane Shadel, and Frantz, Susanne K. Frantz. *Masterpieces of American Glass*. New York, N.Y.: Crown Publishers Inc., 1990.

Stevens, Gerald. *Early Canadian Glass*. Toronto, Canada: The Ryerson Press, 1967.

Stout, Sandra McPhee. *The Complete Book of Mckee Glass*. North Kansas City, Mo.: Trojan Press Inc., 1972.

———. *Depression Glass, Vol. 1, Vol. 2, Vol. 3*. Des Moines, Iowa: Wallace-Homestead Book Co., 1970, 1971, 1976.

Stuart, Sheila. *Small Antiques for the Small House*. Cranberry, N.J.: A.S. Barnes & Co. Inc., 1968.

Swan, Martha Louise. *American Cut & Engraved Glass: The Brilliant Period in Historical Perspective*. Radnor, Pa.: Wallace-Homestead, 1986.

Tait, Hugh, ed. *Glass: 5000 Years*. New York: Harry N. Abrams Inc., 1991.

Toledo Museum of Art. *A Guide to the Glass Collections, Art in Glass*. Toledo, Ohio: Toledo Museum of Art, 1969.

Toohey, Marlena. *A Collector's Guide to Black Glass*. Marietta, Ohio: Antique Publications, 1988.

Truitt, Robert & Deborah. *Collectible Bohemian Glass: 1880-1940*. Kensington, Md.: B & D Glass, 1995.

———. *Mary Gregory Glassware, 1880-1990*. Kensington, Md.: Robert Truitt, 1998.

Utt, Mary Lou & Glenn. *Lalique Perfume Bottles*. New York, N.Y.: Crown Publishers Inc., 1990.

Van Tassel, Valentine. *American Glass*. New York: M. Barrows & Company Inc., Publishers, 1950.

Von Zweck, Dina, gen. ed. *The Woman's Day Dictionary of Glass*. Secaucus, N.J.: Citadel Press, 1983.

Vose, Ruth Hurst. *A Collector's Guide to Antique Glass*. London, England: Leopard, a Division of Random House UK Ltd., 1996.

Waterford Glass Limited. *Waterford Crystal*. Dublin, Ireland: Brown & Nolan Ltd.

Watkins, Lura Woodside. *Cambridge Glass—1818 to 1888 (The Story of the New England Glass Company)*. New York: Bramhall House, 1930.

———. *American Glass & Glassmaking*. New York, N.Y.: Chanticleer Press, 1950.

Watson, Lucilla. *Understanding Antiques*. New York, N.Y.: Viking Penguin Inc., 1987.

Weatherman, Hazel Marie. *Colored Glassware of the Depression Era*. Springfield, Mo.: Weatherman Glassbooks, 1970.

Weiss, Jeffery. *Cornerstone Collector's Guide to Glass*. New York: Simon & Schuster, 1981.

Weitman, Stan & Arlene. *Crackle Glass: Identification & Value Guide*. Paducah, Ky.: Collector Books, 1996.

Wheaton Glass Company. *The Wheaton Story*. Millville, N.J.: Wheaton Glass Company, 1960.

Whitehouse, David, compiler. *Glass: A Pocket Dictionary of Terms Commonly Used to Describe Glass & Glassmaking*. Corning, N.Y.: The Corning Museum of Glass, 1993.

Whitehouse, David. *Glass of the Roman Empire*. Corning, N.Y.; Corning Museum of Glass,1988.

Whitmyer, Margaret and Kenn. *Bedroom & Bathroom Glassware of the Depression Years*. Paducah, Ky.: Collectors Books, 1990.

Wiener, Herbert, and Freda Lipkowitz. *Rarities in American Cut Glass*. Houston, Texas: The Collectors House of Books Publishing Co., 1975.

Wiggins, Berry. *Stretch in Color*. Elkton, Va.: Berry Wiggins, 1994?.

Wilkinson, R. *Hallmarks of Antique Glass*. London: Richard Madley Ltd., 1968.

Wills, Geoffrey. *English & Irish Glass*. Garden City, N.Y.: Doubleday & Company Inc., 1968.

Wilson, Chas West. *Westmoreland Glass*. Paducah, Ky.: Collector Books, 1996.

Wilson, H. Weber. *Great Glass in American Architecture*. New York: E.P. Dutton, 1986.

Wilson, Jack D. *Phoenix & Consolidated Art Glass (1926-1980)*. Marietta, Ohio: Antique Publications, 1989.

Wilson, Kenneth M. *New England Glass & Glassmaking*. New York: Thomas Y. Crowell Company, 1975.

Winchester, Alice, editor. *The Antiques Book*. New York, N.Y.: Bonanza Books, a Division of Crown Publishers Inc., 1950.

Wray, Christopher. *Art Nouveau Lamps and Fixtures of James Hinks & Sons*. New York, N.Y.: Arch Cape Press, 1989.

Yalom, Libby. *Shoes of Glass*. Marietta, Ohio: Antique Publications, 1988.

Zerwick, Chloe. *A Short History of Glass*. Corning, N.Y.: The Corning Museum of Glass, 1980.

Dorflinger, Christian: A Miracle in Glass. White Mills, Pa.: Dorflinger Glass Museum Committee, 1989.

The Sandwich Collector, Vol.II, Issue I, Jan.1985. East Sandwich, Mass.: McCue Publications, 1983.

The Victorian Glass & China Book. New York, N.Y.: Arch Cape Press, 1990.

Additional References for Glass Collectors

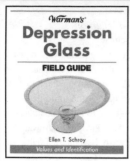